Child, Family, and State

ASPEN PUBLISHERS

Child, Family, and State

Problems and Materials on Children and the Law

Sixth Edition

Robert H. Mnookin
Samuel Williston Professor of Law
Harvard University

D. Kelly Weisberg
Professor of Law
Hastings College of the Law
University of California

Wolters Kluwer
Law & Business

AUSTIN   BOSTON   CHICAGO   NEW YORK   THE NETHERLANDS

To contact Customer Care, e-mail customer.care@aspenpublishers.com, call 1-800-234-1660, fax 1-800-901-9075, or mail correspondence to:

> Aspen Publishers
> Attn: Order Department
> PO Box 990
> Frederick, MD 21705

Printed in the United States of America.

1 2 3 4 5 6 7 8 9 0

ISBN 978-0-7355-7926-2

Library of Congress Cataloging-in-Publication Data

Mnookin, Robert H.
   Child, family, and state : problems and materials on children and the law / Robert H. Mnookin, D. Kelly Weisberg.—6th ed.
      p. cm.
   Includes bibliographical references and index.
   ISBN 978-0-7355-7926-2 (casebound : alk. paper)
   1. Children—Legal status, laws, etc.—United States—Cases. 2. Parent and child (Law)—United States—Cases. 3. Child abuse—Law and legislation—United States. 4. Custody of children—Law and legislation—United States. I. Weisberg, D. Kelly. II. Title.

KF479.M543 2009
346.7301'35—dc22   2009011234

About Wolters Kluwer Law & Business

Wolters Kluwer Law & Business is a leading provider of research information and workflow solutions in key specialty areas. The strengths of the individual brands of Aspen Publishers, CCH, Kluwer Law International and Loislaw are aligned within Wolters Kluwer Law & Business to provide comprehensive, in-depth solutions and expert-authored content for the legal, professional and education markets.

CCH was founded in 1913 and has served more than four generations of business professionals and their clients. The CCH products in the Wolters Kluwer Law & Business group are highly regarded electronic and print resources for legal, securities, antitrust and trade regulation, government contracting, banking, pension, payroll, employment and labor, and healthcare reimbursement and compliance professionals.

Aspen Publishers is a leading information provider for attorneys, business professionals and law students. Written by preeminent authorities, Aspen products offer analytical and practical information in a range of specialty practice areas from securities law and intellectual property to mergers and acquisitions and pension/benefits. Aspen's trusted legal education resources provide professors and students with high-quality, up-to-date and effective resources for successful instruction and study in all areas of the law.

Kluwer Law International supplies the global business community with comprehensive English-language international legal information. Legal practitioners, corporate counsel and business executives around the world rely on the Kluwer Law International journals, loose-leafs, books and electronic products for authoritative information in many areas of international legal practice.

Loislaw is a premier provider of digitized legal content to small law firm practitioners of various specializations. Loislaw provides attorneys with the ability to quickly and efficiently find the necessary legal information they need, when and where they need it, by facilitating access to primary law as well as state-specific law, records, forms and treatises.

Wolters Kluwer Law & Business, a unit of Wolters Kluwer, is headquartered in New York and Riverwoods, Illinois. Wolters Kluwer is a leading multinational publisher and information services company.

In memory of I.J. Mnookin, whose parental love illumined a
sovereignty the law must reflect.

—*R. H. M.*

To my husband, George, and my children, Aaron and Sarah.

—*D. K. W.*

SUMMARY OF CONTENTS

Contents	*xi*
Preface	*xxv*
Acknowledgments	*xxxi*

1. The Child, the Family, and the State	1
2. The Legal Framework for a Child's Economic Relationship Within the Family	149
3. Protecting the Child from Abuse and Neglect	227
4. Medical Treatment: Who Speaks for the Child?	371
5. Child Custody	451
6. State-Enforced Limitations on the Liberty of Minors	651
7. Juvenile Delinquency	753

Table of Cases	*881*
Index	*891*

CONTENTS

Preface		*xxv*
Acknowledgments		*xxxi*

1	*The Child, the Family, and the State*	*1*

	A.	Introduction	1
		John E. Coons, Law and the Sovereigns of Childhood	3
	B.	Is a Fetus a Child?	4
		Roe v. Wade	*4*
		Note: Dissenters' Views in *Roe*	12
		Gonzales v. Carhart	*13*
		Notes and Questions: *Roe* and *Gonzales*	21
		Legal Paternalism: Forcing Medical Treatment on Pregnant Women	31
		Jefferson v. Griffin Spalding County Hospital Authority	*31*
		Questions on Intervention During Pregnancy	34
		Spousal Notification	39
		Planned Parenthood of Southeastern Pennsylvania v. Casey	*40*
		Questions on Spousal Consent	44
		The Legal Treatment of a Fetus	47
	C.	The Judicial Allocation of Power Between Parents and the State	49
		Meyer v. Nebraska	*49*
		Pierce v. Society of Sisters	*51*
		Notes and Questions on *Meyer* and *Pierce:* A Constitutional Framework for Education	53
		Prince v. Massachusetts	*58*
		Questions on Prince v. Massachusetts	62
		Wisconsin v. Yoder	*63*
		Notes and Questions	67
		Roger W. McIntire, Parenthood Training or Mandatory Birth Control: Take Your Choice	70

Problem: Should the Government License
    Parents?   77
D.   What Voice for the Child?   78
    Wisconsin v. Yoder   78
    Questions on *Yoder* Dissent   81
    Troxel v. Granville   *81*
    Note on Juvenile Court Jurisdiction   83
    Ginsberg v. New York   *83*
    ACLU v. Mukasey   *90*
    Note: U.S. Commission on Obscenity and
       Pornography, Report: Draft of Proposed
       Legislation — Sale and Display of Explicit
       Sexual Material to Young Persons (1970)   96
    Discussion of *Ginsberg* and *ACLU v. Mukasey*:
       State Regulation of Sexually Explicit
       Materials   97
    Problem   104
    Note: Protection of Children from Sexual
       Exploitation: Child Pornography   104
    Note: Restricting Minors' Access to Other
       Materials in the Modern Era   106
    Tinker v. Des Moines Independent Community
       School District   *114*
    Morse v. Frederick   *120*
    Questions on *Tinker* and *Morse*   126
    Note: Students' Right to Information —
       Schoolbooks and the Internet   132
    Note: Procedural Rights and the Punishment of
       Students for Expressive Activity   133
    Some Queries: Corporal Punishment in Schools   135
    In re Doe   *135*
    Questions: Privacy Rights of Minors   141

2 *The Legal Framework for a Child's Economic*
   Relationship Within the Family   ***149***

A.   Common Law Background   149
    William Blackstone, Commentaries on the Laws
       of England   149
    Yale Diagnostic Radiology v. Estate of Fountain   *154*
    Notes and Comments: Common Law   157
    William Blackstone, Commentaries on the Laws
       of England   160
    Michael H. v. Gerald D.   *161*
    Note: Nonmarital Children   167

	B.	The Parental Support Obligation	178
		1. Who Has the Legal Duty of Support?	178
		Elisa B. v. Superior Court	*178*
		Wallis v. Smith	*181*
		Harmon v. Department of Social Services	*184*
		Notes and Questions: Who Should Have the Support Obligation?	187
		2. The Scope of the Parental Support Obligation	191
		Introductory Problem	191
		Wagner v. Wagner	*192*
		Discussion: Child Support After Divorce	194
		3. Modification of Child Support Decrees and Enforcement Problems	199
		Introductory Problem — Modification and Enforcement	199
		Note: Modification of Child Support After Divorce	199
	C.	A Child's Inheritance Rights	207
		Gillett-Netting v. Barnhart	*207*
		Discussion: The Inheritance Rights of Children	210
	D.	Management and Control of the Property of a Minor	213
		Introductory Problem	213
		Discussion: Alternative Means to Hold and Control the Property of a Minor	214
	E.	Governmental Income Transfer Programs that Affect Children	216
		Introductory Note	216
		Note: The Personal Responsibility and Work Opportunity Reconciliation Act (PRWORA)	221

3	***Protecting the Child from Abuse and Neglect***	**227**
	A. Problems and Introduction	227
	B. The Parental Privilege to Discipline Children	228
	1. Limitations on Parents' Use of Force	228
	Willis v. State	*228*
	ALI Model Penal Code §3.08	232
	Restatement (Second) of Torts §§147, 150, 151	233
	Dennis Alan Olson, Comment, The Swedish Ban of Corporal Punishment	234
	Notes and Questions	235
	2. Corporal Punishment in Schools	238
	Restatement (Second) of Torts §§152-155	239
	Baker v. Owen	*239*
	Questions on Corporal Punishment in Schools	243
	Note: Ingraham v. Wright	245

C. Child Abuse   247
    1. Scope of the Problem   247
            Child Maltreatment 2006   247
            Note on CAPTA   248
    2. Definitions, Causes, and Consequences of Child Abuse   248
            Diana J. English, The Extent and Consequences
                of Child Maltreatment   248
    3. Discovery of Abuse: Reporting Laws   252
            Ham v. Hospital of Morristown   *252*
            Questions on Reporting Requirements   255
    4. The Central Registry   257
            Humphries v. County of Los Angeles   *258*
            Notes and Questions on Central Registries   263
            Note: Sanctions for Failure of State to Act After
                Report: DeShaney v. Winnebago County   264
    5. An Agenda for Reform   265
            Douglas J. Besharov, Child Abuse Realities:
                Over-Reporting and Poverty   265
    6. The Problem of Sexual Abuse   269
            *M.W. v. Department of Children & Family
                Services*   *269*
            Child Sexual Abuse: Intervention and Treatment
                Issues (1993)   272
            Lindsay C. Arthur, Child Sexual Abuse: Improv-
                ing the System's Response   275
            D. Kelly Weisberg, The "Discovery" of Sexual
                Abuse: Experts' Role in Legal Policy
                Formulation   277
    7. Child Rape and the Death Penalty   283
            Kennedy v. Louisiana   *283*
            Notes and Questions   289
    8. The Child Victim as Witness   292
            People v. Vigil   *292*
            Notes and Questions   297
D. Standard for Intervention and Dispositional Alternatives   304
    1. When Should the State Remove?   305
            Roe v. Conn   *305*
            Notes and Questions   310
            *In re Deborah G., Georgia G., Bruce G., and
                Elizabeth G.*   *314*
            Questions   317
            California Welfare & Institutions Code §§300,
                361 (West 2008)   318
            Michael S. Wald et al., Protecting Abused and
                Neglected Children   321
            Problems   323

2. The State as Parent: The Foster Care System 328
   a. Introduction 328
      Robert H. Mnookin, Foster Care — In Whose Best
         Interest? 328
      Sandra Bass et al., Children, Families and Foster
         Care: Analysis and Recommendations 331
   b. Standards to Guide the Operation of a Foster Care
      System After Removal 334
      Smith v. Organization of Foster Families for
         Equality and Reform 334
      Notes and Questions 345
      The Aftermath and Effects of Smith v. OFFER 347
      David L. Chambers & Michael S. Wald, "Smith v.
         OFFER" 347
   c. Exit from Foster Care: The Aging Out of Older Foster
      Children 349
      Occean v. Kearney 349
      Note on Aging Out of Foster Care 351
3. Foster Care Reform 352
   a. Statutory Reform: AACWA and ASFA 352
   b. The Role of Litigation 354
   c. Criticisms and Proposals for Reform 355
      Dorothy E. Roberts, Is There Justice in Children's
         Rights?: The Critique of Federal Family
         Preservation Policy 355
      Elizabeth Bartholet, The Challenge of Children's
         Rights Advocacy: Problems and Progress in
         the Area of Child Abuse and Neglect 359
4. Termination of Parental Rights: Procedural Safeguards 361
   a. Reasonable Efforts Requirements 361
      In re Ty M. 361
      Notes and Questions 366
   b. Standard of Proof 368
   c. Right to Counsel 369

4 Medical Treatment: Who Speaks for the Child? **371**

A. Introduction 371
B. The Legal Context for the Medical Treatment of Children 372
   1. Battery and the Requirement of Informed Consent 372
   2. Statutory Materials: When May a Minor Consent to
      Medical Treatment? 374
      Ark. Stat. Ann. §20-9-602 (2005) 374
      Ala. Code §§22-8-3 to 22-8-7 (1997) 375
      Minn. Stat. Ann. §§144.341 to 144.347
         (2005 & Supp. 2008) 376

3. Model Statute   379
    Institute of Judicial Administration and the
        American Bar Association, Juvenile Justice
        Standards: Standards Relating to Rights of
        Minors 9-12 (1980)   379
4. Who Pays for Medical Treatment?   381
C. Exceptions and Limitations to Parental Consent
    Requirements   383
    1. Introductory Issues   383
        Problems   383
    2. State-Imposed Health Requirements Applicable to All
        Children   385
    3. The Neglect Limitation   388
        In re Phillip B.   *388*
        Note: Medical Neglect and the Juvenile Court   391
        Parham v. J.R.   *393*
        Notes and Questions   398
    4. Emergencies   400
        Notes and Questions   400
    5. Who Decides If the Parents Disagree and Based on What
        Standard?   400
        In re K.I.   *400*
        Questions   405
    6. Exceptions Where the Minor Alone May Consent to
        Medical Treatment   405
        Preliminary Questions   405
        Lois A. Weithorn, Children's Capacities in Legal
            Contexts   407
D. Disabled Newborns   409
    1. Introduction   409
        Problems   409
    2. Relevant Materials   410
        Miller ex rel. Miller v. HCA, Inc.   *410*
        Notes and Questions   414
        Note: Federal Legislation   416
        Steven R. Smith, Disabled Newborns and the
            Federal Child Abuse Amendments: Tenuous
            Protection   416
    3. Philosophy   420
        Robert H. Mnookin, Two Puzzles   420
        Discussion and Queries   422
        Raymond S. Duff & August B. Campbell, Moral
            and Ethical Dilemmas in the Special-Care
            Nursery   422
        John A. Robertson, Involuntary Euthanasia of
            Defective Newborns: A Legal Analysis   423

President's Commission for the Study of Ethical
        Problems in Medicine and Biomedical and
        Behavioral Research: Deciding to Forgo
        Life-Sustaining Treatment   424
    Problems   426
E. Adolescent Health Care   427
  1. Introduction   427
        Centers for Disease Control and Prevention,
          Youth Risk Behavior Surveillance — United
          States, 2007   428
  2. Suicide   428
        State v. Scruggs   *429*
        Notes and Questions   433
        Note on Other Adolescent Health Issues   436
F. Medical Experimentation on Children   437
  1. Introductory Problem   437
  2. Historical Background   438
        Ross G. Mitchell, The Child and Experimental
          Medicine   438
  3. Is Medical Experimentation on Children Essential?   441
        Ann E. Ryan, Comment, Protecting the Rights of
          Pediatric Research Subjects in the Interna-
          tional Conference of Harmonisation of
          Technical Requirements for Registration of
          Pharmaceuticals for Human Use   441
  4. May Parents Under Existing Law Consent to Medical
        Procedures Not Undertaken for the Treatment of the
        Child in Question?   442
        Grimes v. Kennedy Krieger Institute, Inc.   *442*
        Notes and Questions   448

5 *Child Custody*   **451**

A. Introduction   451
        In re Baby M   *451*
        Questions on *Baby M*   460
        Postscript on *Baby M*   460
        Guardianship of Phillip B., a Minor   *461*
        Robert H. Mnookin, The Guardianship of Phillip B.:
          Jay Spears' Achievement   467
  1. The Problem of Delay   469
  2. Varieties of Custody Law   470
      a. Juvenile Court Child Neglect Laws   470
      b. Involuntary Termination of Parental Rights —
            Adoption   471
      c. Divorce Custody Law   472
      d. Guardianship Custody Law   472

3. Two Functions of Custody Law: Private Dispute Settlement and Child Protection   473
4. What Role Should Psychological Evidence Play in
   Deciding Custody Disputes? Should the Insights of
   Psychology and Psychiatry Be Used for Reformula-
   tion of Custody Standards?   474
5. How Much Weight Should Be Given to the Interests of
   the Biological Parents in Custody Disputes Involving
   Third Parties?   477
6. What Role Should the Child Have in the Resolution of a
   Custody Dispute?   477
         Robert H. Mnookin, The Guardianship of
            Phillip B.: Jay Spears' Achievement   478
7. To What Degree Should the Legal Standards for the
   Resolution of Custody Disputes Be Discretionary?   479
8. One Set of Standards?   480
9. The Indeterminacy of Present-Day Standards   481
         Robert H. Mnookin, Child-Custody Adjudication:
            Judicial Functions in the Face of
            Indeterminacy   481

B. Adoption   487
         Introductory Problems   487
1. Adoption: The Prerequisite of Consent or Involuntary
   Termination of Parental Rights   488
         In re Adoption of Williams   489
         Questions and Notes   491
2. Adoption and the Unwed Father   495
         Stanley v. Illinois   495
         Notes and Questions   498
         Uniform Parentage Act (2000, as
            amended in 2002)   500
         Lehr v. Robertson   505
         Questions and Notes   513
3. Independent Adoption Versus Agency Adoption   518
4. Adoption Failure   520
5. Baby Selling   522
         Richard A. Posner, The Regulation of the Market
            in Adoptions   523
6. Adopted Children's Right to Learn Their Origins   526
7. The Relevance of Sexual Orientation to Adoption   528
         In re Adoption of Doe   528
         Notes and Questions   534
8. The Relevance of Race to Adoption   537
         Adoption of Vito   538
         Notes and Questions   541

Cynthia G. Hawkins-León & Carla Bradley, Race
and Transracial Adoption: The Answer Is
Neither Simply Black or White Nor Right or
Wrong   545
C.   Parental Custody After Divorce   548
  1.   Introduction   548
         Introductory Problem   548
         Notes and Questions on Contested Child Custody   549
  2.   Effects of Parental Divorce   550
         Judith S. Wallerstein, Child of Divorce: An
           Overview   550
         E. Mavis Hetherington & John Kelly, For Better
           or For Worse: Divorce Reconsidered   552
         Eleanor E. Maccoby et al., Custody of Children
           Following Divorce   555
         Eleanor E. Maccoby & Robert H. Mnookin,
           Dividing the Child: Social and Legal
           Dilemmas of Custody   558
  3.   Limits on Private Ordering   559
  4.   Parental Disputes Concerning Child Custody   560
     a.   Standards for Selecting the Custodial Parent: What
          Should the Standard Be?   560
          Note on Separating Siblings   562
     (1) Best Interests of the Child   562
          Robert H. Mnookin, Child-Custody Adjudication:
            Judicial Functions in the Face of
            Indeterminacy   562
     (a) Fitness   564
          Hollon v. Hollon   *564*
          Notes and Questions   569
     (b) Wealth   572
          In re Custody of Tara Marie Pearce   *572*
          Notes and Questions   575
          David L. Chambers, Rethinking the Substantive
            Rules for Custody Disputes in Divorce   575
     (c) Race   580
          Palmore v. Sidoti   *580*
          Notes and Questions   582
     (2) Joint Custody   584
          Problems   584
          Taylor v. Taylor   *584*
          Notes on Joint Custody   592
     b.   Standards Regarding the Noncustodial Parent:
          Visitation   597
     (1) No Visitation?   598
          Peterson v. Jason   *598*
          Notes and Questions   599

Jessica Pearson & Nancy Thoennes, The Denial
of Visitation Rights: A Preliminary Look at Its
Incidence, Correlates, Antecedents and
Consequences   600
Eleanor E. Maccoby & Robert H. Mnookin,
Dividing the Child: Social and Legal
Dilemmas of Custody   602
(2) Conditions on Visitation   604
Khalsa v. Khalsa   *604*
Notes and Questions   607
(3) Third-Party Visitation Rights   609
Troxel v. Granville   *609*
Notes and Questions   613
5. Process: What Process Should Be Used to Resolve
Disputes?   617
a. Adversarial Process   617
Donald T. Saposnek, Mediating Child Custody
Disputes   617
b. Mediation   619
(1) Roles of the Mediator   620
(2) Degrees of Intervention   621
(3) Children's Role in Mediation   621
c. Collaborative Law   623
d. Coin-Flipping   623
Robert H. Mnookin, Child Custody Adjudication:
Judicial Functions in the Face of
Indeterminacy   623
e. What Role for the Child in Custody Decisionmaking? 625
(1) Consideration of the Child's Preference   625
(2) Procedures for Ascertaining a Child's Preference 626
(3) Counsel for the Child?   627
6. Postdecree Problems   628
a. Modification   628
b. Jurisdiction Over and Enforcement of Custody Decrees 631
Problem   631
Notes and Questions on Jurisdiction and
Enforcement   632
D. Custody and the New Reproductive Techniques   637
Introductory Problems   637
In re Baby M   *638*
Notes and Questions on *Baby M*   638
Uniform Parentage Act §§702-704   639
Uniform Parentage Act §§801, 806, 807, 809   645
Note on In Vitro Fertilization   646
American Bar Association, Model Act Governing
Assisted Reproductive Technology (2008)   648

6 State-Enforced Limitations on the Liberty of Minors 651

A. Introduction   651
B. Child Labor   652
    1. Historical Perspective   653
        State Reform   654
        Federal Reform   655
    2. Contemporary Regulation of Child Labor   656
        Fair Labor Standards Act   657
        Notes and Questions Concerning the Conse-
          quences of Child Labor Violations   659
C. Driving Privileges   662
    1. Introduction   662
        Age Limits   663
        Special Rules for Minors Old Enough to Be
          Eligible for Licenses   663
    2. The Necessity of Parental Consent and Implied Parental
        Liability   664
        Jackson v. Houchin   *664*
        Notes and Questions   666
    3. Parental Negligence and Other Special Liability Provisions   667
        Dortman v. Lester   *667*
        Note: Other Special Liability Provisions   669
    4. The Minor's Liability: Standard of Care for Adult
        Activities   670
        Dellwo v. Pearson   *670*
    5. The Standard of Care for the Negligence of Minors   671
        Problem   672
    6. The Power of Minors to Make Contracts and the Defense
        of Infancy   673
D. Drinking   676
        Introductory Problem   676
    1. State Controls on Consumption of Alcoholic Beverages
        by Minors   677
        a. Legal Drinking Age: Background   677
        b. The Variety of Sanctions   678
        (1) Criminal Sanctions Against the Minor   678
        (2) Criminal Sanctions Against the Adult Supplier   678
        (3) Exemptions for Parents Who Supply Liquor to Their
          Children   678
        (4) Regulatory and Civil Provisions   679
        (5) Enforcement   680
    2. Teenagers and Alcohol: Research Findings   681
        James Mosher, The History of Youthful-Drinking
          Laws: Implications for Public Policy   682

		3.	Drinking and Driving Among Teenagers	686
			Some Final Questions on Teenage Drinking	688
			Review Problem: Drinking, Driving, and Obscenity	689
	E.	Contraception		689
			Carey v. Population Services International	*689*
			Notes and Questions	696
	F.	Juvenile Curfews		702
			Hodgkins v. Peterson (*Hodgkins II*)	*702*
			Notes and Questions on Curfews	709
	G.	"Status" Offenses		713
		1.	Status Offense Jurisdiction of the Juvenile Court	713
			In re Walker	*713*
			District of Columbia v. B.J.R.	*719*
			Note: Runaways — Where Do They Go?	722
		2.	Should Status Offenses Be Abolished?	724
			Randy Frances Kandel & Anne Griffiths, Reconfiguring Personhood: From Ungovernability to Parent Adolescent Autonomy Conflict Actions	724
		3.	Status Offenders	729
			Notes and Questions	729
		4.	Dispositions in PINS Cases	733
			State v. Damian R.	*733*
			Notes and Questions	737
			Juvenile Justice and Delinquency Prevention Act	737
		5.	Should Children Be Able to Divorce Their Parents?	742
			In re Snyder	*742*
			Notes and Questions	746
			Bruce C. Hafen, Children's Liberation and the New Egalitarianism: Some Reservations About Abandoning Youth to Their "Rights"	748
			Written Review Problems	750

| **7** | ***Juvenile Delinquency*** | | | ***753*** |

	A.	Introduction		753
			Introductory Problem	754
	B.	Background		755
		1.	The Purposes of Punishment and Juvenile Justice	755
			a. Rehabilitation	755
			b. Deterrence	758
			c. Incapacitation	760
			d. Retribution	761

		Andrew R. Strauss, Note, Losing Sight of the Utilitarian Forest for the Retributivist Trees: An Analysis of the Role of Public Opinion in a Utilitarian Model of Punishment	762
	2.	The Problem of Juvenile Crime	764
		Howard N. Snyder, Juvenile Arrests 2004, Juvenile Justice Bulletin	764
		Note: Youth Gangs and Anti-Gang Legislation	767
	3.	The Early Juvenile Court: Historical Origins and Philosophy	769
		a. Historical Origins of the Juvenile Court	769
		The Invention of the Juvenile Court (Frederic L. Faust & Paul J. Brantingham eds.)	769
		b. Philosophy of the Early Juvenile Court	771
		Rehabilitative Ideal	771
		Procedural Informality	772
		Individualization	772
		Separation of Juvenile and Adult Offenders	772
	4.	The Juvenile Justice System Today: The Bureaucratic Process	772
		Howard N. Snyder, The Juvenile Court and Delinquency Cases	773
C.		Jurisdiction and Disposition in the Juvenile Court	775
	1.	Who Is Subject to the Delinquency Jurisdiction of the Juvenile Court?	775
		In re Michael B.	775
		Note: Jurisdictional Requirements	776
	2.	Disposition and Treatment	784
	3.	Segregation of Juvenile Offenders from Adult Offenders	787
	4.	Capital Punishment for Persons Who Commit Crimes as Juveniles	789
		Roper v. Simmons	789
		Notes and Questions	796
D.		Procedural Differences Between the Delinquency Process and the Adult Criminal Process	798
		In re Gault	798
		Notes and Questions	811
		McKeiver v. Pennsylvania	815
		Notes and Questions	819
	1.	Arrest	824
	2.	Pretrial Detention	825
	3.	Searches	827
		New Jersey v. T.L.O.	827
		Board of Education v. Earls	834
		Notes and Questions on *T.L.O.* and *Earls*	840

4.	Notice of Charges	849
5.	The Voluntariness of Juvenile Confessions	850
6.	*Miranda* Rights	852
	a. When Is a Juvenile in Custody in Order to Trigger *Miranda* Warnings?	853
	b. Parental Role	854
	c. *Miranda* and the Possibility of Transfer to Adult Court	856
	d. Additional *Miranda* Issues	856
7.	Waiver of a Juvenile's Rights	857
	In re S.H.	*857*
	ABA, Institute of Judicial Administration, Juvenile Justice Standards Project, Pretrial Court Proceedings (1980)	861
	Waiver of the Juvenile's Rights	861
	The Role of Parents and Guardians ad Litem in the Delinquency Proceedings	862
	a. Competence to Waive a Juvenile's Rights	864
	b. Applicable Standard	865
	c. Incompetence as a Matter of Law	867
	d. Mandatory Counsel	868
E.	The Role of the Lawyer in the Juvenile Court Process	869
	Problem	869
	Discussion	871
	ABA, Model Code of Professional Responsibility (1978)	873
	ABA, Annotated Model Rules of Professional Conduct	874
	ABA, Institute of Judicial Administration, Juvenile Justice Standards, Standards Relating to Counsel for Private Parties	874
F.	The Future of the Juvenile Court	879
	Barry C. Feld, The Transformation of the Juvenile Court	879

Table of Cases	*881*
Index	*891*

PREFACE

A single overarching question lies at the core of this sixth edition, as in the previous editions: Who decides on behalf of the child? More precisely, how does law allocate power and responsibility for children in our society, and how should it do so? This question reflects the belief that the primary function of law in relation to children is to outline a framework for the distribution of decisional power among the child, the family, and various agencies of the state. Thus, the title of the book.

What makes the study of children and the law particularly intriguing is the fact that as children grow up they acquire an increasing capacity for making decisions for themselves. Babies and very young children are incapable of making decisions about many important questions affecting their lives. It is not simply unwise to emancipate a two-and-a-half-year-old; it is impossible. Therefore, for the very young, the question is not whether the child should decide, but rather which adult should decide on behalf of the child. As the child grows older, however, it becomes increasingly possible for the child to assume responsibility. Consequently, a critical issue that recurs in many contexts throughout the book concerns the degree to which law should recognize the autonomy of older children — that is, the extent to which the law gives power to children to decide for themselves.

Another core issue explored in various contexts throughout the book concerns the appropriate role of government vis-à-vis children and their families. The parens patriae tradition reflects a deep-rooted notion that government has a special responsibility to protect children even from their parents. Delineating the scope of the government's role necessarily poses profound questions of political and moral philosophy concerning the proper relationship of children to their family and of the family to the state.

Note on the Sixth Edition. This sixth edition of the casebook continues the basic design and emphasis of the former editions. At the same time, this edition takes into account many timely and fascinating changes in the law.

Chapter 1 provides a discussion of legal developments wrought by the Internet, specifically federal and state regulation of sexually explicit material (including the new case of ACLU v. Mukasey that invalidates the Child Online Protection Act), federal legislation expanding criminal law enforcement to protect children from sexual victimization on the Internet, and regulation of student library access to the Internet. The chapter also provides updates regarding the legal regulation of minors' access to violent materials in movies, television, music, and video games; and the extension of "zero-tolerance policies" to include a broader range of conduct and harsher sanctions.

In addition, Chapter 1 explores many contemporary educational issues that reflect state and federal regulation of the family, such as home schooling, school vouchers, regulation of student speech (including the new case of Morse v. Frederick that upholds regulation of students' First Amendment rights), and corporal punishment in the schools.

Finally, the chapter includes the latest developments on abortion, such as partial-birth abortion bans (including the new case of Gonzales v. Carhart that upholds the federal Partial-Birth Abortion Ban Act), state and federal health care conscience refusal laws that allow health care providers to refuse to provide abortion services, the global gag rule, the expansion of abortion-specific informed-consent laws, and other recent state and federal restrictions on abortion. The chapter gives special attention to minors' sexual privacy rights as well as minors' rights in the abortion context including such issues as parental notification requirements (including the new case of In re Doe that highlights the application of a parental notification statute), the operation of judicial bypass proceedings, and the application of parental involvement laws to minors' access to the "abortion pill" and emergency contraception.

Chapter 2 includes an update on federal welfare reform legislation, as well as legal developments regarding the parental obligation for necessaries, state and federal enforcement of child support obligations, postmajority support (including the new case of Wagner v. Wagner), the legal status of nonmarital children, paternity disestablishment, and stepparent support obligations. Cutting-edge topics include the legal status of children born of assisted reproduction, such as disputes involving same-sex couples (including the new case of Elisa B. v. Superior Court), as well as posthumously conceived children's right to government survivorship benefits.

Chapter 3 covers updates on the parental privilege to discipline children (including the new case of Willis v. State), the constitutionality of central registries (including the new case of Humphries v. County of Los Angeles), corporal punishment in the schools and at home (including international developments), the constitutionality of the death penalty for child rape (including the new case of Kennedy v. Louisiana), evidentiary concerns involving the child sexual abuse victim as witness (including the new case of People v. Vigil that addresses the implications of Crawford v. Washington), and representation for abused children. The chapter also highlights developments regarding foster care, such as foster parents' rights, problems stemming from exiting from foster care for older children, and foster care reforms.

Chapter 4 incorporates a discussion of current developments regarding state-imposed health requirements applicable to all children, recent litigation concerning the contested link between childhood vaccines and autism, the controversy surrounding the new HPV vaccine (Gardisil) for adolescent girls, and the resolution of disputes about the medical treatment of infants with severe physical and mental impairments. The chapter also features the issue of parents' refusal of treatment in the context of severely premature newborns whose prognosis is uncertain, and the issue of whether parents may consent to nontherapeutic medical procedures for their children. The chapter concludes with a section highlighting some of the legal issues that are implicated in the context of adolescent health, such as antibullying legislation, adolescent suicide (including the new case of State v. Scruggs), and obesity.

Chapter 5 addresses legal developments in the custody and visitation rights of stepparents, grandparents, same-sex parents, and unwed fathers; the child's preference in custody decisionmaking; legal representation for children in child custody cases; relocation disputes; child custody jurisdiction and enforcement; and alternative dispute resolution. The chapter also covers the role of sexual orientation in adoption (including the new case of In re Adoption of Doe), and new developments in the law of assisted reproduction, such as postdissolution disputes over ''ownership'' of embryos, surrogate parenting (including international developments), and access to reproductive technology by gay and lesbian couples. Finally, the chapter explores provisions of the new ABA Model Act Governing Assisted Reproductive Technology.

Revisions to Chapter 6 include updates on state regulation of teenage drinking and driving, sex education in the schools (i.e., abstinence-based sex education programs), teenagers' access to contraception, juvenile curfews, status offenders (i.e., changes in the standard of proof, entitlement to counsel, and developments in the reinstitutionalization movement to detain status offenders in secure facilities), and emancipation (i.e., juveniles ''divorcing'' their parents).

Finally, Chapter 7 explores several major legal developments in juvenile justice. The chapter provides updates on the law of search and seizure (including recent developments on the topic of strip searches), the voluntariness of juvenile confessions, the right to jury trial, anti-gang legislation, *Miranda* rights for juveniles, and the juvenile death penalty. The chapter also highlights developments and criticisms regarding the practice of juvenile waiver to adult court. Finally, the chapter explores suggestions for reform of the juvenile justice system.

Like the previous editions, this sixth edition places considerable emphasis on empirical psychological and sociological research. This edition highlights data on minors' exercise of abortion rights; corporal punishment; the effects of divorce on children; the changing foster care population; gay and lesbian parenting issues in custody, adoption, and foster care; state compliance with deinstitutionalization requirements for status offenders and runaways; juvenile drinking and driving; teenage sexual activity (rates of intercourse and pregnancy) and contraceptive practices; juvenile curfews; differential treatment of male and female status offenders; juvenile crime rates; transfer to adult criminal court; juvenile capacity and maturity in the contexts of confessions and the juvenile death penalty; searches and seizures; and the legal representation of juveniles in the delinquency context.

Note on the First Edition. This book is designed for a law school course on children and the law. The first edition grew out of a conviction that critical questions relating to children could not be adequately addressed in the traditional family law or juvenile justice course and that there were intellectual and pedagogical advantages in a more systematic examination of the legal treatment of childhood. Juvenile law courses typically concentrate on the juvenile court — its jurisdiction and its procedures. Family law courses, on the other hand, are primarily concerned with questions relating to marriage and divorce. Existing casebooks for such courses seemed either too narrow or too broad to allow a systematic examination of what it means to be a child for purposes of the law.

In approaching the task of writing this book, it was obvious that an extraordinarily broad range of law might affect or be relevant to children. It was decided that the primary objective would be to write a book that would provide students with the opportunity of learning how to think about children and the law and how to develop a framework that might then prove useful in exploring a broad variety of issues, including many that are not touched on in the book.

Note to Instructors. Because the book is designed for law school teaching, a few paragraphs addressed primarily to law school instructors are in order. The Questions and Problems sections in each chapter are the heart of the book. More questions are included than could possibly be discussed with any thoroughness in the available class time. It is hoped, however, that questions not discussed in class may nonetheless stimulate student thought, be useful to generate student research that can result in law review notes and comments, and encourage scholarship by lawyers and nonlawyers alike.

In addition to the questions, there are a number of problems. In fact, this sixth edition includes many more problems than previous editions. These problems can serve either as vehicles for classroom discussion or as written exercises for students; in our teaching we use them for both. The problems exhibit considerable variety not only in subject areas, but also in terms of the lawyering skills required.

Some background in psychology, human development, and sociology is extremely helpful in the study of children and the law. Instructors might wish to assign background reading concerning children and families at the beginning of the course. In this respect we would like to recommend Arlene S. Skolnick's *The Intimate Environment: Exploring Marriage and the Family* (6th ed. 1996) and Arlene S. Skolnick and Jerome Skolnick's *The Family in Transition: Rethinking Marriage, Sexuality, Child Rearing and Family Organization* (15th ed. 2008). These books provide a lucid introduction to and summary of a great deal of theoretical and empirical research relating to the social context of childhood, the psychology of socialization, child development, and the child's social relationships within the family. Other excellent areas for background reading are the history of childhood and the history of the family. Recommended sources include the chapter "Inducting Children into the Social Order" in Carl N. Degler's *At Odds: Women and the Family in America from the Revolution to the Present* (1980) and the introductory chapter, "The Evolution of Childhood," in *The History of Childhood* (Lloyd deMause ed., 1974). For more recent works, see Paula S. Fass and Mary Ann Mason eds., *Childhood in America* (2000), and Steven Mintz, *Huck's Raft: A History of American Childhood* (2004). Several collections of materials relating to the history of childhood merit special mention, including Robert H. Bremner ed., *Children and Youth in America: A Documentary History* (3 vols., 1970-1974) and Paula S. Fass ed., *Encyclopedia of Children and Childhood in History and Society* (3 vols., 2003).

Many students will undoubtedly wish to do outside reading on the questions, problems, and cases presented in the book. For this purpose, we have included references to helpful articles and books. Several additional collections of essays are particularly useful: Margaret K. Rosenheim et al. eds., *A Century of Juvenile Justice* (2001), S. Randall Humm et al. eds., *Child, Parent, and State: Law and Policy Reader* (1994), and the journals in the series "The Future of Children" (on such topics as adoption, child abuse, divorce, firearms, foster care, health care, and the juvenile court), published by the David and Lucile Packard Foundation, Center for the Future of Children, Los Altos, California. Finally, a number of recent law review symposia have focused on interesting issues relevant to children. See

Symposium, Caring for Our Children: Delivery of Mental Health Services to Children and Adolescents, 25 J. Legal Med. 1 (2004); *Symposium, Defending Childhood,* 14 U. Fla. J.L. & Pub. Pol'y 125 (2003); *Symposium: The Relationship Rights of Children,* 11 Wm. & Mary Bill Rts. J. 843 (2003); *Symposium, Therapeutic Jurisprudence and Research,* 71 U. Cin. L. Rev. 13 (2002); *Symposium, Research with Children: The New Legal and Policy Landscape,* 6 J. Health Care L. & Pol'y 1 (2002).

This edition of the casebook continues to allow instructors considerable flexibility in designing courses or seminars of varying lengths and emphasis. The book as a whole is intended for a one-semester course that meets three hours a week. The book also could be used, however, for shorter courses such as in-depth seminars. For example, a seminar might focus on the juvenile justice system, emphasizing Chapters 3, 6, and 7. For law schools that offer a separate course in juvenile delinquency or in which delinquency issues are covered in criminal law courses, the instructor might use Chapters 1 through 6 and omit Chapter 7. Particular chapters will also provide a focus for specialized seminars. Chapters 3, 4, and 5 certainly could form the core materials for in-depth seminars: Chapter 3 on child abuse and neglect, Chapter 4 on medical treatment of children, and Chapter 5 on custody law. Apart from the first chapter, which introduces major themes that are explored in the remainder of the book, the chapters may be rearranged to suit the needs of the instructor.

Editorial Matters. This sixth edition incorporates significant editorial revisions. Judicial opinions often tend to be long and redundant. Instructors will note that many of the cases and excerpts in previous editions have been shortened markedly for the sake of brevity and clarity. Throughout the book, deletions are indicated by ellipses, with the following exceptions: citations have been modified or eliminated, footnotes have been eliminated, and paragraphs have been modified to make edited excerpts coherent without indication. When retained, footnotes in reprinted materials have the original footnote numbers. Our own footnotes are indicated by footnote numbers in brackets. These bracketed footnotes are numbered consecutively throughout each chapter. Additions to reprinted materials are indicated by brackets as well.

Acknowledgments for the Sixth Edition. We would like particularly to acknowledge the valuable research assistance provided by the following students: Kimberly Liu, Caroline Rothert, and Grace Spulak of Harvard Law School; and Kristen Driskell and Matthew Garfinkle of Hastings College of the Law. Thanks also are due to Carmen Corral-Reid and Teresa Horton of Aspen Publishers for their superb editorial assistance.

Robert H. Mnookin
Harvard Law School

D. Kelly Weisberg
Hastings College of the Law

April 2009

ACKNOWLEDGMENTS

We wish to thank the authors and copyright holders of the following works who permitted their inclusion in this book:

ABA, Institute of Judicial Administration, Juvenile Justice Standards. Copyright 1980, Ballinger Publishing Company.

"ABA, Model Act Governing Assisted Reproductive Technology," (pp. 18-19), published by the ABA Section of Family Law Committee on Reproductive & Genetic Technologies, 2008. ©2008 by the American Bar Association. Reprinted with permission.

ABA, Model Code of Professional Responsibility (1986). Reprinted with permission of the American Bar Association. Copies of *ABA Model Code of Professional Responsibility* are available from Service Center, American Bar Association, 321 North Clark Street, Chicago, IL 60610, 1-800-285-2221.

American Law Institute, Model Penal Code §3.08 (Tent. Draft No. 8). Copyright 1958 by the American Law Institute. Reprinted with permission. All rights reserved.

American Law Institute, Restatement (Second) of Torts, §§147, 150-155 (1965). Copyright 1965 by the American Law Institute. Reprinted with permission. All rights reserved.

Andrews, R. Hale, Jr. & Andrew H. Cohn, Note, Ungovernability: The Unjustifiable Jurisdiction, 83 Yale L.J. 1383 (1974). Reprinted by permission of The Yale Law Journal Company and Fred B. Rothman & Company.

Annas, George J., Mandatory PKU Screening: The Other Side of the Looking Glass, 72 Am. J. Public Health 1401 (1986). Reprinted with permission of the author.

Arthur, Lindsay G., Child Sexual Abuse: Improving the System's Response, 37 Juv. & Fam. Ct. J. (No. 2) 1-14 (1986). Reprinted with permission of the author and the National Council of Juvenile and Family Court Judges, Reno, NV.

Bartholet, Elizabeth, The Challenge of Children's Rights Advocacy: Problems and Progress in the Area of Child Abuse and Neglect, 3 Whittier J. Child & Fam. Advoc. 215, 218-221 (2004). Used by permission of Whittier Journal of Child and Family Advocacy.

Bass, Sandra, et al., Children, Families and Foster Care: Analysis and Recommendations, The Future of Children, v. 14 no. 1 (Winter 2004), pp. 6-8. From The Future of Children, a publication of the David and Lucile Packard Foundation.

Belgum, Eunice, Book Review, 89 Harv. L. Rev. 823. Copyright © 1976 by Harvard Law Review Association.

Bennett, Robert, Allocation of Child Medical Decision-Making Authority: A Suggested Interest Analysis, 62 Va. L. Rev. 285 (1976). Reprinted with permission of Fred B. Rothman & Company.

Hafen, Bruce C., Children's Liberation and the New Egalitarianism: Some Reservations about Abandoning Youth to Their "Rights", 1976 B.Y.U. L. Rev. (No. 3) 605. Copyright 1976 by the Brigham Young University Law Review. Reprinted by permission.

Hawkins-León, Cynthia G., & Carla Bradley, Race and Transracial Adoption: The Answer Is Neither Simply Black or White Nor Right or Wrong, 51 Cath. U. L. Rev. 1227, 1255-1267 (2002). Work used with permission of Catholic University Law Review. Excerpts from Carla Bradley & Cynthia Hawkins-León, The Transracial Adoption Debate: Counseling and Legal Implications, Journal of Counseling & Development, 80(4), 433-440 (2002). ACA. Reprinted with permission. No further reproduction authorized without written permission from the American Counseling Association.

Hetherington, E. Mavis, & John Kelly, For Better or For Worse: Divorce Reconsidered, W.W. Norton & Co., 228-229 (2002). Copyright © 2002 by E. Mavis Hetherington and John Kelly. Used by permission of W.W. Norton & Company, Inc.

Kandel, Randy Frances, & Anne Griffiths, Reconfiguring Personhood: From Ungovernability to Parent Adolescent Autonomy Conflict Actions, 53 Syracuse L. Rev. 995, 1002-1003, 1032-1042, 1059-1063 (2003).

Keith-Spiegel, Patricia C., Children and Consent to Participate in Research, in Children's Competence to Consent (G. Melton et al. eds., 1983).

Kempe, C. Henry & Ray E. Helfer, eds., Helping the Battered Child and His Family (1972).

Krugman, Richard D., The Coming Decade: Unfinished Tasks and New Frontiers, 9 Child Abuse & Neglect 119 (1985). Copyright 1985, Pergamon Press.

Langer, Dennis H., Medical Research Involving Children: Some Legal and Ethical Issues, 36 Baylor L. Rev, 1, 11-16 (1984).

Levine, Robert J., Ethics and Regulation of Clinical Research 239-241 (2d ed. 1986). Copyright 1986 Urban and Schwarzenberg, Baltimore-Munich.

Maccoby, Eleanor E. & Robert H. Mnookin, Dividing the Child: Social and Legal Dilemmas of Custody 274-275 (1992). Reprinted by permission of Harvard University Press. Copyright © 1992 by the President and Fellows of Harvard College.

Maccoby, Eleanor E. et al., Custody of Children Following Divorce, in The Impact of Divorce, Single-Parenting and Step-Parenting on Children (E. Mavis Hetherington & Josephine D. Arasteh eds., 1988).

McIntire, Roger W., Parenthood Training or Mandatory Birth Control: Take Your Choice, Psychology Today 34 (Oct. 1973). Reprinted from Psychology Today Magazine, © 1973 Sussex Publishers, Inc.

McIvor, Greg, Human Rights: Swedish Parents Demand Right to Smack Children, Inter Press Service, Feb. 5, 1993. Inter Press Service, available from Global Information Network, NY, NY.

Mitchell, Ross G., The Child and Experimental Medicine, 1 Brit. Med. J. 721-722 (1964). Published by permission of British Medical Journal.

Mnookin, Robert H., Child-Custody Adjudication: Judicial Functions in the Face of Indeterminacy, 39 Law & Contemp. Probs. (No. 3) 226 (Summer 1975).

Mnookin, Robert H., Foster Care — In Whose Best Interest? 43 Harv. Ed. Rev. 4 (Nov. 1973). Copyright © 1973 by President and Fellows of Harvard College.

Mnookin, Robert H., Two Puzzles, 1984 Arizona State Law Journal 667, 668-671, 677-679.

Mnookin, Robert H., The Guardianship of Phillip B.: Jay Spears' Achievement, 40 Stan. L. Rev. 841 (1988). Copyright 1988 by the Board of Trustees of the Leland Stanford Junior University.

Mnookin, Robert H. & Lewis Kornhauser, Bargaining in the Shadow of the Law: The Case of Divorce, 88 Yale L.J. 950 (1979).

Mosher, James, The History of Youthful-Drinking Laws: Implications for Public Policy, in Minimum-Drinking-Age Laws: An Evaluation (Henry Wechsler ed., 1980). Reprinted by permission of the author.

National Research Council, Risking the Future: Adolescent Sexuality, Pregnancy, and Childbearing, vol. 1 (1986). Copyright 1986 by the National Academy of Sciences.

Nelson, F. Kirk & Joel E. Bernstein, Consent in Pediatric Medical Experimentation, 3 J. Legal Med. 15 (March 1975).

Olson, Dennis Alan, Comment, The Swedish Ban of Corporal Punishment, 1984 B.Y.U. L. Rev. 447.

O'Malley, Patrick M. & Alexander C. Wagenaar, Effects of Minimum Age Drinking Laws, 52 J. Stud. Alcohol 478-491 (1991). Reprinted with permission from Journal of Studies on Alcohol. Copyright by Alcohol Research Documentation, Inc., Rutgers Center of Alcohol Studies, Piscataway, NJ 08855.

Pearson, Jessica & Nancy Thoennes, The Denial of Visitation Rights: A Preliminary Look at Its Incidence, Correlates, Antecedents and Consequences, 10 Law and Policy (No. 4) 363-380 (1988).

Posner, Richard A., The Regulation of the Market in Adoptions, 67 B.U. L. Rev. 59 (1987).

President's Commission for the Study of Ethical Problems in Medicine and Biomedical and Behavioral Research: Deciding to Forgo Life-Sustaining Treatment (Pub. No. 83-17978) 197-204, 217-223 (1983).

President's Commission for the Study of Ethical Problems in Medicine and Biomedical and Behavioral Research: Screening and Counseling for Genetic Conditions 12-15 (1983).

President's Commission on Law Enforcement and Administration of Justice, Task Force Report: Juvenile Delinquency and Youth Crime 4-6 (1967).

Ramsey, Paul, A Reply to Richard McCormick: The Enforcement of Morals: Nontherapeutic Research on Children, 6 Hastings Center Rep. (No. 4) 21 (Aug. 1976). © Institute of Society, Ethics and the Life Sciences, 360 Broadway, Hastings-on-Hudson, NY 10706.

Roberts, Dorothy E., Is There Justice in Children's Rights?: The Critique of Federal Family Preservation Policy, 2 U.PA. J. Const. L. 112, 118-138 (1999).

Robertson, John A., Involuntary Euthanasia of Defective Newborns: A Legal Analysis, 27 Stan. L. Rev. 213 (1975). Copyright 1975 by the Board of Trustees of the Leland Stanford Junior University.

Ryan, Ann E., Comment, Protecting the Rights of Pediatric Research Subjects in the International Conference of Harmonisation of Technical Requirements for Registration of Pharmaceuticals for Human Use, 23 Fordham Int'l L.J. 848, 855-857 (2000).

Saposnek, Donald T., Mediating Child Custody Disputes 7-16 (rev. ed. 1998).

Schultz, J. Lawrence & Fred Cohen, Isolationism in Juvenile Court Jurisprudence, in Pursuing Justice for the Child (Margaret Kenney Rosenheim ed. 1976). © The University of Chicago 1976. All rights reserved.

Schwartz, Harold L. & Arthur Hirsh, Child Abuse and Neglect: A Survey of the Law, 28 Medical Trial Technique Quarterly 293, 306-308 (1982). Reprinted with permission from Clark Boardman Callaghan, 50 Broad Street East, Rochester, NY 14694.

Simpson, Anna Louise, Comment, Rehabilitation as the Justification of a Separate Juvenile Justice System, 64 Cal. L. Rev. 984 (1976). Copyright © California Law Review, Inc. Reprinted by permission.

Smith, Steven R., Disabled Newborns and the Federal Child Abuse Amendments: Tenuous Protection, 37 Hastings L.J. 765-825 (1986). Copyright 1986 Hastings College of the Law. Reprinted with permission.

Snyder, Howard, Juvenile Arrests 2001, Juvenile Justice Bulletin, Office of Juvenile Justice and Delinquency Prevention. (Dec. 2003), pp. 1, 4, 5, 7-10. From The Future of Children, a publication of the David and Lucile Packard Foundation.

Steinman, Susan, Joint Custody: What We Know, What We Have Yet to Learn, and the Judicial and Legislative Impact, 16 U.C. Davis L. Rev. 739 (1983). Copyright 1983 by The Regents of the University of California. Reprinted with permission.

Strauss, Andrew R., Note, Losing Sight of the Utilitarian Forest for the Retributivist Trees: An Analysis of the Role of Public Opinion in a Utilitarian Model of Punishment, 23 Cardozo L. Rev. 1549, 1571-1581 (2002).

ten Bensel, Robert W., The Scope of the Problem, 35 Juv. & Fam. Ct. J. 1 (Winter 1984). Reprinted with permission of the author and the National Council of Juvenile and Family Court Judges.

UCLA Medicine and Society Forum, Would It Have Been Ethical to Give Swine Flu Vaccine to Children Without Prior Testing? (Jan. 27, 1977).

Uniform Parentage Act, §§201, 204, 301, 302, 402, 403, 404, 405. Copyright © 2002 by National Conference of Commissioners on Uniform State Laws.

Wagenaar, Alexander C., Alcohol, Young Drivers and Traffic Accidents (1983). Reprinted by permission of Lexington Books, Lexington, MA. Copyright 1983 D.C. Heath and Company.

Wald, Michael S. et al., Protecting Abused and Neglected Children 9-12 (1988). Reprinted with the permission of the publishers, Stanford University Press. Copyright © 1988 by the Board of Trustees of the Leland Stanford Jr. University.

Wallerstein, Judith S., Children of Divorce: An Overview, 4 Behav. Sci. & L. 105-116 (1986). Reproduced by permission of John Wiley & Sons Limited.

Weir, Robert F., Life-and-Death Decisions in the Midst of Uncertainty, in Compelled Compassion: Government Intervention in the Treatment of Critically Ill Newborns 25-29 (Arthur L. Caplan et al. eds., 1992).

Weisberg, D. Kelly, The "Discovery" of Sexual Abuse: Experts' Role in Legal Policy Formulation, 18 U.C. Davis L. Rev. 1 (1984). Copyright 1984 by the Regents of the University of California. Reprinted with permission.

Child, Family, and State

CHAPTER **1**

The Child, the Family, and the State

A. INTRODUCTION

Over a century ago, John Stuart Mill observed that "[t]he existing generation is master both of the training and the entire experience of the generation to come."[1] Mill thought this to be true and proper. Our generation appears to be the first in which Mill's proposition will encounter serious challenge in what may prove a long intellectual and ultimately legal and political campaign.

The idea that adults "master" the "training and the entire experience" of children seems empirically wrong, both from the perspective of the child's individual psychology and as a matter of social roles. While an infant obviously comes into the world dependent for its survival on adults, experimental psychologists suggest that even the very young child selectively perceives and interprets situations and events.[2] There is no way for adults to make sure that children will receive or accept a particular message because children contribute to what they experience.[3] For this reason, and because environmental events and cultural determinants beyond the purposeful control of adults bear so heavily on the child's experience, the notion that adults somehow control the socialization of the next generation seems dubious. Arguably, the present-day social reality in America would be as accurately described by turning Mill's assertion on its head — children and youth may dominate the experience of their elders. The victims of intergenerational confrontation may include adults as well as children. In all events, Mill's description is strangely one-sided: The older and younger generations seem in fact inextricably intertwined in a reciprocal relationship in which the unique experience of each affects the other.

---

[1] John Stuart Mill, On Liberty 77 (David Spitz ed. 1975). This part of the introduction has been adapted from Robert H. Mnookin, Foreword — Symposium on Children and the Law, 39 Law & Contemp. Probs. (No. 3) 1-3 (1975).

[2] See H. Rudolph Schaffer, The Growth of Sociability (1971).

[3] See Arlene S. Skolnick, The Intimate Environment 372-374 (4th ed. 1987).

Apart from the accuracy of Mill's description, could it possibly describe a just relationship among human beings? For children, Mill explicitly rejected his own principle of individual liberty on a variety of grounds, the most important of which related to the notion that the child was incapable of self-improvement by means of rational discussion.[4] Limiting the freedom of children was therefore, by his lights, necessary both to protect children against "their own actions as well as against external injury"[5] and to protect society from the untutored.[6] Mill rejected, however, the prevalent nineteenth-century notion that parents should have unfettered dominion over their children. He instead thought that the state was justified in using law to limit parental liberty when necessary for the good of the child or society.[7]

How the family and the state dominate the lives of children and whether they should are questions that provide a useful starting point for an examination of children and the law. Law outlines a framework for the distribution of decisional power among the child, the family, and various agencies of the state. Although the pattern of the law is complex, it seems plain that children generally have less liberty than adults and are often less accountable. Within the family, parents have legal power to make a wide range of important decisions that affect the life of the child, but the state holds them responsible for the child's care and support.[8] Children have the special power to avoid contractual obligations[9] but are not normally entitled to their own earnings[10] and cannot manage their own property.[11] Moreover, in accordance with age-based lines, persons younger than certain statutory limits are not allowed to vote,[12] hold public office,[13] work in various occupations,[14] drive a car,[15] buy liquor,[16] or be sold certain kinds of reading material,[17] quite apart from what they or their parents may wish.

Because of such legally imposed limitations on the child's power to decide, some reformers suggest that a children's liberation movement should follow the trail blazed by the civil rights and women's movements.[18] At the core of these

---

[4] See Mill, supra note 1, at 11.

[5] Id. See also id. at 75.

[6] See id. at 100.

[7] See id. at 96-101.

[8] See Chapters 2 and 3.

[9] See Chapter 6, p. 673.

[10] See Chapter 2, p. 158.

[11] See Chapter 2, p. 214.

[12] See, e.g., Cal. Const. art. II, §2 (West 2002); cf. Oregon v. Mitchell, 400 U.S. 112 (1970) (upholding congressional power to lower voting age from 21 to 18 for federal but not for state elections).

[13] See, e.g., Cal. Govt. Code §1020 (West 1995) ("A person is incapable of holding a civil office if at the time of his election or appointment he is not 18 years of age.").

[14] See, e.g., Fair Labor Standards Act, 29 U.S.C. §212 (2000); Cal. Lab. Code §§1285-1312 (West 2003 & Supp. 2008). See generally Chapter 6, section B.

[15] See Chapter 6, p. 662.

[16] See, e.g., Cal. Const. art. XX, §22 (West 1996); Cal. Bus. & Prof. Code §§25658-65 (West 1997 & Supp. 2008). See Chapter 6, p. 676.

[17] See Ginsberg v. New York, p. 83 infra.

[18] See, e.g., Virginia Coigney, Children Are People Too (1975); Richard E. Farson, Birthrights (1974).

other movements, however, is the rather straightforward notion that a person's legal autonomy should not be made dependent on race or sex, at least without some compelling justification. Any broad assertion that age is also irrelevant to legal autonomy inescapably collides with certain biological and economic realities.[19]

Because the young are necessarily dependent for some period after birth, the relevant question often is which adult should have the power to decide on behalf of the child. That an element of domination of children by adults is inevitable gives no license to ignore the moral dimension implicit in the advocates' challenge. Moreover, for older children, the emancipators' rhetoric has raised questions worthy of serious examination: In what circumstances should the law give children the power to decide certain things for themselves and to be responsible for their own actions? Are some of the age-based lines drawn too high? What are the advantages and disadvantages of arbitrary lines as opposed to more flexible alternatives? In addressing all these questions, it must be recognized that the legal system reflects at least as much as it shapes the social context in which children grow up. The law's assignment of roles and authority for children of various ages gives expression to society's perception of the child's humanity and importance as an individual.

John E. Coons, Law and the Sovereigns of Childhood
58 Phi Delta Kappan (No. 1) 19 (Sept. 1976)

The common law and statutory structures that affect childhood come in three styles which can be labeled rules, minimums, and sovereignties. Rules are more or less specific standards of conduct and may take a positive or negative form. Thus children under 15 are forbidden to drive automobiles or work in factories and are commanded to attend school. Parents are limited in their choice of punishments and are commanded to provide adequate nourishment. Minimums are legal devices which in various ways assure that the level of goods and services necessary to the child's protection, control, and preparation for adult life will not fall below some floor. For example, where the family is unable to supply the basics of nutrition, protection, dress, or housing, law provides money, goods, or services sufficient to raise its performance to the standard; if the family's failure is beyond the help of material resources, law places the child in a foster family for which it provides a modest subsidy. And, recognizing the child's need for a substantial period of formal education and the family's frequent incapacity to provide it by itself, law also supplies a school meeting at least some basic criteria. Here we see that minimums and rules often become indistinguishable; the rule that a child must be a student for 180 days a year is part of the guarantee that he will enjoy the social minimum of education.

However, by far the law's most significant intervention is of the third type, one which occupies and pre-empts that vast area of child rearing which is above the

---

[19] See generally Martin Guggenheim, What's Wrong with Children's Rights (2005) (exploring the ways in which the children's rights movement has been invoked in such contexts as abortion, adoption, custody, and foster care).

guaranteed minimum and not covered by specific rules. Here the law's way is to recognize in someone or some institution a residual authority and discretion to protect, control, and prepare the child. Law, in short, ordains the petty sovereignties of childhood.

But petty only in the sense that each of these infant hegemonies is itself subject in theory to substantial regulation by the overarching government; the actual scope of its authority often is anything but petty. . . .

B.   IS A FETUS A CHILD?

Roe v. Wade
410 U.S. 113 (1973)

Mr. Justice BLACKMUN delivered the opinion of the Court. . . .

I

The Texas statutes that concern us here are Arts. 1191-1194 and 1196 of the State's Penal Code,[1] Vernon's Ann. P.C. These make it a crime to "procure an abortion," as therein defined, or to attempt one, except with respect to "an abortion procured

---

[1] **Article 1191. Abortion**

If any person shall designedly administer to a pregnant woman or knowingly procure to be administered with her consent any drug or medicine, or shall use towards her any violence or means whatever externally or internally applied, and thereby procure an abortion, he shall be confined in the penitentiary not less than two nor more than five years; if it be done without her consent, the punishment shall be doubled. By 'abortion' is meant that the life of the fetus or embryo shall be destroyed in the woman's womb or that a premature birth thereof be caused.

Art. 1192. Furnishing the means

Whoever furnishes the means for procuring an abortion knowing the purpose intended is guilty as an accomplice. . . . [Article 1193 punishes attempted abortion.]

Art. 1194. Murder in producing abortion

If the death of the mother is occasioned by an abortion so produced or by an attempt to effect the same, it is murder.

Art. 1196. By medical advice

Nothing in this chapter applies to an abortion procured or attempted by medical advice for the purpose of saving the life of the mother. . . .

or attempted by medical advice for the purpose of saving the life of the mother."
Similar statutes are in existence in a majority of the States. . . .

II

Jane Roe, a single woman who was residing in Dallas County, Texas, instituted this
federal action in March 1970 against the District Attorney of the county. She
sought a declaratory judgment that the Texas criminal abortion statutes were
unconstitutional on their face, and an injunction restraining the defendant from
enforcing the statutes.

Roe alleged that she was unmarried and pregnant; that she wished to terminate
her pregnancy by an abortion "performed by a competent, licensed physician,
under safe, clinical conditions"; that she was unable to get a "legal" abortion
in Texas because her life did not appear to be threatened by the continuation of
her pregnancy; and that she could not afford to travel to another jurisdiction in
order to secure a legal abortion under safe conditions. She claimed that the Texas
statutes were unconstitutionally vague and that they abridged her right of personal
privacy, protected by the First, Fourth, Fifth, Ninth, and Fourteenth Amendments.
By an amendment to her complaint Roe purported to sue "on behalf of herself and
all other women" similarly situated. [The district court held that the Ninth and
Fourteenth Amendments protected the fundamental right of single women and
married persons to choose to have children, and that the Texas abortion legislation
was vague and overbroad. The Supreme Court concurred with the district court that
Jane Roe had standing and that the case was not rendered moot by the termination
of her pregnancy prior to its decision.]

V

The principal thrust of appellant's attack on the Texas statutes is that they improperly invade a right, said to be possessed by the pregnant woman, to choose to
terminate her pregnancy. Appellant would discover this right in the concept of
personal "liberty" embodied in the Fourteenth Amendment's Due Process Clause;
or in personal, marital, familial, and sexual privacy said to be protected by the Bill
of Rights or its penumbras, see Griswold v. Connecticut, 381 U.S. 479 (1965);
Eisenstadt v. Baird, 405 U.S. 438 (1972) (White, J., concurring); or among those
rights reserved to the people by the Ninth Amendment, Griswold v. Connecticut,
381 U.S., at 486 (Goldberg, J., concurring), Before addressing this claim, we feel it
desirable briefly to survey, in several aspects, the history of abortion, for such
insight as that history may afford us, and then to examine the state purposes and
interests behind the criminal abortion laws.

VI

It perhaps is not generally appreciated that the restrictive criminal abortion laws in
effect in a majority of States today are of relatively recent vintage. [T]hey derive
from statutory changes effected, for the most part, in the latter half of the 19th
century. . . .

VII

Three reasons have been advanced to explain historically the enactment of criminal abortion laws in the 19th century and to justify their continued existence.

It has been argued occasionally that these laws were the product of a Victorian social concern to discourage illicit sexual conduct. Texas, however, does not advance this justification in the present case, and it appears that no court or commentator has taken the argument seriously. . . .

A second reason is concerned with abortion as a medical procedure. When most criminal abortion laws were first enacted, the procedure was a hazardous one for the woman. . . . Thus it has been argued that a State's real concern in enacting a criminal abortion law was to protect the pregnant woman, that is, to restrain her from submitting to a procedure that placed her life in serious jeopardy.

Modern medical techniques have altered this situation. Appellants and various amici refer to medical data indicating that abortion in early pregnancy that is, prior to the end of first trimester, although not without its risk, is now relatively safe. Mortality rates for women undergoing early abortions, where the procedure is legal, appear to be as low as or lower than the rates for normal childbirth. Consequently, any interest of the State in protecting the woman from an inherently hazardous procedure, except when it would be equally dangerous for her to forgo it, has largely disappeared. Of course, important state interests in the area of health and medical standards do remain. The State has a legitimate interest in seeing to it that abortion, like any other medical procedure, is performed under circumstances that insure maximum safety for the patient. This interest obviously extends at least to the performing physician and his staff, to the facilities involved, to the availability of after-care, and to adequate provision for any complication or emergency that might arise. The prevalence of high mortality rates at illegal "abortion mills" strengthens, rather than weakens, the State's interest in regulating the conditions under which abortions are performed. Moreover, the risk to the woman increases as her pregnancy continues. Thus the State retains a definite interest in protecting the woman's own health and safety when an abortion is proposed at a late stage of pregnancy.

The third reason is the State's interest — some phrase it in terms of duty — in protecting prenatal life. Some of the argument for this justification rests on the theory that a new human life is present from the moment of conception. The State's interest and general obligation to protect life then extends, it is argued, to prenatal life. Only when the life of the pregnant mother herself is at stake, balanced against the life she carries within her, should the interest of the embryo or fetus not prevail. Logically, of course, a legitimate state interest in this area need not stand or fall on acceptance of the belief that life begins at conception or at some other point prior to live birth. In assessing the State's interest, recognition may be given to the less rigid claim that as long as at least *potential* life is involved, the State may assert interests beyond the protection of the pregnant woman alone.

Parties challenging state abortion laws have sharply disputed in some courts the contention that a purpose of these laws, when enacted, was to protect prenatal life. Pointing to the absence of legislative history to support the contention, they claim that most state laws were designed solely to protect the woman. Because medical advances have lessened this concern, at least with respect to abortion in early pregnancy, they argue that with respect to such abortions the laws can no longer be justified by any state interest. There is some scholarly support for this view of original purpose. The few state courts called upon to interpret their laws in the late 19th and early 20th centuries did focus on the State's interest in protecting the woman's health rather than in preserving the embryo and fetus. Proponents of this view point out that in many States, including Texas, by statute or judicial interpretation, the pregnant woman herself could not be prosecuted for self-abortion or for cooperating in an abortion performed upon her by another. They claim that adoption of the "quickening" distinction through received common law and state statutes tacitly recognizes the greater health hazards inherent in late abortion and impliedly repudiates the theory that life begins at conception.

It is with these interests, and the weight to be attached to them, that this case is concerned.

VIII

The Constitution does not explicitly mention any right of privacy. In a line of decisions, however, going back perhaps as far as Union Pacific R. Co. v. Botsford, 141 U.S. 250, 251 (1891), the Court has recognized that a right of personal privacy, or a guarantee of certain areas or zones of privacy, does exist under the Constitution. In varying contexts the Court or individual Justices have indeed found at least the roots of that right in the First Amendment, . . . in the Fourth and Fifth Amendments, . . . in the penumbras of the Bill of Rights, Griswold v, Connecticut, 381 U.S. 479, 484-485 (1965); in the Ninth Amendment, id., at 486 (Goldberg, J., concurring); or in the concept of liberty guaranteed by the first section of the Fourteenth Amendment, see Meyer v. Nebraska, 262 U.S. 390, 399 (1923). These decisions make it clear that only personal rights that can be deemed "fundamental" or "implicit in the concept of ordered liberty" are included in this guarantee of personal privacy. They also make it clear that the right has some extension to activities relating to marriage, Loving v. Virginia, 388 U.S. 1, 12 (1967), procreation, Skinner v. Oklahoma, 316 U.S. 535, 541-542 (1942), contraception, Eisenstadt v. Baird, 405 U.S. 438, 453-454 (1972); id., at 460, 463-465 (White, J., concurring), family relationships, Prince v. Massachusetts, 321 U.S. 158, 166 (1944), and child rearing and education, Pierce v. Society of Sisters, 268 U.S. 510, 535 (1925), Meyer v. Nebraska, supra.

This right of privacy, whether it be founded in the Fourteenth Amendment's concept of personal liberty and restrictions upon state action, as we feel it is, or, as the District Court determined, in the Ninth Amendment's reservation of rights to the people, is broad enough to encompass a woman's decision whether or not to terminate her pregnancy. The detriment that the State would impose upon the pregnant woman by denying this choice altogether is apparent. Specific and direct harm medically diagnosable even in early pregnancy may be involved. Maternity, or additional offspring, may force upon the woman a distressful life and future. Psychological harm may be imminent. Mental and physical health may be taxed by child care. There is also the distress, for all concerned, associated with the unwanted child, and there is the problem of bringing a child into a family already unable, psychologically and otherwise, to care for it. In other cases, as in this one, the additional difficulties and continuing stigma of unwed motherhood may be involved. All these are factors the woman and her responsible physician necessarily will consider in consultation.

On the basis of elements such as these, appellants and some amici argue that the woman's right is absolute and that she is entitled to terminate her pregnancy at whatever time, in whatever way, and for whatever reason she alone chooses. With this we do not agree. Appellants' arguments that Texas either has no valid interest at all in regulating the abortion decision, or no interest strong enough to support any limitation upon the woman's sole determination, is unpersuasive. The Court's decisions recognizing a right of privacy also acknowledge that some state regulation in areas protected by that right is appropriate. As noted above, a state may properly assert important interests in safeguarding health, in maintaining medical standards, and in protecting potential life. At some point in pregnancy, these respective interests become sufficiently compelling to sustain regulation of the factors that govern the abortion decision. The privacy right involved, therefore, cannot be said to be absolute. In fact, it is not clear to us that the claim asserted by some amici that one has an unlimited right to do with one's body as one pleases bears a close relationship to the right of privacy previously articulated in the Court's decisions. The Court has refused to recognize an unlimited right of this kind in the past. Jacobson v. Massachusetts, 197 U.S. 11 (1905) (vaccination); Buck v. Bell, 274 U.S. 200 (1927) (sterilization).

We therefore conclude that the right of personal privacy includes the abortion decision, but that this right is not unqualified and must be considered against important state interests in regulation. . . .

Where certain "fundamental rights" are involved, the Court has held that regulation limiting these rights may be justified only by a "compelling state interest," and that the legislative enactments must be narrowly drawn to express only the legitimate state interests at stake. . . .

IX

The District Court held that the appellee failed to meet his burden of demonstrating that the Texas statute's infringement upon Roe's rights was necessary to support a compelling state interest, and that, although the defendant presented "several compelling justifications for state presence in the area of abortions," the statutes outstripped these justifications and swept "far beyond any areas of compelling state interest." 314 F. Supp., at 1222-1223. Appellant and appellee both contest that holding. Appellant, as has been indicated, claims an absolute right that bars any state imposition of criminal penalties in the area. Appellee argues that the State's determination to recognize and protect prenatal life from and after conception constitutes a compelling state interest. As noted above, we do not agree fully with either formulation.

A

The appellee and certain amici argue that the fetus is a "person" within the language and meaning of the Fourteenth Amendment. In support of this they outline at length and in detail the well-known facts of fetal development. If this suggestion of personhood is established, the appellant's case, of course, collapses, for the fetus' right to life is then guaranteed specifically by the Amendment. . . .

The Constitution does not define "person" in so many words. Section I of the Fourteenth Amendment contains three references to "person." The first, in defining "citizens," speaks of "persons born or naturalized in the United States." The word also appears both in the Due Process Clause and in the Equal Protection Clause. "Person" is used in other places in the Constitution: in the listing of qualifications for representatives and senators, Art. I, §2, cl. 2, and §3, cl. 3; in the Apportionment Clause, Art. I, §2, cl. 3;[53] in the Migration and Importation provision, Art. I, §9, cl. 1; in the Emolument Clause, Art. I, §9, cl. 8; in the Electors provisions, Art. II, §1, cl. 2, and the superseded cl. 3; in the provision outlining qualifications for the office of President, Art. II, §1, cl. 5; in the Extradition provisions, Art. IV, §2, cl. 2, and the superseded Fugitive Slave Clause 3; and in the Fifth, Twelfth, and Twenty-second Amendments as well as in §§2 and 3 of the Fourteenth Amendment. But in nearly all these instances, the use of the word is such that it has application only postnatally. None indicates, with any assurance, that it has any possible prenatal application.[54]

All this, together with our observation, supra, that throughout the major portion of the 19th century prevailing legal abortion practices were far freer than they are today, persuades us that the word "person," as used in the Fourteenth Amendment, does not include the unborn. . . .

This conclusion, however, does not of itself fully answer the contentions raised by Texas, and we pass on to other considerations.

B

The pregnant woman cannot be isolated in her privacy. She carries an embryo and, later, a fetus. . . . The situation therefore is inherently different from marital intimacy, or bedroom possession of obscene material, or marriage, or procreation, or education, with which *Eisenstadt, Griswold, Stanley, Loving, Skinner, Pierce,* and *Meyer* were respectively concerned. As we have intimated above, it is

---

[53] We are not aware that in the taking of any census under this clause, a fetus has ever been counted.

[54] When Texas urges that a fetus is entitled to Fourteenth Amendment protection as a person, it faces a dilemma. Neither in Texas nor in any other State are all abortions prohibited. Despite broad proscription, an exception [exists] for an abortion procured or attempted by medical advice for the purpose of saving the life of the mother. . . . But if the fetus is a person who is not to be deprived of life without due process of law, and if the mother's condition is the sole determinant, does not the Texas exception appear to be out of line with the Amendment's command?

There are other inconsistencies between Fourteenth Amendment status and the typical abortion statute. It has already been pointed out, supra, that in Texas the woman is not a principal or an accomplice with respect to an abortion upon her. If the fetus is a person, why is the woman not a principal or an accomplice? Further, the penalty for criminal abortion . . . is significantly less than the maximum penalty for murder. . . . If the fetus is a person, may the penalties be different?

reasonable and appropriate for a State to decide that at some point in time another interest, that of health of the mother or that of potential human life, becomes significantly involved. The woman's privacy is no longer sole and any right of privacy she possesses must be measured accordingly.

Texas urges that, apart from the Fourteenth Amendment, life begins at conception and is present throughout pregnancy, and that, therefore, the State has a compelling interest in protecting that life from and after conception. We need not resolve the difficult question of when life begins. When those trained in the respective disciplines of medicine, philosophy, and theology are unable to arrive at any consensus, the judiciary, at this point in the development of man's knowledge, is not in a position to speculate as to the answer.

It should be sufficient to note briefly the wide divergence of thinking on this most sensitive and difficult question. There has always been strong support for the view that life does not begin until live birth. This was the belief of the Stoics. It appears to be the predominant, though not the unanimous, attitude of the Jewish faith. It may be taken to represent also the position of a large segment of the Protestant community, . . . As we have noted, the common law found greater significance in quickening. Physicians and their scientific colleagues have regarded that event with less interest and have tended to focus either upon conception or upon live birth or upon the interim point at which the fetus becomes "viable," that is, potentially able to live outside the mother's womb, albeit with artificial aid. Viability is usually placed at about seven months (28 weeks) but may occur earlier, even at 24 weeks. The Aristotelian theory of "mediate animation," that held sway throughout the Middle Ages and the Renaissance in Europe, continued to be official Roman Catholic dogma until the 19th century, despite opposition to this "ensoulment" theory from those in the Church who would recognize the existence of life from the moment of conception. The latter is now, of course, the official belief of the Catholic Church [and] is a view strongly held by many non-Catholics as well and by many physicians. Substantial problems for precise definition of this view are posed, however, by new embryological data that purport to indicate that conception is a "process" over time, rather than an event, and by new medical techniques such as menstrual extraction, the "morning-after" pill, implantation of embryos, artificial insemination, and even artificial wombs.

In areas other than criminal abortion the law has been reluctant to endorse any theory that life, as we recognize it, begins before live birth or to accord legal rights to the unborn except in narrowly defined situations and except when the rights are contingent upon live birth. For example, the traditional rule of tort law had denied recovery for prenatal injuries even though the child was born alive. That rule has been changed in almost every jurisdiction. In most States recovery is said to be permitted only if the fetus was viable. . . . In a recent development, generally opposed by the commentators, some States permit the parents of a stillborn child to maintain an action for wrongful death because of prenatal injuries. Such an action, however, would appear to be one to vindicate the parents' interest and is thus consistent with the view that the fetus, at most, represents only the potentiality of life. Similarly, unborn children have been recognized as acquiring rights or interests by way of inheritance or other devolution of property, and have been represented by guardians ad litem. Perfection of the interests involved, again, has generally been contingent upon live birth. In short, the unborn have never been recognized in the law as persons in the whole sense.

X

In view of all this, we do not agree that, by adopting one theory of life, Texas may override the rights of the pregnant woman that are at stake. We repeat, however, that the State does have an important and legitimate interest in preserving and protecting the health of the pregnant woman, whether she be a resident of the State or a nonresident who seeks medical consultation and treatment there, and that it has still *another* important and legitimate interest in protecting the potentiality of human life. These interests are separate and distinct. Each grows in substantiality as the woman approaches term and, at a point during pregnancy, each becomes "compelling."

With respect to the State's important and legitimate interest in the health of the mother, the "compelling" point, in the light of present medical knowledge, is at approximately the end of the first trimester. This is so because of the now established medical fact . . . that until the end of the first trimester mortality in abortion is less than mortality in normal childbirth. It follows that, from and after this point, a State may regulate the abortion procedure to the extent that the regulation reasonably relates to the preservation and protection of maternal health. Examples of permissible state regulation in this area are requirements as to the qualifications of the person who is to perform the abortion; as to the licensure of that person; as to the facility in which the procedure is to be performed, that is, whether it must be a hospital or may be a clinic or some other place of less-than-hospital status; as to the licensing of the facility; and the like.

This means, on the other hand, that, for the period of pregnancy prior to this "compelling" point, the attending physician, in consultation with his patient, is free to determine, without regulation by the State, that in his medical judgment the patient's pregnancy should be terminated. If that decision is reached, the judgment may be effectuated by an abortion free of interference by the State.

With respect to the State's important and legitimate interest in potential life, the "compelling" point is at viability. This is so because the fetus then presumably has the capability of meaningful life outside the mother's womb. State regulation protective of fetal life after viability thus has both logical and biological justifications. If the State is interested in protecting fetal life after viability, it may go so far as to proscribe abortion during that period except when it is necessary to preserve the life or health of the mother.

Measured against these standards, Art. 1196 of the Texas Penal Code, in restricting legal abortions to those "procured or attempted by medical advice for the purpose of saving the life of the mother," sweeps too broadly. The statute makes no distinction between abortions performed early in pregnancy and those performed later, and it limits to a single reason, "saving" the mother's life, the legal justification for the procedure. The statute, therefore, cannot survive the constitutional attack made upon it here.

This conclusion makes it unnecessary for us to consider the additional challenge to the Texas statute asserted on grounds of vagueness.

XI

To summarize and to repeat:

1. A state criminal abortion statute of the current Texas type, that excepts from criminality only a *life saving* procedure on behalf of the mother, without regard to pregnancy stage and without recognition of the other interests involved, is violative of the Due Process Clause of the Fourteenth Amendment.

(a) For the stage prior to approximately the end of the first trimester, the abortion decision and its effectuation must be left to the medical judgment of the pregnant woman's attending physician.

(b) For the stage subsequent to approximately the end of the first trimester, the State, in promoting its interest in the health of the mother, may, if it chooses, regulate the abortion procedure in ways that are reasonably related to maternal health.

(c) For the stage subsequent to viability the State, in promoting its interest in the potentiality of human life, may, if it chooses, regulate, and even proscribe, abortion except where it is necessary, in appropriate medical judgment, for the preservation of the life or health of the mother.

2. The State may define the term "physician," . . . to mean only a physician currently licensed by the State, and may proscribe any abortion by a person who is not a physician as so defined.

In Doe v. Bolton, [410 U.S. 179 (1973)], procedural requirements contained in one of the modern abortion statutes are considered. That opinion and this one, of course, are to be read together.[20]

This holding, we feel, is consistent with the relative weights of the respective interests involved, with the lessons and example of medical and legal history, with the lenity of the common law, and with the demands of the profound problems of the present day. The decision leaves the State free to place increasing restrictions on abortion as the period of pregnancy lengthens, so long as those restrictions are tailored to the recognized state interests. The decision vindicates the right of the physician to administer medical treatment according to his professional judgment up to the points where important state interests provide compelling justifications for intervention. Up to those points the abortion decision in all its aspects is inherently, and primarily, a medical decision, and basic responsibility for it must rest with the physician. . . .

NOTE: DISSENTERS' VIEWS IN *ROE*

Justices Rehnquist and White, dissenting in both *Roe* and its companion Doe v. Bolton, criticized the Court for usurping the function of the legislature. According to Justice White, "The Court . . . values the convenience of the pregnant mother more than the continued existence and development of the life or potential life that

---

[20] Doe v. Bolton, a companion case to *Roe,* invalidated Georgia's statute (inspired by the American Law Institute's Model Penal Code provision permitting abortion in limited cases), including its procedural requirements of hospitalization in an accredited facility, committee approval, two-doctor concurrence, and state residency.

she carries. . . . I find no constitutional warrant for imposing such an order of priorities on the people and legislatures of the States." 410 U.S. at 222.

Justice Rehnquist did not think the right of privacy was involved in the abortion cases. He stated, however, that freedom from "unwanted state regulation of consensual transactions" is a form of liberty recognized in earlier Supreme Court decisions; moreover, "[t]he Due Process Clause of the Fourteenth Amendment undoubtedly does place a limit, albeit a broad one, on legislative power to enact laws such as this. If the Texas statute were to prohibit abortion even where the mother's life is in jeopardy, I have little doubt that such a statute would lack a rational relation to a valid state objective." 410 U.S. at 172-173.

Gonzales v. Carhart
550 U.S. 124 (2007)

Justice KENNEDY delivered the opinion of the Court.

[We consider here] the validity of the Partial-Birth Abortion Ban Act of 2003, 18 U.S.C. §1531 (2000 ed., Supp. IV), a federal statute regulating abortion procedures. . . . The Act proscribes a particular manner of ending fetal life. . . .

Abortion methods vary depending to some extent on the preferences of the physician and, of course, on the term of the pregnancy and the resulting stage of the unborn child's development. Between 85 and 90 percent of the approximately 1.3 million abortions performed each year in the United States take place in the first three months of pregnancy, which is to say in the first trimester. The most common first-trimester abortion method is vacuum aspiration (otherwise known as suction curettage) in which the physician vacuums out the embryonic tissue. Early in this trimester an alternative is to use medication, such as mifepristone (commonly known as RU-486), to terminate the pregnancy. The Act does not regulate these procedures.

Of the remaining abortions that take place each year, most occur in the second trimester. The surgical procedure referred to as "dilation and evacuation" or "D&E" is the usual abortion method in this trimester. . . . A doctor must first dilate the cervix at least to the extent needed to insert surgical instruments into the uterus and to maneuver them to evacuate the fetus. The steps taken to cause dilation differ by physician and gestational age of the fetus. [Then, the] woman is placed under general anesthesia or conscious sedation. The doctor, often guided by ultrasound, inserts grasping forceps through the woman's cervix and into the uterus to grab the fetus. The doctor grips a fetal part with the forceps and pulls it back through the cervix and vagina, continuing to pull even after meeting resistance from the cervix. The friction causes the fetus to tear apart. . . . Some doctors, especially later in the second trimester, may kill the fetus [by chemical injection] a day or two before performing the surgical evacuation. . . . Other doctors refrain from injecting chemical agents, believing it adds risk with little or no medical benefit.

The abortion procedure that was the impetus for the numerous bans on "partial-birth abortion," including the Act, is a variation of this standard D&E. . . . [T]his D&E variation will be referred to as intact D&E. The main difference between the two procedures is that in intact D&E a doctor extracts the fetus intact or largely intact with only a few passes. There are no comprehensive statistics indicating what percentage of all D&Es are performed in this manner. . . . Intact D&E gained public notoriety when, in 1992, Dr. Martin Haskell gave a presentation describing his method of performing the operation. In the usual intact D&E the fetus' head lodges in the cervix, and dilation is insufficient to allow it to pass. Haskell explained the next step as follows:

> . . . [While] lifting the cervix and applying traction to the [fetal] shoulders with the fingers of the left hand, the surgeon takes a pair of blunt curved Metzenbaum scissors in the right hand. He carefully advances the tip, curved down, along the spine and under his middle finger until he feels it contact the base of the skull under the tip of his middle finger.
>   The surgeon then forces the scissors into the base of the skull or into the foramen magnum. Having safely entered the skull, he spreads the scissors to enlarge the opening.
>   The surgeon removes the scissors and introduces a suction catheter into this hole and evacuates the skull contents. With the catheter still in place, he applies traction to the fetus, removing it completely from the patient.
>   . . .

[Dr. Haskell's approach is not the only method of killing the fetus once its head lodges in the cervix. Other doctors use different techniques. Further, other second-trimester abortion methods exist, including medical induction and surgical procedures, hysterotomy and hysterectomy, although they present risks of complications.]

After Dr. Haskell's procedure received public attention, with ensuing and increasing public concern, bans on "partial-birth abortion" proliferated. By the time of [Stenberg v. Carhart, 530 U.S. 914 (2000), in which a 5-4 majority invalidated a Nebraska partial-birth abortion ban], about 30 States had enacted bans designed to prohibit the procedure. [Congress passed this ban in 2003, which President Bush signed into law.]

The Act responded to *Stenberg* in two ways. First, Congress made factual findings [among other things] that "[a] moral, medical, and ethical consensus exists that the practice of performing a partial-birth abortion . . . is a gruesome and inhumane procedure that is never medically necessary and should be prohibited." Second, and more relevant here, the Act's language differs from that of the Nebraska statute struck down in *Stenberg* [by specifying that delivery must occur to one of two anatomical landmarks and then requiring the physician's fatal overt act to occur after delivery of the entire fetal head outside the woman's body]. The operative provisions of the Act provide in relevant part:

> (a) Any physician who, in or affecting interstate or foreign commerce, knowingly performs a partial-birth abortion and thereby kills a human fetus shall be fined under this title or imprisoned not more than 2 years, or both. This subsection does not apply to a partial-birth abortion that is necessary to save the life of a mother whose life is endangered by a physical disorder, physical illness, or physical injury, including a life-endangering physical condition caused by or arising from the pregnancy itself. . . .

(b) As used in this section —

(1) the term "partial-birth abortion" means an abortion in which the person performing the abortion —

(A) deliberately and intentionally vaginally delivers a living fetus until, in the case of a head-first presentation, the entire fetal head is outside the body of the mother, or, in the case of breech presentation, any part of the fetal trunk past the navel is outside the body of the mother, for the purpose of performing an overt act that the person knows will kill the partially delivered living fetus; and

(B) performs the overt act, other than completion of delivery, that kills the partially delivered living fetus. . . .

[Three district courts held the federal ban unconstitutional under *Stenberg*, and the courts of appeals affirmed. Two of these cases are before the United States Supreme Court here.]

[A central premise in Planned Parenthood of Southeastern Pa. v. Casey, 505 U.S. 833 (1992) (upholding portions of Pennsylvania's informed consent abortion statute)] — that the government has a legitimate and substantial interest in preserving and promoting fetal life — would be repudiated were the Court now [to invalidate the federal partial-birth abortion ban]. *Casey* involved a challenge to Roe v. Wade, 410 U.S. 113 (1973). [*Casey*, supra, at 846] contains this summary:

> It must be stated at the outset and with clarity that *Roe*'s essential holding, the holding we reaffirm, has three parts. First is a recognition of the right of the woman to choose to have an abortion before viability and to obtain it without undue interference from the State. Before viability, the State's interests are not strong enough to support a prohibition of abortion or the imposition of a substantial obstacle to the woman's effective right to elect the procedure. Second is a confirmation of the State's power to restrict abortions after fetal viability, if the law contains exceptions for pregnancies which endanger the woman's life or health. And third is the principle that the State has legitimate interests from the outset of the pregnancy in protecting the health of the woman and the life of the fetus that may become a child. These principles do not contradict one another; and we adhere to each.

Though all three holdings are implicated in the instant cases, it is the third that requires the most extended discussion; for we must determine whether the Act furthers the legitimate interest of the Government in protecting the life of the fetus that may become a child. To implement its holding, *Casey* rejected both *Roe*'s rigid trimester framework and the interpretation of *Roe* that considered all previability regulations of abortion unwarranted. . . .

. . . We assume the following principles for the purposes of this opinion. Before viability, a State "may not prohibit any woman from making the ultimate decision to terminate her pregnancy." 505 U.S., at 879 (plurality opinion). It also may not impose upon this right an undue burden, which exists if a regulation's "purpose or effect is to place a substantial obstacle in the path of a woman seeking an abortion before the fetus attains viability." Id., at 878. On the other hand, "regulations which do no more than create a structural mechanism by which the State, or the parent or guardian of a minor, may express profound respect for the life of the unborn are permitted, if they are not a substantial obstacle to the woman's exercise of the right to choose." Id., at 877. *Casey*, in short, struck a balance. The balance was central to its holding. We now apply its standard to the cases at bar. . . .

The Act punishes "knowingly performing" a "partial-birth abortion." It defines the unlawful abortion in explicit terms. First, the person performing the abortion must "vaginally deliver a living fetus." Second, the Act's definition of partial-birth abortion [specifies "anatomical landmarks," requiring] the fetus to be delivered "until, in the case of a head-first presentation, the entire fetal head is outside the body of the mother, or, in the case of breech presentation, any part of the fetal trunk past the navel is outside the body of the mother." . . . Third, to fall within the Act, a doctor must perform an "overt act, other than completion of delivery, that kills the partially delivered living fetus." For purposes of criminal liability, the overt act causing the fetus' death must be separate from delivery. And the overt act must occur after the delivery to an anatomical landmark. . . . Fourth, . . . the physician must have "deliberately and intentionally" delivered the fetus to one of the Act's anatomical landmarks. If a living fetus is delivered past the critical point by accident or inadvertence, the Act is inapplicable. In addition, the fetus must have been delivered "for the purpose of performing an overt act that the [doctor] knows will kill [it]." If either intent is absent, no crime has occurred. . . .

[The Court rejects Respondents' contention the Act is unconstitutionally vague on its face.] Unlike the statutory language in *Stenberg* that prohibited the delivery of a "substantial portion" of the fetus — where a doctor might question how much of the fetus is a substantial portion — the Act defines the line between potentially criminal conduct on the one hand and lawful abortion on the other. Doctors performing D&E will know that if they do not deliver a living fetus to an anatomical landmark they will not face criminal liability. This conclusion is buttressed by the intent that must be proved to impose liability [because] scienter requirements alleviate vagueness concerns. . . .

We next determine whether the Act imposes an undue burden, as a facial matter, because its restrictions on second-trimester abortions are too broad. . . . Under the principles accepted as controlling here, the Act [which applies pre- and postviability], as we have interpreted it, would be unconstitutional "if its purpose or effect is to place a substantial obstacle in the path of a woman seeking an abortion before the fetus attains viability." *Casey*, 505 U.S., at 878 (plurality opinion). . . . The Act's purposes are set forth in recitals preceding its operative provisions. [It] proscribes a method of abortion in which a fetus is killed just inches before completion of the birth process. Congress stated as follows: "Implicitly approving such a brutal and inhumane procedure by choosing not to prohibit it will further coarsen society to the humanity of not only newborns, but all vulnerable and innocent human life, making it increasingly difficult to protect such life." The Act expresses respect for the dignity of human life. Congress was concerned, furthermore, with the effects on the medical community and on its reputation caused by the practice of partial-birth abortion [as its findings show].

Casey reaffirmed these governmental objectives. The government may use its voice and its regulatory authority to show its profound respect for the life within the woman. A central premise of the opinion was that the Court's precedents after *Roe* had "undervalued the State's interest in potential life." 505 U.S., at 873. . . . Where it has a rational basis to act, and it does not impose an undue burden, the State may use its regulatory power to bar certain procedures and substitute others, all in furtherance of its legitimate interests in regulating the medical profession in order to promote respect for life, including life of the unborn. The Act's ban on abortions that involve partial delivery of a living fetus furthers the Government's objectives.

Respect for human life finds an ultimate expression in the bond of love the mother has for her child. The Act recognizes this reality as well. Whether to have an abortion requires a difficult and painful moral decision. While we find no reliable data to measure the phenomenon, it seems unexceptionable to conclude some women come to regret their choice to abort the infant life they once created and sustained. See Brief for Sandra Cano et al. as Amici Curiae in No. 05-380, pp. 22-24. Severe depression and loss of esteem can follow.

In a decision so fraught with emotional consequence some doctors may prefer not to disclose precise details of the means that will be used, confining themselves to the required statement of risks the procedure entails. From one standpoint this ought not to be surprising. Any number of patients facing imminent surgical procedures would prefer not to hear all details, lest the usual anxiety preceding invasive medical procedures become the more intense. This is likely the case with the abortion procedures here in issue.

It is, however, precisely this lack of information concerning the way in which the fetus will be killed that is of legitimate concern to the State. *Casey*, supra, at 873 (plurality opinion) ("States are free to enact laws to provide a reasonable framework for a woman to make a decision that has such profound and lasting meaning"). The State has an interest in ensuring so grave a choice is well informed. It is self-evident that a mother who comes to regret her choice to abort must struggle with grief more anguished and sorrow more profound when she learns, only after the event, what she once did not know: that she allowed a doctor to pierce the skull and vacuum the fast-developing brain of her unborn child, a child assuming the human form.

It is a reasonable inference that a necessary effect of the regulation and the knowledge it conveys will be to encourage some women to carry the infant to full term, thus reducing the absolute number of late-term abortions. The medical profession, furthermore, may find different and less shocking methods to abort the fetus in the second trimester, thereby accommodating legislative demand. The State's interest in respect for life is advanced by the dialogue that better informs the political and legal systems, the medical profession, expectant mothers, and society as a whole of the consequences that follow from a decision to elect a late-term abortion.

It is objected that the standard D&E is in some respects as brutal, if not more, than the intact D&E, so that the legislation accomplishes little. What we have already said, however, shows ample justification for the regulation. Partial-birth abortion, as defined by the Act, differs from a standard D&E because the former occurs when the fetus is partially outside the mother to the point of one of the Act's anatomical landmarks. It was reasonable for Congress to think that partial-birth abortion, more than standard D&E, "undermines the public's perception of the appropriate role of a physician during the delivery process, and perverts a process during which life is brought into the world." . . .

[The next question is] whether the Act has the effect of imposing an unconstitutional burden on the abortion right because it does not allow use of the barred procedure where " 'necessary, in appropriate medical judgment, for [the] preservation of the . . . health of the mother.' " [Ayotte v. Planned Parenthood of Northern New Eng., 546 U.S. 320, 327-328 (2006).] The prohibition in the Act would be unconstitutional, under precedents we here assume to be controlling, if it "subjected [women] to significant health risks." *Ayotte*, supra, at 328; see also *Casey*, supra, at 880 (opinion of the Court). . . . Respondents presented evidence that intact D&E may be the safest method of abortion, for reasons similar to those adduced in *Stenberg*. Abortion doctors testified, for example, that intact D&E decreases the risk of cervical laceration or uterine perforation because it requires fewer passes into the uterus with surgical instruments and does not require the removal of bony fragments of the dismembered fetus, fragments that may be sharp. [Respondents presented additional evidence on safety advantages.] These contentions were contradicted by other doctors who testified in the District Courts and before Congress. They concluded that the alleged health advantages were based on speculation without scientific studies to support them. They considered D&E always to be a safe alternative.

There is documented medical disagreement whether the Act's prohibition would ever impose significant health risks on women. [According to precedents, medical uncertainty] does not foreclose the exercise of legislative power in the abortion context any more than it does in other contexts. The medical uncertainty over whether the Act's prohibition creates significant health risks provides a sufficient basis to conclude in this facial attack that the Act does not impose an undue burden.

The conclusion that the Act does not impose an undue burden is supported by other considerations. Alternatives are available to the prohibited procedure. As we have noted, the Act does not proscribe [the standard] D&E. If the intact D&E procedure is truly necessary in some circumstances, it appears likely an injection that kills the fetus is an alternative under the Act that allows the doctor to perform the procedure. . . .

In reaching the conclusion the Act does not require a health exception, we [note that, as respondents pointed out,] and the District Courts recognized, some recitations in the Act are factually incorrect. Whether or not accurate at the time, some of the important findings have been superseded. [For example, despite Congress's findings, intact D&E is taught at medical schools, and a medical consensus does not exist that the procedure is never medically necessary.]

The considerations we have discussed support our further determination that these facial attacks should not have been entertained in the first instance. In these circumstances the proper means to consider exceptions is by as-applied challenge [in which the] nature of the medical risk can be better quantified and balanced than in a facial attack. . . . [Reversed.]

Justice GINSBURG, with whom Justice STEVENS, Justice SOUTER, and Justice BREYER join, dissenting. . . .

. . . Today's decision is alarming. It refuses to take *Casey* and *Stenberg* seriously. It tolerates, indeed applauds, federal intervention to ban nationwide a procedure found necessary and proper in certain cases by the American College of Obstetricians and Gynecologists (ACOG). It blurs the line, firmly drawn in *Casey*, between previability and postviability abortions. And, for the first time since *Roe*, the Court blesses a prohibition with no exception safeguarding a woman's health. . . .

. . . As *Casey* comprehended, at stake in cases challenging abortion restrictions is a woman's "control over her [own] destiny." 505 U.S., at 869 (plurality opinion). "There was a time, not so long ago," when women were "regarded as the center of home and family life, with attendant special responsibilities that precluded full and independent legal status under the Constitution." Id., at 896-897. Those views, this Court made clear in *Casey*, "are no longer consistent with our understanding of the family, the individual, or the Constitution." Women, it is now acknowledged, have the talent, capacity, and right "to participate equally in the economic and social life of the Nation." Their ability to realize their full potential, the Court recognized, is intimately connected to "their ability to control their reproductive lives." Thus, legal challenges to undue restrictions on abortion procedures do not seek to vindicate some generalized notion of privacy; rather, they center on a woman's autonomy to determine her life's course, and thus to enjoy equal citizenship stature.

In keeping with this comprehension of the right to reproductive choice, the Court has consistently required that laws regulating abortion, at any stage of pregnancy and in all cases, safeguard a woman's health. . . . In *Stenberg*, we expressly held that a statute banning intact D&E was unconstitutional in part because it lacked a health exception. [D]ivision in medical opinion "at most means uncertainty, a factor that signals the presence of risk, not its absence." "[A] statute that altogether forbids [intact D&E]. . . . consequently must contain a health exception." . . .

. . . The Court offers flimsy and transparent justifications for upholding a nationwide ban on intact D&E sans any exception to safeguard a women's health. [T]he Act scarcely furthers [the state's interest in preserving fetal life]: The law saves not a single fetus from destruction, for it targets only a method of performing abortion. . . . As another reason for upholding the ban, the Court emphasizes that the Act does not proscribe the nonintact D&E procedure. But why not, one might ask. Nonintact D&E could equally be characterized as "brutal," involving as it does "tearing [a fetus] apart" and "ripping off" its limbs. "The notion that either of these two equally gruesome procedures . . . is more akin to infanticide than the other, or that the State furthers any legitimate interest by banning one but not the other, is simply irrational." *Stenberg*, 530 U.S., at 946-947 (Stevens, J., concurring).

Delivery of an intact, albeit nonviable, fetus warrants special condemnation, the Court maintains, because a fetus that is not dismembered resembles an infant.

But so, too, does a fetus delivered intact after it is terminated by injection a day or two before the surgical evacuation, or a fetus delivered through medical induction or Caesarean. Yet, the availability of those procedures — along with D&E by dismemberment — the Court says, saves the ban on intact D&E from a declaration of unconstitutionality. Never mind that the procedures deemed acceptable might put a woman's health at greater risk.

Ultimately, the Court admits that "moral concerns" are at work, concerns that could yield prohibitions on any abortion. . . . By allowing such concerns to carry the day and case, overriding fundamental rights, the Court dishonors our precedent. See, e.g., *Casey*, 505 U.S., at 850 ("Some of us as individuals find abortion offensive to our most basic principles of morality, but that cannot control our decision. Our obligation is to define the liberty of all, not to mandate our own moral code."); Lawrence v. Texas, 539 U.S. 558, 571 (2003) (Though "for many persons [objections to homosexual conduct] are not trivial concerns but profound and deep convictions accepted as ethical and moral principles," the power of the State may not be used "to enforce these views on the whole society through operation of the criminal law." (citing *Casey*, 505 U.S., at 850)).

Revealing in this regard, the Court invokes an antiabortion shibboleth for which it concededly has no reliable evidence: Women who have abortions come to regret their choices, and consequently suffer from "severe depression and loss of esteem." Because of women's fragile emotional state and because of the "bond of love the mother has for her child," the Court worries, doctors may withhold information about the nature of the intact D&E procedure. The solution the Court approves, then, is not to require doctors to inform women, accurately and adequately, of the different procedures and their attendant risks. Instead, the Court deprives women of the right to make an autonomous choice, even at the expense of their safety.

This way of thinking reflects ancient notions about women's place in the family and under the Constitution — ideas that have long since been discredited.

. . . One wonders how long a line that saves no fetus from destruction will hold in face of the Court's "moral concerns." The Court's hostility to the right [that] *Roe* and *Casey* secured is not concealed. [T]he opinion refers to obstetrician-gynecologists and surgeons who perform abortions not by the titles of their medical specialties, but by the pejorative label "abortion doctor." A fetus is described as an "unborn child" and as a "baby". . . .

. . . As the Court wrote in *Casey*, "overruling *Roe*'s central holding would not only reach an unjustifiable result under principles of stare decisis, but would seriously weaken the Court's capacity to exercise the judicial power and to function as the Supreme Court of a Nation dedicated to the rule of law." 505 U.S., at 865. . . . Though today's opinion does not go so far as to discard *Roe* or *Casey*, the Court, differently composed than it was when we last considered a restrictive abortion regulation, is hardly faithful to our earlier invocations of "the rule of law" and the "principles of stare decisis." Congress imposed a ban despite our clear prior holdings that the State cannot proscribe an abortion procedure when its use is necessary to protect a woman's health. . . .

NOTES AND QUESTIONS: *ROE* AND *GONZALES*

(1) Significance of **Roe.**   What are the conflicting interests at stake in Roe v. Wade? How does the Court accommodate those interests? On what grounds does Justice Blackmun conclude that a woman's right to privacy "is broad enough to encompass a woman's decision whether or not to terminate her pregnancy"? Does Justice Blackmun recognize that the state has a legitimate interest in protecting "potential life," or does he assume that the state may only protect the life of a child after birth? How does Justice Blackmun determine when the state's interest in protecting prenatal life becomes a compelling interest? What justification does Blackmun give for concluding that the state's interest in protecting prenatal life grows "substantially as the woman approaches term"?

To what extent does *Gonzales* follow *Roe*? To what extent does it depart from it? Does abortion remain a "fundamental right"? Does it still rest on the right of privacy? What is the standard of review for restrictions on abortion in *Roe*? In *Gonzales*? How does Justice Kennedy's treatment in *Gonzales* of the conflicting interests at stake compare with *Roe*'s treatment of those interests? At what point in pregnancy does the state develop a substantial interest in protecting potential life, according to *Gonzales*? How does that differ from the point at which the state has an interest in protecting potential life, according to *Roe*?

(2) Viability as the Standard.   What is the definition of viability? What is its significance, according to *Roe*? On what ground does Justice Blackmun determine that the "compelling" point is at viability? How long will an infant born at full term be "viable" without human intervention and help? How does the legal significance of viability differ from its moral significance?

Under *Roe*'s trimester framework, virtually no regulation was permitted during the first trimester. Regulations designed to protect the woman's health were permitted during the second trimester until the point of viability. Finally, regulations designed to protect the potential life of the fetus were permitted only in the third trimester. The Court's adoption of viability as a benchmark in *Roe* was extremely controversial. See, e.g., John H. Ely, The Wages of Crying Wolf: A Comment on Roe v. Wade, 82 Yale L.J. 920, 924 n.1 (1973) (suggesting that the Court has mistaken "a definition for a syllogism"). Should the capacity to live independently be a reason to force a woman to allow the fetus's continued dependency on her? Cf. Judith J. Thompson, A Defense of Abortion, 1 Phil. & Pub. Aff. 47 (1971) (arguing that abortion should be morally permissible because a woman's right of bodily autonomy legitimates her right to deny the continued and traumatic use of her body for a nine-month period).

To what extent does *Gonzales* raise questions about the continued validity of the viability standard? Consider the majority's statement in *Gonzales* that "[t]he Act does apply both previability and postviability because, by common understanding and scientific terminology, a fetus is a living organism while within the womb, whether or not it is viable outside the womb." *Gonzales*, 127 S. Ct. at 1627.

Note that, at the time of Roe v. Wade, viability occurred at approximately 28 weeks. By the time of Planned Parenthood of Southeastern Pennsylvania v. Casey,

500 U.S. 833 (1992) (discussed infra), viability occurred at 23 to 24 weeks. Id. at 860. More recently, physicians set viability at 23 weeks. See Bill Would Establish Fetus Viability at 20 Weeks, Ft. Wayne News Sentinel, Feb. 18, 2005, at L3 (explaining viability and criticizing proposed Indiana legislation that set viability at 20 weeks as creating a standard lower than "medical science's ability to sustain a fetus").

(3) Fetal Rights.   In *Roe*, Justice Blackmun points out that the "unborn have never been recognized by the law as persons in the whole sense." Why does Justice Blackmun reject the contention that the fetus is a "person" for purposes of the Fourteenth Amendment? What difference does it make if a fetus is a "person" for these purposes?

Since *Roe*, the federal government and several states have recognized the unborn as "persons" in various legislation. For example, in 2004, Congress enacted the Unborn Victims of Violence Act (UVVA), Pub. L. No. 108-212, 118 Stat. 568 (codified at 18 U.S.C. §1841), criminalizing the act of killing or injuring an unborn child (at any period of gestation) during the commission of a federal crime involving a pregnant woman (i.e., recognizing two victims of the crime). The federal government also conferred legal rights on a fetus by revisions to the State Children's Health Insurance Program (SCHIP), 67 Fed. Reg. 61, 956 (Oct. 2, 2002) (codified at 42 C.F.R. pt. 457). SCHIP provides health insurance coverage to states for uninsured children whose families are at the poverty level. Regulations redefine "child" to include all children, from conception until age 19, regardless of a pregnant woman's immigration status.

Further, several states now have laws protecting the fetus in a variety of contexts. See, e.g., Tex. Civ. Prac. & Rem. Code Ann. §71.001(4) (Vernon Supp. 2006) (defining an "individual" for purposes of wrongful death liability as "an unborn child at every stage of gestation from fertilization until birth"). What are the implications of such legislation for abortion? See also the discussion of fetal homicide laws, infra p. 47. For a recent discussion of the tension between abortion prohibitions and statutes recognizing the fetus as a child, see Nora Christie Sandstad, Pregnant Women and the Fourteenth Amendment: A Feminist Examination of the Trend to Eliminate Women's Rights During Pregnancy, 26 Law & Ineq. J. 171 (2008).

(4) Sex Discrimination.   Abortion regulation raises obvious questions of sex discrimination. Only women get pregnant, and only women seek abortions.

> Laws restricting abortion so dramatically shape the lives of women, and only of women, that their denial of equality hardly needs detailed elaboration. While men retain the right to sexual and reproductive autonomy, restrictions on abortion deny that autonomy to women. Laws restricting access to abortion thereby place a real and substantial burden on women's ability to participate in society as equals. Even a woman who is not pregnant is inevitably affected by her knowledge of the power relationships created by a ban on abortion.

Laurence H. Tribe, Abortion: The Clash of Absolutes 105 (1990). Does equal protection doctrine provide a better rationale than privacy doctrine for the right to an abortion? What does Justice Ginsburg respond in her dissent in *Gonzales*?

See also Ruth Bader Ginsburg, Some Thoughts on Autonomy and Equality in Relation to Roe v. Wade, 63 N.C. L. Rev. 375, 386 (1985); Catharine A. MacKinnon, Privacy v. Equality: Beyond Roe v. Wade, in Feminism Unmodified: Discourses on Life and Law 93, 97 (1987).

(5) Abortion Regulation: The Road from **Roe** *to* **Gonzales.** Roe v. Wade produced a variety of hostile reactions, including efforts to enact constitutional amendments to prohibit abortion. Although abortion foes have been unsuccessful thus far in overturning *Roe*, they have enjoyed more success in attempts to place significant restrictions on abortion. Congress as well as many states have enacted numerous laws (discussed infra) that regulate abortion rights.

a. Public Funding for Abortion. If a woman lacks funds for an abortion, must a state provide one free? Not according to a trilogy of cases decided by the Supreme Court that permit states to refuse to provide Medicaid coverage for nontherapeutic abortions. See Beal v. Doe, 432 U.S. 438 (1977); Maher v. Roe, 432 U.S. 464 (1977); Poelker v. Doe, 432 U.S. 519 (1977). Also, in Harris v. McRae, 448 U.S. 297 (1980), the Supreme Court sustained the Hyde Amendment, a federal statute prohibiting the expenditure of federal Medicaid money for abortions except to preserve the woman's life. Further, in Webster v. Reproductive Health Servs., 491 U.S. 490 (1989), the Court relied on Harris v. McRae to uphold a statute prohibiting the use of public hospitals and medical staff in the performance of abortions.

Subsequently in 1993, Congress amended the Hyde Amendment to permit abortion services when a pregnancy resulted from rape or incest. More than one-third of the states refused to comply with that amendment. Federal courts ordered 11 states into compliance. National Abortion and Reproductive Rights Act League (NARAL), Fact Sheet: The Appropriations Process and Discriminatory Abortion Funding Restrictions 3 (Jan. 1, 2004). Currently, 32 states and the District of Columbia now follow the Hyde Amendment by funding abortions for Medicaid recipients only when the woman's life is endangered or the pregnancy results from rape or incest. Guttmacher Institute, State Politics in Brief: State Funding of Abortion Under Medicaid (July 1, 2008).

In 1997, Congress applied the Hyde Amendment to Medicaid recipients enrolled in managed care plans and, the following year, banned publicly funded abortions for the disabled (under the Medicare Program) except to preserve the life of the mother or in cases of rape or incest. NARAL Fact Sheet, supra, at 2-3. Similar funding restrictions currently apply to Native American women on reservations, military personnel (prohibiting even services paid for by private funds at military facilities overseas), and federal inmates. Id. at 4-6.

After Roe v. Wade and until 1976, all legal abortions performed annually at public hospitals were funded by Medicaid. Tribe, supra, at 151. By withdrawing Medicaid funding and permitting bans on abortion in public hospitals, has the state effectively deprived indigent women of the right to terminate a pregnancy? For indigent women, are these restrictions any different in effect from an outright prohibition?

b. Refusals to Provide Abortion Services: Conscience Clauses. In the wake of Roe v. Wade, states enacted "refusal clauses" that protect institutional and individual health care providers that wish to refuse to provide abortion services (or to provide referrals or abortion *counseling*, as discussed later). Currently, almost all states have laws that allow health care providers (both public and private) to refuse to provide abortion services on the basis of their moral or religious objections. See Guttmacher Institute, State Policies in Brief: Refusing to Provide Health Services 1 (Aug. 1, 2008) (stating that 46 states allow individual health care providers to refuse to provide abortion services). These refusal clauses have gradually been expanded to include a broader range of health care providers and health care services (such as contraception and sterilization), and to provide these "conscientious objectors" with immunity from any adverse employment action stemming from their refusals to provide services. See generally Maxine M. Harrington, The Ever-Expanding Health Care Conscience Clause: The Quest for Immunity in the Struggle Between Professional Duties and Moral Beliefs, 34 Fla. St. U. L. Rev. 779 (2007).

On the federal level, Congress enacted the Federal Refusal Clause (Consolidated Appropriations Act, 2005, Pub. L. No. 108-447, §508(d), 118 Stat. 2809, 3163, reenacted as Departments of Labor, Health and Human Services, and Education, and Related Agencies Appropriations Act, 2006, Pub. L. No. 109-149, §508(d), 119 Stat. 2833, 2879-2880; Continued in the Revised Continuing Appropriations Resolution, 2007, Pub. L. No. 110-5). The Federal Refusal Clause, commonly known as the Weldon Amendment (because it amended an appropriations bill funding health and human services and educational programs) denies federal funding to any federal or state agency or program that subjects an "institutional or individual health care entity" (defined broadly to include health care providers, health maintenance organizations, and health insurance plans) to "discrimination" because of the latter's refusal to provide abortion services or referrals. The Act was challenged by an organization representing federally funded family planning programs in National Family Planning and Reproductive Health Assn, Inc. v. Gonzales, 468 F.3d 826 (D.C. Cir. 2006), on the ground that the legislation's vagueness constituted a violation of the First Amendment and also that the legislation exceeded the limits of Congress's spending powers. The Court of Appeals remanded the case to the district court to dismiss for lack of jurisdiction, reasoning that the organization lacked standing because it did not face imminent injury.

Before leaving office, former President George W. Bush expanded the federal refusal law by eliminating federal funding for any health care provider who refuses to accommodate employees' right to refuse care (including services, information and counseling even in emergencies) based on their personal beliefs. Rob Stein, Rule Shields Health Workers Who Withhold Care Based on Beliefs, Dec. 19, 2008, at A10. However, shortly after President Barack Obama took office, he announced plans to rescind the Bush administration's Department of Health and Human Services policy expanding the provider conscience rule. David Stout, Moving Toward Undoing Rule on Abortion, N.Y. Times, Feb. 28, 2009, at A15.

c. Speech: Restrictions on Abortion Counseling.   Federal and state laws also regulate the provision of *information* about abortion by health care providers. Title X of the Public Health Service Act, 42 U.S.C. §§300-300a-6 (2000) provides public funding for family planning clinics that serve low-income clients. As enacted in 1970, the legislation prohibited funding of abortion but was silent with respect to abortion counseling and referral. In 1988, the Secretary of Health and Human Services promulgated regulations prohibiting service providers from providing abortion counseling and referral services (a so-called gag rule). In Rust v. Sullivan, 500 U.S. 173 (1991), the Supreme Court upheld the challenged regulations, rejecting claims that the regulations violated petitioners' (i.e., Title X grantees' and physicians') First Amendment rights. In response to plaintiffs' argument that the gag rule infringed on the fundamental right to abortion, the Court relied on the principle announced in *Maher*, *McRae*, and *Webster* to reiterate that there is no right to public funds to secure access to a particular benefit even if the right to such benefit is protected by the government.

Former President Bill Clinton rescinded the gag rule upon taking office. However, by 1999, anti-choice legislators forced him to reinstate it and to make it a global rule. In 2000, Congress repealed the global gag rule, but President George W. Bush reimposed it. The global gag rule prohibits the U.S. Agency for International Development (USAID), which supports family-planning services worldwide, from granting family-planning funds to any overseas health center unless the center promises that it will not spend its private, non-U.S. funds for abortions or abortion counseling and referrals. See NARAL, Global Gag Rule: A Flawed Policy That Sacrifices Women's Lives 1-2 (Jan. 1, 2008). President Barack Obama rescinded the global gag rule after taking office. Noam N. Levey, Obama Halts Abortion "Gag Rule" for Global Aid, Chi. Trib. Jan. 24, 2009, at 4.

d. Informed Consent Laws. A majority of states have enacted a special type of restriction on abortion counseling — a content-based restriction that takes the form of an abortion-specific informed consent law. (Prior to undergoing any medical procedure, physicians must secure a patient's informed consent by providing accurate, unbiased information about the risks, benefits, and alternatives to help the patient make an informed judgment about the proposed treatment.) In Planned Parenthood of Southeastern Pennsylvania v. Casey, 505 U.S. 833 (1992), the Supreme Court upheld the constitutionality of several provisions of Pennsylvania's content-specific informed consent law, including a 24-hour waiting period that followed on the heels of a physician's providing the woman with detailed information about the procedure, risks and alternatives, "probable gestational age of the unborn child," and the availability of printed materials on various alternatives to abortion (i.e., information on child support, adoption, and other services). Currently, 33 states have abortion-specific informed consent laws, and 24 states mandate a waiting period before an abortion. Guttmacher Institute, State Policies in Brief: Counseling and Waiting Period for Abortion 1 (July 1, 2008).

According to a recent 50-state study by the Guttmacher Institute, several states with content-based restrictions on abortion counseling mandate the disclosure of biased information based on an anti-abortion rationale. For example, five states furnish abortion counseling materials that include warnings about the disputed link between breast cancer and abortion. Seven states provide extremely negative views of the mental health consequences that women experience after an abortion (i.e., suicidal thoughts, eating disorders, posttraumatic stress disorder, etc.). Five states require that the woman be told that the state favors childbirth over abortion. Finally, five states require that the woman be informed about the fetus's ability to feel pain. Chinue Turner Richardson, Misinformed Consent: The Medical Accuracy of State-Developed Abortion Counseling Materials, Guttmacher Policy

Review (Fall 2006). According to the American Medical Association, medical researchers are not able to determine at what point in development, if at all, a fetus perceives pain. See id. at 3 (citing research).

South Dakota has the most extreme of the abortion-specific informed consent laws (S.D.C.L. §34-23A-10.1), requiring a physician to inform the patient that "the abortion will terminate the life of a whole, separate, unique living human being" and that "her existing constitutional rights with regards to that relationship will be terminated" by the abortion, and also that abortion poses risks of "depression and related psychological distress [and] increased risk of suicide ideation and suicide." Planned Parenthood of South Dakota, the only abortion provider in the state, challenged the law as a violation of physicians' right to free speech and an "undue burden" (discussed infra) on the woman's right to seek an abortion. In Planned Parenthood of Minnesota, North Dakota, South Dakota v. Rounds, 530 F.3d 724 (8th Cir. 2008), the Eighth Circuit overturned the preliminary injunction that prevented the law from taking effect, finding that the plaintiffs had not demonstrated a fair chance of success in challenging the statute as infringing on First Amendment grounds because it could not be shown that the disclosure was untruthful, misleading, or irrelevant to the patient's decision to have an abortion. In contrast, South Dakota voters twice rejected ballot measures that would have proscribed virtually all abortions. See Key Ballot Measures Nationwide, Orlando Sentinel, Nov. 6, 2008, at A14.

Another form of informed consent law is a fetal ultrasound law. For example, a proposed bill in South Carolina (H.B. 3355) would modify the state informed consent law ("Woman's Right to Know Act") to require that, prior to performing an abortion, the physician must perform an ultrasound that must be "reproduced and reviewed with the mother." Failure to follow these requirements would result in misdemeanor liability. See Matthew Gordon, State Attempts to Expand Abortion Informed Consent Requirements: New Life after Gonzales v. Carhart, 35 J.L. Med. & Ethics 751 (2007) (discussing the constitutionality of the South Carolina bill and the South Dakota statute).

Congress also considered the enactment of federal content-specific informed consent abortion counseling laws. In 2004, the "Unborn Child Pain Awareness Act of 2005" was first introduced in Congress. The proposed legislation includes a congressionally approved informed consent provision that requires abortion providers to notify patients about congressional findings on fetal pain as well as the option of administering anesthesia to the fetus. The measure was subsequently reintroduced in Congress (H.R. 3442, S. 356, 110th Cong. (2007)).

(6) The Undue Burden Standard. *Casey* announced the adoption of a new "undue burden" standard in place of *Roe*'s strict scrutiny test. After *Casey*, only those regulations that impose an "undue burden" on the woman's right to an abortion will be invalidated. How does the "undue burden" standard differ from *Roe*'s strict scrutiny test? According to the Court in *Casey* and *Gonzales*, what constitutes an "undue burden"? Why does the majority in *Gonzales* conclude that the federal partial-birth abortion ban does *not* impose an undue burden? How subjective is the "undue burden" standard? Is the adoption of the undue burden standard likely to help states draft regulations that are constitutionally permissible or to open the door to more litigation?

Did the challenged regulations in *Casey* (i.e., the requirements of mandatory pre-abortion counseling script and a 24-hour waiting period) constitute an undue burden on a woman's right to an abortion? What are the likely effects of a mandated disclosure requirement and a mandatory waiting period? Does the latter requirement, if it necessitates a woman making two trips to the abortion facility, impose an undue burden on a woman who must travel from another county or state for the abortion? On a woman with limited funds? On a battered woman who does not wish family members to discover the pregnancy? See Ted Joyce & Robert Kaestner, The Impact of Mississippi's Mandatory Delay Law on the Timing of Abortion, 32 Fam. Plan. Persp. 4 (2000) (finding that mandatory waiting periods result in women traveling to neighboring states to evade restrictions and to delay having the abortion performed, which may lead to health complications).

In the Court's evaluation in *Gonzales* of whether the partial-birth abortion ban constitutes an undue burden, the majority and dissenting justices disagree regarding the percentage of women for whom the ban was relevant (i.e., the correct denominator for the fraction). Justice Kennedy asserts that the question is how many women would be burdened out of "all instances in which the doctor proposes to use the prohibited procedure," and finds that fraction small enough to impose no undue burden overall. *Gonzales*, 127 S. Ct. at 1639. In contrast, Justice Ginsburg believes that the relevant denominator is "women who, in the judgment of their doctors, require an intact D&E because other procedures would place their health at risk," which led her to conclude that the "absence of a health exception burdens *all* women for whom it is relevant." Id. at 1651 (Ginsburg, J., dissenting). Whose views are more persuasive?

Recently, federal courts applied the undue burden standard to invalidate some state abortion restrictions. See, e.g., Northland Family Planning Clinic, Inc. v. Cox, 487 F.3d 323 (6th Cir. 2007) (striking down Michigan's "Legal Birth Definition Act," which banned previability abortion procedures); Richmond Med. Ctr. for Women v. Herring, 527 F.3d 128 (4th Cir. 2008) (invalidating Virginia's "partial-birth infanticide" ban).

Does state fetal pain legislation (discussed supra) constitute an undue burden? For contrasting views, see Hannah Stahle, Two Views on Fetal Pain Legislation: Fetal Pain Legislation: An Undue Burden, 10 Quinnipiac Health L.J. 251 (2007); Katherine E. Engelman, Two Views on Fetal Pain Legislation: Fetal Pain Legislation: Protection Against Pain Is Not an Undue Burden, 10 Quinnipiac Health L.J. 279 (2007).

(7) Maternal Health Exception. *Roe* required that restrictions on abortion contain exceptions to preserve the life or health of the mother. How does the Court in *Gonzales* accommodate the state's interest in protecting women's health in abortion decision making? How can the Court's decision in *Gonzales* be reconciled with *Roe* regarding the issue of the preservation of the health of the mother? How does the majority in *Gonzales* treat the absence of a health exception in the statute? How does the dissent? Does the majority's seeming reliance on congressional findings that the procedure in question is never medically necessary provide adequate justification for their decision? Even when there were errors in Congress's findings, as noted by both the majority and the dissent?

(8) Partial-Birth Abortion Bans.   Prior to *Gonzales*, more than half the states had partial-birth abortion bans. See Guttmacher Institute, State Policies in Brief: Bans on "Partial-Birth" Abortion 1 (July 1, 2008) (pointing to 31 states with bans that apply either throughout pregnancy or after viability; of these 31 bans, 27 do not contain a health exception). In a precursor to *Gonzales*, the U.S. Supreme Court considered a Nebraska partial-birth abortion ban statute. Stenberg v. Carhart, 530 U.S. 914 (2000). *Stenberg* found that the Nebraska ban was unconstitutional because, inter alia, the law lacked a health exception for the mother. Why did *Gonzales* uphold the federal partial-birth abortion ban despite the lack of such an exception? How does *Gonzales* distinguish the state partial-birth abortion ban that the Supreme Court invalidated in *Stenberg*? Does *Gonzales* inappropriately sanction legislative intrusion into the realm of medical decision making? See generally Comment, Gonzales v. Carhart, 121 Harv. L. Rev. 265 (2007) (arguing that the Court deferred too greatly to congressional medical findings regarding the necessity of the abortion procedure). Why does *Gonzales* conclude with the assertion of a preference for as-applied changes instead of facial challenges to abortion restrictions? Do you agree with Justice Kennedy that the availability of as-applied challenges to the Act is sufficient to protect exceptions for women's health? *Gonzales*, 127 S. Ct. at 1638-1639.

(9) Physicians' Role.   Note how the role of the physician evolved from *Roe* to *Gonzales*. How does the Supreme Court in *Roe* and *Gonzales* regard the role of the physician in the woman's decision to have an abortion? What should be the role of the physician in such an important decision? What is the likely impact of partial-birth abortion bans on health care providers who perform abortions? See Michael F. Green, The Intimidation of American Physicians — Banning Partial Birth Abortion, 356 New Eng. J. Med. 2128 (2007). Some states have now "privatized" bans on abortion by enacting tort remedies for provision of an abortion — creating a tort for which there can be no defense and no cap on the amount of liability (thereby giving women who obtain abortions a civil cause of action against their abortion providers). What is the likely impact of these new tort actions? See Maya Manian, Privatizing Bans on Abortion: Eviscerating Constitutional Rights Through Tort Remedies, 80 Temp. L. Rev. 123 (2007).

The number of physicians who perform abortions is dwindling. Since 1982, the number of abortion providers nationally has diminished by 37 percent. "Of the remaining practitioners, 57 percent are older than 50 and are expected to retire within the next decade." Grace Hammond, Last of the Old Guard: Abortion Providers Retire in the West, Leaving Their Posts Empty, Planet News, July 30, 2008, available at *http://planetjh.com/news/A_103980.aspx* (last visited Aug. 1, 2008). Eighty-seven percent of all U.S. counties lacked an abortion provider in 2005. Guttmacher Institute, Facts on Induced Abortion in the United States (July 2008).

(10) Technological Advances, Birth Control and Abortion.   What role do modern medical advances play in a woman's right to an abortion? Consider the "abortion pill" (RU-486, or mifepristone), which can be taken to induce an abortion during the first two months of pregnancy. In 2000, the Food and Drug Administration approved RU-486 for general use as a method of medical abortion (i.e., an abortion accomplished through medication). How does the availability of an "abortion pill" change the debate over abortion? Under *Gonzales*, can the

government ban abortions accomplished through medical means, such as RU-486, so long as surgical abortions remain available? Must there be a health exception? Can the government ban the use of modern methods of emergency contraception that prevent pregnancy by inhibiting ovulation, fertilization, or implantation of fertilized ova?

(11) Morality. Philosophers and moralists have long debated the morality of abortion and the legitimacy of state intervention to protect prenatal life. Compare John T. Noonan, A Private Choice (1979) (arguing that a fetus, as a human organism, should be accorded full moral status from conception) with Michael Tooley, Abortion and Infanticide, 2 Phil. & Pub. Aff. 37 (1972) (contending that the moral significance of personhood lies in conscious experience, a stance that makes abortion (and infanticide) morally permissible).

In *Gonzales*, the Court asserts that "[w]hether to have an abortion requires a difficult and painful moral decision," 127 S. Ct. at 1634, and that the "additional ethical and moral concerns" implicated in the procedure thus justified Congress's prohibition. Id. at 1633. Consider also the rhetoric of the Court's graphic descriptions of partial-birth abortion (some of which were omitted). In Lawrence v. Texas, 539 U.S. 558 (2003), the Supreme Court invalidated a state sodomy statute by holding that substantive due process protects the right to make decisions about private sexual conduct. In so doing, the Court asserted that "this Court's obligation is to define the liberty of all, not to mandate its own moral code" and cited *Casey*, 505 U.S. at 850. How are *Gonzales*'s moral overtones in tension with *Casey* and *Lawrence*? Cf. Steven G. Calabresi, Substantive Due Process After Gonzales v. Carhart, 106 Mich. L. Rev. 1517, 1521 (2008) ("Clearly, the *Gonzales* Court takes a different view from the *Casey* and *Lawrence* Courts when it comes to government enforcement of morals legislation"). Who should decide moral issues such as these about abortion: the family, legislature, or courts?

(12) The Court's Characterization of Women's Role in Abortion. The *Gonzales* majority justifies abortion restrictions, in part, as a means of protecting women from decisions they do not understand and might later come to regret. To what extent does the majority's reasoning in *Gonzales* indicate that protecting women from postabortion regret is a more important value than protecting them from other health risks? How does the new abortion rationale differ from the state's rationale in protecting women according to *Roe*? What does this protective rationale reveal about the Court's assumptions about women and motherhood? In her dissent, how does Justice Ginsburg respond to this rationale and these assumptions? Does this new characterization of abortion restrictions deny women the equal protection of the law? See Reva B. Siegel, The New Politics of Abortion: An Equality Analysis of Women-Protective Abortion Restrictions, 2007 U. Ill. L. Rev. 991 (arguing that the Equal Protection Clause restrains the government from enforcing gender-based assumptions in the regulation of abortion).

(13) Clinic Violence. Clinic violence also affects access to abortion. Since 1977, there have been 5,600 reported acts of violence against abortion providers (i.e., bombings, arsons, death threats, kidnappings, and assaults) and 132,000 reported acts of distruption (i.e., bomb threats and harassing phone calls). Since 1993, anti-abortion protests have resulted in the deaths of three doctors, two clinic employees, a clinic escort, and a security guard. NARAL, Fact Sheet: Clinic

Violence and Intimidation 1 (Dec. 1, 2007). In response to such violence, Congress enacted the Freedom of Access to Clinic Entrances Act of 1994 (FACE), 18 U.S.C. §248 (2000), which bars force, threat of force, or physical obstruction aimed at injuring, intimidating, or interfering with any patients or providers of reproductive health services. Violators face criminal and civil penalties. States also have enacted legislation modeled after the federal act. NARAL, Fact Sheet, supra (listing 16 states and the District of Columbia).

In Planned Parenthood of the Columbia/Williamette, Inc. v. American Coalition of Life Activists, 290 F.3d 1058 (9th Cir. 2002), a federal court of appeals upheld a permanent injunction enjoining the posting by "wanted posters" on the Internet, listing personal information (i.e., addresses, license plates) of health care providers. The court determined that the posters constituted "true threats" in light of prior incidents when physicians identified on the Web site were murdered. In addition, the court upheld a jury verdict ordering the creators of the Web site to pay compensatory damages to the abortion providers. See Adam Liptak, Posters by Abortion Foes Posed Threat, Court Rules, N.Y. Times, May 17, 2002, at A20.

Several federal courts have upheld the constitutionality of FACE against challenges based on the First Amendment, vagueness and overbreadth, equal protection, the Commerce Clause, and the Tenth Amendment. See, e.g., U.S. v. Kopp, 2005 WL 839672 (W.D.N.Y. 2005); Norton v. Ashcroft, 298 F.3d 547 (6th Cir. 2002). But cf. U.S. v. Bird, 401 F.3d 633 (5th Cir. 2005) (holding that passage of FACE was beyond Congress's authority under the Commerce Clause).

The Supreme Court also has addressed clinic protests. See Scheidler v. National Organization for Women, 537 U.S. 393 (2003) (holding that pro-life activities aimed at disrupting clinic access, although unlawful, did not amount to extortion, a predicate offense for liability under the Racketeer Influenced and Corrupt Organizations Act, 18 U.S.C. §1961 (2000)); Hill v. Colorado, 530 U.S. 703 (2000) (upholding the constitutionality of a restriction on protestors to more than eight feet from any person near a health care facility, absent consent, as a permissible content-neutral regulation).

(14) Epilogue.   Several years after Roe v. Wade, Norma McCorvey (identified as the plaintiff "Jane Roe"), was working at a Texas abortion clinic when the anti-abortion group Operation Rescue moved in next door. Influenced by her contacts with the pro-life staff, McCorvey experienced a change of heart, leading to her conversion to Catholicism, and her decision to join the opponents of legalized abortion. Today, she is a mother of three with two grandchildren and "100 percent pro-life." Matt VandeBunte, Roe v. Wade Figure Brings Story to GR, Grand Rapids Press, Mar. 25, 2008, at B4. In McCorvey v. Hill, 385 F.3d 846 (5th Cir. 2004), she filed a motion for relief from judgment in which she sought to have the district court revisit Roe v. Wade, based on "new" scientific data that abortion harms women. The Fifth Circuit Court of Appeals affirmed the district court's denial of her motion, finding that plaintiff lacked standing because the case was moot. The Supreme Court denied certiorari. 543 U.S. 1154 (2005).

Abortion regulation is relevant also to other issues of reproductive control. For a discussion of minors' contraceptive rights, see Chapter 6, and new reproductive technologies, see Chapter 5.

Legal Paternalism: Forcing Medical Treatment on Pregnant Women

The Supreme Court, in *Roe, Casey,* and *Gonzales,* recognizes that the state has an interest in protecting potential life during pregnancy. To what extent should the state be able to assert its interest in protecting potential life as a justification for influencing the behavior of a mother during pregnancy? Should the state be able to compel the pregnant woman to take actions thought necessary to protect the health, present and future, of the unborn child? Even before the point of viability?

Jefferson v. Griffin Spalding County Hospital Authority
274 S.E.2d 457 (Ga. 1981)

Per Curiam.

On Thursday, January 22, 1981, the Griffin Spalding County Hospital Authority petitioned the Superior Court of Butts County, as a court of equity, for an order authorizing it to perform a caesarean section and any necessary blood transfusions upon the defendant . . . in the event she presented herself to the hospital for delivery of her unborn child, which was due on or about Monday, January 26. The superior court conducted an emergency hearing on Thursday, January 22, and entered the following order:

> Defendant is in the thirty-ninth week of pregnancy. In the past few weeks she has presented herself to Griffin Spalding County Hospital for pre-natal care. The examining physician has found and defendant has been advised that she has a complete placenta previa; that the afterbirth is between the baby and the birth canal; that it is virtually impossible that this condition will correct itself prior to delivery; and that it is a 99% certainly that the child cannot survive natural childbirth (vaginal delivery). The chances of defendant surviving vaginal delivery are no better than 50%.
>
> The examining physician is of the opinion that a delivery by cesarean section prior to labor beginning would have an almost 100% chance of preserving the life of the child, along with that of defendant.
>
> On the basis of religious beliefs, defendant has advised the Hospital that she does not need surgical removal of the child and will not submit to it. Further, she refuses to take any transfusion of blood.
>
> The Hospital is required by its own policies to treat any patient seeking emergency treatment. It seeks authority of the Court to administer medical treatment to defendant to save the life of herself and her unborn child.
>
> The child is, as a matter of fact, viable and fully capable of sustaining life independent of the mother (defendant). The issue is whether this unborn child has any legal right to the protection of the Court. . . .
>
> Because the life of defendant and of the unborn child are, at the moment, inseparable, the Court deems it appropriate to infringe upon the wishes of the mother to the extent it is necessary to give the child an opportunity to live.
>
> Accordingly, the plaintiff hospitals are hereby authorized to administer to defendant all medical procedures deemed necessary by the attending physician to preserve the life of defendant's unborn child. This authority shall be effective

only if defendant voluntarily seeks admission to either of plaintiff's hospitals for the emergency delivery of the child.

The Court has been requested to order defendant to submit to surgery before the natural childbirth process (labor) begins. The Court is reluctant to grant this request and does not do so at this time. However, should some agency of the State seek such relief through intervention in this suit or in a separate proceeding, the Court will promptly consider such request.

On Friday, January 23, the Georgia Department of Human Resources, acting through the Butts County Department of Family and Children Services, petitioned the Juvenile Court of Butts County for temporary custody of the unborn child, alleging that the child was a deprived child without proper parental care necessary for his or her physical health (see Code Ann. §24A-401(h)(1)), and praying for an order requiring the mother to submit to a caesarean section. After appointing counsel for the parents and for the child, the court conducted a joint hearing in both the superior court and juvenile court cases and entered the following order on the afternoon of January 23:

At the proceeding held today, Jessie Mae Jefferson and her husband, John W. Jefferson were present and represented by counsel, Hugh Glidewell, Jr. Richard Milam, Attorney at Law, represented the interests of the unborn child.

Based on the evidence presented, the Court finds that Jessie Mae Jefferson is due to begin labor at any moment. There is a 99 to 100 percent certainty that the unborn child will die if she attempts to have the child by vaginal delivery. . . . There is a 50 percent chance that Mrs. Jefferson herself will die if vaginal delivery is attempted. There is an almost 100 percent chance that [the baby and] Mrs. Jefferson will survive if a delivery by Caesarean section is done prior to the beginning of labor. . . .

Mrs. Jefferson and her husband have refused and continue to refuse to give consent to a Caesarean section. This refusal is based entirely on the religious beliefs of Mr. and Mrs. Jefferson. They are of the view that the Lord has healed her body and that whatever happens to the child will be the Lord's will.

Based on these findings, the Court concludes and finds as a matter of law that this child is a viable human being and entitled to the protection of the Juvenile Court Code of Georgia. The Court concludes that this child is without the proper parental care and subsistence necessary for his or her physical life and health.

Temporary custody of the unborn child is hereby granted to the State of Georgia Department of Human Resources and the Butts County Department of Family and Children Services. The Department shall have full authority to make all decisions, including giving consent to the surgical delivery appertaining to the birth of this child. The temporary custody of the Department shall terminate when the child has been successfully brought from its mother's body into the world or until the child dies, whichever shall happen.

Because of the unique nature of these cases, the powers of the Superior Court of Butts County are invoked and the defendant, Jessie Mae Jefferson, is hereby Ordered to submit to a sonogram (ultrasound). . . . Should said sonogram indicate to the attending physician that the complete placenta previa is still blocking the child's passage into this world, Jessie Mae Jefferson, is Ordered to submit to a Caesarean section and related procedures. . . .

The Court finds that the State has an interest in the life of this unborn, living human being. The Court finds that the intrusion involved into the life of Jessie Mae Jefferson and her husband, John W. Jefferson, is outweighed by the duty of the State to protect a living, unborn human being from meeting his or her death before being given the opportunity to live.

This Order shall be effective at 10:00 a.m. on Saturday, January 24, 1981, unless a stay is granted by the Supreme Court of Georgia or some other Court having the authority to stay an Order of this Court.

[The parents filed a motion for a stay, which was denied.]

HILL, Presiding Justice, concurring.

The power of a court to order a competent adult to submit to surgery is exceedingly limited. Indeed, until this unique case arose, I would have thought such power to be nonexistent. Research shows that the courts generally have held that a competent adult has the right to refuse necessary lifesaving surgery and medical treatment (i.e., has the right to die) where no state interest other than saving the life of the patient is involved. Anno. Patient's Right to Refuse Treatment, 93 A.L.R.3d 67, §3 (1979).

On the other hand, one court has held that an expectant mother in the last weeks of pregnancy lacks the right to refuse necessary life saving surgery and medical treatment where the life of the unborn child is at stake. Raleigh Fitkin-Paul Morgan Memorial Hospital v. Anderson, [201 A.2d 537 (N.J. 1964)]; see also Re Melideo, 88 Misc.2d 974, 390 N.Y.S.2d 523 (1976); Re Yetter, 62 Pa. D. & C.2d 619, 623 (1973).

The Supreme Court has recognized that the state has an interest in protecting the lives of unborn, viable children (viability usually occuring at about 7 months, or 28 weeks). Roe v. Wade, 410 U.S. 113, 160, 164-165 (1973). . . .

In denying the stay of the trial court's order and thereby clearing the way for immediate reexamination by sonogram and probably for surgery, we weighed the right of the mother to practice her religion and to refuse surgery on herself, against her unborn child's right to live. We found in favor of her child's right to live.

Although we are not called upon here to decide whether the intervention of the juvenile court was necessary, I for one approve the trial court's action in exercising jurisdiction over the unborn child as juvenile judge and over the mother as judge of a court of equity. According to the testimony, this child was facing almost certain death, and was being deprived of the opportunity to live. For this reason, Code Ann. §24A-401(h) (5) is inapplicable.[1] . . .

SMITH, Justice, concurring.

The free exercise of religion is, of course, one of our most precious freedoms. . . . The courts have, however, drawn a distinction between the free exercise of religious belief which is constitutionally protected against any infringement and religious practices that are inimical or detrimental to public health or welfare which are not. . . .

---

[1] According to newspaper reports, "a third ultrasound test performed Friday night showed the placenta had moved — a most unusual occurrence . . ." Atlanta Journal/Constitution, January 25, 1981.

In the instant case, it appears that there is no less burdensome alternative for preserving the life of a fully developed fetus than requiring its mother to undergo surgery against her religious convictions. Such an intrusion by the state would be extraordinary, presenting some medical risk to both the mother and the fetus. However, the state's compelling interest in preserving the life of this fetus is beyond dispute. See Roe v. Wade, supra; Code §26-1202 et seq. Moreover, the medical evidence indicates that the risk to the fetus and the mother presented by a Caesarean section would be minimal, whereas, in the absence of surgery, the fetus would almost certainly die and the mother's chance of survival would be no better than 50 percent. Under these circumstances, I must conclude that the trial court's order is not violative of the First Amendment, notwithstanding that it may require the mother to submit to surgery against her religious beliefs. See Raleigh Fitkin-Paul Memorial Hospital v. Anderson, supra; see also Green v. Green, 448 Pa. 338, 292 A.2d 387 (1972).

We deal here with an apparent life and death emergency; questions relating to the jurisdiction of the lower court are not our primary concern.

Code §24A-301 sets forth the jurisdiction of the juvenile courts. It provides in pertinent part: "(a) The court shall have exclusive original jurisdiction over *juvenile* matters and shall be the sole court for initiating action: (1) Concerning any *child* . . . (C) Who is alleged to be deprived . . ." (Emphasis supplied.). Code §24A-401 defines the term "child" as "any individual under the age of 17 years." I believe the legislature intended that the juvenile courts exercise jurisdiction only where a child has seen the light of day. I am aware of no "child deprivation" proceeding wherein the "child" was unborn.

This is a case of first impression, and the trial court, in an attempt to cover all possible ground, rendered its judgment "both as a Juvenile Court and under the broad powers of the Superior Court of Butts County." As the trial court's action was a proper exercise of its equitable jurisdiction with respect to both the mother and the fetus and its decision on the merits a correct one, I fully concur in the denial of appellant's motion for stay. . . .

QUESTIONS ON INTERVENTION DURING PREGNANCY

(1) Epilogue. A few days after the Georgia Supreme Court's order, Ms. Jefferson delivered a healthy baby without any need for surgical intervention. The "99% certainty that the child cannot survive natural childbirth" was probably an inaccurate estimate. See George J. Annas, Forced Cesareans: The Most Unkindest Cut of All, Hastings Center Rep. 16 (June 1982) (also citing another case where the woman was forced to undergo a Caesarean because a fetal monitor indicated signs of fetal distress which turned out in fact to be significantly overstated). If it is difficult to predict the risks to the woman and the fetus, should physicians (and courts) defer to the woman's preference?

How is a judge, faced with an emergency request for an order compelling a Caesarean section, to evaluate the physician's claims of benefits and risks? See generally Joel J. Finer, Toward Guidelines for Compelling Cesarean Surgery: Of Rights, Responsibility, and Decisional Authenticity, 76 Minn. L. Rev. 239 (1991) (proposing guidelines for compulsory Caesarean sections balancing the mother's decision, the net gain or loss in human life, bodily integrity, and privacy rights).

(2) Justifications for Intervention. Is a state justified in requiring a Caesarean section, or in regulating abortion, to protect a woman's health if she is prepared to accept the risks? As Justice Hill's concurring opinion indicates, ordinarily a state cannot compel a competent adult to accept medical treatment. See, e.g., Cruzan v. Director, Missouri Dept. of Health, 497 U.S. 261, 262 (1990) ("a competent person has a liberty interest under the Due Process Clause in refusing unwanted medical treatment"). Should it matter that a woman is pregnant?

Can you think of other examples of legal paternalism (i.e., where the state prohibits individuals from engaging in conduct that is harmful only to themselves or that requires individuals to take self-protective measures)? For example, some states require motorists to wear seat belts and compel motorcyclists to wear helmets. See, e.g., Ohio Rev. Code Ann. §4513.263 (West 1999 & Supp. 2007) (seat belts); N.Y. Veh. & Traf. §381 (McKinney 2005 & Supp. 2008); Wash. Rev. Code Ann. §46.37.530 (West 2001 & Supp. 2008) (helmets). Although arguably the state's interest in preserving life is even greater than its interest in protecting health and safety, the underlying justifications for the religious objection cases (of which *Jefferson* is an example) are unclear. Although there are numerous cases in which courts have compelled unwilling patients to submit to medical treatment, the decisions often rely not on a compelling state interest to protect the health or life of the individual but on a desire to protect others. Courts have intervened typically "only when the lives of third parties were jeopardized or when the patient was not competent to refuse care." Barry Nobel, Religious Healing in the Courts: The Liberties and Liabilities of Patients, Parents, and Healers, 16 U. Puget Sound L. Rev. 599, 617 (1993). Does this suggest that there are few situations where a course of action only affects the actor? Or that legal paternalism is an accepted justification for state action, John Stuart Mill notwithstanding?[21]

(3) Problem. Simmone Ikerd pleads guilty to welfare fraud. Simmone is a drug addict who is 11 weeks pregnant and is undergoing treatment at a methadone clinic. She is sentenced to five years' probation, conditioned upon completion of drug treatment. Subsequently, she appears in court for a probation violation, i.e., failure to appear for a drug test (she claims she had to leave the test site to take an older child to the doctor). Believing that the only place where Simmone's addiction and the health of her fetus could be addressed is a correctional facility, the judge sentences her to prison for the duration of her pregnancy. The judge explains that if Simmone loses the baby, he will reconsider the sentence. She appeals. What result? See State v. Ikerd, 850 A.2d 516 (N. J. Super. Ct. App. Div. 2004). See generally April L. Cherry, The Detention, Confinement, and Incarceration of Pregnant Women for the Benefit of Fetal Health, 16 Colum. J. Gender & Law 147 (2007).

Given the important influence of prenatal care, consider the range of ways that conduct during pregnancy may affect the baby's well-being. Could a state require prenatal care for all pregnant women? Even during the first six months? Regulate

---

[21] For two classic articles analyzing the philosophical justifications for legal paternalism, see Joel Feinberg, Legal Paternalism, 1 Canadian J. Phil. 105 (1971); Gerald Dworkin, Paternalism, in Morality and the Law (Richard A. Wasserstrom ed. 1971).

the diet of pregnant women or prohibit them from using certain drugs (e.g., caffeine) not otherwise illegal? Make it a criminal offense to smoke or drink alcohol? Compel a diabetic to accept insulin to protect the fetus? Make public health benefits contingent on a pregnant woman's submission to physical examination or abstention from drugs or alcohol? What guidance do *Roe, Casey*, and *Gonzales* provide?

Suppose that surgery on the fetus before birth could correct a severe birth defect. Could a state order a pregnant woman to undergo fetal surgery? See Krista L. Newkirk, Note, State-Compelled Fetal Surgery: The Viability Test Is Not Viable, 4 Wm. & Mary J. Women & L. 467 (1997). Could a state compel prenatal genetic testing of a pregnant woman at risk of giving birth to a child with a defect? See Wendy E. Roop, Note, Not in My Womb: Compelled Prenatal Genetic Testing, 27 Hastings Const. L.Q. 397 (2000). Similarly, could a state force a pregnant woman who is HIV-positive to take medicine that would protect her unborn fetus? See Andrea Marsh, Testing Pregnant Women and Newborns for HIV: Legal and Ethical Responses to Public Health Efforts to Prevent Pediatric AIDS, 13 Yale J.L. & Feminism 195 (2001).

Should a court be able to appoint a guardian ad litem to represent the interests of the unborn child if the mother is unable to provide proper prenatal care or to make decisions to protect the fetus's health? See In re Guardianship of J.D.S. v. Department of Children and Families, 864 So. 2d 534 (Fla. Dist. Ct. App. 2004) (concluding that the state guardianship statute did not cover fetuses and adequate safeguards existed to ensure that J.D.S.'s guardian did not "act capriciously or cavalierly when considering the health of the incapacitated mother and fetus"). Id. at 539.

(4) Benefit vs. Risk.   In *Jefferson,* the court believed that requiring a Caesarean in the circumstances would save the baby and reduce a perceived risk to the mother's life. The intervention was seen, in other words, as benefiting both the mother and the child. Suppose a mother refused a Caesarean in circumstances where her refusal created no risks to her own life or health but grave risks for the unborn child. In such circumstances, would it be appropriate to require a Caesarean, which itself creates some risk for the mother?

In Baby Boy Doe v. Mother Doe, 632 N.E.2d 326 (Ill. App. Ct. 1994), a pregnant woman refused, on religious grounds, a Caesarean section that was recommended because the placenta of her 35-week fetus was receiving insufficient oxygen. The Illinois appellate court denied the state's request to order the forced Caesarean. Refusing to balance fetal rights versus the woman's rights, the court held that a woman's competent choice to refuse "medical treatment as invasive as a cesarean" must be honored, even in circumstances where the choice may be harmful to her fetus. Id. at 330.

Baby Boy Doe, supra, left open the question whether blood transfusions (considerably less invasive than Caesarean sections) could be ordered for a pregnant woman. In In re Fetus Brown, 689 N.E.2d 397 (Ill. App. Ct. 1997), a woman who was 34 weeks pregnant lost more blood than anticipated during an operation, posing a life-threatening risk to the patient and her fetus. The patient refused, on religious grounds, the recommended transfusion. The circuit court ordered the blood transfusion. The appellate court reversed. Applying *Baby Boy Doe,* the appellate court reiterated that the state may not balance interests and may not override a competent woman's treatment decision to save the life of her viable fetus. These cases may signify a change in judicial attitudes toward legal intevention for pregnant women.

See also David M. Caruso, Childbirth Choices Debated, L.A. Times, May 30, 2004, at A19 (citing a survey by University of Chicago researchers in 2002 finding that 4 percent of directors of maternal-fetal medicine fellowship programs believe pregnant women should be required to undergo Caesareans for the sake of their fetuses compared to 47 percent in 1987). But cf. Pemberton v. Tallahassee Regional Med. Ctr., 66 F. Supp. 2d 1247 (N.D. Fla. 1999) (holding that mother's constitutional rights were not violated by court-ordered Caesarean when she insisted on vaginal delivery against medical advice).

(5) Religious Justification. Reported cases suggest that the most common reason for refusal of treatment by pregnant women is religious belief. See, e.g., *Jefferson,* supra; Taft v. Taft, 446 N.E.2d 395 (Mass. 1983); Raleigh Fitkin-Paul Morgan Memorial Hosp. v. Anderson, 201 A.2d 537 (N.J. 1964), *cert. denied,* 377 U.S. 985 (1964). Should the religious beliefs of a pregnant woman matter when the survival of the fetus is at risk? See generally April L. Cherry, The Free Exercise Rights of Pregnant Women Who Refuse Medical Treatment, 69 Tenn. L. Rev. 563 (2002). Should it be easier to intervene if the woman's justification is not religious? Or if she refuses to give a reason? See Caruso, supra (citing case of hospital that obtained a court order to compel a Caesarean for a woman with a normal history of delivering large babies who chose natural childbirth).

(6) Applicable Standard. By what standard should a court consider and balance the risks and benefits for the mother and child in deciding whether to intervene? May the state then intervene solely on the fetus's behalf without regard to the mother? Or order a procedure that creates a serious risk to the mother's life to save the child? In In re A.C., 533 A.2d 611 (D.C. 1987), *reh'g granted, vacated,* 539 A.2d 203 (D.C. 1988), a judge ordered a Caesarean section on a terminally ill woman, A.C., who was 26 weeks pregnant, without her consent and despite the objections of her family, physicians, and the hospital obstetric staff. The baby died almost immediately, and two days later A.C. died. The surgery was listed as a contributing cause of her death. On appeal, a three-judge panel of the District of Columbia Court of Appeals held that in the constitutionally mandated balancing test between the life of the women and the life of the fetus, a pregnant women's wishes may be overridden if she is not in "good health," stating that the "Caesarean section would not significantly affect A.C.'s condition because she had, at best, two days left. . . ." 533 A.2d at 617.

Vacating the earlier opinion and granting a rehearing en banc, the Court of Appeals held that a terminally ill pregnant woman has the right to determine the course of her own medical treatment unless she is incompetent or unable to provide informed consent, in which case her decision must be ascertained via substituted judgment. In re A.C., 573 A.2d 1235 (D.C. 1990).

(7) Autonomy vs. Equality. What implication does recognition of fetal rights, and thereby overriding the pregnant woman's autonomy to control her life during her pregnancy, have for women's equality? An empirical study of 21 court-ordered obstetrical procedures reveals that orders are obtained in 86 percent

of the cases (most frequently in cases involving minority women in teaching hospitals or on public assistance). The authors conclude: "Clearly court orders force women to assume medical risks and forfeit their legal autonomy in a manner not required of competent men or non-pregnant women. . . ." Veronica B. Kolder et al., Court-Ordered Obstetrical Interventions, 316 N. Eng. J. Med. 1192, 1194 (May 7, 1987). Also, what is the implication of framing the issue as a "maternal-fetal" conflict? See April L. Cherry, *Roe's* Legacy: The Nonconsensual Medical Treatment of Pregnant Women and Implications for Female Citizenship, 6 U. Pa. J. Const. L. 723 (2004) (suggesting that compelled medical treatment of pregnant women subordinates women to their reproductive capacity and state-sanctioned mothering roles); Michelle Oberman, Mothers and Doctors' Orders: Unmasking the Doctor's Fiduciary Role in Maternal-Fetal Conflicts, 94 Nw. U. L. Rev. 451 (2000) (arguing that this paradigm ignores the role played by doctors in undermining the autonomy rights of their pregnant patients).

A related problem is the inability of pregnant women to execute living wills. All 50 states and the District of Columbia authorize the use of either a living will or power of attorney (or both) for incompetent patients. However, a majority of states prohibit the withdrawal of life support in cases of pregnant women. Does the state's interest in protecting the unborn child justify limiting the mother's exercise of her "right to die"? Are such limits constitutional? See Emma Murphy Sisti, Note, Die Free or Live: The Constitutionality of New Hampshire's Living Will Pregnancy Exception, 30 Vt. L. Rev. 143 (2005).

(8) Discriminatory Application?   There is some evidence to suggest that physicians are more likely to intervene to compel Caesareans and other invasive procedures if the mother is a woman of color or a member of a lower socioeconomic class. See Deborah J. Krauss, Regulating Women's Bodies: The Adverse Effect of Fetal Rights Theory on Childbirth Decisions and Women of Color, 26 Harv. C.R.-C.L. L. Rev. 523 (1991). As Krauss reports:

> Physicians seek court-ordered obstetrical interventions most often when the pregnant woman is a member of a racial minority or disadvantaged socioeconomic group. A national study found that in eighty-one percent of the court-ordered obstetrical interventions reported (including Caesarean sections, hospital detentions and intrauterine transfusions), the woman was African-American, Asian-American or Latina. One-quarter of the women ordered to undergo unwanted treatment did not speak English as their primary language. Specifically in cases of court-ordered Caesarean sections, eighty percent of the patients were members of minority groups, and twenty-seven percent were not native English speakers. Every request for a court order involved a woman who was a patient at a teaching hospital or who received public assistance. None of the patients in the study were deemed incompetent by a psychiatrist. [Id. at 531.]

See also Dorothy Roberts, Killing the Black Body: Race, Reproduction, and the Meaning of Liberty (1997).

(9) Imposition of Criminal Sanctions.   After the fact, should the state ever be able to impose criminal sanctions on a mother if her child dies or is severely harmed because of the mother's failure to protect the "child" during the pregnancy? In State v. McKnight, 576 S.E.2d 168 (S.C. 2003), Regina McKnight was

convicted of homicide by child abuse after giving birth to a stillborn girl with cocaine in her system. The South Carolina Supreme Court held that the prosecution did not violate due process or the right to privacy and that the 20-year sentence was not cruel and unusual punishment. In May 2008, the South Carolina Supreme Court reversed McKnight's conviction based on ineffective assistance of counsel. McKnight v. State, 661 S.E. 2d 354 (S.C. 2008). *McKnight* represents the minority approach that imposes criminal liability on pregnant substance abusers.

Two years before *McKnight,* the United States Supreme Court addressed the constitutionality of a hospital policy of testing pregnant women for the purpose of fetal protection. In Ferguson v. City of Charleston, 532 U.S. 67 (2001), a state hospital developed a policy of testing pregnant patients suspected of substance abuse without their knowledge or consent. Patients who tested positive were arrested. When patients challenged the policy as a violation of the Fourth Amendment, the United States Supreme Court held that the tests constituted unreasonable searches absent consent, in view of the policy's law enforcement purpose.

See also News, Mom in Caesarean Case Gets Probation, Chi. Trib., Apr. 30, 2004, at 18 (describing case of substance abuser who was sentenced to probation for child endangerment for refusing to have a Caesarean). See generally Linda C. Fentiman, The New "Fetal Protection": The Wrong Answer to the Crisis of Inadequate Health Care for Women and Children, 84 Denv. U.L. Rev. 537 (2006) (detailing the rise in intrusive and punitive government actions against pregnant women, including criminal prosecutions).

(10) Fetal Protection Policies.   Should concern for the unborn child justify barring pregnant women or women of child-bearing age from employment that exposes a woman to toxic agents with mutagenic or teratogenic effects? In International Union, UAW v. Johnson Controls, 499 U.S. 187 (1991), a lead battery manufacturer adopted a fetal protection policy barring *all* female employees except those who could document infertility from working in jobs with potential lead exposure in excess of OSHA standards. The United States Supreme Court held that the policy was facially discriminatory under Title VII because it barred only female employees, despite evidence showing the debilitating effects of lead exposure on the male reproductive system as well. On the legacy of *Johnson Controls,* see Elaine Draper, Reproductive Hazards and Fetal Exclusion Policies After *Johnson Controls,* 12 Stan. L. & Pol'y Rev. 117 (2001).

Spousal Notification

So far, the analysis has centered on the extent to which the state is justified in interfering with the pregnant woman's decision, in order to protect the woman or to preserve the life or well-being of the fetus. This involves the allocation of decisional power between the state, on the one hand, and the woman, on the other. But what about the interest of the father? There is, of course, the possibility that the mother and father of the fetus might not agree. In that case, there remains the issue of which private individual shall have the power to decide on an abortion: the mother acting alone? Or, only if the father consents as well? If spousal consent is not required, should the woman at least have to notify her husband of her plan to have an abortion? Should it make any difference if the mother and father are married?

In the wake of *Roe*, several states passed abortion statutes that conditioned abortion by a married woman on spousal consent or spousal notification. Such provisions were challenged on constitutional grounds in a number of cases. The Supreme Court decided the question of spousal consent in Planned Parenthood of Central Missouri v. Danforth, 428 U.S. 52 (1976), invalidating a Missouri statute that required the husband's prior written consent for a first-trimester abortion unless the abortion was necessary to preserve the life of the mother. However, *Danforth* left open the issue of spousal notification—that issue was decided by Planned Parenthood of Southeastern Pennsylvania v. Casey, an extract from which follows.

Planned Parenthood of Southeastern Pennsylvania v. Casey[22]
505 U.S. 833 (1992)

Justice O'CONNOR, Justice KENNEDY, and Justice SOUTER delivered the opinion of the Court with respect to Part V-C [below]:

Section 3209 of Pennsylvania's abortion law provides, except in cases of medical emergency, that no physician shall perform an abortion on a married woman without receiving a signed statement from the woman that she has notified her spouse that she is about to undergo an abortion. The woman has the option of providing an alternative signed statement certifying that her husband is not the man who impregnated her; that her husband could not be located; that the pregnancy is the result of spousal sexual assault which she has reported; or that the woman believes that notifying her husband will cause him or someone else to inflict bodily injury upon her. A physician who performs an abortion on a married woman without receiving the appropriate signed statement will have his or her license revoked, and is liable to the husband for damages.

The District Court heard the testimony of numerous expert witnesses, and made detailed findings of fact regarding the effect of this statute. These included:

> 273. The vast majority of women consult their husbands prior to deciding to terminate their pregnancy. . . .
>
> 281. Studies reveal that family violence occurs in two million families in the United States. This figure, however, is a conservative one that substantially under-states (because battering is usually not reported until it reaches life-threatening proportions) the actual number of families affected by domestic violence. In fact, researchers estimate that one of every two women will be battered at some time in their life. . . .
>
> 282. A wife may not elect to notify her husband of her intention to have an abortion for a variety of reasons, including the husband's illness, concern about her own health, the imminent failure of the marriage, or the husband's absolute opposition to the abortion. . . .

---

[22] That portion of the *Danforth* opinion relating to Missouri's parental consent requirement for an abortion for a minor is discussed at p. 142, infra.

283. The required filing of the spousal consent form would . . . force women to reveal their most intimate decision-making on pain of criminal sanctions. The confidentiality of these revelations could not be guaranteed, since the woman's records are not immune from subpoena. . . .

284. Women of all class levels, educational backgrounds, and racial, ethnic and religious groups are battered. . . .

285. Wife-battering or abuse can take on many physical and psychological forms. The nature and scope of the battering can cover [murder, marital rape, and child abuse].

289. Mere notification of pregnancy is frequently a flashpoint for battering and violence within the family. The number of battering incidents is high during the pregnancy and often the worst abuse can be associated with pregnancy. . . . The battering husband may deny parentage and use the pregnancy as an excuse for abuse. . . .

290. Secrecy typically shrouds abusive families. Family members are instructed not to tell anyone, especially police or doctors, about the abuse and violence. Battering husbands often threaten their wives or her children with further abuse if she tells an outsider of the violence and tells her that nobody will believe her. A battered woman, therefore, is highly unlikely to disclose the violence against her for fear of retaliation. . . .

298. Because of the nature of the battering relationship, battered women are unlikely to avail themselves of the exceptions to section 3209 of the Act. . . .

These findings are supported by studies of domestic violence. [Recent research] and the District Court's findings reinforce what common sense would suggest. In well-functioning marriages, spouses discuss important intimate decisions such as whether to bear a child. But there are millions of women in this country who are the victims of regular physical and psychological abuse at the hands of their husbands. Should these women become pregnant, they may have very good reasons for not wishing to inform their husbands of their decision to obtain an abortion. . . . Many may fear devastating forms of psychological abuse from their husbands, including verbal harassment, threats of future violence, the destruction of possessions, physical confinement to the home, the withdrawal of financial support, or the disclosure of the abortion to family and friends. These methods of psychological abuse may act as even more of a deterrent to notification than the possibility of physical violence, but women who are the victims of the abuse are not exempt from §3209's notification requirement. And many women who are pregnant as a result of sexual assaults by their husbands will be unable to avail themselves of the exception for spousal sexual assault, §3209(b)(3), because the exception requires that the woman have notified law enforcement authorities within 90 days of the assault, and her husband will be notified of her report once an investigation begins, §3128(c). If anything in this field is certain, it is that victims of spousal sexual assault are extremely reluctant to report the abuse to the government. . . .

The spousal notification requirement is thus likely to prevent a significant number of women from obtaining an abortion. It does not merely make abortions a little more difficult or expensive to obtain; for many women, it will impose a substantial obstacle. We must not blind ourselves to the fact that the significant number of women who fear for their safety and the safety of their children are likely to be deterred from procuring an abortion as surely as if the Commonwealth had outlawed abortion in all cases.

Respondents attempt to avoid the conclusion that §3209 is invalid by pointing out that it imposes almost no burden at all for the vast majority of women seeking abortions. They begin by noting that only about 20 percent of the women who obtain abortions are married. They then note that of these women about 95 percent notify their husbands of their own volition. Thus, respondents argue, the effects of §3209 are felt by only one percent of the women who obtain abortions. Respondents argue that since some of these women will be able to notify their husbands without adverse consequences or will qualify for one of the exceptions, the statute affects fewer than one percent of women seeking abortions. For this reason, it is asserted, the statute cannot be invalid on its face. We disagree with respondents' basic method of analysis. . . . The proper focus of constitutional inquiry is the group for whom the law is a restriction, not the group for whom the law is irrelevant. . . . The unfortunate yet persisting conditions we document above will mean that in a large fraction of the cases in which §3209 is relevant, it will operate as a substantial obstacle to a woman's choice to undergo an abortion. It is an undue burden, and therefore invalid. . . .

We recognize that a husband has a "deep and proper concern and interest . . . in his wife's pregnancy and in the growth and development of the fetus she is carrying." *Danforth*, supra, at 69. With regard to the children he has fathered and raised, the Court has recognized his "cognizable and substantial" interest in their custody. Stanley v. Illinois, 405 U.S. 645, 651-652 (1972). . . . Before birth, however, the issue takes on a very different cast. It is an inescapable biological fact that state regulation with respect to the child a woman is carrying will have a far greater impact on the mother's liberty than on the father's. The effect of state regulation on a woman's protected liberty is doubly deserving of scrutiny in such a case, as the State has touched not only upon the private sphere of the family but upon the very bodily integrity of the pregnant woman. The Court has held that "when the wife and the husband disagree on this decision, the view of only one of the two marriage partners can prevail. Inasmuch as it is the woman who physically bears the child and who is the more directly and immediately affected by the pregnancy, as between the two, the balance weighs in her favor." *Danforth*, supra, 428 U.S., at 71. This conclusion rests upon the basic nature of marriage and the nature of our Constitution: "[T]he marital couple is not an independent entity with a mind and heart of its own, but an association of two individuals each with a separate intellectual and emotional makeup. If the right of privacy means anything, it is the right of the *individual*, married or single, to be free from unwarranted governmental intrusion into matters so fundamentally affecting a person as the decision whether to bear or beget a child." Eisenstadt v. Baird, 405 U.S., at 453 (emphasis in original). The Constitution protects individuals, men and women alike, from unjustified state interference, even when that interference is enacted into law for the benefit of their spouses.

There was a time, not so long ago, when a different understanding of the family and of the Constitution prevailed. In Bradwell v. State, 16 Wall. 130, 21 L. Ed. 442 (1873), three Members of this Court reaffirmed the common-law principle that "a woman had no legal existence separate from her husband, who was regarded as her head and representative in the social state; and, notwithstanding some recent modifications of this civil status, many of the special rules of law flowing from and dependent upon this cardinal principle still exist in full force in most States." Id., at 141 (Bradley, J., joined by Swayne and Field, JJ., concurring in judgment). Only one generation has passed since this Court observed that "woman is still regarded as the center of home and family life," with attendant "special responsibilities" that precluded full and independent legal status under the Constitution. Hoyt v. Florida, 368 U.S. 57, 62 (1961). These views, of course, are no longer consistent with our understanding of the family, the individual, or the Constitution.

In keeping with our rejection of the common-law understanding of a woman's role within the family, the Court held in *Danforth* that the Constitution does not permit a State to require a married woman to obtain her husband's consent before undergoing an abortion. 428 U.S., at 69. The principles that guided the Court in *Danforth* should be our guides today. For the great many women who are victims of abuse inflicted by their husbands, or whose children are the victims of such abuse, a spousal notice requirement enables the husband to wield an effective veto over his wife's decision. Whether the prospect of notification itself deters such women from seeking abortions, or whether the husband, through physical force or psychological pressure or economic coercion, prevents his wife from obtaining an abortion until it is too late, the notice requirement will often be tantamount to the veto found unconstitutional in *Danforth*. . . .

The husband's interest in the life of the child his wife is carrying does not permit the State to empower him with this troubling degree of authority over his wife. . . . A husband has no enforceable right to require a wife to advise him before she exercises her personal choices. If a husband's interest in the potential life of the child outweighs a wife's liberty, the State could require a married woman to notify her husband before she uses a postfertilization contraceptive. Perhaps next in line would be a statute requiring pregnant married women to notify their husbands before engaging in conduct causing risks to the fetus. After all, if the husband's interest in the fetus' safety is a sufficient predicate for state regulation, the State could reasonably conclude that pregnant wives should notify their husbands before drinking alcohol or smoking. Perhaps married women should notify their husbands before using contraceptives or before undergoing any type of surgery that may have complications affecting the husband's interest in his wife's reproductive organs. And if a husband's interest justifies notice in any of these cases, one might reasonably argue that it justifies exactly what the *Danforth* Court held it did not justify — a requirement of the husband's consent as well. A State may not give to a man the kind of dominion over his wife that parents exercise over their children.

Section 3209 embodies a view of marriage consonant with the common-law status of married women but repugnant to our present understanding of marriage and of the nature of the rights secured by the Constitution. Women do not lose their constitutionally protected liberty when they marry. The Constitution protects all individuals, male or female, married or unmarried, from the abuse of governmental power, even where that power is employed for the supposed benefit of a member of the individual's family. These considerations confirm our conclusion that §3209 is invalid. . . .

Chief Justice Rehnquist, with whom Justice White, Justice Scalia, and Justice Thomas join . . . dissenting in part . . .

Section 3209 of the Act contains the spousal notification provision. [We] first emphasize that Pennsylvania has not imposed a spousal consent requirement of the type the Court struck down in Planned Parenthood of Central Mo. v. Danforth, 428 U.S., at 67-72. Missouri's spousal consent provision was invalidated in that case because of the Court's view that it unconstitutionally granted to the husband "a veto power exercisable for any reason whatsoever or for no reason at all." Id., at 71. But the provision here involves a much less intrusive requirement of spousal notification, not consent. . . .

The question before us is therefore whether the spousal notification requirement rationally furthers any legitimate state interests. We conclude that it does. First, a husband's interests in procreation within marriage and in the potential life of his unborn child are certainly substantial ones. The State itself has legitimate interests both in protecting these interests of the father and in protecting the potential life of the fetus, and the spousal notification requirement is reasonably related to advancing those state interests. By providing that a husband will usually know of his spouse's intent to have an abortion, the provision makes it more likely that the husband will participate in deciding the fate of his unborn child, a possibility that might otherwise have been denied him. This participation might in some cases result in a decision to proceed with the pregnancy. As Judge Alito observed in his dissent below, "[t]he Pennsylvania legislature could have rationally believed that some married women are initially inclined to obtain an abortion without their husbands' knowledge because of perceived problems — such as economic constraints, future plans, or the husbands' previously expressed opposition — that may be obviated by discussion prior to the abortion." 947 F.2d, at 726 (opinion concurring in part and dissenting in part).

The State also has a legitimate interest in promoting "the integrity of the marital relationship." 18 Pa. Cons. Stat. §3209(a) (1990). . . . In our view, the spousal notice requirement is a rational attempt by the State to improve truthful communication between spouses and encourage collaborative decisionmaking, and thereby fosters marital integrity. . . .

QUESTIONS ON SPOUSAL CONSENT

(1) Spousal consent vs. spousal notification.   What is the difference between a spousal consent requirement and a spousal notification requirement? Should courts treat the two requirements similarly? Or, are there important differences between the requirements? Do you agree with the plurality in *Casey* that in many cases the spousal notification requirement will be "tantamount to the veto found unconstitutional in *Danforth*"? 505 U.S. at 897-898.

(2) Father's Interests.   After *Danforth* and *Casey*, does the father possess any legal interest in decisions regarding his unborn child? Does the father's interest grow as the mother approaches term? Is it reasonable to allow the state, but not the father, to intervene on behalf of the unborn child to prohibit abortions? Do you agree with the plurality in *Casey* that the spousal notification requirement should

be rejected because "a husband's interest in the potential life of the child [should not outweigh] a wife's liberty"? 505 U.S. at 897-898.

One legal commentator suggests that we should consider the harms (both to the individual and the community) that the abortion restriction was designed to prevent. S. Dresden Brunner, Cultural Feminism: It Sounds Good, But Will It Work? Application to a Husband's Interest in His Wife's Abortion Decision, 22 U. Dayton L. Rev. 101 (1996). What are the possible harms to the marital parties if the wife does not inform her husband of her plan to have an abortion? To society? That analysis leads the preceding commentator to conclude that the husband should have input into abortion decision making in a nonabusive marriage. What do you think of this approach?

What does *Casey* signify about whether the state could require a mother to notify a father about other marital decisions regarding children, such as providing a living child with necessary medical care, allowing a child to enroll in a private school, or consenting to a daughter's abortion?

Several fathers' rights cases took place in the years following *Roe* when fathers tried unsuccessfully to enjoin their wives from undergoing abortions, or to enjoin their wives' physicians from conducting abortions. See, e.g., Coe v. Cook County, No. 96C2636, 1997 WL 797662 (N.D. Ill. Dec. 24, 1997) (dismissing father's claim against a health professional for damages for violation of his right to equal protection based on his girlfriend's abortion). See generally Adrienne D. Gross, Note, A Man's Right to Choose: Searching for Remedies in the Face of Unplanned Parenthood, 55 Drake L. Rev. 1015 (2007).

(3) Empirical Data. Data from abortion clinics reveal that as many as 86 percent of women inform their male partners about their abortion plans. Married women are as likely as single women to inform the biological father. Marcelle Christian Holmes, Reconsidering a "Woman's Issue": Psychotherapy and One Man's Postabortion Experiences, 58 Am. J. Psychotherapy 103 (Jan. 2004). How do the plurality and the dissent in *Casey* view empirical data? For an empirical study of men's role in the abortion decision, see Arthur B. Shostak, The Role of Unwed Fathers in the Abortion Decision, in Young Unwed Fathers, Changing Roles and Emerging Policies 292 (Robert I. Lerman & Theodora J. Ooms eds. 1995).

(4) Undue Burden Test. Under the undue burden test, is it clear that Pennsylvania's statute requiring a woman to sign a statement of notification is so burdensome? What course of action do you suppose most women would take if they did not desire to notify their husbands?

What reasons does the Court give for suggesting that the requirement constitutes an undue burden? Are those reasons persuasive? Recall, for example, Justice O'Connor's statement that "The unfortunate yet persistent condition we document above will mean that in a large fraction of the cases in which §3209 is relevant, it will operate as a substantial burden. . . ." 505 U.S. at 895. What data support this "large fraction"? Is the spousal notification requirement more or less burdensome than a 24-hour waiting period? If you were advising a Pennsylvania legislator, how would you suggest the statute be changed to address the Court's objections?

(5) Compelling Fetal Surgery or Embryo Transfers. Suppose a couple discovers that the viable fetus that the wife is carrying has a serious birth defect. The

problem is correctable by fetal surgery. Does the husband have any right to compel the wife to undergo the surgery? How is the husband's right similar to, or different from, his right in the abortion context? See David C. Blickenstaff, Comment, Defining the Boundaries of Personal Privacy: Is There a Paternal Interest in Compelling Therapeutic Fetal Surgery?, 88 Nw. U. L. Rev. 1157 (1994).

It may soon be possible to transplant an embryo from a pregnant woman to a carrier who can bear the child. If the transplant involves no more substantial risk to the mother than an abortion, would the state have the right to compel a transplant rather than allow an abortion? Would the father?

(6) Comatose Pregnant Wife. How should a court balance a pregnant woman's interests against the father's interests if the woman is severely disabled? Marie Odette Henderson, when six and one-half months pregnant, was put on life support due to a brain tumor. Her parents asked the physicians to remove her from the equipment that was keeping her and her fetus alive. The father of the unborn child, who was Ms. Henderson's fiancé, obtained a court order naming him the fetus's guardian and directing the hospital not to remove the equipment. Almost two months later, a healthy and apparently normal child was delivered by Caesarean section, and physicians disconnected Ms. Henderson's life support system. See Brain-Dead Woman Kept Alive for Fetus, San Jose Mercury News, April 23, 1993, at 1B (describing several such cases). See also Matter of Klein, 538 N.Y.S.2d 274 (App. Div. 1989) (appointing husband of comatose pregnant woman to be her guardian to sign informed-consent abortion authorization forms), *appeal denied*, 536 N.E.2d 627 (N.Y. 1989), *stay denied sub nom.* Short v. Klein, 489 U.S. 1003 (1989). On the moral and legal aspects of maintaining a brain-dead woman on life support for the successful delivery of her fetus, see Daniel Sperling, Maternal Brain Death, 30 Am. J.L. & Med. 453 (2004).

(7) Vision of Family and Gender Roles. What vision of marriage, the family, and gender roles does the preceding opinion in *Casey* reflect? Are the views of women and their decision-making capacity that influenced the *Casey* approach to the spousal notification requirement consistent with *Casey*'s ruling upholding the informed consent and 24-hour waiting period requirements?

(8) Standing to Intervene. Do the husbands of pregnant women have standing to intervene as parties to challenge a state ban on partial-birth abortions? See Planned Parenthood v. Doyle, 162 F.3d 463 (7th Cir. 1998) (holding that plaintiff husbands have no significant interest in the litigation other than an ideological one, which is not an adequate basis for standing).

(9) Husband's Support Obligation. Should the scope of the father's rights be affected by his duty of support? Should a woman's right to decide whether to have an abortion affect a man's obligation to support the child if the woman chooses instead to have the baby? Suppose the man asks that she have a first-trimester abortion for which he offers to pay? See Erika M. Heister, Note, Child Support Statutes and the Father's Right Not to Procreate, 2 Ave Maria L. Rev. 213 (2004). Do paternity statutes (that subject men to support obligations for nonmarital children) constitute a denial of equal protection by requiring men to support their unwanted children in view of the fact that the state permits women to choose to abort their unwanted children? See Dubay v. Wells, 506 F.3d 422 (6th Cir. 2007).

The Legal Treatment of a Fetus

(1) At common law, it was not a crime to abort or kill a fetus prior to quickening. The abortion or killing of a "quick" fetus was a crime, but the commentators were split over whether it was a felony or instead some lesser crime. Bracton, writing in the thirteenth century, took the position that it was a homicide "if the foetus is already formed or quickened." Henry de Bracton, 2 On the Laws and Customs of England 341 (Thorne ed. 1968). According to Coke, the abortion of a woman "quick with childe" was "a great misprision and no murder." 3 Coke Institutes 50 (1648). Blackstone suggested that at ancient common law the abortion of a quickened fetus had been considered homicide or manslaughter. 1 William Blackstone, Commentaries 129-130 (1765). In an omitted portion of the *Roe* opinion, Justice Blackmun wrote that in America, "it now appear[s] doubtful that abortion was ever firmly established as a common-law crime even with respect to the destruction of a quick fetus." 410 U.S. at 136.

(2) Fetal Homicide Legislation. The courts of several states have wrestled with whether the killing of an unborn fetus is homicide. A majority of states now follow the federal Unborn Victims of Violence Act (UVVA) of 2004, 18 U.S.C. §1841 (Supp. IV 2004)[23] (discussed supra p. 22) by their enactment of fetal homicide laws that impose dual criminal liability based on the injury or death of a child in utero during the commission of certain crimes against the mother. See Luke M. Milligan, A Theory of Stability: John Rawls, Fetal Homicide, and Substantive Due Process, 87 B.U. L. Rev. 1177, 1183 (2007) (stating that 36 states have incorporated this "double-victim approach into their penal codes"). Statutes vary in terms of the protection and stage of pregnancy at which criminal liability attaches.

The expanding legal status of the fetus is further reflected by other federal legislation (such as the State Children's Health Insurance Program, 67 Fed. Reg. 61, 956 (Oct. 2, 2002), codified at 42 C.F.R. pt. 457) as well as state legislative definitions of the term "person" in various contexts that include a child in utero (both developments are discussed supra p. 22). See also Milligan, supra, at 1186 (citing similar legislation in Kentucky, Ohio, and Pennsylvania). What will be the likely impact of such legislation on abortion rights?

(3) Postpartum Psychosis Defense. In England, the Infanticide Act, 1938, 1 & 2 Geo. 6, ch. 36, provides that if a woman kills her baby within one year of birth while disturbed by the effects of giving birth, she shall be charged with manslaughter, not murder. Postpartum psychosis has been used as a defense in American courts, such as in the much publicized trial of Andrea Yates, a mother who drowned her five children in the bathtub. A Texas jury recommended a life sentence. Jim Yardley, Mother Who Drowned 5 Children in Tub Avoids a Death Sentence, N.Y Times, Mar. 16, 2002, at A1. See generally Michelle Oberman, "Lady Madonna, Children at Your Feet": Tragedies at the Intersection of Motherhood, Mental Illness and the Law, 10 Wm. & Mary J. Women & L. 33 (2003).

---

[23] The UVVA was dubbed "Laci and Conner's Law" in memory of a California woman who was murdered by her husband when she was eight months pregnant.

(4) Tort Law: Wrongful Death.   For purposes of tort law, if a child was not born alive because of injuries inflicted during the pregnancy, the traditional rule refused to permit recovery on behalf of the fetus because the fetus was considered part of the mother — only the mother could sue for injuries to herself. Dietrich v. Northampton, 138 Mass. 14 (1884). The "born-alive" rule developed at common law because of the inability of early medical science to determine if a fetus was alive. The majority rule now permits recovery under state wrongful death statutes for prenatal injuries even if a child is stillborn. Elisabeth H. Sperow, Redefining Child Abuse Under the State Children's Health Insurance Program: Capable of Repetition, Yet Evading Results, 12 Am. U.J. Gender Soc. Pol'y & L. 137, 145 (2004).

(5) Tort Actions Against Parents for Prenatal Injuries.   The "born-alive" rule permitted a child to recover damages from *third parties* for prenatal injuries. Should a child have an action against a *parent* for a prenatal injury? Jurisdictions are split on this issue. Compare Remy v. MacDonald, 801 N.E.2d 260 (Mass. 2004) (rejecting plaintiff's negligence suit against her mother for prenatal injuries sustained during an automobile accident), with National Cas. Co. v. Northern Trust Bank of Florida, 807 So. 2d 86 (Fla. 2001) (permitting a suit in similar circumstances). Should such suits be permitted? What are the implications of this expansion of liability? Should it matter whether the prenatal injury is caused by the mother's negligence or intentional infliction of prenatal injuries (e.g., stemming from substance abuse during the pregnancy)?

(6) Additional Birth-Related Torts: Wrongful Life, Wrongful Birth. Wrongful life claims are asserted by a *child* who suffers from birth defects, claiming that the physician's negligence in failing to inform the mother of potential birth defects deprived the mother of the option of avoiding conception or terminating the pregnancy (i.e., but for the defendant's negligence, the child would not have been born). Claims for wrongful birth and wrongful pregnancy are pursued by *parents* to recover damages for expenses and emotional distress resulting from the birth of a disabled or unwanted child, respectively. Deana A. Pollard, Wrongful Analysis in Wrongful Life Jurisprudence, 55 Ala. L. Rev. 327, 327-328 (2004).

Only a small number of jurisdictions recognize wrongful life actions. In contrast, many jurisdictions allowed parents' claims for wrongful birth. Id. at 328 n.8. However, beginning in 1988, several state legislatures enacted laws (stemming from anti-abortion sentiment) that prohibit claims for wrongful life and wrongful birth if such claims were based on the argument that the woman would have obtained an abortion but for the health care professional's negligence. Courts have consistently upheld the constitutionality of such statutes. Michael T. Murtaugh, Wrongful Birth: The Courts' Dilemma in Determining a Remedy for a "Blessed Event," 27 Pace L. Rev. 241, 275 (2007). Do such statutes prevent a woman from giving informed consent to terminate a pregnancy? Do they constitute an undue burden on a woman's right to an abortion? See Christine Intromasso, Reproductive Self-Determination in the Third Circuit: The Statutory Proscription of Wrongful Birth and Wrongful Life Claims as an Unconstitutional Violation of

Planned Parenthood v. Casey's Undue Burden Standard, 24 Women's Rts. L. Rep. 101 (2003) (so arguing).

(7) Inheritance Rights. Both at common law and under modern statutes, an infant *en ventre sa mère* who is subsequently born alive is regarded as a life in being for purposes of inheritance. California Civil Code §43.1 (West 2007) provides that "(a) child conceived, but not yet born, is deemed an existing person, so far as necessary for the child's interests in the event of the child's subsequent birth." Many states today have statutes regulating inheritance by posthumous children. E.g., Mass. Gen. Laws Ann. ch. 190 §8 (West 2004); N.Y. Est., Powers & Trusts Law §4-1.1(c) (Consol. 2006); Ohio Rev. Code Ann. §2105.14 (West 2005). See also Uniform Probate Code §2-108 which provides "relatives of the decedent conceived before his death but born thereafter inherit as if they had been born in the lifetime of the decedent."

(8) Is a fetus a "child" for purposes of civil child abuse and neglect statutes? There are a number of cases, like *Jefferson*, supra, in which state officials have sought to use such statutes to protect unborn children by intervening in the life of a pregnant woman. See, e.g., Kilmon v. State, 905 A.2d 306 (Md. 2006); State v. Martinez, 137 P.3d 1195 (N.M. Ct. App. 2006) (both refusing to apply state child abuse statutes to a fetus). But cf. State v. McKnight, 576 S.E.2d 168 (S.C. 2003) (holding that such a prosecution for "homicide by child abuse" did not violate due process or the right to privacy, and that a sentence of 20 years, suspended to 12 years, was not cruel and unusual punishment), *reversed on other grounds*, McKnight v. State, 661 S.E.2d 354 (S.C. 2008). For further discussion of child abuse and neglect, see Chapter 3.

(9) Posthumously Conceived Children. With the advent of the new reproductive technology, children can be born more than nine months after the death of a biological father. Do such children have inheritance rights? See discussion of Gillett-Netting v. Barnhart, infra p. 207. Child support issues are considered more generally in Chapter 2.

C. THE JUDICIAL ALLOCATION OF POWER BETWEEN PARENTS AND THE STATE

Meyer v. Nebraska
262 U.S. 390 (1923)

Mr. Justice MCREYNOLDS delivered the opinion of the Court.

Plaintiff in error was tried and convicted . . . under an information which charged that on May 25, 1920, while an instructor in Zion Parochial School, he unlawfully taught the subject of reading in the German language to Raymond Parpart, a child of ten years, who had not attained and successfully passed the eighth grade. The information is based upon "An act relating to the teaching of foreign languages in the State of Nebraska," approved April 9, 1919, which follows [Laws 1919, c. 249]:

> Section 1. No person, individually or as a teacher, shall, in any private, denominational, parochial or public school, teach any subject to any person in any language other than the English language.
>
> Sec. 2. Languages, other than the English language, may be taught as languages only after a pupil shall have attained and successfully passed the eighth grade as evidenced by a certificate of graduation issued by the county superintendent of the county in which the child resides.
>
> Sec. 3. Any person who violates any of the provisions of this act shall be deemed guilty of a misdemeanor and upon conviction, shall be subject to a fine of not less than twenty-five dollars ($25), nor more than one hundred dollars ($100) or be confined in the county jail for any period not exceeding thirty days for each offense.
>
> Sec. 4. Whereas, an emergency exists, this act shall be in force from and after its passage and approval.

The Supreme Court of the State affirmed the judgment of conviction. It declared the offense charged and established was "the direct and intentional teaching of the German language as a distinct subject to a child who had not passed the eighth grade," in the parochial school maintained by Zion Evangelical Lutheran Congregation, a collection of Biblical stories being used therefor. . . .

The problem for our determination is whether the statute as construed and applied unreasonably infringes the liberty guaranteed to the plaintiff in error by the Fourteenth Amendment. "No State shall . . . deprive any person of life, liberty, or property, without due process of law."

While this Court has not attempted to define with exactness the liberty thus guaranteed, the term has received much consideration. . . . Without doubt, it denotes not merely freedom from bodily restraint but also the right of the individual to contract, to engage in any of the common occupations of life, to acquire useful knowledge, to marry, establish a home and bring up children, to worship God according to the dictates of his own conscience, and generally to enjoy those privileges long recognized at common law as essential to the orderly pursuit of happiness by free men. The established doctrine is that this liberty may not be interfered with, under the guise of protecting the public interest, by legislative action which is arbitrary or without reasonable relation to some purpose within the competency of the State to effect. Determination by the legislature of what constitutes proper exercise of police power is not final or conclusive but is subject to supervision by the courts.

The American people have always regarded education and acquisition of knowledge as matters of supreme importance which should be diligently promoted. . . . Corresponding to the right of control, it is the natural duty of the parent to give his children education suitable to their station in life; and nearly all the States, including Nebraska, enforce this obligation by compulsory laws.

Practically, education of the young is only possible in schools conducted by especially qualified persons who devote themselves thereto. The calling always has been regarded as useful and honorable, essential, indeed, to the public welfare. Mere knowledge of the German language cannot reasonably be regarded as harmful. Heretofore it has been commonly looked upon as helpful and desirable. Plaintiff in error taught this language in school as part of his occu-pation. His right thus to teach and the right of parents to engage him so to instruct their children, we think, are within the liberty of the Amendment. . . .

It is said the purpose of the legislation was to promote civic development by inhibiting training and education of the immature in foreign tongues and ideals before they could learn English and acquire American ideals. . . . It is also affirmed that the foreign born population is very large, that certain communities commonly . . . move in a foreign atmosphere, and that the children are thereby hindered from becom-ing citizens of the most useful type and the public safety is imperiled.

That the State may do much, go very far, indeed, in order to improve the quality of its citizens, physically, mentally and morally, is clear; but the individual has certain fundamental rights which must be respected. The protection of the Con-stitution extends to all, to those who speak other languages as well as to those born with English on the tongue. Perhaps it would be highly advantageous if all had ready understanding of our ordinary speech, but this cannot be coerced by methods which conflict with the Constitution — a desirable end cannot be promoted by prohibited means. . . .

The desire of the legislature to foster a homogeneous people with American ideals prepared readily to understand current discussions of civic matters is easy to appreciate. Unfortunate experiences during the late war and aversion toward every characteristic of truculent adversaries were certainly enough to quicken that aspi-ration. But the means adopted, we think, exceed the limitations upon the power of the State and conflict with rights assured to plaintiff. . . . No emergency has arisen which renders knowledge by a child of some language other than English so clearly harmful as to justify its inhibition with the consequent infringement of rights long freely enjoyed. We are constrained to conclude that the statute as applied is arbitrary and without reasonable relation to any end within the competency of the State.

As the statute undertakes to interfere only with teaching which involves a modern language, leaving complete freedom as to other matters, there seems no adequate foundation for the suggestion that the purpose was to protect the child's health by limiting his mental activities. It is well known that proficiency in a foreign language seldom comes to one not instructed at an early age, and experience shows that this is not injurious to the health, morals or understanding of the ordinary child. *no justification*

The judgment of the court below must be reversed. . . .

Pierce v. Society of Sisters
268 U.S. 510 (1925)

Mr. Justice MCREYNOLDS delivered the opinion of the Court.

These appeals are from decrees . . . which granted preliminary orders restrain-ing appellants from threatening or attempting to enforce the Compulsory Education Act. . . . *affirmed*

The challenged Act, effective September 1, 1926, requires every parent, guard-ian or other person having control or charge or custody of a child between eight and sixteen years to send him "to a public school for the period of time a public school shall be held during the current year" in the district where the child resides; and failure so to do is declared a misdemeanor. There are exemptions—not specially important here—for children who are not normal, or who have completed the eighth grade, or who reside at considerable distances from any public school, or whose parents or guardians hold special permits from the County Superintendent. The manifest purpose is to compel general attendance at public schools by normal children, between eight and sixteen, who have not completed the eighth grade. And without doubt enforcement of the statute would seriously impair, perhaps destroy, the profitable features of appellees' business and greatly diminish the value of their property.

Appellee, the Society of Sisters, is an Oregon corporation, organized in 1880, with power to care for orphans, educate and instruct the youth, establish and maintain academies or schools, and acquire necessary real and personal property. It has long devoted its property and effort to the secular and religious education and care of children, and has acquired the valuable good will of many parents and guardians. . . . The Compulsory Education Act of 1922 has already caused the withdrawal from its schools of children who would otherwise continue, and their income has steadily declined. . . .

[T]he Society's bill alleges that the enactment conflicts with the right of parents to choose schools where their children will receive appropriate mental and religious training, the right of the child to influence the parents' choice of a school, the right of schools and teachers therein to engage in a useful business or profession, and is accordingly repugnant to the Constitution and void. And, further, that unless enforcement of the measure is enjoined the corporation's business and property will suffer irreparable injury.

Appellee, Hill Military Academy, is a private corporation organized in 1908 under the laws of Oregon, engaged in owning, operating and conducting for profit an elementary, college preparatory and military training school for boys between the ages of five and twenty-one years. . . . By reason of the statute and threat of enforcement appellee's business is being destroyed and its property depreciated; parents and guardians are refusing to make contracts for the future instruction of their sons, and some are being withdrawn.

[The Academy alleges that the Act violates its Fourteenth Amendment rights and seeks an injunction.]

[The matter was heard] by three judges on motions for preliminary injunctions. . . . The court ruled that the Fourteenth Amendment guaranteed appellees against the deprivation of their property without due process of law consequent upon the unlawful interference by appellants with the free choice of patrons, present and prospective. It declared the right to conduct schools was property and that parents and guardians, as a part of their liberty, might direct the education of children by selecting reputable teachers and places. Also, that these schools were not unfit or harmful to the public, and that enforcement of the challenged statute would unlawfully deprive them of patronage and thereby destroy their owners' business and property. . . .

No question is raised concerning the power of the State reasonably to regulate all schools, to inspect, supervise and examine them, their teachers and pupils; to require that all children of proper age attend some school, that teachers shall be of good moral character and patriotic disposition, that certain studies plainly essential to good citizenship must be taught, and that nothing be taught which is manifestly inimical to the public welfare.

The inevitable practical result of enforcing the Act under consideration would be destruction of appellees' primary schools, and perhaps all other private primary schools for normal children within the State of Oregon. These parties are engaged in a kind of undertaking not inherently harmful, but long regarded as useful and meritorious. Certainly there is nothing in the present records to indicate that they have failed to discharge their obligations to patrons, students or the State. And there are no peculiar circumstances or present emergencies which demand extraordinary measures relative to primary education.

Under the doctrine of Meyer v. Nebraska, 262 U.S. 390, we think it entirely plain that the Act of 1922 unreasonably interferes with the liberty of parents and guardians to direct the upbringing and education of children under their control. As often heretofore pointed out, rights guaranteed by the Constitution may not be abridged by legislation which has no reasonable relation to some purpose within the competency of the State. The fundamental theory of liberty upon which all governments in this Union repose excludes any general power of the State to standardize its children by forcing them to accept instruction from public teachers only. The child is not the mere creature of the State; those who nurture him and direct his destiny have the right, coupled with the high duty, to recognize and prepare him for additional obligations. . . .

The decrees below are affirmed.

NOTES AND QUESTIONS ON *MEYER* AND *PIERCE*: A CONSTITUTIONAL FRAMEWORK FOR EDUCATION

(1) Whose Rights Are Vindicated? The constitutional importance of *Meyer* and *Pierce,* especially in establishing the constitutional framework for American education, would be difficult to exaggerate. Both opinions are opaque, however, and subject to various interpretations. Whose rights are being vindicated? In *Meyer,* is the Court concerned with the liberty of the teacher, the child, or the child's parents? In *Pierce,* is the concern with the private school's proprietary rights or parents' rights to rear their children or both?

(2) In her "revisionist" account of *Meyer* and *Pierce,* Barbara Woodhouse claims that the right vindicated in both cases is the right of parents to control their children, which the Court finds protected by the "liberty" clause of the Fourteenth Amendment. Barbara B. Woodhouse, Who Owns the Child?: *Meyer* and *Pierce* and the Child as Property, 33 Wm. & Mary L. Rev. 995 (1992). Woodhouse argues that it only makes sense to locate the right to control children in the liberty clause if children are viewed as parental property:

> Ironically, the Court in *Meyer* and *Pierce* chose to hang parental control of children on the branch of Fourteenth Amendment "liberty." Courts before *Meyer* had generally been slow to extend Fourteenth Amendment protection to the

> parent's rights over the child. Pierce himself observed that "it is a strange per-
> version of the word 'liberty' to apply it to a right to control the conduct of others."
> Yet adopt, for a moment, the perspective that children are patriarchal property.
> Suddenly, the right of parental control in *Meyer* and *Pierce* — authored and joined
> by the court's most inflexible laissez-faire conservatives and grounded on eco-
> nomic substantive due process precedents — acquires a logical framework. Prop-
> erty and ownership were indeed a powerful subtext of parental rights rhetoric in
> the era of *Pierce* and *Meyer*. [Id. at 1041-1042.]

Given our long history of treating children as the property of their parents (usually
of their father), do you find this view compelling? Or, do you think that if the Court
viewed children as parental property, it would have located the parents' right to
control children in the Fourteenth Amendment's "property" clause, rather than in
its "liberty" clause?

(3) Principle of Family Autonomy.   *Meyer* and *Pierce* establish broad liberal
principles of family autonomy in the face of government intervention. Subsequently, the U.S. Supreme Court reaffirmed parents' fundamental liberty interest
in childrearing in Troxel v. Granville, 530 U.S. 57 (2000). *Troxel,* relying on *Meyer*
and *Pierce,* held that a court order compelling visitation between children and their
grandparents violated a mother's due process rights to control the upbringing of her
children by failing to give sufficient deference to the mother's wishes. (*Troxel* is
reprinted infra p. 609.)

Are there negative implications for children by virtue of the recognition of
broad principles of family autonomy? Professor Barbara Woodhouse suggests
that *Pierce* presents two "faces": protection of children via principles of liberty, family privacy, and pluralism versus endangerment of those children who
are "held hostage in the child welfare system by a distorted vision of the family
and Constitution." See Barbara Bennett Woodhouse, Child Abuse, the Constitution, and the Legacy of Pierce v. Society of Sisters, 78 U. Det. Mercy L. Rev.
479, 489 (2001). Another commentator criticizes that the concept of parental
rights today is different from that of the 1923 family. She then queries: "Is it,
then, a good idea to breathe new life into [parental rights] at a time when the
underlying Blackstone/Kent assumption that parents act in the best interests
of their children is open to question in far too many cases?" Susan E. Lawrence,
Substantive Due Process and Parental Rights: From Meyer v. Nebraska to
Troxel v. Granville, 8 J.L. & Fam. Stud. 71, 111 (2006). What do you think
of these criticisms?

(4) Historical Background.   The legislation at issue in both *Meyer* and *Pierce*
stemmed from anti-Bolshevist and xenophobic fears. The statute at issue in *Meyer*
was one of 22 such state restrictions on the teaching of foreign languages in public
and private elementary schools. Lawrence, supra, at 73-74. No state other than
Oregon had a requirement that children attend only *public* schools. The Oregon
legislature adopted the provision following a referendum campaign promoted by
the Ku Klux Klan and the Scottish Rite Masons, who claimed to want to "Amer-
icanize" the schools, with the support of public school teachers who feared a
negative vote would hurt public education. For historical background, see Paula
Abrams, The Little Red Schoolhouse: *Pierce,* State Monopoly of Education and

the Politics of Intolerance, 20 Const. Comment. 61, 66-70 (2003); Woodhouse, Who Owns the Child, supra, at p. 51.

(5) Pluralism. Several commentators characterize *Pierce* as a triumph of pluralism both in terms of family values and educational decision making. See, e.g., Peggy Cooper Davis, Contested Images of Family Values: The Role of the State, 107 Harv. L. Rev. 1348, 1363 (1994); Martha Minow, Before and After *Pierce,* A Colloquium on Parents, Children, Religion and Schools, 78 U. Det. Mercy L. Rev. 407, 408-409 (2001).

Does pluralism in education promote children's interests? What justifications exist for a public school monopoly? Might not a common public education best ensure critical common values? At the other extreme, what would the world look like if there were no compulsory education? What reasons would parents have to invest in their children's education? What public or state interests exist to justify compelling parents who would choose not to provide for their children's education? Does *Pierce* represent a workable compromise between these two extremes? Does *Pierce* strike an appropriate balance among the competing interests of the child, family, private schools, and the state? See Barbara Bennett Woodhouse, Speaking Truth to Power: Challenging "The Power of Parents to Control the Education of Their Own," 11 Cornell J.L. & Pub. Pol'y 481 (2002) (questioning the deference given to parents' educational choices).

(6) Could the state, after Meyer v. Nebraska, prohibit parents from sending their children to a private school where *all* instruction was in a foreign language? Put another way, could a state constitutionally require a school to offer some English instruction? Could "too much" foreign language instruction interfere with the child's ability to learn English?

(7) What if parents claim that substantial foreign language instruction is essential to preserve their children's ethnic heritage? Cf. Wisconsin v. Yoder, infra, p. 63. Are there circumstances in which the state should be under an affirmative obligation to offer instruction in a foreign language? Cf. Lau v. Nichols, 414 U.S. 563 (1974) (failure of San Francisco school system to provide English language instruction to students of Chinese ancestry who did not speak English denied them a meaningful opportunity to participate in the public educational program, in violation of §601 of the Civil Rights Act of 1964).

(8) After *Pierce,* would it be possible for the state to require the registration of children at birth and the compulsory placement of children in state-controlled day care and nursery schools?

(9) Home schooling is the education of children in the home as opposed to in an institutional setting such as a public or private school. Do *Meyer* and *Pierce* guarantee the right of parents to educate their children at home? (Home schooling is also discussed infra pp. 68-69.)

(10) Who should decide whether and where a child should go to school? Who should pay for a child's education? If the principle of *Pierce* is that the state cannot compel parents to send their children to state schools, what does this imply for the rights of parents who lack the funds to send their children to private schools? Is the *Pierce* principle only important for those who can afford private school alternatives?

(11) School Vouchers.   Can you imagine a school system where parents have the right to choose public or private education for their children — and their choice would be funded by the state? The "parental choice" movement has been gaining in popularity. Stemming from intense criticism of the public school system, parents increasingly have been advocating passage of legislation that provides "vouchers" or "school choice grants." Under such legislation, parents receive state financial assistance to fund the tuition costs of their children's attendance at sectarian schools. Several publicly funded voucher programs exist across the country.

The "parental choice" movement met with its first success at the federal level in 2004 when President George W Bush signed an appropriations bill creating a federally financed school voucher program in the District of Columbia. Consolidated Appropriations Act, 2004, Pub. L. No. 108-199, 118 Stat. 3 (2004). In addition, several municipalities have implemented voucher programs. In 1999, Florida became the first state to enact a statewide voucher law. However, the Florida Supreme Court invalidated the program as a violation of the state constitution's education clause. Bush v. Holmes, 919 So.2d 393 (Fla. 2006) (holding that the voucher program undermined the public school system by diverting funds previously earmarked for public schools to private schools and also violated the requirement that the school system be uniform). A subsequent attempt to resurrect the Florida voucher program by amending the state constitution failed when the state supreme court ruled that the proposed amendments were improperly placed on the ballot. Ford v. Browning, 992 So. 2d 132 (Fla. 2008).

Do voucher programs violate the Establishment Clause? In Zelman v. Simmons-Harris, 536 U.S. 639 (2002), the U.S. Supreme Court addressed the constitutionality of a school voucher program established by the state of Ohio. The program provided tuition aid to students residing within failing school districts. Parents of eligible students received tuition aid to send their children to a public or private school of their choosing within the district. The majority of students participating in the program enrolled in sectarian schools. A group of Ohio taxpayers sought to enjoin the program, claiming that it violated the Establishment Clause. The Supreme Court disagreed:

> In sum, the Ohio program is entirely neutral with respect to religion. It provides benefits directly to a wide spectrum of individuals, defined only by financial need and residence in a particular school district. It permits such individuals to exercise genuine choice among options public and private, secular and religious. Id. at 662.

See also Locke v. Davey, 540 U.S. 712 (2004) (holding that prohibition on state aid to students pursuing devotional theology degrees did not violate Free Exercise Clause); Mitchell v. Helms, 530 U.S. 793 (2000) (holding that a program under which local school districts may use federal funds to provide equipment to private schools, including religious schools, did not violate the Establishment Clause).

Some commentators speculated that *Zelman* would have a profound impact on the relationship between education and religion. See, e.g., Klint Alexander, The Road to Vouchers: The Supreme Court's Compliance and the Crumbling of the Wall of Separation Between Church and State in American Education, 92 Ky. L.J. 439 (2003/2004). In fact, *Zelman* triggered a rash of lawsuits focusing on the validity of state constitutional and statutory bans against public aid for sectarian education. Such provisions, called Blaine Amendments, exist in 37 states. Tresa Baldas, School Voucher Suits Hitting States, Natl. L.J., Dec. 13, 2003, at A1.

Criticisms of public education also led to major reform legislation, the No Child Left Behind Act (NCLB) of 2001, Pub. L. No. 107-110, 115 Stat. 1425 (2002) (codified at 20 U.S.C. §§6301-7941). NCLB attempts to increase account-ability for student performance by rewarding states and schools that improve educational achievement and requiring all children to reach proficiency in state educational standards.

(12) Public Duty to Educate.   Consider whether a state has the constitutional duty to provide the opportunity for free public education, at least for children whose parents could not otherwise afford to send them to school. For example, could a state close its public schools or charge tuition?

In the United States, history and custom have created the expectation that all children, regardless of parental resources, are entitled to an education. Every state provides for free public education, typically through high school. Many state constitutions require as much. See, e.g., Mich. Const. Art. VIII, §2. The Supreme Court observed in Brown v. Board of Education, 347 U.S. 483, 493 (1954), that "education is perhaps the most important function of state and local govern-ments." Nevertheless, the Supreme Court held that education is not a "fundamental" right; i.e., the right to education is not explictly or implicitly guaranteed for purposes of requiring strict judicial scrutiny under the Equal Pro-tection Clause. See San Antonio Indep. Sch. Dist. v. Rodriguez, 411 U.S. 1 (1973). The Court left open in *Rodriguez,* however, the possibility that a state would violate equal protection if it adopted a system that absolutely denied all educational opportunities to any of its children. See 411 U.S. at 36-37.

This issue was squarely faced by the Court in Plyler v. Doe, 457 U.S. 202 (1982) (holding unconstitutional a Texas statute that denied funds for a free edu-cation of undocumented school-age alien children). In *Plyler,* the Court reaffirmed its position that "[p]ublic education is not a 'right' granted to individuals by the Constitution." But, the Court went on to point out, "neither is it merely some governmental 'benefit' indistinguishable from other forms of social welfare leg-islation." Id. at 220. Noting the lifetime hardship and stigma connected with illit-eracy, the Court found that the statute denied to a discrete class of children (illegal aliens) a basic education, and by so doing, "foreclosed any realistic possibility that they will contribute in even the smallest way to the progress of our Nation" Id. at 223.

(13) Problem.   Recently, a nationwide "parental rights" movement has been gaining momentum to persuade legislators to amend state constitutions or to enact legislation to provide increased parental authority over children's education and discipline. The movement stems in part from concerns about controlling the teaching of sex education, AIDS, and homosexuality.

You are a legislator in a state legislature that is considering passage of the following state constitutional amendment:

Be It Resolved by the Legislature of Our State that the amendment proposed herein shall appear on the ballot as follows: Section 26 of Article 1 of the

State Constitution shall provide that parents have a fundamental right to raise, educate, and care for their children; require the Legislature to protect parental rights by appropriate legislation; and exclude application of the new section to minors emancipated by general law or laws protecting minors from neglect, abuse, or criminal wrongdoing.

The amendment addresses the relative rights of parents and children when such rights come into legal conflict, specifically by providing that parental rights supersede children's rights, including any rights claimed by minors under the privacy provision of the state constitution. This would allow the legislature to protect parental rights in all matters affecting their children, including, but not limited to, the decision of a minor to obtain an abortion. Minors would retain all of the rights guaranteed under the U.S. Constitution.

What arguments would you make in favor of the proposed legislation? Against? Does such legislation merely reaffirm *Meyer* and *Pierce* or does it grant parents additional rights?

Prince v. Massachusetts
321 U.S. 158 (1944)

Mr. Justice RUTLEDGE delivered the opinion of the Court.

The case brings for review another episode in the conflict between Jehovah's Witnesses and state authority. This time Sarah Prince appeals from convictions for violating Massachusetts' child labor laws, by acts said to be a rightful exercise of her religious convictions.

[T]he only questions for our decision [are] whether §§80 and 81 [of chapter 149, Gen. Laws of Mass.], as applied, contravene the Fourteenth Amendment by denying or abridging appellant's freedom of religion and by denying to her the equal protection of the laws.

Sections 80 and 81 form parts of Massachusetts' comprehensive child labor law. They provide methods for enforcing the prohibitions of §69, which is as follows:

> No boy under twelve and no girl under eighteen shall sell, expose or offer for sale any newspapers, magazines, periodicals or any other articles of merchandise of any description, or exercise the trade of bootblack or scavenger, or any other trade, in any street or public place.

Sections 80 and 81, so far as pertinent, read:

> Whoever furnishes or sells to any minor any article of any description with the knowledge that the minor intends to sell such article in violation of any provision of sections sixty-nine to seventy-three, inclusive, or after having received written notice to this effect from any officer charged with the enforcement thereof, or knowingly procures or encourages any minor to violate any provisions of said sections, shall be punished by a fine of not less than ten nor more than two hundred dollars or by imprisonment for not more than two months, or both.

Any parent, guardian or custodian having a minor under his control who compels or permits such minor to work in violation of any provision of sections sixty to seventy-four, inclusive, . . . shall for a first offense be punished by a fine of not less than two nor more than ten dollars or by imprisonment for not more than five days, or both; . . .

. . . Mrs. Prince, living in Brockton, is the mother of two young sons. She also has legal custody of Betty Simmons [a niece, age 9], who lives with them. The children too are Jehovah's Witnesses and both Mrs. Prince and Betty testified they were ordained ministers. The former was accustomed to go each week on the streets of Brockton to distribute "Watchtower" and "Consolation," according to the usual plan. She had permitted the children to engage in this activity previously, and had been warned against doing so by the school attendance officer, Mr. Perkins. But, until December 18, 1941, she generally did not take them with her at night.

That evening, as Mrs. Prince was preparing to leave her home, the children asked to go. She at first refused. Childlike, they resorted to tears; and, motherlike, she yielded. Arriving downtown, Mrs. Prince permitted the children "to engage in the preaching work with her upon the sidewalks." That is, with specific reference to Betty, she and Mrs. Prince took positions about twenty feet apart near a street intersection. Betty held up in her hand, for passers-by to see, copies of "Watchtower" and "Consolation." From her shoulders hung the usual canvas magazine bag on which was printed: "Watchtower and Consolation 5cts. per copy." No one accepted a copy from Betty that evening and she received no money. Nor did her aunt. But on other occasions, Betty had received funds and given out copies.

Mrs. Prince and Betty remained until 8:45 P.M. A few minutes before this, Mr. Perkins approached Mrs. Prince. A discussion ensued. He inquired and she refused to give Betty's name. However, she stated the child attended the Shaw School. Mr. Perkins referred to his previous warnings and said he would allow five minutes for them to get off the street. Mrs. Prince admitted she supplied Betty with the magazines and said, "[N]either you nor anybody else can stop me. . . . This child is exercising her God-given right and her constitutional right to preach the gospel, and no creature has a right to interfere with God's commands." However, Mrs. Prince and Betty departed. She remarked as she went, "I'm not going through this any more. We've been through it time and time again. I'm going home and put the little girl to bed." It may be added that testimony, by Betty, her aunt and others, was offered at the trials, and was excluded, to show that Betty believed it was her religious duty to perform this work and failure would bring condemnation "to everlasting destruction at Armageddon."

[T]he questions are no longer open whether what the child did was a "sale" or an "offer to sell" within §69 or was "work" within §81. . . . The only question remaining therefore is whether, as construed and applied, the statute is valid. . . .

[Appellant's argument] rests squarely on freedom of religion under the First Amendment, applied by the Fourteenth to the states. She buttresses this foundation, however, with a claim of parental right as secured by the due process clause of the latter Amendment. Cf. Meyer v. Nebraska, 262 U.S. 390. These guaranties, she thinks, guard alike herself and the child in what they have done. Thus, two claimed liberties are at stake. One is the parent's, to bring up the child in the way he should go, which for appellant means to teach him the tenets and the practices of their faith. The other freedom is the child's, to observe these; and among them is "to preach the gospel . . . by public distribution" of "Watchtower" and "Consolation," in conformity with the scripture: "A little child shall lead them." . . .

To make accommodation between these freedoms and an exercise of state authority always is delicate. . . . On one side is the obviously earnest claim for freedom of conscience and religious practice. With it is allied the parent's claim to authority in her own household and in the rearing of her children. The parent's conflict with the state over control of the child and his training is serious enough when only secular matters are concerned. It becomes the more so when an element of religious conviction enters. Against these sacred private interests, basic in a democracy, stand the interests of society to protect the welfare of children, and the state's assertion of authority to that end, made here in a manner conceded valid if only secular things were involved. . . . It is the interest of youth itself, and of the whole community, that children be both safeguarded from abuses and given opportunities for growth into free and independent well-developed men and citizens. . . .

The rights of children to exercise their religion, and of parents to give them religious training and to encourage them in the practice of religious belief, as against preponderant sentiment and assertion of state power voicing it, have had recognition here, most recently in West Virginia State Board of Education v. Barnette, 319 U.S. 624 [(1943)].[24] Previously in Pierce v. Society of Sisters, 268 U.S. 510, this Court had sustained the parent's authority to provide religious with secular schooling, and the child's right to receive it, as against the state's requirement of attendance at public schools. And in Meyer v. Nebraska, 262 U.S. 390, children's rights to receive teaching in languages other than the nation's common tongue were guarded against the state's encroachment. It is cardinal with us that the custody, care and nurture of the child reside first in the parents, whose primary function and freedom include preparation for obligations the state can neither supply nor hinder. Pierce v. Society of Sisters, supra. And it is in recognition of this that these decisions have respected the private realm of family life which the state cannot enter.

But the family itself is not beyond regulation in the public interest, as against a claim of religious liberty. Reynolds v. United States, 98 U.S. 145 [(1878)]; Davis v. Beason, 133 U.S. 333 [(1890)]. And neither rights of religion nor rights of parenthood are beyond limitation. Acting to guard the general interest in youth's well being, the state as parens patriae may restrict the parent's control by requiring school attendance, regulating or prohibiting the child's labor and in many other ways. Its authority is not nullified merely because the parent grounds his claim

[24] In West Virginia Board of Education v. Barnette, the Supreme Court upheld an injunction restraining the enforcement against Jehovah's Witnesses of a regulation requiring public school students to recite the Pledge of Allegiance under pain of expulsion. The Court based its decision on the First Amendment free speech guarantee that prohibited a compulsory rite "touching matters of opinion and political attitude," 319 U.S. at 636, although the plaintiffs were Jehovah's Witnesses parents bringing suit for themselves, their children, and others for whom the salute and pledge offended religious beliefs. Cf. Elk Grove Unified Sch. Dist. v. Newdow, 542 U.S. 1 (2004) (ruling that a noncustodial father lacked standing to challenge recitation of the Pledge of Allegiance).

to control the child's course of conduct on religion or conscience. Thus, he cannot claim freedom from compulsory vaccination for the child more than for himself on religious grounds. [Jacobson v. Massachusetts, 197 U.S. 11 (1905).] The right to practice religion freely does not include liberty to expose the community or the child to communicable disease or the latter to ill health or death. The catalogue . . . is sufficient to show what indeed appellant hardly disputes, that the state has a wide range of power for limiting parental freedom and authority in things affecting the child's welfare; and that this includes, to some extent, matters of conscience and religious conviction.

But it is said the state cannot do so here. This, first, because when state action impinges upon a claimed religious freedom, it must fall unless shown to be necessary for or conducive to the child's protection against some clear and present danger, and, it is added, there was no such showing here. The child's presence on the street, with her guardian, distributing or offering to distribute the magazines, it is urged, was in no way harmful to her, nor in any event more so than the presence of many other children at the same time and place, engaged in shopping and other activities not prohibited. Accordingly, in view of the preferred position the freedoms of the First Article occupy, the statute in its present application must fall. . . . And, finally, it is said, the statute is, as to children, an absolute prohibition, not merely a reasonable regulation, of the denounced activity.

Concededly a statute or ordinance identical in terms with §69, except that it is applicable to adults or all persons generally, would be invalid. But the mere fact a state could not wholly prohibit this form of adult activity, whether characterized locally as a "sale" or otherwise, does not mean it cannot do so for children. . . .

The state's authority over children's activities is broader than over like actions of adults. This is peculiarly true of public activities and in matters of employment. A democratic society rests, for its continuance, upon the healthy, well-rounded growth of young people into full maturity as citizens, with all that implies. It may secure this against impeding restraints and dangers within a broad range of selection. Among evils most appropriate for such action are the crippling effects of child employment, more especially in public places, and the possible harms arising from other activities subject to all the diverse influences of the street. It is too late now to doubt that legislation appropriately designed to reach such evils is within the state's police power, whether against the parent's claim to control of the child or one that religious scruples dictate contrary action.

It is true children have rights, in common with older people, in the primary use of highways. But even in such use streets afford dangers for them not affecting adults. And in other uses, whether in work or in other things, this difference may be magnified. This is so not only when children are unaccompanied but certainly to some extent when they are with their parents. What may be wholly permissible for adults therefore may not be so for children, either with or without their parents' presence.

[T]he validity of [the street preaching] prohibition applied to children not accompanied by an older person hardly would seem open to question. The case reduces itself therefore to the question whether the presence of the child's guardian puts a limit to the state's power. That fact may lessen the likelihood that some evils the legislation seeks to avert will occur. But it cannot forestall all of them. The zealous though lawful exercise of the right to engage in propagandizing the community, whether in religious, political or other matters, may and at times does create situations difficult enough for adults to cope with and wholly inappropriate for children, especially of tender years, to face. . . . Parents may be free to become martyrs themselves. But it does not follow they are free, in identical circumstances, to make martyrs of their children before they have reached the age of full and legal discretion when they can make that choice for themselves. Massachusetts has determined that an absolute prohibition, though one limited to streets and public places and to the incidental uses proscribed, is necessary to accomplish its legitimate objectives. Its power to attain them is broad enough to reach these peripheral instances in which the parent's supervision may reduce but cannot eliminate entirely the ill effects of the prohibited conduct. We think that with reference to the public proclaiming of religion, upon the streets and in other similar public places, the power of the state to control the conduct of children reaches beyond the scope of its authority over adults, as is true in the case of other freedoms, and the rightful boundary of its power has not been crossed in this case.

In so ruling we dispose also of appellant's argument founded upon denial of equal protection. [T]he contention is that the street, for Jehovah's Witnesses and their children, is their church . . . and to deny them access to it for religious purposes as was done here has the same effect as excluding altar boys, youthful choristers, and other children from the edifices in which they practice their religious beliefs and worship. . . . However Jehovah's Witnesses may conceive them, the public highways have not become their religious property merely by their assertion. And there is no denial of equal protection in excluding their children from doing there what no other children may do. . . .

The judgment is affirmed.

QUESTIONS ON PRINCE v. MASSACHUSETTS

(1) State's Power.   The Court states that a child labor prohibition, such as §69 applied in *Prince,* would not be constitutional if applied to adult Jehovah's Witnesses, and the cases cited by the Court support that conclusion. Why should the state's power be greater vis-à-vis children? What reasons does the Court give for its conclusion that the "validity of such a prohibition applied to children not accompanied by an older person hardly would seem open to question" (supra p. 61)? Do you agree with the conclusion? What reasons can you give? Do these reasons apply if the child is accompanied by an adult? A parent or guardian?

(2) Actual Harm.   Was there a showing in *Prince* of actual risk or harm to this particular child? Do the justifications for preventing child labor apply to the facts of this case? See Chapter 6. Is there any harm on the facts of *Prince* to any substantial state interest?

(3) Limits of State's Power.   Does the Court in *Prince* define the outer limits of the state's power to constrict parental freedom because of the state's interest in protecting the child? What do you think those limits are?

Wisconsin v. Yoder
406 U.S. 205 (1972)

Mr. Chief Justice BURGER delivered the opinion of the Court. . . .

. . . Respondents Jonas Yoder and Adin Yutzy are members of the Old Order Amish Religion, and respondent Wallace Miller is a member of the Conservative Amish Mennonite Church. . . . Wisconsin's compulsory school attendance law required them to cause their children to attend public or private school until reaching age 16 but the respondents declined to send their children, ages 14 and 15, to public school after completing the eighth grade. The children were not enrolled in any private school, or within any recognized exception to the compulsory attendance law, and they are conceded to be subject to the Wisconsin statute.

On complaint of the school district administrator for the public schools, respondents were charged, tried, and convicted of violating the compulsory attendance law in Green County Court and were fined the sum of $5 each. Respondents defended on the ground that the application of the compulsory attendance law violated their rights under the First and Fourteenth Amendments. . . .

In support of their position, respondents presented as expert witnesses scholars on religion and education [who] expressed their opinions on the relationship of the Amish belief concerning school attendance to the more general tenets of their religion, and described the impact that compulsory high school attendance could have on the continued survival of Amish communities. . . . The history of the Amish sect was given in some detail, beginning with the Swiss Anabaptists of the 16th century who rejected institutionalized churches and sought to return to the early, simple, Christian life de-emphasizing material success, rejecting the competitive spirit, and seeking to insulate themselves from the modern world. As a result of their common heritage, Old Order Amish communities today are characterized by a fundamental belief that salvation requires life in a church community separate and apart from the world and worldly influence. This concept of life aloof from the world and its values is central to their faith.

A related feature of Old Order Amish communities is their devotion to a life in harmony with nature and the soil, as exemplified by the simple life of the early Christian era which continued in America during much of our early national life. Amish beliefs require members of the community to make their living by farming or closely related activities. . . .

Amish objection to formal education beyond the eighth grade is firmly grounded in these central religious concepts. They object to the high school and higher education generally because the values it teaches are in marked variance with Amish values and the Amish way of life; they view secondary school education as an impermissible exposure of their children to a "worldly" influence in conflict with their beliefs. . . .

Formal high school education beyond the eighth grade is contrary to Amish beliefs not only because it places Amish children in an environment hostile to Amish beliefs with increasing emphasis on competition in class work and sports and with pressure to conform to the styles, manners and ways of the peer group, but because it takes them away from their community, physically and emotionally, during the crucial and formative adolescent period of life. [H]igh school attendance with teachers who are not of the Amish faith — and may even be hostile to it — interposes a serious barrier to the integration of the Amish child into the Amish religious community. . . .

The Amish do not object to elementary education through the first eight grades as a general proposition because they agree that their children must have basic skills in the "three R's" in order to read the Bible, to be good farmers and citizens and to be able to deal with non-Amish people when necessary in the course of daily affairs.

[However, as Dr. John Hostetler, an expert on Amish society, testified,] compulsory high school attendance could not only result in great psychological harm to Amish children, because of the conflicts it would produce, but would, in his opinion, ultimately result in the destruction of the Old Order Amish church community as it exists in the United States today. The testimony of Dr. Donald A. Erickson, an expert witness on education, also showed that the Amish succeed in preparing their high school age children to be productive members of the Amish community. He described their system of learning-through-doing the skills directly relevant to their adult roles in the Amish community as "ideal" and perhaps superior to ordinary high school education. . . .

In sum, the unchallenged testimony of acknowledged experts in education and religious history, almost 300 years of consistent practice, and strong evidence of a sustained faith pervading and regulating respondents' entire mode of life support the claim that enforcement of the State's requirement of compulsory formal education after the eighth grade would gravely endanger if not destroy the free exercise of respondents' religious beliefs.

III . . .

We turn then to the State's broader contention that its interest in its system of compulsory education is so compelling that even the established religious practices of the Amish must give way. . . .

The State advances two primary arguments in support of its system of compulsory education. It notes, as Thomas Jefferson pointed out early in our history, that some degree of education is necessary to prepare citizens to participate effectively and intelligently in our open political system if we are to preserve freedom and independence. Further, education prepares individuals to be self-reliant and self-sufficient participants in society. We accept these propositions.

However, the evidence adduced by the Amish in this case is persuasively to the effect that an additional one or two years of formal high school for Amish children in place of their long established program of informal vocational education would do little to serve those interests. . . . It is one thing to say that compulsory education for a year or two beyond the eighth grade may be necessary when its goal is the preparation of the child for life in modern society as the majority live, but it is quite another if the goal of education be viewed as the preparation of the child for life in the separated agrarian community that is the keystone of the Amish faith.

The State attacks respondents' position as one fostering "ignorance" from which the child must be protected by the State. No one can question the State's duty to protect children from ignorance but this argument does not square with the facts disclosed in the record. [T]he Amish community has been a highly successful social unit within our society even if apart from the conventional "mainstream." Its members are productive and very law-abiding members of society; they reject public welfare in any of its usual modern forms. . . .

The State, however, supports its interest in providing an additional one or two years of compulsory high school education to Amish children because of the possibility that some such children will choose to leave the Amish community, and that if this occurs they will be ill-equipped for life. [T]hat argument is highly speculative. There is no specific evidence of the loss of Amish adherents by attrition, nor is there any showing that upon leaving the Amish community Amish children, with their practical agricultural training and habits of industry and self-reliance would become burdens on society because of educational shortcomings. . . .

The requirement of compulsory schooling to age 16 must therefore be viewed as aimed not merely at providing educational opportunities for children, but as an alternative to the equally undesirable consequence of unhealthful child labor displacing adult workers, or, on the other hand, forced idleness. The two kinds of statutes — compulsory school attendance and child labor laws — tend to keep children of certain ages off the labor market and in school; this in turn provides opportunity to prepare for a livelihood of a higher order than that children could perform without education and protects their health in adolescence.

In these terms, Wisconsin's interest in compelling the school attendance of Amish children to age 16 emerges as somewhat less substantial than requiring such attendance for children generally. For, while agricultural employment is not totally outside the legitimate concerns of the child labor laws, employment of children under parental guidance and on the family farm from age 14 to age 16 is an ancient tradition which lies at the at the periphery of the objectives of such laws.[19] There is no intimation that the Amish employment of their children on family farms is in any way deleterious to their health or that Amish parents exploit children at tender years. . . . Moreover, employment of Amish children on the family farm does not present the undesirable economic aspects of eliminating jobs which might otherwise be held by adults.

IV

Finally, the State, on authority of Prince v. Massachusetts, argues that a decision exempting Amish children from the State's requirement fails to recognize the substantive right of the Amish child to a secondary education, and fails to give due regard to the power of the State as parens patriae to extend the benefit of secondary education to children regardless of the wishes of their parents. Taken at its broadest sweep, the Court's language in *Prince,* might be read to give support to

---

[19] . . . The Federal Fair Labor Standards Act of 1938 excludes from its definition of "oppressive child labor" employment of a child under age 16 by "a parent . . . employing his own child . . . in an occupation other than manufacturing or mining or an occupation found by the Secretary of Labor to be particularly hazardous for the employment of children between the ages of sixteen and eighteen years or detrimental to their health or well- being." 29 U.S.C. §203(1).

the State's position. However, the Court was not confronted in *Prince* with a situation comparable to that of the Amish as revealed in this record; this is shown by the Court's severe characterization of the evils which it thought the legislature could legitimately associate with child labor, even when performed in the company of an adult. 321 U.S., at 169-170. . . .

This case, of course, is not one in which any harm to the physical or mental health of the child or to the public safety, peace, order, or welfare has been demonstrated. The record is to the contrary, and any reliance on that theory would find no support in the evidence. . . .

[O]ur holding today in no degree depends on the assertion of the religious interest of the child as contrasted with that of the parents. It is the parents who are subject to prosecution here for failing to cause their children to attend school, and it is their right of free exercise, not that of their children, that must determine Wisconsin's power to impose criminal penalties on the parent. The dissent argues that a child who expresses a desire to attend public high school in conflict with the wishes of his parents should not be prevented from doing so. There is no reason for the Court to consider that point since it is not an issue in the case. The children are not parties to this litigation. The State has at no point tried this case on the theory that respondents were preventing their children from attending school against their expressed desires, and indeed the record is to the contrary.[21] The State's position from the outset has been that it is empowered to apply its compulsory attendance law to Amish parents in the same manner as to other parents — that is, without regard to the wishes of the child. That is the claim we reject today.

Our holding in no way determines the proper resolution of possible competing interests of parents, children, and the State in an appropriate state court proceeding in which the power of the State is asserted on the theory that Amish parents are preventing their minor children from attending high school despite their expressed desires to the contrary. Recognition of the claim of the State in such a proceeding would, of course, call into question traditional concepts of parental control over the religious upbringing and education of their minor children recognized in this Court's past decisions. It is clear that such an intrusion by a State into family decisions in the area of religious training would give rise to grave questions of religious freedom comparable to those raised here and those presented in Pierce v. Society of Sisters. On this record we neither reach nor decide those issues. . . .

However read, the Court's holding in *Pierce* stands as a charter of the rights of parents to direct the religious upbringing of their children. And, when the interests of parenthood are combined with a free exercise claim of the nature revealed by this record, more than merely a "reasonable relation to some purpose within the competency of the state" is required to sustain the validity of the State's requirement under the First Amendment. To be sure, the power of the parent, even when linked to a free exercise claim, may be subject to limitation under *Prince* if it appears that parental decisions will jeopardize the health or safety of the child,

---

[21] The only relevant testimony in the record is to the effect that the wishes of the one child who testified corresponded with those of her parents. Testimony of Frieda Yoder, Tr. 92-94, to the effect that her personal religious beliefs guided her decision to discontinue school attendance after the 8th grade. The other children were not called by either side.

or have a potential for significant social burdens. But in this case, the Amish have introduced persuasive evidence undermining the arguments the State has advanced to support its claims in terms of the welfare of the child and society as a whole. . . .

For the reasons stated we hold, with the Supreme Court of Wisconsin, that the First and Fourteenth Amendments prevent the State from compelling respondents to cause their children to attend formal high school to age 16. . . . Nothing we hold is intended to undermine the general applicability of the State's compulsory school attendance statutes. . . .

Affirmed.

Mr. Justice POWELL and Mr. Justice REHNQUIST took no part in the consideration or decision of this case.

Mr. Justice STEWART, with whom Mr. Justice BRENNAN joins, concurring. . . .

This case in no way involves any questions regarding the right of the children of Amish parents to attend public high schools, or any other institutions of learning, if they wish to do so. As the Court points out, there is no suggestion whatever in the record that the religious beliefs of the children here concerned differ in any way from those of their parents. Only one of the children testified. The last two questions and answers on her cross-examination accurately sum up her testimony.

> Q. So I take it then, Frieda, the only reason you are not going to school, and did not go to school since last September, is because of *your* religion?
> A. Yes.
> Q. That is the only reason?
> A. *Yes.* (Emphasis supplied.)

It is clear to me, therefore, that this record simply does not present the interesting and important issue discussed in Part II of the dissenting opinion of Mr. Justice Douglas. With this observation, I join the opinion and the judgment of the Court. [Justice Douglas's dissenting opinion is at p. 78 infra.]

NOTES AND QUESTIONS

(1) Justification. Does *Yoder* overrule *Prince?* How is *Prince* characterized and distinguished in *Yoder?* Does absence from public school risk "harm" to the "health" of the child, "public safety, peace, order or welfare"? If not, what then is the justification for compulsory secondary education?

(2) Conflict of Interests. Unlike *Pierce, Yoder* poses the question of whether there are constitutional interests of children and parents that outweigh the state's interest in compelling all children to attend school. What is at stake for (1) the Amish community; (2) Amish parents; (3) the state; and (4) the child?

Yoder presumes that the parents are in agreement about the child's religious and educational upbringing. Suppose that the parents disagree. How should such conflicts be resolved? In Elk Grove Unified School District v. Newdow, 542 U.S. 1 (2004), the United States Supreme Court ruled that a *noncustodial* father lacked standing to challenge under the Free Exercise and Establishment Clauses the required daily recitation at his daughter's public school of the phrase "under God" in the Pledge of Allegiance. The Court also rejected the father's argument that the Pledge recitation impaired his own right to instruct his daughter in his religious views. But cf. Circle Schools v. Pappert, 381 F.3d 172 (3d Cir. 2004) (holding that requirement that school students recite Pledge of Allegiance or national anthem at beginning of school day violated First Amendment and that parental notification clause, requiring parental notification of students who declined to recite pledge or refrained from saluting flag, constituted viewpoint discrimination in violation of First Amendment).

(3) State's Interest.   Does the state have a legitimate interest in "seeking to develop the latent talents of its children" and "in seeking to prepare them for the life style that they may *later choose,*" as Justice White, in an omitted concurring opinion, suggests (406 U.S. at 240)? Does an Amish child with only an eighth-grade education have a real chance to "later choose" to live outside the Amish community? Does the majority deal with this issue? The Wisconsin Supreme Court squarely decided that to "force a worldly education on all Amish children, the majority of whom do not want or need it, in order to confer a dubious benefit on the few who might later reject their religion is not a compelling interest." State v. Yoder, 182 N.W.2d 539 (Wis. 1971).

(4) *Yoder* can be seen as a case in which there is a conflict between the state and the Amish parents over how the children would be socialized. Are eight years of schooling sufficient to satisfy the two interests advanced by the state to justify compulsory education: the need to prepare children for citizenship and economic self-reliance? Will two years matter?

(5) Home Schooling.   Suppose parents have sincere religious or academic objections to sending their children to public school but they are not part of a self-contained and self-sufficient religious community for which an eighth-grade education and on-the-job training will suffice. Should they be allowed to educate their children at home?

Over the past several decades, an increasing number of parents have opted to educate their children at home. Home schooling is currently legal in all states. Some estimates place the number of home-schooled children at 2 percent of the total school age children in the country. Kimberly A. Yuracko, Education Off the Grid: Constitutional Constraints on Homeschooling, 96 Cal. L. Rev. 123, 125 (2008). Whereas the original home schooling movement was dominated by liberal progressive reformers, the modern movement is influenced by conservative Christians who desire to shield their children from harmful secular values. Id. at 126-127. Federal and state courts have upheld parents' right to home school. However, states retain the power to regulate home schooling, including the qualifications of the instructors, curriculum, number of days of instruction, administration of standardized tests, and parental reporting obligations. See, e.g., Mass. Gen. Laws. Ann. ch. 76, §1 (West 1996 & Supp. 2008); Mich. Comp. Laws Ann. §380.1561 (West 2005 & Supp. 2007).

A California appellate court recently held that parents do not have a constitutional right to home school their children and that the state compulsory education law requires that children (ages 6 to 18) attend either a full-time public or private school or be taught by credentialed tutors at home. In re Rachel L., 73 Cal.Rptr.3d 77 (Ct. App. 2008). The ruling was met with such criticism that the court agreed to reconsider. On reconsideration, the court ruled that state law does permit home schooling (even without a teaching credential). However, the court added that the right to home school may be overridden to protect the safety of a child who has been abused or neglected. Jonathan L. v. Superior Court, 81 Cal.Rptr.3d 571 (Ct. App. 2008). How does this ruling square with *Meyer, Pierce, Prince*, and *Yoder*? Note that the California home schooling cases stemmed from a Department of Social Services investigation regarding possible child abuse and neglect. How should the state accommodate parents' right to educate their children at home versus the state's policy of ensuring that children are protected from abuse and neglect? For further discussion of child abuse and neglect, see Chapter 3.

(6) Special Public School District.   Should self-contained, self-sufficient religious communities be able to establish their own public school districts if they are opposed, for religious reasons, to their children attending regular public schools? In Kiryas Joel Village School District v. Grumet, 512 U.S. 687 (1994), a public school district was created by special legislative act in an exclusive Hasidic community. The religious group, adherents of a strict sect of Judaism, had plenary authority over education in the district. The Supreme Court held that the creation of such a district violated the Establishment Clause.

Immediately after the decision, the New York state legislature abolished the special district and enacted a new law attempting to re-establish the district under more religiously neutral grounds. That statute and another subsequent statute reestablishing the special school district were declared unconstitutional. Grumet v. Cuomo, 625 N.Y.S.2d 1000 (N.Y Sup. Ct. 1995), *rev'd,* 647 N.Y.2d 565 (N.Y. App. Div. 1996), *aff'd,* 681 N.E.2d 340 (N.Y. 1997). See also Grumet v. Pataki, 675 N.Y.S.2d 662 (N.Y. App. Div. 1998); *motion to vacate denied,* 702 N.E.2d 837 (N.Y. 1998), *aff'd,* 720 N.E.2d 66 (N.Y. 1999), *stay granted,* 527 U.S. 1019 (1999), *cert, denied,* 528 U.S 946 (1999). However, the fourth attempt of the state legislature was upheld, thus ending the 12-year effort to create a separate school district for the community. See Tamar Lewin, Controversy Over, Enclave Joins School Board Group, N.Y. Times, Apr. 20, 2002, at B4.

(7) Federal Legislation.   Subsequent to *Yoder,* the Supreme Court decided Employment Division v. Smith, 494 U.S. 872 (1990), in which two employees were terminated for smoking peyote, a ritual of their Native American religion. They claimed that their termination constituted a violation of their right to free exercise of their religion. Rejecting this argument, the Court held that free exercise can bar application of a generally applicable law only when joined with a violation of some other constitutional protection, such as freedom of speech or press, or a parental right (citing *Yoder*). In 1993, Congress rejected this interpretation and enacted the Religious Freedom Restoration Act (RFRA), 42 U.S.C. §2000bb (1994), requiring states to provide religious exemptions from generally applicable laws. In City of Boerne v. Flores, 521 U.S. 507 (1997), the Supreme Court ruled RFRA unconstitutional on the ground that it exceeded Congress's enforcement powers under the Fourteenth Amendment. Three years later, Congress enacted a narrower version of the RFRA. The Religious Land Use and Institutionalized Persons Act of 2000 (RLUIPA), 42 U.S.C. §§2000cc to 2000cc-5 (2000), exempts

religious institutions from regulations that impose a "substantial burden" on religious exercise. The Supreme Court upheld RLUIPA in Cutter v. Wilkinson, 544 U.S. 709 (2005).

(8) Epilogue.   Economic pressures and the scarcity of farmland have contributed to a transformation in the nature of Amish labor from farming to sawmills and woodworking. See Joe Milicia, Outside World Touches Amish; Many Have Left Farming and Operate Small Businesses. Farm Machinery and Telephones Have Become Part of Their Lives, L.A. Times, May 16, 2004, at A26; S. 974, 108th Cong. (2003) (remarks of Sen. Specter (R.-Pa.)) As a result, the Amish have incurred fines for violating the Fair Labor Standards Act of 1938, 29 U.S.C. §213(c) (2000), which gives the U.S. Department of Labor the authority to set child labor standards to prohibit children from working in hazardous occupations.

In 2004, to address the issue of Amish labor, Congress enacted an amendment to the Fair Labor Standards Act exempting a minor from child labor restrictions if the minor is "supervised by an adult relative of the entrant or is supervised by an adult member of the same religious sect or division as the entrant" and does not himself operate the woodworking machinery. See Consolidated Appropriations Act, 2004; Pub. L. No. 108-199, §108, 118 Stat. 3, 236 (2004). Critics pointed out that the fatality rate for the lumber and wood products industry is five times the national average. See H.R. 4257, 105th Cong. (1998) (remarks of Rep. Bill Clay (D.-Mo.)). Does such legislation violate the Establishment Clause?

Roger W. McIntire, Parenthood Training or Mandatory Birth Control: Take Your Choice
Psychology Today 34 (Oct. 1973)

Few parents like to be told how to raise their children, and even fewer will like the idea of someone telling them whether they can have children in the first place. But that's exactly what I'm proposing — the licensing of parenthood. Of course, civil libertarians and other liberals will claim this would infringe the parents' rights to freedom of choice and equal opportunity. But what about the rights of children? Surely the parents' competence will influence their children's freedom and opportunity. Today, any couple has the right to try parenting, regardless of how incompetent they might be. No one seems to worry about the unfortunate subjects of their experimenting.

The idea of licensing parenthood is hardly new. But until recently, our ignorance of environmental effects, our ignorance of contraception, and our selfish bias against the rights of children have inhibited public discussion of the topic. In recent years, however, psychologists have taught us just how crucial the effect of the home environment can be, and current research on contraception appears promising.

Contraception by Capsule

Successful control of parenthood will require a contraceptive that remains in effect until it is removed or counteracted by the administration of a second drug. . . .

The Child Victim

Clearly, we will soon have the technology necessary to carry out a parenthood licensing program, and history tells us that whenever we develop a technology, we inevitably use it. We should now be concerned with developing the criteria for good parenthood. In some extreme cases we already have legal and social definitions. We obviously consider child abuse wrong, and look upon those who physically mistreat their children as bad parents. In some states the courts remove children from the custody of parents convicted of child abuse.

In a recent review of studies of child-abusing parents, John J. Spinetta and David Rigler concluded that such people are generally ignorant of proper child-rearing practices. They also noted that many child-abusing parents had been victims of abuse and neglect in their own youth. Thus our lack of control over who can be parents magnifies the problem with each generation.

In the case of child-abusing parents, the state attempts to prevent the most obvious physical mistreatment of children. At this extreme, our culture does demand that parents prove their ability to provide for the physical well-being of their children. But our culture makes almost no demands when it comes to the children's psychological well-being and development. Any fool can now raise a child anyway he or she pleases, and it's none of our business. The child becomes the unprotected victim of whoever gives birth to him.

Ironically, the only institutions that do attempt to screen potential parents are the adoption agencies, although their screening can hardly be called scientific. Curiously enough, those who oppose a parent-licensing law usually do not oppose the discriminating policies practiced by the adoption agencies. It seems that our society cares more about the selection of a child's second set of parents than it does about his original parents. In other words, our culture insists on insuring a certain quality of parenthood for adopted children, but if you want to have one of your own, feel free.

Screening and selecting potential parents by no means guarantees that they will in fact be good parents. Yet today we have almost no means of insuring proper child-rearing methods. The indiscriminate "right to parent" enables everyone, however ill-equipped, to practice any parental behavior they please. Often their behavior would be illegal if applied to any group other than children. But because of our prejudice against the rights of children, we protect them only when the most savage and brutal parental behavior can be proved in court. Consider the following example:

Supermarket Scenario

A mother and daughter enter a supermarket. An accident occurs when the daughter pulls the wrong orange from the pile and 37 oranges are given their freedom. The mother grabs the daughter, shakes her vigorously, and slaps her. What is your reaction? Do you ignore the incident? Do you consider it a family squabble and none of your business? Or do you go over and advise the mother not to hit her child? If the mother rejects your advice, do you physically restrain her? If she persists, do you call the police? Think about your answers for a moment.

Now let me change one detail. *The girl was not that mother's daughter.* Do you feel different? Would you act differently? Why? Do "real" parents have the right to abuse their children because they "own" them? Now let me change another detail. Suppose the daughter was 25 years old, and yelled, "Help me! Help me!" Calling the police sounded silly when I first suggested it. How does it sound with a mere change in the age of the victim?

Now let's go back to the original scene where we were dealing with a small child. Were you about to advise the mother or insist? Were you going to say she shouldn't or couldn't? It depends on whose rights you're going to consider. If you think about the mother's right to mother as she sees fit, then you advise; but if you think about the child's right as a human being to be protected from the physical assault of this woman, then you insist. The whole issue is obviously tangled in a web of beliefs about individual rights, parental rights, and children's rights. We tend to think children deserve what they get, or at least must suffer it. Assault and battery, verbal abuse, and even forced imprisonment become legal if the victims are children.

When I think about the issue of children's rights, and the current development of new contraceptives, I see a change coming in this country. I'm tempted to make the following prediction in the form of a science-fiction story:

Motherhood in the [Future]

"Lock" was developed as a kind of semipermanent contraceptive. . . . One dose of Lock and a woman became incapable of ovulation until the antidote "Unlock" was administered. As with most contraceptives, Lock required a prescription, with sales limited by the usual criteria of age and marital status.

Gradually, however, a subtle but significant distinction became apparent. Other contraceptives merely allowed a woman to protect herself against pregnancy at her own discretion. Once Lock was administered, however, the prescription for Unlock required an active decision to allow the *possibility* of pregnancy.

[Soon,] the two drugs were being prescribed simultaneously, leaving the Unlock decision in the hands of the potential mother. Of course, problems arose. Mothers smuggled Lock to their daughters and the daughters later asked for Unlock. Women misplaced the Unlock and had to ask for more. Faced with the threat of a black market, the state set up a network of special dispensaries for the contraceptive and its antidote. When the first dispensaries opened . . . , they dispensed Lock rather freely, since they could always regulate the use of Unlock. But it soon became apparent that special local committees would be necessary to screen applicants for Unlock. "After all," the dispensary officials asked themselves, "how would you like to be responsible for this person becoming a parent?"

Protect Our Children

That same year, [when the dispensaries opened], brought the school-population riots. Overcrowding had forced state education officials to take some action.

Thanks to more efficient educational techniques, they were able to consider reducing the number of years of required schooling. This, however, would have thrown millions of teenagers out onto the already overcrowded job market, which would make the unions unhappy. Thus, rather than shortening the entire educational process, the officials decided to shorten the school day into two half-day shifts. That led to the trouble.

Until then, people had assumed that schools existed primarily for the purpose of education. But the decision to shorten the school day exposed the dependence of the nation's parents on the school as the great baby sitter of their offspring. Having won the long struggle for daycare centers, and freedom from diapers and bottles, mothers were horrified at the prospect of a few more hours of responsibility every day until their children reached 18 or 21. They took to the streets.

In Richmond, Virginia, a neighborhood protest over the shortened school day turned into a riot. One of the demonstrators picked up a traffic sign near the school that cautioned drivers to "Protect Our Children," and found herself leading the march toward city hall. Within a week that sign became the national slogan for the protesters, as well as for the Lock movement. It came to mean not only protecting our children from overcrowding and lack of supervision, but also protecting them from pregnancy.

Because of the school-population riots, distribution of Lock took on the characteristics of an immunization program under the threat of an epidemic. With immunization completed, the state could control the birth rate like a water faucet by the distribution of Unlock. However, this did not solve the problem of deciding who should bear the nation's children.

Congress Takes Over

To settle the issue, Congress appointed a special blue-ribbon commission of psychologists, psychiatrists, educators, and clergymen to come up with acceptable criteria for parenthood, and a plan for a licensing program. The commission issued its report. . . . Based upon its recommendations, Congress set up a Federal regulatory agency to administer a national parenthood-licensing program similar to driver-training and licensing procedures.

The agency now issues study guides for the courses, and sets the required standards of child-rearing knowledge. Of course, the standards vary for parents, teachers, and childcare professionals, depending upon the degree of responsibility involved. The courses and exams are conducted by local community colleges, under the supervision of the Federal agency. Only upon passing the exams can prospective parents receive a prescription for Unlock.

Distribution of Lock and Unlock is now strictly regulated by the Federal agency's local commissions. Since the records of distribution are stored in Federal computer banks, identification of illegitimate pregnancies (those made possible by the unauthorized use of Unlock) has become a simple matter. Parents convicted of this crime are fined, and required to begin an intensive parenthood-training program immediately. If they do not qualify by the time their child is born, the child goes to a community childcare program until they do.

Drawing the Battle Lines

As might be expected, the parent-licensing program has come under attack from those who complain about the loss of their freedom to create and raise children according to their own choice and beliefs. To such critics, the protect-our-children or Lock faction argues: "It's absurd to require education and license to drive a car, but allow anybody to raise our most precious possession or to add to the burden of this possession without demonstrating an ability to parent."

"But the creation of life is in the hands of God," says the freedom-and-right-to-parent-faction (referred to by their opposition as the "far-right-people").

"Nonsense," say the Lock people. "Control over life creation was acquired with the first contraceptive. The question is whether we use it with intelligence or not."

"But that question is for each potential parent to answer as an individual," say the far-right-people.

The Lock people answer: "Those parents ask the selfish question of whether they want a child or not. We want to know if the child will be adequately cared for — by them and by the culture."

The far right respond, "God gave us bodies and all their functions. We have a right to the use of those functions. Unlock should be there for the asking. Why should the Government have a say in whether I have a child?"

"Because the last century has shown that the Government will be saddled with most of the burden of raising your child," say the Lock people. "The schools, the medical programs, the youth programs, the crime-prevention programs, the colleges, the park and planning commissions — they will be burdened with your child. That's why the Government should have a say. The extent of the Government's burden depends on your ability to raise your child. If you screw it up, the society *and* Government will suffer. That's why they should screen potential parents."

From the right again: "The decision of my spouse and myself is sacred. It's none of their damn business."

But the Locks argue: "If you raised your child in the wilderness and the child's malfunctions punished no one but yourselves, it would be none of their damn business. But if your child is to live with us, be educated by us, suffered by us, add to the crowd of us, we should have a say."

Face of the Future

I can understand how some people might find this story either far-fetched or frightening, but I don't think any prediction in it is too far in the future. Carl Djerassi suggested the possibility of a semipermanent contraceptive such as "Lock" and "Unlock" (although he didn't use those brand names) as early as 1969, in an article in Science. [O]ther scientists are currently making significant strides in contraceptive research.

Throughout history, as knowledge has eroded away superstition about conception and birth, humans have taken increasing control over the birth of their offspring. Religious practices, arranged marriages, mechanical and biochemical contraception have all played a role in this regulation of procreation. Until now, however, such regulation has dealt only with the presence or absence of children, leaving their development to cultural superstitions. Anyone with normal biology may still produce another child, and, within the broadest limits, treat it anyway he or she chooses.

We have taken a long time in coming to grips with this problem because our society as a whole has had no demonstrably better ideas about child-rearing than any individual parent. And until now, people couldn't be stopped from having children because we haven't had the technology that would enable us to control individual fertility.

How to Rear a Child

The times are changing. With the population problem now upon us, we can no longer afford the luxury of allowing any two fools to add to our numbers whenever they please. We do have, or soon will have, the technology to control individual procreation. And, most important, psychology and related sciences have by now established some child-rearing principles that should be part of every parent's knowledge. An objective study of these principles need not involve the prying, subjective investigation now used by adoption agencies. It would merely insure that potential parents would be familiar with the principles of sound child-rearing. Examinations and practical demonstrations would test their knowledge. Without having state agents check every home (and of course, we would never accept such "Big Brother" tactics) there could be no way to enforce the use of that knowledge. But insistence on the knowledge would itself save a great deal of suffering by the children.

The following list suggests a few of the topics with which every parent should be familiar:

1. Principles of sound nutrition and diet.
2. Changes in nutritional requirements with age.
3. Principles of general hygiene and health.
4. Principles of behavioral development: normal range of ages at which behavioral capabilities might be expected, etc.
5. Principles of learning and language acquisition.
6. Principles of immediacy and consistency that govern parents' reactions to children's behavior.
7. Principles of modeling and imitation: how children learn from and copy their parents' behavior.
8. Principles of reinforcement: how parent and peer reactions reward a child's behavior, and which rewards should be used.
9. Principles of punishment: how parents' reactions can be used to punish or discourage bad behavior.
10. Response-cost concept: how to "raise the cost" or create unpleasant consequences in order to make undesirable behavior more "expensive" or difficult.

11. Extinction procedures and adjunctive behavior: if rewards for good behavior cease, children may "act up" just to fill the time.
12. Stimulus-control generalization: children may act up in some situations, and not in others, because of different payoffs. For example, Mommy may give the child candy to stop a tantrum, whereas Daddy may ignore it or strike the child.

Most of us have some familiarity with the principles at the beginning of this list, but many parents have little knowledge of the other topics. Some psychologists would obviously find my list biased toward behavior modification, but their revisions or additions to the list only strengthen my argument that our science has a great deal to teach that would be relevant to a parenthood-licensing program.

Misplaced Priorities

Of course the word licensing suggests that the impersonal hand of Government may control individual lives, and that more civil servants will be paid to meddle in our personal affairs. But consider for a moment that for our safety and well-being we already license pilots, salesmen, scuba divers, plumbers, electricians, teachers, veterinarians, cab drivers, soil testers and television repairmen. To protect pedestrians, we accept restrictions on the speed with which we drive our cars. Why, then, do we encourage such commotion, chest thumping, and cries of oppression when we try to protect the well-being of children by controlling the most crucial determiner of that well-being, the competence of their parents? Are our TV sets and toilets more important to us than our children? Can you imagine the public outcry that would occur if adoption agencies offered their children on a first-come-first-served basis, with no screening process for applicants? Imagine some drunk stumbling up and saying, "I'll take that cute little blond-haired girl over there."

We require appropriate education for most trades and professions, yet stop short at parenthood because it would be an infringement on the individual freedom of the parent. The foolishness of this position will become increasingly apparent the more confident we become in our knowledge about child-rearing.

The first step toward a parenthood law will probably occur when child-abuse offenders will be asked or required to take "Lock" as an alternative to, or in addition to, being tried in court. Or the courts may also offer the child abuser the alternative of a remedial training program such as the traffic courts now use. The next step may be the broadening of the term "child abuse" to include ignorant mistreatment of a psychological nature. Some communities may add educational programs to marriage-license requirements, while others may add parenthood training to existing courses in baby care.

When the Government gets around to setting criteria for proper childrearing, these must be based upon a very specific set of principles of nutrition, hygiene, and behavior control. They cannot be based on bias and hearsay. Some of the criteria now used by adoption agencies, such as references from neighbors and friends, cannot be considered objective. We don't interview your neighbors when you apply for a driver's license, and it shouldn't be done for a parent's license either. But just as a citizen must now demonstrate knowledge and competence to drive a car, so ought he to demonstrate his ability to parent as well. Proof of exposure to education is not enough. We are not satisfied merely with driver training courses, but demand a driver's test as well. We should require the same standards of parents.

We can hope that as progress occurs in the technology of contraception and the knowledge of child-rearing principles, the current "right to parent" will be re-evaluated by our society. Perhaps we can construct a society that will also consider the rights that children have to a humane and beneficial upbringing.

PROBLEM: SHOULD THE GOVERNMENT LICENSE PARENTS?

Assume it is the year 2020, and you are legislative counsel to a United States Senator. A bill has been drafted setting up a federal regulatory agency to administer a national parenthood-licensing program incorporating the ideas put forward in the McIntire article. Would such a bill be constitutional in light of *Roe, Pierce, Prince,* and *Yoder?* If not, which provisions are invalid? As applied to whom? What changes would make the bill valid? Could there be compulsory contraception? Compulsory adult education in parenting? Would either make sense in terms of policy?

With the benefit of hindsight, do McIntire's predictions seem so outlandish? Consider the following:

(1) The fictional "Lock" was intended as a semipermanent contraceptive, requiring a prescription. Once "Lock" was administered, a prescription for "Unlock" necessitated an affirmative decision to procreate. Do we now possess the technology to implement a parenthood licensing program? Various semiper-manent contraceptives (e.g., implantable as well as injectable methods) currently provide effective birth control for periods ranging from three months to five years. Are these contraceptives the nonfictional equivalents of "Lock"?

(2) McIntire also suggests that the "first step toward a parenthood law" would occur with the imposition of "Lock" as an alternative to trial. In In re Bobbijean P., No. NN 03626-03, 2005 WL 127048 (N.Y. Fam. Ct. Jan. 10, 2005), a family court judge ordered two parents, after a finding of neglect, not to conceive additional children until the parents were able to obtain custody of their children currently in foster care. The court did not mandate a particular birth control method, pointing instead to the variety of methods (including injections, Norplant, and the patch, among others). The family court judge subsequently denied plantiffs' motion to vacate the restriction on procreation. See also State v. Oakley, 629 N.W.2d 200 (Wis. 2001), *reconsideration denied & opinion clarified,* 635 N.W.2d 760 (Wis. 2001) (holding that a condition of probation, that defendant avoid having another child unless he showed that he could support that child and current children, was valid despite its infringement upon the fundamental right to pro-create). Do these cases suggest that we have taken "the first step toward a parent-hood law"?

Several states considered legislation mandating use of the implantable contra-ceptive Norplant by convicted child abusers. Other states considered legislation to make Norplant mandatory for female drug addicts or welfare recipients. Are such measures sound policy? Are they constitutional? See generally Kimberly A. Smith,

Note, Conceivable Sterilization: A Constitutional Analysis of a Norplant/Depo-Provera Welfare Condition, 77 Ind. L.J. 389 (2002). In August 2002, the manu-facturer of Norplant suspended sales of the contraceptive after settling the claims of 30,000 women who claimed that they had not been warned adequately about the drug's side effects. Andrew Harris, Ruling Finishes Off Norplant Suits, Nat'l. L.J., Sept. 30, 2002, at B6.

McIntire also suggests that another "next step" will be broadening of the term "child abuse" to include psychological abuse. Since his article, many states have expanded the definition in this manner. See, e.g., Alaska Stat. §47.17.010 (2006) (definition includes mental injury); 23 Pa. Cons. Stat. Ann. §6303 (West 2001 & Supp. 2007). Issues of child abuse are explored further in Chapter 3. For thought-provoking essays about parental licensing, see Claudia Mangel, Licensing Parents: How Feasible?, 22 Fam. L.Q. 17 (1988); Michael J. Sandmire & Michael S. Wald, Licensing Parents: A Response to Claudia Mangel's Proposal, 24 Fam. L.Q. 53 (1990). See also Jack C. Westman, Licensing Parents: Can We Prevent Child Abuse and Neglect? (2001).

D. *WHAT VOICE FOR THE CHILD?*

The majority in *Yoder* sidestepped analyzing the possible conflict between the views of the Amish children and the views of their parents about the children's best interests. Should the majority have sought to identify the independent interests of the children? How? Should the children have been separately represented in the litigation? Are there disadvantages to this sort of inquiry? Consider the approach advocated by Justice Douglas in his dissenting opinion in *Yoder,* which follows.

Wisconsin v. Yoder
406 U.S. 205, 241 (1972)

. . . Mr. Justice Douglas, dissenting in part:

I

I agree with the Court that the religious scruples of the Amish are opposed to the education of their children beyond the grade schools, yet I disagree with the Court's conclusion that the matter is within the dispensation of parents alone. The Court's analysis assumes that the only interests at stake in the case are those of the Amish parents on the one hand, and those of the State on the other. The difficulty with this approach is that, despite the Court's claim, the parents are seeking to vindicate not only their own free exercise claims, but also those of their high-school-age children.

It is argued that the right of the Amish children to religious freedom is not presented by the facts of the case, as the issue before the Court involves only the

Amish parents' religious freedom to defy a state criminal statute imposing upon them an affirmative duty to cause their children to attend high school.

First, respondents' motion to dismiss in the trial court expressly asserts, not only the religious liberty of the adults, but also that of the children, as a defense to the prosecutions. It is, of course, beyond question that the parents have standing as defendants in a criminal prosecution to assert the religious interests of their children as a defense.[1] Although the lower courts and the majority in this Court assume an identity of interest between parent and child, it is clear that they have treated the religious interest of the child as a factor in the analysis.

Second, it is essential to reach the question to decide the case not only because the question was squarely raised in the motion to dismiss, but also because no analysis of religious liberty claims can take place in a vacuum. If the parents in this case are allowed a religious exemption, the inevitable effect is to impose the parents' notions of religious duty upon their children. Where the child is mature enough to express potentially conflicting desires, it would be an invasion of the child's rights to permit such an imposition without canvassing his views. As in *Prince,* it is an imposition resulting from this very litigation. As the child has no other effective forum, it is in this litigation that his rights should be considered. And, if an Amish child desires to attend high school, and is mature enough to have that desire respected, the State may well be able to override the parents' religiously motivated objections.

Religion is an individual experience. It is not necessary, nor even appropriate, for every Amish child to express his views on the subject in a prosecution of a single adult. Crucial, however, are the views of the child whose parent is the subject of the suit. Frieda Yoder has in fact testified that her own religious views are opposed to high-school education. I therefore join the judgment of the Court as to respondent Jonas Yoder. But Frieda Yoder's views may not be those of Vernon Yutzy or Barbara Miller. I must dissent, therefore, as to respondents Adin Yutzy and Wallace Miller as their motion to dismiss also raised the question of their children's religious liberty.

II

This issue has never been squarely presented before today. Our opinions are full of talk about the power of the parents over the child's education. See Pierce v. Society of Sisters, 268 U.S. 510; Meyer v. Nebraska, 262 U.S. 390. And we have in the past analyzed similar conflicts between parent and State with little regard for the views

---

[1] Thus, in Prince v. Massachusetts, 321 U.S. 158, a Jehovah's Witness was convicted for having violated a state child labor law by allowing her nine-year-old niece and ward to circulate religious literature on the public streets. There, as here, the narrow question was the religious liberty of the adult. There, as here, the Court analyzed the problem from the point of view of the State's conflicting interest in the welfare of the child. But, as Mr. Justice Brennan, speaking for the Court, has so recently pointed out, "The Court [in *Prince*] implicitly held that the custodian had standing to assert alleged freedom of religion . . . rights of the child that were threatened in the very litigation before the Court and that the child had no effective way of asserting herself." Eisenstadt v. Baird, 405 U.S. 446, n. 6. Here, as in *Prince*, the children have no effective alternate means to vindicate their rights. The question, therefore, is squarely before us.

of the child. See Prince v. Massachusetts, 321 U.S. 158. Recent cases, however, have clearly held that the children themselves have constitutionally protective interests.

These children are "persons" within the meaning of the Bill of Rights. We have so held over and over again. . . .

On this important and vital matter of education, I think the children should be entitled to be heard. While the parents, absent dissent, normally speak for the entire family, the education of the child is a matter on which the child will often have decided views. He may want to be a pianist or an astronaut or an ocean geographer. To do so he will have to break from the Amish tradition.[2]

It is the future of the student, not the future of the parents, that is imperilled in today's decision. If a parent keeps his child out of school beyond the grade school, then the child will be forever barred from entry into the new and amazing world of diversity that we have today. The child may decide that that is the preferred course, or he may rebel. It is the student's judgment, not his parent's, that is essential if we are to give full meaning to what we have said about the Bill of Rights and of the right of students to be masters of their own destiny.[3] If he is harnessed to the Amish way of life by those in authority over him and if his education is truncated, his entire life may be stunted and deformed. The child, therefore, should be given an opportunity to be heard before the State gives the exemption which we honor today.

The views of the two children in question were not canvassed by the Wisconsin courts. The matter should be explicitly reserved so that new hearings can be held on remand of the case.[4] . . .

[2] A significant number of Amish children do leave the Old Order. Professor Hostetler notes that "the loss of members is very limited in some Amish districts and considerable in others." Amish Society, 210. In one Pennsylvania church, he observed a defection rate of 30%. Id. Rates up to 50% have been reported by others. Casad, Compulsory High School Attendance and the Old Order Amish: A Commentary on State v. Garber, 16 Kan. L. Rev. 423, 434 n.51 (1968).

[3] The court below brushed aside the students' interests with the off-hand comment that "when a child reaches the age of judgment, he can choose for himself his religion." 49 Wis. 2d 430, 182 N.W.2d 549. But there is nothing in this record to indicate that the moral and intellectual judgment demanded of the student by the question in this case is beyond his capacity. Children far younger than the 14- and 15-year-olds involved here are regularly permitted to testify in custody and other proceedings. Indeed, the failure to call the affected child in a custody hearing is often reversible error. See, e.g., Callicott v. Callicott, 364 S.W.2d 455 (Tex. Civ. App. 1963) (reversible error for trial judge to refuse to hear testimony of eight-year-old in custody battle). Moreover, there is substantial agreement among child psychologists and sociologists that the moral and intellectual maturity of the fourteen-year-old approaches that of the adult. See, e.g., J. Piaget, The Moral Judgment of the Child (1948); Elkind, Children and Adolescents 75-80 (1970); L. Kohlberg, Moral Education in the Schools: A Developmental View, in R. Muuss, Adolescent Behavior and Society 199-200 (1971); W. Kay, Moral Development 172-183 (1968); A. Gesell & R Ilg, Youth: The Years From Ten to Sixteen 175-182 (1956). The maturity of Amish youth, who identify with and assume adult roles from early childhood, see M. Goodman, The Culture of Childhood 92-94 (1970), is certainly not less than that of children in the general population.

[4] Canvassing the views of all school-age Amish children in the State of Wisconsin would not present insurmountable difficulties. A 1968 survey indicated that there were at that time only 256 such children in the entire State. Comment, 1971 Wis. L. Rev. 832, 852 n. 132 (1971).

QUESTIONS ON *YODER* DISSENT

(1) Is Justice Douglas correct that the children's rights are necessarily implicated in this case? If the parent is being criminally prosecuted, why are the religious views of the child "crucial"? On the other hand, under the majority opinion, how would a child who disagreed with his parents' views vindicate his rights? If the parent kept the child home after eighth grade, would the child bring suit against his parents? Who would pay for the suit? Who would be guardian ad litem? Is Douglas correct that if the children's views are not canvassed in this suit against their Amish parents, "the children have no effective alternate means to vindicate their rights"? See n.1 of Douglas' dissent, p. 79 supra.

(2) If the denial of a high school education can, as Douglas asserts, lead to a "stunted and deformed" life, why is not the state's interest in requiring *all* children to stay in school past eighth grade a compelling one?

(3) Justice Douglas asserts that "where the child is mature enough to express potentially conflicting desires, it would be an invasion of the child's rights to permit . . . an imposition" of parents' notions of religious duty "without canvassing [the child's] views." When is the child "mature enough"? Is the child "mature enough" by definition if able "to express" disagreement? Or does Justice Douglas have in mind an independent evaluation, perhaps case-by-case, of each Amish child's maturity? See n.4 of Douglas's dissent, p. 80 supra.

(4) If an Amish child were to express disagreement with parental notions of religious duty, what would Douglas's view require the lower court to do? Do as the child wants? Apply the Wisconsin compulsory education statute? Or have the court evaluate what is best for the child? What if the parents said they would not want the child living at home if he were to attend a secular high school?

(5) Compare the approach to the identification of the children's interests of the majority and dissent in *Yoder* with Justice Stevens's dissent in Troxel v. Granville, which follows. In *Troxel,* the United States Supreme Court found unconstitutional a broad Washington state statute (allowing any person to petition for visitation at any time based on the child's best interests) as a violation of substantive due process when applied to a mother's decision to limit the visitation rights of grandparents following the death of her children's father. (Justice Stevens, dissenting, would have denied certiorari.) The plurality opinion in *Troxel* is reprinted at page 609 in Chapter 5. (Issues concerning religion also arise in connection with custody and adoption. See Chapter 5, sections B and C.)

Troxel v. Granville
530 U.S. 57, 86-91 (2000)

. . . Justice STEVENS, dissenting.

. . . The presumption that parental decisions generally serve the best interests of their children is sound, and clearly in the normal case the parent's interest is paramount. But even a fit parent is capable of treating a child like a mere possession.

Cases like this do not present a bipolar struggle between the parents and the State over who has final authority to determine what is in a child's best interests. There is at a minimum a third individual, whose interests are implicated in every case to which the statute applies — the child. . . .

A parent's rights with respect to her child have thus never been regarded as absolute, but rather are limited by the existence of an actual, developed relationship with a child, and are tied to the presence or absence of some embodiment of family. These limitations have arisen, not simply out of the definition of parenthood itself, but because of this Court's assumption that a parent's interests in a child must be balanced against the State's long-recognized interests as parens patriae, and, critically, the child's own complementary interest in preserving relationships that serve her welfare and protection.

While this Court has not yet had occasion to elucidate the nature of a child's liberty interests in preserving established familial or family-like bonds, it seems to me extremely likely that, to the extent parents and families have fundamental liberty interests in preserving such intimate relationships, so, too, do children have these interests, and so, too, must their interests be balanced in the equation. At a minimum, our prior cases recognizing that children are, generally speaking, constitutionally protected actors require that this Court reject any suggestion that when it comes to parental rights, children are so much chattel. . . .

This is not, of course, to suggest that a child's liberty interest in maintaining contact with a particular individual is to be treated invariably as on a par with that child's parents' contrary interests. Because our substantive due process case law includes a strong presumption that a parent will act in the best interest of her child, it would be necessary, were the state appellate courts actually to confront a challenge to the statute as applied, to consider whether the trial court's assessment of the "best interest of the child" incorporated that presumption. . . .

But presumptions notwithstanding, we should recognize that there may be circumstances in which a child has a stronger interest at stake than mere protection from serious harm caused by the termination of visitation by a "person" other than a parent. The almost infinite variety of family relationships that pervade our ever-changing society strongly counsel against the creation by this Court of a constitutional rule that treats a biological parent's liberty interest in the care and supervision of her child as an isolated right that may be exercised arbitrarily. It is indisputably the business of the States, rather than a federal court employing a national standard, to assess in the first instance the relative importance of the conflicting interests that give rise to disputes such as this. Far from guaranteeing that parents' interests will be trammeled in the sweep of cases arising under the statute, the Washington law merely gives an individual — with whom a child may have an established relationship — the procedural right to ask the State to act as arbiter, through the entirely well-known best-interests standard, between the parent's protected interests and the child's. It seems clear to me that the Due Process Clause of the Fourteenth Amendment leaves room for States to consider the impact on a child of possibly arbitrary parental decisions that neither serve nor are motivated by the best interests of the child. . . .

NOTE ON JUVENILE COURT JURISDICTION

As explained earlier, Justice Douglas in his *Yoder* dissent does not clarify how a child who disagreed with parental views could vindicate his or her rights. Because various sorts of juvenile proceedings are considered throughout this book, it is useful at this point to identify the typical juvenile court proceedings.

(1) Child Neglect or Abuse: Dependency Jurisdiction.   Every state has as part of its jurisdictional statute a provision allowing the court to assume jurisdiction over children who are thought to be endangered because of parental neglect or abuse. Once jurisdiction is established, the court is empowered to remove the child from parental custody or take other steps to protect the child. Typically these statutory standards are broad and vague. The question of when it is appropriate for the state to intervene coercively in the family to protect children is analyzed in various contexts later in the book. The physical abuse of children and the general issues of when the state should remove children from parental custody and what should happen to such children are considered in Chapter 3. In all events, neglect or abuse cases focus primarily on the parents, not on the child's conduct. Problems of neglect in connection with the medical treatment of children are considered in Chapter 4.

(2) Delinquency Jurisdiction.   Courts may also take jurisdiction over a young person who is shown to have violated criminal law — i.e., to have committed an act that, for an adult, would have been a crime. A variety of questions relating to delinquency are considered in Chapter 7.

(3) Noncriminal Misbehavior of Minors: Children in Need of Supervision. Juvenile courts may also hear claims that a young person is "unruly" or "in need of supervision" or is engaged in vaguely defined types of conduct regarded as improper or quasi-criminal — e.g., truancy, refusal to obey parental commands, or hanging around in places that are thought inappropriate for young persons. A number of modern juvenile statutes have a separate jurisdictional heading for such young people, who are determined to be "Persons In Need of Supervision" (PINS) or "Children In Need of Supervision" (CHINS). See Chapter 6 infra. Older statutes simply include such noncriminal misbehavior within the definition of delinquency. In all events, these "offenses" are sometimes called "status offenses" or "crimes for children alone," for they typically permit a court to assume jurisdiction over a young person in circumstances where there could be no state intervention in the life of an adult. These aspects of juvenile court jurisdiction are considered in Chapter 6, which deals generally with various state-imposed constraints on the liberties of young people.

Ginsberg v. New York
390 U.S. 629 (1968)

Mr. Justice Brennan delivered the opinion of the Court.

This case presents the question of the constitutionality on its face of a New York criminal obscenity statute which prohibits the sale to minors under

17 years of age of material defined to be obscene on the basis of its appeal to them whether or not it would be obscene to adults.

Appellant and his wife operate "Sam's Stationery and Luncheonette" in Bellmore, Long Island. They have a lunch counter, and, among other things, also sell magazines including some so-called "girlie" magazines. Appellant was prosecuted under two informations, each in two counts, which charged that he personally sold a 16-year-old boy two "girlie" magazines on each of two dates in October 1965, in violation of §484-h of the New York Penal Law, McKinney's Consol. Laws, c. 40. He was . . . found guilty on both counts. The judge found (1) that the magazines contained pictures which depicted female "nudity" in a manner defined in subsection 1(b), that is "the showing of . . . female . . . buttocks with less than a full opaque covering, or the showing of the female breast with less than a fully opaque covering of any portion thereof below the top of the nipple . . . ," and (2) that the pictures were "harmful to minors" in that they had, within the meaning of subsection 1(f) "that quality of . . . representation . . . of nudity . . . [which] . . . (i) predominantly appeals to the prurient, shameful or morbid interest of minors, and (ii) is patently offensive to prevailing standards in the adult community as a whole with respect to what is suitable material for minors, and (iii) is utterly without redeeming social importance for minors." He held that both sales to the 16-year-old boy therefore constituted the violation under §484-h of "knowingly to sell . . . to a minor" under 17 of "(a) any picture . . . which depicts nudity . . . and which is harmful to minors," and "(b) any . . . magazine . . . which contains . . . [such pictures] . . . and which, taken as a whole, is harmful to minors." . . . We affirm.

I

The "girlie" picture magazines involved in the sales here are not obscene for adults. . . . Section 484-h does not bar the appellant from stocking the magazines and selling them to persons 17 years of age or older, and therefore the conviction is not invalid under our decision in Butler v. State of Michigan, 352 U.S. 380.

Obscenity is not within the area of protected speech or press. Roth v. United States, 354 U.S. 476, 485. The three-pronged test of subsection I(f) for judging the obscenity of material sold to minors under 17 is a variable from the formulation for determining obscenity under *Roth*. . . . Appellant's primary attack upon §484-h is leveled at the power of the State to adapt this . . . formulation to define the material's obscenity on the basis of its appeal to minors, and thus exclude material so defined from the area of protected expression. He makes no argument that the magazines are not "harmful to minors" within the definition in subsection I(f). Thus "[n]o issue is presented . . . concerning the obscenity of the material involved." *Roth,* 354 U.S., at 481.

The New York Court of Appeals "upheld the Legislature's power to employ variable concepts of obscenity"[4] in a case in which the same challenge to state power to enact such a law was also addressed to §484-h. Bookcase, Inc. v. Broderick, 18

---

[4] People v. Tannenbaum, 18 N.Y.2d 268, 270, 274 N.Y.S.2d 131, 133, 220 N.E.2d 783, 785, dismissed as moot, 388 U.S. 439. The concept of variable obscenity is developed in Lockhart &

N.Y.2d 71, 271 N.Y.S.2d 947, 218 N.E.2d 668, appeal dismissed for want of a properly presented federal question, *sub nom.* Bookcase, Inc. v. Leary, 385 U.S. 12. In sustaining state power to enact the law, the Court of Appeals said, Bookcase, Inc. v. Broderick, 18 N.Y.2d, p. 75, 271 N.Y.S.2d, p. 952, 218 N.E.2d, p. 671:

> [M]aterial which is protected for distribution to adults is not necessarily constitutionally protected from restriction upon its dissemination to children. In other words, the concept of obscenity or of unprotected matter may vary according to the group to whom the questionable material is directed or from whom it is quarantined. Because of the State's exigent interest in preventing distribution to children of objectionable material, it can exercise its power to protect the health, safety, welfare and morals of its community by barring the distribution to children of books recognized to be suitable for adults.

Appellant's attack is not that New York was without power to draw the line at age 17. Rather, his contention is the broad proposition that the scope of the constitutional freedom of expression secured to a citizen to read or see material concerned with sex cannot be made to depend upon whether the citizen is an adult or a minor. He accordingly insists that the denial to minors under 17 of access to material condemned by §484-h, insofar as that material is not obscene for persons 17 years of age or older, constitutes an unconstitutional deprivation of protected liberty.

We have no occasion in this case to consider the impact of the guarantees of freedom of expression upon the totality of the relationship of the minor and the State. It is enough for the purposes of this case that we inquire whether it was constitutionally impermissible for New York, insofar as §484-h does so, to accord minors under 17 a more restricted right than that assured to adults. . . . We conclude that we cannot say that the statute invades the area of freedom of expression constitutionally secured to minors.

Appellant argues that there is an invasion of protected rights under §484-h constitutionally indistinguishable from the invasions under the Nebraska statute forbidding children to study German, which was struck down in Meyer v. State of Nebraska, 262 U.S. 390; the Oregon statute interfering with children's attendance at private and parochial schools, which was struck down in Pierce v. Society of Sisters of the Holy Names of Jesus and Mary, 268 U.S. 510; and the statute compelling children against their religious scruples to give the flag salute, which was struck down in West Virginia State Board of Education v. Barnette, 319 U.S. 624. We reject that argument. We do not regard New York's regulation in defining obscenity on the basis of its appeal to minors under 17 as involving an invasion of such minors' constitutionally protected freedoms. Rather §484-h simply adjusts the definition of obscenity "to social realities by permitting the appeal of this type

---

McClure, Censorship of Obscenity: The Developing Constitutional Standards, 45 Minn. L. Rev. 5 (1960). At 85 the authors state:

> Variable obscenity . . . furnishes a useful analytical tool for dealing with the problem of denying adolescents access to material aimed at a primary audience of sexually mature adults. For variable obscenity focuses attention upon the make-up of primary and peripheral audiences in varying circumstances, and provides a reasonably satisfactory means for delineating the obscene in each circumstance.

of material to be assessed in term of the sexual interests . . ." of such minors. Mishkin v. State of New York, 383 U.S. 502, 509; Bookcase, Inc. v. Broderick, supra, 18 N.Y.2d, at 75, 271 N.Y.S.2d, at 951, 218 N.E.2d, at 671. That the State has power to make that adjustment seems clear, for we have recognized that even where there is an invasion of protected freedoms "the power of the state to control the conduct of children reaches beyond the scope of its authority over adults. . . ." Prince v. Commonwealth of Massachusetts, 321 U.S. 158, 170.[6] . . .

[T]wo interests justify the limitations in §484-h upon the availability of sex material to minors under 17, at least if it was rational for the legislature to find that the minors' exposure to such material might be harmful. First of all, constitutional interpretation has consistently recognized that the parents' claim to authority in their own household to direct the rearing of their children is basic in the structure of our society. "It is cardinal with us that the custody, care and nurture of the child reside first in the parents, whose primary function and freedom include preparation for obligations the state can neither supply nor hinder." Prince v. Commonwealth of Massachusetts, supra, at 166. The legislature could properly conclude that parents and others, teachers for example, who have this primary responsibility for children's well-being are entitled to the support of laws designed to aid discharge of that responsibility. . . . Moreover, the prohibition against sales to minors does not bar parents who so desire from purchasing the magazines for their children.

The State also has an independent interest in the well-being of its youth. . . . Judge Fuld . . . emphasized its significance in the earlier case of People v. Kahan, 15 N.Y.2d 311, 258 N.Y.S.2d 391, 206 N.E.2d 333, which had struck down the first version of §484-h on grounds of vagueness. In his concurring opinion, 15 N.Y.2d, at 312, 258 N.Y.S.2d, at 392, 206 N.E.2d, at 334, he said:

> While the supervision of children's reading may best be left to their parents, the knowledge that parental control or guidance cannot always be provided — and society's transcendent interest in protecting the welfare of children justify reasonable regulation of the sale of material to them. It is, therefore, altogether fitting

---

[6] Many commentators, including many committed to the proposition that "[n]o general restriction on expression in terms of 'obscenity' can . . . be reconciled with the first amendment," recognize that "the power of the state to control the conduct of children reaches beyond the scope of its authority over adults," and accordingly acknowledge a supervening state interest in the regulation of literature sold to children, Emerson, Toward a General Theory of the First Amendment, 72 Yale L.J. 877, 938, 939 (1963):

> Different factors come into play, also, where the interest at stake is the effect of erotic expression upon children. The world of children is not strictly part of the adult realm of free expression. The factor of immaturity, and perhaps other considerations, impose different rules. Without attempting here to formulate the principles relevant to freedom of expression for children, it suffices to say that regulations of communication addressed to them need not conform to the requirements of the first amendment in the same way as those applicable to adults.

. . . Prince v. Commonwealth of Massachusetts is urged to be constitutional authority for such regulation. See, e.g., [R. Kuh, Foolish Figleaves? 258-260 (1967)]; Comment, Exclusion of Children from Violent Movies, 67 Col. L. Rev. 1149, 1159-1160 (1967); Note, Constitutional Problems in Obscenity Legislation Protecting Children, 54 Geo. L.J. 1379 (1966).

and proper for a state to include in a statute designed to regulate the sale of pornography to children special standards, broader than those embodied in legislation aimed at controlling dissemination of such material to adults.

In Prince v. Commonwealth of Massachusetts, supra, 321 U.S., at 165, this Court, too, recognized that the State has an interest "to protect the welfare of children" and to see that they are "safeguarded from abuses." . . . The only question remaining, therefore, is whether the New York Legislature might rationally conclude, as it has, the exposure to the materials proscribed by §484-h constitutes such an "abuse."

Section 484-e of the law states a legislative finding that the material condemned by §484-h is "a basic factor in impairing the ethical and moral development of our youth and a clear and present danger to the people of the state." It is very doubtful that this finding expresses an accepted scientific fact. But obscenity is not protected expression and may be suppressed without a showing of the circumstances which lie behind the "clear and present danger" in its application to protected speech. Roth v. United States, supra, 354 U.S., at 486-487.[9] To sustain state power to exclude material defined as obscenity by §484-h requires only that we be able to say that it was not irrational for the legislature to find that exposure to material condemned by the statute is harmful to minors. In Meyer v. State of Nebraska, supra, 262 U.S., at 400, we were able to say that children's knowledge of the German language "cannot reasonably be regarded as harmful." That cannot be said by us of minors' reading and seeing sex material. To be sure, there is no lack of "studies" which purport to demonstrate that obscenity is or is not "a basic factor in impairing the ethical and moral development of . . . youth and a clear and present danger to the people of the state." But the growing consensus of commentators is that "while these studies all agree that a causal link has not been demonstrated, they are equally agreed that a causal link has not been disproved either."[10] We do not demand of legislatures "scientifically certain criteria of legislation." Noble

[9] Our conclusion in *Roth,* 354 U.S., at 486-487, that the clear and present danger test was irrelevant to the determination of obscenity made it unnecessary in that case to consider the debate among the authorities whether exposure to pornography caused antisocial consequences.

[10] Magrath, [The Obscenity Cases: Grapes of *Roth,* 1966 Sup. Ct. Rev. 1, 52]. See, e.g., id., at 49-56; Dibble, Obscenity: A State Quarantine to Protect Children, 39 So. Cal. L. Rev. 345 (1966); Wall, Obscenity and Youth: The Problem and a Possible Solution, Crim. L. Bull., Vol. 1, No. 8, pp. 28, 30 (1965); Note, 55 Cal. L. Rev. 926, 934 (1967); Comment, 34 Ford. L. Rev. 692, 694 (1966). See also J. Paul & M. Schwartz, Federal Censorship: Obscenity in the Mail 191-192; Blakey, Book Review, 41 Notre Dame Law. 1055, 1060, n.46 (1966); Green, Obscenity, Censorship, and Juvenile Delinquency, 14 U. Toronto L. Rev. 229, 249 (1962); Lockhart & McClure, Literature, The Law of Obscenity, and the Constitution, 38 Minn. L. Rev. 295, 373-385 (1954); Note, 52 Ky. L.J. 429, 447 (1964). But despite the vigor of the ongoing controversy whether obscene material will perceptibly create a danger of antisocial conduct, or will probably induce its recipients to such conduct, a medical practitioner recently suggested that the possibility of harmful effects to youth cannot be dismissed as frivolous. Dr. Gaylin of the Columbia University Psychoanalytic Clinic, reporting on the views of some psychiatrists in 77 Yale L.J., at 592-593, said:

> It is in the period of growth [of youth] when these patterns of behavior are laid down, when environmental stimuli of all sorts must be integrated into a workable sense of self, when sensuality is being defined and fears elaborated, when pleasure confronts security and

State Bank v. Haskell, 219 U.S. 104, 110. We therefore cannot say that §484-h, in defining the obscenity of material on the basis of its appeal to minors under 17, has no rational relation to the objective of safeguarding such minors from harm.

[The Court also rejected appellant's claims that subsections (f) and (g) of §484-h were void for vagueness, and that the statute lacked a sufficient scienter requirement.]

Affirmed.

Mr. Justice STEWART, concurring in the result.

A doctrinaire, knee-jerk application of the First Amendment would, of course, dictate the nullification of this New York statute. But that result is not required, I think, if we bear in mind what it is that the First Amendment protects.

The First Amendment guarantees liberty of human expression in order to preserve in our Nation what Mr. Justice Holmes called a "free trade in ideas." To that end, the Constitution protects more than just a man's freedom to say or write or publish what he wants. It secures as well the liberty of each man to decide for himself what he will read and to what he will listen. The Constitution guarantees, in short, a society of free choice. Such a society presupposes the capacity of its members to choose.

When expression occurs in a setting where the capacity to make a choice is absent, government regulation of that expression may co-exist with and even implement First Amendment guarantees. . . .

I think a State may permissibly determine that, at least in some precisely delineated areas, a child — like someone in a captive audience — is not possessed of that full capacity for individual choice which is the presupposition of First Amendment guarantees. It is only upon such a premise, I should suppose, that a State may deprive children of other rights — the right to marry, for example, or the right to vote — deprivations that would be constitutionally intolerable for adults.

I cannot hold that this state law, on its face, violates the First and Fourteenth Amendments.

Mr. Justice FORTAS dissenting.

This is a criminal prosecution. Sam Ginsberg and his wife operate a luncheonette at which magazines are offered for sale. A 16-year-old boy was enlisted by his mother to go the luncheonette and buy some "girlie" magazines so that Ginsberg

---

impulse encounters control — it is in this period, undramatically and with time, that legalized pornography may conceivably be damaging.

Dr. Gaylin emphasizes that a child might not be as well prepared as an adult to make an intelligent choice as to the material he chooses to read:

[P]sychiatrists . . . made a distinction between the reading of pornography, as unlikely to be per se harmful, and the permitting of the reading of pornography, which was conceived as potentially destructive. The child is protected in his reading of pornography by the knowledge that it is pornographic, i.e., disapproved. It is outside of parental standards and not a part of his identification processes. To openly permit implies parental approval and even suggests seductive encouragement. If this is so of parental approval, it is equally so of societal approval — another potent influence on the developing ego. Id., at 594.

could be prosecuted. He went there, picked two magazines from a display case, paid for them, and walked out. Ginsberg's offense was duly reported. . . . Ginsberg was prosecuted and convicted. The court imposed only a suspended sentence. But as the majority here points out, under New York law this conviction may mean that Ginsberg will lose the license necessary to operate his luncheonette.

The two magazines that the 16-year-old boy selected are vulgar "girlie" periodicals. However tasteless and tawdry they may be, we have ruled (as the Court acknowledges) that magazines indistinguishable from them in content and offensiveness are not "obscene" within the constitutional standards heretofore applied. These rulings have been in cases involving adults.

The Court avoids facing the problem whether the magazines in the present case are "obscene" when viewed by a 16-year-old boy, although not "obscene" when viewed by someone 17 years of age or older. It says that Ginsberg's lawyer did not choose to challenge the conviction on the ground that the magazines are not "obscene." He chose only to attack the statute on its face. Therefore, the Court reasons, we need not look at the magazines and determine whether they may be excluded from the ambit of the First Amendment as "obscene" for purposes of this case. . . .

In my judgment, the Court cannot properly avoid its fundamental duty to define "obscenity" for purposes of censorship of material sold to youths, merely because of counsel's position. By so doing the Court avoids the essence of the problem; for if the State's power to censor freed from the prohibitions of the First Amendment depends upon obscenity, and if obscenity turns on the specific content of the publication, how can we sustain the conviction here without deciding whether the particular magazines in question are obscene?

The Court certainly cannot mean that the States and cities and counties and villages have unlimited power to withhold anything and everything that is written or pictorial from younger people. But it here justifies the conviction of Sam Ginsberg because the impact of the Constitution, it says, is variable, and what is not obscene for an adult may be obscene for a child. This it calls "variable obscenity." I do not disagree with this, but I insist that to assess the principle — certainly to apply it — the Court must define it. We must know the extent to which literature or pictures may be less offensive than *Roth* requires in order to be "obscene" for purposes of a statute confined to youth. See Roth v. United States, 354 U.S. 476 (1957).

I agree that the State in the exercise of its police power — even in the First Amendment domain — may make proper and careful differentiation between adults and children. But I do not agree that this power may be used on an arbitrary, free-wheeling basis. This is not a case where, on any standard enunciated by the Court, the magazines are obscene, nor one where the seller is at fault. . . .

The conviction of Ginsberg on the present facts is a serious invasion of freedom. To sustain the conviction without inquiry as to whether the material is "obscene" . . . in face of this Court's asserted solicitude for First Amendment values is to give the State a role in the rearing of children which is contrary to our traditions and to our conception of family responsibility. It begs the question to present this undefined, unlimited censorship as an aid to parents in the rearing of their children. This decision does not merely protect children from activities which all sensible parents would condemn. Rather, its undefined and unlimited approval of state censorship in this area denies to children free access to books and works of art to which many parents may wish their children to have uninhibited access. For denial of access to these magazines, without any standard or definition of their allegedly distinguishing characteristics, is also denial of access to great works of art and literature. . . .

[Justice Douglas, joined by Justice Black, dissented in an opinion that is omitted.]

ACLU v. Mukasey
534 F.3d 181 (3rd Cir. 2008), *cert. denied,* **129 S.Ct. 1032 (2009)**

GREENBERG, Circuit Judge.

This matter comes on before this Court on an appeal from an order of the District Court [finding] that the Child Online Protection Act ("COPA"), 47 U.S.C. §231, facially violates the First and Fifth Amendments of the Constitution and permanently enjoining the Attorney General [Michael Mukasey] from enforcing COPA. The Government challenges the District Court's conclusions that: (1) COPA is not narrowly tailored to advance the Government's compelling interest in protecting children from harmful material on the World Wide Web; (2) there are less restrictive, equally effective alternatives to COPA; and (3) COPA is impermissibly overbroad and vague. . . .

Congress enacted COPA to protect minors from exposure to sexually explicit material on the Web. The Web is just one portion of the Internet [which also consists of e-mails, instant messages, online chatting, streaming audio and video, etc.] The District Court indicated that "[a] little more than 1 percent of all Web pages on the Surface Web (amounting to approximately 275 million to 700 million Web pages) are sexually explicit" [ACLU v. Gonzales, 478 F. Supp.2d 775, 788 (E.D. Pa. 2007) [hereinafter *Gonzales*]. COPA provides for civil and criminal penalties — including up to six months imprisonment — for anyone who knowingly posts "material that is harmful to minors" on the Web "for commercial purposes." 47 U.S.C. §231(a)(1). "Intentional" violations result in heavier fines. Id. at §231(a)(2). "[M]aterial that is harmful to minors" includes any communication that is obscene or that:

> (A) the average person, applying contemporary community standards, would find, taking the material as a whole and with respect to minors, is designed to appeal to, or is designed to pander to, the prurient interest; (B) depicts, describes, or represents, in a manner patently offensive with respect to minors, an actual or simulated sexual act or sexual contact, an actual or simulated normal or perverted sexual act, or a lewd exhibition of the genitals or post-pubescent female breast; and (C) taken as a whole, lacks serious literary, artistic, political, or scientific value for minors.

Id. at §231(e)(6). "The term 'minor' means any person under 17 years of age." Id. at §231(e)(7). [A] web publisher can assert an affirmative defense to prosecution under COPA if he or she [restricts access by minors to "material that is harmful to minors" by requiring use of a credit or debit card, accepting a digital certificate that verifies age, or using any other reasonable age verification measures].

Congress enacted COPA after the Supreme Court declared Congress's first attempt to protect minors from exposure to sexually explicit materials on the Web [the Communications Decency Act] to be unconstitutional. See Reno v. American Civil Liberties Union, 521 U.S. 844 (1997). [The day after COPA became law, plaintiffs (content providers and users of the Web) filed this action seeking an injunction barring COPA's enforcement. The District Court granted a preliminary injunction, and the Third Circuit Court of Appeals affirmed (ACLU v. Reno, 217 F.3d 162 (3d Cir. 2000)(*ACLU I*)). The United States Supreme Court vacated and remanded, disagreeing that the "community standards" language made the statute unconstitutionally overbroad. Ashcroft v. ACLU, 535 U.S. 564 (2002). On remand, the Third Circuit again affirmed the preliminary injunction (ACLU v. Ashcroft, 322 F.3d 240 (3d Cir. 2003) (*ACLU II*)). This time, the Supreme Court affirmed, but remanded the case for a trial on the merits in light of current technological developments regarding filtering technologies (Ashcroft v. ACLU, 542 U.S. 656 (2004)). After a bench trial, the District Court issued a permanent injunction, holding COPA unconstitutional. Here, the Government appeals.]

... COPA criminalizes a category of speech — "harmful to minors" material — that is constitutionally protected for adults. Because COPA is a content-based restriction on protected speech, it is presumptively invalid and the Government bears the burden of showing its constitutionality. [T]he parties agree that the Government has a compelling interest to protect minors from exposure to harmful material on the Web. Inasmuch as we agree with them on that point, we turn to the question of whether COPA is narrowly tailored to effectuate its purpose. ...

In its decision made after the trial on the merits now on appeal before us, the District Court concluded that COPA is not narrowly tailored because it is both overinclusive and underinclusive. First, the court determined that COPA is impermissibly overinclusive because it "prohibits much more speech than is necessary to further Congress' compelling interest. For example, ... the definitions of 'commercial purposes' and 'engaged in the business' apply to an inordinate amount of Internet speech and certainly cover more than just commercial pornographers [such as Web publishers who sell advertising containing material harmful to minors on an otherwise noncommercial Web site]" *Gonzales*, 478 F.Supp.2d at 810 (citations omitted). The court also concluded that COPA is overinclusive because it "applies to speech that is obscene as to all minors from newborns to age sixteen, and not just to speech that is obscene as to older minors. . . ." Id. [In *ACLU II*] we found there is nothing in the text of COPA to limit its application solely to "commercial pornographers" or to limit the phrase "material that is harmful to minors" to include material that only is harmful to "older" minors. Our prior decision is binding on these issues on this appeal.

The District Court also found that COPA is not narrowly tailored because it is underinclusive [for the reason that it does not apply to foreign sexually explicit Web sites]. The Government contends that the District Court erred by construing COPA not to apply to foreign Web sites, and thus the Government argues that COPA is not underinclusive. [W]e think that it is likely that Congress would have desired to place COPA's restrictions on foreign Web sites available for access in this country but chose not to do so because [enforcement of COPA against overseas Web site owners would be burdensome and impractical]. [However] there are numerous other grounds that require us to find that COPA is not narrowly tailored and is unconstitutional. Accordingly, we will refrain from deciding [that] matter.

The District Court also found that COPA's affirmative defenses "do not aid in narrowly tailoring COPA to Congress's compelling interest." *Gonzales*, 478 F.Supp.2d at 813. Specifically, the court found that:

> there is no evidence of age verification services or products available on the market to owners of Web sites that actually reliably establish or verify the age of Internet users. Nor is there evidence of such services or products that can effectively prevent access to Web pages by a minor.

Id. at 800. . . . The court further found that the minimum information required by a data verification services company "can easily be circumvented by children who generally know the first and last name, street address and zip codes of their parents or another adult." Id. . . .

The Government argues that the District Court erred in rejecting the limiting effect of COPA's affirmative defenses. It contends that "[t]he possibility that some minors may have access to credit cards merely demonstrates that no system of age verification is foolproof. It does not call into question the availability of credit card screening as an affirmative defense that tailors COPA more narrowly." The Government also argues that "the court ignored testimony that minors do not have access to traditional payment cards under their own control but simply have access to cards supervised by adults." But the District Court found that even if there is parental supervision of payment card use, the supervision does not prevent access to harmful material by minors because parents "may not be able to identify transactions on sexually explicit Web sites because the adult nature of such transactions is often not readily identifiable. . . ." *Gonzales*, 478 F.Supp.2d at 802. . . .

The Government also argues that the District Court incorrectly determined that the affirmative defenses present their own First Amendment concerns. [However] [w]e conclude that the District Court correctly found that implementation of COPA's affirmative defenses by a Web publisher so as to avoid prosecution would involve high costs and also would deter users from visiting implicated Web sites. It is clear that these burdens would chill protected speech and thus that the affirmative defenses fail a strict scrutiny analysis. . . .

In addition to failing the strict scrutiny test because it is not narrowly tailored, COPA does not employ the least restrictive alternative to advance the Government's compelling interest in its purpose. . . . The District Court discussed Internet content filters at length in its Findings of Fact. We will review these findings in detail, as the need to determine whether filters are more effective than COPA to effectuate Congress's purpose in enacting that statute was the primary reason the Supreme Court remanded the case. According to the District Court:

> Internet content filters are computer applications which, inter alia, attempt to block certain categories of material from view that a Web browser or other

Internet application is capable of displaying or downloading, including sexually explicit material. Filters categorize and block Web sites or pages based on their content. By classifying a site or page, and refusing to display it on the user's computer screen, filters can be used to prevent children from seeing material that might be considered unsuitable.

Gonzales, 478 F.Supp.2d at 789. The court explained:

Filters can be programmed or configured in a variety of different ways according to, inter alia, the values of the parents using them and the age and maturity of their children. . . . [F]ilters can be set up to restrict materials available on Web pages and other Internet applications based on numerous factors including the type of content they contain, the presence of particular words, the address of the Web site, the Internet protocol used, or computer application used. Some filters can also restrict Internet access based on time of day, day of week, how long the computer has been connected to the Internet, or which user is logged onto a computer.

Id. at 790. The court then described in detail how filters operate [by using "black lists" that target certain Web addresses, "white lists" that exempt certain Web addresses, and "dynamic filtering" that analyzes different parts of the content, such as file names, URLs, links, sizes of images, and formatting]:

. . . In addition to analyzing the content of Web pages, dynamic filters also take the context of the page into consideration, to ensure that the determinations are as accurate as possible. For example, many companies will develop templates that provide additional context to teach the software how to recognize certain contexts — for example, to block the word 'breast' when used in combination with the word 'sexy,' but not when used in combination with the words 'chicken' or 'cancer.' . . .

Id. at 790-91. . . . The court then described the flexible nature of filters:

Some filtering programs offer only a small number of settings, while others are highly customizable, allowing a parent to make detailed decisions about what to allow and what to block. Filtering products do this by, among other things, enabling parents to choose which categories of speech they want to be blocked (such as sexually explicit material, illicit drug information, information on violence and weapons, and hate speech) and which age setting they want the product to apply. . . . Filtering products can be used by parents even if they have more than one child. For example, if a family has four children, many filtering products will enable the parent to set up different accounts for each child, to ensure that each child is able to access only the content that the parents want that particular child to access.

Id. . . .

The District Court found that "[f]ilters are widely available and easy to obtain," and that "[f]iltering programs are fairly easy to install, configure, and use and require only minimal effort by the end user to configure and update." Id. at 793. The court found that "[i]nstalling and setting up a filter will usually take a typical computer user no more than ten or fifteen minutes. The installation and set-up process is not technically complex and does not require any special training or knowledge." Id. at 794. The court then considered the evidence regarding the effectiveness of filters. It found that:

> [f]iltering products have improved over time and are now more effective than ever before. This is because, as with all software, the filtering companies have addressed problems with the earlier versions of the products in an attempt to make their products better. Another reason the effectiveness of filtering products has improved is that many products now provide multiple layers of filtering. Whereas many filters once only relied on black lists or white lists, many of today's products utilize black lists, white lists, and real-time, dynamic filtering to catch any inappropriate sites that have not previously been classified by the product. There is a high level of competition in the field of Internet content filtering. That factor, along with the development of new technologies, has also caused the products to improve over time.

Id. at 794-95. [The District Court also found that filtering programs have built-in mechanisms to prevent children from circumventing the filters, including password protection and other devices to prevent children from uninstalling the product or changing the settings]. Finally, the court found that "filters generally block about 95% of sexually explicit material." Id. . . .

[The Government contends] that the District Court erred in concluding that filters are a less restrictive alternative. . . . We agree with the District Court's conclusion that filters and the Government's promotion of filters are more effective than COPA. The Supreme Court already has written how the Government could act to promote and support the use of filters:

> Congress undoubtedly may act to encourage the use of filters. We have held that Congress can give strong incentives to schools and libraries to use them. It could also take steps to promote their development by industry, and their use by parents. It is incorrect, for that reason, to say that filters are part of the current regulatory status quo. The need for parental cooperation does not automatically disqualify a proposed less restrictive alternative. In enacting COPA, Congress said its goal was to prevent the 'widespread availability of the Internet' from providing 'opportunities for minors to access materials through the World Wide Web in a manner that can frustrate parental supervision or control.' COPA presumes that parents lack the ability, not the will, to monitor what their children see. By enacting programs to promote use of filtering software, Congress could give parents that ability without subjecting protected speech to severe penalties.

Id. at 669-70. [Further, given] the vast quantity of speech that COPA does not cover [such as foreign sexually explicit Web sites] but that filters do cover, it is apparent that filters are more effective in advancing Congress's interest. . . .

At oral argument, the Government made much of a study that found that only 54 percent of parents use filters. But the Government has neglected the fact that this figure represents a 65 percent increase from a prior study done four years earlier, which indicates that significantly more families are using filters. Furthermore, the circumstance that some parents choose not to use filters does not mean that filters are not an effective alternative to COPA. Though we recognize that some of those parents may be indifferent to what their children see, others may have decided to use other methods to protect their children — such as by placing the family computer in the living room, instead of their children's bedroom — or trust that their children will voluntarily avoid harmful material on the Internet. Studies have shown that the primary reason that parents do not use filters is that they think they are unnecessary because they trust their children and do not see a need to block content. The Government simply has not carried its burden of showing that COPA is a more effective method than filters in advancing the Government's compelling interest as evidenced in COPA.

In addition to being more effective, it is clear that filters are less restrictive than COPA. As the Supreme Court has stated:

> [Filters] impose selective restrictions on speech at the receiving end, not universal restrictions at the source. Under a filtering regime, adults without children may gain access to speech they have a right to see without having to identify themselves or provide their credit card information. Even adults with children may obtain access to the same speech on the same terms simply by turning off the filter on their home computers. Above all, promoting the use of filters does not condemn as criminal any category of speech, and so the potential chilling effect is eliminated, or at least much diminished. All of these things are true, moreover, regardless of how broadly or narrowly the definitions in COPA are construed.

Ashcroft, 542 U.S. at 667. . . . Unlike COPA, filters permit adults to determine if and when they want to use them and do not subject speakers to criminal or civil penalties.

During oral argument, the Government [also] contended that the First Amendment does not prohibit Congress from adopting a "belt-and-suspenders" approach to addressing the compelling government interest of protecting minors from accessing harmful material on the Web, with filters acting as the "belt" and COPA as the "suspenders." But as counsel for plaintiffs correctly pointed out, under the First Amendment, if the belt works at least as effectively as the suspenders, then the Government cannot prosecute people for not wearing suspenders. Here, based on the prior litigation in the Supreme Court and this Court in *ACLU II* and the District Court's findings on the remand, the Government has not shown that COPA is a more effective and less restrictive alternative to the use of filters and the Government's promotion of them in effectuating COPA's purposes. . . .

[The Third Circuit Court of Appeals also concludes that COPA is impermissibly vague for the reasons that (1) the phrase "communication for commercial purposes" as modified by the phrase "engaged in the business" is not limited to commercial pornographers; (2) the definition of "minor" as any person under 17 years of age creates vagueness because materials that could have "serious literary, artistic, political, or scientific value" for a 16-year-old would not necessarily have the same value for a three-year-old; and (3) COPA's use of the phrase "as a whole" is vague because it is unclear how that phrase would apply to the Web. Finally, the court finds that COPA is impermissibly overbroad because its application of the term "community standards" widens the spectrum of protected speech that COPA affects, requiring every Web publisher to abide by the most restrictive and conservative state's community standards to avoid criminal liability.]

COPA, like the Communications Decency Act before it, "effectively suppresses a large amount of speech that adults have a constitutional right to receive and to address to one another" [Reno v. ACLU, 521 U.S. 844, 874 (1997)], and thus is overbroad. For this reason, COPA violates the First Amendment. . . .

NOTE: U.S. COMMISSION ON OBSCENITY AND PORNOGRAPHY, REPORT: DRAFT OF PROPOSED LEGISLATION—SALE AND DISPLAY OF EXPLICIT SEXUAL MATERIAL TO YOUNG PERSONS (1970)[25]

The purpose of the Commission's proposed legislation is "to regulate the direct commercial distribution of certain explicit sexual materials to young persons in order to aid parents in supervising and controlling the access of children to such materials. The legislature finds that whatever social value such material may have for young persons can adequately be served by its availability to young persons through their parents." Id. at 66.

The proposed statute prohibits the knowing distribution or display for sale of "explicit sexual material" to young persons. However, if the material has "artistic, literacy, historical, scientific, medical, educational or other similar social values for adults," it is not prohibited. The statute covers pictorial or three-dimensional material including but not limited to books, magazines, films, photographs and statuary, but it does not include broadcasts or telecasts by facilities licensed under the Federal Communications Act, 47 U.S.C. §§30 et seq. Distribution with a parent's consent or to a married young person is not prohibited. Id. at 66-67.

In its Report, the Commission limited its obscenity regulation to "young persons" because of the lack of empirical proof that a causal relationship exists between adult exposure to sexual material and crime or emotional abnormalities. Id. at 52. Due to the serious ethical problems involved in experimentally exposing children to sexual materials, no such conclusion can be reached in regard to children. Also, the Commission was influenced, to a considerable degree, by its finding that a large majority of Americans believe that children should not be exposed to certain sexual materials. Therefore, the Commission leaves the ultimate decision to parents as to whether their children should be exposed to sexual material. Id. at 57.

The proposed legislation is limited to pictorial material because of the existence of many textual works that are explicit, yet valuable to young people. The Commission believes it could not create a clear legal distinction between harmful text and valuable text. Further, commercial distributors and dealers might seriously curtail their distribution for fear of violating a vague law. Id. at 58. "The speculative risk of harm to juveniles from some textual material does not justify these dangers," said the Commission. Id. at 60.

---

[25] The federal government established two commissions to study pornography and issue recommendations. In 1967 President Lyndon Johnson created the U.S. Commission on Obscenity and Pornography (sometimes termed the "Lockhart Commission" after its chairperson, constitutional scholar William Lockhart). In 1985 President Ronald Reagan requested the Attorney General to establish a second commission—the U.S. Attorney General's Commission on Pornography (commonly referred to as the "Meese Commission" after then-Attorney General Edwin Meese). For a discussion of these commissions, see generally Gordon Hawkins & Franklin E. Zimring, Pornography in a Free Society (1988).

DISCUSSION OF *GINSBERG* AND *ACLU v. MUKASEY*: STATE REGULATION OF SEXUALLY EXPLICIT MATERIALS

(1) The Role of the State

a. A Different Standard for Children? Why does *Ginsberg* uphold a statute regulating minors' access to sexually explicit materials (permitting a variable standard for obscenity) whereas *ACLU v. Mukasey* enjoins enforcement of such a statute? What rationale does the majority in *Ginsberg* offer to explain why the standard for obscenity should be different for adults and children? Why does *ACLU v. Mukasey* find that the statute violates the First Amendment?

The U.S. Commission on Obscenity and Pornography (supra p. 96) in 1970 also advocated different standards for adults and children. What rationale does the Commission offer for its "two-tier" proposals — the repeal of all obscenity laws for adults but some limitations for children? Are you persuaded by the Commission's justification?

Compare the following theories about a variable standard. Professor Thomas Emerson, who wrote extensively on the First Amendment, suggests that for adults there should be no governmental restriction of expression on grounds of obscenity. As footnote 6 of the *Ginsberg* opinion indicates, however, Professor Emerson thought differently with regard to children. He subsequently elaborated:

> A system of freedom of expression . . . cannot and does not treat children on the same basis as adults. The world of children is not the same as the world of adults, so far as a guarantee of untrammeled freedom of the mind is concerned. The reason for this is, as Justice Stewart said in *Ginsberg,* that a child "is not possessed of that full capacity for individual choice which is the presupposition of the First Amendment guarantees." He is not permitted that measure of independence, or able to exercise that maturity of judgment, which a system of free expression rests upon. This does not mean that the First Amendment extends no protection to children; it does mean that children are governed by different rules. This differentiation concerns one of the most delicate aspects of the obscenity problem and embodies a key concept for dealing with that problem. . . .

Thomas Emerson, The System of Freedom of Expression 496-497 (1970).

On the other hand, why should the "world of children" not be included fully in the system of free expression? Is it so clear that immaturity requires the imposition of different rules? Consider the following:

> If one of the core purposes of the First Amendment is to prevent the government from using censorship to impose its own political and moral values on the population, then entirely exempting children from that protection would create a gaping hole in that purpose, since after all, most people's values, beliefs, and world views are formed during childhood. Permitting the State to completely control "the ethical and moral development" of minors threatens to produce the worst kind of tyranny — a point made by Judge Posner [in American Amusement Mach. Assn. v. Kendrick, 244 F.3d 572, 576-577 (7th Cir. 2001) (enjoining the enforcement of a municipal ordinance limiting minors' access to violent video games)] using the example of the Hitler Jugend during World War II.

Ashutosh Bhagwat, What If I Want My Kids to Watch Pornography? Protecting Children from "Indecent" Speech, 11 Wm. & Mary Bill Rts. J. 671, 690 (2003).

Beginning in 1996, Congress enacted several statutes to protect children from harmful material on the Internet. The Child Online Protection Act (COPA), at issue here, addressed the constitutional infirmities of its predecessor statute (the Communications Decency Act of 1996 or CDA) in several ways: targeting only commercial pornographers (rather than both commercial and noncommercial Web site publishers), applying only to Web-based communications (rather than to all Internet communications including e-mails and chat rooms), and defining essential terms (e.g., "by means of the World Wide Web," "commercial purposes," "engaged in business" and limiting the definition of "minor" to those 17 and under). Finally, COPA narrowed the vague "indecent" and "patently offensive" standard of the CDA to a "harmful to minors" community-based standard incorporating the three-prong Miller v. California test [413 U.S. 15 (1973)] (i.e., appealing to the prurient interest of minors; patently offensive to minors; and lacking serious literary, artistic, political, or scientific value for minors).

The difficulty of defining "harmful to minors" has been a shortcoming of both COPA and its predecessor, CDA. Is COPA's standard an improvement compared to the CDA standard? What do the terms "prurient interest," "patently offensive," and "lacking serious literary, artistic, political, or scientific value" mean *with respect to minors?* How does one determine what is "patently offensive" to a 6-year-old as opposed to a 14-year-old? To a 12-year-old girl as opposed to a 16-year-old boy? As one commentator notes:

> It is not clear whether COPA prohibits material that lacks value for all minors, for some minors, or for some variation of the "average" or "reasonable" sixteen-year-old. It is unclear whether minors of a certain age can discern any "value," whether social, political, or literary, in certain materials. A speaker who attempts to satisfy COPA's "harmful to minors" standard may be assigned the hopelessly difficult task of determining whether its content contains "value" for an eight-year-old. . . .

Timothy Zick, Congress, The Internet, and the Intractable Pornography Problem: The Child Online Protection Act of 1998, 32 Creighton L. Rev. 1147, 1194-1195 (1999).

Several European nations have enacted statutes aimed at protecting minors from harmful or unsuitable materials on the Internet. For a discussion of European regulation, see Eva Lievens et al., The Co-Protection of Minors in New Media: A European Approach to Co-Regulation, 10 UC Davis J. Juv. L. & Pol'y 97 (2006). After ACLU v. Mukasey, would the U.S. Supreme Court be likely to uphold a standard incorporating a variable standard for harmful materials on the Internet? Could a sufficiently narrow statute be drafted to surmount a challenge on the ground of vagueness? What should such a statute encompass? Who will determine what material is harmful to minors? Would material be harmful to any minor or only those below a certain age? Would the Court be likely to uphold a standard that varies according to both the age and gender of the minor?

The Supreme Court in Miller v. California, supra (establishing constitutional standards for obscenity) permitted community standards to govern the determination of obscenity. If community standards are relevant in the determination of materials that are harmful to minors, which "community" would apply to the Internet? Compare Justice Stevens's concurring opinion in Ashcroft v. American Civil Liberties Union (*Ashcroft II*), 542 U.S. 656, 674 (2004), in which he criticizes "community standards" as a constitutional deficiency that permits the least tolerant community to determine Internet content.

Ginsberg and *ACLU v. Mukasey* address different media and different rules. Is such different context-specific regulation justifiable in an age when the forms of communication are converging? For example, personal computers now have sound and graphic capabilities to display video games, music, movies, and Internet access. What are the implications of this convergence in terms of the standard to be applied to minors' access to sexually explicit materials? Note that broadcasting has received the most limited First Amendment protection. See, e.g., FCC v. Pacifica Foundation, 438 U.S. 726 (1978) (holding that the broadcast of a monologue featuring "Filthy Words" could be subject to administrative sanctions because of its use in an afternoon broadcast when children were in the audience). If sexually explicit materials from the Internet are accessible at any time of day, does that dictate a different result in *ACLU v. Mukasey*? See also Reno v. ACLU, 521 U.S. 844, 868-870 (1997) (distinguishing the Internet from broadcasting by suggesting that the former is not invasive).

b. The State's Dual Interests: Effects on Children. According to *Ginsberg*, two interests justify limitation on the availability of sexually explicit materials to minors: (1) the importance of the parental role in the rearing of their children and (2) the state's "independent interest in the well-being of its youth," specifically youth's "ethical and moral development." In terms of the second interest, did the Court in *Ginsberg* and/or *ACLU v. Mukasey* actually find that exposure to sexually explicit materials is harmful to minors? What evidence of harm was considered by the Court in the respective cases? Might such exposure have positive impact? Did the Court in *Ginsberg* and/or *ACLU v. Mukasey* presume that the protection of minors was a compelling interest? Or did the Court merely decide that it was rational for the legislature to find such exposure harmful? Does the government have an appropriate role in protecting the well-being of its youth in terms of inculcating moral and ethical values?

The Effects Panel of the first U.S. Commission on Obscenity and Pornography summarized its findings regarding the evidence on the relationship between erotic materials and antisocial behavior as follows:

> In its assignment to the Commission "to study the effect of obscenity and pornography upon the public," Congress added for emphasis "and particularly minors, and its relationship to crime and other antisocial behavior" (P.L. 90-100). This emphasis reflects: (a) a long-standing concern that has been voiced by many officials and (b) the state of scientific knowledge at the time the Commission was established.
>
> The paucity of research information regarding the effects of pornography on the antisocial behavior of adults and youth is partly a function of a general

sensitivity about the scientific study of private behavior — especially sexual behavior and specifically as it concerns children. The Commission was not immune to social forces restricting research in this area nor to the logistical and methodological difficulties inherent in pioneering efforts. Research that the Commission initiated is, therefore, somewhat more restricted in quantity and in the quality of rigor than that required for unequivocal conclusions. . . .

Two important findings emerge from the studies reviewed:

(a) experience with erotic materials is widespread among American youth; and (b) the experiences of delinquent and nondelinquent youth, though not identical, are generally similar. The small differences which appear to be in the amount of exposure and the reactions to it, seem to be attributable to age and subcultural variables. Taken together, these data provide no particular support for the thesis that experience with sexual materials is a significant factor in the causation of juvenile delinquency.

There is some evidence that both juvenile misbehavior and certain dimensions of experience with erotic materials may be explained by the subcultural and social processes operative in the home, neighborhood, and school peer groups. . . .

. . . Available research concerning the effects of erotic material upon juveniles has not included experimental studies in which the direction of relationships is more systematically assessed. Continuing fears about the consequences of controlled exposure studies have precluded the accumulation of strong evidence. The generally wide experience of adolescents with sexual materials, however, suggests that concerns about detrimental effects of experimentation may well be unwarranted. . . .

The subsequent Commission on Pornography (established in 1985) also addressed the issue of the effects of pornography. After extensive study, the Meese Commission reported several general findings: (1) extended exposure to pornography increases the belief that less common sexual practices are common; (2) pornography that portrays sexual aggression as pleasurable for the victim increases the acceptance of coercive sexual practices; (3) acceptance of coercive sexuality appears to be related to sexual aggression; and (4) exposure to violent pornography, at least in the laboratory setting, increases punitive behavior toward women. Michael J. McManus, Introduction, Final Report of the Attorney General's Commission on Pornography xviii (1986).

What explains the difference in the findings of the two Commissions? Does the evidence of harm to minors found by the Commission(s) justify proposed restrictions? The first commission draws a distinction between pictorial materials and written materials, in terms of both enforcement and harm. Are these distinctions justified? Are they distinctions of constitutional dimension? Given that exposure to violent pornography appears to foster harmful behavior toward women, do such materials violate women's right to equal protection? See generally Catharine A. MacKinnon, Only Words (1993).

Considering the relevance of the uncertain state of the social science evidence to the questions facing the Supreme Court in *Ginsberg* and *ACLU v. Mukasey*, does uncertainty justify a separate standard for children? Or does such a question "miss the point" because it "fail[s] to address the true question: whether the State has a legitimate or compelling interest in inculcating moral and ethical values in children by controlling their access to indecent materials as a step towards creating a morally virtuous citizenry." Bhagwat, supra, at 685. Who should decide whether children should be exposed to sexually explicit materials — parents, children, the legislature, the courts?

(2) The Role of Parents

a. The State versus Parental Role.　　As explained earlier, *Ginsberg* recognizes that the state has a legitimate interest in the regulation of indecent speech in order to support the parental role in childrearing. Does the Court's suggestion in *Ginsberg* that "constitutional interpretation" has consistently recognized the parent's claim to authority in childrearing place *Ginsberg* in the *Pierce-Yoder* tradition that parents decide for children? Or does the suggestion that the state has an independent interest in the well-being of its youth align *Ginsberg* with *Prince* in asserting the power of the state to protect children even over parental opposition?

May the state intervene to prevent a child's access to such materials when: The parents deliberately provide the child with "objectionable" reading? Leave such reading matter lying around the house? Accompany the child to buy such material selected by the child? Give the child a note addressed to a store clerk, saying that the child has their permission to buy sexually oriented reading? Purchase, but fail to install, blocking and filtering software on the home computer? Should any of these situations provide grounds for a child neglect proceeding? See Chapter 3. Could such parental conduct be made criminal? Suppose the parents' permissive conduct was discovered because the child was selling (or downloading and distributing) the objectionable materials to classmates? Are criminal sanctions an appropriate method of protecting minors from the harm of exposure to sexually explicit materials?

b. Protection of Parents' Rights.　　Under the New York statute in *Ginsberg*, parents have the power to permit access to soft-core magazines for their children. Under COPA, children are able to access pornographic and sexually explicit sites and images on the Internet with parental consent. Does such parental power create an inevitable conflict between parents who wish their children to be free to choose and parents who want to protect their children from sexual materials? Effective protection for parents who do not want their children to be exposed might require a flat prohibition on minors' possession of, and Internet access to, objectionable material: Children might otherwise show the material to each other. On the other hand, allowing parents to buy material for their children, or to install blocking or filtering software, does not enable permissive parents to allow *the child* free choice to decide what material is of interest. Children may be inhibited from revealing to the permissive parent their interest in material because of embarrassment or fear of parental disapproval. Compare *Ginsberg's* resolution with the recommendation of the first United States Commission on Obscenity and Pornography.

c. Is Parental Regulation Effective?　　In *ACLU v. Mukasey,* the Third Circuit Court of Appeals favors blocking and filtering software as less restrictive alternatives than COPA to regulate speech. Is reliance on parental control and supervision justified to regulate minors' access to sexually explicit materials on the

Internet? To what extent should the state assume that parents are capable and/or willing to regulate children's access to inappropriate materials on the Internet? If the state can demonstrate that parents who are aware of their children's exposure to sexually explicit materials are failing to act, may the state nonetheless regulate such materials in the interests of child protection?

Can parental or state regulation ever be effective? The first Commission on Pornography found widespread violation of *Ginsberg-type* laws. As long as sexually explicit materials are available to adults (and indeed are constitutionally protected), is it possible to control effectively children's access? Children can be refused admission to movies, but denial of access to books, printed matter, and the Internet is obviously more difficult. Indeed, a system that is so restrictive that bookstore owners tend not to carry books that are banned for children would probably violate Butler v. Michigan, 352 U.S. 380, 383 (1957), where the Supreme Court unanimously invalidated a Michigan law that prohibited the distribution to the general public of material "tending to incite minors to violent or depraved or immoral acts, manifestly tending to the corruption of the morals of youth." Justice Frankfurter characterized the legislation as "quarantining the general reading public against books not too rugged for grown men and women in order to shield juvenile innocence." Id. at 383. This would result, he suggested, in reducing "the adult population of Michigan to reading only what is fit for children." Id.

Is it legitimate to adopt legislation that will probably be ineffective in controlling the access of youth, but that will nevertheless express social disapproval? See Lawrence v. Texas, 539 U.S 558, 571 (2003) (finding unconstitutional as a violation of substantive due process a state sodomy statute, reasoning that the Court's obligation is to "define the liberty of all, not to mandate our own moral code").

What are the appropriate roles of parents and the state in regulating children's access to the Internet? Consider the following view:

> [T]he widespread availability of [indecent] material in the larger society makes it virtually impossible for parents to act effectively on their own. Instead, if parents are to have meaningful rights in this area, the community must have the power to regulate the manner in which such material is distributed. . . . Although liberalism presumes that adults are sufficiently autonomous to resist harmful social and cultural influences, this assumption cannot be made with respect to children.

Steven J. Heyman, Ideological Conflict and the First Amendment, 78 Chi.-Kent L. Rev. 531, 608-609 (2003).

Do you agree? Compare Nadine Strossen, William O. Douglas Lecture: Current Challenges to the First Amendment, 36 Gonz. L. Rev. 279 (2000-01) (opposing governmental regulation of the Internet) with Robert Peters, Problems of Censorship in a New Technological Age: It Will Take More than Parental Use of Filtering Software to Protect Children from Internet Pornography, 31 N.Y.U. Rev. L. & Soc. Change 829 (2007) (favoring regulation).

Alternatively, should the industry (the content providers and/or service providers) regulate itself? Is cyberspace "so different from other communication media that it will, or should, resist all government regulation"? Jack L. Goldsmith,

Against Cyberanarchy, 65 U. Chi. L. Rev. 1199 (1998) (arguing that it is not). What are the advantages and disadvantages of parental, state, and industry regulation? If the state facilitates parental control, should it also facilitate the control of those in loco parentis, such as teachers? For example, should it require public schools and libraries to use filtering software on their computers to prevent children's access to sexually explicit materials? See the discussion at p. 132.

(3) The Role of the Child. Regarding both *Ginsberg* and *ACLU v. Mukasey,* to what extent do a minor's own First Amendment rights constrain the state's power to limit access to sexually explicit materials? Minors might desire "girlie" magazines for entertainment purposes; however, children access the Internet not only for entertainment but also for research purposes. Sexually explicit materials on anatomy that are posted on the Internet, for example, might serve as a resource for biology students.

Because of the nature of the respective challenges in *Ginsberg* and *ACLU v. Mukasey,* the Supreme Court did not concern itself with this issue. Several decades ago, however, the Court conceded that minors might possess such an interest. In Erznoznik v. Jacksonville, 422 U.S. 205 (1975), the Court invalidated a Jacksonville, Florida, ordinance making it illegal for drive-in movies to show films containing nudity. Rejecting the city's argument that the ordinance was for the protection of children, the Court indicated that minors do have a "significant measure" (id. at 212) of First Amendment protection. See id. at 214 ("In most circumstances, the values protected by the First Amendment are no less applicable when government seeks to control the flow of information to minors").

Subsequently, a federal district court in Michigan affirmed that view in Cyberspace, Communications, Inc. v. Engler, 55 F. Supp. 2d 737 (E.D. Mich. 1999) (enjoining enforcement of amendments to a state statute that criminalized use of computers or the Internet to disseminate sexually explicit materials to minors). In holding that the amendments would have had an adverse effect on public policy by stifling discussions and were not narrowly tailored, Judge Tarnow vigorously defended the rights of children to information:

> The Defendants failed to satisfy that the Act will further a compelling interest of the State. Plaintiffs though did submit testimony and documentation that such an Act could produce a result contrary to the desires of society. The free flow of information on the Internet enables a teenager to ask about premarital sex or sexually transmitted diseases with anonymity. Plaintiffs at the hearing read into the record an example of a teenager asking Dr. Marty Klein, a sex therapist in California and plaintiff in this case, who operates a website entitled "Ask Me Anything," about an encounter with her boyfriend that she incorrectly reasoned was not sexual intercourse. Other examples offered at the hearing include submitted transcripts of chat room discussions concerning contraceptives and abstention. Sometimes words were utilized in these discussions which could be construed as "sexually explicit" and "harmful to a minor," which theoretically could subject the disseminator to criminal prosecution.
>
> This would have an adverse effect on public policy. With all Internet participants fearful of criminal prosecution if certain terminology is utilized, the discussions would be stifled to the point that a teenager seeking answers to curious questions concerning a subject foremost on their mind, could not find answers via

this medium. Without open discussion of how to prevent being raped or birth control or abstention, there would quite possibly be greater numbers of teenage pregnancy or sexually transmitted diseases. This would be contrary to the interests of the State. [Id. at 749.]

See also American Amusement Machine Assn. v. Kendrick, 244 F.3d 572 (7th Cir. 2001) (Posner, J.) (enjoining a municipal ordinance that limited minors' access to violent video games by pointing out that children must be provided access to the world of ideas and opinions). For further discussion of minors' access to violent materials, see infra p. 106.

PROBLEM

Congress enacted the Family Movie Act (FMA), H.R. 4586, 109th Cong. 1st Sess. (2005), as part of the Family Entertainment and Copyright Act (FECA) (codified at 15 U.S.C. §1114), which inter alia protects technology that filters sex, violence, and profanity on DVD movies by exempting such technology from federal copyright laws. The legislation permits technology companies to sell DVD players for home use that produce "sanitized" versions of DVDs that delete or mute sexually explicit and violent audio or video content that some persons find objectionable. Several major movie studios, civil liberties associations, and parents' groups challenge the FMA as unconstitutional. What result? Does the FMA create a variable standard of obscenity that would be constitutional based on *Ginsberg* and/or *ACLU v. Mukasey*?

NOTE: PROTECTION OF CHILDREN FROM SEXUAL EXPLOITATION: CHILD PORNOGRAPHY

Both Congress and the Supreme Court have upheld the government's right to protect minors from such forms of sexual exploitation as child pornography. Congress first enacted the Protection of Children Against Sexual Exploitation Act of 1977, 18 U.S.C. §§2251-2257 (2000), prohibiting any person from "knowingly" transporting, shipping, receiving, or distributing material in interstate commerce that shows minors engaged in sexually explicit conduct. Id. at §2252(a). The Act was designed to remedy gaps in existing federal legislation and to provide more efficient enforcement among the various federal agencies (i.e., Department of Justice, FBI, postal and custom services).

In New York v. Ferber, 458 U.S. 747 (1982), the United States Supreme Court upheld a New York statute prohibiting distribution of materials that depict a sexual performance of a child under age 17. The Court held that child pornography, even if not technically obscene, falls outside First Amendment protection for several reasons. The Court found a compelling state interest in protecting the children's physical and psychological welfare by preventing their use in making pornography and also reasoned that the distribution of child pornography is directly linked to the sexual abuse of children because it provides a record of the abuse and encourages the production of such materials. *Ferber* limited the application of child pornography statutes to depictions of *live performances* and required that any ban on the material must have a *scienter* requirement.

Both the Protection of Children Against Sexual Exploitation Act and *Ferber,* supra, addressed *distribution* of pornographic materials. In Osborne v. Ohio, 495 U.S. 103 (1990), the United States Supreme Court upheld a state statute prohibiting the *possession* of child pornography. Relying on a policy rationale similar to that of *Ferber,* the Court reasoned that prohibiting possession of child pornography would reduce supply and demand.

The scienter requirement in the Protection of Children Against Sexual Exploitation Act was at issue in United States v. X-Citement Video, 982 F.2d 1285 (9th Cir. 1992). A defendant argued that the statute violated the First Amendment because it lacked the necessary element of knowledge regarding the minority of the performer. Disagreeing, the Ninth Circuit held (based on legislative intent) that the scienter requirement applied to both the knowledge of the performer's minority and the nature of its contents.

In 1986, Congress enacted the Child Sexual Abuse and Pornography Act, Pub. L. No. 99-628, 100 Stat. 3510 (codified as 18 U.S.C. §§2251, 2255-2256, 2421-2423 (2000)). That legislation banned the production and use of advertisements for child pornography and clarified the term "visual depiction" to include undeveloped film and videotape.

The development of computer networks capable of transmitting child pornography to a worldwide audience resulted in the passage of additional federal legislation. Congress amended the Protection of Children Against Sexual Exploitation Act with the Child Protection and Obscenity and Enforcement Act of 1988, 18 U.S.C. §§2251-2256 (2000), to make it a federal crime to transmit computerized advertisements for or visual depictions of child pornography. Congress again amended the Protection of Children Against Sexual Exploitation Act in 1996 with the Child Pornography Prevention Act (CPPA), 18 U.S.C. §2252(A) (2000), to criminalize computer-generated child pornography. Prior to the CPPA, a work was considered pornographic if it depicted an *actual* minor, under age 18, engaging in actual or simulated sexually explicit conduct. (Recall that *Ferber,* supra, limited First Amendment protection to conduct involving *live* performances.) However, advances in computer technology necessitated broadening the definition of "child pornography" to include virtual pornography — pictures that *appear* to be of minors engaging in sexually explicit conduct that are virtually indistinguishable from pictures of actual children. In Ashcroft v. Free Speech Coalition, 535 U.S. 234 (2002), the United States Supreme Court declared key provisions of the CPPA unconstitutionally overbroad. The Court reasoned that the CPPA banned protected speech because of its prohibition on speech that recorded no crime and created no victims in its production.

Congress next enacted the Protection of Children Against Sexual Predators Act of 1998, 18 U.S.C. §1470 (2000), to punish sex offenders who lure children by means of the Internet. The Act permits sentence enhancements for the use of computers in the sexual exploitation of children, creates liability on Internet service providers to report violations of federal child pornography laws to law enforcement, and directs the U.S. Sentencing Commission to review sentencing guidelines to ensure that penalties for acts of sexual child exploitation are consistent and reflective of congressional intent to punish child sex offenders severely. Also, in 1998, Congress passed the Child Online Privacy Protection Act (COPPA), 15 U.S.C. §6501 (2000), to protect children's safety online by placing restrictions on the solicitation of personal information from children online without parental consent.

In 2000, Congress enacted the Children's Internet Protection Act (CIPA), Pub. L. No. 106-554, §1701, 114 Stat. 2763A-335 (2000). CIPA requires the installation of filtering software on computers in public schools and libraries that receive federal technology funds (discussed infra p. 132). In 2003, Congress enacted the Prosecutorial Remedies and Other Tools to End the Exploitation of Children Today Act (PROTECT), Pub. L. No. 108-21, §151, 117 Stat. 650 (2003), to provide authorization for wiretapping in regard to child pornography and sexual exploitation of children (as well as other sexual offenses).

Finally, in 2006, Congress enacted several pieces of protective legislation. The Truth in Domain Names Act (TDNA), 18 U.S.C. §2252B(a)-(b) (2006), makes it illegal to knowingly use a misleading domain name to "deceive a person into viewing material constituting obscenity" or to "deceive a minor into viewing material that is harmful to minors." In addition, Congress enacted the Adam Walsh Child Protection Safety Act of 2006, 42 U.S.C.A. §16901 (2006), to improve federal criminal law enforcement that protects children from victimization by sex offenders by means of such provisions as: reformulating the federal standards for sex offender registration and notification; increasing the number of Internet Crimes Against Children Task Forces; enhancing the penalties for the distribution of materials involving the sexual exploitation of children or child pornography, and using misleading Internet domain names to direct children to harmful material; and directing the Attorney General to expand training and technology efforts to respond to the threat posed by sex offenders who use the Internet to solicit or exploit children.

NOTE: RESTRICTING MINORS' ACCESS TO OTHER MATERIALS IN THE MODERN ERA

The second governmental commission on pornography (the Meese Commission) was formed in 1985 to determine the "nature, extent, and impact" of pornography and to make recommendations concerning more effective enforcement. Final Report of the Attorney General's Commission on Pornography 3 (1986). In issuing its report, the Meese Commission explained the need for such a study of pornography by pointing to technological changes affecting society. "Nor have the changes been solely technological," stated the report.

> In sixteen years [since the first commission] there have been numerous changes in the social, political, legal, cultural, and religious portrait of the United States, and many of these changes have undeniably involved both sexuality and the public portrayal of sexuality. With reference to the question of pornography, therefore, there can be no doubt that we confront a different world than that confronted by

the 1970 Commission. [Final Report of the Attorney General's Commission on Pornography 6-7 (1986).]

Another aspect of this "different world" is an increasingly violent youth culture. Beginning in 1997, several incidents of school violence erupted in schools across the country.[26] Youth violence, once limited to inner cities, spread to rural areas and affluent suburbs.

The most serious incident took place in April 1999 at Columbine High School in the upper-middle-class Denver suburb of Littleton, Colorado. Two students dressed in black trench coats killed 17 students and a teacher, and wounded 23 other students. Shortly afterward, reports emerged in the media about the gunmen's fascination with violent movies, heavy-metal music, and violent video games.[27] Some attributed the violence to the influence of the Internet.[28] In response to the massacre, the public demanded increasing regulation of violence in the entertainment industry and stricter gun control regulation.[29]

Consider the implications of *Ginsberg* and *ACLU v. Mukasey* for other forms of sexually explicit materials as well as materials that are violent (rather than sexually explicit). Historically, regulation of minors' access to sexually explicit and violent materials has focused on several areas, including:

(1) Dial-a-Porn. "Dial-a-porn," or "phone sex," is the telephonic transmission of pornography. Dial-a-porn became nationally available in 1983. There are two types of dial-a-porn: Either the customer converses with a live paid performer who talks in a sexually explicit manner or, alternatively, the customer listens to a sexually explicit prerecorded message. In either case, the customer incurs substantial telephone or credit-card bills. In 1988, Congress placed a complete ban on the transmission of obscene and indecent messages by telephone by means of an amendment to the Communications Act of 1934, 47 U.S.C. §223 (as amended).

In Sable Communications, Inc. v. FCC, 492 U.S. 115 (1989), a dial-a-porn provider challenged the constitutionality of the ban. The United States Supreme Court held that Congress could prohibit the transmission of obscene but not indecent telephone messages because the latter are protected by the First Amendment. The Court reasoned that, although Congress had a compelling interest in child protection, the statute was overbroad because the FCC could limit minors' access

---

[26] In 1997, in Pearl, Mississippi, a 16-year-old killed his mother and two classmates, and wounded seven others; and in West Paducah, Kentucky, a 14-year-old killed three students and wounded five others. In 1998, in Jonesboro, Arkansas, two boys, ages 11 and 13, called in a false fire alarm and then killed four girls and a teacher and wounded ten others; and in Springfield, Oregon, a 15-year-old first killed his parents and then two students, and wounded 22 others in a high school cafeteria. See Valerie Richardson, A Massacre in Colorado, Students Killed, Injured in Blood Bath, Wash. Times, Apr. 21, 1999, at A1. In another school shooting, a 16-year-old boy killed nine people and wounded 14 others in Redlake, Minnesota. Amanda Paulson et al., School Shooting: Familiar Echoes, New Concerns, Christian Sci. Monitor, Mar. 23, 2005, at 1.

[27] See Ellen Barry, Games Feared as Violent Youths' Basic Training, Boston Globe, Apr. 29, 1999, at A1; Richard Corliss, Bang, You're Dead, Time Magazine, May 3, 1999, at 49; Marilyn Manson's Music Blamed in Colorado Shooting (NBC television broadcast, Apr. 29, 1999).

[28] Do Not Enter, PC Mag., June 22, 1999 (comments of former Vice President Al Gore).

[29] Jeffrey Taylor, House GOP Tries to Curb Violent Fare, Wall St. J., June 8, 1999, at A20.

to indecent dial-a-porn messages by less restrictive means (e.g., by regulatory methods that had been proposed by the FCC such as credit cards, access codes, and scrambled messages). Further, the Court ruled that a total ban on indecent, sexually explicit messages would impermissibly restrict adults' access to such materials:

> Under our precedents, §223(b), in its present form, has the invalid effect of limiting the content of adult telephone conversations to that which is suitable for children to hear. It is another case of "burn[ing] up the house to roast the pig." [Id. at 130-131.]

In response to *Sable,* Congress again attempted to regulate the dial-a-porn industry with the Helms Amendment, 47 U.S.C. §223(c)(2) (2000), requiring telephone companies to block access to dial-a-porn services unless customers affirmatively requested access in writing. The Second and Ninth Circuits upheld these opt-in restrictions in Dial Information Servs. v. Thornburgh, 938 F.2d 1535 (2d Cir. 1991), and Information Providers' Coalition v. FCC, 928 F.2d 866 (9th Cir. 1991), on the basis that the restrictions did not amount to a complete ban.

(2) Movie Ratings.   In the 1960s, films began reflecting pervasive societal changes in sexual mores that were triggered by the women's liberation movement, the greater availability of contraceptives, and criticisms of the institution of marriage. As films displayed more nudity and sex, the public voiced increasing demands for regulation.

The city of Dallas in 1965 enacted the first ordinance aimed at protecting children. That ordinance, which served as a model for other municipalities, authorized an administrative board to classify films as "suitable" for children under age 16. Statutory grounds for classification as "not suitable" included portrayal of "sexual promiscuity [so as] to incite or encourage delinquency or sexual promiscuity on the part of young persons or to appeal to their prurient interests." Revised Code of Civil and Criminal Ordinance of the City of Dallas, 1960, Ch. 46A-1 (cited in Interstate v. Dallas, 390 U.S. 676, 681 (1968)). The board could consider a film "likely to incite or encourage" such conduct if the film created "the impression on young persons that such conduct is profitable, desirable, acceptable, respectable, praiseworthy or commonly accepted." Id.

The Supreme Court invalidated the Dallas ordinance on grounds of vagueness. The majority opinion, authored by Justice Marshall, stated that vagueness in the standards for regulation of expression was not excused by the "salutary purpose of protecting children" (id. at 689), and further, that constitutional standards for vagueness did not vary according to the age of the persons protected by a statute. However, recognizing the dangers of motion pictures, particularly for youth, the Court (citing *Ginsberg*) affirmed the desirability of age classifications in regulating the dissemination to minors of objectionable material. Id. at 690.

Fearing a rash of legislative reform in response to Interstate v. Dallas, officials in the Motion Picture Association of America (MPAA) moved quickly to regulate the movie industry themselves. The resultant MPAA rating system, adopted in 1968, still forms the basis for movie-viewing standards.

The MPAA system has four rating categories: "G" for general audiences (all ages admitted); "PG" for "parental guidance suggested"; "R" for "restricted" (those under age 16 must be accompanied by a parent or guardian); and "X" for "X-rated" (no one under age 17 admitted).[30] The MPAA subsequently added a "PG-13" category (parental guidance suggested for those under age 13), in reaction to protests over violence contained in "Indiana Jones and the Temple of Doom." Further, the MPAA later substituted the term "NC-17" for the "X" rating to signify that no children under 17 will be admitted. (Thus, ratings for "X-rated" movies currently are applied by other organizations and not the MPAA.) On the history of movie regulation, see Angela J. Campbell, Self-Regulation and the Media, 51 Fed. Comm. L.J. 711, 750-752 (1999); Swopes v. Lubbers, 560 F. Supp. 1328, 1335-1337 (W.D. Mich. 1983) (background statement by MPAA President Jack Valenti).

The MPAA failed to copyright its rating system, so the producers of pornographic films were able to commandeer the "X" rating for use in their movies. Because the "X" rating came to be associated with pornographic films, which many theaters refused to play and many publications refused to advertise, a non-pornographic adult movie that received a rating of "X", rather than "R", suffered severe economic losses.

In 1990, the producers of one such film, "Tie Me Up! Tie Me Down!," filed suit against the MPAA to compel a change in the film's rating from "X" to "R." Miramax Films Corp. v. Motion Picture Assn. of America, 560 N.Y.S.2d 730 (Sup. Ct. 1990). The Supreme Court of New York County refused to grant the filmmakers' request. The opinion, however, is noteworthy for its candid expression of reservations regarding the MPAA rating system:

> Although each of the categories which the rating system uses is cloaked in terms which suggest that they are fashioned to protect America's children, the inference of concern for the welfare of children is not borne out by any scrutiny of the standard and the guidance given to the rating board members. The standard is not scientific. There are no physicians, child psychiatrists or child care professionals on the board, nor is any professional guidance sought to advise the board members regarding any relative harm to minor children. Id. at 733.

The court continued:

> If the MPAA chooses to rate films for the benefit of children, it is its duty to do so with standards that have a rational and professional basis. . . . The respondent is strongly advised either to consider proposals for a revised rating system that permits of a professional basis for rating films or to cease the practice altogether. Id. at 736.

---

[30] Originally, MPAA President Jack Valenti urged that the industry adopt only three categories, ending in "R" ratings. "It was my view that a parent ought to have the right to accompany children to any movie the parent chose without the movie industry or the government denying that right." Swopes v. Lubbers, 560 F. Supp. 1328, 1336-1337 (W.D. Mich. 1983) (citing background statement). However, the movie exhibitor organization advocated the X rating, stemming from fear of possible legal repercussions, and Valenti acquiesced.

Do you agree with the *Miramax* court's assessment? Should the MPAA hire psychologists or other experts to rate movies? Or should the MPAA "cease the practice altogether"?

If a 16-year-old desires to see an "X-rated" movie, or an "NC-17"-rated movie (no children under 17), who should decide whether the child views the film? By prohibiting minors under the age of 17 from attending "NC-17"-rated movies, does the MPAA infringe on the rights of the child to choose? Does the MPAA infringe on the rights of parents under *Meyer, Pierce,* and *Yoder* to raise that child as they see fit? If someone other than the child or parents makes decisions about the child's movie attendance, should it be a private organization such as the MPAA? Would your answers differ if the MPAA rated novels rather than movies?

Does the state have a role to play in regulating minors' movie viewing? How effective is the rating system? How easy is it for minors to evade the rating system? Two common ways to evade such restrictions, of course, are the rental of videotapes (rather than viewing films in movie theaters) and viewing of airline movies. In Video Software Dealers Assn. v. Webster, 773 F. Supp. 1275 (W.D. Mo. 1991), *aff'd,* 982 F.2d 684 (8th Cir. 1992), the Eighth Circuit Court of Appeals declared unconstitutional, as overbroad, a state statute that prohibited the sale or rental of violent videotapes to minors under 17 years of age. And, in response to parental complaints to the airline industry regarding sex and violence in airline movies, some airlines have responded by showing less violent and sexually explicit films. See Joe Garofoli, The Film-Unfriendly Skies; Major Airlines Struggle to Find Good Movies That Are Appropriate for Passengers of All Ages, S.F. Chron., Aug. 26, 2001, at 48.

Congressional concern about the impact of television violence on children dates to the dawn of television. Despite numerous hearings from 1952 to 1985, Congress has adopted only two legislative proposals addressing the problem. In the Television Program Improvement Act of 1990, 47 U.S.C. §303c (2000), Congress provided for an antitrust exemption to allow (but not require) the industry to hold discussions or formulate agreements to limit violent material on television. That exemption expired in 1993 with little effect, except for influencing broadcast and cable networks to air parental advisories before programs with violent content.

Next, as part of the Telecommunications Act of 1996, 47 U.S.C. §303(x) (2000), Congress authorized the V-chip, a set of internal controls that can read ratings transmitted by television networks to block programming with violence and sexually explicit content. The legislation mandated a "voluntary" television rating system that was similar to movie ratings and also required all television sets with a screen 13 inches or greater to be equipped with the device. The V-chip enables parents to block programs or entire channels. As a result of V-chip legislation, many broadcast and cable networks formulated policies to rate programs by age and contents. Is the V-chip constitutional? See Denver Area Telecomms. Consortium, Inc. v. FCC, 518 U.S. 727, 756 (1996) (suggesting in dicta that it is). How effective is the approach of parental monitoring in this context? Does it alter your view to learn that only 15 percent of parents have used the V-chip and only 42 percent of those who have a V-chip-equipped television say they have used it? See Robert Peters, It Will Take More Than Parental Use of Filtering Software to Protect Children from Internet Pornography, 31 N.Y.U. Rev. L. & Soc. Change

829, 837 (2007) (citing Henry J. Kaiser Family Foundation, Parents, Media and Public Policy 7 (2004)).

The Supreme Court addressed the constitutionality of another provision of the Telecommunications Act (§505) (limiting sexually explicit adult cable television programming to nighttime hours) in United States v. Playboy Entertainment Group, 529 U.S. 803 (2000). Invalidating the legislation as a violation of the First Amendment, the Court reasoned that a different provision of the Telecommunications Act provided a less restrictive means for achieving the same end by requiring cable operators to block channels *upon request* by a customer.

Congress again devoted attention to the subject of television violence with congressional hearings following the shootings at Columbine High School in 1999. This time, attention was focused on the marketing of violent entertainment to children in several different media — music lyrics, movies, video games, and the Internet. Congress considered, but never adopted, various legislative proposals to restrict the marketing of violent entertainment to children. Proposals included: a requirement that the FCC establish a toll-free number and a Web site to log complaints about television violence; a "safe harbor proposal" to require airing violent programming when children were least likely to watch; the establishment of a national commission to determine the causes of youth violence; a permanent antitrust exemption for the industry to develop voluntary guidelines on television violence; criminalizing the sale of extremely violent movies, video games, and books to minors; and a requirement that the industry develop a universal labeling system for violent television programs, movies, video games, and records. Also, former President Clinton called on the movie industry itself to regulate the violence in films and broadcasts. Clinton Challenges Hollywood to Curb Violence in Movies and on Television (CNN television broadcast, May 16, 1999). Subsequently, the National Association of Theatre Owners (representing two-thirds of the nation's movie screens) announced that they would require teenage viewers to present photo identification when they show up without an adult to see an R-rated film. David E. Rosenbaum, Theaters Will Ask to See Photo ID's for R-Rated Films: A Response to Violence, N.Y. Times, June 9, 1999, at A1.

Congress subsequently enacted the Family Entertainment and Copyright Act (FECA), 109 Pub. L. 9, 119 Stat. 218. One section of FECA is the Family Movie Act (codified at 17 U.S.C. §110), which legalizes electronic filtering technology designed to modify DVDs by "sanitizing" (i.e., skipping or muting) their sexually explicit or violent audio/video content. The legislation exempts both the filtering technology and the resultant "sanitized" DVDs from federal copyright laws provided the filtering software and resultant DVDs are for home use. See Jon Healey, Anti-Piracy Legislation Also Has a Bitter Pill for Studios, L.A. Times, Apr. 19, 2005.

What do you think of these various proposals to regulate minors' access to sexually explicit and violent materials? Why do you suppose Congress has faced such difficulty enacting any of these proposals?

(3) Music Labels.   Efforts to censor music in the interests of child protection began in the 1980s. In 1984, the National Parent Teachers Association of America (NPTA) requested that the Recording Industry Association of America (RIAA) adopt a voluntary rating system similar to that of the movie industry. The RIAA,

however, delayed until an influential citizen group led by Tipper Gore (wife of former Vice President Al Gore) and other politicians' wives formed the Parents' Music Resource Center (PMRC) to lobby the music industry. Specifically, the PMRC urged a rating system to inform parents of objectionable content in albums (i.e., violence, sex, references to drugs and alcohol, etc.); lyrics and ratings on album covers; and ratings for music concerts. See Deborah Cazan, Concerts: Rated or Raided? First Amendment Implications of Concert-Rating, 2 Vand. J. Ent. L. & Prac. 170, 171 (2000) (tracing history of regulation).

The PMRC took its concerns to Congress, and the Senate Committee on Commerce, Science, and Transportation held hearings. See Contents of Music and Lyrics of Records: Hearings Before the Senate Comm. on Commerce, Science and Transportation, 99th Cong., 1st Sess. (1985). The PMRC's lobbying efforts netted two results: The RIAA finally agreed to place a voluntary warning label on all albums containing sexually explicit lyrics or violent imagery (saying "Explicit Lyrics — Parental Advisory"), and several state legislatures initiated measures to require parental advisory labels.

Stemming from similar concerns, the Washington state legislature enacted a statute that subjected distributors of music sound recordings to civil and criminal penalties for distribution of "erotic" sound recordings to minors. In Soundgarden v. Eikenberry, 871 P.2d 1050 (Wash. 1994), the Washington Supreme Court held the statute unconstitutional. Although the court concluded that the statutory definition of "erotic material" satisfied the *Ginsberg* test of variable obscenity, the court nonetheless held that the statute was overbroad and a violation of due process as a prior restraint on protected speech and for lack of proper notice to distributors before subjecting them to sanctions.

Two decades after the voluntary adoption of warning labels, critics of the music industry continue to maintain that it has not done enough to protect children from objectionable lyrics. In 2001, the Federal Trade Commission released a report (discussed infra at p. 113) castigating the music recording industry for its marketing tactics to children of albums with sexually explicit and violent lyrics. Although the industry had made some progress in self-regulation, according to the report, it continued to promote to children irresponsibly such music on television, radio, the Internet and teen magazines. Congressional hearings in 2001 and 2002 examined the entertainment industry's self-regulatory efforts. Legislators criticized the music recording industry for refusing to use more descriptive parental advisory labels. Industry reforms, effective April 1, 2002, introduced a label saying "Edited Version" to identify albums with modified versions of albums that contain parental advisories as well as the label "Edited Version Also Available" to alert consumers of the availability of a modified version of an album. See Lynette Holloway, Industry Is Resisting Tougher Label Standards, N.Y. Times, Oct. 21, 2002, at C7. Many state legislatures also have proposed another regulatory measure originally proposed by the PMRC — rating concerts for sexually explicit and violent lyrics. See generally Cazan, supra.

Yet another approach to limiting minors' access to recordings that advocate violence is through the imposition of tort liability on record manufacturers and/or performers. Several parents initiated such suits unsuccessfully after their children's suicides or homicidal acts. See, e.g., Davidson v. Time Warner, Inc., No. Civ.A.

V-94-006, 1997 WL 405907 (S.D. Tex. Mar. 31, 1997); Waller v. Osbourne, 958 F.2d 1084 (11th Cir. 1992); Vance v. Judas Priest, Nos. 86-5844, 86-3939, 1990 WL 130920 (Nev. Dist. Ct. Aug. 24, 1990). Should the First Amendment be a defense to tort liability?

(4) Video Games. Video games (played on home video game systems, portable hand-sized machines, cell phones, personal computers, and coin-operated machines in arcades and stores) comprise a major component of the entertainment industry. Originally targeted to children, the games' audience now includes large numbers of adults as well. Currently, sales of video games constitute a $27.5 billion industry. Roxanne Christ and Farnaz Alemi, Clean Games, Los Angeles Lawyer 12 (May 2008).

Congress first became concerned about violent video games in 1993 after the launch of the popular "Mortal Kombat" (featuring a tournament in which players kill their opponents to yells of "Finish him!" and the sight of spurting blood). Following congressional hearings, Senators Joseph Lieberman (D.-Conn.) and Herb Kohl (D.-Wis.) introduced the Video Game Rating Act of 1994, S. 1823, 103rd Cong. (1994), which proposed the establishment of a commission to create a rating system for video games. To avert the possibility of governmental regulation, the Interactive Digital Software Association used the MPAA ratings to establish the Entertainment Software Rating Board (ESRB) in 1994 that created letter ratings for video games. The seven ratings include EC for Early Childhood (ages 3 and older), E for Everyone, T for Teen (suitable for ages 13 and older), M for Mature (ages 17 and older), AO for Adults Only, RP for Rating Pending, and E10$^+$ for games rated between E and T to designate games that are slightly more violent and mature for children approaching their teens. The ESRB also uses content descriptors to reveal the presence of violence, strong sexual content or strong language, mature sexual themes, use of drugs, or other potentially offensive content. The American Amusement Machine Association drafted similar ratings for coin-operated video arcade machines.

Video games came under increasing scrutiny following the school violence at Littleton, Colorado, in April 1999. Media reports highlighted the teen gunmen's fascination with the violent video games "Quake" and "Doom." Shortly thereafter, former President Bill Clinton announced the initiation of a federal study into the marketing strategies of the movie, music, and video game industries. Betty Streisand & Angie Cannon, Lawyers, Guns, Money, Hollywood, Under New Probe, May Have a Lot to Hide, U.S. News & World Report, June 14, 1999, at 56. After an 18-month study, the Federal Trade Commission released a report, "Marketing Violent Entertainment to Children: A Review of Self-Regulation and Industry Practices in the Motion Picture, Music Recording and Electronic Game Industries," available at *www.ftc.gov/opa/2000/09/youthviol* (last visited Aug. 30, 2008). The report finds that companies in the motion picture, music recording, and electronic game industries routinely target children under 17 in marketing products that their own rating systems deem inappropriate or that warrant parental caution due to violent content, and also that retailers make little effort to restrict youths' access to violent material. Rather than suggest specific legislative proposals, the FTC recommended additional self-regulation by the industry, including the improvement of the usefulness of the movie, music, and video game industries' ratings and labels by the establishment or expansion of codes that prohibit target marketing to children under 17; an increase in compliance at the retail level by checking identification or requiring parental permission; and an effort to increase parental understanding about the meanings of the ratings and labels.

Since 2003, legislators in various states have introduced numerous anti-video-game bills. Lillian R. BeVier, Controlling Communications That Teach or Demonstrate Violence: "The Movie Made Them Do It," 32 J.L. Med. & Ethics 47, 47 (2004). Video game manufacturers have filed suit to enjoin enforcement of the resulting legislation. To date, no state regulation has passed constitutional muster. See, e.g., Video Software Dealers' Assn. v. Schwarzenegger, 2009 WL 415582 (9th Cir. 2009); Entertainment Software Assn. (ESA) v. Swanson, 519 F.3d 768 (8th Cir. 2008); American Amusement Machine Assn. v. Kenrick, 244 F.3d 572 (7th Cir. 2001). For a discussion of recent case law, see Kevin W. Saunders, Shielding Children from Violent Video Games Through Ratings Offender Lists, 41 Ind. L. Rev. 55, 56-67 (2008).

Suits seeking to establish tort liability based on harm to children and others resulting from dissemination of violent video games have similarly been unsuccessful. See, e.g., James v. Meow Media, Inc., 300 F.3d 683 (6th Cir. 2002); Sanders v. Acclaim Entertainment, Inc., 188 F. Supp. 2d 1264 (D. Colo. 2002).

Congress is presently considering legislation, the Protect Children from Video Game Sex and Violence Act of 2003, H.R. 669, 108th Cong. (2003), prohibiting the sale or rental of adult video games to minors. Retail stores would be subject to increasing fines for selling or renting, or attempting to sell or rent "to a minor any video game that depicts nudity, sexual conduct, or other content harmful to minors." The bill was reintroduced in 2007 by Representative John Dingell (D-Mich.), and referred to the Subcommittee on Higher Education, Lifelong Learning, and Competitiveness. For a discussion of the proposed legislation, see Patrick R. Byrd, It's All Fun and Games Until Someone Gets Hurt: The Effectiveness of Proposed Video-Game Legislation on Reducing Violence in Children, 44 Hous. L. Rev. 401 (2007).

Why have reformers focused so much attention on the threat to youth from video games? Is the interactive nature of the media a factor? The portability of the game machines? Are movies and television, in fact, more harmful to minors? Or, as some cynics suggest, is the attention attributable to the fact that the video game industry has no lobby in Washington and fails to provide significant campaign contributions? See Jeffrey Taylor & Bob Davis, Clinton Picks an Easy Target for His Campaign Against Youth Violence: Makers of Video Games, Wall St. J., June 3, 1999, at A28 (so suggesting).

Tinker v. Des Moines Independent Community School District
393 U.S. 503 (1969)

Mr. Justice FORTAS delivered the opinion of the Court.

Petitioner John F. Tinker, 15 years old, and petitioner Christopher Eckhardt, 16 years old, attended high schools in Des Moines, Iowa. Petitioner Mary Beth Tinker, John's sister, was a 13-year-old student in junior high school.

In December 1965, a group of adults and students in Des Moines held a meeting at the Eckhardt home. The group determined to publicize their objections to the hostilities in Vietnam and their support for a truce by wearing black armbands during the holiday season and by fasting on December 16 and New Year's Eve. Petitioners and their parents had previously engaged in similar activities, and they decided to participate in the program.

The principals of the Des Moines schools became aware of the plan to wear armbands. On December 14, 1965, they met and adopted a policy that any student wearing an armband to school would be asked to remove it, and if he refused he would be suspended until he returned without the armband. Petitioners were aware of the regulation that the school authorities adopted.

On December 16, Mary Beth and Christopher wore black armbands to their schools. John Tinker wore his armband the next day. They were all sent home and suspended from school until they would come back without their armbands. They did not return to school until after the planned period for wearing armbands had expired — that is, until after New Year's Day.

This complaint was filed in the United States District Court by petitioners, through their fathers, under §1983 of Title 42 of the United States Code. It prayed for an injunction restraining the respondent school officials and the respondent members of the board of directors of the school district from disciplining the petitioners, and it sought nominal damages. After an evidentiary hearing the District Court dismissed the complaint. It upheld the constitutionality of the school authorities' action on the ground that it was reasonable in order to prevent disturbance of school discipline. 258 F. Supp. 971 (1966). The court referred to but expressly declined to follow the Fifth Circuit's holding in a similar case [forbidding students to wear freedom buttons] that the wearing of symbols like the armbands cannot be prohibited unless it "materially and substantially interfere[s] with the requirements of appropriate discipline in the operation of the school." Burnside v. Byars, 363 F.2d 744, 749 (1966).

[The Court of Appeals for the Eighth Circuit affirmed. 383 F.2d 988 (1967).]

The District Court recognized that the wearing of an armband for the purpose of expressing certain views is the type of symbolic act that is within the Free Speech Clause of the First Amendment. . . . As we shall discuss, the wearing of armbands in the circumstances of this case was entirely divorced from actually or potentially disruptive conduct by those participating in it. It was closely akin to "pure speech" which, we have repeatedly held, is entitled to comprehensive protection under the First Amendment.

First Amendment rights, applied in light of the special characteristics of the school environment, are available to teachers and students. It can hardly be argued that either students or teachers shed their constitutional rights to freedom of speech or expression at the schoolhouse gate. This has been the unmistakable holding of this Court for almost 50 years. . . .

On the other hand, the Court has repeatedly emphasized the need for affirming the comprehensive authority of the States and of school officials, consistent with fundamental constitutional safeguards, to prescribe and control conduct in the schools. Our problem lies in the area where students in the exercise of First Amendment rights collide with the rules of the school authorities.

The problem posed by the present case does not relate to regulation of the length of skirts or the type of clothing, to hair style, or deportment. Cf. Ferrell v. Dallas Independent School District, 392 F.2d 697 (C.A. 5th Cir. 1968); Pugsley v. Sellmeyer, 158 Ark. 247, 250 S.W. 538, 30 A.L.R. 1212 (1923). It does not concern aggressive, disruptive action or even group demonstrations. Our problem involves direct, primary First Amendment rights akin to "pure speech."

The school officials banned and sought to punish petitioners for a silent, passive expression of opinion, unaccompanied by any disorder or disturbance on the part of petitioners. There is here no evidence whatever of petitioners' interference, actual or nascent, with the schools' work or of collision with the rights of other students to be secure and to be let alone. Accordingly, this case does not concern speech or action that intrudes upon the work of the schools or the rights of other students.

Only a few of the 18,000 students in the school system wore the black armbands. Only five students were suspended for wearing them. There is no indication that the work of the schools or any class was disrupted. Outside the classrooms, a few students made hostile remarks to the children wearing armbands, but there were no threats or acts of violence on school premises.

The District Court concluded that the action of the school authorities was reasonable because it was based upon their fear of a disturbance from the wearing of the armbands. But, in our system, undifferentiated fear or apprehension of disturbance is not enough to overcome the right to freedom of expression. Any departure from absolute regimentation may cause trouble. Any variation from the majority's opinion may inspire fear. Any word spoken, in class, in the lunchroom, or on the campus, that deviates from the views of another person may start an argument or cause a disturbance. But our Constitution says we must take this risk, and our history says that it is this sort of hazardous freedom — this kind of openness — that is the basis of our national strength and of the independence and vigor of Americans who grow up and live in this relatively permissive, often disputatious, society.

In order for the State in the person of school officials to justify prohibition of a particular expression of opinion, it must be able to show that its action was caused by something more than a mere desire to avoid the discomfort and unpleasantness that always accompany an unpopular viewpoint. Certainly where there is no finding and no showing that engaging in the forbidden conduct would "materially and substantially interfere with the requirements of appropriate discipline in the operation of the school," the prohibition cannot be sustained. Burnside v. Byars, supra, 363 F.2d at 749.

In the present case, the District Court made no such finding, and our independent examination of the record fails to yield evidence that the school authorities had reason to anticipate that the wearing of the armbands would substantially interfere with the work of the school or impinge upon the rights of other students. Even an official memorandum prepared after the suspension that listed the reasons for the ban on wearing the armbands made no reference to the anticipation of such disruption.

On the contrary, the action of the school authorities appears to have been based upon an urgent wish to avoid the controversy which might result from the expression, even by the silent symbol of armbands, of opposition to this Nation's part in the conflagration in Vietnam. It is revealing, in this respect, that the meeting at which the school principals decided to issue the contested regulation was called in response to a student's statement to the journalism teacher in one of the schools that he wanted to write an article on Vietnam and have it published in the school paper. (The student was dissuaded.)

It is also relevant that the school authorities did not purport to prohibit the wearing of all symbols of political or controversial significance. The record shows that students in some of the schools wore buttons relating to national political campaigns, and some even wore the Iron Cross, traditionally a symbol of Nazism. The order prohibiting the wearing of armbands did not extend to these. Instead, a particular symbol — black armbands worn to exhibit opposition to this Nation's involvement in Vietnam — was singled out for prohibition. Clearly, the prohibition of expression of one particular opinion, at least without evidence that it is necessary to avoid material and substantial interference with schoolwork or discipline, is not constitutionally permissible.

In our system, state-operated schools may not be enclaves of totalitarianism. School officials do not possess absolute authority over their students. Students in school as well as out of school are "persons" under our Constitution. They are possessed of fundamental rights which the State must respect, just as they themselves must respect their obligations to the State. In our system, students may not be regarded as closed-circuit recipients of only that which the State chooses to communicate. They may not be confined to the expression of those sentiments that are officially approved. In the absence of a specific showing of constitutionally valid reasons to regulate their speech, students are entitled to freedom of expression of their views. . . .

The classroom is peculiarly the "marketplace of ideas." The Nation's future depends upon leaders trained through wide exposure to that robust exchange of ideas which discovers truth "out of a multitude of tongues, [rather] than through any kind of authoritative selection."

The principle of these cases is not confined to the supervised and ordained discussion which takes place in the classroom. The principal use to which the schools are dedicated is to accommodate students during prescribed hours for the purpose of certain types of activities. Among those activities is personal intercommunication among the students. This is not only an inevitable part of the process of attending school; it is also an important part of the educational process. A student's rights, therefore, do not embrace merely the classroom hours. When he is in the cafeteria, or on the playing field, or on the campus during the authorized hours, he may express his opinions, even on controversial subjects like the conflict in Vietnam, if he does so without "materially and substantially interfer[ing] with the requirements of appropriate discipline in the operation of the school" and without colliding with the rights of others. Burnside v. Byars, supra, 363 F.2d at 749. But conduct by the student, in class or out of it, which for any reason — whether it stems from time, place, or type of behavior — materially disrupts classwork or involves substantial disorder or invasion of the rights of others is, of course, not immunized by the constitutional guarantee of freedom of speech. . . .

As we have discussed, the record does not demonstrate any facts which might reasonably have led school authorities to forecast substantial disruption of or material interference with school activities, and no disturbances or disorders on the school premises in fact occurred. These petitioners merely went about their ordained rounds in school. Their deviation consisted only in wearing on their sleeve a band of black cloth, not more than two inches wide. They wore it to exhibit their disapproval of the Vietnam hostilities and their advocacy of a truce, to make their views known, and, by their example, to influence others to adopt them. They neither interrupted school activities nor sought to intrude in the school affairs or the lives of others. They caused discussion outside of the classrooms, but no interference with work and no disorder. In the circumstances, our Constitution does not permit officials of the State to deny their form of expression. . . .

Reversed and remanded.

[Concurring opinions of Justice Stewart and Justice White omitted.]

Mr. Justice BLACK, dissenting.

The Court's holding in this case ushers in what I deem to be an entirely new era in which the power to control pupils by the elected "officials of state supported public schools . . ." in the United States is in ultimate effect transferred to the Supreme Court. The Court brought this particular case here on a petition for certiorari urging that the First and Fourteenth Amendments protect the right of school pupils to express their political views all the way "from kindergarten through high school." . . .

Assuming that the Court is correct in holding that the conduct of wearing armbands for the purpose of conveying political ideas is protected by the First Amendment, the crucial remaining questions are whether students and teachers may use the schools at their whim as a platform for the exercise of free speech — "symbolic" or "pure" — and whether the courts will allocate to themselves the function of deciding how the pupils' school day will be spent. . . .

While the record does not show that any of these armband students shouted, used profane language, or were violent in any manner, detailed testimony by some of them shows their armbands caused comments, warnings by other students, the poking of fun at them, and a warning by an older football player that other, non-protesting students had better let them alone. There is also evidence that a teacher of mathematics had his lesson period practically "wrecked" chiefly by disputes with Mary Beth Tinker, who wore her armband for her "demonstration." Even a casual reading of the record shows that this armband did divert students' minds from their regular lessons, and that talk, comments, etc., made John Tinker "self-conscious" in attending school with his armband. While the absence of obscene remarks or boisterous and loud disorder perhaps justifies the Court's statement that the few armband students did not actually "disrupt" the classwork, I think the record overwhelmingly shows that the armbands did exactly what the elected school officials and principals foresaw they would, that is, took the students' minds off their classwork and diverted them to thoughts about the highly emotional subject of the Vietnam war. [I]f the time has come when pupils of state-supported schools, kindergartens, grammar schools, or high school, can defy and flout orders of school officials to keep their minds on their own schoolwork, it is the beginning of a new revolutionary era of permissiveness in this country fostered by the judiciary. . . .

I deny, therefore, that it has been the "unmistakable holding of this Court for almost 50 years" that "students" and "teachers" take with them into the "school-house gate" constitutional rights to "freedom of speech or expression." Even *Meyer* did not hold that.

. . . In my view, teachers in state-controlled public schools are hired to teach there. [C]ertainly a teacher is not paid to go into school and teach subjects the State does not hire him to teach as a part of its selected curriculum. Nor are public school students sent to the schools at public expense to broadcast political or any other views to educate and inform the public. The original idea of schools, which I do not believe is yet abandoned as worthless or out of date, was that children had not yet reached the point of experience and wisdom which enabled them to teach all of their elders. It may be that the Nation has outworn the old-fashioned slogan that "children are to be seen not heard," but one may, I hope, be permitted to harbor the thought that taxpayers send children to school on the premise that at their age they need to learn, not teach.

[M]embers of this Court like all other citizens, know, without being told, that the disputes over the wisdom of the Vietnam war have disrupted and divided this country as few other issues ever have. Of course students, like other people, cannot concentrate on lesser issues when black armbands are being ostentatiously displayed in their presence to call attention to the wounded and dead of the war, some of the wounded and dead being their friends and neighbors. It was, of course, to distract the attention of other students that some students insisted up to the very point of their own suspension from school that they were determined to sit in school with their symbolic armbands.

. . . We cannot close our eyes to the fact that some of the country's greatest problems are crimes committed by the youth, too many of school age. School discipline, like parental discipline, is an integral and important part of training our children to be good citizens — to be better citizens. Here a very small number of students have crisply and summarily refused to obey a school order designed to give pupils who want to learn the opportunity to do so. One does not need to be a prophet or the son of a prophet to know that after the Court's holding today some students in Iowa schools and indeed in all schools will be ready, able, and willing to defy their teachers on practically all orders. . . .

. . . Turned loose with lawsuits for damages and injunctions against their teachers as they are here, it is nothing but wishful thinking to imagine that young, immature students will not soon believe it is their right to control the schools rather than the right of the States that collect the taxes to hire the teachers for the benefit of the pupils. This case, therefore, wholly without constitutional reasons in my judgment, subjects all the public schools in the country to the whims and caprices of their loudest-mouthed, but maybe not their brightest, students. I, for one, am not fully persuaded that school pupils are wise enough, even with this Court's expert help from Washington, to run the 23,390 public school systems in our 50 States. I wish, therefore, wholly to disclaim any purpose on my part to hold that the Federal Constitution compels the teachers, parents, and elected school officials to surrender control of the American public school system to public school students. I dissent.

Morse v. Frederick
127 S. Ct. 2618 (2007)

Chief Justice ROBERTS delivered the opinion of the Court.

. . . On January 24, 2002, the Olympic Torch Relay passed through Juneau, Alaska, on its way to the winter games in Salt Lake City, Utah. The torchbearers were to proceed along a street in front of Juneau-Douglas High School (JDHS) while school was in session. Petitioner Deborah Morse, the school principal, decided to permit staff and students to participate in the Torch Relay as an approved social event or class trip. Students were allowed to leave class to observe the relay from either side of the street. Teachers and administrative officials monitored the students' actions.

Respondent Joseph Frederick, a JDHS senior, [joined his friends] across the street from the school to watch the event. . . . As the torchbearers and camera crews passed by, Frederick and his friends unfurled a 14-foot banner bearing the phrase: "BONG HiTS 4 JESUS." The large banner was easily readable by the students on the other side of the street.

Principal Morse immediately crossed the street and demanded that the banner be taken down. Everyone but Frederick complied. Morse confiscated the banner and told Frederick to report to her office, where she suspended him for 10 days. Morse later explained that she told Frederick to take the banner down because she thought it encouraged illegal drug use, in violation of established school policy. Juneau School Board Policy No. 5520 states: "The Board specifically prohibits any assembly or public expression that . . . advocates the use of substances that are illegal to minors. . . ." In addition, Juneau School Board Policy No. 5850 subjects "[p]upils who participate in approved social events and class trips" to the same student conduct rules that apply during the regular school program.

Frederick administratively appealed his suspension, but the Juneau School District Superintendent upheld it. [H]e then filed suit under 42 U.S.C. §1983, alleging that the school board and Morse had violated his First Amendment rights. . . . We granted certiorari on two questions: whether Frederick had a First Amendment right to wield his banner, and, if so, whether that right was so clearly established that the principal may be held liable for damages. We resolve the first question against Frederick, and therefore have no occasion to reach the second.

At the outset, we reject Frederick's argument that this is not a school speech case. . . . The event occurred during normal school hours. It was sanctioned by Principal Morse "as an approved social event or class trip," and the school district's rules expressly provide that pupils in "approved social events and class trips are subject to district rules for student conduct." Teachers and administrators were interspersed among the students and charged with supervising them. The high school band and cheerleaders performed. Frederick, standing among other JDHS students across the street from the school, directed his banner toward the school, making it plainly visible to most students. Under these circumstances, we agree with the superintendent that Frederick cannot "stand in the midst of his fellow students, during school hours, at a school-sanctioned activity and claim he is not at school." . . .

The message on Frederick's banner is cryptic. It is no doubt offensive to some, perhaps amusing to others. To still others, it probably means nothing at all. Frederick himself claimed "that the words were just nonsense meant to attract television cameras." But Principal Morse thought the banner would be interpreted by those viewing it as promoting illegal drug use, and that interpretation is plainly a reasonable one.

As Morse later explained in a declaration, when she saw the sign, she thought that "the reference to a 'bong hit' would be widely understood by high school students and others as referring to smoking marijuana." She further believed that "display of the banner would be construed by students, District personnel, parents and others witnessing the display of the banner, as advocating or promoting illegal drug use" — in violation of school policy. . . .

We agree with Morse. At least two interpretations of the words on the banner demonstrate that the sign advocated the use of illegal drugs. First, the phrase could be interpreted as an imperative: "[Take] bong hits . . ." — a message equivalent, as Morse explained in her declaration, to "smoke marijuana" or "use an illegal drug." Alternatively, the phrase could be viewed as celebrating drug use — "bong hits [are a good thing]," or "[we take] bong hits" — and we discern no meaningful distinction between celebrating illegal drug use in the midst of fellow students and outright advocacy or promotion.

The pro-drug interpretation of the banner gains further plausibility given the paucity of alternative meanings the banner might bear. The best Frederick can come up with is that the banner is "meaningless and funny." The dissent similarly refers to the sign's message as "curious," "ambiguous," "nonsense," "ridiculous," "obscure," "silly," "quixotic," and "stupid." Gibberish is surely a possible interpretation of the words on the banner, but it is not the only one, and dismissing the banner as meaningless ignores its undeniable reference to illegal drugs. . . . The dissent mentions Frederick's "credible and uncontradicted explanation for the message — he just wanted to get on television." But that is a description of Frederick's *motive* for displaying the banner; it is not an interpretation of what the banner says. . . .

The question thus becomes whether a principal may, consistent with the First Amendment, restrict student speech at a school event, when that speech is reasonably viewed as promoting illegal drug use. We hold that she may.

In *Tinker*, this Court made clear that "First Amendment rights, applied in light of the special characteristics of the school environment, are available to teachers and students" [393 U.S. 503, 506 (1969)]. . . . *Tinker* held that student expression may not be suppressed unless school officials reasonably conclude that it will "materially and substantially disrupt the work and discipline of the school." Id., at 513. The essential facts of Tinker are quite stark, implicating concerns at the heart of the First Amendment [i.e., disapproval of the war in Vietnam]. The only interest the Court discerned underlying the school's actions was the "mere desire to avoid the discomfort and unpleasantness that always accompany an unpopular viewpoint," or "an urgent wish to avoid the controversy which might result from the expression." *Tinker*, 393 U.S., at 509. That interest was not enough to justify banning "a silent, passive expression of opinion, unaccompanied by any disorder or disturbance." Id., at 508.

This Court's next student speech case was [Bethel v. Fraser, 478 U.S. 675 (1986)]. Matthew Fraser was suspended for delivering a speech before a high school assembly in which he employed what this Court called "an elaborate, graphic, and explicit sexual metaphor." Id. at 678. Analyzing the case under *Tinker*, the District Court and Court of Appeals found no disruption, and therefore no basis for disciplining Fraser. This Court reversed, holding that the "School District acted entirely within its permissible authority in imposing sanctions upon Fraser in response to his offensively lewd and indecent speech." Id. at 685.

[We] distill from *Fraser* two basic principles. First, *Fraser*'s holding demonstrates that "the constitutional rights of students in public school are not automatically coextensive with the rights of adults in other settings." Id., at 682. Had Fraser delivered the same speech in a public forum outside the school context, it would have been protected. In school, however, Fraser's First Amendment rights were circumscribed "in light of the special characteristics of the school environment." *Tinker*, supra, at 506. Second, *Fraser* established that the mode of analysis set forth in *Tinker* is not absolute. Whatever approach *Fraser* employed, it certainly did not conduct the "substantial disruption" analysis prescribed by *Tinker*.

Our most recent student speech case [Hazelwood School Dist. v. Kuhlmeier, 484 U.S. 260, 271 (1998)] concerned "expressive activities that students, parents, and members of the public might reasonably perceive to bear the imprimatur of the school." [This Court held] that "educators do not offend the First Amendment by exercising editorial control over the style and content of student speech in school-sponsored expressive activities so long as their actions are reasonably related to legitimate pedagogical concerns." *Kuhlmeier*, supra, at 273. *Kuhlmeier* does not control this case because no one would reasonably believe that Frederick's banner bore the school's imprimatur. The case is nevertheless instructive because it confirms both principles cited above. . . .

Drawing on the principles applied in our student speech cases, we have held in the Fourth Amendment context that "while children assuredly do not 'shed their constitutional rights . . . at the schoolhouse gate,' . . . the nature of those rights is what is appropriate for children in school." Vernonia School Dist. 47J v. Acton, 515 U.S. 646, 655-656 (1995) (quoting *Tinker*, supra, at 506). In particular, "the school setting requires some easing of the restrictions to which searches by public authorities are ordinarily subject." New Jersey v. T.L.O., 469 U.S. 325, 340 (1985); Board of Ed. of Independent School Dist. No. 92 of Pottawatomie Cty. v. Earls, 536 U.S. 822, 829-830 (2002) (" 'special needs' inhere in the public school context" . . .).

Even more to the point, these cases also recognize that deterring drug use by schoolchildren is an "important-indeed, perhaps compelling" interest. Drug abuse can cause severe and permanent damage to the health and well-being of young people:

> School years are the time when the physical, psychological, and addictive effects
> of drugs are most severe. Maturing nervous systems are more critically impaired

> by intoxicants than mature ones are; childhood losses in learning are lifelong and profound; children grow chemically dependent more quickly than adults, and their record of recovery is depressingly poor. And of course the effects of a drug-infested school are visited not just upon the users, but upon the entire student body and faculty, as the educational process is disrupted. [*Vernonia*, supra, at 661-662.]

Just five years ago, we wrote: "The drug abuse problem among our Nation's youth has hardly abated since *Vernonia* was decided in 1995. In fact, evidence suggests that it has only grown worse." *Earls*, supra, at 834, and n. 5.

The problem remains serious today. About half of American 12th graders have used an illicit drug, as have more than a third of 10th graders and about one-fifth of 8th graders [National Institute on Drug Abuse, National Institutes of Health, Monitoring the Future: National Survey Results on Drug Use, 1975-2005, Secondary School Students 99 (2006)]. Nearly one in four 12th graders has used an illicit drug in the past month. Some 25% of high schoolers say that they have been offered, sold, or given an illegal drug on school property within the past year.

Congress has declared that part of a school's job is educating students about the dangers of illegal drug use. It has provided billions of dollars to support state and local drug-prevention programs, and required that schools receiving federal funds under the Safe and Drug-Free Schools and Communities Act of 1994 certify that their drug prevention programs "convey a clear and consistent message that . . . the illegal use of drugs [is] wrong and harmful." 20 U.S.C. §7114(d)(6) (2000 ed., Supp. IV).

Thousands of school boards throughout the country — including JDHS — have adopted policies aimed at effectuating this message. Those school boards know that peer pressure is perhaps "the single most important factor leading schoolchildren to take drugs," and that students are more likely to use drugs when the norms in school appear to tolerate such behavior. Student speech celebrating illegal drug use at a school event, in the presence of school administrators and teachers, thus poses a particular challenge for school officials working to protect those entrusted to their care from the dangers of drug abuse.

The "special characteristics of the school environment," and the governmental interest in stopping student drug abuse — reflected in the policies of Congress and myriad school boards, including JDHS — allow schools to restrict student expression that they reasonably regard as promoting illegal drug use. *Tinker* warned that schools may not prohibit student speech because of "undifferentiated fear or apprehension of disturbance" or "a mere desire to avoid the discomfort and unpleasantness that always accompany an unpopular viewpoint" [*Tinker*, supra, at 508]. The danger here is far more serious and palpable. The particular concern to prevent student drug abuse at issue here, embodied in established school policy extends well beyond an abstract desire to avoid controversy.

. . . School principals have a difficult job, and a vitally important one. When Frederick suddenly and unexpectedly unfurled his banner, Morse had to decide to act — or not act — on the spot. It was reasonable for her to conclude that the banner promoted illegal drug use — in violation of established school policy — and that failing to act would send a powerful message to the students in her charge, including Frederick, about how serious the school was about the dangers of illegal drug use. The First Amendment does not require schools to tolerate at school events student expression that contributes to those dangers. . . .

Justice STEVENS, with whom Justice SOUTER and Justice GINSBURG join, dissenting.

A significant fact barely mentioned by the Court sheds a revelatory light on the motives of both the students and the principal of Juneau-Douglas High School (JDHS). On January 24, 2002, the Olympic Torch Relay gave those Alaska residents a rare chance to appear on national television. As Joseph Frederick repeatedly explained, he did not address the curious message — "BONG HiTS 4 JESUS" — to his fellow students. He just wanted to get the camera crews' attention. . . .

. . . I would hold [that] the school's interest in protecting its students from exposure to speech "reasonably regarded as promoting illegal drug use," cannot justify disciplining Frederick for his attempt to make an ambiguous statement to a television audience simply because it contained an oblique reference to drugs. The First Amendment demands more, indeed, much more. . . .

. . . Two cardinal First Amendment principles animate both the Court's opinion in *Tinker* and Justice Harlan's dissent [in *Tinker*]. First, censorship based on the content of speech, particularly censorship that depends on the viewpoint of the speaker, is subject to the most rigorous burden of justification. . . . Second, punishing someone for advocating illegal conduct is constitutional only when the advocacy is likely to provoke the harm that the government seeks to avoid.

[T]oday the Court fashions a test that trivializes the two cardinal principles upon which *Tinker* rests. The Court's test invites stark viewpoint discrimination. In this case, for example, the principal has unabashedly acknowledged that she disciplined Frederick because she disagreed with the pro-drug viewpoint she ascribed to the message on the banner, incidentally, that Frederick has disavowed. [T]he Court's holding in this case strikes at "the heart of the First Amendment" because it upholds a punishment meted out on the basis of a listener's disagreement with her understanding (or, more likely, misunderstanding) of the speaker's viewpoint. . . .

The Court rejects outright these twin foundations of *Tinker* because, in its view, the unusual importance of protecting children from the scourge of drugs supports a ban on all speech in the school environment that promotes drug use. Whether or not such a rule is sensible as a matter of policy, carving out pro-drug speech for uniquely harsh treatment finds no support in our case law and is inimical to the values protected by the First Amendment.

[I]t is one thing to restrict speech that advocates drug use. It is another thing entirely to prohibit an obscure message with a drug theme that a third party subjectively — and not very reasonably — thinks is tantamount to express advocacy. . . . On its face, then, the [school] rule gave Frederick wide berth "to express [his] ideas and opinions" so long as they did not amount to "advoca[cy]" of drug use. . . . Therefore, just as we insisted in *Tinker* that the school establish some likely connection between the armbands and their feared consequences, so too JDHS must show that Frederick's supposed advocacy stands a meaningful chance of making otherwise-abstemious students try marijuana.

But instead of demanding that the school make such a showing, the Court punts. . . . To the extent the Court defers to the principal's ostensibly reasonable judgment, it abdicates its constitutional responsibility. The beliefs of third parties, reasonable or otherwise, have never dictated which messages amount to proscribable advocacy. Indeed, it would be a strange constitutional doctrine that would allow the prohibition of only the narrowest category of speech advocating unlawful conduct, yet would permit a listener's perceptions to determine which speech deserved constitutional protection. . . .

To the extent the Court independently finds that "BONG HiTS 4 JESUS" objectively amounts to the advocacy of illegal drug use — in other words, that it can most reasonably be interpreted as such — that conclusion practically refutes itself. This is a nonsense message, not advocacy. The Court's feeble effort to divine its hidden meaning is strong evidence of that. Frederick's credible and uncontradicted explanation for the message — he just wanted to get on television — is also relevant because a speaker who does not intend to persuade his audience can hardly be said to be advocating anything. But most importantly, it takes real imagination to read a "cryptic" message (the Court's characterization, not mine) with a slanting drug reference as an incitement to drug use. Admittedly, some high school students (including those who use drugs) are dumb. Most students, however, do not shed their brains at the schoolhouse gate, and most students know dumb advocacy when they see it. The notion that the message on this banner would actually persuade either the average student or even the dumbest one to change his or her behavior is most implausible. That the Court believes such a silly message can be proscribed as advocacy underscores the novelty of its position, and suggests that the principle it articulates has no stopping point. . . .

Although this case began with a silly, nonsensical banner, it ends with the Court inventing out of whole cloth a special First Amendment rule permitting the censorship of any student speech that mentions drugs, at least so long as someone could perceive that speech to contain a latent pro-drug message. [T]wo personal recollections [have] no doubt influenced my conclusion that it would be profoundly unwise to create special rules for speech about drug and alcohol use.

The Vietnam War is remembered today as an unpopular war. During its early stages, however, "the dominant opinion" that Justice Harlan mentioned in his *Tinker* dissent regarded opposition to the war as unpatriotic, if not treason. . . . As we now know, the then-dominant opinion about the Vietnam War was not etched in stone.

Reaching back still further, the current dominant opinion supporting the war on drugs in general, and our anti-marijuana laws in particular, is reminiscent of the opinion that supported the nationwide ban on alcohol consumption. . . . While alcoholic beverages are now regarded as ordinary articles of commerce, their use was then condemned with the same moral fervor that now supports the war on drugs. . . . But just as prohibition in the 1920's and early 1930's was secretly questioned by thousands of otherwise law-abiding patrons of bootleggers and speakeasies, today the actions of literally millions of otherwise law-abiding users of marijuana, and of the majority of voters in each of the several States that tolerate medicinal uses of the product, lead me to wonder whether the fear of disapproval by those in the majority is silencing opponents of the war on drugs.

Surely our national experience with alcohol should make us wary of dampening speech suggesting — however inarticulately — that it would be better to tax and regulate marijuana than to persevere in a futile effort to ban its use entirely.

Even in high school, a rule that permits only one point of view to be expressed is less likely to produce correct answers than the open discussion of countervailing views. In the national debate about a serious issue, it is the expression of the minority's viewpoint that most demands the protection of the First Amendment. Whatever the better policy may be, a full and frank discussion of the costs and benefits of the attempt to prohibit the use of marijuana is far wiser than suppression of speech because it is unpopular. . . .

QUESTIONS ON *TINKER* AND *MORSE*

(1) Are **Ginsberg** *and* **Tinker** *consistent?* *Ginsberg* expressly adopts a notion of "variable" First Amendment rights and upholds the legitimacy of a different legal standard of obscenity for young people. Does *Tinker* hold that high school students have the same First Amendment rights as adults?

(2) **Tinker** *Test.* According to *Tinker*, schools may not restrict student speech unless necessary to avoid a material and substantial interference with the work of the school or school discipline. The applicability of *Tinker* depends in large part on the definition of these terms. What is meant by the "work of the school"? "Disruption"? "Material and substantial interference"?

How relevant in the determination of "disruption" is the reaction of the recipient of the student's speech? See, e.g., J.S. ex rel. H.S. v. Bethlehem Area Sch. Dist., 807 A.2d 847 (Pa. 2002) (holding that student's offensive remarks posted on his Internet Web site did not constitute "true threat" for purposes of regulation under the First Amendment despite the fear experienced by the teacher who was the target of the speech); Smith v. Novato Unified Sch. Dist., 59 Cal. Rptr.3d 508 (Ct. App. 2007) (adopting an objective test for "incitement," pursuant to state statute protecting student speech, that focuses on the words of the speaker rather than the reaction of the intended audience).

(3) **Tinker** *Trilogy.* *Tinker* represents the apex of constitutional protection for student speech. Subsequent Supreme Court cases upheld exceptions to *Tinker*. In Bethel v. Fraser, 478 U.S. 675 (1986), a high school senior gave a nominating speech at a school assembly (in favor of a classmate running for office) that contained an elaborate sexual metaphor. The student speaker was suspended for three days and his name was removed from the list of approved graduation speakers for violating the school's "disruptive-conduct rule." The Supreme Court held that the student's conduct was not entitled to First Amendment protection and that the school acted within its authority in imposing sanctions, reasoning that the inculcation of proper values and the protection of minors are appropriate functions of public education. The case thereby permitted a school to regulate student speech that was not disruptive but merely offensive.

In Hazelwood v. Kuhlmeier, 484 U.S. 260 (1998), a high school principal deleted two articles in the school newspaper concerning teen pregnancy and divorce, stemming from his concern about the privacy of pregnant students and that of a divorced parent. The Supreme Court disagreed that student staff members' First Amendment rights were violated by the school's censorship. The Court reasoned that a school paper published by students in a journalism class does not qualify as a "public forum," and that school officials retain the right to impose reasonable restrictions on school-sponsored activities provided that the officials' actions are reasonably related to legitimate pedagogical concerns. *Tinker* does not apply, according to the Court, because *Tinker* involved a school's mere tolerance of student speech, whereas *Hazelwood* involved a school's active promotion of particular student speech.

What result would an application of the *Tinker* test dictate in *Morse*? Why didn't *Tinker* control the result in *Morse*? Why didn't *Hazelwood*? Is *Morse* another exception to *Tinker*? If so, have the exceptions swallowed the rule?

(4) Parental Role. In an omitted concurrence in *Morse*, Justice Thomas advocates broad disciplinary authority for public school educators based on the doctrine of in loco parentis (the common law doctrine that refers to the legal responsibility of a person or organization to assume parental functions and responsibilities). "If students in public schools were originally understood as having free-speech rights, one would have expected 19th-century public schools to have respected those rights and courts to have enforced them. They did not." *Morse*, 127 S. Ct. at 2630 (Thomas, J., concurring). His historical analysis leads him to conclude that *Tinker* significantly impaired the authority of educators and should be overturned.

On the other hand, in a separate concurring opinion (also omitted here), Justice Alito rejects the argument that school officials stand in loco parentis as the basis for regulation of student speech. He called it "a dangerous fiction to pretend that parents simply delegate their authority — including their authority to determine what their children may say and hear — to public school authorities." *Morse*, 127 S. Ct. at 2637 (Alito, J., concurring). "It is even more dangerous to assume that such a delegation of authority somehow strips public school authorities of their status as agents of the State. Most parents, realistically, have no choice but to send their children to a public school and little ability to influence what occurs in the school." Id. He concludes that, although public schools may ban speech advocating illegal drug use due to the threat to student safety, any further restrictions are undesirable based on First Amendment grounds. Which view of the school's "parental" role do you find more persuasive?

In *Tinker*, what role did the children's parents play in the minors' decision to wear armbands? Should that matter in the Court's decision? Justice Black points out in an omitted portion of his dissent that the Tinkers' father was a Methodist minister who was paid a salary by the American Friends Service Committee, and Christopher Eckhardt's mother was an official in the Women's International League for Peace and Freedom. As Robert Burt has queried: "From this record, is it crystal clear whose political expression rights were being protected — the children's or their parents'?" Robert Burt, Developing Constitutional Rights of, in, and for Children? 39 Law & Contemp. Probs. (No. 3) 118, 122 (1975). Burt then adds:

> *Tinker*, from this perspective, is no different from the parental-rights cases [*Yoder* and *Prince*] considered earlier. In general, it is false psychology to portray a

dispute between children and the state without acknowledging the direct —
implicit or explicit — role of parents in that dispute. Id. at 12.

Is there a tension between the parental rights doctrine asserted in *Meyer, Pierce,*
and *Yoder* and the custodial role of the public school officials? If so, how should
that tension be resolved? For example, what power does a parent have to punish or
constrain a child in activities that might be constitutionally protected from state
intrusion?

(5) Political Speech.   Does *Tinker* turn in important part on the fact that the
school prohibited some, but not all, student speech that involved political expression? What type of student speech constitutes "political expression" that is constitutionally protected under *Tinker*? In *Morse,* why does Chief Justice Roberts
reject the Ninth Circuit's conclusion that "BONG HiTS 4 JESUS" is political
speech? Does Frederick's banner constitute advocacy of illegal drug use? Contrast
the views of the majority and the dissent on this point.

Consider the nature of the following student conduct as "political speech."
May a school ban student displays of the Confederate flag? Would a student's
display of that flag be likely to lead to a material and substantial disruption of
school discipline or invade the rights of others under *Tinker*? See Barr v. Lafon,
538 F.3d 554 (6th Cir. 2008). May a school ban the display of symbols or slogans
that advocate support for gay rights? Would student advocacy of gay rights — for
example, on clothing — constitute a material and substantial interference with
appropriate discipline or interfere with the rights of others? See Gillman v. ex rel.
Gillman v. School Bd., 567 F. Supp.2d 1359 (N.D. Fla. 2008).

In addition to students' rights under the First Amendment, federal law (the
Equal Access Act, 20 U.S.C. §4071(a)(2007)) requires schools that have adopted a
limited open forum to allow noncurricular student groups to use school facilities
regardless of the religious, political, or philosophical content of the group's speech.
Would a high school violate the Equal Access Act by refusing to allow a gay and
lesbian student group to *advertise* its meetings via flyers distributed at school and
via the school's intercom system — even though the school would allow the group
to hold the meeting? Compare Gay-Straight Alliance of Okeechobee High Sch. v.
Sch. Bd., 483 F. Supp.2d 1224 (S.D. Fla. 2007), with Caudillo v. Lubbock Indep.
Sch. Dist., 311 F. Supp. 2d 550 (N.D. Tex. 2004). See generally Alice Riener,
Comment: Pride and Prejudice: The First Amendment, the Equal Access Act, and
the Legal Fight to Gay Student Groups in High Schools, 14 Am. U.J. Gender Soc.
Pol'y & L. 613 (2006).

(6) What Is School-Related Speech?   In *Morse,* why did the Supreme Court
determine that Frederick's expression was school-related speech? One commentator contends that Frederick's speech took place on a "public forum" (a sidewalk)
and was therefore entitled to constitutional protection. Erwin Chemerinsky, How
Will Morse v. Frederick Be Applied?, 12 Lewis & Clark L. Rev. 17 (2008). What
arguments support and refute that view?

How far does the school's authority extend to censor student speech off-
campus? How does the student use of the Internet affect the determination of
the limits of school administrators' authority? Suppose a student — in the privacy
of his home during nonschool hours — drafts offensive remarks about a school

administrator and then circulates them on an Internet site that can be viewed by other students in the school? Compare Doninger v. Niehoff, 527 F.3d 41 (2d Cir. 2008) (holding that school had authority to punish student for her offensive blog entry because her derogatory comments about school administrators and her incitement to students to protest to administration created foreseeable risk of substantial disruption and led to school authorities taking considerable time to answer students) with Layshock v. Harmitage Sch. Dist., 496 F. Supp.2d 587 (W.D. Pa. 2007) (holding that because no nexus existed between student's creation of Internet parody of principal and a substantial disruption of school environment that suspension violated student's free speech rights, where no classes were canceled, no widespread disorder occurred, and the only in-school conduct in which student engaged in relation to parody was showing it to other students in classroom).

(7) Viewpoint Discrimination. Viewpoint discrimination is constitutionally impermissible. Constitutional doctrine dictates that speech restrictions must be made without regard to the viewpoint expressed in the speech. *Hazelwood* left open the question of whether viewpoint discrimination is permissible for student school-sponsored speech. Following *Hazelwood*, the federal circuit courts split on whether the Supreme Court created a constitutional exception to viewpoint restrictions on student expression. See Susannah Barton Tobin, Note, Divining *Hazelwood*: The Need for a Viewpoint Neutrality Requirement in School Speech Cases, 39 Harv. C.R.-C.L. L. Rev. 217, 231-238 (2004) (pointing out that First, Third, and Tenth Circuits read *Hazelwood* to permit viewpoint restrictions of school-sponsored speech, whereas the Sixth, Ninth, and Eleventh Circuits read *Hazelwood* to require viewpoint neutrality).

Does the majority in *Morse* uphold viewpoint discrimination? Would Frederick have been disciplined if his banner condemned the use of drugs? Would the Court have ruled differently if the banner had read "LEGALIZE BONG HITS"? Note that Justices Breyer and Stevens each dissented, largely stemming from their concerns with viewpoint discrimination. See *Morse*, 127 S. Ct. at 2637 (Breyer, J., dissenting) (fearing that the majority's opinion "would give public school authorities a license to suppress speech on political and social issues based on disagreement with the viewpoint expressed"); id. at 2645 (Stevens, J., dissenting) (asserting that "the Court's holding in this case strikes at 'the heart of the First Amendment' because it upholds a punishment meted out on the basis of a listener's disagreement with her understanding (or, more likely, misunderstanding) of the speaker's viewpoint").

Are the dissenters correct that the holding in *Morse* gives school officials too much discretion to ban speech asserting a controversial or unpopular position? To avoid authorizing viewpoint restrictions, should the Court have ruled merely that the principal had qualified immunity from liability for damages, as Justice Breyer suggests in his separate, omitted, concurring decision? See *Morse*, 127 S. Ct. at 2741 (Breyer, J., concurring) (contending that the principal did not clearly violate the law because the First Amendment tests of *Tinker* and its progeny are complex and difficult to apply).

What is the appropriate role of schools in dictating the viewpoints that students may express? Is there a plausible distinction between requiring viewpoint neutrality for students' own speech and for school-sponsored student speech? Is the

Hazelwood Court's argument convincing that in the latter instance, there is a danger of attribution of students' viewpoints to the school?

(8) School's Educational Mission.   In a symposium on the 25th anniversary of *Tinker*, one legal commentator contrasts the *Tinker*'s majority and dissenting views of "school work," by pointing out that the majority (Justice Fortas) defines the term narrowly (i.e., teaching), whereas the dissent (Justice Black) believes that schools are instruments of socialization. Mark Yudof, *Tinker* Tailored: Good Faith, Civility, and Student Expression, 69 St. John's L. Rev. 365 (1995). How does the Court in *Hazelwood* regard the school's educational mission? How do the majority and dissent in *Morse* regard it? What do you think the school's educational mission should be?

(9) Special Characteristics of the School Environment.   According to the Supreme Court, students' First Amendment rights must be evaluated based on the "special characteristics of the school environment." Hazelwood v. Kuhlmeier, 484 U.S. 260, 266 (1988) (quoting *Tinker*, 393 U.S. at 506). Recent history has been marked by a number of high-profile school shootings, beginning in 1999 with the Columbine High School shooting and including recent tragedies like the 2007 Virginia Tech massacre. With this in mind, consider Justice Alito's sole justification for restrictions on speech in *Morse* that the school environment poses a "special danger" to the physical safety of students due to the lack of parental protection and the close proximity of students to each other. *Morse*, 127 S. Ct. at 2638 (Alito, J., concurring). Given this unique environment, "school officials must have greater authority to intervene before speech leads to violence." Id. Although the facts of *Morse* concern incitement to illegal drug use, does the holding also justify restrictions on speech that is reasonably regarded as promoting physical violence?

At least one court has extended *Morse* to apply to potential school violence. In Ponce v. Socorro Indep. Sch. Dist., 508 F.3d 765 (5th Cir. 2007), a high school student kept a diary, written in the first-person perspective, in which he detailed the creation of a pseudo-Nazi group and the group's plan to commit a "Columbine shooting." The assistant principal suspended the student, after determining that his writing posed a threat to safety and security. The Fifth Circuit upheld the decision pursuant to *Morse*. Relying on Justice Alito's concurrence in *Morse*, the Court explained, "it was reasonable for [the school] to conclude that failing to respond to [the student's] diary would not only place [the student] and other students at risk of physical danger if the intent expressed in the diary was actualized, but would also send a message to [the student who wrote the diary] and to the informing student that the school administration would tolerate violent threats against the student body." Id. at 771 fn.3.

Could a restriction on speech that threatens school violence be justified alternatively by the *Tinker* test? In a case preceding *Morse*, the Ninth Circuit upheld a school's decision to discipline a student who showed his teacher a poem he wrote that described him shooting other students. Lavine v. Blaine Sch. Dist., 257 F.3d 981 (9th Cir. 2001). Applying *Tinker*, the court found that "[t]aken together and given the backdrop of actual school shootings, we hold that these circumstances were sufficient to have led school authorities reasonably to forecast substantial disruption of or material interference with school activities — specifically, that [the student] was intending to inflict injury upon himself or others." Id. at 990.

(10) Legacy of **Morse.** What is the likely impact of *Morse* on regulation of student expression in the public schools? Is *Morse* likely to lead to an expansion of school authority concerning student speech or be limited to the regulation of only pro-drug messages? See Chemerinsky, supra (expressing the hope that Justice Alito's concurring opinion will be influential in limiting further restrictions on students' First Amendment rights); John Dayton & Anne Proffitt Dupre, *Morse* Code: How School Speech Takes a ("Bong") Hit, 233 Ed. Law Rep. 503 (2008) (speculating that post-*Morse* case law suggests that *Morse* will promote further litigation to clarify its scope); Melinda Cupps Dickler, The *Morse* Quartet: Student Speech and the First Amendment, 53 Loy. L. Rev. 355, 358 (2007) (pointing out that post-*Morse* case law is split about the breadth of its holding).

(11) Problems. Public schools, increasingly, are establishing dress codes. Some schools ban certain types of clothing; others prohibit the wearing of gang apparel. Are the types of student conduct in the following examples expressive speech? If so, are the following regulations constitutional? Are *Tinker, Fraser, Hazelwood,* and *Morse* applicable? Do the following regulations serve legitimate pedagogical objectives?

a. A high school student is asked to turn inside-out his T-shirt portraying a three-faced Jesus with the wording "See No Truth, Hear No Truth, Speak No Truth" and "Marilyn Manson" printed on the front. The word "Believe," emphasizing the letters "l-i-e," is printed on the back. The rock band Marilyn Manson promotes violence and pro-drug views in their lyrics. The school dress and grooming policy forbids "clothing with offensive illustrations, drug, alcohol, or tobacco slogans." See Boroff v. Van Wert City Bd. of Educ., 220 F.3d 465 (6th Cir. 2000).

b. A student is asked to remove his T-shirt displaying a picture of then-President George W. Bush with the phrase "international terrorist" printed on the front. Barber ex rel. Barber v. Dearborn Pub. Sch., 286 F. Supp. 2d 847 (E.D. Mich. 2003).

c. A student is asked to remove her pin of the Palestinian flag. Tamar Lewin, High School Tells Student to Remove Antiwar Shirt, N.Y. Times, Feb. 26, 2003, at A12.

d. A school bans the wearing of Muslim head scarves by female students. Derek H. Davis, Reacting to France's Ban: Headscarves and Other Religious Attire in American Public Schools, 46 J. Church & State 221 (2004).

e. A school prohibits a transgender high school student from wearing clothes and accessories that are consistent with her gender identity. See Doe ex rel. Doe v. Yunits, 2000 WL 33162199 (Mass. Super. Ct. 2000).

f. A school regulates hair length of male students. See Alabama & Coushatta Tribes of Texas v. Trustees of Big Sandy Indep. Sch. Dist., 817 F. Supp. 1319 (E.D. Tex. 1993). Or the school prohibits the wearing of "sagging pants." See Bivens exrel. Green v. Albuquerque Pub. Sch., 899 F. Supp. 556 (D.N.M. 1995), *aff'd without opinion,* 131 F.3d 151 (10th Cir. 1997).

See generally Todd A. DeMitchell et al., Dress Codes in the Public Schools: Principals, Policies, and Precepts, 29 J.L. & Educ. 31 (2000); Rob Killen, Note,

The Achilles' Heel of Dress Codes: The Definition of Proper Attire in Public Schools, 36 Tulsa L.J. 459 (2000).

NOTE: STUDENTS' RIGHT TO INFORMATION — SCHOOLBOOKS AND THE INTERNET

First Amendment issues concerning the censorship of school libraries and texts have been the focus of controversy since *Tinker.* The Supreme Court first addressed censorship of public school libraries in Board of Education v. Pico, 457 U.S. 853 (1982). In *Pico,* a local school board removed nine books (including Kurt Vonnegut's *Slaughterhouse Five,* Langston Hughes' *Best Short Stories of Negro Writers* and the anonymous memoir of a young addict, *Go Ask Alice*) from the high school and junior high school libraries on the ground that the books were "anti-American, anti-Christian, anti-Semitic, and just plain filthy." Id. at 857 (quoting the Board's press release). In response to the students' suit challenging the constitutionality of the school board's policy, the Supreme Court held that the First Amendment imposes limitations on a local school board's ability to censor information. Although local school boards have a legitimate role in the determination of school library content, they may not remove books from school libraries merely because they dislike the ideas contained therein.

After *Pico,* school libraries broadened student access to information by the installation of computers. In 1994, Congress enacted legislation to provide sectarian and nonsectarian schools with the necessary funds to do so. Improving America's Schools Act of 1994, Pub. L. No. 103-382, 108 Stat. 3518 (codified at 20 U.S.C. §§7351(a), (b)) (2000 & Supp. 2005). In 2000, Congress responded to calls for child protection from harmful material on the Internet by the passage of the Children's Internet Protection Act (CIPA), Pub. L. No. 106-554, 114 Stat. 2763A-335 (2000) (codified as amended in 47 U.S.C. §254 and scattered sections of 20 U.S.C.). CIPA conditions federal Internet access subsidies to elementary and secondary schools and libraries on the installation of filtering technology to prevent minors from obtaining access to harmful material.

When a group of public libraries, library associations, library patrons, and Web site publishers challenged the constitutionality of CIPA, the Supreme Court held that CIPA did not impose an impermissible condition in violation of the First Amendment. According to Chief Justice Rehnquist (with three Justices concurring and two Justices concurring in result), federal subsidies were intended to help libraries fulfill their traditional role of obtaining material of appropriate quality for educational purposes, and Congress could validly insist that public funds be spent for the purposes for which they were authorized, even though filtering software tended to erroneously block some constitutionally protected speech. United States v. American Library Assn., 539 U.S. 194 (2003). See generally Steven D. Hinckley, Your Money or Your Speech: The Children's Internet Protection Act and the Congressional Assault on the First Amendment in Public Libraries, 80 Wash. U.L.Q. 1025, 1099 (2002) (criticizing CIPA as an attempt to "end-run constitutional roadblocks" to content-based regulation by means of the spending power).

NOTE: PROCEDURAL RIGHTS AND THE PUNISHMENT
OF STUDENTS FOR EXPRESSIVE ACTIVITY

Following *Tinker*, there was some question as to whether *Tinker* applied not only to prior restraints of student speech but also to subsequent punishment of students for expressive activity. The Supreme Court addressed this issue in subsequent cases. In both Bethel v. Fraser and Morse v. Frederick (discussed supra), the Supreme Court held that *Tinker* did not prevent the school from disciplining a student for either vulgar remarks or a pro-drug message, respectively.

However, only Bethel v. Fraser raised the issue whether the circumstances of the particular punishment (a three-day suspension) violated the student's due process rights. The student argued that he had no way of knowing that delivery of his speech would subject him to sanctions. Rejecting that argument, the Supreme Court ruled that the school disciplinary rule proscribing "obscene" language, as well as the admonition of several teachers prior to the speech, gave adequate warning to the student that his lewd speech could subject him to sanctions. Further, the Supreme Court held that the three-day suspension was sufficiently brief that it did not give rise to full procedural due process rights.

Earlier, the Supreme Court had held that minimum procedural due process requirements apply (i.e., notice of the charges, an explanation of the evidence and an opportunity to present the student's version of the facts) prior to a student's ten-day suspension. Goss v. Lopez, 419 U.S. 565, 581 (1975). *Goss* determined that the ten-day suspension implicated both the student's "property" and "liberty" interests.

Compare Laney v. Farley, 501 F.3d 577 (6th Cir. 2007) (holding that a one-day in-school suspension of a student, for letting a cell phone ring in class, violates neither the student's due process property interest in public education nor her due process liberty interest in her reputation), with Mahaffey ex rel. Mahaffey v. Aldrich, 236 F.Supp.2d 779 (E.D. Mich. 2002) (holding that a student's right to due process was violated when he was suspended for one semester for posting objectionable material on an Internet Web site without his being afforded due process protections). On the legacy of Goss v. Lopez, see Youssef Chouhoud & Perry A. Zirkel, The *Goss* Progeny: An Empirical Analysis, 45 San Diego L. Rev. 353 (2008) (concluding that case law over the past two decades favors school authorities rather than student-plaintiffs).

In the late 1980s and early 1990s, states adopted a strict approach to school discipline, known as a "zero-tolerance policy," in response to perceptions of increasing school violence. Zero-tolerance policies received approbation at the federal level when Congress enacted the Gun-Free Schools Act of 1994, 20 U.S.C. §8921(b), which conditioned federal funding on the enactment of state laws imposing at least a one-year expulsion on any student who brought a firearm to school and requiring referrals of the student to law enforcement. In United States v. Lopez, 514 U.S. 549 (1995), the Supreme Court held the Act unconstitutional, concluding that it exceeded congressional authority under the Commerce Clause because possession of a gun in a local school zone is not an economic activity that substantially affects interstate commerce. Congress repealed the Act subsequently in the No Child Left Behind Act of 2001, Pub. L. No. 107-110, 115 Stat. 1425 (codified as amended in scattered sections of 20 U.S.C.). Nonetheless, all states enacted zero-tolerance laws in compliance with federal law and continued to enforce them.

Schools extended zero-tolerance policies far beyond the federal requirements to include a broader range of behaviors and harsher sanctions. The number of students who were subject to suspension and expulsion "exploded." Christina L. Anderson, Comment, Double Jeopardy: The Modern Dilemma for Juvenile Justice, 152 U. Pa. L. Rev. 1181, 1192 (2004). Schools punished a variety of allegedly disruptive expressions, including those that were written, verbal, artistic, gestural, fashion related, and Internet based. Louis P. Nappen, School Safety v. Free Speech: The Seesawing Tolerance Standards for Students' Sexual and Violent Expressions, 9 Tex. J. on C.L. & C.R. 93, 101-114 (2003).

In the post-Columbine era, these policies led to strict punishments for verbal expression that was even slightly threatening. For example, (1) a Louisiana middle school student received two weeks in a juvenile detention center for saying to another student in the lunch line, "If you take all the potatoes, I'm gonna get you"; (2) a Massachusetts student was suspended indefinitely for telling a boy that the latter was "on his list" (he meant to say "shit list" but refrained from profanity because of a teacher's presence); (3) an Oklahoma student received a 15-day suspension for casting a magic spell that caused a teacher to become sick; and (4) a Nevada girl received a ten-day suspension for compiling a list of classmates with whom she was "frustrated." Nappen, supra, at 108. Schools punished violent expressions more severely than sexual expressions. "To contrast, delivering a speech with sexual innuendos to an entire student body in 1988 results in a suspension for three days (*Bethel*); whereas, reading a violent story to a creative writing class in 2001 may result in mandatory suspension or expulsion." Id. at 109.

Cases examining the constitutionality of punishment for Internet-based expressive activity have proliferated in recent years. Some courts assess a student's statements according to the "true threat" standard of Watts v. United States, 394 U.S. 705, 708 (1969) (per curiam) (holding that a particular threat against the president was not a "true threat" but merely a "crude offensive method of stating political opposition"). See, e.g., Riehm v. Engelking, 538 F.3d 952 (8th Cir. 2008) (holding that a student essay depicting a Columbine-type fantasy shooting qualified as a true threat that was not protected by the First Amendment). Others courts apply the *Tinker* standard, based on the belief that school authorities have broader authority to sanction student speech than the *Watts* standard allows. See, e.g., Wisniewski v. Board of Educ. of Weedsport Cent. Sch. Dist., 494 F.3d 34 (2d Cir. 2007) (holding that a student's Internet-based drawing depicting his shooting of his English teacher posed a reasonably foreseeable risk that it would come to the attention of school authorities and would materially and substantially disrupt the work of school).

Litigation challenging zero-tolerance policies generally has proven unsuccessful. Courts have held that the zero-tolerance sanctions of suspension and expulsion comport with due process requirements. One commentator explains that procedural due process challenges are futile because most schools currently provide notice and some form of hearing. She adds that substantive due process challenges, similarly, have not met with much success because of the high standard (an "extraordinary departure from established norms" that is "wholly arbitrary") as well as judicial deference to local school systems regarding disciplinary decisions. Alicia C. Insley, Comment, Suspending and Expelling Children from Educational Opportunity: Time to Reevaluate Zero Tolerance Policies, 50 Am. U. L. Rev. 1039, 1056 (2001). "In conclusion, both procedural and substantive due process challenges are likely to be successful only in cases of blatant omissions of minimum procedures or extreme policies that present no rational connection [with pedagogical purposes]." Id. at 1057.

SOME QUERIES: CORPORAL PUNISHMENT IN SCHOOLS

Many schools have traditionally used corporal punishment to discipline students. Should parents have the power to prohibit use of corporal punishment on their child in a public school? What do the cases considered in this chapter imply? See Baker v. Owen, p. 239, infra. From the child's perspective, could corporal punishment ever offend the constitutional prohibition against cruel and unusual punishment? If corporal punishment is permitted, does the Due Process Clause (particularly in light of Goss v. Lopez) require some sort of hearing before punishment is imposed? See Note on Ingraham v. Wright, p. 245, infra. Chapter 3 considers generally the parental right to discipline children and legal limitations on the physical mistreatment of children. Corporal punishment in schools is considered in that context. See pp. 238-246, infra.

In re Doe
973 So.2d 548 (Fla. Dist. Ct. App. 2008)

KELLY, Judge.

The appellant, a minor, challenges the final order dismissing her petition for judicial waiver of the statutory requirement that her physician notify her parent or guardian prior to terminating her pregnancy. We affirm because the minor has failed to carry her burden of proving the grounds for a waiver under section 390.01114, Florida Statutes (2007), alleged in her petition.

Section 390.01114(2)(a) requires a physician to notify a minor's parent or legal guardian at least forty-eight hours before performing an abortion on that minor. A minor may petition a circuit court to waive the notification requirement. Subsections (4)(c) and (d) of the statute establish three grounds for granting a waiver, two of which are pertinent here. Subsection (4)(c) provides for a waiver if the court finds, by clear and convincing evidence, that the minor is sufficiently mature to decide whether to terminate her pregnancy. Subsection (4)(d) provides for a waiver if the court finds, by a preponderance of the evidence, that the notification of a parent or guardian is not in the best interests of the minor.

[In the transcript of the hearing on the minor's petition,] we learn that she is seventeen years old, lives with her parents, attends high school, plans to attend junior college and then transfer to a university "for maybe a pharmaceutical degree or a pediatrician," and earns grades that are "[a]verage, like A, B, and Cs." We also know that she has worked part-time at two different restaurants during the past year and a half. She explained to the court that she and the father of her child were using condoms when she became pregnant and she answered affirmatively when asked by her attorney whether in her mind she was "doing everything . . . under the circumstances to try and prevent this from happening."

The minor testified that she and her parents are Catholic and attend church every Sunday. She stated that if her parents knew that she was pregnant, "they would be upset with me" and that if they knew she had an abortion, "they would feel better that I took it into my own hands and showed responsibility." She did not want to tell them about the abortion now because she did not think they would understand "right now," but she planned to tell them in the future when she "felt comfortable with telling them what she did." The father of the child no longer speaks to the minor and has no interest in raising the child. When asked about abortion versus having the child and perhaps giving it up for adoption, she explained that she "probably" would have to go to "some pregnancy school" rather than her regular school if she did that. She answered "yes" and "mm hm" when asked by her attorney whether she had "considered all alternatives to terminating her pregnancy" and had "given that long and thoughtful consideration."

As the party seeking an exception to the notification provision of the statute, the minor bears the burden of proof. After hearing the testimony outlined above, the trial court found that the minor had not adduced sufficient evidence to prove any of the criteria that would permit a judicial waiver of the parental notification requirement. We agree.

In arguing for reversal, the minor asserts that she is sufficiently mature to decide whether to terminate her pregnancy. The statute requires that she establish maturity by clear and convincing evidence. . . . The maturity of a pregnant minor must be determined on a case-by-case basis. Bellotti v. Baird, 443 U.S. 622, 643, n. 23 (1979) (*Bellotti II*). In attempting to define maturity for the application of a bypass statute one court noted:

> Maturity is "difficult to define, let alone determine. . . ." Bellotti v. Baird, 443 U.S. 622, 643-44 n. 23 (1979) (commonly referenced as *Bellotti II*). Notwithstanding, determine it we must. While the U.S. Supreme Court has not explicitly defined "maturity" in the context of parental notification or consent statutes, it has observed that "minors often lack the *experience, perspective, and judgment* to recognize and avoid choices that could be detrimental to them." (Emphasis supplied.) Id., 443 U.S. at 635.

In re Petition of Anonymous 1, 251 Neb. 424, 558 N.W.2d 784, 787-88 (1997). . . .

Similarly, another court has stated that when evaluating maturity, pertinent factors include, but are not limited to, the minor's physical age, her understanding of the medical risks associated with the procedure as well as emotional consequences, her consideration of options other than abortion, her future educational and life plans, her involvement in civic activities, any employment, her demeanor and her seeking advice or emotional support from an adult. In re Doe, 924 So.2d 935, 939 (Fla. 1st DCA 2006). . . .

Further, in assessing maturity, the trial court "may draw inferences from the minor's composure, analytic ability, appearance, thoughtfulness, tone of voice, expressions, and her ability to articulate her reasoning and conclusions." Ex parte Anonymous, 806 So.2d 1269, 1274 (Ala. 2001). The criteria suggested by these cases, while not exhaustive, is consistent with the statutory mandate that the trial court hear evidence relating to "the emotional development, maturity, intellect, and understanding of the minor, and all other relevant evidence" and at a minimum, provides a sound starting point in attempting to determine whether a minor is sufficiently mature to decide whether to have an abortion. §390.01114(4)(e).

The minor's testimony in this case tells us virtually nothing about her level of maturity. Significantly, the minor failed to demonstrate any knowledge regarding any specific immediate or long-term physical, emotional, or psychological risks of having an abortion. The record contains no evidence indicating that the minor was aware of, appreciated, or had seriously considered those risks. Nor is there any evidence that she sought advice or emotional support from any adult or that she had considered what she would do should any physical or emotional complications arise from the abortion. The minor responded affirmatively to her attorney's conclusory questions regarding whether she had thoughtfully considered alternatives to having an abortion. However, because she did not elaborate, it is impossible to evaluate what alternatives she considered, how she weighed those alternatives, or how she arrived at her decision. The minor still lives at home with her parents, she works but she gave no indication as to what her job involves, and she did not indicate that she had assumed any other responsibilities, financial or otherwise, that one would associate with maturity. In light of the myriad deficiencies in the evidence offered by the minor, no reasonable fact finder could conclude that she had proven by clear and convincing evidence that she was sufficiently mature to decide whether to terminate her pregnancy.

The minor alternatively asserts that notification of a parent or guardian is not in her best interest. The statute requires that this exception to the notification requirement be proven by a preponderance of the evidence. In determining whether notification would not be in the minor's best interests, the trial court should weigh the advantages and disadvantages of parental notification in the minor's specific situation. Some factors to be considered are: the minor's emotional or physical needs; the possibility of intimidation, other emotional injury, or physical danger to the minor; the stability of the minor's home and the possibility that notification would cause serious and lasting harm to the family structure; the relationship between the parents and the minor and the effect of notification on that relationship; and the possibility that notification may lead the parents to withdraw emotional and financial support from the minor.

Here, the minor did not present evidence pertinent to any of these factors. When asked why she did not want to tell her parents about the abortion, her only stated concern was that she thought they would not understand. She was also concerned that they would be upset if they knew she was pregnant. This amounts to nothing more than a generalized fear of telling her parents and does not, by itself, establish that notification would not be in her best interests. Accordingly, we conclude that the trial court correctly determined that the minor's reason for not wanting to tell her parents about the abortion was not sufficient to establish that notification was not in her best interest.

The minor also argues that reversal is required because the judge based his decision on his personal views rather than facts of record. We reject this contention as unsupported by the record. Admittedly, the judge, in response to statements made by the minor's attorney, made some comments that at least by implication reflected his personal views regarding abortion. However, read in context, it is evident that the judge understood that the sole question he was to decide was whether the minor's parents should be notified, not whether the minor should have an abortion. . . . Even if we agreed that the judge's comments suggested that he was influenced by his personal beliefs rather than the facts of record, we would nevertheless be constrained to affirm. Such an error is harmless in a case such as this where the record is devoid of any factual basis upon which the judge could have concluded that the minor had satisfied her burden to prove any of the criteria supporting a judicial waiver of the parental notification requirement. . . .

NORTHCUTT, Chief Judge, dissenting.

. . . [T]he law requires a reversal in this case. [T]he acting circuit judge was improperly influenced by nonrecord personal considerations revealed by his remarks at the hearing; he violated the law by failing to rule on one of the statutory grounds alleged in the petition within 48 hours of its filing; and he violated the law by failing to issue an order that contained specific factual findings and legal conclusions in support of the one inadequate ruling that he did make. . . .

The judge was charged with determining whether the law permits this petitioner to exercise her constitutional right to terminate her pregnancy without first notifying her parents. She was entitled to have him make that determination as an impartial, neutral judicial officer, based solely on the evidence before him. Instead, the judge cast himself in the role of the young woman's parents and speculated about how upset they would be upon learning that their daughter had "committed an abortion." He discussed his own religious affiliation and personal history and mused about what would have happened if the young birth mother of his adopted daughter had "decided to do something different." With no evidence to support him — and despite his own observation that, as Catholics, the young woman's parents would be highly upset to discover that she had terminated her pregnancy — the judge speculated that if they were notified of her intention to do so beforehand, they would react with the same understanding and give her the same support that the judge had promised his own daughters. [These] remarks by themselves warranted a reversal.

The judge's decision must also be reversed for his failure to abide by the statutory requirement that the court's written order contain "specific factual findings and legal conclusions supporting its decision." §390.01114(4)(e). The judge employed a form order prescribed by Florida Rule of Juvenile Procedure 8.991. The form language of the order stated: "The minor has not proven by sufficient evidence any of the criteria that would permit a judicial waiver of the parental notification requirement of Section 390.01114(3), Florida Statutes, for the following reasons: . . ." Beneath this printed passage the judge wrote in his own hand, simply: "Based on testimony of Petitioner the Court believes the request is for expediency and not in best interest of Petitioner."

This order was plainly inadequate. Obviously, it made no reference whatever to the petitioner's allegation that she is sufficiently mature to decide whether to terminate her pregnancy. The judge's belief that the petitioner's request was "for expediency" was irrelevant and merely begged the question; all requests for waivers of parental notification are for expedience in one way or another. Finally, the conclusory assertion that a waiver would not be in the young woman's best interest was not founded on specific factual findings as required by the statute. . . .

Moreover, the judge's total failure to rule on one of the grounds alleged in the bypass petition violated the 48-hour deadline imposed by law. The statute is clear . . . "*The court shall rule, and issue written findings of fact and conclusions of law, within 48 hours after the petition is filed*, except that the 48-hour limitation may be extended at the request of the minor. *If the court fails to rule within the 48-hour period* and an extension has not been requested, *the petition is granted, and the notice requirement is waived*." §390.01114(b) (emphases supplied). . . .

[Another issue was omitted from the trial judge's order: consideration of the minor's maturity.] [T]he judge's failure to address this issue in his order suggests the possibility that he mistakenly thought that in order to obtain a judicial bypass the petitioner was required to prove *both* that she was sufficiently mature and that notifying her parents would not be in her best interest. We cannot be certain of this because the judge did not comply with the statutory directive to specifically set out his legal conclusions in his order. But there is no other logical reason why the order dismissing the petition mentioned only one of the statutory grounds alleged in the petition and omitted any reference to the other. The judge must have believed that his rejection of just one ground required him to dismiss the petition. . . .

On the question of the petitioner's maturity — which the judge did not bother to address either at the hearing or in his order — the panel supported its assertion syllogistically by quoting from cases that recite "nonexhaustive" lists of factors that can bear on a minor's maturity level, then focusing on factors that the panel members felt were not sufficiently addressed in the evidence. In so doing the panel ignored the obvious truth that the presence or absence of any of those factors is not determinative. . . . The same is true of all of the factors the panel found wanting in this case. The alleged absence of proof on those matters did not mean that this young woman could not be found to be sufficiently mature to determine whether to terminate her pregnancy based on the proof that she did submit.

[The panel cites eight "maturity" factors.] The record in this case included evidence of five of them:

Physical age: Unlike that of, say, a thirteen- or fourteen-year-old child's, this young woman's disability of nonage was very near its end. At the time of the hearing she was just four months shy of her eighteenth birthday . . .

Consideration of other options: The petitioner testified that her decision had been a difficult one, to which she had given long and thoughtful consideration. This included consideration of keeping the child and the impact this would have on her family life, her current education, and her future plans. The panel dismissed this evidence [saying she merely responded affirmative to her attorney's conclusory questions whether she had thoughtfully considered alternatives to having an abortion]. [Her answers] reflected perfectly reasonable, mature considerations, and they constituted evidence on this factor that the judge was entitled to credit and that the panel was not entitled to arbitrarily ignore.

Education and life plans: [The petitioner] had given thought to her future and she had developed specific educational and professional aspirations.

Employment: She had been employed at two restaurants over the previous one and a half years, working "at least" twenty to twenty-five hours per week while attending school. The panel opinion quibbled with this evidence as well: "she works but she gave no indication as to what her job involves. . . ." 973 So.2d at 552.

Demeanor: The young woman's demeanor was certainly apparent at the hearing. Tellingly, the judge — charged by law with detailing his reasons for dismissing the bypass petition — did not comment that this factor contributed to his decision. The panel opinion did not mention it, either. It couldn't, of course, even though several of the cases it cited on the maturity issue describe this as one of the most important considerations. On this basis alone, the panel's claim that the record is devoid of evidence that the petitioner is sufficiently mature to determine whether to terminate her pregnancy was unwarranted.

I acknowledge that the record does not contain a great deal of evidence bearing on the other ground in the petition, that it would not be in the petitioner's best interest to give her parents advance notice that she was terminating her pregnancy. But the judge's improper and openly argumentative personal assertions likely would have intimidated most adults — indeed, most attorneys. It is not difficult to imagine the chilling effect that his behavior had on this young woman's ability to elaborate on her situation.

Still, even as it was, her evidence did not prove merely that she had a "generalized fear" of telling her parents of her plan, as the panel opinion suggested. To the contrary, the evidence disclosed specific reasons for her concern. Not quite finished with her secondary schooling, she lived in her parents' home. The family actively practiced Catholicism: they attended church every Sunday; the petitioner's mother opposed her efforts to obtain birth control pills. . . .

Given the likely reaction of the petitioner's parents — with whom she was living at a time when she had only a part-time job and had not yet completed the high school education upon which all of her future plans depended — an unbiased fact finder certainly could conclude that informing them of her intention to terminate her pregnancy was not in her best interest.

In sum, the panel disregarded the judge's expressed reliance on his personal history and attitudes when dismissing the petition, disregarded the judge's violation of the statutory deadline for ruling, and disregarded the judge's violation of the statute requiring him to make specific findings in support of his ruling. The panel's decision to affirm notwithstanding these errors was unprecedented. It was founded on the panel's misconstruction of the record and its adoption of an evidentiary standard that virtually no petitioner could ever meet. . . .

QUESTIONS: PRIVACY RIGHTS OF MINORS

(1) Background. The principal case takes place in Florida where the state supreme court twice invalidated laws mandating parental involvement laws. See, e.g., North Florida Women's Health & Counseling Servs. v. State, 866 So. 2d 612 (Fla. 2003); In re T.W., 551 So. 2d 1186 (Fla. 1989). Nonetheless, in November 2004, Florida voters overwhelmingly approved an amendment to the state constitution that exempts parental notification for purposes of abortion from the state constitutional right to privacy. A federal district court refused to grant a temporary injunction to block enforcement of the law. Jackie Hallifax, Parent-Notice Law OK'd by Federal Judge, Miami Herald, July 8, 2005, at 7B.

(2) Different Treatment of Minors' Abortion Rights. The United States Supreme Court permits greater regulation of minors' abortion rights compared to those of adults. The juvenile abortion cases are fascinating because they involve a conflict between the juvenile's own privacy interests (which are entitled to at least some constitutional protection) and parents' interests in childrearing (which *Pierce* and *Yoder* suggest are also constitutionally protected from state intrusion). What should the state's role be?

The Supreme Court in Bellotti v. Baird (*Bellotti II*), 443 U.S. 622 (1979) explains the differences between adults and teenagers that allow states to regulate minors' abortion decisions to an extent that would be impermissible if applied to adults. According to *Bellotti II*, a state can require a minor to obtain parental consent prior to undergoing an abortion provided that the law authorizes an alternative to parental consent — a judicial "bypass" procedure. The Court reasoned that minors' constitutional rights to an abortion are not coextensive with adults because of three factors: "the peculiar vulnerability of children; their inability to make critical decisions in an informed, mature manner; and the importance of the parental role in child rearing." Id. at 634.

a. With respect to vulnerability, is the Supreme Court's assumption correct that the psychological effects of abortion are more severe for teenagers than adults? Psychological evidence refutes that assumption: Studies reveal that few women or adolescents experience severe psychological problems after abortion. See Wendy J. Quinton et al., Adolescents and Adjustment to Abortion: Are Minors at Greater Risk?, 7 Psychol. Pub. Pol'y & L. 491 (2001) (presenting empirical findings that minors do not experience greater adjustment difficulties following abortion in either the short or long term).

b. Are adolescents less able to make informed, mature decisions? What does an informed and mature abortion decision entail? Studies that have examined decision-making processes of adolescents and adults find few, if any, differences in cognitive abilities, at least for adolescents who are age 14 and older. J. Shoshanna Ehrlich, Grounded in the Reality of Their Lives: Listening to Teens Who Make the Abortion Decision Without Involving Their Parents, 18 Berkeley Women's L.J. 61, 150 (2003). See also Shoshanna Ehrlich, Who Decides? The Abortion Rights of Teens (2006).

c. Consider the importance of the parental role. How might involvement of parents be helpful? How should parents' and minors' rights be accommodated, according to the majority and dissent in In re Doe? In your opinion?

(3) Parental Role Generally.   Currently, a majority of states require parental involvement in a minor's decision to have an abortion. Of the 34 states with parental involvement laws, 22 require parental consent and 10 require parental notification. Most states require consent or notification of only one parent. However, two states require consent of both parents; one state requires both parents to be notified; and two states require both parental consent and notification. Guttmacher Institute, State Policies in Brief: Parental Involvement in Minors' Abortion (Oct. 2008), available at www.guttmacher.org/statecenter/spibs/spib_PIMA (last visited Oct. 3, 2008). Many states with parental involvement laws make exceptions in cases of medical emergency, abuse, assault, incest, or neglect.

(4) Federal Protection of Parental Rights: Child Custody Protection Act. The Supreme Court in *Bellotti II* emphasized the importance of the parental role in childbearing, especially the parents' ability to help their daughter make critical decisions. May states mandate that this counseling function be fulfilled only by parents? Data reveal that virtually all minors who refuse to involve their parents do consult at least one adult (relative, boyfriends' parents, foster parent, or health care professional). Ehrlich, Grounded in the Reality, supra, at 98-100. A few states permit adult relatives to serve as a substitute for parents' consent. Guttmacher, State Policies, supra.

Does the involvement of other adults in a minor's abortion decision interfere with parental control? Proposed federal legislation, the Child Custody Protection Act, S. 403, 109th Cong. (passed by Senate, July 25, 2006), introduced by Sen. John Ensign (R-Nev.), would make it a federal offense for a nonparent to knowingly transport a minor across a state line with the intent that she obtain an abortion in circumvention of a state's parental consent or notification law. The bill does not apply if the abortion is necessary to save the minor's life. The bill would also subject physicians to criminal liability for performing an abortion in violation of parental notification requirements. Many states are enacting similar laws. See, e.g., Planned Parenthood of Kan. & Mid-Mo. v. Nixon, 220 S.W.3d 732 (Mo. 2007) (upholding a statute that subjects to civil liability those persons who "cause, aid, or assist" a minor to obtain an abortion without the requisite parental consent).

What is the purpose of such legislation? To strengthen the family by protecting parental rights to custody? To make abortion more difficult to obtain? If such a law were enacted, what would be its effect? To prevent abortion? Decrease teenage sexual activity? Promote better communication among family members? Would such legislation be constitutional? Does the prohibited conduct fall within Congress's constitutional authority to regulate the transportation of individuals in interstate commerce? Does it interfere with the constitutionally protected right to travel? Place an undue burden on women's right to an abortion?

(5) Parental Consent.   The United States Supreme Court has delivered several pronouncements on parental involvement laws. In Planned Parenthood of Central Missouri v. Danforth, 428 U.S. 52 (1976), the Court invalidated a Missouri blanket parental consent requirement that would have required all minors to involve their parents in abortion decision making unless a physician certified that the abortion was necessary to preserve the mother's life. In *Bellotti II*, supra, the Court set forth the requirements for parental consent laws, including the judicial bypass proceeding. In Planned Parenthood of Southeastern

Pennsylvania v. Casey, 505 U.S. 833 (1992), the Court upheld a one-parent consent requirement with a judicial bypass procedure, reasoning that the provision was consistent with prior case law and furthered the state's legitimate interest in "the welfare of its young citizens, whose immaturity, inexperience, and lack of judgment may sometimes impair their ability to exercise their rights wisely." Id. at 970-971 (citing Hodgson v. Minnesota, 497 U.S. 417, 444 (1990)).

(6) Parental Notification. The Supreme Court has examined the constitutionality of parental notification statutes as well. See, e.g., Lambert v. Wicklund, 520 U.S. 292 (1997) (upholding a one-parent notification statute with judicial bypass allowing waiver when notification was not in the minor's best interests); Hodgson v. Minnesota, supra (upholding a two-parent notification requirement because of the presence of the judicial bypass procedure); Akron v. Akron Center for Reproductive Health (*Akron II*), 462 U.S. 416 (1983) (upholding a one-parent notification statute containing a judicial bypass procedure because it satisfied the *Bellotti II* criteria for a parental consent statute); Ayotte v. Planned Parenthood of Northern New England, 546 U.S. 320 (2006) (remanding a challenge to New Hampshire's parental notification law, for failure to contain a health exception, to determine if it was possible to devise a narrower remedy than a permanent injunction against enforcement of law). Although the United States Supreme Court has not explicitly required a judicial bypass proceeding for notification statutes, the Court has held that the presence of such a provision guaranteeing this proceeding renders parental notification statutes constitutional. Are notification and consent requirements distinguishable where minors are concerned?

(7) Bypass Procedure.

a. Burden of Proof. Virtually all states with parental involvement laws require bypass proceedings to enable minors to obtain an abortion without parental consent. According to *Bellotti II*, supra, the minor has the burden of showing that she is sufficiently mature to make the abortion decision or, if not, that an abortion nonetheless would be in her best interests.

Data in the 1980s and 1990s suggested that courts in many jurisdictions granted virtually all petitions by minors who sought judicial authorization for abortion. See Margaret C. Crosby & Abigail English, Mandatory Parental Involvement/Judicial Bypass Laws: Do They Promote Adolescent Health?, 12 J. Adolescent Health 143 (1991); Robet H. Mnookin, Bellotti v. Baird: A Hard Case, in In the Interest of Children 242 (1985). More recent data suggest that a conservative political climate has led to more frequent denials of minors' petitions. See, e.g., Helena Silverstein, Girls on the Stand: How Courts Fail Pregnant Minors (2007) (concluding, based on a survey of bypass proceedings in Alabama, Pennsylvania, and Tennessee, that some judges reject minors' waivers because the judges oppose abortion; some judges insist that the minor receive counseling from a pro-life Christian ministry; still others appoint a lawyer to represent the interests of the fetus). See also In re Anonymous, 964 So.2d 1239 (Ala. Civ. Ct. App. 2007) (denying minor's petition for waiver based on a finding that she failed to carry her burden of proof that she was sufficiently mature or that an abortion would be in her best interests).

b. Determination of Maturity. The Supreme Court has not clarified the meaning of "maturity" for abortion decision making. How is a trial court to make such a determination? How relevant are factors such as grades, school attendance, extracurricular activities, employment history, future plans, financial situation, prior court involvement, health, history of substance abuse, prior contraceptive history, future plans to use contraception, and prior consultation with health professionals? How relevant is the minor's composure (or lack thereof) during her testimony? See, e.g., Ex parte Anonymous, 812 So. 2d 1234 (Ala. 2001) (affirming a finding of immaturity based on minor's lack of emotion and "rehearsed" testimony).

Given the difficulties in determining maturity on a case-by-case basis, should states adopt age-based lines that provide that a girl above or below a certain age is presumed mature (or immature) in terms of requiring parental consent? Professors Suellyn Scarnecchia and Julie Kunce Field have proposed such guidelines for judges to use in the determination of maturity in the abortion context. For example, they suggest a presumption that minors aged sixteen and above be treated as sufficiently mature to obtain judicial waiver, and a presumption that an abortion is in the best interest of a minor under age thirteen due to the serious health risks associated with young childbearing. For minors aged thirteen to fifteen, Scarnecchia and Field recommend the use of factors regarding the ability to give informed consent (such as the minor's process of gathering medical information from health care providers) rather than minors' academic performance or general plans for the future. Suellyn Scarnecchia & Julie Kunce Field, Judging Girls: Decision Making in Parental Consent in Abortion Cases, 3 Mich. J. Gender & L. 75, 99-112 (1995). What do you think of such suggestions?

What role might socioeconomic class play in a judge's determination of "maturity" for abortion decision making? See id. at 87 (suggesting that judges may determine that teenagers from low-income backgrounds who seek judicial waivers display a low level of moral maturity). Is "maturity" too subjective a standard to be reliable? See Anna C. Bonny, Parental Consent and Notification Laws in the Abortion Context: Rejecting the "Maturity" Standard in Judicial Bypass Proceedings, 11 U.C. Davis J. Juv. L. & Pol'y 311 (2007) (so arguing).

c. Evidentiary Standard.   What should be the evidentiary standard for proof of maturity — clear and convincing evidence? A preponderance? See, e.g., In re B.C., 74 P.3d 285 (Ariz. Ct. App. 2003) (holding that minor bears burden of proving entitlement to abortion by clear and convincing evidence). Does a clear-and-convincing standard constitute an undue burden under *Casey*? In In re Doe, what evidentiary standard does the Florida trial court apply for the determination of maturity? What standard does the court apply for proof that notification of a parent is not in the minor's best interests? Does such a distinction make sense?

d. Judicial Role.   Do judges have the requisite expertise to assess maturity and competence? Should judges delegate this duty to mental health personnel? To what extent is the judgment about maturity shaped by the judge's ideology and values? Will a liberal or conservative judge think it mature or immature for a young woman to become pregnant? Not to want to talk to her parents? To choose to assume responsibility for the decision herself? What other value judgments may be influential? See Nanette Dembitz, The Supreme Court and a Minor's Abortion Decision, 80 Colum. L. Rev. 1251, 1255-1256 (1980) (arguing that the minor's very decision to seek an abortion shows deliberation and responsibility).

Did the trial judge's ideology and values in In re Doe influence his decision? Contrast the appellate court's majority and dissenting views on this point. See also Ex parte Anonymous, 806 So.2d 1269 (Ala. 2001) (upholding the denial of a minor's petition to waive parental notification).

Some judges are recusing themselves from bypass proceedings based on their moral or religious beliefs that abortion is murder. See Adam Liptak, On Moral Grounds, Some Judges Are Opting out of Abortion Cases, N.Y. Times, Sept. 4, 2005, at 21 (citing examples in Alabama, Minnesota, Pennsylvania, and Tennessee). Do recusals create an undue burden on the minor's right to choose? See Lauren Treadwell, Note, Informal Closing of the Bypass: Minors' Petitions to Bypass Parental Consent for Abortion in an Age of Increasing Judicial Recusals, 58 Hastings L.J. 869 (2007).

If a judge decides that a teenager is not mature but that an abortion is nonetheless in her best interests, may the judge still require the minor to consult with her parent(s)? See In re Moe, 423 N.E.2d 1038, 1042 (Mass. App. Ct. 1981) (holding that, after a determination that an abortion is in the minor's best interests, the judge may not decide it would be "in her even better interest" to consult with one or both parents).

e. Representation in Bypass Proceedings. In some bypass proceedings, judges have the option to appoint a guardian ad litem for the fetus. Are such guardianship appointments constitutional? Do they constitute an undue burden on the minor's right to an abortion? See Linda C. Fentiman, The "New Fetal Protection": The Wrong Answer to the Crisis of Inadequate Health Care for Women and Children, 84 Denv. L. Rev. 537, 571 (2006) ("Such fetal guardianships turn what may already be an intimidating but paternalistic proceeding into an adversarial one, effectively changing the burden of proof established by the legislature in authorizing a judicial bypass proceeding.").

(8) Physician's Role. What should be the role of the physician in the minor's abortion decision? Should judges delegate the determination of maturity to the physicians who perform the abortions? Would this create a conflict of interest?

Should physicians who fail to verify the minor's age be subject to tort liability? In a Texas lawsuit, a woman and her father alleged that the physician who performed the woman's abortion was negligent and violated the Texas parental notification statute by accepting a grocery card as proof that the minor was old enough to have the abortion without parental consent. The jury allocated liability 90 percent to the minor and 10 percent to the physician but awarded zero damages. Subsequently, the state Department of Health established strict guidelines about the requisite forms of identification that abortion clinics can accept. Scott E. Williams, Plaintiffs Take Nothing in Suit Against Doctor Who Performed Abortion, Tex. Law., Apr. 19, 2004, at 10.

Should physicians be required to give medical records of minors who have had abortions to law enforcement on the basis that such records may provide evidence of rape or statutory rape? Or would disclosure of such records violate minors' right to privacy? See Planned Parenthood of Indiana v. Carter, 854 N.E.2d 853 (Ind. Ct. App. 2006). See generally Jessica Ansley Bodger, Taking the Sting out of Reporting Requirements: Reproductive Health Clinics and the Constitutional Right to Informational Privacy, 56 Duke L.J. 583 (2006).

(9) Vision of the Family.   What vision of the family is reflected in parental consent and notification statutes? How is that vision articulated in In re Doe? See generally Anne C. Dailey, Constitutional Privacy and the Just Family, 67 Tul. L. Rev. 955 (1993).

(10) State Constitutional Right to Abortion.   Minor plaintiffs have sometimes been more successful in securing abortion rights under state constitutions. Why? See Planned Parenthood of Central N.J. v. Farmer, 762 A.2d 620 (N.J. 2000) (parental notification statute absent judicial waiver, without corresponding limitation on minors who seek medical care related to pregnancy, violates state constitution's equal protection provision); American Academy of Pediatrics v. Lungren, 940 P.2d 797 (Cal. 1997) (parental consent statute violates state constitutional right to privacy). California voters rejected an effort to amend the state constitution (Proposition 4) to require parental notification in November 2008. See also J. Shoshanna Ehrlich, Minors as Medical Decision Makers: The Pretextual Reasoning of the Court in the Abortion Cases, 7 Mich. J. Gender & L. 65 (2000) (criticizing the Supreme Court for ignoring the equal protection argument that minors possess significant self-consent rights in medical contexts other than abortion).

(11) Application of Parental Involvement Laws to RU-486.   At the time parental involvement legislation was enacted, only surgical abortions existed. Since 2000, abortions can be accomplished by medication. In that year, the Food and Drug Administration approved RU-486 or mifepristone, common known as the "abortion pill," for termination of early pregnancies. Should parental consent and notification laws apply to regulate minors' access to RU-486? Would application of such laws constitute an undue burden on minors' right to an abortion? See Amanda C. Scuder, The Inapplicability of Parental Involvement Mifepristone (RU 486) to Minors, 10 Am. U. J. Gender Soc. Pol'y & L. 711, 714-715 (2002) (contending that some states are applying parental involvement legislation to the distribution of mifepristone).

Should different requirements apply to regulate minors' access to the "abortion pill" compared to emergency contraception? The "abortion pill" differs from emergency contraception (i.e., birth control pills taken in sufficiently large doses within 72 hours of intercourse to prevent implantation of fertilized ova). In 2006, the Food and Drug Administration approved over-the-counter sales of emergency contraception but only for individuals 18 years and older. Why did the FDA impose an age requirement? What problems does it create? See Barbara Chevalier, The Constitutionality of the FDA's Age-Based Plan B Regulations: Why the FDA Made the Wrong Decision, 22 Wis. Women's L.J. 235 (2007).

(12) Medical Emergencies.   Some states provide that parental consent or notification is not required in cases of a medical emergency. According to Roe v. Wade, regulations must contain adequate provision for abortion if the pregnancy poses a threat to the mother's life *or health*. Courts have addressed the constitutionality of the medical emergency exception in the context of minors' decision making. See, e.g., Planned Parenthood of Idaho v. Wasden, 376 F.3d 908 (9th Cir. 2004) (invalidating state statute because the definition of "medical emergency" was so narrow as to preclude minors with conditions that, although medically necessitating an abortion, were not "sudden, unexpected" and "abnormal"); Planned Parenthood of Northern New England v. Heed, 390 F.3d 53 (1st Cir. 2004) (holding that an

exception to notification only to prevent *death* of a minor was unconstitutionally narrow), *vacated and remanded sub nom.* Ayotte v. Planned Parenthood of Northern New England, 546 U.S. 320 (2006) (holding that the notification statute was invalid absent a health exception, but remanding to determine if legislative intent would allow only unconstitutional applications to be enjoined). To what extent does Gonzales v. Carhart, supra, raise questions about the current status of the health exception in parental involvement statutes?

(13) Empirical Data.

a. Reasons for Nondisclosure. Why would a teenager choose not to notify her parent(s) of a pending abortion? Ehrlich points out multiple reasons: fear that parents would have a severe adverse reaction (leading to infliction of physical harm or ejecting the minor from the home); anticipation of parental opposition to the abortion, pressure to have the baby or to get married; and anticipation of ensuing problematic family dynamics. Ehrlich, Grounded in the Reality, supra, at 94-95 (noting also that for minors living with one or both parents, 30 percent feared a severe adverse reaction, such as abuse). Would a statute providing for a bypass proceeding only for abused and neglected minors (whose abuse or neglect has been reported) be constitutional? See Planned Parenthood, Sioux Falls Clinic v. Miller, 63 F.3d 1452 (8th Cir. 1995) (invalidating statute for failure to consider the mature minor and best-interests test). See also Planned Parenthood of Blue Ridge v. Camblos, 155 F.3d 352 (4th Cir. 1998) (holding that bypass was not required in all notification statutes if the statute contained appropriate exceptions, such as for victims of abuse and neglect).

b. Reasons for Choosing Abortion. Minors have many reasons for choosing to have an abortion, including feeling unprepared for motherhood; interference with future plans; difficult life circumstances (already having a child, not having a place to live, or health problems); concerns about ability to support the child; and issues related to pregnancy, abortion, and adoption. Ehrlich, Grounded in Reality, supra, at 97.

c. Consequences of Parental Involvement Laws. What are the consequences of parental involvement laws? Some research suggests that parental involvement laws negatively impact minors' health by causing delays in medical care — i.e., increasing the incidence of abortions late in pregnancy. Jennifer Blasdell, Mother, May I? Ramifications for Parental Involvement Laws for Minors Seeking Abortion Services, 10 Am. U. J. Gender Soc. Pol'y & L. 287, 288-290 (2002) (reviewing data). Other research suggests that parental involvement laws decrease birth rates and abortion rates. James L. Rogers et al., Impact of the Minnesota Parental Notification Law on Abortion and Birth, 81 Am. J. Pub. Health 294 (1991). Can you think of an alternative explanation for the decrease in birth rates and abortion rates in a given jurisdiction (e.g., forum shopping)?

(14) Problem. Assess the constitutionality of the following provisions in a proposed parental notification statute that would (1) permit notification of a substitute adult relative in cases of child abuse and (2) impose civil liability on physicians for failure to notify parents of a minor's abortion.

> Notice to a parent shall not be required if, at least 48 hours prior to performing the abortion, the attending physician has delivered notice in the manner

prescribed and on the form prescribed to an adult family member designated by the unemancipated minor and has made a written report of known or suspected child abuse concerning the unemancipated minor to the appropriate law enforcement or public child protective agency. Such report shall be based on a minor's written statement that she fears physical, sexual, or severe emotional abuse from a parent who would otherwise be notified and that her fear is based on a pattern of physical, sexual, or severe emotional abuse of her exhibited by a parent. The physician shall include the minor's statement with his or her report and shall also retain a copy of the statement and the report in the minor's medical records. The physician shall also include with the notice a letter informing the adult family member that a report of known or suspected child abuse has been made concerning the minor and identifying the agency to which the report was made.

Any person who performs an abortion on an unemancipated minor and in so doing knowingly or negligently fails to comply with the provisions of this Section shall be liable for damages in a civil action brought by the unemancipated minor, her legal representative, or by a parent wrongfully denied notification. The time for commencement of the action shall be within four years of the date the minor attains majority or four years of the date a parent wrongfully denied notification discovers or reasonably should have discovered the failure to comply with this Section, whichever period expires later. A person shall not be liable under this Section if the person establishes by written or documentary evidence that the person relied upon evidence sufficient to convince a careful and prudent person that the representations of the unemancipated minor or other persons regarding information necessary to comply with this Section were bona fide and true. In addition to any damages awarded under this subdivision, the plaintiff shall be entitled to an award of reasonable attorney fees. (California, Proposition 4)

See also Scofield v. Sibley, 874 So.2d 611 (Fla. Dist. Ct. App. 2004) (holding that a civil cause of action by a parent for violation of a parental involvement law may not be predicated on an unconstitutional statute). See generally Jennifer L. Achilles, Comment, Using Tort Law to Circumvent Roe v. Wade and Other Pesky Due Process Decisions: An Examination of Louisiana's Act 825, 78 Tul. L. Rev. 853 (2004).

CHAPTER 2

The Legal Framework for a Child's Economic Relationship Within the Family

This chapter explores the legal framework for the child's economic relationship to the family. Its primary focus is the parental support obligation, and the state's role to enforce this obligation. It also briefly examines the state's role in supplementing the family's income where the parents lack adequate resources to care for the child. The extract from Blackstone's Commentaries highlights the common law background. After you have finished this chapter, reread the Blackstone extract and ask yourself how the law has changed, and perhaps more interestingly, what doctrinal relics still remain, and how our present-day law reflects its historical antecedents.

In studying the material in this chapter, keep the following questions in mind: To what extent is the duty to support children a legal obligation? A moral one? Who has the legal duty of support? To whom is the duty owed? What is included in support and how is it determined? What are the legal mechanisms for enforcing a support obligation? What are the sanctions? Who may sue? Are the child's economic claims affected by the marital status of his or her parents? What is the parents' support obligation to children who are born via assisted reproduction? What role should law and courts have in allocating resources within the ongoing family? If the parents should separate or divorce? If a parent dies? When does (and should) the state provide the resources for the support of children?

A. COMMON LAW BACKGROUND

William Blackstone, Commentaries on the Laws of England
Vol. 1, 446-454

The next, and the most universal relation in nature, is immediately derived from the preceding, being that between parent and child.

Children are of two sorts; legitimate and spurious, or bastards; each of which we shall consider in their order; and, first of legitimate children.

Legitimate Children

A legitimate child is he that is born in lawful wedlock, or within a competent time afterwards. *"Pater est quem nuptiae demonstrant,"* [The nuptials show who the father is.] is the rule of the civil law; and this holds with the civilians, whether the nuptials happen before, or after, the birth of the child. With us in England the rule is narrowed, for the nuptials must be precedent to the birth; of which more will be said when we come to consider the case of bastardy. At present let us inquire into, 1. The legal duties of parents to their legitimate children. 2. Their power over them. 3. The duties of such children to their parents.

And, first, the duties of parents to legitimate children: which principally consist in three particulars; their maintenance, their protection, and their education.

Duty to Support

The duty of parents to provide for the *maintenance* of their children, is a principle of natural law: an obligation, says Puffendorf, laid on them not only by nature herself, but by their own proper act, in bringing them into the world: for they would be in the highest manner injurious to their issue, if they only gave their children life, that they might afterwards see them perish. By begetting them, therefore, they have entered into a voluntary obligation, to endeavour, as far as in them lies, that the life which they have bestowed shall be supported and preserved. And thus the children will have a perfect *right* of receiving maintenance from their parents. And the president Montesquieu has a very just observation upon his head: that the establishment of marriage in all civilized states is built on this natural obligation of the father to provide for his children: for that ascertains and makes known the person who is bound to fulfil this obligation: whereas, in promiscuous and illicit conjunctions, the father is unknown; and the mother finds a thousand obstacles in her way; — shame, remorse, the constraint of her sex, and the rigour of laws; — that stifle her inclinations to perform this duty; and besides, she generally wants ability.

The municipal laws in all well-regulated states have taken care to enforce this duty though Providence has done it more effectually than any laws, by implanting in the breast of every parent that natural $\sigma\tau o\rho\gamma\eta$ or insuperable degree of affection, which not even the deformity of person or mind, not even the wickedness, ingratitude, and rebellion of children can totally suppress or extinguish.

The civil law obliges the parent to provide maintenance for his child: and, if he refuses, *"judex de ea re cognoscet."* [The judge shall take cognizance of the matter.] Nay, it carries this matter so far, that it will not suffer a parent at his death totally to disinherit his child, without expressly giving his reason for so doing; and there are fourteen such reasons reckoned up, which may justify such disinherison. If the parent alleged no reason, or a bad, or a false one, the child might set the will aside, *tanquam testamentum inofficiosum,* [as an undutiful will] a testament contrary to the natural duty of the parent. And it is remarkable under what colour the children were to move for relief in such a case; by suggesting that the parent had lost the use of his reason, when he made the *inofficious* testament. And this, as Puffendorf observes, was not to bring into dispute the testator's power of disinheriting his own offspring; but to examine the motives upon which he did it: and, if they were found defective in reason, then to set them aside. But perhaps this is going rather too far; every man has, or ought to have, by the laws of society, a power over his own property: and, as Grotius very well distinguishes, natural right obliges to give a *necessary* maintenance to children; but what is more than that they have no other right to, than as it is given them by the favour of their parents, or the positive constitutions of the municipal law. [See p. 210 infra, for present-day limitations on parental power to disinherit minor children in civil law countries as well as the United States.]

Let us next see what provisions our own laws have made for this natural duty. It is a principle of law, that there is an obligation on every man to provide for those descended from his loins; and the manner, in which this obligation shall be performed, is thus pointed out. The father and mother, grandfather and grandmother of poor impotent persons shall maintain them at their own charges, if of sufficient ability, according as the quarter session shall direct: and if a parent runs away, and leaves his children, the church-wardens and overseers of the parish shall seize his rents, goods, and chattels, and dispose of them toward their relief.[1] By the interpretations which the courts of law have made upon these statutes, if a mother or grandmother marries again, and was before such second marriage of sufficient ability to keep the child, the husband shall be charged to maintain it for this being a debt of hers, when single, shall like others extend to charge the husband. But at her death, the relation being dissolved, the husband is under no farther obligation.

No person is bound to provide a maintenance for his issue, unless where the children are impotent and unable to work, either through infancy, disease, or accident; and then is only obliged to find them with necessaries, the penalty on refusal being no more than 20s. a month. For the policy of our laws, which are ever watchful to promote industry, did not mean to compel a father to maintain his idle and lazy children in ease and indolence: but thought it unjust to oblige the parent against his will to provide them with superfluities, and other indulgences of fortune; imagining they might trust to the impulse of nature, if the children were deserving of such favours. . . .

Our law has made no provision to prevent the disinheriting of children by will: leaving every man's property in his own disposal, upon a principle of liberty in this, as well as every other action; though perhaps it had not been amiss, if the parent had been bound to leave them at the least a necessary subsistence. Indeed, among persons of any rank or fortune, a competence is generally provided for younger children, and the bulk of the estate settled upon the eldest, by the marriage-articles. Heirs also and children are favourites of our courts of justice, and cannot be disinherited by any dubious or ambiguous words; there being required the utmost certainty of the testator's intentions to take away the right of an heir.

---

[1] [In support of this proposition, Blackstone cited the Poor Laws, 43 Eliz., c. 2 (Poor Relief, 1601) described further at p. 157 infra.]

Duty to Protect

From the duty of maintenance we may easily pass to that of *protection,* which is also a natural duty, but rather permitted than enjoined by any municipal laws: nature, in this respect, working so strongly as to need rather a check than a spur. . . .

Duty to Educate

The last duty of parents to their children is that of giving them an *education* suitable to their station in life; a duty pointed out by reason, and of far the greatest importance of any. For, as Puffendorf very well observes, it is not easy to imagine or allow, that a parent has conferred any considerable benefit upon his child by bringing him into the world, if he afterwards entirely neglects his culture and education, and suffers him to grow up like a mere beast, to lead a life useless to others, and shameful to himself. Yet the municipal laws of most countries seem to be defective in this point, by not constraining the parent to bestow a proper education upon his children. Perhaps they thought it punishment enough to leave the parent, who neglects the instruction of his family, to labour under those griefs and inconveniences, which his family, so uninstructed, will be sure to bring upon him. Our laws, though their defects in this particular cannot be denied, have, in one instance made a wise provision for breeding up the rising generation; since the poor and laborious part of the community, when past the age of nurture, are taken out of the hands of their parents, by the statutes for apprenticing poor children; and are placed out by the public in such a manner, as may render their abilities, in their several stations, of the greatest advantage to the commonwealth. The rich indeed are left at their own option, whether they will breed up their children to be ornaments or disgraces to their family. . . .

Parental Power

The *power* of parents over their children is derived from the former consideration, their duty: this authority being given them, partly to enable the parent more effectually to perform his duty, and partly as a recompence for his care and trouble in the faithful discharge of it. And upon this score the municipal laws of some nations have given a much larger authority to the parents than others. The ancient Roman laws gave the father a power of life and death over his children; upon this principle, that he who gave had also the power of taking away. But the rigour of these laws was softened by subsequent constitutions; so that we find a father banished by the emperor Hadrian for killing his son, though he had committed a very heinous crime, upon this maxim, that *"patria potestas in pietate debet, non in atrocitate, consistere."* [Paternal power shall consist of kindness, not cruelty.] But still they maintained to the last a very large and absolute authority: for a son could not acquire any property of his own during the life of his father; but all his acquisitions belonged to the father, or at least the profits of them for his life.

The power of a parent by our English laws is much more moderate; but still sufficient to keep the child in order and obedience. He may lawfully correct his child, being under age, in a reasonable manner; for this is for the benefit of his education.

The consent or concurrence of the parent to the marriage of his child under age was also *directed* by our ancient law to be obtained: but now it is absolutely *necessary;* for without it the contract is void. And this also is another means, which the law has put into the parent's hands, in order the better to discharge his duty; first, or protecting his children from the snares of artful and designing persons: and next, of settling them properly in life, by preventing the ill consequences of too early and precipitate marriages. A father has no other power over his son's *estate,* than as his trustee or guardian; for though he may receive the profits during the child's minority, yet he must account for them when he comes of age. He may indeed have the benefit of his children's labour while they live with him, and are maintained by him; but this is no more than he is entitled to from his apprentices or servants. The legal power of a father (for a mother, as such, is entitled to no power, but only to reverence and respect), the power of a father, I say, over the persons of his children ceases at the age of twenty-one: for they are then enfranchised by arriving at years of discretion, or that point which the law has established (as some must necessarily be established), when the empire of the father, or other guardian, gives place to the empire of reason. Yet, till that age arrives, this empire of the father continues even after his death; for he may by his will appoint a guardian to his children. He may also delegate part of his parental authority, during his life, to the tutor or schoolmaster of his child; who is then *in loco parentis,* and has such a portion of the power of the parent committed to his charge, viz. that of restraint and correction, as may be necessary to answer the purposes for which he is employed.

Duties of Children

The *duties* of children to their parents arise from a principle of natural justice and retribution. For to those who gave us existence, we naturally owe subjection and obedience during our minority, and honour and reverence ever after: they, who protected the weakness of our infancy, are entitled to our protection in the infirmity of their age; they, who by sustenance and education have enabled their offspring to prosper, ought in return to be supported by that offspring in case they stand in need of assistance. Upon this principle proceed all the duties of children to their parents which are enjoined by positive laws. And the Athenian laws carried this principle into practice with a scrupulous kind of nicety; obliging all children to provide for their father, when fallen into poverty; with an exception to spurious children, to those whose chastity has been prostituted by consent of the father, and to those whom he had not put in any way of gaining a livelihood. The legislature, says baron Montesquieu, considered, that in the first case the father, being uncertain, had rendered the natural obligation precarious; that in the second case, he had sullied the life he had given, and done his children the greatest of injuries, in depriving them of their reputation; and that in the third case he had rendered their life (so far as in him lay) an insupportable burden, by furnishing them with no means of subsistence.

Our laws agree with those of Athens with regard to the first only of these particulars, the case of spurious issue. In the other cases the law does not hold the tie of nature to be dissolved by any misbehaviour of the parent; and therefore a child is equally justifiable in defending the person, or maintaining the cause or suit of a bad parent, as a good one; and is equally compellable, if of sufficient ability, to maintain and provide for a wicked and unnatural progenitor, as for one who has shewn the greatest tenderness and parental piety.

Yale Diagnostic Radiology v. Estate of Fountain
838 A.2d 179 (Conn. 2004)

BORDEN, J.

The sole issue in this appeal is whether a medical service provider that has provided emergency medical services to a minor may collect for those services from the minor when the minor's parents refuse or are unable to make payment. . . .

The following facts and procedural history are undisputed. In March, 1996, [Harun Fountain, a 13-year-old unemancipated minor] was shot in the back of the head at point-blank range by a playmate. As a result of his injuries, including the loss of his right eye, Fountain required extensive lifesaving medical services from a variety of medical services providers, including the plaintiff. The expense of the services rendered by the plaintiff to Fountain totaled $17,694. The plaintiff billed Tucker, who was Fountain's mother,[2] but the bill went unpaid and, in 1999, the plaintiff obtained a collection judgment against her. In January, 2001, however, all of Tucker's debts were discharged pursuant to an order of the Bankruptcy Court for the District of Connecticut. Among the discharged debts was the judgment in favor of the plaintiff against Tucker.

During the time between the rendering of medical services and the bankruptcy filing, Tucker, as Fountain's next friend, initiated a tort action against the boy who had shot him. Among the damages claimed were "substantial sums of money [expended] on medical care and treatment. . . ." A settlement was reached, and funds were placed in the estate established on Fountain's behalf under the supervision of the Probate Court. Tucker was designated the fiduciary of that estate. Neither Fountain nor his estate was involved in Tucker's subsequent bankruptcy proceeding.

Following the discharge of Tucker's debts, the plaintiff moved the Probate Court for payment of the $17,694 from the estate. The Probate Court denied the motion, reasoning that, pursuant to General Statutes §46b-37(b),[3] parents are liable for medical services rendered to their minor children, and that a parent's refusal or inability to pay for those services does not render the minor child liable. The Probate Court further ruled that minor children are incapable of entering into a

---

[2] There is no reference to Fountain's father in the record or briefs of either party. We therefore assume that he is not available as a viable source of payment of the plaintiff's bill for services rendered to Fountain.

[3] General Statutes §46b-37(b) provides: "Notwithstanding the provisions of subsection (a) of this section, it shall be the joint duty of each spouse to support his or her family, and both shall be liable for: (1) The reasonable and necessary services of a physician or dentist; (2) hospital expenses rendered the husband or wife or minor child while residing in the family of his or her parents; (3) the rental of any dwelling unit actually occupied by the husband and wife as a residence and reasonably necessary to them for that purpose; and (4) any article purchased by either which has in fact gone to the support of the family, or for the joint benefit of both." . . .

legally binding contract or consenting, in the absence of parental consent, to medical treatment. The Probate Court held, therefore, that the plaintiff was barred from seeking payment from the estate. [On appeal, the superior court reversed and entered judgment for the plaintiff-provider.]

. . . Connecticut has long recognized the common-law rule that a minor child's contracts are voidable. Under this rule, a minor may, upon reaching majority, choose either to ratify or to avoid contractual obligations entered into during his minority. See 4 S. Williston, Contracts (4th Ed. 1992) §8:14, pp. 271-72. The traditional reasoning behind this rule is based on the well established common-law principles that the law should protect children from the detrimental consequences of their youthful and improvident acts, and that children should be able to emerge into adulthood unencumbered by financial obligations incurred during the course of their minority. The rule is further supported by a policy of protecting children from unscrupulous individuals seeking to profit from their youth and inexperience.

The rule that a minor's contracts are voidable, however, is not absolute. An exception to this rule, eponymously known as the doctrine of necessaries, is that a minor may not avoid a contract for goods or services necessary for his health and sustenance. See 5 S. Williston, Contracts (4th Ed. 1993) §9:18, pp. 149-57. Such contracts are binding even if entered into during minority, and a minor, upon reaching majority, may not, as a matter of law, disaffirm them. Id.

The parties do not dispute the fact that the medical services rendered to Fountain were necessaries; rather, their dispute centers on whether Connecticut recognizes the doctrine of necessaries. As evidenced by the following history, the doctrine of necessaries has long been a part of Connecticut jurisprudence.

In Strong v. Foote [42 Conn. 203, 205 (1875)], this court affirmed a judgment in favor of a dentist against a minor for services rendered to the minor, who had an estate and who was an orphan for whom a guardian had been appointed. This court stated: "In suits against minors, instituted by persons who have rendered services or supplied articles to them, the term 'necessaries' is not invariably used in its strictest sense, nor is it limited to that which is requisite to sustain life, but includes whatever is proper and suitable in the case of each individual, having reference to his circumstances and condition in life." Id. The court further noted that the services were "within the legal limitations of the word 'necessaries,' " and that the plaintiff was not required to inquire as to the minor's guardianship before rendering the services because the services were "necessary to meet an unsupplied want." Id.

Furthermore, from 1907 to 1959, statutory law regarding minors and the doctrine of necessaries remained unchanged. General Statutes §42-2 [codified] the common law doctrine of necessaries. We recognize that §42-2 was repealed in 1959, when Connecticut adopted the Uniform Commercial Code. That repeal was not intended, however, to eliminate the doctrine because the statute was replaced by General Statutes §42a-1-103, which contemplated that the Uniform Commercial Code would continue to be supplemented by the general principles of contract law regarding minors.

In light of these precedents, we conclude that Connecticut recognizes the doctrine of necessaries. We further conclude that, pursuant to the doctrine, the defendants are liable for payment to the plaintiff for the services rendered to Fountain.

We have not heretofore articulated the particular legal theory underlying the doctrine of necessaries. We therefore take this occasion to do so, and we conclude that the most apt theory is that of an implied in law contract, also sometimes referred to as a quasi-contract. We further conclude that based on this theory, the defendants are liable.

[W]hen a medical service provider renders necessary medical care to an injured minor, two contracts arise: the primary contract between the provider and the minor's parents; and an implied in law contract between the provider and the minor himself. The primary contract between the provider and the parents is based on the parents' duty to pay for their children's necessary expenses, under both common law and statute. Such contracts, where not express, may be implied in fact and generally arise both from the parties' conduct and their reasonable expectations. The primacy of this contract means that the provider of necessaries must make all reasonable efforts to collect from the parents before resorting to the secondary, implied in law contract with the minor.

The secondary implied in law contract between the medical services provider and the minor arises from equitable considerations, including the law's disfavor of unjust enrichment. Therefore, where necessary medical services are rendered to a minor whose parents do not pay for them, equity and justice demand that a secondary implied in law contract arise between the medical services provider and the minor who has received the benefits of those services. These principles compel the conclusion that, in the circumstances of the present case, the defendants are liable to the plaintiff, under the common-law doctrine of necessaries, for the services rendered by the plaintiff to Fountain.

The present case illustrates the inequity that would arise if no implied in law contract arose between Fountain and the plaintiff. Fountain was shot in the head at close range and required emergency medical care. Under such circumstances, a medical services provider cannot stop to consider how the bills will be paid or by whom. Although the plaintiff undoubtedly presumed that Fountain's parent would pay for his care and was obligated to make reasonable efforts to collect from Tucker before seeking payment from Fountain, the direct benefit of the services, nonetheless, was conferred upon Fountain. Having received the benefit of necessary services, Fountain should be liable for payment for those necessaries in the event that his parents do not pay.

Furthermore, in the present case, we note, as did the trial court, that Fountain received, through a settlement with the boy who caused his injuries, funds that were calculated, at least in part, on the costs of the medical services provided to him by the plaintiff in the wake of those injuries. Fountain, through Tucker, brought an action against the tortfeasor and, in his complaint, cited "substantial sums of money [expended] on medical care and treatment. . . ." This fact further supports a determination of an implied in law contract under the circumstances of the case.

The defendants claim, however, that the doctrine of necessaries has been legislatively abrogated by §46b-37(b)(2). We disagree. Section 46b-37(b)(2) governs the joint liability of parents for the support and maintenance of their family, and, in doing so, merely codifies the common-law principle, long recognized in Connecticut, that both parents are primarily responsible for providing necessary goods and services to their children. Section 46b-37(b)(2), however, is silent as to a child's secondary liability. That statute neither promotes nor prohibits a determination of secondary liability on the part of a minor when the minor has received emergency medical services and the parents are either unwilling or unable to pay for those services. . . . Nothing in either the language or the purpose of §46b-37(b)(2) indicates an intent on the part of the legislature to absolve minors of their secondary common-law liability for necessaries.

To the contrary, the purposes behind the statutory rule that parents are primarily liable and the common-law rule, pursuant to the doctrine of necessaries, that a minor is secondarily liable, when read together, serve to encourage payment on contracts for necessaries. Those purposes are (1) to reinforce parents' obligation to support their children, and (2) to provide a mechanism for collection by creditors when, nonetheless, the parents either refuse or are unable to discharge that obligation.

The defendants further contended, at oral argument before this court, that, even if we were to conclude that the doctrine of necessaries is applicable, the defendants are not liable to the plaintiff because there has been no showing that Tucker was unwilling or unable to provide necessaries to Fountain. . . . We disagree.

The undisputed facts show that Tucker had four years to pay the plaintiff's bill for the services rendered to Fountain. She did not pay that bill even when the plaintiff pursued a collection action against her. These facts are sufficient to show that Tucker was unwilling or unable to pay for Fountain's necessary medical services. . . . The judgment is affirmed.

NOTES AND COMMENTS: COMMON LAW

(1) Moral or Legal Obligation?   Early English cases, such as Mortimore v. Wright, 151 Eng. Rep. 502 (Exch. Ch. 1840), suggest that there was a moral but not a legal obligation on the part of parents to support their children. What does this mean? That the child had no power to sue the parent for support? That a creditor could not recover from the parent the cost of providing goods or services to a child even if they were "necessaries"? That there would be no legal sanctions brought against a father who failed to support his child?

(2) Elizabethan Poor Laws.   The Elizabethan "Poor Laws" did in effect create a legal obligation to exhaust parental resources for the support of a child before the local parish was obligated to provide relief.

The Act for Relief of the Poor, 43 Eliz., c. 2, §1 (1601) provided:

[T]hat the church wardens of every parish, and four . . . substantial householders there . . . shall be called overseers of the poor of the same parish; and they . . . shall take order from time to time, by and with the consent of two or more . . . justices of peace . . . for setting to work all such persons, married or unmarried, having no means to maintain them, and use no ordinary and daily trade of life to get their living by: and also to raise . . . by taxation of every inhabitant . . . and every occupier of lands, houses . . . or salable underwoods in the same parish . . . a convenient stock of flax, hemp, wool, thread, iron and other necessary ware and stuff, to set the poor on work: and also competent sums of money towards the necessary relief of the lame, impotent, old, blind, and such others among them, being poor and not able to work, and also for the putting out of such children to be apprentices. . . .

Section 7 of the same act made it plain that primary responsibility for the indigent was with the family, not the state:

> That the father and grandfather, mother and the grandmother, and the children of every poor, old, blind, and impotent person, or other poor person not able to work, being of a sufficient ability, shall at their own charges relieve and maintain every such person. . . .

It was only when the family was unable to support the child that the local parish was called upon to provide assistance. The statute contemplated that if a parent was a recipient of aid, his or her children would be apprenticed or indentured to some other person to provide the child with a trade. As Blackstone suggests, however, where the child was able to work, a father had no support obligation under the poor laws. See supra p. 151.

(3) Parental Right to a Minor's Services and Earnings. Whereas the parental support obligation at common law was not well established, a parent's common law right to a child's services was clear. This meant that the parent could take the earnings of an unemancipated child. See Blackstone p. 153 supra. This common law tradition remains part of the law today and is incorporated in the statutory provisions of most states. See, e.g., Cal. Fam. Code §7500 (West 2004).

At common law "emancipation denoted the release of a minor from parental control, and the acquisition by the minor of the right to dispose of his own earnings." 5 Chester Garfield Vernier, American Family Laws §282 (1938). Emancipation was normally thought to require parental consent, or assent (which sometimes would be implied), and this too is also reflected in present-day statutes. "The parent, whether solvent or insolvent, may relinquish to the child the right of controlling the child and receiving the child's earnings. Abandonment by the parent is presumptive evidence of that relinquishment." Cal. Fam. Code §7504 (West 2004).

(4) "Necessaries" Doctrine. At common law, a husband had an obligation to provide support for his wife and children. Related to that support obligation was the necessaries doctrine — the husband's duty to provide *necessary goods and services* to his wife and children, and if he failed to do so, the creditor's ability to sue the husband to recover the cost. This gender-based common law doctrine largely has been abrogated based on the Equal Protection Clause and state equal rights amendments. Many jurisdictions render each spouse liable for expenses incurred by the other spouse. (Sometimes, one spouse is primarily liable and the other is secondarily liable.) Similarly, jurisdictions now hold, by case law or statute, that both parents have equal obligations to contribute to their children's support.

Yale Diagnostic illustrates current American law regarding parents' obligation to provide necessaries to their children. In most jurisdictions today, both parents are liable for "necessaries" purchased by unemancipated minors living with the family. Minors ordinarily may disaffirm their own contracts prior to, or within, a reasonable time after reaching majority. However, an exception to this rule exists for necessaries. As *Yale Diagnostic* explains: "a minor may not avoid a contract for goods or services necessary for his health and sustenance." Also, the necessaries doctrine in effect permits self-help, for the parents' credit or the minor's own credit may be used by the minor to purchase essential goods and services.

The most frequently litigated issue is: were the goods or services "necessaries"? If not, the doctrine does not apply. Also, was the minor emancipated at the time of the purchase? If so, the parents are not responsible.

Yale Diagnostic, in announcing principles of primary (parents') and secondary (minors') liability for the costs of necessary medical treatment of minors, is consistent with the trend in recent case law. See, e.g., Williams v. Baptist Health Systems, Inc., 857 So. 2d 149 (Ala Civ. App. 2003); Layton Phys. Therapy Co. v. Palozzi, 777 N.E.2d 306 (Ohio Ct. App. 2002). See also American Law Institute, Restatement (Third) of the Law of Restitution & Unjust Enrichment, §20 (Illustration 2) (Tentative Draft No. 2, April 1, 2002 (accord)).

(5) Changes in the Child's Economic Contributions to the Family — Some Broader Issues. Until the late nineteenth century, young people often assumed adult work roles and contributed to the family's support. The twentieth century has seen, however, a substantial increase in the period of dependence of youth on their families. It is now difficult for a minor either to contribute substantially to the family's economic well-being or to be economically self-sufficient. Indeed, many young people are now economically dependent on their parents for a number of years after they reach the age of majority.

These historical changes in the work role of children are described in David Stern et al., How Children Used to Work, 39 Law & Contemp. Probs. (No. 3) 93 (1975). This article suggests that in the past, children were economic assets to their parents: Young people could work and thus contribute to family support. Grown children frequently contributed to the support of their elderly parents. Now these economic benefits to parents have largely disappeared.[2] Although parents still have the legal right to the earnings of their minor children, few children can have earnings that substantially contribute to the family pot, given the constraints imposed by compulsory education, child labor prohibitions (see Chapter 6 infra), and the increased specialization of work roles. Moreover, social security and pension funds appear to be displacing the family as the primary source of old-age assistance.

Consider the broader implications of these changes. Thomas Hobbes asserted that "there is not reason why any man should desire to have children or to take care to nourish them if afterwards to have no other benefit from them than from other men." Leviathan 329 (William Molesworth ed. 1939-1945). The disappearance of these economic benefits poses difficult questions. In an age when the economic benefits to parents of having children are largely gone, should society bear a larger share of the cost of child raising? Are parents as a group more trustworthy, given the absence of opportunities for economic exploitation of their children and the primacy of noneconomic motivation to have them in the first place? Or must the state assume a more active role because of the diminution of an economic motive for parents themselves to "invest" in their own children?

---

[2] The exception is filial support legislation in many jurisdictions that imposes a duty on adult children to support *indigent* elderly parents. See generally Seymour Moskowitz, Filial Responsibility Statutes: Legal and Social Policy Considerations, 9 J.L. & Pol'y 709 (2001).

William Blackstone, Commentaries on the Laws of England
Vol. 1, 454-459

Illegitimate Children

We are next to consider the case of illegitimate children, or bastards; with regard to whom let us inquire, 1. Who are bastards. 2. The legal duties of the parents towards a bastard child. 3. The rights and incapacities attending such bastard children.

Who Are Bastards

A bastard, by our English laws, is one that is not only begotten, but born, out of lawful matrimony. The civil and canon laws do not allow a child to remain a bastard, if the parents afterwards intermarry: and herein they differ most materially from our law; which, though not so strict as to require that the child shall be *begotten,* yet makes it an indispensable condition that it shall be *born,* after lawful wedlock. And the reason of our English law is surely much superior to that of the Roman, if we consider the principal end and design of establishing the contract of marriage, taken in a civil light; abstractedly from any religious view, which has nothing to do with the legitimacy or illegitimacy of the children. The main end and design of marriage, therefore, being to ascertain and fix upon some certain person, to whom the care, the protection, the maintenance, and the education of the children should belong; . . .

Children born during wedlock may in some circumstances be bastards. As if the husband be out of the kingdom of England (or, as the law somewhat loosely phrases it, *extra quatuor maria* — beyond the four seas), for above nine months, so that no access to his wife can be presumed, her issue during that period shall be bastards. But, generally, during the coverture access of the husband shall be presumed, unless the contrary can be shown; which is such a negative as can only be proved by showing him to be elsewhere: for the general rule is, *praesumitur pro legitimatione* [the presumption is in favor of legitimacy].

Support of Bastards

Let us next see the duty of parents to their bastard children, by our law; which is principally that of maintenance. For, though bastards are not looked upon as children to any civil purposes, yet the ties of nature, of which maintenance is one, are not so easily dissolved: and they hold indeed as to many other intentions; as, particularly, that a man shall not marry his bastard sister or daughter. The civil law, therefore, when it denied maintenance to bastards begotten under certain atrocious circumstances, was neither consonant to nature, nor reason; however profligate and wicked the parents might justly be esteemed.

The method in which the English law provides maintenance for them is as follows: When a woman is delivered, or declares herself with child, of a bastard, and will by oath before a justice of peace charge any person having got her with child, the justice shall cause such person to be apprehended, and commit him till he gives security, either to maintain the child, or appear at the next quarter sessions to dispute and try the fact. But if the woman dies, or is married before delivery, or miscarries, or proves not to have been with child, the person shall be discharged: otherwise the sessions, or two justices out of sessions, upon original application to them, may take order for the keeping of the bastard, by charging the mother or the reputed father with the payment of money or other sustentation for that purpose. And if such putative father, or lewd mother, run away from the parish, the overseers by direction of two justices may seize their rents, goods, and chattels, in order to bring up the said bastard child. Yet such is the humanity of our laws, that no woman can be compulsively questioned concerning the father of her child, till one month after her delivery: which indulgence is, however, very frequently a hardship upon parishes, by giving the parents opportunity to escape.

The Rights and Incapacities of Bastards

I proceed next to the rights and incapacities which appertain to a bastard. . . .

The incapacity of a bastard consists principally in this, that he cannot be heir to anyone, neither can he have heirs, but of his own body; for, being *nullius filius,* he is therefore of kin to nobody, and has no ancestor from whom any inheritable blood can be derived. A bastard was also, in strictness, incapable of holy orders; and, though that were dispensed with, yet he was utterly disqualified from holding any dignity in the church: but this doctrine seems now obsolete; and in all other respects, there is no distinction between a bastard and another man. And really any other distinction, but that of not inheriting, which civil policy renders necessary, would, with regard to the innocent offspring of his parents' crimes, be odious, unjust, and cruel to the last degree, and yet the civil law, so boasted of for its equitable decisions, made bastards in some cases incapable even of a gift from their parents. A bastard may, lastly, be made legitimate and capable of inheriting, by the transcendent power of an act of parliament, and not otherwise, as was done in the case of John of Gaunt's bastard children, by a statute of Richard the Second.

Michael H. v. Gerald D.
491 U.S. 110 (1989)

Justice Scalia announced the judgment of the Court and delivered an opinion, in which The Chief Justice joins, and in all but note 6 of which Justice O'Connor and Justice Kennedy join.

Under California law, a child born to a married woman living with her husband is presumed to be a child of the marriage. Cal. Evid. Code Ann. §621 (West Supp. 1989). The presumption of legitimacy may be rebutted only by the husband or wife, and then only in limited circumstances. The instant appeal presents the claim that this presumption infringes upon the due process rights of a man who wishes to establish his paternity of a child born to the wife of another man, and the claim that it infringes upon the constitutional right of the child to maintain a relationship with her natural father.

The facts of this case are, we must hope, extraordinary. On May 9,1976, in Las Vegas, Nevada, Carole D., an international model, and Gerald D., a top executive in a French oil company, were married. The couple established a home in Playa del Rey, California, in which they resided as husband and wife when one or the other was not out of the country on business. In the summer of 1978, Carole became involved in an adulterous affair with a neighbor, Michael H. In September 1980, she conceived a child, Victoria D., who was born on May 11, 1981. Gerald was listed as father on the birth certificate and has always held Victoria out to the world as his daughter. Soon after delivery of the child, however, Carole informed Michael that she believed he might be the father.

In the first three years of her life, Victoria remained always with Carole, but found herself within a variety of quasi-family units. In October 1981, Gerald moved to New York City to pursue his business interests, but Carole chose to remain in California. At the end of that month, Carole and Michael had blood tests of themselves and Victoria, which showed a 98.07% probability that Michael was Victoria's father. In January 1982, Carole visited Michael in St. Thomas, where his primary business interests were based. There Michael held Victoria out as his child. In March, however, Carole left Michael and returned to California, where she took up residence with yet another man, Scott K. Later that spring, and again in the summer, Carole and Victoria spent time with Gerald in New York City, as well as on vacation in Europe. In the fall, they returned to Scott in California.

In November 1982, rebuffed in his attempts to visit Victoria, Michael filed a filiation action in California Superior Court to establish his paternity and right to visitation. In March 1983, the court appointed an attorney and guardian ad litem to represent Victoria's interests. Victoria [through her guardian ad litem] then filed a cross-complaint asserting that if she had more than one psychological or de facto father, she was entitled to maintain her filial relationship, with all of the attendant rights, duties, and obligations, with both. In May 1983, Carole filed a motion for summary judgment. During this period, from March through July 1983, Carole was again living with Gerald in New York. In August, however, she returned to California, became involved once again with Michael, and instructed her attorneys to remove the summary judgment motion from the calendar.

For the ensuing eight months, when Michael was not in St. Thomas he lived with Carole and Victoria in Carole's apartment in Los Angeles and held Victoria out as his daughter. In April 1984, Carole and Michael signed a stipulation that Michael was Victoria's natural father. Carole left Michael the next month, however, and instructed her attorneys not to file the stipulation. In June 1984, Carole reconciled with Gerald and joined him in New York, where they now live with Victoria and two other children since born into the marriage.

In May 1984, Michael and Victoria, through her guardian ad litem, sought visitation rights for Michael *pendente lite*. To assist in determining whether visitation would be in Victoria's best interests, the Superior Court appointed a psychologist to evaluate Victoria, Gerald, Michael, and Carole. The psychologist recommended that Carole retain sole custody, but that Michael be allowed continued contact with Victoria pursuant to a restricted visitation schedule. The court concurred and ordered that Michael be provided with limited visitation privileges *pendente lite*.

On October 19, 1984, Gerald, who had intervened in the action, moved for summary judgment on the ground that under Cal. Evid. Code §621 there were no triable issues of fact as to Victoria's paternity. This law provides that "the issue of a wife cohabiting with her husband, who is not impotent or sterile, is conclusively presumed to be a child of the marriage." Cal. Evid. Code Ann. §621(a) (West Supp. 1989). The presumption may be rebutted by blood tests, but only if a motion for such tests is made, within two years from the date of the child's birth, either by the husband or, if the natural father has filed an affidavit acknowledging paternity, by the wife. §621(c) and (d).

On January 28, 1985, having found that affidavits submitted by Carole and Gerald sufficed to demonstrate that the two were cohabiting at conception and birth and that Gerald was neither sterile nor impotent, the Superior Court granted Gerald's motion for summary judgment, rejecting Michael's and Victoria's challenges to the constitutionality of §621. The court also denied their motions for continued visitation pending the appeal under Cal. Civ. Code §4601, which provides that a court may, in its discretion, grant "reasonable visitation rights . . . to any . . . person having an interest in the welfare of the child." Cal. Civ. Code Ann. §4601 (West Supp. 1989). It found that allowing such visitation would "violat[e] the intention of the Legislature by impugning the integrity of the family unit." Supp. App. to Juris. Statement A-91.

On appeal, Michael asserted, inter alia, that the Superior Court's application of §621 had violated his procedural and substantive due process rights. Victoria also raised a due process challenge to the statute, seeking to preserve her de facto relationship with Michael as well as with Gerald. She contended, in addition, that as §621 allows the husband and, at least to a limited extent, the mother, but not the child, to rebut the presumption of legitimacy, it violates the child's right to equal protection. Finally, she asserted a right to continued visitation with Michael under §4601. After submission of briefs and a hearing, the California Court of Appeal affirmed the judgment of the Superior Court and upheld the constitutionality of the statute. . . .

The Court of Appeal denied Michael's and Victoria's petitions for rehearing, and, . . . the California Supreme Court denied discretionary review. [W]e noted probable jurisdiction of the present appeal. 485 U.S. 903. Before us, Michael and Victoria both raise equal protection and due process challenges. We do not reach Michael's equal protection claim, however, as it was neither raised nor passed upon below. . . .

We address first the claims of Michael. At the outset, it is necessary to clarify what he sought and what he was denied. California law, like nature itself, makes no provision for dual fatherhood. Michael was seeking to be declared the father of Victoria. The immediate benefit he evidently sought to obtain from that status was visitation rights. . . . But if Michael were successful in being declared the father, other rights would follow — most importantly, the right to be considered as the parent who should have custody, Cal. Civ. Code Ann. §4600 (West 1983), a status which "embrace[s] the sum of parental rights with respect to the rearing of a child, including the child's care; the right to the child's services and earnings; the right to direct the child's activities; the right to make decisions regarding the control, education, and health of the child; and the right, as well as the duty, to prepare the child for additional obligations, which includes the teaching of moral standards, religious beliefs, and elements of good citizenship." 4 California Family Law §60.02[l][b] (C. Markey ed. 1987) (footnotes omitted). All parental rights, including visitation, were automatically denied by denying Michael status as the father. . . .

Michael contends as a matter of substantive due process that, because he has established a parental relationship with Victoria, protection of Gerald's and Carole's marital union is an insufficient state interest to support termination of that relationship. This argument is, of course, predicated on the assertion that Michael has a constitutionally protected liberty interest in his relationship with Victoria. . . .

In an attempt to limit and guide interpretation of the [Due Process] Clause, we have insisted not merely that the interest denominated as a "liberty" be "fundamental" (a concept that, in isolation, is hard to objectify), but also that it be an interest traditionally protected by our society. As we have put it, the Due Process Clause affords only those protections "so rooted in the traditions and conscience of our people as to be ranked as fundamental." Snyder v. Massachusetts, 291 U.S. 97 (1934) (Cardozo, J.). . . .

This insistence that the asserted liberty interest be rooted in history and tradition is evident, as elsewhere, in our cases according constitutional protection to certain parental rights. Michael reads the landmark case of Stanley v. Illinois, 405 U.S. 645 (1972), and the subsequent cases of Quilloin v. Walcott, 434 U.S. 246 (1978), Caban v. Mohammed, 441 U.S. 380 (1979), and Lehr v. Robertson, 463 U.S. 248 (1983), as establishing that a liberty interest is created by biological fatherhood plus an established parental relationship — factors that exist in the present case as well. We think that distorts the rationale of those cases. As we view them, they rest not upon such isolated factors but upon the historic respect — indeed, sanctity would not be too strong a term — traditionally accorded to the relationships that develop within the unitary family.[3] . . .

Thus, the legal issue in the present case reduces to whether the relationship between persons in the situation of Michael and Victoria has been treated as a protected family unit under the historic practices of our society, or whether on any other basis it has been accorded special protection. We think it impossible to find that it has. In fact, quite to the contrary, our traditions have protected the marital family (Gerald, Carole, and the child they acknowledge to be theirs) against the sort of claim Michael asserts.[4]

[3] Justice Brennan asserts that only "a pinched conception of 'the family' " would exclude Michael, Carole, and Victoria from protection. We disagree. The family unit accorded traditional respect in our society, which we have referred to as the "unitary family," is typified, of course, by the marital family, but also includes the household of unmarried parents and their children. Perhaps the concept can be expanded even beyond this, but it will bear no resemblance to traditionally respected relationships — and will thus cease to have any constitutional significance — if it is stretched so far as to include the relationship established between a married woman, her lover, and their child, during a 3-month sojourn in St. Thomas, or during a subsequent 8-month period when, if he happened to be in Los Angeles, he stayed with her and the child.

[4] Justice Brennan insists that in determining whether a liberty interest exists we must look at Michael's relationship with Victoria in isolation, without reference to the circumstance that Victoria's mother was married to someone else when the child was conceived, and that that woman and her husband wish to raise the child as their own. We cannot imagine what compels this strange procedure of looking at the act which is assertedly the subject of a liberty interest in isolation from its effect upon other people — rather like inquiring whether there is a liberty interest in firing a gun where the case at hand happens to involve its discharge into another person's body. The logic of Justice Brennan's

The presumption of legitimacy was a fundamental principle of the common law. Traditionally, that presumption could be rebutted only by proof that a husband was incapable of procreation or had had no access to his wife during the relevant period. As explained by Blackstone, nonaccess could only be proved "if the husband be out of the kingdom of England (or, as the law somewhat loosely phrases it, *extra quatuor maria* [beyond the four seas]) for above nine months. . . ." I Blackstone's Commentaries 456 (J. Chitty ed. 1826). And, under the common law both in England and here, "neither husband nor wife [could] be a witness to prove access or nonaccess." J. Schouler, Law of the Domestic Relations §225, p. 306 (3d ed. 1882); R. Graveson & F. Crane, A Century of Family Law: 1857-1957, p. 158 (1957). The primary policy rationale underlying the common law's severe restrictions on rebuttal of the presumption appears to have been an aversion to declaring children illegitimate, thereby depriving them of rights of inheritance and succession, 2 J. Kent, Commentaries on American Law *175, and likely making them wards of the state. A secondary policy concern was the interest in promoting the "peace and tranquillity of States and families," Schouler, supra, §225, at 304, quoting Boullenois, Traite des Status, bk. 1, p. 62, a goal that is obviously impaired by facilitating suits against husband and wife asserting that their children are illegitimate. . . .

We have found nothing in the older sources, nor in the older cases, addressing specifically the power of the natural father to assert parental rights over a child born into a woman's existing marriage with another man. Since it is Michael's burden to establish that such a power (at least where the natural father has established a relationship with the child) is so deeply embedded within our traditions as to be a fundamental right, the lack of evidence alone might defeat his case. But the evidence shows that even in modern times — when, as we have noted, the rigid protection of the marital family has in other respects been relaxed — the ability of a person in Michael's position to claim paternity has not been generally acknowledged. . . .

Moreover, even if it were clear that one in Michael's position generally possesses, and has generally always possessed, standing to challenge the marital child's legitimacy, that would still not establish Michael's case. As noted earlier, what is at issue here is not entitlement to a state pronouncement that Victoria was begotten by Michael. It is no conceivable denial of constitutional right for a State to decline to declare facts unless some legal consequence hinges upon the requested declaration. What Michael asserts here is a right to have himself declared the natural father *and thereby to obtain parental prerogatives.* What he must establish, therefore, is not that our society has traditionally allowed a natural father in his circumstances to establish paternity, but that it has traditionally accorded such a father parental rights, or at least has not traditionally denied them. Even if the law in all States had always been that the entire world could challenge the marital presumption and obtain a declaration as to who was the natural father, that would not advance Michael's claim. Thus, it is ultimately irrelevant, even for purposes of determining current social attitudes towards the alleged substantive right Michael asserts, that the present law in a number of States appears to allow the natural father — including the natural father who has not established a relationship with

---

position leads to the conclusion that if Michael had begotten Victoria by rape, that fact would in no way affect his possession of a liberty interest in his relationship with her.

the child—the theoretical power to rebut the marital presumption, see Note, Rebutting the Marital Presumption: A Developed Relationship Test, 88 Colum. L. Rev. 369, 373 (1988). What counts is whether the States in fact award substantive parental rights to the natural father of a child conceived within, and born into, an extant marital union that wishes to embrace the child. We are not aware of a single case, old or new, that has done so. This is not the stuff of which fundamental rights qualifying as liberty interests are made.[6] . . .

We do not accept Justice Brennan's criticism that this result "squashes" the liberty that consists of "the freedom not to conform." It seems to us that reflects the erroneous view that there is only one side to this controversy — that one disposition can expand a "liberty" of sorts without contracting an equivalent "liberty" on the other side. Such a happy choice is rarely available. Here, to provide protection to an adulterous natural father is to deny protection to a marital father, and vice versa. If Michael has a "freedom not to conform" (whatever that means), Gerald must equivalently have a "freedom to conform." One of them will pay a price for asserting that "freedom" — Michael by being unable to act as father of the child he has adulterously begotten, or Gerald by being unable to preserve the integrity of the traditional family unit he and Victoria have established. Our disposition does not choose between these two "freedoms," but leaves that to the people of California. Justice Brennan's approach chooses one of them as the constitutional imperative, on no apparent basis except that the unconventional is to be preferred.

We have never had occasion to decide whether a child has a liberty interest, symmetrical with that of her parent, in maintaining her filial relationship. We need not do so here because, even assuming that such a right exists, Victoria's claim must fail. Victoria's due process challenge is, if anything, weaker than Michael's. Her basic claim is not that California has erred in preventing her from establishing that Michael, not Gerald, should stand as her legal father. Rather, she claims a due process right to maintain filial relationships with both Michael and Gerald. This assertion merits little discussion, for, whatever the merits of the guardian ad litem's belief that such an arrangement can be of great psychological benefit to a child, the claim that a State must recognize multiple fatherhood has no support in the history or traditions of this country. Moreover, even if we were to construe Victoria's argument as forwarding the lesser proposition that, whatever her status vis-à-vis Gerald, she has a liberty interest in maintaining a filial relationship with her

---

[6] Justice Brennan criticizes our methodology in using historical traditions specifically relating to the rights of an adulterous natural father, rather than inquiring more generally "whether parenthood is an interest that historically has received our attention and protection." . . . We do not understand why, having rejected our focus upon the societal tradition regarding the natural father's rights vis-à-vis a child whose mother is married to another man. Justice Brennan would choose to focus instead upon "parenthood." Why should the relevant category not be even more general—perhaps "family relationships"; or "personal relationships"; or even "emotional attachments in general"? Though the dissent has no basis for the level of generality it would select, we do: We refer to the most specific level at which a relevant tradition protecting, or denying protection to, the asserted right can be identified. If, for example, there were no societal tradition, either way, regarding the rights of the natural father of a child adulterously conceived, we would have to consult, and (if possible) reason from, the traditions regarding natural fathers in general. But there is such a more specific tradition, and it unqualifiedly denies protection to such a parent. . . .

natural father, Michael, we find that, at best, her claim is the obverse of Michael's and fails for the same reasons.

Victoria claims in addition that her equal protection rights have been violated because, unlike her mother and presumed father, she had no opportunity to rebut the presumption of her legitimacy. We find this argument wholly without merit. We reject, at the outset, Victoria's suggestion that her equal protection challenge must be assessed under a standard of strict scrutiny because, in denying her the right to maintain a filial relationship with Michael, the State is discriminating against her on the basis of her illegitimacy. See Gomez v. Perez, 409 U.S. 535, 538 (1973). Illegitimacy is a legal construct, not a natural trait. Under California law, Victoria is not illegitimate, and she is treated in the same manner as all other legitimate children: she is entitled to maintain a filial relationship with her legal parents.

[A]llowing a claim of illegitimacy to be pressed by the child — or, more accurately, by a court-appointed guardian ad litem — may well disrupt an otherwise peaceful union. Since it pursues a legitimate end by rational means, California's decision to treat Victoria differently from her parents is not a denial of equal protection.

The judgment of the California Court of Appeal is affirmed.

[The separate concurring opinions of Justices O'Connor and Stevens are omitted, as is the dissenting opinion by Justice Brennan, in which Justices Marshall and Blackman joined].

NOTE: NONMARITAL CHILDREN

(1) Introduction: English Common Law Backdrop. Should a child's support or inheritance rights be affected by whether his or her parents were married when the child was born? The common law answer to this question in England was harsh and reasonably clear cut. A child born "out-of-wedlock" (now termed a "nonmarital child") was illegitimate; that status affected both inheritance and support rights.

The most clear-cut consequence at common law of birth "out-of-wedlock" was the denial of all inheritance rights. Sometimes called *filius nullius* (nobody's child), the child could not be the lawful heir of either the mother or father.[3] Support rights were less clear. Such a child was said not to have a legally enforceable common law right to support from either its mother or its father. Nevertheless, it appears that both parents might be held economically responsible for the child by the local parish under the Poor Laws.[4] Moreover, even before the enactment of the Poor Laws in the seventeenth century, there is historical evidence that the courts of the Church of England enforced support obligations against fathers of such children.[5]

Although the common law treatment of the nonmarital child in England was comparatively straightforward, the status of nonmarital children has undergone considerable transformation in the United States. First, state and federal law

---

[3] Ralph C. Brashier, Inheritance Law and the Evolving Family 125 (2004).

[4] R.H. Helmholz, Support Orders, Church Courts, and the Rule of *Filius Nullius:* A Reassessment of the Common Law, 63 Va. L. Rev. 431, 432 (1977).

[5] Id.

gradually eliminated distinctions between nonmarital and marital children. Second, federal law as well as the revised Uniform Parentage Act (discussed infra) established new frameworks for legal recognition of nonmarital children's relationships with their fathers.

What follows is only a brief introduction to the complicated subject of how being born outside marriage affects a child's legal rights concerning various economic issues. Marital status of a child's parents may also affect questions relating to custody and adoption. These issues are considered in Chapter 5.

(2) Contemporary Definitions: What Is a "Nonmarital Child"?

a. Presumption of Legitimacy in Marriage. For children both begotten and born in wedlock, biology makes it easy to determine who the child's mother is, and there usually is not much difficulty in determining whether she is married at the time the child is born. But how can one ever be sure who the father is? As *Michael H.* reveals, there is a long-standing presumption that treats a child born to a married woman as the offspring of the woman and her husband. In some states this presumption is irrebuttable. Other states reach the same result by applying "Lord Mansfield's Rule," which denies the spouses the right to testify concerning the illegitimacy of a child born during the marriage. In some states the presumption is rebuttable on clear and convincing evidence to the contrary. State laws typically provide that a child is considered born within a marriage if born within a certain period (usually ten months or 300 days) following divorce. E.g., Kan. Stat. Ann. §38-1114(a)(1), (b) (2000); Mass Gen. Laws Ann. ch. 209C §6(a)(1) (2007 & Supp. 2008). See also Unif. Parentage Act §204(a), 9B U.L.A. 311 (2001 & Supp. 2008) reprinted infra p. 501.

Do the stated policy rationales in *Michael H.* continue to justify the presumption of legitimacy? How relevant to the continued vitality of the presumption are the increased accuracy of genetic testing and the decreasing stigma of illegitimacy? Are presumptions of paternity necessary or should they be discarded in favor of case-by-case determinations of paternity? How should courts resolve conflicting presumptions of paternity?

Increasingly, jurisdictions treat the presumption as rebuttable and undertake case-by-case determinations. In some jurisdictions, courts determine putative fathers' claims to paternity based on either the best-interests-of-the-child standard or the substantial relationship test. See, e.g., N.A.H. v. S.L.S., 9 P.3d 354, 357 (Colo. 2000) ("best interest of the child must be considered as part of the policy and logic analysis used to decide legal fatherhood"); Randy A.J. v. Norma I.J., 677 N.W.2d 630 (Wis. 2004) (putative father was unable to establish paternity in part because he failed to establish that he had a substantial relationship with child). For a criticism of the application of the best interests standard to biological fathers' paternity claims, see Debi McRae, Evaluating the Effectiveness of the Best Interests Marital Presumption of Paternity: Is It Actually in the Best Interests of Children to Divorce the Current Application of the Best Interests Marital Presumption of Paternity?, 5 Whittier J. Child & Fam. Advoc. 345 (2006) (pointing out the dangers of excluding genetic evidence).

Because *Michael H.* was based in large part on judicial reluctance to disrupt an intact marriage, should the presumption be applicable if the married couple has separated or divorced when the putative father makes a claim? See, e.g., Fish v.

Behers, 741 A.2d 721 (Pa. 1999) (holding that presumption of paternity does not apply where husband and wife have divorced, as the underlying policy rationale is not advanced). Should the presumption be applicable if the married couple divorces, and then the mother *remarries* the putative father? See Boone v. Ballinger, 228 S.W.3d 1 (Ky. App. 2007) (holding that the equitable waiver doctrine precludes the biological father, now married to the biological mother, from challenging the parental rights of the former husband, who had been married to the mother at the time of birth and acted as the primary parent).

Reaction to *Michael H.* has been mixed.[6] Some jurisdictions follow *Michael H.* and hold that statutes denying rights to a putative father are constitutional under state or federal constitutions. See, e.g., Aichele v. Hodge, 673 N.W.2d 452 (Mich. Ct. App. 2003); In re Adoption of Baby Girl H., 635 N.W.2d 256 (Neb. 2001). Other jurisdictions hold that such statutes violate state constitutions. See, e.g., Callender v. Skiles, 591 N.W.2d 182 (Iowa 1996) (statute denied putative father due process rights under state constitution); In re J.W.T., 872 S.W.2d 189 (Tex. 1994) (same) (superseded by Tex. Fam. Code Ann. §160.101(a)(3) (West 2002 & Supp. 2008) (replaced with the revised Uniform Parentage Act permitting biological father to contest a claim by presumed father).

Similarly, the legislature and judiciary in California (where *Michael H.* arose) have not been completely receptive to the operation of the presumption. Indeed, several California state courts refused to follow *Michael H.* See, e.g., Steven W. v. Matthew S., 39 Cal. Rptr. 2d 535 (Ct. App. 1995); Comino v. Kelly, 30 Cal. Rptr. 2d 728 (Ct. App. 1994); Brian C. v. Ginger K., 92 Cal. Rptr. 2d 294 (Ct. App. 2000). But cf. In re Jesusa V., 10 Cal. Rptr. 3d 205 (Cal. 2004) (holding that factors supporting husband's claim to be presumed father outweighed those of biological father); Dawn D. v. Superior Court, 72 Cal. Rptr. 2d 871 (Cal. 1998) (relying on *Michael H.* to reject putative father's claim as against husband on the basis that alleged father's "mere desire" to establish parental relationship does not constitute a protected interest).

Also, dissatisfaction with *Michael H.* led the California legislature to amend the conclusive presumption of legitimacy to allow a putative father in some cases (i.e., if the man who is not the husband has received the child into his home and openly held out the child as his child) to move for blood tests within two years of birth (Cal. Fam. Code §7541(b) (West 2004 & Supp. 2008), enacted by Stats. 1992, c. 162 (A.B. 2650), §10, amending former Cal. Evid. Code §621). Currently, eight states (Alabama, Delaware, North Dakota, Oklahoma, Texas, Utah, Washington, and Wyoming) have adopted the new UPA.[7] The new UPA incorporates the two-year limitation on the putative father's ability to request blood tests, subject to estoppel principles that operate to preserve the child's ties to a nonbiological father who held the child out as his. U.P.A. §608.

---

[6] Following the Supreme Court decision, plaintiff Michael Hirschensohn formed an advocacy group for unmarried fathers (Equality Nationwide for Unwed Fathers, or ENUF) and successfully lobbied to change California law. Then, at age 47, Hirschensohn enrolled at the University of West Los Angeles School of Law. Marcia Coyle, After the Gavel Comes Down, Natl. L.J., Feb. 25, 1991, at 1.

[7] UPA, Legislative Fact Sheet, *http://www.nccusl.org/Update/uniformact_factsheets/ uniformacts-fs-upa.asp* (last visited Oct. 15, 2008).

On California paternity law, see Courtney Poel, Fathers Needed: Paternity Not Necessary, 16 J. Contemp. Legal Issues 23 (2007). On unwed fathers' rights generally, see Leslie Joan Harris, A New Paternity Law for the Twenty-First Century: Of Biological, Social Function, Children's Interests, and Betrayal, 44 Willamette L. Rev. 297 (2007); Melanie B. Jacobs, My Two Dads: Disaggregating Biological and Social Paternity, 38 Ariz. St. L.J. 809 (2006); David D. Meyer, Parenthood in a Time of Transition: Tensions Between Legal, Biological, and Social Conceptions of Parenthood, 54 Am. J. Comp. L. 125 (2006).

b. Assisted Reproduction.   Traditionally, if a married woman became pregnant via artificial insemination, statutes provided that the child was treated as the legitimate offspring of the marriage, especially if the artificial insemination occurred with the husband's knowledge or consent. See, e.g., Unif. Parentage Act §5, 9B U.L.A. 301 (1973). Revised UPA provisions apply to nonmarital as well as marital children who are born via assisted reproductive techniques. Specifically, a man is the father of a child created by assisted reproduction if the man "provides sperm for, or consent to, assisted reproduction by a woman with the intent to be the parent of her child." Unif. Parentage Act, §703, 9B U.L.A. 356 (2001 & Supp. 2008). The man must consent in writing "in a record signed by the woman and the man." Id. at §704(a). Failure to provide written consent will not necessarily preclude a finding of paternity, provided that the man resided together in the same household with the woman and child during the first two years of the child's life and the couple openly held out the child as theirs. Id. at §704(b). Thus, the evidentiary fact of "holding out" substitutes for the written consent.

According to the new UPA, a husband who does *not* consent to assisted reproduction before or after the child's birth may challenge paternity. Such a challenge is permitted within two years of the husband's discovery of the child's birth. Id. at §705(a). An exception ("at any time") is permitted to this two-year rule in several circumstances: if the husband did not provide the sperm, the couple has not cohabited since the use of assisted reproduction, and the husband never openly held out the child as his. Id. at §705(b).

Occasionally, an ex-wife may proceed with assisted reproduction *following a divorce.* In such a case, the former husband is not the father of the resulting child unless the man previously provided written consent to postdivorce assisted reproduction. Id. at §706(a). In addition, both a woman and a man have the ability to withdraw consent by so stating in writing. Id. at §706(b). Presumably, such a writing would be filed with the fertility laboratory. Id. (cmt.). The new UPA envisions, therefore, that a child may be without a legally recognized father if the woman's husband establishes nonpaternity by proof of lack of consent to assisted reproduction, if he fails to authorize postdivorce assisted reproduction, or withdraws his consent before placement of eggs, sperm, or embryos.

c. Legitimation.   Although the practice was unknown at common law, states provided mechanisms for a child to be "legitimated" subsequent to birth. Historically, the "legitimated" nonmarital child was placed on an equal legal footing with the marital child. Requirements for legitimation varied from state to state (e.g., marriage after the birth, acknowledgment, etc.).

Beginning in the late 1960s, the United States Supreme Court invalidated state legislation that discriminated against nonmarital children or their parents by denying them benefits granted to legitimate children and their parents.[8] In response, states began abrogating distinctions between illegitimate and legitimate children. See, e.g., N.C. Gen. Stat. §49-15 (2005) (enacted in 1967) ("[A]fter the establishment of paternity of an illegitimate child . . . , the rights, duties, and obligations of the mother and the father so established, with regard to support and custody of the child, shall be the same . . . as if the child were the legitimate child").

Influenced by the original Uniform Parentage Act of 1973, many states adopted rebuttable "presumptions of paternity." That is, presumptions of paternity arose if the child's mother and father married subsequent to the birth (even if the attempted marriage is invalid) (UPA §4(1), (2), (3)); if formal written acknowledgment was properly filed and not disputed by the child's mother within a reasonable time (UPA §4(5)); or based on the father's conduct (i.e., taking the child into his home and holding out the child as his) (UPA §4(4)). The new UPA of 2000, as amended in 2002, revises these methods by requiring a time frame for establishment of paternity by conduct — the reception and holding out must be during the first two years of the child's life (UPA §204(a)(5)) — and by eliminating the acknowledgment requirement because it conflicts with a subsequent UPA provision (Article 3 on Voluntary Acknowledgment of Paternity), under which a valid acknowledgment establishes paternity rather than a presumption of paternity.

Such changes blurred the lines between establishment of paternity (i.e., the biological relationship) and legitimacy (i.e., the legal relationship of father and child). Because law reform effectuated similarities in the effects of paternity acknowledgment, judicial determination of paternity, and legitimation proceedings, most distinctions regarding the consequences of paternity establishment versus legitimation (in terms of such legal rights as custody, inheritance, support, and notice for adoption, for example) have been eliminated.

(3) Births of Nonmarital Children in the United States: Demographics.   In 2006, there were 4,265,996 live births registered in the United States. Of these live births, 38.5 percent were to unmarried women.[9]

Birth rates of nonmarital children differ according to the mother's race and ethnicity. In 2005, the birth rate of nonmarital children to Hispanic women was highest (at 100.3 per 1,000), followed by African-American women (67.8), non-Hispanic white women (30.1), and Asian or Pacific Islander women (24.9).[10]

(4) Support of Nonmarital Children in the United States.   In the United States, absent a statute to the contrary, the mother but not the father was traditionally said to have a common law duty of support for nonmarital children. Allen v. Hunnicut, 52 S.E.2d 18 (N.C. 1949); Baugh v. Maddox, 95 So. 2d 268 (Ala. 1957). The Supreme Court established in Gomez v. Perez, 409 U.S. 535 (1973), that a

---

[8] See, e.g., Glona v. American Guarantee & Liability Ins. Co., 391 U.S. 73 (1968) (holding unconstitutional a statute under which the mother of an illegitimate child was not permitted to recover for her child's wrongful death); Levy v. Louisiana, 391 U.S. 68 (1968) (holding unconstitutional a statute under which illegitimate children were denied the right to recover for the wrongful death of their mother).

[9] National Center for Health Statistics, National Vital Statistics Report, Births: Preliminary Data for 2006, vol. 56, no. 17, Dec. 5, 2007, p. 2.

[10] National Center for Health Statistics, National Vital Statistics Report, Births: Final Data for 2005, vol. 56, no. 6, Dec. 5, 2007, p. 11.

state cannot grant children born within marriage a statutory right to paternal support and maintenance while denying this right to nonmarital children. Today, every state has statutes under which both parents can be compelled to contribute to the support of nonmarital children.

(5) Inheritance Rights Involving Nonmarital Children in the United States.

a. The Nonmarital Child's Right to Inherit from a Father.   The laws in most states traditionally provided that a nonmarital child occupied the same position as a child born within marriage with regard to inheritance rights vis-à-vis the child's *mother.*[11] However, although a father could include a nonmarital child as a named beneficiary in a will, the child would receive nothing if the father died intestate (without a will). The nonmarital child's right to inherit intestate from the biological father was problematic because of concerns about proof of paternity.

In the late 1970s, the United States Supreme Court began examining whether states could impose a higher standard of proof or require particular kinds of proof for nonmarital children to inherit via intestate succession from their fathers. The Court held that, for a nonmarital child to inherit from a noncustodial biological father, a state could require a higher level of proof in the form of a judicial declaration of paternity (Lalli v. Lalli, 439 U.S. 259 (1978)), but could not require that the child's parents subsequently marry after the child's birth (Trimble v. Gordon, 430 U.S. 762 (1977)).

Today, states have expanded the inheritance rights of nonmarital children. Many states have done so by adopting the original UPA, declaring equal treatment for all children without regard to the marital status of their parents so long as the father can be identified by presumptions of parentage. When the Uniform Probate Code underwent substantial revision in 1990, it adopted similar language. UPC §2-114(a). The new UPA, as amended in 2002, reaffirms the original policy of equality of treatment (providing that "A child born to parents who are not married to each other has the same rights under the law as a child born to parents who are married to each other." UPA §202. See generally Ralph C. Brashier, Inheritance Law and the Evolving Family 125-147 (2004).

b. The Parent's Right to Inherit from a Nonmarital Child.   At common law, parents could not inherit *from* their nonmarital children. Because a nonmarital child *was filius nullius* (a child of no one), the child was deemed to have no heirs if the child died without issue. Today, many jurisdictions have liberalized this rule. However, in some states, whereas mothers can inherit from a nonmarital child, fathers must prove that they have supported and acknowledged a nonmarital child to inherit from the child. Do statutes conditioning a father's ability to inherit from his nonmarital child violate the Equal Protection Clause? See Rainey v. Cheever, 510 S.E.2d 823 (Ga. 1999) (so holding). See generally Eleanor Mixon, Note, Deadbeat Dads: Undeserving of the Right to Inherit from Their Illegitimate Children and Undeserving of Equal Protection, 34 Ga. L. Rev. 1773, 1775-1776 (2000).

c. The Child's Right to Inherit from Two Different Fathers.   *Michael H.* reveals that changing norms in the American family are challenging the long-standing assumption that a child can have only one father. Suppose in *Michael H.*

---

[11] See generally Brashier, supra note [3], at 125.

that Michael and Gerald both died intestate (without a will). Victoria unquestionably would have a right to inherit from Gerald based on the marital presumption of legitimacy. Under what circumstances might she also inherit from Michael?

States take different approaches to this question. Some jurisdictions would allow Victoria to inherit from Michael regardless of whether he played a role in her upbringing. Other states preclude a child with a presumed father from establishing a claim to a biological parent — even in cases in which the presumed father did not play a role in the child's upbringing. Megan Pendleton, Intestate Inheritance Claims: Determining a Child's Right to Inherit When Biological and Presumptive Paternity Overlap, 29 Cardozo L. Rev. 2823, 2826 (2008). See also In re Estate of Burden, 53 Cal. Rptr.3d 390 (Ct. App. 2007) (permitting a child to establish rights to his biological father's intestate estate, even though the father did not participate in the child's upbringing or provide financial support, reasoning that the decedent's acknowledgment of paternity satisfied the probate code condition for establishment of a father-child relationship for intestate succession purposes when father "openly held out child as his own").

(6) Identifying the Father: Paternity Proceedings. For support purposes, and sometimes for inheritance purposes, it is important to identify the child's biological father. We have seen that, according to traditional law, there is a presumption applicable to a marital child — in some states irrebuttable — that the mother's husband is the child's father. Now, in a majority of states, the presumption is rebuttable.[12] Paula Roberts, Truth and Consequences: Part I. Disestablishing the Paternity of Non-Marital Children, 37 Fam. L.Q. 35, 36 n.5 (2003). On the other hand, for a child whose mother is not married, the father can be legally identified and made subject to a support obligation through a paternity proceeding.

Paternity actions, rooted in the English bastardy proceeding, historically were quasi-criminal proceedings characterized by short statutes of limitations, proof beyond a reasonable doubt, and trial by jury. Increasing social awareness on the federal level of the problems of child support enforcement prompted a reformulation of these elements. In the 1980s, the United States Supreme Court invalidated several state statutes of limitations on paternity suits. See Clark v. Jeter, 486 U.S. 456 (1988) (six-year statute); Pickett v. Brown, 462 U.S. 1 (1983) (two-year statute); Mills v. Habluetzel, 456 U.S. 91 (1982) (one-year statute). Under federal welfare reform legislation enacted in 1996 (the Personal Responsibility and Work Opportunity Reconciliation Act or PRWORA), states now must allow paternity suits to be brought at any time before the child attains 18 years of age. 42 U.S.C. §666(a)(5)(A) (2000 & Supp. 2005).

Historically, states justified short statutory periods to prevent the filing of stale claims and discourage fraud. Concerns about blackmail and fraudulent claims of paternity have been eliminated, however, by advances in scientific proof of paternity. Formerly, test results were admitted into evidence to exclude a putative father, i.e., the human leukocyte antigens (HLA) blood-test system produced a

---

[12] Federal child support legislation gives states the option of making the presumption rebuttable or conclusive depending on genetic testing results' indicating a threshold probability that the alleged father is the father of the child. 42 U.S.C. §666(a)(5)(G) (2000 & Supp. 2005).

97.3 percent exclusion rate. Today, scientific advances in DNA testing yield a 99 percent probability that a given man is the child's father. Roberts, supra, at 37 n. 16.

Inroads have also been made on several other quasi-criminal elements of paternity establishment. By 1990, many jurisdictions began lowering the standard of proof in determinations of paternity. See, e.g., Rivera v. Minnich, 483 U.S. 574 (1987) (holding that due process was satisfied by a standard of preponderance of the evidence to establish paternity). In addition, federal legislation (explained infra) provides that the parties in paternity procedures are not entitled to a trial by jury. States now commonly view paternity actions as civil proceedings.

Federal welfare reform legislation established new procedures for paternity establishment. According to PRWORA, states must adopt new paternity provisions to receive federal funds for child support enforcement programs and welfare programs. Paternity can be established by: (1) either parent bringing a paternity suit; (2) both parents in a voluntary acknowledgment of paternity.

a. Paternity Suits and Genetic Testing.   According to federal law (42 U.S.C. §§654(20) and 602(a)(2)), either parent may bring a paternity suit at any time until the child attains 18 years of age. Id. at §666(a)(5)(A). On either parent's request (provided that the request is supported by a sworn statement "establishing a reasonable possibility of the requisite sexual contact between the parties") (id. at §666(a)(5)(B)(I)(1), a court must order genetic tests. Paternity is established on the basis of these tests. (If one party refuses to undergo such tests, a court will establish paternity based on other evidence or by default.) Once paternity is established, the court enters an appropriate order that often includes an award of child support. These paternity establishment procedures may create either a rebuttable or a conclusive presumption of paternity (at the state's option). Id. at §666(a)(5)(G).

b. Voluntary Paternity Establishment.   A significant development in paternity establishment is the transformation from judicial proceedings to voluntary affidavits. Beginning in 1992, a few states adopted voluntary programs that targeted mothers at birthing facilities, providing that in-hospital affidavits established a rebuttable presumption of paternity. These programs were so successful that Congress included a requirement in the Omnibus Budget Reconciliation Act of 1993, 42 U.S.C. §666(a)(5)(C) (2000), that all states adopt voluntary paternity establishment programs. PRWORA in 1996 expanded the scope of these programs by providing that (1) a valid, unrescinded, unchallenged acknowledgment of paternity is equivalent to a judicial determination of paternity (rather than merely a presumption of paternity) and is entitled to full faith and credit; (2) parents must be advised of the legal consequences before signing a voluntary acknowledgment; and (3) either parent has the option to rescind within 60 days, but may challenge the voluntary acknowledgment thereafter only judicially and only on limited grounds (fraud, duress, or material mistake of fact). Id. at §666(a)(5). If a parent desires a support order, he or she must petition in a separate proceeding. See Paul K. Legler, The Coming Revolution in Child Support Policy: Implications of the 1996 Welfare Act, 30 Fam. L.Q. 519, 532-534 (1996). The revised UPA of 2002 also complies with the federal mandate by providing for voluntary establishment of paternity and specifies that voluntary affidavits serve as judgments for enforcement purposes. UPA, Article 3 (cmt).

c. Paternity Establishment by Conduct.   Under the original version of the Uniform Parentage Act, paternity could also be established by conduct — i.e., a man's receiving the child (during the child's minority) into his home and openly holding out the child as his own child. UPA §4(a)(4), 9B U.L.A. 295 (2001). Provided that this presumption was not challenged, the man achieved presumed fatherhood status. As previously explained, the revised UPA required such conduct to occur within the first two years of life. UPA §204(a)(5).

Occasionally, a man's conduct might give rise to conflicting presumptions of paternity under the original UPA. For example, whereas one man might enjoy a presumption of paternity arising from having accepted the child into his home and having held the child out as his own, another man might enjoy a presumption of paternity arising from the child's being born during marriage or from genetic testing revealing that he is the child's biological father. The original UPA provided that in the case of competing presumptions, "the presumption which on the facts is founded on the weightier considerations of policy and logic controls." UPA §4(b).

The revised UPA eliminates this manner of resolution of competing presumptions. According to the Prefatory Note to the new UPA: "Nowadays the existence of modern genetic testing obviates this old approach to the problem of conflicting presumptions when a court is to determine paternity." However, under the new UPA, courts may deny requests for genetic testing based on estoppel principles "in the interests of preserving a child's ties to the presumed or acknowledged father who openly held himself out as the child's father regardless of whether he is in fact the genetic father." UPA §608.

d. Interstate Paternity Establishment.   Historically, establishing paternity was difficult when the mother and father resided in different states. Personal jurisdiction could be obtained under a long-arm statute only if the child's father had "minimum contacts" within the state of the mother's residence. In an effort to address this problem, the National Conference of Commissioners on Uniform State Laws promulgated the Uniform Interstate Family Support Act (UIFSA), 9 U.L.A. (pt. IB), 159 (2005 & Supp. 2008), in 1992. UIFSA replaced two previous uniform interstate support acts, the Uniform Reciprocal Enforcement of Support Act (URESA), and the Revised Uniform Reciprocal Enforcement of Support Act (RURESA). UIFSA facilitates interstate enforcement by utilizing long-arm jurisdiction without the necessity for the intervention of a court or agency in the obligor's state (abrogating the reciprocity requirement that was the hallmark of previous legislation), eliminates the possibility of conflicting support orders, and extends recognition to support orders entered by administrative agencies. Federal welfare legislation (PRWORA, discussed infra, pp. 221-225), enacted in 1996, mandates that all states adopt UIFSA as a condition of state eligibility for federal funding of child support enforcement. By 1998 all jurisdictions had complied with the federal mandate. John J. Sampson & Barry J. Brooks, Uniform Interstate Family Support Act (2001) with Prefatory Note and Comments (with Still More Unofficial Annotations), 36 Fam. L.Q. 329, 338 (2002).

UIFSA was amended in 2001. The most important amendments recognize that jurisdictions may extend comity to foreign support orders and, in addition, clarify jurisdictional rules regarding modification of support orders (e.g., providing that nonresident parties may voluntarily agree, even if the parties and child have moved from the issuing state, that the original forum will continue to exercise exclusive jurisdiction to avoid relitigating issues).

Do paternity statutes violate equal protection by permitting a man to be adjudged a father and ordered to pay child support without according him the same parental rights that automatically inure to the mother of that child? See Dubay v. Wells, 506 F.3d 422 (6th Cir. 2007).

e. Paternity Disestablishment.   Many jurisdictions, by either case law or statute, now recognize the disestablishment of paternity, generally on grounds of paternity fraud. Increasingly, former husbands and unwed fathers are seeking to disestablish paternity to avoid child support obligations after genetic testing reveals that their "children" are not biologically related to them. Some states require that the man act within a prescribed time. A few states impose criminal penalties for those women who intentionally establish the paternity of the wrong man. Paula Roberts, Part III, Who Pays When Paternity Is Disestablished?, 37 Fam. L.Q. 69, 69 (2003). Are these approaches sound policy?

Should a father be permitted to disestablish paternity if he has *already* assumed the role of the child's father? Courts sometimes deny a parent's disestablishment claim based on principles of equitable estoppel. See, e.g., Hubbard v. Hubbard, 44 P.3d 153 (Alaska 2002). Other courts bar paternity disestablishment based on res judicata principles — i.e., the divorce decree or child support order establishing paternity is regarded as a final judgment. See, e.g., People v. R.L.C., 47 P.3d 327 (Colo. 2002). See also Paula Roberts, Part II: Questioning the Paternity of Marital Children, 37 Fam. L.Q. 55 (2003).

If a father is permitted to disestablish paternity, who becomes responsible for child support? The biological father? The state? Can the presumed father recover past child support from the biological father or the state? See, e.g., R.A.C. v. P.J.S, 927 A.2d 97 (N.J. 2007) (holding that presumed father cannot seek child support reimbursement from the biological father, and declining to apply equitable tolling to the state Parentage Act); Bouchard v. Frost, 840 A.2d 109 (Me. 2004) (holding that sovereign immunity barred father's recovery of support payments to state agency). See generally Andrew S. Epstein, Note, The Parent Trap: Should a Man Be Allowed to Recoup Child Support Payments if He Discovers He Is Not the Biological Father of the Child?, 42 Brandeis L.J. 655 (2004).

Although disestablishment of paternity terminates the current obligation to pay child support, some jurisdictions are reluctant to discharge *child support arrearages.* Roberts, Part III, supra, at 73. What policy reasons support such judicial reluctance?

(7) *Nonmarital Children and Other Dependency Benefits.* In a variety of contexts, benefits may be available to a child because the decedent is the parent. For example, dependency benefits may be available to a child under a pension plan, or a governmental program (e.g., the Social Security Act, 42 U.S.C. §§301-1397f (2000 & Supp. 2005)), or a statute (e.g., as the Copyright Act, 17 U.S.C. §§101-1101 (2000)). Thus, in a variety of areas it is important to determine whether a young person is a "child" or a "dependent" of a particular adult. These issues can be particularly troublesome for nonmarital children, as illustrated here:

a. May a nonmarital child recover for the wrongful death of the father under a state wrongful death statute? Does barring a nonmarital child from recovery violate equal protection? See Levy v. Louisiana, 391 U.S. 68 (1968); Brookbank v. Gray, 658 N.E.2d 724 (Ohio 1996) (so holding). Conversely, should parents of a nonmarital child be able to recover for the wrongful death of the child? Does barring such a parent from recovery violate the right to equal protection? See Glona v. American Guarantee & Liability Ins. Co., 391 U.S. 73 (1968) (so holding).

b. May a nonmarital child recover under a state workers' compensation act? Does barring a nonmarital child from recovery violate equal protection? See Weber v. Aetna Casualty & Surety Co., 406 U.S. 164 (1972) (so holding); Findaya W., by and through Theresa W. v. A.-T.E.A.M. Co., 546 N.W.2d 61 (Neb. 1996) (holding that requiring nonmarital children to prove actual dependency on decedent while presuming dependency for legitimate children violates the right to equal protection).

c. May a mother of a nonmarital child be denied "mother's insurance benefits" because she was never married to the wage earner on whom her claim is based? Would a denial of these benefits violate equal protection? See Califano v. Boles, 443 U.S. 282 (1979) (holding constitutional a Social Security Act provision granting "mother's benefits" to a widow or divorced wife but not to the mother of the deceased's nonmarital child because Congress could reasonably conclude that the mother of the nonmarital child was less likely to be a dependent).

d. The Social Security Act provides death benefits for minor dependents of a decedent wage earner. For children born within the marriage, the Act simply assumes the requisite dependency. However, benefits are available to nonmarital children: (1) who would be entitled to take an intestate share of the deceased's property under the laws of the state in which the decedent resided at death; (2) who have been acknowledged in writing; (3) where the insured was subject to a child support order; or (4) where there is sufficient evidence to demonstrate that the father was living with the child or contributing to the child's support. 42 U.S.C. §§416(h)(2), (3) (2000). Do such provisions violate the nonmarital child's right to equal protection? See, e.g., Mathews v. Lucas, 427 U.S. 495 (1976) (upholding differential treatment of nonmarital children against an equal protection attack based on rational basis review).

On the issue of whether posthumous children who are conceived after the father's death qualify for Social Security survivor's benefits, see Gillett-Netting v. Barnhart, infra, p. 207.

(8) Nonmarital Children and Immigration Status. Nonmarital children merit special treatment in immigration law. In Nguyen v. INS, 533 U.S. 53 (2001), a nonmarital child (Nguyen) born to a Vietnamese mother and American father faced deportation following a criminal conviction for sexual assault. His deportation order was pursuant to an immigration provision (8 U.S.C. §1409) that specified different requirements for the acquisition of citizenship by nonmarital children born to an alien mother and a citizen father compared to nonmarital children born to an alien father and citizen mother. Nguyen and his father alleged that the provision violated the Equal Protection Clause by imposing stricter requirements for nonmarital children with citizen fathers. The Supreme Court rejected their argument, reasoning that the stricter provisions for establishment of citizenship in cases involving a citizen father served important governmental

interests (i.e., facilitating the identification of a parent–child relationship and ensuring that parent and child have the opportunity to develop a significant relationship). See generally Aubry Holland, Comment, The Modern Family Unit: Toward a More Inclusive Vision of the Family in Immigration Law, 96 Calif. L. Rev. 1049 (2008).

The application of paternity laws to same-sex couples is discussed below.

B. THE PARENTAL SUPPORT OBLIGATION

The introductory materials suggest that at common law in England there was some question whether there was a legal (as opposed to a moral) obligation to support minor children. Today, the legal nature of the parental support obligation is plain. Statutes in every jurisdiction impose a duty of support on *both* parents to support their minor children.

Disputes relating to child support arise in a variety of circumstances and in many different legal contexts. A parent who is not living with a child (typically the father) may be ordered by a court to make periodic payments (typically to the mother) to defer the costs of supporting the child. The parents may or may not have ever been married, or even lived together. The absent parent may have deserted the child or may be apart because of parental divorce or separation not of his or her choosing. Both civil and criminal sanctions may be imposed on a noncustodial parent in a variety of proceedings for the failure to make required child support payments.

Today, imposition of the duty of child support is complicated by the rise of diverse family forms as well as the increasing use of assisted reproduction. The cases in this chapter highlight the variety of proceedings and contexts as they relate to child support. *Yale Diagnostic,* supra, involves the common law "necessaries" doctrine and a creditor's claim against the parents. *Elisa B.* and *Harmon,* infra, are cases in which a child support issue arose in the context of dissolution of the parental relationship (a same-sex relationship in one case and a marital relationship in the other). Wallis v. Smith explores the issue of a father's obligation to pay child support when the mother has committed contraceptive fraud. *Gillett-Netting,* infra, raises the issue of the inheritance rights of children who were conceived and born after their father's death.

1.   Who Has the Legal Duty of Support?

Elisa B. v. Superior Court
117 P.3d 660 (Cal. 2005)

MORENO, J. . . .

On June 7, 2001, the El Dorado County District Attorney filed a complaint in superior court to establish that Elisa B. is a parent of two-year-old twins Kaia B.

and Ry B., who were born to Emily B., and to order Elisa to pay child support. [Elisa denied being the twins' parent.] Elisa testified that she entered into a lesbian relationship with Emily in 1993. They began living together six months later. Elisa obtained a tattoo that read "Emily, por vida," which in Spanish means Emily, for life. They introduced each other to friends as their "partner," exchanged rings, opened a joint bank account, and believed they were in a committed relationship.

Elisa and Emily discussed having children and decided that they both wished to give birth. Because Elisa earned more than twice as much money as Emily, they decided that Emily "would be the stay-at-home mother" and Elisa "would be the primary breadwinner for the family." At a sperm bank, they chose a donor they both would use so the children would "be biological brothers and sisters." [Each attended the other's insemination procedures, prenatal medical appointments, labor, and delivery.] Elisa gave birth to Chance in November, 1997, and Emily gave birth to Ry and Kaia prematurely in March, 1998. Ry had medical problems; he suffered from Down's Syndrome, and required heart surgery.

They jointly selected the children's names, joining their surnames with a hyphen to form the children's surname. They each breast fed all of the children. Elisa claimed all three children as her dependents on her tax returns and obtained a life insurance policy on herself naming Emily as the beneficiary so that if "anything happened" to her, all three children would be "cared for." Elisa believed the children would be considered both of their children.

Elisa's parents referred to the twins as their grandchildren and her sister referred to the twins as part of their family and referred to Elisa as their mother. Elisa treated all of the children as hers and told a prospective employer that she had triplets. Elisa and Emily identified themselves as coparents of Ry at an organization arranging care for his Down's Syndrome.

Elisa supported the household financially. Emily was not working. Emily testified that she would not have become pregnant if Elisa had not promised to support her financially, but Elisa denied that any financial arrangements were discussed before the birth of the children. Elisa later acknowledged in her testimony, however, that Emily "was going to be an at-home mom for maybe a couple of years and then the kids were going to go into day care and she was going to return to work."

They consulted an attorney regarding adopting "each other's child," but never did so. Nor did they register as domestic partners or execute a written agreement concerning the children. Elisa stated she later reconsidered adoption because she had misgivings about Emily adopting Chance.

Elisa and Emily separated in November, 1999. Elisa promised to support Emily and the twins "as much as I possibly could" and initially paid the mortgage payments [and later the rent for Emily and the twins. Then she stopped providing such support.] At the time of trial, Elisa was earning $95,000 a year. . . .

We must determine whether the Court of Appeal erred [in ruling under California's version of the original Uniform Parentage Act (UPA), Cal. Fam. Code §7600 et seq.] that Elisa could not be a parent of the twins born to her lesbian partner, and thus had no obligation to support them. . . . The UPA defines the " '[p]arent and child relationship' " as "the legal relationship existing between a child and the child's natural or adoptive parents. . . . The term includes the mother and child relationship and the father and child relationship" (§7601). One purpose of the UPA was to eliminate distinctions based upon whether a child was born into a marriage, and thus was "legitimate," or was born to unmarried parents, and thus was "illegitimate." Thus, the UPA provides that . . . : "The parent and child relationship extends equally to every child and to every parent, regardless of the marital status of the parents" (§7602.) . . .

Section 7611 provides several circumstances in which "[a] man is presumed to be the natural father of a child," including: if he is the husband of the child's mother, is not impotent or sterile, and was cohabiting with her (§7540); if he signs a voluntary declaration of paternity stating he is the "biological father of the child" (§7574, subd. (b)(6)); and if "[h]e receives the child into his home and openly holds out the child as his natural child" (§7611, subd. (d)). [Although] the UPA contains separate provisions defining who is a mother and who is a father, it expressly provides that in determining the existence of a mother and child relationship, "[i]nsofar as practicable, the provisions of this part applicable to the father and child relationship apply." (§7650.)

The Court of Appeal correctly recognized that, under the UPA, Emily has a parent and child relationship with each of the twins because she gave birth to them. (§7610, subd. (a)). . . . Relying upon our statement in Johnson v. Calvert, [851 P.2d 776 (Cal. 1993)], that "for any child California law recognizes only one natural mother," the Court of Appeal reasoned that Elisa, therefore, could not also be the natural mother of the twins and thus "has no legal maternal relationship with the children under the UPA."

The Attorney General, appearing pursuant to section 17406 to "represent the public interest in establishing, modifying, and enforcing support obligations," argues that the Court of Appeal erred, stating: "*Johnson*'s one-natural-mother comment cannot be thoughtlessly interpreted to deprive the child of same-sex couples the same opportunity as other children to two parents and to two sources of child support when only two parties are eligible for parentage." As we shall explain, the Attorney General is correct that our statement in *Johnson* that a child can have "only one natural mother" does not mean that both Elisa and Emily cannot be parents of the twins [because this case is distinguishable].

We perceive no reason why both parents of a child cannot be women. That result now is possible under the current version of the domestic partnership statutes [providing that: "The rights and obligations of registered domestic partners with respect to a child of either of them shall be the same as those of spouses." Cal. Fam. Code §297.5(d)]. Prior to the effective date of the current domestic partnership statutes, we recognized in an adoption case that a child can have two parents, both of whom are women. [Sharon S. v. Superior Court, 73 P.3d 554 (Cal. 2003).] If both parents of an adopted child can be women, we see no reason why the twins in the present case cannot have two parents, both of whom are women.

[W]e proceed to examine the UPA to determine whether Elisa is a parent to the twins in addition to Emily. . . . Subdivision (d) of section 7611 states that a man is presumed to be the natural father of a child if "[h]e receives the child into his home and openly holds out the child as his natural child." The Court of Appeal in [In re Karen C., 124 Cal. Rptr.2d 677 (Ct. App. 2002)], held that subdivision (d) of section 7611 "should apply equally to women." [W]e must determine whether Elisa received the twins into her home and openly held them out as her natural children [pursuant to Cal. Fam. Code §7611]. There is no doubt that Elisa satisfied the first part of this test. . . . Our inquiry focuses, therefore, on whether she openly held out the twins as her natural children.

The circumstance that Elisa has no genetic connection to the twins does not necessarily mean that she did not hold out the twins as her "natural" children under section 7611. . . . It is undisputed that Elisa actively consented to, and participated in, the artificial insemination of her partner with the understanding that the resulting child or children would be raised by Emily and her as coparents, and they did act as coparents for a substantial period of time. Elisa received the twins into her home and held them out to the world as her natural children. . . . Rebutting the presumption that Elisa is the twins' parent would leave them with only one parent and would deprive them of the support of their second parent. Because Emily is financially unable to support the twins, the financial burden of supporting the twins would be borne by the county, rather than Elisa.

In establishing a system for a voluntary declaration of paternity in section 7570, the Legislature declared: "There is a compelling state interest in establishing paternity for all children. Establishing paternity is the first step toward a child support award, which, in turn, provides children with equal rights and access to benefits, including, but not limited to, social security, health insurance, survivors' benefits, military benefits, and inheritance rights. . . ." By recognizing the value of determining paternity, the Legislature implicitly recognized the value of having two parents, rather than one, as a source of both emotional and financial support, especially when the obligation to support the child would otherwise fall to the public. . . .

Although Elisa presently is unwilling to accept the obligations of parenthood, this was not always so. . . . We conclude, therefore, that Elisa is a presumed mother of the twins under section 7611, subdivision (d). . . .

Wallis v. Smith
22 P.3d 682 (N.M. Ct. App. 2001)

BOSSON, Judge.

. . . [Peter] Wallis and [Kellie Rae] Smith began an intimate, sexual relationship some time before April 1997. They discussed contraceptive techniques and agreed that Smith would use birth control pills. Wallis and Smith further agreed that their sexual intimacy would last only as long as Smith continued to take birth control pills because Wallis made it clear that he did not want to father a child. Wallis participated in contraception only passively; he relied on Smith to use birth control and took no precautions himself.

As time went by, Smith changed her mind. She chose to stop taking birth control pills, but never informed Wallis of her decision. Wallis continued their intimate relationship, and Smith became pregnant. Smith carried the fetus to term and gave birth to a normal, healthy girl on November 27, 1998. [Wallis sued Smith for money damages, asserting four causes of action — fraud, breach of contract, conversion, and prima facie tort. The district court dismissed for failure to state a claim on which relief may be granted. Wallis appealed.]

Wallis alleges that he has suffered, and will continue to suffer, substantial economic injury as a proximate result of his unintended fatherhood because New Mexico law requires him to pay child support for the next eighteen years. See NMSA 1978, §40-11-15 (1997). Due to his statutory obligations, Wallis asserts that he has been injured by Smith's conduct, and requests compensatory and punitive damages from her. The district court determined that public policy prohibited the relief sought by Wallis, and dismissed the case with prejudice.

Contraceptive Fraud

. . . At the onset of our discussion it is important to distinguish the factual allegations of this case from other kinds of related lawsuits, and thus underscore the limited reach of this opinion. Wallis's complaint is not about sexually-transmitted disease, e.g., McPherson v. McPherson, 712 A.2d 1043 (Me. 1998), nor does it concern the damages arising from an unwanted pregnancy that led to an abortion, e.g., Alice D. v. William M., 450 N.Y.S.2d 350 (Civ. Ct. 1982), or an undesired pregnancy resulting in medical complications, e.g., Barbara A. v. John G., 193 Cal. Rptr. 422 (Ct. App. 1983). This case is not even brought to recover the expense of giving birth. E.g., Chrystal R.M. v. Charlie A.L., 459 S.E.2d 415, 417 (W. Va. 1995); see also §40-11-15(C) (providing recovery for the "reasonable expenses of the mother's pregnancy, birth and confinement"). Wallis's complaint is limited to compensatory damages for the "economic injury" of supporting a normal, healthy child.

Although Wallis insists that he is not attempting to circumvent his child support obligations, we cannot agree. It is self-evident that he seeks to recover for the very financial loss caused him by the statutory obligation to pay child support. At oral argument when pressed by the Court to clarify what damages Wallis was seeking, his counsel stated that Wallis was seeking not punitive, but compensatory damages measured by his "out of pocket loss." Therefore, this case boils down to whether sound public policy would permit our courts to require Smith to indemnify Wallis for child support under the circumstances of this case.

Our legislature has spoken to the public policy that governs the economic consequences of sexual relationships that produce children, and that policy is reflected in New Mexico child support laws. See NMSA 1978, §§40-11-1 to-23 (1986, as amended through 1997). In 1986, our legislature adopted, with minor revisions, the Uniform Parentage Act (UPA), which outlines the legal procedure to establish a parent–child relationship and the corresponding obligation of child support. See 1986 N.M. Laws, ch. 47, §§1-23; Unif. Parentage Act §§1-30, 9B U.L.A. 287 (West 1987). The UPA imposes a form of strict liability for child support, without regard to which parent bears the greater responsibility for the child's being.

Making each parent financially responsible for the conception and birth of children also illuminates a strong public policy that makes paramount the interests of the child. Our jurisprudence has abandoned the notion that the father of an "illegitimate" child could decline to accept the financial responsibility of raising that child. . . . Placing a duty of support on each parent has the added benefit of insulating the state from the possibility of bearing the financial burden for a child. In our view, it is difficult to harmonize the legislative concern for the child, reflected in the immutable duty of parental support, with Wallis's effort in this lawsuit to shift financial responsibility for his child solely to the mother.

New Mexico is not alone in its view of parental responsibility and the conflict created by lawsuits such as this. To our knowledge, no jurisdiction recognizes contraceptive fraud or breach of promise to practice birth control as a ground for adjusting a natural parent's obligation to pay child support. . . .

Some courts have dismissed contraceptive fraud cases on the ground that the claims tread too far into the realm of an individual's privacy interests. [Stephen K. v. Roni L., 164 Cal. Rptr. 618 (Ct. App. 1980).] We agree that individuals are entitled a sphere of privacy into which courts should not tread. A person's choice whether or not to use contraceptives understandably fits into this sphere. We also believe that the "privacy interests involved . . . require a cautious approach," and therefore we elect to rely primarily on the prevailing public policy of child support, while at the same time recognizing the serious privacy concerns implicated and threatened by the underlying lawsuit.

Wallis's attempt to apply traditional contract and tort principles to his contraceptive agreement is unconvincing and, in the end, futile. The contract analogy fails because children, the persons for whose benefit child support guidelines are enacted, have the same needs regardless of whether their conception violated a promise between the parents. Further, a parent being sued for causing the conception and birth of a child is no ordinary tortfeasor; a defendant under these circumstances is legally entitled to collect financial support on behalf of the child. We will not re-enter the jurisprudence of illegitimacy by allowing a parent to opt out of the financial consequences of his or her sexual relationships just because they were unintended. Nor will we recognize a cause of action that trivializes one's personal responsibility in sexual relationships. Indeed, permitting "such actions while simultaneously encouraging paternity actions for support flies in the face of all reason." [Welzenbach v. Powers, 660 A.2d 1133 (N.H. 1995).] We also observe that if Wallis did not desire children, he was free and able to practice contraceptive techniques on his own.

Wallis tries to make the basis for liability not so much the birth of the child, but the fact that Smith lied, and perpetrated a fraud on him. But not all misrepresentations are actionable. . . . Finally, Wallis argues that our courts have recognized tort claims which measure damages by the economic injury of supporting an unwanted child. See Lovelace Med. Ctr. v. Mendez, 111 N.M. 336, 345, 805 P.2d 603, 612 (1991) [holding that a couple who sought to protect their financial resources by limiting the size of their family through sterilization could sue a negligent physician for economic damages measured by the cost of raising an additional child to the age of majority]. Because *Lovelace* does not speak to the issue of inter-parental liability, which is the crux of Wallis's appeal, it has no bearing on our decision.

Accordingly, we hold that the actions asserted here cannot be used to recoup the financial obligations of raising a child. . . .

Harmon v. Department of Social Services
951 P.2d 770 (Wash. 1998)

GUY, Justice.

. . . Appellant Edward Harmon married Darlene Dooley in 1985. At that time Darlene was the custodial parent of two daughters, ages eight and nine years old, who were born during her marriage to Tom Dooley. After living with their mother and stepfather for almost seven years, both children left the Harmon home in February 1992 and moved into the home of their father and stepmother, Tom and Linda Dooley.

On March 31,1992, the superior court modified custody of the children, ordering the primary residential placement of the children be changed from the mother's home to the father's home. The modification order did not address child support. In April 1992, the children's father requested the Department of Social and Health Services (hereafter Department) to calculate and collect support payments for the children. . . . The Administrative Law Judge (ALJ) determined the mother was permanently disabled and had no ability to earn income. Based on this state's child support schedule, RCW 26.19.020, the ALJ ordered the mother to pay $25 per child per month. Shortly after the proceeding against the mother was concluded, the Department served the stepfather, Appellant Edward Harmon, with a "Notice and Finding of Financial Responsibility."

[B]ased on the net incomes of the stepfather and father, the ALJ computed the stepfather's total monthly support obligation (should he be found to be liable on appeal) to be $486.10. The stepfather is disabled and unemployed. His monthly net income of $1,320.20 is received from Department of Labor and Industries and Social Security Administration disability payments. [The stepfather appealed.]

Does RCW 26.16.205 impose an obligation upon a stepparent which is equal to that of the natural mother and father for the purpose of calculating and paying child support for stepchildren who have moved from the stepparent's home?

[RCW 26.16.205, the family expense statute that dates from 1881] was enacted in derogation of the common law, under which a husband was primarily responsible and a wife only secondarily responsible for the expenses of the family. Under this statute, a mother and a father were equally obligated for the necessary expenses of child rearing, and this obligation survived the termination of the marriage. [The statute] remained unchanged for nearly 90 years, until 1969, when, at the request of the Department of Public Assistance, the law was amended as follows:

> The expenses of the family and the education of the children, *including stepchildren,* are chargeable upon the property of both husband and wife, or either of them, and in relation thereto they may be sued jointly or separately: *PROVIDED, That with regard to stepchildren, the obligation shall cease upon the termination of the relationship of husband and wife.*

The Department explained to the Legislature that the purpose of the [amendment] was to comply with federal regulations governing allocation of federal public assistance funds to the State. In determining eligibility for public assistance, the Department treated a child who lived with a stepparent and one of his or her parents in the same manner as it treated a child who lived with both natural parents. [F]ederal regulations required that all stepparents, not just those on public assistance, be treated the same, under a law of general application. . . .

The Legislature again amended RCW 26.16.205 in 1990. [The amended statute provides:]

> The expenses of the family and the education of the children, including stepchildren, are chargeable upon the property of both husband and wife, or either of them, and they may be sued jointly or separately. When a petition for dissolution of marriage or a petition for legal separation is filed, the court may, upon motion of the stepparent, terminate the obligation to support the stepchildren. The obligation to support stepchildren shall cease upon the entry of a decree of dissolution, decree of legal separation, or death.

. . . In the present case, the Court of Appeals held that while RCW 26.16.205 does not, in clear and unambiguous language, set forth a new rule redefining how the stepparent's duty of support arises, "the statute does, in clear and unambiguous language, redefine the events that terminate the duty of support once it has arisen: 'entry of a decree of dissolution, decree of legal separation, or death.' " [Harmon v. Dept. of Soc. & Health Servs., 922 P.2d 201 (Wash. Ct. App. 1996)].

With this background in mind, we begin our analysis of the issue before us. . . . One of the overriding policies and a standard of the statewide child support schedule is that the obligation to support a child should be equitably apportioned between the parents of the child. Another aim of the law is to provide uniformity throughout the state for calculating support obligations. To that end, the law requires worksheets and instructions that must be used in every case. . . . The basic child support obligation is determined under Part I and is based on the monthly incomes of the parents of the child whose support is being determined. Once the combined net monthly income is determined pursuant to RCW 26.19.071, a presumptive amount of child support is calculated, based on the child support economic table contained in RCW 26.19.020.

RCW 26.19.071(1) sets the standard for determining the income, upon which the basic child support obligation is based, as follows: All income and resources of each parent's household shall be disclosed and considered by the court when the court determines the child support obligation of each parent. *Only the income of the parents of the children whose support is at issue shall be calculated for purposes of calculating the basic support obligation. Income and resources of any other person shall not be included in calculating the basic support obligation.* (Emphasis added.)

A new spouse's, or stepparent's, income must be listed under Part VI (Additional Factors for Consideration) but may not be used to calculate the presumptive basic support obligation. In the present case, under the child support statute, only the mother's income and the father's income should have been used to determine the presumptive basic support obligation.

A court may deviate from the presumptive amount, but deviations are the exception to the rule and should not be used routinely. Additionally, the income of a new spouse is not, by itself, a sufficient reason for deviation. RCW 26.19.075(1)(a)(i).

In making its recommendation to the Legislature, the Child Support Schedule Commission considered the use of the support schedule in families involving stepparents. The Commission reported to the Legislature that it was guided in part by the principle that the child support schedule "should not create extraneous negative effects on the major life decisions of either parent. The schedule should avoid creating economic disincentives for remarriage. . . ." Report at 8. . . . In a special report on the use of the schedule for blended families, the Commission recommended that the "income of spouses [of the child's parents] should be disregarded in any formula approach." Washington State Child Support Schedule Comm'n Rep. On Use of Support Schedule for Blended Families 3 (Dec. 1989). [The Legislature accepted the Commission's recommendations.]

Two questions are considered in our analysis. The first is whether the statute imposes a child support obligation on a stepparent that is equal to that of the child's parents. The second is whether the statute provides the only means of ending whatever obligation is created by RCW 26.16.205. We answer both questions in the negative.

First, to interpret the family expense statute in a manner that makes stepparents equally responsible, with parents, for child support would require us to disregard the language and the impact of our child support schedule and to judicially create an exception to RCW 26.19. We cannot construe RCW 26.16.205 to conflict with the language or the purposes of RCW 26.19.

The family expense statute is not a child support statute but, rather, a statute that makes both parties to a marriage equally responsible for the necessary expenses of the family. The family includes stepchildren who are part of the family unit, who reside in the family home, or who are in the residential care of one of the adults in this family unit. It does not include children who are in the primary residential care of the other parent.

With respect to the language regarding termination of a stepparent's obligation under the family expense statute, we believe the Legislature intended only to distinguish between parents and stepparents to the extent that the obligation, once assumed, would not continue for stepparents beyond the termination of the marriage. The parent's obligation for the support of a child continues and is not dependent on the continuation of the marital relationship. The provision for terminating a stepparent's obligation under the statute is not the exclusive means for terminating the obligation. Notwithstanding the statute's specific and limiting language, any support obligation for a child may terminate when the child reaches the age of majority, is married, emancipated or otherwise no longer dependent. Because we hold the stepfather in this appeal was not primarily liable for the support of his wife's children after the court ordered the placement of the children be changed to their father, we do not determine what other ways the obligations that arise under the family expense statute might terminate. . . .

NOTES AND QUESTIONS: WHO SHOULD HAVE THE SUPPORT OBLIGATION?

(1) Biological or Social Relationship as the Basis for Child Support.   Children of same-sex couples challenge traditional notions of child support obligations based on biological relationships. Historically, the legal obligation to pay child support was entwined with paternity establishment. For a nonmarital child, a court order establishes paternity as well as child support. Alternatively, paternity of a nonmarital child can be established through voluntary acknowledgment (and child support orders sometimes follow). For a marital child, both parents have the duty of support during the marriage; on dissolution, the divorce court generally awards child support. As we have seen, competing claims of paternity may arise *(Michael H.*, supra). Increasingly, competing claims of maternity are emerging. Competing claims of either paternity or maternity have implications for child support obligations.

Should the child support obligation be based on an adult's biological or social relationship to the child? Should either relationship alone be enough? Should the child support obligation be based on the parties' relationship (i.e., marriage or domestic partnership)? A few states (e.g., California, Connecticut, Hawaii, Maine, New Hampshire, New Jersey, Oregon, Vermont, and Washington) now confer legal rights on domestic partners provided that the couple registers as such. In *Elisa B.*, were Elisa and Emily domestic partners according to California law? Should that fact make a difference in the court's determination? Should registration be a prerequisite to the imposition of liability for child support for same-sex couples? See Grace Ganz Blumberg, Legal Recognition of Same-Sex Conjugal Relationships: The 2003 California Domestic Partner Rights and Responsibilities Act in Comparative Civil Rights and Family Law Perspective, 51 UCLA L. Rev. 1555 (2004) (advocating recognition of registered and stable unregistered cohabitation). To what extent does a system that turns on the formal actions of adults, such as registering as domestic partners, replicate the inequality problems that the traditional preference for marital children created?

Massachusetts became the first state to permit same-sex marriage. See Goodridge v. Department of Pub. Health, 798 N.E.2d 941 (Mass. 2003). In 2008, supreme courts in California and Connecticut also legalized same-sex marriage. See In re Marriage Cases, 183 P.3d 384 (Cal. 2008); Kerrigan v. Commissioner of Public Health, 957 A.2d 407 (Conn. 2008). Subsequently, California voters approved an amendment to the state constitution (Proposition 8) to ban same-sex marriage. Gay rights advocates filed suit, contending that Proposition 8 could not be enacted as an initiative amendment, but rather only by a constitutional "revision," thereby requiring either a two-thirds vote of the legislature (rather than a simple majority popular vote) or a state Constitutional Convention. Strauss v. Horton, No. S168047 (Cal. filed Nov. 5, 2008). If the couple in the principal case had been married, how would that fact have altered the result?

As *Elisa B.* reveals, courts increasingly are wrestling with the resolution of disputes involving parental rights (child support as well as custody and visitation) on the dissolution of same-sex relationships. Some courts, like *Elisa B.*, apply the UPA's paternity provisions to former lesbian partners. Which provision(s) of the UPA does *Elisa B.* apply? Why? What are the advantages and disadvantages of this approach? How might the application of the UPA differ for members of lesbian versus gay relationships? If genetic evidence is increasingly permitted to rebut parentage presumptions, what will that development signify for same-sex couples?

Is the recognition of a same-sex partner's parental status a prerequisite to the imposition of a child support obligation? Conversely, does the contribution of financial support ensure recognition of a same-sex partner's parental status on dissolution of the relationship? See Wakeman v. Dixon, 921 So.2d 669 (Fla. Dist. Ct. App. 2006) (holding that partners' coparenting agreements were unenforceable, even though former partner had supported and been a de facto parent of the children); A.H. v. M.P., A.H. v. M.P., Mass., 857 N.E.2d 1061 (Mass. 2006) (holding that a partner's financial contribution to the family was a parenting function that did not rise to the level of creating "de facto" parental status). See generally Caroline P. Blair, It's More Than a One-Night Stand: Why a Promise to Parent Should Obligate a Former Lesbian Partner to Pay Child Support in the Absence of a Statutory Requirement, 39 Suffolk L. Rev. 465 (2006). For discussion of custody and visitation issues involving same-sex couples, see Chapter 5.

Does *Elisa B.* suggest that two parents are always better than one? To what extent is the two-parent preference based on economic issues? Might *more* than two parents be better still? See Jacob v. Schultz-Jacob, 923 A.2d 473 (Pa. Super. Ct. 2007) (holding that a child could have three parents subject to parental rights and responsibilities, including the lesbian partners who raised the child and the sperm donor who was involved in their lives). A Canadian court of appeal reached the same conclusion in A.A. v. B.B., 83 O.R.3d 561 (2007). See generally Laura Nicole Althouse, Three's Company? How American Law Can Recognize a Third Social Parent, in Same-Sex Headed Families, 19 Hastings L.J. 171 (2007).

(2) Mother's Refusal to Enforce Support.   Suppose a mother does not choose to enforce the support obligation against the father (or her partner, as the case may be). Does the child have a right to child support from that party nonetheless? Should it matter whether the mother would otherwise require public assistance to support the child? Does it affect your opinion regarding Elisa's support obligation to learn that Emily's baby, who was premature and had Down's syndrome, required considerable medical assistance?

(3) Child Support Obligations of Gamete Donors.   The original Uniform Parentage Act (§5b) provided that a sperm donor was not considered the child's natural father (and therefore was relieved of parental obligations such as child support liability) if he donated sperm to a licensed physician for purposes of insemination of a married woman who was not the donor's wife. The revised UPA of 2002 (§702) flatly provides that "A donor is not a parent of a child conceived by means of assisted reproduction." The new provision thereby eliminates the requirements that the sperm donation be made to a licensed physician and inseminated in a married woman (because of concerns about protecting the procreative rights of the unmarried). Further, intent to be a parent under the revised UPA is determinative: The father–child relationship is established if a man provides sperm for, or consents to, assisted reproduction by a woman with the *intent to be the parent* of her child (§703).

How would the revised UPA provisions apply to the determination of the support obligations of a man who donates sperm to a lesbian couple? Does it matter if he is an anonymous donor or a known party? Would it matter if the donor decides to assume a parental role toward the ensuing child? See Mintz v. Zoernig, 198 P.3d 861 (N.M. Ct. App. 2008) (holding that a known sperm donor who agreed with lesbian partners that he would serve merely as a male role model for their child cannot disavow his support obligation despite the parties' agreement that he have no financial obligations).

Cases involving disputed maternity sometimes also arise. For example, suppose one same-sex partner serves as the egg donor but the other partner carries the resulting embryo. When the child is born, who is (are) the child's mother(s)? Which parent or parents bear(s) responsibility for child support? What light on this issue is shed by new UPA §106: "Provisions of this [Act] relating to determination of paternity apply to determinations of maternity"? See also K.M. v. E.G., 117 P.3d 673 (Cal. 2005) (holding that a woman who had donated her eggs so that her former lesbian partner could bear a child was a parent of the resulting twins, reasoning that the woman's genetic relationship to the twins constituted evidence of a mother–child relationship under the UPA).

(4) Contraceptive Fraud. Should a father's child support obligations be affected by the fact that the mother deceived him about her use of birth control? *Wallis* illustrates the general rule that the mother's contraceptive fraud does not serve as a defense to a father's support obligation. See also L. Pamela P. v. Frank S., 449 N.E.2d 713 (N.Y. Ct. App. 1983). Should the father be permitted to maintain a tort action for fraud or infliction of emotional distress instead? See Day v. Heller, 653 N.W.2d 475 (Neb. 2002) (rejecting husband's suit). Should support obligations in cases of fraud, if not dismissed, at least be reduced?

Should the mother's wrongful conduct *ever* relieve the father of liability for child support? That is, should the general rule apply when the woman acquires the "purloined sperm" from (a) a man who is unconscious? See, e.g., S.F. v. State ex rel. T.M., 695 So. 2d 1186 (Ala. Civ. App. 1996); (b) a male who is a victim of statutory rape? See, e.g., State ex rel. Hermesmann v. Seyer, 847 P.2d 1273 (Kan. 1993); (c) a fertility clinic (from deposited sperm intended for an earlier use), but long after the couple's intimate relationship terminates? See, e.g., In re Parentage of J.M.K., supra.

See generally Donald C. Hubin, Daddy Dilemmas: Untangling the Puzzles of Paternity, 13 Cornell J.L. & Pub. Pol'y 29, 52-61 (2003); Michelle Oberman, Sex, Lies, and the Duty to Disclose, 47 Ariz. L. Rev. 871 (2005).

(5) Support Obligations of Stepparents. Suppose a child's mother remarries after a divorce or after the father dies. If her new husband adopts the child, he clearly has a legal support obligation. What financial responsibility does he have if he does not adopt the child? As a matter of policy, should a stepparent have a legal support obligation? Suppose the natural father is alive, as in the *Harmon* case. Should the child support obligation be apportioned between the two fathers? How should the obligation be affected if the stepfather and mother later separate or divorce? Should any other circumstances terminate the stepparent's financial obligation — for example, if the children leave the stepparent's household, as in *Harmon?* Faced with the fact that approximately one-fourth of all children will live with a stepparent before the age of majority, many courts and legislatures have

reformulated the rules affecting stepparent support obligations. Mary Ann Mason & Nicole Zayac, Rethinking Stepparent Rights: Has the ALI Found a Better Definition?, 36 Fam. L.Q. 227, 227 (2002).

a. Stepparent Obligation During the Marriage.   Most states follow the common law rule that stepparents have no obligation to support their stepchildren during the stepparent's marriage to the child's custodial parent. This general rule is subject to two exceptions. In a few jurisdictions, *stepparent support statutes* impose a duty on stepparents (although sometimes only if the stepchildren are, or will be, likely to become public charges). John C. Mayoue, Stepping In to Parent, 25 Fam. Advoc. 36, 42 (2002) (listing 16 states with stepparent support statutes). In addition, some jurisdictions impose a duty based on the "in loco parentis" doctrine (i.e., the stepparent has voluntarily taken the child into the home and assumed parental obligations). Margaret M. Mahoney, Stepparents as Third Parties in Relation to Their Stepchildren, 40 Fam. L.Q. 81, 107 (2006).

b. Stepparent Obligation Postdivorce.   A stepparent has no legal duty to support a former stepchild after the termination of the stepparent's marriage to the child's custodial parent. Thus, none of the stepparent support statutes continue the obligation postdivorce. Id. Moreover, the in loco parentis doctrine does not apply after divorce, even if the stepparent continues his or her relationship with the stepchild (for example, by visitation). Id. However, in limited cases, courts may impose a postdivorce duty of support on stepparents by means of the equitable estoppel doctrine or principles of implied contract. Id. at 39. Equitable estoppel might arise, for example, if a stepparent interferes with a biological parent's efforts to visit or provide support to a child.

c. New Mate Income Excluded.   Are a stepparent's financial resources taken into account in determining the custodial or noncustodial parent's support obligation? Some states explicitly exclude the stepparent's resources from such consideration. See, e.g., Cal. Fam. Code §4057.5 (West 2004) (excluding income of a subsequent spouse or nonmarital partner except in cases of "extreme and severe hardship" to the child).

d. Federal Legislation.   Federal treatment of stepparents' support obligations lacks consistency, although "there is more coherence in federal than state law." Mason & Zayac, supra, at 231. For example, eligibility for purposes of Social Security survivor benefits is based on the child's "dependency" on the stepparent (defined by percentage of support and duration of co-residence). See generally Mary Ann Mason & David Simon, The Ambiguous Stepparent: Federal Legislation in Search of a Model, 29 Fam. L.Q. 445 (1995).

e. ALI Principles.   The American Law Institute (ALI), an influential group of lawyers, law professors and judges, completed a decade-long project to promote uniformity in family law. See ALI, Principles of the Law of Family Dissolution: Analysis and Recommendations (2002). The ALI Principles, although they recognize two new types of parents (parents by estoppel and de facto parents) for purposes of custody and visitation rights, do not significantly alter the rules regarding stepparent support obligations. Mason & Zayac, supra, at 246. Thus, for example, the ALI Principles (§3.12) provide that the income of a stepparent (or steppartner) should not be considered in calculating the custodial parent's support obligation postdivorce. Custody and visitation rights are discussed in Chapter 5.

(6) Relative Responsibility.   A majority of states have statutes that for some purposes extend support obligations beyond the traditional obligations of parents to support their minor children. (As noted in Blackstone, earlier, the Elizabethan Poor Laws themselves made grandparents responsible.) "Family expense statutes" generally provide that the expenses of the family are chargeable against the property of both spouses. (Such statutes are similar to, but broader than, the common law doctrine of necessaries.) In addition, many state "filial responsibility" laws make adult children responsible for the support of elderly parents in some circumstances, thereby relieving governmental authorities from the burden of doing so.

Filial responsibility statutes differ in scope and duration of liability, responsible relatives, and penalties. Standing is accorded to different persons or institutions, such as the indigent parent, a public agency, the welfare authority, or creditors furnishing necessaries. The laws, however, are similar in terms of imposing financial responsibility only for the benefit of relatives who are indigent and only when the responsible adult has adequate resources for his or her own spouse and dependents. Relative responsibility laws have withstood constitutional challenges. See, e.g., Americana Healthcare v. Randall, 513 N.W.2d 566 (S.D. 1994). However, such laws are rarely enforced.

See generally, Seymour Moskowitz, Adult Children and Indigent Parents: Intergenerational Responsibilities in International Perspective, 86 Marq. L. Rev. 401 (2002); Allison E. Ross, Note, Taking Care of Our Caretakers: Using Filial Responsibility Laws to Support the Elderly Beyond the Government's Assistance, 16 Elder L.J. 167 (2008).

2.   The Scope of the Parental Support Obligation

INTRODUCTORY PROBLEM

Ann Wriggins graduated from Berkeley High School this past June at the age of 16 because she accumulated extra credits by taking summer school courses. She has been admitted to junior college for this fall, but her father claims that she would learn more by going to work. Ann is willing to continue living at home but wants to go to junior college. Because her parents are unwilling to pay her fees, she will not be able to attend college even if she lives at home. The fees amount to $4,500 per year, and her parents (whose annual income is $90,000 per year) acknowledge that they could afford the cost. Should Ann be able to sue her parents for nonsupport? How long should Ann's parents be required to support her? Until she reaches 18? She obtains a bachelor's degree? If she decides to attend law school? Suppose Ann's parents divorce. Are her chances of obtaining educational support better?

Suppose that Ann's father finally agrees to pay for her college expenses, and Ann enrolls in the junior college. Then Ann decides she prefers living with her boyfriend rather than at home. Can her father condition his educational support on Ann's continuing to live at home? After Ann completes her education, at age 22, she becomes completely incapacitated in an automobile accident. Do her parents have an obligation to continue to pay for her support?

Wagner v. Wagner
989 So.2d 572 (Ala. Civ. App. 2008)

THOMAS, Judge.

John Scott Wagner appeals from a judgment [ordering him] to make payments for the postminority educational expenses of the parties' older child. . . .

The father and the mother were divorced on August 30, 1999. Pursuant to the divorce judgment, the mother was awarded custody of the parties' two children and the father was ordered to pay the mother $875 per month in child support and $350 per month in alimony. Soon thereafter, the father petitioned the trial court to modify his child-support payments due to his substantially decreased income. The trial court granted the father's petition on October 27, 1999, and reduced the father's monthly child-support obligation to $510 per month. Approximately five and a half years later, on March 27, 2006, the mother filed a petition to modify child support, seeking postminority educational support for the parties' older child, who was 18 years old at the time. . . . The father answered the mother's petitions, alleging [that] he should not be responsible for postminority educational support for the older child. . . .

After the parties divorced, the father remarried in 1999. He has a daughter born of that marriage and a stepson from his current wife's previous relationship. The father testified that he also supports his sister-in-law's two children. At trial, the mother testified that she had not remarried. . . .

At the time of trial, the older child had graduated from high school and was attending Mississippi College, a private college, as a full-time student. The mother testified that the older child was planning to earn a degree in ministerial studies and wanted to become a youth counselor after she graduated. . . . According to the mother's calculations, the total estimated cost of the older child's attending Mississippi College for the 2006-2007 academic school year, after deducting the scholarships the child received, was $16,060.

Although the mother and the father both have college degrees, the father testified that if the parties had remained married he would not have been able to afford to contribute to the older child's college education. The father also testified that neither the mother nor the older child had consulted him when making the decision to attend Mississippi College and that contributing to the educational expenses of the older child's attending Mississippi College would unduly burden his ability to provide for the children he is currently supporting. The father did admit, however, that he wanted all of his children to have the best education possible and that he could contribute some money toward the older child's college expenses. . . .

The father next asserts that the trial court erred in ordering him to make payments for the postminority educational expenses of the parties' older child. The father claims that the trial court's determination was contrary to the factors set forth in Ex parte Bayliss, 550 So.2d 986 (Ala. 1989), and other pertinent caselaw regarding postminority educational support. We disagree.

In Ex parte Bayliss, the Alabama Supreme Court held that, in determining whether to award postminority educational support, a trial court "shall consider all relevant factors that shall appear reasonable and necessary, including primarily the financial resources of the parents and the child and the child's commitment to, and aptitude for, the requested education." 550 So.2d at 987. The court then held that the trial court may also consider "the standard of living that the child would have enjoyed if the marriage had not been dissolved and the family unit had been preserved and the child's relationship with his parents and responsiveness to parental advice and guidance." Id. Additionally, this court has held that the trial court "must also determine if the noncustodial parent has 'sufficient estate, earning capacity, or income to provide financial assistance without undue hardship' " and that "[u]ndue hardship does not imply the absence of personal sacrifice, because many parents sacrifice to send their children to college." Penney v. Penney, 785 So.2d 376, 379 (Ala. Civ. App. 2000) (quoting Thrasher v. Wilburn, 574 So.2d 839, 841 (Ala. Civ. App. 1990)).

[W]e cannot hold that the trial court's award of postminority educational support was plainly or palpably wrong. The parties did not dispute the older child's commitment to, or aptitude for, college. She had performed well in school, had obtained academic scholarships, and, by the time of trial, had already begun attending classes at Mississippi College as a full-time student. Further, although the father generally asserted in testimony that contributing substantial funds toward the older child's postminority education would impair his ability to provide the children he is currently supporting with finances for a college education, the father presented no evidence indicating that he would, in fact, face an "undue" hardship by being obligated to provide the court-ordered financial assistance for the older child's postminority educational support. The record clearly indicates that the parties struggled financially while they were married and that the father struggled financially in the years immediately following the parties' divorce. However, the record also indicates that, at the time of trial, the father was financially stable. At the time of trial, the father was earning a substantial income of approximately $8,000 per month and had approximately $50,000 in equity in his residence.

The trial court also considered what the parties' standard of living would likely have been if they had not divorced and whether the older child would have had the opportunity to pursue a college education with the parents' financial assistance. The trial court determined that the mother and the father would have financially contributed and encouraged their child to attend college. The father argues that, when the parties were married, the family barely survived and was ridden with bankruptcy debt from the children's illnesses; that the mother did not work or contribute financially towards the family; and that, if the parties had remained married, he would not have been able to better himself financially, much less afford to make college-education payments for the older child. Again, however, we cannot hold that the trial court exceeded its discretion in ordering the father to provide postminority educational support for the older child. Both the mother and the father had obtained a college education; most of the parties' financial hardships during their marriage were due to the children's serious, but temporary, health problems; and the father presented no evidence, other than his speculation, indicating that the mother would not have later obtained employment if the parties had remained married.

[Finally, the father] contends that the trial court erred by including costs for various "living expenses," including transportation costs and automobile maintenance, in its postminority educational support award. . . . In Waddell v. Waddell, 904 So.2d 1275 (Ala. Civ. App. 2004), a majority of this court upheld a trial court's judgment ordering a father to pay health-insurance costs as a part of a postminority educational support award under Ex parte Bayliss. The court reasoned that, in some cases, health insurance might be just as necessary as other educational expenses, such as room and board, "to enable children of divorced parents to devote themselves to the pursuit of college educations." *Waddell*, 904 So.2d at 1283. The court further noted that, under the analysis in Ex parte Bayliss, " '[e]ducational expenses involve more than tuition and books; therefore, the trial court should also consider 'evidence on the reasonable necessaries . . . for the child to attend college.' Thrasher [v. Wilburn, 574 So.2d 839, 841 (Ala. Civ. App. 1990)." Additionally, in Stinson v. Stinson, 729 So.2d 864, 868 (Ala. Civ. App. 1998), this court upheld a judgment ordering the father to pay telephone expenses and "additional living expenses" over and above the cost of tuition, room, board, books, and supplies.

Thus, contrary to the father's assertion, we hold that postminority educational support may include more than the costs of tuition and books, and may include other expenses that the trial court, acting within its discretion, determines to be reasonably necessary for the child to attend college. In light of this determination, we further hold that the trial court did not commit plain or palpable error by incorporating monthly allotments for various automobile and personal expenses in its postminority educational support award, which included $227.50 per month for automobile insurance, fuel, and maintenance; $150 per month for food in addition to the meal plan provided by the college; $60 per month for toiletries; and $8.75 per month for the student health and recreation center. From the evidence contained in the record, we conclude that a reasonable fact finder could have determined that these expenses were reasonably necessary for the parties' older child to attend Mississippi College. . . .

DISCUSSION: CHILD SUPPORT AFTER DIVORCE

(1) The Transformation from Discretion to Guidelines.   When granting a divorce, courts establish whether the noncustodial parent should pay child support, and if so, the amount. In making this determination, the trial court considers the financial resources of each parent and the family's prior standard of living. Until comparatively recently, courts accomplished this discretionary determination using imprecise statutory standards. For example, the Uniform Marriage and Divorce Act (UMDA) §309, 9A U.L.A. (pt. 1) 159, 573 (1998 & Supp. 2008), provides:

> In a proceeding for dissolution of marriage, legal separation, maintenance, or child support, the court may order either or both parents owing a duty of support to a child of the marriage to pay an amount reasonable or necessary for his support, without regard to marital misconduct, after considering all relevant factors including:
>> (1) the financial resources of the child;
>> (2) the financial resources of the custodial parent;

(3) the standard of living the child would have enjoyed had the marriage not been dissolved;

(4) the physical and emotional condition of the child and his educational needs; and

(5) the financial resources and needs of the noncustodial parent.

However, beginning in the late 1960s, Congress became increasingly involved in child support enforcement (see discussion of historical background pp. 203-206, infra). Initially, federal involvement was confined to welfare cases, but subsequently expanded to all child support cases. As a consequence of federal legislative reform, the former regime of discretionary standards gave way to enforcement by guidelines. In the Child Support Enforcement Amendments of 1984, 42 U.S.C. §§651 et seq. (2000 & Supp. 2005), Congress mandated that states establish definite numerical formulas ("child support guidelines") to assist courts in determining child support. States were required to have these guidelines in place by 1987 or risk losing a percentage of federal welfare (i.e., Aid to Dependent Children) funds. Subsequent federal legislation (the Family Support Act of 1988, 42 U.S.C. §667 (2000)) specified that states must use these guidelines as a rebuttable presumption *in all cases* and required states to update their guidelines regularly. The intent of these federal laws was to remedy several shortcomings: the inadequacy of awards compared to the actual cost of child rearing, inconsistent orders among those parents with similar economic circumstances, and delays in processing.[13]

The federal mandate did not require that states adopt any particular model for the calculation of child support. As a result, states implemented the guidelines according to three models: (1) the most popular Income Shares Model (adopted by approximately three-fourths of the states), which relies on the combined income of both parents on the assumption that a child should receive the same proportion of parental income as if the family had remained intact; (2) the Percentage-of-Income Approach (adopted by approximately ten states), which bases support on a percentage of the noncustodial parent's income (i.e., the obligor's income alone); and (3) the Melson Formula (now virtually abandoned), which is based on the idea that parents should keep income for their basic needs first, and then additional income should flow to the child. Jo Michelle Beld & Len Biernat, Federal Intent for State Child Support Guidelines: Income Shares, Cost Shares, and the Realities of Shared Parenting, 37 Fam. L.Q. 165, 167 (2003).

This variation in treatment has resulted in considerable statewide rules regarding

> [t]he income basis for the determination of support; the estimates of spending on children upon which the guidelines are based; the treatment of child care costs; the treatment of medical insurance and out-of-pocket expenditures for medical care; provisions for other children to whom the parent owes a duty of support; adjustments for parenting time; and provisions for adjusting support when the obligor is low-income. [Id. at 166.]

---

[13] Nancy Thoennes et al., The Impact of Child Support Guidelines on Award Adequacy, Award Variability, and Case Processing Efficiency, 25 Fam. L.Q. (No. 3) 325, 326 (1991).

Was Congress wise to require the establishment of child support schedules? What are the advantages and disadvantages of the new system, compared with the former practice of allowing courts to exercise discretion on a case-by-case basis? How effective do you think the models are in meeting the needs of contemporary families and accomplishing the preceding goals? For example, is the percentage-of-income model "based on outdated assumptions about parental roles and resources"? Id. at 200. Should more generous adjustments take into account the noncustodial parent's visitation expenses? William V. Fabricius & Sanford L. Braver, Non-Child Support Expenditures on Children by Nonresidential Divorced Fathers, 41 Fam. Ct. Rev. 321 (2003) (so arguing). But cf. Irwin Garfinkel et al., Visitation and Child Support Guidelines: A Comment on Fabricius & Braver, 42 Fam. Ct. Rev. 342 (2004) (rebuttal). See also Marygold S. Melli, Guideline Review: The Search for an Equitable Child Support Formula, in Child Support: The New Frontier 113-127 (J. Thomas Oldham & Marygold S. Melli eds., 2000) (critiquing state guideline reviews as inadequate).

Empirical evidence has explored the effectiveness of the guidelines in accomplishing their objectives. One study (of award rates, award levels, variation in awards and deviations from guidelines formulas) concludes: (1) guidelines increase the probability of obtaining an award for many women who previously would not have received an award, especially for mothers of nonmarital children; (2) guidelines may also increase the size of the awards for these particular mothers; (3) guidelines do appear to achieve greater uniformity of treatment — primarily by eliminating extreme awards — but have not resulted in identical awards for families with similar circumstances; and (4) deviations from the guidelines occur in a significant percent of the awards.[14] See also Andrea H. Beller & John W. Graham, Small Change: The Economics of Child Support (1993) (finding little improvement in child support enforcement in states with guidelines, based on a study conducted prior to the federal support legislation of 1996).

(2) Postmajority Support for Education.   *Wagner* illustrates the problem of whether a parent is liable for support after the child reaches majority. Traditionally, a parent's duty of support ceased upon the child's reaching the age of majority (or upon emancipation, discussed infra). Although the age of majority used to be 21, most states now have lowered the age to 18. This development has given rise to the issue whether a noncustodial parent is liable for postmajority child support for college expenses.

Jurisdictions have responded to this issue in several ways. Some states rigidly enforce the statutory age limitation (18 years) and refuse to award postmajority educational support. Other states permit such support by either statute or case law. See, e.g., Conn. Gen. Stat. §46b-56c (West 2004 & Supp. 2008) (authorizing educational support orders for four years of higher education for any child who has not attained age 23). Some states also extend eligibility for postmajority support to children who reach the age of majority while still enrolled in high

---

[14] Laura M. Argys et al., Can the Family Support Act Put Some Life Back into Deadbeat Dads? An Analysis of Child Support Guidelines, Award Rates, and Levels, 36 J. Hum. Resources 250-251 (2001).

school. Ariz Rev. Stat. §25-501A (West 2007 & Supp. 2008) (permitting educational support only until age 19).

Some jurisdictions require that children's eligibility for postmajority educational support depends on their maintenance of at least a "C" average and full-time student status. Occasionally, a statute has an additional reporting requirement (e.g., the student must submit documentation of grades and credit to the parent each semester) for continued eligibility. See, e.g., Spencer v. Spencer, 126 S.W.3d 770 (Mo. Ct. App. 2004) (finding that child's noncompliance with statute caused by grandmother's mailing transcripts to child's father did not disqualify child from support).

a. Constitutionality. Do statutes requiring divorced parents to pay for postmajority educational support violate equal protection by treating divorced parents differently than married parents? Most courts reject attacks on the constitutionality of statutes requiring divorced parents to provide postmajority educational support for their children, reasoning that such statutes further a legitimate governmental objective. See, e.g., In re Marriage of Grittman, 730 N.W.2d 209 (Iowa Ct. App. 2008); Kohring v. Snodgrass, 999 S.W.2d 228 (Mo. 1999); In re Crocker, 22 P.3d 759 (Ore. 2001). But cf. Curtis v. Kline, 666 A.2d 265 (Pa. 1995).

b. Definition of "Educational Expenses." If noncustodial fathers are required to pay for "educational expenses," it becomes important to know what is included in the term. Is the term limited to tuition and books? Does it include living expenses? Extracurricular activities? Entertainment? Transportation costs (i.e., a car)? Clothing? Laundry? A cash allowance? What light does *Wagner* shed on the matter?

Suppose the statute (or marital agreement) provides for postmajority education support for "reasonable" expenses. Can the father be ordered to pay tuition at a college of the child's choice? Or is "reasonable" limited by the payor's circumstances? If the latter, are circumstances measured at the time of the divorce or the child's enrollment in college? The majority view requires determining whether the child's choice of college is "reasonable" (for settlement agreements with no explicit limitation) in consideration of both the child's needs and the parent's ability to pay at the time of the divorce. Hathaway v. Hathaway, 98 S.W.3d 675, 680 (Tenn. Ct. App. 2002) (adopting majority view). See generally Linda J. Ravdin, Prenups to Protect Children, 24 Fam. Advoc. 33 (2002) (urging that parents' agreements better define the term "college expenses").

c. Conditioning Postmajority Educational Support on Conduct. May a parent condition continuance of the support obligation on the student's conduct? See Waddell v. Waddell, 904 So.2d 1275 (Ala. Civ. App. 2004) (holding that a trial court "may" consider the child's responsiveness to parental guidance in deciding to what extent a noncustodial parent should be obligated for postminority educational support). According to the general rule, parents do not have financial responsibility for children who are emancipated. At common law, emancipation could occur by marriage or military service (or today, pursuant to statute). Some courts find that a minor may "constructively emancipate" himself or herself (and thereby end the parents' support duty) by withdrawing from parental control and supervision without cause. See, e.g., Roe v. Doe, 272 N.E.2d 567 (N.Y. 1971) (father no longer had support obligation for daughter who refused to live in dorm against father's wishes). Alternatively, constructive emancipation might occur if the child abandons the noncustodial parent by refusing all contact without justification. See, e.g., Chambers v. Chambers, 742 N.Y.S.2d 725 (App. Div. 2002) (daughter became emancipated, thereby forfeiting support, when she chose to defy father's wishes and leave home to evade his rules about dating).

How much control should a noncustodial parent be allowed to exert over an adult child's lifestyle when the parent is contributing to the child's financial support? Should the answer depend on a determination of the reasonableness of the parent's conduct? The minor's conduct? Or a judicial assessment of comparative fault? See generally Leslie J. Harris et al., Making and Breaking Connections Between Parents' Duty to Support and Right to Control Their Children, 69 Or. L. Rev. 689 (1990). Emancipation is discussed further in Chapter 6.

d. Separation Agreements Requiring Postmajority Educational Support. Spouses can obligate themselves to pay for child support for longer than a jurisdiction requires. Courts have more latitude to permit postmajority support if the parties provide for that eventuality in a separation agreement. See, e.g., Wood v. Wood, 667 N.W.2d 235 (Neb. 2003) (holding that court has authority to order postmajority support where support was included in approved settlement agreement). What rights does a child as a third-party beneficiary have to enforce the parents' separation agreement? See Chen v. Chen, 893 A.2d 87 (Pa. 2006) (finding that mother not daughter was beneficiary of agreement).

e. ALI Principles.   The ALI Principles (§3.16) suggest that postmajority educational support be determined on a case-by-case basis. That judicial determination should depend on the availability of parental resources and the likelihood of such support had the parents remained together. What factors does *Wagner* consider?

f. Empirical Research.   For policy purposes, it would be useful to learn how frequently noncustodial fathers voluntarily contribute toward their children's college expenses. Although empirical research is limited, one study that followed 49 children in Marin County, California, found that after high school, many middle-class fathers ceased financial support, maintained it at minimal levels, or attached burdensome strings. Judith S. Wallerstein & Shauna B. Corbin, Father-Child Relationships After Divorce: Child Support and Educational Opportunity, 20 Fam. L.Q. (No. 2) 109 (1986). A subsequent study found that mothers and fathers voluntarily contribute a similar proportion of their financial resources to their children's college education, but fathers with joint legal custody provide more voluntary assistance than fathers without custody. See William V. Fabricius et al., Divorced Parent's Financial Support of their Children's College Expenses, 41 Fam. Ct. Rev. 224 (2003) (study of 368 college students measuring the amount that both divorced parents contributed to college education).

(3) Postmajority Support for Adult Disabled Children.   Most jurisdictions recognize another exception to the common law rule (that the parental support obligation terminates at majority) for a disabled child who has reached majority but is unable to become self-supporting. However, courts are divided about financial liability for a child who becomes disabled *after* majority. Although the common law did not impose a parental support obligation in the latter case, many courts currently do so. Compare Riggs v. Riggs, 578 S.E.2d 3 (S.C. 2003) with In re Jacobson, 842 A.2d 77 (N.H. 2004).

3.   Modification of Child Support Decrees and Enforcement Problems

INTRODUCTORY PROBLEM — MODIFICATION AND ENFORCEMENT

In May 2005 Mary Jones and Thomas Jones were divorced. At that time Thomas earned $46,000 a year, Mary did not work, and they had one child, age three. Their divorce decree provided that Thomas was to pay Mary $250 a month for spousal support for a period of three years (until she could complete her nursing degree and be self-supporting), and $350 a month for child support. Thomas paid Mary the $600 a month at the beginning of every month from May 2005 until September 2008, when Thomas married Evelyn, who has a child by an earlier marriage.

(1) What effect should Thomas's remarriage have on his child support payments?

(2) What remedies are available to Mary to collect support if Thomas simply stops making payments?

(3) Suppose Thomas and Evelyn are about to move to Ohio from California, where Mary lives. What would you recommend to Mary in terms of insuring payment of support? After the move, if she were to sue, how would she enforce the support order?

(4) Suppose Thomas and Evelyn move away and leave no forwarding address. How can Mary find out where Thomas now lives?

NOTE: MODIFICATION OF CHILD SUPPORT AFTER DIVORCE

It is generally recognized that provisions for child support in divorce decrees are modifiable on a showing of changed circumstances. The primary concern in making the order is the welfare of the child. Most courts allow modification to provide for support, even though the original decree contained neither a provision for child support nor a reservation of the power to include one.

Jurisdictions vary on the degree of change necessary to justify modification. The majority require that the change be substantial and permanent, at the same time allowing a good deal of discretion to the trial judge to determine whether that standard has been met. The Uniform Marriage and Divorce Act §316, 9A U.L.A. (pt. II) 102 (1998 & Supp. 2008), does not allow for modification of child support provisions unless there is a showing of "changed circumstances so substantial and continuing as to make the terms unconscionable."

Many of the grounds for modification can be classified under the general heading of changes in the financial condition or needs of the parent or the child. A reduction in the income of a father paying support is usually grounds for reducing the obligation, unless the reduction was "voluntary." Suppose the ex-husband-father is a tax lawyer earning $200,000 a year. Should his decision to give up his practice and work for a legal aid clinic for $60,000 a year be sufficient grounds to authorize reduction of his child support obligation? Or suppose the father decides to quit his full-time job and go to law school? See Little v. Little, 975 P.2d 108 (Ariz. 1999).

Several jurisdictions have considered the effect on child support obligations of a parent's voluntary decision to forgo employment. Courts apply one of three tests to determine modification in such circumstances: (1) the good faith test (whether the obligor acted in good faith and not to evade support); (2) the strict rule test, which considers the obligor's earning capacity; and (3) a balancing test that weighs various factors. Lewis Becker, Spousal and Child Support and the "Voluntary Reduction of Income" Doctrine, 29 Conn. L. Rev. 647, 658 (1997).

An increase in the income of the obligor may also be grounds for modification, particularly where the needs of the child have also increased. Another obvious ground for a modification is a change in the needs of the child. Most of the cases involve increased needs, the strongest ones for increase being increased educational or medical costs. DeArriba v. DeArriba, 100 S.W.3d 134 (Mo. Ct. App. 2003) (education); In re Marriage of Ford, 100 Cal. Rptr. 817 (Ct. App. 1972) (medical).

Remarriage of an obligor and the birth of additional children are often rejected as a ground for reduction of support. See, e.g., In re Marriage of Potts, 696 N.E.2d 1263 (Ill. App. Ct. 1998). Similarly, remarriage of an obligee-wife is not normally an adequate ground for modification. (Note that if the obligee-wife's new husband adopts the children, then he assumes the duty of support.) Some states specifically exclude from consideration, for child support purposes, the obligor's or obligee's subsequent spouses. See, e.g., Cal. Fam. Code §4057.5 (West 2004 & Supp. 2008).

An agreement between the husband and wife to change support payments will usually be accepted as a ground for modification, but the court will examine the agreement to determine whether it is consistent with the child's welfare.

A number of circumstances result in termination of a parent's support duty, including the child's reaching the age of majority, emancipation, the child's adoption by a stepparent, or paternity disestablishment. In addition, at common law the duty of support terminated upon the obligor's death unless the obligor bound himself contractually to continue child support payments after death. Therefore, courts generally do not have the power to make a support order against an obligor's estate. Benson ex rel. Patterson v. Patterson, 830 A.2d 966 (Pa. 2003).

Can support orders be modified retroactively? The majority rule is that a court is not authorized to increase or decrease child support payments retroactively, on the theory that the right to support payments is vested as payments become due. See, e.g., Aguero v. Aguero, 976 P.2d 1088 (Okla. Ct. App. 1999) (holding that trial court erred when it allowed father to assert equitable defenses of laches, waiver, and estoppel to mother's claim for child support arrearages). See generally Susan L. Thomas, Death of Obligor Parent as Affecting Decree for Support of Child, 14 A.L.R.5th 557 (1993).

(1) The Problem: Policy Perspectives. Existing studies indicate that a high percentage of fathers fail to make child support payments. According to recent census data, of custodial mothers who are due child support, 77.2 percent receive some payment, but only 46.2 percent receive the full amount due.[15] The finding that only about half of women who are due child support receive full payment is

---

[15] Census Bureau, Custodial Mothers and Fathers and Their Child Support: 2005, p. 7.

confirmed by earlier studies.[16] One study of single mothers points out that despite improvement in child support enforcement over the last few decades, the proportion overall of those mothers who receive child support has remained largely unchanged.[17] The specific child support enforcement tools are discussed infra, pp. 203-206.

(2) Remedies for Enforcement of Child Support.

a. Money Judgments: Sequestration, Attachment of Property.   The economic obligation imposed by the divorce decree can be enforced as a money judgment. If the wife can get personal jurisdiction over the husband, then the decree can be enforced like any other money judgment. Traditionally, state statutes also provide various remedies even without personal jurisdiction over the obligor. For example, attachment and sequestration of the husband's money or property within a state may provide the wife with remedies even if the husband is no longer in the state.

b. Contempt Power.   When a child support order arises out of divorce, the courts have broad equitable enforcement powers; most important is the contempt power. By holding in contempt a father who fails to pay support, a court may send the father to jail until he pays or agrees to pay. Studies reveal increased rates of compliance for delinquent noncustodial parents who are exposed to the *possibility* of jail time.[18]

Some limitations exist on the ability to use the contempt power. A distinction is normally made between spousal support and child support, on the one hand, and property settlements, on the other. Property settlements, often included in the decree of divorce, may not normally be enforced by contempt proceedings. See Danielson v. Evans, 36 P.3d 749 (Ariz. Ct. App. 2001).

c. Criminal Nonsupport Proceedings.   The most drastic sanction available to enforce support is a criminal proceeding. This can often be a powerful weapon, because in some jurisdictions a criminal nonsupport claim filed by a wife can lead to the immediate police arrest of the husband. There are sometimes limitations that make this remedy unavailable. Some courts will not entertain a criminal complaint if the husband makes any support payments at all, no matter how inadequate. Moreover, the pendency of a contempt enforcement provision is sometimes used to decline jurisdiction. Unlike civil contempt, if a husband is in prison, payment does not lead to automatic release. Often, however, the husband is put on probation if he keeps up support payments.

(3) Problems with the Enforcement of Child Support: Interstate Enforcement.

There are basically three reasons child support is difficult to enforce. First, the father may not have the resources to make the payments. Second, the mother may have great difficulty in locating the father. Third, even if the father can be located,

---

[16] Andrea H. Beller & John W. Graham, Small Change: The Economics of Child Support 18, 41 (1993).

[17] Elaine Sorensen & Ariel Halpern, Child Support Enforcement Is Working Better Than We Think, Urban Institute, New Federalism Series, No. A-31 (Mar. 1999), at 1.

[18] David Chambers, Making Fathers Pay: The Enforcement of Child Support Enforcement (1979); Drew A. Swank, The National Child Non-Support Epidemic, 2003 Mich. St. DCL L. Rev. 357, 375.

if he now resides in a state different from that where the mother and child are found, there may be substantial difficulties relating to interstate enforcement.

The United States Supreme Court has interpreted the scope of the Full Faith and Credit Clause very narrowly as it applies to the enforcement of spousal support and child support. The Court has held that the constitutional obligation of full faith and credit is limited to *final* as distinguished from modifiable decrees. Consequently, a spousal support or child support decree, which is subject to modification in the future by the court that rendered it, need *not* be given full faith and credit. See Sistare v. Sistare, 218 U.S. 1 (1910); Barber v. Barber, 323 U.S. 77 (1944). Full faith and credit can apply, however, with regard to the amount that has been reduced to judgment for sums past due.

It was not until the National Conference of Commissioners on Uniform State Laws (NCCUSL) promulgated the Uniform Reciprocal Enforcement of Support Act (URESA), 9B U.L.A. 273 (2001), in 1950 that there was a widely adopted solution to the enforcement of child support decrees in sister states. URESA provided an effective two-step process to reach nonresident obligors, allowing the filing of a complaint in the *obligee's home state* that could be heard, processed, and collected in the *obligor's home state.* URESA also contained criminal provisions and a method of permanently registering a foreign support order in the state where the obligor resided.

Nonetheless, URESA and its 1968 successor, the Revised Uniform Reciprocal Enforcement of Support Act (RURESA), 9B U.L.A. 81 (2001), had significant shortcomings, specifically the potential to create multiple support orders in varying amounts in different jurisdictions. In part, the lack of uniformity among states (in terms of their adoption of the different versions) complicated the enforcement process. The acts also were dependent on the courts for enforcement, rather than taking advantage of administrative procedures such as wage withholding. In response to these and other problems, NCCUSL replaced the earlier models with the Uniform Interstate Family Support Act (UIFSA), 9 U.L.A. (pt. IB) 159 (2005 & Supp. 2008), in 1992. Although based on URESA and RURESA, UIFSA contains new procedures for establishing, enforcing, and modifying support orders.

UIFSA replaces the former two-state approach (under URESA and RURESA) with a one-state proceeding under which a tribunal in one state only may issue or modify a support order. UIFSA provides uniform rules for child support enforcement by setting basic jurisdictional standards, by requiring that one state exercise continuing exclusive jurisdiction, by establishing rules for determining which state issues the controlling order in the event of multistate proceedings, and by providing rules for modifying or refusing to modify another state's child support order. UIFSA's eight bases for expanded long-arm jurisdiction over absent obligors include when the individual resided with the child in the state, the child resides in the state "as the result of acts or directives of the individual," the individual engaged in intercourse in the state and the child may have been conceived therefrom, and there is any other basis consistent with the Constitution for the exercise of personal jurisdiction. UIFSA §201, 9 U.L.A. (pt. IB) 185 (2005 & Supp. 2008).

Amendments to UIFSA in 2001 clarify jurisdictional rules limiting modification in the nonissuing state (e.g., all parties and the child must have left the issuing state and the petitioner must be a nonresident of the state where modification is sought). The amendments explain that UIFSA is not the exclusive method of establishing or enforcing a support order (i.e., a nonresident may voluntarily submit to jurisdiction). The amendments explain in greater specificity how a controlling order is to be determined and reconciled if multiple orders are issued. The amendments also provide that a party who submits to jurisdiction for support purposes does not automatically submit to jurisdiction for custody or visitation purposes, specify the applicability of the local law of a responding state with regard to enforcement procedures and remedies, and fix the duration of a support order to that required under the law of the issuing state (i.e., a second state cannot modify an order to extend support to age 21 if the issuing state limits support to age 18). Finally, the amendments expand UIFSA to include coverage of support orders from foreign countries.

To ensure acceptance by the states, Congress made enactment of UIFSA a condition for federal funding for child support enforcement under PRWORA, 42 U.S.C. §666(f) (2000). PRWORA is discussed infra.

(3) Federal Child Support Enforcement Efforts.

a. Background: AFDC.   The early 1970s were marked by a recognition of the relationship between high welfare costs and the inadequacy of child support. By 1973, the federal Aid for Dependent Children program, or AFDC, was costing taxpayers $7.6 billion a year. A large percentage of this money went to support children who should have been covered by child support. Although many delinquent fathers could afford to pay, they evaded responsibility because state welfare agencies were lax in collection efforts. Congress responded by passing the Child Support Enforcement Act of 1974, 42 U.S.C. §§651-669 (2000 & Supp. 2005), which added Part D (Child Support and Establishment of Paternity) to Title IV of the Social Security Act (Public Law 93-647), and which marked the first federal involvement in a matter that had formerly been left to the states. Title IV-D created a cooperative state and federal program (Office of Child Support Enforcement or OCSE) to locate wayward fathers and collect child support money due to AFDC recipients.

During 1976, the program's first full year of operation, IV-D agencies throughout the United States collected over $600 million in child support.[19] After that time, the amount of money collected under the program increased each year, reaching $7 billion in 1991.[20] Federal child support enforcement efforts resulted in over $18 billion in total collections by 2002.[21] Nonetheless, increases in collection were marked by the ever-increasing number of women with children who were in need of support.

b. Child Support Enforcement Amendments of 1984.   The Child Support Enforcement Amendments of 1984, Pub. L. No. 98-378, 98 Stat. 1305 (1984) (codified as amended in scattered sections of 42 U.S.C.), amended Title IV-D to make child support enforcement services available to all families, not merely

---

[19] Beller & Graham, supra note [16], at 4, 163; Joseph I. Lieberman, Child Support in America 6 (1986).

[20] Lieberman, supra note [19], at 8.

[21] Census Bureau, Statistical Abstract of the United States 2003, Table 567 ("Child Support Enforcement Program — Caseload and Collections: 1990-2002").

to those on welfare. The core provisions of the legislation were mandatory wage attachment and an extension of the tax intercept program created in 1982. The 1984 bill required all support orders to include a conditional order for wage with-holding. Withholding was to begin when payments were one month in arrears or when a noncustodial parent voluntarily requested that payments be withheld. The legislation specifically provided for the interception of federal and state tax refunds of nonwelfare obligors. Prior to this enactment, tax refund withholding was allowed only for families receiving welfare.

The 1984 Amendments encouraged the imposition of liens against property and the posting of bonds to guarantee overdue payment, and extend provisions for bonds and liens to out-of-state orders. States were required to provide information on past-due child support to consumer credit agencies, and might impose late-payment penalties on overdue support payments. In addition, the amendments required states to establish specific nonbinding guidelines for child support awards. The amendments also required states, as a condition for receipt of federal funds, to extend their statutes of limitations to permit paternity establishment until 18 years postbirth.

The legislation provided the noncustodial parent with procedural protection. The parent was to be notified in advance if either wage withholding or a tax refund offset was to go into effect. The obligor was then given an opportunity to prove that his support obligations had been fulfilled.

c. Family Support Act of 1988.   In 1988 Congress enacted the Family Support Act (FSA), Pub. L. No. 103-485, 102 Stat. 2343 (codified in scattered sections of titles 5, 26, and 42 U.S.C.). The FSA addressed child support awards and enforcement mechanisms. The Act provided that the standardized guide-lines that states were required to adopt by the Child Support Enforcement Amendments of 1984 should serve as a rebuttable presumption. In addition, the FSA provided for periodic review and adjustment of child support awards under Title IV-D, state review of guidelines every four years, mandatory wage withholding for all child support orders, and time limits within which state child support enforcement agencies must take various actions. Wage withholding was to be instituted absent a judicial finding of good cause or a parental agreement to a different effect. The FSA also enacted reforms regarding paternity establish-ment (discussed infra).

d. Child Support Recovery Act and the Full Faith and Credit for Child Support Orders Act.   Congress enacted the Child Support Recovery Act (CSRA) of 1992, 28 U.S.C. §228 (2000). CSRA created a new federal remedy for interstate child support enforcement by criminalizing the willful failure to pay child support owed to a child in another state. The Supreme Court's decision in United States v. Lopez, 514 U.S. 549 (1995) (holding unconstitutional the Gun Free School Zone Act for exceeding Congress's power to regulate interstate commerce), subsequently raised questions about congressional regulation of matters (such as child support) that were traditionally regulated by the states. Almost all of the federal courts that considered challenges to the CSRA on this basis later determined the CSRA to be constitutional. See, e.g., United States v. King, 276 F.3d 109 (2d Cir. 2002); United States v. Crawford, 115 F.3d 1397 (8th Cir. 1997).

In 1994, Congress enacted the Full Faith and Credit for Child Support Orders Act (FFCCSOA), 28 U.S.C. §1738B (2000), based on Article IV (the Full Faith and Credit Clause) of the Constitution. FFCCSOA requires states to recognize those child support orders of other states (including those decrees of the District of Columbia, Puerto Rico, U.S. possessions and territories, but not including foreign jurisdictions), and prohibits states from modifying such orders. Congress passed the FFCCSOA to promote uniformity in the face of the proliferation of conflicting child support orders in different states.

Subsequently, Congress passed the Deadbeat Parents Punishment Act (DPPA) of 1998, 18 U.S.C. §228 (2000). Aimed at strengthening the CSRA, DPPA provides that any person can be charged with a felony who (1) travels across state lines with the intent to evade a child support obligation over $5,000 or one that has remained unpaid for longer than one year, or (2) willfully fails to pay support for a child living in a different state if that obligation is greater than $10,000 or if the obligation remains unpaid for more than two years.

Critics charged that DPPA, like CSRA, constituted an invalid congressional attempt to regulate interstate commerce. The Supreme Court renewed the debate in United States v. Morrison, 529 U.S. 598 (2000) (holding unconstitutional, as an overextension of congressional powers under the Commerce Clause, a provision of the Violence Against Women Act that provided a federal remedy for victims of gender-motivated violence). However, in United States v. King, 276 F.3d 109 (2d Cir. 2002), the Second Circuit Court of Appeals upheld the DPPA as a legitimate exercise of congressional power under the Commerce Clause.

e. Personal Responsibility and Work Opportunity Reconciliation Act (PRWORA) and Child Support Enforcement.   In 1996 Congress enacted PRWORA, Pub. L. No. 104-193, 110 Stat. 2105 (codified in scattered sections of 42 U.S.C. and 8 U.S.C.). Several of PRWORA's provisions address child support enforcement.

By January 1, 1998, PRWORA §321 required all states to adopt the Uniform Interstate Family Support Act (UIFSA) to facilitate interstate child support enforcement. PRWORA improves full faith and credit for child support orders by revising procedural guidelines for courts to follow in determining which order to recognize when multiple orders have been issued. For example, the Act defines a child's "home state" as the place where a child has lived with a parent for six consecutive months preceding the time of petitioning for support. The support order from the home state is given preference in determining continuing and exclusive jurisdiction for purposes of modification and enforcement of the support order (§322).

PRWORA requires the establishment and maintenance of statewide case registries for collection and disbursement of support payments (§312). Specifically, PRWORA expands the Federal Parent Locator Service to require states to maintain automated case registries containing records of all cases in which the state provides services pertaining to collection or modification of child support payments, and for recording any support order established or modified after October 1, 1998. Among other things, the registries are to be used for transmitting orders or notices regarding income withholding (one of the child support enforcement mechanisms authorized by the Act).

PRWORA also requires states to adopt certain methods for child support enforcement, specifically procedures for automated directories for new hires (§313) and mandatory income withholding (§314). That is, states must maintain automated directories containing information on all newly hired employees. This directory of new hires may be used for locating parents who owe support, verifying eligibility for programs, and administering employment security or worker's compensation programs. States may impose monetary fines on employers who fail to comply with these requirements (§316).

PRWORA requires states to have procedures for mandatory income withholding to collect support payments subject to state enforcement, and specifies that income withholding will also apply to support arrearages on orders issued prior to October 1, 1996, without need for a judicial or administrative hearing. Income is defined as any periodic payment to an individual and includes worker's compensation, disability payments, or interest. PRWORA revises the procedural guidelines for income withholding, primarily ensuring that it is carried out in compliance with due process requirements. Further, PRWORA insulates employers from liability for complying with a notice for withholding that appears regular on its face (§314).

In addition, the Act authorizes recording of the social security numbers of all applicants for professional or occupational licenses, drivers' licenses, and marriage licenses for the purpose of tracking those individuals owing support (§317). PRWORA permits restricting these licenses for individuals owing support arrearages, and provides that states must have plans in place to provide for liens against property for such individuals (§365). The Act amends bankruptcy laws so that debts for child support are nondischargeable. Also PRWORA requires states to prescribe procedures for child support orders relating to children of minor parents to be enforceable against grandparents (§§300-375). Other provisions of PRWORA (regarding work requirements, paternity establishment, and unwed teenage mothers) are discussed infra pp. 222-223.

(4) Proposed Federal Legislation: "Responsible Fatherhood" Bill. In 1999, Congress introduced the Father's Count Act, H.R. 3073, 106th Cong. (1999), to amend the Social Security Act (Title IV, Part A) to provide for grants to public and private organizations to promote "responsible fatherhood." The proposed legislation was designed to encourage young fathers to marry the mothers of their children and become financially responsible. The bill would have provided $150 million in grants to promote marriage and successful parenting, and to supply assistance to fathers and their families to avoid or leave welfare. Critics questioned the need for the bill, claiming that the majority of men owing child support are financially stable and do not need government assistance. They also questioned the policy of encouraging marriage in all cases, contending that the bill provided no protection for victims of domestic violence. The bill passed the House but not the Senate. Congress renewed efforts to pass the legislation in 2003 and in 2004. In September 2004, the Healthy Marriages and Responsible Fatherhood Act (S.B. 2830) was introduced in Congress by Senators Santorum (R-Pa.) and Bayh (D-In.). However, the bill did not move forward in the Senate.

C.   A CHILD'S INHERITANCE RIGHTS

Gillett-Netting v. Barnhart
371 F.3d 593 (9th Cir. 2004)

Betty FLETCHER, Circuit Judge:

Plaintiff-Appellant Rhonda Gillett-Netting, on her own behalf and on behalf of her minor children Juliet O. Netting and Piers W. Netting, appeals the district court's grant of summary judgment for the Commissioner of Social Security. The district court affirmed the Commissioner's decision holding that Juliet and Piers are not entitled to child's insurance benefits based on the earnings of their deceased father, Robert Netting. . . . [1]

In December 1994, Netting was diagnosed with cancer. At the time, he and his wife, Gillett-Netting, were trying to have a baby together, but Gillett-Netting suffered from fertility problems that had caused her to miscarry twice. Because doctors advised Netting that chemotherapy might render him sterile, he delayed the start of his treatment for several days so that he could deposit his semen at the University of Arizona Health Sciences Center, where it was frozen and stored for later use by his wife. Netting quickly lost his battle with cancer. He died on February 4, 1995, before his wife was able to conceive. Earlier, Netting confirmed that he wanted Gillett-Netting to have their child after his death using his frozen sperm. In-vitro fertilization of Gillett-Netting's eggs with Netting's sperm was undertaken successfully on December 19, 1995. . . . Juliet and Piers Netting were born on August 6, 1996.

On August 19, 1996, Gillett-Netting filed an application on behalf of Juliet and Piers for Social Security child's insurance benefits based on Netting's earnings. The Social Security Administration (SSA) denied the claim initially and upon reconsideration, and Gillett-Netting timely filed a request for a hearing before an Administrative Law Judge (ALJ) [who also denied her claim].

Developing reproductive technology has outpaced federal and state laws, which currently do not address directly the legal issues created by posthumous conception. Neither the Social Security Act nor the Arizona family law that is relevant to determining whether Juliet and Piers have a right to child's insurance benefits makes clear the rights of children conceived posthumously. Our task is to determine whether Juliet and Piers have a right to child's insurance benefits under the law as currently formulated.

Under the Act, every child is entitled to benefits if the claimant is the child, as defined in 42 U.S.C. §416(e), of an individual who dies fully or currently insured; the child or the child's representative files an application for benefits; the child is unmarried and a minor (or meets disability requirements) at the time of application; and the child was dependent on the insured wage earner at the time of his death.

---

[1] Gillett-Netting also argues that applying the Act to preclude the award of child's insurance benefits to posthumously conceived children violates the children's right to equal protection of the laws. Because we conclude that Juliet and Piers are entitled to benefits under the Act, we do not reach Gillett-Netting's equal protection claim.

42 U.S.C. §402(d)(1). It is undisputed that Netting was fully insured under the Act when he died, that Juliet and Piers are his biological children and are unmarried minors, and that Gillett-Netting filed an application for child's insurance benefits on their behalf. . . .

The Act defines "child" broadly to include any "child or legally adopted child of an individual," as well as a stepchild who was the insured person's stepchild for at least nine months before the insured person died, and a grandchild or stepgrandchild of the insured person under certain circumstances. See 42 U.S.C. §416(e). Courts and the SSA have interpreted the word "child" used in the definition of "child" to mean the natural, or biological, child of the insured.

The Commissioner argues and the district court held that "child" is further defined by 42 U.S.C. §§416(h)(2), (3) [set forth infra], and that Juliet and Piers cannot be considered the children of Netting unless they meet the requirements of one of these provisions. These sections were added to the Act to provide various ways in which children could be entitled to benefits even if their parents were not married or their parentage was in dispute. They have no relevance to the issue before us. . . .

Under the current version of §416(h), a claimant whose parentage is disputed is deemed to be the child of an insured individual if: (1) the child would be entitled to take an intestate share of the individual's property under the laws of the state in which the individual resided at death; (2) the child's parents went through a marriage ceremony resulting in a purported marriage between them that, but for a legal impediment unknown to them at the time, would have been a valid marriage; (3) the deceased wage earner acknowledged the claimant as his or her child in writing; (4) the deceased wage earner, before dying, had been decreed by a court to be the parent of the claimant; (5) the deceased wage earner, before dying, had been ordered by a court to contribute to the support of the claimant because the claimant was his or her child; or (6) the insured individual is shown by evidence satisfactory to the Commissioner to have been the parent of the claimant and to have been living with or contributing to the support of the claimant at the time that he died. See U.S.C. §§416(h)(2), (3).

Although these provisions offer means of "determining whether an applicant is the child . . . of a fully or currently insured individual," id. at §416(h)(2)(A), when parentage is disputed, nothing in the statute suggests that a child must prove parentage under §416(h) if it is not disputed. We conclude that these provisions do not come into play for the purposes of determining whether a claimant is the "child" of a deceased wage earner unless parentage is disputed. In this case, the Commissioner concedes that Juliet and Piers are Netting's biological children. Therefore, we conclude that the district court erred by holding that Juliet and Piers are not Netting's children for the purposes of the Act.

. . . The only remaining issue is whether Juliet and Piers, the undisputed biological children of a deceased, insured individual, are statutorily deemed dependent on Netting without proof of actual dependency.

Under the Act, a claimant must show dependency on an insured wage earner in order to be entitled to child's insurance benefits. 42 U.S.C. §402(d)(1). However, the Act statutorily deems broad categories of children to have been dependent on a deceased, insured parent without demonstrating actual dependency. It is well-settled that all legitimate children automatically are considered to have been dependent on the insured individual, absent narrow circumstances not present in this case.

Similarly, "illegitimate" children who prove parentage under 42 U.S.C. §§416(h)(2), (3) are "deemed to be the legitimate child of such individual" and, therefore, are deemed to have been dependent on the insured wage earner. 42 U.S.C. §402(d)(3). Thus, the provisions of §416(h) described above typically come into play to prove dependency rather than parentage. . . .

. . . Dependency is a broad concept under the Act, whereby the vast majority of children are statutorily deemed dependent on their deceased parents, and only completely unacknowledged, illegitimate children must prove actual dependency in order to be entitled to child's insurance benefits. Moreover, the Act is construed liberally to ensure that children are provided for financially after the death of a parent.

Juliet and Piers are indisputably Netting's legitimate children under the law of the state in which they reside. "Arizona has eliminated the status of illegitimacy[.]" State v. Mejia, 97 Ariz. 215, 399 P.2d 116 (1965). In Arizona, "[e]very child is the legitimate child of its natural parents and is entitled to support and education as if born in lawful wedlock." Ariz. Rev. Stat. §8-601. "It has long been the policy of th[e] state to protect innocent children from the omissions of their parents" by abolishing legal distinctions based on legitimacy. Hurt v. Superior Court, 124 Ariz. 45, 601 P.2d 1329, 1331 (1979). Under Arizona law, Netting would be treated as the natural parent of Juliet and Piers and would have a legal obligation to support them if he were alive, although they were conceived using in-vitro fertilization, because he is their biological father and was married to the mother of the children. See Ariz. Rev. Stat. §25-501(providing that children have a right to support from their natural parents; the biological father of a child born using artificial insemination is considered a natural parent if the father is married to the mother). Although Arizona law does not deal specifically with posthumously-conceived children, *every* child in Arizona, which necessarily includes Juliet and Piers, is the legitimate child of her or his natural parents.[7]

The Commissioner nevertheless argues that Juliet and Piers do not satisfy the "legitimate child" requirement, and therefore cannot be deemed dependent under §402(d)(3), unless they also are able to inherit from Netting under state intestacy laws or meet one of the other provisions of §416(h). This is not the case. Legitimacy in §402(d)(3) is determined in accordance with state law. See Jimenez v. Weinberger, 417 U.S. 628, 635-36 (1974) (noting that children who are considered legitimate under state law are entitled to child's insurance benefits without proving dependency). While §416(h) provides alternative avenues for children to be

---

[7] This is not to say that every posthumously-conceived child in Arizona would be eligible for survivorship benefits on the basis of the earnings of the deceased sperm donor. If the sperm donor had not been married to the mother, Arizona would not treat him as the child's natural parent, and he likely would have no obligation to support the child if he were alive. In such circumstances, no eligibility for benefits would exist unless the Commissioner made a determination that the claimant was the dependent child of the deceased wage earner for purposes of the Act by virtue of satisfying one of the requirements in §416(h).

deemed legitimate, nothing in the Act suggests that a child who is legitimate under state law separately must prove legitimacy under the Act. It would make little sense to require a child whose parents were married to demonstrate legitimacy by showing she meets a test set forth in §416(h), for example by showing that her parent acknowledged her in writing or that a court determined her parentage prior to the parent's death.[8]

Because Juliet and Piers are Netting's legitimate children under Arizona law, they are deemed dependent under §402(d)(3), and need not demonstrate actual dependency nor deemed dependency under the provisions of §416(h). As Netting's legitimate children, Juliet and Piers are conclusively deemed dependent on Netting under the Act and are entitled to child's insurance benefits based on his earnings. . . .

DISCUSSION: THE INHERITANCE RIGHTS OF CHILDREN

(1) Intestate Share for a Child.   If parents die without a will, legislation in every state provides for an intestate share for the child. For example, the Illinois statute provides:

> (a) If there is a surviving spouse and also a descendant of the decedent: ½ of the entire estate to the surviving spouse and ½ to the decedent's descendants per stirpes.

> (b) If there is no surviving spouse but a descendant of the decedent: the entire estate to the decedent's descendants per stirpes. 755 Ill. Comp. Stat. Ann. 5/2-1 (West 2007).

States also protect against unintentional disinheritance by means of "pretermitted heir" legislation, which provides a share for an omitted child born to (or adopted by) a testator *after* the testator executes a will. The rationale underlying such legislation is presumed intent (i.e., the idea that the testator would have wanted to provide a share for an accidentally omitted child).

(2) Do Parents Have the Legal Power to Disinherit Minor Children?   Every state except Louisiana empowers a parent to disinherit a child by will. As pointed out by Blackstone, the parent had this power at common law. Louisiana, whose law is influenced by the civil law tradition, has a system of "forced heirship." This requires, in effect, that children receive a minimum portion of a parent's estate unless certain conditions exist. Specifically, a parent in Louisiana has just cause to disinherit a child if:

> (1) The child has raised his hand to strike a parent, or has actually struck a parent, but a mere threat is not sufficient.

---

[8] Because Juliet and Piers are Netting's legitimate children under Arizona state law, we need not consider whether they could be deemed dependent for another reason, such as their ability to inherit property from their deceased father under Arizona intestacy laws. See generally [Woodward v. Commissioner of Social Security, 760 N.E.2d 257 (Mass. 2002)]. As a practical matter, in most cases legitimate children would be able to inherit under state intestacy laws, but they need not *demonstrate* their ability to do so in order to be entitled to child's insurance benefits.

(2) The child has been guilty, toward a parent, of cruel treatment, crime, or grievous injury.

(3) The child has attempted to take the life of a parent.

(4) The child, without any reasonable basis, has accused a parent of committing a crime for which the law provides that the punishment could be life imprisonment or death.

(5) The child has used any act of violence or coercion to hinder a parent from making a testament.

(6) The child, being a minor, has married without the consent of the parent.

(7) The child has been convicted of a crime for which the law provides that the punishment could be life imprisonment or death.

(8) The child, after attaining the age of majority and knowing how to contact the parent, has failed to communicate with the parent without just cause for a period of two years, unless the child was on active duty in any of the military forces of the United States at the time. [La. Civ. Code Ann. Art. 1621 (West Supp. 2008).]

May a parent evade this system of "forced heirship"? A Louisiana statute restricts parental evasion in some circumstances: "Donations inter vivos and mortis causa may not exceed three-fourths of the property of the donor if he leaves, at his death, one forced heir; and one-half if he leaves at his death, two or more forced heirs. . . . La. Civ. Code Ann. Art. 1495 (West 2000 & Supp. 2008). The Louisiana legislature subsequently restricted its forced share to those children who were 23 years old or younger or who were incapacitated; however, the state supreme court declared these restrictions unconstitutional. Succession of Lauga, 624 So. 2d 1156 (La. 1993); Succession of Terry, 624 So. 2d 1201 (La. 1993). In 1995, the voters approved a state constitutional amendment that required the legislature to implement legislation reinstating the above restrictions on testamentary freedom in terms of children's ages (23 and younger) and competency. Katherine Shaw Spaht, The Remnant of Forced Heirship: The Interrelationship of Undue Influence, What's Become of Disinherison, and The Unfinished Business of the Stepparent Usufruct, 50 La. L. Rev. 637, 641-643 (2000) (explaining background).

(3) Should Legislation Limit the Power of Disinheritance?   The United States is almost alone among nations in allowing disinheritance of children by their parents.[22] Countries employ two different methods to protect children from intentional disinheritance: forced heirship (followed by civil law countries, and Louisiana, discussed supra, based on the Napoleanic Code) and the family maintenance system (followed by many common law countries), which permits the court to exercise its discretion to provide for the needs of the heirs. Should other states in the United States adopt one of these two schemes? If so, which?

May a father disinherit a child to defeat his child support obligation? See L.W.K. v. E.R.C., 735 N.E.2d 359 (Mass. 2000) (holding that a testator charged with an obligation to support his child cannot nullify that obligation by

---

[22] Ronald Chester, Should American Children Be Protected Against Disinheritance?, 32 Real Prob. Prob. & Tr. J. 405, 406 (1997).

disinheriting the child because child support obligations should take precedence over testamentary dispositions).

(4) Special Family Protection Statutes.   The general power of disinheritance is alleviated by statutory provisions protecting the surviving spouse and minor children. For example, homestead exemptions and personal property exemptions allow the setting apart of property to be exempt from execution for the decedent's debts. See, e.g., Cal. Prob. Code §6510 (West 1991). Also, during the period of probate administration, a family support allowance can be granted from the probate estate to a surviving spouse and minor children (sometimes also to adult children who were dependent on the decedent). See, e.g., Cal. Prob. Code §6540(a)(2) (West 1991 & Supp. 2008). More important, although minor children can be disinherited, the spouse ordinarily cannot. Because a surviving spouse has a legal duty to support the child and because the survivor generally receives property from the estate based on minimum share legislation (or through the operation of community property laws), some protection is provided indirectly for the children.

(5) Posthumous Children.   A posthumous child is a child who was conceived while the intestate was alive but born after the deceased parent's death. What are the inheritance rights of a posthumous child? At common law, and according to the Uniform Probate Code (§2-108), posthumous children inherit as if they had been born during the decedent's lifetime. State intestacy statutes generally include similar provisions. See generally Joseph H. Karlin, "Daddy, Can You Spare a Dime?" Intestate Heir Rights of Posthumously Conceived Children, 79 Temp. L. Rev. 1317 (2006).

(6) Assisted Conception.   New reproductive technologies, combined with cryopreservation of genetic material, have made possible the birth of an increasing number of children who are *conceived* posthumously. Cases like *Gillett-Netting* explore the extent of a posthumously conceived child's inheritance rights in the context of government benefits. On what basis did the court hold that the Netting children qualified for survivors' benefits under the Social Security Act?

Some states grant rights to posthumously conceived children if the decedent left written consent to be a parent. See, e.g., In re Estate of Kolacy, 753 A.2d 1257 (N.J. Super. Ct. 2000) (holding that twins conceived by in-vitro fertilization and born nearly 18 months after their father's death qualified as father's legal heirs under state intestacy law). But cf. Finley v. Astrue, 270 S.W.3d 849 (Ark. 2008) (holding that child was not legal heir under state intestacy statute because statute did not specifically refer to implantation after death). Should consent of the deceased be a requirement for the child to succeed to governmental benefits? If so, what should be the scope of that consent — an intention to be a parent? To support the child? Both? How should that consent be manifested?

Gillett-Netting involves the right to governmental benefits. Should a posthumously conceived child be permitted to inherit from a father via intestate succession (i.e., state laws applicable to decedents who died without a will)? Several states recently have amended their intestacy laws to include such children. Some of these states (e.g., Colorado, Delaware, Texas, Virginia, and Washington) permit these children to inherit if the decedent left written consent to be a parent. Other states add a requirement that the birth occur within a stated time following death (e.g., three years in Louisiana). Lindsay Fortado, Children Born Into Legal Limbo,

Natl. L.J., July 19, 2004, at 1. See also Cal. Prob. Code §249.5 (West 2007) (requiring written parental consent and child being in being within 2 years of parent's death). Are these requirements sound policy? Why require the birth to occur within a stated time after the father's death? What period of time is preferable?

Although the father in *Gillett-Netting* supplied the genetic material, is a biological relationship essential to the child's right to inherit? Would a posthumously conceived child qualify as a dependent if the husband, prior to his death, consented to the wife's artificial insemination by means of third-party sperm? What light does *Gillett-Netting* shed on this question?

(7) New Model Act. The ABA approved new model legislation (the Model Act Governing Assisted Reproductive Technology) in February 2008 that addresses parentage issues arising from the use of reproductive technology. The Act clarifies the concept of "parental status" based on whether the individual consented in writing during his or her lifetime to the use of his gametes, before their use, and also specified that his or her consent would apply to their use after death. See Model Act Governing Assisted Reproductive Technology §607 (2008). The new Model Act would regulate posthumously-conceived children's right to inherit (as well as issues of informed consent, donor identity, control of cryopreserved gametes, mental-health consultation, privacy, gamete and embryo donation, and isurance). For background on the Act, see Charles P. Kindregan, Jr. & Steven H. Snyder, Clarifying the Law of ART: The New American Bar Association Model Act Governing Assisted Reproductive Technology, 42 Fam. L.Q. 203 (2008).

(8) Problem. Gaby and Bruce Vernoff are a married couple. When Bruce dies unexpectedly in an accident, Gaby asks his physician to extract Bruce's sperm. Four years later, Gaby gives birth to a daughter using Bruce's genetic material. Gaby then files a claim for Social Security survivor benefits for the daughter. What are the daughter's inheritance rights? See Robert Salladay, Advancing the Issue: Reproduction and the Law; Controversy Continues to Dog a Procedure That Allows Human Embryos to Be Frozen for Use at a Later Date: "Dead Dads" Create Legal Issues, Daily Press, June 16, 2004, at A3.

D.   MANAGEMENT AND CONTROL OF THE PROPERTY OF A MINOR[23]

INTRODUCTORY PROBLEM

Ann Douglas is the 16-year-old daughter of Mr. and Mrs. Thomas Douglas. The Douglases are extremely wealthy, and it is clear that some day Ann will inherit a great fortune. Her parents wish to provide her now with the practical experience of managing her own investments and money. They therefore wish to give her

---

[23] For an introduction to this topic, see generally Jesse Dukeminier et al., Wills, Trusts, and Estates 116-120 (7th ed. 2005); William M. McGovern & Sheldon F. Kurtz, Wills, Trusts and Estates Including Taxation and Future Interests 315 (2d ed. 2001).

$50,000 to invest, spend, or use in any way she wishes. Is there any way as a practical matter this can be accomplished? What would you advise?

DISCUSSION: ALTERNATIVE MEANS TO HOLD AND CONTROL THE PROPERTY OF A MINOR

One element of the child's economic relationship to his or her family that is often overlooked has to do with the child's own property. A child may inherit stocks or bonds or real estate from a relative, or may receive as a gift a property that requires management. What are the child's powers to deal with his or her own property? What are the parents' powers with respect to the child's property? What are the alternative ways a child may "own" property?

What follows is a brief discussion of the four basic alternatives.

(1) Property Held in the Minor's Own Name: Practical Problems.   Property is sometimes simply held in the child's name without any indication of minority status. For example, a child may be the grantee in a real estate deed. Also, corporate securities or bank accounts may simply be registered in a child's name with no indication of age. Although holding title directly in the name of a minor is sometimes said to be against public policy, there are no criminal or civil sanctions — only substantial practical problems.

These practical difficulties arise because neither the child nor his or her parents may be able to manage the property or effectuate a transfer or sale. Apart from questions of maturity and competence, the child himself or herself may have severe practical difficulties because the contracts of minors are voidable — i.e., a minor may disavow a contract because of minority. See pp. 673-676, infra, for discussion of the power of disavowal of contract. This makes it risky for someone to do business with a minor. For example, if a minor owns real estate and signs a five-year lease with a tenant, the tenant risks having the lease set aside if the minor chooses to disavow. When property is sold or transferred by a minor, a title insurance company or a stock agent may decline to insure title or to transfer stock if the transferor is a minor. Indeed, special legislation has been enacted to protect banks against claims that might arise when they deal directly with a minor in connection with a bank account. See, e.g., Cal. Fin. Code §850 and §6751 (West 2004).

Nor do a child's parents as such have the legal power to manage or transfer a child's property. Although parents are said to be the "natural guardians" of a child's person (and as a consequence have broad powers and responsibilities with regard to custody, education, discipline, etc.), parents have no legal power *as parents* over the property of their children. This long-standing common law tradition persists to this day and is now sometimes expressed in state statutes. California Family Code §7502 (West 2004) provides, for example, "The parent, as such, has no control over the property of the child." In all events, if property is held simply in the name of the child, the child's parents lack the legal power to convey the property, or the right to manage or control the property, or even take the income and spend it on the child.

(2) Guardian of the Estate of a Child.   At common law, if a child inherited property or was given property requiring management, a court could appoint a

guardian of the child's estate. This feudal relic is still available and at times required today. Even where the court-appointed guardian is a parent, the guardian of a child's estate is empowered to manage the child's assets and spend the income for the benefit of the child only with court supervision and approval and subject to inflexible and restrictive rules. Consequently guardianships are inconvenient, inefficient, and expensive.

There are a number of basic problems with guardianship administration. First, a guardianship is expensive to administer. Court supervision and approval is required for almost every action that the guardian takes, and this imposes court costs, attorneys' fees, and delays. In addition, a guardian must typically post a bond, pay an annual bond premium out of the income of the property, and file "accountings" in court. These all add to the administration costs. Second, the investment powers of the guardian are very limited, even with court approval. As a consequence, particularly in inflationary times, it is often extremely difficult for a guardian to obtain a decent return on the child's property. Third, a guardianship automatically terminates when a child reaches the age of majority, which is now typically 18. Where substantial property is involved, this may be undesirable because the 18-year-old may lack the maturity to manage his or her own property. Indeed, the disadvantages of guardianship for a child's estate are so substantial that a primary reason for parents of young children to write a will is to create alternative arrangements that avoid this necessity.[24]

(3) Trusts.[25]   The most flexible method of holding property on behalf of minors involves the use of a trust. With a trust, properties are held in the name of the trustee, who then has a fiduciary responsibility to manage, invest the property, and spend the proceeds in a manner consistent with the trust instrument. The trustee must be a competent adult or a responsible institution — like a bank. Management and control by the trustee is possible without going to court, and thus the inconvenience and expense of a guardianship can be avoided. Within very broad limits, the trust instrument itself may define the powers of the trustee, how the money is to be invested and expended, and the term of the trust. Thus, provision can be made for the distribution of the corpus or income of the trust in any manner that the trustor designates. There is no requirement that properties automatically be distributed to a young person when he or she reaches 18 or 21. Indeed, the trust instrument can permit the rights of several intended beneficiaries to be tailored to the precise wishes of the trustor, and can even provide for the interests of the beneficiaries to be limited or adjusted according to changed circumstances.

(4) Uniform Transfers to Minors Act.[26]   Every state now has some form of Uniform Transfers to Minors Act or its predecessor, the Uniform Gifts to Minors Act. These statutory provisions allow certain kinds of property (e.g., stocks, bonds, bank accounts) to be registered in the name of a qualified custodian, who then has

[24] Dukeminier et al., supra note [23], at 118.

[25] See generally George G. Bogert, The Law of Trusts and Trustees (rev. 2d ed. 1993); Austin Wakeman Scott & William Fratcher, Trusts (4th ed. 1988).

[26] The Uniform Gifts to Minors Act (UGMA), 8A U.L.A. 297 (2003), was revised in 1983 as the Uniform Transfers to Minors Act (UTMA), 8C U.L.A. 1 (2001).

broad powers to deal with the property, without court supervision. The act's provisions are triggered when property is put in the name of a custodian with an appropriate legend invoking the Uniform Act. Some states allow bequests to be subject to the act as well. In all events, the act provides a "canned trust" with standard provisions. The custodian, like a trustee, has fiduciary responsibilities to the minor and has broad statutory power to invest and reinvest the property and to spend the proceeds (whether income or principal) for the minor's support, maintenance, education, and benefit. The custodian has nearly complete discretion as to the time and amount of any such payments.

The age of distribution depends on the manner in which the property is transferred. If property is transferred by means of a gift, the exercise of a power of appointment, a will, or the terms of a trust, then the property may be distributed to a minor at age 21. The age of distribution for other transfers (e.g., employee benefit plans) is tied to the age of majority in the enacting state. Some states allow the transferor to vary the age of distribution within a fixed range (from 18 to 25 years). At the age designated for distribution, the custodianship terminates, and the custodian may distribute the property. Although not as flexible as a custom-made trust, the act generally provides a convenient and inexpensive method of holding property for a minor.

E.   GOVERNMENTAL INCOME TRANSFER PROGRAMS THAT AFFECT CHILDREN

INTRODUCTORY NOTE

The initial topics in this chapter primarily concern how law provides a framework for private ordering as well as standards and a legal mechanism for the enforcement of certain rights. This section highlights the more active role of government in providing financial resources for child support. Specifically, many public programs provide money, goods, or services that help families fulfill their private support obligations.

In some programs, the benefits do not depend on whether there is a child in the family. For example, unemployment insurance, first enacted in 1935 as part of the Social Security Act, provides income security for a limited period of time for employees who are out of work regardless of whether they have children. Similarly, workers' compensation provides income maintenance to workers injured in the course of employment without regard to the size of their families. Of course, children within these families may benefit substantially from the extra resources provided during hard times faced by their parents.

Other income maintenance programs base the amount of benefits on the presence or number of children. For example, the Old Age Survivors and Disability Insurance Program (OASDI), under Title II of the Social Security Act, is a federal program that provides benefits for (1) retired workers, (2) workers who are totally disabled, and (3) surviving dependents of workers. Although the amount of family benefits is based in part on the worker's past earnings, benefits are increased by the presence of children under 18 (or under 22, if in school). The case of Jimenez v. Weinberger, 417 U.S. 628 (1974), established that nonmarital children born after the disability of a worker are eligible for benefits under this program. In 2003, approximately 3.1 million children received benefits as survivors of deceased workers or dependents of disabled or retired workers.[27]

In addition, in 1972 Congress enacted the Supplemental Security Income (SSI) program, 42 U.S.C. §§1381-1383d (2000 & Supp. 2005), to assist needy aged, blind, and disabled persons.[28] In Sullivan v. Zebley, 493 U.S. 521 (1990), the Supreme Court invalidated, as contrary to congressional intent, Social Security Administration regulations that applied a different standard for determination of disability for children and adult claimants. *Sullivan* contributed to an increase in the number of children who were recipients of SSI.[29] In 1996, however, PRWORA §211 made the definition of "disability" more restrictive by establishing a new and separate disability definition for children under age 18 that requires a child to have a "medically determinable physical or mental impairment, which results in marked and severe functional limitations, and which can be expected to result in death or which has lasted or can be expected to last for a continuous period of not less than 12 months."[30] As a result, an estimated 135,000 children (13 percent of SSI child recipients) who were receiving aid no longer qualified. The number of children receiving SSI payments, and the percentage of the caseload they represent, has declined from 955,174 (14.4 percent) in December 1996 to 847,063 (12.9 percent) in December 1999.[31] To help remedy this problem, Congress mandated in the Balanced Budget Act of 1997, Pub. L. No. 105-33, §4913, 111 Stat. 251, 573 (1997), that states must continue Medicaid coverage for those children who were previously receiving SSI benefits but who failed to meet the more restrictive definition of "disability."

The food stamp program is another example of an income transfer program in which benefits are increased if there are children in the household. First enacted in 1964, the Food Stamp Act, 7 U.S.C. §§2011-2032, was amended in 1977 to permit low-income households to acquire stamps that may be used to purchase food. The coupon allotment of food stamps is based on the cost of a thrifty food plan, reduced by a fraction of the household's net income. For these purposes, the household includes all persons who are living as one economic unit and who customarily purchase food and prepare meals together (other than boarders, roomers, and certain unrelated live-in attendants). See United States Dept. of Agriculture v. Moreno, 413 U.S. 528 (1973) (invoking the equal protection component of the Fifth Amendment to strike the statutory exclusion of households containing a nonrelative). Eligibility depends on the household's monthly income, and the

[27] Social Security Administration, Fact Sheet on the Old-Age, Survivors, and Disability Insurance Program: 2003.

[28] House Comm. on Ways & Means, 106th Cong., 2d Sess., Background Material and Data on Programs Within the Jurisdiction of the Committee on Ways and Means ("2000 Green Book") 51 (Comm. Print. 2000).

[29] Id.

[30] 42 U.S.C. §1382c(a)(3)(C)(i) (2000).

[31] House Comm. on Ways & Means, 2000 Green Book, supra note [28], at 251.

amount of allowable monthly income is influenced by the number of persons included in the household. Therefore, the presence of children in the household can affect the maximum allowable monthly income and the coupon allotment of stamps.

Beginning in 1985 Congress enacted legislation significantly changing food stamp regulations. The Food Security Act, 7 U.S.C. §1281, required states to implement employment and training programs for recipients, provided automatic eligibility for recipients on Aid to Families with Dependent Children (AFDC) and SSI, prohibited collection of sales taxes on food stamp purchases, and increased benefits for those with high shelter costs and dependent care costs. Legislation in 1986 and 1987 increased benefits for the homeless and again for those with high shelter costs.[32] Subsequent legislation, the Hunger Prevention Act of 1988, Pub. L. No. 100-435, 102 Stat. 1645 (codified as amended in scattered sections of 7 U.S.C.), further expanded eligibility, increased benefits, and restructured the employment and training program. The 1990 Farm Bill, Pub. L. No. 101-624, 104 Stat. 3359 (codified in scattered sections of 7 U.S.C.) permitted states to authorize restaurants to accept food stamps from homeless households; authorized grants to organizations to conduct food stamps outreach targeted to rural, elderly, homeless, non-English-speaking and low-income working families with children; and provided that all persons applying for SSI at social security offices be given food stamp applications.[33]

The 1990 Farm Bill also gave authority to the USDA to establish electronic benefits transfer systems, by which recipients could receive electronic cards (similar to automatic bank teller cards) rather than food stamps. 7 U.S.C. §2016(i)(1)(A) (2000). Purchases would be made with these cards and the amount deducted automatically from an account balance. The expansion of the use of electronic banking technology to deliver welfare benefits was intended to reduce welfare fraud and abuse.[34]

The Mickey Leland Childhood Hunger Relief Act, 7 U.S.C. §§2011 et seq. (2000), enacted August 10, 1993, as part of the Omnibus Budget Reconciliation Act (OBRA), provided for increased food stamp benefits to especially vulnerable recipients, such as those facing high shelter costs. In addition, the Act increased the penalties for fraud.

PRWORA, the federal welfare reform legislation enacted in 1996 (discussed infra), instituted major reductions in the food stamp program, cutting approximately $20 billion from the program over six years. As a result, between September 1996 and September 1997, the number of persons receiving food stamps decreased dramatically by 3.9 million.[35] Two-thirds of these reductions affected families with children. The Center on Budget and Policy Priorities estimated that in 1998

---

[32] House Comm. on Ways & Means, 103d Cong., 1st Sess., Overview of Entitlement Programs ("1993 Green Book") 1630 (Comm. Print 1993).

[33] Carrie Lewis, Recent Developments Affecting the Food Stamp Program, 26 Clearinghouse Rev. 1069, 1070 (Jan. 1993).

[34] See Electronic Food Stamps Prove Vulnerable to Fraud, S.F. Chron., July 13, 1994, at A3 (discussing use of the electronic technology by retailers in Maryland, the first state to implement the system).

[35] Children's Defense Fund, The State of America's Children, 1998 Yearbook 54-55 (1998).

more than 5 million families with children lost an average of $36 per month in food stamp benefits.[36] The spending cuts led to a significant increase in requests for emergency food assistance.[37]

In May 2002, Congress enacted the Farm Security and Rural Investment Act, 7 U.S.C. §§7901 et seq., including reauthorization of the food stamp program. Program alterations restored food stamp eligibility for immigrant children under age 18, regardless of how long the children have been living in this country, and adjusted the standard deduction to varying household sizes.

In 2002, the food stamp program served approximately 4.4 million households, including 10 million children, each month.[38] The characteristics of married-couple households with children varied considerably from those of single-adult households with children.[39] The average monthly food stamp benefit for single-adult households was lower than that of married-couple households ($248 versus $303), due to the smaller size of single-adult households.[40] The per capita benefit was higher for people in single-adult households than for people in married-couple households ($80 versus $65) in part because single-adult households were poorer. Among all households with children, 15 percent received child support, and 8 percent had no income.[41]

In 2006, the recent reform effort regarding government benefits began as a privatization movement that sought to dismantle the organizations at the state level that deliver federal benefits by replacing them with private contractors. The privatization movement was motivated by concerns about the significant fiscal constraints on state budgets. As a result, by July 2007, approximately twenty states had contracted out some portions of food stamp eligibility determination, and several other states were considering similar efforts.[42]

Several other programs provide nutritional assistance to children. The National School Lunch Act, 42 U.S.C. §§1751 et seq. (2000 & Supp. 2005), provides federal matching funds for public and private schools that serve meals to children. The program provides a reimbursement system for meals served to children based on household income; and children in the Temporary Assistance for Needy Families Program (TANF) and those in the food stamp program automatically receive free meals.[43] In 2001, more than 25.4 million children each day received their lunch through the National School Lunch Program at a cost of $6.4 billion.[44] In addition, the Special Supplemental Nutrition Program for Women, Infants, and Children (WIC) serves to safeguard the health of low-income women, infants, and children

---

[36] Id. at 545.

[37] Id.

[38] Office of Analysis, Nutrition & Evaluation, FSP-03-CHAR02, Characteristics of Food Stamp Households: Fiscal Year 2002, 15, 22.

[39] Id. at 15.

[40] Id. at 18.

[41] Id.

[42] David A. Super, Privatization, Policy Paralysis, and the Poor, 96 Cal. L. Rev. 393, 395-396 (2008).

[43] House Comm. on Ways & Means, 2000 Green Book, supra note [28], at 957.

[44] Office of Analysis, Nutrition, and Evaluation, Statistics on the National School Lunch Program (Aug. 2003).

up to age five who are at nutritional risk by providing nutritious foods to supplement diets, information on healthy eating, and referrals to health care.[45] As of April 2002, approximately 8 million women, infants, and children were enrolled in the WIC program. Among these enrollees, approximately half are children; infants and women account for one-fourth, respectively.[46] Additional child nutrition programs receiving federal funds include a surplus commodity program, a special milk program, the nonschool food program, and the school breakfast program.[47] In 2008, the U.S. Department of Agriculture Secretary announced $9 million in grants for state agency technology improvements to the WIC program. The funds will facilitate the implementation of new computer systems to modernize the delivery of electronic benefits.[48]

Medicaid is another federal program that provides in-kind benefits to children from low-income families. Medicaid Act, 42 U.S.C. §§1396 et seq. (2000 & Supp. 2005). Currently, more than 44 million people in low-income families receive health care services through the Medicaid program. Medicaid spending is expected to be about $216 billion in FY 2009, rising to $287 billion in 2013. A recent Kaiser Foundation report details projected federal cuts in the President's FY 2009 budget proposal that would reduce Medicaid spending by $17.4 billion over the next five years and by $46.7 billion over the next ten years. The cuts would be accomplished by reducing the federal match rate for certain services and by making changes to managed care, long-term care, reimbursement for prescription drugs, and other Medicaid administration functions.[49] Begun in 1965, the Medicaid program is jointly funded by the federal and state governments to assist states in providing medical long-term care assistance to eligible individuals. Medicaid enables states, inter alia, to furnish (1) medical assistance on behalf of needy families with dependent children and needy individuals, as well as those who are aged, blind, or permanently and totally disabled; and (2) rehabilitation and other services to help such families. For an eligible family, Medicaid can provide for full or partial payment for a child's medical care services. Traditionally, Medicaid eligibility depended on eligibility under the Aid to Families with Dependent Children (AFDC) or Supplemental Security Income (SSI) programs. This changed as eligibility was extended in 1986 to groups of low-income pregnant women and children without ties to the welfare system. Further, states were required, as of July 1, 1991, to cover all children under age 19 and whose family income was below 100 percent of the federal poverty level.[50]

---

[45] 42 U.S.C. §§1771 et seq. (2000 & Supp. 2005). The Child Nutrition Act of 1966 was amended through Pub. L. No. 107-249 (2002).

[46] Office of Analysis, Nutrition, and Evaluation, WIC Participant and Program Characteristics 2002 (Sept. 2003).

[47] Id.

[48] USDA Speeds Help for 'Women, Infants, and Children' Nutrition Delivery, US Fed. News, Sept. 18, 2008 (available at 2008 WLNR 17792737).

[49] Kaiser Foundation, The Kaiser Commission on Medicaid and the Uninsured, Feb. 2008, p. 1 (available at www.kff.org/kcmu).

[50] House Comm. on Ways & Means, Overview of Entitlement Programs, supra note [32], at 1633-1635 (coverage mandatory for pregnant women, for services related to the pregnancy, and full

Welfare reform legislation (PRWORA), enacted in 1996, established the conditional work program TANF (discussed infra) to replace AFDC. Unlike AFDC, TANF does not confer automatic Medicaid eligibility. However, PRWORA maintains Medicaid eligibility for those individuals who met AFDC standards but who do not qualify for assistance under TANF.[51] Further, to remedy some of the hardships caused by PRWORA, the Balanced Budget Act of 1997, Pub. L. No. 205-33, 111 Stat. 251, 573 (1997), created a new health insurance program under Title XXI of the Social Security Act called the State Children's Health Insurance Program (SCHIP). This program enabled states to initiate and expand health insurance coverage for uninsured children through an option of providing 12 months of Medicaid coverage regardless of whether the children met income eligibility tests and by allowing states to presume eligibility until it has been determined.[52] Congress reauthorized SCHIP (H.R. 2) in 2009 for an additional four years.

For over 60 years, the primary means by which the federal government assisted needy children was the AFDC program. First enacted in 1935 as part of the Social Security Act, 42 U.S.C. §§601-617 (2000 & Supp. 2004), this program involved a partnership among the federal, state, and local governments. The program provided welfare payments for those needy children (and others in the child's household) who were deprived of support because a parent was absent, incapacitated, deceased, or unemployed. Under this program, federal statutes determined eligibility. States, however, decided the amount of benefits and administered the program. AFDC was replaced by PRWORA in 1996 (discussed below).

NOTE: THE PERSONAL RESPONSIBILITY AND WORK OPPORTUNITY RECONCILIATION ACT (PRWORA)

In 1996, Congress enacted the Personal Responsibility and Work Opportunity Reconciliation Act of 1996 (PRWORA), Pub. L. No. 104-193, 110 Stat. 2105 (codified primarily in scattered sections of 7 U.S.C. and 42 U.S.C.). As the first major reform of the welfare system since the New Deal, PRWORA aimed to: (1) aid needy families so that children may be cared for in their homes or those of relatives; (2) end dependency of needy parents on government benefits by promoting job preparation, work, and marriage; (3) prevent and reduce out-of-wedlock pregnancies and establish goals for preventing and reducing their incidence; and (4) encourage formation and maintenance of two-parent families.[53]

PRWORA abolished several federally funded programs, including AFDC (the primary cash assistance program for families), Emergency Assistance for Needy

---

coverage to children under age six with family incomes below 133 percent of the federal poverty income guidelines).

[51] House Comm. on Ways & Means, 105th Cong., 2d Sess., Background Material and Data on Programs Within the Jurisdiction of the Committee on Ways & Means (1998 Green Book) 952 (Comm. Print 1998).

[52] Id. at 953.

[53] Id. at 495.

Families (EA; emergency help to families with children for a maximum of one month per year), and the Job Opportunities and Basic Skills (JOBS) Training Program (the work and training program). In their place, PRWORA substitutes the Temporary Assistance for Needy Families Program (TANF). Unlike former law that *entitled* individuals and families to receive welfare assistance, TANF provides a block grant to the states for programs that are time-limited and conditioned on work.[54] TANF combined the funding for the repealed programs (AFDC, EA, and JOBS) into a single annual grant of $16.5 billion through the year 2002. (Presently, block grant funding remains at $16.5 billion annually.) Instead of receiving unlimited federal funds like under AFDC, states receive a "capped" block grant under PRWORA that had limited potential to increase following inflation, growth, or economic recession.

TANF significantly enlarged states' discretion in operating their welfare systems. No longer required to provide matching state grants to receive federal funding, states instead only need to meet a "maintenance of effort" provision (MOE) requiring them to maintain spending equal to at least 75 percent of their 1994 spending level for AFDC, EA, and JOBS. (Those states that do not meet mandatory work requirements must satisfy an 80 percent maintenance requirement.) States may also choose to offer vouchers or services to recipients rather than cash assistance. In addition, states may decide which categories of needy families to assist, may choose to adopt financial rewards or penalties to induce work, and can continue to set benefit levels.[55] States also have the ability to transfer up to 30 percent of welfare block grant funds into other social service programs.

TANF imposes conditions of the receipt of federal funds. States must achieve certain minimum participation rates in the work program. For example, 50 percent of all recipients have to be working (or participating in work-related activities) by the year 2002 or the state's block grant would decrease. However, the "caseload reduction credit" allows states to have fewer than 50 percent of recipients in these activities if their welfare caseloads decrease. States must also spend a certain amount of state funds on behalf of eligible families, must impose a time limit on benefits, and must limit funds to unwed teenage mothers (discussed infra).

Some of the major provisions of the 1996 welfare reform legislation include the following:

a. Work requirements (PRWORA §103).   PRWORA requires states to impose work requirements and time-limited TANF grants. The head of every family must find work within two years of receiving aid or the family loses benefits. States may choose to impose more strict work requirements and time limits than those required by the Act.

Recipients in single-parent families must participate in a "qualifying work activity" for a minimum number of hours per week. Work requirements are increased for two-parent families. Recipients may not be penalized for failure to meet work requirements if their failure is based on their inability to find child care. Thus, the work requirement may be waived, at the option of the state, for parents with children under 12 months. For parents with children under age six, hours may be limited to 20 per week.

[54] Id. at 494.
[55] Id. at 495.

Payments to families are limited to two years for any one period of time. Further, adults are subject to a five-year lifetime cap for the receipt of welfare. If families' benefits are terminated because the head of the family is unwilling or unable to find work within the two-year period, states are not required to provide other services to meet the family's or children's needs. PRWORA also amended the Food Stamp Act (§801 et seq.) to link food stamp eligibility to work requirements (§824).

b. Unwed Teenage Mothers (PRWORA §§103, 905).   PRWORA prohibits states from providing benefits to unwed teenage mothers (under age 18) unless the young women meet certain conditions. First, they must live at home or in another adult-supervised setting. Certain exceptions exist for teenage parents who have no parent, guardian, or other adult relative, or who are victims of abuse (§103). Second, as soon as her child is three months old, the mother must attend high school or an alternative educational or training program. PRWORA also instituted family caps, permitting states to deny aid to children who are born more than ten months after the family goes on welfare (§103(a)). States receive bonuses (supplemental federal funds) if they show a decrease in the numbers of illegitimate births and pregnancies to teenage mothers (§103(a)).

The Act also provides for monitoring states' progress toward the goal of preventing teenage pregnancy. The Secretary of Health and Human Services must establish a plan for assuring that at least 25 percent of communities impose a teenage pregnancy prevention program. The Secretary is required to report annually on the success of preventing out-of-wedlock teenage pregnancies (§905).

c. Paternity Establishment (PRWORA §§301, 331, 332).   PRWORA amended the Social Security Act, Title IV, Part D (Child Support and Establishment of Paternity), to require states to expand services relating to paternity establishment with the goal of increasing collection of child support payments. States must continue these services for families no longer eligible for aid under TANF (§301). Also, states must have procedures to require a child and other parties to submit to genetic testing in contested cases, and must establish a threshold probability level beyond which the genetic results create a rebuttable or conclusive presumption of paternity.

PRWORA expands the focus on *voluntary* paternity acknowledgment, requiring states to have in-hospital programs that attempt to establish paternity immediately at birth. Voluntary establishment programs must also be available from the state agency responsible for maintaining birth records. Such programs must inform the mother and father of the rights, legal consequences, and responsibilities that arise from signing a paternity acknowledgment. A voluntary acknowledgment of paternity is considered a legal finding of paternity (§331). Finally, states are also required to publicize and encourage the use of procedures for voluntary establishment of paternity and child support (§332).

d. Sanctions (PRWORA orders §103).   PRWORA provided that states may sanction families for failure to comply with requirements of the Act, including the failure to ensure that minor children attend school. Similarly, the federal government may also sanction states for failure to comply with requirements of the Act and for failure to meet minimum participation rates.

Before PRWORA was set to expire on October 1, 2002, Congress made several unsuccessful attempts to reauthorize TANF. Congressional attention to the War on

Terror and military action in Iraq led to postponement of the reauthorization. TANF continued to operate by continuing resolution until February 2006, when Congress enacted the Deficit Reduction Act (DRA) of 2005, Pub. L. No. 109-171, to reauthorize TANF through federal FY 2010. TANF continues to emphasize work as a condition of aid and to grant states discretion over program eligibility and administration.

However, the most significant change is the imposition of tougher work participation requirements on the states. Although the number of work hours and the percentage of recipients who must meet work participation goals are unchanged from the original legislation, the reauthorized program limits the range of activities that qualify as "work," reduces state flexibility in meeting work participation benchmarks, imposes tighter restrictions on job search activities that count toward "weekly work hours," and requires state agencies to verify reported hours of work activities. Moreover, states have less flexibility to exclude parents of young children from the work requirements.[56]

Since its passage, commentators have highlighted shortcomings of the Act. Some question the ability of PRWORA to decrease poverty levels, arguing that the lack of focus on education merely moves recipients to low-salaried jobs that leave them unable to support a family. Instead, commentators suggest shifting the focus to education, subsidized salaries, and improved child care.[57] Others highlight the problems that develop in a recession, particularly in central cities that have a concentration of welfare recipients.[58]

The most prevalent criticisms, however, focus on the work requirements. Specifically, many former welfare recipients and low-income workers struggle to keep their jobs because of lack of education and poor job skills.[59] Critics argue as well that programs do not help welfare recipients handle possible family problems (e.g., financial stress, lack of child care, or caring for disabled family members) while trying to maintain employment.[60]

Commentators generally commend the increased emphasis on paternity establishment and enforcement of child support obligations. However, many caution that these provisions alone do not result in decreased poverty levels. Instead, PRWORA must advocate expanded education and training opportunities, tax credits, a higher minimum wage, and, ideally, adequate paying jobs in the private

---

[56] Scott W. Allard, The Changing Face of Welfare During the Bush Administration, 37 Publius 304, June 22, 2007, np (available at 2007 WLNR 12785563).

[57] Lindsay Mara Schoen, Note, Working Welfare Recipients: A Comparison of the Family Support Act and the Personal Responsibility and Work Opportunity Reconciliation Act, 24 Fordham Urb. L.J. 635, 658-661 (1997).

[58] John Accordino, The Consequences of Welfare Reform for Central City Economies, 64 J. Am. Plan. Assn. 11, 11-14 (1998). See also Margaret Weir, The Uncertain Future of Welfare Reform in the Cities, 15 Brookings Rev. 30 (1997).

[59] Nancye Campbell et al., Job Retention and Advancement in Welfare Reform (Brookings Institute, 2002). See also Joel Handler, "Ending Welfare as We Know It": The Win/Win Spin or the Stench of Victory, 5 J. Gender Race & Just. 131 (2001).

[60] Courtney Jarchow, Job Retention and Advancement Strategies (Natl. Conf. of State Legislatures, 2003).

sector.[61] In addition, others worry that the tougher measures toward paternity establishment and child support enforcement may have a negative impact for victims of domestic violence by alerting fathers to the location of mothers and forcing women to remain in abusive relationships because of the federal emphasis on self-sufficiency with its limitations on benefits.[62]

What are the long-term effects of the welfare reforms? Statistics reveal that welfare caseloads have declined dramatically during the past several years. In 2001, the average monthly number of TANF recipients was 5.4 million persons, 57 percent lower than the average monthly AFDC caseload in 1996 and the smallest number of people on welfare since 1968.[63] This decrease has been attributed to the PRWORA provisions of work requirements and time limits.[64] Whereas studies confirm that welfare reforms have increased employment and earnings, particularly for single mothers, they also indicate that the favorable economy of the late 1990s was partly responsible for these effects.[65]

One commentator concludes:

> One key difference between welfare retrenchment in the late 1990s and the retrenchment that may occur over the next few years, however, is that the late 1990s were a time of unprecedented economic expansion. Both poverty and unemployment were at historic lows, and low-skill workers were having an easier time finding work than in the previous decades. Today, poverty rates are on the rise, increasing by 12 percent since 1999, and the low-skill labor market is tighter than before. Future caseload reduction and withdrawal of welfare assistance will occur in an environment where low-income households have fewer labor market options, which will lead to greater unmet needs for communities to address.[66]

For further analysis of welfare reform policy, see Rebecca M. Blank & Ron Haskins, The New World of Welfare (2002); Andrea Kave et al., Welfare Reform and Beyond: The Future of the Safety Net (2002); Frances F. Piven et al., Work, Welfare and Politics: Confronting Poverty in the Wake of Welfare Reform (2002); Alvin L. Schorr, Welfare Reform: Failures and Remedies (2001).

---

[61] Paul K. Legler, The Coming Revolution in Child Support Policy: Implications of the 1996 Welfare Act, 30 Fam. L.Q. 519, 562-563 (1996). See also Stacy L. Brustin, The Intersection Between Welfare Reform and Child Support Enforcement: D.C.'s Weak Link, 52 Cath. U.L. Rev. 621 (2003); Sheila Rafferty Zedlewski, Family Economic Resources in the Post-Reform Era, 12 The Future of Children: Children and Welfare Reform 121 (Winter/Spring 2002).

[62] Shelley Kintzel et al., Comments, The Effects of Domestic Violence on Welfare Reform: An Assessment of the Personal Responsibility and Work Opportunity Reconciliation Act as Applied to Battered Women, 50 U. Kan. L. Rev. 591 (2002). See also Jessica Pearson et al., Child Support and Domestic Violence: The Victims Speak Out, 5 Violence Against Women 427 (1999).

[63] Dept. of Health & Hum. Servs., Indicators of Welfare Dependence: 2003, Annual Report to Congress (2003).

[64] House Comm. on Ways & Means, 2000 Green Book, supra note [28], at 251.

[65] See, e.g., Jeffrey Grogger et al., Consequences of Welfare Reform: A Research Synthesis 98 (Rand Corp. 2002).

[66] Allard, supra note [56].

CHAPTER 3

Protecting the Child from Abuse and Neglect

A. PROBLEMS AND INTRODUCTION

(1) Eleanor Papillon is a 20-year-old single parent. She is a devoted member of a fundamentalist religious sect, one of the tenets of which is to strongly disapprove nonmarital sex. Eleanor's son Danny is four years old. When Eleanor took Danny in for an annual medical check-up, the pediatrician — Dr. Thomas Stein — noticed that Danny had bruise marks on his arms, stomach, back, and buttocks. The doctor asked Eleanor what had happened. Eleanor said that during a visit to his aunt's house three days before, Danny had been discovered under a bed with his pants off with a little girl, also aged four, who had her pants off. Eleanor reported that she had beaten Danny that night at home, after she became enraged by his refusal to admit what he had done.

a. Does Danny have a tort action for assault and battery against his mother? Under the standards of the Restatement (Second) of Torts, reprinted infra p. 233, would the mother's spanking be privileged? Would the doctrine of parental tort immunity prevent a suit? See infra p. 237. Are tort remedies appropriate?

b. Could Eleanor be criminally liable for the spanking she inflicted on Danny under the standards of the ALI Model Penal Code? (Reprinted p. 232, infra.) Are penal remedies appropriate?

c. What legal advice would you give to Dr. Stein? Is he obligated to make a report of this case to the police under the California reporting statute? See Ham v. Hospital of Morristown, p. 252, infra. What purposes are served by requiring a report?

d. Based on Eleanor's behavior, could a juvenile court assume jurisdiction over Danny as a neglected child? The California jurisdictional provisions, Welf. & Inst. Code §300, are reprinted at pp. 318-320, infra. Would it be appropriate for a juvenile court to take jurisdiction over Danny and to remove Danny from maternal custody and put him in foster care? To take jurisdiction and to leave Danny at home with supervision by a social worker? These issues are considered further in section E of this chapter, which deals more generally with the neglect jurisdiction of the juvenile court and the foster care system.

(2) Mission School, a public junior high school in Little Rock, Arkansas, has regulations that permit a classroom teacher to paddle a student if the teacher determines that (a) the student has behaved in a disruptive way and (b) the paddling is likely to improve class decorum. Four days ago Toby Rockland, a 13-year-old eighth grader, was paddled by his English teacher, Mr. Klaus. Klaus told Toby that Toby had disrupted the class by failing to raise his hand before speaking out in class and by whispering to other students during a study period. The paddling caused Toby considerable pain and has resulted in a large black and blue mark on his buttocks. As a consequence Toby visited a doctor and had to stay home from school for two days to recover.

a. Does Toby have any claim against the teacher under the tort law of your jurisdiction? Would he have a claim if the standards of the Restatement (Second) of Torts applied? See p. 239, infra. Could this paddling offend the prohibition against cruel and unusual punishment? See Ingraham v. Wright, p. 245, infra.

b. Suppose Toby's parents object on principle to corporal punishment. As parents, do they have the right to prohibit the use of corporal punishment in school? Under the standards of the Restatement, would it be different if Mission School were a private school? What do the *Pierce, Meyer*, and *Yoder* cases, found in Chapter 1, suggest about parental prerogatives? See Baker v. Owen, p. 239, infra.

c. Does the Constitution require that Toby be given a hearing of some sort before he is paddled? See the Note on Procedural Due Process in school, p. 245, supra, and the material on Ingraham v. Wright, pp. 245-246, infra.

This chapter explores the tension generated by (1) the privilege of parents and those standing in loco parentis to use corporal punishment to discipline children; (2) the important social interest in protecting children (who ordinarily are in no position to defend themselves) from physical abuse from adults; and (3) the value our society places on family privacy. In studying the materials in this chapter, you should focus on the questions of what legal standards should be used to evaluate the use of parental force toward children, whether the remedies of tort law or criminal law provide adequate protection, and what methods are available to discover parental excesses.

B.   THE PARENTAL PRIVILEGE TO DISCIPLINE CHILDREN

1.   Limitations on Parents' Use of Force

Willis v. State
888 N.E.2d 177 (Ind. 2008)

RUCKER, Justice.

This case requires us to examine the balance that must be struck in determining when a parent's use of physical force as a form of discipline crosses the line into criminal conduct. . . .

Sophia Willis is a single mother raising her eleven-year-old son, J.J., who has a history of untruthfulness and taking property belonging to others. [On Friday, February 3, 2006] J.J.'s fifth grade teacher, Ms. McCuen, saw J.J. giving a bag of women's clothing to a classmate. Finding this to be an "odd exchange," Ms. McCuen contacted J.J.'s mother. Willis met with Ms. McCuen and identified the clothing as hers.

Experiencing ongoing disciplinary problems with J.J., Willis sent him to her sister's home over the next two days to ponder her options. When J.J. returned on Sunday Willis had a long conversation with her son and questioned him about his conduct. J.J. denied taking the clothing and instead concocted a story that shifted blame to other students. Willis warned that if he did not tell the truth he would be punished. J.J. again gave the same story. In response Willis instructed J.J. to remove his pants and place his hands on the upper bunk bed. J.J. complied, and Willis proceeded to strike him five to seven times with either a belt or an extension cord.[1] Although trying to swat J.J. on the buttocks, his attempt to avoid the swats resulted in some of them landing on his arm and thigh leaving bruises. J.J. testified that during this exchange his mother was "mad." Willis countered that she was not angry but "disappointed."

The following Monday J.J. returned from gym class and asked to see the school nurse. Showing the nurse the bruises, J.J. told her that he received a "whooping" from his mother "[b]ecause I had took some clothes and I had lied." The nurse contacted child protective services that in turn contacted the Indianapolis Police Department.

Willis was arrested and charged with battery as a Class D felony.[3] After a bench trial she was found guilty as charged. . . . Contending that she had the legal authority to discipline her son, Willis appealed on grounds that the evidence was not sufficient to sustain the conviction. . . .

A parent has a fundamental liberty interest in maintaining a familial relationship with his or her child. This fundamental interest includes the right of parents "to direct the upbringing and education of children," Pierce v. Soc'y of Sisters, 268 U.S. 510, 534-35 (1925). However, the potential for child abuse cannot be taken lightly. Consequently, the State has a powerful interest in preventing and deterring the mistreatment of children. The difficult task of prosecutors and the courts is to determine when parental use of physical force in disciplining children turns an otherwise law-abiding citizen into a criminal.

A parental privilege to use moderate or reasonable physical force, without criminal liability, was recognized at common law. For example, Blackstone observed, "[B]attery is, in some cases, justifiable or lawful; as where one who

---

[1] The evidence on this point is in conflict. Willis testified she used a belt and introduced it as Defendant's Exhibit C. Tr. at 57. J.J. testified that his mother used an extension cord. Id. at 8. For purposes of determining guilt and imposing sentence, the trial court declared, "I think it wouldn't matter if it was a belt or an extension cord." Id. at 65.

[3] Sometimes referred to as "battery on a child," the statute provides that "[a] person who knowingly or intentionally touches another person in a rude, insolent, or angry manner commits battery, a Class B misdemeanor," Ind. Code §35-42-2-1(a), and the offense is a Class D felony "if it results in bodily injury to . . . a person less than fourteen (14) years of age and is committed by a person at least eighteen (18) years of age." I.C. §35-42-2-1(a)(2)(B).

hath authority, a parent or master, gives moderate correction to his child, his scholar, or his apprentice." William Blackstone, 3 Blackstone's Commentaries on the Laws of England 120 (Oxford reprint 1992). A similar view has been expressed in this state's jurisprudence. See e.g., Hinkle v. State, 127 Ind. 490, 26 N.E. 777, 778 (1891) ("[F]ather has the right to administer proper and reasonable chastisement to his child without being guilty of an assault and battery, but he has no right to administer unreasonable chastisement, or to be guilty of cruel and inhuman treatment of his child. . . ."). . . .

A number of jurisdictions have specifically codified a parental discipline privilege. [Indiana has not yet done so.] Over several decades our courts have addressed parental claims of legal authority. [Citations omitted]. Nonetheless, as the Court of Appeals has observed, there is still "precious little Indiana case law providing guidance as to what constitutes proper and reasonable parental discipline of children, and there are no bright-line rules." Mitchell v. State, 813 N.E.2d 422, 427 (Ind. Ct. App. 2004).

As a matter of judicial declaration or legislative enactment, several jurisdictions have embraced some, parts, or all of either the Model Penal Code or the Restatement (Second) of Torts to identify permissible parental conduct in the discipline of children. We think it helpful to take a look at these sources. The Model Penal Code provides in relevant part that a parent's use of force is justifiable if:

> (a) the force is used for the purpose of safeguarding or promoting the welfare of the minor, including the prevention or punishment of his misconduct; and
> (b) the force used is not designed to cause or known to create a substantial risk of causing death, serious bodily injury, disfigurement, extreme pain or mental distress or gross degradation.

Model Penal Code §3.08(1) (1985). We make two observations. First, the Code does not explicitly demand that the use of force be reasonable. Second, under the Code, so long as a parent acts for the purpose of safeguarding or promoting the child's welfare (including the specific purpose of preventing or punishing misconduct), the parent is privileged in using force, unless the force creates a substantial risk of death or excessive injuries. Neither of these two propositions finds support in Indiana's common law. We conclude therefore that the Model Penal Code is not a helpful source to inform our decision on the law in this area.

In contrast, the Restatement provides, "A parent is privileged to apply such reasonable force or to impose such reasonable confinement upon his [or her] child as he [or she] reasonably believes to be necessary for its proper control, training, or education." Restatement of the Law (Second) Torts, §147(1) (1965). We adopt the Restatement view. Not only is it entirely consistent with the law in this jurisdiction, but also it provides guidance on the factors that may be considered in determining the reasonableness of punishment. It reads:

> In determining whether force or confinement is reasonable for the control, training, or education of a child, the following factors are to be considered: (a) whether the actor is a parent; (b) the age, sex, and physical and mental condition of the child; (c) the nature of his offense and his apparent motive;

(d) the influence of his example upon other children of the same family or group; (e) whether the force or confinement is reasonably necessary and appropriate to compel obedience to a proper command; (f) whether it is disproportionate to the offense, unnecessarily degrading, or likely to cause serious or permanent harm. Restatement, supra, §150.

We hasten to add that this list is not exhaustive. There may be other factors unique to a particular case that should be taken into consideration. And obviously, not all of the listed factors may be relevant or applicable in every case. But in either event they should be balanced against each other, giving appropriate weight as the circumstances dictate, in determining whether the force is reasonable.

The defense of parental privilege, like self-defense, is a complete defense. [T]o sustain a conviction for battery where a claim of parental privilege has been asserted, the State must prove that either: (1) the force the parent used was unreasonable or (2) the parent's belief that such force was necessary to control her child and prevent misconduct was unreasonable. See Restatement, supra, §147. . . .

Several of the factors suggested by the Restatement are helpful in evaluating the facts in this case. Although we know that J.J. is an eleven-year-old male child, there is nothing in the record concerning his physical or mental condition. In any event, "A punishment which would not be too severe for a boy of twelve may be obviously excessive if imposed upon a child of four or five." Restatement, supra, §150 cmt. c. As for the nature of the offense and J.J.'s apparent motive, the record is not clear as to why J.J. took his mother's clothing to school and then lied about it. That aside, most parents would likely consider as serious their eleven-year-old child's behavior in being untruthful and taking property of others. At the very least, a parent might consider that such behavior could set the stage for more aberrant behavior later in life. Willis expressed her concerns in this regard, "[H]e's going to do it again. . . . [H]e's already done it again. . . . And I hate to say it, but I know my son will end up back in the court system." [Trial Transcript] at 75. Comments to the Restatement provide, "[A] more severe punishment may be imposed for a serious offense, or an intentional one, than for a minor offense, or one resulting from a mere error of judgment or careless inattention. The fact that the child has shown a tendency toward certain types of misconduct may justify a punishment which would be clearly excessive if imposed upon a first offender." Restatement, supra, §150 cmt. c. Clearly J.J. was not a first offender.

Concerning whether the force Willis employed against J.J. was reasonably necessary and appropriate to compel obedience to her insistence that he tell the truth, again the Restatement is instructive. "As in all cases in which the question arises as to whether there has been excessive means of carrying out the privilege [to use force], the actor is not privileged to use a means to compel obedience if a less severe method appears to be likely to be equally effective." Restatement, supra, §150 cmt. d. The record shows that Willis has used progressive forms of discipline. Typical punishment was to send J.J. to his room, ground him, or withhold privileges such as television, games, and time spent outdoors. According to Willis, after grounding failed the last time J.J. was caught stealing, she decided harsher punishment — swatting with a belt — would be more effective. As Willis explained, "I thought about it over the entire weekend and I even tried to talk to him again. And he continued to lie. . . . I didn't know what else to do."

Considering whether the punishment J.J. received was unnecessarily degrading, disproportionate to the offense J.J. committed, or likely to cause J.J. serious or permanent harm, we make the following observations. J.J. received five to seven swats on his buttocks, arm, and thigh for what many parents might reasonably consider a serious offense. We find nothing particularly degrading about this manner of punishment. Nor, in context, is it readily apparent that the punishment was disproportionate to the offense. The question is whether the manner of punishment was "likely to cause [J.J.] serious or permanent harm." Restatement, supra, §150(f). The best answer to this question is J.J.'s own testimony which indicated that the swats hurt "[f]or a minute" but did not hurt the next day when he returned to school. To be sure the bruising was still apparent, but there is no indication that the school nurse provided any medical attention or even suggested that medical attention was necessary. In essence it appears from the record that the bruises were neither serious nor permanent. This fact militates against a conclusion that the punishment was unreasonable. . . . Considering the totality of the circumstances, we are not persuaded that the State disproved the defense beyond a reasonable doubt. We therefore set aside Willis' conviction.

ALI Model Penal Code §3.08

§3.08 Use of Force by Persons with Special Responsibility for Care, Discipline or Safety of Others

The use of force upon or toward the person of another is justifiable if:

(1) the actor is the parent or guardian or other person similarly responsible for the general care and supervision of a minor or a person acting at the request of such parent, guardian or other responsible person and:

(a) the force is used for the purpose of safeguarding or promoting the welfare of the minor, including the prevention or punishment of his misconduct; and

(b) the force used is not designed to cause or known to create a substantial risk of causing death, serious bodily harm, disfigurement, extreme pain or mental distress or gross degradation; or

(2) the actor is a teacher or a person otherwise entrusted with the care or supervision for a special purpose of a minor and:

(a) the actor believes that the force used is necessary to further such special purpose, including the maintenance of reasonable discipline in a school, class or other group, and that the use of such force is consistent with the welfare of the minor; and

(b) the degree of force, if it had been used by the parent or guardian of the minor, would not be unjustifiable under paragraph (1)(b) of this Section; or

(3) the actor is the guardian or other person similarly responsible for the general care and supervision of an incompetent person; and:

(a) the force is used for the purpose of safeguarding or promoting the welfare of the incompetent person, including the prevention of his misconduct, or, when such incompetent person is in a hospital or other institution for his care and custody, for the maintenance of reasonable discipline in such institution; and

(b) the force used is not designed to cause or known to create a substantial risk of causing death, serious bodily harm, disfigurement, extreme or unnecessary pain, mental distress, or humiliation . . .

Restatement (Second) of Torts §§147, 150, 151

§147. General Principle

(1) A parent is privileged to apply such reasonable force or to impose such reasonable confinement upon his child as he reasonably believes to be necessary for its proper control, training, or education.

(2) One other than a parent who has been given by law or has voluntarily assumed in whole or in part the function of controlling, training, or educating a child, is privileged to apply such reasonable force or to impose such reasonable confinement as he reasonably believes to be necessary for its proper control, training, or education, except in so far as the parent has restricted the privilege of one to whom he has entrusted the child.

§150. Factors Involved in Determining Reasonableness of Punishment

In determining whether force or confinement is reasonable for the control, training, or education of a child, the following factors are to be considered:

(a) whether the actor is a parent;

(b) the age, sex, and physical and mental condition of the child;

(c) the nature of his offense and his apparent motive;

(d) the influence of his example upon other children of the same family or group;

(e) whether the force or confinement is reasonably necessary and appropriate to compel obedience to a proper command;

(f) whether it is disproportionate to the offense, unnecessarily degrading, or likely to cause serious or permanent harm.

§151. Purpose of Punishment

Force applied or confinement imposed primarily for any purpose other than the proper training or education of the child or for the preservation of discipline is not privileged although applied or imposed in an amount and upon an occasion which would be privileged had it been applied for such purpose.

Dennis Alan Olson, Comment, The Swedish Ban of Corporal Punishment
1984 B.Y.U. L. Rev. 447-456

On July 1, 1979, Sweden became the first nation to prohibit corporal punishment of children by their parents. The Swedish Parenthood and Guardianship Code was amended to provide: "A child may not be subjected to corporal punishment or other injurious or humiliating treatment." The new Swedish law is distinctive because it allows greater intrusion into family life than the laws of other countries that have considered the relationship between corporal punishment and child abuse specifically and children's rights generally. The law also represents the final step in an attempt by lawmakers to change societal views without coercion. . . .

The 1979 law prohibiting corporal punishment reflects the major transformation of Swedish attitudes against the punishment of children that has occurred over the past thirty years. Traditionally, the right of parents to use corporal punishment in raising their children was wholly accepted in Sweden. Both religious and legal codes reiterated the proverbial dictum that sparing the rod spoils the child.

When Swedish family law was codified in 1920, it expressly gave parents the right to punish their children. This language of the statute was extensively criticized because it resulted in the widespread use of severe corporal punishment. In an effort to discourage the use of harsh punishments, the Parenthood and Guardianship Code was amended in 1949 to replace the word "punish" with reprimand. However, this change in the code was not accompanied by comparable changes in the criminal law. The Penal Code preserved the parental right to punish children and protected parents from criminal prosecution for actions against those under their supervision, as long as the injuries inflicted were not long-term. This exception from criminal liability for parents and guardians made child abuse cases difficult to prosecute until the exception was eliminated from the Penal Code in 1957.

In 1965, the rising number of child abuse cases led the justice minister to call for stronger statutory condemnation of corporal punishment. . . .

[I]n response to the Ministry's proposal to amend the code, the Riksdag adopted [a] proposal in 1966 [which] neither called for an acknowledgement of the right to punish nor expressly banned physical punishment. Despite the passive nature of simply removing all references to corporal punishment from the Code, the Riksdag considered this action a ban on corporal punishment. Even later, when the Riksdag expressly banned corporal punishment in 1979, it insisted that its action was merely a codification of the existing law.

The ban of corporal punishment was contrary to the prevailing public opinion in Sweden concerning corporal punishment. A public opinion poll in 1965 showed that 54% of all adult Swedes considered physical punishment occasionally necessary in child rearing. However, by 1968 the percentage of persons supporting physical punishment had fallen from 53% to 42% while opposition to corporal punishment had increased from 35% to 54%. This shift of opinion continued through 1971 when a survey indicated that support for corporal punishment had decreased to 35%. The 1971 survey also asked whether people thought the law prohibited corporal punishment. Sixty-one percent of the respondents felt that it was prohibited, while the remaining 39% either felt physical punishment was permitted by law or had no opinion on the issue. . . .

In preparation for the International Year of the Child, the Riksdag established the Commission on Children's Rights on February 24,1977. The Commission was charged with investigating ways of strengthening the legal position of children. In 1978 the Commission issued its first report, entitled *Children's Rights: A Ban Against Corporal Punishment.* The report proposed the enactment of an explicit ban of physical punishment. Corporal punishment was viewed as "a form of degrading treatment" which results in a "lack of self-esteem and a personality change" that could affect the child for life. The report found that "[c]hild psychiatrists and psychologists have long been in agreement that physical punishment of children is inappropriate."

Influenced by such opinions and the need for society to "work against all forms of violence," the Commission found an express ban of corporal punishment necessary in order for children to grow up realizing that violence is not socially acceptable behavior. The Commission noted that, while most Swedes felt corporal punishment was prohibited, many people continued to violate the law. The Commission felt greater public knowledge of the law would result in increased compliance. However, the Commission recognized the difficulty of publicizing the mere absence of permission to reprimand or punish. Unless the ban were explicitly expressed, it would be difficult to increase public knowledge concerning the illegality of corporal punishment beyond the 1971 level. . . . The Commission's proposal was introduced in the Riksdag. In a report of its own, the government emphasized the role of the law in changing the attitudes of parents and guardians. The Riksdag's Law Committee proposed slight changes in some sections of the law but did not substantively alter the ban. A nearly unanimous vote of the Riksdag adopted the government proposal.

The law prohibiting corporal punishment of children was not intended to include criminal sanctions requiring changes in the Penal Code. The legislation was consciously designed as a prohibition "without teeth." The Commission on Children's Rights noted in its first report that no changes in the Penal Code were proposed. The remittance comments also made reference to the noncriminal nature of the ban and suggested use of a strong advertising campaign to increase public awareness and obedience to the law. The government adopted this suggestion as part of its own report. . . .

NOTES AND QUESTIONS

(1) Physical Abuse or Discipline?   Virtually all American states, either by statute or case law, permit "reasonable" corporal punishment by parents or guardians.[1] What distinguishes abuse from discipline according to Willis v. State?

---

[1] Elizabeth T. Gershoff & Susan H. Bitensky, The Case Against Corporal Punishment of Children, 13 Psychol. Pub. Pol'y & L. 231, 247 (2007).

(2) Reasonableness.   What factors determine whether the parent's degree of force was "reasonable"? According to the American Law Institute Model Penal Code? The Restatement (Second) of Torts? Why did the Indiana Supreme Court adopt the Restatement approach in *Willis*? Should the law take into account a "cultural defense" in the determination of reasonableness (i.e., cultural practices among immigrant populations that permit various forms of corporal punishment)? See generally Michael Futterman, Comment, Seeking a Standard: Reconciling Child Abuse and Condoned Child Rearing Practices Among Different Cultures, 34 U. Miami Inter-Am. L. Rev. 491 (2003).

(3) Swedish Reform Movement.   How likely is Congress to enact a ban similar to the Swedish legislation? How would parents in the United States react to a ban similar to the Swedish legislation? Are American parents likely to respond to a prohibition without criminal penalties? If not, what penalties would be necessary to enforce the ban? Are criminal penalties, such as those for child abuse or assault, appropriate as redress for spanking or slapping?[2] See Calif. Welf. & Inst. Code §300, reprinted infra, pp. 318-320. Could an American ban on corporal punishment be reconciled with the Supreme Court's decisions in *Meyer, Pierce*, and *Prince?* Note that Congress unsuccessfully attempted to enact legislation that would have authorized a federal parental right to use "reasonable" corporal discipline (the Parental Rights and Responsibilities Act of 1995, S. 984, 104th Cong. §3 (1995)).

As the earlier excerpt explains, the Swedish ban of 1979 was actually the third stage of legislative reform. The first reform occurred in 1957, when the Swedish Parliament eliminated the parental privilege from the Penal Code — that is, removing parental physical punishment as a defense to criminal assault. In the second stage, in 1966, the Swedish Parliament removed references to even mild forms of corporal punishment from the Parents' Code.

(4) Effects of the Swedish Ban.

a. Attitudinal Change.   The Swedish ban significantly changed attitudes toward corporal punishment. Before the ban, 54 percent of all adult Swedes considered such punishment necessary occasionally. Attitudes began to change following an aggressive public awareness campaign. By 2000, 92 percent of Swedish parents reported that they had not struck their children during the prior year.[3]

b. International Law.   The Swedish ban initiated a worldwide trend: 22 countries later banned corporal punishment of children in all settings, including

---

[2] In 2007, the Massachusetts legislature considered the first statewide ban on corporal punishment by parents on children under age 18 (H. 3922). Laurel J. Sweet, Bay State Going Slap-Happy, House to Debate Ban on Spanking, Boston Herald, Nov. 27, 2007, at 2. The bill was referred to a study committee. Beacon Hill Roll Call, Telegram & Gazette (Worcester), May 2, 2008, at 14 (available at 2008 WLNR 8370702).

[3] Joan E. Durrant, From Mopping up the Damage to Preventing the Flood: The Role of Social Policy in Preventing Violence Against Children, Soc. Pol'y J. New Zealand, July 1, 2006, at 1 (available at 2006 WLNR 16807689). See also Joan E. Durrant, Legal Reform and Attitudes Toward Physical Punishment in Sweden, 11 Int'l J. Children's Rts. (No. 2) 147 (2003).

the home.[4] But cf. Canadian Foundation for Children, Youth & Law v. Canada, [2004] 1 S.C.R. 76, 234 D.L.R. (4th) 257 (Can.) (allowing parents and teachers to use spanking, except for babies and teenagers, provided the force is "reasonable"); R. v. Swan, 0215/07, [2008] O.J. 1055 WESTLAW (O.S.C.J. Mar. 13, 2008) (Can.) (upholding a father's right to use force to *restrain* a teenager). The Canadian Parliament is presently considering a bill that would prohibit corporal punishment of children.[5]

c. *Convention on the Rights of the Child.*   The Swedish ban also influenced international human rights law. Article 19 of the 1989 United Nations Convention on the Rights of the Child (which imposes human rights obligations on signatory nations) requires governments to protect children from all forms of maltreatment.

Moreover, Article 37 provides that no child shall be subjected to cruel, inhuman, or degrading punishment. Although the Convention does not contain an explicit prohibition of "physical punishment," the international committee that interprets the Convention has emphasized that corporal punishment of children is "incompatible with the Convention" and recommended its prohibition.[6] (The United States has not yet ratified the U.N. Convention on the Rights of the Child.) In addition, several international organizations (e.g., the U.N. Committee on the Rights of the Child, the Council of Europe's Parliamentary Assembly, and the Council of Europe's Commissioner for Human Rights) now provide that corporal punishment of children is a violation of international human rights law.[7]

(5) *Challenges to the Ban.* Several Swedish parents challenged the ban as a violation of the European convention for the Protection of Human Rights and Fundamental Freedoms respecting family life and freedom of religion (church tenets that support corporal punishment). The European Court of Human Rights rejected their challenge in X, Y, and Z v. Sweden, 5 Eur. Ct. H.R. 147 (1983). Subsequently, the European Court of Human Rights held that a stepfather's beating of a nine-year-old boy with a bamboo garden stake violated his human rights. A. v. United Kingdom, 27 Eur. Ct. H.R. 611 (1999). In response, the British government promised to amend the law. In 2004, Parliament considered a total ban on corporal punishment but decided instead merely to limit the scope of "reasonable chastisement" to exclude assaults resulting in actual bodily harm.[8]

(6) *Parental Tort Immunity.* Virtually all jurisdictions have abolished the parental tort immunity doctrine, prohibiting an unemancipated child from suing a parent for negligent injuries. The doctrine was first recognized in Hewellette v. George, 9 So. 885 (1891). By the 1950s, almost all states had adopted the doctrine. California started the trend toward abrogation with Gibson v. Gibson, 479 P.2d 648 (Cal. 1971), replacing the doctrine with the "reasonable parent standard" (i.e., the

[4] Global Initiative to End All Corporal Punishment of Children, Countdown to Universal Prohibition, States with Full Abolition (Sept. 2008) (available at *http:www.endcorporalpunishment.org*).

[5] Tim Naumetz, Spare the Rod — or Face Criminal Charges?, Hamilton Spectator, June 19, 2008, at A9.

[6] Cited in Linda Rose-Krasnor et al., Physical Punishment and the U.N. Convention on the Rights of the Child, Int'l Soc. Study of Behav. Dev. Newsletter, No. 2, Serial No. 38 (2001), at 9.

[7] Gershoff & Bitensky, supra note [1], at 232.

[8] Alan Cowell, The House of Lords Restrains the Hand That Hits the Child, N.Y. Times, July 6, 2004, at A4.

standard of care required by a "reasonable and prudent parent"). Is tort law an effective means of protecting children from physical abuse?

(7) Problem. T.A. is a 12-year-old special needs child with Tourette syndrome (a motor disorder characterized by involuntary movements and vocal outbursts) and attention deficit hyperactivity disorder (ADHD) (a genetic dysfunction characterized by inattention, hyperactivity, and impulsivity). On the day that his family moves to a new home, T.A. is disobedient and defiant, and refuses to be helpful. When his mother asks him to retrieve a trash can, he empties the contents onto the kitchen floor. He later denies the act and begins crying and screaming. Determining that T.A. is "out of control," his stepfather spanks him eight to ten times with a belt, leaving bruises that remain for several days. T.A.'s sister tells their biological father, who reports the incident to the authorities. The state statute provides:

> [t]o use or attempt or offer to use force upon or toward the person of another is not unlawful if committed by a parent . . . in the exercise of a lawful authority to restrain or correct his child or ward and if restraint or correction has been rendered necessary by the misconduct of such child or ward, or by his refusal to obey the lawful command of such parent . . . and the force used is reasonable in manner and moderate in degree.

Should T.A. be adjudicated an abused or neglected child, or did the stepfather's spanking constitute "reasonable force"? See In re T.A., 663 N.W.2d 225 (S.D. 2003).

2. Corporal Punishment in Schools

Anglo-American law has permitted the use of physical force for disciplining children in schools as well as the home. In England, the basis of the teacher's right to administer corporal punishment was found in the doctrine of in loco parentis. That is, the school's authority derived from a partial delegation of the parental right to discipline. Blackstone wrote:

> [The father] may also delegate part of his parental authority, during his life, to the tutor or schoolmaster of his child; who is then in loco parentis, and has such a portion of the power of the parent committed to his charge, viz. that of restraint and correction, as may be necessary to answer the purposes for which he is employed. [2 Commentaries on the Laws of England *453 (Thomas M. Cooley ed. 1884).]

With the advent of compulsory education, it became difficult to find either a delegation or consent in the relation between parent and teacher, especially where the parent expressly objected to the use of corporal punishment. American courts have therefore emphasized maintenance of public order and control of the classroom in analyzing the teacher's right to administer corporal punishment. This analysis requires the court to weigh the parent's right to choose between means of discipline against the school's need to restrain or correct pupils. Note, in this regard, the balance struck by the Restatement (Second) of Torts §153, infra.

Restatement (Second) of Torts §§152-155

§152. Partial Control of Child

One who is charged only with the education or some other part of the training of a child has the privilege of using force or confinement to discipline the child only in so far as the privilege is necessary for the education or other part of the training which is committed or delegated to the actor.

§153. Power of Parent to Restrict Privilege

(1) One who is in charge of the control, training, or education of a child solely as the delegate of its parent is not privileged to inflict a punishment which the parent has forbidden or to punish the child for doing or refusing to do that which the parent has directed the child to do or not to do.

(2) One who is in charge of the education or training of a child as a public officer is privileged to inflict such reasonable punishments as are necessary for the child's proper education or training, notwithstanding the parent's prohibitions or wishes.

§154. Privilege of One in Charge of Group

One who is in charge of the training or education of a group of children is privileged to apply such force or impose such confinement upon one or more of them as is reasonably necessary to secure observance of the discipline necessary for the education and training of the children as a group.

§155. Effect of Excessive Force

If the actor applies a force or imposes a confinement upon a child which is in excess of that which is privileged, (a) the actor is liable for so much of the force or confinement as is excessive; (b) the child has the privilege stated in §§63-75 to defend himself against the actor's use or attempted use of the excessive force or confinement.

Baker v. Owen
395 F. Supp. 294 (M.D.N.C. 1975), *aff'd without opinion*, **423 U.S. 907 (1975)**

CRAVEN, Circuit Judge.

    This three-judge court was convened to consider the claims of Russell Carl Baker and his mother that their constitutional rights were violated when Russell Carl was corporally punished by his teacher over his mother's objections and without procedural due process. Russell Carl, a sixth-grader, was paddled on December 6, 1973, for allegedly violating his teacher's announced rule against throwing kickballs except during designated play periods. Mrs. Baker had previously requested of Russell Carl's principal and certain teachers, that Russell Carl not be corporally punished, because she opposed it on principle. Nevertheless, shortly after his alleged misconduct her son received two licks in the presence of a second teacher and in view of other students.

Mrs. Baker alleges that the administration of corporal punishment after her objections violated her parental right to determine disciplinary methods for her child. Russell Carl charges that the circumstances in which the punishment was administered violated his right to procedural due process, and that the punishment itself in this instance amounted to cruel and unusual punishment. This special court was convened because both Mrs. Baker in her claim and Russell Carl in his procedural due process claim have challenged the constitutionality of North Carolina General Statutes §115-146. They claim that this statute, which empowers school officials to "use reasonable force in the exercise of lawful authority to restrain or correct pupils and to maintain order,"[1] is unconstitutional insofar as it allows corporal punishment over parental objection and absent adequate procedural safeguards.

We hold that fourteenth amendment liberty embraces the right of parents generally to control means of discipline of their children, but that the state has a countervailing interest in the maintenance of order in the schools, in this case sufficient to sustain the right of teachers and school officials to administer reasonable corporal punishment for disciplinary purposes. We also hold that teachers and school officials must accord to students minimal procedural due process in the course of inflicting such punishment. We further hold that the spanking of Russell Carl in this case did not amount to cruel and unusual punishment. . . .

The Supreme Court first acknowledged the constitutional stature of parental rights over half a century ago in Meyer v. Nebraska, 262 U.S. 390 (1923). . . . Two years later the Court in Pierce v. Society of Sisters, 268 U.S. 510 (1925), struck down another state statute requiring public school attendance because it "unreasonably interfere[d] with the liberty of parents and guardians to direct the upbringing and education of children under their control," id. at 534-535.

---

[1] N.C. Gen. Stat. §115-146 reads as follows:

> *Duties of teachers generally: principals and teachers may use reasonable force in exercising lawful authority.* — It shall be the duty of all teachers, including student teachers, substitute teachers, voluntary teachers, teachers' aides and assistants when given authority over some part of the school program by the principal or supervising teacher, to maintain good order and discipline in their respective schools. . . .
>
> Principals, teachers, substitute teachers, voluntary teachers, teachers' aides and assistants and student teachers in the public schools of this State may use reasonable force in the exercise of lawful authority to restrain or correct pupils and maintain order. No county or city board of education or district committee shall promulgate or continue in effect a rule, regulation or bylaw which prohibits the use of such force as is specified in this section.

The *Meyer* and *Pierce* decisions have since been interpreted by the Court as recognizing that, under our constitutional scheme, "the custody, care and nurture of the child reside first in the parents." Mrs. Baker urges that the right to determine disciplinary methods for Russell Carl is part of her primary right to and responsibility for his "custody, care and nurture"; that as such it is a fundamental right; and that the state therefore must show a compelling interest in order to punish Russell Carl corporally against her wishes.

... We agree with Mrs. Baker that the fourteenth amendment concept of liberty embraces the right of a parent to determine and choose between means of discipline of children, but few constitutional rights are absolute. Our inquiry does not end with the conclusion that Mrs. Baker has such a right but we must go on to consider the nature and extent of the state's interest in school discipline. . . .

We reject Mrs. Baker's suggestion that this right is fundamental and that the state can punish her child corporally only if it shows a compelling interest that outweighs her parental right. We do not read *Meyer* and *Pierce* to enshrine parental rights so high in the hierarchy of constitutional values. In each case the parental right prevailed not because the Court termed it fundamental and the state's interest uncompelling, but because the Court considered the state's action to be arbitrary, without reasonable relation to an end legitimately within its power. . . .

A finding that Mrs. Baker's power of decision regarding corporal punishment is fundamental would require the state to show both a compelling interest and the unavailability of alternative means of fulfilling that interest before it could contravene her decision. A sensitive consideration of the nature of Mrs. Baker's right to preclude corporal punishment, and the context in which she seeks to assert it, simply forecloses the imposition of such a burden upon the state.

Insight into the nature of Mrs. Baker's right, for the purpose of deciding whether it should receive ultimate protection, can best be gained by comparing it to the parental rights at stake in *Meyer, Pierce*, and *Prince*. The Court in *Meyer* spoke of "the natural duty of the parent to give his children education," . . . 262 U.S. at 400; . . . In *Pierce* the Court was faced with a claim invoking "the right of parents to choose schools where their children will receive appropriate mental and religious training," 268 U.S. at 532, . . . And in *Prince* the parental right was the inculcation of one's religious beliefs in one's children. . . .

The common characteristic of the parental interests in all three cases is their venerability. In each instance the Court started with a premise that could provoke no quarrel — that the specific parental concern implicated was worthy of great deference due to its unquestioned acceptance throughout our history. Mrs. Baker's opposition to corporal punishment, on the other hand, enjoys no such universal approbation in our society even today, and certainly not historically. Quite the contrary, it bucks a settled tradition of countenancing such punishment when reasonable. See generally F. Harper & F. James, The Law of Torts §3.20 (1956); 68 Am. Jur. 2d, Schools §258 (1973). And though we accept Mrs. Baker's assertion that corporal punishment of children is today discouraged by the weight of professional opinion, we are also cognizant that the issue is unsettled and probably incapable of categorical resolution. We simply cannot foresee a parent's absolute disapproval of reasonable corporal punishment soon achieving the kind of societal respect that is clearly accorded the desire to expose one's child to certain fields of knowledge, to send him to a private or parochial school, or to pass on one's religious heritage to him. Thus, regardless whether the specific parental interests involved in _Meyer, Pierce_, and _Prince_ should be considered fundamental, and without disparaging one whit Mrs. Baker's right to decide the methods of punishment to be employed with Russell Carl by herself or other private parties, we cannot say that her right of total opposition to his corporal punishment is fundamental in a constitutional sense.

We believe, therefore, that defendants can justify their corporal punishment of Russell Carl by showing that it furthered a legitimate state end. . . .

There can be no doubt about the state's legitimate and substantial interest in maintaining order and discipline in the public schools. Education may not be a fundamental interest, see [San Antonio School Dist. v. Rodriguez], 411 U.S. at 29-40, but the people of our states have long recognized its vital importance and provided it to their young people at public expense. It should be clear beyond peradventure, indeed self-evident, that to fulfill its assumed duty of providing an education to all who want it a state must maintain order within its schools. . . .

There are many, of course, including Mrs. Baker and the experts upon whose testimony and writings she relies, who believe that school officials can and should maintain [order] without using corporal punishment. We are aware that their view is shared by many professional educators, parents and others. But as we noted above, opinion on the merits of the rod is far from unanimous. On such a controversial issue, where we would be acting more from personal preference than from constitutional command, we cannot allow the wishes of a parent to restrict school officials' discretion in deciding the methods to be used in accomplishing the not just legitimate, but essential purpose of maintaining discipline. So long as the force used is reasonable — and that is all that the statute here allows — school officials are free to employ corporal punishment for disciplinary purposes until in the exercise of their own professional judgment, or in response to concerted pressure from opposing parents, they decide that its harm outweighs its utility. . . .

[The court then discussed whether corporal punishment was consistent with the child's rights under the Fourteenth Amendment.]

We believe that Russell Carl does have an interest, protected by the concept of liberty in the fourteenth amendment, in avoiding corporal punishment. . . . We believe that the concept must include, in appropriate instances, personal security in the seemingly small things of life as well as in the obviously momentous. . . . Secondly, the legal system, once quite tolerant of physical punishment in many contexts, has become less so. See generally Jackson v. Bishop, 404 F. 2d 571 (8th Cir. 1968) (prohibiting use of the strap on prisoners); 18 U.S.C. §2191 (1970) (outlawing flogging of sailors on United States ships); 1 F. Harper & P. James, The Law of Torts §3.20, at 289 (1956) (discussing husband's loss of the privilege of corporally disciplining his wife, and employer's similar loss of the privilege as to domestic employees). Indeed, it is questionable at best whether the law would now privilege any degree of corporal punishment of an adult. While the state historically has been granted broader powers over children than over adults, see, e.g., _Prince_, supra, 321 U.S. at 167-170, the Supreme Court has explicitly recognized that children have rights, too. Goss v. Lopez, supra, 419 U.S. at 570-576; _Tinker_, supra, 393 U.S. at 506, 511. Thus, although the weight of legal authority still permits corporal punishment of public school children, see Restatement (Second) of Torts §153(2) (1965), it seems uncontrovertible that the child has a legitimate interest in avoiding unnecessary or arbitrary infliction of a punishment that probably would be completely disallowed as to an adult. Moreover, North Carolina has itself given school children reasonable expectation of freedom from excessive or pointless corporal punishment by writing into section 115-146 the requirements that such punishment be reasonable and used for specific purposes only. Yet it has failed to provide any procedural protection to insure that those acting under the statutory authority will adhere to its dictates and neither punish arbitrarily nor use unreasonable force.

Having concluded . . . that North Carolina school children have a liberty interest, we must decide what procedural safeguards should protect it. . . . Our task is to fashion procedures that accommodate as best as possible the child's interest with the state's unquestioned interest in effective discipline. There is no dispute about the state's assertion that elaborate, time-consuming procedures antecedent to infliction of corporal punishment would destroy its value, as the essence of corporal punishment is swift and tangible wages for one's transgression. Plaintiffs concede, as we believe they must, that this basic consideration precludes our requiring the full panoply of procedural due process rights, i.e., such things as formal notice, right to counsel, right of confrontation and cross-examination.

Instead, plaintiffs request only those minimal procedures necessary to protect the student's interest without undercutting the disciplinary value of the punishment. We believe such procedures are few in number, but that is not to downplay their importance. First, except for those acts of misconduct which are so anti-social or disruptive in nature as to shock the conscience, corporal punishment may never be used unless the student was informed beforehand that specific misbehavior could occasion its use, and, subject to this exception, it should never be employed as a first line of punishment for misbehavior. The requirements of an announced possibility of corporal punishment and an attempt to modify behavior by some other means — keeping after school, assigning extra work, or some other punishment — will insure that the child has clear notice that certain behavior subjects him to physical punishment. Second, a teacher or principal must punish corporally in the presence of a second school official (teacher or principal), who must be informed beforehand and in the student's presence of the reason for the punishment. The student need not be afforded a formal opportunity to present his side to the second official; the requirement is intended only to allow a student to protest, spontaneously, an egregiously arbitrary or contrived application of punishment. And finally, an official who has administered such punishment must provide the child's parent, upon request, a written explanation of his reasons and the name of the second official who was present.

QUESTIONS ON CORPORAL PUNISHMENT IN SCHOOLS

(1) Who Decides on School Discipline?   Are you convinced by the way the *Baker* court squares *Meyer, Pierce*, and *Prince?* The court seems to knock down a straw man in rejecting Mrs. Baker's total opposition to corporal punishment.

Isn't the real issue whether the parent or the state gets to decide on the means of discipline? Note that Mrs. Baker would apparently not strip the school of all disciplinary power, such as holding Russell Clark after school. Should this have made any difference to the court? What sources does the court draw on in fixing the content of students' due process rights?

(2) Effectiveness of Corporal Punishment in Schools.   Approximately half of the states permit the use of corporal punishment in public schools as a means of discipline.[9] Are such disciplinary measures effective? Many commentators and social scientists are doubtful, arguing

> that corporal punishment is an ineffective disciplinary tool, causing more behavioral problems than it cures. Second, corporal punishment may produce many harmful side-effects — physical, sexual, emotional, and racial — that result even from its judicious application.[10]

Critics contend that teachers and administrators are more likely to punish the economically disadvantaged, minorities, and males.[11] Some suggest that corporal punishment in the schools perpetuates notions of the acceptability of physical punishment.[12]

(3) Permission vs. Preclusion.   Unlike the North Carolina statute at issue in Baker v. Owen that permitted school officials to inflict corporal punishment notwithstanding a parent's request, a few states specifically allow parents to forbid corporal punishment of their child. See, e.g., Utah Code Ann. §53A-11-802 (2006). See also Rinehart v. Board of Educ., 621 N.E.2d 1365 (Ohio Ct. App. 1993) (holding that *Baker* imposes a procedural requirement on a teacher before inflicting corporal punishment to verify the absence of a note from a parent forbidding it).

(4) North Carolina Post-Baker.   North Carolina still permits corporal punishment in the schools. However, in 1991 the legislature replaced N.C. Gen. Stat. §115-146 with a statutory delegation of authority to local school boards. Whereas the former law permitted the use of reasonable force "to restrain or correct pupils and maintain order" and expressly precluded local regulations "which prohibit[ ] the use of such force," the subsequent revision (N.C. Gen. Stat. §115C-390 (2005))

---

[9] Gershoff & Bitensky, supra note [1] at 246 (explaining that 22 states permit corporal punishment in the schools although some of these states allow local school districts to ban the practice). See also Center for Effective Discipline, Discipline and the Law, State Laws, available at *www.stophitting.com/laws/legalInformation.php* (last visited Nov. 12, 2008).

[10] John M. Bylsma, Comment, Hands Off! New North Carolina General Statutes Section 115C-390 Allows Local School Boards to Ban Corporal Punishment, 70 N.C. L. Rev. 2058, 2069 (1992). See also Gershoff & Bitensky, supra note [1], at 233-240 (reviewing research findings regarding adverse outcomes of corporal punishment such as increased aggression, criminal and antisocial conduct, and risk of abusing one's own child or spouse).

[11] Data from the U.S. Department of Education support the disproportionate nature of corporal punishment in the schools. For example, in 2006-2007, African-American students received 36 percent of the paddlings, although such students comprised only 17 percent of public school students. Center for Effective Discipline, U.S. Statistics on Corporal Punishment by State and Race, Corporal Punishment and Paddling Statistics by State and Race, available at *http:www.stophitting.com/disatschool* (last visited on Nov. 12, 2008).

[12] Katherine Hunt Federle, Violence Is the Word, 37 Hous. L. Rev. 97, 106 (2000).

increases local autonomy by permitting school boards to restrict or prohibit the use of reasonable force. Seven months after passage of the law, one-third of North Carolina's school districts had banned the use of corporal punishment.[13]

(5) Nationwide Trend.   The change in North Carolina law is illustrative of a trend toward decreasing acceptance of corporal punishment in the public schools. Data reveal that 223,190 students were subjected to corporal punishment in 2006-2007, compared to 1,521,896 students in 1976 (after *Baker*).[14] Following a legal setback in Ingraham v. Wright (discussed infra), opponents of corporal punishment directed their attention to legislative efforts to prohibit the practice in schools. Teachers, pediatricians, child abuse experts, and members of national organizations, such as the PTA and the AMA, lobbied legislators to enact protective legislation.[15]

Of the states that prohibit corporal punishment in schools, some dilute the prohibition by drawing a technical distinction between "corporal punishment" and "reasonable force" (permitting the latter in specified circumstances). See, e.g., Iowa Code Ann §280.21 (West Supp. 2008) (permitting use of reasonable force not designed to cause pain but for the protection of the employee, the student, or other students); Mass. Gen. Laws Ann. ch. 71 §37G(b) (West Supp. 2008) (permitting reasonable force to protect pupils, teachers, and others from assault).

NOTE: INGRAHAM v. WRIGHT

In Ingraham v. Wright, 430 U.S. 651 (1977), the United States Supreme Court upheld the constitutionality of corporal punishment of school children. Two junior high students who alleged that their paddling by school officials limited their physical capacity for a week brought an individual action for damages and sought declaratory and injunctive relief on behalf of all public school students. The students claimed that (1) paddling constitutes cruel and unusual punishment in violation of the Eighth Amendment, and (2) if paddling were allowed, the Due Process Clause would require prior notice and an opportunity to be heard before the imposition of punishment. The Court, dividing 5 to 4, rejected both claims.

(1) Eighth Amendment Claim.   The Court held that the Eighth Amendment did not apply to the public school setting based on the history of the Eighth Amendment, precedent, and a comparison with other institutions. The Court reasoned that students have little need for such protection because a school, unlike a

---

[13] Bylsma, supra note [10], at 2006. Currently, slightly more than half of North Carolina's school systems still impose corporal punishment. Venita Jenkins, Harnett Removes Paddling Option, Fayetteville (N.C.) Observer, Sept. 15, 2008, available at 2008 WLNR 17498826.

[14] Center for Effective Discipline, supra note [11]. States with the highest percentage of students who are struck by educators are Georgia, Mississippi, and Texas (comprising nearly three-quarters of all cases). Id.

[15] John Dayton, Corporal Punishment in Public Schools: The Legal and Political Battle Continues, 89 Educ. L. Rep. 727, 729 (May 19, 1994).

prison, is an open institution in which other adults or pupils may witness and protest any mistreatment.

(2) Procedural Due Process Claim.   Conceding that the child had a liberty interest under the Fourteenth Amendment (at least where the school punishment inflicts "appreciable physical pain" id. at 674), the majority held, however, that procedural due process was satisfied by the existence of civil remedies and criminal sanctions. A hearing prior to the imposition of corporal punishment was unnecessary and burdensome and would "entail a significant intrusion into an area of primary educational responsibility." Id. at 682.

Justice White, in a dissenting opinion joined by Justices Brennan, Marshall, and Stevens, argued that the remedy of a tort action was "utterly inadequate to protect against erroneous infliction of punishment"(id. at 693) and in all events could not undo the "infliction of physical pain." Id. at 695. Justice White (who wrote the Court's majority opinion in *Goss*, described at p. 133, supra) added:

> The majority emphasizes, as did the dissenters in *Goss*, that even the "rudimentary precautions" required by that decision would impose some burden on the school disciplinary process. But those costs are no greater if the student is paddled rather than suspended; the risk of error in the punishment is no smaller; and the fear of "a significant intrusion" into the disciplinary process . . . is just as exaggerated. Id. at 700.

(3) Substantive Due Process.   The Supreme Court declined to review the question of whether the infliction of severe corporal punishment on public school students violates students' substantive due process rights under the Fourteenth Amendment. However, virtually every federal circuit court that has addressed this issue has allowed such claims.[16]

(4) Other Legal Approaches.   Subsequent to *Ingraham*, some courts moved away from reliance on substantive due process, in preference to resort to other constitutional guarantees, in cases of excessive punishment by school officials. For example, in Preschooler II v. Clark County School Board of Trustees, 479 F.3d 1175, 1177 (9th Cir. 2007), the mother of an autistic preschool child alleged constitutional violations of her son's rights pursuant to 42 U.S.C. §1983, for a teacher's repeated acts of beating and slapping, and slamming her son into a chair. The Ninth Circuit Court of Appeal, although relying on *Ingraham*, explained that allegations of excessive force by school officials based on civil rights actions should be analyzed under a more specific constitutional provision (i.e., the Fourth Amendment here), rather than generalized notions of substantive due process. *Preschooler*, supra, at 1182 (citing Graham v. Connor, 490 U.S. 386, 394 (1989)).

---

[16] Diane Heckman, Constitutional Due Process and Corporal Punishment Involving Athletes, 158 West Educ. L. Rep. 513 (2002) (analyzing substantive due process claims by circuit). See also Kirkland ex rel. Jones v. Greene Cty Bd. of Educ., 347 F.3d 903 (11th Cir. 2003) (holding that principal's repeated strikes of 13-year-old with metal cane to teen's head, neck, and ribs violated his substantive due process right).

C. CHILD ABUSE

1. Scope of the Problem

Child Maltreatment 2006
U.S. Dept. of Health & Human Services, Administration for Children & Families,
available at *http://www.acf.hhs.gov/programs/cb/pubs/cm06*

... During [federal fiscal year] 2006, an estimated 905,000 children were determined to be victims of abuse or neglect. . . .

Children in the age group of birth to 1 year had the highest rate of victimization at 24.4 per 1,000 children of the same age group in the national population. More than one-half of the child victims were girls (51.5 percent) and 48.2 percent were boys. Approximately one-half of all victims were White (48.8 percent); one-quarter (22.8 percent) were African-American; and 18.4 percent were Hispanic.

[N]eglect was the most common form of child maltreatment. CPS investigations determined that [m]ore than 60 percent (64.1 percent) of victims suffered neglect; [m]ore than 15 percent (16.0 percent) of the victims suffered physical abuse; [l]ess than 10 percent (8.8 percent) of the victims suffered sexual abuse; and [l]ess than 10 percent (6.6 percent) of the victims suffered from emotional maltreatment.

Child fatalities are the most tragic consequence of maltreatment. . . . During 2006, [a]n estimated 1,530 children died due to child abuse or neglect. The overall rate of child fatalities was 2.04 deaths per 100,000 children. More than 40 percent (41.1 percent) of child fatalities were attributed to neglect. [P]hysical abuse also was a major contributor to child fatalities. More than three-quarters (78 percent) of the children who died due to child abuse and neglect were younger than 4 years old. Infant boys (younger than 1 year) had the highest rate of fatalities, at 18.5 deaths per 100,000 boys of the same age in the national population; and [i]nfant girls had a rate of 14.7 deaths per 100,000 girls of the same age.

In 2006, nearly 80 percent (79.4 percent) of perpetrators of child maltreatment were parents, and another 6.7 percent were other relatives of the victim. Women comprised a larger percentage of all perpetrators than men, 57.9 percent compared to 42.1 percent. More than 75 percent (77.5 percent) of all perpetrators were younger than age 40. Of the perpetrators who maltreated children, less than 10 percent (7.0 percent) committed sexual abuse, while 60.4 percent committed neglect. Of the perpetrators who were parents, more than 90 percent (91.5 percent) were the biological parent of the victim. . . .

For 2006, more than one-half of all reports (56.3 percent) of alleged child abuse or neglect were made by professionals. . . . This term includes teachers, police officers, lawyers, and social services staff. The remaining reports were made by nonprofessionals, including friends, neighbors, and relatives. The three largest percentages of report sources were from such professionals as teachers (16.5 percent), lawyers or police officers (15.8 percent), and social services staff (10 percent). . . .

NOTE ON CAPTA

The preceding report is based on an annual data collection effort that was mandated by the first comprehensive federal legislation on the subject of child abuse and neglect. In 1974 Congress enacted the Child Abuse Prevention and Treatment Act of 1974 (CAPTA), 42 U.S.C. §§5101-5106 (2000 & Supp. 2005), to provide funding for state child protective services. To qualify for federal funds, CAPTA requires states to adopt procedures for reporting and investigating reports of abuse, provide immunity from prosecution to persons who make good-faith reports, provide for confidentiality of records, and provide for the appointment of a guardian ad litem (who is not required to be an attorney) to represent children in judicial proceedings.

Congress reauthorized CAPTA by the Keeping Children and Families Safe Act of 2003 (Pub. L. No. 108-36, 117 Stat. 800 (2003)). Recent amendments mandate that states require health care providers to report infants who are prenatally exposed to drug abuse to child protective services; disclose confidential information to governmental agencies if necessary for the purpose of child protection; promptly inform perpetrators of allegations of maltreatment; develop background checks of adults in prospective adoptive and foster care homes; and adopt procedures to improve the training and supervision of caseworkers.

2. Definitions, Causes, and Consequences of Child Abuse

Diana J. English, The Extent and Consequences of Child Maltreatment

The Future of Children, vol. 8, no. 1 (Spring 1998), 40-42, 45-48

Defining Child Maltreatment

The concept of child maltreatment is relatively new in Western society, although there is historical evidence that children have long been murdered, abandoned, incarcerated, mutilated, sexually exploited, beaten, and forced into labor by their parents and caregivers. For instance, in colonial America, children were flogged to instill discipline, and in the early twentieth century, children routinely worked 14-hour days in mills and mines. Such actions were not formally defined as maltreatment, however, and public authorities seldom interceded on the children's behalf.

The emergence of official definitions of unacceptable treatment of children has helped to trigger and sustain efforts by authorities to protect children. Because they have important policy implications, however, definitions of maltreatment have been hotly debated. Despite efforts to create uniform approaches, the definitions used by state legislatures, agency officials, and researchers remain ambiguous and inconsistent. Some of the key differences are discussed below.

By the mid-twentieth century, legislation defining child maltreatment was introduced into many state statutes, and some states required physicians to report abuse or neglect. In 1974, the U.S. Congress passed the Child Abuse Prevention and Treatment Act (CAPTA), Public Law 93-247, to give a national definition of child maltreatment and prescribe actions states should take to protect children. That law established a broad definition of maltreatment as: "The physical and mental injury, sexual abuse, neglected treatment or maltreatment of a child under age 18 by a person who is responsible for the child's welfare under circumstances which indicate the child's health and welfare is harmed and threatened thereby, as determined in accordance with regulations prescribed by the Secretary of Health, Education, and Welfare."

This definition of child maltreatment specifies that only parents or care-givers can be perpetrators of child abuse and neglect. Abusive behavior by other individuals, whether known to the child or strangers, is considered assault. Of particular note, this national definition includes both mental injury and neglect. . . .

The federal CAPTA legislation sets minimum definitional standards for the states receiving federal funds, but the details of defining maltreatment fall to the states, and specific definitions vary considerably. For example, some states include educational neglect (when a child consistently fails to attend school) in their definition of child maltreatment, while others do not. States also vary in the criteria and procedures they use to first screen and later validate reports of alleged maltreatment. . . .

Debates over how broadly to define maltreatment began with the drafting of the CAPTA legislation, and they have continued. Underlying the debate is the difficulty of identifying an appropriate government role in the lives of children and families. Advocates for a narrow definition of child abuse and neglect argue that before the government has a right to intervene in the privacy of the family, the parental action should have resulted in observable harm or pose an imminent risk of such harm. Others stress the damage that persistent neglect or psychological abuse can do to children, even if that damage appears only later. Thus, arguments center on whether to include mental injury and neglect, whether cumulative harm should be considered, and whether threatened as well as actual harm should count as maltreatment. [S]upporters of a broad definition prevailed when the federal definition [in CAPTA] was established. . . .

Factors Associated with Abuse and Neglect

[U]nderstanding the factors that contribute to maltreatment and that shape its consequences for children is crucial to the development of prevention and treatment approaches. For instance, the likelihood that an individual child will experience abuse or neglect may be influenced by the characteristics of the parent or caregiver. . . .

Caregiver Characteristics

A wide variety of characteristics of the child's parents or caregivers have been linked to an increased likelihood of child abuse or neglect. For instance, individual attributes such as low self-esteem, poor impulse control, aggressiveness, anxiety, and depression often characterize maltreating parents of caregivers. Inaccurate knowledge of child development, inappropriate expectations of the child, and negative attitudes toward parenting contribute to child-rearing problems, as well. . . .

Domestic violence involving the child's caregiver is a problem that is more likely to contribute to physical abuse than neglect. [B]etween 1.5 and 3.3 million children in the United States witness domestic violence each year. Not only is the experience of witnessing violence likely to be psychologically harmful, but several studies have found that male batterers are more likely than other men to physically abuse their children. Women who are victims of domestic violence are also more likely to be reported for maltreating their children.

Substance abuse by the parent or caregiver is strongly associated with child maltreatment. Current estimates indicate that between 50 and 80% of families involved with child protective services are dealing with a substance-abuse problem. . . .

Socioeconomic Characteristics

[R]esearchers have focused on the relationship between child maltreatment and [poverty]. Although child abuse and neglect occur in families of all income brackets, cases of child maltreatment are drawn disproportionately from lower-income families. . . .

No one fully understands the links between poverty and maltreatment. The stress and frustrations of living in poverty may combine with attitudes toward the use of corporal punishment to increase the risk of physical violence. For instance, researchers have found that unemployment can lead to family stress and to child abuse. When a family lacks the basic resources needed to provide for a child, neglect is likely, although researchers suggest that dynamics over and above poverty (such as disorganization and social isolation) differentiate neglecting families from others. Indeed, most poor people do not mistreat their children. The effects of poverty appear to interact with other risk factors such as unrealistic expectations, depression, isolation, substance abuse, and domestic violence to increase the likelihood of maltreatment.

Child Characteristics

Studies suggest that young children, girls, premature infants, and children with more irritable temperaments are more vulnerable to abuse and neglect. Girls are more likely to suffer from sexual abuse than boys, but other types of maltreatment affect both sexes about equally. Maltreated infants and young children are significantly more likely to be reported to CPS agencies than are older children. About 16 per 1,000 children under age one were involved in substantiated reports in 1994, compared to only 9 per 1,000 adolescents ages 16 to 18. The youngest children, whose bodies are fragile, more often die from maltreatment: 45% of the maltreatment-related fatalities from 1993 to 1995 involved infants, and 85% involved children under age five.

Consequences of Child Maltreatment

. . . The psychological, emotional, or physical damage that a child suffers as a result of maltreatment depends on aspects of the abuse itself and on the child's stage of development. It should be noted that most research on maltreated children comes through clinical studies of young children who have been referred for treatment, who are typically those exhibiting the most serious behavioral problems. Moreover, most of the children studied are involved with public child welfare agencies and come from families of lower socioeconomic status and minority populations. For both reasons, the findings summarized below may not reflect the consequences of child maltreatment for the entire population of abused and neglected children.

In some cases, children do not appear to exhibit significant effects from maltreatment. These children may have been buffered by personal characteristics such as optimism, high self-esteem, high cognitive ability, or a sense of hopefulness despite their circumstances. Damaging effects may be limited if the abuse occurs only once, or if a supportive adult is available who lets the child feel he or she is believed and will be protected. In some cases, however, effects of abuse may surface long after the experience. For example, some preadolescent sexual-abuse victims do not exhibit the effects of the abusive relationship until adolescence or adulthood, when they become involved in intimate relationships.

Other children who suffer maltreatment evidence signs of serious emotional or physical harm. . . . Lasting growth retardation may result when the caregiver's feeding of an infant becomes disturbed; this response to neglect is called nonorganic failure to thrive. Other physical sequelae can affect victims of sexual abuse, who may become infected with sexually transmitted diseases.

Psychological problems are prevalent among victims of maltreatment. Physically abused children tend to be aggressive toward peers and adults, to have difficulty with peer relations, and to show a diminished capacity for empathy toward others. Studies of neglected toddlers show that their ability to trust others is often impaired. This may lead to feelings of being unloved and unwanted, and may inhibit the development of the social skills needed to form healthy relationships with peers and adults. When a child cannot master developmental tasks (like learning to trust) at the appropriate age, the accomplishment of later tasks becomes more difficult throughout the life span.

As they get older, children who have been abused and neglected are more likely to perform poorly in school and to commit crimes against persons. They more often experience emotional problems, depression, suicidal thoughts, sexual problems, and alcohol/substance abuse. Some children internalize reactions to maltreatment by becoming depressed or experiencing eating disorders, sleep disruption, and alcohol/drug abuse. Others externalize their reactions by engaging in physical aggression, shoplifting or committing other crimes, or attempting suicide. Retrospective studies of adults who were mistreated as children reveal a similar array of short- and long-term impairments.

As can be seen from this brief description, the effects of maltreatment on children are often severe and long-lasting, although for any given child, the consequences of abuse or neglect will be shaped by the intensity, duration, and type of abuse; the presence of supportive adults; and the age of the child at the time. The fact that each child and maltreatment experience is unique means that each child requires individual assessment and tailored supports. . . .

3.   Discovery of Abuse: Reporting Laws

Ham v. Hospital of Morristown
917 F. Supp. 531 (E.D. Tenn. 1995)

JARVIS, Chief Judge.

. . . Plaintiffs allege that on March 21, 1993, the minor plaintiff, Desiree Levon Ham, who was then 16 months old, was brought to the emergency room of defendant Lakeway Regional Hospital in Morristown, Tennessee, by her mother Claudine D. Griffin. Ms. Griffin informed the hospital personnel that Desiree had been experiencing nausea and vomiting over the two to three preceding days. Desiree was then admitted to the hospital under the primary care of defendant Dan E. Hale, O.D. On March 22, Desiree was seen in consultation by defendant David V. Willbanks, M.D., a pediatrician, and by defendant Everett G. Lynch, M.D., a family practice physician. Plaintiffs further allege that, during the course of Desiree's hospitalization, the defendants or their representatives all observed the child and noted that she had blisters on the palms and fingers of both hands. She also had an abrasion on her forehead. Desiree's mother was at a loss to explain these injuries, except to say that there was a mouse in the house and to speculate that Desiree might have been bitten by that mouse. At any rate, Desiree was treated for acute gastroenteritis for the next few days, improved, and was discharged on March 26 to her mother.

Two days later, on March 28, Ms. Griffin brought Desiree to the emergency room of the Morristown-Hamblen Hospital in an "unresponsive state and suffering seizures." Desiree was subsequently transferred to the East Tennessee Children's Hospital in Knoxville, Tennessee, where she was evaluated and placed in intensive care, apparently the victim of extreme child abuse. Desiree is presently afflicted with severe, irreversible brain damage as a result of this abuse. The complaint alleges that these injuries were sustained by Desiree after she was released from Lakeway Regional Hospital into the custody of her mother on March 26.

Ms. Griffin was subsequently charged with child abuse, although those charges have now been dismissed. The Hamblen County grand jury has since returned an indictment against Charles Ryan Dixon [the mother's boyfriend] for aggravated child abuse involving Desiree. Desiree has now been placed in the physical and legal custody of her paternal grandmother, Daisy Nadine Ham, who has brought this action on Desiree's behalf. [Physicians and hospital personnel moved to dismiss or for summary judgment.]

Before addressing whether Tenn. Code Ann. §37-1-403 creates a private cause of action, the court will turn briefly to defendants' contention that there is no common law duty to report suspected child abuse to anyone. The law is well settled in Tennessee that, in a cause of action for negligence, there must first be a duty of care owed by the defendant to the plaintiff. Thus, where there is no duty, then there can be no negligence. [T]he common law of Tennessee does not impose a duty on a treating physician to either report suspected child abuse or to prevent any such child abuse. This void in the common law was filled by the Tennessee legislature when it enacted Part 4 of the chapter in the [Tenn. Code Ann. §§37-1-101 through 616, which summarizes] the duty owed by the defendants in this case . . . :

"*Mandatory* Child Abuse Reports." T.C.A. §37-1-401 (emphasis added). The specific subsection relied upon by plaintiffs is set forth in T.C.A. §37-1-403 ("Reporting of brutality, abuse, neglect or child sexual abuse"). This statute provides in pertinent part as follows:

> (a) Any person, including, but not limited to, any:
>   (1) Physician, osteopath, medical examiner, chiropractor, nurse or hospital personnel engaged in the admission, examination, care or treatment of persons;
>   . . . having knowledge of or called upon to render aid to any child who is suffering from or has sustained any wound, injury, disability, or physical or mental condition which is of such a nature as to reasonably indicate that it has been caused by brutality, abuse or neglect or which on the basis of available information reasonably appears to have been caused by brutality, abuse or neglect, shall report such harm immediately, by telephone or otherwise, to the judge having juvenile jurisdiction or to the county office of the department or to the office of the sheriff or the chief law enforcement official of the municipality where the child resides. . . .

There is no question, therefore, that this statute creates a duty on the part of these defendants; however, the issue to be determined by this court with respect to the pending motions is whether this statute creates a private cause of action.

In support of their position, defendants rely on a number of cases from other jurisdictions which clearly hold that similar reporting statutes do not create a private cause of action. See, e.g., Thelma D. v. Board of Education of City of St. Louis, 669 F. Supp. 947,950 (E.D. Mo. 1987) (following Doe "A" v. Special School District of St. Louis County, 637 F. Supp. 1138 (E.D. Mo. 1986)). In fact, only one jurisdiction has held that a mandatory child abuse reporting statute creates a private cause of action under common law. See Landeros v. Flood, 551 P.2d 389 (Cal. 1976). There is also dicta in Doran v. Priddy, 534 F. Supp. 30, 33 (D. Kan. 1981), which indicates that court's willingness to follow *Landeros* had the issue been raised. Otherwise, there are no other courts outside of Tennessee which have held that a private cause of action is created for a child by a statute requiring a professional to report physical injuries to children which appear to have been inflicted other than by an accident.* Thus, if this court were to be persuaded simply by the weight of the authority on one side or the other of this issue from other jurisdictions, then defendants would readily prevail on their motion to dismiss.

However, as previously noted, the law of this case is controlled by Tennessee case law which interprets this reporting statute. [I]n Doe v. Coffee County Board of Education, 852 S.W.2d 899 (Tenn. Ct. App. 1992), the Court of Appeals for the Middle Section appears to have answered [affirmatively] the question presently confronting this court. In *Coffee County*, four students and their parents filed suit against the boys' basketball coach of the Manchester Central High School ("MCHS"), because of the coach's improper sexual activities with the students.

---

* Cases which interpret Michigan's child protection law, Mich. Comp. Laws §§722.621, et seq., are easily distinguishable because that statute specifically provides that the failure to report may result in civil liability.

Suit was also filed against the school board and four school employees [for failure to report the sexual misconduct and take appropriate action].

Finally, defendants contend that no private right of action can be created by the reporting statute because it is not designed to protect any particular class of people — rather, it is designed to protect the general public. The court disagrees. T.C.A. §37-1-402(a) sets forth the purpose and the focus of the reporting statute:

> The purpose of this part is to protect children whose physical or mental health and welfare are adversely affected by brutality, abuse or neglect by requiring reporting of suspected cases by any person having cause to believe that such case exists. It is intended that, as a result of such reports, the protective services of the state shall be brought to bear on the situation to prevent further abuses, to safeguard and enhance the welfare of children, and to preserve family life. This part shall be administered and interpreted to provide the greatest possible protection as promptly as possible for children.

The reporting statute, therefore, is not intended for the protection of the general public. It is intended to protect children only and, more specifically, those children who are the victims of brutality, neglect, and physical and sexual abuse. . . . In sum, while the court acknowledges that the defendants have raised many forceful arguments in support of their position that the reporting statute does not create a private cause of action, the court concludes that these arguments do not circumvent the clear import of the *Coffee County* case: the reporting statute creates a legal obligation to report suspected brutality, neglect, or physical or sexual abuse of children and the failure to report "can give rise to liability. . . ." *Coffee County*, 852 S.W.2d at 909. Defendants' motions to dismiss on this basis must therefore be denied.

[T]he inquiry now becomes whether, as with any other negligence claim, plaintiffs can establish that the failure to report the child abuse has proximately caused the injury to Desiree. If there is no proximate causation, then there can be no civil damage liability. . . . In support of their motion for summary judgment, the defendant doctors have filed their affidavits. The doctors admit that they saw blisters on Desiree's hands; however, they further opined that there was nothing about those blisters which indicated that they were caused by trauma. Rather, in the doctors' opinions, they were caused by Desiree's documented internal problems, i.e., viral gastroenteritis. The doctors also admit that Desiree had a bruise or abrasion on the left side of her forehead.

In response, plaintiffs have filed the affidavits of Carol M. White, a registered nurse, and Dr. Larry E. Wolfe, a family practitioner who has emergency room experience. In the court's opinion, these affidavits easily raise a genuine issue of material fact as to whether the defendant doctors should have been put on notice that Desiree was the victim of abuse. For example, Dr. Wolfe testifies that, within a reasonable degree of medical certainty, Desiree's "diarrhea could have been caused due to the stress from trauma." Dr. Wolfe further testifies as follows:

> No lab work was ordered in the Emergency Room, thus there was no monitoring of electrolytes. After admission, the lab work showed an elevated white blood cell count with lymphocytes being significantly elevated, indicative of an

> inflammatory process. Desiree Ham's hepatic enzymes were elevated which led Dr. Lynch to document "suspect hepatitis." The hepatitis survey showed no antibiotics or viruses detected. Possible liver trauma was not noted. In my professional opinion, within a reasonable degree of medical certainty, liver function studies are not this high in viremia. An elevation in liver function studies, which is as significant as this, is indicative of soft tissue injury.

Thus, Dr. Wolfe concludes that Desiree's injuries could have been caused by external trauma. This conclusion therefore creates a genuine issue of material fact as to the reasonableness of the doctors' conclusions that there was no child abuse and, consequently, no duty to report these injuries to one of the authorities enumerated by statute. Thus, defendants' motion for summary judgment must be denied.

QUESTIONS ON REPORTING REQUIREMENTS

(1) Mandatory Reporting Laws. Currently, all 50 states have mandatory reporting statutes that require designated individuals to report child abuse to specified authorities (e.g., law enforcement and/or social service agencies). When reporting laws were first enacted in the 1960s, the legislation mandated reporting of *physical* abuse by *physicians.* Since that time, states have broadened the definition of "abuse" and the mandated reporters (to include a variety of professionals). Some states include "any" individual as a designated reporter. See, e.g., N.J. Stat. Ann. §9:6-8.10 (2002).

How broadly should legislatures define "abuse?" Should statutory definitions include prenatal abuse? Compare Kilmon v. State, 905 A.2d 306 (Md. 2006) (holding that a potential injury to a fetus caused by the mother's ingestion of cocaine could not be the basis for a conviction for reckless endangerment to a child), with State v. McKnight, 576 S.E.2d 168 (S.C. 2003) (holding that a homicide-by-child-abuse statute applied to a stillbirth caused by the mother's ingestion of cocaine), *rev'd on other grounds*, McKnight v. State, 661 S.E.2d 354 (S.C. 2008). See generally Linda C. Fentiman, The "New Fetal Protection": The Wrong Answer to the Crisis of Inadequate Health Care for Women and Children, 84 Denv. U. L. Rev. 537 (2006).

Should statutory definitions include *witnessing* abuse? Many states now incorporate the act of childhood exposure to domestic violence into their statutory definitions of abuse and neglect. See generally Linda Quigley, Note, The Intersection Between Domestic Violence and the Child Welfare System: The Role Courts Can Play in the Protection of Battered Mothers and their Children, 13 Wm. & Mary J. Women & L. 867 (2007) (examining research on the adverse effects of witnessing domestic violence and discussing legislative responses).

Should statutory definitions include prospective abuse of other siblings? See M.W v. Department of Children & Family Services, p. 269 infra.

Are such broad definitions and the standard that evokes a report ("reasonable cause to suspect" or "reasonable cause to believe") void for vagueness? See State v. Brown, 140 S.W.3d 51 (Mo. 2004).

What is the purpose of reporting statutes? Given the preceding purpose(s), what are the advantages and disadvantages of enumerating each of the following report recipients (e.g., law enforcement, courts, and social service agencies)? Should the state mandate or merely encourage reporting of child abuse? See Marc A. Franklin & Matthew Ploeger, Of Rescue and Report: Should Tort Law Impose a Duty to Help Endangered Persons or Abused Children?, 40 Santa Clara L. Rev. 991 (2000) (questioning whether a mandate is appropriate).

(2) Liability for Failure to Report.   All reporting statutes impose criminal penalties for failure to report child abuse. Only a few jurisdictions, by statute or case law, provide for additional civil liability. Curt Richardson, Comment, Physician/Hospital Liability for Negligently Reporting Child Abuse, 23 J. Legal Med. 131, 135 (2002). The judicial trend rejects a private cause of action. See, e.g., Cuyler v. United States, 362 F.3d 949 (7th Cir. 2004); Becker v. Mayo Fdn., 737 N.W.2d 200 (Minn. 2007).

Is civil and/or criminal liability the appropriate legal response for a designated professional's failure to report child abuse? What purpose of tort law is served by the imposition of liability on reporters? What purposes of the criminal law (e.g., deterrence, rehabilitation) are served by the imposition of penal sanctions against reporters? What are the advantages and disadvantages of invoking civil liability and/or criminal sanctions?

(3) Protection for Failure to Report.   What professionals should be subject to civil and/or criminal sanctions for nonreporting? Should liability extend to psychotherapists, clergy, and attorneys? See generally Katharyn I. Christian, Comment, Putting Legal Doctrines to the Test: The Inclusion of Attorneys as Mandated Reporters of Child Abuse, 32 J. Legal Prof. 215 (2008). Should the reporting obligation take precedence over the evidentiary privilege that attaches to confidential communications made during relationships with these professionals? Does the importance of the evidentiary privilege outweigh the potential benefit to be gained in child protection?

(4) Clergy Privilege and the Sex Abuse Scandal.   States adopt different approaches to the role of clergy in child abuse reporting. Many states exempt clergy from reporting, whereas some states abrogate the clergy privilege for reporting purposes. In 2002, a large number of claims surfaced that involved sexual molestation of parishioners (mostly adolescent boys) by Catholic priests; claims included allegations of a cover-up by church authorities who simply relocated offending priests.[17] In response, many states revised their child abuse laws to strengthen criminal and civil penalties and extended criminal statutes of limitations to facilitate litigation of "stale" claims by victims. At the same time, many states amended their reporting laws to include clergy among mandated reporters. How can the tension between a child's right to be protected from abuse and the constitutional right of free exercise be reconciled? See Norman Abrams, The

---

[17] See Fox Butterfield, 789 Children Abused by Priests Since 1940, Massachusetts Says, N.Y. Times, July 23, 2003, at A1. Currently, members of the clergy are required to report child abuse in 26 states. See Child Welfare Information Gateway, Clergy as Mandatory Reporters of Child Abuse and Neglect (2008), available at *www.childwelfare.gov/systemwide/laws_policies/statutes/clergymandated.cfm*.

Impact of Clergy Sexual Misconduct Litigation on Religious Liberty: Addressing the Tension Between the Clergy Communicant Privilege and the Duty to Report Child Abuse in State Statutes, 44 B.C. L. Rev. 1127 (2003).

(5) Immunity for Erroneous Reports. Persons who file reports that are subsequently determined to be erroneous often are granted immunity from civil liability. Whereas a few states grant absolute immunity, most provide for immunity only where the report was made either from "reasonable cause" or in "good faith." Compare Cal. Penal Code §11172 (West 2000 & Supp. 2008) (absolute immunity) with Rine v. Chase, 765 N.Y.S.2d 648 (App. Div. 2003) ("good faith"). What are the advantages and disadvantages of granting absolute immunity from liability?

(6) Sanctions for a Parent's Failure to Protect. In the *Ham* case, note that Ms. Griffin and her boyfriend originally were both charged with the crime of child abuse (although the charges against her were later dropped). Considerable controversy exists about the extent of liability for a mother who fails to protect her child from an abuser. If the mother fails to act, should she be liable for neglect or "passive" abuse? If so, should it matter if she is a victim of abuse herself? What should be the disposition in such cases? Should the child be removed from the mother's custody? See Nicholson v. Williams, 203 F. Supp. 2d 153 (E.D.N.Y. 2002) (finding that state agency's procedure of removal of children from battered mothers' custody solely on the ground of neglect violates substantive and procedural due process). Should the mother's parental rights be terminated? If the child dies as a result of the abuse, should the passive mother be charged with murder? See Justine A. Dunlap, Judging Nicholson: An Assessment of Nicholson v. Scoppetta, 82 Denv. U. L. Rev. 671 (2005); Maureen K. Collins, Comment, Nicholson v. Williams: Who Is Failing Whom? Collaborating the Agendas of Child Welfare Agencies and Domestic Violence Services to Better Protect and Support Battered Women and Their Children, 38 New Eng. L. Rev. 725 (2004).

Most states designate parents as "permissive" reporters of child abuse. Some commentators suggest making parents mandatory reporters, thereby providing a statutory basis for the imposition of civil or criminal liability on parents who do not intervene to protect children from abusers. See Suzanne M. Nicholls, Note, Responding to the Cries of the Innocent: Holding Non-Offending Parents Criminally Responsible for Failure to Protect the Abused Child, 30 T. Jefferson L. Rev. 309 (2007). What do you think of this suggestion?

Keep in mind that a juvenile court may assume jurisdiction over an abused or neglected child and may remove such a child from parental custody. Indeed, child abuse can lead to the termination of parental rights. These issues are explored, infra.

4. The Central Registry

Most states have incorporated into their reporting law a requirement that some state agency maintain a register of all reported cases of suspected child abuse. The central registry originally was designed to act both as a central warehouse for statistical data to help ascertain the incidence and nature of child abuse, and as a practical tool for assisting professionals, allowing them to determine whether a particular child has been previously abused or neglected and to keep track of parents previously suspected of child abuse. More recently, social service agencies also rely on child abuse registries to identify and preclude individuals with abusive propensities from working in the field of child care. Central registries are not without their problems, as the following case reveals.

Humphries v. County of Los Angeles
2009 WL 102101 (9th Cir. 2009)

BYBEE, Circuit Judge:

Appellants Craig and Wendy Humphries are living every parent's nightmare. Accused of abuse by a rebellious child, they were arrested, and had their other children taken away from them. . . . Notwithstanding the findings of two California courts that the Humphries were "factually innocent" and the charges "not true," the Humphries were identified as "substantiated" child abusers and placed on California's Child Abuse Central Index (CACI), a database of known or suspected child abusers. As the Humphries quickly learned, California offers no procedure to remove their listing on the database as suspected child abusers, and thus no opportunity to clear their names. . . . This case presents the question of whether California's maintenance of the CACI violates the Due Process Clause of the Fourteenth Amendment because identified individuals are not given a fair opportunity to challenge the allegations against them. . . .

California maintains a database of "reports of suspected child abuse and severe neglect," known as the Child Abuse Central Index or CACI. [M]aintenance of the CACI has been governed by the Child Abuse and Neglect Reporting Act (CANRA) (Cal. Penal Code §11170(a)(2)). . . . There are many different ways a person can find [himself or herself] listed in the CACI. CANRA mandates that various statutorily enumerated individuals report instances of known or suspected child abuse and neglect either to a law enforcement agency or to a child welfare agency. These agencies, in turn, are required to conduct "an active investigation," which involves investigating the allegation and determining whether the incident is . . . (1) "substantiated," meaning it is more likely than not that child abuse or neglect occurred; (2) "inconclusive," meaning there is insufficient evidence to determine whether child abuse and/or neglect occurred; or (3) "unfounded," meaning the report is false, inherently improbable, an accidental injury, or does not constitute child abuse or neglect. . . . The agency must submit both "substantiated" and "inconclusive" reports for inclusion in the CACI.

Given the high standard of proof required for a report to be dismissed as "unfounded" — false or inherently improbable — and the low standard of proof required for a report to be categorized as "substantiated" — more likely than not — with "inconclusive" presumably encompassing everything in between, we understand the minimum evidence required for CANRA to compel the submission of a report to be something less than a preponderance, but more than a scintilla. . . .

The Humphries' nightmarish encounter with the CANRA system began on March 17, 2001, when S.H., Craig's fifteen-year-old daughter from a previous marriage, took their car and drove to her biological mother's home in Utah.

S.H. had previously lived in Utah with her biological mother and stepfather and their three younger children. In June 2000, S.H's biological mother called Craig and said she wanted S.H. to live with the Humphries in Valencia, California, on a trial basis. The night of March 17, S.H. took the Humphries' car without their knowledge, drove to her mother's home in Utah, and reported that the Humphries had been abusing her for several months. An emergency room physician diagnosed "non-accidental trauma, with extremity contusions. . . ."

Based on an investigation from the Utah police, the victim's statement, and emergency room records describing the victim's allegations, on April 11, 2001, Michael L. Wilson, a detective for the Family Crimes Bureau of the Los Angeles County Sheriff's Department ("LASD"), obtained probable cause warrants to arrest the Humphries for cruelty to a child, Cal. Penal Code §273a(a), and torture, id. §206. On April 16, Detective Wilson, accompanied by fellow detective Charles Ansberry, arrested Craig and Wendy Humphries, and booked them on the single charge of felony torture under California Penal Code §206. The same day, a Sheriff's deputy, without a warrant, picked up the Humphries' two other children from their schools and placed them in protective custody. Both children denied any fear of abuse or mistreatment and indicated their desire to return home. . . .

[T]he day after the Humphries were arrested, Detective Wilson completed a child abuse investigation report identifying the Humphries' case as a "substantiated report" of child abuse. Pursuant to CANRA, this information was sent to the CA DOJ, which in turn created a CACI listing identifying Craig and Wendy Humphries as child abuse suspects with a "substantiated" report. . . . On August 29, 2001, the Humphries' criminal case was dismissed. The prosecutor had learned that in November 2000, Dr. Isaac Benjamin Paz surgically removed a melanoma on S.H.'s shoulder. S.H. had follow-up visits with Dr. Paz in December 2000 and March 2001, periods that corresponded with S.H.'s claims of abuse. On all these occasions, Dr. Paz examined S.H.'s entire body, and saw no sign of abuse. The prosecutor determined that this information "contradict[ed] the basic part of [S.H's] testimony that she was injured during the entire time" and agreed that the Humphries' criminal case [should be dismissed]. The Humphries then successfully petitioned the criminal court under California Penal Code §851.8 for orders finding them "factually innocent" of the felony torture charge, and requiring the arrest records pertaining to that charge be sealed and destroyed. . . .

[Meanwhile], in separate, non-criminal proceedings, Detective Wilson requested that Los Angeles County file a juvenile court dependency petition to have the Humphries' two children declared dependent children of the juvenile court based on the fact that their "sibling has been abused or neglected." [After a hearing], the juvenile court ordered that the Humphries retain custody of their children, and dismissed all counts as "not true." . . .

As required by CANRA, in May 2001, the Humphries were notified that they were listed in the CACI. The notice informed them that if they believed the report was unfounded, and they desired a review, that they should address their request to Detective Wilson. [T]he Humphries contacted LASD's Family Crimes Bureau through their attorney. They discovered that Detective Wilson no longer worked at the Bureau and there was no available procedure for them to challenge their listing in the CACI. On May 9, 2002, LASD Sergeant Michael Becker advised the

Humphries' attorney that after conducting an investigation, the LASD would not reverse its report labeling the Humphries as "substantiated" child abusers for the purposes of the CACI. Becker indicated that the fact that charges were filed "would indicate to us that some sort of crime did occur" and the fact that the case was dismissed "would not negate the entries" into the CACI. . . . Despite the fact that two independent California tribunals had found that the allegations underlying the Humphries' CACI listing were "not true" and that the Humphries are "factually innocent," the CA DOJ continues to list the Humphries in the CACI as substantiated child abusers. Furthermore, because the Humphries were listed pursuant to a "substantiated report," they will remain listed on the CACI indefinitely.

[The Humphries fear] that the CACI listing will both influence their ability to obtain certain benefits and further injure their already damaged reputation. . . . Wendy currently works as a special education teacher and resource specialist at a public school in California. She possesses a number of teaching credentials that must be periodically renewed in order to maintain her current employment — a renewal process that requires her to apply to the California Commission on Teacher Credentialing. The Humphries have introduced evidence indicating that the information available on the CACI might have an impact on her ability to obtain educational credentials. Wendy has also indicated a desire to pursue a degree in psychology from the University of California at Los Angeles. Two courses of interest within the psychology department place all of the students in a child care program licensed by the state of California. To enroll in these classes, all potential students must pay for and submit to a CACI check. . . .

The Humphries argue that Appellees violated their Fourteenth Amendment right to procedural due process by listing and continuing to list them on the CACI, without any available process to challenge that listing. . . . The Humphries contend that they have a liberty interest under the "stigma-plus" test of Paul v. Davis, 424 U.S. 693 (1976). [They] argue that the stigma of being listed in the CACI as substantiated child abusers, plus the various statutory consequences of being listed on the CACI constitutes a liberty interest, of which they may not be deprived without process of law. We agree.

. . . In Paul v. Davis, the Supreme Court clarified that procedural due process protections apply to reputational harm only when a plaintiff suffers stigma from governmental action plus alteration or extinguishment of "a right or status previously recognized by state law." 424 U.S. 693, 711 (1976). This holding has come to be known as the "stigma-plus test." [B]eing labeled a child abuser by being placed on the CACI is "unquestionably stigmatizing." . . . The more difficult issue is whether the Humphries can satisfy the "plus" test. The Humphries must show that, as the result of being listed in the CACI, "a right or status previously recognized by state law was distinctly altered or extinguished." *Paul*, 424 U.S. at 711. . . .

The Humphries allege [that] being listed on the CACI alters their rights in two general ways. First, state statutes mandate that licensing agencies search the CACI and conduct an additional investigation prior to granting a number of rights and benefits. These rights include gaining approval to care for children in a day care center or home (Cal. Health & Safety Code §1596.877(b)), obtaining a license or employment in child care (id. §1522.1(a)), volunteering in a crisis nursery (id. §1526.8(b)(2)), receiving placement or custody of a relative's child (Cal. Welf. & Inst. Code §361.4(c)), or qualifying as a resource family (id. §16519.5(d)(1)(A)(i)). These benefits are explicitly conditioned on the agency checking the CACI and conducting an additional investigation. Second, information in the CACI is specifically made available to other identified agencies: state contracted licensing agencies overseeing employment positions dealing with children (Cal. Penal Code §11170(b)(4)); persons making pre-employment investigations for "peace officers, child care licensing or employment, adoption, or child placement" (id. §11170(b)(8)); individuals in the Court Appointed Special Advocate program conducting background investigations for potential Court Appointed Special Advocates (id. §11170(b)(5)), and out-of-state agencies making foster care or adoptive decisions (id. §11170(e)(1)). . . .

We hold that where a state statute creates both a stigma and a tangible burden on an individual's ability to obtain a right or status recognized by state law, an individual's liberty interest has been violated. A tangible burden exists in this context where a law effectively requires agencies to check a stigmatizing list and investigate any adverse information prior to conferring a legal right or benefit. . . .

The Humphries must show [also] that the procedural safeguards of their liberty interest established by the state are constitutionally insufficient to protect their rights. . . . We evaluate the process that California provides persons listed on the CACI under the three-part test set out in Mathews v. Eldridge, 424 U.S. 319 (1976) [balancing:] (1) the private interest affected by the official action; (2) the risk of erroneous deprivation and the probable value of additional procedural safeguards; and (3) the governmental interest, including the fiscal and administrative burdens of additional procedures. . . .

[T]he Humphries have an interest in not being stigmatized by having their names included in a child abuse database that places a tangible burden on legal rights, if they have not committed the acts underlying the reports that led to their inclusion. Thus, they have an interest in pursuing employment and adoption, seeking to obtain custody of a relative's children, and securing the appropriate licenses for working with children without having to be subject to an additional investigation, delays, and possible denial of a benefit under California law due to an incorrect listing on the CACI.

There is no doubt that California has a vital interest in preventing child abuse and that the creation or maintenance of a central index, such as the CACI, is an effective and responsible means for California to secure its interest. [Nevertheless,] California can have no interest in maintaining a system of records that contains incorrect or even false information. First, the effectiveness of a system listing individuals that pose a danger to children becomes less effective if a larger and larger percentage of the population erroneously becomes listed due to unsubstantiated claims. . . . In addition, there is a great human cost in California, as elsewhere, to being falsely accused of being a child abuser. These costs are not only borne by the individuals falsely accused, but by their children and extended families, their neighbors and their employers. Indeed, with the same passion that California condemns the child abuser for his atrocious acts, it has an interest in protecting its citizens against such calumny. . . .

The final, and perhaps most important, *Mathews* factor is the risk of erroneous deprivation and the probable value of additional procedural safeguards. [W]e ask . . . "[A]fter examining the process by which persons are listed on the CACI, what is the risk of someone being erroneously listed?" In light of the Humphries' allegations . . . the answer is "quite likely." . . . A determination that the report is "not unfounded" is a very low threshold. [T]he accused is presumed to be a child abuser and listed in CANRA unless the investigator determines that the report is false, improbable, or accidental. Incomplete or inadequate investigations must be reported for listing on the CACI.

We have no evidence in the record that indicates exactly how many "false positives" reporting agencies receive. However, given the high stakes in child abuse cases, presumably an agency investigation and child abuse report can be triggered by as little as an anonymous phone call. It is apparent in such a system there is a real danger of prank and spite calls. California should investigate such reports, and it can — and perhaps should — retain records on any reports it cannot determine to be "unfounded." When it retains all reports that are "not unfounded," it assumes a substantial risk that some of its reports are false. . . .

The record is devoid of any systematic study of the error rate in the CACI. We do note that in a 2004 self-study of CANRA, a California task force reported on a pilot program in San Diego County, where "DOJ discovered that approximately 50 percent of CACI listings originating from [one agency] should be purged because the supporting documentation was no longer maintained at the local level." Child Abuse and Neglect Reporting Act Task Force Report 24 (2004). . . .

Any errors introduced at the time information is posted to the CACI arguably can be corrected. [T]he CA DOJ must notify the known or suspected child abuser that he has been reported to the CACI. At that point, if the person believes he has been reported in error, he has three options. First, he can try to informally persuade the investigator who reported it in the first place. Second, he can wait until an agency or other entity that is required to consult the CACI receives the information and rely on the agency or other entity's "independent conclusions regarding the quality of the evidence disclosed, and its sufficiency for making decisions." Third, once an agency makes an adverse decision, some persons have a right to appeal the decision in court. None of these means for correcting erroneous information in the CACI is well designed to do so. We consider each in turn.

1. *Persuading the investigator.* First, attempting to persuade the investigating officer is not a satisfactory way to correct the records. [T]he only recourse offered to the Humphries was to try to get the investigator who had made the original determination that their case was "substantiated" to change his mind. Nothing in CANRA instructs Detective Wilson how to deal with the Humphries. He is not required to respond to the Humphries or address their concerns or pleas in any way, he has been given no standard for reevaluating his initial judgment, and no one else other than Detective Wilson is required to respond to the Humphries. If Detective Wilson refuses to reconsider his original evaluation, the Humphries have no statutory recourse elsewhere within the LASD. . . .

2. *Reaching an independent agency conclusion.* Appellees also argue that there is little risk of erroneous deprivation because an agency that has consulted the CACI must base its decision regarding the listed person on its own "independent

conclusions." (Cal. Penal Code §11170(b)(9)(A)). . . . First, we note that by the time the decision maker has referenced the CACI and become charged with undertaking an additional investigation, the individual liberty interest in avoiding stigma and alteration of a legal right has already occurred. . . . Second, even if the agency conducts a thorough investigation, nothing the agency decides affects the CACI listing; that is, even if an agency, conducting its own investigation, decides that the claims against a listed person are unfounded, the agency has no power to correct the CACI listing. The person is stuck in CACI-limbo. . . .

Disregarding these limitations temporarily, it is not clear to us that an agency, in reality, can or will regularly engage in the process required to determine that charges against an individual are unfounded. . . . An agency with a limited budget, presented with the choice of thoroughly investigating allegations of child abuse so that it can issue a license, or simply denying the license after a cursory investigation so that it can spend its resources elsewhere, can reasonably be expected to choose the latter. . . .

3. *Seeking court review.* Finally, Appellees argue that some persons adversely affected by decisions resulting from their listing on the CACI may seek redress in the legal system on a case-by-case basis. The administrative review process offers some check on the system. As we know from our own experience, court review of agency decisions can be a cumbersome process. What is most troubling about the states' argument, however, is that even court review cannot solve the problem. [T]he Humphries' experience is instructive. The Humphries have taken advantage of every procedure available to them, including the California courts. They went to the dependency court, which found that the allegations were "not true" and returned their children to them. They went to the prosecutor, who dropped all the charges against them. They went to the criminal court, which declared them "factually innocent" and sealed their arrest records. None of this had any effect on their CACI listing. They will remain on the CACI until the investigating agency submits corrected information to the system. . . .

In the end, this is not a difficult case. The lack of any meaningful, guaranteed procedural safeguards before the initial placement on CACI combined with the lack of any effective process for removal from CACI violates the Humphries' due process rights. . . .

NOTES AND QUESTIONS ON CENTRAL REGISTRIES

(1) Existing Shortcomings.   Soon after the enactment of central registries, commentators recognized their shortcomings, including the lack of an opportunity to challenge inclusion, broad criteria for inclusion, a limited right of access to included information, and the inadequacy of expungement procedures.[18] Some early defects were corrected by statutory amendments. However, substantial problems persisted, including significant delays in the expungement process, the lack of predeprivation hearings, the low standard of proof for inclusion, inadequate

---

[18] Gail Garringer & James N. Hyde, Child Abuse and the Central Registry, in Child Abuse: Intervention and Treatment 171-175 (Nancy B. Ebeling & Deborah A. Hill eds. 1975).

notice of inclusion, and the existence of a conflict of interest if the same official functions as investigator and adjudicator.[19] Which of these problems characterize the child abuse registry in *Humphries*?

(2) Constitutionality of Central Registries.

a. Substantive Due Process. *Humphries* is one of several substantive and procedural due process challenges to registry statutes. To date, most courts agree that inclusion in a registry that is accessible to employers implicates the individual's due process rights to employment and reputation. See, e.g., Dupuy v. Samuels, 397 F.3d 493 (7th Cir. 2005); Valmonte v. Bane, 18 F.3d 992 (2d Cir. 1994).

b. Procedural Due Process: Standard of Proof. When Detective Wilson filed his report on the Humphries, the standard of proof for determination of a "substantiated" report of child abuse required the investigator to find "credible evidence" of abuse (Cal. Penal Code §11165.12(b)(2001). The state legislature subsequently amended the statute to require evidence "that makes it more likely than not that child abuse or neglect . . . occurred." Id. What should be the standard of proof to determine whether there is sufficient evidence to include an individual in the registry? How does the large number of unsubstantiated reports affect your opinion?

c. Procedural Due Process: Expungement. CAPTA provides for expungement of records of child maltreatment in cases that are unsubstantiated or false. See 42 U.S.C. §5106(b)(2)(A)(xii) (2000 & Supp. 2005) (requiring "prompt expungement of any records that are accessible to the general public or are used for purposes of employment or other background checks in cases determined to be unsubstantiated or false, except that nothing in this section shall prevent State child protective services agencies from keeping information on unsubstantiated reports in their casework files to assist in future risk and safety assessment"). How long should states maintain records of unsubstantiated cases before expungement? How long would the Humphries' records remain in the state database?

(3) Equal Protection Challenges. Some courts criticize child abuse procedures as a violation of equal protection, claiming that the procedures discriminate on the basis of gender, race, and class. See, e.g., People United for Children, Inc. v. City of New York, 108 F. Supp. 2d 275 (2000), Yuan v. Rivera, 48 F. Supp. 2d 335 (1999). Do you agree that strenthening procedural protections, such as central registries, "may reduce the incidence of racial, gender, and socioeconomic bias in child abuse investigations"?[20] If you were advising a state legislator, how would you suggest the registry statute be improved?

NOTE: SANCTIONS FOR FAILURE OF STATE TO ACT AFTER REPORT: DESHANEY v. WINNEBAGO COUNTY

Once a case of child abuse has been reported, does the child have a constitutional right to protection from the State? The Supreme Court addressed this issue in DeShaney v. Winnebago County Department of Social Services, 489

---

[19] Kate Hollenbeck, Between a Rock and a Hard Place: Child Abuse Registries at the Intersection of Child Protection, Due Process, and Equal Protection, 11 Tex. J. Women & L. 1, 16 (2001).
[20] Id. at 34.

U.S. 189 (1989). A report of paternal abuse of two-year-old Joshua was made to the Wisconsin Department of Social Services (DSS) in January 1982. After the father denied the charges, DSS dropped the case. However, after more reports of abuse, a caseworker was assigned to make monthly home visits. During those visits, she noted numerous injuries to the child, although she never took any action to remove the child from the home. Two years later the child was beaten so severely by his father that the resulting brain damage left him retarded. Joshua and his mother filed an action under 42 U.S.C. §1983 claiming that the child had been deprived of his liberty without due process because of DSS's failure to protect him.

In an opinion by Chief Justice Rehnquist, the Court held that a State does not have a duty to protect an individual unless the State has taken him into custody against his will. Some active interference by the State is required because "[t]he affirmative duty to protect arises not from the State's knowledge of the individual's predicament or from its expressions of intent to help him, but from the limitation which it has imposed on his freedom to act on his own behalf." 489 U.S. at 200. No such limitation was found in this case because "[t]he most that can be said of the state functionaries . . . is that they stood by and did nothing when suspicious circumstances dictated a more active role." Id. at 203.

In the dissent, Justice Brennan (joined by Justices Marshall and Blackmun) found that DSS *had* limited Joshua's ability to act on his own behalf because, under Wisconsin law, only DSS handles child abuse cases. Once DSS receives a report, citizens and other governmental agencies feel their job is done. "If DSS ignores or dismisses . . . suspicions, no one will step in to fill the gap." Id. at 210. As the dissent stated, "[u]nfortunately for Joshua DeShaney, the buck effectively stopped with the Department." Id. at 209.

DeShaney left unresolved the question of which custodial relationships, short of incarceration, might trigger an affirmative obligation on the part of the state to protect children from abuse. For example, does the state have an affirmative duty to protect children placed in foster care? Many courts have concluded, after *DeShaney*, that "foster children have the requisite special relationship with the state to trigger potential due process protections."[21] For further discussion of issues regarding foster care, see section E, infra.

5. An Agenda for Reform

Douglas J. Besharov, Child Abuse Realities: Over-Reporting and Poverty
8 Va. J. Soc. Pol'y & L. 165, 188-192, 196-203 (2000)

For thirty years, advocates, program administrators, and politicians have joined the cause to encourage even more reports of suspected child abuse and neglect. [T]heir efforts have been spectacularly successful, with about three million children now

---

[21] Mark Strasser, Deliberate Indifference, Professional Judgment, and the Constitution: On Liberty Interests in the Child Placement Context, 15 Duke J. Gender L. & Pol'y 223, 231 (2008) (discussing different standards in determining liability to foster children in state care).

reported each year. . . . All states now have specialized child protective agencies to receive and investigate reports, and treatment services for maltreated children and their parents have been expanded substantially. [However, at the present time] concerns other than non-reporting should come to the fore.

A. The Costs of Inappropriate Reports

The determination that a report is unfounded can only be made after an unavoidably traumatic investigation that is, inherently, a breach of parental and family privacy. To determine whether a particular child is in danger, caseworkers must inquire into the most intimate personal and family matters. Often, it is necessary to question friends, relatives, and neighbors, as well as school teachers, day care personnel, doctors, clergy, and others who know the family.

Laws against child abuse are an implicit recognition that family privacy must give way to the need to protect helpless children. But in seeking to protect children, it is all too easy to ignore the legitimate rights of parents. Each year, about 700,000 families are put through investigations of unfounded reports. This is a massive and unjustified violation of parental rights. . . .

The current flood of unfounded reports is overwhelming the limited resources of child protective agencies. For fear of missing even one abused child, workers perform extensive investigations of vague and apparently unsupported reports. Even when a home visit based on an anonymous report turns up no evidence of maltreatment, workers usually interview neighbors, schoolteachers, and day-care personnel to make sure that the child is not abused. And even repeated anonymous and unfounded reports do not prevent a further investigation. But all of this takes time.

As a result, children in real danger are getting lost in the press of inappropriate cases. Forced to allocate a substantial portion of their limited resources to unfounded reports, child protective agencies are less able to respond promptly and effectively when children are in serious danger. Some reports are left uninvestigated for a week and even two weeks after they are received. Investigations often miss key facts because workers rush to clear cases. Dangerous home situations receive inadequate supervision, as workers must ignore pending cases as they investigate the new reports that arrive daily on their desks. Decision-making also suffers. With so many cases of insubstantial or unproven risk to children, caseworkers are desensitized to the obvious warning signals of immediate and serious danger. [A] relatively clear agenda for reform emerges. . . .

1. Clarify child abuse reporting laws

Existing laws are often vague and overbroad. They should be rewritten to provide real guidance about what conditions should, and should not, be reported. This can be accomplished without making a radical departure from present laws or practices. The key is to describe reportable conditions in terms of specific parental behaviors or conditions that are tied to severe and demonstrable harms (or potential harms) to children.

It would help, for example, to make a distinction between (1) direct evidence, meaning firsthand accounts or observations of seriously harmful parental behavior, and (2) circumstantial evidence, meaning concrete facts, such as the child's physical condition, which suggest that the child has been abused or neglected. (Behavioral indicators, however, should not, by themselves, be considered a sufficient basis for a report.) . . .

2. Provide continuing public education and professional training

Few people fail to report because they want children to suffer abuse and neglect. Likewise, few people make deliberately false reports. Most involve an honest desire to protect children coupled with confusion about what conditions are reportable. Thus, educational efforts should emphasize the conditions that do not justify a report, as well as those that do.

3. Screen reports

No matter how well professionals are trained and no matter how extensive public education efforts are, there will always be a tendency for persons to report cases that should not be investigated. Until recently, most states did not have formal policies and procedures for determining whether to accept a call for investigation. Such policies should be adopted by all states and they should provide explicit guidance about the kinds of cases that should not be assigned for investigation.

Reports should be rejected when the allegations fall outside the agency's definitions of "child abuse" and "child neglect," as established by state law. Often, the family has a coping problem for which they would be more appropriately referred to another social service agency. Prime examples include children beyond the specified age, alleged perpetrators falling outside the legal definition, and family problems not amounting to child maltreatment. Reports should also be rejected when the caller can give no credible reason for suspecting that the child has been abused or neglected. . . . Anonymous reports, reports from estranged spouses, and even previous unfounded reports from the same source should not be automatically rejected, but they need to be carefully evaluated. Rejected reports should be referred to other agencies that can provide services needed by the family.

4. Modify liability laws

Current laws provide immunity for anyone who makes a report in good faith, but give no protection to those who, in a good faith exercise of professional judgment, decide that a child has not been abused or neglected and, hence, should not be reported. This combination of immunities and penalties encourages the over-reporting of questionable situations.

5. Give feedback to persons who report

If persons who report are not told what happened, they may conclude that the agency's response was ineffective or even harmful to the child, and the next time they suspect that a child is maltreated, they may decide not to report. In addition, finding out whether their suspicions were valid also refines their diagnostic skills and thus improves the quality and accuracy of their future reports. Reporters also need such information to interpret subsequent events and to monitor the child's condition.

6. Adopt an agency policy

Appropriate reporting of suspected child maltreatment requires a sophisticated knowledge of many legal, administrative, and diagnostic matters. To help ensure that staffs respond properly, an increasing number of public and private agencies are adopting formal agency policies about reporting. Some state laws mandate them. The primary purpose of these policies, or agency protocols, is to inform staff members of their obligation to report and of the procedures to be followed. . . .

B. Address Poverty-Related Neglect

In the wake of welfare reform, the ways in which child protective agencies respond to the condition of poverty takes on added importance. [Social agencies] overreact to cases of social deprivation in poor families. In fact, poor, socially deprived children are more likely to be placed in foster care than are abused children. These disadvantaged children, in no real danger of physical injury, languish for years in foster care. Living in emotionally traumatic conditions, hundreds of thousands of poor children suffer more harm than if they were simply left at home.

To say that poor children are inappropriately included in programs for abused and neglected children is not the same as saying that they do not have pressing needs, nor that they should not be the concern of public and private programs. But the nature of the intervention should be different — and it should be voluntary. Child protective agencies have not been established as society's response to poverty, and for them to assume this role misdirects their resources from their proper mission. . . .

Helping these families, usually involving single mothers, does not require mandatory reporting laws, involuntary investigations, central registers of reports, or psychologically oriented "treatment" interventions. In too many instances, such efforts are ineffectual, and even harmful.

Society should acknowledge the overlap between child maltreatment and poverty and adopt intervention strategies that address the families' broader problems. Such strategies might include compensatory child development programs housed in integrated service centers for teen mothers. But, even in the absence of such specialized services, society would do better if it did nothing in poverty-related cases, rather than the wrong — and often harmful — something. . . .

[T]he following factors [are] prone to over-reporting:

- Clothing neglect: Examples are wearing torn pants, wearing cast-off clothing, or not having a raincoat or gloves.
- Nutritional neglect: Examples are eating unbalanced meals, eating too many "junk foods," or cultural food preferences. Even skipping breakfast can be normal if it's the child's choice. We must remember that approximately one third of adults prefer not to eat breakfast.

- Hygiene neglect: Examples are coming to school with a dirty face, dirty hair, or dirty clothing. If the child is not malodorous and the problem is periodic, it is probably of minimal importance.
- Home environment neglect: Mildly unsanitary homes are quite common. We should not be over critical of housekeeping below standards, such as poorly washed dishes or a house that is covered with dog hair and needs vacuuming.
- Cultural deprivation or intellectual stimulation neglect: This term is often directed at families whose children allegedly are not talked to enough or presented with sufficient creative toys. All too often this term is applied to children with developmental delays due to normal variation or prematurity.
- Safety neglect: Many normal accidents are called safety neglect to the detriment of the parents, for example, blaming the parents for burns that occur on space heaters despite numerous precautions the parents have taken. On a practical level, some unsafe environments cannot be changed.
- Minor acute illness neglect: Insect bites, lice, scabies, and impetigo occur in children from all socioeconomic groups. Often parents are blamed for diaper rashes and cradle cap. Parents may be criticized because they have not given their child antipyretics before bringing them to the physician for a fever. Parents may be blamed for not coming to the clinic soon enough for an ear infection that they did not know existed. . . .

[I]n assessing such cases, a two-pronged inquiry is appropriate:

(1) Does the care of the child fall below commonly accepted community standards? To justify a report, the deviation must be clear and unambiguous, and should not be the product of responsible differences in culture or lifestyle. . . .

(2) Has the child's physical or mental condition been impaired or is it in danger of being impaired? [U]sing nutrition as an example, if the child seems hungry and emaciated, a report should be made.

Conclusion

This paper has proposed a broad agenda for reform. [M]uch more needs to be done if the nation's child protective system is to meet the high responsibilities assigned to it, without harming some of the children and families entrusted to its care.

6. The Problem of Sexual Abuse

M.W. v. Department of Children & Family Services
881 So. 2d 734 (Fla. Ct. App. 2004)

Cope, J.

M.W. appeals an order adjudicating his three natural daughters dependent. [O]n July 1, 2001, M.W. was arrested for sexual battery on his stepdaughter,

J.G. The petition alleges that M.W. had sexual intercourse with his stepdaughter over a three-year period, beginning when the child was ten years old. As to the criminal charges, M.W. was released on bail and the criminal charges remain pending.

The Department filed a petition for dependency as to the stepdaughter J.G. (also referred to as "the stepdaughter") and M.W.'s natural daughters, J.W 1, J.W 2, and J.W 3 (also referred to as "the natural daughters"). With regard to the stepdaughter, M.W. entered a consent plea to the dependency petition. Pursuant to this consent, the stepdaughter was adjudicated dependent as to M.W.

Four days later, the trial court conducted an adjudicatory hearing on the petition for dependency as to M.W.'s natural daughters. They were eight, seven, and three years old at the time of the dependency hearing. M.W. was present at the hearing and represented by counsel, but did not testify.

The trial court received testimony from a psychologist who had evaluated M.W., and took judicial notice of the consent order relating to the stepdaughter. The court entered an order adjudicating the natural daughters dependent as to M.W. The order states, in part:

> . . . 4b. Dr. Schzechowicz testified that there would be a high risk of sexual abuse re-occurring if [M. W.] had access to the Child [J.G.]. As such, no contact with [J.G.] was recommended. Dr. Schzechowicz further recommended that [M.W.] be ordered to attend and successfully complete the Mentally Disordered Sex Offender (MDSO) Program.
>
> 4c. Dr. Schzechowicz testified that even though according to the testing [M.W.] had exhibited a low risk of recidivism [as to the natural daughters], there were concerns regarding his psychological functioning and he presented as a psychological[ly] maladjusted individual. [M.W.] showed no remorse and blamed the victim-child for any alleged misconduct. Hence, the risk to the Children [the natural daughters] according to Dr. Schzechowicz, was increased by [M.W.'s] commission of a similar act on another Child, to-wit: [J.G.], the Children's half-sister.
>
> . . . 6. The Court finds, that based on the totality of the circumstances, and after reviewing the documents admitted into evidence as well as hearing expert testimony on the matter, the risk of imminent sexual abuse to the above captioned Children [the natural daughters] is increased by the Father's commission of a similar act on another Child, to-wit, the Children's half-sibling, [J.G.], his lack of remorse and his psychological functioning.
>
> It is hereby ORDERED and ADJUDGED that the above captioned Children be adjudicated dependent within the meaning and intent of Florida Statutes Chapter 39.

[On appeal] M.W. argues that the evidence was legally insufficient to support the dependency order. He argues that his sexual abuse of his stepdaughter is insufficient to support a dependency adjudication as to his natural daughters. He contends that the psychologist's testimony defeats the Department's petition. We disagree.

The Florida Supreme Court has said, "The purpose of a dependency proceeding is not to punish the offending parent but to protect and care for a child who has been neglected, abandoned, or abused." M.F. v. Florida Department of Children and Families, 770 So. 2d 1189, 1193 (Fla. 2000).

In administering the child protection system, "The health and safety of the children served shall be of paramount concern." Fla. Stat. §39.001(1)(b)1.

Under the statute, a dependent child includes one who is "at substantial risk of imminent abuse, abandonment, or neglect by the parent or parents or legal custodians." Id. §39.01(14)(f). In making that determination, the trial court is to look at the totality of the circumstances.

M.W. relies on the *M.F.* decision, but that reliance is misplaced. In *M.F.*, the father had sexually abused one of his children, K.F. The father was convicted of sexual battery and imprisoned for fifteen years. K.F. was adjudicated dependent as to the father.

In further proceedings, the trial court found M.F.'s other children dependent, on the theory that the other children were at risk of prospective abuse. Rejecting that rationale for the dependency order, the Florida Supreme Court reasoned that since the father was imprisoned for fifteen years and presumably would have no contact with the children, it would follow that there was no risk of prospective abuse.

The present case differs from *M.F.* In the present case the father is at liberty on bail and there is thus no physical impediment to his having contact with the children. The remaining children are all younger daughters, who are plainly not old enough to protect themselves.

The *M.F.* court ruled that an adjudication of dependency based on the fact that a parent has sexually abused one child is a factor which can be considered in deciding whether the remaining children are at prospective risk. Id. The father has admitted to having repeated sexual intercourse with his stepdaughter and an adjudication of dependency as to that child has been entered.

M.W. argues, however, that the following testimony of the psychologist supports his position that the instant order should be reversed:

Q: Do you have an opinion regarding whether M.W. is at high risk to re-engage in sexually illegal behavior in the future?

A: If you're talking about M.W., and I'm going to make an assumption here that he did engage in the behavior he's charged with, if he actually did this, then if you were to give him unfettered access to the alleged victim in this case, then my opinion is there would be a very high risk to his stepdaughter. If we're talking about the other children, the signs would indicate that he is not a high risk and if these are his natural children. Based on both the Static Actuarial and Dynamic Risk Factors.

Q: Just so that we can be clear. Supposing, let's assume that M.W. is found guilty of this offense that he was arrested and charged with. Is there an increased risk for his natural children?

A: Of course, ma'am. Any time someone engages in sexually inappropriate behavior, the likelihood of future behavior increases. The results of the testing would indicate that the likelihood in terms of his sexually abusing his natural children *is below base rates, but it's not zero, by any means.* [Transcript, Mar. 27, 2003, at 19-20 (emphasis added).]

M.W. argues that since the psychologist said M.W. is not a high risk to his natural children, it follows that the legal standard for a dependency order has not been satisfied. We disagree.

In deciding whether there is a substantial risk of imminent abuse, the trial court is to examine all of the circumstances. This includes the severity of potential harm as well as the likelihood it will occur.

In this case the risk to be protected against is sexual abuse of minor children. It is among the greatest of harms that can be inflicted on children. It is physical harm which is serious criminal conduct.

Because the nature of the harm is so great, it is intolerable to allow even a low probability that M.W. will sexually abuse the other children. The psychologist here testified that while the danger to the natural children was below base rates, *"it's not zero, by any means."* (Emphasis added).

As we interpret M.W.'s position, he wants us to rule that the trial court cannot order protective services unless there is reason to believe that, more probably than not, he will sexually abuse his other children. The contention apparently is that if the likelihood is below fifty percent, then the young children must be left to fend for themselves. That analysis is incorrect under the statute and under the *M.F.* decision.

Quite apart from the psychological evaluation results, in M.W.'s own statements to the psychologist he denied responsibility and blamed the victim. Further, at the time of the proceeding below, treatment in the MDSO program had been recommended, but it is not clear whether treatment had begun. In any event, M.W. had completed no such program. These factors, too, support the conclusion that M.W. cannot be left to his own devices.

The trial court applied the correct legal standard and the dependency order is fully supported by the evidence. Affirmed.

Child Sexual Abuse: Intervention and Treatment Issues (1993)
U.S. Department of Health and Human Services,
National Clearinghouse on Child Abuse and Neglect

Definitions, Scope, and Effects of Child Sexual Abuse . . .

There are two types of statutes in which definitions of sexual abuse can be found — child protection (civil) and criminal. The purposes of these laws differ. Child protection statutes are concerned with sexual abuse as a condition from which children need to be protected. Thus, these laws include child sexual abuse as one of the forms of maltreatment that must be reported by designated professionals and investigated by child protection agencies. Courts may remove children from their homes in order to protect them from sexual abuse. Generally, child protection statutes apply only to situations in which offenders are the children's caretakers.

Criminal statutes prohibit certain sexual acts and specify the penalties. Generally, these laws include child sexual abuse as one of several sex crimes. Criminal statutes prohibit sex with a child, regardless of the adult's relationship to the child, although incest may be dealt with in a separate statute.

Definitions in child protection statutes are quite brief and often refer to State criminal laws for more elaborate definitions. In contrast, criminal statutes are frequently quite lengthy.

Child Protection Definitions

The Federal definition of child maltreatment is included in the Child Abuse Prevention and Treatment Act. Sexual abuse and exploitation is a subcategory of child abuse and neglect. The statute does not apply the maximum age of 18 for other types of maltreatment, but rather indicates that the age limit in the State law shall apply. Sexual abuse is further defined to include:

''(A) the employment, use, persuasion, inducement, enticement, or coercion of any child to engage in, or assist any other person to engage in, any sexually explicit conduct or simulation of such conduct for the purpose of producing a visual depiction of such conduct; or

(B) the rape, molestation, prostitution, or other form of sexual exploitation of children, or incest with children; . . .''

In order for States to qualify for funds allocated by the Federal Government, they must have child protection systems that meet certain criteria, including a definition of child maltreatment specifying sexual abuse.

Criminal Definitions

With the exception of situations involving Native American children, crimes committed on Federal property, interstate transport of minors for sexual purposes, and the shipment or possession of child pornography, State criminal statutes regulate child sexual abuse. Generally, the definitions of sexual abuse found in criminal statutes are very detailed. The penalties vary depending on:

- the age of the child, crimes against younger children being regarded as worse;
- the level of force, force making the crime more severe;
- the relationship between victim and offender, an act against a relative or household member being considered more serious; and
- the type of sexual act, acts of penetration receiving longer sentences.

Often types of sexual abuse are classified in terms of their degree (of severity), first degree being the most serious and fourth degree the least, and class (of felony), a class A felony being more serious than a class B or C, etc. . . .

Prevalence of Child Sexual Abuse

. . . Rates of victimization for females range from 6 to 62 percent, with most professionals estimating that between one in three and one in four women are sexually abused in some way during their childhoods. The rates for men are somewhat lower, ranging from 3 to 24 percent, with most professionals believing that 1 in 10 men and perhaps as many as 1 in 6 are sexually abused as children. As noted earlier, many believe that male victimization is more underreported than female, in part because of societal failure to identify the behavior as abusive. However, the boy himself may not define the behavior as sexual victimization but as sexual experience, especially if it involves a woman offender. Moreover, he may be less likely to disclose than a female victim, because he has been socialized not to talk about his problems. This reticence may be increased if the offender is a male, for he must overcome two taboos, having been the object of a sexual encounter with an adult and a male. Finally, he may not be as readily believed as a female victim. . . .

The Impact of Sexual Abuse

Regardless of the underlying causes of the impact of sexual abuse, the problems are very real for victims and their families. Finkelhor, whose conceptualization of the traumatogenic effects of sexual abuse is the most widely employed, divides sequelae into four general categories, each having varied psychological and behavioral effects.

- *Traumatic sexualization.* Included in the psychological outcomes of traumatic sexualization are aversive feelings about sex, overvaluing sex, and sexual identity problems. Behavioral manifestations of traumatic sexualization constitute a range of hypersexual behaviors as well as avoidance of or negative sexual encounters.
- *Stigmatization.* Common psychological manifestations of stigmatization are what Sgroi calls "damaged goods syndrome" and feelings of guilt and responsibility for the abuse or the consequences of disclosure. These feelings are likely to be reflected in self-destructive behaviors such as substance abuse, risk-taking acts, self-mutilation, suicidal gestures and acts, and provocative behavior designed to elicit punishment.
- *Betrayal.* Perhaps the most fundamental damage from sexual abuse is its undermining of trust in those people who are supposed to be protectors and nurturers. Other psychological impacts of betrayal include anger and borderline functioning. Behavior that reflects this trauma includes avoidance of investment in others, manipulating others, re-enacting the trauma through subsequent involvement in exploitive and damaging relationships, and engaging in angry and acting-out behaviors.
- *Powerlessness.* The psychological impact of the trauma of powerlessness includes both a perception of vulnerability and victimization and a desire to control or prevail, often by identification with the aggressor. As with the trauma of betrayal, behavioral manifestations may involve aggression and exploitation of others. On the other hand, the vulnerability effect of powerlessness may be avoidant responses, such as dissociation and running away; behavioral manifestations of anxiety, including phobias, sleep problems, elimination problems, and eating problems; and revictimization.

[A] variety of factors influence how sexual maltreatment impacts on an individual. These factors include the age of the victim (both at the time of the abuse and the time of assessment), the sex of the victim, the sex of the offender, the extent of the sexual abuse, the relationship between offender and victim, the reaction of others to knowledge of the sexual abuse, other life experiences, and the length of time between the abuse and information gathering. For example, the findings for child victims and adult survivors are somewhat different.

It is important for professionals to appreciate both the incomplete state of knowledge about the consequences of sexual abuse and the variability in effects. . . .

Lindsay C. Arthur, Child Sexual Abuse: Improving the System's Response
37 Juv. & Fam. Ct. J. (No. 2) 1, 11-14 (1986)

. . . When a child is sexually abused there are two immediate and strong reactions; the abuser must be punished, the child must be helped. If the abuser is a stranger, there is no problem. The child and her family can be worked with and the abuser can be sent to prison with no one else hurt. . . . But if the abuser is a parent of the child, a choice may have to be made. Either treat the child or punish the abuser, usually not both. If the abusing parent is put in jail, the abused child will feel guilty, a parent who may be otherwise a valuable member of the family is gone, the family loses a paycheck, its standard of living tumbles, the abused child may be blamed by the rest of the family. The best treatment requires the whole family, the abuser and the abused, the mother who may be an enabler, the other children who are necessarily involved. Without the abuser, the treatment circle is not complete, the problems cannot be fully resolved, the children may yet grow up to be abusers themselves. . . .

Severe Punishment or Effective Prevention

The decision to punish severely or to concentrate on treatment is not simple. It requires legal input as to the probabilities of getting a conviction and what evidence is needed for the family members. It involves social input as to the possibilities and effectiveness of treatment and the impact on the family of participation in the criminal processes. It requires political input as to the demands of the public for punishment, for revenge and the political impact of not prosecuting.

Children who are abused will probably abuse their own children or stand by while others abuse them, and their children in turn will abuse or enable the abuse of their own children, and on and on. Children who are abused are likely to become status offenders, delinquents, and criminals. Children who are abused are likely to have unstable marriages with the consequent trauma to themselves and their children. But children who are abused can usually be treated. The impact of the abuse can be reduced. The cycle of abuse can be broken.

The purpose of the intervention is to remove the guilt feelings. To remove the insecurity, to remove the anger. If the impact of abuse can be ended, if this cycle can be broken, intervention can be of major significance.

The impact of the abuse can be treated, a sufficient degree of normalcy can be restored. But the treatment of intra-family abuse will usually require that the abuser, be it parent or sibling, be apart of the treatment, freely discussing what happened and why and working out understanding and relationships that can prevent a recurrence. But an abuser facing trial and a long term in prison is surely going to be advised by his lawyer not to discuss any part of what happened. He may harbor too much fear and resentment to truly participate in any understandings. An abuser facing a short term in prison upon condition of cooperation in treatment may be more than willing to assist the rehabilitative process.

And so the problem. If the only options are either to use mild punishment in order to rehabilitate the family or to punish the abuser severely and lose his cooperation, which should it be? A decision must be made, and early, as to whether there will be treatment including [the] abuser with his participation insured by the continuing threat of punishment, or whether there will be immediate heavy punishment of the abuser and treatment without his participation. There must be a professional assessment of both the possibilities of conviction and the possibilities of rehabilitation. All of the various options must be canvassed and weighed. . . .

Assessment

Very early in cases of intra-family sexual abuse an assessment must be made to determine:

— If the evidence is sufficient for a conviction,

— If convicted, what is the probable sentence,

— How well can the family be rehabilitated if the abuser is not punished,

— How well can the family be rehabilitated if the abuser is punished,

— Is it politically possible not to punish. . . .

There are, of course, numerous options [including] prosecution for a felony, prosecution for a misdemeanor, prosecution in a plea bargained support of a rehabilitation process, a protective order, an action for neglect, even a civil action by the victim for damages or injunctive relief.

There are various possible felonies: rape, incest, carnal knowledge, aggravated assault, and their more modern and more sterile names: criminal sexual conduct in the first degree, etc. The choice depends on the credibility of the victim as a witness, the chances for conviction, the possible sentences, the public outcry, and the goals set for final disposition of the abuser, the abused, and the family. An incidental consideration is the unwillingness of the child to testify against a parent if it may result in a prison sentence but her willingness to testify if only a short jail sentence is possible.

There are also possible misdemeanors. [In addition], [a]n increasingly common remedy is the protective order. It is frequently based upon a statute and is prosecuted at no cost to the victim. It has the flexibility of an injunction and can usually be obtained, at least in preliminary form, in a matter of hours.

For maximum flexibility, an action for neglect probably allows the widest possible scope in developing and monitoring a rehabilitation plan. The procedure was statutorily designed precisely for rehabilitation. The caselaw requires a preliminary plan and progress reports. It can be backed up by contempt. And if the plan fails, it can be converted to an action to terminate parental rights.

If there is a sexual abuse, there is a possibility of a divorce or action with the consequent powers of the court to determine and monitor custody and visitation, though the divorce monitoring procedures are usually rather more clumsy than monitoring a neglect rehabilitation plan. Spouses, however, are not usually interested in divorce even though their children have been sexually molested.

Civil actions are a possibility. Unless, however, it can somehow involve the family's liability insurance, there seems little point to it. . . .

Coordination of Intervention

In sexual abuse cases there are often several agencies involved. . . . When abuse is reported, it is usually to the police. It may be required to notify the welfare agency. Both may send out investigators, each looking at the facts from a different perspective: the police need to decide if a crime was committed and to preserve the evidence for a prosecution; the welfare agency needs to know if a child is in danger and the steps needed to protect it. . . .

There may be actions started in juvenile court, in family court, in criminal court, and some judge may be asked for a protective order. There may even be different lawyers for different family members, each making different motions for different purposes. In larger communities, there may be three or four judges, each unaware of what the other is doing, each getting slightly differently focussed versions of the same facts, each issuing orders which may well conflict with each other. . . .

The prosecutor will usually be involved in any neglect or criminal procedures. The police and the welfare agency are usually responsive to the prosecutor. The prosecutor, being usually elected, is aware of public sentiment. And the prosecutor is usually able to communicate well with the judges. Coordination thus seems best to lie with the prosecutor. Supported by the rationale and decisions of an assessment team, a reasonable amount of coordination should be possible. . . .

D. Kelly Weisberg, The "Discovery" of Sexual Abuse: Experts' Role in Legal Policy Formulation
18 U.C. Davis L. Rev. 1-2, 5, 6-10, 18-19, 25, 27-43, 45-56 (1984)

Despite evidence of sexual abuse of children throughout history,[1] the labeling of this phenomenon as a pervasive social problem is relatively recent. The phenomenon has received so much attention that it has been labeled several times in the past half century. . . . Legal policy directed at sexual abuse of children has undergone several successive reformulations in the past half century. In each stage, a new definition of criminal behavior and proscribed sanctions were enacted into law. Different participants were involved in each successive stage of the labeling process. . . .

---

[1] Sexual abuse of children has been noted to occur as far back in history as ancient Greece and Rome. See L. DeMause, The History of Childhood 43-47 (1974). . . .

I.   Era of the Sexual Psychopath: From "Badness to Sickness"[15]

The first comprehensive legal labeling of child molestation appeared in the 1930s, and psychiatrists were the first experts relied upon to define the problem. Their initial reaction was to label such sexual crimes as indicative of an "illness," one they were uniquely qualified to treat. The impetus for this labeling came from several sexually-motivated murders of children in the late 1930s. . . .

The incomprehensibility of sexual crimes involving children spurred the call for experts — qualified to understand and assess the situation, to study the problem, and to make recommendations for its solution. The experts selected to make sense of both the criminal act and the offender were psychiatrists. . . .

The psychiatrists diagnosed child molestation as a form of mental illness, terming the illness "sexual psychopathy." They suggested a treatment for the patient: the patient should be hospitalized until "well" or normal again. . . .

Statutes utilized medical terminology and labeled the offender with psychiatric nomenclature. The terminology was made applicable specifically to child molesters.

Proper identification of the mental illness of sexual psychopathy necessitated the use of trained experts. Psychiatrists were required to interview the alleged perpetrator to determine both the malady's existence and the proper treatment. These dual functions of the psychiatric expert were embodied in the sexual psychopath legislation. . . .

The psychiatrist's role in the enactment of sexual psychopath legislation in the 1930s to 1940s has been previously noted in the literature. However, two important questions remain unanswered. First, why did these specific experts, rather than other scientists or behaviorists, play such an important role in the formulation of this legislation? Second, why was the role of psychiatrists enacted at this time in history? . . .

In short, the call for these experts came at a time when the public was increasingly aware of the promise of psychiatry. Social conditions made the public receptive to psychiatrists' input. Specifically, Freud's writings in the early twentieth century stimulated interest in the use of psychiatry to explain the irrational. World War I increased public awareness of psychiatry's value in treating war casualties. The Leopold-Loeb[22] trial revealed that psychiatry could have specific application to criminal law. These factors contributed to the emergence of psychiatrists in legal policymaking. When the public voiced concern about sex crimes, [t]he stage had been set for these experts to enact their roles.

II.   The First Relabeling: The 1950s

Legislation in the 1950s reflects the reconstruction and relabeling of child molestation by psychiatrists. Several states repealed or amended their sexual psychopath

---

[15] The term was coined by two sociologists in their social historical analysis of the transformation from religious and criminal to medical designations of deviance. See generally P. Conrad & J. Schneider, Deviance and Medicalization: From Badness to Sickness (1980).

[22] This trial in 1924 of two middle-class youths for murder was the first time psychiatrists testified as expert witnesses to explain criminal behavior. See Simon Baatz, For the Thrill of It: Leopold, Loeb, and the Murder That Shocked Jazz Age Chicago (2009).

statutes and enacted different legislation dealing with sex offenses. The new legislation renamed the patient's "illness." . . .

The sexual psychopath became the "mentally disordered sex offender" in California, the "sexually dangerous person" in Illinois, and the "sexual deviate" in Wisconsin. Not all jurisdictions adopted an entirely new label. Some jurisdictions merely modified and shortened the former label to "psychopathic offenders." One trend was evident: [m]edical nomenclature was deemphasized, and criminal terminology became more prominent. . . .

Several factors explain the relabeling of this social problem in the 1950s. First, the 1950s reflected a resurgence of interest in the application of psychiatry to legal problems. [S]ocietal recognition of psychiatry's shortcomings may also explain the relabeling process. Psychiatry was in a more advanced stage of development than in the 1930s; the legislation of the 1950s reflected a more realistic appraisal of the answers psychiatry could and could not supply. The realization was dawning that psychiatry was not an exact science nor one able to furnish precise solutions upon demand. The act of diagnosing an offender was not as simple as the weighing of a chemical compound. Nor could psychiatry permanently and completely "cure" sex offenders. With inadequate facilities, psychiatrists could barely hope to treat even a small number of patients.

The acute shortage of psychiatric personnel in public institutions after World War II frustrated hopes of treatment for sex offenders. . . . The second wave of legislation clearly recognized the problem of psychiatric supply and demand. . . .

Another explanation for the relabeling process may be found in sexual behavior research. An important influence on policymakers was Alfred Kinsey. . . . The reconstruction of the child molestation problem in the 1950s was . . . aided by research debunking the "old" social problem of the 1930s. The accumulation of research, especially that conducted by Kinsey's Institute for Sex Research, helped dispel certain widespread beliefs about sex offenders. These myths included the following: sex criminals progressed from minor sex crimes (exhibitionism and voyeurism) to major sex crimes (forcible rape and child molestation), and sex crimes were increasing. Sexual psychopathy had not proved to be of the magnitude and seriousness as first thought; a different approach was in order. The efforts of psychiatrists could be devoted best to treating only the serious sexual offenders. . . .

III.   The Third Label: Policy making in the 1970s

In the early 1970s child molestation received yet another label: "sexual abuse," or "child sexual abuse." The new label appeared in both federal and state legislation. The federal Child Abuse Prevention and Treatment Act, enacted in 1974, required each state to adopt a uniform definition of abuse that included "physical or mental injury, sexual abuse or exploitation, negligent treatment, or maltreatment" in order to qualify for federal monies for the prevention and treatment of abuse. The new nomenclature appeared also in state legislation on abused children.

New experts played a role in the labeling process: psychologists and social workers became preeminent in this period. These experts focused on the familial offender — the father or stepfather molester. Instead of hospitalization or civil commitment for the patient, the recommended treatment was family counseling. The experts viewed the entire family, rather than merely the perpetrator, as the source of the problem. For the first time attention was also focused on the child victim, for whom counseling was also recommended.

A. The Role of Psychologists and Social Workers in Relabeling

The definitional process of sexual abuse . . . began simultaneously by psychologists and social workers. A West Coast psychologist, Henry Giarretto, played a prominent role in this development. . . .

This new label of child sexual abuse was effectively promoted from its West Coast origins. [Giarretto] published articles discussing the problem. The media highlighted [his treatment center], and staff members appeared on local and national television and radio programs. The staff disseminated child sexual abuse information [and] also conducted presentations and training seminars for professionals. . . .

The director-psychologist also wanted [his treatment program] to serve as a model for similar centers in other communities. Not surprisingly, with such national publicity, similar programs were soon established in Washington, Connecticut, Georgia, New York, and Pennsylvania to provide services to sexually abused children and their parents. . . .

Social workers as well as psychologists influenced the construction of this "new" social problem. One social worker in particular, Vincent DeFrancis, played a prominent role. DeFrancis, a lawyer with post-graduate training in social work and Director of the American Humane Association, a prominent child protection organization, broadened the focus of national attention from battered children to sexually abused children. Early federal legislation defined child abuse as intentional physical injury. DeFrancis' efforts helped expand this definition to include sexual abuse.

DeFrancis, long interested in child protective services, had a special interest in child sexual abuse. In 1965, he became Project Director of a research project to study sexual abuse funded by the Children's Bureau of the Department of Health, Education and Welfare. . . .

DeFrancis' influence soon extended into the federal level. When Congress considered enacting national child abuse legislation. DeFrancis testified before the Senate. [He] attempted to put the battered child problem in its proper perspective, pointing to the lesser incidence of intentionally inflicted injuries compared with other types of abuse: "Based upon an estimate . . . there must be somewhere between 30,000 and perhaps 40,000 at the outside of truly battered children but there must be at least 100,000 children each year who are sexually abused. . . ." Largely because of his influence, Congress broadened the federal definition of child abuse from physical injury to include sexual abuse. . . .

B. Reasons for Acceptance of Psychology and Social Work Theories

The work of the social worker-lawyer DeFrancis, as well as that of psychologist Giarretto, came during a time that was receptive to the influence of their disciplines. [W]hy were the helping professions, especially psychology and social work, the primary labelers of the "new" social problem in the 1960s and 1970s?

The answer may be found in important developments taking place in these two disciplines that led to increasing interest in the contribution of social work and psychology to legal problems.

First, the occurrence of several social conditions increased political activism by social workers. These conditions included: 1) an American foreign policy that highlighted discrepancies between affluent and poorer nations; 2) President John F. Kennedy's approach to social problems; 3) a mass urban movement by ethnic and racial minorities that swelled the relief rolls in the cities; 4) the civil rights movement; and 5) race riots in American cities that were fueled by unemployment and housing conditions. . . .

Social workers began to recognize the importance of utilizing the law to affect social change. . . .

Social workers also increased social action directed at child welfare reform, especially child abuse. Renewed interest developed in child protective services. Although the child welfare movement originally swept through America in the mid-nineteenth century,[180] the movement abated in the twentieth century until medical and social science research uncovered the abused child. . . .

[S]ocial workers played a central role in legal policymaking directed at the abused child. Two child welfare organizations historically interested in child protective services, the Children's Division of the American Humane Society and the United States Children's Bureau, contributed model legislation. Social workers not only called attention to physical abuse by conducting research and writing articles, but they also lobbied for passage of reporting statutes. . . . Social workers had developed an expertise in child abuse legislation and consequently were regarded as experts when the problem of sexual abuse was addressed. The social welfare emphasis on protective services, specifically for the child, contributed to the shift in focus of legal policy to the young victim.

The liaison between social work, psychology, and law provided for the expanded role of psychologists and social workers in child abuse legislation. The federal Child Abuse Prevention and Treatment Act authorized funding to public agencies and nonprofit organizations with training programs for professional and paraprofessional personnel in the fields of "medicine, law, education, *social work*, and other related fields." (Emphasis added.) State legislation mandated reports of child abuse by psychologists and social workers, among other professionals. State departments of social services absorbed an increasing number of tasks. . . .

Professional interest in abuse was reflected in the law by the insertion of the social welfare and psychological objectives of prevention and treatment. This dual

---

[180] Protective services and programs for child abuse victims existed in America since the mid-nineteenth century. Early child protective services developed after the cause célèbre case of Mary Ellen in New York in 1866. For a description of this case, see V. DeFrancis, The Fundamentals of Child Protection 19 (1955). Several social conditions combined to generate a widespread interest in child protection. These conditions included industrialization, urbanization, immigration, and a changing concept of childhood. The early child protection movement took several forms, including the removal of dependent, neglected, and delinquent children from almshouses and other institutions and their placement in private homes; the creation of juvenile courts and probation systems; the passage of compulsory school attendance laws; and crusades against child labor. See generally W. Trattner, Social Welfare in America, ch. 6 ("Child Welfare") (1974).

emphasis is apparent both from the title of the new legislation and its language. Moreover, the legislation voiced a concern for . . . the entire family unit. Broad purpose clauses of state legislation were directed at strengthening the family. . . .

A constant refrain of the federal and state legislation was the emphasis on treatment and counseling. This emphasis may be traced to the growth and acceptance of family therapy in legal circles. In the mid-1960s social work professionals first advocated treating the whole family with conjoint family therapy techniques. These techniques were rapidly adopted in legal settings. . . . Social workers began advocating its use not only for delinquent children, but also for abused children and their families.

Thus, the new legal label emerging in the 1970s depended on the influence of both psychologists and social workers. The social problem was constructed in the 1970s, after it had been labeled initially in the 1930s and again in the 1950s. Now the problem was termed "child sexual abuse." Attention was focused for the first time on the child victim. To help the child victim and prevent recurrent abuse, the entire family and not merely the criminal offender received treatment.

IV. *Reform in the 1980s: From "Sickness to Badness"*

In the 1980s the social problem [was again] relabeled. Beginning in the late 1970s, a number of states repealed their sex offender legislation and replaced it with more punitive statutes. New experts advocated law-and-order interests as primary goals for the new legislation. Psychiatrists no longer occupy a central role in policymaking or in handling of sex offenders. The pendulum's swing has reversed; current legal policy signals a movement away from rehabilitation and treatment and a return to more severe punishment of the sex offender. . . . Law reform was fueled by public and legislative concern about these crimes, as well as concern that existing legislation allowed parole of still dangerous persons. . . .

B. The Punitive Approach of the New Legislation

The most recent legislation reflects a harsher approach to the sex offender. Punishment has become the focus with treatment and rehabilitation receding into the background. In California, the legislature replaced the mentally disordered sexual offender statutes with long mandatory imprisonment terms for convicted child molesters and allowed hospitalization only during these prison terms. Hospitalization is no longer an alternative to a prison sentence. . . .

With the new legislation, psychiatric treatment of sex offenders is significantly curtailed. Child molestation is now being redefined by the criminal label of "sexual assault."[253] Medical influence over child molesters has yielded to criminal jurisdiction. Child molestation, originally defined as "badness," and later as "sickness," has been labeled again as "badness."

---

[253] See, e.g., Colo. Rev. Stat. §18-3-405 (1978 & Supp. 1983) ("sexual assault on a child"); N.H. Rev. Stat. Ann. §632-A:2 (1983) ("aggravated felonious sexual assault" — if actor is member of the same household of victim, or with victim less than 13 years of age); id. §632-A:3 ("felonious sexual assault" — if victim is between 13 and 16 years of age).

C. Factors Behind the Emerging Punitive Policy

The emergence of the new legal policy on sex offenses . . . may be explained in part by the growing reform movement to curtail the influence of psychiatrists in the law. [A] number of events have contributed to the waning of their influence. First, psychiatric testimony on evaluation of defendants' mental state, in general, has come under increasing attack. A burgeoning literature has assailed psychiatry and psychiatrists. . . .

Criticisms of psychiatry and psychiatrists have also come from another front. The insanity defense has been under increasing attack, and with it, greater attention has been focused on the proper role of psychiatry and psychiatrists in the criminal law. . . .

The current trend in sex offender legislation heralds a movement from treatment and rehabilitation and a return to more punitive dispositions. . . . However, the reversal of the pendulum from rehabilitation and treatment to punishment has not been without gains. The differentiation among sex offenders which was first urged by Kinsey has been recognized. Legal dispositions now reflect the impact of social workers and psychologists in terms of a different and more "humanistic" approach towards intrafamilial offenders compared to stranger perpetrators. Specifically, incest offenders are more likely than stranger molesters to benefit in many jurisdictions from the rehabilitation model: they are more likely to receive shorter sentences, probation, and counseling. In addition, legal personnel now question whether commitment under sexual psychopath statutes is appropriate for intrafamilial offenders, and urge out-patient family treatment instead.

Advances have also been made in treatment of sex offenders. Pioneering programs, many headed by psychiatrists, have been established across the country to treat sex offenders. Institutional and community-based programs work to change the attitudes and behaviors of sex offenders. Such programs aim to reduce recidivism rates of convicted offenders and to increase knowledge about sex offenders in general to prevent future attacks.

Further, the child victims of sex offenders receive more attention. Many jurisdictions have adopted reforms minimizing the trauma of child victims in the investigation and hearing stages of the criminal process. Such reforms include special training for police, child protective service workers, and prosecutors for interviewing child victims; a team approach to interviewing children (utilizing social welfare and legal personnel); fewer investigative interviews; and videotaped testimony of the child victim. This humane response is the legacy of the intervention by members of the helping professions.

7. Child Rape and the Death Penalty

Kennedy v. Louisiana
128 S. Ct. 2641 (2008)

Justice KENNEDY delivered the opinion of the Court.

. . . This case presents the question whether the Constitution bars respondent from imposing the death penalty for the rape of a child where the crime did not result, and was not intended to result, in death of the victim. . . . Petitioner's crime was one that cannot be recounted in these pages in a way sufficient to capture in full the hurt and horror inflicted on his victim or to convey the revulsion society, and the jury that represents it, sought to express by sentencing petitioner to death.

At 9:18 A.M. on March 2, 1998, petitioner called 911 to report that his stepdaughter, referred to here as L.H., had been raped. He told the 911 operator that L.H. had been in the garage while he readied his son for school. Upon hearing loud screaming, petitioner said, he ran outside and found L.H. in the side yard. Two neighborhood boys, petitioner told the operator, had dragged L.H. from the garage to the yard, pushed her down, and raped her. . . . When police arrived at petitioner's home between 9:20 and 9:30 A.M., they found L.H. on her bed, wearing a T-shirt and wrapped in a bloody blanket. She was bleeding profusely from the vaginal area. Petitioner told police he had carried her from the yard to the bathtub and then to the bed. Consistent with this explanation, police found a thin line of blood drops in the garage on the way to the house and then up the stairs. Once in the bedroom, petitioner had used a basin of water and a cloth to wipe blood from the victim. This later prevented medical personnel from collecting a reliable DNA sample. L.H. was transported to the Children's Hospital. An expert in pediatric forensic medicine testified that L.H.'s injuries were the most severe he had seen from a sexual assault in his four years of practice. . . .

At the scene of the crime, at the hospital, and in the first weeks that followed, both L.H. and petitioner maintained in their accounts to investigators that L.H. had been raped by two neighborhood boys. . . . Eight days after the crime, and despite L.H's insistence that petitioner was not the offender, petitioner was arrested for the rape. The State's investigation had drawn the accuracy of petitioner and L.H.'s story into question. [P]olice found blood on the underside of L.H.'s mattress. This convinced them the rape took place in her bedroom, not outside the house. Police also found that petitioner made two telephone calls on the morning of the rape. Sometime before 6:15 A.M., petitioner called his employer and left a message that he was unavailable to work that day. Petitioner called back between 6:30 and 7:30 A.M. to ask a colleague how to get blood out of a white carpet because his daughter had "just become a young lady." At 7:37 A.M., petitioner called B & B Carpet Cleaning and requested urgent assistance in removing bloodstains from a carpet. Petitioner did not call 911 until about an hour and a half later.

About a month after petitioner's arrest, L.H. was removed from the custody of her mother, who had maintained until that point that petitioner was not involved in the rape. On June 22, 1998, L.H. was returned home and told her mother for the first time that petitioner had raped her. . . . [At trial L.H., then 13 years old] testified that she "woke up one morning and Patrick was on top of [her]." . . . L.H. acknowledged that she had accused two neighborhood boys but testified petitioner told her to say this and that it was untrue.

The jury having found petitioner guilty of [aggravated rape of a child under twelve years old, pursuant to La. Stat. Ann. §14:42], the penalty phase ensued. The State presented the testimony of S.L., who is the cousin and goddaughter of petitioner's ex-wife. S.L. testified that petitioner sexually abused her three times when she was eight years old and that the last time involved sexual intercourse. . . . The jury unanimously determined that petitioner should be sentenced to death. The Supreme Court of Louisiana affirmed. . . . We granted certiorari.

The Eighth Amendment, applicable to the States through the Fourteenth Amendment, provides that "[e]xcessive bail shall not be required, nor excessive fines imposed, nor cruel and unusual punishments inflicted." The Amendment proscribes all excessive punishments, as well as cruel and unusual punishments that may or may not be excessive. . . . Whether this requirement has been fulfilled is determined not by the standards that prevailed when the Eighth Amendment was adopted in 1791 but by the norms that currently prevail. The Amendment "draw[s] its meaning from the evolving standards of decency that mark the progress of a maturing society." . . .

Evolving standards of decency must embrace and express respect for the dignity of the person, and the punishment of criminals must conform to that rule. [P]unishment is justified under one or more of three principal rationales: rehabilitation, deterrence, and retribution. It is the last of these, retribution, that most often can contradict the law's own ends. This is of particular concern when the Court interprets the meaning of the Eighth Amendment in capital cases. When the law punishes by death, it risks its own sudden descent into brutality, transgressing the constitutional commitment to decency and restraint.

[W]e have explained that capital punishment must be limited to those offenders who commit a narrow category of the most serious crimes and whose extreme culpability makes them the most deserving of execution. . . . Applying this principle, we held in [Roper v. Simmons, 543 U.C. 551 (2005) and Atkins v. Virginia, 536 U.S. 304 (2002)] that the execution of juveniles and mentally retarded persons are punishments violative of the Eighth Amendment because the offender had a diminished personal responsibility for the crime. The Court further has held that the death penalty can be disproportionate to the crime itself where the crime did not result, or was not intended to result, in death of the victim. In [Coker v. Georgia, 433 U.S. 584 (1977)], for instance, the Court held it would be unconstitutional to execute an offender who had raped an adult woman. . . .

. . . The history of the death penalty for the crime of rape is an instructive beginning point. In 1925, 18 States, the District of Columbia, and the Federal Government had statutes that authorized the death penalty for the rape of a child or an adult. [Furman v. Georgia, 408 U.S. 238 (1972)] invalidated most of the state statutes authorizing the death penalty for the crime of rape; and in *Furman*'s aftermath only six States reenacted their capital rape provisions. . . . All six statutes were later invalidated under state or federal law.

Louisiana reintroduced the death penalty for rape of a child in 1995. . . . Five States have since followed Louisiana's lead [i.e., Georgia, Montana, Oklahoma, South Carolina, and Texas]. By contrast, 44 States have not made child rape a capital offense. As for federal law, Congress in the Federal Death Penalty Act of 1994 expanded the number of federal crimes for which the death penalty is a permissible sentence, including certain nonhomicide offenses; but it did not do the same for child rape or abuse. See 108 Stat.1972 (codified as amended in scattered sections of 18 U.S.C.). . . .

. . . The evidence of a national consensus with respect to the death penalty for child rapists, as with respect to juveniles, mentally retarded offenders, and vicarious felony murderers, shows divided opinion but, on balance, an opinion against it. Thirty-seven jurisdictions — 36 States plus the Federal Government — have the death penalty. [O]nly six of those jurisdictions authorize the death penalty for rape of a child. . . . The small number of States that have enacted this penalty, then, is relevant to determining whether there is a consensus against capital punishment for this crime.

Respondent insists that the six States where child rape is a capital offense, along with the States that have proposed but not yet enacted applicable death penalty legislation, reflect a consistent direction of change in support of the death penalty for child rape. Consistent change might counterbalance an otherwise weak demonstration of consensus. See *Atkins*, 536 U.S. at 315 ("It is not so much the number of these States that is significant, but the consistency of the direction of change"). But . . . no showing of consistent change has been made in this case.

Respondent and its *amici* identify five States where, in their view, legislation authorizing capital punishment for child rape is pending. It is not our practice, nor is it sound, to find contemporary norms based upon state legislation that has been proposed but not yet enacted. There are compelling reasons not to do so here. Since the briefs were submitted by the parties, legislation in two of the five States has failed. . . .

There are measures of consensus other than legislation. Statistics about the number of executions may inform the consideration whether capital punishment for the crime of child rape is regarded as unacceptable in our society. These statistics confirm our determination from our review of state statutes that there is a social consensus against the death penalty for the crime of child rape. [N]o individual has been executed for the rape of an adult or child since 1964, and no execution for any other nonhomicide offense has been conducted since 1963. Louisiana is the only State since 1964 that has sentenced an individual to death for the crime of child rape. . . . After reviewing the authorities informed by contemporary norms, including the history of the death penalty for this and other nonhomicide crimes, current state statutes and new enactments, and the number of executions since 1964, we conclude there is a national consensus against capital punishment for the crime of child rape. . . .

It must be acknowledged that there are moral grounds to question a rule barring capital punishment for a crime against an individual that did not result in death. These facts illustrate the point. Here the victim's fright, the sense of betrayal, and the nature of her injuries caused more prolonged physical and mental suffering than, say, a sudden killing by an unseen assassin. The attack was not just on her but on her childhood. For this reason, we should be most reluctant to rely upon the language of the plurality in *Coker*, which posited that, for the victim of rape, "life may not be nearly so happy as it was" but it is not beyond repair. 433 U.S. at 598. Rape has a permanent psychological, emotional, and sometimes physical impact on the child. We cannot dismiss the years of long anguish that must be endured by the victim of child rape.

It does not follow, though, that capital punishment is a proportionate penalty for the crime. The constitutional prohibition against excessive or cruel and unusual punishments mandates that the State's power to punish be exercised within the limits of civilized standards. Evolving standards of decency that mark the progress of a maturing society counsel us to be most hesitant before interpreting the Eighth Amendment to allow the extension of the death penalty, a hesitation that has special force where no life was taken in the commission of the crime. It is an established principle that decency, in its essence, presumes respect for the individual and thus moderation or restraint in the application of capital punishment. . . .

. . . Consistent with evolving standards of decency and the teachings of our precedents we conclude that, in determining whether the death penalty is excessive, there is a distinction between intentional first-degree murder on the one hand and nonhomicide crimes against individual persons, even including child rape, on the other. The latter crimes may be devastating in their harm, as here, but in terms of moral depravity and of the injury to the person and to the public, they cannot be compared to murder in their severity and irrevocability.

In reaching our conclusion we find significant the number of executions that would be allowed under respondent's approach. . . . Approximately 5,702 incidents of vaginal, anal, or oral rape of a child under the age of 12 were reported nationwide in 2005; this is almost twice the total incidents of intentional murder for victims of all ages (3,405) reported during the same period [citations omitted]. [U]nder respondent's approach, the 36 States that permit the death penalty could sentence to death all persons convicted of raping a child less than 12 years of age. This could not be reconciled with our evolving standards of decency and the necessity to constrain the use of the death penalty. . . .

Our decision is consistent with the justifications offered for the death penalty. [Gregg v. Georgia, 428 U.S. 153, 173 (1976)] instructs that capital punishment is excessive when it is grossly out of proportion to the crime or it does not fulfill the two distinct social purposes served by the death penalty: retribution and deterrence of capital crimes. . . . The goal of retribution, which reflects society's and the victim's interests in seeing that the offender is repaid for the hurt he caused, does not justify the harshness of the death penalty here. In measuring retribution, as well as other objectives of criminal law, it is appropriate to distinguish between a particularly depraved murder that merits death as a form of retribution and the crime of child rape.

There is an additional reason for our conclusion that imposing the death penalty for child rape would not further retributive purposes. . . . In considering the death penalty for nonhomicide offenses this inquiry necessarily also must include the question whether the death penalty balances the wrong to the victim.

It is not at all evident that the child rape victim's hurt is lessened when the law permits the death of the perpetrator. Capital cases require a long-term commitment by those who testify for the prosecution, especially when guilt and sentencing determinations are in multiple proceedings. In cases like this the key testimony is not just from the family but from the victim herself. During formative years of her adolescence, made all the more daunting for having to come to terms with the brutality of her experience, L.H. was required to discuss the case at length with law enforcement personnel. In a public trial she was required to recount once more all the details of the crime to a jury as the State pursued the death of her step-father. . . . Society's desire to inflict the death penalty for child rape by enlisting the child victim to assist it over the course of years in asking for capital punishment forces a moral choice on the child, who is not of mature age to make that choice. . . .

There are, moreover, serious systemic concerns in prosecuting the crime of child rape that are relevant to the constitutionality of making it a capital offense. The problem of unreliable, induced, and even imagined child testimony means there is a special risk of wrongful execution in some child rape cases. This undermines, at least to some degree, the meaningful contribution of the death penalty to legitimate goals of punishment. Studies conclude that children are highly susceptible to suggestive questioning techniques like repetition, guided imagery, and selective reinforcement. See Ceci & Friedman, The Suggestibility of Children: Scientific Research and Legal Implications, 86 Cornell L.Rev. 33, 47 (2000) (there is strong evidence that children, especially young children, are suggestible to a significant degree — even on abuse-related questions); Gross, Jacoby, Matheson, Montgomery, & Patil, Exonerations in the United States 1989 Through 2003, 95 J.Crim. L. & C. 523, 539 (2005) (discussing allegations of abuse at the Little Rascals Day Care Center); see also Quas, Davis, Goodman, & Myers, Repeated Questions, Deception, and Children's True and False Reports of Body Touch, 12 Child Maltreatment 60, 61-66 (2007) (finding that 4- to 7-year-olds were able to maintain [a] lie about body touch fairly effectively when asked repeated, direct questions during a mock forensic interview). . . .

With respect to deterrence, if the death penalty adds to the risk of non-reporting, that, too, diminishes the penalty's objectives. Underreporting is a common problem with respect to child sexual abuse. Although we know little about what differentiates those who report from those who do not report, one of the most commonly cited reasons for nondisclosure is fear of negative consequences for the perpetrator, a concern that has special force where the abuser is a family member. The experience of the *amici* who work with child victims indicates that, when the punishment is death, both the victim and the victim's family members may be more likely to shield the perpetrator from discovery, thus increasing underreporting. See Brief for National Association of Social Workers et al. as *Amici Curiae* 11-13. As a result, punishment by death may not result in more deterrence or more effective enforcement.

In addition, by in effect making the punishment for child rape and murder equivalent, a State that punishes child rape by death may remove a strong incentive for the rapist not to kill the victim. . . . Each of these propositions, standing alone, might not establish the unconstitutionality of the death penalty for the crime of child rape. Taken in sum, however, they demonstrate the serious negative consequences of making child rape a capital offense. These considerations lead us to conclude, in our independent judgment, that the death penalty is not a proportional punishment for the rape of a child. . . .

The rule of evolving standards of decency with specific marks on the way to full progress and mature judgment means that resort to the penalty must be reserved for the worst of crimes and limited in its instances of application. . . . [Reversed.]

NOTES AND QUESTIONS

(1) Epilogue. Both the state of Louisiana and the Bush administration urged the Supreme Court to reconsider its decision in light of the Court's failure to take into account a recently enacted federal law imposing the death penalty for the crime of child rape by a member of the military, arguing that the existence of the law undermined the Court's conclusion that there was a "national consensus" against authorizing the death penalty for a nonhomicide crime. The Court declined to reconsider, instead adding a footnote in the majority opinion explaining that the military law did not change its analysis. In contrast, Justice Scalia, although voting against rehearing, made clear his opinion that the new law "utterly destroys the majority's claim to be discerning a national consensus and not just giving effect to the majority's own preference."[23]

Following the Court's opinion in *Kennedy*, the Louisiana governor promised to support a new bill that would meet constitutional muster on the death penalty in child rape cases.[24] The defendant currently faces life in prison without the possibility of parole. State v. Kennedy, 994 So. 2d 1287 (La. 2008).

(2) History of Child Rape Laws. In the wake of a sensational child rape case in which a defendant raped and shot a 13-year-old in the head, the Louisiana legislature enacted the child rape statute at issue in *Kennedy*.[25] Although a few state legislatures enacted similar laws, no state had sentenced a defendant to death for a nonhomicide crime until Patrick Kennedy's case. *Kennedy*, 128 S. Ct. at 2651. At the time *Kennedy* was pending, only two individuals, both from Louisiana, awaited imposition of the death penalty for child rape.

(3) Data on Child Rape Victims and Offenders. According to Department of Justice statistics, slightly over two-thirds of the victims of reported sexual assaults are under the age of 18, even though juveniles comprise only 25 percent of the total population. In addition, most child victims are raped by a family member or family friend — only 4 percent of child rape victims report that the rapist was a stranger. (By contrast, 33 percent of adult rape victims report that the rapist was a stranger.)[26] Note that both men sentenced to death in Louisiana for child rape knew their victims: Patrick Kennedy was convicted of raping his 8-year-old stepdaughter; Richard Davis was convicted of repeatedly raping a 5-year-old girl that he and his girlfriend looked after.[27]

(4) Recidivism. The Department of Justice reports that 3.3 percent of child molesters are rearrested for another sex crime against a child within three years of

---

[23] Kennedy v. Louisiana, 129 S. Ct. 1 (2008). See also Adam Liptak, Justices' Ban on Executing Child Rapists Will Stand, N.Y. Times, Oct. 2, 2008, at A21.

[24] Ed Anderson, Jindal Urging Death Penalty for Child Rapists, New Orleans Times Picayune, Aug. 10, 2008, at 17; James Oliphant, Court Curbs Death Penalty, Chi. Trib., June 26, 2008, at 3.

[25] Monica C. Bell, Note, Grassroots Death Sentences?: The Social Movement for Capital Child Rape Laws, 98 J. Crim. L. & Criminology 1, 3-6 (2007).

[26] Howard N. Snyder, Bureau of Justice Statistics, Sexual Assault of Young Children as Reported to Law Enforcement: Victim, Incident, and Offender Characteristics 2 (July 2000), available at *http://www.ojp.usdoj.gov/bjs/pub/pdf/saycrle.pdf.*

[27] Cain Burdeau, Associated Press, Supreme Court to Decide Whether Child Rapists Can Be Put to Death, Virginian-Pilot & Ledger Star (Norfolk, Va.), Apr. 15, 2008, at 3.

release. In fact, sex offenders are four times more likely than nonsex offenders to be arrested for another sex crime after release.[28] Do these statistics change the analysis of the penological goals of a statute imposing the death penalty?

What are alternative ways (other than the death penalty) by which a state can prevent sex offenders from perpetrating additional sex crimes against children? Lifetime registration as a sex offender? Longer sentences? Some states require repeat sex offenders to be treated with medroxyprogesterone acetate (MPA), a chemical that can diminish the person's "deviant" sexual behavior and help to control sexual urges. See, e.g., Cal. Penal Code §645 (West 2008) (restricting its use to offenders whose victim is a child under the age of 13); Fla. Stat. §794.0235 (2008); Iowa Code §903B.10 (2008). Side effects of MPA can include such inconveniences as weight gain, but are also linked to cancer in laboratory animals.[29] Do these laws raise Eighth Amendment concerns? Note that at least one state court has found that *surgical* castration violates the prohibition on cruel and unusual punishment. See State v. Brown, 326 S.E.2d 410 (S.C. 1985). Does chemical castration raise similar concerns, or is it sufficiently distinguishable? Does chemical castration raise other constitutional concerns? See, e.g., Tran v. State, 965 So.2d 226 (Fla. Dist. Ct. App. 2007) (administration of MPA violated double jeopardy).

(5) Child Rape Versus the Rape of an Adult Woman. The Louisiana Supreme Court found in an earlier case that its capital child rape statute was within the bounds of the Eighth Amendment, distinguishing *Coker* as having left open the question whether the death penalty might be appropriate in a case of child rape. Thus, according to the state supreme court, although the Eighth Amendment prohibited the death penalty for the rape of an *adult* woman, it did not do so for the rape of a *child*. State v. Wilson, 685 So.2d 1063 (La. 1996), *cert. denied sub nom.*, Bethley v. Louisiana, 520 U.S. 1259 (1997). In State v. Kennedy, 957 So.2d 757 (2007), the decision in which the Supreme Court granted certiorari, the Louisiana supreme court cited its prior holding in *Wilson*. Do you agree with the United States Supreme Court in *Coker* or with the Louisiana Supreme Court as to the appropriateness of distinguishing between the rape of a child and the rape of an adult when imposing the death penalty? Is there a difference in terms of the offender's culpability between the sexual assault of a 17-year-old victim and that of an 8-year-old victim? What reasons does the Supreme Court give in *Kennedy* for rejecting the distinction? Do you find the Court's reasoning persuasive?

(6) Prosecutions. What were the "serious systemic concerns," according to the Supreme Court in *Kennedy*, that are inherent in prosecutions of the crime of child rape and that are relevant in the determination of the constitutionality of a child rape statute? How much weight, do you think, should be given to a child victim's statements during investigation of accusations of child rape and at trial?

---

[28] Bureau of Justice Statistics, Department of Justice, Criminal Offender Statistics (1994), available at *http://www.ojp.usdoj.gov/bjs/crimoff.htm#recidivism.*

[29] Matthew V. Daley, Note, A Flawed Solution to the Sex Offender Situation in the United States: The Legality of Chemical Castration for Sex Offenders, 5 Ind. Health L. Rev. 87, 92-93 (2008).

Why? (Issues of the defendant's constitutional right to confrontation are explored in the next case infra.)

(7) Evolving Standards of Decency.   In deciding death penalty cases, the Supreme Court considers six factors to determine the "evolving standards of decency":

> (1) history — whether this class of defendants had been historically subjected to the death penalty; (2) judicial precedent — what has the Court previously said or presumed about the treatment of this class of defendants; (3) statutes — have the states subjected these defendants to the death penalty; (4) jury verdicts — have juries voted to impose a death sentence on these defendants in capital prosecutions; (5) penological goal — would deterrence or retribution be achieved by the execution; and (6) international and comparative law — how do other countries and international organizations deal with or suggest how this class of defendants should be treated?[30]

How does the Court in *Kennedy* address each of these factors? Are there some factors it ignores? How objective is this six-standard test?

a. History.   As discussed in *Kennedy*, between 1930 and 1964, 18 states authorized the death penalty for child rape (128 S. Ct. at 2651). Only recently had states begun to enact capital child rape laws. Did the Court give adequate time for "history" to develop? Is it significant that only 13 years passed between the first state statute to authorize the death penalty for child rape and the case that struck it down?

b. Judicial Precedent.   Two recent Supreme Court cases, Atkins v. Virginia, 536 U.S. 304 (2002) and Roper v. Simmons, 543 U.S. 551 (2005), previously limited the application of the death penalty. *Atkins* struck down a law permitting execution of the mentally retarded; *Roper* prohibited seeking the death penalty for youth who were under the age of 18 when they committed the crime. How does the Supreme Court use these precedents to support its conclusion in *Kennedy*?

c. Statutes.   Based on an analysis of existing statutes addressing child rape, why does the Court conclude that there is a national consensus against capital punishment for the crime?

d. Jury Verdicts.   In *Kennedy*, a jury initially sentenced the defendant to death. To what extent does the reliability of child witnesses weigh in the Supreme Court's decision to hold the statute unconstitutional? Does the Court appear concerned that the horrific nature of the crime of child rape might bias juries to favor the death penalty?

e. Penological Goal.   What are the principal rationales for punishment? How do child rape statutes fulfill these goals? For example, as the Court in *Kennedy* points out, some scholars question whether capital child rape statutes might actually create an incentive for the attacker to kill the child after the rape (because the child is the only witness to the crime), whereas others suggest that child rapists are not likely to be deterred by a capital punishment statute because such a crime does

---

[30] Dwight Aarons, The Abolitionist's Dilemma: Establishing the Standards for the Evolving Standards of Decency, 6 Pierce L. Rev. 441, 445 (2008).

not usually stem from rational or calm thinking but instead is impulsive or uncontrollable.

f. International and Comparative Law.   Currently, 137 countries, either by law or practice, have abolished the death penalty. This number includes all Western European nations. Many other countries still permit capital punishment — including China, Iran, Pakistan, Iraq, and Sudan, which, together with the United States, account for 91 percent of all such executions. However, more than half of these countries do not impose the death penalty for the crime of child rape. On the other hand, some countries, such as China, Iran, Jordan, and Mongolia, among others, still impose the death penalty for child rape.[31]

Although the Court in *Kennedy* could have relied on international law to support its holding, the majority almost completely ignores the international perspective on the death penalty. This neglect may be a response to criticism of the Court's decisions in *Roper* and Lawrence v. Texas, 539 U.S. 558 (2003) (declaring a state sodomy statute unconstitutional), both of which depended heavily on international law.[32] Other scholars find such constitutional comparativism extremely helpful to the development of human rights.[33] What role should international human rights law play in the interpretation of our constitutional rights?

8.   The Child Victim as Witness

In addition to the fundamental issue of how society ought to intervene in cases of child sexual abuse, many interesting procedural issues emerge during the prosecution of sexual abuse cases. These issues arise from the desire to protect a child victim from the trauma of the judicial process while safeguarding the defendant's constitutional rights. The following materials explore these conflicting interests.

People v. Vigil
127 P.3d 916 (Colo. 2006)

RICE, Justice.

Joe E. Vigil was convicted of sexual assault on a child. . . . Defendant Vigil and John Kohl were visiting the home of Brett Brown. All the men were drinking

---

[31] Joanna H. D'Avella, Note, Death Row for Child Rape? Cruel and Unusual Punishment under the *Roper-Atkins* "Evolving Standards of Decency" Framework, 92 Cornell L. Rev. 129, 154 (2006); Frederick C. Millett, Note, Will the United States Follow England (and the Rest of the World) in Abandoning Capital Punishment?, 6 Pierce L. Rev. 547, 634 (2008). See also Amnesty International USA, Recent Death Penalty Trends: Fact Sheet, *http://www.amnestyusa.org/abolish/factsheets/FactSheets.pdf* (last visited Nov. 18, 2008).

[32] Roger P. Alford, Four Mistakes in the Debate on "Outsourcing Authority," 69 Alb. L. Rev. 653 (2006).

[33] David S. Law, Globalization and the Future of Constitutional Rights, 102 Nw. U. L. Rev. 1277 (2008). See also Holly Arnould, Note, Lawrence v. Texas and Roper v. Simmons: Enriching Constitutional Interpretation with International Law, 22 St. John's J. Legal Comment. 685 (2008) (describing both sides of the argument).

alcohol. While Brown and Kohl were on the Internet, Vigil sat in another room and played a game with Brown's seven-year-old son, JW, the victim in this case. [The father testified at trial that he went to check on his child.] When the father attempted to open the bedroom door, he encountered resistance. The father pushed his head into the room and saw Vigil positioned over the child. Vigil and the child both were partially undressed, and the father saw "skin to skin" contact. While the father comforted his child, Vigil fled the house. The child, who had tears in eyes and appeared scared and confused, told his father that Vigil "stuck his winkie in his butt" and that his "butt hurt."

Upon hearing this, the father ran outside after Vigil and watched Vigil run down the street, simultaneously pulling up his pants. Next, the child's father called 911. While the father was on the phone, Kohl, the father's friend, observed the child curled up, crying, and shaking. The father's friend asked the child if he were hurt. Two or three times the child told his father's friend that his "butt hurt."

A police officer responding to the father's call saw Vigil walking on a sidewalk near the father's home. When the police officer stepped out of his car, Vigil pulled out a knife and held it to his own throat. When the officer asked Vigil what he was doing, Vigil responded, "I done bad." Then Vigil stabbed himself in the throat and chest. At the hospital, Vigil told emergency room personnel that he wanted to die and that he "did a bad thing."

Later, the child and his mother went to the hospital with another police officer. Around 3:00 A.M. the police officer asked a doctor to perform a victim sexual assault kit. Before examining the child, the doctor spoke with the police officer to learn why the child was at the hospital and how law enforcement was involved. Next, the doctor performed a forensic sexual abuse examination on the child. When the doctor asked the child whether anyone had hurt him, the child said that someone had hurt him. When the doctor asked if the child felt pain, the child said, "It felt like a poop." During the examination, the doctor found bruising around the child's anus, and he took an anal swab. A forensic scientist analyzed the swab and discovered the presence of semen but did not identify the source of the semen. A few days after the alleged assault, a police officer conducted a videotaped interview of the child.

[Vigil was subsequently charged with one count of sexual assault on a child. A jury found him guilty. At trial, the judge ruled that the child was unavailable to testify.] On appeal Vigil argued that the trial court violated his constitutional right of confrontation by admitting . . . the child's statements to his father and his father's friend, and the child's statements to the doctor. . . .

In Crawford v. Washington, [541 U.S. 36 (2004)], the United States Supreme Court held that admitting testimonial hearsay at trial, absent the unavailability of the declarant and a prior opportunity for cross-examination by the defendant, violates the accused's confrontation right under the Sixth Amendment to the United States Constitution. The *Crawford* majority did not adopt a precise definition of the term "testimonial." The Court, however, did provide some guidance. Specifically, *Crawford* held that, at a minimum, statements are testimonial if the declarant made them at a "preliminary hearing, before a grand jury, or at a former trial; and [in] police interrogations." [Id. at 68.] Beyond this explicit guidance, the Supreme Court discussed three formulations of statements that might qualify as testimonial, namely: 1) "ex parte in-court testimony or its functional equivalent — that is material such as affidavits, custodial examinations, prior testimony that the defendant was unable to cross-examine, or similar pretrial statements that declarants would reasonably expect to be used prosecutorially"; 2) "extrajudicial statements . . . contained in formalized testimonial materials, such as affidavits, depositions, prior testimony or confessions"; and 3) "statements that were made under circumstances which would lead an objective witness reasonably to believe that the statement would be available for use at a later trial." [Id. at 51-52.]

We start our analysis by determining whether the child's statements to the doctor are testimonial in nature, and specifically, whether the statements fit into any of the clearly proscribed areas of testimonial evidence, as delineated by *Crawford*. Clearly, the child did not make his statements in the course of a preliminary hearing, in front of a grand jury, or at a prior trial; therefore, these formulations of testimonial evidence are not at issue. However, the defendant contends that the child made his statement in the course of a police interrogation, the fourth clearly defined area of testimonial evidence in *Crawford*, and therefore the statements are testimonial in nature.

Ordinarily, if a law enforcement official is involved during the course of questioning, such questioning would be considered a "police interrogation." Because the questioning in this case was done by a doctor as a part of a sexual assault examination, we must decide whether this questioning constituted police interrogation. Unfortunately, we are not helped in our determination of this issue by *Crawford*, as the Court explained that it used the term "interrogation" in a colloquial sense. . . . [D]icta does suggest, however, that police "interrogation" may extend beyond the type of structured police questioning at issue in *Crawford*, particularly in light of *Crawford*'s stated concern that the "[i]nvolvement of government officers in the production of testimony with an eye toward trial presents a unique potential for prosecutorial abuse." [Id. at 56 n. 7.]

We must determine, therefore, whether the doctor's questioning, as part of a sexual assault examination, constituted the functional equivalent of police interrogation. In light of the concerns stated in *Crawford*, we examine first, whether and to what extent government officials were involved in producing the statements and second, whether their purpose was to develop testimony for trial. Courts from other jurisdictions which have considered this issue are divided in their conclusions. The supreme courts in Oregon and Maryland [State v. Mack, 101 P.3d 349 (Or. 2004); State v. Snowden, 867 A.2d 314 (Md. 2005)] have analyzed this issue and determined that questioning by social workers, at the behest of the police, constitutes police interrogation and that, therefore, the Confrontation Clause bars the testimony. In addition, courts which have analyzed the police interrogation issue in terms of questioning by doctors have reached the opposite conclusion, reasoning that a doctor is questioning the child for the purpose of providing a diagnosis and treatment, rather than eliciting the child's testimony for trial.

Although each factual situation must be judged on its own merits, the facts of this case are more like those in the cases where courts found a child's statements to a doctor to be non-testimonial. As the doctor testified at trial, his purpose in questioning the child was to determine whether the child would "say something that could help [the medical personnel] understand what the potential injuries were." The child's responses helped the doctor develop his opinion regarding whether a sexual assault had occurred and how best to treat the child. Thus, rather than being an agent of the police, the doctor's job involved identifying and treating sexual abuse. The fact that the doctor was a member of a child protection team does not, in and of itself, make him a government official absent a more direct and controlling police presence. . . . In fact, the police officer in the instant case testified that she was not involved in the medical examination or in the room when the doctor performed the examination. . . . Accordingly, we conclude that, under *Crawford*'s explicit guidance, the child's statements to the doctor are not testimonial evidence. . . .

[W]e must also determine whether the child's statements fall into one of the three formulations of the "core class" of testimonial statements at which the Confrontation Clause was directed and are therefore testimonial. *Crawford*, 541 U.S. 36, 51-52. In this regard, Vigil argues that these statements are testimonial because the child made the statements to the doctor under circumstances which would have led an objective witness reasonably to believe that the statements would be available for use at a later trial. In addition, Vigil argues that the phrase "objective witness" must be defined as an objectively reasonable adult observer educated in the law. The People disagree with this construction and argue that the phrase "objective witness" should be defined as an objectively reasonable person in the position of the declarant.

Based on our reading of *Crawford* and our review of other courts deciding this issue, we hold that the "objective witness" language in *Crawford* refers to an objectively reasonable person in the declarant's position. . . . Turning now to the application of the objective witness test to the statements the child made to the doctor, we analyze the circumstances surrounding the statements to determine whether an objective witness in the position of the child would believe that his statements would be used at trial. We hold that no objective witness in the position of the child would believe that his statements to the doctor would be used at trial. Rather, an objective seven-year-old child would reasonably be interested in feeling better and would intend his statements to describe the source of his pain and his symptoms. In addition, an objectively reasonable seven-year-old child would expect that a doctor would use his statements to make him feel better and to formulate a medical diagnosis. He would not foresee the statements being used in a later trial.

Thus, from the perspective of an objective witness in the child's position, it would be reasonable to assume that this examination was only for the purpose of medical diagnosis, and not related to the criminal prosecution. No police officer was present at the time of the examination, nor was the examination conducted at the police department. The child, the doctor, and the child's mother were present in the examination room. Accordingly, we reverse the court of appeals and conclude that the child's statements to the doctor were not testimonial. . . .

. . . Since we find that the child's statements to the doctor are nontestimonial, we must next [analyze the constitutionality of nontestimonial statements under the federal confrontation clause as set forth in Ohio v. Roberts, 448 U.S. 56 (1980)]. To satisfy the *Roberts* test, the child's statements must bear sufficient indicia of reliability by falling within a "firmly rooted hearsay exception" or bearing "particularized guarantees of trustworthiness." A statement made for the purpose of medical diagnosis or treatment qualifies as a firmly rooted exception to the hearsay rule. Where a firmly rooted hearsay exception is at issue, reliability is implied and it is not necessary for the declarant to be unavailable. . . .

Colorado Rule of Evidence 803(4) excepts from the hearsay rule "statements made for purposes of medical diagnosis or treatment and describing medical history, or past or present symptoms, pain, or sensations, or the inception or general character of the cause or external source thereof insofar as reasonably pertinent to diagnosis or treatment." CRE 803(4) (2005). [O]nce the proponent establishes that the statements were made to a physician for purposes of diagnosis or treatment, that the statements were reasonably pertinent to diagnosis or treatment, and that the physician relied on the statements in reaching an expert opinion, then the statements qualify for admission without regard to an independent demonstration of trustworthiness.

In its written order, the trial court found all the facts necessary to admit the child's statements to the doctor as statements made for purposes of medical diagnosis or treatment. [T]he child's mother and the police officer took the child to the doctor so that he could offer a diagnosis regarding whether the child was sexually assaulted; the statements regarding the history as to where the child was hurt were reasonably pertinent to diagnosing the cause of the child's bruising and redness; the doctor relied on the statements in reaching the opinion that the child had been hurt by a penis. Therefore, the trial court properly found that the history the doctor elicited from the child was admissible under CRE 803(4) and that the People provided an adequate foundation.

Accordingly, we conclude that the child's statements for purposes of medical diagnosis and treatment bore sufficient indicia of reliability. Admission of these statements did not violate Vigil's federal constitutional right to confront the witnesses against him. . . .

[Additionally,] Vigil argues that the child's statements to his father and his father's friend are testimonial and, therefore, the trial court violated his federal constitutional right to confrontation because he did not have a prior opportunity to cross-examine the child. To address this argument, we must determine whether the child's excited utterances to the father and the father's friend are testimonial statements. [Under *Crawford*,] the child's statements to his father and his father's friend do not constitute testimonial evidence because the child did not make the statements at a preliminary hearing, before a grand jury, at a former trial, or during a police interrogation. The facts do not suggest that any government officials were involved when the child made the statements to his father and his father's friend; thus, we need not further examine whether the situation presented the dangers of police interrogation.

Next, we examine the child's statements under *Crawford*'s other three formulations of potentially testimonial evidence. Like the statements to the doctor, the child's statements to his father and his father's friend clearly do not fall within the first two formulations of testimonial evidence. The child did not make the statements to his father and his father's friend ex parte, in an affidavit, a custodial examination, prior testimony that Vigil was unable to cross-examine, or a pretrial statement that the child would reasonably expect to be used prosecutorially. The statements were not formal extrajudicial statements made in an affidavit, a deposition, prior testimony, or a confession.

Finally, we analyze the statements under the third formulation in an effort to determine whether an objectively reasonable witness in the child's position would believe that his statement would be used at a later trial. When the child made these statements, he was at home speaking informally to his father and his father's friend. An objectively reasonable seven-year-old boy would make statements expressing pain and explaining what had happened with an interest in seeking comfort and help. The facts do not indicate the child was making these statements in an attempt to develop testimony for trial.

Similarly, nothing in the circumstances surrounding the making of the statements would suggest that the child's father or the child's father's friend were questioning the boy with a view toward developing testimony. To an objectively reasonable seven-year-old child, it would appear that the child's father and the father's friend were interested in learning what happened, determining whether the child was hurt, and comforting the child. An objectively reasonable seven-year-old child would foresee his father and his father's friend using his statements to comfort and protect him. In sum, since the child's statements were not made under circumstances which would lead an objectively reasonable seven-year-old boy to believe that his statements would be available for use at a later trial, the child's statements are not testimonial.

Because the child's statements to his father and his father's friend are non-testimonial, we must assess whether the statements bear sufficient indicia of reliability to satisfy the federal Confrontation Clause. As discussed above, a hearsay statement that falls within a firmly rooted exception satisfies this test. An excited utterance is a firmly rooted hearsay exception. Where an excited utterance is at issue, reliability is implied and it is not necessary for the declarant to be unavailable. Vigil does not contest the trial court's determination that the child's statements to his father and his father's friend constitute excited utterances. Therefore, we conclude that the child's excited utterances bore sufficient indicia of reliability and that admission of these statements did not violate Vigil's federal constitutional right to confront the witnesses against him. . . .

NOTES AND QUESTIONS

(1) Constitutional Issues. Two primary constitutional issues arise in regard to the admission of a child abuse victim's testimony. *Vigil* addresses the admissibility of the victim's *out-of-court statements* about abuse. State and federal courts also have addressed the constitutionality of *in-court procedures* involving child abuse victims. Both types of cases implicate the defendant's right of confrontation under the Sixth Amendment.

(2) Child's Out-of-Court Statements. Reports of child abuse frequently come from teachers, law enforcement, social services personnel, family members, and friends. When the out-of-court statement of a child ("a declarant") to such a person is offered at trial to establish the fact of the abuse ("the proof of the

matter asserted"), the statement is termed "hearsay." Hearsay is generally not admissible because of its lack of reliability, although there are many exceptions to the hearsay rule. To whom did the child in *Vigil* make his statements about the sexual abuse?

a. Impact of Crawford.   *Vigil* raises the issue of the constitutionality of the admission of a child's hearsay evidence under the Confrontation Clause. Hearsay evidence is particularly useful in child abuse prosecutions because the child victim may be unavailable to testify. What are some of the reasons that sexually abused child victims might be unavailable to testify?

Vigil explains and applies the rule announced by the Supreme Court in Crawford v. Washington, 541 U.S. 36 (2004), a case that has major implications for Confrontation Clause analysis. In *Crawford*, the defendant's wife made a recorded statement during a police investigation that contradicted her husband's subsequent claim of self-defense. The trial court admitted the wife's recorded statement (her in-court testimony was barred by the marital privilege) as an exception to the hearsay rule, reasoning that the statement bore sufficient indicia of reliability. Reversing, the United States Supreme Court held that the use of her recorded statement violated the Confrontation Clause because a defendant must have a prior opportunity for cross-examination when out-of-court testimonial statements are at issue. *Crawford* has had a dramatic impact on prosecution of battering and child abuse by severely limiting the admission of victims' and witnesses' out-of-court statements.

b. Testimonial vs. Nontestimonial.   After *Crawford*, the admissibility of hearsay evidence depends on whether the out-of-court statement is deemed "testimonial." Testimonial statements will not be admitted unless the declarant is available for cross-examination at trial or, if the declarant is unavailable, the statement was previously subject to cross-examination. Should the determination of whether a statement is "testimonial" depend on the *recipient* of the statement? If so, are statements to a police officer always testimonial? Should it matter if the statements are part of informal questioning rather than formal interrogations? See People v. Bradley, 799 N.Y.S.2d 472 (App. Div. 2005). Are statements to family members always nontestimonial? Compare State v. Brigman, 615 S.E.2d 21 (N.C. Ct. App. 2005), with In re E.H., 823 N.E.2d 1029 (Ill. Ct. App. 2005), *reversed on other grounds*, 863 N.E.2d 231 (Ill. 2006).

The Supreme Court subsequently decided two consolidated cases to address gaps left by *Crawford* concerning the meaning of "testimonial hearsay." In Davis v. Washington, 547 U.S. 813 (2006), the Court held that statements to 911 operators are not testimonial and therefore admissible because they are elicited to resolve an emergency. However, in Hammon v. Indiana, (id.) the Court ruled that admission of a victim's statement to a responding police officer violates the defendant's right to confrontation, absent the opportunity for cross-examination, because the officer was investigating a possible crime. Although neither case involves children's hearsay, the decision has significant implications for child abuse prosecutions.

c. A Special Test for Children's Testimonial Statements?   As *Vigil* explains, *Crawford* asserted that the determination of a statement as "testimonial" depends, in part, on whether the statement was made under circumstances that would lead a witness to believe that the statement would be available for use at a later trial. Why did the court in *Vigil* determine that some of the child's statements were nontestimonial and therefore should have been admissible?

Should the admissibility of a child's out-of-court statement depend on whether *the child* reasonably believed that the statement could be used later for trial? That is, should the testimonial determination view the declarant's intention or expectation of a child from the perspective of an objective person or an objective child of the victim's age? How does *Vigil* respond to this issue? Is such a rule appropriate to characterize children's expectations? Compare State v. Snowden, 867 A.2d 314, 329 (Md. 2005). Should a prosecutorial purpose "trump" the expectation of the child? See Robert P. Mosteller, Testing the Testimonial Concept and Exceptions to Confrontation: "A Little Child Shall Lead Them," 82 Ind. L.J. 917, 984 (2007) (suggesting that this result is dictated "historically, doctrinally, and as a matter of policy" by the concern with the defendant's rights).

One commentator has proposed a special test for determining whether a child's statement is testimonial: From the child-declarant's perspective, a statement is testimonial not only if the child understood its potential for formal prosecutorial use, but also "if the child understood that she was reporting wrongdoing and that some adverse consequences—including that Mommy would get mad—would be visited on the wrongdoer." Daniel E. Monnat, The Kid Gloves Are Off: Child Hearsay After Crawford v. Washington, 30 Champion 18, 20 (Jan/Feb. 2006) (citing view of Professor Richard D. Friedman). What do you think of such a test?

If a child makes a statement about the abuse to a person who is a statutorily designated reporter (i.e., physician, teacher, or social worker), does the child's statement thereby become testimonial because of the nature of the government involvement (i.e., the statutory duty to report)? See Myrna Raeder, Remember the Ladies and the Children Too, *Crawford*'s Impact on Domestic Violence and Child Abuse Cases, 71 Brook. L. Rev. 311, 377 (2005) ("mandatory reporting arguably makes any reporter a government proxy, virtually excluding all hearsay of unavailable children"). But cf. Mosteller, Testing the Testimonial Concept, supra, at 952 (finding that no lower courts post-*Crawford* have ruled that the reporting requirement makes a statement automatically testimonial).

(3) Exceptions to the Hearsay Rule.   Beginning in the 1980s, many states responded to the problem of child sexual abuse by expanding exceptions to the hearsay rule: codifying "tender years" hearsay exceptions, expanding two "firmly rooted" hearsay exceptions (the excited utterance and the medical diagnosis or treatment exception), and increasing the use of residual or catch-all hearsay exceptions (which are admissible if the statements have sufficient indicia of trustworthiness). The Federal Rules of Evidence, enacted in 1975, codify many of the preceding hearsay exceptions.

a. Tender Years Hearsay Statutes.   In response to the failure of traditional hearsay exceptions to permit admission of children's statements, many states created special "tender years" hearsay exceptions to permit the admission of a sexually abused child's previous out-of-court statements (e.g., to a parent, friend, therapist). Note that many statements of children that previously were admissible under these tender years hearsay exceptions would violate *Crawford*'s restrictions on testimonial hearsay because of the lack of an opportunity for prior cross-examination.

b. Excited Utterances or Spontaneous Declaration. In another exception to the hearsay rule, an out-of-court statement is admissible provided that it was spontaneous and made under circumstances of shock or excitement. See Fed. R. Evid. 803(2). The rationale for this exception is that statements made while the declarant is in the throes of excitement are less likely to be fabricated. Many courts have expanded this exception for child sexual abuse victims to permit admission of a child's statement even if considerable time has elapsed between the abuse and the statement because children often delay reporting due to "fear, loyalty or lack of comprehension." Melissa Lloyd, Comment, Juridical Hubris: A Comment on Baugh v. State of Florida, 5 Barry L. Rev. 129, 135 (2005). Did statements of the child in *Vigil* qualify as excited utterances? Why?

c. Medical Diagnosis and Treatment. A statement is admissible under the medical diagnosis or treatment exception if the statement describes a medical condition and is pertinent to diagnosis or treatment. See Fed. R. Evid. 803(4). The rationale for this exception is that patients are likely to provide truthful information to health care providers because they know that false statements will affect their treatment. (Note that general statements about the abuse are admissible under this exception but not those relating to the identity of the perpetrator.) Robert G. Marks, Should We Believe the People Who Believe the Children?: The Need for a New Sexual Abuse Tender Years Hearsay Exception Statute, 32 Harv. J. on Legis. 207, 230-231 (1995). In response to the difficulties of prosecuting child sexual abuse, states have expanded the medical diagnosis and treatment exception. Did the child's statements to the doctor in *Vigil* qualify under this exception? Why?

d. Residual Hearsay Exception. Finally, a residual hearsay exception is sometimes used in child sexual abuse cases to admit statements that are not covered by another rule, provided that such statements have equivalent guarantees of trustworthiness. See Fed. R. Evid. 803(24) (for a declarant regardless of availability), 804(b)(5) (for a declarant who is unavailable).

Both excited utterance and medical diagnosis exceptions are considered "firmly rooted" hearsay exceptions. The residual exception and tender years statutory exception are not so considered. Marks, supra, at 219. What is the likely impact of *Crawford* on the various hearsay exceptions? For an in-depth discussion of the hearsay rule and its exceptions in child abuse litigation, see John E. B. Myers, 2 Evidence in Child, Domestic and Elder Abuse Cases 473-660 (2005).

(4) The Supreme Court: Children's Statements to Physicians. Prior to *Crawford*, the United States Supreme Court decided two cases concerning the admissibility of a child's out-of-court statement to a physician. In Idaho v. Wright, 497 U.S. 805 (1990), the defendant was convicted of molesting his five-year-old and two-year-old daughters based on the younger child's statements to a pediatrician. The child's statements to the pediatrician were admitted under the state's "residual exception." (Resort to this exception was necessitated, rather than the exception for medical diagnosis and treatment, because the child incriminated her father as her *sister's* abuser.) According to the residual hearsay exception, to satisfy the Confrontation Clause, the prosecution has to produce the victim or, if he or she is unavailable, the statement has to manifest sufficient guarantees of reliability. Reversing, the Supreme Court held inadmissible the child's statements to her pediatrician because they lacked the requisite guarantees of trustworthiness for

the reasons that the interview was conducted without procedural safeguards, it contained leading questions, and the statements were based on the doctor's preconceived ideas. In a subsequent case, White v. Illinois, 502 U.S. 346 (1992), the Supreme Court held that statements about her sexual abuse made by a four-year-old to her mother, babysitter, police officer, emergency room nurse, and doctor were all admissible (and that the prosecution was not required to produce the child at trial) under the spontaneous declaration and medical examination exceptions to the hearsay rule. Note that *Wright* relied on a trustworthiness and reliability test that was abandoned after *Crawford*. Mosteller, Testing the Testimonial Concept, supra, at 956. See also State v. Buda, 949 A.2d 761 (N.J. 2008) (noting that the appellate court had refused to rely on *White*, reasoning that it was no longer good law).

(5) Special Testimonial Procedures: Background. Many states have enacted legislation providing for special testimonial in-court procedures to protect child abuse victims as witnesses. The United States Supreme Court first examined the issue of whether a special testimonial procedure violated the defendant's Sixth Amendment right in Coy v. Iowa, 487 U.S. 1012 (1988), in which the defendant was charged with sexually assaulting two 13-year-old neighbors. Iowa law permitted a complaining witness to testify either via one-way closed-circuit television or behind a screen. The trial judge approved the use of a screen blocking the defendant from the girls' sight but permitting him to see them dimly and hear them. Nonetheless, the Supreme Court, emphasizing the importance of a defendant's face-to-face meeting with witnesses, held that this procedure violated the defendant's right of confrontation. (In dicta, the Court stated that exceptions would be allowed when necessary to further an important public policy. Id. at 1021.)

In Maryland v. Craig, 497 U.S. 836 (1990), involving a prosecution of a preschool director for child abuse and sexual abuse, the Supreme Court held that the right of confrontation does not prohibit a procedure by which a child victim testifies via one-way closed-circuit television. Despite the procedure preventing the child from seeing the accused, the Court reasoned that the existence of other requisites of confrontation preserved the defendant's rights: the establishment of the child's competence; testimony under oath; cross-examination; and the witness's visibility to the judge, jury, and defendant. The majority also determined that the state's interest in the well-being of abuse victims "may be sufficiently important to outweigh, at least in some cases, a defendant's right to face his or her accusers in court." Id. at 853. Are statutes constitutional that provide for two-way closed circuit television of children's testimony? Compare U.S. v. Yates, 438 F.3d 1307 (11th Cir. 2006), with U.S. v. Gigante, 166 F.3d 75 (2d Cir. 1999). See generally Marc Chase McAllister, Two-Way Video Trial Testimony and the Confrontation Clause: Fashioning a Better *Craig* Test in Light of *Crawford*, 34 Fla. St. U. L. Rev. 835 (2007).

Note that some commentators question the viability of *Craig* after *Crawford*. See, e.g., Robert P. Mosteller, *Crawford*'s Impact on Hearsay Statements in Domestic Violence and Child Sexual Abuse Cases, 71 Brook. L. Rev. 411 (2005). The Supreme Court recently denied certiorari in a case to resolve this question. See Petition for Writ of Certiorari, Vogelsberg v. Wis., 127 S. Ct. 2265 (May 14, 2007) (No. 06-1243).

(6) Determination of Necessity. *Coy*, supra, ruled unconstitutional a statute incorporating a *legislatively imposed* presumption of trauma and suggested the

need for *individualized hearings* to support testimonial protection. How should the trial judge determine "necessity" to find a child "unavailable" for testifying? Should the trial judge personally interview the victim? See U.S. v. Rouse, 111 F.3d 561 (8th Cir. 1997) (holding that a judge may make such a finding based on questioning). Should the judge admit expert testimony? See Lomholt v. Iowa, 327 F.3d 748 (8th Cir. 2003) (finding that expert testimony by a sexual abuse counselor, based on observations of child's behavior, was sufficient to establish case-specific findings to allow closed-circuit television). What should be the standard of proof for necessity? See, e.g., Cal. Penal Code §1347(b)(2) (West 2004 & Supp. 2008) (requiring clear and convincing evidence of trauma). What relevance, if any, should the following factors play in the determination of necessity: the child's age, gender, severity and frequency of the abuse, threats?

In the determination of necessity, to what extent is a court's reliance on *predictive* evidence by expert witnesses justified? What are the psychological effects of testifying on children? Might the experience of testifying actually have beneficial effects for child victims? Existing research fails to state conclusively whether testifying is harmful or beneficial to sexually abused children. See John E.B. Myers, 1 Evidence in Child, Domestic and Elder Abuse 134-141 (2005); Gail Goodman et al., Innovations for Child Witnesses: A National Survey, 5 Psychol. Pub. Pol'y & L. 255, 258 (1999) (summarizing data).

Vigil, Craig, Coy, and *White* involve molestation by an unrelated adult. Most sexual abuse is perpetrated by family members rather than strangers. In the determination of "necessity" for child victims to qualify for special protective procedures, would victims of familial abuse be likely to suffer more or less trauma from testifying than other victims?

(7) Law Reform.

a. Federal Legislation. In response to *Craig,* supra, Congress enacted the Child Victims' and Child Witnesses' Rights Act (CVCWR), 18 U.S.C. §3509 (2000 & Supp. 2005). The Act provides, as an alternative to children's courtroom testimony, that a child witness may testify by means of two-way closed-circuit television or by videotaped depositions provided that: (1) the child is unable to testify because of fear, (2) there is a substantial likelihood (established by expert testimony) that the child will suffer emotional trauma from testifying, (3) the child suffers a mental or other infirmity, and (4) conduct by the defendant or defense counsel causes the child to be unable to continue testifying.

CVCWR goes further than *Craig* by permitting testimony via two-way closed-circuit television (in contrast to the one-way closed-circuit procedure authorized by statute in *Craig*). CVCWR also provides such other protections as requiring that competency exams be appropriate in light of the child's age and development, protecting confidentiality, requiring the use of multidisciplinary child abuse teams, permitting the appointment of a guardian ad litem and the use of an adult support person, and allowing the use of testimonial aids, such as anatomical dolls. Janet Leach Richards, Protecting the Child Victim in Abuse Cases, 34 Fam. L.Q. 393, 400-401 (2000). Several federal courts upheld the constitutionality of CVCWR prior to *Crawford*. See, e.g., United States v. Etimani, 328 F.3d 493 (9th Cir. 2003).

b. Uniform Law. The Uniform Law Commissioners approved the Uniform Child Witness Testimony by Alternative Methods Act (UCWTAMA) in 2002.

The Act gives authority to civil and criminal judges to order a hearing to determine whether a child should be allowed to testify by an alternative method. The child's presence is not required at this hearing. Upon a showing of good cause, the judge will permit the child to testify outside the courtroom and outside the defendant's presence. To date, the Act has been approved by three states. See Uniform Child Witness Testimony by Alternative Methods Act, Legislative Fact Sheet, available at *http://nccusl.org/Update/uniformact_factsheets/uniformacts-fs-ucwtbama.asp* (last visited Nov. 18, 2008).

Some commentators criticize the Act, claiming (1) it violates the federal Confrontation Clause, as interpreted by *Craig*, by encompassing *any* shielding procedure, by failing to limit the considerations by which judges permit shielding, and by not limiting the types of cases in which shielding is permissible; (2) it violates many state constitutional provisions requiring face-to-face confrontation; and (3) it has negative consequences from a public policy perspective by diminishing the presumption of innocence. See Katherine W. Grearson, Note, Proposed Uniform Child Witness Testimony Act: An Impermissible Abridgement of Criminal Defendants' Rights, 45 B.C. L. Rev. 467, 491-496 (2004) (discussing criticisms).

(8) Constitutionality of Other Protective Procedures. State legislatures have enacted a number of protective mechanisms for child victims of sexual abuse.

a. Videotaping. Many states authorize preservation of a child's testimony on videotape for later presentation at trial as a substitute for the presence of the child. Videotaping testimony also eliminates the need for repeated interviews of the child. Some videotaping statutes require that the defendant be present and cross-examination allowed at the videotaping session. Other statutes permit the videotape to be used subject to an opportunity for subsequent cross-examination at a judicial hearing. Are these statutes constitutional after *Crawford*? How should videotaping be conducted to ensure that children's statements are considered nontestimonial and therefore admissible? See Mosteller, Testing the Testimonial Concept, supra, at 966-975 (suggesting videotaping for a nonprosecutorial purpose, by non-law-enforcement interviewers, and without police involvement).

b. Courtroom Closure. Despite the Sixth Amendment guarantee of a "public trial" in criminal prosecutions, trial judges have the discretion to close the courtroom to spectators and the press to lessen trauma to witnesses. The Supreme Court examined the constitutionality of one closure statute in Globe Newspaper v. Superior Court, 457 U.S. 596 (1982). Although finding mandatory courtroom closure unconstitutional, the Court permitted closure subject to a particularized finding on a case-by-case basis (taking into account the victim's age, maturity and understanding, the nature of the crime, desires of the victims, and the interests of parents and relatives). Note that the Child Victims' and Child Witnesses' Rights Act, supra, permits judges to close their courtrooms, at the judge's discretion, when child victims testify. See 18 U.S.C. §3509(e) (2000) (court may exclude all persons who do not have an interest in the case if the court determines that requiring the child to testify in open court would cause "substantial psychological harm to the child or would result in the child's inability to effectively communicate").

(9) Other Protective Mechanisms. States have developed additional protective evidentiary rules.

a. Abrogation of Marital Privilege.   Some states have statutory provisions eliminating the marital disqualification privilege (disqualifying a spouse as a witness against the other spouse) in cases of child sexual abuse. See, e.g., Mass. Gen. Laws, ch. 233, §20 (West 2000 & Supp. 2008).

b. Extensions of the Statute of Limitations; Delayed Discovery Rules.   Many states have adopted delayed discovery rules that extend the statute of limitations for tort recovery in child sexual abuse cases because victims may repress memories of the abuse for years afterward. See generally Elizabeth A. Wilson, Suing for Lost Childhood: Child Sexual Abuse, the Delayed Discovery Rule, and the Problem of Finding Justice for Adult-Survivors of Child Abuse, 12 UCLA Women's L.J. 145 (2003). The clergy sexual abuse scandal (discussed supra) led many states to extend their statutes of limitations. See Peter E. Smith, The Massachusetts Discovery Rule and Its Application to Non-Perpetrators in "Repressed Memory" Child Sexual Abuse Cases, 30 New Eng. J. on Crim. & Civ. Confinement 179 (2004) (citing Mass. Gen. Laws ch. 260, §4C).

(10) Policy.   Are these aforementioned protections necessary for child victims of sexual abuse? Should child witnesses be treated differently from adults by being accorded special treatment? In all cases? Or, only in sexual abuse cases? How far should courts extend the rationale for special protective procedures for child victim witnesses? To child eyewitnesses? To child victims of crimes of a nonsexual nature?

(11) Competency.   Competency rules provide an additional judicial check on the reliability of child witnesses. How does a court determine a child's competency to testify? At early common law, children under age 14 were presumed to be incompetent as witnesses. Case law gradually liberalized this rule, holding that capacity is determined not by age, but rather by the ability to differentiate truth from falsehood and an understanding of the duty to tell the truth. See Rex v. Brasier, 168 Eng. Rep. 202 (1770); Wheeler v. United States, 159 U.S. 523 (1895). The Federal Rules of Evidence bolstered the movement to abolish the presumption of incompetence for young children. Eliminating the distinctions between child and adult witnesses, Fed. R. Evid. 601, provides that "[e]very person is competent to be a witness except as otherwise provided in these rules." In response to the adoption of the federal rules in 1975, many states liberalized their competency requirements for child witnesses. Further, some state statutes have special competency rules for child victims and child eyewitnesses in child abuse litigation. Myers, supra, at 77-81. See generally Aviva A. Orenstein et al., Children as Witnesses: A Symposium on Child Competence and the Accused's Right to Confront Child Witnesses, 82 Ind. L.J. 809 (2007).

D. STANDARD FOR INTERVENTION AND DISPOSITIONAL ALTERNATIVES

This section focuses on when the state should assume primary responsibility for the care and custody of children by intervention in the parent-child relationship. It examines the standard for intervention, which includes broad statutory definitions of parental neglect, and explores that standard in the context of both short-term summary removal, as well as long-term state-sponsored foster care. It presents criticisms of the foster care system as well as foster care reform. Finally, it discusses the remedy of termination of parental rights.

1. When Should the State Remove?

Roe v. Conn
417 F. Supp. 769 (M.D. Ala. 1976)

Before RIVES, Circuit Judge, JOHNSON, Chief District Judge, and VARNER, District Judge.

[These class actions challenge the constitutionality of Alabama's child neglect law. Ala. Code Tit. 13, §350 et seq. (1958). Plaintiff Wambles represents the class of mothers and plaintiff Roe represents the class of children who have been or may be subject to the removal provisions without a prior hearing where there was no showing of immediate or threatened harm.]

Findings of Fact

Margaret Wambles is a 25-year-old white woman who has never married. On September 15, 1971, Plaintiff Wambles gave birth to a son, Richard Roe, who lived with her continuously until June 2, 1975, when he was seized by Officer L. T. Conn of the Montgomery Police Department and placed in the custody of the Montgomery County Department of Pensions and Security. This seizure was ordered by Judge Thetford of the Montgomery County Family Court without affording Plaintiff Wambles prior notice and a hearing. Such authority as exists for this action is provided by Alabama Code, Title 13, §350(2) and 352(4), which purports to permit a juvenile court judge to summarily remove a "neglected child" from its home if the judge believes the child's welfare so warrants.[1]

---

[1] Title 13, §350(2) reads in pertinent part:

> The words "neglected child" shall mean any child, who, while under sixteen years of age . . . has no proper parental care or guardianship or whose home by reason of neglect, cruelty, or depravity, on the part of his parent or parents, guardian or other person in whose care he may be, is an unfit and improper place for such child . . . or is under such improper or insufficient guardianship or control as to endanger the morals, health or general welfare of such child . . . or who for any other cause is in need of the care and protection of the state.

Sec. 350(4) provides that any child described as neglected shall be subject to the guardianship of the state and entitled to its care and protection. Sec. 352 sets forth the procedure to be followed in a child neglect case. A verified complaint is first filed with the juvenile court of the county of the child's residence by any person having knowledge of, or information concerning, the child. It is sufficient for the petition, after briefly stating the relevant facts, to aver that the named child is neglected and in need of the care and protection of the state. Upon the filing of the petition, the judge, clerk, or chief probation officer of the court shall cause an examination to be made and shall issue a summons requiring the child to appear before the court. Sec. 352(4) provides that, "If it appears from the

The investigation which led to termination of Plaintiff Wambles' parental rights was prompted by Defendant Coppage. Mr. Coppage, who is white, lived intermittently with Plaintiff Wambles from 1970 until March, 1975, and claims to have fathered Richard Roe. On June 1, 1975, Mr. Coppage contacted the Montgomery Police Department and reported that Plaintiff Wambles might be neglecting Richard Roe, that she had been evicted from her former residence because she was keeping company with black males, and that she had moved to Highland Village (a black neighborhood) where she was living with a black man. On the basis of this information, Police Officer Conn initiated an investigation of Plaintiff Wambles. The records of the Montgomery Police Department were checked but revealed no previous complaints of child neglect against Plaintiff Wambles and no adult file on her.

Officer Conn went to the Wambles' residence . . . at approximately 7:30 P.M. on June 2,1975. Plaintiff Wambles permitted Officer Conn to enter and inspect her dwelling, which the officer found was a two-bedroom apartment, where Plaintiff Wambles and her son were living with a black man to whom she was not married. Richard Roe was clothed, clean, and in "fairly good" physical condition with no signs of physical abuse. The home was "relatively clean" and stocked with "adequate food." Upon completing his inspection, Defendant Conn left the home and called Defendant Ward [director of the county youth facility] and reported his findings. He was then instructed by Defendant Ward to go to the Youth Facility and get a pick-up order. The only facts about Margaret Wambles known to Judge Thetford before he issued the pick-up order were that she was unemployed and that she and her child are white and were living with a black man in a black neighborhood. Judge Thetford had no information as to how long Margaret Wambles had lived in Montgomery, where she had worked, or how long she had been unemployed. He had no evidence that Richard Roe was being physically abused and no information as to the condition of the Wambles' home. Judge Thetford knew nothing about the man with whom Margaret Wambles was living, other than his race and the fact that he was not married to her. Judge Thetford testified that the race of the man with whom Plaintiff Wambles was living was relevant to his decision to order Richard Roe removed from his mother's custody, particularly because they were living in a black neighborhood. Judge Thetford concluded that this habitation in a black neighborhood could be dangerous for a child because it was his belief that "it was not a healthy thing for a white child to be the only [white] child in a black neighborhood."

At approximately 8:30 P.M. on June 2, 1975, after obtaining the pick-up order, Defendant Conn, accompanied by two other Montgomery police officers, returned to Plaintiff Wambles' home. When Defendant Conn announced that he had come to take Richard Roe, Plaintiff Wambles picked up her child and ran to the back of the apartment. After Defendant Conn showed Plaintiff Wambles the pick-up order,

---

petition that . . . the child is in such condition that its welfare requires that custody be immediately assumed, the judge of the court may endorse upon the summons a direction that the officer serving said summons shall at once take said child into his custody." The statute further provides that the custody of any child who has been summarily seized is subject to the discretion of the judge pending hearing of the case.

[The Alabama neglect provisions have been amended, effective January 15, 1977.]

she still refused to surrender the child. Thereupon, with the child crying, "No, mama, don't let him take me," Defendant Conn grabbed Plaintiff Wambles by the arm and pulled her back into the living room, took Richard Roe from her arms, and left without leaving a copy of the pick-up order. After the seizure, Defendant Conn took Richard Roe to a DPS-licensed shelter home in Montgomery.

No hearing was scheduled or held following Richard Roe's removal until July 10, 1975. No attorney was requested or appointed to represent Richard Roe at the July 10 hearing. At the hearing in the Family Court of Montgomery County, both Defendant Coppage and Plaintiff Wambles were present and represented by counsel. Judge Thetford entered an order on July 11, 1975, wherein he awarded Defendant Coppage custody of Richard Roe after making a finding that he was the natural father of the child. . . .

Expert Testimony

Plaintiffs Wambles and Roe have submitted the testimony of witnesses Dr. Sally A. Provence and Dr. Albert J. Solnit as experts in the field of child care and development. Drs. Provence and Solnit summarized their views as follows:

1. Summary removal of a young child from a parent who has been his major caregiver is a severe threat to his development. It disrupts and grossly endangers what he most needs, that is, the continuity of affectionate care from those to whom he is attached through bonds of love.

2. Summary removal should be allowed only under conditions in which physical survival is at stake.

3. In situations in which some interference is indicated because parents are unable to take good care of their child, there are alternatives to summary removal which should be used either singly or in combination. Among these are the following: (a) the provision in the child's home of assistance to parents with child care and with managing a household; (b) the provision of counselling to parents about how to care for a child in ways that enhance his development and well-being; (c) the provision of a day care center or day care family in which assistance to child and parent can be provided which is addressed to their specific needs; (d) the provision of a residential facility or foster family in which both parent and child can receive the nurture and guidance they may need (in extended families, relatives often supply such benevolent help, and when they are unavailable, it is one of society's responsibilities to organize and make available such assistance); and (e) the provision of 24-hour substitute care for a child, which does not cut him off from contact with his parents. . . .

Conclusions of Law

The Fundamental Right to Family Integrity

A district court in Iowa recently reviewed the long line of Supreme Court cases addressed to the constitutional interests at stake where various aspects of family life are threatened and concluded that there is a fundamental right to family integrity protected by the Fourteenth Amendment to the United States Constitution.

Alsager v. District Court of Polk County, Iowa, 406 F. Supp. 10, 15 (S.D. Iowa 1975). . . .

This Court is in full agreement . . . that the Constitution recognizes as fundamental the right of family integrity. This means that in our present case the state's severance of Plaintiff Wambles' parent-child relationship and of Plaintiff Roe's child-parent relationship will receive strict judicial scrutiny. Recognizing that fundamental right, this Court will now apply the pertinent constitutional principles to the facts of the present case.

Summary Seizure

This Court holds that Alabama Code, Title 13, §352(4), which authorizes summary seizure of a child "if it appears that . . . the child is in such condition that its welfare requires," violates procedural due process under the Fourteenth Amendment of the United States Constitution.

To determine the nature of the procedural safeguards that the Constitution mandates, the administrative needs of the State must be carefully balanced against the interests of the affected citizens. There is no question that the family members will suffer a grievous loss if the State severs the parent-child relationship; an interest, we have held, that is part of the liberty concept of the Fourteenth Amendment. The State of Alabama, on the other hand, does have a legitimate interest in protecting children from harm as quickly as possible. Normally, before intrusion into the affairs of the family is allowed, the State should have reliable evidence that a child is in need of protective care. In the absence of exigent circumstances, this fact-finding process, as a matter of basic fairness, should provide notice to the parents and child of the evidence of abuse and provide them with an opportunity for rebuttal at a hearing before an impartial tribunal.

The facts of this case dispel any notion that the State was faced with an emergency situation. As we earlier found, Officer Conn's investigation revealed that Richard Roe was clothed, clean, and in "fairly good" physical condition with no signs of physical abuse. The Wambles' home was "relatively clean" and stocked with "adequate food." Without danger of immediate harm or threatened harm to the child, the State's interest in protecting the child is not sufficient to justify a removal of the child prior to notice and a hearing. Additionally, even in the event summary seizure had been justified, a hearing would have had to follow the seizure "as soon as practicable" and not six weeks later as it did in the present case. . . . For these reasons, this Court is of the opinion that Alabama Code Title 13, §352(4) violates the procedural due process clause of the Fourteenth Amendment. . . .

Removal Upon a Finding of "Neglect"

After the hearing on July 10, 1975, Judge Thetford ordered the termination of the parental rights of Plaintiff Wambles to Richard Roe on the basis that the child was "a dependent or neglected child as defined by the laws of Alabama." . . .

. . . It is not disputed that the State of Alabama has a legitimate interest in the welfare of children. Minor intrusions into the affairs of the family may be permitted when the State has reason to believe that a child's best interest is at stake. In such cases, various options and alternatives are available to the State to achieve its objective of child protection. One possibility might be a requirement that the parents attend seminars and weekly counselling sessions on child care and the responsibilities of parenthood. Another situation might warrant supervision of the parents by a welfare counselor or the placing of a neutral person — such as an aunt — in the home to serve as a bridge between the parents and the child. The State's interest, however, would become "compelling" enough to sever entirely the parent-child relationship only when the child is subjected to real physical or emotional harm and less drastic measures would be unavailing.

Here, the State offered no assistance to Plaintiff Wambles, who was faced with the troubling predicament of raising a young child without the aid of a husband, nor did it explore the possibility of accomplishing its objective of protecting Richard Roe's welfare by use of alternatives other than termination of custody.

The Alabama statute defining "neglected" children sweeps far past the constitutionally permissible range of interference into the sanctity of the family unit. The fact that a home is "improper" in the eyes of the state officials does not necessarily mean that a child in that home is subject to physical or emotional harm.

[T]he state's burden is not only to show that the child is being disadvantaged but also to show that the child is being harmed in a real and substantial way. Accordingly, this Court declares Alabama Code, Title 13, §§350 and 352 unconstitutional, because it violates the family integrity of Margaret Wambles and all other mothers in the class represented by her and the family integrity of Richard Roe and all other children in the class represented by him.

This Court holds, as an alternative ground, that the challenged statutory provisions are unconstitutionally vague. . . . In the present case, not only is the statutory definition of neglect circular (a neglected child is any child who has no proper parental care by reason of neglect), but it is couched in terms that have no common meaning. . . . When is a home an "unfit" or "improper" place for a child? Obviously, this is a question about which men and women of ordinary intelligence would greatly disagree. Their answers would vary in large measure in relation to their differing social, ethical, and religious views. Because these terms are too subjective to denote a sufficient warning to those individuals who might be affected by their proscription, the statute is unconstitutionally vague. . . .

Appointment of Counsel for the Child

The Plaintiffs maintain that the Alabama child custody procedure violates the due process clause of the Constitution because that procedure does not provide for the appointment of independent counsel to represent a child in a neglect proceeding, and none was appointed here. We agree. . . .

. . . The juvenile court judge should, however, independently appoint counsel for the child, requiring the parents, if they are financially able, to pay for this legal representation. If the parents are indigent, free counsel should be afforded the child.

Consideration of Race

Plaintiffs contend that there was a racial animus behind the decision to remove Richard Roe from his mother's custody. It is undisputed that Judge Thetford, at the time he signed the pick-up order, knew only that Margaret Wambles was unemployed, that she and her child are white, and that they were living in a black neighborhood with a black man to whom Plaintiff Wambles was not married.

While a white child who is part of an interracial family unit and lives in a black neighborhood may be disadvantaged socially or culturally, this fact alone does not rise to the level of harm to the child that is required before the State can terminate the parent's right to custody of the child.[16] Since race per se can never amount to sufficient harm to justify a constitutional termination, this Court finds it unnecessary to decide whether consideration of racial factors by a juvenile court judge represents prohibited racial discrimination. . . .

[I]t is Ordered, Adjudged and Decreed by this Court that:

1. Defendants are hereby enjoined from enforcing the summary removal provision of Alabama Code, Title 13, §352(4) (1958), insofar as it permits summary removal of the child in the absence of the danger of immediate or threatened harm to the child.

2. Defendants are hereby enjoined from enforcing the standards of "neglect" found in Alabama Code, Title 13, §350(2) insofar as the statute permits removal of a child from parental custody in the absence of a showing of physical or emotional harm to the child.

3. Defendants are enjoined from instituting change of custody proceedings without independent counsel appointed to represent the child.

Since the State proceedings that terminated Margaret Wambles' custody over Richard Roe and the award of custody to Cecil Coppage are tainted with unconstitutionality, the rights of the parties should be returned to the status quo ante. This Court, however, believes that, when the interest of a young child is at stake, we should proceed cautiously, not unmindful of the changed circumstances of the child even though these changes were unconstitutionally accomplished. Accordingly, it is further ordered, adjudged and decreed by the Court that:

4. The State Department of Pensions and Security immediately reassume custody of Richard Roe pending further action in regard to his custody. If the State has not initiated within 30 days neglect proceedings consistent with the dictates of the United States Constitution, Defendants are further enjoined to deliver Richard Roe back to the custody of Margaret Wambles. . . .

NOTES AND QUESTIONS

(1) Stages of Intervention.   Roe v. Conn reveals the stages of juvenile court intervention in cases of child abuse and neglect. Initial intervention takes two forms: *summary seizure* or the assertion of *temporary custody.* If the court determines that an emergency exists, the court may order (in an ex parte hearing) that the child be immediately removed from the home. On the other hand, the adversarial

---

[16] Neither is the fact that the parent is living with someone to whom he or she is not married. "Immorality" of the parent, without a showing that the child is being physically or emotionally harmed in a real way, is not sufficient justification for the State to terminate a parent-child relationship.

proceeding regarding temporary custody (termed a "jurisdictional hearing") determines whether the child falls within the statutory definition of an abused or neglected child. The next stage occurs after this jurisdictional determination when the court conducts a "dispositional hearing." At that time, the court chooses among various dispositions (e.g., conditions on custody, foster care, termination of parental rights).

(2) Threshold for Removal. According to Roe v. Conn, what is the standard for summary seizure of a child from the home? What is the standard for termination of parental rights? How do the standards differ?

Roe v. Conn enjoined removal from parental custody under a neglect statute in the absence of a showing of "physical or emotional harm." How does one show emotional abuse or neglect? Should emotional maltreatment be a basis for removing a child via summary seizure or via termination of parental rights? Is it possible to predict when a child is emotionally endangered? Or does such an inquiry invite predictions beyond the capacity of the behavioral sciences? Can an inquiry requiring predictions of future emotional harm to the child do more harm than good? If there is a showing of physical or emotional harm, should removal be permitted even if there are reasonable means of protecting the child at home?

For a criticism that the practice of emergency removal is used far more frequently than necessary to protect children from harm and causes emotional damage to children, see Paul Chill, Burden of Proof Begone: The Pernicious Effect of Emergency Removal in Child Protective Proceedings, 42 Fam. Ct. Rev. 540 (2004).

(3) Emotional Maltreatment. Courts have been slow to recognize emotional maltreatment as child abuse, in part because emotional maltreatment (unlike physical abuse) leaves no *physical* marks. Early definitions of "abuse" emphasized serious physical injuries. CAPTA, in requiring a minimal definition by states as a condition of their receiving federal funds, defines "child abuse" and "neglect" as

> the physical or *mental injury*, sexual abuse or exploitation, negligent treatment, or maltreatment of a child under the age of eighteen, or the age specified by the child protection law of the State, by a person including any employee of a residential facility or any staff person providing out of home care who is responsible for the child's welfare under circumstances indicating harm or threatened harm to the child's health or welfare. The term encompasses both acts and omissions on the part of a responsible person. [45 C.F.S. §1340.2(d) (2003) (originally codified at 42 U.S.C. §5106(g)) (emphasis added).]

States subsequently refined their definitions, thereby permitting considerable variation.

(4) In an omitted footnote, the court suggests that in a divorce proceeding, the more open-ended "best interest" standard would be "entirely appropriate." How is this case different from a divorce custody fight? Is this case not simply a private dispute between the child's mother and a man who claims to be the child's father? The case makes plain that "race per se" and "parental immorality in itself can never amount to sufficient harm" to justify state removal from parental custody in a neglect proceeding. In a divorce custody dispute, is it

appropriate to take race and sexual conduct into consideration? For discussion of this issue, see Chapter 5.

(4) Counsel for the Abused Child.   Do you agree that independent counsel for the child is constitutionally compelled in a child abuse and neglect proceeding? If so, is counsel required because the child's interest may not coincide with that of either the state or the parents? See discussion of Lassiter v. Department of Social Services, p. 369, infra. How should the child's representative decide what the child's interests are? By asking the child what he or she wants? By deciding on behalf of the child what is best for the child?

a. CAPTA and the GAL.   Federal legislation spurred the adoption of guardian ad litem (GAL) programs for abused and neglected children. The Child Abuse Prevention and Treatment Act (CAPTA) of 1974, 42 U.S.C. §§5101-5707 (2000 & Supp. 2005), requires that for states to qualify for federal funds for the prevention and treatment of abuse

> in every case involving an abused or neglected child which results in a judicial proceeding, a guardian ad litem, who has received training appropriate to the role, and who may be an attorney or a court appointed special advocate who has received training appropriate to that role (or both), shall be appointed to represent the child. . . ." [42 U.S.C. §5106a(b)(2)(A)(xiii) (2000 & Supp. 2005).]

The Act does not require that the GAL be an attorney. Only about one-third of the states require the appointment of a lawyer for the child in abuse or neglect proceedings. Katherine Hunt Federle, Righting Wrongs: A Reply to the Uniform Law Commission's Uniform Representation on Children in Abuse, Neglect, and Custody Proceedings, 42 Fam. L.Q. 103, 106 (2008). See also Kenny A. ex rel. Winn v. Perdue, 356 F. Supp.2d 1353 (N.D. Ga. 2005) (holding that foster children had right to counsel pursuant to state statute and Due Process Clause). Do you agree that the child's representative should be an attorney? Why or why not?

b. ABA Standards of Practice.   The ABA approved the Standards of Practice for Lawyers Who Represent Children in Abuse and Neglect Cases in 1996. See Standards of Practice for Lawyers Who Represent Children in Abuse and Neglect Cases (reprinted in 29 Fam. L.Q. 375 (1995)). The ABA approved separate guidelines for children's representatives in custody proceedings in 2003 (discussed in Chapter 5, infra). See American Bar Association, Standards of Practice for Lawyers Representing Children in Custody Cases, 37 Fam. L.Q. 129 (2003). To integrate the two different set of ABA standards (those for the abuse/neglect context and those for the custody context), the National Conference of Commissioners on Uniform State Laws (NCCUSL) approved the Uniform Representation of Children in Abuse, Neglect, and Custody Proceedings Act in 2006 and amended the Act in 2007. See Uniform Representation of Children in Abuse, Neglect, and Custody Proceedings Act, 42 Fam. L.Q. 1 (2008).

The new Uniform Act provides for two types of lawyer representatives for children — a "child's attorney" and a "best interests attorney." The Act explicitly rejects the combined role of attorney/guardian ad litem. The child's attorney adopts the traditional attorney-client relationship with the child, directed by the client (rather than by what the lawyer believes to be in the child's best interests), and bound by ethical obligations. On the other hand, the best interests attorney, although also in an attorney-client relationship with the child, advocates for the child's best interests "based on an objective assessment of the available evidence, including the circumstances and needs of the child, and according to applicable legal principles." Id. at 11. The latter representative is important for children who are unable or unwilling to direct counsel. Id.

For critical commentary on the new Uniform Act, see Barbara Ann Atwood, The Uniform Representation of Children in Abuse, Neglect, and Custody Proceedings: Bridging the Divide Between Pragmatism and Idealism, 42 Fam. L.Q. 63 (2008); Federle, supra. See also Jean Koh Peters, How Children Are Heard in Child Protective Proceedings, in the United States and Around the World in 2005: Survey Findings, Initial Observations, and Areas for Further Study, 6 Nev. L.J. 966 (2006) (surveying state standards in child protection proceedings).

(5) Child Abandonment as Neglect. The rising incidence of abandonment of newborns prompted legislatures to enact "Baby Moses" statutes. These statutes permit mothers who have given birth to surrender their newborn within the first hours of life to a hospital employee, anonymously and without fear of criminal prosecution. Are these safe haven laws an appropriate response to the problem of child abandonment? See Carol Sanger, Infant Safe Haven Laws: Legislating in the Culture of Law, 106 Colum. L. Rev. 753 (2006). Do these laws violate the father's due process rights? See Jeffrey A. Parness, Lost Paternity in the Culture of Motherhood: A Different View of Safe Haven Laws, 42 Val. U. L. Rev. 81 (2007).

(6) Problem. In the predawn hours of April 6, 2008, a caravan of K-9 unit vehicles arrived at the "Yearning for Zion Ranch" in Eldorado, Texas, a 1,700-acre polygamist compound of the Fundamentalist Church of Jesus Christ of Latter Day Saints. Texas law enforcement authorities, together with child protective service workers, conducted a house-to-house search and forcibly removed more than 400 children from their homes in the largest child welfare operation in state history.

The authorities were acting in response to a late-night phone call to a family violence shelter from a 16-year-old girl ("Jane Doe"). Speaking in a whisper to avoid being overhead, the teenager said that she was the seventh "wife" of 50-year-old Dale Barlow. She explained that she had given birth to his child when she was only 15 years old and that she was currently pregnant with his second child. She also described vicious beatings by him. Texas law prohibits girls younger than 16 from marrying, even with parental approval. (The constitutionality of the state ban on plural marriage has been upheld by the state supreme court.) The rural compound was built by followers of polygamist leader Warren Jeffs, who was recently sentenced to two consecutive sentences of five years to life in prison in Utah for being an accomplice to the rape of a 14-year-old girl who wed her cousin in an arranged marriage in 2001. Dale Barlow, the alleged "husband" of the teenage complainant, is currently on probation in Utah for conspiracy to commit sexual conduct with a minor. He denies having married Jane Doe and even denies having been in Texas recently.

The children (and some of the mothers who were allowed to accompany them) were loaded into buses going to a larger town 45 miles away and placed by law enforcement officials and social workers in a church and civic center. There, they remained for several weeks while investigators interviewed them about the whereabouts of the 16-year-old girl and also attempted to determine what charges should be brought. Jane Doe's phone call was later determined to be a hoax perpetrated by a Colorado woman who had previously been arrested for making false reports of abuse.

Suppose that you are an intern in the office of the state Child Protective Services (CPS) Department who has been asked by your supervisor to review the actions taken by state officials in the case. You have been asked to address the following questions in light of prevailing case law and statutory law: (1) Was the Texas Child Protective Services Department acting within its statutory authority in removing these children from their homes? (2) Were the actions of CPS officials following the raid in compliance with their statutory duties? (3) What is the likelihood that a Texas juvenile court will be able to assert jurisdiction over these children? (4) Suppose that CPS does determine that protective action on behalf of these children is warranted. What action(s) should CPS take? Does each child have the right to an attorney? (5) What legal response should CPS anticipate from the parents' attorneys if the court asserts jurisdiction and what should CPS attorneys respond to the parents' argument(s)? In your view, what should be the appropriate disposition of this case? See In re Texas Dept. of Family & Protective Services, 255 S.W.3d 613 (Tex. 2008).

In re Deborah G., Georgia G., Bruce G., and Elizabeth G.
2d Civil No. 40391, Cal. Ct. App., June 29, 1973 (unpublished opinion)

Wood, J. . . .

George and Patricia G. are the parents of five children: Michael, age 15;[1] Deborah, age 11; Georgia, age 7; Bruce, age 5; and Elizabeth, age 2. . . . Deborah and Georgia had been adjudged dependent children in Alameda County in 1969, approximately two years prior to the herein proceedings; however, they remained in the family home.

The petitions herein were filed in 1971. In each petition, it is alleged that the child is under 21 years of age, and comes within the provisions of "Section 600b of the Juvenile Court Law of California" (Welf. & Inst. Code, §600, subd. (b)) in that the home of said minor "is an unfit place for him in that his home has become and is an unkempt and unsanitary place of living."

Evidence at the hearing of the petitions included testimony by a probation officer, a school nurse, the director of the housing authority, the maintenance foreman of the housing authority, a neighbor of the Gibsons, and a deputy sheriff. Some of that testimony . . . follows:

Prior to 1970, two of respondents' children had been adjudged dependent children of the juvenile court in Alameda County. In early 1970 respondents moved into San Luis Obispo County, and resided there with five of the children. Commencing in early 1970 employees of various governmental agencies visited

---

[1] Michael is not a party in this appeal. Apparently Mrs. G. is also the mother of three other children who were previously placed in foster homes.

the family home. In substance, they noticed that the house was "very filthy" and a strong odor emanated therefrom; the floors were "sticky" with food particles and dog hairs; the children were dirty and had body odors; lice were removed from the head of one child; garbage and litter were in the backyard; trash was in the living room; the bathroom was "terribly dirty" and "full of flies"; the kitchen floor was encrusted with food and dirt; pans of grease were on the stove, and there was an odor of stale food; the bedding was dirty; and the children were frequently absent from school.

The nurse testified that on several occasions she requested that respondents clean the house and that in her opinion the family was not being handled well and it would take a "superhuman" effort for respondents to become adequate parents through counseling. The director of the housing authority continuously urged respondents to clean their house; and the maintenance foreman of the housing authority testified that the condition of the kitchen was so filthy that he hated to go in there before his noon meal.

Respondents (parents) testified and called five witnesses, including a social worker. Such testimony was in part as follows:

Each of the respondents was overweight and in poor health (diabetes and gout), and their disabilities made it difficult to keep the house clean. They loved their children, and the children were not dirtier than ordinary children; the house (according to the social worker) was not dirtier than the average house;[2] there was mutual affection between the parents and the children; conditions of the home improved after the first visit by the social worker; a homemaker employed by the county visited the home on 20 or more occasions since 1970 to give Mrs. Gibson training and help; the homemaker did not think that the home presented a health hazard; the children were in good health, except for minor ailments; the children were happy; and there was no evidence of unkindness or cruelty by the parents.

Some of the petitioner's evidence was presented at a hearing on November 29, 1971, to determine jurisdiction of the juvenile court over Bruce and Elizabeth, and to consider the issue of dependent status of Deborah and Georgia (who had previously been adjudged dependent children of the juvenile court in Alameda County). The juvenile court temporarily removed the four children from the family home; and continued the hearing to December 6, 1971. Further evidence was presented by the parties on that date, and the matter was continued to December 13, 1972, at which time the parties presented further evidence.

The court found that Bruce and Elizabeth were dependent children within the provisions of section 600, subdivision (b), of the Juvenile Court Law (Welf. & Inst. Code, §600, subd. (b)), and that they should be removed from custody of the parents pursuant to section 726, subdivisions (a) and (c) of said code; and ordered that each of them be placed in the home of foster parents under supervision of the

---

[2] The testimony of that witness regarding the condition of the house was contradicted by a report which that witness had written previously. Also, testimony of another social worker was presented by respondents (parents) in the form of a letter; and on cross-examination that witness testified that in a previous letter he had stated that "this is a long-term case of a multiproblem family. The physical home environment has been a long-term chronic problem and does not appear to be improved."

county, with arrangements for the parents to visit them. As to Deborah and Georgia, the court found that an order continuing the status of each of them as a dependent child for one year was necessary; and the provisions of said section 726, subdivisions (a) and (c), required that their custody be taken from the parents. It was ordered that the previous commitment of said children to the home of foster parents remain in effect, with arrangements for visits by their parents.

As to appellants' contention that the petitioner did not sustain the burden of proving the allegations of the petition, they argue: The allegations of the petition did not give fair notice of the grounds for adjudicating that the children were dependent children under section 600, subdivision (b), of said code; and petitioner (probation officer) did not present sufficient evidence to establish the alleged grounds for such adjudication.

In wardship proceedings the welfare of the child is of paramount concern. [T]he findings of the juvenile court will not be disturbed on appeal where there is substantial evidence to support them. . . .

In the present case each petition alleged in part that the minor came within the provisions of section "600b" of the Juvenile Court Law of California in that the home of the minor "is an unfit place for him in that his home has become and is an unkempt and unsanitary place of living." [T]he court said that there was "clear, competent and credible testimony . . . that the home of the parents is not a suitable place of abode for any said minors and that the home provided by the parents is an unfit place by reason of neglect." Findings (as to each minor) were in part that "all of the allegations of the petition are true, and that said minor is a person described by and coming within the provisions of Section 600(b) of the Juvenile Court Law." In the circumstances, the allegations of each petition gave the respondents reasonable notice of the grounds upon which deprivation of custody of the child was sought, evidence was presented on those grounds, and there was no material variance between the allegations of the petition and the findings. Respondents were not denied due process of law.

Also, there was substantial evidence to support the findings that each child was a dependent child within the provisions of said section 600, subdivision (b). . . . There was sufficient evidence to the effect that the home was unkempt and unsanitary so as to be an unfit place, by reason of neglect, and not a suitable abode for the children; efforts were made by various officials to help respondents remedy such neglect; such efforts were of no avail; such neglect continued for a substantial period of time; each parent was ill and overweight to the extent that it was difficult for them to keep the house clean; and extraordinary efforts would be required in order to improve the situation by counseling the parents. Petitioner was not required, as appellants assert, to prove that the conditions of the abode cause "sickness and disease of mind or body" in order to establish "neglect" within the meaning of said section 600, subdivision (b). As above stated, the welfare of the child is of paramount concern, and a purpose of the juvenile court law is to secure for each minor such care and guidance as will serve the spiritual, emotional, mental, and physical welfare of the minor and the best interests of the state. . . .

[T]he unfitness of a home for a particular child (as provided in said section 600, subd. (b)) is a relative concept, and it cannot be determined except by judicial appraisal of all available evidence bearing on the child's best interests. In the present case the findings that each child was a dependent child, under said section 600, subdivision (b), were supported by substantial evidence. . . .

Appellant further contends that the court erred in ordering removal of the children from the family home (dispositional orders). As to each child, the court made a finding and order that the child be removed from the family home pursuant to section 726, subdivisions (a) and (c), of the Welfare and Institutions Code, which provides in part: "In all cases wherein a minor is adjudged a ward or dependent child of the court, the court may limit the control to be exercised over such . . . dependent child by any parent . . . but no ward or dependent child shall be taken from the physical custody of a parent . . . unless upon the hearing the court finds one of the following facts: (a) That the parent . . . is incapable of providing or has failed or neglected to provide proper maintenance, training and education of the minor. . . . (c) That the welfare of the minor requires that his custody be taken from his parent."

Appellants argue that the court, in making its findings under the above cited provisions, failed to consider uncontradicted evidence that the family, when furnished with homemaking and other services to which they were entitled by law, were capable of maintaining a sanitary home. Although there was testimony to the effect that improvements in condition of the home occurred after home-making and other social services were provided, there was also testimony (by nurse) that the improvements did not last longer than a month, then there would be another complaint. Appellants also argue that the court in making its order was influenced "erroneously" by references in the probation report to services which the parents had received for many years. It is to be noted, however, that section 706 of the Welfare and Institutions Code provides that the juvenile court, with reference to the question of the proper disposition of the minor, "shall receive in evidence the social study of the minor made by the probation officer . . . and in any judgment and order of disposition, shall state the social study made by the probation officer has been read and considered by the court." As to the court's rejection of further proposed testimony as to availability of additional services, no offer of proof was made as to such testimony, and in view of the continuing inability of the parents to remedy conditions of the home when services had been provided, it appears that the court could properly reject further evidence of services which might be available. The evidence was sufficient to support the findings that the minors should be removed from the home and to support the orders removing them.

The orders are affirmed.

QUESTIONS

(1) Do you think there was evidence that the children's health was seriously endangered? Without such a showing, should the state be allowed to remove the children from parental custody? Even if the filth did not endanger the children's health? Is this constitutional?

(2) Do you believe it is a good thing for the evaluation of parental attitudes and behavior to depend on a judge's (or social worker's) personal values?

Most foster children come from poor families. The foster care system has long been criticized as being class biased.[34] Even though there are other plausible explanations for the high proportion of foster children from poor families, present day juvenile court standards allow a judge to impart his personal values into the decision-making process and therefore leave considerable scope for imposition of middle-class biases.

(3) If the parents are prepared to cooperate, should removal ever be allowed where the children can be protected in the home with reasonable services? Why shouldn't the state be required to provide services to protect children within the home rather than removing the children? Foster care is extremely expensive.[35] Wouldn't it be much cheaper simply to send in a housecleaning service to clean up the house at regular intervals? Consider the excerpt below on the policy dilemmas of home versus foster care placement. See also In re A.H., 842 A.2d 674 (D.C. 2004) (affirming removal of five children from parental custody for an unsanitary home environment).

(4) In *Deborah G.* note how vague, open-ended, and subjective the statutory standard of Welfare and Institutions Code §600(b) is. When is a home an "unfit place"? How is a judge to decide what is proper? Would section 600 be unconstitutional under the standards of Roe v. Conn?

Section 600 has since been amended to provide more specific standards for removal. It is now Welfare and Institutions Code §300, infra. Would *Deborah G.* have been decided differently under this new statutory standard?

California Welfare & Institutions Code §§300, 361 (West 2008)

§300. Children Subject to Jurisdiction . . .

Any child who comes within any of the following descriptions is within the jurisdiction of the juvenile court which may adjudge that person to be a dependent child of the court:

> (a) The child has suffered, or there is a substantial risk that the child will suffer, serious physical harm inflicted nonaccidentally upon the child by the child's parent or guardian. For the purposes of this subdivision, a court may find there is a substantial risk of serious future injury based on the manner in which a less serious injury was inflicted, a history of repeated inflictions of injuries on the child or the child's siblings, or a combination of these and other actions by the parent or guardian which indicate the child is at risk of serious physical harm. For purposes of this subdivision, "serious physical

---

[34] See Daan Braveman & Sarah Ramsey, When Welfare Ends: Removing Children from the Home for Poverty Alone, 70 Temple L. Rev. 447 (1997); Candra Bullock, Comment, Low-Income Parents Victimized by Child Protective Services, 11 Am. U. J. Gender Soc. Pol'y & L. 1023 (2003).

[35] The average monthly cost of foster care is $387 for children age 2, $404 for children age 9, and $462 for those age 16. U.S. Dept. of Health and Human Services, Foster Care, Basic Monthly Maintenance Rates for Children Ages 2, 9, and 16, Selected Years 1994-2000 (cited in Comm. on Ways & Means., 108th Cong., 2d Sess., Background Material and Data on Programs Within the Jurisdiction of the Committee on Ways and Means (2004 Green Book 11-29 (Comm. Print 2004))).

harm" does not include reasonable and age-appropriate spanking to the buttocks where there is no evidence of serious physical injury.

(b) The child has suffered, or there is a substantial risk that the child will suffer, serious physical harm or illness, as a result of the failure or inability of his or her parent or guardian to adequately supervise or protect the child, or the willful or negligent failure of the child's parent or guardian to adequately supervise or protect the child from the conduct of the custodian with whom the child has been left, or by the willful or negligent failure of the parent or guardian to provide the child with adequate food, clothing, shelter, or medical treatment, or by the inability of the parent or guardian to provide regular care for the child due to the parent's or guardian's mental illness, developmental disability, or substance abuse. No child shall be found to be a person described by this subdivision solely due to lack of an emergency shelter for the family. Whenever it is alleged that a child comes within the jurisdiction of the court on the basis of the parent's or guardian's willful failure to provide adequate medical treatment or specific decision to provide spiritual treatment through prayer, the court shall give deference to the parent's or guardian's medical treatment, nontreatment, or spiritual treatment through prayer alone in accordance with the tenets and practices of a recognized church or religious denomination, by an accredited practitioner thereof, and shall not assume jurisdiction unless necessary to protect the child from suffering serious physical harm or illness. . . .

(c) The child is suffering serious emotional damage, or is at substantial risk of suffering serious emotional damage, evidenced by severe anxiety, depression, withdrawal, or untoward aggressive behavior toward self or others, as a result of the conduct of the parent or guardian or who has no parent or guardian capable of providing appropriate care. No child shall be found to be a person described by this subdivision if the willful failure of the parent or guardian to provide adequate mental health treatment is based on a sincerely held religious belief and if a less intrusive judicial intervention is available.

(d) The child has been sexually abused, or there is a substantial risk that the child will be sexually abused, as defined in Section 11165.1 of the Penal Code, by his or her parent or guardian or a member of his or her household, or the parent or guardian has failed to adequately protect the child from sexual abuse when the parent or guardian knew or reasonably should have known that the child was in danger of sexual abuse.

(e) The child is under the age of five years and has suffered severe physical abuse by a parent, or by any person known by the parent, if the parent knew or reasonably should have known that the person was physically abusing the child. . . .

(f) The child's parent or guardian caused the death of another child through abuse or neglect.

(g) The child has been left without any provision for support; physical custody of the child has been voluntarily surrendered pursuant to Section 1255.7 of the Health and Safety Code [newborn abandonment provision] and the child has not been reclaimed within the 14-day period specified in subdivision (e) of that section; the child's parent has been incarcerated or institutionalized and cannot arrange for the care of the child; or a relative or other adult custodian with whom the child resides or has been left is unwilling or unable to provide care or support for the child, the whereabouts of the parent are unknown, and reasonable efforts to locate the parent have been unsuccessful. . . .

(i) The child has been subjected to an act or acts of cruelty by the parent or guardian or a member of his or her household, or the parent or guardian has failed to adequately protect the child from an act or acts of cruelty when the parent or guardian knew or reasonably should have known that the child was in danger of being subjected to an act or acts of cruelty.

(j) The child's sibling has been abused or neglected . . . and there is a substantial risk that the child will be abused or neglected . . . . The court shall consider the circumstances surrounding the abuse or neglect of the sibling, the age and gender of each child, the nature of the abuse or neglect of the sibling, the mental condition of the parent or guardian, and any other factors the court considers probative in determining whether there is a substantial risk to the minor.

It is the intent of the Legislature that nothing in this section disrupt the family unnecessarily or intrude inappropriately into family life, prohibit the use of reasonable methods of parental discipline, or prescribe a particular method of parenting. . . . The Legislature further declares that a physical disability, such as blindness or deafness, is no bar to the raising of happy and well-adjusted children and that a court's determination pursuant to this section shall center upon whether a parent's disability prevents him or her from exercising care and control. . . .

§361. Grounds for Removal of Child

. . . (c) A dependent child may not be taken from the physical custody of his or her parents or guardian or guardians with whom the child resides at the time the petition was initiated, unless the juvenile court finds clear and convincing evidence of any of the following circumstances . . . :

(1) There is or would be a substantial danger to the physical health, safety, protection, or physical or emotional well-being of the minor or if the minor were returned home, and there are no reasonable means by which the minor's physical health can be protected without removing the minor from the minor's parent's or guardian's physical custody. . . .

(2) The parent or guardian of the minor is unwilling to have physical custody of the minor . . . .

(3) The minor is suffering severe emotional damage, as indicated by extreme anxiety, depression, withdrawal, or untoward aggressive behavior towards himself or herself or others, and there are no reasonable means by which the minor's emotional health may be protected without removing the minor from the physical custody of his or her parent or guardian.

(4) The minor or a sibling of the minor has been sexually abused, or is deemed to be at substantial risk of being sexually abused, by a parent, guardian, or member of his or her household, or other person known to his or her parent . . . .

(5) The minor has been left without any provision for his or her support, or a parent who has been incarcerated or institutionalized cannot arrange for the care of the minor, or a relative or other adult custodian with whom the child has been left by the parent is unwilling or unable to provide care or support for the child and the whereabouts of the parent is unknown and reasonable efforts to locate him or her have been unsuccessful . . . .

(d) The court shall make a determination as to whether reasonable efforts were made to prevent or to eliminate the need for removal of the minor from his or her home or, if the minor is removed for one of the reasons stated in paragraph (5) of subdivision (c), whether it was reasonable under the circumstances not to make any of those efforts . . . .

Michael S. Wald et al., Protecting Abused and Neglected Children
9-12 (1988) (references omitted)

The Policy Dilemma

Policy preferences for or against the use of foster care to protect abused or neglected children rest ultimately on value judgments. Leaving such a child at home, even if the best treatment program is available, always entails some risk. Against that risk a legislature drafting a statute, or a judge in an individual case, must weigh any costs associated with placement. Critics of foster placement tend to focus on three factors: a preference for preserving biological ties or minimizing government intrusion in the family; concern over the financial cost of placement; and concern that foster care may actually be worse for children than living at home would be, even taking into account the risk of reabuse or continued neglect for children at home. . . .

The hard problem is how to evaluate the third concern. What is meant when it is said that foster care may be *worse* for children? It certainly does not mean that children are more likely to be abused or physically neglected in foster care: it appears clear that removal lowers the chances of reabuse or neglect. Although some children are injured by foster parents, the rate of reported abuse by foster parents is lower than that of the general population and far lower than the rate of reabuse by those who have once abused a child. Foster parents also are less likely to neglect children's physical needs. For the most part, they do not leave children unattended; they virtually always provide adequate food or shelter; they send foster children to school; their households tend to be stable and their care of the child regular. The attraction of foster care as a means of protecting children from further abuse or neglect is heightened by the relatively poor results of programs attempting to prevent reabuse by providing special services to parents. Several studies report reabuse in as many as 50 percent of all cases, even where the services to parents were intensive. Changing the behavior of neglectful parents may be even more difficult. Thus, if the major goal is to protect children from further *physical* harm, this is most likely achieved through foster care.

If one is concerned with *emotional* harm, however, the calculus may change. A number of researchers have reported problems in the emotional development of foster children. If placement with foster parents does have a significant negative impact on the emotional or social development of children, a policy designed only to avoid the risk of further abuse or physical neglect may be unwise. It is of interest, therefore, to review the research on the impact of foster care in order to identify particular possible harms to children. . . .

A. The Case Against Foster Care

Awareness of the psychological impact of placement had its roots in the theoretical work of child analysts, especially that of John Bowlby, who asserted that separation from parents might have a negative impact on children, even children from "bad" homes. Bowlby was instrumental in identifying the importance to every child of having an emotional bond with her parents (or other primary caretaker). He labelled this relationship "attachment." It now has been well demonstrated that separation from attachment figures is extremely painful to children and, more significantly, may have long-term negative consequences, at least if the child is not able to establish an adequate new relationship.

Attachment theory predicts several different ways in which removal from home may be harmful to a child. In addition to the pain of separation, which often is very profound, a lengthy separation from a primary caretaker may permanently impair the child's attachment to that person, even if the separation is not permanent. Perhaps the greatest threat, however, occurs when the child is separated permanently from an attachment figure and is either unable to develop a new relationship or is denied the opportunity to do so. Deprivation of a secure attachment relationship with a primary caretaker may impair a child's ability to form other adequate relationships, both as a child, and as an adult. Deprivation of any attachment relationship also has been associated with diminished school performance and increased delinquency, though "causal" connections are still undetermined. Moreover, the quality as well as the existence of an attachment relationship may be important to the child's development. Several studies have found that a child's intellectual curiosity, personality development, and ability to get along with peers (up to age five) are related to how *secure* an attachment she has to a primary caretaker.

It is well documented that foster care frequently neither lends itself to maintaining ties with the biological parent nor facilitates establishment of emotional bonds with new caretakers. Foster care *is supposed to be temporary* — a way station until the child's home can be made safe. Yet if foster parents are told their custody of the child is only temporary, it seems unlikely they will allow themselves to become emotionally involved with the child. Adults, like children, suffer pain upon separation. A foster mother who has cared for many children may protect herself against that pain by limiting emotional involvement. Foster fathers may be even less involved. Thus, the foster families may act in ways that impede the development of a secure attachment relationship between the child and foster parents. . . .

Foster care may put children at risk in other ways. Many commentators assert that children need continuity and stability of environment in order to have normal emotional development. There also is clinical evidence that some children view foster home placement as punishment for wrongdoing or as rejection by their parents. . . . As a result, children placed in foster homes may experience identity problems, conflicts of loyalty, and anxiety about their future.

There also are studies showing high rates of behavioral problems, school problems, and delinquency among foster children, though none of these studies compared rates of such behavior in non-foster children or presented evidence about the children's behavior prior to placement. In addition, several studies find that children in foster care retain strong emotional bonds to their biological parents, even after lengthy stays in care. Even if foster children do not show developmental or social deficits, their preferences require some consideration.

Despite methodological problems with the research, there is reason to be concerned with the social, emotional, and academic development of children after they are placed in foster care, given the theoretical literature and the consistency of the clinical findings. If foster placement leads to substantial deterioration in these areas, it may be better to forgo foster placement and run the risk of further physical abuse or neglect by the biological parents, at least in situations where abuse or neglect is not life-threatening or likely to lead to permanent impairment.

PROBLEMS

Barbara Cardell. Barbara Cardell, who was four months pregnant when she entered prison, recently gave birth to a child while serving a prison term for armed robbery. She is unmarried, has no immediate family, says that she does not know who the father is, and that she wishes to keep the child with her in prison. Should a juvenile court assume jurisdiction over the infant and place the child in foster care? If her expected prison term is six years, should her parental rights be terminated and the infant placed for adoption?

Eleanor Papillon. Eleanor Papillon first came to the attention of the County Department of Social Services in 2007, when the parole agent from the California Youth Authority called the department to refer Eleanor, then 16 years old, because she was pregnant and needed to apply for welfare benefits. Eleanor, a Youth Authority parolee, had been in and out of institutions. Her main problems had been as a runaway. She could not get along with her mother and stepfather (who were observant Catholics) and would not stay in any placement, such as the Catholic Convent at the Good Shepherd, where she had been placed most recently. She was not precisely estranged from her mother, but her mother considered her incorrigible and always inclined to choose the wrong boyfriends.

After Danny was born, in February 2008, Eleanor and Danny were placed together in a foster home where the foster mother could take care of Danny while Eleanor was attending school. Eleanor did attend high school, did very well, and eventually went into a medical assistant training program for which she had won a scholarship. Meanwhile she continued to live in the foster home with Danny. Eleanor had an excellent record on parole, and the record contained many references from the social worker to the effect that she was very mature for her age. She obtained a job as a medical technician, and both mother and child were placed in foster care.

About a year after placement, the receptionist in Eleanor's place of employment called the social worker to say that when she, the receptionist, had returned from work she found Eleanor chanting to herself in the office of one of the doctors. Eleanor was on her knees, and the receptionist could not get her to stop chanting or to get up. When the doctor returned, he also tried to get through to her but with no success. Finally Eleanor was sent to San Francisco General Hospital, where she was sedated. Doctors there discovered Eleanor was in a religious trance. After sedating her, they sent her home.

Eleanor's religion evidently had become an important part of her life. It was a fundamentalist religion, and Eleanor felt its strict and specific code had shown her "the way." This religion eschewed short skirts, cosmetics, and other things, including sex. At the time of the chanting incident when the caseworker spoke to Eleanor about her seizure, psychiatric help was suggested. Eleanor rejected this idea completely because she felt her religion had given her the answers that others might seek through psychiatry. She believed so firmly in her religion that she felt certain she did not need psychiatric help.

In the early part of 2008 Eleanor moved out of the foster home and made an arrangement for her mother to care for Danny while she was working. In September of 2008 a telephone report from the maternal grandmother was received in the agency to the effect that the maternal grandmother had noted Danny to be covered with bruise marks on his arms, stomach, and back. The caseworker immediately made a home visit, but Eleanor was not at home. The landlord stated that Eleanor and Danny usually left in the early morning and did not return until early evening.

That evening the caseworker and an officer from the Community Relations Department of the Police Department went to the home, and an examination of the child was made. It showed Danny to be covered with bruise marks and discoloration from his waist to his ankles. The only area not bruised was the genital area, although the insides of his thighs were also heavily discolored. Eleanor and Danny were taken to the Mount Zion emergency room, where a doctor examined Danny, and took x-rays. Eleanor was also seen by the attending psychiatrist, who recommended that an immediate psychiatric appointment be made by her for ongoing therapy.

Eleanor gave the following account of her beating of Danny. She was in her sister's home when one of the other children told her that Danny was under the bed with his panties off with a little girl, also aged four, who also had her panties off. Embarrassed and ashamed, Eleanor took Danny home immediately, but because she was so enraged she did not punish him then. However, that evening, the next day, and the day following she continually questioned him as to who had taken down his panties. At first Danny admitted that he had taken down his own pants, but with the continual emotional harassment left the question unanswered. It was three days later that she beat Danny for this incident, the reason being that he must be trained now not to let anyone pull his pants down until he was married. She stated that she did not do this out of anger, but out of love for him. She also stated that she knew sex play among children her son's age was normal, but she would not allow it anyway. She told the caseworker that she would do so again if this incident or a like one was repeated, although again she knew this to be a normal learning experience for all children.

The next day the maternal grandmother explained to the caseworker that her daughter had joined the Pentecostal religion two years earlier, telling her mother that she was doing this to save Danny because he was born in sin, and she was a sinner.

What would you have recommended regarding Danny and Eleanor? Should a neglect petition be filed? Should Danny be removed from Eleanor's custody?

Ritchie Adams. Four weeks ago Ritchie Adams, six years old, was brought to Juvenile Hall by a baby-sitter. The child's mother told the baby-sitter to take him there because she had no way of caring for him.

When contacted by the Probation Officer, Ritchie's mother said she was unable to care for Ritchie. She told of her own unhappy childhood with quarrelsome parents, a sharp sibling rivalry, with preference given to boys in the family, and an early and unhappy marriage following her pregnancy with Ritchie. She described Ritchie as subject to temper tantrums beyond her control, hateful like his father, and hyperactive.

Ritchie's mother is in her late twenties. She talked of her wish to marry again and was very much involved with a new male friend. She reported that she had had no recent contact with Mr. Adams and did not know where he was living. Mrs. Adams explained that Ritchie's sister, Sheryl Adams, birthdate January 18, 2004, lived with her. An older brother, Dickie, born June 30, 2002, was in a mental hygiene foster home, having been placed through the Community Service Division of the Department of Social Welfare with a family in Fresno County.

Ritchie is large for his age, with light brown, somewhat wavy hair, fair complexion, and a moderately prominent nose. He is rough and somewhat aggressive in manner. He responds quickly to the attention and interest shown by cottage staff. However, the staff at Juvenile Hall, where Ritchie has been kept since he was brought in by the baby-sitter, vary somewhat in the way they describe him. One staff member described him as having temper tantrums and a short attention span, and as being difficult at school, impulsive, and quite a handful. When first at the detention hall, he threw food around and was generally difficult, although he was responsive to attention. Another staff member saw him as determined but not unusually different from other children.

The psychiatrist at the Probation Department was asked to see Ritchie. Ritchie was seen once and the following report was rendered by Ralph Weiner, M.D., dated nearly seven months after Ritchie had first arrived at the Hall. The report stated:

> He is certainly disturbed. He is belligerent, a sourpuss and does not evoke a great deal of affection from others; plays poorly with other children; is selfish, demanding and easily frustrated. The ideal setting for him would be one in which he would receive individual attention plus some kind of small group activity, supervised by someone trained in dealing with emotionally disturbed youngsters.

The usual school and the usual foster home would not be workable. He requires a treatment setting. He does not appear retarded but an intelligence test score will be forthcoming.

Mrs. Adams has not initiated any contact with Ritchie during his past month at Juvenile Hall and has seen him only when she came in for an interview. Mrs. Adams is willing and indeed appears eager to have Ritchie placed in foster care. She says she wants what is best for Ritchie.

Should Ritchie be returned to his mother or accepted into care? Does it matter whether placement is by court order, under a neglect statute, or by voluntary placement? Which, if any, would you recommend? What alternatives are there to placement? If your recommendation is for placement, what type of placement would you recommend?

Robert Doe.   Jeff and Wanda Doe were arrested on a public street for being under the influence of crack cocaine. Their 17-month-old son, Robert, was with them. Wanda was detained at the Elmwood Rehabilitation Center, and Jeff was released on his own recognizance. Robert was taken into temporary protective custody.

Robert was born June 4, 2007 with a toxicology screen positive for cocaine. At that time his father (Jeff) was incarcerated in the Santa Clara County Jail. Robert was made a dependent of the court on the basis of a petition filed June 15, 2007, which stated that no parent or guardian was exercising proper care and control. Consequently, he was ordered into relative/foster home placement with his maternal grandparents. Robert had been returned to his parents about six months before the present incident.

Both parents gave accounts of the circumstances leading up to their arrest. According to Wanda, she had asked Jeff to buy some "rock." She "took a hit," then said to herself, "What are you doing?" She said that they were walking through the parking lot with Robert when the police arrested them. She also said she had been depressed about their current financial situation, which had resulted in Jeff leaving home so she could regain her welfare benefits, and she wanted to "sneak a hit." Wanda appeared remorseful after her arrest and said she knew she had "blown it."

Prior to this arrest it had appeared that Wanda was making progress in dealing with her drug problem. According to a counselor in the Santa Clara County Outpatient Drug Free Program, Wanda had been admitted into their program in July 2008, and had since attended nine sessions and missed only two. She was tested for drugs on 10 occasions between July 18 and October 2, 2008, and all test results were negative. She was attending NA/AA meetings. Wanda was very serious about regaining custody of Robert and stated that she had not been involved in drugs since July 2007. Although Wanda had made excellent progress, the Drug Free Program continued to provide services as a support system.

Jeff claimed that he had not used crack cocaine immediately prior to the arrest but admitted that Wanda had. He is currently employed full-time. Prior to this incident he completed an alcohol residential rehabilitation program and had undergone random drug testing on a monthly basis for the past six months. The results of all these tests were negative.

Robert was placed in the home of his maternal grandparents after this incident. He is an energetic, outgoing 17-month-old who appears to have adjusted well to the reunion with his grandparents.

Both parents have expressed interest in reuniting with Robert. How should a court deal with this situation?

Mona Stay. The family consists of a transracial couple, Mona Stay, 23, and her common law husband Frank Brown, aged 26. There are three children: Frank, three and a half; Sylvia, 18 months; and Wilma, 7 months. The couple has been together over five years. Although they quarrel and separate periodically, they seem very mutually dependent and likely to remain a couple.

Their original referral was from a nurse who had become aware of the eldest child's, Frank's, condition. He was difficult to discipline, was eating dirt and paint chips, and seemed hyperactive. Although over three, he was not speaking. His father reacted to him with impatience. He was often slapped and hardly ever spoken to with fondness. The caseworker persuaded Mona to cooperate in taking young Frank in for a test for lead poisoning and for a full developmental evaluation. This child had had several bouts with impetigo, had been bitten through the eyelid by a stray dog, and had a series of ear infections resulting in a slight hearing loss. Although physically normal, developmentally he appeared already nearly a year retarded.

Often this child was found outside the house alone when the caseworker came to see the family. On one occasion he was seen hanging from a broken fire escape on the second floor. The worker was unable to rouse his mother or to enter the house until she got help from the nearby landlord, after which she ran upstairs and rescued the child. Only then did the sleeping Mona awaken.

With much effort expended on his behalf, this child has been attending a therapeutic nursery. His speech has already developed after four or five months, and his hyperactivity has calmed. He comes through as a lovable little boy.

Sylvia is surprisingly pale for a transracial child and indeed suffers from severe anemia. This child has had recurrent eye infections and a bout with spinal meningitis at three months, which, fortunately, seems to have left no effects. Much effort has gone into working with Mona concerning Sylvia's need for proper diet and iron supplement. After a year of contact this is still a problem.

The baby was born after the family had become known to the agency. Despite the agency's urging, Mona refused to go for prenatal care until she was in her second trimester, but she did maintain a fairly good diet, helped by small "loans" from the agency when her money for food ran out. When Wilma was born, she was left to lie most of the time in her bassinet, receiving very little attention from either parent. At four months of age, Wilma weighed only five pounds and was tentatively diagnosed as exhibiting "failure to thrive" by the hospital. Thereafter the mother avoided going to the clinic, and the caseworker spent much effort concerning the feeding and sheer survival of Wilma. The baby is now slowly gaining weight but is still limp and inactive.

In addition to an active caseworker, a homemaker was assigned to this family for months. Much more was involved than trying to help Mona learn to organize her day: she had almost no motivation to get started. Rather than learning how to manage, she tried to manipulate the homemaker into doing her housework for her. However, with time and patience, Mona has been persuaded to go with the caseworker on shopping trips, is learning how to buy groceries to best advantage, and from time to time manages to get the laundry into and out of the laundromat. So far as her plans for herself. Mona has talked of seeking training as a beauty operator, but has never followed through on this or on other positive plans.

The family's sole support is public assistance. Frank Brown, the father, was on drugs earlier in their relationship, but managed to get off them. Now, however, he drinks heavily, and although he manages to work, he never contributes to the household.

Mona, apparently, was herself a neglected child and was removed from her parents in infancy. Placed with an adoptive family, there was constant friction during her growing up, and she ran away from home several times. During her teens, she was placed in an institution for incorrigible girls. Later she spent a period in a mental hospital, during which she was withdrawn from heroin addiction. It is a commentary on her life that she regards this period in the adolescent ward as one of her happiest ever. Her adoptive mother is now dead, and her father wants nothing more to do with her, so she was more or less living on the streets when she met with Frank and set up their present establishment.

Mona and Frank, despite his obvious exploitativeness, seem to love each other and their children, and to want to keep the family together. They are able to relate to those who try to help them, so at least one is not operating constantly against hostile resistance. Mona is an intelligent woman and now shows adequate ability to handle the children. She can be an excellent cook — when there is food. Yet this remains a disorganized household. Bills are never paid, clothes are thrown around, the children never sleep on clean sheets, and trash is piled around the house so that flies and maggots abound. Mona still leaves the youngsters alone for brief periods. There is no heat in the house, and the family will soon have to move, with neither any idea where to go nor funds for rent deposits and the like.

What new action, if any, should the agency take with regard to the family? Is removal of the children appropriate? What specific facts should be determinative when deciding whether or not to remove?

2. The State as Parent: The Foster Care System

a. Introduction

Robert H. Mnookin, Foster Care — In Whose Best Interest?
43 Harv. Educ. Rev. 599 (1973) (footnotes omitted)

Most American parents raise their children free of intrusive legal constraints or major governmental intervention. Although compulsory education and child labor laws indicate there are some conspicuous legal limitations on parents, it is the family, not the state, which has primary responsibility for child rearing. Despite this predominant pattern, there are about [496,000 children among the nation's

72 million][36] for whom the state has assumed primary responsibility. These children live in state sponsored foster care, a term [used here] to include foster family homes, group homes, and child welfare institutions. For a number of the children in foster care, the state has assumed responsibility because no one else is available. Some children are orphans; others have been voluntarily given up by a family no longer willing or able to care for them. A significant number of children, however, are placed in foster care because the state has intervened and coercively removed the child from parental custody.

. . . When parents oppose foster care placement, a court can nevertheless order removal after a judicial proceeding if the state can demonstrate parental abuse or neglect. But if parents consent to foster care placement, no judicial action is necessary. Many foster care placements, perhaps one-half or more, are arranged by state social welfare departments without any court involvement.

A substantial degree of state coercion may be involved in many so-called voluntary placements, making the distinction between voluntary and coercive placement illusory. Many social welfare departments routinely ask parents to agree to give up their children before initiating neglect proceedings in court. Some parents who would have been willing to keep their children may consent to placement to avoid a court proceeding against them. If one were to use the legal standards of voluntariness and informed consent applied in the criminal law to confessions and to the waiver of important legal rights, many cases of relinquishment after state intervention might not be considered voluntary. On the other hand, not all court-ordered foster care placements involve coercion of the parents. Some take place with their full concurrence.

How the State Removes Children from Their Parents

Source of the Power

The power of government to protect children by removing them from parental custody has roots deep in American history. And in colonial times just as today, the children of the poor were the most affected. Seventeenth century laws of Massachusetts, Connecticut, and Virginia, for example, specifically authorized magistrates to "bind out" or indenture children *of the poor* over parental objections. . . .

By the early nineteenth century, the parens patriae power of the state, i.e., the sovereign's ultimate responsibility to guard the interests of children and others who lacked legal capacity, was thought sufficient to empower courts to remove a child from parental custody. Significantly, the reinforcement of public morality, and not simply the protection of children from cruelty, was seen as sufficient justification for the exercise of this power. Joseph Story, the renowned Massachusetts legal scholar who sat on the Supreme Court from 1811 to 1845, stated in his treatise on equity courts:

---

[36] Data are current as of 2007. U.S. Children's Bureau, Administration for Children, Youth and Families, Trends in Foster Care and Adoption-FY 2002-FY 2007, available at *http://www.acf.hhs. gov/programs/cb/stats_research/afcars/trends.htm.*

Although, in general, parents are intrusted with the custody of the persons, and the education of their children, yet this is done upon the natural presumption, that the children will be properly taken care of, and will be brought up with a due education in literature, and morals, and religion; and that they will be treated with kindness and affection. But, whenever this presumption is removed; whenever (for example,) it is found, that a father is guilty of gross ill-treatment or cruelty towards his infant children; or that he is in constant habits of drunkenness and blasphemy, or low and gross debauchery, or that he professes atheistical or irreligious principles; or that his domestic associations are such as tend to the corruption and contamination of his children; or that he otherwise acts in a manner injurious to the morals and interests of his children; in every such case, the Court of Chancery will interfere, and deprive him of the custody of his children, and appoint a suitable person to act as guardian, and to take care of them, and to superintend their education. [Story, 2 Equity Jurisprudence Sec. 1341 (1857)].

The Process of Removal

[Compared to practices of] 100 years ago, far more complex administrative processes are involved. [A century ago] social workers and probation departments did not exist. Today a case usually reaches court after weaving through a complicated welfare bureaucracy where numerous officials including social workers, probation officers, and court personnel, may have had contact with the family.

... The process is usually initiated by a report from a social worker or the police, or less frequently from a neighbor, medical professional, or school staff member. Although practices vary, a member of a special unit of the social welfare or probation department is usually responsible for an initial investigation of the report. Customarily this investigation [involves] a visit to the home and a telephone conversation with the person who turned in the report. The investigator, sometimes together with a supervisor, then must decide whether to close the case, to suggest that the welfare agency informally (and non-coercively) provide services or supervision, or to file a petition in court.

Filing a petition initiates a judicial inquiry that usually has two stages. First, the court must determine whether it has jurisdiction over the child. This involves deciding on the basis of exceedingly broad and ill-defined statutory provisions whether the parents have failed to live up to acceptable social standards for child rearing. If it is determined that they have, then such jurisdiction empowers the court to intervene into the family. . . . The second stage involves a dispositional hearing, where the judge decides the manner of intervention. Removal from the home is by no means mandatory. The court can instead require supervision within the child's own home, psychological counseling for the parents and/or the child, or periodic home visits by a social worker, probation officer, or homemaker. . . .

After a court decides to remove a child from home, a public agency, often the social welfare or probation department, is assigned responsibility for placing the child. [Some children live in foster care under the auspices of voluntary agencies, while others are under the supervision of state social service agencies. Of state-supervised children, some live in foster family homes, group homes, or child welfare institutions.]

Foster family homes are usually licensed by the state, with regulations regarding aspects such as the size of the home, number of children, and age of foster parents. Under a contract, foster parents are paid a monthly fee for each child in their care. . . . Although foster parents are responsible for the day-to-day care of the children, the contract between the agency and the foster parents usually requires the foster parents to acknowledge that "the legal responsibility for the foster child remains with the Agency," and to "accept and comply with any plans the Agency makes for the child," including "the right to determine when and how the child leaves" the foster home.

[The author identifies three principles that should govern the operation of the foster care system:

(1) Removal should be a last resort to be used only when the child cannot be protected within the home;

(2) The decision to require foster care placement should be based on legal standards that can be applied in a consistent and evenhanded way, and not be profoundly influenced by the values of the particular deciding judge; and

(3) If removal is necessary, the state should actively seek, when possible, to help the child's parents overcome the problems that led to removal so that the child can be returned home as soon as possible. If the child cannot be returned home in a reasonable time despite efforts by the state, the state should find a stable alternative arrangement, such as adoption, for the child. A child should not be left in foster care for an indefinite period of time.

The above article was influential in the passage of federal legislation (discussed infra) that addresses the problem of "foster care drift" by facilitating the movement of children more promptly from foster care to either adoptive placements or reunification with their families.]

Sandra Bass et al., Children, Families and Foster Care: Analysis and Recommendations

The Future of Children
vol. 14, no. 1 (Winter 2004), pp. 6-8

The Current State of Foster Care

Foster care is intended to serve as a temporary haven for abused and neglected children who cannot safely remain with their families. However for some children, the journey through foster care is characterized by further trauma and abuse; and even in the best situations, foster care is inherently fraught with uncertainty, instability, and impermanence. The number of children and families who require foster care services has grown substantially over the past two decades, and these families are typically contending with a multitude of complex and interrelated life challenges such as mental illness, unemployment, substance abuse, and domestic violence. . . .

Children enter foster care for a number of reasons. For some children, the journey begins at birth, when it is clear that a mother cannot care for her newborn infant. Other children come to the attention of child welfare when a teacher, a social worker, a police officer, or a neighbor reports suspected child maltreatment to child protective services. Some of these children may have experienced physical or sexual abuse at the hands of a loved and trusted adult. More often, parents battling poverty, substance addiction, or mental illness woefully neglect their children's needs.

In 2001, approximately 3 million referrals were made to child protective services, and more than 900,000 children were found to be victims of maltreatment. When child maltreatment is unsubstantiated, caseworkers and courts must decide whether the child can safely remain home if the family is provided with in-home services, or whether the child should be placed into state care. In 2001, 290,000 children entered the foster care system.

The term *foster care* commonly refers to all out-of-home placements for children who cannot remain with their birth parents. Children may be placed with non-relative foster families, with relatives, in a therapeutic or treatment foster care home, or in some form of congregate care, such as an institution or group home. Nearly half of all children in foster care live with non-relative foster families, and about one-quarter reside with relatives. More than 800,000 children spent some time in the foster care system in 2001, with approximately 540,000 children in foster care at any one time.

After children are removed from their homes and placed in foster care, caseworkers develop a permanency plan based on an assessment of the child's individual needs and family circumstances. The plan is then reviewed by the court. For most children, the primary permanency plan is reunification with their birth parents. According to federal law [discussed infra p. 366], states must make "reasonable efforts" to provide birth parents with the services and supports they need to regain custody of their children. However, there are exceptions to this requirement. States are not required to pursue reunification under certain circumstances. In these circumstances, alternative permanency options such as adoption or legal guardianship are the goal for these children.

Under current law, if children are in foster care for 15 out of the previous 22 months, states are to recommend that parental rights be terminated and the child be made available for adoption. In 2001, there were 126,000 children who were no longer legally connected to their parents awaiting adoption. However, the child welfare agency can waive the termination requirement if birth parents are making progress in their case plans and workers believe they can *reunify* with their children soon, or if workers believe that another placement that does not require termination of parental rights, such as legal guardianship, is in the child's best interests.

The average length of stay for children in foster care is approximately 33 months, but some children stay a much shorter time and some much longer. According to 2001 data from the Adoption and Foster Care Analysis and Reporting System (AFCARS), approximately 38% of children who exited foster care in 2001 had spent 11 months or less in the system. At the other end of the spectrum, however, approximately 32% of children had been in care for 3 years or longer. The longer a child remains in care, the greater the likelihood that he or she will experience multiple placements. On average, approximately 85% of children who are in foster care for less than 1 year experience 2 or fewer placements, but placement instability increases with each year a child spends in the system.

More than half (57%) of the children in foster care exit through reunification with their birth parents, although in recent years, reunification rates have declined.

Children who entered the system in 1997 had a 13% slower rate to reunification than those who entered in 1990. During this same period, the number of children who were adopted from foster care increased substantially. [M]ost states have more than doubled the number of adoptions from foster care over the last seven years and some states reported tripling the number. Additionally, many states have increased the number of children achieving permanence by offering caregivers the option of becoming legal guardians.

The Child Welfare System

When entering foster care, or the "child welfare system," a child does not enter a single system, but rather multiple systems that intersect and interact to create a safety net for children who cannot remain with their birth parents. State and local child welfare agencies, courts, private service providers, and public agencies that administer other government programs (such as public assistance or welfare, mental health counseling, substance abuse treatment), and Medicaid all play critical roles in providing supports and services to children and families involved in foster care. Indeed, families often find themselves juggling the requirements and paperwork of multiple systems.

Child welfare agencies are central to the system, but their policies and practices vary significantly from state to state. For example, each state determines its own definition of maltreatment, its own laws based on federal regulations, and its own level of investment in child welfare services. The organization of child welfare agencies also varies significantly across states. In some states the child welfare system is administered at the state level, whereas in others it is administered at the county level.

In every state, the courts also play a significant role in child welfare cases, from the initial decision to remove a child to the development of a permanency plan to the decision to return a child home or terminate parental rights and make the child available for adoption. . . .

Many jurisdictions rely on volunteer court appointed special advocates (CASAs) to ensure that children in foster care have a voice in the legal decision-making process. CASAs are assigned to one child (or a sibling group) for an extended period of time and are trained to serve as mentors and advocates. . . . Currently, more than 900 CASA programs operate in 45 states, and more than 250,000 children have been assigned CASAs. . . .

The emergence and convergence of several significant social problems in the mid-1980s had a tumultuous effect on the child welfare system. The crack epidemic, homelessness, the rapidly growing incarceration rate, and HIV/AIDS proved devastating for poor families and communities. In turn, families contending with multiple problems were unable to appropriately care for their children, and the number of children entering foster care rose. In 1980 approximately 300,000 children were in foster care; by 1998 that number had climbed to an unprecedented 568,000.

Today, children and families who enter the foster care system continue to wrestle with these complex and interrelated problems. Additionally, the population of children in the system has shifted. Children of color compose the majority of children in foster care, with disproportionate representation of African-American and American-Indian children. The changes in the severity of the needs of children in the system and in the diversity of populations that are represented, tax the system to provide appropriate services, delivered by trained workers, and in foster care homes that are tailored to children's individual needs. . . .

b. Standards to Guide the Operation of a Foster Care System After Removal

This section concerns what happens and should happen to a child who is in foster care, and the respective rights and responsibilities of the natural parents, foster parents, and state officials. Two ways a minor can leave foster care are (1) to be returned to his natural parents; or (2) to be adopted, which requires either the consent of the natural parents or termination of parental rights. In reading the cases that follow, keep in mind the following questions:

(1) Once a juvenile court assumes responsibility for a neglected or dependent child, when should its jurisdiction over the child end and the child be returned home? (a) When the original circumstances that gave rise to the intervention in the first place no longer exist? (b) When there are no longer any statutory grounds, old or new, for establishing jurisdiction? or (c) When a court thinks it is in the best interest of the child for jurisdiction to terminate?

(2) Under what circumstances should parental rights be terminated to free a foster child for adoption? Statutes traditionally allowed termination for "abandonment" of children by their biological parents or for egregious acts of child maltreatment. What additional circumstances should give rise to termination of parental rights?

Smith v. Organization of Foster Families for Equality and Reform
431 U.S. 816 (1977)

Mr. Justice BRENNAN delivered the opinion of the Court.

Appellees, individual foster parents[1] and an organization of foster parents, brought this civil rights class action pursuant to 42 U.S.C. §1983 . . . on their

---

[1] Appellee Madeleine Smith is the foster parent with whom Eric and Danielle Gandy have been placed since 1970. The Gandy children, who are now 12 and 9 years old respectively, were voluntarily placed in foster care by their natural mother in 1968, and have had no contact with her at least since being placed with Mrs. Smith. The foster care agency has sought to remove the children from Mrs. Smith's care because her arthritis, in the agency's judgment, makes it difficult for her to continue to provide adequate care. . . .

Appellees Ralph and Christiane Goldberg were the foster parents of Rafael Serrano, now 14. His parents placed him in foster care voluntarily in 1969 after an abuse complaint was filed against them. [The Goldbergs eventually separated, placing Rafael in residential care.]

Appellees Walter and Dorothy Lhotan were foster parents of the four Wallace sisters, who were voluntarily placed in foster care by their mother in 1970. The two older girls were placed with the Lhotans in that year, their two younger sisters in 1972. In June 1974, the Lhotans were informed that the agency had decided to return the two younger girls to their mother and transfer the two older girls to another foster home. The agency apparently felt that the Lhotans were too emotionally involved with the girls and were damaging the agency's efforts to prepare them to return them to their mother. The state courts have ordered that all the Wallace children be returned to their mother. [The children eventually were returned to their mother.]

own behalf and on behalf of children for whom they have provided homes for a year or more. They sought declaratory and injunctive relief . . . alleging that the procedures governing the removal of foster children from foster homes provided in New York Social Services Law §§383(2) and 400, and in Title 18, New York Codes Rules and Regulations §450.14 violated the Due Process and Equal Protection Clauses of the Fourteenth Amendment. . . . A group of natural mothers of children in foster care[5] were granted leave to intervene on behalf of themselves and others similarly situated.

[The district court determined that the preremoval procedures unconstitutionally deprived the foster child of a hearing before being either transferred to another foster home or returned to the natural parents, 418 F. Supp. 277 (1976).]

I . . .

The expressed central policy of the New York system is that "it is generally desirable for the child to remain with or be returned to the natural parent because the child's need for a normal family life will usually best be met in the natural home and . . . parents are entitled to bring up their own children unless the best interests of the child would be thereby endangered," Soc. Serv. L. §384-b(1)(a)(ii). But the State has opted for foster care as one response to those situations where the natural parents are unable to provide the "positive, nurturing family relationships" and "normal family life in a permanent home" that "offer the best opportunity for children to develop and thrive." Id., §384-b(1)(b), (1)(a)(i).

Foster care has been defined as "[a] child welfare service which provides substitute family care for a planned period for a child when his own family cannot care for him for a temporary or extended period and when adoption is neither desirable nor possible." Child Welfare League of America, Standards for Foster Family Care, 5 (1959). Thus, the distinctive features of foster care are first, "that it is care in a *family*, it is noninstitutional substitute care," and second, "that it is for a *planned* period — either temporary or extended. This is unlike adoptive placement, which implies a *permanent* substitution of one home for another." [Alfred Kadushin, Child Welfare Services 355 (1967).]

Under the New York scheme children may be placed in foster care either by voluntary placement or by court order. Most foster care placements are voluntary. They occur when physical or mental illness, economic problems, or other family crises make it impossible for natural parents, particularly single parents, to provide a stable home life for their children for some limited period. Resort to such placements is almost compelled when it is not possible in such circumstance to place the child with a relative or friend, or to pay for the services of a homemaker or boarding school.

---

[5] Intervenor Naomi Rodriguez, who is blind, placed her newborn son Edwin in foster care in 1973 because of marital difficulties. When Mrs. Rodriguez separated from her husband three months later, she sought return of her child. Her efforts over the next nine months to obtain return of the child were resisted by the agency, apparently because it felt her handicap prevented her from providing adequate care. [She] finally prevailed, three years after she first sought return of the child. . . .

Voluntary placement requires the signing of a written agreement by the natural parent or guardian, transferring the care and custody of the child to an authorized child welfare agency. Although by statute the terms of such agreements are open to negotiation, it is contended that agencies require execution of standardized forms. . . .

The agency may maintain the child in an institutional setting, but more commonly acts under its authority to "place out and board out" children in foster homes. Foster parents, who are licensed by the State or an authorized foster care agency, provide care under a contractual arrangement with the agency, and are compensated for their services. The typical contract expressly reserves the right of the agency to remove the child on request. Conversely, the foster parent may cancel the agreement at will.

The New York system divides parental functions among agency, foster parents and natural parents, and the definitions of the respective roles are often complex and often unclear. The law transfers "care and custody" to the agency, Soc. Serv. L. §384-a, but day-to-day supervision of the child and his activities, and most of the functions ordinarily associated with legal custody, are the responsibility of the foster parent. Nevertheless, agency supervision of the performance of the foster parents takes forms indicating that the foster parent does not have the full authority of a legal custodian.[18] Moreover, the natural parent's placement of the child with the agency does not surrender legal guardianship; the parent retains authority to act with respect to the child in certain circumstances.[20] The natural parent has not only the right but the obligation to visit the foster child and plan for his future; failure of a parent with capacity to fulfill the obligation for more than a year can result in a court order terminating the parent's rights on the ground of neglect.

Children may also enter foster care by court order. . . . The consequences of foster care placement by court order do not differ substantially from those for children voluntarily placed, except that the parent is not entitled to return of the child on demand . . . ; termination of foster care must then be consented to by the court.

The provisions of the scheme specifically at issue in this case come into play when the agency having legal custodianship determines to remove the foster child from the foster home, either because it has determined that it would be in the child's best interests to transfer him to some other foster home, or to return the

---

[18] "The agency sets limits and advances directives as to how the foster parents are to behave toward the child — a situation not normally encountered by natural parents. The shared control and responsibility for the child is clearly set forth in the instruction pamphlets issued to foster parents." Kadushin, supra, at 394. Agencies frequently prohibit corporal punishment; require that children over a certain age be given an allowance; forbid changes in the child's sleeping arrangements or vacations out-of-State without agency approval; require the foster parent to discuss the child's behavioral problems with the agency. Id., at 394-395. Furthermore, since the cost of supporting the child is borne by the agency, the responsibility, as well as the authority, of the foster parent is shared with the agency. Ibid.

[20] "[A]lthough the agency usually obtains legal custody in foster family care, the child still legally 'belongs' to the parent and the parent retains guardianship. This means that, for some crucial aspects of the child's life, the agency has no authority to act. Only the parent can consent to surgery for the child, or consent to his marriage, or permit his enlistment in the armed forces, or represent him at law." Kadushin, supra, at 355. But see Soc. Serv. L. §383-b.

child to his natural parents in accordance with the statute or placement agreement. Most children are removed in order to be transferred to another foster home.[23] The procedures by which foster parents may challenge a removal made for that purpose differ somewhat from those where the removal is made to return the child to his natural parent.

Soc. Serv. L. §383(2) provides that the "authorized agency placing out or boarding [a foster] child . . . may in its discretion remove such child from the home where placed or boarded." Administrative regulations implement this provision. The agency is required, except in emergencies, to notify the foster parents in writing 10 days in advance of any removal. The notice advises the foster parents that if they object to the child's removal they may request a "conference" with the social services department. The department schedules requested conferences within 10 days of the receipt of the request. The foster parent may appear with counsel at the conference, where he will "be advised of the reasons [for the removal of the child], and be afforded an opportunity to submit reasons why the child should not be removed." 18 N.Y.C.R.R. §450.10(a). The official must render a decision in writing within five days after the close of the conference, and send notice of his decision to the foster parents and the agency. The proposed removal is stayed pending the outcome of the conference.

If the child is removed after the conference, the foster parent may appeal to the department of social services for a "[full adversary administrative hearing which is subject to judicial review]; however, the removal is not automatically stayed pending the hearing and judicial review.

This statutory and regulatory scheme applies statewide.[28] In addition, regulations . . . provide even greater procedural safeguards [in the form of a *preremoval* trial, upon request of the foster parents, if a child is being transferred to another foster home]. One further preremoval procedural safeguard is available. [Soc. Serv. Law §392] provides a mechanism whereby a foster parent may obtain preremoval judicial review of any agency's decision to remove a child who has been in foster care for 18 months or more.

Foster care of children is a sensitive and emotion-laden subject. . . . The New York regulatory scheme is no exception. . . .

From the standpoint of natural parents, such as the appellant intervenors here, foster care has been condemned as a class-based intrusion into the family life of the

---

[23] The record shows that in 1973-1974 approximately eighty percent of the children removed from foster homes in New York State after living in the foster home for one year or more were transferred to another foster placement. Thirteen percent were returned to the biological parents, and seven percent were adopted. Tr. of Oral Arg., at 34; Brief for Appellees, at 20.

[28] There is some dispute whether the procedures set out in 18N.Y.C.R.R. §450.10 and Soc. Serv. L. §400 apply in the case of a foster child being removed from his foster home to be returned to his natural parents. Application of these procedures to children who have been placed voluntarily, for example, arguably conflicts with the requirements of Soc. Serv. L. §384a(2)(a) that children in that situation be returned to the natural parent as provided in the placement agreement or within 20 days of demand. . . .

Nevertheless, nothing in either the statute or the regulations limits the availability of these procedures to transfers within the foster-care system. Each refers to the decision to *remove* a child from the foster family home, and thus on its face each would seem to cover removal for the purpose of returning the child to its parents. . . .

poor. See, e.g., Jenkins, Child Welfare as a Class System, in Children and Decent People, 3 (Schorr ed. 1974). It is certainly true that the poor resort to foster care more often than other citizens. . . .

The extent to which supposedly "voluntary" placements are in fact voluntary has been questioned on other grounds as well. For example, it has been said that many "voluntary" placements are in fact coerced by threat of neglect proceedings and are not in fact voluntary in the sense of the product of an informed consent. Mnookin, Foster Care — In Whose Best Interest? 43 Harv. Educ. Rev. 599, 601 (1973). Studies also suggest that social workers of middle-class backgrounds, perhaps unconsciously, incline to favor continued placement in foster care with a generally higher-status family rather than return the child to his natural family, thus reflecting a bias that treats the natural parents' poverty and life-style as prejudicial to the best interests of the child. This accounts,[35] it has been said, for the hostility of agencies to the efforts of natural parents to obtain the return of their children.

Appellee foster parents as well as natural parents . . . note that children often stay in "temporary" foster care for much longer than contemplated by the theory of the system. . . . The District Court found as a fact that the median time spent in foster care in New York was over four years. Indeed, many children apparently remain in this "limbo" indefinitely. Mnookin, Child-Custody Adjudication: Judicial Functions in the Face of Indeterminacy, 39(3) Law and Contemp. Probs. 226, 273 (1975). The District Court also found that the longer a child remains in foster care, the more likely it is that he will never leave. . . . It is not surprising then that many children, particularly those that enter foster care at a very early age and have little or no contact with their natural parents during extended stays in foster care, often develop deep emotional ties with their foster parents.[40]

Yet such ties do not seem to be regarded as obstacles to transfer of the child from one foster placement to another. The record in this case indicates that nearly 60% of the children in foster care in New York City have experienced more than one placement, and about 28% have experienced three or more. [E]ven when it is clear that a foster child will not be returned to his natural parents, it is rare that he achieves a stable home life through final termination of parental ties and adoption into a new permanent family.

---

[35] Other factors alleged to bias agencies in favor of retention in foster care are the lack of sufficient staff to provide social work services needed by the natural parent to resolve their problems and prepare for return of the child; policies of many agencies to discourage involvement of the natural parent in the care of the child while in foster care; and systems of foster care funding that encourage agencies to keep the child in foster care. Wald, [State Intervention on Behalf of 'Neglected' Children], 28 Stan. L. Rev. 623, 677-679 (1976).

[40] The development of such ties points up an intrinsic ambiguity of foster care that is central to this case. The warmer and more home-like environment of foster care is intended to be its main advantage over institutional care, yet because in theory foster care is intended to be only temporary, foster parents are urged not to become too attached to the children in their care. Mnookin, supra, 43 Harv. Educ. Rev., at 613. Indeed, the New York courts have upheld removal from a foster home for the very reason that the foster parents had become too emotionally involved with the child. In re Jewish Child Care Assn. (Sanders), 5 N.Y.2d 222 (1959). See also the case of the Lhotans, named appellees in this case, supra, n.l. . . .

[W]e present this summary in the view that some understanding of those criticisms is necessary for a full appreciation of the complex and controversial system with which this lawsuit is concerned. But [o]ur task is only to determine whether the District Court correctly held that the present procedures preceding the removal from a foster home of children resident there a year or more are constitutionally inadequate. . . .

II

Our first inquiry is whether appellees have asserted interests within the Fourteenth Amendment's protection of "liberty." [A]ppellees' basic contention is that when a child has lived in a foster home for a year or more, a psychological tie is created between the child and the foster parents which constitutes the foster family the true "psychological family" of the child. That family, they argue, has a "liberty interest" in its survival as a family protected by the Fourteenth Amendment. . . . Upon this premise they conclude that the foster child cannot be removed without a prior hearing satisfying due process. Appointed counsel for the children, . . . however, disagrees, and has consistently argued that the foster parents have no such liberty interest independent of the interests of the foster children, and that the best interest of the children would not be served by procedural protections beyond those already provided by New York law. The intervening natural parents of children in foster care . . . also oppose the foster parents, arguing that recognition of the procedural right claimed would undercut both the substantive family law of New York, which favors the return of children to their natural parents as expeditiously as possible . . . and their constitutionally protected right of family privacy, by forcing them to submit to a hearing and defend their rights to their children before the children could be returned to them. . . .

We [now] turn to appellees' assertion that they have a constitutionally protected liberty interest . . . in the integrity of their family unit. This assertion clearly presents difficulties. . . . There does exist a "private realm of family life which the state cannot enter," Prince v. Massachusetts, 321 U.S. 158, 166 (1944), that has been afforded both substantive and procedural protection. But is the relation of foster parent to foster child sufficiently akin to the concept of "family" recognized in our precedents to merit similar protection?[48] Although considerable difficulty has attended the task of defining "family" for purposes of the Due Process Clause, we are not without guides to some of the elements that define the concept of "family" and contribute to its place in our society.

First, the usual understanding of "family" implies biological relationships, and most decisions treating the relation between parent and child have stressed this element. Stanley v. Illinois, 405 U.S. 645, 651 (1972), for example, spoke of "[t]he rights to conceive and raise one's children" as essential rights. . . . A biological relationship is not present in the case of the usual foster family. But biological

---

[48] Of course, recognition of a liberty interest in foster families for purposes of the procedural protections of the Due Process Clause would not necessarily require that foster families be treated as fully equivalent to biological families for purposes of substantive due process review. Cf. Moore v. City of East Cleveland, supra, at 6 (White, J., dissenting).

relationships are not exclusive determination of the existence of a family. [T]he importance of the familial relationship, to the individuals involved and to the society, stems from the emotional attachments that derive from the intimacy of daily association, and from the role it plays in "promot[ing] a way of life" through the instruction of children, Wisconsin v. Yoder, 406 U.S. 205, 231-233 (1972), as well as from the fact of blood relationship. No one would seriously dispute that a deeply loving and interdependent relationship between an adult and a child in his or her care may exist even in the absence of blood relationship. At least where a child has been placed in foster care as an infant, has never known his natural parents, and has remained continuously for several years in the care of the same foster parents, it is natural that the foster family should hold the same place in the emotional life of the foster child, and fulfill the same socializing functions, as a natural family.[52] For this reason, we cannot dismiss the foster family as a mere collection of unrelated individuals.

But there are also important distinctions between the foster family and the natural family. First, unlike the earlier cases recognizing a right to family privacy, the State here seeks to interfere not with a relationship having its origins entirely apart from the power of the State, but rather with a foster family which has its source in state law and contractual arrangements. . . . Here, however, whatever emotional ties may develop between foster parent and foster child have their origins in an arrangement in which the State has been a partner from the outset. . . .

A second consideration related to this is that ordinarily procedural protection may be afforded to a liberty interest of one person without derogating from the substantive liberty of another. Here, however, such a tension is virtually unavoidable. Under New York law, the natural parent of a foster child in voluntary placement has an absolute right to the return of his child in the absence of a court order obtainable only upon compliance with rigorous substantive and procedural standards, which reflect the constitutional protection accorded the natural family. Moreover, the natural parent initially gave up his child to the State only on the express understanding that the child would be returned in those circumstances. These rights are difficult to reconcile with the liberty interest in the foster family relationship claimed by appellees. It is one thing to say that individuals may acquire a liberty interest against arbitrary governmental interference in the family-like associations into which they have freely entered, even in the absence of biological connection or state-law recognition of the relationship. It is quite another to say that one may acquire such an interest in the face of another's constitutionally recognized liberty interest that derives from blood relationship, state law sanction, and basic human right — an interest the foster parent has recognized by contract from the outset. Whatever liberty interest might otherwise

---

[52] The briefs dispute at some length the validity of the "psychological parent" theory propounded in Goldstein, Freud and Solnit, Beyond the Best Interests of the Child (1973). The book, on which appellee foster parents relied to some extent in the District Court, is indeed controversial. See, e.g., Strauss and Strauss, Book Review, 74 Colum. L. Rev. 996 (1974); Kadushin, Beyond the Best Interests of the Child: An Essay Review, 48 Soc. Sci. Rev. 508, 512 (1974). But this case turns not on the disputed validity of any particular psychological theory, but on the legal consequences of the undisputed fact that the emotional ties between foster parent and foster child are in many cases quite close, and undoubtedly in some as close as those existing in biological families.

exist in the foster family as an institution, that interest must be substantially atten-uated where the proposed removal from the foster family is to return the child to his natural parents.

As this discussion suggests, appellees' claim to a constitutionally protected liberty interest raises complex and novel questions. It is unnecessary for us to resolve those questions definitively in this case, however, for, like the District Court, we conclude that "narrower grounds exist to support" our reversal. We are persuaded that, even on the assumption that appellees have a protected "liberty interest," the District Court erred in holding that the preremoval procedures presently employed by the State are constitutionally defective.

III

Where procedural due process must be afforded because a "liberty" or "property" interest is within the Fourteenth Amendment's protection, there must be deter-mined "what process is due" in the particular context. . . .

Consideration of the procedures employed by the City and State of New York [in light of the factors set forth in Mathews v. Eldridge, 414 U.S. 319 (1976), i.e., the private interest affected, the risk of an erroneous deprivation of such interest by the procedures, and the government's interest, including fiscal or administrative burdens that additional or substitute procedural requirements would entail] requires the conclusion that those procedures satisfy constitutional standards.

Turning first to the procedure applicable in New York City, SSC Procedure No. 5 provides that before a child is removed from a foster home, the foster parents may request an "independent review." . . . Such a procedure would appear to give a more elaborate trial-type hearing to foster families than this Court has found required in other contexts of administrative determinations. The District Court found the procedure inadequate on four grounds, none of which we find sufficient to justify the holding that the procedure violates due process.

First, the court held that the "independent review" administrative proceeding was insufficient because it was only available on the request of the foster parents. In the view of the District Court, the proceeding should be provided as a matter of course, because the interests of the foster parents and those of the child would not necessarily be coextensive, and it could not be assumed that the foster parents would invoke the hearing procedure in every case in which it was in the child's interest to have a hearing. . . . We disagree. As previously noted, the constitutional liberty, if any, sought to be protected by the New York procedures is a right of *family* privacy or autonomy, and the basis for recognition of any such interest in the foster family must be that close emotional ties analogous to those between parent and child are established when a child resides for a lengthy period with a foster family. If this is so, necessarily we should expect that the foster parents will seek to continue the relationship to preserve the stability of the family; if they do not request a hearing, it is difficult to see what right or interest of the foster child is protected by holding a hearing. [C]onsideration of the interest to be protected and the likelihood of erroneous deprivations, . . . do not support the District Court's imposition of [automatic hearings]. Moreover, automatic provision of hearings [would impose] a substantial additional administrative burden on the state. . . .

Second, the District Court faulted the city procedure on the ground that participation is limited to the foster parents and the agency, and the natural parent and the child are not made parties to the hearing. This is not fatal in light of the nature of the alleged constitutional interests at stake. When the child's transfer from one foster home to another is pending, the interest arguably requiring protection is that of the foster family, not that of the natural parents. Moreover, the natural parent can generally add little to the accuracy of factfinding concerning the wisdom of such a transfer. . . . Much the same can be said in response to the District Court's statement that ". . . it may be advisable, under certain circumstances, for the agency to appoint an adult representative better to articulate the interests of the child. In making this determination, the agency should carefully consider the child's age, sophistication and ability effectively to communicate his own true feelings." But nothing in the New York City procedures prevents consultation of the child's wishes. . . . Such consultation, however, does not require that the child or an appointed representative must be a party with full adversary powers in all pre-removal hearings.

The other two defects in the city procedure found by the District Court must also be rejected. One is that the procedure does not extend to the removal of a child from foster care to be returned to his natural parent. But as we have already held, whatever liberty interest may be argued to exist in the foster family is significantly weaker in the case of removals preceding return to the natural parent, and the balance of due process interests must accordingly be different. . . . Similarly, the District Court pointed out that the New York City procedure coincided with the informal "conference" and postremoval hearings provided as a matter of state law. This overlap in procedures may be unnecessary or even to some degree unwise, but a State does not violate the Due Process Clause by providing alternative or additional procedures beyond what the Constitution requires.

Outside New York City, where only the statewide procedures apply, foster parents are provided not only with the procedures of a preremoval conference and postremoval hearing provided by 18 N.Y.C.R.R. §450.10 and Soc. Serv. L. §400, but also with the preremoval *judicial* hearing available on request to foster parents who have in their care children who have been in foster care for 18 months or more, Soc. Serv. L. §392. [A] foster parent in such case may obtain an order that the child remain in his care.

The District Court found three defects in this full judicial process. First, a §392 proceeding is available only to those foster children who have been in foster care for 18 months or more. . . . We do not think that the 18-month limitation on §392 actions renders the New York scheme constitutionally inadequate. The assumed liberty interest to be protected in this case is one rooted in the emotional attachments that develop over time between a child and the adults who care for him. But there is no reason to assume that those attachments ripen at less than 18 months or indeed at any precise point. Indeed, testimony in the record, . . . as well as material in published psychological texts, suggests that the amount of time necessary for the development of the sort of tie appellees seek to protect varies considerably depending on the age and previous attachments of the child. . . .

The District Court's other two findings of infirmity in the §392 procedure have already been considered and held to be without merit. . . . Finally, the §392 hearing is available to foster parents, both in and outside New York City, even where the removal sought is for the purpose of returning the child to his natural parents. Since this remedy provides a sufficient constitutional preremoval hearing to protect whatever liberty interest might exist in the continued existence of the foster family when the State seeks to transfer the child to another foster home, a fortiori the procedure is adequate to protect the lesser interest of the foster family in remaining together at the expense of the disruption of the natural family.

. . . Since we hold that the procedures provided by New York State in §392 and by New York City's SSC Procedure No. 5 are adequate to protect whatever liberty interests appellees may have, the judgment of the District Court is reversed.

Mr. Justice STEWART, with whom The Chief Justice and Mr. Justice REHNQUIST join, concurring in the judgment.

The foster parent-foster child relationship involved in this litigation is, of course, wholly a creation of the State. New York law defines the circumstances under which a child may be placed in foster care, prescribes the obligations of the foster parents, and provides for the removal of the child from the foster home. . . . The agency compensates the foster parents, and reserves in its contracts the authority to decide as it sees fit whether and when a child shall be returned to his natural family or placed elsewhere. . . . Were it not for the system of foster care that the State maintains, the relationship for which constitutional protection is asserted would not even exist.

The New York Legislature and the New York courts have made it unmistakably clear that foster care is intended only as a temporary way station until a child can be returned to his natural parents or placed for adoption. . . .

In these circumstances, I cannot understand why the Court thinks itself obliged to decide these cases on the assumption that either foster parents or foster children in New York have some sort of "liberty" interest in the continuation of their relationship.[1] Rather than tiptoeing around this central issue, I would squarely

---

[1] The Court's opinion seems to indicate that there is no reason to distinguish between the claims of the foster parents and the foster children, either because the parents have standing to assert the rights of the children or because the parents' interest is identical to that of the children. I cannot agree.

First, it is by no means obvious that foster parents and foster children have the same interest in a continuation of their relationship. When the child leaves the foster family, it is because the agency with custody of him has determined that his interests will be better served by a new home, either with his natural parents, adoptive parents, or a different foster family. Any assessment of the child's alleged deprivation must take into account not only what he has lost, but what he has received in return. Foster parents, on the other hand, do not automatically receive a new child with whom they will presumably have a more profitable relationship.

Second, . . . this is not a case where the failure to grant the parents their requested relief will inevitably tend to "dilut[e] or adversely affec[t]" the alleged constitutional rights of the children. Denying the parents a hearing simply has no effect whatever on the children's separate claim to a hearing, and does not impair their alleged constitutional rights. There is therefore no standing in the parents to assert the children's claims.

I would nevertheless consider both the parents' and the children's claims in these cases, but only because the suit was originally brought on behalf of both the parents and the children, all of whom were parties plaintiff. While it is true that their interests may conflict, there was no reason not to allow counsel for the parents to continue to represent the children to the extent that their interests may be

hold that the interests asserted by the appellees are not of a kind that the Due Process Clause of the Fourteenth Amendment protects.

[T]he predicate for invoking the Due Process Clause — the existence of state-created liberty or property — [is] missing here. New York confers no right on foster families to remain intact, defensible only upon proof of specific acts or circumstances. . . . Similarly, New York law provides no basis for a justifiable expectation on the part of foster families that their relationship will continue indefinitely. . . .

What remains of the appellees' argument is the theory that the relation of the foster parent to the foster child may generate emotional attachments similar to those found in natural families. The Court surmises that foster families who share these attachments might enjoy the same constitutional interests in "family privacy" as natural families. . . .

But under New York's foster care laws, any case where the foster parents had assumed the emotional role of the child's natural parents would represent not a triumph of the system, to be constitutionally safeguarded from state intrusion, but a failure. The goal of foster care, at least in New York, is not to provide a permanent substitute for the natural or adoptive home, but to prepare the child for his return to his real parents or placement in a permanent adoptive home by giving him temporary shelter in a family setting. Thus, the New York Court of Appeals has recognized that the development of close emotional ties between foster parents and a child may hinder the child's ultimate adjustment in a permanent home, and provide a basis for the *termination* of the foster family relationship. In re Jewish Child Care Assn. (Sanders), supra.[2] Perhaps it is to be expected that children who spend unduly long stays in what should have been temporary foster care will develop strong emotional ties with their foster parents. But this does not mean, and I cannot believe, that such breakdowns of the New York system must be protected or forever frozen in their existence by the Due Process Clause of the Fourteenth Amendment.

One of the liberties protected by the Due Process Clause, the Court has held, is the freedom to "establish a home and bring up children." Meyer v. Nebraska, supra, at 399. . . . But this constitutional concept is simply not in point when we deal with foster families as New York law has defined them. The family life upon which the State "intrudes" is simply a temporary status which the State itself has

---

compatible. The conflict was avoided by the District Court's appointment of independent counsel, who took a position opposite to that of the foster parents as to where the children's welfare lay. The appointment of independent counsel, however, should not have left the children without advocacy for the position, right or wrong, that they are entitled to due process hearings. That position should have been left to be asserted by the counsel who originally brought the suit for the children. My view, therefore, is that the parents and the children are properly before the Court and entitled to assert their own separate claims, but that neither group has standing to assert the claims of the other.

[2] "That the Sanders have given Laura a good home and have shown her great love does not stamp as an abuse of discretion the Trial Justice's determination to take her from them. Indeed, it is the extreme of love, affection, and possessiveness manifested by the Sanders, together with the conduct which their emotional involvement impelled, that supplies the foundation of reasonableness and correctness for his determination. The vital fact is that Mr. and Mrs. Sanders are not, and presumably will never be, Laura's parents by adoption. Their disregard of that fact and their seizure of full parental status in the eyes of the child might well be, or so the Trial Justice was entitled to find, a source of detriment to the child in the circumstances presented." 5 N.Y.2d, at 229, 156 N.E.2d, at 703.

created. It is a "family life" defined and controlled by the law of New York, for which New York pays, and the goals of which New York is entitled to and does set for itself.

NOTES AND QUESTIONS

(1) Constitutional Procedures. Are the procedures provided in New York constitutionally compelled? Suppose a state did not have any procedures to allow foster parents either a trial-type hearing before removal or a preremoval conference and a postremoval hearing procedure? Would the Constitution be satisfied? Does the Constitution require some sort of trial-type hearing for foster parents *before* removal when (a) the child is not returning to his natural parents; (b) the foster parents and child have a substantial psychological relationship; (c) the child has lived with the foster parents more than 18 months; or (d) the foster parents request a hearing?

(2) Contractual Relationship. What effect do the terms of a contract between the state and foster parents have on the foster parents' constitutional rights? If the foster parents' "contractual relationship with the state" had said nothing about the state's removal rights, would the foster parents then have had a constitutionally protected liberty interest? Would the outcome be different?

(3) Suppose the foster parents were the child's aunt and uncle (or grandparents), who had signed a contract with the state and received foster care payments from the state. Would they be entitled to greater constitutional protection? Would there be a "relationship having its origins entirely apart from the power of the state"?

(4) Where a child has no biological parents (either because they have died or abandoned the child), would foster parents have a constitutional liberty interest in the relationship with the child after the child had lived with them for some period of time?

(5) Sibling Relationships. Do foster children have a liberty interest in sibling relationships? Compare Adoption of Pierce, 790 N.E.2d 680 (Mass. App. Ct. 2003) (holding that the best interests standard prevails over a foster child's right to maintain a sibling relationship), with Cal. Welf. & Inst. Code §366.26 (West 2008) (establishing a "sibling relationship exception" that prohibits a court from ordering the termination of parental rights when evidence shows that such termination would substantially interfere with the child's relationship with a sibling). See generally Ellen Marrus, Fostering Family Ties: The State as Maker and Breaker of Kinship Relationships, 2004 U. Chi. Legal F. 319 (2004) (arguing for maintenance of sibling relationships in dependency decisions); Meghann M. Seifert, Note, Sibling Visitation After Adoption: The Implications of the Massachusetts Sibling Visitation Statute, 84 B.U. L. Rev. 1467 (2004) (case note on *Pierce*).

(6) Are the constitutional rights of the foster parents any greater in a case where the children have been placed in foster care by a juvenile court because of parental neglect? Does anything turn on the fact that the natural parents in these cases "voluntarily" place their children in foster care?

(7) Psychological Parent. Does OFFER adequately protect the relationship of the child to a "psychological parent"? Where it can be shown that a foster child

has substantial psychological ties to foster parents who wish to adopt the child, should it be possible to terminate the parental rights of a biological parent who is not a "psychological parent"? The concept of the "psychological parent" was developed by Joseph Goldstein, Anna Freud, and Alfred Solnit in Beyond the Best Interests of the Child (1973) to denote an individual, who may or may not be the child's biological parent, who has strong emotional bonds with the child. See In re Phillip B., pp. 461-467 infra. Also see In re Emiliano M., 2008 WL 5220944 (Conn. Super. Ct. 2008) (terminating parental rights in favor of psychological parent). Would giving children a greater voice in dependency proceedings result in more protection for the psychological parent-child relationship? See Jaclyn Jean Jenkins, Listen to Me! Empowering Youth and Courts Through Increased Youth Participation in Dependency Hearings, 46 Fam. Ct. Rev. 163 (2008).

(8) Kinship Care. An increasing number of children (especially African-American children) live with relatives (kinship care) either by informal agreement or formal child welfare arrangement. Kinship care became especially popular in the late 1980s with the AIDS epidemic and maternal substance abuse. What are the advantages of kinship care for children? For biological parents? For the state?

Federal child welfare policy promotes kinship foster care. For example, PRWORA, 42 U.S.C. §671(a)(19) (2000), encourages states to give preference to relative caregivers. And, for children who are in kinship care, the Adoption and Safe Families Act (ASFA) (discussed infra p. 353) allows states to waive the rule requiring termination if children have been in out-of-home placements for 15 of the last 24 months. 42 U.S.C. §675(5)(E)(i) (2000). And, Congress reauthorized the Older Americans Act in 2000, 42 U.S.C. §§3001-3058 (2000) (originally passed in 1987) to make funds available to state offices on aging to aid older caregivers who raise children related to the caregivers.

What is the extent of constitutional protection for the kinship foster family? See Safia Hussain, Note, Safeguarding Liberty Interests in New York's Kinship Foster Care System, 59 Rutgers L. Rev. 637, 653 (2007) (discussing a few cases in which a court ruled that kinship foster parents and children possess a liberty interest requiring adequate due process protection). See generally David J. Herring, Kinship Foster Care: Implications of Behavioral Biology Research, 56 Buff. L. Rev. 495 (2008); Dorothy E. Roberts, Kinship Care and the Price of State Support for Children, 76 Chi.-Kent L. Rev. 1619 (2001).

(9) Voluntary Foster Care Placement. OFFER reveals that parents, rather than the state, often initiate foster care placement. What does OFFER reveal about the problems posed by such voluntary surrenders? See also In re Sanjivini K., 391 N.E.2d 1316 (N.Y. Ct. App. 1979) (finding that best interests of child were not served by freeing her for adoption by foster parents where mother voluntarily surrendered child to agency but made considerable effort to preserve parental ties throughout child's life). See generally Deborah Paruch, The Orphaning of Underprivileged Children: America's Failed Child Welfare Law & Policy, 8 J. L. Fam. Stud. 119 (2006) (discussing voluntary placements in foster care and the failure to consider adequately these children's needs in termination of parental rights proceedings).

(10) Foster Care Subsidies for Children with Special Needs. Some children in foster care may be hard to place because of a disability. ASFA §201 (codified at

42 U.S.C. §673A) provides financial incentives for states to increase adoptions of children with special needs. Is subsidized adoption like baby selling (discussed in Chapter 5)? Why is it that the symbolic repugnance of paying people to adopt a child seems to be less substantial than baby selling, where a biological mother is paid to give up a newborn? See generally Barbara L. Seaton, Promoting the Adoption of Special Needs Children, 17 Widener L.J. 469 (2008).

(11) Liberty Interest: Other Jurisdictions.   The Supreme Court in Smith v. OFFER refused to reach the question of whether foster parents can have a constitutionally protected "liberty" interest in the continued placement of a foster child in their home, but merely held that even if such a liberty interest existed, the New York agency had given the foster parents adequate procedural protection. Several circuits have since squarely held that foster parents do not possess a constitutionally protected liberty interest in the maintenance of the foster family relationship, because of the distinguishing factors mentioned by the majority in Smith v. OFFER. See, e.g., Rodriguez v. McLoughlin, 214 F.3d 328 (2d Cir. 2000); Gibson v. Merced County Dept. of Human Resources, 799 F.2d 582, 586 (9th Cir. 1986); Procopio v. Johnson, 994 F.2d 325 (7th Cir. 1993).

(12) Gay and Lesbian Foster Parents.   Does Smith v. OFFER offer any protection for the relationship of the child to a gay and lesbian foster parent? According to one study, same-sex couples have adopted about 65,000 children nationwide, and an additional 14,000 children (4 percent of all foster children) live with lesbian or gay foster parents. See Editorial, End Adoption for Same-Sex Couples, Chi. Sun-Times, Sept. 26, 2008, at 23. Yet, several states prohibit gay and lesbian couples from serving as foster parents or adopting foster children. See Amanda Ruggeri, A Quiet Fight Over Gay Adoption, U.S. News & World Rep., Nov. 3, 2008, at 29. In Lofton v. Sec'y of the Dept. of Children & Family Servs., 358 F.3d 804 (11th Cir. 2004), a gay foster parent challenged a Florida law that banned him, on the basis of his sexual orientation, from adopting his foster children (although Florida law permits gays and lesbians to become foster parents or legal guardians of children). Rejecting his claim, the Eleventh Circuit refused to read *Smith* sufficiently broadly to find that parental rights could be extended to foster parents based on the emotional ties between foster parent and child. However, in a more recent case, In re Adoption of Doe, 2008 WL 5006172 (Fla. Cir. Ct. 2008), a Florida Circuit Court held that the statutory ban on gays and lesbians from adopting children violates foster children's constitutional right to permanency and fails to meet the rational basis test. (For further discussion of *Doe*, see Chapter 5, infra.) See generally Michael S. Wald, Adults' Sexual Orientation and State Determinations Regarding Placement of Children, 40 Fam. L.Q. 381 (2006).

The Aftermath and Effects of Smith v. OFFER

David L. Chambers & Michael S. Wald, "Smith v. OFFER"
In the Interest of Children 114-117 (Robert H. Mnookin ed., 1985)

Despite the reversal by the Supreme Court the case was not without some impact. Beginning with the smallest but clearest impact of all, the Gandy children [see n. 1 of the opinion] stayed with Mrs. Smith. By the time that the Supreme Court had decided that New York's procedures were constitutionally permissible and vacated the restraining order that had been in effect for over three years, the Catholic Guardian Society had long abandoned its plans to move the children. The children seem to have thrived with Mrs. Smith. On May 7, 1981, seven years after the restraining order was entered, a New York state court approved a petition by Mrs. Smith to adopt the children.

In addition, . . . the litigation did result in New York City adopting new regulations providing for formal hearings prior to intra-foster-care transfers. These hearings, which are not available if the child is being returned home, must be requested by the foster parents. The placing agencies are required to notify all foster parents of their rights. The hearings are conducted in a far more formal manner than those held under the prior regulations. The foster parents can bring counsel and witnesses are sworn and subject to cross-examination. There is often expert testimony and several people from the agency, as well as the biological parents and their representatives, attend. These hearings generally last less than one day although some go on for several days. Occasionally, it takes months to complete the process.

Thus, for intra-foster-care moves, Lowry [the attorney representing the foster parents in *Smith*] obtained her goal in *New York City.* [However, the] New York State Department of Social Services declined to adopt the new regulations, and the New York State legislature has rejected bills that would have mandated New York City's approach across the state. . . .

We cannot determine whether children are "better off" as a result of the hearings that are held. Retta Friedman, who hears all these cases, is a former caseworker. She believes that hearings, although time-consuming and frequently subject to delays, have resulted in better information being gathered, and as a result, in more protection for children.

She believes that the effectiveness of the hearings is due to the fact that the agency worker must be present and is subject to cross-examination by the foster parent, who may be represented by counsel. In the past all the hearing officer had was a written report from the agency. Now the agencies do a much better job of substantiating the reasons for their actions and in providing documentation to the hearing officer. Friedman also believes that the hearings facilitate understanding and acceptance among foster parents. . . .

In addition to the actual requests for hearings, it may be that the regulations act to deter some inappropriate agency actions. . . . Most of the people we interviewed thought that there had been little change in agency behavior as a result of the new regulations. However, at least some people, including Gans [the attorney representing the interests of the natural parents in *Smith*], felt that the litigation did contribute to opening up the process in New York City to public attention and that this had led to some improvement in the system.

It may also be that the case accomplished the NYCLU's goals in some other ways. [T]he majority did indicate that there might be constitutionally-protected interests in permanence and stability in some foster care relationships. They implied that procedures similar to those in New York might be constitutionally required. States that did not afford foster parents any preremoval conferences or hearings were put on notice that their process might be unconstitutional.

The *OFFER* decision has been cited by a few courts as a basis for protecting a *very* long-term foster relationship, although most of the ten to fifteen published opinions that have cited the case, for more than a passing reference in a string citation, have used it to deny foster parents any rights.

c. Exit from Foster Care: The Aging Out of Older Foster Children

Occean v. Kearney
123 F. Supp. 2d 618 (S.D. Fla. 2000)

DIMITROULEAS, District Judge.

... Plantiff brings these claims for injunctive and declaratory relief under Title 42 U.S.C. Section 1983, alleging that his substantive due process and procedural due process rights were violated when Defendants, in their official capacities as executives in a state agency, the Florida Department of Children and Family Services (hereinafter "DCF"), ended Plaintiff's foster care benefits when Plaintiff reached the age of eighteen without previously affording Plaintiff notice and an opportunity to be heard. ...

The Amended Complaint alleges that Plaintiff, now nineteen years old, was born in the Bahamas and arrived thereafter in the United States with his mother. In March 1992, DCF removed Plaintiff from his parents' custody and placed him in foster care because he and his siblings were being left in their home inappropriately. On August 20,1994, DCF transferred Plaintiff to Mel Blount Youth Home of Georgia, a behavioral modification facility, contracted to the Florida DCF to provide 24 hour, seven day a week care and education to juveniles under DCF control. In March 1995, the juvenile court in Fort Lauderdale entered an order providing that if DCF was to change the Plaintiff's placement, it shall present to the court a written report outlining what treatment plan is proposed for the Plaintiff and DCF's basis for such a recommendation. In June, 1995, the juvenile court changed the case plan goal for Plaintiff to long term foster care, and Plaintiff was given an Independent Living Skills Assessment to complete. Plaintiff stated that he wished to get his GED, attend technical school, and secure employment. According to the Amended Complaint, on May 6,1997, Plaintiff met the eligibility criteria for receipt of Special Immigrant Status from the INS.

The Amended Complaint further alleges that according to the reports and recommendations to the juvenile court and from the Mel Blount facility's files, Plaintiff seemed to be making significant progress in this program and was working towards his GED. One month before his benefits were terminated, DCF recommended that Plaintiff continue individual and group counseling and explore vocational options for positive transition from youth home into the community. Furthermore, Plaintiff expressed his desire to remain in the youth home until he obtained his GED. On December 26,1998, Plaintiff's eighteenth birthday, without any notice or an opportunity to be heard, his case was closed by DCF. Plaintiff was told on March 16, 1999 to immediately pack and leave on the next bus to Fort Lauderdale with only a few of his belongings and fifty dollars. Upon arrival in Fort Lauderdale, Plaintiff was unable to work because he never received legal immigration status from INS while in custody of the DCF nor his GED. While in

South Florida, Plaintiff was arrested and incarcerated. Before his release from state custody, INS placed a hold on Plaintiff and he was transferred to an INS contract facility where he awaits deportation. . . .

Defendant argues that Plaintiff has no substantive due process claim because the continuance of foster care benefits after the age of eighteen and the assistance in obtaining a green card are not the type of liberty or property interest traditionally afforded due process. Defendants allege that the liberty interests the Plaintiff asserts are not those that are "objectively, deeply rooted in this Nation's history and tradition." Washington v. Glucksberg, 521 U.S. 702, 720-21 (1997). The Due Process Clause does not obligate states to provide its citizens with substantive services, even if those services are necessary to secure citizens' life, liberty, or property interest. However, a State owes a duty under the Due Process Clause to take care of those who have already been deprived of their liberty.

. . . When a person is institutionalized and wholly dependent on the state, a special relationship is created that requires a certain minimal standard of care. Youngberg v. Romeo, 457 U.S. 307, 317 (1982). In *Youngberg*, the Supreme Court held that the state was under a duty to provide respondent, a mentally retarded individual involuntarily committed to a state institution, with such training as an appropriate professional would consider reasonable to ensure safety and to facilitate his ability to function free from bodily restraint. The United States Court of Appeals for the Second Circuit has extended the meaning of *Youngberg* to children who are the responsibility of the state.

Defendants argue that Plaintiff has no substantive due process right to continued foster care benefits or assistance in obtaining a green card because no special relationship was created between Plaintiff and Defendants, and Plaintiff's claim simply does not rise to the level of a fundamental right secured by the Constitution. In the case at bar, Plaintiff argues Defendants accepted the responsibility of providing Plaintiff a residential placement in which he would be prepared to enter the adult world, thereby creating a special relationship, but instead abandoned the Plaintiff without a GED and without the legal ability to work because the Defendants did not obtain legal immigration status for Plaintiff while in foster care. Plaintiff, therefore, argues that Defendants deprived Plaintiff of his federal liberty interest in a humane and decent existence as a foster child in the care of the state, by not providing him with continued benefits in the form of participation in a GED program and legal immigration status.[3] However, if such a special relationship existed, when Plaintiff turned 18, such special relationship terminated for purposes of a substantive due process analysis. Moreover, Plaintiff is in INS custody due to his committing a crime while he was 18 years old and no longer in DCF care. Plaintiff's own intervening cause leads this Court to conclude that no substantive due process violation occurred in this case.

Ultimately, the Court is left with a claim that simply does not rise to the level of a fundamental right protected by the Due Process Clause of the Constitution. Even

---

[3] Florida Statutes Section 409.145(a) authorizes the DCF to continue to provide the services of the children's foster care program to individuals 18 to 21 years of age who are enrolled in a program to obtain a high school equivalency diploma. In 2000, the statute was apparently amended to allow for such benefits until the age of 23.

if Defendants' conduct in summarily terminating Plaintiff's foster care benefits upon turning age 18 was arbitrary and capricious, this Court concludes that such post-age 18 foster care benefits are not a fundamental right that merits protection under the substantive due process clause.

The Court reaches a different conclusion as to Plaintiff's procedural due process claim. Defendant alleges that Plaintiff has no property right in continued foster care benefits and therefore, has failed to state a state procedural due process claim. There are two questions in the analysis of a procedural due process claim: first, did the plaintiff have a property interest of which he was deprived by state action, and if so, did the plaintiff receive sufficient process regarding that deprivation. Plaintiff alleges that he has a property interest in securing legal immigration status through the assistance of DCF, and in continued foster care as provided by Section 409.165(4) of the Florida Statutes. Plaintiff further alleges that once he turned eighteen he was entitled to the benefits until the age of twenty-one, that Defendants provided Plaintiff a plan calling for him to remain in foster care through May 31, 1999, and that Defendants violated the juvenile court judge's prohibition on terminating Plaintiff's existing foster placement without a court order. Finally, Plaintiff argues that the Florida Administrative Codes provides a procedure to be followed for mandatory administrative review, including notice of the conference, for children reaching age 18 but eligible for continued foster care benefits. See Florida Administrative Code Sections 65C-13.019 and 65C-16.003.

Defendants argue that Plaintiff's attainment of age 18 automatically terminates any property rights held by Plaintiff to continued benefits. Once reaching this "magic age," Defendants argue that Plaintiff's property rights ended, since Florida law allows DCF the discretion to continue benefits. However, the Defendants conceded at oral argument that there is an issue as to whether they failed to provide Plaintiff, prior to his turning 18, the assistance mandated by the Florida Administrative Code regarding aid in obtaining legal immigration status. Plaintiff also alleges that he never received a hearing or any type of process informing him of his denial of the extended foster care benefits.

When limitations exist on agency discretion to terminate or extend benefits, procedural due process must be afforded. In this case, both Florida Administrative Code and the continuing order of the juvenile court arguably provided such limitations on the discretion of Defendants in terminating Plaintiff's benefits. Taking Plaintiff's allegations as true, Plaintiff has sufficiently stated for purposes of defeating a motion to dismiss that he has a property interest entitled to procedural due process in these foster care benefits and immigration status assistance. Therefore, Plaintiff's allegations meet both requirements for a procedural due process claim and state a claim upon which relief can be granted. . . .

NOTE ON AGING OUT OF FOSTER CARE

Occean v. Kearney, supra, highlights the plight of the older foster care child who exits from foster care. Many foster children, particularly those who are not adopted or reunified with their families, exit foster care at the age of 18. These children "age out," i.e., they are no longer eligible for foster care benefits regardless of whether they have sufficient skills or resources to live on their own.

Approximately 20,000 teens leave foster care each year because they have reached the age of majority. Susan Vivian Mangold, Extending Non-Exclusive Parenting and the Right to Protection for Older Foster Children: Creating Third Options in Permanency Planning, 48 Buff. L. Rev. 835, 863 (2000) (citing congressional findings, H.R. 3443, 106th Cong. (1999)). According to empirical studies, many of these youths face unemployment, homelessness, incarceration, and nonmarital pregnancy. Mangold, supra, at 863-866.

In the mid-1980s federal legislation first recognized the needs of older foster care children. As a result, Congress enacted the Independent Living Initiative (ILI) 42 U.S.C. §677, in 1986, requiring specific planning to help these youth before their exit from foster care. The ILI required states to provide services to foster care children to prepare them for independent living.

Then, in 1999, Congress passed the Foster Care Independence Act (FCIA), 42 U.S.C. §677 (2000), to provide additional funding for improved services to these older youths who leave the foster care system. Specifically, FCIA offers programs in education, training or postsecondary education, employment, and financial support that may continue until age 21 if necessary. FCIA also allows Medicaid coverage to youths between the ages of 18 and 21 who were in foster care on their 18th birthday. FCIA also authorizes additional funding to assist states to find permanent homes for foster care youths. In 2001, Congress increased total funding for services targeted at youth aging out of foster care to $200 million. Promoting Safe and Stable Families Amendments of 2001, Pub. L. No. 107-133, §§201-02, 115 Stat. 2413, 2422-25 (2001). See generally Katherine M. Swift, A Child's Right: What Should the State Be Required to Provide to Teenagers Aging Out of Foster Care?, 15 Wm. & Mary Bill Rts. J. 1205 (2007).

3. Foster Care Reform

a. Statutory Reform: AACWA and ASFA

Foster care was envisaged as a temporary solution to family disfunction or disruption. However, in the 1970s, public attention began focusing on the problem of "foster care drift." The term signifies the experience of foster care children who suffer multiple foster care placements, moving endlessly from foster home to foster home without any hope of family reunification or adoption. Many commentators criticized the practice and highlighted its psychological harm to children.[37] The United States Supreme Court added fuel to the debate with its criticism of foster care drift in Smith v. OFFER (supra, pp. 334-345).

---

[37] See, e.g., Joseph Goldstein et al., Beyond the Best Interests of the Child (1973); Robert H. Mnookin, Child-Custody Adjudication: Judicial Functions in the Face of Indeterminacy, 39 Law & Contemp. Probs. 226 (1975); Robert H. Mnookin, Foster Care — In Whose Best Interest?, 43 Harv. Educ. Rev. 599 (1973); Michael S. Wald, State Intervention on Behalf of "Neglected" Children, 28 Stan. L. Rev. 623 (1976).

Concern about the "limbo" of foster care motivated substantial legislative reform on the federal and state level. In 1980 Congress passed the Adoption Assistance and Child Welfare Act (AACWA), 42 U.S.C. §§620-28, 670-79(a). The primary objective of the AACWA was to facilitate finding permanent homes for children (by preventing the need for removal, returning children to their families, or placing them for adoption). AACWA emphasizes preventive and reunification services.

The Act provides federal matching funds to states for foster care and adoptive services if states adopt certain standards. Specifically, AACWA requires that: (1) states must formulate case plans ("permanency planning") that are designed to achieve placement in the least possible restrictive setting, (2) states must conduct periodic case reviews, and (3) states must make "reasonable efforts" to prevent removal of children from the home and to reunify the family following removal (42 U.S.C. §671(a)(15)). Through these provisions Congress attempted to shift resources from temporary out-of-home care and to focus on channeling resources either to a child's natural family or to other permanent care alternatives.

Even before Congress passed the AACWA, individual states were acting independently to adopt legislation that pointed in the same direction. After 1980, states adopted legislation to conform to the minimum requirements for federal funding set out by the AACWA.

Following federal legislative reform, several problems remained. The AACWA failed to define the term "reasonable efforts." That reform would be addressed in subsequent legislation (the Adoption and Safe Families Act, discussed infra). And, compliance with the AACWA varied considerably from state to state. Under the regulatory scheme contemplated by the Department of Health and Human Services (HHS), if a state asserted compliance with the AACWA, the state was automatically granted federal funding, and its practices were subject to only minimal scrutiny by HHS. As a result, many states received funding without in fact complying with the minimum requirements of the AACWA.

Congress turned again to address foster care reform with the enactment of the Adoption and Safe Families Act of 1997 (ASFA), Pub. L. No. 105-89, 111 Stat. 2115 (codified in scattered sections of 42 U.S.C.). ASFA strengthens the requirements of AACWA. One of ASFA's most important reforms is to clarify the meaning of the AACWA's "reasonable efforts" standard, 42 U.S.C. §672(a)(15)(D). Under AACWA, states had to make reasonable efforts to prevent the need for foster care and to reunify families after placement. However, AACWA failed to specify the extent of the efforts that were required.

In contrast, ASFA recognizes that reunification is not possible or advisable in all cases. Thus, ASFA eliminates the reasonable efforts requirement in the AACWA for the most severe cases (torture, sexual abuse, a parent murders another child, or a parent loses parental rights to a sibling), 42 U.S.C. §675(a)(15)(D). In addition, ASFA aims to facilitate adoption by reducing the amount of time that children spend in foster care. Thus, ASFA shortens the period triggering permanency hearings to no later than 12 months after the child's entry into foster care and also requires states to seek termination of parental rights for children who have been in foster care for 15 of the last 22 months (42 U.S.C. §675(5)(E)).

b. The Role of Litigation

Following the enactment of AACWA, class action lawsuits were brought by foster children against state and local agencies to secure regulatory enforcement of the Act. This effort began with Lynch v. King, 550 F. Supp. 324 (D. Mass. 1982), *aff'd sub nom.* Lynch v. Dukakis, 719 F.2d 504 (1st Cir. 1983), where a federal court for the first time recognized a private right of action against a state agency for the failure to live up to federal foster care requirements (specifically requiring the Massachusetts Department of Social Services to reduce caseloads, provide detailed case plans for each foster child, and periodically review each foster child's status). Several federal courts followed by similarly recognizing a private right of enforcement of the statutory provisions of the AACWA. See, e.g., LaShawn v. Dixon, 762 F. Supp. 959 (D.D.C. 1991).

The Supreme Court called an abrupt halt in 1992 to this movement. Suter v. Artist M., 503 U.S. 347 (1992), involved a class action against the Illinois Department of Children and Family Services for failure to use "reasonable efforts" to assign caseworkers to child clients. Finding no congressional intent to permit private enforcement of the AACWA, the Court reasoned that the Act constituted only a vague directive that failed to provide guidance as to measurement of "reasonable efforts." Following *Suter*, compliance with the AACWA remains dependent on monitoring by HHS. As one commentator criticizes:

> By refusing to recognize a right to private enforcement of the AACWA, the Court has restricted enforcement of the Act to the one entity that consistently has refused to exercise its authority in the face of substantial statutory violations and systemic state failures to provide for children in its care.[38]

Congress subsequently disapproved the Supreme Court's holding in *Suter*. By an amendment to the Social Security Act, 42 U.S.C. §1320a-2, -10 (2000), Congress limited the Supreme Court's holding (that precluded private causes of action) to the "reasonable efforts" provision of the AACWA (§671(a)(15)). Further, one commentator[39] has speculated that children whom the state places in foster care (as opposed to those who are merely retained in their homes under state supervision) may still be able to seek redress after *DeShaney* (see discussion supra p. 264) for substantive due process violations. Several federal courts have recognized such a cause of action;[40] however, the Supreme Court has yet to address the issue.

Litigation to reform state child protective services continues. To avoid dismissal under *Suter*, lawsuits have relied on other constitutional, state statutory, and federal statutory causes of action. See, e.g., Kenny A. ex rel. Winn. v. Perdue, 532 F.3d 1209 (11th Cir. 2008) (class action suit pursuant to 42 U.S.C. §1983, alleging that foster care services in select Georgia counties were inadequate); Occean v.

---

[38] Arlene E. Fried, The Foster Child's Avenue of Redress: Questions Left Unanswered, 26 Colum. J.L. & Soc. Probs. 465 (1993).

[39] Id. at 479.

[40] See, e.g., Burton v. Richmond, 276 F.3d 973 (8th Cir. 2002); Olivia Y. ex rel Johnson v. Barbour, 351 F. Supp. 2d 543 (S.D. Miss. 2004); Charlie H. v. Whitman, 83 F. Supp. 2d 476 (D.N.J. 2000).

Kerney, *supra* (recognizing a private cause of action under a different AACWA provision, §671(a)(16)).

Nonetheless, litigation has been a major vehicle for foster care reform. To date, courts have ordered 27 states to improve their child welfare systems. Jill K. Jensen, Notes & Comments, Fostering Interdependence: A Family-Centered Approach to Help Youth Aging Out of Foster Care, 3 Whittier J. Child & Fam. Advoc. 329, 338 (2004).

For critical commentary on the AACWA and AFSA, see Will L. Crossley, Defining Reasonable Efforts: Demystifying the State's Burden Under Federal Child Protection Legislation, 12 B.U. Pub. Int. L.J. 259 (2003); Terry Lyons, When Reasonable Efforts Hurt Victims of Abuse: Five Years of the Adoption and Safe Families Act of 1997, 26 Seton Hall Legis. J. 391 (2002); Amy Willinson-Hagen, Note: The Adoption and Safe Families Act of 1997: A Collision of Parens Patriae and Parent's Constitutional Rights, 11 Geo. J. on Poverty L. & Pol'y 137 (2004).

c. Criticisms and Proposals for Reform

Dorothy E. Roberts, Is There Justice in Children's Rights?: The Critique of Federal Family Preservation Policy
2 U. Pa. J. Const. L. 112, 118-138 (1999)

In November 1997 President Clinton signed the Adoption and Safe Families Act. . . . ASFA represents a dramatic shift in federal child welfare philosophy from an emphasis on the reunification of children in foster care with their biological families toward support for the adoption of these children into new families. . . .

A. *ASFA's New Focus Cannot Solve the Foster Care Problem*

ASFA's promotion of adoption is unlikely to improve the situation of most children in foster care. There are insufficient adoptive homes for the increasing number of children removed from their biological families. Moreover, unnecessarily separating children from their biological parents does not advance children's interests, but rather destroys family bonds that usually benefit children. . . .

The policy of promoting adoption at the expense of terminating parental rights assumes that adoption will significantly reduce the large numbers of children in out-of-home placements. The key supporters of ASFA operated according to the premise that the foster care problem stems from barriers to adoption. They criticized family preservation policies that made it difficult to terminate parental rights. They implied that if states removed these barriers — if courts terminated parental rights sooner — the foster care problem would dissipate and even disappear.

This is a false hope. There are not enough people wishing to adopt to absorb the high volume of children already pouring into foster care. Data on the foster care system over the last twenty years show that the number of parental rights terminations far outpaces the number of adoptions. Martin Guggenheim's study of statistics gathered from Michigan and New York over the period from 1987 to 1993 showed a dramatic increase in the number of children who become "state wards" — children whose parents' rights have been terminated and who are waiting in foster care to be adopted. . . . ASFA's accelerated deadlines for termination of parental rights will probably increase the state ward population; its adoption incentives, on the other hand, even if they achieve congressional goals, will probably fail to provide enough new homes for these children. This shortfall is exacerbated by the fact that the children most likely affected by ASFA's expedited termination process are the very ones least likely to be adopted. Black parents' rights are already terminated sooner than those of white parents, yet black children are less likely than white children to be adopted.

It is difficult to see how these children's interests are furthered by the extinction of their legal connection to their parents. "State governments appear to be destroying family ties of a large, and continually increasing number of children," Guggenheim charges, "with no concomitant benefit to children." Termination weakens family stability for many foster children by disrupting their relationship with their parents, while failing to result in permanent placement. . . .

There are alternatives to adoption that could ensure family stability while preserving the parent-child relationship. For example, children can often be safely placed in the long-term care of relatives or neighbors with parental visitation, leaving open the possibility of parents regaining custody if circumstances improve. In a 1994 survey of children in Illinois state custody who had been living with a relative for more than one year, 85% of relatives reported that the best plan for the children was to remain with them until the children were grown. . . .

ASFA's focus on terminating parental rights reflects the judgment that the risk of wrongful reunifications outweighs that of wrongful disruptions of families. This judgment, too, is misguided. The priority ASFA placed on child safety was cast as a correction of the 1980 Act's reasonable efforts requirement, which encouraged the return of foster children to violent homes. The reasonable efforts requirement, however, was itself enacted in response to evidence that agency caseworkers offered families minimal assistance and even obstructed parents' attempts to reunite with their children.

Even under the Child Welfare Act's reasonable efforts requirement, state agencies continued to make anemic efforts to prevent out-of-home placements and reunify families. Family preservation programs often fail because they do not address the needs of families, are inadequately funded, and do not last long enough. Caseworkers caught in the dual role of supporting families while recruiting foster and adoptive parents sometimes sabotage parents' quest to reunite with their children. A 1997 report issued by the General Accounting Office stated that more than half of the family support programs it surveyed "were not able to serve all families who needed services primarily due to the lack of funds and staff."

Services for families in California, for example, are permitted to continue for a maximum of six months and, on average, end after only half this time. How can agencies expect to solve problems arising from any combination of deplorable conditions — chronic poverty, dangerous neighborhoods, shoddy housing, poor health, drug addiction, profound depression, lack of childcare — with a three month parenting course or ephemeral crisis intervention? . . .

B. ASFA Mischaracterizes the Foster Care Problem

The pragmatic problems with ASFA's emphasis on adoption are related to a more fundamental philosophical flaw. Congress has misidentified the foster care problem. The injustice of the American foster care system does not stem from the small number of children being adopted. It stems, rather, from the large number of children removed from their homes.

The class and race dimensions of foster care magnify this problem — virtually all of the parents who lose custody of their children are poor, and a startling percentage are black. More than 200,000 children are removed from their homes and placed in foster care annually. In 1998, black children made up 45% of the foster care population while comprising only 15% of the general population under age eighteen. In the nation's urban centers, the racial disparity is even greater. Chicago's foster care population, for example, is almost 90% black. Of 42,000 children in foster care in New York City in 1997, only 1300 were white. Moreover, once black children enter foster care, they remain there longer, are moved more often, and receive less desirable placements than white children. . . .

The focus on adoption as the solution to the foster care problem directs attention away from the wide scale removal of poor black children from their homes. When Congress stated that its aim was "to make sure that every child has the opportunity to live in a safe, stable, loving and permanent home," it had in mind terminating parents' rights, not reducing poverty or building stronger supports for families. . . .

By promoting adoption so myopically, we forget that our ultimate goal should be to reduce the need for adoptions. [W]e can support adoption while working to curtail its causes. By combating poverty and its dangers to children, an ideal society would radically decrease its need for adoption. . . .

C. ASFA Disparages Biological Bonds

Perhaps the most disturbing aspect of ASFA's focus on adoption and its rescue mentality is the message it sends about the poor and minority families whose children have been placed in foster care. Throughout congressional testimony regarding the Act, adoption was portrayed as safer than the reunification of children with their biological families. Virtually every mention of biological families was negative, while adoptive homes were referred to as loving and stable. . . .

Perhaps the major reason for preferring extinction of parental ties in foster care is society's centuries-old depreciation of the relationship between poor parents and their children, especially those who are black. Most Americans can grasp a white middle-class child's emotional attachment to her biological father even though she is being raised by a stepfather. No one doubts the immediate re-connection of a wealthy child with his family when he returns from a year at boarding school. The public has a harder time, however, imagining a strong emotional bond between black parents and their children. . . . Poor black mothers are stereotyped as deviant and uncaring; they are blamed for transferring a degenerate lifestyle of welfare dependency and crime to their children. Black fathers are simply thought to be absent. When parents of children in foster care are portrayed as deranged and violent monsters, it becomes even more difficult for the public to believe that their children would want to maintain a relationship with them. . . .

Race and class politics are critical to understanding ASFA's impact because ASFA's emphasis on adoption was influenced by concurrent trends in federal welfare reform. ASFA was passed on the heels of the overhaul of federal welfare policy. The Personal Responsibility and Work Opportunity Reconciliation Act of 1996 ended the federal guarantee of cash assistance to America's children and allowed states to implement extensive welfare reform programs. State welfare reform measures hinder the ability of many poor mothers to care for their children: they reduce cash assistance to families, eliminate payments to some families altogether, and require mothers, often without adequate child care, to work and participate in job training, counseling, and other programs. What will happen to the children of mothers who fail to meet new work rules because of child care or transportation problems, who are unable to find work within the two-year time limit, or who leave their children at home without adequate care while they participate in required work programs? . . . Welfare-to-work programs may not rescue enough families from poverty to offset the numbers forced into the child welfare system by time limits, sanctions, and working conditions. In short, welfare reform may cause a net increase in the number of children entering foster care. . . .

The shift in federal policy from family preservation toward adoption also corresponded with the change in the federal position on trans-racial adoption. For decades, the federal government permitted public adoption agencies to enforce race-matching policies that sought to place black children exclusively with black adoptive families. In 1994 and 1996, however, Congress prohibited agencies receiving federal funding from placing children according to race or even from taking race into account in placement decisions. Federal support of trans-racial adoption has been championed as a critical step in increasing the numbers of adoptions of black children, the population with the lowest rate of permanent placements. Race-matching policies, it is argued, damage black children by not only denying them placements with white adoptive parents, but also by causing them to languish in foster care. . . .

The emphasis on freeing children for adoption heightens the tension between foster parents and biological parents, a contest that increasingly takes on a racial cast. . . . These contests bring to the surface a theme that runs more subtly through some of the discourse supporting trans-racial adoption — the belief that black children fare better if raised by white adoptive families than if returned home. Advocates of trans-racial adoption frequently assert the benefits of racial assimilation that black children and white parents experience by living together. In *Family Bonds*, for example, Elizabeth Bartholet rejects the claim that black children belong with black parents not only because "there is no evidence that black parents do a better job than white parents of raising black children with a sense of pride in their racial background," but also because black children reap substantial advantages from a white environment. Unlike black children "living in a state of relative isolation or exclusion from the white world," Bartholet contends, "black children raised in white homes are comfortable with their blackness and also uniquely comfortable in dealing with whites." As in the rhetoric promoting ASFA, the rhetoric promoting trans-racial adoption promotes the disruption of

poor minority families by depicting adoptive homes as superior to children's existing family relationships.

In sum, ASFA's emphasis on adoption and its popularity stemmed largely from
concurrent developments in government policy related to welfare and trans-racial
adoption. Determining whether ASFA furthers children's rights must take into
account this political context. . . .

Elizabeth Bartholet, The Challenge of Children's Rights Advocacy: Problems and Progress in the Area of Child Abuse and Neglect
3 Whittier J. Child & Fam. Advoc. 215, 218-221 (2004)

A.   *Early Intensive Home Visitation*

Early home visitation programs have developed in recent years as a way of addressing the problems of fragile families, typically first-time mothers whose children
are identified as being at risk of child abuse and neglect because of the mothers'
low socio-economic status and other factors. Inspired by Europe, where home
visitation for young mothers is often provided as part of universal health care,
some of the American programs have developed a more intensive visitation model
better suited to a high risk population, with mothers visited on a regular basis both
during pregnancy and through the first couple of years of the child's infancy.

I see this intensive form of home visitation as enormously promising. David
Olds has demonstrated, through his careful research methodology, that his model,
which uses nurse practitioners as the home visitors, works to reduce child abuse
and neglect and is cost effective, at least when targeted to relatively high risk
populations. His cost effectiveness research shows that his home visitation
program saves the government money over the short term by reducing repeat
pregnancies and helping to move young mothers into employment and off welfare.

This is an extremely conservative measure of cost effectiveness, since it does
not even take into account the long term savings anticipated from reducing child
abuse and neglect, and the enormous social costs associated with it. A comprehensive recent report on home visitation program research by an independent
group of experts assembled by the U.S. Department of Health and Human Services
constitutes a powerful endorsement of home visitation's success in reducing child
abuse and neglect. The report concludes: "On the basis of strong evidence of
effectiveness, the Task Force recommends early childhood home visitation for
the prevention of child abuse and neglect." The Task Force's highest standard
of effectiveness was met. The Task Force recommended home visitation for all at
risk populations, including all disadvantaged and low-birthweight infants. It found
that home visitation reduced the incidence of child abuse and neglect by about
40%, as compared with control populations, and concluded, as has David Olds, that
the impact on child abuse and neglect was likely even greater because of the
"surveillance" effect — the fact that the very presence of home visitors increases
the likelihood that child abuse and neglect will be observed. The Task Force also
endorsed Olds' cost effectiveness research and his conclusion that programs using
nurse practitioners appeared to work better than those using paraprofessionals.

The kind of intensive and expensive home visitation programs which have actually been shown to be effective are the kind of general family support that our country has traditionally been reluctant to finance. Our politicians are all too ready to focus on the immediate expense of family support and ignore the horrendous long-term costs of child abuse and neglect — the costs associated with foster care and with the lives of crime, substance abuse, domestic violence, and unemployment that all too many victims of child maltreatment will live.

Also, our current early home visitation model is not likely to reach the families that are most at risk for child abuse and neglect. The model is voluntary not mandatory, offering home visitation to parents but not forcing it upon them. This is no surprise since the model has been built within the political realities of our deference to parental autonomy. The problem is that the parents who are most likely to be maltreating their children are those least likely to be willing to open the door to the home visitor who might witness the substance abuse and the child abuse and neglect that will put the parents at risk for criminal prosecution and child protective service intervention. Even the most enthusiastic home visitation advocates admit that a high percentage of parents refuse to participate and that the hard core problem parents are likely to be in this group. Yet as best I know I am virtually alone in advocating for mandatory home visitation, which seems to me essential if we are to reach the hard core group. . . .

C. *Family Preservation*

. . . Our child welfare policies place a high priority on family preservation even after serious child abuse and neglect has been identified. The Adoption and Safe Families Act (ASFA) passed by Congress in 1997 constitutes a major attempt to rebalance our society's priorities, placing a higher value on children's interests in safety and in moving on to permanent adoptive homes if their birth parents can not demonstrate within a reasonable period of time that they are capable of providing a nurturing home. ASFA is paralleled by numerous state and local policy initiatives placing a higher priority on children's interests when they seem in conflict with family preservation, such as expedited termination of parental rights (TPR) programs, and concurrent planning.

I have been an enthusiastic advocate for ASFA, for expedited TPR in egregious cases of child abuse and neglect, and for concurrent planning. I think we need to place a higher priority on children's interests than we have traditionally, and be more skeptical than we have traditionally as to whether those interests are always served by keeping them in their birth families. We need to recognize that what children victimized by child abuse and neglect, like battered women, often need is liberation from their families, rather than family preservation.

Critics of ASFA and other adoption-friendly policies argue that they are an unfair attack upon poor families. They are right that we don't do enough to enable poor families to succeed. We need to do more up front to support these families through intensive home visitation and other supportive programs. But once serious child abuse and neglect has been identified, many of the families at issue have fallen into such serious dysfunction that family support services are not likely to help create families that will really work for children. Research, including the most recent research, demonstrates that even well-funded, model family preservation programs have not succeeded in transforming dangerous family environments into ones that are safe and nurturing.

The critics of ASFA and other adoption-friendly policies are, like the critics of transracial adoption, both numerous and powerful. And ASFA leaves much discretion to state and other decision-makers: it is designed to set a new policy direction, but unlike MEPA [Multiethnic Placement Act, discussed in Chapter 5, infra] it mandates relatively little, and it contains many loopholes providing opportunities for those resistant to ASFA's spirit. The evidence to date indicates that some important ASFA provisions are having little impact. States are making liberal use of the exceptions to ASFA's requirement that parental rights be terminated for children held in foster care for 15 of the prior 22 months. States are generally not taking advantage of the opportunity ASFA provides to move children in egregious child abuse and neglect cases onto a fast track to adoption, bypassing any family preservation efforts. And after ASFA, as before, roughly one-third of all foster care children reunited with their birth families will reenter foster care, a statistic that speaks volumes about the harm we are doing to children in our efforts to keep them with their birth families.

Nonetheless, careful observers of ASFA see in their research evidence that this law, together with adoption-friendly state and local initiatives, is making a difference. There has been a dramatic increase in the number of adoptions from foster care. And many child welfare experts testify that ASFA has helped create a new pressure to expedite cases to permanency and to focus more on child safety. . . .

[The author also advocates the elimination of racial barriers to adoption placements and enforcement of federal legislation to that effect (discussed in Chapter 5). Finally, she advocates the enforcement of deadlines (one year) for substance-abusing parents to demonstrate that they are free of drugs and are able to parent before their parental rights are terminated.]

What do you think of the preceding criticisms and proposals of Professors Roberts and Bartholet?

4. Termination of Parental Rights: Procedural Safeguards

a. Reasonable Efforts Requirements

In re Ty M.
655 N.W.2d 672 (Neb. 2003)

WRIGHT, J.

Shawn M. and Holly M. each appeal from a judgment of the county court for Dodge County, sitting as a juvenile court, which terminated their parental rights to Ty M., born March 23, 1997, and Devon M., born June 10, 1998. . . . Ty and Devon were placed in the care, custody, and control of the Nebraska Department of Health and Human Services (DHHS) on November 20, 1998, after police were sent to the home to investigate a report that the children were in danger based on neglect. At the time, Ty was approximately 1 1/2 years old and Devon was approximately 5 months old. . . .

A petition to terminate parental rights was filed on February 27, 2001. The petition alleged that grounds for termination existed under Neb. Rev. Stat. §43-292(6) (Reissue 1998) because (1) the children had been determined to be children under §43-247(3)(a) [authorizing jurisdiction of any juvenile who lacks proper parental care] and (2) following that determination, reasonable efforts had been made to preserve and reunify the family, and the efforts had failed to correct the conditions which led to that determination. The petition also alleged that [distinct] grounds for termination existed under §43-292(7) [providing that] termination would be in the best interests of the children [for the reason that they] had been in out-of-home placement for 15 or more of the most recent 22 months. . . .

Best Interests of Children

Holly argues that the juvenile court erred in finding that it is in the best interests of the children to terminate her parental rights. She asserts that none of the witnesses could identify anything other than minor negative events which occurred while the children were in the parents' care. . . .

The children were initially removed from the home based upon the uncleanliness of the home. The home was filthy, and the conditions were inappropriate for children. Bottles contained spoiled formula or milk. Feces stains were seen on the carpet. The children's room had a strong odor of urine and spoiled formula or milk. The breathing treatment apparatus used by Devon was filthy and unusable, and no medication for the machine was found in the home.

The case plans that were implemented were not adopted merely to teach the parents how to clean a house. If cleanliness was the sole issue to be addressed prior to reuniting the family, it would not have been necessary for DHHS to expend more than $ 111,000 in resources trying to reunite the parents with the children. The conditions observed in the house were only a symptom of the problems which led to the adjudication and the subsequent plans for reunification. They did not represent a situation which could be remedied by simply hiring a cleaning service. . . .

The juvenile court agreed to a modified case plan received on April 21, 1999, which included goals for each parent. . . . Additional case plans were filed and received by the juvenile court on April 20 and October 20, 1999, April 21 and August 31, 2000, and January 12,2001. At a hearing on November 30,2001, Mary Goodwin, a protection and safety worker for DHHS who had been the caseworker for the parents since April 2000, testified as to the goals outlined in the final case plan for reunification of the family.

The first goal was for Holly to acquire skills to provide a clean and safe environment for the children. While Shawn was incarcerated between October 1999 and October 2000, Holly lived in various places, but did not have a residence of her own. In September 2000, Holly had obtained her own residence, but she said she was not ready to have the children returned to her. Holly had requested that the children be removed from the home in February 1999 because she was afraid of Shawn, who had broken a car window and "thrown the other son, Nicki, around."

A second goal was for Holly to address her mental health issues and comply with all mental health recommendations. Holly dropped out of therapy between August and November 2000 and again in May 2001.

The third goal called for Holly to acquire the skills needed to protect her children from domestic violence by participating in a domestic violence support group and to demonstrate an ability to assert herself in a way that would protect her and the children. Holly attended three sessions on domestic violence in November and December 2000. She received a psychiatric evaluation on July 31, 2000, and was given medication for depression. Psychological evaluations were later scheduled, but neither Holly nor Shawn appeared, and they did not reschedule the appointments.

The fourth goal was for Holly to demonstrate the ability to manage her children's behavior at all times during visits. Goodwin said the children's behavior was chaotic during visits, and Holly admitted that she could not control the children, who would be aggressive toward each other and would not listen to Holly. At times, she would "zone out" and would not notice that the children were "tearing up" the visitation room. On one occasion, they pulled down the drapes. They jumped off tables and climbed up on a file cabinet and jumped off. On another occasion, one boy jumped onto a pile of blankets, injuring another boy who was underneath the blankets. Goodwin stated that these problems were ongoing.

The fifth goal was for Holly to address her marital situation and determine whether it is in the best interests of her children to continue her relationship with Shawn. In September 2000, Holly reported that Shawn had threatened to break her hips, and in October 2000, she reported that she was hiding from Shawn because he was getting out of jail and she was afraid of him. However, the couple reunited when Shawn was released from jail.

The sixth goal was for Holly to learn to manage her finances to demonstrate that she can provide for the basic needs of her children and herself. Holly obtained her own home in September 2000.

The seventh goal was for Shawn to acquire the skills needed to provide a clean environment for his children. Goodwin said he was not able to work on the goal because he was incarcerated for a year.

The eighth goal was for Shawn to address mental health issues and to comply with mental health recommendations. Shawn completed a psychological evaluation in July 1999, which resulted in a finding that Shawn had an issue with anger management. It was recommended that Shawn receive counseling for anger management, parenting issues, and marital issues. After the parents missed appointments for counseling, they were referred to Susan Rippke, an in-home therapist. Shawn had several sessions with Rippke before Shawn was incarcerated. Holly missed approximately five appointments between August and November 1999. She was then scheduled to travel to Omaha for counseling, but dropped out after one appointment. Shawn received some therapy while in jail and was in therapy at the time of the November 2001 hearing.

The ninth goal was for Shawn to gain control over his temper and learn to manage his anger in appropriate ways. When he was released from jail in October

2000, he was referred to a men's group to address domestic violence, but he did not take part.

The 10th goal was for Shawn to increase his parenting knowledge and skills, demonstrate an understanding of child development, learn and utilize nonphysical ways to discipline, and respond to his children in a nurturing manner. Goodwin said the parents had taken advantage of parenting assistance on only a few occasions. Problems with managing the children's behavior during visits continued, and Goodwin reported occasions when Shawn yelled at Ty. Shawn countermanded consequences given by Holly and told the children they did not have to follow her directions. The parents continued to neglect safety issues by allowing the children to ride on the bottom of carts at stores, which resulted in injury to one of the children. The parents allowed Ty to ride a toy motorcycle into the street when a car was approaching. . . .

The 11th goal was for Shawn to learn to manage his finances to demonstrate an ability to provide for his and the children's needs. Shawn worked at one job from December 2000 to June 2001. At the end of June, he began working at another job, where he reported earning about $1,500 every 2 weeks and working "a lot" of overtime. Holly worked part-time jobs between February 1999 and June 2000, when she began working a full-time job, where she worked until September. She was unemployed between September and November 2000. She worked at another job from November 2000 until September 2001, was unemployed for a while, and then began working again.

Goodwin's testimony indicates that the parents have continued to behave in ways which are not in the best interests of the children. They have received various forms of assistance from DHHS staff, yet they have not been able to meet the goals set for them over a 2-year period.

While it appears that the parents have addressed some of the issues in the case plans, we have held that

> " 'participation in certain elements of the court ordered plan does not necessarily prevent the court from entering an order of termination where the parent has made no progress toward rehabilitation. A parent is required not only to follow the plan of the court to rehabilitate herself but also to make reasonable efforts on her own to bring about rehabilitation.' " [In re Interest of L.H. et al., 487 N.W.2d 279, 289 (Neb. 1992), quoting In re Interest of M., 453 N.W.2d 589 (Neb. 1990).]

This court has also held that partial compliance with one provision of a rehabilitation plan does not prevent termination of parental rights.

In addition, this court has held that the juvenile court is not limited to reviewing the efforts of the parent under the plan last ordered by the court; rather, the court looks at the entire reunification program and the parent's compliance with the various plans involved in the program, as well as any effort not contained within the program which would bring the parent closer to reunification. . . .

[W]e conclude that the record shows by clear and convincing evidence that it is in the best interests of the children to terminate the parental rights of Shawn and Holly. The parents have been provided many reasonable opportunities to rehabilitate, and they have failed to do so. The condition of the home was merely a manifestation of the parents' inability to properly care for their children. The evidence clearly and convincingly shows that the parents willfully failed to comply in whole or in part with the material provisions of the rehabilitation plans. . . .

Reasonable Efforts

Shawn argues that the juvenile court erred in finding that reasonable efforts had been made to preserve and reunify the family in the juvenile action and in the termination proceedings. He asserts that the State did not meet its burden because it relied on certified copies of prior court orders and did not elicit testimony on the reasonable efforts which had been made. . . . Holly argues that the State did not meet its burden to show that reasonable efforts would not result in reunification of the family. She suggests that the parents' opportunity to work toward reunification was thwarted by the actions of DHHS to decrease visitation. . . .

Section 43-292 identifies the grounds for termination of parental rights. It provides that termination may be ordered when it is in the best interests of the children and another condition exists. Subsection (6) allows for termination after a determination that the juveniles fall under §43-247(3)(a) and reasonable efforts to preserve and reunify the family if required under Neb. Rev. Stat. §43-283.01 (Reissue 1998), under the direction of the court, have failed to correct the conditions leading to the determination. Subsection (7) allows for termination after the juveniles have been in an out-of-home placement for 15 or more months of the most recent 22 months.

The parties stipulated to the dates of the children's out-of-home placement, which clearly showed that they had been out of the parental home for all but 2 of the approximately 36 months before the termination hearing. They were in foster care with nonrelatives for more than 24 months immediately preceding the hearing. Thus, §43-292(7) applies to these children, and if it is in their best interests to be removed from the home on this basis, the juvenile court may so order.

The record shows that DHHS worked with the family for almost 3 years before parental rights were terminated. The case plans in evidence and the court hearings and orders in the record support a finding that reasonable efforts were made to reunify the family. As we have held on numerous occasions, children cannot, and should not, be suspended in foster care or be made to await uncertain parental maturity. The assignment of error concerning reasonable efforts has no merit.

Unconstitutionality of §43-292(7)

The parents assert that §43-292(7) is unconstitutional because it uses an arbitrary and vague standard to terminate parental rights based solely on the length of time a child has been placed outside the home. The parents' arguments concerning the constitutionality of §43-292(7) are stated in broad terms and suggest only that the statute violates due process because it provides an arbitrary standard.

We have frequently held that where a parent is unable or unwilling to rehabilitate himself or herself within a reasonable time, the best interests of the children require termination of the parental rights. [S]ubsection (7) merely provides a guideline for the "reasonable time" given to the parents to rehabilitate themselves. . . . Section 43-292(7) is not unconstitutional. Adequate safeguards are provided to ensure that parental rights are not terminated based solely upon the length of time children are in an out-of-home placement.

Conclusion

The children in this case were initially removed from the home because it was filthy and unlivable. Although these conditions were apparently corrected at a later date, they were not the only basis upon which parental rights were terminated. The uncleanliness of the home was a manifestation of a lack of parenting skills on the part of Shawn and Holly. During a period of more than 2 years, the parents were unable to correct these deficiencies.

We find no error on the part of the juvenile court in its judgment terminating the parental rights of Shawn and Holly to Ty and Devon. The judgment is affirmed.

NOTES AND QUESTIONS

(1) Federal Mandate.   Every state has statutory provisions authorizing the permanent removal of an endangered child from the home. Before termination of parental rights, however, the state must provide rehabilitation services, including reunification efforts. Federal legislation mandates the provision of these services. The Adoption Assistance and Child Welfare Act of 1980 (AACWA), 42 U.S.C. §§620 et seq., 670 et seq. (2000 & Supp. 2005), provides that, to qualify for federal funding, states have to make *"reasonable efforts"* (id. at §671(a)(15)) to prevent placement of a child in foster care and to reunify a foster child with his or her parents. Some state statutes contained "reasonable efforts requirements" prior to the enactment of AACWA, but the AACWA triggered widespread adoption of such requirements.

Some jurisdictions (like Nebraska in In re Ty) now specify that a ground for termination of parental rights is the failure of the state's "reasonable efforts" to remedy the condition leading to the determination of the child as abused or neglected. See Neb. Rev. Stat. §43-292 (2004) (requiring best interests test plus failure of reasonable efforts).

(2) "Reasonable Efforts" Defined.   What constitutes "reasonable efforts"? Because neither the AACWA nor many state statutes define the term, courts must interpret whether the provision of certain services satisfies the requirement. What services did the state provide in In re Ty? How does the court determine whether the provision of these services constituted "reasonable efforts"?

Federal legislation currently defines the nature of reunification services. The Adoption and Safe Families Act (ASFA) defines such services to include: (i) Individual, group, and family counseling; (ii) Inpatient, residential, or outpatient substance abuse treatment services; (iii) Mental health services; (iv) Assistance to address domestic violence; (v) Services designed to provide temporary child care and therapeutic services for families, including crisis nurseries. 42 U.S.C. §629a(a) (2000 & Supp. 2005).

(3) Time-Limited Services.   How much time must the state devote to providing reasonable efforts before terminating parental rights? ASFA currently emphasizes the time-limited nature of rehabilitation services, restricting services to those provided within a 15-month period following placement of a child into foster care. See 42 U.S.C. §629a(a)(7) (2000). See also State ex rel. Children, Youth & Families Dept., 47 P.3d 859 (N.M. Ct. App. 2002) (declaring that states are not required to make reunification efforts for an indefinite period of time, reasoning that ASFA's 15-month period provides a measure of the state's duty).

Is ASFA's 15-month period sufficient time for the state to provide meaningful services? See Will L. Crossley, Defining Reasonable Efforts: Demystifying the State's Burden Under Federal Child Protection Legislation, 12 B.U. Pub. Int. L.J. 259, 292 (2003) (arguing that it is not sufficient, especially for parents who are substance abusers or serving jail sentences).

(4) Exceptions to "Reasonable Efforts" Requirement.   Are "reasonable efforts" required even when they are likely to be futile? ASFA removed the "reasonable efforts" requirement in cases in which (1) the child has been the victim of aggravated circumstances, such as torture, abandonment, or sexual abuse; (2) the parent has killed another child or attempted to do so; or (3) the state has terminated the parent's rights with respect to a sibling. 42 U.S.C. §§671 (a)(15)(D)(i), (ii), (iii) (2000).

(5) Duration in Foster Care as Ground for Termination.   To what extent can states rely on the duration that a child has spent in foster care to trigger termination proceedings? Note that the duration that Ty and his brother spent in out-of-home placement was a separate statutory ground for termination of parental rights (provided that the best interests test was also satisfied). The Nebraska statutory provision for termination of parental rights adopts ASFA's requirement that states must seek termination of parental rights for any child who has been in foster care for 15 of the last 22 months. 42 U.S.C. §675(5)(E) (2000).

Is the child's stay in foster care an appropriate indicator of parental unfitness? How does In re Ty respond to the parents' argument that the durational requirement violates their due process rights? Cf. In re H.G., 757 N.E.2d 864 (Ill. 2001) (holding that the statutory presumption of parental unfitness based on child's duration in foster care is not narrowly tailored to serve the compelling state interest in child protection and thus violates due process).

(6) Incarceration as Ground for Termination.   In In re Ty, the father had been incarcerated for approximately one year. Should incarceration of a parent be a sufficient ground for termination of a parent's rights? Many states have such provisions, although the details vary considerably. Compare Tex. Fam. Code Ann. §161.001(1)(Q)(ii) (Vernon 2002 & Supp. 2008) (terminating parental rights in cases of confinement and inability to care for the child for at least two years) with Fla. Stat. Ann. §39.806(1)(d) (West 2003 & Supp. 2008) (incarceration is grounds for termination, provided that prison term comprises a substantial portion of the child's minority; parent comes within statutory designation of "violent career criminal"; or the court determines by clear and convincing evidence that continuation of the parent-child relationship would be harmful to the child). See generally Philip M. Genty, Damage to Family Relationships as a Collateral Consequence of Parental Incarceration, 30 Fordham Urb. L.J. 1671 (2003) (suggesting that ASFA

has had a disproportionate impact on incarcerated parents who have children in foster care by increasing the rates of termination of parental rights.

(7) "Reasonable Efforts" for Mentally Ill Children.   Is ASFA's requirement that states make "reasonable efforts" for family preservation and reunification being met for mentally ill children? Recent research reveals that state welfare officials increasingly are informing parents of children with serious mental illness that parents must transfer custody of their children to the state, pursuant to state statutes, as a condition of receiving mental health services because children in foster care can more easily obtain mental health resources. Do such statutes violate a family's constitutional due process right to family integrity? See generally Tracy J. Simmons, Relinquishing Custody in Exchange for Mental Healthcare Services: Undermining the Adoption and Safe Families Act's Promise of Reasonable Efforts Towards Family Preservation and Reunification, 10 J. L. & Fam. Stud. 377 (2008).

(8) "Reasonable Efforts" and Cultural Context.   A considerable number of child welfare cases involve families from different cultural backgrounds. Should the "reasonable efforts" requirement take into account cultural context in terms of the definition of whether services are "reasonable"? See Nell Clement, Do "Reasonable Efforts" Require Cultural Competence? The Importance of Culturally Competent Reunification Services in the California Child Welfare System, 5 Hastings Race & Poverty L.J. 397 (2008) (so arguing).

(9) Does inclusion of "reasonable efforts" requirements before termination contribute to harm to children by creating unnecessary obstacles to termination of parental rights, as some commentators argue? Compare Elizabeth Bartholet, Nobody's Children: Abuse and Neglect, Foster Care Drift, and the Adoption Alternative (1999) with Martin Guggenheim, Somebody's Children: Sustaining the Family's Place in Child Welfare Policy, 113 Harv. L. Rev. 1716 (1999) (rebutting Bartholet's assumptions and conclusions).

b. Standard of Proof

The United States Supreme Court resolved the standard of proof issue for termination of parental rights in Santosky v. Kramer, 455 U.S. 745 (1982). In *Santosky*, the Court held that the New York Family Court Act's "fair preponderance of the evidence" standard for determining "permanent neglect" denied due process to parents where termination of rights was at stake.

In writing for the majority, Justice Blackmun emphasized that the fundamental liberty interest of natural parents in the care, custody, and control of their child does not disappear simply because they have not been model parents or have temporarily lost custody of their child to the state. For this reason, the Court held that before a state may sever completely and irrevocably the rights of parents in their natural child, due process requires the state to support its allegations by at least "clear and convincing" evidence. The Court declined to require the even more stringent "beyond a reasonable doubt" standard, but noted that state legislatures and courts are free to adopt the higher standard.

Justice Rehnquist, joined by three other Justices, dissented and argued that the standard of proof chosen by New York reflected a constitutionally permissible balance of the competing interests of the parents, the child, and the state. He emphasized the state's earnest efforts to aid the parents in regaining custody of their children and the numerous procedural protections afforded by other provisions of New York law. According to Justice Rehnquist, the majority's "obsessive focus on the standard of proof" was not required by the Due Process Clause and constituted a worrisome intrusion into an area of law traditionally entrusted to the states.

States have adopted different approaches to the standard of proof required by *Santosky*. See Brian C. Hill, Comment, The State's Burden of Proof at the Best Interests Stage of a Termination of Parental Rights, 2004 U. Chi. Legal F. 557, 565-566 (surveying jurisdictions). Most states follow *Santosky* and require clear and convincing evidence. However, some states hold that *Santosky* applies only to the initial determination of parental unfitness in a termination-of-parental-rights hearing but not to the dispositional stage of the proceeding (sometimes called the "best interests" stage after the standard used to decide whether a child should be removed from parental custody). These states apply a preponderance-of-the-evidence standard in the latter stage. An occasional state requires the strictest standard of beyond a reasonable doubt. Is the dispositional stage sufficiently different from the evidentiary stage to require the use of a different standard of proof? See Hill, supra (arguing that courts should apply the *Santosky* standard to both stages).

c. Right to Counsel

The Supreme Court has determined that an indigent parent has no constitutional right to counsel in a termination of parental rights proceeding. In Lassiter v. Department of Social Services, 452 U.S. 18 (1981), the Court held that the Due Process Clause does not give biological parents a right to counsel in every parental termination proceeding. Rather, according to the Court, the decision to appoint counsel should be made by the trial court on a case-by-case balancing test in light of the parents' interests, the state interests, and the risk of error. The Court reasoned that the failure to appoint counsel to petitioner did not deprive her of due process in light of the circumstances — i.e., the termination petition contained no allegations on which criminal charges could be based, the case presented no complicated points of law, and the presence of counsel would not have made a difference for the petitioner (who had been sentenced to 25 to 40 years' incarceration for second-degree murder).

However, most states reject *Lassiter*, either by case law or statute. Currently, about 40 states provide counsel for parents in termination-of-parental-rights proceedings. Bruce A. Boyer, Justice, Access to the Courts, and the Right to Free Counsel for Indigent Parents: The Continuing Scourge of Lassiter v. Department of Social Services of Durham, 36 Loy. U. Chi. L.J. 363, 367 (2005) (pointing out the increase in jurisdictions following *Lassiter*, when 33 states had provisions for a right to counsel). See also Clare Pastore, Life after *Lassiter*: An Overview of State-Court Right-to-Counsel Decisions, 40 Clearinghouse Review 186 (July-Aug. 2006).

Does a statutory right to counsel in parental rights termination cases require a right to *effective* counsel? See New Jersey Div. of Youth and Family Services v.

B.R., 929 A. 2d 1034 (N.J. 2007); In re M.S., 115 S.W.3d 534 (Tex. 2003) (both so holding). See generally Michele R. Forte, Notes and Comments, Making the Case for Effective Assistance of Counsel in Involuntary Termination of Parental Rights Proceedings, 28 Nova L. Rev. 193 (2003).

CHAPTER 4

Medical Treatment: Who Speaks for the Child?

A. *INTRODUCTION*

As a general rule, informed parental consent is both a necessary and sufficient condition for the medical treatment of minors. This chapter examines the reasons for this general rule and its exceptions. It explores in several different contexts how power and responsibility to decide about the medical care of minors is now allocated among the child, the family, various medical professionals, and state officials, and asks how power *should* be allocated. What voice should the child have? What is the appropriate role of parents, doctors, and the state?

This chapter begins with some background material on the general requirement of parental consent and its exceptions. Excerpts from several statutes are provided, and questions are posed concerning the relationship of the consent requirement to the issue of who is and should be financially responsible for paying for a child's medical care. Next, some standard common law and statutory limitations and exceptions to the general parental consent requirement are explored. These relate to mandatory immunizations and screening procedures (applicable to all children), the neglect limitation (where a court may override a parental decision for an individual child), the emergency treatment of children (where no parental consent is required if the parent is unavailable), and various exceptions that allow minors themselves to consent to treatment.

The chapter then examines the parental consent requirement in the context of the decision to withhold or discontinue life-sustaining procedures for a newborn with birth defects. Materials are provided to explore the legal, ethical, and policy issues relating to when the state should overrule parental decisions in an extreme context. Adults may, under some circumstances, decide to withhold treatment for themselves (such as by the use of advance directives). Is it ever acceptable to withhold essential treatment from a severely handicapped newborn who cannot decide for itself? If so, what should the standards be? Who should decide? What procedure should be followed?

The same issues are examined in the context of medical experimentation on children. Should an exception to the general rule that allows parents to consent to the medical treatment of their child be made when the treatment is experimental, or when the child is exposed to a procedure that is not even for his or her therapeutic benefit?

The chapter also explores some of the legal issues that are implicated in the context of adolescent health. In particular, the chapter explores how power and responsibility for adolescent health decision making should be allocated among the child, the family, medical professionals, and the state.

The focus of this chapter is how power and responsibility should be allocated. It does not include materials addressing the state of children's health in the United States or the broad range of health policy issues relating to how the American health delivery system might better serve children.

B.   *THE LEGAL CONTEXT FOR THE MEDICAL TREATMENT OF CHILDREN*

1.   Battery and the Requirement of Informed Consent

As a general proposition, the primary legal principles governing the relationship of doctors to their adult patients are found in the tort law of battery and negligence. The tort of negligence is committed when the patient is harmed because a doctor's conduct falls below the standard of care reasonably to be expected from persons possessing the doctor's professional qualifications. For the most part, the standard of care is unaffected by whether the patient is an adult or a minor.

For battery, on the other hand, the legal framework for children is quite different from that for adults. Battery, in the most general terms, is committed when there is the touching of another without express consent.[1] A successful suit for battery does not require that the plaintiff be physically injured, that the plaintiff suffer a financial loss, or that medical treatment be unsuccessful. Moreover, once a battery has been established, the defendant is responsible for any and all damages that are a consequence of the nonprivileged touching. For negligence, in contrast to battery, the plaintiff must establish substantial injuries, typically with financial implications, and the defendant is in no event responsible for injuries that are not reasonably foreseeable.

For battery, "the central concept is the offense to personal dignity which occurs when another impinges on one's bodily integrity without full and valid consent."[2] In the medical context, to avoid committing a battery, a physician may ordinarily treat an adult patient only after the patient has given informed voluntary consent.[3]

---

[1] Bryan J. Warren, Pennsylvania Medical Informed Consent Law: A Call to Protect Patient Autonomy Rights by Abandoning the Battery Approach, 38 Duq. L. Rev. 917, 928 (2000) (citing William L. Prosser, Law of Torts §10 (4th ed., 1971)).

[2] Charles Fried, Medical Experimentation: Personal Integrity and Social Policy 16 (1974).

[3] On the history of the legal doctrine of informed consent, see Warren, supra note [1], at 927-935.

As a general proposition this requires that the doctor must give the patient the information necessary to make an informed choice. Typically, the diagnosis and prognosis of an illness must be evaluated and the benefits and risks of alternative treatments must be disclosed. There are limitations to the consent requirement for adults. These relate to emergencies (where consent may not be necessary), and the so-called therapeutic privilege (which allows a doctor to withhold information if the doctor reasonably believes that disclosure would not be in the patient's interest and would interfere with the best treatment).

A primary justification for this requirement of informed consent is protection of an adult's right of self-determination.[4] It also may serve to protect patients against depersonalized, authoritarian medical treatment.[5] Are these justifications any less important for children?

Because it was thought that children lacked the capacity to provide consent for purposes of avoiding a battery,[6] courts at common law held that until children reached majority, only a parent or legal guardian could give effective consent to medical treatment.[7] What policies does this rule serve? It protects the child from the responsibility of deciding for himself or herself. For infants or children who lack the maturity to evaluate alternatives and to make an informed choice, someone must decide on the child's behalf. But why parents? The general rule of parental consent is in accordance with broad notions of family privacy, parental autonomy, and the importance of familial bonds. But at the root of the common law rule was the narrower notion that parents are legally responsible for the care and support of their children. Among other things, the parental consent requirement protects parents from having to pay for unwanted or unnecessary medical care and from the possible financial consequences of supporting the child if unwanted treatment is unsuccessful. Indeed, as an Ohio court declared:

> [The rule that parents must consent for minors] is not based upon the capacity of a minor to consent, so far as he is personally concerned . . . but is based upon the right of parents whose liability for support and maintenance of their child may be greatly increased by an unfavorable result from [a surgeon's operation]. [Lacey v. Laird, 139 N.E.2d 25, 30 (Ohio 1956).]

Is there an alternative to the general rule of parental consent? One commentator advocates another approach: a bright-line rule that permits all adolescents over age 16 to have the right to make their own decisions regarding routine medical

---

[4] Pratt v. Davis, 118 Ill. App. 161, 166 (1905), *aff'd*, 79 N.E. 562 (Ill. 1906): ". . . the free citizen's first and greatest right, which underlies all others — the right to the inviolability of his person. . . ."

[5] Robert A. Burt, Taking Care of Strangers: The Rule of Law in Doctor-Patient Relations (1979); Raymond S. Duff & August B. Hollingshead, Sickness and Society (1968); Jay Katz, The Silent World of Doctor and Patient (1984).

[6] Commonwealth v. Nickerson, 87 Mass. (5 Allen) 518 (1863); William L. Prosser & W. Page Keeton, Handbook of the Law of Torts 115 (5th ed. 1984).

[7] Moss v. Rishworth, 222 S.W. 225 (Tex. Civ. App. 1920) (holding that father could recover from surgeon for child's death during operation to remove badly diseased tonsils and adenoids); Zoski v. Gaines, 260 N.W. 99 (Mich. 1935) (holding surgeon liable for operation without parental consent when boy was sent to hospital with note from city physician requesting removal of tonsils).

and surgical treatment.[8] What do you think of this suggestion? How capable are minors of various ages to understand a diagnosis, nature and risks of treatment (and risks of nontreatment), and alternatives to treatment, and then to give their opinions?

2.   Statutory Materials: When May a Minor Consent to Medical Treatment?

Ark. Stat. Ann. §20-9-602 (2005)

§20-9-602. Consent Generally

It is recognized and established that, in addition to such other persons as may be so authorized and empowered, any one of the following persons is authorized and empowered to consent, either orally or otherwise, to any surgical or medical treatment or procedures not prohibited by law which may be suggested, recommended, prescribed, or directed by a licensed physician:

(1) Any adult, for himself or herself;

(2) Any parent, whether an adult or a minor, for his or her minor child or for his or her adult child of unsound mind whether the child is of the parent's blood, an adopted child, a stepchild, or a foster child. However, the father of an illegitimate child cannot consent for the child solely on the basis of parenthood;

(3) Any married person, whether an adult or a minor, for himself or herself;

(4) Any female, regardless of age or marital status, for herself when given in connection with pregnancy or childbirth, except the unnatural interruption of a pregnancy;

(5) Any person standing in loco parentis, whether formally serving or not, and any guardian, conservator or custodian, for his or her ward or other charge under disability;

(6) Any emancipated minor, for himself or herself;

(7) Any unemancipated minor of sufficient intelligence to understand and appreciate the consequences of the proposed surgical or medical treatment or procedures, for himself or herself;

(8) Any adult, for his or her minor sibling or his or her adult sibling of unsound mind;

(9) During the absence of a parent so authorized and empowered, any [grandparent]. . . .

---

[8] Andrew Newman, Adolescent Consent to Routine Medical and Surgical Treatment, 22 J. Legal Med. 501 (2001). See also Andrew Popper, Averting Malpractice by Information: Informed Consent in the Pediatric Treatment Environment 819, 831 (1998) (advocating a middle ground, between a rule of parental consent and a rule allowing unconditional veto power by the minor, which enables a child who is capable of meaningful speech and discussion to hear information and express an opinion).

Ala. Code §§22-8-3 to 22-8-7 (1997)

§22-8-3. *When Physician May Proceed Without Consent of Parent*

Any legally authorized medical, dental, health or mental health services may be rendered to minors of any age without the consent of a parent or legal guardian when, in the physician's judgment, an attempt to secure consent would result in delay of treatment which would increase the risk to the minor's life, health or mental health.

§22-8-4. *When Minor May Give Consent Generally*

Any minor who is 14 years of age or older, or has graduated from high school, or is married, or having been married is divorced or is pregnant may give effective consent to any legally authorized medical, dental, health or mental health services for himself or herself, and the consent of no other person shall be necessary.

§22-8-5. *Consent of Minor for Self and Child*

Any minor who is married, or having been married is divorced or has borne a child may give effective consent to any legally authorized medical, dental, health or mental health services for himself or his child or for herself or her child.

§22-8-6. *Consent of Any Minor as to Pregnancy, Venereal Disease, Drug Dependency, Alcohol Toxicity and Reportable Diseases*

Any minor may give effective consent for any legally authorized medical, health or mental health services to determine the presence of, or to treat, pregnancy, venereal disease, drug dependency, alcohol toxicity or any reportable disease, and the consent of no other person shall be deemed necessary.

§22-8-7. *Effect of Minor's Consent; Liability of Physicians, etc.; Waiver of Rights or Causes of Action*

(a) The consent of a minor who professes to be, but is not, a minor whose consent alone is effective to medical, dental, health or mental health services shall be deemed effective without the consent of the minor's parent or legal guardian if the physician or other person relied in good faith upon the representations of the minor.

(b) Any physician or other person who has relied in good faith upon the representations of any persons under any of the provisions of this chapter or who acts in good faith under any of the provisions of this chapter shall not be liable for not having consent. . . .

Minn. Stat. Ann. §§144.341 to 144.347 (2005 & Supp. 2008)

Consent of Minors for Health Services

144.341. Living Apart from Parents and Managing Financial Affairs, Consent for Self

Notwithstanding any other provision of law, any minor who is living separate and apart from parents or legal guardian, whether with or without the consent of a parent or guardian and regardless of the duration of such separate residence, and who is managing personal financial affairs, regardless of the source or extent of the minor's income, may give effective consent to personal medical, dental, mental and other health services, and the consent of no other person is required.

144.342. Marriage or Giving Birth, Consent for Health Service for Self or Child

Any minor who has been married or has borne a child may give effective consent to personal medical, mental, dental and other health services, or to services for the minor's child, and the consent of no other person is required.

144.343. Pregnancy, Venereal Disease, Alcohol or Drug Abuse, Abortion

Subd. 1. Minor's consent valid.

Any minor may give effective consent for medical, mental and other health services to determine the presence of or to treat pregnancy and conditions associated therewith, venereal disease, alcohol and other drug abuse, and the consent of no other person is required.

Subd. 2. Notification concerning abortion.

Notwithstanding the provisions of section 13.02, subdivision 8, no abortion operation shall be performed upon an unemancipated minor or upon a woman for whom a guardian has been appointed pursuant to sections 524.5-101 to 524.5-502 because of a finding of incapacity, until at least 48 hours after written notice of the pending operation has been delivered in the manner specified in subdivisions 2 to 4.

> (a) The notice shall be addressed to the parent at the usual place of abode of the parent and delivered personally to the parent by the physician or an agent.

(b) In lieu of the delivery required by clause (a), notice shall be made by certified mail addressed to the parent at the usual place of abode of the parent with return receipt requested and restricted delivery to the addressee which means postal employee can only deliver the mail to the authorized addressee. . . .

Subd. 3. Parent, abortion; definitions.

For purposes of this section, "parent" means both parents of the pregnant woman if they are both living, one parent of the pregnant woman if only one is living or if the second one cannot be located through reasonably diligent effort, or the guardian or conservator if the pregnant woman has one. . . .

Subd. 4. Limitations.

No notice shall be required under this section if:
(a) The attending physician certifies in the pregnant woman's medical record that the abortion is necessary to prevent the woman's death and there is insufficient time to provide the required notice; or
(b) The abortion is authorized in writing by the person or persons who are entitled to notice; or
(c) The pregnant minor woman declares that she is a victim of sexual abuse, neglect, or physical abuse as defined in section 626.556. Notice of that declaration shall be made to the proper authorities as provided in section 626.556, subdivision 3.

Subd. 5. Penalty.

Performance of an abortion in violation of this section shall be a misdemeanor and shall be grounds for a civil action by a person wrongfully denied notification. A person shall not be held liable under this section if the person establishes by written evidence that the person relied upon evidence sufficient to convince a careful and prudent person that the representations of the pregnant woman regarding information necessary to comply with this section are bona fide and true, or if the person has attempted with reasonable diligence to deliver notice, but has been unable to do so.

Subd. 6. Substitute notification provisions . . .

(c)(i) If such a pregnant woman elects not to allow the notification of one or both of her parents or guardian or conservator, any judge of a court of competent jurisdiction shall, upon petition, or motion, and after an appropriate hearing, authorize a physician to perform the abortion if said judge determines that the pregnant woman is mature and capable of giving informed consent to the proposed abortion. If said judge determines that the pregnant woman is not mature, or if the pregnant woman does not claim to be mature, the judge shall determine whether the performance of an abortion upon her without notification of her parents, guardian, or conservator would be in her best interests and shall authorize a physician to perform the abortion without such notification if said judge concludes that the pregnant woman's best interests would be served thereby.

(ii) Such a pregnant woman may participate in proceedings in the court on her own behalf, and the court may appoint a guardian ad litem for her. The court shall, however, advise her that she has a right to court appointed counsel, and shall, upon her request, provide her with such counsel.

(iii) Proceedings in the court under this section shall be confidential and shall be given such precedence over other pending matters so that the court may reach a decision promptly and without delay so as to serve the best interests of the pregnant woman. . . .

144.344. Emergency Treatment

Medical, dental, mental and other health services may be rendered to minors of any age without the consent of a parent or legal guardian when, in the professional's judgment, the risk to the minor's life or health is of such a nature that treatment should be given without delay and the requirement of consent would result in delay or denial of treatment.

144.3441. Hepatitis B Vaccination

A minor may give effective consent for a hepatitis B vaccination. The consent of no other person is required.

144.345. Representations to Persons Rendering Service

The consent of a minor who claims to be able to give effective consent for the purpose of receiving medical, dental, mental or other health services but who may not in fact do so, shall be deemed effective without the consent of the minor's parent or legal guardian, if the person rendering the service relied in good faith upon the representations of the minor.

144.346. Information to Parents

The professional may inform the parent or legal guardian of the minor patient of any treatment given or needed where, in the judgment of the professional, failure to inform the parent or guardian would seriously jeopardize the health of the minor patient.

144.347. Financial Responsibility

A minor so consenting for such health services shall thereby assume financial responsibility for the cost of said services.

3.   Model Statute

Institute of Judicial Administration and the American Bar Association, Juvenile Justice Standards: Standards Relating to Rights of Minors 9-12 (1980)

4.1. Prior Parental Consent

A. No medical procedures, services, or treatment should be provided to a minor without prior parental consent, except as specified in Standards 4.4-4.9.

B. Circumstances where parents refuse to consent to treatment are governed by the Abuse and Neglect volume.

4.2. Notification of Treatment

A. Where prior parental consent is not required to provide medical services or treatment to a minor, the provider should promptly notify the parent or responsible custodian of such treatment and obtain his or her consent to further treatment, except as hereinafter specified.

B. Where the medical services provided are for the treatment of chemical dependency, Standard 4.7, or venereal disease, contraception, and pregnancy, Standard 4.8, the physician should first seek and obtain the minor's permission to notify the parent of such treatments.

   1. If the minor-patient objects to notification of the parent, the physician should not notify the parent that treatment was or is being provided unless he or she concludes that failing to inform the parent could seriously jeopardize the health of the minor, taking into consideration

      a. the impact that such notification could have on the course of treatment;

      b. the medical considerations which require such notification;

      c. the nature, basis, and strength of the minor's objections;

      d. the extent to which parental involvement in the course of treatment is required or desirable.

   2. A physician who concludes that notification of the parent is medically required should:

      a. indicate the medical justifications in the minor-patient's file; and

      b. inform the parent only after making all reasonable efforts to persuade the minor to consent to notification of the parent.

C. Where the medical services provided are for the treatment of a mental or emotional disorder pursuant to Standard 4.9, after three sessions the provider should notify the parent of such treatment and obtain his or her consent to further treatment.

4.3. Financial Liability

A. A parent should be financially liable to persons providing medical treatment to his or her minor child if the parent consents to such services, or if the services are provided under emergency circumstances pursuant to Standard 4.5.

B. A minor who consents to his or her own medical treatment under Standard 4.6-4.9 should be financially liable for payment for such services, and should not disaffirm the financial obligation on account of minority.

C. A public or private health insurance policy or plan under which a minor is a beneficiary should allow a minor who consents to medical services or treatment to file claims and receive benefits, regardless of whether the parent has consented to the treatment.

D. A public or private health insurer should not inform a parent or policy holder that a minor has filed a claim or received a benefit under a health insurance policy or plan of which the minor is a beneficiary, unless the physician has previously notified the parent of the treatment for which the claim is submitted.

4.4. Emancipated Minor

A. An emancipated minor who is living separate and apart from his or her parent and who is managing his or her own financial affairs may consent to medical treatment on the same terms and conditions as an adult. Accordingly, parental consent should not be required, nor should there be subsequent notification of the parent, or financial liability.

   1. If a physician treats a minor who is not actually emancipated, it should be a defense to a suit basing liability on lack of parental consent, that he or she relied in good faith on the minor's representations of emancipation. . . .

4.5. Emergency Treatment

A. Under emergency circumstances, a minor may receive medical services or treatment without prior parental consent.

   1. Emergency circumstances exist when delaying treatment to first secure parental consent would endanger the life or health of the minor.

   2. It should be a defense to an action basing liability on lack of parental consent, that the medical services were provided under emergency circumstances.

B. Where medical services or treatment are provided under emergency circumstances, the parent should be notified as promptly as possible, and his or her consent should be obtained for further treatment.

C. A parent should be financially liable to persons providing emergency medical treatment.

D. Where the emergency medical services are for treatment of chemical dependency (Standard 4.7); venereal disease, contraception, or pregnancy (Standard 4.8); or mental or emotional disorder (Standard 4.9), questions of notification of the parent and financial liability are governed by those provisions and Standards 4.2 B., 4.2 C., and 4.3.

4.6. Mature Minor

A. A minor of [16] or older who has sufficient capacity to understand the nature and consequences of a proposed medical treatment for his or her benefit may consent to that treatment on the same terms and conditions as an adult.

B. The treating physician should notify the minor's parent of any medical treatment provided under this standard, subject to the provisions of Standard 4.2 B.

4.7. Chemical Dependency

A. A minor of any age may consent to medical services, treatment, or therapy for problems or conditions related to alcohol or drug abuse or addiction.

B. If the minor objects to notification of the parent, the person or agency providing treatment under this standard should notify the parent of such treatment only if he or she concludes that failing to inform the parent would seriously jeopardize the health of the minor, and complies with the provisions of Standard 4.2.

4.8. Venereal Disease, Contraception, and Pregnancy

A. A minor of any age may consent to medical services, therapy, or counseling for:

    1. treatment of venereal disease;

    2. family planning, contraception, or birth control other than a procedure which results in sterilization; or

    3. treatment related to pregnancy, including abortion.

B. If the minor objects to notification of the parent, the person or agency providing treatment under this standard should notify the parent of such treatment only if he or she concludes that failing to inform the parent would seriously jeopardize the health of the minor, and complies with the provision of Standard 4.2.

4.9. Mental or Emotional Disorder

A. A minor of fourteen or older who has or professes to suffer from a mental or emotional disorder may consent to three sessions with a psychotherapist or counselor for diagnosis and consultation.

B. Following three sessions for crisis intervention and/or diagnosis, the provider should notify the parent of such sessions and obtain his or her consent to further treatment.

4. Who Pays for Medical Treatment?

Parents generally have the primary responsibility for paying for a child's medical treatment. Child support statutes in many jurisdictions are very broadly written (see Chapter 2) and have readily been construed to require the payment of necessary medical expenses. The common law made little provision for civil enforcement by the child or a third party of the parents' obligation to pay medical expenses; the modern trend, however, has been to allow third parties to sue the neglectful parent in quasi-contract.

Government also plays an important role in paying for medical care when parents are too poor to provide necessary medical treatment. For example, the Medicaid program was created expressly to provide health care and services to people who cannot afford them. There were over 55 million people receiving Medicaid benefits in 2004. Approximately 20 million of them were under age 12.[9]

Formerly, Medicaid entitlement was automatic for people receiving Aid to Families with Dependent Children (AFDC). When welfare reform legislation (PRWORA) replaced AFDC with the Temporary Assistance for Needy Families (TANF) program in 1996, Congress severed the automatic eligibility provision between welfare and Medicaid. Under PRWORA, states may deny Medicaid to heads of households who lose TANF benefits because of their refusal to work. However, states must continue to provide Medicaid benefits to pregnant women and children.[10] (PRWORA is discussed in Chapter 2, pp. 221-225.)

The Balanced Budget Act of 1997, Pub. L. No. 105-33, 111 Stat. 251 (1997), established the State Children's Health Insurance Program (SCHIP), 42 U.S.C. §§1397 et seq. (2000), to provide health insurance coverage to states for uninsured children in eligible low-income families. Revisions to SCHIP, 67 Fed. Reg. 61,956 (Oct. 2, 2002) (codified at 42 C.F.R. pt. 457 (2003)), redefine "child" (formerly those under 19 years of age) to include the unborn.[11]

As you can see from the preceding materials, some states provide statutory authority for young people in some circumstances to consent to their own medical treatment. See, e.g., pp. 374-378. When the child, not the parent, is providing the only consent for treatment, who should pay? Is it fair to impose the financial responsibility on the parents, especially in circumstances where parents can plausibly claim they would not have approved of treatment? Would not requiring parents to pay jeopardize the possible confidentiality interests of the minor? If parents are required to pay, would this create substantial risks that the parents might obstruct the young person's access to care?

If parents are not to pay directly, would it nonetheless be possible for the minor to be able to make use of his or her parent's health insurance? Without parental knowledge? Should the minor be able to bind himself or herself contractually to be obligated for payment, notwithstanding his or her minority? Would the "necessaries" doctrine so provide? See p. 158, supra. Should the state guarantee payment by the minor? Note how Section 4.3 of the Juvenile Justice Standards Relating to the Rights of Minors resolves these issues. See p. 379, supra.

---

[9] Centers for Medicare and Medicaid Services, FY 2004 National MSIS Tables (2007), available at *http://www.cms.hhs.gov/Medicaid DataSourcesGenInfo/02-MSISData.asp.*

[10] House Comm. on Ways & Means, 108th Cong., 2d Sess., Background Material and Data on Programs Within the Jurisdiction of the Committee on Ways & Means (2004 Green Book) 15-33 (Comm. Printing 2004). On the history of Medicaid, see id. at 15-26 to 15-45.

[11] See generally Elisabeth H. Sperow, Redefining Child Abuse Under the State Children's Health Insurance Program: Capable of Repetition, Yet Evading Results, 12 Am. U. J. Gender Soc. Pol'y & L. 137, 139 (2004).

C. EXCEPTIONS AND LIMITATIONS TO PARENTAL CONSENT REQUIREMENTS

1. Introductory Issues

PROBLEMS

Consider these problems in light of the preceding statutory materials:

(1) Twelve-year-old Jacqueline Parker fell off her bike after school at 3:15 P.M. while playing with a friend. Because Jacqueline appeared to be in extreme pain, the friend's mother took Jacqueline to the hospital emergency room. The friend's mother attempted unsuccessfully to contact Jacqueline's mother, who was out shopping and was not expected to return home until after 6:00 P.M. Jacqueline's father was away on a business trip. Whose consent, if any, should be required before:

a. The hospital may take x-rays to determine if her arm is broken?

b. The doctor may set the fracture, assuming he knows her arm is broken?

c. The physician may administer some pain-killing drug to make the child more comfortable until her mother is located? May the friend's mother consent? Would it make any difference if the adult accompanying Jacqueline had been her aunt? A paid baby-sitter? A camp counselor? A teacher? Suppose her parents were on a safari and might not be reached for a week or more? Would Jacqueline's consent be sufficient? Suppose Jacqueline's parents are divorced and she is injured during visitation with her noncustodial father. May he give effective consent?

(2) Karen is a 13-year-old suffering from irreversible kidney malfunction. She has had a kidney transplant, but the transplant has failed. Karen now has hemodialysis three times a week. She is tolerating dialysis poorly, and typically has severe headaches, chills, nausea, and weakness. Apart from dialysis, she is also on medication and has an extremely restricted diet. She is unable to attend school, is socially isolated, and always feels tired and uncomfortable.

On May 10, Karen was hospitalized after having had a high fever for ten days. With her parents' consent, the doctors operated and removed the transplanted kidney, the pathology of which indicated that any subsequent transplant would in all probability also fail.

Two weeks later, the arteriovenous shunt that had been placed in Karen's arm for hemodialysis was found to be infected. Part of her vein wall was removed, and the placement of the shunt was revised. Three days later, however, the shunt clotted and closed. This meant that the shunt would have to be further revised if dialysis were to continue. This would require minor (but uncomfortable) surgery. Without dialysis, Karen will die. With dialysis, she can be kept alive, but her condition will never improve.

a. If Karen and her parents together refuse to permit shunt revision and any further dialysis, must the medical staff accept their decision? Would it constitute battery if they were to proceed with treatment anyway?

b. Suppose Karen's parents insist on continuing the life-supporting treatment, but Karen objects? What would you advise the medical staff to do?

c. Suppose Karen's parents refuse to consent to further treatment, but Karen insists on continuing the treatment? What would you advise?[12]

(3) Kevin is a 15-year-old who suffers from extensive neurofibromatosis, or Von Recklinghausen's disease. It has caused a massive deformity of the right side of his face and neck involving a large overgrowth of facial tissue that has created a fold or flap which in turn has distorted his cheek, mouth, and right ear. The disease has not affected Kevin's sight or hearing and does not endanger his life.

Kevin's teachers and doctors all believe that Kevin should have surgery to correct this condition. The surgery will not cure the disease, for there is no known cure. But a plastic surgeon has indicated that an operation will improve both the "function and appearance" of his face. The surgery does involve substantial risks, however. A surgeon who is in favor of the operation has stated, "I think it is a dangerous procedure. I think it involves considerable risk. It is a massive surgery of six to eight hours duration with great blood loss." A psychiatrist has examined Kevin and has reported that he is not psychotic, that there is no evidence of any thinking disorder, but that he is extremely dependent on his mother, has feelings of inferiority and a "low self-concept." The doctors believe this is in part because of his grotesque appearance. Delaying the operation until Kevin is older will, if anything, decrease surgical risks but may increase the psychological risks to Kevin. Kevin's mother is a Jehovah's Witness. The mother is not opposed to have the recommended surgery performed upon her son, but she steadfastly refuses to give her consent to the administration of any blood transfusions during the course of the surgery, without which the proposed surgery may not safely be performed.

The county health commissioner and doctors petitioned the juvenile court to declare Kevin a "neglected child" so that a guardian may consent to the operation with a transfusion. Assume the relevant state statute permits the juvenile court to take jurisdiction when a parent "neglects or refuses when able to do so to provide or allow medical, surgical, or other care necessary for a child's health." You are the judge. What would you decide?[13]

(4) Helena is eight years old and has a malignant brain tumor. She is unlikely to survive more than another year. Her parents, who are married and live together, disagree about her treatment. Her father wants her to have more chemotherapy. Her mother feels this would put Helena through needless pain and suffering. Each

---

[12] See generally Joseph Goldstein et al., Before the Best Interests of the Child 91-110 (1979); Joseph Goldstein, Medical Care for the Child at Risk: On State Supervention of Parental Autonomy, 86 Yale L.J. 645, 658-661 (1977).

Two highly publicized cases address problems of minors' consent. In the first case, a 16-year-old cancer patient ran away from Massachusetts to Texas to avoid chemotherapy (to which her parents had consented). In the second case, a 15-year-old girl fled her home in California after police, paramedics, and social workers compelled her to undergo chemotherapy for ovarian cancer (despite the fact that the girl and her parents refused their consent). See Susan D. Hawkins, Note, Protecting the Rights and Interests of Competent Minors in Litigated Medical Treatment Disputes, 64 Fordham L. Rev. 2075, 2075 (1996).

[13] See In re Sampson, 317 N.Y.S.2d 641 (Fam. Ct. 1970), *aff'd*, 323 N.Y.S.2d 253 (App. Div. 1971), *aff'd*, 278 N.E.2d 918 (N.Y. 1972).

parent now seeks a judicial declaration that will give that parent unilateral authority to grant or refuse consent to the treatment.

Is it appropriate to grant either parent this authority? If so, how would you decide which parent should have the power? If not, should the parents continue to share authority? Should decision making be delegated to a third party? What role in the decision making should Helena's opinions play? If she were 14 years old, would that alter your opinion? What special problems are posed by securing consent to medical treatment in cases involving dying children?[14]

2. State-Imposed Health Requirements Applicable to All Children

Some medical procedures are required for all children and in this sense represent generally applicable limitations on parental prerogatives. For example, the Supreme Court has upheld a compulsory state smallpox vaccination law as a reasonable and proper exercise of the police power. Jacobson v. Massachusetts, 197 U.S. 11 (1905). Vaccination requirements act to protect society from public health hazards created by communicable diseases where a parental decision may endanger not only a particular child but society at large. Consider circumstances where there is no risk of contagion — for example, a child with poor hearing or eyesight. In light of *Prince, Yoder, Pierce*, and *Meyer*, do you think there are any constitutional limitations on the state's power to impose generally applicable medical screening procedures without parental consent because it is thought to be beneficial for individual children? As a matter of policy, apart from constitutional law, what limit should there be?

The range of compulsory public interventions for children encompasses immunizations, school and newborn screening, and fluoridation of public water supplies. All states require that school children be immunized against certain contagious diseases, such as diphtheria, whooping cough, tetanus, measles, mumps, polio, Haemophilus influenzae type b (hib), and hepatitis B. The first mandatory smallpox vaccination requirements date from the mid-1800s.[15] Schools also generally require tuberculosis tests. All states offer medical exemptions when vaccination would have an adverse effect on the child's life or health. Virtually all states offer religious exemptions where vaccination is contrary to the individual's religious beliefs. Less than half the states provide for exemptions on philosophical or moral grounds.[16]

[14] See generally Ann Eileen Driggs, The Mature Minor Doctrine: Do Adolescents Have the Right to Die?, 11 Health Matrix 687 (2001); Martin T. Harvey, Adolescent Competency and the Refusal of Medical Treatment, 13 Health Matrix 297 (2003). On the related problem of securing consent for research involving dying children, see Michael A. Grodin & Leonard H. Glantz, Children as Research Subjects 217 (1994).

[15] Steve P. Calandrillo, Vanishing Vaccinations: Why Are So Many Americans Opting out of Vaccinating Their Children?, 37 U. Mich. J.L. Reform 353, 365 (2004).

[16] Sean Coletti, Note, Taking Account of Partial Exemptors in Vaccination Law, Policy, and Practice, 36 Conn. L. Rev. 1341, 1343 (2004).

Congress addressed the issue of immunization beginning in the 1980s. In the 1970s and 1980s, parents whose children had been harmed allegedly by vaccines filed several lawsuits against vaccine manufacturers. In response, Congress enacted the National Vaccine Injury Compensation Act (NVICP) of 1986, 42 U.S.C. §§300aa-1 to -34 (2000 & Supp. 2005), to compensate children who were injured by vaccines and also to protect vaccine manufacturers from the threat of bankruptcy. At the same time, declining immunization rates resulted in epidemics of certain childhood diseases. For example, a measles epidemic in 1990 affected 55,000 children and caused 132 deaths.[17] To improve vaccination rates, Congress enacted a vaccine entitlement program (as part of the Omnibus Budget Reconciliation Act of 1993, Pub. L. No. 103-166, 107 Stat. 312), to provide free immunizations to uninsured children, children covered by Medicaid, and insured children whose health insurance failed to cover immunizations.

Recently, the United States Court of Federal Claims (the designated tribunal under the NVICP) held hearings to decide whether thimerosal, a mercury-based preservative in childhood vaccines, led thousands of children to develop autism.[18] The Court found no basis for the claim. Major studies have failed to document the existence of a link between the preservative and autism. In addition, the removal of thimerosal from childhood vaccines in 2001 appears to have had no effect on the rate of autism.[19]

Immunization of adolescents against sexually transmitted infections has also provoked considerable recent controversy. In 2006, the Food and Drug Administration (FDA) approved the first vaccine (Gardisil) against the human papillomavirus (HPV), a sexually transmitted infection that can cause cervical cancer and genital warts. In response, many states introduced legislation mandating vaccination of all young girls against HPV, requiring insurance companies to cover HPV vaccination, promoting awareness of the HPV vaccine, or establishing research groups to study the vaccine.[20] At the same time, some commentators questioned the necessity and constitutionality of these laws, and other commentators urged that legislatures await the development of research to determine the efficacy of the vaccine and its long-term side effects.[21]

States also require medical screening of school children, although screening procedures vary from state to state (e.g., hearing and vision tests, etc.). In addition, states mandate screening of newborns. States screen 4 million newborns annually

---

[17] Calandrillo, supra note [15], at 373.

[18] Cedillo v. Secretary of Health and Human Servs., 2009 WL 331968 (Fed. Ct. 2009). See also Regina Moreland, The Potential Impact of *Cedillo* for Vaccine-Related Autism Cases, 29 J. Legal Med. 363 (2008).

[19] Gardiner Harris, Court Hears More Claims of Vaccine-Autism Link, N.Y. Times, May 13, 2008, at A14.

[20] See National Conference of State Legislatures, HPV: State Legislation, available at *http://www.ncsl.org/programs/health/HPVvaccine.htm* (last visited Sept. 5, 2008).

[21] See generally Gail Javitt et al., Assessing Mandatory HPV Vaccination: Who Should Call the Shots?, 36 J.L. Med. & Ethic 384 (2008); Sylvia Law, Human Papillomavirus Vaccination, Private Choice, and Public Health, 41 U.C. Davis L. Rev. 1731 (2008); Pauline Self, Note, The HPV Vaccination: Necessary or Evil?, 19 Hastings Women's L.J. 149 (2008).

for particular disorders.[22] No federal guidelines require the inclusion of particular disorders; however, federal recommendations exist to screen newborns for phenylketonuria (PKU), congenital hypothyroidism, and sickle cell anemia. Many states expanded the number of blood tests for newborns based on new mass spectrometry equipment as well as new computer software and more comprehensive training of technicians. For example, New York state officials recently quadrupled the number of tests for newborns from 11 to 44.[23]

Statutes generally do not require parental consent for newborn screening. Most states provide medical exemptions from screening; several states allow exemptions for any reason. Many states require that results remain confidential, subject to exemptions for the purposes of research, law enforcement, and paternity establishment.[24]

Some states require HIV testing of newborns. Pediatric AIDS cases among children younger than age 13 represent 1.1 percent of all reported cases.[25] The majority of cases result from perinatal transmission (before or during birth). Because of concerns about invasion of the mother's privacy (e.g., a positive result for a newborn signifies that the mother is HIV-positive), the HIV screening initially was only for data collection purposes to determine the nationwide prevalence of infection. Unlike many other newborn screening programs, however, the HIV screening led to the release of newborns from the hospital without their parents being informed of abnormal results. The ethics of this approach led the New York legislature to pass the AIDS Baby Bill, N.Y. Pub. Health §2500-f (2002) (effective in 1996), to allow for screening of newborns for HIV status and to provide for disclosure of this status to the babies' mothers.[26] In the 1990s, the number of children with AIDS declined dramatically due to implementation of guidelines for counseling, voluntary HIV testing of pregnant women, the use of medication for pregnant women with AIDS, and the administering of medication to affected newborns.[27] The incidence of pediatric AIDS continues to decline. From 2002 to 2006, the number of AIDS cases among children under age 13 decreased 64 percent.[28]

Yet another public intervention is the fluoridation of public waters to prevent and retard tooth decay. Courts have upheld the public power to fluoridate the water

---

[22] U.S. General Accounting Office Report, Newborn Screening: Characteristics of State Programs, GAO 03-449 (Mar. 2003), available at *http://www.gao.gov/new.items/d03449.pdf* (last visited Oct. 26, 2004).

[23] Al Baker, State Will Expand Blood Tests That Seek Out Defects in Newborn Babies, N.Y. Times, Oct. 28, 2004, at A25.

[24] GAO Report, Newborn Screening, supra note [22].

[25] NCCAN, Trends in the Well-Being of America's Children and Youth 2002, Health Conditions and Health Care, Children and Youth with HIV/AIDS, p. 148.

[26] Michele M. Contreras, Note, New York's Mandatory HIV Testing of Newborns: A Positive Step Which Results in Negative Consequences for Women and Their Children, 20 Women's Rts. L. Rep. 21 (1998). See also Gina A. Angelletta, New York Public Health Law §2500-F: The Hand That Robbed the Cradle of Privacy, 8 St. John's J. Legal Comment 175 (2003).

[27] NCCAN, Trends in Well-Being of America's Children, supra note [25].

[28] Centers for Disease Control and Prevention, Cases of HIV Infection and AIDS in the United States and Dependent Areas, 2006, at 7, available at *http://cdc.gov/hiv/topics/surveillance/resources/reports/2006report/pdf/2006SurveillanceReport.pdf*.

supply. See, e.g., Ill. Pure Water Comm. v. Director of Pub. Health, 470 N.E.2d 988 (Ill. 1984) (upholding constitutionality of statute requiring mandatory fluoridation of drinking water).

3.   The Neglect Limitation

In re Phillip B.
156 Cal. Rptr. 48 (Ct. App. 1979)

CALDECOTT, Presiding Justice.

A petition was filed by the juvenile probation department in the juvenile court, alleging that Phillip B., a minor, came within the provision of [California] Welfare and Institutions Code section 300, subdivision (b), because he was not provided with the "necessities of life."

The petition requested that Phillip be declared a dependent child of the court for the special purpose of ensuring that he receive cardiac surgery for a congenital heart defect. Phillip's parents had refused to consent to the surgery. The juvenile court dismissed the petition. The appeal is from the order.

Phillip is a 12-year-old boy suffering from Down's Syndrome. At birth his parents decided he should live in a residential care facility. Phillip suffers from a congenital heart defect — a ventricular septal defect that results in elevated pulmonary blood pressure. Due to the defect, Phillip's heart must work three times harder than normal to supply blood to his body. When he overexerts, unoxygenated blood travels the wrong way through the septal hole reaching his circulation, rather than the lungs.

If the congenital heart defect is not corrected, damage to the lungs will increase to the point where his lungs will be unable to carry and oxygenate any blood. As a result, death follows. During the deterioration of the lungs, Phillip will suffer from a progressive loss of energy and vitality until he is forced to lead a bed-to-chair existence.

Phillip's heart condition has been known since 1973. At that time Dr. Gathman, a pediatric cardiologist, examined Phillip and recommended cardiac catheterization to further define the anatomy and dynamics of Phillip's condition. Phillip's parents refused.

In 1977, Dr. Gathman again recommended catheterization and this time Phillip's parents consented. The catheterization revealed the extensive nature of Phillip's septal defect, thus it was Dr. Gathman's recommendation that surgery be performed.

Dr. Gathman referred Phillip to a second pediatric cardiologist, Dr. William French of Stanford Medical Center. Dr. French estimates the surgical mortality rate to be five to ten percent, and notes that Down's Syndrome children face a higher than average risk of postoperative complications. Dr. French found that Phillip's pulmonary vessels have already undergone some change from high pulmonary artery pressure. Without the operation, Phillip will begin to function less physically until he will be severely incapacitated. Dr. French agrees with Dr. Gathman that Phillip will enjoy a significant expansion of his life span if his defect is surgically corrected. Without the surgery, Phillip may live at the outside 20 more years. Dr. French's opinion on the advisability of surgery was not asked.

It is fundamental that parental autonomy is constitutionally protected. The United States Supreme Court has articulated the concept of personal liberty found in the Fourteenth Amendment as a right of privacy which extends to certain aspects of a family relationship [citing Roe v. Wade, Wisconsin v. Yoder, Eisenstadt v. Baird, Griswold v. Connecticut, Meyer v. Nebraska, and Pierce v. Society of Sisters]. "It is cardinal with us that the custody, care and nurture of the child reside first in the parents, whose primary function and freedom include preparation for obligations the state can neither supply nor hinder." (Prince v. Massachusetts (1944) 321 U.S. 158, 166.) . . .

Parental autonomy, however, is not absolute. The state is the guardian of society's basic values. Under the doctrine of *parens patriae*, the state has a right, indeed, a duty, to protect children. (See, e.g., Prince v. Massachusetts, supra, 321 U.S. 158 at p. 166.) State officials may interfere in family matters to safeguard the child's health, educational development and emotional well-being.

One of the most basic values protected by the state is the sanctity of human life. (U.S. Const., 14th Amend., §1.) Where parents fail to provide their children with adequate medical care, the state is justified to intervene. However, since the state should usually defer to the wishes of the parents, it has a serious burden of justification before abridging parental autonomy by substituting its judgment for that of the parents.

Several relevant factors must be taken into consideration before a state insists upon medical treatment rejected by the parents. The state should examine the seriousness of the harm the child is suffering or the substantial likelihood that he will suffer serious harm; the evaluation for the treatment by the medical profession; the risks involved in medically treating the child; and the expressed preferences of the child. Of course, the underlying consideration is the child's welfare and whether his best interests will be served by the medical treatment.

Section 300, subdivision (b), permits a court to adjudge a child under the age of 18 years a dependent of the court if the child is not provided with the "necessities of life."

The trial judge dismissed the petition on the ground that there was "no clear and convincing evidence to sustain this petition."

The rule is clear that the power of the appellate court begins and ends with a determination as to whether there is any substantial evidence, contradicted or uncontradicted, which will support the conclusion reached by the trier of fact. . . . The "clear and convincing evidence" standard for proof applies only to the trial court, and is not the standard for appellate review. . . .

Turning to the facts of this case, one expert witness testified that Phillip's case was more risky than the average for two reasons. One, he has pulmonary vascular changes and statistically this would make the operation more risky in that he would be subject to more complications than if he did not have these changes. Two, children with Down's Syndrome have more problems in the postoperative period. This witness put the mortality rate at five to ten percent, and the morbidity would be somewhat higher. When asked if he knew of a case in which this type of operation had been performed on a Down's Syndrome child, the witness replied that he did, but could not remember a case involving a child who had the degree of pulmonary vascular change that Phillip had. Another expert witness testified that one of the risks of surgery to correct a ventricular septal defect was damage to the nerve that controls the heart beat as the nerve is in the same area as the defect. When this occurs a pacemaker would be required.

The trial judge, in announcing his decision, cited the inconclusiveness of the evidence to support the petition.

On reading the record we can see the trial court's attempt to balance the possible benefits to be gained from the operation against the risks involved. The court had before it a child suffering not only from a ventricular septal defect but also from Down's Syndrome, with its higher than average morbidity, and the presence of pulmonary vascular changes. In light of these facts, we cannot say as a matter of law that there was no substantial evidence to support the decision of the trial court.

In denying the petition the trial court ruled that there was no clear and convincing evidence to sustain the petition. The state contends the proper standard of proof is by a preponderance of the evidence and not by the clear and convincing test. The state asserts that only when a permanent severance of the parent-child relationship is ordered by the court must the clear and convincing standard of proof be applied. Since the petition did not seek permanent severance but only authorization for corrective heart surgery, the state contends the lower standard of proof should have been applied. . . . [However,] the "clear and convincing standard" was proper in this case.

Section 353 requires that at the beginning of the hearing on a petition, "[t]he judge shall ascertain whether the minor and his parent or guardian or adult relative, as the case may be, has been informed of the right of the minor to be represented by counsel, and if not, the judge shall advise the minor and such person, if present, of the right to have counsel present and where applicable, of the right to appointed counsel."

Amicus Curiae contends the judge erred in failing to notify Phillip of his right to counsel, thus Phillip was not properly represented. . . .

In the present case, the facts show that a deputy district attorney was representing Phillip at the hearing. He was introduced to the judge as Phillip's attorney. The deputy district attorney proceeded to make an opening statement and continued to represent Phillip throughout the entire hearing.

The judge was under no statutory duty to inform Phillip of his right to counsel when it was evident to the court that Phillip was, in fact, represented by counsel.

The order dismissing the petition is affirmed.

A petition for a rehearing was denied. Appellants' petition for a hearing by the California Supreme Court was also denied. Justice Mosk was of the opinion that the petition should be granted. For the fascinating aftermath of this case, see infra p. 461.

NOTE: MEDICAL NEGLECT AND THE JUVENILE COURT

A very important legal constraint on parental prerogatives relates to child neglect laws. Although there are historical antecedents related to the parens patriae power of equity courts, every state now has a statute allowing a court (typically a juvenile court) to assume jurisdiction over a child to override individual parental judgments concerning the medical treatment of their child.[29] As you can see from the materials in Chapter 3 on child abuse and neglect, neglect statutes are typically extremely vague and give courts substantial discretion to intervene to protect a child's health.

When should courts intervene? Only when a child's life is threatened? Whenever a judge believes the parents are not acting in the child's best interest? Many cases (e.g., *In re Sampson*)[30] represent expansive notions of the appropriate judicial role. Problem (3), supra p. 384, is based on *Sampson*, in which a New York family court judge declared Kevin Sampson, age 15, "a neglected child" to override Kevin's mother's decision — based on her religious objections — not to permit blood transfusions for Kevin during surgery. In ordering the operation, the court in effect assumed the parental role:

> [To] postpone the surgery merely to allow the boy to become of age so that he may make the decision himself as suggested by the surgeon and urged by both counsel for the mother and the Law Guardian . . . totally ignores the developmental and psychological factors stemming from his deformity which the Court deems to be of the utmost importance in any consideration of the boy's future welfare and begs the whole question.[31]

Many have argued that the neglect standard should impose only minimum standards and should be very narrowly construed. Professor Goldstein, for example, argues that:[32]

> State supervention of parental judgment would be justified to provide any proven, nonexperimental, medical procedure when its denial would mean *death* for a child who would otherwise have an opportunity for either a *life worth living* or a *life of relatively normal healthy growth* toward adulthood[18] — to majority when a person is freed of parental control and presumed competent to decide for himself. The state

---

[29] In many jurisdictions, parents are guilty of a criminal homicide if their failure to provide medical attention results in the child's death. Failure to provide medical attention can also result in felony or misdemeanor criminal neglect charges.

[30] 317 N.Y.S.2d 641 (Fam. Ct. 1970), *aff'd*, 323 N.Y.S.2d 253 (App. Div. 1971), *aff'd*, 278 N.E.2d 918 (N.Y. 1972).

[31] 317 N.Y.S.2d at 655. For additional cases in which a parent objects to a child's medical treatment on religious grounds, see James G. Dwyer, The Children We Abandon: Religious Exemptions to Child Welfare and Education Laws as Denials of Equal Protection to Children of Religious Objectors, 74 N.C.L. Rev. 1321 (1996).

[32] Goldstein, Medical Care, supra note [12], at 651-654.

[18] While a life of relatively normal healthy growth is assumed to be a life worth living, it is not assumed that all lives worth living from a societal-consensus point of view could be characterized as relatively normal or healthy. For example, a quadriplegic child, in need of a blood transfusion for reasons unrelated to that condition might, for society, be a "life worth living" though not a life of normal healthy growth.

would overcome the presumption of parental autonomy in health-care matters only if it could establish: (a) that the medical profession is in agreement about what non-experimental medical treatment is right for the child; (b) that the expected outcome of that treatment is what society agrees to be right for any child, a chance for normal healthy growth toward adulthood or a life worth living; *and* (c) that the expected outcome of denial of that treatment would mean death for the child. . . .

There would be no justification, however, for coercive intrusion by the state in those life-or-death situations (a) in which there is no proven medical procedure, *or* (b) in which parents are confronted with conflicting medical advice about which, if any, treatment procedure to follow, *or* (c), in which, even if the medical experts agree about treatment, there is less than a high probability that the nonexperimental treatment will enable the child to pursue either a life worth living or a life of relatively normal healthy growth toward adulthood. . . .

Outside of narrow central core of agreement, "a life worth living" and "a life of relatively normal healthy growth" are highly personal terms about which there is no societal consensus. There can thus be no societal consensus about the "rightness" of always deciding for "life," or of always preferring the predicted results of the recommended treatment over the predicted result of refusing such treatment. It is precisely in those cases in which reasonable and responsible persons can and do disagree about whether the "life" after treatment would be "worth living" or "normal," and thus about what is "right," that parents must remain free of coercive state intervention in deciding whether to consent to or reject the medical program proffered for their child. . . .

Phillip B., supra p. 388, represents one of few reported cases in which a trial court decision refusing to require life-sustaining care was affirmed on appeal. In *Phillip B.*, Phillip's father testified that he would have no reluctance to authorize surgery for either of his other sons if they had the same physical problem. Is the result justified because Phillip was a mentally disabled child? Would this be a sufficient justification under Professor Goldstein's standard? Does Phillip have a chance toward "normal healthy growth toward adulthood or a life worth living"?[33]

There is now federal legislation that requires child protection agencies to have a broader notion of when they should protect children. See section D, infra, on disabled newborns.

Most neglect cases are not appealed. Some commentators believe that the vague statutory standards frequently permit intervention at the trial level under circumstances where the child's life is not threatened, and the judge simply substitutes his or her judgment (or confirms a doctor's judgment) concerning the child's best medical interests. The neglect limitation in effect poses the critical question of defining when the state should coercively intervene into the family to override parental judgment concerning the health care of a child. Are special procedural safeguards necessary when the parent and child may have "conflicting interests"? The materials later in this chapter concerning disabled newborns and the medical experimentation on children provide further opportunities to explore these questions.

---

[33] For a discussion *of Phillip B.*, see Wesley Sokolosky, The Sick Child and the Reluctant Parent — A Framework for Judicial Intervention, 20 J. Fam. L. 69 (1981-82); Yolanda V. Vorys, The Outer Limits of Parental Autonomy: Withholding Medical Treatment from Children, 42 Ohio St. L.J. 813 (1981).

Parham v. J.R.
442 U.S. 584 (1979)

Mr. Chief Justice Burger delivered the opinion of the Court.

The question presented in this appeal is what process is constitutionally due a minor child whose parents or guardian seek state administered institutional mental health care for the child and specifically whether an adversary proceeding is required prior to or after the commitment.

[Appellees J.R. and J.L., children being treated in a Georgia state mental hospital, were plaintiffs in this class action, based on 42 U.S.C. §1983, against the state mental health authorities. Appellees sought a declaratory judgment that Georgia's voluntary commitment procedures for children under the age of 18 violated the Due Process Clause and requested an injunction against their future enforcement.

J.R. was declared a neglected child by the county and removed from his natural parents when he was three months old. He was placed in seven different foster homes prior to his admission to the state mental hospital at the age of seven. J.L., now deceased, was admitted to the state mental hospital at the age of six years. Prior to his admission, he had received out-patient treatment at the hospital for over two months. His natural parents were divorced, and his mother had remarried. He had been expelled from school because he was aggressive and uncontrollable. He was returned to his mother and stepfather two years later but the parents, unable to control J.L. to their satisfaction, requested his readmission. J.L.'s parents relinquished their parental rights two years later.]

Georgia Code §88-503.1 (1975) provides for the voluntary admission to a state regional hospital of children such as J.L. and J.R. Under that provision, admission begins with an application for hospitalization signed by a "parent or guardian." Upon application, the superintendent of each hospital is given the power to admit temporarily any child for "observation and diagnosis." If, after observation, the superintendent finds "evidence of mental illness" and that the child is "suitable for treatment" in the hospital, then the child may be admitted "for such period and under such conditions as may be authorized by law."

Georgia's mental health statute also provides for the discharge of voluntary patients. Any child who has been hospitalized for more than five days may be discharged at the request of a parent or guardian. Even without a request for discharge, however, the superintendent of each regional hospital has an affirmative duty to release any child "who has recovered from his mental illness or who has sufficiently improved that the superintendent determines that hospitalization of the patient is no longer desirable." §88-503.2 (1975). . . .

II

In holding unconstitutional Georgia's statutory procedure for voluntary commitment of juveniles, the District Court first determined that commitment . . . constitutes a severe deprivation of a child's liberty . . . in terms of both freedom from bodily restraint and freedom from the "emotional and psychic harm" caused by the institutionalization. Having determined that a liberty interest is implicated by a child's admission to a mental hospital, the court considered what process is required to protect that interest. It held that the process due "includes at least the right after notice to be heard before an impartial tribunal." [412 F. Supp. 112, 139 (M.D. Ga. 1976).]

In requiring the prescribed hearing, the court rejected Georgia's argument that no adversary-type hearing was required since the State was merely assisting parents who could not afford private care by making available treatment similar to that offered in private hospitals and by private physicians. The court acknowledged that most parents who seek to have their children admitted to a state mental hospital do so in good faith. It, however, relied on one of appellees' witnesses who expressed an opinion that "some still look upon mental hospitals as a 'dumping ground.' " Id., at 138. No specific evidence of such "dumping," however, can be found in the record.

The District Court also rejected the argument that review by the superintendents of the hospitals and their staffs was sufficient to protect the child's liberty interest. . . .

III

In an earlier day, the problems inherent in coping with children afflicted with mental or emotional abnormalities were dealt with largely within the family. . . . While some parents no doubt were able to deal with their disturbed children without specialized assistance, others especially those of limited means and education, were not. Increasingly, they turned for assistance to local, public sources or private charities. Until recently, most of the states did little more than provide custodial institutions for the confinement of persons who were considered dangerous.

As medical knowledge about the mentally ill and public concern for their condition expanded, the states, aided substantially by federal grants, have sought to ameliorate the human tragedies of seriously disturbed children. Ironically, as most states have expanded their efforts to assist the mentally ill, their actions have been subjected to increasing litigation and heightened constitutional scrutiny. . . .

. . . Assuming the existence of a protectible property or liberty interest, the Court has required a balancing of a number of factors [including the private interest affected, the risk of an erroneous deprivation of such interest, the value of other procedural safeguards, and the government's interest that other procedural requirements might entail. Mathews v. Eldridge, 424 U.S. 319 (1976)]. In applying these criteria, we must consider first the child's interest in not being committed. Normally, however, since this interest is inextricably linked with the parents' interest in and obligation for the welfare and health of the child, the private interest at stake is a combination of the child's and parents' concerns. Next, we must examine the State's interest in the procedures it has adopted for commitment and treatment of children. Finally, we must consider how well Georgia's procedures protect against arbitrariness in the decision to commit a child to a state mental hospital.

(a)

It is not disputed that a child, in common with adults, has a substantial liberty interest in not being confined unnecessarily for medical treatment and that the state's involvement in the commitment decision constitutes state action under the

Fourteenth Amendment. . . . We also recognize that commitment sometimes produces adverse social consequences for the child because of the reaction of some to the discovery that the child has received psychiatric care. . . . For purposes of this decision, we assume that a child has a protectible interest not only in being free of unnecessary bodily restraints but also in not being labeled erroneously by some persons because of an improper decision by the state hospital superintendent.

(b)

We next deal with the interests of the parents who have decided, on the basis of their observations and independent professional recommendations, that their child needs institutional care. Appellees argue that the constitutional rights of the child are of such magnitude and the likelihood of parental abuse is so great that the parents' traditional interests in and responsibility for the upbringing of their child must be subordinated at least to the extent of providing a formal adversary hearing prior to a voluntary commitment.

Our jurisprudence historically has reflected Western civilization concepts of the family as a unit with broad parental authority over minor children. Our cases have consistently followed that course [and] asserted that parents generally "have the right, coupled with the high duty, to recognize and prepare [their children] for additional obligations." Pierce v. Society of Sisters, 268 U.S. 510, 535 (1925). See also Wisconsin v. Yoder, 406 U.S. 205, 213 (1972); Prince v. Massachusetts, 321 U.S. 158, 166 (1944); Meyer v. Nebraska, 262 U.S. 390, 400 (1923). Surely, this includes a "high duty" to recognize symptoms of illness and to seek and follow medical advice. The law's concept of the family rests on a presumption that parents possess what a child lacks in maturity, experience, and capacity for judgment required for making life's difficult decision. More important, historically it has recognized that natural bonds of affection lead parents to act in the best interests of their children. 1 W Blackstone, Commentaries *447; 2 J. Kent, Commentaries on American Law *190.

As with so many other legal presumptions, experience and reality may rebut what the law accepts as a starting point. . . . That some parents "may at times be acting against the interests of their children" as was stated in Bartley v. Kremens, 402 F. Supp. 1039, 1047-1048 (E.D. Pa. 1975), vacated and remanded, 431 U.S. 119 (1977), creates a basis for caution, but is hardly a reason to discard wholesale those pages of human experience that teach that parents generally do act in the child's best interests. . . .

Nonetheless, we have recognized that a state is not without constitutional control over parental discretion in dealing with children when their physical or mental health is jeopardized. See Wisconsin v. Yoder, supra, 406 U.S., at 230; Prince v. Massachusetts, supra, 321 U.S., at 166. . . . Appellees urge that these precedents limiting the traditional rights of parents, if viewed in the context of the liberty interest of the child and the likelihood of parental abuse, require us to hold that the parents' decision to have a child admitted to a mental hospital must be subjected to an exacting constitutional scrutiny, including a formal, adversary, preadmission hearing.

Appellees' argument, however, sweeps too broadly. Simply because the decision of a parent is not agreeable to a child or because it involves risks does not automatically transfer the power to make that decision from the parents to some agency or officer of the state. The same characterizations can be made for a tonsillectomy, appendectomy, or other medical procedure. Most children, even in adolescence, simply are not able to make sound judgments concerning many decisions, including their need for medical care or treatment. Parents can and must make those judgments. Here, there is no finding by the District Court of even a single instance of bad faith by any parent of any member of appellees' class. . . . The fact that a child may balk at hospitalization . . . does not diminish the parents' authority to decide what is best for the child . . . Neither state officials nor federal courts are equipped to review such parental decisions. . . .

In defining the respective rights and prerogatives of the child and parent in the voluntary commitment setting, we conclude that our precedents permit the parents to retain a substantial, if not the dominant, role in the decision, absent a finding of neglect or abuse, and that the traditional presumption that the parents act in the best interests of their child should apply. We also conclude, however, that the child's rights and the nature of the commitment decision are such that parents cannot always have absolute and unreviewable discretion to decide whether to have a child institutionalized. They, of course, retain plenary authority to seek such care for their children, subject to a physician's independent examination and medical judgment.

(c)

The State obviously has a significant interest in confining the use of its costly mental health facilities to cases of genuine need. . . . To accomplish this purpose, the State has charged the superintendents of each regional hospital with the responsibility for determining, before authorizing an admission, whether a prospective patient is mentally ill and whether the patient will likely benefit from hospital care. . . .

The State in performing its voluntarily assumed mission also has a significant interest in not imposing unnecessary procedural obstacles that may discourage the mentally ill or their families from seeking needed psychiatric assistance. [M]any parents who believe they are acting in good faith would forgo state-provided hospital care if such care is contingent on participation in an adversary proceeding designed to probe their motives and other private family matters in seeking the voluntary admission. . . .

(d)

[T]he risk of error inherent in the parental decision to have a child institutionalized for mental health care is sufficiently great that some kind of inquiry should be made by a "neutral factfinder" to determine whether the statutory requirements for admission are satisfied. . . . That inquiry must carefully probe the child's background using all available sources, including, but not limited to, parents, schools, and other social agencies. Of course, the review must also include an interview with the child. It is necessary that the decisionmaker have the authority to refuse to admit any child who does not satisfy the medical standards for admission. Finally, it is necessary that the child's continuing need for commitment be reviewed periodically by a similarly independent procedure. . . .

Due process has never been thought to require that the neutral and detached trier of fact be law trained or a judicial or administrative officer. Surely, this is the case as to medical decisions, for "neither judges nor administrative hearing officers are better qualified than psychiatrists to render psychiatric judgments." In re Roger S., 19 Cal. 3d 921, 942, 569 P.2d 1286, 1299 (1977) (Clark, J., dissenting). Thus, a staff physician will suffice, so long as he or she is free to evaluate independently the child's mental and emotional condition and need for treatment.

It is not necessary that the deciding physician conduct a formal or quasi-formal, hearing. A state is free to require such a hearing, but due process is not violated by use of informal traditional medical investigative techniques. . . . Another problem with requiring a formalized, factfinding hearing lies in the danger it poses for significant intrusion into the parent-child relationship. Pitting the parents and child as adversaries often will be at odds with the presumption that parents act in the best interests of their child. It is one thing to require a neutral physician to make a careful review of the parents' decision in order to make sure it is proper from a medical standpoint; it is a wholly different matter to employ an adversary contest to ascertain whether the parents' motivation is consistent with the child's interests. [Moreover,] there is a risk that it would exacerbate whatever tensions already exist between the child and the parents. . . .

It has been suggested that a hearing conducted by someone other than the admitting physician is necessary in order to detect instances where parents are "guilty of railroading their children into asylums" or are using "voluntary commitment procedures in order to sanction behavior of which they disapprov[e]." Ellis, Volunteering Children: Parental Commitment of Minors to Mental Institutions, 62 Calif. L. Rev. 840, 850-851 (1974). Curiously, it seems to be taken for granted that parents who seek to "dump" their children on the state will inevitably be able to conceal their motives and thus deceive the admitting psychiatrists and the other mental health professionals. . . . It is unrealistic to believe that trained psychiatrists, skilled in eliciting responses, sorting medically relevant facts, and sensing motivational nuances will often be deceived about the family situation surrounding a child's emotional disturbance. . . .

Georgia's statute envisions a careful diagnostic medical inquiry to be conducted by the admitting physician at each regional hospital [as well as periodic reviews and a duty to discharge a child who is no longer mentally ill].

We are satisfied that the voluminous record as a whole supports the conclusion that the admissions staffs of the hospitals have acted in a neutral and detached fashion in making medical judgments in the best interests of the children. The State, through its mental health programs, provides the authority for trained professionals to assist parents in examining, diagnosing, and treating emotionally disturbed children. Through its hiring practices, it provides well-staffed and well-equipped hospitals and — as the District Court found — conscientious public employees to implement the State's beneficent purposes. . . .

IV

Our discussion [above] was directed at the situation where a child's natural parents request his admission to a state mental hospital. Some members of appellees' class, including J.R., were wards of the State of Georgia at the time of their admission. Obviously their situation differs from those members of the class who have natural parents. While the determination of what process is due varies somewhat when the state, rather than a natural parent, makes the request for commitment, we conclude that the differences in the two situations do not justify requiring different procedures at the time of the child's initial admission to the hospital. [The Court then suggests that, on remand, the district court consider the need for more rigorous review procedures for wards of the state so they will not get "lost in the shuffle."]

On this record, we are satisfied that Georgia's medical factfinding processes are reasonable and consistent with constitutional guarantees. . . . The judgment is therefore reversed, and the case is remanded to the District Court for further proceedings consistent with this opinion.

NOTES AND QUESTIONS

The Mental Hospitalization of Troublesome Youth

(1) Vision of Family.   Commentators on child mental health policy point out that the majority opinion in *Parham* "represents a construction of the supposed reality of how hospitalization occurs, derived from idyllic notions of how the family and the mental health professions should be." Gary B. Melton et al., No Place to Go: The Civil Commitment of Minors 126 (1998). What are the Court's assumptions about the family, mental health institutions, and the effects of formal, adversarial commitment procedures? See id. at 127-141.

(2) Procedures.   What procedures does the majority in *Parham* require before a juvenile can be committed to a mental hospital? What limits, if any, are placed on the discretion of parents and doctors to decide what is best for the child?

(3) Due Process.   *Parham* focuses on the due process question of what procedures are required. Consider the substantive question of what standards should define when a young person should be committed. When is it appropriate to institutionalize a juvenile in a psychiatric hospital? In most states, an adult can be committed in one of two ways: (1) by voluntarily consenting to his own commitment; or (2) through an involuntary process that typically requires a showing that the person is a danger to himself or others by reason of a mental disorder. Are you persuaded that the substantive standards for juveniles should be different?

(4) Involuntary Commitment.   When a young person does not wish to be committed, how would you define the circumstances when commitment is appropriate? Would you require a demonstration that the young person is suffering from a classic mental disorder, such as a psychosis, a severe depression, or an organic disorder? Would you require a showing that outpatient treatment is likely to be less effective? That commitment is likely to improve the young person's condition?

More broadly, what benefits and risks do you see associated with committing a young person? What did the Court require?

(5) Troublemakers? Do you agree with the Court that the questions presented in the case are "essentially medical in character" and therefore are best resolved by medical personnel rather than judicial or administrative officers? Evidence suggests that most youths who are committed to inpatient psychiatric treatment have typically been given one of a number of vague labels that identify either "conduct disorders," which involve chronic violations of rules at home or school; or "personality disorders," which may involve uncertainty about a variety of issues relating to identity or long-term goals, excessive shyness, or overreactions to stressful situations such as parental fighting or divorce. Lois A. Weithorn, Mental Hospitalization of Troublesome Youth: An Analysis of Skyrocketing Admission Rates, 40 Stan. L. Rev. 773, 789 (1988). Further, a large proportion of children hospitalized in psychiatric facilities are considered "troublemakers" who disobey their parents, run away, miss school, take drugs, and engage in sexual activity. Some may even present a threat to persons or property or a psychological threat to family stability. Id. at 792.

(6) Trans-Institutionalization. In the late 1970s and 1980s the rates of juvenile admissions to psychiatric hospitals — particularly private psychiatric hospitals — increased substantially. At the same time, the number of young persons institutionalized as status offenders declined substantially. Could it be that the strict procedures in the delinquency process (see Chapter 7) and the move toward deinstitutionalizing status offenders (see Chapter 6) have resulted, as some commentators argue, in a "trans-institutionalization"? The argument is essentially that the population of teenagers cared for by the welfare system, the juvenile justice system, and the mental health system are substantially interchangeable. Pressure to reduce the rate of institutionalization in one system will simply increase the rate of institutionalization in the other systems. See Weithorn, supra, at 805-807.

(7) Role of Insurance. Commentators have argued that the Court's failure to impose substantial procedural safeguards in *Parham* has contributed to the increase in psychiatric populations — particularly in private mental hospitals for which in many states there are no safeguards imposed at all. There are other important factors at work as well, such as insurance. Both public and private insurance funding favors inpatient over outpatient treatment. State resources available for the juvenile justice system are often quite limited; however, insurance funding can pay for institutionalization in the mental health system. Weithorn, supra, at 826.

(8) State Protections. State laws vary considerably in the protections they offer minors for whom psychiatric hospitalization is sought. One commentator points out some of these protections:

> In California, for example, minors ages fourteen and older have the right to a hearing before confinement in a public mental hospital [In re Roger S., 569 P.2d 1286 (Cal. 1977)] or an independent clinical review after hospitalization in a private facility. Illinois gives committed minors age twelve or older the right to seek judicial review of their hospitalization. Upon petition by the legal rights services, private or otherwise appointed counsel, a relative, or one acting as next

friend, Ohio provides a right to judicial determination whether "voluntary" hospitalization is in the best interests of the minor. Beyond such statutory due process
protections, minors held in public facilities or pursuant to state commitment laws
may also seek review of their confinement by petition for a writ of habeas corpus.
[Jan C. Costello, "The Trouble Is They're Growing, The Trouble Is They're
Grown": Therapeutic Jurisprudence and Adolescents' Participation in Mental
Health Care Decisions, 29 Ohio N.U. L. Rev. 607 (2003).]

4. Emergencies

NOTES AND QUESTIONS

(1) At common law a doctor may treat a child without parental consent in the
event of an emergency, at least where the parent is unavailable and where delay
endangers the child's life. Many states have express statutory exceptions from the
parental consent requirement for emergencies. If the child's parents are available but
refuse to consent, may the doctors proceed with life-saving treatment anyway? Or
must the hospital first have the child declared "neglected" and secure a court order?
See Miller ex rel. Miller v. HCA, infra p. 410. Where it would be neglect to withhold
consent, why should a hospital delay treatment while reasonable efforts are made to
contact the child's parents? More generally, what purposes are served by a consent
requirement under circumstances where it would be neglect to withhold consent
altogether? Would the "consent" of a second doctor serve as well or better?

(2) In an emergency situation where the child's parents are unavailable and the
child is conscious, should the child have the capacity to refuse treatment? Can a
rational adult refuse treatment that is essential to preserve his or her life?

(3) If doctors can be trusted in emergencies to act without parental consent,
why can't they be trusted to act without such consent in more routine medical
circumstances?

(4) In light of the fact that state law allows doctors to proceed without parental
consent in emergencies, why do you think schools, summer camps, and youth
organizations like the Boy Scouts regularly request parents to sign consent
forms stating that their child may be treated in an emergency if the parent cannot
be located?

5. Who Decides If the Parents Disagree and Based on What Standard?

In re K.I.
735 A.2d 448 (D.C. 1999)

REID, Associate Judge:

This poignant matter involves a "do not resuscitate" order ("the DNR")
entered by the Superior Court of the District of Columbia in the case of a neglected
child, K.I., who, since birth approximately two years ago, has suffered

continuously from several serious medical problems. Currently the child is in a comatose state and has been described as "neurologically devastated." . . .

The record before us shows the following facts. On June 15,1997, K.I. was born prematurely at twenty-six weeks gestation. K.I.'s treating physician at the Hospital for Sick Children, Dr. Glenn Hornstein, who testified at the DNR hearing, stated that as a result of the premature birth, K.I. "developed BPD; or broncho-pulmonary dysplasia," an abnormal condition of the lung cells which requires the child to use oxygen. In addition, K.I. suffered from "hemoglobin SC disease, which is similar [to] or it is sickle cell disease, just a mild variance"; "reactive airways disease," characterized by wheezing; and "gastro-esophageal refl[u]x."

K.I. was released from the neonatal intensive care unit of the hospital in November 1997 to the biological mother, B.I. Beginning on November 24, 1997, for a period of five weeks, B.I. and K.I. stayed in an apartment in the Northwest sector of the District of Columbia with D.M., K.I.'s putative father who claims to be K.I.'s biological father. K.I. was required to wear a heart monitor and an apnea monitor, take medication for the lungs, and use oxygen continuously. D.M. became concerned when B.I. would take K.I. off the oxygen and heart monitor and fail to give the child the lung medication. He also was troubled when he saw B.I. consume about three "40-ounce . . . very strong beer[s]" every day. He stated, at the August 26,1998 neglect proceeding, that B.I. became intoxicated and would "start stumbling and falling and get very silent and have a nasty attitude." B.I. would "leave the house and leave [D.M.] there with the baby and come back a day later or two days later." On December 28, 1997, B.I. left D.M.'s home. She carried K.I. with her but failed to take the oxygen. D.M. alerted Howard University that K.I. was without her oxygen.

On December 29, 1997, in response to D.M.'s alert, Edmond Lahai, then an employee of the District of Columbia Department of Human Services, Children and Family Services Administration, searched for B.I. and K.I. When he located B.I., she initially denied that K.I. was with her. Mr. Lahai found two Metropolitan Police officers, and when he returned with the police to the abode where B.I. was staying, she admitted that K.I. was with her. K.I. had no oxygen and no monitors.

A neglect petition was filed against B.I. on December 31,1997, under D.C. Code §16-2301(9)(B), (C), and (F). The petition alleged that B.I. failed to: (1) provide K.I. with the requisite medical care; (2) schedule appointments for K.I.; and (3) use K.I.'s monitoring devices or tube feeding procedure. [At the hearing, K.I. was found to be a neglected child.]

On December 29, 1997, Mr. Lahai took K.I. to Howard University Hospital. Later, K.I. was transferred to the Hospital for Sick Children. When K.I. began to experience respiratory distress at the Hospital for Sick Children and her condition worsened, Dr. Hornstein transferred the child to Children's Hospital on July 21, 1998. On that same day, K.I. went into cardiac arrest and suffered hypoxia, which involves "a deprivation of oxygen to the cells and to the brain." Resuscitation efforts lasted for approximately twenty-five minutes. After the resuscitation efforts ceased, K.I.'s heart began to function again. However, the following day she experienced a seven-hour seizure which terminated only after the administration of "phenobarbital medication which . . . put K.I. into a pentobarb-like coma . . . to control the seizure."

On August 22, 1998, K.I. was returned to the Hospital for Sick Children, where she continued to experience severe medical problems. At the DNR hearing, Dr. Hornstein described the child's current condition — no "purposeful movements," persistent "myochronic jerks" [involving] "shaking of [the] arms and legs." In addition, according to Dr. Hornstein, K.I. "withdraws to pain or . . . feels discomfort when people do interventions such as . . . when [he] attempted to place [an] IV in [K.I.'s] . . . hand, [K.I.] actually was grimacing and sort of writhing and moving around as if in discomfort."

Due to K.I.'s persistent medical problems, the trial court "held ahearing to determine the propriety of aggressive resuscitation efforts in the event that [K.I.] suffered pulmonary or respiratory arrest." Several persons testified, including experts in pediatric critical care, bioethics, and ethics as well as B.I. and D.M. . . . Dr. Gabriel Jacob Hauser, a professor of bioethics at Georgetown University, the Chief of Pediatric Critical Care Service at the Georgetown University Hospital, and the former chair of the hospital's ethics committee, testified that: "While [K.I.] is capable of feeling pain and discomfort, [the child] responds to no other stimuli; . . . is unable to react to [the] environment, cannot contemplate events taking place [in close proximity], and is incapable of giving or receiving love." Furthermore, "the possible resuscitation efforts that would be used on [K.I.] in the event of cardiac arrest or respiratory failure, assuming no DNR order is in place . . . [w]ould entail substantial amounts of pain and discomfort."

[The trial court concluded that it had jurisdiction and that the best interests, rather than the substituted judgment, standard applied. Based on an application of that standard, the trial court granted the medical guardian ad litem's request to issue the DNR. The mother appealed.]

B.I. argues that, as a parent, she has the right to determine whether, and in what manner, K.I. should be resuscitated, and thus, the court erred by applying the best interests of the child instead of the substituted judgment standard in deciding whether to issue the DNR. She also maintains that the court based its judgment upon the preponderance of the evidence, the standard governing neglect proceedings, rather than clear and convincing evidence. . . . D.M. asserts that the DNR should be upheld . . .

. . . Finally, the amici curiae, consisting of the Hospital for Sick Children where K.I. receives medical care, the Medical Society of the District of Columbia, the American Medical Association . . . , two professors of law from the Georgetown University Law Center, and the Metropolitan Washington Bioethics Network, also support the DNR because "the best interest of [K.I.] is served by the establishment of a reasonable plan of medical care which is premised on the very limited benefits available to [K.I.] from medical science."

. . . We turn first to the issue of the trial court's jurisdiction over this matter. . . . The Family Division of the Superior Court ("the Division") has jurisdiction over cases pertaining to neglected children. . . . There is substantial evidence in the record showing that while K.I. was under the care of B.I., B.I. frequently consumed alcohol, took away K.I.'s required oxygen and monitors for apnea and the heart, and failed to provide adequate care for the child; thus, K.I. was properly adjudicated a neglected child.

Given the lack of appropriate attention and care by B.I., the trial court assumed its role as parens patriae "to promote [K.I.'s] best interest," and to provide necessary relief. . . . The court's exercise of its discretion as parens patriae was essential since the District government took no position on the resuscitation issue and because B.I. and D.M. had a fundamental disagreement concerning resuscitation — D.M. supported the need for the DNR, while B.I. opposed the DNR and favored the use of a variety of medical techniques, "including intubation, defibrillation (shock with electric paddles), and interosseous efforts at introducing medication into [K.I.'s] system" in an effort to reverse any cardiac arrest or respiratory distress. B.I.'s goal is to keep K.I. "breathing." Moreover, in light of the fact that K.I. has been described as "neurologically devastated," feels and reacts to pain and discomfort but not to other stimuli, has no reaction to the surrounding environment, cannot give or receive love or express a view; and because some of the resuscitation techniques engender substantial pain and discomfort, we cannot fault the trial court's decision to issue the DNR based upon guidance from medical experts and consistent with the best interests of K.I., rather than abiding by B.I.'s wishes.

Although biological parents have a "fundamental liberty interest . . . in the care, custody, and management of their child [which] does not evaporate simply because they have not been model parents or have lost temporary custody of their child to the State[,]" Santosky v. Kramer, 455 U.S. 745, 753 (1982), that interest is not absolute since "[t]he paramount concern is the child's welfare and all other considerations, including the rights of a parent to a child, must yield to its best interests and well-being." Davis v. Jurney, 145 A.2d 846, 849 (D.C. 1958). Although B.I. clearly has a liberty interest "in the care, custody and management of [K.I.]," *Santosky*, supra, 455 U.S. at 753, K.I.'s well-being takes precedence over B.I.'s parental rights.

In short, the trial court did not err in exercising jurisdiction over the DNR issue rather than yielding to B.I.'s wishes as a parent.

B.I. insists that, after the trial court decided to exercise jurisdiction over the DNR matter, the court should have applied the substituted judgment rather than the best interests of the child standard in determining whether to issue the DNR. . . .

Historically, the substituted judgment standard arose in estate cases involving incompetent persons, and generally has been invoked in cases of adults who at one time were competent but later became incompetent. In applying the doctrine, "[t]he court, as surrogate for the incompetent, is to determine as best it can what choice [the] individual, if competent, would make with respect to medical procedures." In re Boyd, 403 A.2d 744, 750 (D.C. 1979) (footnote omitted). "[T]he substituted judgment inquiry is primarily a subjective one," [In re A.C., 573 A.2d 1235, 1249 (D.C. 1990)], and in both In re A.C. and In re Boyd, *supra*, we set forth factors to be followed in ascertaining the decision that the incompetent person would make. These factors include giving "the greatest weight . . . to the previously expressed wishes of the patient." In re A.C., *supra*, 573 A.2d at 1249-50. As we said in In re A.C.,

> to determine the subjective desires of thepatient, the court must consider the totality of the evidence, focusing particularly on written or oral directions

concerning treatment to family, friends, and health-care professionals. The court should also take into account the patient's past decisions regarding medical treatment, and attempt to ascertain from what is known about the patient's value system, goals, and desires what the patient would decide if competent. [Id. at 1251 (citations omitted).]

In In re Barry, 445 So.2d 365,371 (Fla. App. 2 Dist. 1984), the court noted that: "The [substituted judgment] doctrine has been helpful in the case of adults, but it is difficult to apply to children or young adults." Indeed, most of the substituted judgment cases cited by B.I., including those from this jurisdiction, concerned adults. Moreover, unlike K.I.'s situation, in one of the cases cited by B.I. which involved a minor, there was no neglect adjudication, and both parents agreed to petition the court for approval to remove life support systems. See In re Barry, supra, . . .

To attempt to apply the substituted judgment test in this case where B.I. and D.M. disagree; where K.I., a child born in June 1997, has never been healthy; has issued no oral or written directives as to medical matters or formed any opinions about anything, let alone a value system; not only would be impossible, but also would violate the spirit of the substituted judgment standard, the purpose of which is to implement the wishes of the incompetent individual. Consequently, we hold, consistent with the trial court's memorandum opinion, that "in cases involving minor respondents who have lacked, and will forever lack, the ability to express a preference regarding their course of medical treatment," and where the parents do not speak with the same voice but disagree as to the proper course of action, the best interests of the child standard shall be applied to determine whether to issue a DNR.

[Next, the appellate court held that the correct standard of proof required for issuance of a DNR in the best interests of the child is clear and convincing evidence. The appellate court then turned to whether the trial court appropriately applied that standard.]

Contrary to B.I.'s argument, we are satisfied that the trial court applied the clear and convincing evidence test rather than relying primarily upon factual findings from the neglect adjudication which were made in accordance with the preponderance of the evidence standard. . . .

In this case, the trial court specifically stated that "the issuance of [its] DNR order must be predicated upon a finding by clear and convincing evidence both that it is in [K.I.'s] best interests to forego aggressive revival measures, and that [B.I.'s] refusal to consent to the issuance of the DNR order is unreasonably contrary to [K.I.'s] well-being." Further, the court "[was] satisfied, by clear and convincing evidence, that upon balancing the burdens of continued life against the benefits and rewards of furthering life, [K.I.'s] best interests will be served by issuing a DNR order." Thus, the main focus of the court was on the medical condition of K.I., the impact that aggressive and invasive resuscitation procedures would have on K.I. such as the inducement of pain, discomfort and additional neurological damage. The court did reference the findings of neglect relating to B.I. — her drinking and failure to keep K.I. on oxygen and required monitors. In concluding that B.I.'s "refusal to consent to the entry of [the DNR] is both unreasonable and contrary to

[K.I.'s] best interests," however, the court emphasized B.I.'s lack of cooperation with the hospital staff and her singular goal of keeping K.I. breathing, as evidenced by her statement, "any amount of pain is worth it as long as [K.I.] breathes."

In short, in exercising its role as parens patriae and guided by testimony of several medical, bioethics, and ethics experts in this case where there was a prior adjudication of neglect, the trial court, carefully and thoughtfully, determined by clear and convincing evidence that it was in K.I.'s best interests to avoid use of aggressive resuscitation efforts which cause pain and discomfort. . . . We see no abuse of discretion in this matter. . . .

QUESTIONS

(1) In re K.I. involves medical decision making regarding a child who is subject to the neglect jurisdiction. Suppose B.I. had not been a neglectful parent and that a court had not previously determined K.I. to be neglected. Would the case have been decided the same way? Should courts be the decision maker in cases of parental disagreement about a child's medical treatment? Might there be some alternative manner to resolve the dispute?

(2) In *K.I.*, the medical professionals (expert witnesses and *amici*) concurred that the court should issue the DNR order. Suppose the experts, as well as the parents, disagreed. How should a court adjudicate such a dispute? What factors should a court take into account?

(3) On what basis does the appellate court apply the best interests of the child standard? When should a court apply the substituted judgment standard in cases of medical disputes regarding ill children?

(4) Suppose the parents disagree not about medical treatment but rather about *telling* the child about the nature or consequences of the treatment or illness (e.g., if the illness is terminal). How should such a dispute be resolved? Should a court resort to the "best interests" standard? If so, is the "best interests of the child" a compelling state interest to permit an infringement of one parent's First Amendment rights? For a parental dispute in a related context, see Stephanie L. v. Benjamin L., 602 N.Y.S.2d 80 (N.Y. Sup. Ct. 1993) (refusing to enjoin husband from telling ten-year-old daughter that wife had terminal cancer).

6. Exceptions Where the Minor Alone May Consent to Medical Treatment

PRELIMINARY QUESTIONS

(1) Special Circumstances.   A number of states permit a minor, regardless of age, to give effective consent to the diagnosis or treatment of venereal disease, drug addiction, alcoholism, pregnancy, or for purposes of giving blood. What purposes or interests are served by each of these exceptions? Are young people more likely to make mature decisions about treatment for these conditions? Or do these

exceptions reflect predominant public health interests of society at large? Is the primary purpose to provide for treatment in circumstances where many young people are too embarrassed or fearful to discuss the matter with their parents? If such legislation reflects the privacy interest of minors, why is the doctor often given discretion to inform the young patient's parents that treatment has taken place? For example, see Minn. Stat. Ann. §144.346 (2005), at p. 376 supra.

(2) Emancipation Exception. At common law an "emancipated" minor could consent to medical treatment and a doctor would not be liable for treatment without parental consent. Marriage was considered an act of emancipation. State statutes, in a variety of ways, provide for exceptions for "emancipated" or "mature" minors. Some statutes appear simply to codify the common law. Others modify the common law definition. Minnesota, for example, requires that the minor live "separate and apart from parents or legal guardian" and manage "personal financial affairs," but, unlike common law emancipation, does not require parental assent or consent to living away from home. See p. 376 supra. Still other states allow treatment of a minor without parental consent when the minor is of sufficient intelligence to understand and appreciate the "consequences" of the treatment. See Ark. Stat. Ann. §20-9-602 (2005), supra p. 374. Finally, some states by statute have simply lowered the age of consent. See Ala. Code §22-8-4 (1997), supra p. 375. For an argument in favor of expanding the minor's right to consent, see Andrew Newman, Adolescent Consent to Routine Medical and Surgical Treatment, 22 J. Legal Med. 501 (2001).

(3) Alternative Forms of Consent. Consider these alternative methods of giving young people some say in their medical treatment:

a. Some states use an age-based line and simply adopt a lower age requirement. What are the advantages and disadvantages of age-based lines? Is the normal line today, drawn at 18, too high?

b. What are the advantages of using emancipation as the criterion? When parents no longer are responsible for a young person's support, does it necessarily follow that the self-supporting young person is mature enough to make his or her own medical decisions? Does the emancipation exception simply reflect the idea that parental consent is inconvenient when a young person is no longer living at home? Are 17-year-old college students, living in a dormitory and supported by their parents, emancipated at common law? Is living away from one's parents a better rule of thumb than age for determining when one is mature enough to weigh medical questions properly? If so, why should a "responsible" 17-year-old living at home have fewer rights than a Minnesota runaway?

c. What are the advantages and disadvantages of a more discretionary standard allowing the young person to consent to his own treatment if in a doctor's judgment the young person is sufficiently mature to understand the treatment and its consequences?

(4) Limits of Exception. Where there is an exception for an emancipated or mature minor, should this exception apply to *all* kinds of medical treatment? Suppose a 17-year-old runaway wishes to have a vasectomy. Should an emancipated 14-year-old in Alabama have the same rights to refuse essential medical treatment as an adult? Can an adult refuse essential life-saving treatment? See Chapter 1, p. 35.

(5) Bypass Proceedings.   If parents cannot "veto" a young woman's medical decision to have an abortion, why should parental consent be required for other medical treatment of postpubescent adolescents? Alternatively, if bypass procedures are provided to minors in the abortion context, should such procedures also be available in the mental health context? See Richard E. Redding, Children's Competence to Provide Informed Consent for Mental Health Treatment, 50 Wash. & Lee L. Rev. 695, 719 (1993) (so arguing).

(6) Cognitive Competence.   Do adolescents have the cognitive competence to consent to medical treatment? Do they think the same way adults do? Consider the relevance of the psychological research that follows on the issue of when minors should have the right to consent to their own medical treatment.

Lois A. Weithorn, Children's Capacities in Legal Contexts
Children, Mental Health, and the Law 35-39 (N. Dickon Reppucci et al. eds., 1984)

The doctrine of informed consent requires that three conditions be met in order for a treatment decision to be considered legally valid. The decision must be informed (i. e., the patient must be provided with adequate information about the proposed and alternative treatments), voluntary (i.e., the patient must make the treatment decision free from coercion or unfair inducements), and competent. The predominant legal standard for competency emphasizes that the patient must have an "appreciation" of the nature, extent, and probable consequences of the conduct consented to. Although the notion of appreciation is not clearly defined by the law, it has been viewed by some as a higher level of understanding, requiring the individual to think abstractly and to make inferences about the implications of the proposed treatments for oneself.[3] In practice, however, competency to consent to treatment is typically evaluated by examining the patient's understanding of the basic factual information presented by the attending professional. Consent forms stress such factual information. Roth et al.[4] and Meisel[5] reviewed several additional standards of competency, which may be applied in various contexts. The "rational reasons" or "reasonable decision-making process" standard emphasizes the manner in which the patient arrives at a decision. Did the patient consider the information about the risks and benefits of the various treatments provided by attending professionals? The "evidence of choice" test requires that patients merely express a preference regarding treatment. Finally, the "reasonable

---

[3] P.S. Appelbaum & L.H. Roth, Clinical Issues in the Assessment of Competency, Am. J. of Psychiatry 138(11), 1462-1467 (1981); Weithorn, L.A., Developmental Factors and Competence to Make Informed Treatment Decisions, 5 Child and Youth Services 85-100 (1982).

[4] L.H. Roth, A. Meisel, & C.W. Lidz, Tests of Competency to Consent to Treatment, Am. J. of Psychiatry 134, 279-284 (1977).

[5] A. Meisel, The "Exceptions" to the Informed Consent Doctrine: Striking a Balance Between Competing Values in Medical Decision Making, Wisc. L.J. 413-488 (1979).

outcome" test examines the choice the patient has made to determine whether it is reasonable. This judgment may be made by comparing the patient's choice to prevailing professional opinion as to what are the "best" choices, or to a standard of the choice a "hypothetical reasonable person" might select. . . .

Weithorn[7] and Grisso and Vierling[8] provide discussions of the psychological skills that appear to be required in order to make a competent treatment decision. Based on a Piagetian analysis,[9] these authors predict that most adolescents will have the necessary cognitive skills to demonstrate competency according to the highest standard: appreciation. Since the standard of appreciation requires that individuals understand at a relatively abstract level information about future possibilities resulting from each of several choices, it appears that formal operational thinking would be a prerequisite. Formal operational structures allow individuals to conceptualize multiple abstract possibilities and to hypothesize about the consequences of various courses of action. Since children begin to develop formal operational structures at about age 11, and the stage reaches a point of equilibrium at about age 14, it would appear that 14-year-olds and older adolescents would meet the highest standards of competency.

Weithorn and Campbell[10] investigated the law's presumptions regarding the competency of minors to consent to treatment. Children aged 9 and 14 were compared with adults aged 18 and 21. All subjects were presented with four hypothetical vignettes about individuals suffering from medical or psychological disorders who had to choose among several treatment options. The subjects were presented with detailed information about the nature, purpose, risks, and benefits of the alternative treatments, and were asked to choose among them. The subjects were then asked a series of standardized questions about their decisions, and about the vignettes. The responses were scored according to criteria on several scales, each scale having been designed to measure competency according to one of the legal standards reviewed above.

In general, the findings strongly supported hypothetical predictions. Fourteen-year-olds were found not to differ from adults in most instances according to all scales of competency: inferential understanding (i.e., appreciation), factual understanding, reasoning, reasonable outcome, and evidence of choice. By contrast, 9-year-olds were found to perform significantly less well on the understanding and reasoning scales. However, despite the 9-year-olds' poorer performance on these scales, they did not differ significantly from the adults with respect to the choices they selected (i.e., reasonable outcome test), in three or four instances. This finding suggests that full understanding and the most sophisticated reasoning process may not be prerequisites for reaching a reasonable decision. . . .

[7] [Weithorn, supra note 3].

[8] T. Grisso & L. Vierling, Minors' Consent to Treatment: A Developmental Perspective, Professional Psychology, 9, 412-427 (1978).

[9] Inhelder, B., & Piaget, J., The Growth of Logical Thinking (1958); Piaget, J., Intellectual Evolution From Adolescence to Adulthood, 15 Human Development 1-12 (1972).

[10] L.A. Weithorn & S.B. Campbell, The Competency of Children and Adolescents to Make Informed Treatment Decisions, Child Development 53, 1589-1599 (1982).

D. DISABLED NEWBORNS

1. Introduction

PROBLEMS

(1) Baby *A*, a newborn with Down's syndrome, has an intestinal obstruction that makes food digestion impossible. The chances of a successful operation to correct the obstruction are very good. Without the operation, the baby will starve to death within two weeks. Down's syndrome is a chromosomal disorder that produces mental retardation and several physical characteristics, such as a distinctively shaped head, neck, and abdomen. There is no known treatment. Many such babies can experience physical and mental growth, receive and give love, and be trained to feed and clothe themselves, as well as to perform simple kinds of work. Many live into adulthood. After consulting with family members, attending physicians, their minister, and the hospital geneticist, Baby *A*'s parents decide not to consent to surgery to correct the intestinal blockage. See In re Infant Doe, No. GU 8204-004A (Monroe County Cir. Ct., Ind., Apr. 12, 1982).

(2) Baby *B* is an infant who is born with a medical condition known as anencephaly, a condition characterized by an absence of most of the brain but the presence of a functioning brain stem. Most such babies die within a short time after birth. When Baby *B* is born, she suffers severe respiratory difficulties. The hospital physicians, baby's father, and members of the hospital ethics committee all recommend withholding the use of a mechanical ventilator to help the infant breathe, reasoning that such care would prolong the baby's inevitable death. They want to provide only comfort measures to Baby *B* (not life-sustaining treatment). However, Baby *B's* mother, who is a fundamentalist Christian, insists that the baby be placed on the ventilator. See generally Matter of Baby K., 16 F.3d 590 (4th Cir. 1994), *cert. denied*, 513 U.S. 825 (1994).

(3) Mr. and Mrs. Smith come to the hospital when Mrs. Smith goes into premature labor at 23 weeks of pregnancy. The Smiths' physician tells the Smiths that he has never seen such a premature baby survive and that if their infant did survive, the baby would be likely to suffer from severe physical and mental impairment. The Smiths decide that they do not want the hospital staff to undertake "heroic measures" to save their infant's life. They ask that the hospital not provide any life-sustaining measures. They are concerned about the effect of caring for a severely impaired infant on their two older children, their marriage, and their careers. The hospital administrator is concerned about the extent of the hospital's liability and orders the neonatologist to resuscitate the baby after birth. Baby *C* suffers from severe mental and physical impairment, requires constant operations to be kept alive, and has no prospect of being able to feed himself or of becoming aware of his own existence. Compare Miller ex rel. Miller v. HCA, Inc., 118 S.W.3d 758 (Tex. 2003) (discussed infra) with Preston v. Meriter Hosp., Inc., 678 N.W.2d 347 (Wis. Ct. App. 2004).

a. In these examples, do the parents have the right to withhold consent or insist on treatment? May the doctor and hospital rely on the parents' decision? Must the doctor and hospital rely on the parents' decision? Should the hospital staff ask a juvenile court to take jurisdiction of the baby as a "neglected child"? As an attorney, what would you advise the parents, the attending doctor, and the hospital about potential civil and criminal liability? (See also the federal Child Abuse Amendments of 1984, discussed infra.)

b. Would your answers be different if, rather than permitting the baby to die from nontreatment, a physician gave the baby a lethal injection?

c. What are the moral and legal responsibilities to these children? What factors should make a difference when deciding what treatment to give to a disabled newborn? Survival rate? Life expectancy? Self-awareness? Quality of the baby's life? Burdens on the family? Cost of treatment? Who should decide? By what procedure?

Consider the materials in this chapter in thinking about these questions.

2. Relevant Materials

One of the "miracles" of modern medicine has been the remarkable advances in neonatal care in the past few decades. Beginning in 1970, the neonatal mortality rate decreased significantly. For example, the neonatal mortality rate dropped by half in the next decade — the greatest proportional decrease in any decade since national birth statistics were first gathered in 1915.[34] Particularly dramatic gains have been made in the survival rate of infants weighing less than 1,000 grams (2.2 lbs). However, not all seriously ill newborns will survive or thrive. Of those who do survive, many will suffer severe physical and/or mental impairments — either from their conditions or as a result of medical intervention. The extent of the infants' eventual impairment is often unknown at birth.

The case of Miller ex rel. Miller v. HCA, infra, explores the issue of parents' refusal of treatment in the context of a severely premature newborn whose prognosis is uncertain. The excerpt by Steven Smith explains the origins of the controversy about the ethics of forgoing treatment for seriously disabled newborns and the ensuing federal legislation. Subsequent excerpts highlight the moral and ethical issues raised by the withholding of medical care to disabled newborns.

Miller ex rel. Miller v. HCA, Inc.
118 S.W.3d 758 (Tex. 2003)

Justice Enoch delivered the opinion of the Court.

The narrow question we must decide is whether Texas law recognizes a claim by parents for either battery or negligence because their premature infant, born alive but in distress at only twenty-three weeks of gestation, was provided resuscitative medical treatment by physicians at a hospital without parental consent. . . .

The unfortunate circumstances of this case began in August 1990, when approximately four months before her due date, Karla Miller was admitted to Woman's Hospital of Texas in premature labor. An ultrasound revealed that Karla's fetus weighed about 629 grams or 1 1/4 pounds and had a gestational

---

[34] President's Commission for the Study of Ethical Problems in Medicine and Biomedical and Behavioral Research, Deciding to Forgo Life-Sustaining Treatment, Pub. L. No. 83-17978, at 197-198.

age of approximately twenty-three weeks. Because of the fetus's prematurity, Karla's physicians began administering a drug designed to stop labor.

Karla's physicians subsequently discovered that Karla had an infection that could endanger her life and require them to induce delivery. Dr. Mark Jacobs, Karla's obstetrician, and Dr. Donald Kelley, a neonatologist at the Hospital, informed Karla and her husband, Mark Miller, that if they had to induce delivery, the infant had little chance of being born alive. The physicians also informed the Millers that if the infant was born alive, it would most probably suffer severe impairments, including cerebral palsy, brain hemorrhaging, blindness, lung disease, pulmonary infections, and mental retardation. Mark testified at trial that the physicians told him they had never had such a premature infant live and that anything they did to sustain the infant's life would be guesswork.

After their discussion, Drs. Jacobs and Kelley asked the Millers to decide whether physicians should treat the infant upon birth if they were forced to induce delivery. At approximately noon that day, the Millers informed Drs. Jacob and Kelley that they wanted no heroic measures performed on the infant and they wanted nature to take its course. Mark testified that he understood heroic measures to mean performing resuscitation, chest massage, and using life support machines. Dr. Kelley recorded the Millers' request in Karla's medical notes, and Dr. Jacobs informed the medical staff at the Hospital that no neonatologist would be needed at delivery. Mark then left the Hospital to make funeral arrangements for the infant.

In the meantime, the nursing staff informed other Hospital personnel of Dr. Jacobs' instruction that no neonatologist would be present in the delivery room when the Millers' infant was born. An afternoon of meetings involving Hospital administrators and physicians followed. Between approximately 4:00 P.M. and 4:30 P.M. that day, Anna Summerfield, the director of the Hospital's neonatal intensive care unit, and several physicians, including Dr. Jacobs, met with Mark upon his return to the Hospital to further discuss the situation. Mark testified that Ms. Summerfield announced at the meeting that the Hospital had a policy requiring resuscitation of any baby who was born weighing over 500 grams. Although Ms. Summerfield agreed that she said that, the only written Hospital policy produced described the Natural Death Act and did not mention resuscitating infants over 500 grams.

Moreover, the physicians at the meeting testified that they and Hospital administrators agreed only that a neonatologist would be present to evaluate the Millers' infant at birth and decide whether to resuscitate based on the infant's condition at that time. As Dr. Jacobs testified:

> [W]hat we finally decided that everyone wanted to do was to not make the call prior to the time we actually saw the baby. Deliver the baby, because you see there was this [question] is the baby really 23 weeks, or is the baby further along, how big is the baby, what are we dealing with. We decided to let the neonatologist make the call by looking directly at the baby at birth.

Another physician who attended the meeting agreed, testifying that to deny any attempts at resuscitation without seeing the infant's condition would be inappropriate and below the standard of care. . . .

Mark testified that, after the meeting, Hospital administrators asked him to sign a consent form allowing resuscitation according to the Hospital's plan, but he refused. Mark further testified that when he asked how he could prevent resuscitation, Hospital administrators told him that he could do so by removing Karla from the Hospital, which was not a viable option given her condition. Dr. Jacobs then noted in Karla's medical charts that a plan for evaluating the infant upon her birth was discussed at that afternoon meeting.

That evening, Karla's condition worsened and her amniotic sac broke. Dr. Jacobs determined that he would have to augment labor so that the infant would be delivered before further complications to Karla's health developed. Dr. Jacobs accordingly stopped administering the drug to Karla that was designed to stop labor, substituting instead a drug designed to augment labor. At 11:30 P.M. that night, Karla delivered a premature female infant weighing 615 grams, which the Millers named Sidney. Sidney's actual gestational age was twenty-three and one-seventh weeks. And she was born alive.

[Dr. Eduardo Otero, the neonatologist present in the delivery room when Sidney was born] noted that Sidney had a heart beat, albeit at a rate below that normally found in full-term babies. He further noted that Sidney, although blue in color and limp, gasped for air, spontaneously cried, and grimaced. Dr. Otero also noted that Sidney displayed no dysmorphic features other than being premature. He immediately "bagged" and "intubated" Sidney to oxygenate her blood; he then placed her on ventilation. He explained why:

> Because this baby is alive and this is a baby that has a reasonable chance of living. And again, this is a baby that is not necessarily going to have problems later on. There are babies that survive at this gestational age that — with this birth weight, that later on go on and do well.

Neither Karla nor Mark objected at the time to the treatment provided.

Sidney initially responded well to the treatment. . . . But at some point during the first few days after birth, Sidney suffered a brain hemorrhage — a complication not uncommon in infants born so prematurely. [A]s predicted by Karla's physicians, the hemorrhage caused Sidney to suffer severe physical and mental impairments. At the time of trial, Sidney was seven years old and could not walk, talk, feed herself, or sit up on her own. The evidence demonstrated that Sidney was legally blind, suffered from severe mental retardation, cerebral palsy, seizures, and spastic quadriparesis in her limbs. She could not be toilet-trained and required a shunt in her brain to drain fluids that accumulate there and needed care twenty-four hours a day. The evidence further demonstrated that her circumstances will not change.

[The Millers asserted battery and negligence claims against HCA and the Hospital.] The Millers' claims stemmed from their allegations that despite their instructions to the contrary, the Hospital not only resuscitated Sidney but performed experimental procedures and administered experimental drugs, without which, in all reasonable medical probability, Sidney would not have survived. . . . The jury concluded that HCA and the Hospital were grossly negligent and that the Hospital acted with malice. . . . The trial court rendered judgment jointly and severally against the HCA defendants on the jury's verdict of

$29,400,000 in actual damages for medical expenses, $17,503,066 in prejudgment interest, and $13,500,000 in exemplary damages. HCA appealed.

[The appellate court reversed, holding that parents have the right to withhold life-sustaining treatment (under the state Natural Death Act) only when their baby's condition is certified as terminal. Here, because Sidney's condition was not certified as terminal, the Millers did not have the statutory right to refuse treatment. The appellate court also found that no court order was required to override the parents' refusal because the need for life-sustaining treatment became urgent only when the nonterminally ill baby was under a health provider's care. The dissenting judge disagreed, contending: (1) a court order was required to override the parents' decision; (2) the state Natural Death Act was not mandatory in this context; (3) the parents' choice was protected by the U.S. Constitution; and (4) the court erroneously applied an "emergency exception" when there was no finding of the existence of a medical emergency giving the hospital the right to intervene.]

This case requires us to determine the respective roles that parents and health-care providers play in deciding whether to treat an infant who is born alive but in distress and is so premature that, despite advancements in neonatal intensive care, has a largely uncertain prognosis. [N]either the Texas Legislature nor our case law has addressed this specific situation. . . .

Generally speaking, the custody, care, and nurture of an infant resides in the first instance with the parents. As the United States Supreme Court has acknowledged, parents are presumed to be the appropriate decision-makers for their infants:

> Our jurisprudence historically has reflected Western civilization concepts of the family as a unit with broad parental authority over minor children. Our cases have consistently followed that course; our constitutional system long ago rejected any notion that a child is "the mere creature of the State" and, on the contrary, asserted that parents generally "have the right, coupled with the high duty, to recognize and prepare [their children] for additional obligations." . . . Surely, this includes a "high duty" to recognize symptoms of illness and to seek and follow medical advice. The law's concept of the family rests on a presumption that parents possess what a child lacks in maturity, experience, and capacity for judgment required for making life's difficult decisions. More important, historically it has recognized that natural bonds of affection lead parents to act in the best interests of their children [citing Parham v. J.R., 442 U.S. 584, 602 (1979)].

. . . Of course, this broad grant of parental decision-making authority is not without limits. The State's role as parens patriae permits it to intercede in parental decision-making under certain circumstances. As the United States Supreme Court has noted:

> [A]s persons unable to protect themselves, infants fall under the parens patriae power of the state. In the exercise of this authority, the state not only punishes parents whose conduct has amounted to abuse or neglect of their children but may also supervene parental decisions before they become operative to ensure that the choices made are not so detrimental to a child's interests as to amount to neglect and abuse. [Bowen v. American Hosp. Assn., 476 U.S. 610, 627 n. 13 (1986).]

But the Supreme Court has also pointed out:

> [A]s long as parents choose from professionally accepted treatment options the choice is rarely reviewed in court and even less frequently supervened . . . [Id.].

[W]e now determine whether the Millers can maintain their battery and negligence claims against HCA. [W]e only address whether the Hospital was required to seek court intervention to overturn the lack of parental consent — which it undisputedly did not do — before Dr. Otero could treat Sidney without committing a battery.

The Millers acknowledge that numerous physicians at trial agreed that, absent an emergency situation, the proper course of action is court intervention when health care providers disagree with parents' refusal to consent to a child's treatment. And the Millers contend that, as a matter of law, no emergency existed that would excuse the Hospital's treatment of Sidney without their consent or a court order overriding their refusal to consent. . . . But the Millers' reasoning fails to recognize that, in this case, the evidence established that Sidney could only be properly evaluated when she was born. Any decision the Millers made before Sidney's birth concerning her treatment at or after her birth would necessarily be based on speculation. Therefore, we reject the Millers' argument that a decision could adequately be made pre-birth that denying all post-birth resuscitative treatment would be in Sidney's best interest. Such a decision could not control whether the circumstances facing Dr. Otero were emergent because it would not have been a fully informed one according to the evidence in this case.

The Millers point out that physicians routinely ask parents to make pre-birth treatment choices for their infants including whether to accept or refuse in utero medical treatment and to continue or terminate a pregnancy. While that may be entirely true, the evidence here established that the time for evaluating Sidney was when she was born. The evidence further reflected that Sidney was born alive but in distress. At that time, Dr. Otero had to make a split-second decision on whether to provide life-sustaining treatment. While the Millers were both present in the delivery room, there was simply no time to obtain their consent to treatment or to institute legal proceedings to challenge their withholding of consent, had the Millers done so, without jeopardizing Sidney's life. . . . We agree that, whenever possible, obtaining consent in writing to evaluate a premature infant at birth and to render any warranted medical treatment is the best course of action. And physicians and hospitals should always strive to do so. But if such consent is not forthcoming, or is affirmatively denied, we decline to impose liability on a physician solely for providing life-sustaining treatment under emergent circumstances to a new-born infant without that consent. . . .

NOTES AND QUESTIONS

(1) Who Should Decide?   Miller focuses on the issue: Who should decide whether an extremely premature infant who faces an uncertain prognosis

(regarding the likelihood of suffering severe, permanent physical and mental impairment) should receive life-sustaining treatment? The parents? Medical professionals? The courts? According to what standard(s)? What factors should be taken into account?

(2) Additional Action. What action do you think the hospital should have taken? Should it have sought a court order to override the parents' wishes? One commentator suggests that the physicians should have engaged in a "collaborative medical decisionmaking model" with the Millers, rather than unilaterally deciding to provide life-sustaining treatment. Holly O'Neal Rumbaugh, Miller v. HCA, Inc.: Disempowering Parents from Making Medical Treatment Decisions for Severely Premature Babies, 41 Hous. L. Rev. 675,704 (2004). Do you agree? What additional action might the parents have taken? Could the parents be criminally liable for their nontreatment decision — i.e., the failure to provide necessary medical care to their infant?

(3) Emergency. Was this an emergency situation that would excuse the hospital for treating the infant absent parental consent or a court order? Did the hospital's indecision and delay (between the physicians' meeting and the birth) create the emergency that justified their failure to obtain the parents' consent? *Miller* held that the provision of medical treatment to an infant during "emergent circumstances" (even in the face of parental refusal of consent) is an exception to the general rule that a physician commits battery by providing treatment without parental consent. Does this imply that a parent can never refuse consent to medical treatment for a severely premature infant *prior* to birth?

(4) Applicable Law. Because *Miller* raised an issue of first impression, the state supreme court looked to relevant statutory and case law. How helpful in the determination to permit the withholding of life-sustaining treatment is a given state's Natural Death Act (i.e., giving parents the right to withhold treatment when the infant's condition is certifiably "terminal")? According to Texas law, a terminal condition is one caused "by injury, disease, or illness." Tex. Health & Safety Code §166.002(13) (2001 & Supp. 2008). The Texas Natural Death Act was amended in 1999 and recodified as the Advance Directives Act. See Tex. Health & Safety Code Ann. §§166.001-.166 (2001 & Supp. 2008). Was the Millers' infant in a "terminal" condition? Alternatively, how helpful in the determination is the judicially applied best-interests-of-the-child standard?

(5) Tort Liability. A few states (but not the jurisdiction in *Miller*) recognize a wrongful life cause of action — a tort claim brought on behalf of a child with major disabilities that were caused by another's negligence and that caused the child's severely impaired life. See Carmel Shachar, Assigning and Empowering Moral Decision Making: Acuna v. Turkish and Wrongful Birth and Wrongful Life Jurisprudence in New Jersey, 36 J.L. Med. & Ethics 193, 195 (2008) (pointing out that only three states currently recognize wrongful life claims). The cause of action is premised on the idea that no life is better than a significantly impaired life. Should courts be more willing to recognize such claims? Does recognition of such claims adequately address the issues raised by *Miller*?

On the issue of nontreatment, see also Preston v. Meriter Hosp., Inc., 678 N.W.2d 347 (Wis. Ct. App. 2004) (affirming summary judgment for hospital in suit by mother of infant (born at 23 weeks of gestation) who died shortly after birth when hospital refused to resuscitate or treat the child).

NOTE: FEDERAL LEGISLATION

Steven R. Smith, Disabled Newborns and the Federal Child Abuse Amendments: Tenuous Protection
37 Hastings L.J. 765, 789-804 (1986)

Infant Doe Case

Seldom in American law has such a small case had such an immediate impact as did Indiana's *Infant Doe* case.[88] It lasted less than six days, but led to various lawsuits, several state statutes, a new federal statute, and new federal regulations. *Infant Doe* was the first case of its kind to attract significant national attention.

. . . Infant Doe apparently was born with two serious defects: no connection between the esophagus and the stomach, and a connection between the trachea and the esophagus. Corrective surgery was possible. Without treatment, death was certain either from lack of food and water, which could not be provided because there was no connection to the stomach, or from suffocation. Infant Doe also suffered from Down's syndrome. The child's parents refused to consent to surgery and decided to withhold food and water. The state court refused to order treatment, and the Indiana Supreme Court declined to overturn the lower court's ruling. Six days after birth the infant died, as certiorari was being sought from the United States Supreme Court. This case is notable because it got to court at all. Ordinarily such decisions are made in private. Only if the physician seriously disagrees with the decision to withhold treatment is any court activity likely.

Initial Federal Response

At the time the *Infant Doe* case arose, no federal law explicitly prohibited withholding of treatment from infants. The federal government endeavored to use section 504 of the Rehabilitation Act of 1973, which prohibits discrimination against the disabled by federally funded programs, to fill this void.[95] About a month after Infant Doe's death, the Department of Health and Human Services ("HHS") sent a "Notice to Health Care Providers" concerning "discriminating against the handicapped by withholding treatment or nourishment."[96] The notice warned hospitals that they risked the loss of federal funding by failing to treat infants because of their mental or physical handicap. HHS pointed out current regulations implementing section 504[98] and informed hospitals that they should

---

[88] In re Infant Doe, No. GU 8204-004A (Monroe County Cir. Ct., Ind. Apr. 12, 1982) (declaratory judgment), *cert. denied sub nom.*, Infant Doe v. Bloomington Hosp., 464 U.S. 961 (1983). . . .

[95] 29 U.S.C. §794 (1982) . . . .

[96] Notice to Health Care Providers from Betty Lous Dotson, Director, Office for Civil Rights, Department of Health & Human Services (May 18, 1982).

[98] 45 C.F.R. pt. 84 (1981).

counsel parents against refusing treatment and refuse to aid parents who decide to withhold treatment or nourishment.

This notice was followed in 1983 by a formal HHS "interim final" regulation.[100] The regulation provided that withholding food or customary medical treatment from disabled infants violated section 504 of the Rehabilitation Act. It further required that hospitals post a notice indicating that such discrimination is prohibited by federal law. This notice had to include a "hotline" number that anyone could use to report known or suspected withholding of treatment. The regulations also provided for federal investigation and intervention to protect the life of a disabled individual.

Hospitals and medical groups immediately challenged these regulations in federal court,[101] and the court invalidated the regulations essentially on procedural grounds. HHS had adopted the rule without the public notice or thirty-day delay required by the Administrative Procedure Act and also apparently had neglected to consider a number of important factors, including the disruptive effect of the regulations, the harm that could result from removing an infant from a hospital, the malpractice risks, and the allocation of scarce medical and economic resources.

Shortly after the invalidation of the initial procedure, HHS proposed new procedures that, with very modest changes, were the same as the earlier interim final regulations. After receiving nearly 17,000 comments on the proposed regulations, HHS modified and adopted them early in 1984.[105] The new regulations continued the hotline and posting of notice requirements, but they still suffered from considerable ambiguity about what factors could be considered in deciding to withhold treatment. The regulations permitted medical factors to be taken into account, but prohibited "nonmedical considerations from being injected into the decision-making process." The final regulations also encouraged hospitals to establish infant care review committees ("ICRCs"). These committees were only to be advisory and were not authorized to permit the withholding of treatment from infants.

While the process of adopting federal regulations was underway, another case arose in New York that put them to rest. This case was considerably different from the Indiana *Infant Doe* case. While the New York infant, "Baby Doe," did suffer from a variety of mental and physical abnormalities, her situation was not as clearly life-threatening as had been Infant Doe's situation in Indiana. This child ultimately left the hospital and went home with her parents.[108] Both private individuals and the federal government sought to intervene to require treatment on the child's behalf. These private efforts were unsuccessful, however. The New York court held that, given the record in this case, as a matter of procedure, only the appropriate state agency could bring the action; private individuals could not.[109] The federal government attempted to enter the case under the new federal discrimination provisions contained

---

[100] 48 Fed. Reg. 9630 (1983) (codified at 45 C.F.R. pt. 84 (1985)).

[101] American Academy of Pediatrics v. Heckler, 561 F. Supp. 395 (D.D.C. 1983), *aff'd sub nom.* Bowen v. American Hosp. Ass'n, 106 S. Ct. 2101 (1986).

[105] 49 Fed. Reg. 1622 (1984) (codified at 45 C.F.R. 84 (1985)).

[108] See Vitiello, The Baby Jane Doe Litigation and Section 504: An Exercise in Raw Executive Power, 17 Conn. L. Rev. 95, 106 (1984).

[109] Weber v. Stony Brook Hosp., 60 N.Y.2d 208, 456 N.E.2d 1186, 469 N.Y.S.2d 63, *cert. denied*, 464 U.S. 1026 (1983).

in section 504.[110] After a careful review of the Rehabilitation Act's legislative history, the Second Circuit ultimately rejected this attempt, concluding that Congress had not intended to authorize HHS to become involved in decisions to refuse treatment for seriously ill infants. The Supreme Court has reviewed the issues raised in this case and has agreed with the Second Circuit's holding.[112]

A Change of Focus

With the decision of the Second Circuit in the Baby Jane Doe case, the government's focus has changed from regulatory approaches interpreting section 504 to the establishment of new statutory authority dealing directly with life-saving treatment for infants. Its focus also has changed from protecting newborns under legislation intended to prohibit discrimination against the disabled to legislation intended to reduce the abuse and neglect of children. . . .

The major provision of the legislation regarding withdrawal of life-saving treatment from infants was the addition of a new clause to the federal child abuse law. Existing federal law required states to meet certain criteria to qualify for federal child abuse and neglect prevention funds. The 1984 amendment [codified at 42 U.S.C. §5103(b)(K) (West Supp. 1985)] provided that . . . states must have procedures or programs within the state child protective services to respond to instances of withholding medical treatment from disabled infants. States must provide for the appointment of someone in hospitals with whom the state can deal when nontreat-ment questions arise, who also must provide for prompt notification of instances of suspected medical neglect. Finally, the new law requires that states allow the state child protective services system "to pursue any legal remedies, including the authority to initiate legal proceedings in a court of competent jurisdiction, as may be necessary to prevent the withholding of medically indicated treatment from disabled infants with life-threatening conditions."

Central to the new provision is the term "withholding of medically indicated treatment," defined as the failure to "respond to the infant's life-threatening condition" in a way that is "most likely to be effective in ameliorating or correcting" all life-threatening conditions. Appropriate or necessary treatment must be determined according to the treating physician's "reasonable medical judgment" and specifically includes food, water, and medication. Presumably, treatment also includes surgery and the broad range of all forms of medical intervention.

The statute recognizes several categories in which treatment "other than appropriate nutrition, hydration, or medication" need not be provided to infants. These exceptions to the requirement that lifesaving treatment be given are:

1. When the child is irreversibly comatose.
2. When treatment would "merely prolong dying."
3. When the treatment would not be effective in ameliorating or correcting all of the life-threatening conditions.

---

[110] United States v. University Hosp., 575 F. Supp. 607 (E.D.N.Y. 1983), *aff'd*, 729 F.2d 144 (2d Cir. 1984).

[112] Bowen v. American Hosp. Assn., [476 U.S. 610 (1986)].

4. When the treatment "would otherwise be futile" in terms of the survival of the infant.
5. When imposing the treatment would be "virtually futile" in terms of survival and the treatment itself "under such circumstances would be inhumane."

The statute apparently excludes the provision of "appropriate" food, water, and medication from the treatment permitted to be withdrawn under these exceptions; therefore, these basic necessities must be provided even if one of the above treatment exceptions is present. Of course, by including the qualifying word, "appropriate," the statute implies that there are undefined conditions in which food, water, or medication are "inappropriate."

The Act also does not authorize the government to "establish standards prescribing specific medical treatment for specific conditions" and does not affect any rights or protections under section 504 of the Rehabilitation Act. Neither of these provisions should have a major impact on the Act's implementation. They merely leave open the question of whether the government may continue to push for the treatment of disabled newborns through section 504 of the Rehabilitation Act. The new statute also requires HHS to establish model guidelines concerning infant care review committees. . . .

HHS Regulations

[HHS's final regulations do provide] regulatory definitions of the terms "infant" and "reasonable medical judgment." An "infant" is defined as someone less than one year of age. The regulations also imply that "infant" status extends beyond the first year if the child has been "continuously hospitalized since birth, and was born extremely prematurely or . . . has a long term disability." The definition of "reasonable medical judgment" essentially tracks the common-law tort definition and requires that such judgments "be made by a reasonably prudent physician, knowledgeable about the case and the treatment possibilities with respect to the medical conditions involved." Both of these definitions were taken directly from the congressional conference report.

The appendix to the regulations is four times the length of the interpretive guidelines, and its length suggests the difficulty that HHS had in trying to establish acceptable but clear regulations. In this appendix, HHS notes that it "does not seek to establish these interpretive guidelines as binding rules of law." Instead, the guidelines are "intended to assist in interpreting the statutory definition so that it may be rationally and thoughtfully applied in specific contexts in a manner fully consistent with the legislative intent." . . .

Among the noteworthy points made in the appendix are the following:

(1) Decisions to withhold medically indicated treatment may *not* be based on "subjective opinions about the future 'quality of life' of a retarded or disabled person."
(2) Even when the statute permits the withholding of medically indicated treatment, "the infant must nonetheless be provided with appropriate nutrition, hydration, and medication."

(3) "Life-threatening" conditions include conditions that "significantly increase the risk of the onset of complications that may threaten the life of the infant."

(4) "Treatment" includes adequate evaluation, the referral of the infant to other physicians when necessary, and multiple medical or surgical procedures over a period of time.

(5) "Merely prolong dying" and related provisions that refer to treatments that would extend life only a short time do not apply only when death is "imminent." Treatment must be provided, however, when "many years of life will result from the provision of treatment or where the prognosis is not death in the near future but rather in the more distant future." It is up to the physician's exercise of reasonable medical judgment "to determine whether the prognosis of death, because of its nearness in time, is such that the treatment would not be medically indicated."

(6) The term "virtually futile" treatment means treatment that is highly unlikely to prevent death in the near future.

The regulations also propose model guidelines for establishing infant care review committees. Although the regulations encourage hospitals to establish ICRCs, they are not required to do so. If hospitals do establish them, the committees are not bound to conform to the guidelines suggested by HHS. The purposes of the ICRCs are: to offer counseling in specific cases involving disabled infants; to recommend institutional policies concerning disabled infants; and to educate hospital personnel and families of disabled infants concerning counseling, rehabilitative services, and support organizations. The regulations urge that the ICRC be able to be convened within twenty-four hours or less when there is disagreement between the infant's family and physician concerning withholding treatment or when the decision is made to withhold life-sustaining treatment "in certain categories of cases" identified in ICRC policies. The ICRC may "meet" by telephone when it cannot convene quickly enough in person. . . .

3. Philosophy

Robert H. Mnookin, Two Puzzles
1984 Ariz. St. L.J. 667, 677-679

. . . At a very basic level, there is fundamental disagreement among ethicists concerning the approach and the principles that should inform the analysis of decisions to withhold or withdraw treatment from handicapped newborns.[32] . . .

At one end of the spectrum are those who suggest that all non-dying neonates must be treated, irrespective of handicap, because of the "sanctity of life."[33] Under such an approach, the interests of the infant's family and social burdens are to be

---

[32] For a useful survey of ethical thought with respect to nontreatment issues, see R. Weir, Selective Nontreatment of Handicapped Newborns: Moral Dilemmas in Neonatal Medicine, chs. 6 &7 (1984).

[33] See, e.g., P. Ramsey, Ethics at the Edges of Life: Medical & Legal Intersections (1978). See generally R. Weir, supra note 32, at 146-152.

ignored. Nor is the expected quality of the child's handicapped life relevant. Paul Ramsey has argued, for example, that the severity of an infant's handicaps has no bearing on the decision whether or not to provide treatment: "We have no moral right to choose that some live and others die, when the medical indications for treatment are the same."[34] In more extreme forms, the sanctity of life approach involves a claim that every handicapped infant has an absolute and unwavering right to require that *all* measures be taken to preserve the child's life regardless of the quality of that life, the burdens imposed, the child's suffering, or the cost. This approach permits no balancing: human life, in whatever condition, is the ultimate good.

At the other extreme, there are utilitarians, Peter Singer and Michael Tooley most prominent among them, who find infanticide morally permissible in a wide range of circumstances.[35] Their moral calculus necessarily requires balancing, and it is legitimate and appropriate to consider both the parents' suffering and the social costs involved in raising handicapped children. They argue that it is not membership in the human species that matters, but rather, whether you have certain characteristics of personhood, such as self-consciousness or the ability to feel pain and suffering. If you lack these essential characteristics then your interests need not count in the calculus. "[E]veryday observation strongly suggests that there is no more reason for holding that a newborn baby has these capacities or enjoys these states (of personhood) than there is for holding that this is true of a newborn chimpanzee. [Consequently, the infanticide of newborns] is morally permissible in most cases when it is otherwise desirable."[36] And it makes no moral difference whether euthanasia is active or passive — i.e., whether the death occurs because treatment has been withheld or because a lethal injection has been given to end the neonate's life.

Between these extremes are a number of other approaches. For me the most persuasive is that suggested by Philippa Foot. She distinguishes between active and passive euthanasia, and suggests that withholding treatment is appropriate if, and only if, treatment is not in the patient's best interests. The question to ask is, "Is this death for the sake of the child himself?" If it is, and the doctor and parents are choosing death for that reason alone, then passive euthanasia is morally permissible. She forcefully argues that to take social burdens or familial interests into account is wrong.[37]

While this exclusive focus on the best interests of the child has substantial intuitive appeal, it does not provide a great deal of policy guidance in formulating more precise substantive standards or in deciding what to do in many cases. Even if one believes that the decision to terminate care for a handicapped newborn should be based only upon consideration of the infant's interests, what decision is best for the child? Often the best interests of a child are indeterminate and speculative. To decide what is best for a particular child, a decisionmaker must first make a set of predictions about the outcomes for the child under alternative courses of action. Then the decisionmaker must evaluate these different outcomes in light of some set of values in order to choose the best possible course of action under the circumstances. For reasons I have developed at length in other contexts, making accurate

---

[34] P. Ramsey, supra note 33, at 19. . . .

[35] M. Tooley, Abortion and Infanticide (1983); P. Singer, Practical Ethics 122-157 (1979).

[36] M. Tooley, supra note 35.

[37] Foot, Euthanasia, 6 Phil. & Pub. Affairs 85-87, 109-112 (1977).

predictions and choosing appropriate values are often very problematic.[38] The
same uncertainty appears to hold with respect to handicapped newborns. Doctors
acknowledge how difficult it often is accurately to predict at birth the severity of a
child's eventual handicaps. And even with better predictions, there does not appear
to be much of a social consensus about quality of life issues. An intolerable
handicap for one person may be a challenging and fulfilling opportunity for
another. What values should inform the choice for a particular child? . . .

DISCUSSION AND QUERIES

(1) Criminal prosecution for failure to treat a disabled newborn is rare. What
explains the lack of prosecution of parents, doctors, and hospitals that decide to
withhold treatment of disabled newborns? Is it the low visibility of the practice? Or
is it because there is no social consensus that letting disabled newborns die is
wrong? Or that the sanctions for homicide are too severe?

(2) Does the absence of prosecutions suggest that the criminal homicide laws
should be changed to legalize apparent practices? Or does it suggest that the
problems, if any, created by the possibility of criminal prosecutions are obviated
by nonenforcement? John Robertson has described the present situation "as one in
which prosecuting authorities, through the exercise of their discretion, have informally delegated authority to parents and physicians to decide the fate of defective
newborns."[35] What are the advantages and disadvantages of this "informal
delegation"? Consider the contrasting views that follow.

Raymond S. Duff & August B. Campbell, Moral and Ethical Dilemmas in the Special-Care Nursery
289 New Eng. J. Med. 890, 893-894 (1973)

Can families in the shock resulting from the birth of a defective child understand
what faces them? Can they give truly "informed consent" for treatment or withholding treatment? Some of our colleagues answer no to both questions. In our
opinion, if families regardless of background are heard sympathetically and at
length and are given information and answers to their questions in words they
understand, the problems of their children as well as the expected benefits and
limits of any proposed care can be understood clearly in practically all instances.
Parents *are* able to understand the implications of such things as chronic dyspnea,
oxygen dependency, incontinence, paralysis, contractures, sexual handicaps and
mental retardation. . . .

We do not know how often families and their physicians will make just decisions for severely handicapped children. Clearly, this issue is central in evaluation
of the process of decision making that we have described. But we also ask, if these
parties cannot make such decisions justly, who can?

---

[38] See R. Mnookin, In the Interest of Children (1985).

[35] John A. Robertson, Involuntary Euthanasia of Defective Newborns: A Legal Analysis,
27 Stan. L. Rev. 213, 243 (1975).

We recognize great variability and often much uncertainty in prognoses and in family capacities to deal with defective newborn infants. We also acknowledge that there are limits of support that society can or will give to assist handicapped persons and their families. Severely deforming conditions that are associated with little or no hope of a functional existence pose painful dilemmas for the laymen and professionals who must decide how to cope with severe handicaps. We believe the burdens of decision making must be borne by families and their professional advisers because they are most familiar with the respective situations. Since families primarily must live with and are most affected by the decisions, it therefore appears that society and the health professions should provide only general guidelines for decision making. Moreover, since variations between situations are so great, and the situations themselves so complex, it follows that much latitude in decision making should be expected and tolerated. Otherwise, the rules of society or the policies most convenient for medical technologists may become cruel masters of human beings instead of their servants. [W]e readily acknowledge that the extreme excesses of Hegelian "rational utility" under dictatorships must be avoided. Perhaps it is less recognized that the uncontrolled application of medical technology may be detrimental to individuals and families. . . . Physicians may hold excessive power over decision making by limiting or controlling the information made available to patients or families. It seems appropriate that the profession be held accountable for presenting fully all management options and their expected consequences. Also the public should be aware that professionals often face conflicts of interest that may result in decisions against individual preferences.

John A. Robertson, Involuntary Euthanasia of Defective Newborns: A Legal Analysis
27 Stan. L. Rev. 213, 262-264 (1975)

Duff and Campbell [supra] present the argument for granting parents and physicians final discretion to decide whether a defective infant should be treated and hence live or die. . . .

The logic of this argument, however, is unpersuasive. It rests on the assumption that parents have but two options — to withhold care or to be burdened with the care of the child throughout their lives. But a third option exists — termination of parental rights and obligations. However, while parental discretion to terminate the parental relationship may be justified, it does not follow that parents should also have the right to decide whether the child lives or dies. Clearly, discretion to terminate a relationship of dependency does not mandate that one have the power to impose death on the terminated party. Furthermore, a central element of procedural justice is impartial decisionmaking after full consideration of relevant information. Yet, neither parents nor physicians are impartial or disinterested; both have a strong personal interest in the outcome of their decision. Parents face the decision with the guilt, grief, and damaged image that birth of a defective child brings. They have a strong interest in maintaining previous life plans, and adjustment patterns, and in avoiding the psychic and financial costs of adjusting to care of a defective infant. Moreover, the treatment decision arises in highly emotional circumstances, when their rational faculties are weakest and full information concerning the defect and prognosis is wanting. In addition, the physician's objectivity may be compromised. The obstetrician, for example, may feel guilt or responsibility for the defect, and prefer that the problem be eliminated as soon as possible. He may think that the least he can do for the parents is to relieve them of a potential lifelong burden. Similarly, though less involved, the advice of a pediatrician or consultant is likely to be influenced by his own values concerning care for defective infants. In short, since parents and physicians face the treatment decision with conflicting interests and the pressure of strong emotions, giving them final, unguided discretion to decide whether defective infants live will often lead to hasty, biased choices. . . .

[A]rguably we can depend on the ethical commitments of the medical profession to prevent parental abuses. Physicians perhaps are better equipped than parents to consider these judgments and can intervene when parents misjudge the interests of society and child, thus operating as a check on parental decisionmaking. If the physician challenges the parental choice, . . . , he can seek judicial protection for the child. There is some merit to this claim, but one cannot reliably base a rule on the contingency that physicians will intervene in particularly egregious cases. There is no guarantee that physicians can adequately strike the most socially desirable balance. While nearness to extreme situations often requires physicians to make such judgments, nothing in their training or background qualifies them to identify, assess, and balance all interests involved — in short, to "play judge." In addition, decisions by physicians are likely to reflect specific class, economic, ethical, and cultural biases or interests arising out of prior relationships with the parents. . . .

President's Commission for the Study of Ethical Problems in Medicine and Biomedical and Behavioral Research: Deciding to Forgo Life-Sustaining Treatment
Pub. No. 83-17978, at 217-223 (1983)

. . . The Commission believes that decisionmaking will be improved if an attempt is made to decide which of three situations applies in a particular case — (1) a treatment is available that would clearly benefit the infant, (2) all treatment is expected to be futile, or (3) the probable benefits to an infant from different choices are quite uncertain. . . . The three situations need to be considered separately, since they demand differing responses. . . . [The Commission believes that medical intervention for a baby born with the physical disabilities of Down's syndrome (such as heart obstructions not affecting retardation) should be considered "clearly beneficial therapy."] The Commission has concluded that a very restrictive standard is appropriate: such permanent handicaps justify a decision not to provide life-sustaining treatment only when they are so severe that continued existence would not be a net benefit to the infant. . . . As in all surrogate decisionmaking, the surrogate is obligated to try to evaluate benefits and burdens from the infant's own perspective. The Commission believes that the handicaps of Down syndrome, for example, are not in themselves of this magnitude and do not justify failing to provide medically proven treatment, such as surgical correction of a blocked intestinal tract.

This is a very strict standard in that it excludes consideration of the negative effects of an impaired child's life on other persons, including parents, siblings, and society. Although abiding by this standard may be difficult in specific cases, it is all too easy to undervalue the lives of handicapped infants; the Commission finds it imperative to counteract this by treating them no less vigorously than their healthy peers or than older children with similar handicaps would be treated.

When there is no therapy that can benefit an infant, as in anencephaly or certain severe cardiac deformities, a decision by surrogates and providers not to try predictably futile endeavors is ethically and legally justifiable. Such therapies do not help the child, are sometimes painful for the infant (and probably distressing to the parents), and offer no reasonable probability of saving life for a substantial period. . . .

Just as with older patients, even when cure or saving of life are out of reach, obligations to comfort and respect a dying person remain. Thus infants whose lives are destined to be brief are owed whatever relief from suffering and enhancement of life can be provided, including feeding, medication for pain, and sedation, as appropriate. . . .

Ambiguous Cases

Although for most seriously ill infants there will be either a clearly beneficial option or no beneficial therapeutic options at all, hard questions are raised by the smaller number for whom it is very difficult to assess whether the treatments available offer prospects of benefit — for example, a child with a debilitating and painful disease who might live with therapy, but only a year or so, or a respirator-dependent premature infant whose long-term prognosis becomes bleaker with each passing day.

Much of the difficulty in these cases arises from factual uncertainty. For the many infants born prematurely, and sometimes for those with serious congenital defects, the only certainty is that without intensive care they are unlikely to survive; very little is known about how each individual will fare with treatment. Neonatology is too new a field to allow accurate predictions of which babies will survive and of the complications, handicaps, and potentials that the survivors might have.

The longer some of these babies survive, the more reliable the prognosis for the infant becomes and the clearer parents and professionals can be on whether further treatment is warranted or futile. Frequently, however, the prospect of long-term survival and the quality of that survival remain unclear for days, weeks, and months, during which time the infants may have an unpredictable and fluctuating course of advances and setbacks.

One way to avoid confronting anew the difficulties involved in evaluating each case is to adopt objective criteria to distinguish newborns who will receive life-sustaining treatment from those who will not. Such criteria would be justified if there were evidence that their adoption would lead to decisions more often being made correctly.

Strict treatment criteria proposed in the 1970s by a British physician for deciding which newborns with spina bifida[84] should receive treatment rested upon the location of the lesion (which influences degree of paralysis), the presence of hydrocephalus (fluid in the brain, which influences degree of retardation), and the likelihood of an infection. Some critics of this proposal argued with it on scientific grounds, such as objecting that long-term effects of spina bifida cannot be predicted with sufficient accuracy at birth. Other critics, however, claimed this whole approach to ambiguous cases exhibited the "technical criteria fallacy." They contended that an infant's future life — and hence the treatment decisions based on it — involves value considerations that are ignored when physicians focus solely on medical prognosis.

> The decision (to treat or not) must also include evaluation of the meaning of existence with varying impairments. Great variation exists about these essentially evaluative elements among parents, physicians, and policy makers. It must be an open question whether these variations in evaluation are among the relevant factors to consider in making a treatment decision. When Lorber uses the phrase "contraindications to active therapy," he is medicalizing what are really value choices.[88]

The Commission agrees that such criteria necessarily include value considerations. Supposedly objective criteria such as birth weight limits or checklists for severity of spina bifida have not been shown to improve the quality of decision-making in ambiguous and complex cases. Instead, their use seems to remove the weight of responsibility too readily from those who should have to face the value question — parents and health care providers.

Furthermore, any set of standards, when honestly applied, leaves some difficult or uncertain cases. When a child's best interests are ambiguous, a decision based upon them will require prudent and discerning judgment. . . .

PROBLEMS

(1) If the laws relating to disabled newborns are to be changed, how should they be changed? Should state legislatures define a new type of homicide involving disabled newborns that has a lesser sanction? Or should withholding care from a disabled newborn be legalized?

   a. How would you define the class of disabled newborns for whom it would be legal to withhold care?
   b. How would you take account of advances in medicine over time?
   c. Would you permit "active" euthanasia — such as giving a lethal injection — as well as passive euthanasia, which involves simply withholding care?

---

[84] John Lorber, Early Results of Selective Treatment of Spina Bifida Cystica, 4 Brit. Med. J. 201 (1973); John Lorber, Results of Treatment of Myelomeningocele, 13 Dev. Med. & Child Neurol. 279 (1971). . . .

[88] Robert M. Veatch, The Technical Criteria Fallacy, 7 Hastings Ctr. Rep. 15, 16 (Aug. 1977).

d.   Who would decide which babies would be untreatable? The parents? The attending doctor? A hospital committee? A judge?

e.   By what procedure should the decision to withhold treatment be made?

Draft a statute that would legalize withholding care from disabled newborns.

(2) Two Dutch physicians, Drs. Eduard Verhagen and Pieter J.J. Sauer, have developed guidelines (known as the Groningen Protocol) regarding the use of euthanasia for disabled infants. The physicians divide newborns who are at risk for end-of-life decisions into three groups: (1) infants with no chance of survival, (2) infants whose prognosis is poor and who have a poor quality of life and are dependent on intensive care (such as those with severe brain damage), and (3) infants whose prognosis is hopeless and who experience unbearable suffering but who may not need intensive medical care. According to the Groningen Protocol, the following conditions must be met to end the life of an infant whose suffering cannot be relieved and for whom no improvement can be expected: (a) full and informed consent of the parents regarding whether death would be more humane than continued life, (b) the agreement of a team of physicians, and (c) a subsequent review of each case by an independent legal body to determine whether the decision was justified and all procedures have been followed. What do you think of this proposal? See John Schwartz, When Torment Is Baby's Destiny, Euthanasia Is Defended, N.Y. Times, Mar. 10, 2005, at A3; Peter Singer, Pulling Back the Curtain on the Mercy Killing of Newborns, L.A. Times, Mar. 11, 2005; Eduard Verhagen & Pieter J.J. Sauer, The Groningen Protocol — Euthanasia in Severely Ill Newborns, 352 New Eng. J. Med. 959 (Mar. 20, 2005).

E.   ADOLESCENT HEALTH CARE

This section highlights some of the legal issues that are implicated in the context of adolescent health. In particular, it explores how power and responsibility for adolescent health should be allocated among the child, the family, medical professionals, and state officials. The section begins with background material on adolescent health and then examines particular health issues affecting adolescents.

1.   Introduction

The Centers for Disease Control and Prevention conducts an annual survey of the leading causes of health-risk behaviors among youths. The Youth Risk Behavior Surveillance System (YRBSS) provides information on risk behavior among youths to target and improve health programs.

Centers for Disease Control and Prevention, Youth Risk Behavior Surveillance — United States, 2007

... The Youth Risk Behavior Surveillance System (YRBSS) monitors six categories of priority health-risk behaviors among youth and young adults, including behaviors that contribute to unintentional injuries and violence; tobacco use; alcohol and other drug use; sexual behaviors that contribute to unintended pregnancy and sexually transmitted diseases (STDs), including human immunodeficiency virus (HIV) infection; unhealthy dietary behaviors; and physical inactivity. In addition, YRBSS monitors the prevalence of obesity and asthma. YRBSS includes a national school-based survey conducted by CDC and state and local school-based surveys conducted by state and local education and health agencies. ...

In the United States, 72 percent of all deaths among persons aged 10-24 years result from four causes: motor-vehicle crashes, other unintentional injuries, homicide, and suicide. Results from the 2007 national Youth Risk Behavior Survey (YRBS) indicated that many high school students engaged in behaviors that increased their likelihood of death from these four causes. Among high school students nationwide during 2007, 11.1 percent had never or rarely worn a seat belt when riding in a car driven by someone else. During the 30 days before the survey, 29.1 percent of high school students had ridden in a car or other vehicle driven by someone who had been drinking alcohol, 18 percent had carried a weapon, and 5.5 percent had not gone to school because they felt they would be unsafe at school or on their way to or from school. During the 12 months before the survey, 6.9 percent of high school students had attempted suicide. In addition, 75 percent of high school students had ever drunk alcohol, and 4.4 percent had ever used methamphetamines. Substantial morbidity and social problems among youth also result from unintended pregnancies and STDs, including HIV infection. Results from the 2007 survey indicated that 47.8 percent of students had ever had sexual intercourse, 35 percent of high school students were currently sexually active, and 38.5 percent of currently sexually active high school students had not used a condom during their last sexual intercourse. ... Among high school students nationwide during 2007, 20 percent had smoked cigarettes during the 30 days before the survey, 35.4 percent had watched television 3 or more hours per day on an average school day, and 13 percent were obese. During the 7 days before the survey, 78.6 percent of high school students had not eaten fruits and vegetables five or more times per day, 33.8 percent had drunk soda or pop at least one time per day, and 65.3 percent had not met recommended levels of physical activity. ...

2. Suicide

Suicide is one of the primary causes of death among adolescents. Who, if anyone, should bear responsibility for a juvenile's suicide?

State v. Scruggs
905 A.2d 24 (Conn. 2006)

SULLIVAN, J.

The defendant, Judith Scruggs, was convicted after a jury trial on one charge of risk of injury to a child in violation of General Statutes §53-21(a)(1). [D]efendant claims on appeal that §53-21(a)(1) is unconstitutionally vague as applied to her conduct. . . .

. . . In late 2001, the defendant was a single parent living in a three-bedroom apartment with her two children, Kara Morris and Daniel. Kara was seventeen and Daniel was twelve. The defendant worked approximately sixty hours a week at two jobs — one as a full-time employee of the school that Daniel attended, the other as a part-time employee at Wal-Mart. Daniel was bullied relentlessly at school and, from September through December, 2001, was absent on many days. He frequently exhibited poor hygiene and occasionally defecated in his pants. At home, he slept in his bedroom closet, where he kept knives and a homemade spear to protect himself. The state department of children and families ("department") was aware of Daniel's problems, and had been working with the defendant to have him placed in a different school. At some point in late 2001, the department conducted an inspection of the defendant's apartment in connection with its investigation of Daniel's situation. On December 27, 2001, the department closed its file on Daniel. In the early morning hours of January 2, 2002, Daniel hanged himself in his bedroom closet. . . .

[T]he trial court found the following facts. "The jury heard testimony from several officials who went to the defendant's home on January 2, 2002, after receiving reports of a suicide there. Police testified that they found the dead body of the defendant's twelve-year-old son, Daniel, lying on the floor of a walk-in closet in his bedroom. The defendant and her seventeen-year-old daughter, Kara . . . told the police that Daniel had hung himself. Somewhere in the closet near the body, police found three long kitchen-type knives and a sharp implement affixed to a pole in a spear-like device, but there was no evidence that any of these objects played a role in causing the death.

"The evidence, viewed most favorably to sustaining the verdict, would have reasonably permitted the jury to find that Daniel lived in a home with a foul and offensive odor. [T]he state's witnesses who went there on January 2 described the odor in various terms. . . . [For example, Officer Michael Boothroyd] testified that 'a definite' and 'a bit of offensive' odor 'permeated throughout the whole home.' . . . [Detective Gary Brandl] described the odor as 'very noticeable,' 'as if . . . you . . . stuck your head in a dirty clothes hamper . . . plus an odor of garbage' and said that although he noticed the odor upon entering the apartment, it was even stronger in the back of the house. . . .

"The state's witnesses also described the apartment as very messy and cluttered. Boothroyd said the apartment was 'extremely messy and dirty, very cluttered' and had a 'chaotic atmosphere.' He said that 'it wasn't an easy place to walk through. . . . [Y]ou had to watch your step everywhere you went and [make] sure that you stayed on your feet' because of clothing and other articles piled everywhere on the floors throughout the house. He further testified that he saw dust accumulated on the top of various items. Brandl also said that the clutter made the apartment hard to walk through, with only an eighteen-inch path between piles of debris from the front door to the kitchen. He said he could not even see the floor surface in Daniel's bedroom because of debris on the floor, some piled as high as the bed. When Brandl walked into the bedroom, he had to step on clothing and heard items cracking and breaking underneath. The police had to clear a path in the bedroom for the medical examiner's investigator to walk to the closet where Daniel's dead body lay. . . .

". . . Clothing was strewn in layers on the floors of the three bedrooms. Flat surfaces above floor level — such as tabletops, chairs, and other furniture — were also covered with items, often with no room for any additional items. For example, atop an ironing board in the living room sat an iron, coffee cup, coffee can with Styrofoam cups atop it, pencil, cellophane tape, socks and other clothing, a book, a roll of paper, and other items. There was no clear surface in the kitchen to prepare or eat food. Many items on the kitchen and pantry counters, kitchen table, and stove had additional items inside or on top of them. The only horizontal surfaces above floor level that were free of debris in the photographs taken of the defendant's apartment on January 2, 2002, were the three beds belonging to the defendant and her two children. . . ."

The trial court rejected the defendant's claim that expert testimony was required to establish that the conditions in the apartment likely would result in injury to the mental health of a child. . . . The court concluded that "[a]ny layperson with common sense could conclude that the squalor and home living environment here created a risk to Daniel's emotional health. . . .

[The trial court said further:] "This is not a case about a messy house. No law of which this court is aware regulates the frequency of vacuuming or prescribes specific housekeeping practices. The law, however, does seek to protect children. . . . The evidence here went far beyond messy or disorderly living conditions. The evidence showed extreme clutter and pervasive odor throughout the home, unsanitary bathroom facilities, and a child whose obvious emotional distress manifested itself in severe hygiene problems. It did not take an expert for this jury to conclude that the home living environment was likely to injure the mental, psychological, and emotional health of this troubled and fragile child." Accordingly, the trial court denied the defendant's motions for judgment of acquittal and rendered judgment in accordance with the verdict.

. . . We first address the defendant's claim that §53-21(a)(1) is unconstitutional as applied because it does not require the state to establish that she knew or should have known that her conduct likely would result in injury to a child. Section 53-21(a)(1) provides in relevant part that "[a]ny person who (1) wilfully or unlawfully causes or permits any child under the age of sixteen years to be placed in such a situation that . . . the health of such child is likely to be injured . . . shall be guilty of a class C felony. . . ." Accordingly, we must address the defendant's claim that the statute is unconstitutionally vague because it did not provide her with adequate notice of the line dividing lawful conduct from unlawful conduct in this context. . . . The present matter involves the portion of §53-21(a)(1) relating to the creation of a situation likely to result in injury to the mental health of a child. "Under the 'situation' portion of §53-21[(a)(1)], the state need not prove actual injury to the child. Instead, it must prove that the defendant wilfully created a situation that posed a risk to the child's health or morals. . . . The situation portion of §53-21[(a)(1)] encompasses the protection of the body as well as the safety and security of the environment in which the child exists, and for which the adult is responsible." [In State v. Payne, 695 A.2d 525 (Conn. 1997), the Connecticut supreme court determined that the term "health," as used in the "health is likely to be injured" language of §53-21, includes mental health as well as physical health.]

Before addressing the substance of the defendant's claim that §53-21(a)(1) does not provide adequate notice that her conduct was criminal, we must first address her claim that the trial court improperly applied a subjective standard in determining that the defendant should have known that the conditions in her apartment were likely to injure Daniel's mental health. Specifically, the defendant challenges the trial court's conclusion that Daniel's physical and mental frailty made the risk of injury to his mental health obvious. We agree with the defendant that the court should have applied an objective standard in determining whether the defendant had notice that her conduct fell within the scope of §53-21(a)(1). . . .

After applying this standard, we conclude that the statute is unconstitutionally vague as applied to the defendant's conduct. The state has pointed to no statutes, published or unpublished court opinions in this state or from other jurisdictions, newspaper reports, television programs or other public information that would support a conclusion that the defendant should have known that the conditions in her apartment posed an unlawful risk to the mental health of a child. Rather, the state implicitly relies on an "I know it when I see it" standard. We recognize that there may be generally accepted housekeeping norms and that it may be common knowledge that, all things being equal, a clean and orderly home is preferable to a dirty and cluttered home. The same could be said of any number of conditions and actions that affect a child's well-being. It may be common knowledge, for example, that drinking milk is healthier than a constant diet of soft drinks, reading books is preferable to constant exposure to television programs, large cars are safer than small cars, playing computer games is safer than riding a bicycle, and so on. All of these comparisons, however, involve virtually infinite gradations of conduct, making it extremely difficult, if not impossible, for an ordinary person to know where the line between potentially harmful but lawful conduct and unlawful conduct lies or, indeed, whether that line exists at all. Not all conduct that poses a risk to the mental or physical health of a child is unlawful. Rather, there is an acceptable range of risk.

The trial court appears to have recognized the difficulty in discerning the line between lawful and unlawful conduct in this context. Nevertheless, the court implicitly determined that the jury reasonably could have concluded that the defendant should have known that the extreme clutter and unpleasant odor in her apartment created a situation that was well on the wrong side of that line, particularly in light of Daniel's "troubled and fragile" state of mind.[7] We have

---

[7] Specifically, the trial court focused on the fact that Daniel exhibited poor hygiene and on the conditions of the defendant's home, which discouraged frequent bathing. In support of the latter conclusion, the court noted that clutter prevented the bathroom door from being closed for privacy and was a hindrance to using the bathroom. The court did not appear to find, however, that Daniel's poor hygiene was the direct result of the cluttered condition of the bathroom. There was no evidence,

concluded, however, that the state was obligated to prove beyond a reasonable doubt that the defendant knew or should have known that the conditions would constitute a risk of injury to the mental health of any child. Although the defendant reasonably could have been aware that the conditions were not optimal, we are not persuaded that the nature and severity of the risk were such that the defendant reasonably could not have believed that they were within the acceptable range.

Moreover, although the trial court recognized that the evidence showed that employees of the department had inspected the defendant's apartment during late 2001, and had closed its file on the family only days before Daniel's suicide, it failed to draw the critical inference that the only experts in child safety who had knowledge of the conditions in the defendant's home during the relevant period apparently had concluded that they were not so deplorable as to pose an immediate threat to Daniel's mental health. We do not suggest that the department's failure to take action constituted conclusive evidence that the conditions in the apartment did not pose a risk of injury to the mental health of a child. It does constitute evidence, however, that the conditions in the apartment did not pose such an obvious risk that it would be within the knowledge of an ordinary person.

Finally, the jury unavoidably was made aware during trial that Daniel had exhibited a variety of strange behaviors, was frequently emotionally upset and ultimately had killed himself. There were several possible explanations for Daniel's state of mind and behavior, however, including the relentless bullying that he endured at school and his inherently fragile psyche. Even if it is assumed that the state fairly could rely on evidence of Daniel's suicide to prove that the conditions in the apartment in fact caused injury to Daniel's mental health, that evidence was not competent to prove that such harm was foreseeable. As we have suggested, actual effects are not necessarily foreseeable effects.[10] . . .

We are mindful that §53-21(a)(1) is broadly drafted and was intended to apply to any conduct, illegal or not, that foreseeably could result in injury to the health of a child. We do not rule out the possibility that a home environment could be so squalid that an ordinary person should be expected to know that it poses a risk to the mental health of a child. The testimony in the present case established, however, that there was no sign in the defendant's apartment of rats, mice or other vermin, animal or human waste, or rotting food or garbage. Moreover, the trial court found

---

for example, that the clutter prevented the defendant or Kara from bathing regularly and using the toilet. . . .

   [10] We find the application of hindsight to be particularly troubling in this context. If it is the state's position that the conditions in the defendant's apartment on January 2, 2002, posed a foreseeable risk to the mental health of children, then similar conditions around the state should have been subject to criminal prosecution before now. . . . It seems unfair, and even cruel, both to potential defendants and to potential victims, to prosecute a defendant on the basis of such conditions only when a child actually has suffered some catastrophic harm. Put another way, the state cannot decline to prosecute persons who maintain such conditions because it believes that the risk to children either is within an acceptable range or is speculative and then, only when catastrophic harm actually occurs, use that as evidence that the risk was unacceptable and foreseeable.

that the conditions were not so bad that they would pose a threat to a child's physical health. The evidence showed only that the apartment was extremely cluttered and had an unpleasant odor of uncertain origin.[15] We cannot conclude that the defendant was on notice that these conditions were so squalid that they posed a risk of injury to the mental health of a child within the meaning of §53-21(a)(1). Accordingly, we conclude that the statute is unconstitutionally vague as applied to the defendant's conduct. The judgment is reversed and the case is remanded to the trial court with direction to grant the defendant's motion for judgment of acquittal.

NOTES AND QUESTIONS

(1) Background. The trial court suspended Mrs. Scruggs's 18-month sentence, placed her on probation for five years, and sentenced her to 100 hours of community service. Her arrest occurred two months after she filed suit against the city and the middle school's vice principal and guidance counselor, alleging that they violated her son's civil rights by not providing him the education he was entitled to by law and by not preventing bullying by his classmates. Avi Salzman, Woman Is Spared Prison in Case Tied to Son's Suicide, N.Y. Times, May 15, 2004, at A14; Marc Santora, After Son's Suicide, Mother Is Convicted over Unsafe Home, N.Y. Times, Oct. 7, 2003, at A27. Following her sentencing, Mrs. Scruggs was evicted and lost her two jobs. Scruggs Can't Afford Lawyer, 30 Conn. L. Trib. 11 (June 14, 2004). Her conviction was reversed in the principal case.

(2) Adolescent Suicide.   Suicide is the third leading cause of death among children, after accidents and homicides. In 2001, 2,319 youths ages 10 to 20 committed suicide in the United States. The vast majority of youths who commit suicide are males (83%). Shankar Vedantam, Suicide Alert on Giving Antidepressants to Kids, S.F. Chron., Oct. 16, 2004, at A3. The most frequent manner of committing suicide for youths ages 10 to 20 is the use of a firearm. Id. The youth suicide rate fell dramatically during the past decade, particularly for children ages 10 to 14. Researchers attribute the drop to the passage of firearm laws, as well as the greater acceptance of gays and lesbians. Youth Suicides in U.S. Down by About 25%, S.F. Chron., June 11, 2004, at A3.

(3) Who Should Bear Responsibility?   Who should bear responsibility for Daniel's suicide? Daniel himself? His mother? The school? The students who bullied him? If you believe liability should be imposed, should it take the form of tort damages? Criminal sanctions? Administrative remedies? If Daniel's mother had a younger child still living at home, should her parental rights to that child be terminated? Mrs. Scruggs later claimed that she did not clean the house because, according to her view of childrearing, she believed that adolescents should help with the housekeeping. Salzman, supra, at B4. Does Mrs. Scruggs have a defense to criminal liability based on *Meyer, Pierce*, and *Yoder*?

---

[15] We further note that . . . much of the clutter consisted of Christmas-related items, such as presents, cards, wrapping paper, books, toys, seasonal decorations, knickknacks and other items suggesting that the defendant had attempted to provide a cheerful holiday for her children.

Would your view about the imposition of parental liability be altered if Daniel had killed himself with a loaded gun that his mother kept in the home? Both federal and state law restrict the sale and delivery of firearms and ammunition to minors. See generally Katherine Hunt Federle, The Second Amendment Rights of Children, 89 Iowa L. Rev. 609 (2004). In addition, a number of states have child access prevention (CAP) laws that impose criminal penalties for the negligent storage of a firearm if a child uses the weapon to kill or injure himself or another person. See generally Andrew J. McClurg, Child Access Prevention Laws: A Common Sense Approach to Gun Control, 18 St. Louis U. Pub. L. Rev. 47, 50 (1999). Note that the United States Supreme Court ruled recently in District of Columbia v. Heller, 128 S. Ct. 2783 (2008), that the District of Columbia's handgun ban violated the Second Amendment right to bear arms, thereby raising questions about the constitutionality of other weapons bans and restrictions.

Prior to 1991, no court recognized the legal claims of a suicide victim's family against a school district. However, in Eisel v. Board of Education of Montgomery County, 597 A.2d 447 (Md. 1991), the Maryland supreme court held that a school district can be liable for an adolescent's suicide if the district's employees had knowledge that the student was suicidal and failed to warn the parents or take reasonable preventive action. See also Armijo v. Wagon Mound Public Schools, 159 F.3d 1253 (10th Cir. 1998) (establishing the possibility of school district's liability under §1983 of the Civil Rights Act using a "danger creation" theory, which provides that the state may be liable for an individual's safety if it created the danger that harmed the individual). See generally Richard Fossey & Perry Zirkel, Liability for Student Suicide in the Wake of *Eisel*, 10 Tex. Wesleyan L. Rev. 403 (2004).

(4) Purposes of Criminal Law.   What purposes of the criminal law (general and specific deterrence, incapacitation, rehabilitation, retribution) are served by the imposition of criminal liability in the *Scruggs* case? Are you convinced by the trial court's comment that this case is not about charging the mother "with causing the child's suicide" but rather about "maintaining a situation that endangered the child's mental health"?

(5) Antibullying Legislation.   Should states enact legislation to protect chil dren against peer harassment in the schools? Courts historically have rejected imposing tort liability on school officials for acts of bullying, relying on doctrines of sovereign immunity and proximate cause (viewing the perpetrator's acts as an intervening cause that precludes liability for negligent supervision). Daniel B. Weddle, When Will Schools Take Bullying Seriously?, Trial Mag., Oct. 2003, at 18.

However, school violence at Columbine High School in 1999 triggered a movement for states to pass "antibullying laws," which require schools to institute special procedures to address bullying. Following Daniel Scruggs's death, the Connecticut legislature enacted a bill mandating school officials to place an antibullying policy in student codes of conduct, require teachers and school staff who witness acts of bullying or receive reports to notify school administrators, promise anonymity to reporters, require administrators to investigate such reports, require the school to notify parents of the victim and perpetrator, and require the school to make public a list of verified acts of bullying. "Bullying" is defined as "any overt acts by a student or a group of students directed against another student with the intent to ridicule, harass, humiliate or intimidate the other student while on school grounds, at a school-sponsored activity, or on a school bus, which acts are repeated against the same student over time." Conn. Gen. Stat. Ann. §10-222d (West 2003 & Supp. 2008). If the Connecticut antibullying law had been in effect, do you think it would have prevented Daniel's death? See generally Jill Grim, Note, Peer Harassment in Our Schools: Should Teachers and Administrators Join the Fight, 10 Barry L. Rev. 155, 169-172 (2008) (discussing current state legislation and its effectiveness).

(6) Role of Sexual Orientation. Gay students face a greater risk of bullying in schools. Sharon E. Rush, Lessons From and for "Disabled" Students, 8 J. Gender Race & Just. 75, 82 (2004). In Davis v. Monroe County Board of Education, 526 U.S. 629 (1999), the Supreme Court held that a school may be liable for student sexual harassment under Title IX of the Education Amendments Act of 1972, 20 U.S.C. §§1681-1687 (2000) (prohibiting sexual discrimination in education). Liability attaches when, after receiving notice of the sexual harassment, the school acts with deliberate indifference and the harassment is so severe that it effectively bars the victim's access to an educational opportunity or benefit.

In L.W. ex rel. L.G. v. Toms River Regional Schools Board of Education, 915 A.2d 535 (N.J. 2007), a mother filed a claim with the state Division of Civil Rights alleging that the public school district violated the state antidiscrimination law as a result of the peer harassment of her son based on his perceived sexual orientation. Recognizing the claim based on state law, the court rejected Title IX's "deliberate indifference" standard of review (as too narrow and burdensome for victims) in favor of a standard that imposes liability on a school district when it does not take reasonable measures, judged by the totality of the circumstances, to end the harassment. See generally Gregory M. Attanasio, Case Note, L.W. ex rel. L.G. v. Toms River Regional Schools Board of Education: New Jersey Leads the Way for Harassment-Free Education, 17 Law & Sexuality 163 (2008).

(7) Adolescent Depression and Antipsychotic Drugs. Should medical professionals or drug manufacturers bear any responsibility in cases of adolescent suicide? Controversy has raged concerning the correlation between antidepressant medication and increased risk of suicidal thoughts and behavior in adolescents. Such drugs are commonly prescribed for youth with depression and other psychiatric disorders. Clinical data suggest that children who are taking antidepressants are at increased risk of suicidal thoughts and behavior compared to a comparative sample of youth taking a placebo. In response to such clinical findings, many professionals argue that patients' suicidal thoughts and behavior are attributable to their illness rather than their medications. In October 2004, a scientific advisory panel of the Food and Drug Administration (FDA) ordered several pharmaceutical companies to place "black box" warnings on their antidepressant products disclosing that use of such medication increases suicidal behavior in children. The advisory is the government's strongest warning for dangerous drugs short of an outright ban. Marilyn Elias, Teen Suicide Warnings Going on Drug Labels, Deseret Morning News, Mar. 2, 2005, at A02; Gardiner Harris, Antidepressant Study Seen to Back Expert, N.Y. Times, Aug. 20, 2004, at A18.

Also, parents have attempted to impose liability on drug manufacturers in cases of children's suicides or homicides. See, e.g., Miller v. Pfizer, Inc., 356

F.3d 1326 (10th Cir. 2004) (affirming grant of summary judgment for defendant in suit by parents alleging that medication caused their 13-year-old son to commit suicide). In June 2004, the New York Attorney General sued GlaxoSmithKline, alleging that the company withheld negative results about the effect of the antidepressant Paxil on children and adolescents. In a settlement, the company agreed to post the findings of clinical studies and to pay $2.5 million to the state. Glaxo Settles Legal Dispute, Chemical & Engineering News, Sept. 6, 2004, at 1617.

NOTE ON OTHER ADOLESCENT HEALTH ISSUES

Obesity in children and adolescents is a growing national concern. Research reveals that the percentage of children who are overweight has nearly doubled in the past two decades, whereas the percentage of overweight adolescents has nearly tripled. Eric Bost, Obesity Crisis, Cong. Testimony, 2004 WL 84559038 (Sept. 15, 2004). Obesity increases the likelihood that a child will develop childhood hypertension, heart disease, cancer, and Type 2 diabetes.

Who, if anyone, should bear responsibility for a child's obesity? The child? The parents? The schools? The food and beverage and entertainment industries? What role can the law play in preventing obesity? In 2003, plaintiffs instituted suits against the fast-food industry (modeled after tobacco litigation) charging that the industry has caused consumer obesity. In Pelman v. McDonald's Corp., 237 F. Supp. 2d 512 (S.D.N.Y. 2003), parents of two overweight teenage girls brought a class action suit on behalf of children in New York, alleging violations of state consumer protection laws (misleading and deceptive advertising) and negligence in connection with children's overconsumption of fast-food products that led to their children's health problems. The federal district court granted defendants' motion to dismiss, holding that the parents failed to allege specific deceptive acts or omissions; the defendants owed no duty to warn consumers of products' well-known attributes; and the parents failed to allege facts demonstrating that products were addictive.

Congress responded initially by proposing legislation (dubbed the "Cheeseburger Bill") that would preclude "frivolous lawsuits" in federal or state courts against the manufacturers, distributors, and sellers of fast food. See Personal Responsibility in Food Consumption Act, H.R. 339, 108th Cong. (2003). The bill passed the House of Representatives but never came up for a vote in the Senate. Subsequently, Congress commissioned a study of the problem of childhood obesity.

In the report mandated by Congress, the Institute of Medicine (a private organization associated with the National Academy of Sciences) found that efforts to slow the rise in childhood obesity rates need to involve schools, the food and beverage industries, government, and parents. The Institute's recommendations included having schools ensure that lunches are consistent with federal nutrition guidelines, and put recess and physical-education classes back into the school day; the food, beverage, and entertainment industries should consider a plan to limit advertising of unhealthy products to children; the federal government should convene a task force to explore restrictions on advertising of unhealthy products and improve food labeling to give consumers more information about caloric intake; state and local governments should design communities to provide more opportunities to exercise by providing sidewalks, playgrounds, and other recreational areas; and, finally, parents should provide healthy meals and opportunities to exercise and should limit children's leisure television and computer time to less than two hours a day. Health Advisers Call for Action to Battle Childhood Obesity, Wall St. J., Oct. 1, 2004, at B2. What do you think of these recommendations? See generally Michael Cardin et al., Preventing Obesity and Chronic Disease: Education vs. Regulation vs. Litigation, 35 J.L. Med. & Ethics 120 (2007).

Other adolescent health issues (contraception, sexually transmissible diseases, and drinking) are discussed in Chapter 6.

F.   MEDICAL EXPERIMENTATION ON CHILDREN

As we have seen, informed consent of parents is usually both a necessary and sufficient condition of medical treatment of children. So far, our concern has been with consent to standard medical therapy for a child requiring treatment, as well as the possible consequences if parents fail to provide essential treatment. In this section we explore the limits, if any, of parental power to consent when the child is participating in a medical experiment. Should parental prerogatives be limited when it comes to medical experiments? If so, what is an experiment — that is, how does one define the class of situations where parents should not be able to consent? In addition to parental consent, what other institutional safeguards are essential? As you will see, the legal, ethical, and policy issues posed by medical experimentation on children are profoundly difficult.

Consider the materials that follow in light of the following problems.

1.   Introductory Problem

Eight-year-old Johnny Smith has had leukemia for four years. For the last three years it has been in remission, but his most recent checkup revealed that his white cell count is again above normal, meaning the disease has reappeared. Existing data suggest that the prognosis of Johnny's surviving more than two years with conventional modes of treatment is poor, but not hopeless. Johnny's pediatrician has recommended that Johnny be given a new form of chemotherapy. There have been only a few preliminary tests with it, but the results seem promising. The doctor believes that this new therapy *may* help Johnny more than conventional therapy, and that under the circumstances "it is worth a try." May Johnny's parents consent to the chemotherapy? Should Johnny have any say as well?

Suppose the doctor is a professor at the state university medical school who is running a randomized clinical trial to compare the effectiveness of the new chemotherapy treatment with that of the standard treatment. May Johnny's parents consent to his participation in the experiment, under which the choice of treatment for Johnny will be made by random selection?

May Johnny's parents consent to Johnny's participation in some tests that are not part of Johnny's treatment but for the purpose of increasing knowledge about leukemia? These tests require that blood be taken from Johnny at more frequent intervals and in somewhat greater amounts than would be necessary for treatment.

Suppose that after standard therapy has failed to help Johnny, his doctor recommends an experimental drug that the Food and Drug Administration permits to be used only on a special protocol basis. If the parents refuse permission for the child to enter the study, and most medical professionals would agree that it might well cause a remission, do you think the doctor's petition to a juvenile court to require the drug would succeed? What if Johnny was 16 years old instead of 8 and wanted to try the drug? See Angela R. Holder, Legal Issues in Pediatrics and Adolescent Medicine 159 (2d ed. 1985).

2. Historical Background

> [I]n eighteenth century England . . . Caroline, Princess of Wales, "begged the lives" of six condemned criminals for experimental smallpox vaccination before submitting her own children to the procedure. (She also procured, for further trial, "half a dozen of the charity children belonging to St. James' parish.") [Louis Lasagna, Special Subjects in Human Experimentation, 98 Daedalus (No. 2) 449 (1969).]

Ross G. Mitchell, The Child and Experimental Medicine
1 Brit. Med. J. 721-722 (1964)

Human experimentation is as old as medicine itself, but the experimental method of modern science is comparatively new. . . .

If the notorious experiments ordered by Queen Caroline on "charity children" . . . be excepted, one of the first experiments performed by a physician on living children was the experimental inoculation of young children with measles by Dr. Francis Home, a member of the College of Physicians of Edinburgh, in 1759. Forty years later, as the eighteenth century drew to a close, Edward Jenner made medical and paediatric history by selecting a healthy 8-year-old boy, James Phipps, for the purpose of inoculation with cowpox.

Throughout the nineteenth century paediatrics advanced as a scientific subject, although the concept of the controlled experiment was not yet established. . . .

With the development of bacteriology and biochemistry at the end of the century, the way was clear for the great advances in scientific paediatrics of our own century.

The first attempts at biochemical research in paediatrics were confined to comparatively simple measurements of the constituents of body fluids such as blood and urine. Paediatric journals of the early years of this century contain many reports of studies utilizing blood drawn from the superior sagittal sinus — a vessel first used for this purpose by Marfan in 1898 — or from the jugular vein of infants. Very few articles refer to parental permission for these studies, and there is seldom any expression of doubt about the morality of the work. Children from orphanages and "foundlings" were commonly used as subjects for these investigations. It is perhaps not surprising that this type of research was accepted unquestioningly, for infant and child mortality was still very high and methods of therapy were often drastic. Moreover, medicine had but recently emerged from an era in which children were little regarded, a world where foundlings were bought and sold and child labour was the rule. It is salutary to recall that a hundred years ago the American Society for Prevention of Cruelty to Animals was empowered by the courts to act in a case of cruelty to a child on the grounds that a child is an animal. A society for the prevention of cruelty to children was not founded until 1875 — nearly ten years later. . . . Against such a background, the use of orphans and foundlings for experiments would hardly have seemed to require permission or indeed justification. . . .

Our modern concern with the ethics of human experimentation dates from the Nuremberg trials of war criminals during World War II. The Nuremberg Code was formulated in response to Nazi medical experimentation on concentration camp prisoners. The Nuremberg Code proposes standards for the conduct of nontherapeutic research. It rests on the requirements of: (1) voluntary consent of informed subjects; (2) research that is unprocurable by other means and holds the promise of yielding "fruitful results" to benefit society; and (3) research that is conducted by scientifically qualified persons in a manner that avoids unnecessary physical and mental suffering.

The subsequent Declarations of Helsinki also serve as an international guide for the protection of human subjects in research. The initial Helsinki Declaration was promulgated in 1964 by the World Medical Association to rectify the failure of the Nuremberg Code to address research on subjects who are incapable of providing informed consent, such as children and mentally impaired persons. The Helsinki Declaration required proxy consent for all subjects who are legally incompetent. Subsequent revisions in 1983 (Helsinki Declaration III) emphasize the importance of allowing children's participation in medical decision making, requiring that the researcher obtain not only the consent of a minor's legal guardian but also that of the minor if the minor is able to provide such consent.

The Council for International Organizations of Medical Science, together with the World Health Organization, also developed guidelines for research on children (CIOMS/WHO Guidelines) in 1983. These Guidelines address pediatric research in therapeutic and nontherapeutic contexts. In both cases, the parent must give proxy consent, the child must consent to the extent that he or she is able, and, in the case of nontherapeutic research, the child's refusal to participate must be respected. The level of risk must be low and in proportion to the knowledge that the research is likely to yield.

The first binding international instrument protecting human rights in biomedicine, the Council of Europe Convention of Human Rights and Biomedicine, was adopted by the European Ministers of Justice in 1996. The Biomedical Convention's point of departure, similar to other international protocols, is the requirement that all subjects give voluntary and informed consent. Additional provisions require that research on incompetent persons (such as children) may be performed if: (1) the subject receives direct medical benefit; (2) research cannot be conducted on adults; (3) the subject's legal representative consents; and (4) the subject does not object. (The researcher must consider the child's opinion on whether to participate, based on the child's age and maturity.) Nontherapeutic research that does not benefit the child can be conducted provided it contributes to a greater understanding of the child's condition, will benefit patients of a similar age, and involves minimal risk and minimal burden to the child.

Federal legislation also addresses the protection of children in federally funded research. Beginning in the 1970s the federal government became concerned with the protection of the rights of research subjects. In 1974, Congress enacted the National Research Act (codified at 45 C.F.R. §46 (2001)), establishing a Commission for the Protection of Human Subjects of Biomedical and Behavioral Research, to identify ethical principles to guide research on human subjects. The Commission issued recommendations regarding pediatric research in 1977.

Many of the Commission's recommendations subsequently became the basis of federal regulations (known as the Common Rule) that govern the protection of human subjects generally applicable to federal agencies (codified at 45 C.F.R. §46.101(a) (2001)). For example, the Commission required consent from both parents and the child to participate in research. (The Commission replaced the term "consent" with the term of parental "permission" and the child's "assent.")

The Common Rule departs from the Commission's recommendations in some regards. For example, the Commission Report suggests that the assent of children seven years or older should be required. In contrast, the Common Rule permits a research institution's institutional review board (IRB) to determine a child's capacity to assent (based on the child's age, maturity, and psychological state) and also specifies circumstances in which the child's assent may be overridden (e.g., if the intervention holds out the prospect of increased well-being for the child). Thus, although the Commission Report required the child's refusal to participate to be binding, the Common Rule does not adhere to this recommendation.

Both the Commission Report and the Common Rule distinguish between various risk and benefit categories. For example, both distinguish between research that "poses not greater than minimal risk" and that involving "greater than minimal risk." Also, both distinguish between research that presents a direct benefit to the research subject versus research presenting no such benefit but likely to yield generalized benefit regarding the medical condition. For example,

- research that confers no therapeutic benefit to the child and does not involve greater than minimal risk requires both the child's assent and the parent's permission to participate in research;
- research that may directly benefit the child and that involves greater than minimal risk is permissible, subject to both parental permission and the child's assent, if the potential benefit justifies the risk or if the trial may be as beneficial to the child as an alternative treatment;

- research that will not directly benefit the child but is likely to provide general knowledge about a medical condition and that involves greater than minimal risk is permissible, subject to both parental permission and the child's assent, if the research represents a minor increase over minimal risk or involves approximately the same level of risk as involved in a medical or dental checkup;
- research that would not normally be approved but that presents an opportunity to understand, prevent, or alleviate children's health is subject to external review to ensure that it meets the requisite standards.

On the development of protections for human subjects in medical research, see generally George J. Annas & Michael A. Grodin, The Nazi Doctors and the Nuremberg Code: Human Rights in Human Experimentation (1992); Joanne Roman, Note, U.S. Medical Research in the Developing World: Ignoring Nuremberg, 11 Cornell J.L. & Pub. Pol'y 441, 448-453 (2002).

3. Is Medical Experimentation on Children Essential?

Apart from the benefits or risks to the individual child who is a participant, is medical experimentation, considered in its own right, a social good? Is experimentation on children essential to medical progress? Both experimentation with no therapeutic purpose as well as therapeutic experimentation? What would be the consequences of prohibiting medical experimentation on children?

Ann E. Ryan, Comment, Protecting the Rights of Pediatric Research Subjects in the International Conference of Harmonisation of Technical Requirements for Registration of Pharmaceuticals for Human Use
23 Fordham Intl. L.J. 848, 855-857 (2000)

Even though medical studies that are conducted on children may be controversial, the scientific need for such experimentation is apparent. A child's physiology is significantly different from that of an adult or a child of a different age group. These differences may have a significant impact on whether and how a drug can be used on a pediatric patient. Drug studies conducted on adults, moreover, may not adequately predict whether a drug will be toxic if prescribed to a child. Pharmaceutical companies' failure to test medicines in children may result in death or serious illness. Without adequate pediatric testing, doctors encounter a serious ethical dilemma: either prescribe medication or perform a procedure that potentially may benefit the child, or refrain from this treatment because it has not been adequately tested on children. This problem, commonly referred to as therapeutic orphaning, hampers the development and use of potentially life-saving therapies for pediatric patients.

Pediatric patients are likely to become therapeutic orphans, as many pharmaceutical companies resist conducting research on children because of ethical and legal issues involved in performing pediatric trials, difficulty recruiting subjects, and strains in raising adequate funds to conduct extra protocols. This situation creates grave dangers and risks for pediatric patients, as a large number of medications commonly prescribed for children are not tested on pediatric subjects. The problem is particularly pronounced in medications used to treat serious illnesses, such as the human immunodeficiency virus ("HIV"). Certain age groups are also commonly left out of drug trials, resulting in incomplete and unreliable results concerning the safety and effectiveness of drugs for these patients. . . .

4.   May Parents Under Existing Law Consent to Medical Procedures Not Undertaken for the Treatment of the Child in Question?

Grimes v. Kennedy Krieger Institute, Inc.
782 A.2d 807 (Md. App. 2001)

CATHELL, Judge.

[A] prestigious research institute [Kennedy Krieger Institute or KKI] created a nontherapeutic research program whereby it required certain classes of homes to have only partial lead paint abatement modifications performed[2]. . . . The research institute then encouraged, and in at least one of the cases at bar, required, the landlords to rent the premises to families with young children. . . . Apparently, the children and their parents involved in the cases *sub judice* were from a lower economic stratum and were, at least in one case, minorities. . . .

The purpose of the research was to determine how effective varying degrees of lead paint abatement procedures were. Success was to be determined by periodically, over a two-year period of time, measuring the extent to which lead dust remained in, or returned to, the premises after the varying levels of abatement modifications, and, as most important to our decision, by measuring the extent to which the theretofore healthy children's blood became contaminated with lead, and comparing that contamination with levels of lead dust in the houses over the same periods of time. . . . [Families were compensated $5 initially and $15 subsequently each time they completed a periodic questionnaire.]

Apparently, it was anticipated that the children, who were the human subjects in the program, would, or at least might, accumulate lead in their blood from the dust, thus helping the researchers to determine the extent to which the various partial abatement methods worked. There was no complete and clear explanation in the consent agreements signed by the parents of the children that the research to be conducted was designed, at least in significant part, to measure the success of

---

[2] At least to the extent that commercial profit motives are not implicated, therapeutic research's purpose is to directly help or aid a patient who is suffering from a health condition the objectives of the research are designed to address — hopefully by the alleviation, or potential alleviation, of the health condition.

Nontherapeutic research generally utilizes subjects who are not known to have the condition the objectives of the research are designed to address, and/or is not designed to directly benefit the subjects utilized in the research, but, rather, is designed to achieve beneficial results for the public at large (or, under some circumstances, for profit).

the abatement procedures by measuring the extent to which the children's blood was being contaminated. It can be argued that the researchers intended that the children be the canaries in the mines but never clearly told the parents. (It was a practice in earlier years, and perhaps even now, for subsurface miners to rely on canaries to determine whether dangerous levels of toxic gasses were accumulating in the mines. Canaries were particularly susceptible to such gasses. When the canaries began to die, the miners knew that dangerous levels of gasses were accumulating.)

The researchers and their Institutional Review Board apparently saw nothing wrong with the research protocols that anticipated the possible accumulation of lead in the blood of otherwise healthy children as a result of the experiment, or they believed that the consents of the parents of the children made the research appropriate. [The minor participants in the research program brought negligence actions against the institute. The trial court granted the research institute's motion for summary judgment. The appellate court held, inter alia, that fact issues as to the existence of a duty precluded summary judgment. The appellate court also addressed, infra, the issue of proxy consent for children's participation in nontherapeutic research.]

VI. Parental Consent for Children to Be Subjects of Potentially Hazardous Nontherapeutic Research

The issue of whether a parent can consent to the participation of her or his child in a nontherapeutic health-related study that is known to be potentially hazardous to the health of the child raises serious questions with profound moral and ethical implications. What right does a parent have to knowingly expose a child not in need of therapy to health risks or otherwise knowingly place a child in danger, even if it can be argued it is for the greater good? The issue in these specific contested cases does not relate primarily to the authority of the parent, but to the procedures of KKI and similar entities that may be involved in such health-related studies. The issue of the parents' right to consent on behalf of the children has not been fully presented in either of these cases, but should be of concern not only to lawyers and judges, but to moralists, ethicists, and others. The consenting parents in the contested cases at bar were not the subjects of the experiment; the children were. Additionally, this practice presents the potential problems of children initiating actions in their own names upon reaching majority, if indeed, they have been damaged as a result of being used as guinea pigs in nontherapeutic scientific research. Children, it should be noted, are not in our society the equivalent of rats, hamsters, monkeys, and the like. Because of the overriding importance of this matter and this Court's interest in the welfare of children — we shall address the issue.

Most of the relatively few cases in the area of the ethics of protocols of various research projects involving children have merely assumed that a parent can give informed consent for the participation of their children in nontherapeutic research. The single case in which the issue has been addressed, and resolved, a case with which we agree, will be discussed further, infra.

It is not in the best interest of a specific child, in a nontherapeutic research project, to be placed in a research environment, which might possibly be, or which proves to be, hazardous to the health of the child. We have long stressed that the "best interests of the child" is the overriding concern of this Court in matters relating to children. Whatever the interests of a parent, and whatever the interests of the general public in fostering research that might, according to a researcher's hypothesis, be for the good of all children, this Court's concern for the particular child and particular case over-arches all other interests. It is, simply, and we hope, succinctly put, not in the best interest of any healthy child to be intentionally put in a nontherapeutic situation where his or her health may be impaired, in order to test methods that may ultimately benefit all children.

To think otherwise, to turn over human and legal ethical concerns solely to the scientific community, is to risk embarking on slippery slopes, that all too often in the past, here and elsewhere, have resulted in practices we, or any community, should be ever unwilling to accept.

We have little doubt that the general motives of all concerned in these contested cases were, for the most part, proper, albeit in our view not well thought out. The protocols of the research, those of which we have been made aware, were, in any event, unacceptable in a legal context. One simply does not expose otherwise healthy children, incapable of personal assent (consent), to a nontherapeutic research environment that is known at the inception of the research, might cause the children to ingest lead dust. It is especially troublesome, when a measurement of the success of the research experiment is, in significant respect, to be determined by the extent to which the blood of the children absorbs, and is contaminated by, a substance that the researcher knows can, in sufficient amounts, whether solely from the research environment or cumulative from all sources, cause serious and long term adverse health effects. Such a practice is not legally acceptable.

In Hart v. Brown, 29 Conn. Supp. 368, 289 A.2d 386 (1972), that court was faced, prospectively, with whether to approve the transplant of a kidney from one seven-year-old identical twin to the other twin. The medical information presented to the court indicated that without the transplant, the recipient twin would have to undergo an extensive period of dialysis treatment with the expectation of only a 50% chance that she could survive that treatment for more than five years; the donor twin was expected to live a normal and productive life with one kidney. There were severe rejection problems with the transplant of a kidney from the parents that would have subjected the recipient twin to the possible side effects of immuno-suppressive drugs.

The parents brought an action in behalf of the recipient twin against the doctor and the hospital that had refused to perform the operation absent a court order that the parents or a guardian had the right to consent to the operation. The action, therefore, sought a declaratory judgment concerning whether the parents or a guardian ad litem had the right to consent to the transplant on behalf of the donor twin.

The court first appointed as guardian ad litems an attorney to represent the donor twin, and another person to represent the recipient twin. [The] Connecticut court adopted the "doctrine of substituted judgment." It upheld the giving of the consent of the parents, but only after noting the extensive process that the parties and the court had undertaken. . . . The court then cited the cases of

Strunk v. Strunk, [445 S.W.2d 145 (Ky. 1969)]; Bonner v. Moran, 75 U.S. App. D.C. 156, 126 F.2d 121 (1941) and the unreported Massachusetts cases.

Bonner was an unusual case that involved the grafting of skin from a minor donor cousin to a badly burned donee cousin. In that case, the court did not answer whether a parent, or other appropriate relative or guardian, could give consent for a nontherapeutic (as to the donor cousin) procedure. The issue was whether their consent was necessary under the circumstances, in that the donor cousin had apparently donated the skin without any express consent (and may have already done so when an aunt improperly consented as a surrogate). The trial court found that the minor cousin was sufficiently mature so as to be able to assent to the procedure, thus avoiding a determination as to whether a parent, or appropriate relative, could have given surrogated consent. The trial court gave a "mature minor" instruction to the jury.[40] The trial court's decision was ultimately overturned. The appellate court, reversing, stated:

> "We are constrained, therefore, to feel that the court below should, in the circumstances we have outlined, have instructed that the consent of the parent was necessary. . . . But by his own testimony, it clearly appears that he [the physician] failed to explain, even to the infant, the nature or extent of the proposed first operation." [*Bonner*, 75 U.S. App. D.C. at 156, 126 F.2d at 123.]

As is clear, that court did not say that parental consent would always be sufficient itself, only that it was a necessary ingredient in the equation.

In the *Strunk* case, the proposed donor was a mentally incompetent adult. Her parents sought permission of the court to consent to having one of the incompetent adult's kidneys transplanted to her twenty-six-year-old brother. The court granted permission to the parents, adopting the "doctrine of substituted judgment."

What is of primary importance to be gleaned in the *Hart* and *Strunk* cases is not that the parents or guardians consented to the procedures, but that they first sought permission of the courts, and received that permission, before consenting to a nontherapeutic procedure in respect to some of their minor children, but that was therapeutic to other of their children.

In the case *sub judice*, no impartial judicial review or oversight was sought by the researchers or by the parents. Additionally, in spite of the IRB's improper attempt to manufacture a therapeutic value, there was absolutely no such value of the research in respect to the minor subjects used to measure the effectiveness of the study. In the absence of a requirement for judicial review, in such a circumstance, the researchers, and their scientific based review boards would be, if permitted, the sole judges of whether it is appropriate to use children in nontherapeutic research of the nature here present, where the success of an experiment is to be measured, in substantial part, by the degree to which the research environments cause the absorption of poisons into the blood of children. Science cannot be permitted to be the sole judge of the appropriateness of such research methods on human subjects, especially in respect to children. We hold that in these

---

[40] The doctrine of "mature minor" recognizes that some minors are sufficiently mature to consent.

contested cases, the research study protocols, those of which we are aware, were not appropriate.

When it comes to children involved in nontherapeutic research, with the potential for health risks to the subject children in Maryland, we will not defer to science to be the sole determinant of the ethicality or legality of such experiments. The reason, in our view, is apparent from the research protocols at issue in the case at bar. Moreover, in nontherapeutic research using children, we hold that the consent of a parent alone cannot make appropriate that which is innately inappropriate. . . .

[The court then discusses the case of T.D. v. New York State Office of Mental Health, 626 N.Y.S.2d 1015 (1995), in which a mental health patient in a state facility challenged regulations governing the use of experimental drugs.] In respect to the reasonableness of accepting parental consent for minors to participate in potentially harmful, nontherapeutic research, that court stated:

> "We also find unacceptable the provisions that allow for consent to be obtained on behalf of minors for participation in greater than minimal risk[41] nontherapeutic research from the minor's parent or legal guardian, or, where no parent or guardian is available, from an adult family member involved in making treatment decisions for the child. . . .
>
> We are not dealing here with parental choice among reasonable treatment alternatives, but with a decision to subject the child to nontherapeutic treatments and procedures that may cause harmful permanent or fatal side effects. It follows therefore that a parent or guardian, . . . may not consent to have a child submit to painful and/or potentially life-threatening research procedures that hold no prospect of benefit for the child . . . . We do not limit a parent or legal guardian's right to consent to a child's participation in therapeutic research that represents a valid alternative and may be the functional equivalent of treatment." [T.D. v. New York State Office of Mental Health, 228 A.D.2d 95, 123-124, 650 N.Y.S.2d 173, 191-192 (1996).]

We concur with that assessment.

Additionally, there are conflicting views in respect to nontherapeutic research, as to whether consent, even of a person capable of consenting, can justify a research protocol that is otherwise unjustifiable.

> "This 'justifying' side of consent raises some timeless and thorny questions. What if people consent to activities and results which are repugnant, or even evil? Even John Stuart Mill worried about consensual slavery. . . . Today, we wonder whether a woman's consent to appear in graphic, demeaning, or even violent pornography justifies or immunizes the pornographer. If she appears to consent to a relationship in which she is repeatedly brutalized, does her consent stymie our efforts to stop the brutality or punish the brute?
>
> These problems make us squirm a little, just as they did Mill. We have three ways out: We can say, first, 'Yes, consent justifies whatever is consented to—

---

[41] Minimal risk has been defined as "meaning 'that the probability and magnitude of harm or discomfort anticipated in the research are not greater in and of themselves than those ordinarily encountered in daily life or during the routine physical or psychological examinations or tests.'" . . .

you consented, so case closed;' second, 'This particular consent is deficient — you did not really consent and so the result or action is not justified;' or third, 'You consented, but your consent cannot justify this action or result.' . . .

Note the subtle yet crucial difference between these three options: In the first, consent is king, while the third option assumes a moral universe shaped and governed by extra-consensual considerations. The second option, however, reflects the tension between the other two. We might block the consented-to action, but we pay lip service to consent's justifying role by assuring ourselves that had the consent been untainted, had it been 'informed,' it would have had moral force. In fact, we pay lip service precisely because we often silently suspect that consent cannot and does not always justify. . . . Rather than admit that the consent does not and could not justify the act, we denigrate the consent and, necessarily, the consenter as well.

This is cheating; it is a subterfuge designed to hide our unease and to allow us to profess simultaneous commitment to values that often conflict.'' [Garnett, Why Informed Consent? Human Experimentation and the Ethics of Autonomy, 36 Catholic Lawyer 455, 458-460 (1996) (footnotes omitted).]

The article continues:

"We should worry about the behavior of the experimenter, about our own culpability, and not about the subject's choosing capacities. . . .

Such restrictions on consent, which aim at objective behaviors and results rather than at subjective decision-making processes, are common in the criminal law. For example, guilty pleas must usually be supported by a factual basis, and be knowing and voluntary. We recognize that defendants might quite rationally plead guilty to crimes they did not commit and that prosecutors might be willing to accept such pleas. However, because such pleas embroil the legal system in a monstrous falsehood, we refuse to accept them while admitting that they might indeed be in the defendant's correctly perceived best interests. . . .

Similarly, in contract and consumer law, we often balance our general preference for unfettered respect for consensual arrangements against other concerns. . . . One purpose of these rules is undeniably to substitute the supposedly better judgment of the legislature and the judiciary about what is really in a person's best interest. . . .

. . . The Nuremberg Code explicitly recognized the need to place non-paternalistic limits on the scope of experiments. The Code asks more of an experiment, a researcher, or society than mere consent.'' [Id. at 494-497.][42] . . .

Based on the record before us, no degree of parental consent, and no degree of furnished information to the parents could make the experiment at issue here, ethically or legally permissible. It was wrong in the first instance.

---

[42] "Categorical limitations on human research and experimentation, [would] unavoidably slow us down. . . . Many might die of AIDS who would otherwise be willing to take risks on the slight chance that the next miracle drug might really work. . . . But these losses might be — like the occasionally guilty defendant going free — a price worth paying. The question is not so much whether we can afford to honor our commitment to human dignity, free from subterfuges . . . , but whether we can afford not to, or whether we ought to. . . . The lure of perfectionism and of the all-consuming pursuit of knowledge, both the conceit and the curiosity of the scientist, all conspire to tempt us to play fast and loose with the dignity of our research subjects and ourselves." Id. at 502.

We hold that in Maryland a parent, appropriate relative, or other applicable surrogate, cannot consent to the participation of a child or other person under legal disability in nontherapeutic research or studies in which there is any risk of injury or damage to the health of the subject.

[The court then ruled that informed consent agreements in nontherapeutic research projects, under certain circumstances, can constitute contracts and can evoke "special relationships" that give rise to duties out of the breach of which negligence actions may arise, and also that governmental regulations can create duties on the part of researchers towards human subjects out of which "special relationships" can arise. The court determined there was ample evidence to support a determination of the existence of defendant's duties arising out of contract, or out of a special relationship, or out of regulations and codes.]

We hold that on the present record, the Circuit Courts erred in their assessment of the law and of the facts as pled in granting KKI's motions for summary judgment. . . .

NOTES AND QUESTIONS

(1) How does *Grimes* respond to whether the legal system currently provides adequate protection for children in nontherapeutic experiments? Can parents rely on federal regulations governing institutional review boards to protect their children's interests? Or is medical research flawed by a conflict of interest because research institutions establish IRBs to review their *own* experiments? One commentator elaborates on the magnitude of the problem:

> The failure to protect children in research appears to be more problematic than the few incidents reported in the mainstream press. A study published in 2002 found 65 percent of published research on children did not comply with federal requirements for consent or review. This lack of compliance occurs despite the existence for more than 20 years of federal regulations and voluntary professional guidelines stipulating compliance with the regulations as a requirement for publication. . . .
> [William J. Wenner, Does the Legal System Provide Adequate Protection for Children in Scientific Experiments? The Unanswered Question of Grimes v. Kennedy Krieger Institute, 8 U.C. Davis J. Juv. L. & Pol'y 243 (2004).]

(2) Do you agree with the limitations imposed on parental rights by *Grimes*? How is a court to make the determination? Should the court appoint a guardian ad litem? If so, should the guardian ad litem (a) echo the child's desires; (b) argue against participation, if only as a "devil's advocate"; or (c) make an independent judgment of what is best from the child's perspective and then advocate that result?

Should the doctrine of informed consent apply *more* strictly in the research setting? In a Canadian case involving nontherapeutic research on human subjects, the Saskatchewan Court of Appeal imposed a duty of disclosure on medical researchers "as great as, if not greater than, the duty owed by the ordinary physician or surgeon." Halushka v. Univ. of Sask., [1965] 53 D.L.R. 2d 436, 443-444. If so, how should the informed consent doctrine be changed?

(3) In the case of Hart v. Brown (discussed in *Grimes*), parents asked a court to approve a kidney transplant from one seven-year-old twin to the other. The court considered the transplant as both nonexperimental and nontherapeutic for the donor and then determined that it had the equity power to approve nontherapeutic medical procedures. The court ruled that the parents had the right to consent because the transplant would be of benefit to the healthy twin based on her warm relationship to her sister. Is *Hart* truly an adversarial proceeding? How should a court evaluate the benefits and risks to the donor twin? Is it sound to rest a conclusion on psychological benefits to the donor? Compare Strunk v. Strunk, 445 S.W.2d 149 (Ky. 1969) (reasoning that a transplant was for the benefit of a mental patient donor with the mental age of six) with In re Pescinski, 226 N.W.2d 180 (Wis. 1975) (reasoning that no benefit was established for a prospective donor who was a 39-year-old catatonic schizophrenic with a mental age of 12 who had been institutionalized for 16 years).

(4) The death of a teenager in a biomedical experiment renewed concerns about the dangers of human experimentation. In 1999, a 19-year-old youth suffered a fatal immune-system reaction during a gene therapy experiment at the University of Pennsylvania. See Alice Dembner, Lawsuits Target Medical Research Patient Safeguards, Oversight Key Issues, Boston Globe, Aug. 12, 2002, at A1.

(5) As a society can we ever condone the sacrifice of a child? Remember Prince v. Massachusetts. Why should parents be permitted to make martyrs of their children? With regard to medical experiments on healthy children involving any risks whatsoever, is it too obvious that we are sacrificing children either for the parents' own purposes or for society's purpose? Is this acceptable, even if there is a scheme for compensation funds for those injured by unsuccessful experiments?

Do you agree that because of our commitment to the dignity of the individual and to human life, our society cannot condone the obvious or blatant sacrifice of an individual against his or her will? Is this a reason parents should not be permitted to consent to a medical experiment where it is obvious that the child has not consented, and the child will in no immediate sense benefit? Is there a practical necessity to place some values (i.e., the health of future children) above the health, comfort, and perhaps lives of some living children?

For a classic debate about proxy consent in the experimentation situation, see Richard A. McCormick, Proxy Consent in the Experimental Situation, 18 Persp. in Biology & Med. 2 (Autumn 1974) (arguing that parental consent is morally legitimate because it is a reasonable presumption of what the child would wish because he ought to do so); Paul Ramsey, A Reply to Richard McCormick: The Enforcement of Morals: Nontherapeutic Research on Children, 6 Hastings Center Rep. (No. 4) 21 (Aug. 1976) (arguing that proxy consent, based on the presumptive or implied consent of child, is "a violent and a false presumption" because a child is not a bearer of moral obligations).

CHAPTER 5

Child Custody

A. INTRODUCTION

This chapter is concerned with who should have primary responsibility for the care and custody of children. The introductory section suggests broad questions that cut across the various strands of custody law. A section on adoption follows. The third section, relating to divorce custody, explores a variety of issues relating to the settlement of disputes between biological parents concerning their children. Finally, the last section examines issues involving custody law and the new reproductive technology.

In re Baby M
537 A.2d 1227 (N.J. 1988)

Wilentz, Chief Justice.

In this matter the Court is asked to determine the validity of a contract that purports to provide a new way of bringing children into a family. . . .

In February 1985, William Stern and Mary Beth Whitehead entered into a surrogacy contract. It recited that Stern's wife, Elizabeth, was infertile, that they wanted a child, and that Mrs. Whitehead was willing to provide that child as the mother with Mr. Stern as the father.

The contract provided that through artificial insemination using Mr. Stern's sperm, Mrs. Whitehead would become pregnant, carry the child to term, bear it, deliver it to the Sterns, and thereafter do whatever was necessary to terminate her maternal rights so that Mrs. Stern could thereafter adopt the child. Mrs. Whitehead's husband, Richard, was also a party to the contract; Mrs. Stern was not. Mr. Whitehead promised to do all acts necessary to rebut the presumption of paternity under the Parentage Act. N.J.S.A. 9:17-43a(1), -44a. Although Mrs. Stern was not a party to the surrogacy agreement, the contract gave her sole custody of the child in the event of

Mr. Stern's death. Mrs. Stern's status as a nonparty to the surrogate parenting agreement presumably was to avoid the application of the baby-selling statute to this arrangement. N.J.S.A. 9:3-54.

Mr. Stern, on his part, agreed to attempt the artificial insemination and to pay Mrs. Whitehead $10,000 after the child's birth, on its delivery to him. In a separate contract, Mr. Stern agreed to pay $7,500 to the Infertility Center of New York ("ICNY"). The Center's advertising campaigns solicit surrogate mothers and encourage infertile couples to consider surrogacy. ICNY arranged for the surrogacy contract by bringing the parties together, explaining the process to them, furnishing the contractual form, and providing legal counsel.

The history of the parties' involvement in this arrangement suggests their good faith. William and Elizabeth Stern were married in July 1974, having met at the University of Michigan, where both were Ph.D. candidates. Due to financial considerations and Mrs. Stern's pursuit of a medical degree and residency, they decided to defer starting a family until 1981. Before then, however, Mrs. Stern learned that she might have multiple sclerosis and that the disease in some cases renders pregnancy a serious health risk. . . . Based on the perceived risk, the Sterns decided to forgo having their own children. The decision had a special significance for Mr. Stern. Most of his family had been destroyed in the Holocaust. As the family's only survivor, he very much wanted to continue his bloodline. Initially the Sterns considered adoption, but were discouraged by the substantial delay apparently involved and by the potential problem they saw arising from their age and their differing religious backgrounds. . . . The paths of Mrs. Whitehead and the Sterns to surrogacy were similar. Both responded to advertising by ICNY. The Sterns' response, following their inquiries into adoption, was the result of their long-standing decision to have a child. Mrs. Whitehead's response apparently resulted from her sympathy with family members and others who could have no children (she stated that she wanted to give another couple the "gift of life"); she also wanted the $10,000 to help her family. . . .

. . . On February 6, 1985, Mr. Stern and Mr. and Mrs. Whitehead executed the surrogate parenting agreement. . . . [O]n March 27, 1986, Baby M was born. . . .

Mrs. Whitehead realized, almost from the moment of birth, that she could not part with this child. . . . Nonetheless, Mrs. Whitehead was, for the moment, true to her word. Despite powerful inclinations to the contrary, she turned her child over to the Sterns on March 30 at the Whiteheads' home.

The Sterns were thrilled with their new child [and] looked forward to raising their daughter, whom they named Melissa. While aware by then that Mrs. Whitehead was undergoing an emotional crisis, they were as yet not cognizant of the depth of that crisis and its implications for their newly-enlarged family.

Later in the evening of March 30, Mrs. Whitehead became deeply disturbed, disconsolate, stricken with unbearable sadness. . . . The next day she went to the Sterns' home and told them how much she was suffering. . . . She told them that she could not live without her baby, that she must have her, even if only for one week, that thereafter she would surrender her child. The Sterns, concerned that Mrs. Whitehead might indeed commit suicide, not wanting under any circumstances to risk that, and in any event believing that Mrs. Whitehead would keep her word, turned the child over to her. . . .

The struggle over Baby M began when it became apparent that Mrs. Whitehead could not return the child to Mr. Stern. Due to Mrs. Whitehead's refusal to relinquish the baby, Mr. Stern filed a complaint seeking enforcement of the surrogacy contract. . . . After the order [in favor of Stern] was entered, ex parte, the process server, aided by the police, in the presence of the Sterns, entered Mrs. Whitehead's home to execute the order. Mr. Whitehead fled with the child, who had been handed to him through a window while those who came to enforce the order were thrown off balance by a dispute over the child's current name.

The Whiteheads immediately fled to Florida with Baby M. They stayed initially with Mrs. Whitehead's parents, . . . [later] at roughly twenty different hotels, motels, and homes in order to avoid apprehension. From time to time Mrs. Whitehead would call Mr. Stern to discuss the matter; the conversations, recorded by Mr. Stern on advice of counsel, show an escalating dispute about rights, morality, and power, accompanied by threats of Mrs. Whitehead to kill herself, to kill the child, and falsely to accuse Mr. Stern of sexually molesting Mrs. Whitehead's other daughter.

Eventually the Sterns discovered where the Whiteheads were staying, commenced supplementary proceedings in Florida, and obtained an order requiring the Whiteheads to turn over the child. . . . The prior order of the court, issued ex parte, awarding custody of the child to the Sterns pendente lite, was reaffirmed. . . . Pending final judgment, Mrs. Whitehead was awarded limited visitation with Baby M. . . .

The trial [to enforce the surrogacy contract] took thirty-two days over a period of more than two months [and included testimony by 23 witnesses and 15 expert witnesses. The trial court] held that the surrogacy contract was valid; ordered that Mrs. Whitehead's parental rights be terminated and that sole custody of the child be granted to Mr. Stern; and . . . entered an order allowing the adoption of Melissa by Mrs. Stern. . . . Pending the outcome of the appeal, we granted a continuation of visitation to Mrs. Whitehead, although slightly more limited than the visitation allowed during the trial. . . .

II. Invalidity and Unenforceability of Surrogacy Contract

We have concluded that this surrogacy contract is invalid. Our conclusion has two bases: direct conflict with existing statutes and conflict with the public policies of this State, as expressed in its statutory and decisional law. . . .

A. Conflict and Statutory Provisions

The surrogacy contract conflicts with: (1) laws prohibiting the use of money in connection with adoptions; (2) laws requiring proof of parental unfitness or abandonment before termination of parental rights is ordered or an adoption is granted; and (3) laws that make surrender of custody and consent to adoption revocable in private placement adoptions.

(1) Our law prohibits paying or accepting money in connection with any placement of a child for adoption. N.J.S.A. 9:3-54a. . . . Considerable care was taken in this case to structure the surrogacy arrangement so as not to violate

this prohibition. The arrangement was structured as follows: the adopting parent, Mrs. Stern, was not a party to the surrogacy contract; the money paid to Mrs. Whitehead was stated to be for her services — not for the adoption; the sole purpose of the contract was stated as being that "of giving a child to William Stern, its natural and biological father"; the money was purported to be "compensation for services and expenses and in no way . . . a fee for termination of parental rights or a payment in exchange for consent to surrender a child for adoption"; the fee to the Infertility Center ($7,500) was stated to be for legal representation, advice, administrative work, and other "services." Nevertheless, it seems clear that the money was paid and accepted in connection with an adoption. . . .

Mr. Stern knew he was paying for the adoption of a child; Mrs. Whitehead knew she was accepting money so that a child might be adopted; the Infertility Center knew that it was being paid for assisting in the adoption of a child. The actions of all three worked to frustrate the goals of the statute. It strains credulity to claim that these arrangements, touted by those in the surrogacy business as an attractive alternative to the usual route leading to an adoption, really amount to something other than a private placement adoption for money.

The prohibition of our statute is strong. Violation constitutes a high misdemeanor, N.J.S.A. 9:3-54c, a third-degree crime, N.J.S.A. 2C:43-1b, carrying a penalty of three to five years imprisonment. N.J.S.A. 2C:43-6a(3). The evils inherent in baby bartering are loathsome for a myriad of reasons. The child is sold without regard for whether the purchasers will be suitable parents. The natural mother does not receive the benefit of counseling and guidance to assist her in making a decision that may affect her for a lifetime. In fact, the monetary incentive to sell her child may, depending on her financial circumstances, make her decision less voluntary. . . . Baby-selling potentially results in the exploitation of all parties involved. . . .

(2) The termination of Mrs. Whitehead's parental rights, called for by the surrogacy contract . . . fails to comply with the stringent requirements of New Jersey law. . . . Our statutes, and the cases interpreting them, leave no doubt that where there has been no written surrender to an approved agency or to DYFS [Division of Youth and Family Services], termination of parental rights will not be granted in this state absent a very strong showing of abandonment or neglect. That showing is required in every context in which termination of parental rights is sought, be it an action by an approved agency, an action by DYFS, or a private placement adoption proceeding, even where the petitioning adoptive parent is, as here, a step-parent. . . .

In this case a termination of parental rights was obtained not by proving the statutory prerequisites but by claiming the benefit of contractual provisions. . . .

Since the termination was invalid, it follows, as noted above, that adoption of Melissa by Mrs. Stern could not properly be granted.

(3) The provision in the surrogacy contract stating that Mary Beth Whitehead agrees to "surrender custody . . . and terminate all parental rights" contains no clause giving her a right to rescind. It is intended to be an irrevocable consent to surrender the child for adoption. . . .

Such a provision, however, making irrevocable the natural mother's consent to surrender custody of her child in a private placement adoption, clearly conflicts with New Jersey law.

. . . The provision in the surrogacy contract, agreed to before conception, requiring the natural mother to surrender custody of the child without any right of revocation is one more indication of the essential nature of this transaction: the creation of a contractual system of termination and adoption designed to circumvent our statutes.

B. Public Policy Considerations

The surrogacy contract's invalidity, resulting from its direct conflict with the above statutory provisions, is further underlined when its goals and means are measured against New Jersey's public policy. . . .

The surrogacy contract violates the policy of this State that the rights of natural parents are equal concerning their child, the father's right no greater than the mother's. . . . The whole purpose and effect of the surrogacy contract was to give the father the exclusive right to the child by destroying the rights of the mother.

The policies expressed in our comprehensive laws governing consent to the surrender of a child . . . stand in stark contrast to the surrogacy contract and what it implies. Here there is no counseling, independent or otherwise, of the natural mother, no evaluation, no warning. . . .

Mrs. Whitehead was examined and psychologically evaluated, but if it was for her benefit, the record does not disclose that fact. The Sterns regarded the evaluation as important. . . . Yet they never asked to see it, and were content with the assumption that the Infertility Center had made an evaluation and had concluded that there was no danger that the surrogate mother would change her mind. . . . It is apparent that the profit motive got the better of the Infertility Center. Although the evaluation was made, it was not put to any use, and understandably so, for the psychologist warned that Mrs. Whitehead demonstrated certain traits that might make surrender of the child difficult and that there should be further inquiry into this issue in connection with her surrogacy. . . .

Under the contract, the natural mother is irrevocably committed before she knows the strength of her bond with her child. She never makes a totally voluntary, informed decision, for quite clearly any decision prior to the baby's birth is, in the most important sense, uninformed, and any decision after that, compelled by a pre-existing contractual commitment, the threat of a lawsuit, and the inducement of a $10,000 payment, is less than totally voluntary. Her interests are of little concern to those who controlled this transaction. . . .

Worst of all, however, is the contract's total disregard of the best interests of the child. There is not the slightest suggestion that any inquiry will be made at any time to determine the fitness of the Sterns as custodial parents, of Mrs. Stern as an adoptive parent, their superiority to Mrs. Whitehead, or the effect on the child of not living with her natural mother.

This is the sale of a child, or, at the very least, the sale of a mother's right to her child, the only mitigating factor being that one of the purchasers is the father. Almost every evil that prompted the prohibition of the payment of money in connection with adoptions exists here.

The differences between an adoption and a surrogacy contract should be noted, since it is asserted that the use of money in connection with surrogacy does not pose the risks found where money buys an adoption. First, and perhaps most important, all parties concede that it is unlikely that surrogacy will survive without money. . . . That conclusion contrasts with adoption; for obvious reasons, there remains a steady supply, albeit insufficient, despite the prohibitions against payment. The adoption itself, relieving the natural mother of the financial burden of supporting an infant, is the equivalent of payment.

Second, the use of money in adoptions does not produce the problem—conception occurs, and usually the birth itself, before illicit funds are offered. With surrogacy, the "problem," if one views it as such, consisting of the purchase of a woman's procreative capacity, at the risk of her life, is caused by and originates with the offer of money.

Third, with the law prohibiting the use of money in connection with adoptions, the built-in financial pressure of the unwanted pregnancy and the consequent support obligation do not lead the mother to the highest paying, ill-suited, adoptive parents. She is just as well off surrendering the child to an approved agency. In surrogacy, the highest bidders will presumably become the adoptive parents regardless of suitability, so long as payment of money is permitted.

Fourth, the mother's consent to surrender her child in adoptions is revocable, even after surrender of the child, unless it be to an approved agency, where by regulation there are protections against an ill-advised surrender. In surrogacy, consent occurs so early that no amount of advice would satisfy the potential mother's need, yet the consent is irrevocable.

The main difference, that the plight of the unwanted pregnancy is unintended while the situation of the surrogate mother is voluntary and intended, is really not significant. [T]he essential evil is the same, taking advantage of a woman's circumstances (the unwanted pregnancy or the need for money) in order to take away her child, the difference being one of degree. . . .

Intimated, but disputed, is the assertion that surrogacy will be used for the benefit of the rich at the expense of the poor. In response it is noted that the Sterns are not rich and the Whiteheads not poor. Nevertheless, it is clear to us that it is unlikely that surrogate mothers will be as proportionately numerous among those women in the top twenty percent income bracket as among those in the bottom twenty percent. . . .

The point is made that Mrs. Whitehead agreed to the surrogacy arrangement, supposedly fully understanding the consequences. Putting aside the issue of how compelling her need for money may have been, and how significant her understanding of the consequences, we suggest that her consent is irrelevant. There are, in a civilized society, some things that money cannot buy. . . .

The long-term effects of surrogacy contracts are not known, but feared—the impact on the child who learns her life was bought, that she is the offspring of someone who gave birth to her only to obtain money; the impact on the natural mother as the full weight of her isolation is felt along with the full reality of the sale of her body and her child; the impact on the natural father and adoptive mother once they realize the consequences of their conduct. . . .

In sum, the harmful consequences of this surrogacy arrangement appear to us all too palpable. In New Jersey the surrogate mother's agreement to sell her child is void. . . .

III. Termination

We have already noted that under our laws termination of parental rights cannot be based on contract, but may be granted only on proof of the statutory requirements. . . . Nothing in this record justifies a finding that would allow a court to terminate Mary Beth Whitehead's parental rights under the statutory standard. It is not simply that obviously there was no "intentional abandonment or very substantial neglect of parental duties without a reasonable expectation of reversal of that conduct in the future," N.J.S.A. 9:3-48c(1), quite the contrary, but furthermore that the trial court never found Mrs. Whitehead an unfit mother and indeed affirmatively stated that Mary Beth Whitehead had been a good mother to her other children.

Although the best interests of the child is dispositive of the custody issue in a dispute between natural parents, it does not govern the question of termination. It has long been decided that the mere fact that a child would be better off with one set of parents than with another is an insufficient basis for terminating the natural parent's rights. . . .

IV. Constitutional Issues

Both parties argue that the Constitutions — state and federal — mandate approval of their basic claims. . . . The right asserted by the Sterns is the right of procreation; that asserted by Mary Beth Whitehead is the right to the companionship of her child. . . .

The right to procreate, as protected by the Constitution, has been ruled on directly only once by the United States Supreme Court. See Skinner v. Oklahoma, 316 U.S. 535 (1942) (forced sterilization of habitual criminals violates equal protection clause of fourteenth amendment). . . . The right to procreate very simply is the right to have natural children, whether through sexual intercourse or artificial insemination. It is no more than that. Mr. Stern has not been deprived of that right. Through artificial insemination of Mrs. Whitehead, Baby M is his child. The custody, care, companionship, and nurturing that follow birth are not parts of the right to procreation; they are rights that may also be constitutionally protected, but that involve many considerations other than the right of procreation. To assert that Mr. Stern's right of procreation gives him the right to the custody of Baby M would be to assert that Mrs. Whitehead's right of procreation does not give her the right to the custody of Baby M; it would be to assert that the constitutional right of procreation includes within it a constitutionally protected contractual right to destroy someone else's right of procreation. . . .

Mr. Stern also contends that he has been denied equal protection of the laws by the State's statute granting full parental rights to a husband in relation to the child produced, with his consent, by the union of his wife with a sperm donor. N.J.S.A. 9:17-44. The claim really is that of Mrs. Stern. It is that she is in precisely the same position as the husband in the statute: she is presumably infertile, as is the husband in the statute; her spouse by agreement with a third party procreates with the understanding that the child will be the couple's child. . . .

It is quite obvious that the situations are not parallel. A sperm donor simply cannot be equated with a surrogate mother. The State has more than a sufficient basis to distinguish the two situations — even if the only difference is between the time it takes to provide sperm for artificial insemination and the time invested in a nine-month pregnancy — so as to justify automatically divesting the sperm donor of his parental rights without automatically divesting a surrogate mother. Some basis for an equal protection argument might exist if Mary Beth Whitehead had contributed her egg to be implanted, fertilized or otherwise, in Mrs. Stern, resulting in the latter's pregnancy. That is not the case here, however.

Mrs. Whitehead, on the other hand, . . . claims the right to the companionship of her child. This is a fundamental interest, constitutionally protected. Furthermore, it was taken away from her by the action of the court below. Whether that action under these circumstances would constitute a constitutional deprivation, however, we need not and do not decide. . . . We have decided that both the statutes and public policy of this state require that that termination be voided and that her parental rights be restored. . . .

V. Custody

Having decided that the surrogacy contract is illegal and unenforceable, we now must decide the custody question without regard to the provisions of the surrogacy contract. . . . Under the Parentage Act the claims of the natural father and the natural mother are entitled to equal weight. . . . The applicable rule given these circumstances is clear: the child's best interests determine custody. . . .

. . . The Whiteheads claim that even if the child's best interests would be served by our awarding custody to the Sterns, we should not do so. . . . Their position is that in order that surrogacy contracts be deterred, custody should remain in the surrogate mother unless she is unfit, regardless of the best interests of the child. We disagree. Our declaration that this surrogacy contract is unenforceable and illegal is sufficient to deter similar agreements. We need not sacrifice the child's interests in order to make that point sharper. . . .

The Whiteheads also contend that the award of custody to the Sterns pendente lite was erroneous and that the error should not be allowed to affect the final custody decision. . . .

The argument has considerable force. [However,] [t]he child's interests come first: we will not punish it for judicial errors, assuming any were made. . . . The custody decision must be based on all circumstances, on everything that actually has occurred, on everything that is relevant to the child's best interests. . . .

There were eleven experts who testified concerning the child's best interests, either directly or in connection with matters related to that issue. Our reading of the record persuades us that the trial court's decision awarding custody to the Sterns (technically to Mr. Stern) should be affirmed. . . .

Our custody conclusion is based on strongly persuasive testimony contrasting both the family life of the Whiteheads and the Sterns and the personalities and characters of the individuals. The stability of the Whitehead family life was doubtful at the time of trial. Their finances were in serious trouble (foreclosure by Mrs. Whitehead's sister on a second mortgage was in process). Mr. Whitehead's employment, though relatively steady, was always at risk because of his alcoholism, a condition that he seems not to have been able to confront effectively. Mrs. Whitehead had not worked for quite some time, her last two employments having been part-time. One of the Whiteheads' positive attributes was their ability to bring up two children, and apparently well, even in so vulnerable a household. Yet substantial question was raised even about that aspect of their home life. The expert testimony contained criticism of Mrs. Whitehead's handling of her son's educational difficulties. Certain of the experts noted that Mrs. Whitehead perceived herself as omnipotent and omniscient concerning her children. She knew what they were thinking, what they wanted, and she spoke for them. As to Melissa, Mrs. Whitehead expressed the view that she alone knew what that child's cries and sounds meant. Her inconsistent stories about various things engendered grave doubts about her ability to explain honestly and sensitively to Baby M — and at the right time — the nature of her origin. Although faith in professional counseling is not a sine qua non of parenting, several experts believed that Mrs. Whitehead's contempt for professional help, especially professional psychological help, coincided with her feelings of omnipotence in a way that could be devastating to a child who most likely will need such help. In short, while love and affection there would be, Baby M's life with the Whiteheads promised to be too closely controlled by Mrs. Whitehead. The prospects for a wholesome independent psychological growth and development would be at serious risk.

The Sterns have no other children, but all indications are that their household and their personalities promise a much more likely foundation for Melissa to grow and thrive. There is a track record of sorts — during the one-and-a-half years of custody Baby M has done very well, and the relationship between both Mr. and Mrs. Stern and the baby has become very strong. The household is stable, and likely to remain so. Their finances are more than adequate, their circle of friends supportive, and their marriage happy. Most important, they are loving, giving, nurturing, and open-minded people. They have demonstrated the wish and ability to nurture and protect Melissa, yet at the same time to encourage her independence. Their lack of experience is more than made up for by a willingness to learn and to listen, a willingness that is enhanced by their professional training, especially Mrs. Stern's experience as a pediatrician. They are honest; they can recognize error, deal with it, and learn from it. They will try to determine rationally the best way to cope with problems in their relationship with Melissa. When the time comes to tell her about her origins, they will probably have found a means of doing so that accords with the best interests of Baby M. All in all, Melissa's future appears solid, happy, and promising with them. . . .

Some comment is required on the initial ex parte order awarding custody pendente lite to the Sterns. . . . Any application by the natural father in a surrogacy dispute for custody pending the outcome of the litigation will henceforth require proof of unfitness [of the biological mother], of danger to the child, or the like, of so high a quality and persuasiveness as to make it unlikely that such application will succeed. . . .

VI. Visitation

The trial court's decision to terminate Mrs. Whitehead's parental rights precluded it from making any determination on visitation. . . . We therefore remand the visitation issue to the trial court for an abbreviated hearing and determination as set forth below. . . .

We also note the following for the trial court's consideration: First, this is not a divorce case where visitation is almost invariably granted to the non-custodial spouse. To some extent the facts here resemble cases where the non-custodial spouse has had practically no relationship with the child; but it only "resembles" those cases. In the instant case, Mrs. Whitehead spent the first four months of this child's life as her mother and has regularly visited the child since then. Second, she is not only the natural mother, but also the legal mother, and is not to be penalized one iota because of the surrogacy contract. . . .

In all of this, the trial court should recall the touchstones of visitation: that it is desirable for the child to have contact with both parents; that besides the child's interests, the parents' interests also must be considered; but that when all is said and done, the best interests of the child are paramount.

We have decided that Mrs. Whitehead is entitled to visitation at some point, and that question is not open to the trial court on this remand. The trial court will determine what kind of visitation shall be granted to her, with or without conditions, and when and under what circumstances it should commence. It also should be noted that the guardian's recommendation of a five-year delay is most unusual — one might argue that it begins to border on termination. . . .

Conclusion

This case affords some insight into a new reproductive arrangement: the artificial insemination of a surrogate mother. The unfortunate events that have unfolded illustrate that its unregulated use can bring suffering to all involved. Potential victims include the surrogate mother and her family, the natural father and his wife, and most importantly, the child. Although surrogacy has apparently provided positive results for some infertile couples, it can also, as this case demonstrates, cause suffering to participants, here essentially innocent and well-intended.

We have found that our present laws do not permit the surrogacy contract used in this case. Nowhere, however, do we find any legal prohibition against surrogacy when the surrogate mother volunteers, without any payment, to act as a surrogate and is given the right to change her mind and to assert her parental rights. Moreover, the Legislature remains free to deal with this most sensitive issue as it sees fit, subject only to constitutional constraints. . . . The problem is how to enjoy the benefits of the technology — especially for infertile couples — while minimizing the risk of abuse. The problem can be addressed only when society decides what its values and objectives are in this troubling, yet promising, area. . . .

QUESTIONS ON *BABY M*

See p. 638 infra.

POSTSCRIPT ON *BABY M*

Subsequent to the trial court ruling and by the time of oral argument in the above case, the Whiteheads had separated. Thereafter, Mrs. Whitehead became pregnant by New York accountant Dean Gould, divorced her husband, and married Gould. She has two children from her new marriage as well as the two Whitehead children. The New Jersey Superior Court on remand granted Mary Beth Whitehead liberal visitation rights (542 A.2d 52 (N.J. Super. Ct. Ch. Div. 1988)).

Melissa Stern, who resembles her biological mother, turned 22 in March 2008. She is currently a senior in college, majoring in religion at George Washington University. Susannah Cahalan, Tug O'Love Baby M All Grown Up, N.Y. Post, Apr. 13, 2008, at 9. She continues to visit regularly with her biological mother's family, who now live in Long Island. According to earlier accounts, "[Melissa] is a friendly, happy girl, unaffected by her early fame and the continuing tension between her birth mother and the natural father and the adoptive mother she lives with." Allen Salkin, She's Come a Long Way, Baby M! Gifted Child Born Amid a Two-Family Uproar Thrives, N.Y. Post, Mar. 21, 1999, at 5. For a long time after Baby M's birth, Whitehead voiced strong opposition to surrogacy and expressed the pain it caused her. Elaine D'Aurizio, Whatever Happened to Baby M? Surrogate Mom Still Mourning Loss After 16 Years, Calgary Herald, May 4, 2002. See also Phyllis Chesler, Sacred Bonds: The Legacy of Baby M (1988); Mary Beth Whitehead, A Mother's Story (1989).

Guardianship of Phillip B., a Minor
188 Cal. Rptr. 781 (Ct. App. 1983)

RACANELLI, Presiding Justice.

Few human experiences evoke the poignancy of a filial relationship and the pathos attendant upon its disruption in society's effort to afford every child a meaningful chance to live life to its fullest promise. This appeal, posing a sensitive confrontation between the fundamental right of parental custody and the well being of a retarded child, reflects the deeply ingrained concern that the needs of the child remain paramount in the judicial monitoring of custody. In reaching our decision to affirm, we neither suggest nor imply that appellants' subjectively motivated custodial objectives affront conventional norms of parental fitness; rather, we determine only that on the unusual factual record before us, the challenged order of guardianship must be upheld in order to avert potential harm to the minor ward likely to result from appellants' continuing custody and to subserve his best interests.

On February 23, 1981, respondents Herbert and Patsy H. filed a petition for appointment as guardians of the person and estate of Phillip B., then 14 years of age. Phillip's parents, appellants Warren and Patricia B., appeared in opposition to the petition. . . .

Phillip B. was born on October 16, 1966, with Down's Syndrome, a chromosomal anomaly — usually the presence of an extra chromosome attached to the number 21 pair — resulting in varying degrees of mental retardation and a number of abnormal physical characteristics. Down's Syndrome reportedly occurs in approximately 1/10 of 1 percent of live births.

Appellants, deeply distraught over Phillip's disability, decided upon institutionalization, a course of action recommended by a state social worker and approved by appellants' pediatrician. A few days later, Phillip was transferred from the hospital to a licensed board and care facility for disabled youngsters. Although the facility was clean, it offered no structured educational or developmental programs and required that all the children (up to 8 years of age) sleep in cribs. Appellants initially visited Phillip frequently; but soon their visits became less frequent and they became more detached from him.

When Phillip was three years old a pediatrician informed appellants that Phillip had a congenital heart defect, a condition afflicting half of Down's Syndrome children. Open heart surgery was suggested when Phillip attained age six. However, appellants took no action to investigate or remedy the suspected medical problem.

After the board and care facility had been sold during the summer of 1971, appellants discovered that the condition of the facility had seriously deteriorated under the new management; it had become dirty and cluttered with soiled clothing, and smelled strongly of urine. Phillip was very thin and listless and was being fed watery oatmeal from a bottle. At appellants' request, a state social worker arranged for Phillip's transfer in January, 1972, to We Care, a licensed residential facility for developmentally disabled children located in San Jose, where he remained up to the time of trial. . . . In April 1972, We Care employed Jeanne Haight (later to become program director and assistant administrator of the facility) to organize a volunteer program. . . . Mrs. Haight, who undertook a recruitment program for volunteers, soon recruited respondent Patsy H., who had helped to found a school for children with learning disabilities where Mrs. Haight had once been vice-principal. Mrs. H. began working at We Care on a daily basis. Her husband, respondent Herbert H., and their children, soon joined in the volunteer activities.

Mrs. H., initially assigned to work with Phillip and another child, assisted Phillip in experimenting with basic sensory experiences, improving body coordination, and in overcoming his fear of steps. Mr. H. and one of the H. children helped fence the yard area, put in a lawn, a sandbox, and install some climbing equipment.

Mrs. Haight promptly initiated efforts to enroll Phillip in a preschool program for the fall of 1972, which required parental consent.[4] She contacted Mr. B. who agreed to permit Phillip to participate provided learning aptitude could be demonstrated. Mrs. H. used vocabulary cards to teach Phillip 25 to 50 new words and to comprehend word association. Although Mr. B. failed to appear at the appointed time in order to observe what Phillip had learned, he eventually gave his parental consent enabling Phillip to attend Hope Preschool in October, 1972.

Respondents continued working with Phillip coordinating their efforts with his classroom lessons. Among other things, they concentrated on development of feeding skills and toilet training and Mr. H. and the two eldest children gradually became more involved in the volunteer program.

---

[4] Apparently, Phillip had received no formal preschool education for the retarded even though such training programs were available in the community. Expert testimony established that early introduction to preschool training is of vital importance in preparing a retarded child for entry level public education.

Phillip subsequently attended a school for the trainable mentally retarded (TMR) where the children are taught basic survival words. They are capable of learning to feed and dress themselves appropriately, doing basic community activities such as shopping, and engaging in recreational activities. There is no attempt to teach them academics, and they are expected to live in sheltered settings as adults. . . .

A pattern of physical and emotional detachment from their son was developed by appellants over the next several years. In contrast, during the same period, respondents established a close and caring relationship with Phillip. Beginning in December, 1972, Phillip became a frequent visitor at respondents' home; with appellants' consent, Phillip was permitted to spend weekends with respondents, a practice which continued regularly and often included weekday evenings. At the same time, respondents maintained frequent contact with Phillip at We Care as regular volunteer visitors. Meanwhile, appellants visited Phillip at the facility only a few times a year; however, no overnight home visits occurred until after the underlying litigation ensued.

Respondents played an active role in Phillip's behavioral development and educational training. They consistently supplemented basic skills training given Phillip at We Care.[5]

Phillip was openly accepted as a member of the H. family whom he came to love and trust. He eventually had his own bedroom; he was included in sharing household chores. Mr. H. set up a workbench for Phillip and helped him make simple wooden toys; they attended special Boy Scout meetings together. And Phillip regularly participated in family outings. Phillip referred to the H. residence as "my house." When Phillip began to refer to the Hs. as "Mom" and "Dad," they initially discouraged the familiar reference, eventually succeeding in persuading Phillip to use the discriminate references "Mama Pat" and "Dada Bert" and "Mama B." and "Daddy B."[6] Both Mrs. Haight and Phillip's teacher observed significant improvements in Phillip's development and behavior. Phillip had developed, in Mrs. Haight's opinion, "true love and strong [emotional] feelings" for respondents.

Meanwhile, appellants continued to remain physically and emotionally detached from Phillip. The natural parents intellectualized their decision to treat Phillip differently from their other children. Appellants testified that Phillip, whom they felt would always require institutionalization, should not be permitted to form close emotional attachments which — upon inevitable disruption — would traumatize the youngster.

In matters of Phillip's health care needs, appellants manifested a reluctant — if not neglectful — concern. When Dr. Gathman, a pediatric cardiologist, diagnosed a ventricular septal defect[7] in Phillip's heart in early 1973 and recommended

---

[5] In addition to their efforts to improve Phillip's communication and reading skills through basic sign language and word association exercises, respondents toilet-trained Phillip and taught him to use eating utensils and to sleep in a regular bed (the latter frequently monitored during the night).

[6] At respondents' suggestion, Mrs. Haight requested a photograph of appellants to show Phillip who his parents were; but appellants failed to provide one.

[7] The disease, found in a large number of Down's Syndrome children . . . consists of an opening or "hole" between the heart chambers resulting in elevated blood pressure and impairment of vascular functions. The disease can become a progressive, and ultimately fatal, disorder.

catheterization (a medically accepted pre-surgery procedure to measure pressure and to examine the interior of the heart), appellants refused their consent.

In the spring of 1977, Dr. Gathman again recommended heart catheterization in connection with the anticipated use of general anesthesia during Phillip's major dental surgery. Appellants consented to the pre-operative procedure which revealed that the heart defect was surgically correctable with a maximum risk factor of 5 percent. At a conference attended by appellants and Mrs. Haight in June, 1977, Dr. Gathman recommended corrective surgery in order to avoid a progressively deteriorating condition resulting in a "bed-to-chair existence" and the probability of death before the age of 30.[8] Although Dr. Gathman — as requested by Mrs. B. — supplied the name of a parent of Down's Syndrome children with similar heart disease, no contact was ever made. Later that summer, appellants decided — without obtaining an independent medical consultation — against surgery. Appellants' stated reason was that Dr. Gathman had "painted" an inaccurate picture of the situation. They felt that surgery would be merely life-prolonging rather than life-saving, presenting the possibility that they would be unable to care for Phillip during his later years. A few months later, in early 1978, appellants' decision was challenged in a juvenile dependency proceeding initiated by the district attorney on the ground that the withholding of surgery constituted neglect within the meaning of Welfare and Institutions Code section 300, subdivision (b); the juvenile court's dismissal of the action on the basis of inconclusive evidence was ultimately sustained on appeal (In re Phillip B. (1979) 92 Cal. App. 3d 796, 156 Cal. Rptr. 48, *cert. den. sub nom.* Bothman v. Warren B., 445 U.S. 949 (1980)).

In September, 1978, upon hearing from a staff member of We Care that Phillip had been regularly spending weekends at respondents' home, Mr. B. promptly forbade Phillip's removal from the facility (except for medical purposes and school attendance) and requested that respondents be denied personal visits with Phillip at We Care. Although respondents continued to visit Phillip daily at the facility, the abrupt cessation of home visits produced regressive changes in Phillip's behavior: he began acting out violently when respondents prepared to leave, begging to be taken "home"; he resorted to profanity; he became sullen and withdrawn when respondents were gone; bed-wetting regularly occurred, a recognized symptom of emotional disturbance in children. He began to blame himself for the apparent rejection by respondents; he began playing with matches and on one occasion he set his clothes afire; on another, he rode his tricycle to respondents' residence a few blocks away proclaiming on arrival that he was "home." He continuously pleaded to return home with respondents. Many of the behavioral changes continued to the time of trial.

Appellants unsuccessfully pressed to remove Phillip from We Care notwithstanding the excellent care he was receiving. . . . Meanwhile, Phillip continued living at We Care, periodically visiting at appellants' home. But

---

[8] Dr. Gathman's explicit description of the likely ravages of the disease created anger and distrust on the part of appellants and motivated them to seek other opinions and to independently assess the need for surgery.

throughout, the strong emotional attachment between Phillip and respondents remained intact. . . .

[T]he right of parents to retain custody of a child is fundamental and may be disturbed " 'only in extreme cases of persons acting in a fashion incompatible with parenthood.' " . . . Accordingly, the Legislature has imposed the stringent requirement that before a court may make an order awarding custody of a child to a nonparent without consent of the parents, "it shall make a finding that an award of custody to a parent would be detrimental to the child and the award to a nonparent is required to serve the best interests of the child." (Civ. Code, §4600, subd. (c)). That requirement is equally applicable to guardianship proceedings under Probate Code section 1514, subdivision (b). . . .

The trial court expressly found that an award of custody to appellants would be harmful to Phillip in light of the psychological or 'de facto' parental relationship established between him and respondents. Such relationships have long been recognized in the fields of law and psychology. As Justice Tobriner has cogently observed, "The fact of biological parenthood may incline an adult to feel a strong concern for the welfare of his child, but it is not an essential condition; a person who assumes the role of parent, raising the child in his own home, may in time acquire an interest in the 'companionship, care, custody and management' of that child. The interest of the 'de facto parent' is a substantial one . . . deserving of legal protection" [citing the seminal study of Goldstein, Freud & Solnit, Beyond the Best Interests of the Child (1973) pp. 17-20, hereafter Goldstein]. Persons who assume such responsibility have been characterized by some interested professional observers as "psychological parents": "Whether any adult becomes the psychological parent of a child is based . . . on day-to-day interaction, companionship, and shared experiences. The role can be fulfilled either by a biological parent or by an adoptive parent or by any other caring adult — but never by an absent, inactive adult, whatever his biological or legal relationship to the child may be." (Goldstein, supra, p. 19.)

Appellants vigorously challenge the evidence and finding that respondents have become Phillip's de facto or psychological parents since he did not reside with them full-time. . . . They argue that the subjective concept of psychological parenthood, relying on such nebulous factors as "love and affection" is susceptible to abuse and requires the countervailing element of objectivity provided by a showing of the child's longterm residency in the home of the claimed psychological parent.

We disagree. Adoption of the proposed standard would require this court to endorse a novel doctrine of child psychology unsupported either by a demonstrated general acceptance in the field of psychology or by the record before us. Although psychological parenthood is said to result from "day-to-day attention to [the child's] needs for physical care, nourishment, comfort, affection, and stimulation" (Goldstein, supra, p. 17), appellants fail to point to any authority or body of professional opinion that equates daily attention with full-time residency. To the contrary, the record contains uncontradicted expert testimony that while psychological parenthood usually will require residency on a "24-hour basis," it is not an absolute requirement; further, that the frequency and quality of Phillip's weekend visits with respondents, together with the regular weekday visits at We Care, provided an adequate foundation to establish the crucial parent-child relationship. . . .

Appellants also challenge the sufficiency of the evidence to support the finding that their retention of custody would have been detrimental to Phillip. In making the critical finding, the trial court correctly applied the "clear and convincing" standard of proof necessary to protect the fundamental rights of parents in all cases involving a nonparent's bid for custody. . . .

The record contains abundant evidence that appellants' retention of custody would cause Phillip profound emotional harm. . . . [T]estimony indicated that, as with all children, Phillip needs love and affection, and he would be profoundly hurt if he were deprived of the existing psychological parental relationship with respondents in favor of maintaining unity with his biological parents.

Phillip's conduct unmistakably demonstrated that he derived none of the emotional benefits attending a close parental relationship largely as a result of appellants' individualized decision to abandon that traditional supporting role. Dr. Becking testified that no "bonding or attachment" has occurred between Phillip and his biological parents, a result palpably consistent with appellants' view that Phillip had none of the emotional needs uniquely filled by natural parents. We conclude that such substantial evidence adequately supports the finding that parental custody would have resulted in harmful deprivation of these human needs contrary to Phillip's best interests.

Finally, there was also evidence that Phillip would experience educational and developmental injury if parental custody remains unchanged. At Phillip's functioning level of disability, he can normally be expected to live at least semi-independently as an adult in a supervised residential setting and be suitably trained to work in a sheltered workshop or even a competitive environment (e.g., performing assembly duties or custodial tasks in a fast-food restaurant). Active involvement of a parent figure during the formative stages of education and habilitation is of immeasurable aid in reaching his full potential. Unfortunately, appellants' deliberate abdication of that central role would effectively deny Phillip any meaningful opportunity to develop whatever skills he may be capable of achieving. . . .

Nor can we overlook evidence of potential physical harm to Phillip due to appellants' passive neglect in response to Phillip's medical condition. Although it appears probable that the congenital heart defect is no longer correctable by surgery, the trial court could have reasonably concluded that appellants' past conduct reflected a dangerously passive approach to Phillip's future medical needs.

It is a clearly stated legislative policy that persons with developmental disabilities shall enjoy — inter alia — the right to treatment and rehabilitation services, the right to publicly supported education, the right to social interaction, and the right to prompt medical care and treatment. Moreover, the legislative purpose underlying Civil Code section 4600 is to protect the needs of children generally " '. . . to be raised with love, emotional security and physical safety.' " When a trial court is called upon to determine the custody of a developmentally disabled or handicapped child, as here, it must be guided by such overriding policies rather than by the personal beliefs or attitudes of the contesting parties, since it is the child's interest which remains paramount. Clearly, the trial court faithfully complied with such legislative mandate in exercising its sound discretion based upon the evidence presented. We find no abuse as contended by appellants.

We strongly emphasize, as the trial court correctly concluded, that the fact of detriment cannot be proved solely by evidence that the biological parent has elected to institutionalize a handicapped child, or that nonparents are able and willing to offer the child the advantages of their home in lieu of institutional placement. Sound reasons may exist justifying institutionalization of a handi-capped child. But the totality of the evidence under review permits of no rational conclusion other than that the detriment caused Phillip, and its possible recurrence, was due not to appellants' choice to institutionalize but their calculated decision to remain emotionally and physically detached — abdicating the conventional role of competent decision-maker in times of demonstrated need — thus effectively depriving him of any of the substantial benefits of a true parental relationship. It is the emotional abandonment of Phillip, not his institutionalization, which inevitably has created the unusual circumstances which led to the award of limited custody to respondents. We do not question the sincerity of appellants' belief that their approach to Phillip's welfare was in their combined best interests. But the record is replete with substantial and credible evidence supporting the trial court's determination, tested by the standard of clear and convincing proof, that appel-lants' retention of custody has caused and will continue to cause serious detriment to Phillip and that his best interests will be served through the guardianship award of custody to respondents. . . .

Robert H. Mnookin, The Guardianship of Phillip B.: Jay Spears' Achievement
40 Stan. L. Rev. 841, 852-854 (1988)

[Phillip's heart] catheterization was finally performed in the summer of 1983. . . .[1] It showed that Phillip had miraculously developed a new blockage that had not damaged his heart and yet had protected his lungs from further damage. The doctors reported that surgery was clearly indicated. . . . In September, Phillip underwent open heart surgery at the University of California hospital in San Francisco. [He] came through the surgery beautifully. . . .

Soon after the decision of the appellate court, the Beckers and the Heaths entered into a settlement agreement. The Beckers agreed to dismiss with prejudice the state court actions against the Heaths and further agreed that "unless there is a substantial and material change in the facts and circumstances currently known to the Beckers, the Beckers agree to take no legal action to remove custody of Phillip from the Heaths or to contest, limit or terminate the Heaths' status as Phillip's guardians and/or conservators."[56] The Heaths agreed that they would "provide and

---

[1] For an earlier neglect proceeding brought on behalf of Phillip B. in an unsuccessful effort to compel the Beckers to consent to a heart catheterization, see In re Phillip B., 156 Cal. Rptr. 48 (Ct. App. 1979), reprinted and discussed supra pp. 388-390.

[56] Agreement entered into by Warren and Patricia Becker and Herbert and Patsy Heath at 3 (Aug. 16, 1983). . . .

assume full responsibility for the cost of Phillip's care, and shall relieve the Beckers of and indemnify them against any liability for said costs."[57] They further agreed to permit either the Beckers or Phillip's brothers (after they reached adulthood) to visit Phillip at least two days a year and to provide Phillip with Catholic last rites if he were near death. Each party agreed to assume their own costs on appeal.

The Heaths very much wanted to adopt Phillip; and in early 1984, they filed a petition requesting adoption. The Beckers would neither refuse nor grant consent, so that things remained at a standstill until Phillip turned 18, an event that created new legal options. At 18, the guardianship would, of course, end. Because of Phillip's disabilities, a conservatorship would be necessary. The Heaths promptly petitioned to become Phillip's limited conservators. We also petitioned for a decree of adoption.

Since Phillip was now an adult, it was necessary to proceed under the adult adoption statute, which provides that a court may issue a decree of adoption based on an agreement of adoption executed by the adopting parties. Because it was not clear that Phillip had the capacity to enter into such an agreement himself, we petitioned the court for an order authorizing the conservators to enter into a contract of adult adoption on behalf of their conservatee.

The court ordered an investigation; and the report plainly stated that although Phillip did not understand "the legalities" of the proceedings, he understood "perfectly the question, do you want Mr. and Mrs. Heath to continue to take care of you? His answer, given repeatedly, was that he does. He was most insistent that he wants to live with the Heaths and do things with them. Either as Phillip Heath-Becker or Phillip Becker-Heath." In February 1985, after full notice to the Beckers, who indicated that they did not object, the Heaths adopted Phillip.

Phillip Becker-Heath, a young man with Down syndrome, is now 21 years old. For six years he has lived with his adoptive parents, Pat and Herb Heath, in a comfortable home in San Jose. The Heaths are devoted to Phillip, who is now, more than ever, the center of their lives; their older sons are married, and their daughter is living on her own.

Phillip's life has settled into a comfortable routine. In the morning he gets himself up around 7:00, puts on his glasses and hearing aid, dresses himself, and helps "Mama Pat" with breakfast. The Heaths take him to the bus stop where he catches the county transit bus. The bus drops Phillip a few blocks from the Joseph McKinnon School in San Jose, and he walks the rest of the way on his own.

As part of his school program, Phillip works at the Santa Clara Valley Medical Center where he busses tables in the cafeteria. Earlier this year he worked in the Hewlett Packard cafeteria as part of a special county program for the disabled. He is learning to read, albeit not without a struggle. A tutor works with Phillip at home to supplement the program at McKinnon. Pat expects his reading skills to improve rapidly because Phillip recently began to use a reading program that he runs himself on the Apple computer he received from the Heaths for Christmas.

Phillip loves sports. Because the congenital heart defect that had threatened to cut his life short was corrected by surgery in 1983, Phillip now actively participates

_____

[57] Id. at 3.

in the Special Olympics. He enjoys bowling, basketball, softball, and soccer. Joe Montana's picture hangs in his bedroom, and Phillip and the Heaths look forward to watching the Forty-Niners' games on television. Phillip roots for "number sixteen."

Phillip is a warm, affectionate, and optimistic young man who, according to Pat, is "a little bit cocky, and at times a smart aleck." He is helpful around the house. His chores include taking out the trash and raking the leaves in the yard. The Heaths are committed to seeing that Phillip develops the skills, discipline, and confidence necessary to hold down a job and lead a productive and largely independent life, notwithstanding his handicap. Pat and Herb feel certain that he will do so. "Two aspects of his character," according to Pat, "serve him very well. He wants to be a 'good boy' and he loves to work."

Phillip Becker-Heath recently turned 42 years old. He is doing well. In his young adulthood, he spent two years in a residential group home. However, he returned to the Heaths' home following the death of his girlfriend of 20 years. "They adored each other," says Pat Heath. "He still misses her." For many years, Phillip participated in the Special Olympics in bowling, basketball, and golf. He has given that up, and also given up his favorite hobby, computer art design, because his graphic arts teacher retired. Phillip continues to love music. "His tastes are very eclectic," describes Pat, "from Pavarotti to rock and roll!"

"He's turned out to be the same sweet loving guy as when he was little," she adds. "He's bright and willing to learn new things. His vocabulary is still growing." She says that his language ability has matured recently. "Essentially, he had no language training or schooling during his first five years. That's a critical period for speech development. For a long time, he just spoke words. But, surprisingly, he is now starting to speak more in sentences." She continues, "He has slowed down recently. He is showing his age. He spends his days watching football, working around the house with his dad, going grocery shopping, and sleeping a lot."

No one from Phillip's biological family contacted him since one week after his heart surgery in 1983. Mr. Becker passed away from cancer in 1995. "They don't know what they missed," says Pat Heath. "He's absolutely been the joy of my life. I still smile every time he walks into the room." (Personal communication with Pat Heath, Jan. 4, 2009.)

1. The Problem of Delay

Note the delays involved in *Phillip B.* and *Baby M.* What do you think the effect of this delay is on the lives of the children?

In The Best Interests of the Child: The Least Detrimental Alternative,[2] Goldstein, Freud, and Solnit emphasize that "children have their own built-in time

---

[2] Joseph Goldstein et al., The Best Interests of the Child: The Least Detrimental Alternative 9 (1996).

sense, based on the urgency of their instinctual and emotional needs and on the limits of their cognitive capacities. This results in their intolerance for postponement of gratification and their sensitivity to the length of separations."

What steps do you think might be taken to reduce the time social agencies and courts take in resolving custody disputes? Goldstein, Freud, and Solnit suggest that child placement decisions should be treated as "emergencies." Should appeals be eliminated? What effect would this have had in *Baby M* and *Phillip B.*?

2. Varieties of Custody Law

In many states, custody law reflects a complicated and chaotic multiplicity of such factors as the doctrinal thread invoked, the identity of the disputants, their prior relationship to the child, and the setting from which the dispute arose. Most states have four separate strands of law that can be used to resolve a custody dispute: (a) divorce law, (b) guardianship law, (c) juvenile court child neglect laws, and (d) laws relating to termination of parental rights to free a child for adoption.[3] Typically, no single court has jurisdiction over all four strands. Each strand is invoked most often between particular kinds of parties, but the strands often have overlapping application. Moreover, the term "custody" is itself ambiguous because each of the four strands normally carries different legal implications for the parent-child relationship.

Phillip B. and *Baby M* illustrate the possibility of overlapping application of the various strands of custody law and the complexity of the custody determination. The first action brought on behalf of Phillip was a neglect proceeding (see Chapter 4, p. 388). Later, the Heaths sought custody of Phillip through a guardianship proceeding. Finally, they initiated an action to adopt Phillip. How do the custodial rights of a guardian differ from those of an adoptive parent? *Baby M* was an adoption dispute, but was treated by the lower court much like a divorce custody dispute. Why? How did this affect the court's disposition of the case?

As background for consideration of these sorts of questions, a brief summary of the four dominant strands of custody law follows.

a. Juvenile Court Child Neglect Laws

The power of government to protect children by removing them from parental custody has roots deep in American history. By the early nineteenth century, the parens patriae power of the state was thought sufficient to empower courts of equity to remove a child from parental custody and appoint a suitable person to act as guardian.

Every state today has a statute allowing a court, typically a juvenile court, to assume jurisdiction over an abused or neglected child and to remove the child from parental custody under broad and vague standards reminiscent of those invoked by courts of equity in the nineteenth century. A complex social welfare bureaucracy,

---

[3] See Robert H. Mnookin, Child Custody Adjudication: Judicial Functions in the Face of Indeterminacy, 39 Law & Contemp. Probs. 226 (1975).

however, now is responsible for discovering children in need of protection and initiating appropriate judicial action. A case usually reaches juvenile court only after weaving its way through a process where numerous officials — including social workers, probation officers, and court personnel — may have had contact with the family. The judicial inquiry itself usually contains two stages: first, the court must determine whether it has jurisdiction over the child; if so, the second stage involves a dispositional hearing, where the judge decides the manner of intervention. The court may leave the child at home and require supervision of the home, psychological counseling for the family, or both. But often the court will remove the child from parental custody, subject to some court review of the family situation at a later date.

If the court removes the child from parental custody, it normally orders that the care and custody of the child be supervised by the welfare or probation department, which, in turn, will place the child with relatives, foster parents, or in an institution. Placement does not extinguish the natural parent's duty to support the child financially, although ordinarily the state and the federal governments bear the cost because most affected families are very poor. The state agency and ultimately the court — not the foster parents — are responsible for deciding where the child will live.

This process can generate a variety of custody disputes. The natural parent may object to the initial attempt to remove the child. After removal, the natural parent may seek the return of the child, and the social welfare department or foster parents may object. The foster parents may also object to the transfer of the child to some other foster home. For all of these sorts of disputes, the law of juvenile neglect provides the principal framework for resolution. Initially, most juvenile court neglect proceedings involve the child protection function, for usually an agency of the state is asking a juvenile court to deny custody to a child's parent or parents on the basis of abuse or neglect that is thought to require state intervention to protect the child. Some juvenile court proceedings, however, may involve the private dispute settlement function as well, for there may be competing private claimants.

b. Involuntary Termination of Parental Rights — Adoption

Adoption in this country normally requires that the rights of the natural parent first be extinguished. In most cases, the natural parent or parents consent to the adoption. But if the natural parents withhold consent, state laws provide for adoption without such consent under specified circumstances. Some states have separate proceedings for the involuntary termination of parental rights, and some authorize such termination as a remedy in neglect cases. Apart from contested termination proceedings, a custody dispute may arise if a natural parent challenges the adoption or attempts to withdraw his or her consent.

Termination cases often involve the child protection function: the state may initiate termination proceedings to free for adoption a child already a dependent of the juvenile court on the basis of allegations that the child has been neglected or abandoned by his natural parents. But termination proceedings may also arise out of situations where a stepparent wishes to adopt a spouse's child and therefore seeks to terminate the parental rights of the noncustodial natural parent. Where contested, these cases involve the private dispute settlement as well.

The legal consequences of termination are substantial. Termination extinguishes the natural parent's duty to support the child and may affect the intestate inheritance relationship between the child and his natural parents. More significantly for present purposes, however, the natural parent's custodial rights are completely abolished.

c. Divorce Custody Law

Most child custody disputes requiring judicial resolution arise out of the dissolution of marriage. When a child's parents live together, the issue of which parent has the right to custody does not arise. But when each parent has a separate household, they may disagree about who should have primary responsibility to care for the child. If a divorce is granted, a court at that time normally will determine who will have custody. Courts resolve disputes between parents before or after divorce as well. A substantial body of law (which is here styled "divorce custody law") provides standards for the resolution of such disputes. Although it normally applies to disputes simply between two parents, the occasion of divorce may also lead a relative or friend to ask for custody. In all events the application of divorce custody law nearly always involves the private dispute settlement function, for there are competing private parties — usually the child's parents — seeking custody on the basis of their relationship to the child; but when the court must evaluate a claim that one of the parties would endanger the child, the child-protection function may be involved as well.

When courts award "custody" incident to separation or divorce, the winner usually has less than all the rights included in custody within the on-going two-parent family. In some cases, the parents can have joint custody, with the child periodically living with each parent. In other cases, only one parent has custody, lives with the child, and makes decisions about care and education, including religious training. Such custody is usually subject to the other parent's rights of visitation. Moreover, the divorce decree can provide that the noncustodial parent must be consulted or must consent before certain important decisions are made about the child's education. Finally, the duty of support is often separated from the right to have the child live with the particular parent. In short, divorce custody law permits courts great flexibility in dividing the various legal elements of the parent-child relationship.

d. Guardianship Custody Law

The appointment of a guardian of a child's person (personal guardian) is normally made by a probate court. There are different types of guardians and the term is used to describe very different sorts of relationships, but a personal guardian basically has the exclusive right to decide where the child lives, can control and discipline the child, has the power to consent to the child's medical care, but has no duty to support a child.

Guardianship proceedings typically arise when neither of a child's parents is alive or available and a nonparent wishes to have custodial rights. Most guardianship appointments are probably uncontested, but when there are competing claimants, the dispute is governed by guardianship law. Sometimes a natural parent can be involved in such disputes. This may occur after the death of the parent who has had custody following a divorce. If the child's stepparent (i.e., the spouse of the deceased parent) or some other relative of the deceased parent wishes to become the child's legal guardian, the noncustodial natural parent may object. Sometimes guardianship proceedings are initiated by a noncustodial spouse who wishes appointment to defeat an earlier divorce custody decision. Occasionally, after a neglected child has been placed in foster care by a juvenile court, the foster parents will seek appointment as the guardian. A guardianship custody dispute nearly always involves the private dispute settlement function, for there are competing private litigants; but it may involve the child protection function as well if the court must evaluate a claim that one of the claimants will endanger the child.

3. Two Functions of Custody Law: Private Dispute Settlement and Child Protection

Arguably, courts perform two very different functions in the resolution of custody disputes: private dispute settlement and child protection. The *private dispute settlement* function is involved when the court must choose between two or more private individuals, each of whom claims an associational interest with the child. While such a dispute ordinarily arises between adults, it also affects the child. The characterization of this function as "private" does not imply that a court should treat a child as an "object" and consider only the interests of the adults. By providing a judicial forum, the state protects the substantial public interest in resolving such disputes without resort to private force or violence and also protects the expectations and interests of the individuals directly affected, including the child. The second function, *child protection,* involves the judicial enforcement of standards of parental behavior believed necessary to protect the child. This function is consistent with the well-established principle that the *parens patriae* power of the state empowers courts to remove children from parental custody if such a step is necessary for their protection.

In *Baby M,* what role was the court playing? Was it settling a private dispute between the natural father and the natural mother? Or was it exercising *parens patriae* authority on behalf of a child who was one of its wards? What about in *Phillip B.*? What other interests were at stake in these two cases? What are other purposes and functions of custody law? What are the appropriate roles for the court to play?

As you proceed through this chapter, consider the following questions: In private disputes, what standard should be used in resolving the competing claims of adults who wish to care for the child? What mechanisms, other than adjudication, may be appropriate?

4.   What Role Should Psychological Evidence Play in Deciding Custody Disputes? Should the Insights of Psychology and Psychiatry Be Used for Reformulation of Custody Standards?

Some time ago, a seminal note in the Yale Law Journal argued:

> Optimum custody goals [meeting the standard of the best interests of the child] may be further defined by concentration on the psychological well-being of the child, where "psychological well-being" is used to denote the mental and emotional health of the child — specifically, a process of personality development within the framework of patterns of normal growth as posited by the behavior sciences. [Note, Alternatives to "Parental Right" in Child Custody Disputes Involving Third Parties, 73 Yale L.J. 151, 157 (1963).]

Although suggesting that concern for the psychological welfare of the child, as opposed to the child's physical and material welfare, was implicit in the criteria sometimes referred to in cases applying the best interests of the child test, this note argued that courts should adopt a "psychological best interests test," id. at 162; and that "further inquiry should be made into the fundamental relationship between 'psychological' parent and child." Id. at 160. Under a psychological best interests test, it explained:

> [The] primary aim would be to identify and describe the existing affection-relationship(s), chiefly from the perspective of the particular child who is the subject of the custody dispute. Such relationships might be inferred from evidence shedding light on three questions: the continuity of the relationship between child and adult in terms of proximity and duration; the love of the adult toward the child; and the affection and trust of the child toward the adult. . . . [Id. at 162.]

A few years later, Professor Joseph Goldstein, himself trained in both law and psychiatry, wrote:

> If the law student (who is also hopefully the future judge) were to study the primary sources of psychoanalysis, he would see that at most and at best a psychoanalytically-informed definition of the child's *best interest* would assist court or adoption agency in deciding which disposition among available alternatives is likely to provide the child, whatever his endowments, with the best available opportunity to fulfill his potential in society as a civilized human being. [Joseph Goldstein, Psychoanalysis and Jurisprudence, 77 Yale L.J. 1053, 1076 (1968).]

And Professor Andrew S. Watson has suggested the appropriate roles for expert witnesses, lawyers, and judges in custody disputes and described various factors that would be relevant to the application of a psychological best interests of the child test.

There has been some movement to reformulate juvenile neglect and dependency standards on the basis of psychology as well. Some states have amended their child neglect statutes expressly to include "emotional" neglect. The Minnesota statute, for example, defines a neglected child in part as one whose parents fail to provide the child with "necessary food, clothing, shelter, education, and other care and control necessary for the child's physical, mental or *emotional* health and development, if the parent is physically and financially able." Minn. Stat. Ann. §260C. 301 (2007 & Supp. 2008) (emphasis added). In addition, state legislatures have enacted a broad range of civil and criminal statutes that take into account the negative impact of exposure to domestic violence upon children's psychological development (discussed in Chapter 3, supra).

The best known proposal to use psychology and psychiatry to establish guidelines for the reformulation of custody standards is found in Joseph Goldstein et al., Beyond the Best Interests of the Child (2d ed. 1979). Suggesting that legal standards give too little weight to the psychological well-being of the child, Goldstein, Freud, and Solnit propose "generally applicable guidelines" to govern all "child placement" disputes.[4] And they would require a court to choose for a particular child the "least detrimental available alternative," which the authors define as:

> [T]hat child placement and procedure for child placement which maximizes, in accord with the child's sense of time . . . the child's opportunity for being wanted . . . and for maintaining on a continuous, unconditional, and permanent basis a relationship with at least one adult who is or will become the child's psychological parent.[5]

Any "intervenor" — whether the state, natural parents, or others — who wishes to alter a child's placement would have the burden of establishing that the child is unwanted and if so, that his or her current placement is not "the least detrimental alternative." The focus would be exclusively on the interests of the child, and no preference would be given to the natural parent as such.[6]

In recent years, a new controversial psychological theory has emerged in high-conflict custody disputes. Several courts have considered psychological evidence in custody battles of the "parental alienation syndrome" (PAS). See, e.g., In re Marriage of Bates, 819 N.E.2d 74 (Ill. 2004) (holding that trial court did not abuse its discretion by allowing expert's testimony on parental alienation syndrome). PAS, a theory developed by psychiatrist Richard A. Gardner, identifies a set of conscious and unconscious behaviors by one parent to undermine the child's affection toward the other parent by means of a campaign of vilification and denigration. Dr. Gardner recommends that custody should be transferred to the other parent in severe cases of PAS. PAS has been criticized by many legal and psychological

---

[4] According to Goldstein, Freud, and Solnit, these procedures include "birth certification, neglect, abandonment, battered child, foster care, adoption, delinquency, youth offenses, as well as custody in annulment, separation, and divorce. These labels, in many ways reminiscent of the stultifying common law forms of action, have tended to obscure for scholar, draftsman, and practitioner, a problem common to all such procedures." Goldstein et al., Beyond the Best Interests of the Child 5 (1973).

[5] Id. at 99.

[6] See id. at 100. For a critical review of Goldstein, Freud, and Solnit's proposals, see Michael S. Wald, Thinking About Public Policy Toward Abuse and Neglect of Children: A Review of *Beyond the Best Interests of the Child,* 78 Mich. L. Rev. 645 (1980).

commentators who argue that it lacks any scientific basis and fails to take into account the many possible explanations for parental behavior, such as domestic violence or child abuse, the child's developmental stage, and the parent's caregiving abilities.

See generally Amy J.L. Baker, Adult Children of Parental Alienation Syndrome: Breaking the Ties That Bind (2007); Richard A. Gardner, The Parental Alienation Syndrome (2d ed. 1998); Michele A. Adams, Framing Contests in Child Custody Disputes: Parental Alienation Syndrome, Child Abuse, Gender, and Father's Rights, 40 Fam. L.Q. 315 (2006); Carol S. Bruch, Parental Alienation Syndrome and Parental Alienation: Getting It Wrong in Child Custody Cases, 35 Fam. L.Q. 527 (2001).

Having custody disputes determined by embracing more and more of the niceties of psychological and psychiatric theories requires careful analysis of the limits of these theories, their empirical bases, and the capacity of our legal system to absorb this new doctrine. Can psychologists and psychiatrists consistently differentiate between a situation where an adult and a child have a substantial relationship of the sort we characterize as parent-child and that where there is no such relationship at all? Do existing psychological theories provide a general basis for choosing between two adults when the child has some relationship and psychological attachment to each? In cases where, from the child's perspective, each claimant has a psychological relationship with the child, do you think there would often be widespread consensus among experts about which parent would prove psychologically better (or less detrimental) to the child? In many cases each parent will have a different sort of relationship with the child, with the child attached to each. One may be warm, easygoing, but incapable of discipline. The other may be fair, able to set limits, but unable to express affection. By what criteria is an expert to decide which situation is less detrimental? Moreover, even the proponents of psychological standards have acknowledged how problematic it is to evaluate relationships from a psychological perspective unless a highly trained person spends a considerable amount of time talking to the child or observing the parent and child interact. Superficial examinations by those without substantial training may be worse than nothing. And yet, such problems are surely high risks.

Even with the best trained experts, would the choice often be based on predictions that are beyond the demonstrated capacity of any existing theory?[7]

Note in *Baby M* the role played by experts in the original trial. Are you surprised by the lack of consensus?

---

[7] Numerous authors have criticized the value of psychological testimony for deciding child custody cases. For critiques, see Dana Royce Baerger et al., A Methodology for Reviewing the Reliability and Relevance of Child Custody Evaluations, 18 J. Am. Acad. Matrim. Law. 35 (2002); James N. Bow & Francella A. Quinnell, A Critical Review of Child Custody Evaluations Reports, 40 Fam. Ct. Rev. 164 (2002); Daniel A. Krauss & Bruce D. Sales, Legal Standards, Expertise, and Experts in the Resolution of Contested Child Custody Cases, 6 Psychol., Pub. Pol'y & L. 843 (2000).

5. How Much Weight Should Be Given to the Interests of the Biological Parents in Custody Disputes Involving Third Parties?

Goldstein, Freud, and Solnit in their book, Beyond the Best Interests of the Child (2d ed. 1979), define a "psychological parent" as "one who, on a continuing day-to-day basis, through interaction, companionship, interplay, and mutuality, fulfills the child's psychological needs for a parent, as well as the child's physical needs." Id. at 98.

(1) Should a "psychological parent" who is biologically unrelated to a child prevail in a custody dispute over a natural parent who is a stranger to the child? Third parties who have become "psychological parents" and who seek custody face an obstacle: According to the "natural parent presumption," biological parents are deemed to be the best persons to raise their children absent a showing of unfitness. This was the situation in *Phillip B.* Does it make a difference if the parent is not unfit and is a stranger to the child through no fault of the parent's? For the child, do the risks of removing the child from a "psychological parent" for placement with a psychological stranger outweigh the psychological benefits the child might receive by maintaining a better sense of lineage by living with the natural parent? The court found this to be true in *Phillip B.* Is this always the case? Are courts qualified to make that determination? What evidence is most valuable in helping them decide?

(2) When state officials in the course of child protection treat a child's parents unfairly and violate their rights, what effect (if any) should this have on subsequent judicial proceedings relating to the child? Recall the discussion in *Baby M* about the lower court's error in awarding temporary custody to the father instead of the mother. Did the court adequately address the effect of this error? Should it affect the outcome of the case?

6. What Role Should the Child Have in the Resolution of a Custody Dispute?

Normally, the parties most obviously affected by a dispute have a right to participate in the adjudicatory process. The essential issue in a child custody dispute is what will become of the child, but ordinarily the child is not a true participant in the process. While the best interests principle requires that the primary focus be on the interests of the child, the child ordinarily does not define those interests, nor does the child have representation in the ordinary sense. Even in states that allow for independent representation for the child in the dispute, the role of the child's advocate is different from that in normal adjudication. A lawyer usually looks to the client for instructions about the goals to be pursued. Except in the case of older children, a child's representative in a custody dispute must himself or herself normally define the child's interests.

Many states now require a judge to consider a child's expressed preference in applying the best interests standard in a divorce custody dispute between two parents, and sometimes, when those young persons are 12 to 14 years of age or older, statutes make their choice dispositive. Under California law, once children are 12, they have the right to nominate their own guardian and petition the court for the appointment. The court is to appoint the nominated guardian unless it determines that the nominee is unsuitable. Cal. Prob. Code §§1510, 1514 (West 2002 & Supp. 2008). (The child's preference is considered infra, pp. 625-626.)

California law provides no mechanism for considering the custody preferences of a child who is mentally disabled. However, the trial judge in *Phillip B.* used a hypothetical platonic dialogue between the court and Phillip as a way of considering Phillip's preference. Following is an account of the judge's presentation of this dialogue.

Robert H. Mnookin, The Guardianship of Phillip B.: Jay Spears' Achievement
40 Stan. L. Rev. 841, 849-850 (1988)

During the 10-day trial, the tension in the courtroom was palpable. The case aroused extraordinary emotions, and both sides viewed the stakes as profound. The Heaths believed that they were fighting for Phillip's chance to have a life worth living. The Beckers believed they were defending their integrity as parents.

On August 7, 1981, Judge William Fernandez summoned the parties and their lawyers to the courtroom, which was filled with reporters and well-wishers. When the judge began reading his opinion, [those gathered] had no idea what the result would be because during the trial, the judge had done nothing to tip his hand. Judge Fernandez wrote:

> California does not provide a method by which a mentally retarded child may state a preference. Other states have used a substituted judgment procedure to allow the court to state such a preference for the incompetent. This doctrine requires the court to ascertain as nearly as possible the incompetent person's "actual interests and preferences." . . .
>
> In our case the use of the substituted judgment method to arrive at Phillip's preference may best be stated in the form of a platonic dialogue with the court posing the choices to Phillip and Phillip's preference being ascertained from the more logical choice. The dialogue begins:
>
> *THE COURT:* Phillip . . . your first choice will lead you to a room in an institution where you will live. You will be fed, housed, and clothed but you will not receive any life prolonging medical care. . . . You will not be given an opportunity to add to your basic skills or to your motor skills and . . . will be treated as if you are incapable of learning and not fit to enter into society. You will not be allowed to become attached to any person, in fact efforts will be made to prevent any such attachments. Your biological parents will visit you occasionally, but their love and caring for you will at best be ambivalent. . . .
>
> Your second choice, Phillip, will lead you to a private home where you will be bathed in the love and affection of your psychological parents. . . . You will be given private tutoring and one on one training. . . . Your psychological parents believe that you are educable and will do all in their power to help you receive the education you may need to care for

yourself and to secure work when you are an adult. You will have a chance for life prolonging surgery as well as receiving all the medical care that you need. Even if life prolonging surgery cannot be performed, your psychological parents will always be there to comfort you and care for you in the dark times of your final illness. Best of all, your psychological parents will do all in their power to involve your biological parents in your habilitation and to unite both families together in ensuring for you a life that is worth living.

In my view, the dialogue would end with Phillip choosing to live with the Heaths.

Sad to say the foregoing legal analysis has no precedent in California law.

The judge went on to find that if detriment is defined as harm, then Phillip had suffered harm by the parenting of the Beckers: "severe emotional harm," "physical harm," "medical harm," and "the lasting harm by their stigmatization . . . as permanently mentally ill and disordered." He concluded by reading:

> [T]his is not a hearing to determine surgery for Phillip. That must wait another time and a sound parenting decision. This is a hearing for the purpose of giving Phillip Becker another parenting choice. It is a hearing responsive to Phillip's need for habilitation, and responsive to his desire for a chance to secure a life worth living. *I will give him that chance.*

When Judge Fernandez finished, the court personnel, the reporters in the courtroom, the Heaths, and their attorneys were in tears, not only because of the joyous result, but also because of this extraordinary demonstration of humanity by a courageous judge.

That day the judge signed the guardianship papers, appointing the Heaths guardians. He also authorized a heart catheterization to be done to determine if surgery was still possible. A court order also authorized the Heaths to take Phillip home for reasonable visitation, and later for custody. . . .

7. To What Degree Should the Legal Standards for the Resolution of Custody Disputes Be Discretionary?

Some time ago, Professors Foster and Freed wrote that nowhere has the task of achieving "a workable compromise between the values of flexibility and certainty . . . proved more challenging than in the area of child custody."[8] Although some commentators have attacked the breadth of discretion granted judges in resolving custody disputes, the limited role of appellate review, and the inadequate protection of normal procedural safeguards,[9] courts, legislators, and other commentators have shown enormous hostility toward the development of

[8] Henry H. Foster, Jr. & Doris Jonas Freed, Child Custody (Part I), 39 N.Y.U. L. Rev. 423 (1964).

[9] See, e.g., Robert J. Levy, Uniform Marriage and Divorce Legislation: A Preliminary Analysis 222-246 (1968); David L. Chambers, Rethinking the Substantive Rules for Custody Disputes in Divorce, 83 Mich. L. Rev. 477, 480-486 (1984); Michael Wald, State Intervention on Behalf of "Neglected" Children: A Search for Realistic Standards, 27 Stan. L. Rev. 985 (1975).

rules that provided tight substantive standards for custody disputes. The differences among families generate great pressure to treat each case on its own facts. American custody law has come to require a highly individualized determination of what is in the best interests of a particular child.

Note the sort of evidence the court ultimately relied on in deciding the "best interests" test in *Baby M*. To what degree do the criteria mentioned by the court reflect subjective judgments on the part of the judges about what is in Baby M's best interests?

If the legal standards for resolving a custody dispute are vague and imprecise, will this necessarily mean that a judge will rely on his personal values (and biases) to inform his choice? Is this a bad thing? More generally, what are the benefits and costs of having discretionary legal standards?

8.   One Set of Standards?

To simplify custody law, should there be a single set of legal standards for all custody disputes? As a matter of policy should the legal standards governing a custody dispute depend on the fortuity of which strand of custody law is invoked? Or since the legal consequences of a determination differ under the alternative strands (see pp. 470-473 supra), is there justification for different legal standards?

The distinction offered earlier between the child protection and the private dispute settlement functions helps explain why critics may be impatient with the remaining differences among the standards for the four strands of custody law. Either function can be involved in a judicial proceeding involving the application of any of the four strands of custody law, and a single case may involve both functions. Divorce custody law and guardianship law, for example, nearly always involve the private dispute settlement function, but either can involve the child protection function as well, if a court is required to evaluate a contention that one of the claimants would endanger a child. Cases involving the application of juvenile court child neglect laws or laws relating to termination of parental rights normally involve the child protection function — usually an agency of the state is asking the court to deny custody to a child's parent or parents on the basis of allegations that abuse or neglect endangers the child. The private dispute settlement function may be involved as well, however, if there are competing private parties, each prepared to make a long-term commitment to the child. And both functions are involved where, for example, a noncustodial father initiates a juvenile court child neglect proceeding to remove a child from his former wife's custody and have the child placed with him.[10] Similarly, a proceeding to terminate parental rights may also involve the judicial resolution of a private dispute, when it is initiated by a stepparent who wishes to adopt a child over the objection of a noncustodial natural parent.[11]

Significantly, both *Phillip B.* (see Chapter 4) and the *Rothman* case[12] used by Goldstein, Freud, and Solnit to illustrate their proposed standard, involved a custody fight between a biological parent who had no recent contact with the child and

---

[10] See, e.g., James M.M. v. June O.O., 740 N.Y.S.2d 730 (App. Div. 2002).
[11] See, e.g., In re Adoption of B.M.W., 2 P.3d 159 (Kan. 2000).
[12] Rothman v. Jewish Child Care Assn., 167 N.Y.L.J. 17 (1972).

foster parents who had a substantial relationship with the child and did not wish to give up custody. Thus, both cases encompassed a juvenile court proceeding that was a private dispute involving claimants prepared to make a long-term commitment to the child. In such circumstances, to use a standard different from that employed in private disputes in the divorce or the guardianship context seems anomalous, particularly if one believes that the child's needs should be the primary focus and that biological parenthood should not be dispositive. After all, if one's chief concern is with the child rather than with the impact on the parents or the legal consequences of the proceeding, then the fortuity of the strand of law invoked becomes an unacceptable basis for applying a different legal standard. But does the adoption of a single set of standards confuse the two different judicial functions and risk adverse policy consequences? To illustrate these consequences, the following article analyzes how the highly individualized determinations of what is either detrimental or in the best interests of a particular child contrast with the kinds of determinations usually required of courts in adjudication.

9.   The Indeterminacy of Present-Day Standards

Robert H. Mnookin, Child-Custody Adjudication: Judicial Functions in the Face of Indeterminacy
39 Law & Contemp. Probs. 226, 255-268 (Summer 1975)

When a judge must resolve a custody dispute, he is committed to making a choice among alternatives. The very words of the best-interests-of-the-child principle suggest that the judge should decide by choosing the alternative that "maximizes" what is best for a particular child. Conceived this way, the judge's decision can be framed in a manner consistent with an intellectual tradition that views the decision process as a problem of rational choice. In analyzing the custody decision from this perspective, my purpose is not to describe how judges in fact decide custody disputes nor to propose a method of how they should. Instead, it is to expose the inherent indeterminacy of the best-interests standard.

1. Rational Choice

Decision theorists have laid out the logic of rational choice with clarity and mathematical rigor for prototype decision problems. The decision-maker specifies alternative outcomes associated with different courses of action and then chooses that alternative that "maximizes" his values, subject to whatever constraints the decision-maker faces. This involves two critical assumptions: first, that the decision-maker can specify alternative outcomes for each course of action; the second, that the decision-maker can assign to each outcome a "utility" measure that integrates his values and allows comparisons among alternative outcomes. . . .

2. A Custody Determination Under the Best-Interests-of-the-Child Principle

Assume that a judge must decide whether a child should live with his mother or his father when the parents are in the process of obtaining a divorce. From the perspective of rational choice, the judge would wish to compare the expected utility for the child of living with his mother with that of living with his father. The judge would need considerable information and predictive ability to do this. The judge would also need some source for the values to measure utility for the child. All three are problematic.

a. The Need for Information: Specifying Possible Outcomes

In the example chosen, the judge would require information about how each parent had behaved in the past, how this behavior had affected the child, and the child's present condition. Then the judge would need to predict the future behavior and circumstances of each parent if the child were to remain with that parent and to gauge the effects of this behavior and these circumstances on the child. He would also have to consider the behavior of each parent if the child were to live with the other parent and how this might affect the child. If a custody award to one parent would require removing the child from his present circumstances, school, friends, and familiar surrounding, the judge would necessarily wish to predict the effects these changes would have on the child. These predictions would necessarily involve estimates of not only the child's mutual relationships with the custodial parent, but also his future contacts with the other parent and siblings, the probable number of visits by the noncustodial spouse, the probable financial circumstances of each of the spouses, and a myriad of other factors.

One can question how often, if ever, any judge will have the necessary information. In many instances, a judge lacks adequate information about even the most rudimentary aspects of a child's life with his parents and has still less information available about what either parent plans in the future. . . .

b. Predictions: Assessing the Probability of Alternative Outcomes

Obviously, more than one outcome is possible for each course of judicial action, so the judge must assess the probability of various outcomes and evaluate the seriousness of possible benefits and harms associated with each. But even where a judge has substantial information about the child's past home life and the present alternatives, present-day knowledge about human behavior provides no basis for the kind of individualized predictions required by the best-interests standard. There are numerous competing theories of human behavior, based on radically different conceptions of the nature of man, and no consensus exists that any one is correct.[161] No theory at all is considered widely capable of generating

---

[161] [A] comparison of five sample theories with competing implications [includes:]

1. Physiologically-oriented theories suggest that a child's personality is primarily determined by his physical structure or body type. See, e.g., W. Sheldon, The Varieties of Human Physique: An Introduction to Constitutional Psychology (1940).
2. Behaviorist theories view the child as broadly malleable and suggest that his personality development is shaped by environment through a system of reward and punishment. See, e.g., J. Watson, Behaviorism (1920); B. Skinner, Walden II (1948) (affording an extreme perspective on the implications possible in child rearing).
3. Psychoanalytic theories suggest that the interaction between parent and child sets into motion various developmental and unconscious forces that are the wellsprings of behavior.

reliable predictions about the psychological and behavioral consequences of alternative dispositions for a particular child.

While psychiatrists and psychoanalysts have at times been enthusiastic in claiming for themselves the largest possible role in custody proceedings, many have conceded that their theories provide no reliable guide for predictions about what is likely to happen to a particular child. Anna Freud, who has devoted her life to the study of the child and who plainly believes that theory can be a useful guide to treatment, has warned: "In spite of . . . advances there remain factors which make clinical foresight, i.e., prediction, difficult and hazardous," not the least of which is that "environmental happenings in a child's life will always remain unpredictable since they are not governed by any known laws . . . ."[163]

c. Values to Inform Choice: Assigning Utilities to Various Outcomes

Even if the various outcomes could be specified and their probability estimated, a fundamental problem would remain unsolved. What set of values should a judge use to determine what is in a child's best interests? If a decision-maker must assign some measure of utility to each possible outcome, how is utility to be determined?

For many decisions in an individualistic society, one asks the person affected what he wants. Applying this notion to custody cases, the child could be asked to specify those values or even to choose. In some cases, especially those involving divorce, the child's preference is sought and given weight. But to make the child responsible for the choice may jeopardize his future relationship with the other parent. And we often lack confidence that the child has the capacity and the maturity appropriately to determine his own utility.

Moreover, whether or not the judge looks to the child for some guidance, there remains the question whether best interests should be viewed from a long-term or a short-term perspective. The conditions that make a person happy at age seven to ten may have adverse consequences at age thirty. . . .

Deciding what is best for a child poses a question no less ultimate than the purposes and values of life itself. Should the judge be primarily concerned with the child's happiness? Or with the child's spiritual and religious training? Should the judge be concerned with the economic "productivity" of the child when he grows up? Are the primary values of life in warm, interpersonal relationships, or in

---

Freud stresses the importance of the first few years of life, when the child goes through distinct developmental stages. The parents' response to these stages will be the major determinant of the child's later personality. See generally S. Freud, Beyond the Pleasure Principle, in 18 Collected Works 7, 20-21 (J. Strachey ed. & transl. 1955).

4. Child-development and learning theories present the child as an active participant in the world around him, basically self-generating and activated by innate tendencies towards involving himself with his environment. See, e.g., J. Piaget, The Origins of Intelligence in Children (1952).

5. Interpersonal theories suggest that a child's developing personality is largely determined by the roles and expectations assigned to him by his family. See, e.g., H. Sullivan, The Interpersonal Theory of Psychiatry (1953).

[163] A. Freud, Child Observation and Prediction of Development — A Memorial Lecture in Honor of Ernst Kris, in 13 The Psychoanalytic Study of the Child 92, 97-98 (1958). . . .

discipline and self-sacrifice? Is stability and security for a child more desirable than intellectual stimulation? These questions could be elaborated endlessly. And yet, where is the judge to look for the set of values that should inform the choice of what is best for the child? Normally, the custody statutes do not themselves give content or relative weights to the pertinent values. And if the judge looks to society at large, he finds neither a clear consensus as to the best child rearing strategies nor an appropriate hierarchy of ultimate values. . . .

3. Why Some Custody Cases Are Easy to Decide

An inquiry about what is best for a child often yields indeterminate results because of the problems of having adequate information, making the necessary predictions, and finding an integrated set of values by which to choose. But some custody cases may still be comparatively easy to decide. While there is no consensus about what is best for a child, there is much consensus about what is very bad (e.g., physical abuse); some short-term predictions about human behavior can be reliably made (e.g., chronic alcoholism or psychosis is difficult quickly to modify). . . . Where one alternative plainly risks irreversible effects on the child that are bad and the other does not, there is no need to make longer-term predictions or more complicated psychological evaluations of what is likely to happen to the child's personality.

But to be easy, a case must involve only one claimant who is well known to the child and whose conduct does not endanger the child. If there are two such claimants or none, difficult choices remain. Most custody disputes pose difficult choices. . . . In many private disputes, the court must often choose between parties who each offer advantages and disadvantages, knowing that to deprive the child completely of either relationship will be disruptive. In a divorce custody fight, for example, where the mother is overprotective, possessive, and insecure and the father is demanding, aggressive, and hard-driving, how is the judge to decide where to place a seven-year-old child?

III. Implications of Indeterminacy

A. Would Rules Be Better?

Custody disputes are now decided on the basis of broad, person-oriented principles that ask for highly individualized determinations. The trial judge has broad discretion, but the question asked often has no meaningful answer. What are some of the implications of the use of indeterminate standards in custody disputes? Would more precise standards that ask an answerable question be better? . . .

More rule-like standards would avoid or mitigate some obvious disadvantages of adjudication by an indeterminate principle. For one thing, the use of an indeterminate standard makes the outcome of litigation difficult to predict. This may encourage more litigation than would a standard that made the outcome of more cases predictable. . . .

Indeterminate standards also pose an obviously greater risk of violating the fundamental precept that like cases should be decided alike. Because people differ and no two custody cases are exactly alike, the claim can be made that no process is more fair than one requiring resolution by a highly individualized, person-oriented standard. But with an indeterminate standard, the same case presented to different judges may easily result in different decisions. The use of an indeterminate standard means that state officials may decide on the basis of unarticulated (perhaps even unconscious) predictions and preferences that could be questioned if expressed. Because of the scope of discretion under such a standard, there is a substantial risk that decisions will be made on the basis of values not widely shared in our society, even among judges. . . .

. . . Today, custody disputes are ultimately assigned to courts for resolution, suggesting that a trial judge has the primary authority to decide, although it is not clear how decision-making responsibility is in fact shared by the trial judge with various other professionals (social workers, psychologists, psychiatrists) who also participate in the process. Implicit in some suggested reforms is the notion that the power to decide should be shifted from the judge to some other state official with different professional training. While judges may be ill-equipped to develop and evaluate information about the child, having some other state official decide or making various procedural adjustments (such as giving counsel to the child, providing better staff to courts, or making the proceedings more or less formal) will not cure the root problem. The indeterminacy flows from our inability to predict accurately human behavior and from a lack of social consensus about the values that should inform the decision. Procedural adjustments may make the system fairer and more efficient and may avoid some conspicuously erroneous determinations — goals worth pursuing. But neither greater use of existing expertise nor better procedures will make an indeterminate question answerable for an individual case.

Unlike procedural changes, adjudication by a more determinate rule would confront the fundamental problems posed by an indeterminate principle. But the choice between indeterminate standards and more precise rules poses a profound dilemma. The absence of rules removes the special burdens of justification and formulation of standards characteristic of adjudication. Unfairness and adverse consequences can result. And yet, rules that relate past events or conduct to legal consequences may themselves create substantial difficulties in the custody area. Our inadequate knowledge about human behavior and our inability to generalize confidently about the relationship between past events or conduct and future behavior make the formulation of rules especially problematic. Moreover, the very lack of consensus about values that makes the best-interests standard indeterminate may also make the formulation of rules inappropriate: a legal rule must, after all, reflect some social value or values. An overly ambitious and indeterminate principle may result in fewer decisions that reflect what is known to be desirable. But rules may result in some conspicuously bad decisions that could be avoided by a more discretionary standard. What balance should be struck? . . .

Like the choice in the judicial system of which party is to bear the burden of proof (or the risk of nonpersuasion), one's starting point as to the proper distribution of power can profoundly affect policy conclusions, particularly in the face of factual uncertainties and value clashes. Broadly speaking, there are three basic "starting points" for analyzing policies concerning children: (1) state paternalism, which assumes that the state has primary responsibility for children and ought to exercise full control over their lives, except where delegation to the family is justified; (2) family autonomy, which assumes that power and responsibility for children generally ought to be vested in private hands — essentially the family — except for cases where government rule can be justified; and (3) agnosticism, which rests on no preference and instead approaches individual policy issues on their own merits. . . .

. . . Even if one assumes that the sole criterion for evaluating the three alternative starting points is the interest of the child, there are affirmative justifications for making the family the presumptive locus of decision-making authority, particularly if there is no social consensus about what is best for children. Within the family, the child is more likely to have a voice in the decision, even if his wishes may not be determinative. Family members are more likely to have direct knowledge about a particular child. Affection for the child and mutual self-interest of family members are more likely to inform decisions. In all events, the evaluation of judicial functions in child custody that follows does not require a choice between family autonomy and agnosticism. Some of the policy recommendations do reflect, however, my rejection of state paternalism as a starting point, and it is useful here briefly to summarize the reasons.

First, state paternalism seems inconsistent with our historical and constitutional traditions. Indeed, family autonomy — the notion that those wishing a broader role for coercive governmental intrusion into the family carry a heavy burden of proof — has been the traditional American assumption. . . . The high value placed upon family autonomy . . . suggests a consensus that government may act coercively only when good cause is shown. Such a position would be consistent with our national ideological preference for decentralized decision-making, as generally evidenced by our economic and political system.

Second, state paternalism seems inconsistent with the present distribution of authority and responsibility for children. Most American families today enjoy substantial autonomy with regard to child rearing, and this has important implications for defining the limits of the child-protection function in custody disputes. The responsibility and opportunity of custody is assigned to a child's natural parents, and for the overwhelming majority of children, this simple rule suffices. For only a comparatively small proportion of children must a court resolve a custody dispute and perform either the private dispute-settlement or child-protection function.

Even if one were to accept paternalism as the starting point, broad definition of the child-protection function should be rejected because of its unfortunate consequences. What is best for children is often indeterminate; broad and discretionary standards for child-protection invite decisions based on the values of the particular judges and state officials responsible for a particular case. And apart from the internal integrity of the law, what has happened to children involved in the foster-care system — where the state has primary responsibility for the care of some children — should give pause to those seeking broader state authority. Indeed, even if one assumes that the family is simply a convenient instrument for the exercise of state power, an understanding of limitations with regard to resources, official talent, and what is known about human behavior is essential to the analysis of judicial role.

B. ADOPTION

INTRODUCTORY PROBLEMS

(1) Eloise and Dan Bernheimer divorce when their two children are two and four years old. Eloise is awarded custody of the children, but the father visits regularly every other weekend, and the children stay with him for six weeks in the summer. The children look forward especially to summer visits when their father takes them on camping trips, picnics, and spends a considerable amount of time with them. The children are attached to their father and to their paternal grandparents.

Eloise remarries when the children are four and six years old. Over the next two years, the stepfather, Ben Taylor, develops a close relationship with the children and petitions for adoption. The children say they love both of their fathers, but want to have the same last name as their mother.

a. Where the children's mother favors adoption by the stepparent, should the biological father's consent be an absolute requirement to the adoption? Should termination of the father's rights be permitted if he abandons the children? If he fails to support them? If a judge thinks it is in the children's best interest? Should the children's expressed preference be considered? Should it be dispositive?

b. Is it more to the advantage of the children to have a "complete" and integrated new two-parent family even if that risks the loss of an ongoing relationship of the child to the excluded biological parent?

c. Under the existing laws of most states, if the former husband and natural father does not consent, there must be statutory grounds for termination of his parental rights before the child can be adopted by the stepfather. How would termination of the biological father's rights be possible in such a case?

d. If stepparent adoption is not possible and the mother later dies, what standard should govern a custody dispute between the noncustodial biological father and the stepfather?

e. At the present time, adoption terminates the biological father's duty to support, creates a duty of support in the adopting father, and would extinguish the visitation rights of the biological father. Can you imagine a system of adoption that would make the consequences of adoption less drastic?

(2) Eighteen-year-old Mary Ann Jones wants to relinquish her newborn to the Good Shepherd Adoption Agency but she refuses to tell the agency who the father is. What efforts must the agency make to determine the identity of the father before it can proceed with an adoption? What would be required under the Uniform Parentage Act, infra p. 500?

(3) Barbara and Carol have been in a committed relationship for ten years. One year ago, after being artificially inseminated with sperm from an anonymous donor, Barbara gives birth to a son, Jack. Carol petitions the trial court to adopt Jack in a "second parent" adoption. How should the court decide? If a judge thinks it is in the child's best interests? Should Barbara's approval and consent be required? Should Barbara retain her parental rights, or should the court terminate her parental rights so that Jack will have only one legal mother?

Suppose Barbara and Carol's relationship subsequently breaks up. Barbara moves for court approval to withdraw her own consent to the adoption. Should Barbara's prior consent to the adoption be irrevocable? In the decision-making process, what difference (if any) would it make if Carol was the egg donor of the embryo that was implanted in Barbara's uterus?

(4) An 11-year-old adopted child wants to know who her biological parents are. Should she have the right to learn? In all circumstances? Never? Only if it is persuasively shown that lack of knowledge of her roots is contributing to severe emotional problems? Should it matter whether the child's adoptive parents are willing to have her learn? Whether the natural mother is willing to be identified? Who should decide? By what process? According to what standard?

1. Adoption: The Prerequisite of Consent or Involuntary Termination of Parental Rights

There are two primary methods for freeing a minor for adoption during the lives of the parents: (1) parental consent or (2) involuntary termination of parental rights. Although state statutes vary considerably, "abandonment" of the child by the biological parent is the most common basis for allowing adoption without the parent's consent. Traditionally, such provisions have been rather inflexibly inter-preted to require parental *intent to abandon* — that is, courts were reluctant to terminate parental rights merely because of the parent's demonstrated lack of interest.

However, the Uniform Adoption Act (UAA) facilitates termination in cases of abandonment. UAA was promulgated by the National Conference of Commis-sioners on Uniform State Laws in 1994 as a major reform of adoption law. Unif. Adoption Act §§1-8, 9 U.L.A. 11 (1994). UAA §3-504(c), 9 U.L.A. 86 (West 1999 & Supp. 2008), provides for termination of parental rights if a parent fails to make reasonable and consistent support payments, or to communicate or visit regularly with a child for a consecutive six-month period. In addition, accord-ing to the modern trend, jurisdictions are more supportive of terminating a biological parent's rights in the case of stepparent adoption.

Furthermore, all states allow involuntary termination of parental rights for child maltreatment. Usually the "neglect" standard for termination purposes is somewhat more stringent than for the assertion of juvenile court jurisdiction. Some case law and statutes go so far as to allow adoption without a biological parent's consent if it is in the child's best interests.

Unless parental rights are terminated, adoption requires that both parents consent, and that consent be given without fraud, duress, or undue influence. In addition, consent must be obtained in accordance with prescribed statutory pro-cedures. Some states also require the consent of the child being adopted if he or she is over a stated age, usually age 12 to 14.

This section and the next examine whether the general requirement of parental consent or termination of parental rights should be applied (1) in the case of a stepparent adoption; or (2) for unwed fathers when the mother is willing to relin-quish the child for adoption.

In re Adoption of Williams
766 N.E.2d 637 (Ohio Prob. Ct. 2002)

Wayne F. WILKE, Judge.

This matter came before the court on November 29, 2001, pursuant to Civ. R. 53(E)(4)(b), regarding objections to the decision of the magistrate [which recommended] that the consent of Shawn Williams, the child's biological father, was not necessary for this proposed stepparent adoption petition to proceed. . . .

Facts and Procedural Posture

The child was born on May 22, 1993 in Cincinnati, Ohio. His mother is Ingrid Sandidge and his biological father is Shawn Williams. Ingrid Sandidge and Jeffrey Sandidge were married on September 19, 1998, and Jeffrey Sandidge filed a petition to adopt the child on September 1, 2000.

The magistrate found that Shawn Williams made at least three telephone calls to the child in the year immediately prior to the filing of the adoption petition, although the respondent contends that he made even more calls than that. The magistrate also found that Shawn Williams sent birthday presents, consisting of toys and clothes, in the year immediately preceding the filing of the adoption and that Shawn Williams paid $125 for karate lessons on the child's behalf during that same one-year period. There is presently no court-mandated duty imposed upon Shawn Williams to pay any support. The question is whether Shawn Williams communicated with or supported his son in the year immediately preceding the filing of the adoption petition. If he did communicate with and support his son, then Shawn Williams's consent to the adoption is required. However, if he failed to communicate or to provide support for the child, then Shawn Williams's consent to the proposed adoption is not required.

Conclusions of Law

R.C. 3107.06 provides inter alia that a petition to adopt a minor may be granted only if the minor's biological mother and father consent to the adoption, unless a court finds that their consents are not required. A court may conclude that a biological parent's consent is not required if it finds that the parent has failed without justifiable cause to communicate with the minor or to provide for the maintenance and support of the minor as required by law or judicial decree for a period of at least one year immediately prior to the filing of the adoption petition. Failing to communicate with the minor and failing to provide for the minor are two reasons why a court might find a parent's consent to an adoption is not necessary. One of the problems in this area of law is that of defining what constitutes "failing to communicate" and "failing to support" (R.C. 3107.07[A]), so that a parent's consent is not required.

The seminal case in Ohio on what constitutes a lack of communication is In re Adoption of Holcomb, 481 N.E.2d 613 (Ohio 1985). In *Holcomb,* the court concluded that the legislature, in enacting R.C. 3107.07, opted for certainty. The court determined that a parent's consent is not required if there is a complete absence of communication for the one-year period and if there was no justifiable cause for the failure of communication.

Within a short time, members of the Supreme Court began to disagree about its holding in *Holcomb*. In In re Adoption of Bovett, 33 Ohio St. 3d 102, 515 N.E.2d 919 (Ohio 1987), the court shifted the burden to the parent opposing the adoption to show that any absence of communication or support was justifiable. The court in *Bovett* reaffirmed that it was obliged to strictly construe the statute's language but that it would not adopt a construction "so strict as to turn the statute into a sham." Id. at 106, 515 N.E.2d 919. Justice Douglas applauded the court's decision as a step in the right direction and wrote that trial courts need further guidance as to whether the making of one payment of support during the year or the sending of a Christmas card is enough to frustrate the operation of the statute. Id. at 107, 515 N.E.2d 919 (Douglas, J., concurring). Justice Douglas wrote that a probate court should not be bound "to negate the effect of the statute simply because a natural parent has made a payment or two during the year or has communicated once or twice during the year." Id. Indeed, R.C. 1.47(C) presumes that the intention behind every statute is a just and reasonable result. Several appellate decisions have subsequently followed Justice Douglas's position and have found de minimis efforts at communication and support insufficient to require that parent's consent. No statewide precedent has been established, however.

Recently, the First District Court of Appeals had the opportunity to interpret R.C. 3107.07 with respect to a man who, completely by chance, talked with his son for whom an adoption petition had been filed. The appellate court reversed this court's determination that one encounter was not sufficient "communication" within the meaning of R.C. 3107.07. In re Adoption of Tscheiner, 752 N.E.2d 292 (Ohio Ct. App. 2000). The court in *Tscheiner* stressed that there is an objective test for analyzing the failure of communication required by R.C. 3107.07(A) and that even one event of communication made that parent's consent to an adoption a requirement. In this case, there were at least three instances where the respondent communicated with his son and there was evidence that the respondent paid for some birthday gifts and for karate lessons. Accordingly, Shawn Williams's consent to this adoption is necessary and the objections to the decision of the magistrate are sustained.

Shawn Williams represents one of those parents written of by the Ohio Supreme Court in In re Adoption of Holcomb, supra. He is uncaring, unworthy, and unscrupulous. In this situation, three telephone calls and a petty amount of cash legally define and establish the respondent's relationship with his son and are sufficient to thwart an adoption by a well-meaning stepparent. That is sad and pathetic and reflects the development of case law that is inconsistent with social policy and values.

The underlying premise of adoption law is that a parent's consent to an adoption is required unless a court finds that it is not required. The next step after the consent phase is for a court to determine whether the adoption is in the child's best interest. Adoption proceedings should not, however, become "beauty contests" where a court is forced to make a subjective choice of who would make a better parent, in other words, to make a quasi-determination of the child's best interest at the beginning of the proceedings. On the other hand, a biological parent in many cases is voluntarily so far removed from a child's life that such a choice would be obvious. A chance encounter or single birthday card have been found to be sufficient communication to give standing to a biological parent to oppose an adoption, effectively preventing a child's best interest from ever being considered. Despite this harsh result for the child, this court is bound by the prior decisions of the Ohio Supreme Court and First District Court of Appeals.

There may very well come a time when a court, reviewing the facts in cases such as this, will be able to conclude that a parent's consent to an adoption is not necessary because the parent made only de minimis efforts at either communication or support. Unfortunately, this court is unable to make that determination today. The case law favors a black-letter rule that currently protects a nonconsenting parent's right to thwart an adoption at the expense of a child's best interest. In many cases, a nonconsenting parent is shielded by R.C. 3107.07, although his or her actions are in direct contravention of the common-law obligation of a parent to support a child and, of greater significance, the moral obligation to actually play a role in the child's life. The law should reflect that one's status as a parent requires more than being a name on a birth certificate. It should reflect that parenting is a full-time, on-going endeavor and not something to consider or address only when it is convenient. There seems to be growing recognition that the case law interpreting R.C. 3107.07 is not always beneficial to a child and can cause hardship. In many cases, a child who, through adoption, could have two loving and caring parents is shortchanged and left with one loving and caring parent, and one who gives his or her parental obligations as much thought as a "couch potato" would give in changing a television channel. This court is encouraged that eventually a fairer statute can be crafted (or a body of case law developed) that will more equitably determine whether a parent's consent to an adoption is required. . . .

QUESTIONS AND NOTES

(1) Background.   In 2005, there were approximately four divorces per eight marriages.[13] The high rate of divorce results in an increasing number of steprelationships when custodial parents remarry. Although stepparent and stepchild relationships resemble biological parent-child relationships in many regards, the legal ramifications of the steprelationship are not identical unless the stepparent formally adopts the child.

Stepparent adoption may be completed with the consent of a noncustodial biological parent who voluntarily agrees to a termination of parental rights. The noncustodial parent may be required to file a petition with the court and attend a judicial hearing. The court then makes a finding that the parent's decision is informed and voluntary, and that termination would be in the best interests of the child. However, if the biological parent objects to the adoption and the forfeiture of all rights vis-à-vis the child (including visitation rights), then the stepparent

---

[13] U.S. Bureau of the Census, Statistical Abstract of the United States: 2008 (tab. 121), available at *http://www.census.gov/compendia/statab.*

desiring to effectuate a legal parent-child relationship may have to institute a proceeding for involuntary termination of the noncustodial parent's rights.

In this contested termination proceeding, the noncustodial parent is entitled to constitutional protection. A line of Supreme Court cases, starting with Stanley v. Illinois, infra, pp. 495-498 and including Santosky v. Kramer, supra p. 368, guarantees certain substantive and procedural rights to parents in the face of involuntary termination proceedings. Generally, termination of parental rights requires proof of parental misconduct by clear and convincing evidence (see discussion of Santosky v. Kramer).

Are these substantive and procedural protections, which were developed to protect parental rights in the face of attacks by the state, appropriate in the private dispute context of the steprelationship situation?

(2) Suppose the biological parent refuses to consent to the stepparent adoption, as in *Williams.* The child continues to live in the mother's household with the new stepfather. Several years later the mother dies. What are the rights of the surviving custodial stepparent as against the noncustodial biological parent?

Traditionally, courts would have difficulty awarding custody of children to the surviving stepparent. However, courts have become more willing to assign custody of children to a stepparent involved in a custody dispute with a biological parent after the death of the other biological parent. See, e.g., Doncer v. Dickerson, 81 S.W.3d 349 (Tex. App. 2002) (holding that stepmother had standing to file suit to gain custody of six-year-old boy following the death of the child's father).

Another variation on this theme occurs if the stepparent and the custodial parent divorce. That is, suppose the Williams child lives with his mother and stepfather for several years. Then, the mother's second marriage is dissolved. The stepfather subsequently seeks either custody or postdivorce visitation regarding his former stepchild. How should this dispute be resolved?

Courts occasionally have granted custody in such situations to stepparents. See, e.g., In re Marriage of Riggs, 129 P.3d 601 (Kan. Ct. App. 2006). However, stepparents must overcome a statutory presumption favoring biological preferences as against third parties. Many states now also have statutes that provide explicitly or implicitly for visitation by stepparents. See, e.g., Kan. Stat. Ann. §60-1616 (2006). Some states add the additional requirement for visitation that the stepparent must have contributed to the child's support or stood in loco parentis. (Issues of visitation are discussed infra this chapter at pp. 597-617.) See generally Susan D. Stewart, Brave New Stepfamilies: Diverse Paths Toward Stepfamily Living (2007); Margaret M. Mahoney, Stepparents as Third Parties in Relation to Their Stepchildren, 40 Fam. L.Q. 81 (2006).

(3) Grandparents' Rights. The adoption of the child by a stepparent also raises the issue of grandparents' rights. Suppose Shawn Williams's mother has remarried and after adoption her new husband refuses to let the child's paternal grandparents (the first father's parents) visit. What rights, if any, do the grandparents have? The problem is especially poignant if the noncustodial parent has died and the grandparents' sole connection with that deceased parent is the grandchild.

In response to lobbying by grandparents' rights organizations, all 50 states enacted legislation granting grandparent visitation in limited circumstances. Some statutes permit visitation only in cases of the death or divorce of a parent.

Other statutes permit grandparent visitation even when the children remain in an intact family. Do grandparent visitation statutes unconstitutionally infringe on parental rights? See discussion of Troxel v. Granville, infra, p. 614.

(4) *Support and Inheritance Rights.* What are the consequences for the stepparent-child relationship if the biological parent refuses to give consent to adoption? A stepparent who has not adopted a stepchild generally has no legal obligation of support. Further, stepchildren who are not adopted by a stepparent have no right to inherit the stepparent's property through intestate succession laws — a rule that "undoubtedly is at odds with the wishes of many stepparents who die intestate." Ralph C. Brashier, Inheritance Law and the Evolving Family 157 (2004). In light of the increasing numbers of stepfamilies, should the above rules be changed? If so, how? Should there be an automatic rule of inclusion for stepchildren in intestacy schemes? See generally Peter Wendel, Inheritance Rights and the Step-Partner Adoption Paradigm: Shades of the Discrimination Against Illegitimate Children, 34 Hofstra L. Rev. 351 (2005).

(5) *Problem.* A legislator in the jurisdiction of Whiteacre proposes that the state legislature adopt the following progressive statute:

> A stepchild may inherit from a stepparent if (1) the parent-child relationship began during the stepchild's minority and continued throughout the parties' joint lifetimes and (2) clear and convincing evidence indicates that the stepparent would have adopted the child but for a legal barrier. [Cal. Prob. Code §6454 (West Supp. 2008).]

You are the legislator's intern. Advise the legislator on the merits and shortcomings of the proposed legislation.

(6) *Parental Visitation Following Stepparent Adoption.* How can we accommodate the desires and interests of both the biological noncustodial parent and the stepparent? Must it be an "all or none" situation — either severing the biological parent-child bond or giving the stepparent no real legal status vis-à-vis the child? In a classic law review article, Brigette M. Bodenheimer proposed a form of "weak" adoption — an intermediate form of adoption that permits the continuation of some contact between the biological parent and the child.[14] Courts were slow to adopt this proposal. However, "open adoption," which bears many similarities to Bodenheimer's proposal, has now become the trend. Indeed, adoption agencies that perform only closed adoptions have become the minority because agencies need to offer open adoption to stay competitive in the adoption market.[15]

In an open adoption, the birth mother and adoptive parents know each other's identities prior to the adoption, and the birth mother may exercise significant control over the choice of adoptive parents. The birth mother and adoptive parents then reach an agreement concerning the birth mother's postadoption relationship (often including visitation) with the child. Increasingly, courts are being asked to

---

[14] Brigette M. Bodenheimer, New Trends and Requirements in Adoption Law and Proposals for Legislative Change, 49 S. Cal. L. Rev. 10, 45-51 (1975).

[15] Amy L. Doherty, A Look at Open Adoption, 13 J. Contemp. Legal Issues 591, 592-593 (2000).

enforce such agreements and will generally uphold them if in the best interests of the child. Open adoption is discussed infra p. 527.

(7) Uniform Adoption Act. The UAA includes several innovative provisions regarding stepparent adoptions. The UAA makes a distinction between stepparent adoptions and adoption of a child who is a stranger to the adopted family. Under the UAA, a stepparent adoption does not cut off all rights of the biological parent or the family of the biological parent whose parent-child relationship ends at adoption (as in the stranger adoption). Thus, for example, the child does not lose his or her inheritance rights.

Moreover, UAA does not terminate the visitation rights of the former biological parent (or grandparents). That is, UAA authorizes open adoption in cases of stepparent adoption. Specifically, UAA permits a court to enter a post-adoption visitation order in favor of the former noncustodial parent — either by approving the parties' prior written agreement to that effect or, in the absence of such an agreement, by permitting visitation by a former parent (as well as by a grandparent or sibling of the adoptee) based on a determination of the child's best interests. UAA s4-113, 9 U.L.A. (pt. IA) 110-112 (1999 & Supp. 2008).

What are the advantages and disadvantages of this statutory reform? See generally Margaret M. Mahoney, Open Adoption in Context: The Wisdom and Enforceability of Visitation Orders for Former Parents Under Uniform Adoption Act §4-113, 51 Fla. L. Rev. 89 (1999). To date, UAA has only been adopted in Vermont. Uniform Law Commissioners Web site, *http://nccusl.org/Update/uniformact_factsheets/uniformacts-fs-aa94.asp* (last visited Nov. 12, 2008).

(8) ALI Principles. The American Law Institute, which conducted a decade-long project clarifying underlying principles of family law and making policy recommendations, also addresses the rights of stepparents. See ALI Principles of the Law of Family Dissolution: Analysis and Recommendations (2002). The Principles recognize several types of parents: legal parents (as defined by state law), "parents by estoppel," and "de facto parents." A "parent by estoppel" is a person who acts as a parent in circumstances that would estop the child's legal parent from denying the claimant's parental status. Parent-by-estoppel status may be created when an individual (1) is obligated for child support, or (2) has lived with the child for at least two years and has a reasonable belief that he is the father, or (3) has had an agreement with the child's legal parent since birth (or for at least two years) to serve as a co-parent provided that recognition of parental status would serve the child's best interests. ALI Principles §2.03(1)(b).

In contrast, a de facto parent is a person, other than a legal-parent or a parent by estoppel, who has regularly performed an equal or greater share of caretaking as the parent with whom the child primarily lived, lived with the child for a significant period (not less than two years), and acted as a parent for nonfinancial reasons (and with the agreement of a legal parent) or as a result of a complete failure or inability of any legal parent to perform caretaking functions. Id. at §2.03(1)(c).

If a stepparent qualifies as a parent by estoppel or a de facto parent, an application of the ALI Principles would result in the recognition of that stepparent's right to custody or visitation following the death of a custodial parent or the dissolution of the custodial parent's relationship with the stepparent. For a discussion and critique of these doctrines, see Mary Ann Mason & Nicole Zayac, Rethinking

Stepparent Rights: Has the ALI Found a Better Definition?, 36 Fam. L.Q. 227 (2002); Sarah H. Ramsey, Constructing Parenthood for Stepparents: Parents by Estoppel, and De Facto Parents Under the American Law Institute's Principles of the Law of Family Dissolution, 8 Duke J. Gender L. & Pol'y 285 (2001).

2. Adoption and the Unwed Father

A substantial portion of nonrelative adoptions involve nonmarital children. Before 1972 the fathers of such children had no substantial parental rights. Adoption required only the mother's consent, and the statutory adoption scheme did not require notice to the father that the child was being placed for adoption. In terms of the consent requirement, many states distinguished between unwed fathers who had legitimated their offspring (whose consent was required) and those who had not legitimated their offspring (whose consent was not required). A father may legitimate a child by compliance with statutory requirements (e.g., by marrying the mother after the birth, or acknowledging the child publicly and/or receiving the child into his home).

The picture changed in 1972 with the case of Stanley v. Illinois and the subsequent promulgation of the Uniform Parentage Act in 1973. *Stanley* was proclaimed as a vindication of the rights of unwed fathers. Note that *Stanley* was not an adoption case, but rather a neglect case. Yet, its impressive shadow was cast on adoption as well.

Stanley v. Illinois
405 U.S. 645 (1972)

Mr. Justice WHITE delivered the opinion of the Court.

Joan Stanley lived with Peter Stanley intermittently for 18 years, during which time they had three children. When Joan Stanley died, Peter Stanley lost not only her but also his children. Under Illinois law, the children of unwed fathers become wards of the State upon the death of the mother. Accordingly, upon Joan Stanley's death, in a dependency proceeding instituted by the State of Illinois, Stanley's children were declared wards of the State and placed with court-appointed guardians. Stanley appealed, claiming that he had never been shown to be an unfit parent and that since married fathers and unwed mothers could not be deprived of their children without such a showing, he had been deprived of the equal protection of the laws guaranteed him by the Fourteenth Amendment. . . .

Stanley presses his equal protection claim here. . . . We granted certiorari to determine whether this method of procedure by presumption could be allowed to stand in light of the fact that Illinois allows married fathers — whether divorced, widowed, or separated — and mothers — even if unwed — the benefit of the presumption that they are fit to raise their children.

We must . . . examine [this] question. . . . Is a presumption that distinguishes and burdens all unwed fathers constitutionally repugnant? We conclude that, as a matter of due process of law, Stanley was entitled to a hearing on his fitness as a parent before his children were taken from him and that, by denying him a hearing and extending it to all other parents whose custody of their children is challenged, the State denied Stanley the equal protection of the laws guaranteed by the Fourteenth Amendment.

Illinois has two principal methods of removing nondelinquent children from the homes of their parents. In a dependency proceeding it may demonstrate that the children are wards of the State because they have no surviving parent or guardian. Ill. Rev. Stat., c. 37, §§702-1, 702-5. In a neglect proceeding it may show that children should be wards of the State because the present parent(s) or guardian does not provide suitable care. Ill. Rev. Stat., c. 37, §§702-1, 702-4.

The State's right — indeed, duty — to protect minor children through a judicial determination of their interests in a neglect proceeding is not challenged here. Rather, we are faced with a dependency statute that empowers state officials to circumvent neglect proceedings on the theory that an unwed father is not a "parent" whose existing relationship with his children must be considered. "Parents," say the State, "means the father and mother of a legitimate child, or the survivor of them, or the natural mother of an illegitimate child, and includes any adoptive parent," Ill. Rev. Stat., c. 37, §701-14, but the term does not include unwed fathers.

Under Illinois law, therefore, while the children of all parents can be taken from them in neglect proceedings, that is only after notice, hearing, and proof of such unfitness as a parent as amounts to neglect, an unwed father is uniquely subject to the more simplistic dependency proceeding. By use of this proceeding, the State, on showing that the father was not married to the mother, need not prove unfitness in fact, because it is presumed at law. Thus, the unwed father's claim of parental qualification is avoided as "irrelevant."

In considering this procedure under the Due Process Clause, we recognize, as we have in other cases, that due process of law does not require a hearing "in every conceivable case of government impairment of private interest." Cafeteria Workers v. McElroy, 367 U.S. 886, 894 (1961). That case explained that "[t]he very nature of due process negates any concept of inflexible procedures universally applicable to every imaginable situation" and firmly established that "what procedures due process may require under any given set of circumstances must begin with a determination of the precise nature of the government function involved as well as of the private interest that has been affected by governmental action." . . .

The private interest here, that of a man in the children he has sired and raised, undeniably warrants deference and, absent a powerful countervailing interest, protection. . . . The Court has frequently emphasized the importance of the family. The rights to conceive and to raise one's children have been deemed "essential," Meyer v. Nebraska, 262 U.S. 390, 399 (1923). . . . "It is cardinal with us that the custody, care and nurture of the child reside first in the parents, whose primary function and freedom include preparation for obligations the state can neither supply nor hinder." Prince v. Massachusetts, 321 U.S. 158, 166 (1944). . . .

Nor has the law refused to recognize those family relationships unlegitimized by a marriage ceremony. The Court has declared unconstitutional a state statute denying natural, but illegitimate, children a wrongful-death action for the death of their mother, emphasizing that such children cannot be denied the right of other children because familial bounds in such cases were often as warm, enduring, and important as those arising within a more formally organized family unit. Levy v. Louisiana, 391 U.S. 68, 71-72 (1968). "To say that the test of equal protection should be the 'legal' rather than the biological relationship is to avoid the issue. For the Equal Protection Clause necessarily limits the authority of a State to draw such 'legal' lines as it chooses." Glona v. American Guarantee Co., 391 U.S. 73, 75-76 (1968). These authorities make it clear that, at the least, Stanley's interest in retaining custody of his children is cognizable and substantial.

For its part, the State has made its interest quite plain: Illinois has declared that the aim of the Juvenile Court Act is to protect "the moral, emotional, mental, and physical welfare of the minor and the best interests of the community" and to "strengthen the minor's family ties whenever possible, removing him from the custody of his parents only when his welfare or safety or the protection of the public cannot be adequately safeguarded without removal. . . ." Ill. Rev. Stat., c. 37, §§701-2. These are legitimate interests, well within the power of the State to implement. We do not question the assertion that neglectful parents may be separated from their children.

But we are not asked to evaluate the legitimacy of the state ends, rather, to determine whether the means used to achieve these ends are constitutionally defensible. What is the state interest in separating children from fathers without a hearing designed to determine whether the father is unfit in a particular disputed case? We observe that the State registers no gain towards its declared goals when it separates children from the custody of fit parents. Indeed, if Stanley is a fit father, the State spites its own articulated goals when it needlessly separates him from his family. . . .

It may be, as the State insists, that most unmarried fathers are unsuitable and neglectful parents. It may also be that Stanley is such a parent and that his children should be placed in other hands. But all unmarried fathers are not in this category; some are wholly suited to have custody of their children. This much the State readily concedes, and nothing in this record indicates that Stanley is or has been a neglectful father who has not cared for his children. Given the opportunity to make his case, Stanley may have been seen to be deserving of custody of his offspring. Had this been so, the State's statutory policy would have been furthered by leaving custody in him. . . .

It may be argued that unmarried fathers are so seldom fit that Illinois need not undergo the administrative inconvenience of inquiry in any case, including Stanley's. The establishment of prompt efficacious procedures to achieve legitimate state ends is a proper state interest worthy of cognizance in constitutional adjudication. But the Constitution recognizes higher values than speed and efficiency. . . .

Procedure by presumption is always cheaper and easier than individualized determination. But when, as here, the procedure forecloses the determinative issues of competence and care, when it explicitly disdains present realities in deference to past formalities, it needlessly risks running roughshod over the important interests of both parent and child. It therefore cannot stand.[9]

---

[9] We note in passing that the incremental cost of offering unwed fathers an opportunity for individualized hearings on fitness appears to be minimal. If unwed fathers, in the main, do not care about the disposition of their children, they will not appear to demand hearings. If they do care, under the scheme here held invalid, Illinois would admittedly at some later time have to afford them a properly focused hearing in a custody or adoption proceeding. . . .

. . . The State's interest in caring for Stanley's children is de minimis if Stanley is shown to be a fit father. It insists on presuming rather than proving Stanley's unfitness solely because it is more convenient to presume than to prove. Under the Due Process Clause that advantage is insufficient to justify refusing a father a hearing when the issue at stake is the dismemberment of his family.

The State of Illinois assumes custody of the children of married parents, divorced parents, and unmarried mothers only after a hearing and proof of neglect. The children of unmarried fathers, however, are declared dependent children without a hearing on parental fitness and without proof of neglect. Stanley's claim in the state courts and here is that failure to afford him a hearing on his parental qualifications while extending it to other parents denied him equal protection of the laws. We have concluded that all Illinois parents are constitutionally entitled to a hearing on their fitness before their children are removed from their custody. It follows that denying such a hearing to Stanley and those like him while granting it to other Illinois parents is inescapably contrary to the Equal Protection Clause.

NOTES AND QUESTIONS

(1) Whose rights are being vindicated in *Stanley?* The father's? The children's? Both?

(2) Unnamed Father's Due Process Rights.   Is *Stanley* a procedural case, dealing with the hearing rights of parents? A substantive case, limiting the circumstances when the state may remove children from parental circumstances? Or both? Does *Stanley* mean that a parent has a constitutional right to custody of his children vis-à-vis the state unless unfit? Or only that a parent is entitled to an opportunity to be heard before being deprived of custody? Suppose state law provides that the parental rights of the father of a nonmarital child could be terminated after notice to the father and a full hearing, if a court determines that termination is in the child's best interest. Would *Stanley* speak to this question? See pp. 513-517 infra.

(3) Stanley's Effect on Adoption Law.   Broadly speaking, there are several questions concerning *Stanley's* effect on adoption law:

a. In what circumstances is the consent to adoption by an unmarried father required? Does *Stanley* apply to all fathers of nonmarital children or only to those with some substantial contact with their children?

b. When consent is required, should the adoption necessarily be frustrated by the birth father's refusal?

c. If the unmarried father's consent is not required, does he nevertheless have a right to notice of a pending adoption and a right to participate in the proceedings?

d. What affirmative obligation is there to determine who the father is? Suppose the mother will not say or cannot say who the father is? Should adoption be possible? If a man later shows up claiming that he is the father, what remedies should he have if inadequate steps were taken before the adoption?

(4) Uniform Parentage Act: Paternity Provisions. In the aftermath of *Stanley,* these questions generated conflicting answers, both legislative and judicial. Some answers were provided by the Uniform Parentage Act (UPA) in 1973, which reformed the law regarding parentage, paternity actions, and child support. The UPA was adopted in its entirety by 19 states, but many additional states enacted significant portions of it. Unif. Parentage Act, Prefatory Note, 9B U.L.A. 296-298 (West 2001 & Supp. 2008). According to the original UPA, judicial notice was required to a "presumed father" (as well as to one whose paternity was judicially established) before the father's rights could be terminated. Under the UPA, a man was presumed to be the biological father of a child (1) if he married the mother (before or after the birth) or attempted to do so but the marriage was invalid (§4(a)(1), (2), and (3)); or (2) if he held out the child as his and received the child into his home (id. at (4)); or (3) if he acknowledged paternity in a writing that was filed with the appropriate authorities (id. at (5)). The presumption of paternity could be rebutted by clear and convincing evidence (id. at (b)). If conflicting presumptions arose, the presumption that was founded on "weightier considerations of policy and logic control[led]" (id.).

(5) Revised Uniform Parentage Act: Paternity Provisions. Technological advances in paternity establishment made the original UPA obsolete, and it was revised in 2000 and amended in 2002. The revised UPA replaces two other uniform acts that address parentage: the Uniform Status of Children of Assisted Conception Act (USCACA), created to establish legal parentage for children born via nontraditional means; and the Uniform Putative and Unknown Fathers Act (UPUFA), which allows the identification of putative and unknown fathers and the termination of their parental rights.

The revised UPA makes several improvements to the original Act. The new Act provides for four definitions of "father": (1) an "acknowledged father," who acknowledges paternity in accordance with the requirements established in Article 3 (with the concurrence of the mother and that is treated as an adjudication of paternity); (2) a judicially "adjudicated father"; (3) an "alleged father," who is asserted to be, or asserts himself to be or possibly to be, the father of a child (replacing the former term "putative" father); and (4) a "presumed father," who satisfies the circumstances establishing a presumption of paternity in §204.

For presumed fathers, the revised UPA clarifies the "holding out" requirement. The 1973 UPA neglected to specify a duration for the "holding out" requirement to establish a presumption of paternity (providing merely that any "holding out" was sufficient during a child's minority) (§4(a)(4)). This omission created uncertainty about whether the presumption arose either if the "holding out" occurred for a short time or if it commenced long after birth. The revised UPA requires that the man must reside with the child for the first two years of the child's life to establish the presumption of paternity.

In addition, the original UPA created a presumption of paternity for a man who acknowledged paternity in a writing filed with the appropriate agency (and if the mother failed to dispute that acknowledgment within a reasonable time). The revised UPA omits this presumption because it conflicts with a different provision of the revised Act that allows a valid acknowledgment actually to *establish* paternity rather than to establish a *presumption* of paternity. Because of the advent and accuracy of genetic testing, the revised UPA also omits the clear-and-convincing standard required to rebut the presumption as well as the provision regarding conflicting presumptions of paternity. Moreover, under the revised UPA, a court may use estoppel principles in appropriate circumstances to deny requests for genetic testing in the interest of preserving a child's ties to a presumed or acknowledged father who openly holds himself out as the child's father, regardless of whether he is in fact the genetic father.

The revised UPA also addresses the father's right to notice of a proceeding for adoption or termination of parental rights. Under the new UPA, if the man registers, he may protect his right to notice (assuming that the state of registration is the same state as the birth). The protection of his right to notice in other situations depends on the age of the child. For children aged one year and older at the time of the proceeding for adoption of termination of parental rights, notice must be given to every alleged father whether or not he has registered (§405). To facilitate infant adoptions, the revised UPA places a burden on the father to register if he wants to be notified of an adoption proceeding. The man's failure to register in cases of a child less than one year of age will result in waiver of his rights (§404), unless (1) a father-child relationship has been established under the Act or other law or (2) he has commenced a proceeding to adjudicate his paternity before the court terminates his parental rights.

The revised UPA also takes into account federal legislation regarding the acknowledgment procedure mandated by the Personal Responsibility and Work Opportunity Reconciliation Act (PRWORA) of 1996. Because PRWORA does not preclude the possibility that a child may have both a presumed and acknowledged parent, the new UPA provides that a presumed father must file a denial of paternity for another man's acknowledgment of paternity to be valid.

Eight states currently have adopted the revised Uniform Parentage Act. See Uniform Law Commissioners, A Few Facts About the Uniform Parentage Act, Legislative Fact Sheet, available at *http://www.nccusl.org/Update/uniformact_factsheets/uniformacts-fs-upa.asp* (last visited Jan. 6, 2009). For critiques of the revised UPA, see Nancy E. Dowd, Parentage at Birth: Birth Fathers and Social Fathers, 14 Wm. & Mary Bill Rts. J. 909 (2006) (proposing changes to the UPA); Paula Roberts, Truth and Consequences, Questioning the Paternity of Marital Children, 37 Fam. L.Q. 55 (2003). For further discussion of the requirements to identify unknown fathers, see infra pp. 513-515.

Uniform Parentage Act (2000, as amended in 2002)
9B U.L.A. 309-311, 313-314, 322-324 (2001 & Supp. 2008)

§201. Establishment of Parent-Child Relationship

(a) The mother-child relationship is established between a woman and a child by:

(1) the woman's having given birth to the child[, except as otherwise provided in [Article] 8];

(2) an adjudication of the woman's maternity; [or]

(3) adoption of the child by the woman[; or

(4) an adjudication confirming the woman as a parent of a child born to a gestational mother if the agreement was validated under Article 8 or is enforceable under other law].

(b) The father-child relationship is established between a man and a child by:

(1) an unrebutted presumption of the man's paternity of the child under Section 204;

(2) an effective acknowledgment of paternity by the man under [Article] 3, unless the acknowledgment has been rescinded or successfully challenged;

(3) an adjudication of the man's paternity;

(4) adoption of the child by the man; [or]

(5) the man's having consented to assisted reproduction by a woman under [Article] 7 which resulted in the birth of the child[; or

(6) an adjudication confirming the man as a parent of a child born to a gestational mother if the agreement was validated under [Article] 8 or is enforceable under other law].

§204. Presumption of Paternity

(a) A man is presumed to be the father of a child if:

(1) he and the mother of the child are married to each other and the child is born during the marriage;

(2) he and the mother of the child were married to each other and the child is born within 300 days after the marriage is terminated by death, annulment, declaration of invalidity, or divorce[, or after a decree of separation];

(3) before the birth of the child, he and the mother of the child married each other in apparent compliance with law, even if the attempted marriage is or could be declared invalid, and the child is born during the invalid marriage or within 300 days after its termination by death, annulment, declaration of invalidity, or divorce[, or after a decree of separation];

(4) after the birth of the child, he and the mother of the child married each other in apparent compliance with law, whether or not the marriage is or could be declared invalid, and he voluntarily asserted his paternity of the child, and:

(A) the assertion is in a record filed with [state agency maintaining birth records];

(B) he agreed to be and is named as the child's father on the child's birth certificate; or

(C) he promised in a record to support the child as his own; or

(5) for the first two years of the child's life, he resided in the same household with the child and openly held out the child as his own.

(b) A presumption of paternity established under this section may be rebutted only by an adjudication under [Article] 6.

§301. Acknowledgment of Paternity

The mother of a child and a man claiming to be the genetic father of the child may sign an acknowledgment of paternity with intent to establish the man's paternity.

§302. Execution of Acknowledgment of Paternity

(a) An acknowledgment of paternity must:
    (1) be in a record;
    (2) be signed, or otherwise authenticated, under penalty of perjury by the mother and by the man seeking to establish his paternity;
    (3) state that the child whose paternity is being acknowledged:
        (A) does not have a presumed father, or has a presumed father whose full name is stated; and
        (B) does not have another acknowledged or adjudicated father;
    (4) state whether there has been genetic testing and, if so, that the acknowledging man's claim of paternity is consistent with the results of the testing; and
    (5) state that the signatories understand that the acknowledgment is the equivalent of a judicial adjudication of paternity of the child and that a challenge to the acknowledgment is permitted only under limited circumstances and is barred after two years.
(b) An acknowledgment of paternity is void if it:
    (1) states that another man is a presumed father, unless a denial of paternity signed or otherwise authenticated by the presumed father is filed with the [agency maintaining birth records];
    (2) states that another man is an acknowledged or adjudicated father; or
    (3) falsely denies the existence of a presumed, acknowledged, or adjudicated father of the child.
(c) A presumed father may sign or otherwise authenticate an acknowledgment of paternity.

§402. Registration for Notification

(a) Except as otherwise provided in subsection (b) or Section 405, a man who desires to be notified of a proceeding for adoption of, or termination of parental rights regarding, a child that he may have fathered must register in the registry of paternity before the birth of the child or within 30 days after the birth.
(b) A man is not required to register if [:
    (1)] a father-child relationship between the man and the child has been established under this [Act] or other law [; or

(2) the man commences a proceeding to adjudicate his paternity before the court has terminated his parental rights].

(c) A registrant shall promptly notify the registry in a record of any change in the information registered. The [agency maintaining the registry] shall incorporate all new information received into its records but need not affirmatively seek to obtain current information for incorporation in the registry.

§403. Notice of Proceeding

Notice of a proceeding for the adoption of, or termination of parental rights regarding, a child must be given to a registrant who has timely registered. Notice must be given in a manner prescribed for service of process in a civil action.

§404. Termination of Parental Rights: Child Under One Year of Age

The parental rights of a man who may be the father of a child may be terminated without notice if:

(1) the child has not attained one year of age at the time of the termination of parental rights;

(2) the man did not register timely with the [agency maintaining the registry]; and

(3) the man is not exempt from registration under Section 402.

§405. Termination of Parental Rights: Child at Least One Year of Age

(a) If a child has attained one year of age, notice of a proceeding for adoption of, or termination of parental rights regarding, the child must be given to every alleged father of the child, whether or not he has registered with the [agency maintaining the registry].

(b) Notice must be given in a manner prescribed for service of process in a civil action.

———————————

Subsequent Supreme Court opinions generated additional answers to the many questions left unresolved in the wake of *Stanley.*

Quilloin v. Walcott, 434 U.S. 246 (1978), involved a Georgia statute providing that only the mother of nonmarital child need consent to the adoption of that child unless the father had legitimated the child by marriage and acknowledgment, or by court order. The biological father in *Quilloin* had never lived with the mother and the child, and had never legitimated the child. Shortly after the mother gave birth to the child, she married another man. Adoption was sought by the mother's new husband with whom the child had been living for approximately nine years. The child's biological father, although he had never sought custody before, had made some support payments and had visited the child on numerous occasions. At the time of the dispute, the child himself, then about 11 years old, expressed a desire to be adopted.

The child's biological father was given notice of the adoption petition and participated in a hearing at which he petitioned to be declared the child's legitimate father and to be granted visitation. He also petitioned that the adoption be denied. The Supreme Court affirmed the trial court's opinion granting the adoption on the ground that it was in the child's best interests. The Court rejected both Quilloin's due process and equal protection claims: (1) that due process prohibited termination of his parental rights without a finding of unfitness; and, (2) that the distinction between unmarried and married fathers violated the Equal Protection Clause. The Court held that the father's due process rights were not violated, although it conceded that due process probably would require a showing of unfitness before involuntarily separating a "natural family." Because Quilloin had never had or sought custody, the Court said this requirement was inapplicable to him. The Court also rejected his equal protection argument on the ground that his interests were distinguishable from those of a married father because the latter had borne legal responsibility for the rearing of his children.

Quilloin implied that the extent of an unwed father's rights depended on the nature of his relationship with his child(ren). A year after *Quilloin,* the Court further clarified its views on the rights of unwed fathers in Caban v. Mohammed, 441 U.S. 380 (1979). The New York statute challenged in *Caban* provided that a nonmarital child could be adopted with the consent of the mother alone, without the necessity for the biological father's consent. Although the unwed mother could block the adoption of her child by withholding her consent, the unwed father had no such right — even if his parental relationship was substantial. Such was the case in *Caban.* Abdiel Caban lived with Maria Mohammed for five years, during which time they had two children. When the couple separated, Mohammed went to live with another man whom she thereafter married. Caban continued to see the children frequently and at one point had custody of them. When the Mohammeds petitioned to adopt the children, the natural father and his new wife cross-petitioned for adoption. At the time of the hearing, the children were four and six years old. The trial judge approved the adoption on behalf of the Mohammeds.

In *Caban* the Supreme Court held that the statutory distinction between the rights of mothers and fathers of nonmarital children violated the Equal Protection Clause. The Court stated:

> We find that the distinction in [the statute] between unmarried mothers and unmarried fathers, as illustrated by this case, does not bear a substantial relation to the State's interest in providing adoptive homes for its illegitimate children . . .
> The New York Court of Appeals in In re Malpica-Orsini [331 N.E.2d 486 (N.Y. 1975)] suggested that the requiring of unmarried fathers' consent for adoption would pose a strong impediment for adoption because often it is impossible to locate unwed fathers when adoption proceedings are brought, whereas mothers are more likely to remain with their children. Even if the special difficulties attendant upon

locating and identifying unwed fathers at birth would justify a legislative distinction between mothers and fathers of newborns,[11] these difficulties need not persist past infancy. When the adoption of an older child is sought, the State's interest in proceeding with adoption cases can be protected by means that do not draw such an inflexible gender-based distinction as that made in [the statute]. In those cases where the father never has come forward to participate in the rearing of his child, nothing in the Equal Protection Clause precludes the State from withholding from him the privilege of vetoing the adoption of that child. . . . But in cases such as this, where the father has established a substantial relationship with the child and has admitted his paternity, a State should have no difficulty in identifying the father even of children born out of wedlock. Thus, no showing has been made that the different treatment afforded unmarried fathers and unmarried mothers under [the statute] bears a substantial relationship to the proclaimed interest of the State in promoting the adoption of illegitimate children. [441 U.S. at 391-393.]

Thus, the Court in *Caban* again focused on the nature of the parent-child relationship and required certain indicia of parenthood to extend constitutional protection to the unwed father. Caban, unlike Mr. Quilloin, was a father who had provided support, had lived with his children for a substantial period of time, and visited them frequently after the relationship with their mother disintegrated.

Unanswered by *Quilloin* and *Caban* was the more troublesome question: What was the extent of constitutional protection required for the unwed father who has little more than a biological relationship with his child? Did he have a right to notice and an opportunity to be heard before his child could be adopted? This was the issue framed by the next case to be determined by the Supreme Court.

Lehr v. Robertson
463 U.S. 248 (1983)

Justice STEVENS delivered the opinion of the Court.

The question presented is whether New York has sufficiently protected an unmarried father's inchoate relationship with a child whom he has never supported and rarely seen in the two years since her birth. The appellant, Jonathan Lehr, claims that the Due Process and Equal Protection Clauses of the Fourteenth Amendment, as interpreted in Stanley v. Illinois, give him an absolute right to notice and an opportunity to be heard before the child may be adopted. We disagree.

Jessica M. was born out of wedlock on November 9, 1976. Her mother, Lorraine Robertson, married Richard Robertson eight months after Jessica's birth. On December 21, 1978, when Jessica was over two years old, the Robertsons filed an adoption petition in the Family Court of Ulster County, New York. The court heard their testimony and received a favorable report from the Ulster County Department of Social Services. On March 7, 1979, the court entered an order of adoption. In this proceeding, appellant contends that the adoption order is invalid because he, Jessica's putative father, was not given advance notice of the adoption proceeding.

---

[11] Because the question is not before us, we express no view whether such difficulties would justify a statute addressed particularly to newborn adoptions, setting forth more stringent requirements concerning the acknowledgement of paternity or a stricter definition of abandonment.

The State of New York maintains a "putative father registry." A man who files with that registry demonstrates his intent to claim paternity of a child born out of wedlock and is therefore entitled to receive notice of any proceeding to adopt that child. Before entering Jessica's adoption order, the Ulster County Family Court had the putative father registry examined. Although appellant claims to be Jessica's natural father, he has not entered his name in the registry.

In addition to the persons whose names are listed on the putative father registry, New York law requires that notice of an adoption proceeding be given to several other classes of possible fathers of children born out of wedlock — those who have been adjudicated to be the father, those who have been identified as the father on the child's birth certificate, those who live openly with the child and the child's mother and who hold themselves out to be the father, those who have been identified as the father by the mother in a sworn written statement, and those who were married to the child's mother before the child was six months old. Appellant admittedly was not a member of any of those classes. He had lived with appellee prior to Jessica's birth and visited her in the hospital when Jessica was born, but his name does not appear on Jessica's birth certificate. He did not live with appellee or Jessica after Jessica's birth, he has never provided them with any financial support, and he has never offered to marry appellee. Nevertheless, he contends that the following special circumstances gave him a constitutional right to notice and a hearing before Jessica was adopted.

On January 30, 1979, one month after the adoption proceeding was commenced in Ulster County, appellant filed a "visitation and paternity petition" in the Westchester County Family Court. In that petition, he asked for a determination of paternity, an order of support, and reasonable visitation privileges with Jessica. Notice of that proceeding was served on appellee on February 22, 1979. Four days later appellee's attorney informed the Ulster County Court that appellant had commenced apaternity proceeding in Westchester County; the Ulster County judge then entered an order staying appellant's paternity proceeding until he could rule on a motion to change the venue of that proceeding to Ulster County. On March 3, 1979, appellant received notice of the change of venue motion and, for the first time, learned that an adoption proceeding was pending in Ulster County.

On March 7, 1979, appellant's attorney telephoned the Ulster County judge to inform him that he planned to seek a stay of the adoption proceeding pending the determination of the paternity petition. In that telephone conversation, the judge advised the lawyer that he had already signed the adoption order earlier that day. According to appellant's attorney, the judge stated that he was aware of the pending paternity petition but did not believe he was required to give notice to appellant prior to the entry of the order of adoption.

Thereafter, the Family Court in Westchester County granted appellee's motion to dismiss the paternity petition, holding that the putative father's right to seek paternity ". . . must be deemed severed so long as an order of adoption exists." Appellant did not appeal from that dismissal. On June 22, 1979, appellant filed a petition to vacate the order of adoption on the ground that it was obtained by fraud and in violation of his constitutional rights. The Ulster County Family Court received written and oral argument on the question whether it had "dropped the ball" by approving the adoption without giving appellant advance notice. After deliberating for several months, it denied the petition, explaining its decision in a thorough written opinion. [The Appellate Division of the Supreme Court and the New York Court of Appeals both affirmed.]

Appellant . . . offers two alternative grounds for holding the New York statutory scheme unconstitutional. First, he contends that a putative father's actual or potential relationship with a child born out of wedlock is an interest in liberty which may not be destroyed without due process of law; he argues therefore that he had a constitutional right to prior notice and an opportunity to be heard before he was deprived of that interest. Second, he contends that the gender-based classification in the statute, which both denied him the right to consent to Jessica's adoption and accorded him fewer procedural rights than her mother, violated the Equal Protection Clause.

The Due Process Claim

. . . We therefore first consider the nature of the interest in liberty for which appellant claims constitutional protection and then turn to a discussion of the adequacy of the procedure that New York has provided for its protection. . . .

This Court has examined the extent to which a natural father's biological relationship with his illegitimate child receives protection under the Due Process Clause in precisely three cases: Stanley vs. Illinois, Quilloin v. Walcott, and Caban v. Mohammed. . . .

The difference between the developed parent-child relationship that was implicated in *Stanley* and *Caban,* and the potential relationship involved in *Quilloin* and this case, is both clear and significant. When an unwed father demonstrates a full commitment to the responsibilities of parenthood by "com[ing] forward to participate in the rearing of his child," *Caban,* 441 U.S., at 392, his interest in personal contact with his child acquires substantial protection under the due process clause. At that point it may be said that he "act[s] as a father toward his children." Id., at 389, n.7. But the mere existence of a biological link does not merit equivalent constitutional protection. . . .

The significance of the biological connection is that it offers the natural father an opportunity that no other male possesses to develop a relationship with his offspring. If he grasps that opportunity and accepts some measure of responsibility for the child's future, he may enjoy the blessings of the parent-child relationship and make uniquely valuable contributions to the child's development.[18] If he fails to do so, the Federal Constitution will not automatically compel a state to listen to his opinion of where the child's best interests lie.

In this case, we are not assessing the constitutional adequacy of New York's procedures for terminating a developed relationship. Appellant has never had any

---

[18] Of course, we need not take sides in the ongoing debate among family psychologists over the relative weight to be accorded biological ties and psychological ties, in order to recognize that a natural father who has played a substantial role in rearing his child has a greater claim to constitutional protection than a mere biological parent. New York's statutory scheme reflects these differences, guaranteeing notice to any putative father who is living openly with the child, and providing putative fathers who have never developed a relationship with the child the opportunity to receive notice simply by mailing a postcard to the putative father registry.

significant custodial, personal, or financial relationship with Jessica, and he did not seek to establish a legal tie until after she was two years old.[19] We are concerned only with whether New York has adequately protected his opportunity to form such a relationship.

The most effective protection of the putative father's opportunity to develop a relationship with his child is provided by the laws that authorize formal marriage and govern its consequences. But the availability of that protection is, of course, dependent on the will of both parents of the child. Thus, New York has adopted a special statutory scheme to protect the unmarried father's interest in assuming a responsible role in the future of his child.

After this Court's decision in *Stanley,* the New York legislature [enacted] a statutory adoption scheme that automatically provides notice to seven categories of putative fathers who are likely to have assumed some responsibility for the care of their natural children. If this scheme were likely to omit many responsible fathers, and if qualification for notice were beyond the control of an interested putative father, it might be thought procedurally inadequate. Yet, . . . the right to receive notice was completely within appellant's control. By mailing a postcard to the putative father registry, he could have guaranteed that he would receive notice of any proceedings to adopt Jessica. The possibility that he may have failed to do so because of his ignorance of the law cannot be a sufficient reason for criticizing the law itself. The New York legislature concluded that a more open-ended notice requirement would merely complicate the adoption process, threaten the privacy interests of unwed mothers, create the risk of unnecessary controversy, and impair the desired finality of adoption decrees. Regardless of whether we would have done likewise if we were legislators instead of judges, we surely cannot characterize the state's conclusion as arbitrary.

Appellant argues, however, that even if the putative father's opportunity to establish a relationship with an illegitimate child is adequately protected by the New York statutory scheme in the normal case, he was nevertheless entitled to special notice because the court and the mother knew that he had filed an affiliation proceeding in another court. This argument amounts to nothing more than an indirect attack on the notice provisions of the New York statute. The legitimate state interests in facilitating the adoption of young children and having the adoption proceeding completed expeditiously that underlie the entire statutory scheme also justify a trial judge's determination to require all interested parties to adhere precisely to the procedural requirements of the statute. The Constitution does not require either a

---

[19] This case happens to involve an adoption by the husband of the natural mother, but we do not believe the natural father has any greater right to object to such an adoption than to an adoption by two total strangers. If anything, the balance of equities tips the opposite way in a case such as this. In denying the putative father relief in *Quilloin,* we made an observation equally applicable here:

> Nor is this a case in which the proposed adoption would place the child with a new set of parents with whom the child has never before lived. Rather, the result of the adoption in this case is to give full recognition to a family unit already in existence, a result desired by all concerned, except appellant. Whatever might be required in other situations, we cannot say that the State was required in this situation to find anything more than that the adoption, and denial of legitimation, were in the "best interests of the child." 434 U.S., at 255.

trial judge or a litigant to have special notice to nonparties who are presumptively capable of asserting and protecting their own rights. Since the New York statutes adequately protected appellant's inchoate interest in establishing a relationship with Jessica, we find no merit in the claim that his constitutional rights were offended because the family court strictly complied with the notice provisions of the statute.

The Equal Protection Claim

. . . The legislation at issue in this case, sections 111 and 111a of the New York Domestic Relations Law, is intended to establish procedures for adoptions [that] promote the best interests of the child, protect the rights of interested third parties, and ensure promptness and finality. To serve those ends, the legislation guarantees to certain people the right to veto an adoption and the right to prior notice of any adoption proceeding. The mother of an illegitimate child is always within that favored class, but only certain putative fathers are included. Appellant contends that the gender-based distinction is invidious. . . .

We have held that these statutes may not constitutionally be applied in that class of cases where the mother and father are in fact similarly situated with regard to their relationship with the child. In Caban v. Mohammed, 441 U.S. 380 (1979), the Court held that it violated the Equal Protection Clause to grant the mother a veto over the adoption of a four-year-old girl and a six-year-old boy, but not to grant a veto to their father, who had admitted paternity and had participated in the rearing of the children. The Court made it clear, however, that if the father had not "come forward to participate in the rearing of his child, nothing in the Equal Protection Clause [would] preclude [ ] the State from withholding from him the privilege of vetoing the adoption of that child."

Jessica's parents are not like the parents involved in *Caban*. Whereas appellee had a continuous custodial responsibility for Jessica, appellant never established any custodial, personal, or financial relationship with her. If one parent has an established custodial relationship with the child and the other parent has either abandoned or never established a relationship, the Equal Protection Clause does not prevent a state from according the two parents different legal rights.

The judgment of the New York Court of Appeals is affirmed.

Justice WHITE, with whom Justice MARSHALL and Justice BLACKMUN join, dissenting.

The question in this case is whether the State may, consistent with the Due Process Clause, deny notice and an opportunity to be heard in an adoption proceeding to a putative father when the State has actual notice of his existence, whereabouts, and interest in the child.

I

It is axiomatic that "[t]he fundamental requirement of due process is the opportunity to be heard 'at a meaningful time and in a meaningful manner.' " As Jessica's biological father, Lehr either had an interest protected by the Constitution or he did not. If the entry of the adoption order in this case deprived Lehr of a constitutionally protected interest, he is entitled to notice and an opportunity to be heard before the order can be accorded finality.

According to Lehr, he and Jessica's mother met in 1971 and began living together in 1974. The couple cohabited for approximately 2 years, until Jessica's birth in 1976. Throughout the pregnancy and after the birth, Lorraine acknowledged to friends and relatives that Lehr was Jessica's father; Lorraine told Lehr that she had reported to the New York State Department of Social Services that he was the father [as required for her to receive benefits under Aid to Families with Dependent Children]. Lehr visited Lorraine and Jessica in the hospital every day during Lorraine's confinement. According to Lehr, from the time Lorraine was discharged from the hospital until August, 1978, she concealed her whereabouts from him. During this time Lehr never ceased his efforts to locate Lorraine and Jessica and achieved sporadic success until August, 1977, after which time he was unable to locate them at all. On those occasions when he did determine Lorraine's location, he visited with her and her children to the extent she was willing to permit it. When Lehr, with the aid of a detective agency, located Lorraine and Jessica in August, 1978, Lorraine was already married to Mr. Robertson. Lehr asserts that at this time he offered to provide financial assistance and to set up a trust fund for Jessica, but that Lorraine refused. Lorraine threatened Lehr with arrest unless he stayed away and refused to permit him to see Jessica. Thereafter Lehr retained counsel who wrote to Lorraine in early December, 1978, requesting that she permit Lehr to visit Jessica and threatening legal action on Lehr's behalf. On December 21, 1978, perhaps as a response to Lehr's threatened legal action, appellees commenced the adoption action at issue here. . . .

Lehr's version of the "facts" paints a far different picture than that portrayed by the majority. The majority's recitation, that "[a]ppellant has never had any significant custodial, personal, or financial relationship with Jessica, and he did not seek to establish a legal tie until after she was two years old," obviously does not tell the whole story. Appellant has never been afforded an opportunity to present his case. The legitimation proceeding he instituted was first stayed, and then dismissed, on appellees' motions. Nor could appellant establish his interest during the adoption proceedings, for it is the failure to provide Lehr notice and an opportunity to be heard there that is at issue here. We cannot fairly make a judgment based on the quality or substance of a relationship without a complete and developed factual record. This case requires us to assume that Lehr's allegations are true — that but for the actions of the child's mother there would have been the kind of significant relationship that the majority concedes is entitled to the full panoply of procedural due process protections.[3]

_____

[3] In response to our decision in Caban v. Mohammed, 441 U.S. 380 (1979), the statute governing the persons whose consent is necessary to an adoption has been amended to include certain unwed fathers. The State has recognized that an unwed father's failure to maintain an actual relationship or to communicate with a child will not deprive him of his right to consent if he was "prevented from doing so by the person or authorized agency having lawful custody of the child." N.Y. Dom. Rel. Law §111(1)(d) (as amended by Chap. 575, L. 1980). Thus, even the State recognizes that before a lesser standard can be applied consistent with due process requirements, there must be a determination that there was no significant relationship and that the father was not prevented from forming such a relationship.

I reject the peculiar notion that the only significance of the biological connection between father and child is that "it offers the natural father an opportunity that no other male possesses to develop a relationship with his offspring." A "mere biological relationship" is not as unimportant in determining the nature of liberty interests as the majority suggests.

The "biological connection" is itself a relationship that creates a protected interest. Thus the "nature" of the interest is the parent-child relationship; how well-developed that relationship has become goes to its "weight," not its "nature."[4] Whether Lehr's interest is entitled to constitutional protection does not entail a searching inquiry into the quality of the relationship but a simple determination of the fact that the relationship exists — a fact that even the majority agrees must be assumed to be established.

Beyond that, however, because there is no established factual basis on which to proceed, it is quite untenable to conclude that a putative father's interest in his child is lacking in substance, that the father in effect has abandoned the child, or ultimately that the father's interest is not entitled to the same minimum procedural protections as the interests of other putative fathers. Any analysis of the adequacy of the notice in this case must be conducted on the assumption that the interest involved here is as strong as that of any putative father. That is not to say that due process requires actual notice to every putative father or that adoptive parents or the State must conduct an exhaustive search of records or an intensive investigation before a final adoption order may be entered. The procedures adopted by the State, however, must at least represent a reasonable effort to determine the identity of the putative father and to give him adequate notice.

II

In this case, of course, there was no question about either the identity or the location of the putative father. The mother knew exactly who he was and both she and the court entering the order of adoption knew precisely where he was and how to give him actual notice that his parental rights were about to be terminated by an adoption order. Lehr was entitled to due process, and the right to be heard is one of the fundamentals of that right, which "has little reality or worth unless one is informed that the matter is pending and can choose for himself whether to appear or default, acquiesce or contest."

The State concedes this much but insists that Lehr has had all the process that is due to him. It relies on §111-a, which designates seven categories of unwed fathers to whom notice of adoption proceedings must be given, including any unwed father who has filed with the State a notice of his intent to claim paternity. The State submits that it need not give notice to anyone who has not filed his name, as he is permitted to do, and who is not otherwise within the designated

---

[4] The majority's citation of *Quilloin* and *Caban* as examples that the Constitution does not require the same procedural protections for the interests of all unwed fathers is disingenuous. Neither case involved notice and opportunity to be heard. In both, the unwed fathers were notified and participated as parties in the adoption proceedings.

categories, even if his identity and interest are known or are reasonably ascertainable by the State.

I am unpersuaded by the State's position. In the first place, §111-a defines six categories of unwed fathers to whom notice must be given even though they have not placed their names on file pursuant to the section. Those six categories, however, do not include fathers such as Lehr who have initiated filiation proceedings, even though their identity and interest are as clearly and easily ascertainable as those fathers in the six categories. Initiating such proceedings necessarily involves a formal acknowledgement of paternity, and requiring the State to take note of such a case in connection with pending adoption proceedings would be a trifling burden, no more than the State undertakes when there is a final adjudication in a paternity action. Indeed, there would appear to be more reason to give notice to those such as Lehr who acknowledge paternity than to those who have been adjudged to be a father in a contested paternity action.

The State asserts that any problem in this respect is overcome by the seventh category of putative fathers to whom notice must be given, namely those fathers who have identified themselves in the putative father register maintained by the State. Since Lehr did not take advantage of this device to make his interest known, the State contends, he was not entitled to notice and a hearing even though his identity, location and interest were known to the adoption court prior to entry of the adoption order. I have difficulty with this position. First, it represents a grudging and crabbed approach to due process. The State is quite willing to give notice and a hearing to putative fathers who have made themselves known by resorting to the putative fathers' register. It makes little sense to me to deny notice and hearing to a father who has not placed his name in the register but who has unmistakably identified himself by filing suit to establish his paternity and has notified the adoption court of his action and his interest. [H]e effectively made himself known by other means, and it is the sheerest formalism to deny him a hearing because he informed the State in the wrong manner.

No state interest is substantially served by denying Lehr adequate notice and a hearing. The State no doubt has an interest in expediting adoption proceedings to prevent a child from remaining unduly long in the custody of the State or foster parents. But this is not an adoption involving a child in the custody of an authorized state agency. . . . The State's undoubted interest in the finality of adoption orders likewise is not well served by a procedure that will deny notice and a hearing to a father whose identity and location are known. As this case well illustrates, denying notice and a hearing to such a father may result in years of additional litigation and threaten the reopening of adoption proceedings and the vacation of the adoption. . . .

Because in my view the failure to provide Lehr with notice and an opportunity to be heard violated rights guaranteed him by the Due Process Clause, I need not address the question whether §111-a violates the Equal Protection Clause by discriminating between categories of unwed fathers or by discriminating on the basis of gender.

Respectfully, I dissent.

QUESTIONS AND NOTES

Lehr and prior case law reveal that the unwed father is entitled to constitutional protection of his parental rights so long as he is willing to accept the responsibilities of parenthood. The extent of this constitutional protection varies according to the degree to which the unwed father manifests a willingness to assume a custodial, personal, or financial relationship with his child. Although an unwed father has the right to establish a constitutionally protected relationship with his child, he may lose this right by his failure to act promptly.

(1) Notice. Currently, more than half the states authorize, by statute, the creation of putative father registries.[16] Registries place the burden of protecting the parent-child relationship on the unwed father who has to take the initiative to register with the statutorily designated state agency. If a man fails to take that initiative, state putative father registries eliminate the need for adoption notification and consent. In *Lehr,* the Court held that New York's scheme for providing notice to an unwed father (through the requirement that he enter his name in a putative father's registry entitling him to receive subsequent notice of an adoption proceeding) did not violate the Due Process Clause. According to *Lehr,* if a biological father fails to seize the opportunity to establish a relationship with his child, he may lose his parental rights, including the right to notice of, and to participate in, adoption proceedings.

Lehr, similar to preceding Supreme Court cases *(Quilloin, Caban)* dealt with adoptions of older children. The dilemma left unanswered by *Lehr* and other post-*Stanley* cases concerns their implications for infants. If an unmarried mother is relinquishing a newborn for adoption, what does due process demand if the father is never given an opportunity to comply with the registration requirement for any number of reasons?

Does due process require that the father in the following situations be permitted to show that he never had an opportunity to comply with the requirement of filing a notice in the putative father registry?

a. Unknown Whereabouts of Mother. A man and woman conceive a child out of wedlock. Because of her family's disapproval of her pregnancy, the woman leaves the state and refuses to disclose her whereabouts to the father. He is unable to locate her, although the couple continues to communicate by e-mail. When the mother gives birth in Minnesota, she leaves blank the name of the father on the birth certificate and relinquishes the child for adoption. After the baby is placed with adoptive parents, the father discovers the infant's whereabouts. He then sends the required forms to the Minnesota paternity registry to seek abrogation of the adoption. See Heidibreder v. Carton, 645 N.W.2d 355 (Minn. 2002) (holding that father's parental rights were not violated when he failed to timely register, and registry procedure did not violate his rights to due process and equal protection).

b. False Information that Baby Died. Daniella Janikova and Otakar Kirchner, both Czechoslovakian immigrants, are living together when Daniella

---

[16] Mary Beck, Toward a National Putative Father Registry, 25 Harv. J.L. & Pub. Pol'y 1031, 1036-1037 (2002) ("over thirty states currently have putative father registries" based on state survey).

becomes pregnant. The man leaves for a short visit with a dying relative in Czechoslovakia. Upon being told, falsely, by a meddlesome aunt that Otakar is having an affair with a former girlfriend, Daniella moves out and tells him that their child died at birth. Two months later, he learns that the child was placed for adoption. They subsequently marry and seek the return of the child from the adoptive parents. See In re Petition of John Doe, 638 N.E.2d 181 (Ill. 1994) (setting aside adoption because father had shown sufficient interest to preclude termination of parental rights). The father successfully sought a writ of habeas corpus, requiring the transfer of the four-year-old boy (known as Baby Richard) to the father's custody. In re Petition of Kirchner, 649 N.E.2d 324 (Ill. 1995), *stay denied sub nom.* O'Connell v. Kirchner, 513 U.S. 1138 (1995).

Baby Richard's birth parents subsequently separated, then reconciled and had two daughters. The boy is reportedly doing well. He told his psychologist, "I got stolen when I was a baby. There was a big argument about who I should stay with and about the truth. The other people — I don't know their names — wanted to keep me." Abdon M. Pallash, "Baby Richard," Doing Fine — 7th-Grader Has Straight A's; Psychologist's Book Says Boy Not Scarred by Adoption Ordeal, Chicago Sun-Times, Nov. 18, 2003, at 4. See also Karen Moriarty, Baby Richard: A Four-Year-Old Comes Home (2004).

c. Misrepresentation of Biological Father.   Cara Clausen, an unmarried woman, gives birth to a girl in Iowa, misrepresenting Scott Seefeldt as the father. When Michigan residents Roberta and Jan DeBoer file a petition to adopt Baby Jessica, an Iowa court terminates the parental rights of Clausen and Seefeldt and grants custody during the pendency of the proceeding to the DeBoers, who return to Michigan. Nine days later, Clausen admits that she falsely identified the father and seeks to revoke her consent. Clausen subsequently marries the baby's father, Daniel Schmidt, and they seek the return of the child.

In In re B.G.C., 496 N.W.2d 239 (Iowa 1992), the Iowa Supreme Court held that the biological father's parental rights could not be terminated because his abandonment was not established by clear and convincing evidence. In Michigan, Baby Jessica's prospective adoptive parents unsuccessfully petitioned for modification of the Iowa court order denying their adoption petition and granting custody to the child's biological parents. In re Baby Girl Clausen, 502 N.W.2d 649 (Mich. 1993). The United States Supreme Court refused to stay the order entered pursuant to the Michigan Supreme Court's opinion. 509 U.S. 1301 (1993).

Baby Jessica was returned to the Schmidts and was renamed Anna. Daniel Schmidt was injured in a construction accident in 1998. His subsequent unemployment contributed to the parents' divorce in 2000. Anna and her younger sister reside with their father, although the parents share legal custody. According to her parents, 12-year-old Anna is well adjusted and happy. See "Baby Jessica" Celebrates 10 Years with Birth Family; Her Adoptive Parents in Ann Arbor and Her Birth Parents Fought their Case All the Way to the Supreme Court, Grand Rapids Press, Aug. 3, 2003, at A19; Profile: Effect of Highly Publicized Custody Battles on Children, NBC News: Today, June 3, 2004. The cases of Baby Richard and Baby Jessica spurred many states to enact putative father registries to facilitate newborn adoptions.

d. Ignorance of Pregnancy. On the other hand, suppose that the birth father is not aware of the mother's pregnancy. What due process protection, if any, does the father have?

In Robert O. v. Russell K., 604 N.E.2d 99 (N.Y. 1992), a man and woman live together for a year. When they break up, the woman chooses not to inform the man of her pregnancy and her relinquishment of the child for adoption. Several months later, they reconcile and marry. After the woman informs the father about the child, he registers in the putative father registry and commences proceedings to vacate the adoption (18 months after the child's birth and 20 months after the adoption is finalized). The New York Court of Appeals concludes that the father failed to manifest a willingness to assume full custody within the time provided by statute. The court explains that prompt action was necessary because of the state's legitimate interest in the child's need for stability. "Promptness is measured in terms of the baby's life not by the onset of the father's awareness." Id. at 103. The court limited the time in which a father must act to the six-month period immediately preceding the child's placement for adoption. See also In re Baby Girl U., 638 N.Y.S.2d 253 (App. Div. 1996) (finding that unwed father was not entitled to veto adoption where he failed to seek declaration of paternity until six months after learning of birth and never sought to be financially responsible for the child). Is it realistic to characterize a father as exhibiting no interest in his child if he does not know of its existence?

What does due process require if the identity and/or whereabouts of a father are unknown? The original UPA required that efforts be made to identify the biological father through appropriate inquiries (§25(b)). If such inquiries were unsuccessful, the unknown father's rights could be terminated, subject to a six-month period during which the matter could be reopened if the man came forward and demonstrated that he was the father. However, after the six-month period, the termination was final (§25(d)).

The revised Uniform Adoption Act, 9 U.L.A. 11 (1999 & Supp. 2008), also addresses efforts to identify the father. The revised UAA requires inquiry of the mother. If such inquiry fails to identify the father and there is no reasonable likelihood that publication or posting will lead to actual notice, the Act rules out that method of notice. If the mother refuses to identify the father or his whereabouts, UAA §3-404(e) requires the court to explain to her the importance of disclosure (for finality of adoption and medical history) and to advise her that she may be subject to civil liability for misidentification of the father.

(2) Opportunity to Develop a Relationship. In *Lehr,* the Court noted:

> The significance of the biological connection is that it offers the natural father an opportunity that no other male possesses to develop a relationship with his offspring. If he grasps that opportunity and accepts some measure of responsibility for the child's future, he may enjoy the blessings of the parent-child relationship and make uniquely valuable contributions to the child's development. If he fails to do so, the Federal Constitution will not automatically compel a State to listen to his opinion of where the child's best interests lie. [463 U.S. at 261-262.]

Thus, according to *Lehr,* unwed fathers gain from their biological connection an opportunity interest to develop a relationship that is constitutionally protected.

The opportunity interest can be lost by a parent who fails to develop a relationship, in the case of a father, for example, who shows little interest in his child, fails to visit, or fails to support the child.

It is one case if the father voluntarily abandons his "opportunity interest." But what if he involuntarily does so because of the mother's actions, as in the cases discussed supra, pp. 513-515. May the state deny such a father an opportunity to establish this relationship with the child? In the case of the newborn, how does an unwed father develop a parental relationship with a fetus? How relevant in the evaluation of the father's seizing the "opportunity to develop a relationship" is his prebirth conduct toward the *mother*?

In Bowers v. Pearson, 609 S.E.2d 174 (Ga. Ct. App. 2005), when Margaret Pearson learned that she was pregnant after a brief affair, she informed the father by phone. He made several attempts to speak with her and her parents, but they all refused. Before the child's birth, he filed with the putative father's registry and petitioned to legitimate the child. At the birth, Margaret placed the child for adoption. In the legitimation proceeding, the trial court found that the father abandoned his opportunity to develop a relationship with the child by failing to provide financial or other support during the pregnancy. The Georgia Court of Appeals reversed, concluding that the finding of abandonment was not supported by the evidence because, by the father's registering and instituting the legitimation proceeding, he agreed to assume parental responsibilities and to submit himself to a claim by the mother for expenses. See also In re Adoption of Vest, 2001 WL 242594 (Ohio Ct. App. 2001) (refusing to dispense with consent to adoption of a biological father, finding that he did not willfully abandon the birth mother, in the face of the maternal grandmother's prohibiting him from contacting the birth mother, because he registered with the putative father registry prior to the birth and offered support to both the mother during her pregnancy and to a child support enforcement agency).

Note that in Bowers v. Pearson, supra, the biological father petitioned to legitimate the child prior to the child's birth. Recall that in Lehr v. Robertson, supra, the biological father did not register in New York's putative fathers registry but did file a paternity petition. In the ensuing adoption proceeding, although the trial judge therefore knew Lehr's identity, the court nonetheless granted the adoption and terminated his parental rights without notice. The new UPA §402(b)(2) would accord considerable weight to a father's filing of a paternity action, by exempting an alleged father from the requirement of registration if he "commences a proceeding to adjudicate his paternity before the court has terminated his parental rights."

How promptly does the father have to seize his "opportunity interest"? Does he have to act promptly after the *birth* or upon *learning* of the pregnancy? If the father comes forward long after the adoption, how should a court balance the father's constitutional rights against the child's need for stability in its adoptive placement? See Smith v. Soligon, 561 S.E.2d 850 (Ga. Ct. App. 2002) (six-year delay leads to abandonment of father's opportunity interest to develop parent-child relationship). Should the mother's fraud delay the commencement of any relevant statute of limitations that would terminate the father's parental rights? See McCallum v. Salazar, 636 S.E.2d 486 (Va. Ct. App. 2006) (refusing to authorize delay).

Is there an obligation to ensure that unwed biological fathers know of their rights to file a claim with the state putative father registry? See Heart of Adoptions, Inc. v. J.A., 963 So. 2d 189 (Fla. 2007) (holding that an adoption agency must serve a known unwed father with notice of adoption plan, including his right to file a paternity claim with the state registry prior to seeking termination of his parental rights). For a critical casenote, see Michelle Kaminsky, Note, Excessive Rights for Putative Fathers: Heart of Adoptions Jeopardizes Rights of Mother and Child, 57 Cath. U. L. Rev. 917 (2008).

A student note writer argues that putative father registries do not adequately protect the rights of many unwed fathers. She suggests that states should ensure that the putative fathers (whose rights were terminated) actually knew of the registration requirement and should provide exceptions for genuinely thwarted fathers. See Rebeca Aizpuru, Note, Protecting the Unwed Father's Opportunity to Parent: A Survey of Paternity Registry Statutes, 18 Rev. Litig. 703, 707 (1999). Do you agree with these criticisms?

Another criticism of state putative father registries is that they fail to protect fathers' rights in interstate adoptions because a father's registration in the state of birth will not ensure his notice of an adoption proceeding that takes place in another state. In response to this problem, should federal legislation create a national putative father registry? See Mary Beck, A National Putative Father Registry, 36 Cap. U. L. Rev. 295 (2007). See also Laura Oren, Thwarted Fathers or Pop-Up Pops? How to Determine When Putative Fathers Can Block the Adoption of Their Newborn Children, 40 Fam. L.Q. 153 (2006).

Is tort law (for the intentional interference with parental rights) an appropriate method of protecting the rights of unwed fathers in such cases of thwarting the father's opportunity to develop a relationship with a newborn? See, e.g., Kessel v. Leavitt, 511 S.E.2d 720 (W. Va. 1998) (holding that father could maintain action for fraud against mother's relatives and attorney for concealment of information regarding location and adoption of child).

(3) Standard to Be Applied. What standard should be applied to proceedings terminating the rights of the unwed father for adoption purposes? Suppose the father petitions to establish paternity and requests custody. Should the court apply a best interests standard, or require a finding that a grant of custody would be detrimental to the child, or require a finding of unfitness?

Adoption of Kelsey S., 823 P.2d 1216 (Cal. 1992), examined the constitutionality of the standard to be applied in terminating a father's rights. At the time of Kelsey's birth, the biological father had instituted a paternity action and request for custody, which was consolidated with the prospective adoptive parents' petition for adoption. The prospective adoptive parents alleged that only the mother's consent was required for an adoption because there was no "presumed father" under California law. The California version of the Uniform Parentage Act (Cal. Civ. Code §7004(a), now Cal. Fam. Code §7611 (West 2004 & Supp. 2008)), adopted a different standard in terminating parental rights of "presumed" versus other fathers: "presumed fathers" were permitted, similar to mothers, to withhold consent to adoption. However, the parental rights of other fathers could be terminated more easily based only upon a best interests standard. Kelsey's biological father was unable to establish that he was a "presumed father" because, although he openly held out the child as his own, he was unable to meet the statutory requirement of receiving the child into his home because he was prevented from doing so by the mother.

The trial court ruled, and the appellate court affirmed, that he was not a "presumed father" and that the child's best interest required termination of his parental rights. On appeal, the California Supreme Court held: (1) the statute creating a category of "presumed father" whose consent was required prior to adoption violates federal constitutional guarantees of equal protection and due process for unwed fathers to the extent that the statutes allow a mother's unilateral action to preclude the biological father from becoming a presumed father; and (2) if an unwed father promptly comes forward and demonstrates a full commitment to his parental responsibilities (e.g., emotional, financial), his federal constitutional right to due process prohibits termination of his parental relationship absent a showing of unfitness as a parent. The court remanded the case for a determination of whether the father had demonstrated sufficient commitment to his parental responsibilities. See also In re Raquel Marie X., 559 N.E.2d 418 (N.Y. 1990) (holding a similar statute unconstitutional on equal protection grounds).

(4) Empirical Data.   What are the characteristics of unwed fathers? A national study profiled a large sample of unwed fathers ($n = 12,686$). Robert I. Lerman & Theodora J. Ooms, Young Unwed Fathers: Changing Roles and Emerging Policies (1993). That study reveals: (1) unwed fatherhood is not limited to teens but also occurs among men aged 20-26 who constitute almost 8 percent of unwed fathers (id. at 31); (2) young unwed fatherhood is more prevalent among African Americans (id. at 47); (3) unwed fathers tend to come from families of lower socioeconomic status, be less well educated, have lower academic abilities, and have sexual intercourse at early ages (id.); (4) few unwed fathers have more than one child (id. at 46); and (5) most unwed fathers (80%) remain absent fathers (id. at 32, 46).

Empirical research also suggests that a desire to search for the relinquished child is a common experience of parents who surrender their children for adoption. However, the motivating factor in searching is different for fathers and for mothers. Birth mothers generally search for their children out of a need to alleviate guilt and restore self-esteem through the assurance that the child is well. On the other hand, birth fathers often search for their children with thoughts of taking them back. See Eva Y. Deykin et al., Fathers of Adopted Children: A Study of the Impact of Child Surrender on Birth Fathers, 58 Am. J. Orthopsychiatry 240, 244 (April 1988). What do you think are the implications of such findings for adoption professionals and prospective adoptive parents?

3.   Independent Adoption Versus Agency Adoption

Broadly speaking, if one puts aside cases where children are adopted by a known relative (such as a stepparent), there are two procedures for adoptions: "agency adoptions" and "independent" (or "private") adoptions. Both require that the biological parents' rights be extinguished, either by consent or by termination.

In an agency adoption, a social agency acts as an intermediary between the biological mother and the adoptive family. Often after substantial counseling, the mother typically consensually relinquishes her parental rights and consents to having the agency place the child for adoption. The agency chooses an adoptive family from applicants, after investigating and evaluating alternatives. After placing the child in his or her new home, the agency provides counseling services, may evaluate the family's adjustment during a trial period, and will then assist the family in completing the legal adoption. Should the adoption for some reason fail, the agency will take the child back. Some adoption agencies are actually state agencies. Most are private, often sectarian organizations, licensed by the state.

An independent or private adoption is one where the child is not placed with a new family by an adoption agency. Instead, the biological parent(s) may place the child directly with the adoptive family, or some nonagency intermediary — a friend, a relative, doctor, lawyer, or spiritual advisor — may act as a go-between and place the child. Private adoptions account for a significant amount of domestic adoptions annually.[17] Independent adoptions rose in the 1970s when several factors (i.e., the increased use of contraception, liberalization of abortion, and society's acceptance of women raising nonmarital children) contributed to a shortage of adoptable white infants. In response, many states enacted standards to protect children in independent adoptions.

In a private adoption, if the biological mother receives payment for more than her medical expenses, or if a third-party intermediary who arranges the adoption receives more than an appropriate fee, a crime may be committed. Many states have criminal statutes making baby selling illegal. Concern resulted in congressional hearings over the so-called black market adoptions. There are reports of situations in which adoptive families have paid up to $40,000 for a baby.[18] Despite newspaper articles and congressional hearings decrying the black market for babies, prosecutions for baby selling are infrequent. Complaints rarely arise from the adoptive family, the biological mother, or the go-betweens. Moreover, it is difficult to distinguish cases in which the money that has changed hands is for legitimate expenses and professional fees, from those where a mother is selling her baby. In all events, some proponents of agency adoptions argue that the existence of a black market (and a "gray market," as the intermediary mechanism is called) suggests the need to abolish independent or private adoptions, and allow only agency adoptions.

Proponents of agency adoptions argue that without the safeguards provided by agency adoptions, all parties risk inadequate protection because of lack of concern for (1) the biological mother, (2) the qualifications of the would-be parents, and (3) the safety and welfare of the child. By employing the skills of professionals, agencies investigate the maternal and paternal history of the child; give the child a physical, mental, and psychological examination; and evaluate the health, financial situation, and motivation for adoption of the adoptive parents. In addition, they provide follow-up services, especially during a probationary period when the

---

[17] Kathy S. Stolley, Statistics on Adoption in the United States, in The Future of Children 31 (Packard Foundation, 1993).

[18] Melinda Lucas, Adoption: Distinguishing Between Gray Market and Black Market Activities, 34 Fam. L.Q. 553, 557 (2000).

integration of the child into the adoptive family can be evaluated. The agency also provides for the permanent retention of adoption records and confidentiality.

Opponents of independent adoption not only fear that private adoption fosters a "black market,"[19] but also that several serious risks are augmented by failure to take the safeguards provided by agency adoption. These risks are said to include several dangers: (1) biological parents may be pressured into a hasty and ill-considered decision, particularly because the mother is often unwed and therefore faces social stigma and financial difficulties; (2) adoptive parents may enter the arrangement blindly; (3) adoptive parents may be harassed by biological parents, especially those who change their minds and later regret having consented to the adoption; (4) the adoptive home may not "match" the needs of the particular child; (5) the child is an unprotected pawn if the adoptive parents change their minds about the adoption or are motivated to adopt a child solely to bolster their unsatisfactory marriage; (6) unbeknownst to the adoptive family the child may have some mental or physical disability; (7) there will be no funds or personnel to care for the child if the adoption should fail.

Banning independent adoptions may have its faults as well. Some commentators point to the decrease in adoptions in states that have abolished independent adoption.[20] For example, in Connecticut before a law was passed prohibiting all but agency adoptions, there were 1,092 adoptions in a given year, of which 58 percent were independent. After the law was passed, only 573 adoptions were made, and of these almost half had been made the year before.[21] Moreover, other commentators point to the overall success of independent adoptions.[22] It appears that adoptive parents who have had a private adoption are as happy with their decision years afterwards as those with an agency adoption. Agency practices have also been criticized. Some believe that agency adoptions give too much discretion to professionals to use their personal values to choose among the competing applicants, thus disadvantaging many potential adoptive families. This concern becomes especially acute if adoption agencies are given a monopoly, through the elimination of private adoptions.[23]

4. Adoption Failure

Under the present law of most states, an adoption can be abrogated even after a child is placed with the adoptive family. In some circumstances, it is possible for the biological mother to reclaim the child if she demonstrates that her

---

[19] See L. Jean Emery, Agency Versus Independent Adoption: The Case for Agency Adoption, in The Future of Children 139 (Packard Foundation, 1993).

[20] Pearl S. Buck, Children for Adoption 205-206 (1964).

[21] Id.

[22] William Meezan et al., Adoptions Without Agencies: A Study of Independent Adoptions 42 (1978).

[23] HEW Funds Study of Independent Adoptions (quoting Anne Shyne, Director of the Child Welfare League), 2 Fam. L. Rep. 2149 (1976).

relinquishment of parental rights was induced by force or duress.[24] In addition, it is possible for adoption to be upset upon a demonstration that the required consent of a biological parent was not obtained or that there was a failure to give notice to a parent. These attacks can be made after an adoption has become final, although many states have statutes of limitation that bar attacks on adoption decrees after a certain period of time, typically ranging from six months to three years.[25]

During the probation period, before the adoption decree is entered, the agency placing the child for adoption may also reclaim the child typically upon the discovery of alcoholism, drug abuse, or threatened child abuse in the adoptive family.[26]

Finally, in some states, under certain circumstances, an adoption can be abrogated by the adoptive parents. Adoptive parents may seek abrogation of adoptions on the basis of fraud, misrepresentation, and undue influence, as well as on procedural grounds, including lack of compliance with statutory requirements.[27] The majority of cases involving abrogation by adoptive parents include two common situations: (1) both adoptive parents seek abrogation due to some abnormality or defect in the child; and (2) adoptive fathers seek abrogation, usually after divorcing the child's biological mother. The outcomes of abrogation in each case are quite different: If an adoptive father successfully abrogates an adoption, the child is left in the care of the child's biological mother; however, if the adoptive parents successfully abrogate an adoption, the child effectively is abandoned.

In a famous Rhode Island case, In re Lisa Diane G., 537 A.2d 131 (R.I. 1988), the adoptive parents petitioned to have the adoption of their adoptive daughter set aside on the basis of misrepresentation.

> The gist of the parents' complaint is that the adoption decree was procured by the fraudulent conduct or misrepresentations of certain representatives of the

---

[24] A noted example of a mother changing her mind took place in the famous "Baby Lenore" case. See Scarpetta v. Spence-Chapin Adoption Serv., 269 N.E.2d 787 (N.Y. 1971). For criticisms of the decision, see Henry H. Foster, Revocation of Consent to Adoption: A Covenant Running with the Child?, N.Y.L.J., Aug. 6, 1971, at 1; Sanford N. Katz, The Adoption of Baby Lenore: Problems of Consent and the Role of Lawyers, 5 Fam. L.Q. (No. 4) 405 (1971).

Jurisdictions have assumed a variety of positions regarding withdrawal of parental consent to adoption. Some states focus on the timing of the parents' revocation of consent after the child's birth. See, e.g., Uniform Adoption Act (UAA) §§2-408, 2-409 (1994), 9 U.L.A. pt. IA at 60-62 (1999 & Supp. 2008) (permitting a parent to revoke consent within eight days after the birth); In re Adoption of Anderson, 248 N.W. 657 (Minn. 1993) (consent is revocable until final decree of adoption is issued). Other states invalidate consent that is procured by fraud or duress or based on a parent's immaturity. See, e.g., Ill. Ann. Stat. ch. 750 ¶50/11 (West 1999 & Supp. 2008) (consent is irrevocable absent fraud or duress); Adoption of Thomas, 559 N.E.2d 1230 (Mass. 1990) (immaturity). Still other states differentiate between surrender to an approved agency or to a private adoption, making revocation of consent more difficult for relinquishments to approved agencies. See Sees v. Baber, 377 A.2d 628 (N.J. 1977).

[25] See Homer H. Clark, Law of Domestic Relations 934-935 (2d ed. 1988). For further discussion of adoption consent laws, see Karen D. Laverdiere, Context over Form: The Shifting of Adoption Consent Laws, 25 Whittier L. Rev. 599 (2004).

[26] Agencies supervise the child in the applicant's home for a probationary period, which varies from state to state — usually six months or a year.

[27] See Clark, supra note [25], at 937.

Department of Children and Their Families (DCF). The parents contend that DCF never informed them that the staff at Bradley Hospital, an institution noted for its treatment of the emotionally disturbed, had informed DCF that the child, because of her emotional problems, should not be placed for adoption. In the Family Court the parents sought nullification of the adoption decree and compensation for the expenses they incurred in caring for the child. . . . [Id. at 132.]

Do you think relief should be granted? Does it alter your opinion that the child was eight years old when adopted and now is a teenager? Most states do not permit adoptive parents to rescind an adoption, and most commentators would agree that "adoptors, who voluntarily assumed the responsibility of natural parents, must not expect to be able to give them back again at will any more than they could relieve themselves of the responsibility if the child had been born to them."[28]

However, in response to the problems of misrepresentation by adoption agencies and judicial reluctance to nullify adoption decrees, some states are recognizing a remedy of wrongful adoption. The cause of action does not seek annulment of the adoption but rather damages from the agency for the extraordinary expenses and emotional distress associated with caring for the child. See, e.g., Ross v. Louise Wise Servs., Inc., 836 N.Y.S.2d 509 (N.Y. 2007). See generally Amanda Trefethen, The Emerging Tort of Wrongful Adoption, 11 J. Contemp. Legal Issues 620 (2000); Steve Mulligan, Note, Inconsistency in Illinois Adoption Law: Adoption Agencies' Uncertain Duty to Disclose, Investigate, and Inquire, 39 Loy. U. Chi. L.J. 799 (2008).

5. Baby Selling

At the present time there is a severe shortage of adoptable Caucasian babies, for the demand has remained high while the supply of children available for adoption has substantially diminished. Improvements in contraception techniques, the legalization of abortion, and the decrease in social stigma attached to an unmarried mother raising a child all have contributed to the shrinking supply.

Consider whether a market for baby selling, with appropriate safeguards, might not substantially increase the sum total of human happiness and correct this shortage of adoptable babies. For example, imagine a system where it was legal for a mother (or father?) to be paid any agreed-upon amount for placement of a newborn child in an adoptive home, as long as the adoptive parents met appropriate minimum objective standards that ensured the child would not be cruelly or neglectfully treated.

Who would be harmed by such a system? Would not the adoptive parents (who might otherwise be childless), the child (who might not otherwise be born), and the biological parents (who had received compensation) all be better off? What, then, are the objections to baby selling? Would low-income families who wished to adopt be worse off than today? Would a market for babies lead to overreaching

---

[28] See In re Adoption of a Minor, 214 N.E.2d 281, 282 (Mass. 1966) ("Adoption should create 'a for better, for worse situation' ").

middlemen who would take advantage of "vulnerable" biological and adoptive parents? Should we be fearful of the implications for the eugenic alteration of the human race because baby selling might lead to baby breeding? Or are the primary objections symbolic? By creating a property right of sorts in the biological parents, does baby selling seem too much like slavery? Does baby selling undermine the "best interests of the child" premise of modern child custody law?

At the forefront of the debate over the desirability of a market approach to adoption is Judge Richard A. Posner. In a classic article[29] he considers a "free market theory" of adoption and explores how changes in the law might make the existing market in babies for adoption operate more efficiently and equitably. He further refines his theory in the following article.

Richard A. Posner, The Regulation of the Market in Adoptions
67 B.U. L. Rev. 59, 64-72 (1987)

[In] this article I shall describe briefly how such a market might operate, under what regulatory constraints, and with what likely consequences, and in doing so will try to respond to the most frequently expressed objections to allowing the market to function in this area.

II. Characteristics of and Desirable Constraints on the Baby Market

A. The Question of Price

For heuristic purposes (only!), it is useful to analogize the sale of babies to the sale of an ordinary good, such as an automobile or a television set. We observe, for example, that although the supply of automobiles and of television sets is rationed by price, not all the automobiles and television sets are owned by wealthy people. On the contrary, the free market in these goods has lowered prices, through competition and innovation, to the point where the goods are available to a lot more people than in highly controlled economies such as that of the Soviet Union. There is even less reason for thinking that if babies could be sold to adoptive parents the wealthy would come to monopolize babies. Wealthy people (other than those few who owe their wealth to savings or inheritance rather than to a high income) have high costs of time. It therefore costs them more to raise a child — child rearing still being a time-intensive activity — than it costs the nonwealthy. As a result, wealthy couples tend to have few rather than many children. [Citations omitted.] This pattern would not change if babies could be bought. Moreover, since most people have a strong preference for natural, as distinct from adopted, children, wealthy couples able to have natural children are unlikely (to say the least) to substitute adopted ones.

It is also unlikely that allowing people to bid for babies with dollars would drive up the price of babies, thereby allocating the supply to wealthy demanders.

---

[29] Posner began the debate with an article by Richard A. Posner & Elizabeth Landes, The Economics of the Baby Shortage, 7 J. Legal Stud. 323 (1978).

Today we observe a high black market price conjoined with an artificially low price for babies obtained from adoption agencies and through lawful independent adoptions. . . . The low price in the lawful market is deceptive. . . . Quality-adjusted prices in free markets normally are lower than black market prices, and there is no reason to doubt that this would be true in a free market for adoptions. Thus, while it is possible that "[i]nherent in the baby black market is the unfairness that results from the fact that only the affluent can afford to pay the enormous fees necessary to procure a baby," the words "black market" ought to be italicized. It is not the free market, but unwarranted restrictions on the operation of that market, that has raised the black market price of babies beyond the reach of ordinary people. . . .

B. The Question of Quality

As soon as one mentions quality, people's hackles rise and they remind you that one is talking about a traffic in human beings, not in inanimate objects. The observation is pertinent, and at least five limitations might have to be placed on the operation of the market in babies for adoption. The first, already mentioned and already in place, is that the buyers can have no "right to abuse the thing bought." . . . [The second limitation concerns screening for fitness.] Today, all adoptive parents are, in theory anyway, screened for fitness. Adoption agencies are charged with this responsibility, and if we moved toward a freer market in babies the agencies could be given the additional function of investigating and certifying prospective purchasers, who would pay the price of the service. . . .

The third limitation on a baby market concerns remedies for breach of contract. In an ordinary market a buyer can both reject defective goods and, if the seller refuses to deliver and damages would be an inadequate remedy for the refusal, get specific performance of the contract. Natural parents are not permitted to reject their baby, either when it is born or afterward, because it turns out to be handicapped or otherwise not in conformity with their expectations; no more should adoptive parents who buy their babies. . . . For the welfare of the baby must be considered along with that of the contracting parties. . . . The child is an interested third party whose welfare would be disserved by a mechanical application of the remedies available to buyers in the market for inanimate goods.

For the same reason (the child's welfare) neither natural nor adopting parents should be allowed to sell their children after infancy, that is, after the child has established a bond with its parents. . . .

The last limitation on the baby market that I shall discuss relates to eugenic breeding. Although prospects still seem remote, one can imagine an entrepreneur in the baby market trying to breed a race of *Ubermenschen* who would command premium prices. The external effects of such an endeavor could be very harmful, and would provide an appropriate basis for governmental regulation. . . .

One reason people fear the operation of a free market in babies for adoption is that they extrapolate from experience with the illegal market. Critics who suggest that baby selling offers the promise of huge profits to middlemen — the dreaded "baby brokers" — fail to distinguish between an illegal market, in which sellers demand a heavy premium (an apparent, though not real, profit) in order to defray the expected costs of punishment, and a legal market, in which the premium is eliminated. Seemingly exorbitant profits, low quality, poor information, involvement of criminal elements — these widely asserted characteristics of the black market in babies are no more indicative of the behavior of a lawful market than the tactics of the bootleggers and rum-runners during Prohibition were indicative of the behavior of the liquor industry after Prohibition was repealed.

III. The Objection from Symbolism and the Issue of Semantics

Even if partial deregulation of the baby market might make practical utilitarian sense along the lines just suggested, some will resist on symbolic grounds. If we acknowledge that babies can be sold, the argument goes, we open the door to all sorts of monstrous institutions — including slavery. . . . Allowing parents to sell their children into slavery would be a monstrous idea. Allowing the prospective mother of an illegitimate child to receive money in exchange for giving the child up for adoption, when described in shorthand as "baby selling," seems to many people uncomfortably close to the type of real baby selling that is found in slave societies — that was found in the slave societies of the South before the Civil War. No doubt it requires more thought than most people are willing to give to the problem to hold these quite different concepts separate in their minds. But if they are not held separate we find ourselves condemned to perpetuate the painful spectacle of mass abortion and illegitimacy in a society in which, to a significant extent, children are not available for adoption by persons unwilling to violate the law.

One should always be suspicious of arguments against the market when they are made by people who have no desire to participate in it themselves, people who want to restrict the availability of goods to other people. Most people who invoke vague symbols in opposition to "baby selling" have no interest in or expectation of either adopting a child or conceiving one out of wedlock. They have little empathy with the needs of people who find themselves involuntarily childless or involuntarily pregnant.

The opponents of "baby selling" are unwilling to acknowledge that what we have today, even apart from the black market, is closer to a free market in babies than a free market in babies would be to slavery. . . . As I said at the outset, adoption agencies do lawfully "sell" babies, and many charge thousands of dollars. Moreover, in independent adoptions, the mother herself may "sell" her baby, for it is not considered unlawful to use a part of the fee paid by the adoptive parents to defray the medical and other maintenance costs of the mother during pregnancy. . . .

Two other important examples of legal baby selling should be mentioned. One is the "family compact" doctrine, which allows a woman to enter into an enforceable contract to give up her baby for adoption by a close relative. The other is surrogate motherhood. . . .

So we have legal baby selling today; the question of public policy is not whether baby selling should be forbidden or allowed but how extensively it should be regulated. I simply think it should be regulated less stringently than is done today.

Posner's proposal regarding baby selling has been widely criticized. See, e.g., Tamar Frankel & Francis H. Miller, The Inapplicability of Market Theory to Adoptions, 67 B.U. L. Rev. 99 (1987); Margaret Jane Radin, What, if Anything, Is Wrong with Baby Selling? 26 Pac. L.J. 135 (1995).

6. Adopted Children's Right to Learn Their Origins

There is a tradition in adoptions, particularly agency adoptions, of strict confidentiality. Agencies typically have elaborate safeguards to ensure that (1) the biological parents can never determine the identity of a child relinquished for adoption, and (2) the adopted child, even as an adult, cannot find out the identity of the biological parents. Court adoption records are typically sealed, and allow disclosure only by court order based on some urgent necessity. In independent adoptions, on the other hand, although the court records may be sealed, the adoptive parents often know the identity of the biological mother and sometimes that of both parents. In such circumstances, the adoptive parents decide whether the child will be informed.

An adoption reform movement began in the 1970s to open adoption records and thereby allow the exchange of information between the adopted child and the biological parents. States take different approaches to the provision of identifying information. Most states still require that the original birth certificate and adoption records be sealed, but permit access upon a judicial finding of "good cause." At the other extreme, a few states grant adult adoptees, upon request and without restriction, access to their adoption records or original birth certificates.[30] Other states have created "mutual consent" registries that allow the release of identifying information if both parties register their consent. Still other state statutes provide that, once one party registers, an intermediary will contact the other party to obtain consent to release information. Finally, some state laws honor a party's request for information in the absence of a veto registered by the other party. See Caroline B. Fleming, Note, The Open-Records Debate: Balancing the Interests of Birth Parents and Adult Adoptees, 11 Wm. & Mary J. Women & L. 461, 474-475 (2005) (discussing approaches).

What interests of the adopted child, the adoptive parents, and the biological parents are affected by confidentiality? Should a biological parent's constitutional right to privacy trump a child's right to know? In a case where both the biological parents and an adult adoptee want to find each other (and the adoptive parents have no objection), are there still any arguments for confidentiality? As a practical matter, which of the above approaches should be established?

---

[30] Currently eight states (Alabama, Alaska, Kansas, Maine, Massachusetts, New Hampshire, North Carolina, and Oregon) allow adult adoptees unrestricted access to their birth records. Wendy Koch, As Adoptees Seek Roots, States Unsealing Records, USA Today, Feb. 13, 2008, at 1A. Scotland has permitted unrestricted access to adopted children (after age 17) since 1930. The Adoption of Children (Scotland), 1930, 20 & 21 Geo. 5, ch. 37 §11(9).

What motivates adoptees to search for their birth parents? Empirical data reveal that adoptees' searches are not "a vindictive venture, but an attempt to understand themselves and their situations better."[31] Even when the information they learned was upsetting, a large percentage of adoptees felt they benefited from their searches.

Another aspect of the adoption reform movement is the trend toward open adoption. Whereas the sealed record debate involves the rights of adult adoptees, the open adoption movement generally involves infants. Open adoption signifies the sharing of information and contact between the adoptive and biological parents before and after placement of the child. Open adoption differs from closed adoption because, in an open adoption, the biological mother and adoptive parents know each other's identity; the birth mother may exercise significant control over the choice of adoptive parents; and the parties have an agreement concerning the birth mother's postadoption relationship to the child.

The rise in open adoptions stems from several factors, including the increased number of older adoptees who already have bonds to their birth parent(s); the decrease in adoptable infants (caused by the legalization of abortion) that enabled birth parents to demand conditions in placement; and, finally, data that suggest that open adoption has positive psychological consequences for adoptees, birth parents, and adoptive parents. See Annette Ruth Appell, The Move Toward Legally Sanctioned Cooperative Adoption: Can It Survive the Uniform Adoption Act?, 30 Fam. L.Q. 483, 483 (1996). For a review of applicable statutes and empirical data, see Annette R. Appell, Survey of State Utilization of Adoption with Contact, 6 Adoption Q. 75 (2003).

Because the majority of adoptions are by relatives and stepparents, most adoptions today are not anonymous. The Uniform Adoption Act provides for judicial enforcement of postadoption visitation agreements only for stepparent adoptions. UAA §4-113, 9 U.L.A. (pt. IA) 110-112 (1999 & Supp. 2008). In other cases, the UAA permits "mutually agreed-upon communication between birth and adoptive families," but does not make such agreements enforceable. Id. at 15 (Prefatory Note). Advocates of open adoption emphasize that the practice increases the number of children available for adoption because it comports with many birth parents' desires, eliminates the need for adoptees subsequently to search for their origins, and permits children to avoid the trauma of a complete rupture from their biological parents. In contrast, opponents contend that the practice deters adoption because it creates a fear of disruption of the adoptive family, breaches the traditional principle of confidentiality, and interferes with the establishment of new parent-child relationships. See generally Adam Pertman, Adoption Nation: How the Adoption Revolution Is Transforming America (2000). Which approach do you favor and why?

---

[31] John P. Triseliotis, In Search of Origins: The Experiences of Adopted People 166 (1973). See also Arthur D. Sorosky et al., The Adoption Triangle 121-142 (1978) (finding that the search for biological parents does not indicate a rejection of the adoptive parents and also that the reunions with biological parents do not appear to harm the relationships of the adoptees).

7.   The Relevance of Sexual Orientation to Adoption

What relevance, if any, should be given to the role of sexual orientation in adoption decisionmaking?

In re Adoption of Doe
2008 WL 5006172 (Fla. Cir. Ct. 2008)

LEDERMAN, J.:

This matter came before the Court on Petitioner's sworn Petition for Adoption of John Doe, born June 15, 2000, and his biological half-brother James Doe, born August 2, 2004. [John and James, ages four and four months, respectively] were removed from their home on allegations of abandonment and neglect and placed into the custody of the State. [Petitioner, a licensed foster caregiver, agreed to accept the children.] Twenty months later, upon the termination of parental rights of John and James' [respective biological fathers and mother], the children became available for adoption. [T]he children have now been in Petitioner's care and custody for four years. John is now eight and James is four. . . . Petitioner, the unmarried 45-year old foster care provider of John and James petitioned to adopt the siblings [but the Department of Children and Families] denied Petitioner's application for adoption [because] Petitioner is a homosexual. . . .

Facts

The children arrived at the home of Petitioner and Tom Roe, Sr., domestic partners, and Tom Roe, Sr.'s then eight-year old biological son, Tom Roe, Jr., on the evening of December 11, 2004. John, the elder sibling, arrived with his four-month old brother wearing a dirty adult sized t-shirt and sneakers four sizes too small that seemed more like flip-flops than shoes. Both children were suffering from scalp ringworm. Although John was clearly suffering from a severe case of ringworm, the medication brought from John's home to treat his scalp was unopened and expired. James, too, suffered from an untreated ear infection, as evidenced by the one-month old, nearly unused, medication. John did not speak and had no affect. He had one concern: changing, feeding, and caring for his baby brother. It was clear from the children's first evening at the Petitioner-Roe home that the baby's main caretaker was John, his four-year-old brother.

On that December evening, John and James left a world of chronic neglect, emotional impoverishment and deprivation to enter a new world, foreign to them, that was nurturing, safe, structured and stimulating. Although Petitioner and Roe had fostered other children, caring for John was the most challenging of their foster care experiences. For the first few months, John seemed depressed and presented a void, unresponsive demeanor and appearance. Upon arriving at the Petitioner home, John did not speak a word for about one week. After two weeks, he began to mumble imperceptible utterances. After about one month, John finally began speaking. Petitioner quickly learned that John had never seen a book, could not distinguish letters from numbers, could not identify colors and could not count.

He could not hold a pencil. He had never been in an early childhood program or day care. Nevertheless, John's potential for educational development was apparent. Although he had not had any formal education, John could sing and pick up lyrics very quickly. Early on, Petitioner and Roe noticed that John hoarded food by requesting additional servings at the start of dinnertime and later hiding the extra food in his room. John eventually grew out of this behavior, due in part to a tactic employed by Petitioner and Roe of showing John, in advance of mealtime, the more than sufficient amount of food on the stove prepared and available for the family.

James was a very happy baby and was content with anyone, even strangers. After approximately two months, James began to exhibit signs of attachment to his primary caregivers, Petitioner and Roe. John, however, took about two years to fully bond. At one time, John shunned hugs from Petitioner and Roe. However, in his own time, John developed bonding and today, initiates goodbye hugs each morning before going to school. . . .

Petitioner and Roe met in 1999 and began living together in July 2000. Petitioner, who has a Bachelor in Psychology and Masters Degree in Public Health, has worked as a flight attendant for American Airlines for 17 years. Roe has worked for Amtrak for 10 years. On their second anniversary, the two acknowledged their commitment before friends and family by exchanging matching rings at an informal ceremony at their home. Since that time, they have considered themselves spouses. They support each other financially by pooling their money into joint checking accounts. Both Petitioner and Roe's families support their union. At some point, Petitioner and Roe decided to expand their family. After considering surrogacy and adopting abroad they decided to become foster parents. . . .

The parties tendered experts from all over the country to proffer testimony relating to the social, psychological, interpersonal, and physical effects of same-sex relationships on individuals, families, children, and to some extent, society as a whole. [One of the Department witnesses testified that] the law's restriction serves the best interests of children because when compared to heterosexual behaving individuals, homosexual behaving individuals experience: (1) a lifetime prevalence of significantly increased psychiatric disorders; (2) higher levels of alcohol and substance abuse; (3) higher levels of major depression; (4) higher levels of affective disorder; (5) four times higher levels of suicide attempts; and (6) substantially increased rates of relationship instability and breakup. Such factors, according to the Department, harm children of homosexual parents. Petitioner's expert witnesses countered these conclusions and suggested that: (1) homosexually behaving individuals are no more susceptible to mental health or psychological disorders than their heterosexual counterparts; (2) both heterosexual and homosexual parents can provide nurturing, safe, healthy environments for children; and (3) children of homosexual parents are no more at risk of maladjustment than their counterparts with heterosexual parents. . . .

[Petitioner's expert Dr. Letitia Peplau, Professor of Psychology at the University of California in Los Angeles, California, testified that] research in the field suggests that the relationships of lesbians and gay men are similar in stability, quality, satisfaction, shared experiences and conflict resolution, to that of heterosexual married and unmarried couples. . . . Dr. Susan Cochran, a Professor of Epidemiology and Statistics at the University of California, Los Angeles [testified] as to the effects of sexual orientation on mental health and the prevalence of psychiatric disorders. . . . According to the witness, taken as a whole, the research shows that sexual orientation alone is not a proxy for psychiatric disorders, mental health conditions, substance abuse or smoking; members of every demographic group suffer from these conditions at rates not significantly higher than for homosexuals. . . .

Petitioner's final witness in the area of psychology was Dr. Michael Lamb, Professor of Psychology at the University of Cambridge, London, England [whose] research focuses on the factors relating to children's development and adjustment. . . . The witness testified that based on his 30 years of research and experience in the field, he can say with certainty that children raised by homosexual parents do not suffer an increased risk of behavioral problems, psychological problems, academic development, gender identity, sexual identity, maladjustment, or interpersonal relationship development. . . . Explaining the literature to the contrary, Dr. Lamb offers that such research is unreliable, not methodologically sound, unpublished or published in non-peer review publications, and over-emphasizes non-statistical differences, among other methodological flaws. . . . Moreover, according to the witness, there was no significant difference between the sexual orientation of children with lesbian parents and those with heterosexual parents. . . . With regard to social relationships and peer adjustments, Dr. Lamb reports that children raised by gay parents develop social relationships the same as those raised by heterosexual parents. The research shows that children of gay parents are not ostracized and do not experience discrimination any more than children of heterosexual parents. . . .

Lastly, Dr. Lamb opined that the assumption that children need a mother and a father in order to be well adjusted is outdated and not supported by the research. According to the witness, there is no optimal gender combination of parents; neither men nor women have a greater ability to parent. Additionally, today, two-parent households are less attached to static roles than in the past. Moreover, there is a well established and generally accepted consensus in the field that children do not need a parent of each gender to adjust healthily. The witness opines that the exclusion of homosexuals as adoptive parents is not rationally related to child adjustment. Rather, the witness believes the exclusion hurts children by reducing the number of capable and appropriate parents available and willing to adopt. . . .

Based on the evidence presented from experts from all over this country and abroad, it is clear that sexual orientation is not a predictor of a person's ability to parent. . . . The most important factor in ensuring a well adjusted child is the quality of parenting. [A] child in need of love, safety and stability does not first consider the sexual orientation of his parent. More importantly, sexual orientation, solely, should not interfere with a child's right to enjoy the accoutrements of a legal family. John and James, due to no fault of their own, were removed from an environment perilous to their physical, emotional and educational well being. Their biological parents relinquished them to the State, which in turn placed them into an environment that allowed them, eventually, to heal, and now flourish.

The quality and breadth of research available, as well as the results of the studies performed about gay parenting and children of gay parents, is robust and has provided the basis for a consensus in the field. [R]eports and studies find that there are no differences in the parenting of homosexuals or the adjustment of their children. These conclusions have been accepted, adopted and ratified by the American Psychological Association, the American Psychiatry Association, the American Pediatric Association, the American Academy of Pediatrics, the Child Welfare League of America and the National Association of Social Workers. [T]his Court is satisfied that the issue is so far beyond dispute that it would be irrational to hold otherwise; the best interests of children are not preserved by prohibiting homosexual adoption.

The Guardian Ad Litem, the adoption agency and the assessing professionals agree that Petitioner and his domestic partner's ability to parent is excellent. The quality of parenting, the level of bonding and attachment and the thriving relationship of the children with Petitioner, Roe and Tom Junior is uncontroverted by all parties to this litigation. This Court has presided over John and James case since its inception. This Court has presided over 58 hearings in their case and has had the opportunity to observe the children, Petitioner, and the growing relationship between them. It is clear to this Court that Petitioner is an exceptional parent to John and James who have healed in his care and are now thriving. Accordingly, Petitioner, John and James should be permitted to permanently and legally share the emotional, psychological, and familial bonds of parentage. Nevertheless, based on the law of this state, only a finding that the statute is unconstitutional will permit this Court to grant the petition.

Conclusions of Law

Originally enacted in 1977, Florida Statute §63.042(3)(2008), provides, "No ~~"No Fla. stat.~~ person eligible to adopt under this statute may adopt if that person is a homosexual." Since that time, the statute has survived several challenges. . . . Florida is the only remaining state to expressly ban all gay adoptions without exception. Here, Petitioner attacks the constitutionality of the categorical exclusion of homosexuals as eligible adoptive parents on equal protection and substantive due process grounds. . . .

. . . Florida's statutory framework is explicit that dependent children have the right to permanency and stability in adoptive placements. The legislature has recognized that permanency in an adoptive home is a foster child's right, and that the state has a compelling interest in achieving that result in the most expeditious way. . . .

Here, Fla. Stat. §63.042(3) violates the Children's rights by burdening liberty interests by unduly restraining them in State custody on one hand and simultaneously operating to deny them a permanent adoptive placement that is in their best interests on the other. This Court cannot permit such a double-edged sword to continue to lie dormant in our state law, to the peril of children like John and James, without review. The challenged statute, in precluding otherwise qualified homosexuals from adopting available children, does not promote the interests of children and in effect, causes harm to the children it is meant to protect. Both the state and federal governments recognize the critical nature of adoption to the well-being of children who cannot be raised by their biological parents. There is no question, the blanket exclusion of gay applicants defeats Florida's goal of providing dependent children a permanent family through adoption. The exclusion causes some children to be deprived of a permanent placement with a family that is best suited to meet their needs. As it relates to the case at bar, [t]he record clearly reflects that it is in [the children's] best interests to remain in this placement permanently and to be adopted by Petitioner. However, the statutory exclusion deprives John and James the ability to be adopted by their caregivers, to whom they are strongly bonded. Failure of the State to effectuate a permanent placement for John and James with applicants willing and qualified to assume the task creates the risk of severing the Children's healthy attachments and causing profound long-term negative consequences to their development or relegating them to a childhood and adolescence without a permanent home in foster care.

It is clear that the statutory exclusion of homosexuals as prospective adoptive parents deters permanent placements for children in the care of gay foster parents. Alternative forms of permanency, such as guardianship, deprive children of the significant material benefits appurtenant to adoption including inheritance rights. Such alternate forms of permanency also do not provide the significant psychological benefits afforded by adoption including sharing a common surname or enjoying the sense of belonging to a family adoption provides. In addition to the foregoing, the exclusion exacerbates the shortage of adoptive families, leaving more children, especially dependent children, without a legal family at all.

. . . Petitioner and Children argue that the statute violates their right to equal protection under the law [Article I, §2 of the Florida Constitution] because it singles out homosexuals and children raised by homosexual caregivers for unequal treatment without serving a rational basis. Similarly, the Children posit they are not offered equal protection because one class of children placed by the state with heterosexual caregivers have the potential to be adopted by their caregivers, while other children who are also adoptable, but placed by the state with lesbians and gay men cannot be adopted by their caregivers. . . .

[T]he failure to present any evidence in [D.H.R.S. v. Cox, 627 So. 2d 1210 (Dist. Ct. App. 1993)] 15 years ago and the weight of the evidence presented in [Lofton v. Secretary of Dept. of Children and Family Servs., 358 F.3d 804 (11th Cir. 2004)] nearly five years ago are both cited as the grounds for the courts' inability to find the statute unconstitutional as violative of the equal protection of the U.S. and Florida Constitutions. However, today, based on the developments in the fields of social science, psychology, human sexuality, social work and medicine, the existence of additional studies, the re-analysis and peer review of prior studies, the endorsements by the major psychological, psychiatry, child welfare and social work associations, and the now, consensus based on widely accepted results of respected studies by qualified experts, the issue of whether Fla. Stat. §63.042(3) violates the equal protection of homosexuals and children adoptable by homosexuals, is again ripe for consideration.

. . . This matter does not involve a fundamental right or a suspect class and is thus reviewed under the rational basis test. . . . First, the Department argues that the homosexual adoption restriction serves the legitimate state interests of promoting the well-being of minor children. According to the Department, the law's restriction serves the best interests of children because when compared to heterosexual behaving individuals, homosexual behaving individuals experience higher levels of stressors disadvantageous to children. Second, the State also aims to protect the best interest of children by placing them in an adoptive home which minimizes social stigmatization. A third basis for the State's ban on homosexual adoption is its protection of societal moral interests of the child. . . . The Department argues Fla. Stat. §63.042(3) is rationally related to Florida's interest by protecting children from the undesirable realities of the homosexual lifestyle. However, as thoroughly summarized in the Findings of Fact section of this Final Judgment, the foregoing is, frankly, false. . . . Here, the two witnesses proffered by the Department failed to offer any reasonable, credible evidence to substantiate their beliefs or to justify the legislation. Viewing the statute from this point of view clearly renders it "illogical to the point of irrationality." . . .

The Department next claims that best interests of children are served by placing them in an adoptive home which minimizes the social stigmatization they may experience. Again applying rational basis review, this Court rejects the Department's attempt to justify the statute by reference to a supposed dark cloud hovering over homes of homosexuals and their children. . . . In this regard, the professionals and the major associations now agree there is a well established and accepted consensus in the field that there is no optimal gender combination of parents. As such, the statute is no longer rationally related to serve this interest.

The Department's final rationale is that §63.042(3) rationally relates to Florida's legitimate moral interest to promote public morality. However, public morality per se, disconnected from any separate legitimate interest, is not a legitimate government interest to justify unequal treatment. Lawrence v. Texas, 539 U.S. 558, 582 (2003). . . . Here Petitioner qualifies for approval as an adoptive parent in all respects but one; his sexual orientation. The Department's position is that homosexuality is immoral. Yet, homosexuals may be lawful foster parents in Florida and care for our most fragile children who have been abused, neglected and abandoned. As such, the exclusion forbidding homosexuals to adopt children does not further the public morality interest it seeks to combat. Based on this scenario, there can be no rationally related public morality interest differentiating in the State's support of a homosexual's long-term foster care relationship with a child and a denial of their legal relationship through adoption. Consequently, there is no "morality" interest with regard to one group of individuals permitted to form the visage of a family in one context but prohibited in another. The contradiction between the adoption and foster care statutes defeats the public morality argument and is thus not rationally related to serving a governmental interest.

This Court finds Fla. Stat. §63.042(3) violates the Petitioner and the Children's equal protection rights guaranteed by Article I, §2 of the Florida Constitution without satisfying a rational basis. Moreover, the statutory exclusion defeats a child's right to permanency as provided by federal and state law pursuant to the Adoption and Safe Families Act of 1997. Accordingly, it is ordered and adjudged that John Doe and James Doe be declared the legal children of Petitioner. . . .

NOTES AND QUESTIONS

(1) Background.   Florida was the first state to ban gay and lesbian couples from adopting children. The ban was enacted in the wake of former beauty queen Anita Bryant's "Save Our Children" campaign in 1977 against the repeal of a Miami housing ordinance prohibiting discrimination against gays and lesbians. Subsequently, gay and lesbian couples unsuccessfully challenged the Florida adoption ban at both the federal and state levels. In Lofton v. Secretary of the Department of Children and Family Services, 358 F.3d 804 (11th Cir. 2004), gay and lesbian couples argued that the ban violated equal protection and due process under the *federal* constitution. The Eleventh Circuit upheld the ban, finding a lack of consensus in the medical, sociological, and psychological literature on the effects of a parents' sexual orientation on their children, and deferred to the legislature's determination that sexual orientation had a presumptively negative effect. Plaintiffs also challenged the Florida ban on *state* constitutional grounds. In Cox v. Florida Department of Health and Rehabilitative Services, 656 So. 2d 902 (Fla. 1995), the Florida Supreme Court held that the ban did not violate state constitutional protection against privacy or due process and was not unconstitutionally vague. However, the state supreme court failed to reach the equal protection issue because of an insufficient record. How does the court in *Doe* distinguish *Cox* and *Lofton*?

(2) State Restrictions.   Several jurisdictions expressly take sexual orientation into account in adoption decisionmaking. By 2006, 16 states had taken steps to impose restrictions on adoptions by gay and lesbians through either legislation or ballot initiatives. Andrea Stone, Drives to Ban Gay Adoption Heat Up: In 16 States Laws or Ballot Votes Proposed, USA Today, Feb. 21, 2006, at 1A. Some state proscriptions address an *individual's* sexual orientation, whereas other statutes restrict gay and lesbian *couples* from adopting children. Compare Conn. Gen. Stat. Ann. §45a-726a (West Supp. 2001) (prohibiting placement "with a prospective adoptive or foster parent or parents who are homosexual or bisexual"), with Miss. Code Ann. §93-17-3(2) (Supp. 2002) ("Adoption by couples of the same gender is prohibited"). Which type is the statute in *Doe*? Do such proscriptions manifest an animus toward gays and lesbians that is constitutionally suspect? See Romer v. Evans, 517 U.S. 620 (1996) (invalidating a state constitutional amendment banning the enactment of laws protecting gays and lesbians, based on the Equal Protection Clause, because of anti-gay animosity). In contrast, 12 jurisdictions explicitly prohibit consideration of sexual orientation in adoption.[32]

(3) Sexual Stereotypes.   What are the assumptions and sexual stereotypes that contribute to legislative enactment of proscriptions against adoption by gay and lesbian parents? How does the court in *Doe* respond to them?

---

[32] Angeline Acain, Equal Rights: Anti-Gay Laws Hurt Adoption Advances, Myrtle Beach Sun News, June 3, 2007, at D5 (citing California, Connecticut, the District of Columbia, Illinois, Indiana, Maryland, Massachusetts, Nevada, New Jersey, New York, Pennsylvania, and Vermont). See also Opinion No. 07-140, Tenn. Atty. Gen., Oct. 10, 2007 (interpreting state adoption statute to permit same-sex couples to adopt children, provided that adoption is in the child's best interests).

(4) Foster Parenting Bans Distinguished.   As *Doe* explains, Florida's statutory scheme permitted gays and lesbians to serve as foster parents but not adoptive parents. Does it make sense to permit gays and lesbians to serve as foster parents but to deny them the right to adopt? Do the differences between foster parenting and adoption justify different treatment of the role of sexual orientation? What does the court in *Doe* respond?

(5) Validity of Second-Parent Adoptions.   Some jurisdictions recognize "second-parent adoptions" by members of gay and lesbian couples. Generally, in such adoptions, the biological parent's same-sex partner petitions a court for permission to adopt the child (although such adoptions can occur in situations in which neither prospective adoptive parent has a biological relationship to the child). Currently, 11 jurisdictions permit second-parent adoptions by persons other than stepparents (either by statute or case law). Jason N.W. Plowman, When Second-Parent Adoption Is the Second-Best Option: The Case for Legislative Reform as the Next Best Option for Same-Sex Couples in the Face of Continued Marriage Inequality, 11 Scholar 57, 64-70 (2008). In *Doe*, the petitioner and his partner decided that only the petitioner should seek to adopt John and James, based on their belief that framing the adoption as a two-parent gay adoption would be more difficult. In the event that petitioner's request to adopt was granted, then his partner planned to adopt the children.

In second-parent adoptions, some courts wrestle with the issue of whether granting the adoption requires the court to terminate the parental rights of the biological parent to permit the assumption of parental rights by the second parent. Thus, in S.J.L.S. v. T.L.S., 265 S.W.3d 804 (Ky. Ct. App. 2008), a lesbian domestic partner, who conceived a child via artificial insemination, was able to vacate the adoption decree granted to her same-sex partner because the court concluded that the state statute requiring termination of a biological parent's rights for an adoption to be valid was not estopped due to the biological mother's initial consent to the adoption by her partner. See also In re Adoption of Luke, 640 N.W.2d 374 (Neb. 2002) (holding that a child was not eligible for adoption by the biological mother's companion because the biological mother had not relinquished her parental rights). The underlying rationale is that children should have only one parent of a given gender. Does this rationale make sense in contemporary society, with its high rate of divorce and myriad family forms? See also *Doe*, 2008 WL 5006172, at *10 (discussing expert testimony debunking the assumption that children need a parent of each gender).

Traditionally, the stepparent adoption procedure (which permits a stepparent to adopt a child without terminating the parental rights of the birth parent) has not been available to gay and lesbian couples because they have not been allowed to marry. Some states' domestic partnership laws permit registered same-sex partners to use an expedited stepparent adoption procedure (e.g., Cal. Fam. Code §9000 (West 2007)). See also Stephanie Francis Ward, "Alternative Families" Gaining Acceptance, 31 A.B.A. J. E-Report 2 (2003) (reporting that eight states allow adoption by a nonbiological same-sex parent without termination of the biological parent's rights).

For other recent cases permitting second-parent adoption, see Wheeler v. Wheeler, 642 S.E.2d 103 (Ga. 2007); Goodson v. Castellanos, 214 S.W.3d 741

(Tex. App. 2007). For an empirical study of couples involved in second-parent adoptions, see Catherine Connolly, The Voice of the Petitioner: The Experiences of Gay and Lesbian Parents in Successful Second-Parent Adoption Proceedings, 36 Law & Soc'y Rev. 325 (2002).

(6) Interstate Recognition of Adoption Decrees.   Interstate recognition of adoption decrees is also a problem for gay and lesbian adoptive parents. When a child born in one state is adopted in another state, the adoptive parents may ask an official in the child's state of birth to issue an amended birth certificate listing the out-of-state adoptive parents as the parents. For example, a gay couple in New York jointly adopted a child who was born in Louisiana. When the adoptive parents tried to obtain a birth certificate for their son from the Louisiana state registrar (to obtain medical insurance for the boy), the Louisiana registrar denied their request on the ground that Louisiana did not recognize same-sex adoptions. In Adar v. Smith, 2008 WL 5378130 (E.D. La. 2008), a federal district judge ruled that the New York adoption decree must be given full faith and credit by Louisiana and required issuance of the birth certificate. See also Finstuen v. Crutcher, 496 F.3d 1139 (10th Cir. 2007) (holding unconstitutional an Oklahoma statute banning recognition of out-of-state adoptions by same-sex couples). See generally Rhonda Wasserman, Are You Still My Mother? Interstate Recognition of Adoptions by Gays and Lesbians, 58 Am. U. L. Rev. 1 (2008).

(7) Influence of Same-Sex Marriage Legalization Movement.   What is the impact on adoption law of the movement to legalize same-sex marriage? Of course, in jurisdictions that allow same-sex marriage (currently Massachusetts and Connecticut), gay and lesbian couples have no difficulty adopting children. However, even some jurisdictions that refuse to recognize same-sex marriage appear to reflect a more liberal attitude toward the role of sexual orientation in adoption decisionmaking. See, e.g., In re Adoption of M.A., 930 A.2d 1088 (Me. 2007) (holding that a state statute that allows married couples to file a joint petition for adoption does not prohibit joint adoption by an unmarried same-sex couple because such an adoption promotes the rights of foster children). But cf. S.J.L.S. v. T.L.S., supra (holding that the legal fiction that the relationship between a former domestic partner and the biological mother was equivalent to marriage could not be used to allow the former domestic partner to adopt the child).

On the other hand, the backlash against same-sex marriage has resulted in new strategies by anti-gay advocates. For example, in 2006 the Arkansas Supreme Court invalidated a child welfare restriction (Regulation 200.3.2) that prohibited an individual from becoming a foster parent if an adult member of that person's household was gay or lesbian. Dept. of Human Servs. & Child Welfare Agency Review Bd. v. Howard, 238 S.W.3d 1 (Ark. 2006). In response, anti-gay activists secured passage of a ballot referendum that broadened the ban to prohibit adoption as well as foster care by anyone "cohabitating outside of a valid marriage" (thereby applying the ban to both unmarried opposite-sex couples and same-sex couples). Is the new law susceptible to an equal protection challenge? See Cole v. Arkansas, No. CV 2008-14284 (Ark. Cir. Ct., filed Dec. 30, 2008) (a challenge to the Arkansas law by gay and lesbian couples based on state and federal due process and equal protection guarantees).

(8) Children's Voices. In *Doe*, the children assert their own claims based on equal protection and due process. How do the claims and interests of John and James differ from those of their gay and lesbian prospective adoptive parents? How does the court in *Doe* take into account the children's interests? See generally Tanya M. Washington, Comment, Throwing Black Babies out with the Bath Water: A Child-Centered Challenge to Same-Sex Adoption Bans, 6 Hastings Race & Poverty L.J. 1 (2009).

(9) Relevance of Social Science Data on the Impact of Gay Parenting. How does *Doe* regard the issue of the relevance of the social science data to adoption by gays and lesbians? How does the court evaluate the empirical research under the rational-basis test? Should it matter that some of the existing data refer to outcomes for children in the context of custody rather than adoption? Should it matter that some of the existing data refer to outcomes for children raised by lesbians as opposed to gay men? In studies of foster children, can social science methodology differentiate the impact of a parent's sexual orientation from that of the harm caused by the child's previous home environment? Can it differentiate the impact of sexual orientation from societal stigma? See *Doe*, 2008 WL 5006172, at *9 (discussing expert testimony favoring gay adoption that concludes that the ban will not serve to shield a child from stigma because teasing about parental attributes is universal and "A child that is teased views one reason no less hurtful than another"). See also Susan Golombok, New Family Forms, in Families Count: Effects on Child and Adolescent Development (Alison Clarke-Stewart & Judy Dunn, eds., 2006) (discussing social science research).

(10) Uniform Parentage Act. Should the Uniform Parentage Act (UPA), a model statute that was promulgated originally to adjudicate the paternity of unwed fathers, be applied to same-sex adoption cases? (The UPA is discussed Chapter 2, supra pp. 188-189.) For example, courts have occasionally analogized lesbian second parents to presumptive fathers under the UPA if the second parents have cared for the child and held the child out as their own. What are the advantages and disadvantages of such an approach? See generally Susan Frelich Appleton, Presuming Women: Revisiting the Presumption of Legitimacy in the Same-Sex Couples Era, 86 B.U. L. Rev. 227 (2006); Melanie B. Jacobs, Micah Has One Mommy and One Legal Stranger: Adjudicating Maternity for Nonbiological Lesbian Coparents, 50 Buff. L. Rev. 341 (2002); Nicole N. Parness, Note, Forcing a Square into a Circle: Why Are Courts Straining to Apply the Uniform Parentage Act to Gay Couples and Their Children?, 27 Whittier L. Rev. 893 (2006).

8. The Relevance of Race to Adoption

What relevance, if any, should be given to the role of race in adoption decision making?

Adoption of Vito

728 N.E.2d 292 (Mass. 2000)

MARSHALL, C.J.

This appeal arises from the denial of a petition to dispense with parental consent to adoption. The case concerns a child [who] has lived with his foster parents (also his preadoptive parents) since he was discharged from the hospital one month after his birth. Vito has never lived with his biological mother.[3] He is now eight and one-half years old. [Vito's foster family is from the Dominican Republic; his foster parents speak only Spanish. Vito speaks both Spanish and English. His biological family is African-American.]

We summarize in some detail the findings of fact and conclusions of law made by the judge. In 1990 Vito's biological mother began using crack cocaine, which she continued to do until 1995, with occasional periods of nonuse. Prior to May, 1991, when a judge in the Boston Juvenile Court awarded temporary custody of her three oldest children to the department, she had been trading food stamps and using public welfare benefits to purchase crack cocaine. Her children were often left at home alone. When Vito tested positive for cocaine at birth [in 1992], an abuse and neglect report concerning him was filed. . . .

Vito was discharged from the hospital one month after his birth and was placed in the home of his foster parents; his siblings had been placed in other homes. In March, 1992, the Boston Juvenile Court ordered the department to assume permanent custody of Vito and his three older siblings; the mother's whereabouts were unknown to the department at that time.

From the time of his removal from his mother's care in January, 1992, while in the hospital, until January, 1995, his biological mother visited Vito only once. During that ninety-minute visit, Vito responded minimally to his biological mother, withdrew from her and attached himself to his foster mother. At the end of that visit, the mother agreed to visit Vito again at the end of the month, on his first birthday, but although the foster mother and Vito arrived for the birthday visit, the mother failed to attend; she did not telephone to cancel the visit. Following the failed January, 1993, birthday visit, the biological mother made no request for a visit with her son for the remainder of 1993. During 1994 there were no visits with Vito, and little contact between the biological mother and the department; she told the department she had relocated to Florida.

In 1995, while back in Massachusetts in prison on shoplifting charges, Vito's mother signed a department service plan, entered a drug rehabilitation program and began visits with Vito and his siblings.[10] Vito's mother was released from prison in October, 1995. The judge found that the mother's visits with Vito have been generally consistent since March, 1995, and that she has attended monthly

---

[3] Vito's biological father did not object to the department's petition, nor did he appeal.

[10] Because the department now knew where Vito's biological mother was located, it initiated the effort to begin visits between Vito and her. The first such visit took place in March, 1995, at the Massachusetts Correctional Institution at Framingham. Department regulations provide that the department shall make reasonable efforts to work with incarcerated parents to promote a healthy relationship with their children, such efforts to include regular visitation at the correctional facility.

supervised visits since her release. The judge found that Vito and his biological mother have "no emotional sharing" between them and remain dissociated, despite pleasant play and conversation. The judge found that Vito did not show any genuine interest in his biological siblings and did not appear to have formed any emotional attachment to his biological mother; he did not appear to be excited to see her and separated from her with no difficulties or emotional overtones. The judge nevertheless made an ultimate finding that Vito had formed "a positive relationship" with his biological mother that has developed since visitation began when she was incarcerated.[11] The judge found that Vito's mother, however, had not fully complied with the department's service plan tasks, and concluded that Vito's biological mother cannot now resume care and custody of Vito because "she has not secured adequate stable housing, has not adequately addressed her issues of lengthy substance abuse history and has not acquired any meaningful parenting skills training." She also concluded that Vito's mother's drug abuse and resultant neglect "was severe and of a lengthy duration," although she had improved in the last two years.

In contrast, the judge found that Vito is "fully integrated into his foster family both emotionally and ethnically." The judge found that it was "important" to Vito to belong to his foster family "because that was the only family he had known," and that "[t]he foster parents are invested in adopting [Vito]; they perceive him as their own son." She found that Vito "has a significant attachment to his foster family," and that separating Vito from his foster family could result in a range of negative responses, from severe depression to less severe trauma.

The judge concluded that, by clear and convincing evidence, Vito's mother is currently unfit to parent him. . . . Despite the fact that the biological mother "cares deeply for and has good intentions toward the child," however, "[g]ood intentions . . . are insufficient to establish fitness to parent a child."

The judge further determined that "racial issues *may* at some time in the future" become a problem for Vito (emphasis added). She found that Vito's relationship with his biological mother is "crucial" for his "racial and cultural development and adjustment," that his best interests will be served by continued "significant" contact with her after any adoption, and that under the department's adoption plan Vito would have limited or no connection to his African-American family or culture.[13] She found that the department's plan is not in Vito's "best interest so long as it does not provide for significant ongoing contact with [his] [m]other and [biological] siblings."

[The probate judge therefore denied the petition to dispense with parental consent to adoption but stated that she might enter a new judgment should the

---

[11] During a May, 1995, visit Vito's mother was seen attempting to interact with Vito, talking to him and exchanging toys. During subsequent visits Vito began to direct more conversation to his mother, although he did not refer to her by name or by any version of "mother." One social worker testified that as Vito began to understand English better, between May and September of 1995, he began to relate better to his mother. Another social worker observed that in 1996 Vito referred to his biological mother as his "other mother." The guardian ad litem reported that Vito told her he liked the visits with his mother and that she brings him toys when they visit.

[13] The judge found that there was no evidence that the adoptive family had any significant contacts with the African-American community at this time.

department submit an adoption plan that provided for postadoption contact, including eight yearly visits with his biological mother, as long as the mother is not abusing drugs and the contact continues to be in Vito's best interests. The department appealed. Vacating the probate decree, the Appeals Court directed that the department's petition be granted to dispense with the mother's consent. The Appeals Court further found the judge's proposal for postadoption visitation was permissible but ordered that, given the passage of time, the probate court should rehear any petition for postadoption visitation filed within 30 days. The department petitioned for further appellate review, challenging the judge's requirement of postadoption visitation in the adoption plan and departmental involvement after the adoption.]

Despite numerous appellate decisions to the contrary, the department argues that there is no authority for the judge to enter an order requiring postadoption visitation in a termination proceeding, pursuant to G.L. c. 210, §3, or at least, that such an order cannot be made where there is an identified, pre-adoptive family and the child has no bond with the biological parent. . . . We concluded in [Petition of the Dept. of Social Servs. to Dispense with Consent to Adoption, 467 N.E.2d 861 (Mass. 1984)] that the equitable powers of courts in this area permit a judge, in her discretion, to evaluate an adoption plan proposed by the department [and] decide whether [postadoption] visitation is in the child's best interests. Since our 1984 decision, numerous Appeals Court decisions have expressed an understanding that judges may effect or require postadoption visitation as an outcome of termination proceedings. That was a correct understanding of our law.

A judge's equitable power to order postadoption contact, however, is not without limit. . . . Constitutional considerations also guide the exercise of this equitable power. Adoptive parents have the same legal rights toward their children that biological parents do. Parental rights to raise one's children are essential, basic rights that are constitutionally protected [citing Wisconsin v. Yoder, Stanley v. Illinois, Meyer v. Nebraska, and Prince v. Massachusetts]. State intrusion in the rearing of children by their parents may be justified only in limited circumstances.

At a pragmatic level, unnecessary involvement of the courts in long-term, wide-ranging monitoring and enforcement of the numerous postadoption contact arrangements could result from too ready an application of the court's equitable power to issue contact orders. The postadoption contact arrangements contemplated by the judge in this case were both long term and wide ranging, and necessarily would have involved the court in ongoing arrangements between the biological mother and the adopting family for many years to come. But courts are not often the best place to monitor children's changing needs. . . . We also recognize the concern raised by the department and the amici that untrammeled equitable power used to impose postadoption contact might reduce the number of prospective parents willing to adopt. . . . Where, as here, the child has formed strong, nurturing bonds with his preadoptive family, and there is little or no evidence of a significant, existing bond with the biological parent, judicial exercise of equitable power to require postadoption contact would usually be unwarranted. . . .

Transitional provision for posttermination or postadoption contact in the best interests of the child, however, is a far different thing from judicial meddling in the child's and adoptive family's life, based not on evidence of the emotional ties and current dynamics between the child and the biological parent, but on speculation concerning some hypothetical dynamic between parent and child several years hence, later in adolescence, for example. Parental and familial autonomy cannot be so lightly cast aside. . . .

Looking at the evidence of the actual circumstances of Vito's life and relationships, testimony of the guardian ad litem made clear that Vito's monthly visits with the biological mother had little or no impact on Vito's sense of identity. Rather, the judge's findings reveal that Vito strongly identified with his preadoptive family, emotionally and ethnically. . . .

There was also little in the record before us to suggest that Vito's relationship with his biological mother was likely to become important to Vito's adolescent identity. There was evidence of some possible future significance of the relationship in the guardian ad litem's acknowledgment that, generally, adolescence *may* be a time when a transracial adoptee *may* experience adjustment problems, and that Vito would have little connection to an African-American family or culture living with his adoptive family. Generalities about what may be in the best interests of some children, without more, cannot be the basis of judicial orders concerning postadoption contact of a particular child; the best interests of the child standard is one grounded in the particular needs and circumstances of the individual child in question.

Assuming that it was proper to use racial grounds for determining Vito's best interest, there was no evidence in the record that showed Vito would be deprived of all African-American contacts in his adolescence if regular visits with his biological mother were not mandated. While Vito's foster family "currently" has no significant contacts with the African-American community, that fact says little, if anything, about contacts that his adoptive family might develop in the future, if this becomes important for their son. We discern no support for a determination that Vito's relationship with his biological mother is "crucial" for his "racial and cultural development and adjustment." . . .

We conclude, therefore, that, although the probate judge had a statutory mandate to review the department's adoption plan to determine whether the best interests of the child would be served by a termination decree with that plan, and although the judge had equitable authority to order postadoption contact, including visitation, the judge's determination that such postadoption contact was required was clearly erroneous in this case. . . .

NOTES AND QUESTIONS

(1) Background of Race-Matching Policies. Should African-American children be adopted by white parents? The issue of transracial adoption has evoked controversy for decades. During the 1960s and early 1970s, the Civil Rights Movement led to a supportive climate for transracial adoption. However, the climate changed in 1972 when the National Association of Black Social Workers (NABSW) denounced transracial adoption in an influential statement at their national conference. NABSW contended that white parents could not teach their

African-American children to deal with the prejudice endemic to society. More-over, NABSW argued that transracial adoption constituted a form of genocide and an attack on the African-American family.

In response, the Child Welfare League of America (the nation's oldest and largest child welfare organization) promptly amended their adoption standards to support race matching. This action resulted in a significant decline in transracial adoptions. See Hawley Fogg-Davis, The Ethics of Transracial Adoption 3 (2002) (pointing out that transracial adoption steadily increased following the first docu-mented placement in 1948 until it peaked in 1971, before the NABSW statement); Randall Kennedy, Interracial Intimacies: Sex, Marriage, Identity, and Adoption 450-453 (2003) (similarly explaining the influence of the NABSW position paper).

What are the arguments supporting and opposing transracial adoption? Con-sider the excerpt (reprinted infra) by Cynthia Hawkins-Leon and Carla Bradley, Race and Transracial Adoption: The Answer Is Neither Simply Black or White Nor Right or Wrong, 51 Cath. U. L. Rev. 1227 (2002). For different views of transracial adoption, compare Elizabeth Bartholet, Nobody's Children: Abuse and Neglect, Foster Drift, and the Adoption Alternative (1999); Randall Kennedy, Interracial Intimacies: Sex, Marriage, Identity, and Adoption (2003) (both supporting trans-racial adoption) with Ruth-Arlene W Howe, Transracial Adoption (TRA): Old Prejudices and Discrimination Float Under a New Halo, 6 B.U. Pub. Int. L.J. 409 (1997); Twila L. Perry, Transracial Adoption and Gentrification: An Essay on Race, Power, Family and Community, 26 B.C. Third World L.J. 25 (2006).

(2) The trial judge in Adoption of Vito proposed postadoption visitation with the child's African-American mother and siblings as a method of promoting the child's racial identity. Why did the state supreme court hold that this ruling was erroneous? What is the best way to maintain a transracial adoptee's appreciation of his or her racial heritage? In what circumstances is postadoption visitation appro-priate for transracial adoptees? When is it inappropriate?

(3) Empirical Research. Approximately 15 percent of adoptions from foster care are transracial. Madelyn Freundlich, Transracial and Transcultural Adoptions, 27 Fam. Advoc. 40, 40 (2004). Most research on the effects of transracial adoption has found that transracially adopted children adjust well in their adoptive homes. The most comprehensive longitudinal research concludes that these adoptions serve the children's best interests. That empirical study (spanning three decades and studying 366 children) found no differences in the children's self-esteem or racial self-perception and determined that the children were at ease in both African-American and white worlds. See Rita J. Simon & Howard Altstein, Adop-tion, Race & Identity: From Infancy to Young Adulthood (2d ed. 2002). See also Arnold R. Silverman, Outcomes of Transracial Adoption, in The Future of Chil-dren: Adoption 115 (David & Lucille Packard Foundation ed., 1993). Recent research identifies challenges facing transracial adoptees, such as learning to cope with their different racial or ethnic identity and discrimination. Evan B. Donaldson, Adoption Institute, Finding Families for African American Children: The Role of Race and Law in Adoption from Foster Care — Policy & Practice Perspective 5-6 (2008), available at *http://www.adoptioninstitute.org/publications/MEPApaper20080527.pdf*. For first-person accounts of transracial adoption, see Sharon E. Rush, Loving Across the Color Line: A White Adoptive Mother Learns

About Race (2000); Rita J. Simon & Rhonda M. Roorda, In Their Own Voices: Transracial Adoptees Tell Their Stories (2000).

(4) Federal Legislation. In 1994 Congress enacted the Multiethnic Placement Act (MEPA), 42 U.S.C. §5115a (1994), prohibiting the delay or denial of child placements (in adoption and foster care) by any federally funded agency *solely* on the basis of race, color, or national origin. However, MEPA contained a loophole: Agencies could consider the race, color, or national origin when relevant and in conjunction with other factors. As a result, agencies continued race matching despite the legislation. In response, Congress repealed portions of MEPA in 1996 and substituted new legislation, the Inter-Ethnic Adoption Act (IEAA) (enacted as part of the Small Business Job Protection Act, 42 U.S.C. §§671[a], 674). IEAA strengthened the federal policy against race matching by penalizing federally funded programs that violate the prohibition against race matching by reduction of their federal funds. Following the enactment of IEAA, many commentators contend that race may no longer be considered in placements. See, e.g., Kennedy, supra, at 400; Cynthia Hawkins-León & Carla Bradley, supra, at 1248. That view, however, is not unanimous. Compare Fogg-Davis, supra, at 49. For a recent critique of the federal law, see David J. Herring, The Multiethnic Placement Act: Threat to Foster Child Safety and Well-Being?, 41 U. Mich. J.L. Reform 89 (2007).

In the principal case, did the probate judge's denial of the agency's petition to dispense with the mother's consent — based on the importance of maintaining Vito's racial identity — delay Vito's adoption, in violation of the IEAA? See Adoption of Vito, 728 N.E.2d at 305 (vacating the denial of the petition to dispense with the mother's consent on other grounds, thereby obviating the need to address this question). Might Vito's prospective adoptive parents have a federal cause of action for a potential violation of IEAA? See 42 U.S.C. §674 (d)(3)(A) (S2000) (conferring such a private right or action).

(5) Influence of Palmore v. Sidoti. The United States Supreme Court has not addressed the role of race in adoption decisionmaking. However, in Palmore v. Sidoti (infra, p. 580), the Supreme Court held that consideration of race as the sole basis for the denial of *custody* to a Caucasian mother married to an African-American man violates equal protection. According to some commentators, *Palmore's* application to the context of adoption is unclear. See, e.g., Twila L. Perry, Power, Possibility and Choice: The Racial Identity of Transracially Adopted Children, 9 Mich. J. Race & L. 215, 218 (2003) (book review of Hawley Fogg-Davis, The Ethics of Transracial Adoption (2002)). Following *Palmore,* several state and federal courts upheld consideration of race as one of several factors in adoption. Id. See generally David D. Meyer, *Palmore* Comes of Age: The Place of Race in the Placement of Children, 18 U. Fla. J.L. & Pub. Pol'y 183 (2007).

(6) What are the similarities and differences between legal and societal responses toward adoption by gay and lesbian parents and transracial adoption? See, e.g., Kenneth L. Karst, Law, Cultural Conflict, and the Socialization of Children, 91 Cal. L. Rev. 967 (2003) (pointing out both contexts are dominated by public concerns about the socialization of children).

(7) The Relevance of Religion. Religious-matching laws, which match the religion of the adoptive child (or the biological parents) to that of the adoptive

parents, have long been upheld as constitutional. See, e.g., Dickens v. Ernesto, 281 N.E.2d 153 (N.Y. 1972), *appeal dismissed,* 407 U.S. 917 (1972). Although the modern trend reflects a diminution in the importance of such matching, many states still require religious matching. Amanda C. Pustilnik, Note, Private Ordering, Legal Ordering, and the Getting of Children: A Counterhistory of Adoption Law, 20 Yale L. & Pol'y Rev. 263, 289 nn. 130 & 131 (2002) (pointing out that from 1954 to 1989, the number of states with such provisions diminished from 43 to 17). What constitutional issues do such statutory provisions raise? From the child's perspective, does such a policy make sense?

(8) The Relevance of Ethnicity: the Indian Child Welfare Act. The Indian Child Welfare Act of 1978 (ICWA), 25 U.S.C. §1915(a) (2006), makes ethnic background decisive in the placement of Native American children. The ICWA provides that the Indian tribe has exclusive jurisdiction as against the state concerning any "child custody proceeding" (including adoptive and foster care placements) involving an Indian child. 25 U.S.C. §§1903(1), 1911(a). Thus, upon the petition of either parent, a Native American custodian, or the child's tribe, a state court must transfer the proceeding to the jurisdiction of the tribe.

Congress enacted the legislation in an attempt to reduce the incidence of adoption of Native American children by white families, with the resulting loss of the children's heritage. The purpose of the Act is to "protect the best interests of Indian children and to promote the stability and security of Indian tribes and families by the establishment of minimum federal standards for the removal of Indian children from their families and the placement of such children in foster or adoptive homes which will reflect the unique values of Indian culture." 25 U.S.C. §1902. Absent good cause, preference is given to placement with: (1) a member of the child's extended family; (2) other members of the child's tribe; or (3) other Native American families.

In Mississippi Band of Choctaw Indians v. Holyfield, 490 U.S. 30 (1989) (overturning the adoption of Choctaw twins), the Supreme Court held that state courts lack authority to permit adoption of Native Americans by non-Native Americans, even when the biological parents leave the reservation to give up the children. See generally Solangel Maldonado, Race, Culture, and Adoption: Lessons from Mississippi Band of Choctaw Indians v. Holyfield, 17 Colum. J. Gender & L. 1 (2008) (narrative and exploration of issues of race and cultural identity in adoptions).

A few state courts have adopted an "existing Indian family exception (EIF) doctrine," that rejects application of the ICWA if a child is not being removed from an existing Indian family because the purpose of the Act (to keep Indian children with Indian families) is not served. See, e.g., Ex parte C.L.J., 946 So. 2d 880 (Ala. Civ. App. Ct. 2006) (recognizing the doctrine but refusing to extend it). However, most courts reject it, contending that it is contrary to the language of the ICWA and violates congressional intent. See, e.g., In re Vincent M., 59 Cal. Rptr. 3d 321 (Ct. App. 2007); In re N.B., 2007 WL 2493906 (Colo. Ct. App. 2007). For a recent critique of the ICWA and the exception, see Lorie M. Graham, Reparations, Self-Determination, and the Seventh Generation, 21 Harv. Hum. Rts. J. 47 (2008).

(9) Problem. Sixteen-year-old Tiffany becomes pregnant during an affair with a schoolmate, Christopher, who is a member of the Muscogee Nation tribe. (Tiffany is not a member of any Native American tribe.) Christopher, although

technically a tribal member, does not participate in any tribal activities or live within tribal boundaries. For a short time during the pregnancy, Tiffany moves into Christopher's household. His grandmother provides support, and Christopher begins working at a restaurant to help with expenses. Christopher and Tiffany subsequently break up, and she moves out. Tiffany then tells Christopher that she has miscarried. However, upon deciding to relinquish the baby for adoption, she is advised to notify the father of her plans and that she is still pregnant. After she does, Christopher protests the adoption. Later, he attempts to visit the mother and child at the birth, but the mother and the hospital staff refuse.

Tiffany seeks an order that the child is eligible for adoption without the father's consent and for termination of his parental rights. The father objects to the adoption. The Muscogee Nation files a motion to intervene, contending that the ICWA applies. What result under the ICWA? Irrespective of the ICWA, does dispensing with the father's consent to adoption violate his constitutional rights? See In re Baby Boy L., 103 P.3d 1099 (Okla. 2004).

Consider the following arguments favoring and opposing transracial adoption. Which do you find most persuasive?

Cynthia G. Hawkins-León & Carla Bradley, Race and Transracial Adoption: The Answer Is Neither Simply Black or White Nor Right or Wrong
51 Cath. U. L. Rev. 1227, 1255-1267 (2002)

In Opposition to Transracial Adoption

1. One-Way Nature

One of the primary reasons that African Americans and organizations purporting to represent the interests of African Americans are opposed to transracial adoption is that the phenomenon of transracial adoption occurs unilaterally; the overwhelming trend in transracial adoption is for White adults to adopt African American children. . . .

2. Racial Identity

The earliest adoptions attempted to mimic the biological family. Transracial adoptions make this attempt impossible and are not in the best interests of African American children. It is in the best interests of a child to preserve a child's racial, ethnic, and cultural heritage in adoption placement decisions. . . . It is virtually impossible for White parents to raise African American children in a White environment and have the children retain their African American identity. . . . When an African American child is adopted by White parents who do not have a significant number of African American friends or contacts and who are uninterested in teaching the child about African American culture, the child is left with little or no African American identity. These children struggle unsuccessfully to acquire a positive racial identity; their parents simply cannot provide a same-race role model. This lack of nurturing makes it virtually impossible for the child to develop pride, acceptance, and understanding of his or her heritage. . . .

3. Cultural Genocide

According to some perspective, transracial adoptions actually harm African American children. Taking African American children away from the African American community, it is argued, is a form of "[cultural] genocide." . . . The concern is that African American children are both literally and figuratively stolen from the African American community. . . .

The notion that a parent's love is enough to overcome external racism is naïve. . . . Even in this new millennium, African Americans are victims of racism and are subject to verbal attacks, physical altercations, employment discrimination, higher arrest rates, and discriminatory sentencing guidelines. Without experiencing such discriminatory behavior themselves, White parents do not have and cannot share adequate survival skills to cope with racism. . . .

4. African American Adoptive Parents

To claim that there are many more African American children in foster care awaiting adoption than the number of prospective African American adoptive parents is inaccurate and insults the strength of the African American family. African American adoptive homes can be found for African American children. . . . African American adoptive parents are in short supply because they encounter roadblocks in the adoption process, not because they are disinterested in adopting. [Problems include institutional racism because guidelines are derived from white middle-class perspectives; adoption agencies lack persons of color as staff decision makers; high adoption fees serve as a barrier; prospective adoptive parents of color may possess negative perceptions of adoption agencies; persons of color tend to favor informal adoption; agencies have inflexible standards that favor young, two-parent, wealthier families and disadvantage prospective parents of color; agencies fail to set aside sufficient resources for recruitment of minority parents; and communities of color remain unaware of the need for their services.]

Furthermore, transracial adoption will not relieve the number of African American children in foster care. [W]hile the median age of children in foster care is nine years, the majority of White adoptive parents are not interested in adopting older children (of any race) or children with handicaps. . . . Therefore, even with the phenomenon of transracial adoptions, some hard-to-place children will remain hard-to-place and will continue to linger in the foster care system. Aggressive recruitment of prospective African American adoptive parents will tend to make transracial adoptions unnecessary. . . .

In Support of Transracial Adoption

1. Statistics

Significant support for transracial adoption stems from the existence and effect of race-related statistics for foster care and domestic adoption. [A]pproximately forty-six percent of children who are available for adoption are African American. Meanwhile, sixty-seven percent of American families waiting to adopt are White. . . . [Additionally], African American children remained in foster care thirty-three percent longer than the national median; on average, Black children remain in foster care for two years. Although African Americans adopt at the same rate as Whites, African Americans would have to adopt at a rate many times that of Whites to provide homes for all of the African American children available for adoption. . . .

Evidence demonstrates that children suffer irreparable harm from growing up without permanent parents. Almost thirty percent of children who grow up in unstable circumstances, including foster care, have reported instances of crime, alcoholism, or both. This startling figure is even more disturbing considering that the number of children in fostercare is now double what it was during the 1970s. . . .

2. Race Matching Harms Children

In passing the [MEPA/IEPA], Congress determined that racial matching and same-race placements were responsible, at least in part, for the length of time children spent in foster care. Furthermore, children are less likely to find permanent placements as they age. Thus, race matching decreases the probability that children, particularly African American children, will be placed into permanent homes for adoption. Rather than same-race placement, it is more important that children receive love, attention, and permanency and that they do not languish in foster care.

3. Success Rate

Adoptions are not all successful; however, the failure rate is unrelated to adoptions across racial lines. There is no evidence that transracial adoptions harm children; in fact, transracial adoptions have proven to be successful. Pointedly, research data indicates that transracial adoptees fare well. Over seventy-five percent of transracial adoptions are considered successful — a number comparable to same-race adoptions. Sixty-eight percent of children who were adopted transracially do not feel any discomfort with their appearance compared to their adoptive parents or the community in which they were raised. It can be concluded from these statistics that transracially adopted children are proud of their heritage. Finally, "there is no evidence that adoptive parents form weaker bonds to dissimilar looking children than to similar ones."

4. Self Identity and White Privilege

While identity is admittedly a complex topic, social and cultural attitudes are learned, not inherited. Individuals are not born with a sense of self, but develop self-awareness through social interaction. . . . Most White parents meet the identity needs of their adopted African American children. Many adoptive parents create a multi-racial environment for their children to offset potential identity problems and to provide same-race mentors. Furthermore, White adoptive parents are in a unique position to teach their Black children how to "maneuver in the White world of power and privilege." . . .

C. *PARENTAL CUSTODY AFTER DIVORCE*

1. Introduction

Divorce affects large numbers of children. Approximately 1 million children experience the divorce of their parents annually.[33] How should the opportunities and responsibilities for various aspects of childrearing be allocated in the event of divorce? In Chapter 2 we considered the economic claims a child should have against each of his or her parents in the context of divorce. Here we shall consider issues relating to custody and visitation.

INTRODUCTORY PROBLEM

John and Mary Anderson are legally separated and are in the process of getting divorced. Their only child, Jimmy, is seven years old. Because Mary has been attending law school for the previous three years, Jimmy has spent a great deal of time with John. John, a college teacher who writes fiction, hates doing laundry, housekeeping, and grocery shopping. Despite his strong affection for his son, John agrees that Mary should have custody of Jimmy.

(1) Upon being informed of his parents' decision, Jimmy expresses his strong wish to live with his father. Should the parental agreement nevertheless be dispositive? Before the divorce is made final, should Jimmy have a lawyer? Should the judge consider Jimmy's views? Should Jimmy's views be dispositive? Or should the judge make an independent evaluation? By what standard? Should the judge be able to force Jimmy to live with Mary?

(2) Suppose that upon hearing Jimmy's objection to living with Mary, John and Mary enter into a new agreement providing that Jimmy will spend six months a year with each parent. Suppose that Jimmy objects to this arrangement because he wants to be with his father all the time, because "Mommy has too much work to do and does not like to build model airplanes," and because the arrangement will require that he "move around too much."

(3) Suppose that John changes his mind and decides to seek full custody of Jimmy. Mary then vows to fight such an arrangement. What factors should be taken into consideration for choosing which parent should prevail? Is it relevant that Mary discovered that she is a lesbian and plans to live with her new partner?

(4) Before the divorce Jimmy used to visit Mary's parents for three weeks during the summer. Jimmy is especially fond of his grandfather, who takes him on fishing trips and to baseball games. Mary's parents have never liked John and encouraged Mary to divorce him. Now that he has custody of Jimmy, they are afraid that John will seek revenge by not permitting them to see Jimmy. Suppose

---

[33] Bureau of the Census, Statistical Abstract of the United States 2003 72 (table 83) (23rd ed. 2003). Currently, over 5.7 million children live with a divorced parent. Bureau of the Census, Statistical Abstract of the United States 2008 (table 65), available at *http://www.census.gov/ compendia/statab*.

Jimmy enjoys spending time with his grandparents. Who should decide whether and how often these visits should take place? Should grandparents have a right to see their grandchildren?

(5) Two years after the decree John is offered and accepts the opportunity to teach English literature in France. John plans to take Jimmy with him. Mary is now a well-paid lawyer but considers having to travel to Europe to visit her son outrageous. She seeks modification of the custody decree.

(6) Suppose Jimmy is the child of Mary and Julie, who have been partners for ten years. Mary is Jimmy's biological mother via artificial insemination by an anonymous donor, and Julie has been a parent to Jimmy since his birth. When Jimmy is seven, Mary and Julie's relationship dissolves, and Mary refuses to let Julie have further contact with Jimmy. Does Julie have standing to sue for custody of Jimmy? If a court refuses to grant Julie custody rights, should she be allowed visitation rights even though she has no biological tie to Jimmy? If a court fails to find a legal relationship between Jimmy and Julie, should Julie still be required to pay child support?

For each of the above described circumstances consider the following questions: Should Jimmy have an attorney? Should Jimmy's views be considered? Should they be dispositive? Should the parents' agreement be dispositive? Should the judge make an independent evaluation? By what standard?

NOTES AND QUESTIONS ON CONTESTED CHILD CUSTODY

It appears that in approximately 10 to 20 percent of divorces involving children, the parents cannot agree concerning custody.[34] In these cases, the critical question is how should these disputes be resolved? Through what process? With what standards? Who should decide?

(1) For disputes between parents, what would be the advantage of more precise legal standards? Would it lead to less controversy?

(2) Evaluate critically the advantages and disadvantages of the following standards and compare them to the best interests standard:

   a. A standard that awards custody on the basis of the sex of the parents — e.g., a maternal preference.[35]
   b. A standard that awards custody to the parent of the same sex as that of the child.
   c. A standard that awards custody to the richer parent.
   d. A standard that awards custody to the parent who would be expected to spend more time with the child.
   e. A standard that awards custody to the parent chosen by the child.

---

[34] Eleanor E. Maccoby & Robert H. Mnookin, Dividing the Child: Social and Legal Dilemmas of Custody 103, 134(1992).

[35] For data showing that mothers obtain custody more often, see id. at 112-113 (mothers receive sole physical custody in two out of three cases).

    f.   A standard that awards custody to the parent whose psychological rela-
         tionship to the child would be "less detrimental."

(3) Consider modes of dispute resolution other than traditional adjudication.
What problems do you foresee with each suggestion?

    a.   A system that involved mediators or family counselors who could not
         impose a resolution upon the parents, but who pressed a private resolution
         of the custody dispute.
    b.   A form of adjudication or arbitration that required the disputing parents to
         choose a "judge," who is given the power to resolve the dispute. If the
         judge knows the family, the custody decision might better reflect an intu-
         itive appreciation of the parties' values, psychology, and goals. The
         decision might also be more acceptable to the parents. What problems
         could you foresee with such a mechanism?
    c.   The flip of a coin would avoid the pain associated with an adversarial pro-
         ceeding that requires an open exploration of the intimate aspects of family life
         and an ultimate judgment that one parent is preferable to another.

(4) Although a substantial argument can be made that the primary responsibility
of courts in contesting divorce custody cases is to decide the issue and to decide it
once and for all, the legal system at present allows parents to relitigate these questions over a considerable period of time. For a discussion of the legal standards
relating to modification of custody, see infra, pp. 628-631. Additional complexities
arise when the divorcing parents live in different states; see infra, pp. 631-636.

2.   Effects of Parental Divorce

Both popular and expert opinion agree that divorce affects children in many ways.
As stated above, divorce is an increasingly common experience of childhood. What
are the consequences of divorce for children? What are the psychological effects of
divorce on children? Also, what impact does divorce have on children's day-to-day
reality? Finally, what are the implications of these questions for custody decision
making?
    The past several decades have witnessed considerable social science research
that has increased our understanding of the responses of children to the divorce
process. The excerpts below summarize the findings of some of this research.

Judith S. Wallerstein, Child of Divorce: An Overview
4 Behav. Sci. & L. 105, 112-116 (1986) (citations omitted)

To the child, divorce signifies the collapse of the structure that provides support
and protection. The child reacts as to the anticipated cutting of his or her lifeline. . . .
    Boys are reported to be more vulnerable than girls to the acute stress of the
marital rupture, as well as to the more chronic stresses of the transitional phase in

the preschool and latency ages. Major differences between preschool boys and girls in a wide range of cognitive, social, and developmental measures have been reported. Boys from divorced families perform less well on a range of learning measures than boys in intact families. . . . While boys and girls did not differ in the overall psychological adjustment at the time of the marital breakup, at 18 months later the boys' psychological adjustment had deteriorated markedly, whereas that of the girls had greatly improved, making for a growing gap between the two groups. Other evidence shows that marital turmoil has a greater impact on boys than on girls, both in divorced families and in intact, discordant families. . . .

Developmental factors are critical in the responses of children and adolescents at the time of the marital rupture. Despite significant individual differences in the child, in the family, and in parent-child relations, the child's age and developmental stage appear to be the most important factors governing the initial response. . . .

A major finding in divorce research has been the common patterns of response within different age groups. The age groups which share significant commonalities in perceptions, responses, underlying fantasies, and behaviors are the preschool ages 3-5, early school age or early latency ages 5 1/2-8, later school age or latency ages 8-11, and finally, adolescent ages 12-18. . . .

Preschool children are likely to show regression following one parent's departure from the household. The regression usually occurs in the most recent developmental achievement of the child. Intensified fears are frequent and are evoked by routine separations from the custodial parent during the day and at bedtime. Sleep disturbances are also frequent. The preoccupying fantasy of many of the little children is fear of abandonment by both parents. Yearning for the departed parent is intense. Young children are likely to become irritable and demanding and to behave aggressively with parents, with younger siblings, and with peers.

Children in the 5- to 8-year-old group are likely to show open grieving. They are preoccupied with feelings of concern and longing for the departed parent. Many share the terrifying fantasy of replacement. "Will my daddy get a new dog, a new mommy, a new little boy?" were the comments of several boys in this age group. Little girls wove elaborate Madame Butterfly fantasies, asserting that the departed father would some day return to them, that he loved them "the best." Many of the children in this age group could not believe that the divorce would endure. About half suffered a precipitous decline in their school work.

In the 8 1/2- to 12-year-old group, the central response often seems to be intense anger at one or both parents for causing the divorce. In addition, these children suffer from grief over the loss of the intact family, from anxiety, loneliness, and the humiliating sense of their own powerlessness. Youngsters in this age group often see one parent as the "good" parent and the other as "bad," and they appear especially vulnerable to the blandishments of one or the other parent to engage in marital battles. Children in later latency also have a high potential for assuming a helpful and empathic role in the care of a needy parent. School performance and peer relationships suffer a decline in approximately one-half of these children.

Contrary to community expectations, adolescents are very vulnerable to their parents' divorce. The precipitation of acute depression, accompanied by suicidal preoccupation and acting out, is frequent enough to be alarming. Anger can be intense. . . . Preoccupied with issues of morality, adolescents may judge the parents' conduct during the marriage and the divorce, and they may identify with one parent and do battle against the other. A good number become anxious about their own future entry into adulthood, concerned that they may experience marital failure like their own parents. Researchers have also called attention to the adolescents' impressive capacity to grow to maturity and independence as they respond to the family crisis and the parents' need for help. . . .

. . . No single theme appeared among those children who enhanced or continued their good developmental progress after the divorce crisis had finally ended. . . . Instead, a set of complex configurations was found, in which the relevant components appear to include (1) the extent to which the parent has been able to resolve and put aside conflict and angers and to make use of the relief from conflict provided by the divorce; (2) the course of the custodial parent's handling of the child and the resumption or improvement of parenting within the home; (3) the extent to which the child does not feel rejected by the noncustodial or visiting parent and the extent to which this relationship has continued regularly and kept pace with the child's growth; (4) the extent to which the divorce has helped to attenuate or dilute a psychopathological parent-child relationship; (5) the range of assets and deficits which the child brought to the divorce, including both the child's history in the predivorce family and his or her capacities in the present, particularly intelligence, the capacity for fantasy, social maturity, and the ability to turn to peers and adults; (6) the availability to the child of a supportive human network; (7) the absence in the child of continued anger and depression; and (8) the sex and age of the child at the marital rupture and the remarriage. . . .

The problems that marital rupture poses to children are grave and potentially enduring. The initial responses of children and parents at the height of the crisis during the separation are serious. . . . In the long term, however, the central hazards to the psychological health of children are not the result of the divorce, per se, but rather in the diminished or disputed parenting that so often follows in the wake of marital breakdown. . . .

E. Mavis Hetherington & John Kelly, For Better or For Worse: Divorce Reconsidered
228-229 (2002)

The big headline in my data is that 80 percent of children from divorced homes eventually are able to adapt to their new life and become reasonably well adjusted. A subgroup of girls even become exceptionally competent as a result of dealing with the challenges of divorce, enjoy a normal development, and grow into truly outstanding young adults. The 20 percent who continue to bear the scars of divorce fall into a troubled group, who display impulsive, irresponsible, antisocial behavior or are depressed. At the end of the [study], troubled youths were having difficulty at work, in romantic relationships, and in gaining a toehold in adult life. They had the highest academic dropout rate and the highest divorce rate in the study, and were more likely to be faring poorly economically. In addition, being troubled and a girl made a young woman more likely to have left home early and to have experienced at least one out-of-wedlock pregnancy, birth, or abortion.

However, coming from a non-divorced family did not always protect against growing into a troubled young adult. Ten percent of youths in non-divorced families, compared to 20 percent in divorced and remarried families, were troubled. Most of our troubled young men and women came from families where conflict was frequent and authoritative parenting rare. In adulthood as was found in childhood and adolescence, those who had moved from a highly contentious intact home situation to a more harmonious divorced family situation, with a caring, competent parent, benefited from the divorce and had fewer problems. But the legacy of the stresses and inept parenting associated with divorce and remarriage, and especially with living in a complex stepfamily, are still seen in the psychological, emotional, and social problems in 20 percent of young people from these families. . . .

What about the other 80 percent of young people from divorced and remarried families? While most were not exactly the New Man or New Woman that the divorce revolution's supporters had predicted, they were behaving the way young adults were supposed to behave. They were choosing careers, developing permanent relationships, ably going about the central tasks of young adulthood, and establishing a grown-up life. They ranged from those who were remarkably well adjusted to Good Enoughs and competent-at-a-cost, who were having a few problems but coping reasonably well to very well.

Finally, it should be a reassuring finding for divorced and remarried parents, and their children, that for every young man or woman who emerged from post-nuclear family life with problems, four others were functioning reasonably or exceptionally well . . .

The Wallerstein excerpt above is based on her original study, Surviving the Breakup: How Children and Parents Cope with Divorce (1980) (co-authored with Joan Kelly), which pointed out that the effects of divorce on children vary according to gender, age, and developmental stage at the time of divorce. Wallerstein's study of 60 divorced families with 131 children highlighted many negative consequences of divorce in terms of children's psychological well-being. Her follow-up research, Second Chances: Men, Women, and Children a Decade After Divorce (1989) (co-authored with Sandra Blakeslee), and The Unexpected Legacy of Divorce: A 25-Year Landmark Study) (2000) (co-authored with Julia M. Lewis and Sandra Blakeslee), illuminated the continuing long-term effects of parental divorce, especially in terms of children's relationships with their mothers and fathers, as well as their difficulty in forming and maintaining intimate, adult interpersonal relationships. In contrast, Hetherington's more optimistic findings emphasize the resiliency of the children of divorce. Her longitudinal study of 1,400 families (including divorced and intact families) concludes that the vast majority of the children of divorce become well-adjusted adults.

Social psychologist Paul Amato has attempted to reconcile the two psychologists' seemingly disparate findings. Amato confirms that several of Wallerstein's claims are consistent with the research literature, in particular: (1) children with divorced parents are more likely to experience psychological problems in adulthood than are children with continuously married parents; (2) children of divorced parents, compared with children with continuously married parents, have more problems in forming and maintaining stable intimate relationships; and (3) children of divorce reach adulthood with weaker ties to parents than do children with continuously married parents. Paul R. Amato, Reconciling Divergent Perspectives: Judith Wallerstein, Quantitative Family Research, and Children of Divorce, 52 Fam. Relations 332, 334 (2003).

Nonetheless, based on his longitudinal research of 671 children of divorce (including a control group of intact families), Amato concludes that the long-term effects of divorce are "not as pervasive or as strong as Wallerstein claims." Id. at 336. That is, whereas Wallerstein finds that over one-third of children with divorced parents become psychologically troubled adults, Amato indicates that only 10 percent of such children manifest serious psychological problems in adulthood. Id. at 337. In this regard, Amato's findings more closely approximate those of Hetherington, supra, who found that 20 percent of the children of divorced parents had psychological difficulties as adults. (Wallerstein's more negative findings may be partly attributable to the fact that her sample consisted of families referred to a counseling center by family law attorneys.)

In addition, Amato, like Wallerstein and Hetherington, recognizes that pre-divorce as well as postdivorce factors play an important role in the children's psychological well-being. "Moderating factors may be present in the family prior to marital disruption, or they may exist in postdivorce family arrangements." Id. For example, one important postdivorce factor is a parent's remarriage. Amato notes that the evidence regarding parental remarriage is mixed in terms of its beneficial or harmful effects for children. However, he points out that multiple family transitions (involving multiple divorces and remarriages) are more problematic for children than the experience of a single divorce. Id. at 338.[36]

What is the day-to-day reality for children in the aftermath of divorce? How do legal labels, whether sole custody or joint legal custody, or joint physical custody, translate into contemporary reality for children of divorce? The following study in one jurisdiction of the custodial arrangements of 1,129 families with 1,884 children sheds some light on these questions.

---

[36] For additional discussion of the effects of divorce on children, see Robert E. Emery, The Truth About Children and Divorce: Groundbreaking Research and Advice for Dealing with the Emotions So You and Your Children Can Thrive (2004); Robert E. Emery, Marriage, Divorce, and Children's Adjustment (2d ed. 1999); Paul R. Amato, Children of Divorce in the 1990's: An Update of the Amato & Keith Meta-Analysis, 15 J. of Fam. Psychol. 355 (2001); Paul R. Amato, The Consequences of Divorce for Adults and Children, 62 J. Marriage & Fam. 1269 (2000); Joan B. Kelly, Children's Adjustment in Conflicted Marriage and Divorce: A Decade of Research, 39 J. of Am. Acad. of Child & Adolescent Psychiatry (2000); Kim Leon, Risk and Protective Factors in Young Children's Adjustment to Parental Divorce: A Review of the Research, 52 Fam. Relations 258 (2003); Heidi R. Riggio, Parental Marital Conflict and Divorce, Parent-Child Relationships, Social Support, and Relationship Anxiety in Young Adulthood, 11 Personal Relationships 99 (2004).

Eleanor E. Maccoby et al., Custody of Children Following Divorce
Impact of Divorce, Single-Parenting and Step-Parenting on Children 91, 96-113
(E. Mavis Hetherington & Josephine D. Arasteh eds., 1988)

Although it is possible to document some rapid changes in the nature of the legal labels for the custodial arrangements, little is known concerning the realities that underlie these legal labels. It is possible that some of the changes are more apparent than real. For example, a decree of joint legal custody with maternal physical custody may not mean that families live their lives differently than they did under the traditional pattern of maternal custody with father visitation. On the other hand, having a legitimized role—even a pro forma one—in decisions concerning the child may sustain a father's interests and prevent the "father drop-out" that so commonly occurs [citations omitted].

Further questions concern interspousal conflict. In some number of cases, joint custody—physical or legal—is being settled upon by the couple despite the fact that one of the parents might have preferred an alternative arrangement. It is reasonable to suppose that there may be more conflict, at least initially, in these cases than for the couples who fully agreed on the form of custody they preferred. Some writers assume that joint custody implies more than increased father-child interaction. They present a picture of shared parenting. Furstenberg and Nord (1985) [citation omitted] challenged the assumption of co-parenting, reporting that they found evidence for "parallel parenting" at best. . . . What kind and degree of shared parenting is possible between parents who separate under conditions of high conflict (over custody or other issues)? We need to know more about the conditions under which co-parenting can actually occur, and what role is played in this by the degree of initial agreement or conflict between the divorcing couple. Do hostility and conflict drop away over time? Do they grow faster, or more slowly, if the parents remain in contact because of their mutual involvement with the child? Our study is designed to obtain information relevant to these questions. . . . The purpose of the present chapter is to provide a description of the existing de facto arrangements for physical custody, and to examine how these arrangements vary according to the age and sex of the children and the number of children in the family. The existing studies of divorce give some intriguing indications that the impact of family disruption may be different for children of different ages . . . and has highlighted the possibility that the children's welfare may in part depend on whether they are in the custody of the same-sex versus opposite-sex parent. . . .

Where the Children Were Living at Time 1

. . . We find that over a third of the children in our sample were spending no overnights with father at the time of our Time 1 interview, and 6 percent were spending no overnights with mother. We hasten to point out, however, that the absence of overnights does not imply a total lack of contact with the secondary parent. . . .

Why do most parents continue to choose maternal residence? The reasons are various. . . . Parents make assumptions concerning which of them would be the better parent, and these may be implicitly agreed upon even if never discussed. Beyond the individual skills of the parents involved, many parents of both sexes assume that mothers have a natural talent for child-rearing, especially for children of "tender years," and that fathers do not understand young children as well. Also, there are many parents who seem to assume that it is natural for fathers to give higher priority to their work than mothers will do. . . .

The practicalities of the father's situation often led to maternal custody, at least in the short run. More often than not, it was the fathers who had moved out, leaving the mothers and children in the family dwelling. The father might initially have moved in with relatives or stayed in some other temporary residence where there was no room for the children. . . .

With children of school age, both parents usually saw advantages to keeping them in their familiar school, and the father's residence was seldom close enough to make this convenient. Parents frequently spoke of the importance of maintaining as much stability as possible for the children. As long as the mother stays in the family home, this implies maternal custody. . . .

Custody of Boys and Girls

[T]here is a tilt in the direction of children residing with the same-sex parent. . . . The trend toward living with the same-sex parent is characteristic of all ages, although it is strongest for children age 11 or older. At this age, there are over twice as many boys as girls residing primarily with their fathers. Between the ages of 2 and 11, the numbers of boys and girls residing with father are very similar. . . .

Research conducted when mother custody was the norm showed an overwhelming trend toward father disengagement from the family. This was true uniformly for fathers of sons and daughters. New child-custody options offer fathers the opportunity for greater involvement without assuming sole custody. Our data show that fathers, particularly those with boys, seem to be taking advantage of this option. . . . In our research, we hear respondents expressing related themes of identification with the same-sex parent and the father's superior ability to exercise control over older boys. . . .

Residence of Children of Different Ages

Not surprisingly, [our research] shows that children under the age of 2 are more likely than any other age group to be living with their mothers. . . . Divided residence, where the child regularly spends a substantial number of overnights with each parent, is highest for the children aged 2 through 7, and drops off after that age to a very low level among teenagers. Residence with father is most common among teenagers, although as noted previously this applies to boys only. . . .

We may speculate as to what lies behind these age trends. The low incidence of overnight visits and divided residence for children under 2 reflects a number of logistical problems, such as the need for special equipment for a very young child — crib, stroller, potty chair — all of which would need to be transferred or replicated in a second household. . . .

Why are overnight stays and divided residence most frequent at age 2 through 7, and why do they decline thereafter? The logistics of having children spend time in two households appear to become more complex as children develop their own activity agendas and grow old enough to go back and forth to friends' houses without being accompanied by a parent. We suspect that with increasing age, children have more and more voice in where they will reside, and that when they do have a choice, many prefer to have a single residence for sleeping and to use as a base of operations. . . .

Residential Custody and Family Size

Whether or not children live with their mothers following divorce does not appear to depend on the number of children in the family. The kind and amount of residence with father, however, does vary according to family size. . . .

It appears that maintaining divided residential arrangements for children, where they spend a substantial number of nights in each household, is more difficult for larger families than it is with only one child. Nearly 20 percent of the "only" children have a shared residential pattern, whereas this pattern is found in only 4 percent of the children who have two or more siblings. . . .

About 25 percent of the children in the study have a great deal of contact with their father. Family size is a key determinant of the way in which that contact is affected. In smaller families, divided residence is more common. In larger ones, it is more likely that at least some children in the family will reside with their father. . . .

Summary and Conclusions

. . . Our findings reflect interesting compromises between opposing viewpoints in the joint custody debate. Parents appear to be embracing the norm that fathers should remain involved with their children after divorce. Still, they are not rejecting the idea that children, particularly very young ones, should have their major residence with their mothers. The level of father physical custody is not increasing; but joint physical custody is. Most parents elect an arrangement that assigns physical custody to the mother and legal custody to both parents.

Another key debate about joint custody centers on whether the stability of a single-home environment should be compromised in order to permit frequent contact with each parent. The families in our study seem to weigh stability versus contact differently depending on the age and gender of the child. Very young children are less often alternated between parental households. Divided residence is also less frequent among older children, who have established ties to school and friends. Considerations of parental contact versus a stable environment also seem to be weighted somewhat differently for boys and girls. Boys are more likely than girls to divide their time between two parental households. As boys grow older, however, the need for stability of a single home environment seems to be added to the need for father contact. Consequently, more adolescent boys live with their fathers.

It is important to remember that these findings are drawn from interviews taken shortly after filing for divorce. We do not know whether arrangements that involve the participation of both parents can be sustained over time. . . .

In the following excerpt, Professors Maccoby and Mnookin describe their subsequent findings regarding the participation of parents in custody over a three-year period after divorce (i.e., comparing the period shortly after the divorce petition was filed, one year later, and two years later).

Eleanor E. Maccoby & Robert H. Mnookin, Dividing the Child: Social and Legal Dilemmas of Custody
274-275 (1992)

... For a substantial majority of the families in our study, fathers as well as mothers have remained in regular contact with the children. For those families with dual residence, obviously both parents are deeply involved. For the small minority with father residence, mothers have maintained contact very well indeed. Our most significant finding is that in a majority of families where the children lived with their mother, visitation with the non-residential father was maintained over the period of our study, and the visits most commonly involved overnight stays. At Time 3, only 14% of the children living with their mothers had not seen their fathers within the past year.

The proportion of mother-resident families in which the children had overnight visits with their father remained remarkably constant over three and a half years. On the other hand, when the father had only daytime visits at Time 1, with no overnights, this arrangement proved quite unstable: it often evolved either to no regular visitation at all, or (less commonly) to overnight visitation. Because of this decline in visitation by fathers with only daytime visits, the proportion of mother-resident families having no visits with the father increased from 23 percent at Time 1 to 39 percent at Time 3. On the other hand, almost a quarter of the families who initially had no visitation had established some by Time 3. Thus, within the overall picture of declining visitation with fathers — particularly for those who only had daytime visits — there was a substantial minority of mother-resident families in which visitation was increasing over time.

What factors affect whether children living with their mother maintain contact with the father? A mother's conviction that it is good for the children to sustain their relationship with their father is strongly associated with sustaining contact. Remarriage of the mother has a slight effect; it tends to diminish the amount of time children spend with their father. A residential move of one or both parents has a more powerful effect: when the distance between the two households increases, the children, not surprisingly, see their fathers less.

It is possible, of course, that the amount of contact between children and their fathers will continue to erode, and perhaps at a faster rate, as more time passes. However, we should note that in the follow-up of adolescent children conducted a year after the present study, the large majority of the children in the sample were still seeing their fathers on a fairly regular basis, and very few had not seen him during the past year. In short, during the more than four years following the initial separation, a high proportion of the children in our study maintained "frequent and continuing contact" with both parents.

3. Limits on Private Ordering

A preliminary question is the degree to which the parents themselves should be able to decide who should have custody and to what extent. At the time of separation or dissolution, it is usually possible for parents to agree on these matters and spell out their respective rights and obligations in a separation agreement. Evidence suggests that approximately 80-90 percent of divorced parents agree,[37] although often after difficult bargaining. The traditional doctrine is, however, that when the divorce is granted the court is responsible for independently determining whether a parental agreement serves the child's best interests, and even today parental agreement is not considered binding on the court.[38] Moreover, even if the court at the time of the divorce accepts the parental agreement, the court is free at any time during the child's minority to reopen and modify its decree in light of any change in circumstances. The parties cannot bind themselves by agreement and thus deprive the court of the power to evaluate or reopen custody issues.

What justifications are there for these substantial limitations on parental power? Do they derive from the fact that the child is not normally a meaningful participant in the bargaining process? Can you imagine situations in which a parental agreement concerning custody or visitation reflects the parents' interests rather than the child's?

Do judicial scrutiny of parental agreements and the possibility of subsequent judicial reexamination really safeguard the child's interest? Available empirical evidence suggests that courts typically rubber-stamp parental agreements concerning custody or support. This is less surprising when one considers the general lack of judicial resources for a thorough or independent investigation of the family's circumstances, the vagueness of the applicable legal standards, and the limitations on a court's practical power to control parental behavior once they leave the courtroom. Most courts behave as if their function in the divorce process were private dispute settlement. By the time most divorcing parents reach the courtroom, they no longer have disputes concerning custody, visitation, and child support. Busy judges are typically quite willing to rubber-stamp any private agreement, thus conserving judicial resources for disputed cases.

Provided custody does not go to a parent who endangers the child according to appropriate neglect standards, what interest does the state have, and what function is a court serving by requiring judicial approval of a parental agreement? Is not the function in these cases simply "private dispute settlement"? If so, when there is no dispute, what need is there for judicial intervention or supervision?

[37] Maccoby & Mnookin, supra note [34], at 134.

[38] The Uniform Marriage and Divorce Act, 9A U.L.A. (pt. I) 159 (1998 & Supp. 2008), for example, expressly provides that the terms of a separation agreement not having to do with the children "are binding upon the court unless it finds . . . the separation agreement is unconscionable." There is an express exception, however, for terms "providing for the support, custody, and visitation of children." See UMDA §306(b).

4.   Parental Disputes Concerning Child Custody

a.   Standards for Selecting the Custodial Parent: What Should the Standard Be?

Over the years, courts have applied a variety of presumptions to determine child custody disputes. What are the advantages and disadvantages of presumptions? (The most important standard, the best interests of the child, is explored *infra*, pp. 562-580.)

Traditionally, courts applied the maternal preference, also known as the "tender years" presumption. Under this doctrine, courts gave custody of children of "tender years" (generally preschoolers, but sometimes older children as well) to the mother. Although the United States Supreme Court has never addressed the constitutionality of the doctrine, several state courts in the 1970s and 1980s found that a maternal preference violates equal protection. See, e.g., Watts v. Watts, 350 N.Y.S.2d 285 (Fam. Ct. 1973); Pusey v. Pusey, 728 P.2d 117 (Utah 1986). However, some courts continue to consider it as a relevant factor in custody decision making. See, e.g., Donnelly v. Donnelly, 92 P.3d 298 (Wyo. 2004); Giannaris v. Giannaris, 962 So. 2d 574 (Miss. Ct. App. 2006), *rev'd on other grounds*, 960 So. 2d 462 (Miss. 2007). Note that the American Law Institute (ALI) Principles of the Law of Family Dissolution prohibits a court from considering the gender of either the parent or the child in determining custody arrangements. ALI Principles §2.12(1)(b) (2002).

The "primary caretaker" presumption, which replaced the maternal preference, favors granting custody to the parent who is able to establish that she or he is the child's primary caretaker. West Virginia was the first state to adopt the presumption in Garska v. McCoy, 278 S.E.2d 357, 363 (W. Va. 1981). Primary caretaker status was determined by the performance of such duties as preparation and planning of meals; bathing, grooming, and dressing the children; purchasing, cleaning, and caring for the clothes; medical care; arranging for children's social interactions with peers; arranging alternative care; putting the child to bed at night; discipline; religious, cultural, or social education; and teaching elementary skills. Id. at 363. Minnesota soon followed by adopting the presumption in Pikula v. Pikula, 374 N.W.2d 705 (Minn. 1985), but abrogated it subsequently.

The primary caretaker doctrine generated considerable criticism. Advocates argued that the doctrine was preferable to the maternal preference because it was gender-neutral, encouraged less litigation, and was predictable. Opponents argued that the preference was simply a "tender years" presumption in disguise because the mother is the parent who usually performs caretaking duties and also because it put too much weight on traditional gender roles in society. For discussion of these criticisms, see David L. Chambers, Rethinking the Substantive Rules for Custody Disputes in Divorce, 83 Mich. L. Rev. 477, 527-528 (1984); Martha L. Fineman & Anne Opie, The Uses of Social Science Data in Legal Policy Making: Custody Determinations and Divorce, 1987 Wis. L. Rev. 107; Paul L. Smith, Notes, The Primary Caretaker Presumption: Have We Been Presuming Too Much?, 75 Ind. L. J. 731, 732-733 (2000).

Although only West Virginia and Minnesota adhered to the presumption, many states considered primary caretaker status as a relevant factor in custody decision making. However, criticisms of the doctrine led to abrogation of primary caretaker status as a presumption (although some states continue to consider it as a relevant factor). Minnesota abolished the presumption in 1989 as the sole determinant of custody, replacing it with a hybrid standard in which the status of the child's primary caretaker is one of numerous factors. Minn. Stat. Ann. §518.17 (West 2006 & Supp. 2008). West Virginia also abrogated the presumption and replaced it with the ALI "approximation" standard (explained infra). W. Va. Code Ann. §48-9-206(a) (Michie 2004). Should gender differences have any role in custody decisionmaking? See generally Pamela Laufer-Ukeles, Selective Recognition of Gender Difference in the Law: Revaluing the Caretaker Role, 31 Harv. J.L. & Gender 1 (2008).

The ALI standard creates a presumption that "custodial responsibility" after divorce should be allocated to approximate the parents' caretaking roles in the intact family. ALI Principles §2.08(1). The standard recognizes the variations in parental roles — i.e., that parents' roles and responsibilities often diverge from the primary caretaker model. The ALI standard replaces the traditional physical custody terms of "custody" and "visitation" with the term "custodial responsibility" (to differentiate it from the term "decision making responsibility" for legal custody), in part to abolish the stigma often associated with the noncustodial "visitor" parent. The approximation standard, also known as the "past caretaking standard," may be rebutted by specific factors, such as a prior parental agreement, the child's preference, the need to keep siblings together, harm to the child's welfare (based on emotional attachment to a parent and the parent's ability/availability to meet the child's needs), avoidance of custodial arrangements that would be impractical or interfere with the child's need for stability, and the need to deal with parental relocation (§2.08(1)(a) to (g)). See generally Katharine T. Bartlett, U.S. Custody Laws and Trends in the Context of ALI Principles of the Law of Family Dissolution, 10 Va. J. Soc. Pol'y & L. 16 (2002) (discussion of standard); Elizabeth Scott, Pluralism, Parental Preference, and Child Custody, 80 Cal. L. Rev. 615 (1992) (first proposing approximation standard).

The ALI Principles favor private ordering in custody decision making. According to the Principles, courts should base custody awards on the arrangements to which the parties once agreed (i.e., the approximation standard) in cases in which divorcing parents are unable to agree on a custodial allocation. Moreover, the ALI requires those parents who are able to reach agreement about custody to submit a "parenting plan." This ALI provision mirrors statutory developments in a number of jurisdictions that require parents who seek custody to file a written agreement in which they specify caretaking and decision making authority for their children as well as the manner in which future disputes are to be resolved. According to the Principles, the court should enforce such agreements unless an agreement is not voluntary or would be harmful to the child (§§2.06(1)(a) 2.06(1)(b)).

Finally, some states provide that evidence of domestic violence creates a rebuttable presumption against awards of custody (often including joint custody) to the abusive parent. Other states include such evidence as a factor in the best interests standard. Amy B. Levin, Comment, Child Witnesses of Domestic Violence: How Should Judges Apply the Best Interests of the Child Standard in Custody and Visitation Cases Involving Domestic Violence? 47 UCLA L. Rev. 813, 827 & nn. 31-37 (2000) (state survey). The ALI also addresses the role of domestic violence in custody, providing that batterers may not receive custodial responsibility unless the court orders appropriate measures to ensure protection of the child and the other parent (e.g., by mandating counseling) (§2.11(2)(I)). For further discussion of this presumption, see infra p. 579.

NOTE ON SEPARATING SIBLINGS

Gender issues may also arise in terms of separation of siblings. When more than one child is involved in a custody dispute, some courts separate the siblings — awarding custody of girls to mothers and boys to fathers. Courts may justify such "split" or "divided" custody awards on the rationale that such arrangements allow the child to develop feelings of sexuality. However, the majority of states have a presumption against separating siblings in the event of divorce absent exceptional or compelling circumstances. To meet this standard, courts consider the siblings' proximity in age, relationships between the siblings, and their involvement in similar activities or experiences. See generally Dana E. Prescott, Biological Altruism, Splitting Siblings and the Judicial Process: A Child's Right to Constitutional Protection in Family Dislocation, 71 UMKC L. Rev. 623 (2003).

(1) Best Interests of the Child

The primary consideration in determinations of child custody is the best interests of the child. Judges typically have broad discretion in custody decisionmaking. The best interest standard has been uniformly adopted either by state statutes, which include expanded lists of relevant factors, or by statutes giving courts a general directive. Although state laws vary, certain factors are commonly considered to be relevant in determining the best interests of the child. The following materials first present the historical background on the development of this standard, and next explore several relevant factors.

Robert H. Mnookin, Child-Custody Adjudication: Judicial Functions in the Face of Indeterminacy
39 Law & Contemp. Probs. 226, 235-237 (1975)

The history of the legal standards governing custody disputes between a child's parents reveals a dramatic movement from rules to a highly discretionary principle gradually shorn of narrowing procedural devices. In the early nineteenth century, adjudication of a custody dispute between a husband and wife was controlled by a simple rule: the father, in Lord Ellenborough's words, was "the person entitled by law to the custody of his child."[32] Deciding any custody dispute under these standards required a single factual determination: whether one of the claimants was the biological father of the child who was born while that claimant was married to the child's mother.[33]

An absolute rule of paternal preference does not appear to have been generally applied in nineteenth-century America, and in many jurisdictions courts were authorized to award custody to either parent as part of a divorce proceeding.[34] While some statutes expressed a preference for the father, it appears a rule based on fault emerged: "The children will be best taken care of and instructed by the innocent party."[35] This standard was not as open-ended as first appears because divorce in the nineteenth century required a showing of fault on the part of a spouse. Particularly given the social convention that the wife filed for divorce, courts no doubt awarded custody to the mother more frequently than to the father.

Gradually, in the twentieth century, courts came to acknowledge formally what had perhaps long been the reality. The statutory language, by now putting the wife on an equal footing with the husband, came to be interpreted as giving a substantial preference to the mother, particularly if the children were young. In the words of a New York appellate court, "the child at tender age is entitled to have such care, love, and discipline as only a good and devoted mother can usually give."[39] This maternal-preference rule was achieved in various ways: sometimes by statute, often by a judicially constructed rule that it was in the best interests of the child "of tender years" for the mother — unless shown to be unfit — to have custody.

At the present time, maternal-preference standards are being displaced by a formal insistence on a neutral application of the best-interests standard. . . .

---

[32] King v. DeManneville, 102 Eng. Rep. 1054, 1055 (K.B. 1804).

[33] The force of these rules is illustrated by an early habeas corpus case where a mother's custody claims against an estranged husband were denied even though the child was young, the separation had been forced by the father's ill-treatment of the mother, and there were uncontested allegations of continuing misconduct by the father. King v. DeManneville, 102 Eng. Rep. 1054 (K.B. 1804). Similarly, neither a husband's "cruelty" and "brutality" to his wife nor his cohabitation with another woman after desertion would justify a court of law giving custody to his wife even though he was at the time apparently in jail, where the child was brought to him every day. Ex parte Skinner, 27 Rev. R. 710, 713 (C.P. 1824). See also King v. Greenhill, 111 Eng. Rep. 922 (K.B. 1836).

Early English custody cases suggest that the settlement of such private disputes over custody was kept separate from the child-protection function. The courts of equity and the Chancellor — but not the law courts — were seen as having the power to control an abusive father's legal right to custody or, in an appropriate case, appoint someone else as guardian, if that were necessary to protect the child. See Shelley v. Westbrooke, 37 Eng. Rep. 850 (Ch. 1817). The Chancellor could also enjoin the husband's removal of the child from the Kingdom. See DeManneville v. DeManneville, 32 Eng. Rep. 762 (Ch. 1804). But no discretionary power appears to have existed in courts of law to adjudicate a custody dispute in favor of a wife as against her husband.

[34] . . . Many early cases demonstrate that the mother as well as the father could claim custody [citations omitted]. In 1839, the English Parliament modified the absolute rule of paternal preference for legitimate children by passing the so-called Talfourd's Act, which gave a mother the right to custody of infants under the age of seven years. An Act to Amend the Law Relating to the Custody of Infants, 2 & 3 Vict., c. 54 (1839); and later for infants of any age. An Act to Amend the Law as to the Custody of Infants, 36 & 37 Vict., c. 12 (1873).

[35] [J. Bishop, Commentaries on the Law of Marriage and Divorce 520 (1852).]

[39] Ullman v. Ullman, 151 App. Div. 419, 424-425, 135 N.Y.S. 1080, 1083 (1912).

Divorce custody standards now show the overwhelming dominance of the best-interests principle. A majority of the states provide by statute for a best-interests-of-the-child standard. Other states have no statutory standard but have relied on their courts to develop a best-interests standard. Most of the remaining states have broad and vague statutory standards — calling for determination by such principles as "right and proper," "expedient," or "just and reasonable" — that have been judicially construed as involving the best-interests inquiry. . . .

(a) Fitness

Hollon v. Hollon
784 So. 2d 943 (Miss. 2001)

DIAZ, Justice:

This matter arises from a divorce action decided by the Chancery Court of Jackson County, wherein Timothy Paul Hollon (Tim) and Dorothy Elisabeth Hollon (Beth) were granted a divorce on the grounds of irreconcilable differences. . . . Beth appeals the chancellor's decision to award custody of their son to Tim. . . .

Tim and Beth were married on April 9, 1994, in Jackson County, Mississippi. During the course of the marriage, Zachary Thomas Hollon was born on July, 16, 1996. . . . The family resided in Bonaparte Square Apartment complex in Pascagoula, where Beth served as the on-site manager. The apartment complex owners provided Beth and Tim with a rent-free apartment as part of her compensation package. Tim served the City of Moss Point as a police officer.

Soon after Zach's birth, Tim and Beth's marriage began to deteriorate. They separated in January of 1997, for approximately eight weeks. After reconciling, their marriage again drifted into troubled waters leading to a second separation on January 11, 1998. Tim moved out of the marital apartment and into his parents' home, leaving Zach and Tyler [a son from Beth's previous marriage] in Beth's care. In an effort to alleviate the financial strain placed upon her during her separation, Beth took in a roommate, Beth Dukes (Dukes). Prior to this arrangement, Bonaparte Square Apartment complex also provided Dukes, an officer with the Pascagoula Police department, with a rent-free apartment in exchange for her service as a "courtesy officer." . . .

As roommates, Beth and Dukes split expenses, such as utilities and groceries. In addition, they each served as a baby sitter for the children when one was otherwise occupied. At the time, five people inhabited Beth's three-bedroom apartment; Beth and her two children, Tyler and Zach, as well as Dukes and her son Seth. Tyler, a teenager, was given his own bedroom, while Seth and Zach shared a bedroom as they were both under the age of five. Beth and Dukes shared the third bedroom.

At trial, Beth freely admitted that she and Dukes slept in the same bed. However, she vehemently denied any sexual relationship existed between her and Dukes, continually characterizing their relationship as platonic. Donna Mauldin, a friend of Beth's, testified that Beth told her that she and Dukes were engaged in a sexual relationship. Mauldin further testified that Beth wanted her to deny, if asked, that she ever admitted having a sexual relationship with Dukes. . . .

Tim heard the surfacing allegations surrounding Beth and Dukes' relationship. In order to investigate, Tim borrowed a key to the apartment, his former marital residence, from Donna Mauldin. While Beth and Dukes were away, Tim and Calvin Hutchins entered the apartment without permission and made a photographic record of things Tim felt were "inappropriate." These photographs and rumors led him to become concerned with "the environment that [Zach] would be raised in." Among other things, Tim took photographs of Dukes' clothing and police equipment in the shared bedroom, beer bottles in the refrigerator and wastebasket, liquor bottles on the counter, and one red light bulb in a ceiling fixture. These photographs were admitted into evidence over Beth's objection. . . .

Tim lives with his parents in their four-bedroom house and pays them fifty dollars a month in rent. During the trial, Beth moved out of the apartment complex with her two children and into her parents' five-bedroom house. She initiated this move during the break in the trial because she felt the judge disapproved of her living situation. Beth's plan to reside with her parents is temporary. She and Tyler will move into a newly remodeled three-bedroom house provided, in part, by her new job as the rental property manager for R.J. Homes. Beth no longer lives with Dukes and her son, although they remain friends. . . .

The polestar consideration in child custody cases is the best interest and welfare of the child. [F]actors used to determine what is, in fact, in the "best interests" of a child in regard to custody are as follows: 1) age, health and sex of the child; 2) determination of the parent that had the continuity of care prior to the separation; 3) which has the best parenting skills and which has the willingness and capacity to provide primary child care; 4) the employment of the parent and responsibilities of that employment; 5) physical and mental health and age of the parents; 6) emotional ties of parent and child; 7) moral fitness of parents; 8) the home, school and community record of the child; 9) the preference of the child at the age sufficient to express a preference by law; 10) stability of home environment and employment of each parent; and 11) other factors relevant to the parent-child relationship. [Albright v. Albright, 437 So. 2d 1003, 1005 (Miss. 1983).] It should further be noted that marital fault should not be used as a sanction in custody awards, nor should differences in religion, personal values and lifestyles be the sole basis for custody decisions. Id. at 1005.

[W]e review the evidence and testimony presented at trial under each factor [to determine if the] ruling was supported by the record.

1) The age, health and sex of the child

Although this Court has weakened the "tender years" doctrine in recent years, there is still a presumption that a mother is generally better suited to raise a young child [citations omitted]. [T]he child was barely three years old at the time the trial ended. . . . The chancellor did not explicitly say that this factor favored one party over another. This factor favors Beth because the legal presumption, although weakened, still favors the mother to raise a very small child.

2) The determination of which parent had continuous care of the child prior to the separation

Chancellor Watts was mindful of the fact that since the parties separated, the mother retained primary care of the child, with the father retaining visitation privileges. The chancellor failed to note that Tim did not have custody of Zach during the previous separation, nor express any interest in becoming the custodial parent until the allegations of homosexuality arose. The chancellor did not point out that Tim rarely exercised his visitation rights, nor did he make a specific finding that this favored one parent over the other. Clearly, this factor weighs in favor of Beth.

3) The determination of which parent has the best parenting skills as well as the willingness and capacity to provide primary child care

. . . Prior to the separation, Beth testified that she had the primary responsibility of caring for her two children. She estimated that she provided approximately ninety percent of the direct care for Zach, such as changing, feeding, and supervising him, as well as doing laundry and other housework. Beth shared cooking duties with Tim. Tim testified that he helped change and feed Zach, but qualified his testimony adding that he provided said care in the evenings or on his days off. Tim's work schedule prohibits consistent, in depth care of the child.

The chancellor found that neither parent held an advantage over the other here. From the entirety of the record, it is clear that Beth provided primary child care and if from familiarity or practice alone, holds an advantage over Tim in this area.

4) The employment of the parent and responsibilities of that employment

In his analysis of this factor, the chancellor gave a detailed recitation of the employment circumstances of both Beth and Tim. Although he did not cite a preference for either parent in the record, it is obvious that Beth's working situation is far more conducive to caring for a young child. Tim serves the public as a police officer and thus logs eighty-four hours on duty during his two-week shift. The schedule follows a two days on, two days off, three days on, two days off, two days on, three days off pattern with Tim on duty twelve hours each working day, rotating from a day shift to a night shift every twenty-eight days.

Beth works approximately thirty-five hours a week as a rental property manager in an office environment. Her position requires her to work only during the day, never on weekends and never during the holidays. This is in stark contrast to the regimented schedule that Tim must adhere to, regardless of weekends, holidays, or the hour of the day. . . . Beth also has the option of taking Zach to work with her if she chooses. Without question, this factor weighs heavily in Beth's favor.

5) The physical and mental health and age of the parents

Chancellor Watts noted that, at the time of trial, Beth was 36, Tim was 38, and both were in good physical and mental health. Although not specifically stated by the trial judge, this factor balances equally between Beth and Tim.

6) *The emotional ties of parent and child*

[T]he trial court held that no testimony was presented that showed Zach exhibited a stronger attachment to one parent over the other. Despite this finding, the trial court noted that Zach has been in Beth's continual care throughout both separations and subsequent divorce proceedings. The trial court implied that this factor also balanced equally between Tim and Beth, again never specifying for the record who, if anyone, benefitted from this factor.

7) *The moral fitness of the parents*

The seventh factor, moral fitness, took the lion's share of the chancellor's attention and is essentially what Beth argues dealt the fatal blow to her attempt to retain custody of Zach. Chancellor Watts noted that neither parent attended church regularly, which was "disturbing to the Court to some degree." The chancellor further stated Beth having a red light bulb in a fixture is "somewhat unusual, but not determinative of the issues herein." It is impossible to understand why the color of a light bulb is mentioned under this heading.

The chancellor then dove into the allegations of the homosexual affair. Chancellor Watts found Beth's testimony regarding this issue to be untrustworthy. In fact, because Beth's testimony denying her relationship with Dukes directly contradicted Donna Mauldin's testimony confirming it, he asked the District Attorney's office to consider conducting an investigation into whether or not Beth committed perjury by denying she had a homosexual relationship with Dukes. The chancellor further noted that he ought to have confidence that the custodial parent is a truthful, forthright person, and he stated that he lacked that confidence in Beth. Accordingly, he found that this factor weighed heavily in Tim's favor.

Chancellor Watts also noted that evidence of a homosexual relationship is not, per se, a basis to determine that child custody should be denied. He then went on to rehash, in detail, all of the testimony regarding Beth's alleged sexual relationship with Dukes. This Court has held that:

> In divorce actions, as distinguished from proceedings for modification of custody, sexual misconduct on the part of the wife is not per se grounds for denial of custody. A husband may upon proof of his wife's adultery be granted an absolute divorce on that grounds and yet in the same case custody of the children may be awarded to the mother. Our cases well recognize that it may be in the best interest of a child to remain with its mother even though she may have been guilty of adultery. Cheek v. Ricker, 431 So. 2d 1139, 1144-45 n. 3 (Miss. 1983). . . .

This view of custody arrangements is comparable to that employed in other states in similar fact situations.

The trial court never found the mother unfit to care for Zach, and no evidence was presented regarding any detrimental effects the child may have suffered as a result of living with his mother. The chancellor failed to mention that Tim admitted drinking a couple of beers every other day, that he drank to the point of being under the influence in the past, and formerly gambled every other week, but had not gambled recently because he did not have the money to do so. Beth also admitted to drinking to the point of intoxication in the past, but admitted that she gambled only once every six months.

While this factor is as important as any other and should be given its due consideration, it appears that the allegations offered under this heading were far and away the most scrutinized among the evidence reviewed at trial.

[The chancellor noted that no evidence had been presented with regard to the two factors of "the home, school and community record of the child" and "the preference of the child at an age sufficient to express a preference by law," and therefore did not weigh against either parent.]

10) The stability of home environment and employment of each parent

The chancellor found, after considering the stability of the home environment and employment of each parent, that this factor favored Tim. This reasoning is inexplicable. Beth's current employment situation, discussed above, is clearly more favorable to child-rearing than Tim's schedule.

By the time the second day of the trial arrived, both Tim and Beth lived with their parents, although Beth stated her intention to move into a house of her own. The trial court seemed to hold this relocation and change in employment against her, although a less than subtle warning offered by the chancellor was the sole reason that Beth initiated the change in living situations.

. . . . After considering all of the evidence and weighing the enumerated factors, the trial judge found that it would be in the best interest of the child to be relocated to Tim's care. A cursory glance at the above analysis reveals that the evidence supports a finding that more factors weigh in favor of Beth than Tim. . . .

Tim testified that his only concern with leaving Zach in Beth's permanent custody was the "homosexual environment" in which Zach would be raised. Tim felt that she was qualified in every other way to raise the child. Tim specifically testified that "[i]t's wrong, it's — and I don't care what society says. It's morally wrong. It totally goes against the laws of God. It is wrong, period. I want my son to grow up a healthy, happy, young man." Despite this admonition, he testified that Beth was a good mother. It is clear from the record that the chancellor's defining consideration in determining custody of Zach centered on the allegations of Beth's homosexual affair. In doing so, the chancellor committed reversible error. . . .

Within his analysis of the [best interest] factors, the chancellor abused his discretion by placing too much weight upon the "moral fitness" factor and ignoring the voluminous evidence presented under the remaining factors supporting Beth as the preferred custodial parent. Therefore, we reverse the decision of the Chancery Court of Jackson County and award Beth custody of Zach and remand the case for a determination of Tim's visitation rights. . . .

NOTES AND QUESTIONS

(1) Different Views. Prior to the 1970s few gay and lesbian parents were successful in custody cases.[39] Currently, courts treat the issue of sexual orientation in custody decisionmaking in several different ways: (a) some courts view homosexuality as evidence of parental unfitness per se; (b) other courts employ a "nexus test," which requires proof that the parent's sexual orientation has an adverse impact on the child; and (c) some courts presume adverse impact and require that the gay or lesbian parent has the burden of proof of the absence of adverse impact. The second view, followed by most courts, is also the view supported by most commentators.[40]

(2) Showing of Adverse Impact. Under the majority view, sexual orientation is an issue only insofar as the parent's sexual orientation can be proven to have harmed the child. However, courts differ as to the amount and type of harm required for a showing of adverse impact. For example, is teasing by peers sufficient harm? Compare Jacoby v. Jacoby, 763 So. 2d 410 (Fla. Dist. Ct. App. 2000) (negative thoughts by peers of children not enough to deny or change custody) with Bottoms v. Bottoms, 457 S.E.2d 102 (Va. 1995) (determining that social condemnation is a factor when making a custody determination). What role do judges' values play in custody disputes involving a gay or lesbian parent?

(3) Negative Effects? What are the possible negative effects on a child from having a gay or lesbian parent? Common beliefs include (a) the concern that children raised in homes with gay or lesbian parents are more likely to become homosexual; (b) the fear that a gay or lesbian parent is more likely than a heterosexual parent to molest the children; and (c) children of gay and lesbian parents suffer stigma from peers and the community.

Do the foregoing assumptions have any empirical basis? Studies of children of gay and lesbian parents conclude that sexual orientation of the parent is not an important factor in sex role development.[41] Evidence suggests that child molestation is generally heterosexual in nature.[42] Furthermore, peer pressure may not

[39] Rhonda R. Rivera, Queer Law: Sexual Orientation Law in the Mid-Eighties, 11 U. Dayton L. Rev. 275, 335 (1986). Exact data on the number of gay and lesbian parents are unknown. However, based on the 2000 Census (the most recent data available), of 594,391 households with same-sex couples, 34.3 percent of the female-partner households and 22.3 percent of the male-partner households report at least one child under the age of 18 living with them. U.S. Census Bureau, Married-Couple and Unmarried-Partner Households: 2000 (Feb. 2003), available at *http://www.census.gov/prod/2003pubs/censr-5.pdf*. The census data undoubtedly are low because of under-reporting.

[40] See 2 Child Custody and Visitation: Law and Practice §10.12[2], at 10-216 (Sandra Morgan Little ed., 1999 & Supp. 2007) [hereinafter Little]. This is also the view of the Uniform Marriage and Divorce Act §402.

[41] Charlotte J. Patterson & Anthony R. D'Augelli, Lesbian, Gay, and Bisexual Identities and Youth: Psychological Perspectives (2001); Jennifer L. Wainright et al., Psychosocial Adjustment, School Outcomes, and Romantic Relationships of Adolescents with Same-Sex Parents, 75 Child Development 1886 (Dec. 2004); Fiona L. Tasker & Susan Golombok, Growing up in a Lesbian Family: Effects on Child Development (1998).

[42] Carole Jenny et al., Are Children at Risk for Sexual Abuse by Homosexuals?, 94 Pediatrics 41, 44 (1994).

be as significant a problem as many courts believe.[43] Recall In re Doe, supra p. 530 (expert testimony showing that children of gay parents do not experience discrimination any more than the children of opposite-sex parents).

(4) Effect of Openness. In custody decisions involving gay parents, what other factors should be relevant in the determination of the best interests of the child? Should it matter whether the parent is discreet about his or her sexual relationship(s)? See, e.g., Ex parte J.M.F., 730 So. 2d 1190 (Ala. 1998) (granting change of custody to father when lesbian mother ceased to maintain discreet relationship). Is it clear that a parent's admission of homosexuality to a child is more harmful than secrecy?[44] Whether the parent places the sexual relationship above the children's interests? See, e.g., Charpentier v. Charpentier, 536 A.2d 948 (Conn. 1988) (father awarded custody because lesbian mother neglected children because of partner). How the partner treats the children? See, e.g., Sims v. Sims, 253 S.E.2d 763 (Ga. 1979) (cohabiting partner of lesbian mother physically abused children). Should it matter whether the dispute is between parents or whether the state or a third party is seeking custody? See White v. Thompson, 569 So. 2d 1181 (Miss. 1990) (awarding custody of children of lesbian mother to paternal grandparents based on mother's sexual orientation). Should it matter whether the parent exposes the child to the gay lifestyle? See Marlow v. Marlow, 702 N.E.2d 733 (Ind. Ct. App. 1998) (finding award of paternal custody was not in child's best interests because of father's exposure of child to gay lifestyle).

(5) Risk of Loss of Custody or Visitation. Gay and lesbian parents face the possibility of losing custody not only in initial awards but also in child custody modifications and juvenile court neglect determinations. See, e.g., In re E.C., 609 S.E.2d 381 (Ga. Ct. App. 2004) (reversing a juvenile court finding of neglect that resulted in transfer of custody of children of lesbian mother); L.A.M. v. B.M., 906 So. 2d 942 (Ala. Civ. App. 2004) (holding that evidence was sufficient to warrant change of custody to father when mother was engaged in same-sex affair).

Further, gay and lesbian parents face restrictions on, or loss of, their visitation rights. Such restrictions frequently take the form of prohibitions on gay and lesbian parents from associating with a same-sex partner in the presence of the child. See, e.g., A.O.V. v. J.R.V., 2007 WL 581871 (Va. Ct. App. 2007) (holding that visitation restrictions imposed by the trial court, which limited the children's exposure to father's gay lifestyle, were not an abuse of discretion). Do such judicial decisions implicate the "child protection" and/or "private dispute resolution" strand of custody law? For additional discussion of conditions on visitation, see infra,

---

[43] See, e.g., Richard Green, Sexual Identity of 37 Children Raised by Homosexual or Transsexual Parents, 135 Am. J. Psychiatry 692, 695 (1978) (only 3 out of 21 children recalled being teased by peers because of their mother's homosexuality).

[44] Courts often emphasize the harm to a child stemming from a parent's openness about his or her homosexuality. Paradoxically, researchers conclude that a parent's openness may have a positive influence on parent-child relationships. See Frederick W. Bozett, Gay Fathers: How and Why They Disclose Their Homosexuality to Their Children, 29 Fam. Relations 173, 175-176 (1980) (such gay fathers serve as role models for tolerance of others); Dorothy I. Riddle, Relating to Children: Gays as Role Models, 34 J. Soc. Issues 38, 52-53 (No. 3) (1978) (such parents help set framework for more honest, open, and intimate relationship with their children).

pp. 604-609. For additional discussion of second-parent custody and visitation rights, see infra, pp. 615-616.

(6) Influence of Lawrence v. Texas. The United States Supreme Court held in Lawrence v. Texas, 539 U.S. 558 (2003), that state sodomy laws (which banned homosexual, but not heterosexual, sodomy) violated the individual's constitutional rights to due process and privacy. In holding that the individual had a constitutionally protected right of intimate association, the Court concluded that moral disapproval is not a sufficiently legitimate state interest to justify such differential treatment under the Equal Protection Clause.

What is the impact of *Lawrence* on custody determinations? Compare McGriff v. McGriff, 99 P.3d 111, 117 (Idaho 2004) ("[*Lawrence*] has at least some bearing on the degree to which homosexuality may play a part in child custody proceedings"), with A.O.V. v. J.R.V., supra (rejecting the view that *Lawrence* has any relevance to custody decisions involving same-sex parents and restricting gay father's visitation because of harm to the children). See generally Matt Larsen, Note, Lawrence v. Texas and Family Law: Gay Parent's Constitutional Rights in Child Custody Proceedings, 60 N.Y.U. Annual Survey Am. L. 53 (2004); Jennifer Naeger, Note, And Then There Were None, The Repeal of Sodomy Laws After Lawrence v. Texas and Its Effect on the Custody and Visitation Rights of Gay and Lesbian Parents, 78 St. John's L. Rev. 397 (2004).

ALI Principles. The ALI Principles of the Law of Family Dissolution prohibit a court from considering either the sexual orientation or the extramarital sexual conduct of a parent except upon a showing that such conduct causes harm to the child. ALI Principles §2.12(1)(d) (sexual orientation); §2.12(1)(e) (extramarital sexual conduct) (2002).

(7) Recent Developments. The advent of same-sex marriage in a few states[45] and statutorily created domestic partnerships in other states (California, Connecticut, District of Columbia, Hawaii, Maine, New Jersey, New Hampshire, Oregon, Vermont and Washington) has focused renewed attention on the role of sexual orientation in custody decisionmaking. These jurisdictions provide varying degrees of benefits for gay and lesbian nonbiological parents. Of course, same-sex partners in states that recognize same-sex marriage have the same rights to custody and visitation as opposite-sex marital partners. However, in the remaining states, despite the liberalization of the law regarding same-sex unions, members of same-sex couples continue to experience difficulty in obtaining custody rights. See, e.g., Cook v. Cook, 970 So. 2d 960 (La. 2007) (holding that continuance of mother's relationship with her same-sex partner constituted a change in circumstances that led to custody modification in favor of father); Heatzig v. MacLean, 664 S.E.2d 347 (N.C. Ct. App. 2008) (holding that a former same-sex partner may not invoke parent-by-estoppel doctrine to confer upon her parental status to children born during the relationship). Visitation disputes involving same-sex couples are discussed infra pp. 615-616.

---

[45] In re Marriage Cases, 183 P.3d 384 (Cal. 2008); Kerrigan v. Commissioner of Public Health, 957 A.2d 407 (Conn. 2008); Goodridge v. Department of Public Health, 798 N.E.2d 941 (Mass 2003). The California Supreme Court opinion was abrogated by a voter initiative (Proposition 8) in November 2008. A challenge to the constitutionality of that voter initiative is pending. See Strauss v. Horton, No. S168047 (Cal. Sup. Ct., filed Jan. 7, 2009).

(b) Wealth

In re Custody of Tara Marie Pearce

456 A.2d 597 (Pa. Super. Ct. 1983)

ROWLEY, Judge:

This is an appeal from an order granting custody of the parties' minor child, Tara Marie, to appellee Ernest Pearce.

The parties were married February 29, 1973 and Tara was born August 6, 1977. . . . Tara's parents were divorced on October 25, 1977. . . . Tara resided with her mother, the appellant, from the date of her birth until January of 1981.

On January 15, 1981, appellant entered a hospital for an operation. She arranged for her three children, Michael Knecht, age 11, Shane Wolford, age 8, and Tara to be cared for by her (appellant's) mother and sister. Complications slowed appellant's recovery following the operation and she was unable to care for her children for approximately four weeks. During this period Tara's father, the appellee, offered to care for Tara until appellant's health was improved. Appellant agreed. However, appellee refused to return Tara to appellant when requested to do so.

On February 23, 1981, appellant filed a Petition for a Writ of Habeas Corpus. That same day, the trial court entered an order directing that Tara be returned to appellant. On March 9, 1981, the court entered an order confirming primary custody of Tara in appellant, Judith Pearce, pending a full hearing on her petition for custody. Several hearings were held. . . . A final order, dated June 14, 1982, was entered granting custody of Tara to appellee Ernest Pearce. This appeal followed.

The primary consideration in a custody dispute is the best interest of the child. Therefore, the issue before us is whether the court erred in concluding that placing Tara in appellee's custody would be in Tara's best interest. . . .

In this case, the trial court based its decision granting custody to appellee on three factors: 1) the court concluded that appellee is able to provide better housing facilities for Tara than is appellant; 2) the court found that appellant exhibited unstable behavior characterized by religious delusions; and 3) the court decided that appellant failed to provide adequate supervision for Tara.

We have concluded that these conclusions of the hearing judge are not supported by the record.

The record reveals the following uncontradicted facts. Appellant is thirty-two years old. While pregnant with Tara, she was laid off from her job at Woolrich Woolen Mills and has not worked since. Appellant and her three children live in a three bedroom apartment in Lock Haven Gardens. Tara has her own bedroom and sleeps in a single twin bed. Appellant's income consists of $369.00 a month from Public Assistance. In addition, she has a medical card for the family and receives $157.00 a month in food stamps. Appellant is able to adequately feed, clothe and house her family, including Tara, on her present income.

Appellee is twenty-seven years old and was remarried in June of 1980. Both he and his twenty year old wife are employed at Woolrich Woolen Mills. Appellee has a net income of approximately $135.00 per week. His wife's net income is $115.00 per week. They live in a newly built home on approximately one acre of land. Tara has her own bedroom and a double bed when in appellee's custody. When at appellee's, Tara is cared for at the home of a baby-sitter during the day while appellee and his wife are at work.

The relative wealth of the parties is not a decisive factor in determining custody unless it appears that one parent is unable to provide adequately for the child. In this case, it is undisputed that appellant has been adequately providing for Tara's needs. The home evaluations performed by Clinton County Children and Youth Services concluded that both homes were suitable for a child to grow up in. Therefore, the fact that appellee could provide "somewhat better" living facilities should have been given very little, if any, weight.

The court's finding of mental instability[2] and religious delusions on the part of appellant is unsupported by the record. It is true that appellant's family and friends were concerned about her behavior in late January and early February of 1981 and urged her to seek mental health counseling. The trial court placed great emphasis on one particular incident that occurred in late January of that year. Appellant and a girlfriend entered a bar during the afternoon and ordered cokes. According to witnesses, they were "talking about God" and reportedly left a $15.00 tip.

All of the claimed incidents of "unstable" behavior occurred during the time that appellant admittedly was having difficulty recovering from surgery and was taking medication. She was weak and depressed during that period. There is no evidence, however, that appellant has not fully recovered from her health problems. A psychological evaluation of appellant found no psychosis, no major depressive disorder and no paranoid delusions. While finding some "vague paranoid trends," the report stated that any such feelings had a partial basis in reality in view of recent events. Although appellant was tense and somewhat evasive, this reaction was explained as "normal distress" over the difficulties of obtaining custody of Tara.

Unless it can be shown that a parent's conduct has had harmful effects on a child, it should have little weight in making a custody decision. In this case, there is no evidence that appellant's health problems had any harmful effect on Tara. On the contrary, appellant realized that she could not adequately care for her children following her operation and made satisfactory arrangements for alternate care during that period.

As to appellant's religious beliefs, she is a "born again" Christian who reads the Bible often and admits that religion is an important part of her life. The fact that appellant's family and friends have problems understanding her new beliefs does not establish that she is unfit to raise Tara. There is no evidence that appellant suffers from any delusions or that she has removed herself from reality. Nor is there any evidence that her "intense interest in religion" has had any harmful effect on her children.

---

[2] The trial court did not seem to be overly concerned with appellee's history of past instability. It notes that he was convicted of statutory rape at age eighteen, has a history of alcohol and drug abuse, and is "somewhat prone to violence." However, the court accepted the conclusion in appellee's phychiatric [sic] evaluation that "his most recent marriage and its concomitant stability has tended to ameliorate these faults."

Finally, the court also concluded that appellant did not provide adequate supervision for Tara. The court emphasized that Tara "liberally uses" the playground across the street from her apartment with no apparent adult supervision. The record shows that the playground in question can be seen from appellant's apartment and is surrounded by other apartment buildings. When playing there and in other areas near her home, Tara is in the company of other neighborhood children and often is accompanied by one or both of her older brothers. These facts do not indicate any negligence on the part of appellant. There is no evidence that the playground in the apartment complex poses any special danger. It is not necessary for a normal, healthy four year old to have an adult constantly at her side when she is playing outdoors.

The court seemed especially concerned with an incident which occurred in the summer of 1980 when Tara ran into the street and was almost hit by a car. Appellant acknowledged that the incident occurred and her testimony as to the circumstances was uncontradicted. She had sent Tara downstairs to get a broom, unaware that it was across the street. She did not know that the child had left the house until she looked out the window and saw her returning. The record indicates that appellant was very upset by the incident and responded appropriately. Appellant testified that Tara knows she is not to cross the street alone and that on the few occasions when the child has done so, she had been disciplined.

The final evidence of appellant's "lack of supervision" occurred in September of 1980. Appellant worked for four evenings that month at the Oak Inn, leaving her son Michael in charge of the younger children for three to four hours on each of the four evenings. Michael had instructions to call appellant or Donna, a close neighbor, if there were any problems. This was an isolated incident. The record indicates that at all other times when appellant went out Tara would either have a babysitter or be left with relatives. It is our opinion that none of the above-mentioned evidence supports a finding of lack of adequate supervision on the part of appellant.

Although it is briefly mentioned in the trial court's opinion, we believe that the court failed to give adequate consideration to the effect a change of custody would have on Tara. Continued residence of the child with one parent is a factor which may, in certain cases, be controlling. Tara has resided with appellant since birth. All of the evidence indicates that there is a very close and loving relationship between appellant and her daughter. Tara also has a close relationship with her two half brothers. The psychological evaluation of Tara indicates that she has flourished under appellant's care. She was found to be a typical happy four year old of high average intelligence, with no indication of any emotional problems.

Furthermore, Tara expressed a strong preference for remaining with her mother. While the wishes of the child are not controlling, they do constitute an important factor which must be carefully considered in determining the child's best interest. When asked why she preferred to live with appellant, Tara responded that appellee and his wife always fight when she is there, which upsets her. When Tara was returned to appellant after briefly living with appellee, she was upset, withdrawn and reluctant to leave her mother's side. She initially refused to go on visitations with appellee, and had to be forced to go, kicking and crying. While the situation had improved during the proceedings in the trial court, Tara continued to be reluctant to go on visitations with appellee. On several occasions, Tara asked to be taken back to her mother's home early. While there was inconsistent testimony from Tara herself as to whether she actually enjoyed her visits with appellee once she got there, she made it very clear that she did not desire to live with appellee.

In conclusion, the hearing court's finding that it would be in Tara's best interest to reside with appellee is not supported by the record and therefore constitutes an abuse of discretion. . . . We will remand this case, therefore, for the entry of an appropriate order. . . .

NOTES AND QUESTION

Pearce examines the relevance of various factors in the determination of what constitutes the best interests of the child. Consider the role the following factors should have in custody decisionmaking:

(1) Wealth. What weight, if any, should be given to the superior financial position of one of the parents? The general rule, as *Pearce* reveals, is that the relative wealth of the parties is not a decisive factor unless one parent is unable to provide adequately for the child. See also Kovacs v. Kovacs, 1998 WL 1989809 (Mich. Ct. App. 1998). Although not a decisive factor, should wealth be a relevant factor? Several cases hold that it is. See In re Haley, 1999 WL 1071962 (Ohio Ct. App. 1999) (finding that parent's ability to provide a stable environment and to satisfy child's educational needs are relevant factors); Hammers v. Hammers, 890 So. 2d 944 (Miss. Ct. App. 2004) (finding that stability of employment is relevant factor). Does such a policy raise equal protection issues?

ALI Principles. The ALI Principles prohibit a court from considering parents' relative earning capacities or financial circumstances unless the parents' combined financial resources "set practical limits on the custodial arrangements." ALI Principles §2.12(1)(f).

The following excerpt explores the advantages and disadvantages of reliance on wealth as a factor in custody decisionmaking.

David L. Chambers, Rethinking the Substantive Rules for Custody Disputes in Divorce
83 Mich. L. Rev. 477, 538-540 (1984)

A large income disparity typically exists between divorcing parents. . . . If, in general, secondary caretakers have substantial resources, are there advantages to children from access to such resources that neutralize the advantages of placing children with primary caretakers? Similarly, should the systematic higher earnings of men be considered as yet another reason for rejecting the arguments considered earlier for preferring women as caretakers for very young children?

. . . The disparity in income is, nonetheless, likely to make important differences in the quality of life available to the child in the two [custodial] settings. Studies have shown that in successive income groups of the general population from low to high, the proportion of people who report themselves to be happy rises steadily. For the divorcing family, access to resources can determine whether or not the custodial parent can afford to remain in the home the couple lived in during the marriage and, as it does for all Americans, it can mean access to opportunity for the child — to a more expensive education, summer camp, or music lessons. Moreover, even when most basic needs can be met, a parent accustomed to living at a higher standard is likely to worry a great deal about money, which in turn may produce stress for the child.

At least in the abstract, it would thus appear wholly defensible for courts to give weight in custody decisions to the comparative financial positions of the parties. . . .

The problem with giving substantial weight to resources or income potential is that, in this country today, the effect of doing so is to disadvantage mothers in two ways that many people would consider unfair. First, women in general earn much less than men in general. This disparity in income is widely perceived to be the result of systematic discrimination against women in the labor market. Second, even in families in which the particular parent, usually a woman, could have earned as much as her spouse, a parent who has, with her spouse's concurrence, stayed at home or worked less than full time because of children is at a disadvantage as to resources for reasons that we should applaud, not count against her. For these reasons, it might well be argued that because of the effect it has on mothers, courts should ignore systematic income differences in forming rules. . . .

---

(2) Mental Disability.   *Pearce* also raises the issue of the relevance of a parent's mental disability in custody decision making. In *Pearce* the mother's erratic behavior led family and friends to urge her to seek mental health counseling. Psychological evaluation of the mother revealed some "vague paranoid trends." Why did the court decide not to give much weight to such evidence?

Cases generally hold that the fact of a parent's mental illness per se does not establish unfitness. Rather, as *Pearce* reveals, the focus is the nexus between the mental illness and parenting abilities, specifically whether the parent's mental illness is likely to affect the child adversely. See generally Martha A. Field & Valerie A. Sanchez, Equal Treatment for People with Mental Retardation: Having and Raising Children (2000); Linda A. Francis, Annotation, Mental Health of Contesting Parent as Factor in Award of Child Custody, 53 A.L.R. 5th 375 (2001). Certain factors often influence courts to minimize the importance of mental problems — the effect of medication and treatment, the willingness to look at one's own weaknesses, and the presence of normal stress that anyone might manifest in a similar situation. Are any of these factors present in *Pearce*?

Physical illness or disability is another factor that enters into the determination of the best interests of the child. How should physical disabilities be treated, similarly to mental disability? Should the type of physical disability be relevant? For example, should deafness or blindness be treated differently than motor disabilities? See, e.g., Bednarski v. Bednarski, 366 N.W.2d 69 (Mich. Ct. App. 1985) (inappropriate weight given to mother's deafness).

What relevance, if any, should attach to a parent's terminal illness? For example, should a parent with AIDS, or one infected with HIV (the AIDS virus) be granted custody? See AIDS Patient Gets Custody of Son, S.F. Chron., Oct. 20, 1988, at A-2. See also Pierce J. Reed & Laura Davis Smith, HIV, Judicial Logic and Medical Science: Toward a Presumption of Noninfection in Child-Custody and Visitation Cases, 31 New Eng. L. Rev. 471 (1997).

Until recently, it was often assumed that the severely physically disabled parent could not adequately care for a child. Increasingly, however, appellate courts are rejecting such assumptions and focusing instead on whether the parent's disability will have an adverse effect on the child. See, e.g., Matta v. Matta, 693 N.E.2d 1063 (Mass. App. Ct. 1998); Clark v. Madden, 725 N.E.2d 100 (Ind. Ct. App. 2000).

In In re Marriage of Carney, 598 P. 2d 36 (Cal. 1979), custody was awarded to the father. Five years later the father became a quadriplegic as a result of a Jeep accident while serving in the military reserve, and the mother requested a modification in her behalf. The California Supreme Court reversed the modification award to the mother because the lower court relied solely on the evidence of physical disability. The California Supreme Court noted:

> the essence of parenting is not to be found in the harried rounds of daily carpooling endemic to modern suburban life, or even in the doggedly dutiful acts of "togetherness" committed every weekend by well-meaning fathers and mothers across America. Rather, its essence lies in the ethical, emotional, and intellectual guidance the parent gives to the child throughout his formative years, and often beyond. The source of this guidance is the adult's own experience of life; its motive power is parental love and concern for the child's well-being; and its teachings deal with such fundamental matters as the child's feelings about himself, his relationships with others, his system of values, his standards of conduct, and his goals and priorities in life. Even if it were true, as the court herein asserted that William [the father] cannot do "anything" for his sons except "talk to them and teach them, be a tutor," that would not only be "enough" — contrary to the court's conclusion — it would be the most valuable service a parent can render. Yet his capacity to do so is entirely unrelated to his physical prowess: however limited his bodily strength may be, a handicapped person is a whole person to the child who needs his affection, sympathy, and wisdom to deal with the problems of growing up. Indeed, in such matters, his handicap may well be an asset: few can pass through the crucible of a severe physical disability without learning enduring lessons in patience and tolerance [598 P.2d at 44].

How much difference did it make, do you think, that this was a modification hearing rather than an initial award of custody? See generally Megan Kirshbaum et al., Issues Facing Family Court, Parents with Disabilities, Problems in Family Court Practice, 4 J. Center for Families, Child & Cts. 27 (2003).

(3) Religion.   The mother in *Pearce* was a "born again" Christian who had an "intense interest in religion." What role should religion play in custody decision-making? Although few states have statutes specifically including religion as a factor to consider in awards of custody,[46] many judges do consider religion in

---

[46] See, e.g., Hawaii Rev. Stat. §571-46 (2006 & Supp. 2007); Minn. Stat. Ann. §518.17 (West 2006 & Supp. 2008); S.C. Code Ann. §20-3-160 (1985 & Supp. 2007).

their determination of the child's best interest. The question is complicated by constitutional overlays. The role of religion in custody decisionmaking is considered infra, pp. 607-608.

(4) Other Factors: Time, Daycare, and Breastfeeding.   What other factors should be relevant in determining the best interests of the child? For example, should time be a relevant factor — that is, the amount of time a parent has available to spend with the children? A few cases have held that professionals (specifically, in law and medicine) may be at a disadvantage in custody battles. See, e.g., Prost v. Greene, 652 A.2d 621 (D.C. 1995); In re Rebecca B., 611 N.Y.S.2d 831 (N.Y. App. Div. 1994); Richmond v. Tecklenberg, 396 S.E.2d 111 (S.C. Ct. App. 1990). See also Young v. Hector, 740 So. 2d 1153 (Fla. Dist. Ct. App. 1999) (reversing custody denial to lawyer-mother). See generally Amy D. Ronner, Women Who Dance on the Professional Track: Custody and the Red Shoes, 23 Harv. Women's L.J. 173 (2003); D. Kelly Weisberg, Professional Women and the Professionalization of Motherhood: Marcia Clark's Double Bind, 6 Hastings Women's L.J. 295 (1995).

What might be problematic about utilizing time as a relevant factor in the best interests determination? Consider the following:

> A standard that awards custody to the parent able to spend more time with the child would ignore qualitative differences in time spent with the child and thus might not be justifiable from the perspective of what is good for the child. In all events, because the test would require a prediction of the amount of time each parent would spend with the child, it would be very difficult to apply and would invite exaggeration and dishonesty in litigation. Monitoring the time a parent would actually spend with a child after the custody dispute was resolved would be intrusive and impractical. Moreover, what remedy would there be if a parent later spent less time than expected? . . .[47]

Should a parent's reliance on day care be relevant? In a famous case, a university student was denied custody of her nonmarital child because the mother placed the child in day care while she attended class. The trial court accepted the father's contention that his mother (the child's grandmother) would provide better care for the child while he worked. The Michigan Supreme Court overturned the trial court award of paternal custody. Ireland v. Smith, 547 N.W.2d 686 (Mich. 1996). See also In re Marriage of Loyd, 131 Cal. Rptr. 2d 80 (Ct. App. 2003) (holding that custody modification to mother based on father's reliance on day care was abuse of discretion); Lynda Gorov, California Woman Gets Custody, Harvard; Ruling Allows Single Mother to Return to Studies in Fall, Boston Globe, May 7, 1997, at 3 (awarding custody to single mother who was student at Harvard despite her reliance on day care compared to father whose parents could care for child while he worked in the family restaurant). See generally Cynthia A. McNeely, Comment, Lagging Behind the Times: Parenthood, Custody, and Gender Bias in the Family Courts, 25 Fla. St. U. L. Rev. 891, 955 (1998).

---

[47] Mnookin, Child-Custody Adjudication, supra note [1], at 284-288.

ALI Principles. The ALI Principles of the Law of Family Dissolution provide that placement of a child in day care does not constitute sufficiently changed circumstances to warrant custody modification. ALI Principles §2.15(3)(c).

Should breastfeeding play a role in child custody decisions? Does taking this factor into account resurrect the tender years presumption? See, e.g., Greer v. Greer, 624 S.E.2d 423 (N.C. Ct. App. 2006) (holding that a trial court's finding of fact of a natural bond between a breastfeeding mother and an infant that gives a distinct advantage in parenting was not supported by evidence and not an appropriate matter for judicial notice).

(5) Other Factors: Substance Abuse and Domestic Violence. *Pearce* mentions several additional factors that might play a role in custody decisionmaking. For example, what weight should be given to a parent's history of substance abuse? See, e.g., Beene v. Beene, 997 So. 2d 169 (La. Ct. App. 2008) (affirming modification of child custody agreement to award father sole custody in light of mother's history of substance abuse). Should cigarette smoking be a factor? See Pierce v. Pierce, 860 N.E.2d 1087 (Ohio Ct. App. 2006) (holding that designation of former husband as residential parent was not an abuse of discretion, because former wife and her fiancé each had a pack-a-day smoking habit).

Furthermore, *Pearce* contains allegations of maternal neglect. How relevant should the factors of abuse and neglect be in custody decisionmaking? What about sexual abuse? Most states address abuse as a factor in custody. The majority of these states provide that courts should consider domestic violence in the determination of the best interests of the child. A few states provide that courts may take domestic violence into account in decisions regarding joint custody (e.g., joint custody would not be in the child's best interests in such a case), and some states establish rebuttable presumptions against awards of custody (sole or joint) to perpetrators of domestic violence. See Linda Quigley, Note, The Intersection Between Domestic Violence and the Child Welfare System: The Role Courts Can Play in the Protection of Battered Mothers and Their Children, 13 Wm. & Mary J. Women & L. 867, 886 (2007) (citing research noting that 48 states and the District of Columbia require consideration of domestic violence in custody decisions and 18 of those states have a rebuttable presumption against custody awards to an abuser). Some states now consider exposure to domestic abuse in custody decisionmaking. For a summary of research on children's exposure to domestic violence, see Naomi Cahn, Child Witnessing of Domestic Violence, in Handbook of Children, Culture, and Violence (Nancy E. Dowd et al. eds., 2006). Other statutes address the role of abuse in custody decisionmaking indirectly by providing that if a parent leaves the home to escape spousal abuse, this absence shall not be held against the parent in determining the best interests of the child. See, e.g., Colo. Rev. Stat. §14-10-124(4) (West 2005); Ky. Rev. Stat. §403-270(4) (1999 & Supp. 2007).

Recall (from Chapter 3) that neglect runs the gamut from inadequate supervision to withholding necessary food, clothing, or medical care. Similarly, abuse ranges from isolated acts of physical discipline to more serious acts of beating, burning, and mutilation. Abuse also includes sexual abuse. Where did the alleged acts of the mother in *Pearce* fall on this continuum? How did the court respond?

(6) *Pearce* found both parents to be "fit." Yet, given the record (a mother who allegedly is mentally unstable with religious delusions versus a father who has a history of alcohol and drug abuse), *Pearce* may also be characterized as a case involving two equally "unfit" parents. Cases of equal fitness or unfitness present especially difficult problems for judges. How should such tiebreaker cases be resolved? And by what process — by the courts using rules, preferences, presumptions? By the parties through mediation? Or coin-flipping? See pp. 623-625, infra.

(c) Race

Palmore v. Sidoti
466 U.S. 429 (1984)

Chief Justice BURGER delivered the opinion of the Court.

We granted certiorari to review a judgment of a state court divesting a natural mother of the custody of her infant child because of her remarriage to a person of a different race.

I

When petitioner Linda Sidoti Palmore and respondent Anthony J. Sidoti, both Caucasians, were divorced in May 1980 in Florida, the mother was awarded custody of their 3-year-old daughter.

In September 1981 the father sought custody of the child by filing a petition to modify the prior judgment because of changed conditions. The change was that the child's mother was then cohabiting with a Negro, Clarence Palmore, Jr., whom she married two months later. Additionally, the father made several allegations of instances in which the mother had not properly cared for the child.

After hearing testimony from both parties and considering a court counselor's investigative report, the court noted that the father had made allegations about the child's care, but the court made no findings with respect to these allegations. On the contrary, the court made a finding that "there is no issue as to either party's devotion to the child, adequacy of housing facilities, or respectability of the new spouse of either parent."

The court then addressed the recommendations of the court counselor, who had made an earlier report "in [another] case coming out of this circuit also involving the social consequences of an interracial marriage." From this vague reference to that earlier case, the court turned to the present case and noted the counselor's recommendation for a change in custody because "[t]he wife [petitioner] has chosen for herself and for her child, a life-style unacceptable to the father *and to society. . . .* The child . . . is, or at school age will be, subject to environmental pressures not of choice." (emphasis added).

The court then concluded that the best interests of the child would be served by awarding custody to the father. The court's rationale is contained in the following:

> The father's evident resentment of the mother's choice of a black partner is not sufficient to wrest custody from the mother. It is of some significance, however, that the mother did see fit to bring a man into her home and carry on a sexual

relationship with him without being married to him. Such action tended to place gratification of her own desires ahead of her concern for the child's future welfare. *This Court feels that despite the strides that have been made in bettering relations between the races in the country, it is inevitable that Melanie will, if allowed to remain in her present situation and attains school age and thus more vulnerable to peer pressures, suffer from the social stigmatization that is sure to come* (emphasis added).

The Second District Court of Appeal affirmed without opinion, thus denying the Florida Supreme Court jurisdiction to review the case. We granted certiorari, and we reverse.

II

The judgment of a state court determining or reviewing a child custody decision is not ordinarily a likely candidate for review by this Court. However, the court's opinion, after stating that the "father's evident resentment of the mother's choice of a black partner is not sufficient" to deprive her of custody, then turns to what it regarded as the damaging impact on the child from remaining in a racially mixed household. This raises important federal concerns arising from the Constitution's commitment to eradicating discrimination based on race.

The Florida court did not focus directly on the parental qualifications of the natural mother or her present husband, or indeed on the father's qualifications to have custody of the child. The court found that "there is no issue as to either party's devotion to the child, adequacy of housing facilities, or respectability of the new spouse of either parent." This, taken with the absence of any negative finding as to the quality of the care provided by the mother, constitutes a rejection of any claim of petitioner's unfitness to continue the custody of her child.

The court correctly stated that the child's welfare was the controlling factor. But that court was entirely candid and made no effort to place its holding on any ground other than race. Taking the court's findings and rationale at face value, it is clear that the outcome would have been different had petitioner married a Caucasian male of similar respectability.

A core purpose of the Fourteenth Amendment was to do away with all governmentally imposed discrimination based on race. Classifying persons according to their race is more likely to reflect racial prejudice than legitimate public concerns; the race, not the person, dictates the category. Such classifications are subject to the most exacting scrutiny; to pass constitutional muster, they must be justified by a compelling governmental interest and must be "necessary . . . to the accomplishment" of their legitimate purpose.

The State, of course, has a duty of the highest order to protect the interests of minor children, particularly those of tender years. In common with most states, Florida law mandates that custody determinations be made in the best interests of the children involved. Fla. Stat. §61.13(2)(b)(1) (1983). The goal of granting custody based on the best interests of the child is indisputably a substantial governmental interest for purposes of the Equal Protection Clause.

It would ignore reality to suggest that racial and ethnic prejudices do not exist or that all manifestations of those prejudices have been eliminated. There is a risk that a child living with a stepparent of a different race may be subject to a variety of pressures and stresses not present if the child were living with parents of the same racial or ethnic origin.

The question, however, is whether the reality of private biases and the possible injury they might inflict are permissible considerations for removal of an infant child from the custody of its natural mother. We have little difficulty concluding that they are not.[2] The Constitution cannot control such prejudices, but neither can it tolerate them. Private biases may be outside the reach of the law, but the law cannot, directly or indirectly, give them effect. . . .

The effects of racial prejudice, however real, cannot justify a racial classification removing an infant child from the custody of its natural mother found to be an appropriate person to have such custody.

The judgment of the District Court of Appeal is reversed.

NOTES AND QUESTIONS

(1) Relevance of Race: Different Views.   Prior to *Palmore,* several courts considered the weight to be given to race. Three views appeared to predominate: (1) racial differences are not relevant to custody; (2) racial differences may be considered as one of the factors that would be in the child's best interests; and (3) race may not be used as the determinative factor in awarding custody. See cases cited in Lee R. Ross, Annotation, Race as Factor in Custody Award or Proceedings, 10 A.L.R. 4th 796 (1981). Which view does *Palmore* follow?

(2) Epilogue.   The day the Supreme Court announced its decision, the father, who had moved to Texas with his new wife, filed an application for a temporary restraining order with a Texas court. The mother subsequently filed (1) in Texas, a petition for a writ of habeas corpus to recover possession of the child, and (2) in Florida, a motion to compel return of the child to her custody. The father, in turn, filed a motion to dismiss the mother's motion in the Florida court. Ultimately, the Texas court found that it had jurisdiction for purposes of further interim orders, and the Florida court declined jurisdiction in favor of the Texas court. The mother appealed, arguing that the Florida trial court erred in declining to exercise jurisdiction under the Uniform Child Custody Jurisdiction Act, 9 U.L.A. (pt. 1A) 261 (1999 & Supp. 2008) (see Postdecree Problems, pp. 628-631, infra). The mother also argued that as a result of the Supreme Court's opinion, custody should revert to the situation prior to the order and that she should again have custody.

The court of appeals of Florida replied: "We cannot agree under the particular facts of this child custody case. . . . The Supreme Court's decision was that the modification of custody could not be predicated upon the mother's association with a black man. Its opinion did not direct a reinstatement of the original custody decree and the immediate return of the child. The Supreme Court did not say that a Florida court could not defer to a Texas court. . . ." Palmore v. Sidoti, 472 So. 2d 843, 846 (Fla. Dist. Ct. App. 1985). The court of appeals concluded: "Under

---

[2] In light of our holding based on the Equal Protection Clause, we need not reach or resolve petitioner's claim based on the Fourteenth Amendment's Due Process Clause.

all the circumstances we cannot say that at this time it has been established to be in Melanie's best interest that she be ordered returned to her mother and that the trial court erred in not so ordering. The eight-year-old child appears to have had substantial upheavals of her life, and we find no compelling reason at this point to add a further upheaval. . . ." Id. at 846-847. Do you agree?

(3) Fostering a Child's Racial Identity. Some courts have considered race as a factor in determining which parent would better foster the child's racial identity. In In re Marriage of Gambla, 853 N.E.2d 847 (Ill. App. Ct. 2006), the court found that the African-American mother would be more able to raise the child as a person of color than the Caucasian father, whereas her Caucasian heritage could be taught by the prevailing culture. Other courts have been more reluctant to use race in such a way. See Hamilton v. Hamilton, 42 P.3d 1107 (Alaska Ct. App. 2002); Warford v. Warford, 2004 WL 2940881 (Minn. Ct. App. 2004).

(4) Inappropriate Consideration? How difficult is it to determine whether the court gave inappropriate weight to the role of race? For example, in one of the few post-*Palmore* cases to consider the role of race, Parker v. Parker, 986 S.W.2d 557 (Tenn. Sup. Ct. 1999), a woman who was dating an African-American man (also her employer) sought custody of her child. The trial court awarded custody to the child's father, stating that its decision was not based on race but rather on disapproval of the extramarital relationship and the fact that the relationship was causing the mother to neglect the child. The appellate and state supreme courts upheld the award of paternal custody, accepting the trial court's judgment on the fitness of the parents. See also Parker v. Parker, 986 S.W.2d 557 (Tenn. 1999); Dansby v. Dansby, 189 S.W.3d 473 (Ark. Ct. App. 2004).

See generally Katherine T. Bartlett, Essay, Comparing Race and Sex Discrimination in Custody Cases, 28 Hofstra L. Rev. 877 (2000); Randall Kennedy, Interracial Intimacies: Sex, Marriage, Identity, and Adoption (2003); Rachel F. Moran, Interracial Intimacy: The Regulation of Race and Romance (2001).

(5) ALI Principles. The ALI Principles of the Law of Family Dissolution, §2.12(1)(a), prohibit a court from considering the race or ethnicity of the child, parent, or other member of the household in determining custody arrangements.

(6) Custody vs. Adoption. Compare the treatment of race in the custody and adoption contexts (see The Relevance of Race to Adoption, supra, pp. 537-547). Is the state's interest in adoption proceedings greater than in custody proceedings? If so, should this interest justify differential treatment of the relevance of race? See generally David D. Meyer, *Palmore* Comes of Age: The Place of Race in the Placement of Children, 18 U. Fla. J.L. & Pub. Pol'y 183 (2007) (discussing the influence of *Palmore* in custody and adoption).

(7) Extension of **Palmore.** The Supreme Court based its holding in *Palmore* on the ground that private biases and possible injury therefrom are not permissible considerations for removal from the custody of a biological parent. May this reasoning justify an extension of *Palmore* to other situations? For cases that have extended *Palmore* beyond questions of race, see Jacoby v. Jacoby, 763 So. 2d 410, 413 (Fla. Ct. App. 2000) (holding that perceived community bias against homosexuals is improper basis for a residential custody determination); Inscoe v. Inscoe, 700 N.E.2d 70, 82 (Ohio Ct. App. 1997) (reversing custody award to wife on ground of husband's homosexuality because courts may not consider adverse

impact on a child that flows from the unpopularity of gays and lesbians in our society). Consider also the impact of Lawrence v. Texas, discussed supra p. 571.

(2) Joint Custody

PROBLEMS

(1) Sandra and Rick have been married for ten years. They have two children: Andrew, age six, and Kristin, age four. The past year has been particularly stressful for the family as Sandra and Rick have realized the extent of their marital differences. Finally, the couple decides to obtain a divorce. Both parents have been extremely involved with the children throughout their relationship. Neither is happy at the prospect of losing custody of Andrew and Kristin. The parents consult you, their attorney, to inquire as to the advisability of a "joint custody-type" arrangement.

Sandra and Rick pose several questions to you: What does joint custody mean in terms of future shared responsibilities for childrearing? Is an award of joint custody appropriate if both Sandra and Rick desire this custodial arrangement? What might be the advantages of joint custody for the respective family members — mother, father, and children? What are the disadvantages? What problems might joint custody involve, even in the best possible situation, when both parents agree to it? Is there any "scientific evidence" investigating how joint custody actually works for most families? What else might Sandra and Rick want to know to assist them in making their decision to secure joint custody?

(2) After many discussions with each other and with legal counsel, Sandra and Rick come to a decision. Rick is firm in his desire for joint custody; Sandra, however, would prefer an award of sole custody to her. Each petitions the court. Suppose you are the judge deciding such a case. Is an award of joint custody appropriate in circumstances when one parent does not desire it? What problems might arise if one parent is coerced into accepting a joint custodial arrangement? Are these problems different from the situation in which one parent initially wants sole custody but later agrees to joint custody through negotiation? What are the prospects for such couples to reach consensus in subsequent decisions about child custody?

(3) Alternatively, suppose that after much discussion, Rick and Sandra decide that joint custody is not appropriate for them. Each decides to petition the court for sole custody. Is an award of joint custody ever appropriate in circumstances when neither parent wants it? That is, should a judge ever award joint custody over both parents' objections? If so, in what circumstances?

Consider these questions in light of the materials that follow.

Taylor v. Taylor
508 A.2d 964 (Md. 1986)

McAuliffe, Judge.

... The parties to this appeal are Judith Ann Taylor (Appellant) and Neil Randall Taylor, III (Appellee). The Taylors were married on November 26,

1977, and are the parents of Christina Lee Taylor, born April 9, 1979, and Neil Randall Taylor, IV, born August 5, 1980.

During the summer of 1982, the Taylors began experiencing marital difficulties and on September 10, 1982, they separated. . . . Appellee filed a Bill of Complaint in the Circuit Court for Cecil County seeking an absolute divorce and temporary and permanent custody of the children. Appellant filed an answer in which she requested custody of the children pendente lite and permanently.

On November 24 a "visitation schedule," signed only by counsel, was filed, detailing an apparent agreement between the parties, and specifying the days and times that each party would have the children. On December 7, Judge Donaldson Cole entered a pendente lite order granting the parties "joint custody" of the children "in consideration of the agreement of the parties." The order further provided that the children were to reside with Appellee in the family home, and incorporated by reference the visitation schedule previously filed.

On April 7, 1983, Appellant changed attorneys. Five days later she filed an amended and supplemental answer in which she requested that the order of December 7, 1982, be stricken, and that she be awarded care and custody of the children. Appellant alleged that the order providing joint custody pendente lite was the result of "a meeting with the court without her knowledge," and of action taken by her attorney without her authority. Trial on the merits occurred shortly thereafter, and following a five day trial Judge H. Kenneth Mackey granted Appellee's request for an absolute divorce, and ordered continuation of the arrangement spelled out in the "visitation agreement," which he characterized as "a sort of joint custody." . . . Appellant's Motion for Reconsideration was denied, and she noted an appeal to the Court of Special Appeals. That court affirmed. Taylor v. Taylor, 60 Md. App. 268, 482 A.2d 164 (1984). We granted certiorari to consider the following two questions:

1) Whether a trial judge in Maryland has the authority to grant joint custody; and

2) Whether, if the trial judge did have the authority to grant such an award, he abused his discretion under the facts of this case.

I. Definition of Joint Custody

This dynamic and emotionally charged field of law is unfortunately afflicted with significant semantical problems, described by one writer as a "frightful lack of linguistic uniformity."[3] The inability of courts and commentators to agree on what is meant by the term "joint custody" makes difficult the task of distilling principles and guidelines from a rapidly growing body of literature and case law. What one writer sees as an amorphous concept another sees as a structured legal arrangement. While it is clear that both parents in a joint custody arrangement function as "custodians" in the sense that they are actually involved in the overall welfare of their child, a distinction must be made between sharing parental responsibility in major decision-making matters and sharing responsibility for providing a home for the child.

---

[3] D. Miller, Joint Custody, 13 Fam. L.Q. 345, 376 (1979).

Embraced within the meaning of "custody" are the concepts of "legal" and "physical" custody. Legal custody carries with it the right and obligation to make long range decisions involving education, religious training, discipline, medical care, and other matters of major significance concerning the child's life and welfare.[4] Joint legal custody means that both parents have an equal voice in making those decisions, and neither parent's rights are superior to the other.

Physical custody, on the other hand, means the right and obligation to provide a home for the child and to make the day-to-day decisions required during the time the child is actually with the parent having such custody. Joint physical custody is in reality "shared" or "divided" custody.[5] Shared physical custody may, but need not, be on a 50/50 basis, and in fact most commonly will involve custody by one parent during the school year and by the other during summer vacation months, or division between weekdays and weekends, or between days and nights.

With respect to physical custody, there is no difference between the rights and obligations of a parent having temporary custody of a child pursuant to an order of shared physical custody, and one having temporary custody pursuant to an award of visitation. Thus, a determination to grant legal custody to one parent and to allocate physical custody between the parents may be accomplished either by granting sole custody to one parent and specified rights of visitation to the other, or by granting legal custody to one parent and specified periods of physical custody to each parent. In either instance the effect will be the same.

Proper practice in any case involving joint custody dictates that the parties and the trial judge separately consider the issues involved in both joint legal custody and joint physical custody, and that the trial judge state specifically the decision made as to each.

II. Authority to Award Joint Custody

Appellant argues that "[t]here is no express statutory authority for an award of joint custody in Maryland" and that in the absence of such authority a court of equity lacks jurisdiction to grant joint custody. A strong argument can be made that authority to award joint custody is implicit in the language of the several statutes relating to child custody. We need not decide that issue, for we hold the authority to

---

[4] The parent not granted legal custody will, under ordinary circumstances, retain authority to make necessary day-to-day decisions concerning the child's welfare during the time the child is in that parent's physical custody. Thus, a parent exercising physical custody over a child, whether pursuant to an order of visitation or to an order of shared physical custody, necessarily possesses the authority to control and discipline the child during the period of physical custody. Similarly, that parent has the authority to consent to emergency surgery or emergency major medical care when there is insufficient time to contact the parent having legal custody. We need not here consider the issues that may arise when the parent having legal custody cannot agree with the parent exercising physical custody concerning emergency medical care. . . .

[5] The term "split custody" is generally used to describe the situation in which one parent is given sole custody of some of the children of the parties, with sole custody of the remaining children going to the other parent, and cross rights of visitation. Again, however, the use of terms is not uniform and some courts speak of "divided custody" to describe a situation involving split custody.

grant joint custody is an integral part of the broad and inherent authority of a court exercising its equitable powers to determine child custody. . . .

III. Joint Custody Considerations

This Court last considered the issue of joint custody in McCann v. McCann, 167 Md. 167, 172, 173 A. 7 (1934), in which our predecessors denounced joint control of a child as an arrangement "to be avoided, whenever possible, as an evil fruitful in the destruction of discipline, in the creation of distrust, and in the production of mental distress in the child." Significant societal changes that have occurred over the ensuing half century mandate our reexamination of those views.

Proponents of joint custody point out that it offers an opportunity for a child to enjoy a meaningful relationship with both parents, and may diminish the traumatic effects upon the child that can result from a dissolution of the marriage. While sole custody may reduce the noncustodial parent to the second class status of a visitor, joint custody allows both parties to function as, and be perceived as, parents. The sharing of the burdens as well as the joys of child-rearing may be particularly helpful in the many instances where both parents are employed. Where joint custody has been appropriate, benefits have accrued not only to the child, but to parents as well.

The principal criticism leveled at joint custody is that it creates confusion and instability for children at the very time they need a sense of certainty and finality in their lives. Additionally, it is said to present too great an opportunity for manipulation of the parents by the child. Critics also contend that the option of joint custody creates too great a temptation to the trial judge to avoid choosing one parent and disappointing the other by simply awarding custody to both. Certainly, joint custody is not appropriate in every case. Indeed, it has been suggested that it is appropriate only in a small minority of cases. But when appropriate, joint custody can result in substantial advantages to children and parents alike, and the feasibility of such an arrangement is certainly worthy of careful consideration.

Formula or computer solutions in child custody matters are impossible because of the unique character of each case, and the subjective nature of the evaluations and decisions that must be made. At best we can discuss the major factors that should be considered in determining whether joint custody is appropriate, but in doing so we recognize that none has talismanic qualities, and that no single list of criteria will satisfy the demands of every case.

We emphasize that in any child custody case, the paramount concern is the best interest of the child. . . . The best interest of the child is therefore not considered as one of many factors, but as the objective to which virtually all other factors speak. . . .

Capacity of the Parents to Communicate and to Reach Shared Decisions Affecting the Child's Welfare

This is clearly the most important factor in the determination of whether an award of joint legal custody is appropriate, and is relevant as well to a consideration of shared physical custody. Rarely, if ever, should joint legal custody be awarded in the absence of a record of mature conduct on the part of the parents evidencing an ability to effectively communicate with each other concerning the best interest of the child, and then only when it is possible to make a finding of a strong potential for such conduct in the future. . . .

When the evidence discloses severely embittered parents and a relationship marked by dispute, acrimony, and a failure of rational communication, there is nothing to be gained and much to be lost by conditioning the making of decisions affecting the child's welfare upon the mutual agreement of the parties. Even in the absence of bitterness or inability to communicate, if the evidence discloses the parents do not share parenting values, and each insists on adhering to irreconcilable theories of child-rearing, joint legal custody is not appropriate. The parents need not agree on every aspect of parenting, but their views should not be so widely divergent or so inflexibly maintained as to forecast the probability of continuing disagreement on important matters. In S. Steinman, Joint Custody: What We Know, What We Have Yet to Learn, and the Judicial and Legislative Implications, 16 U.C. Davis L. Rev. 739, 745-46 (1983), the author listed the characteristics of coparental relationships found to be important in a study of successful joint custody arrangements:

> Foremost was the sense of respect for one another as parents, despite the disappointment in each other as marriage partners. Each appreciated the value of the other to the child, and was sensitive to the possible loss of a parent-child relationship. The parents' relationships were characterized by a similarity in basic child-rearing values. There was the capacity to tolerate the minor differences that existed and to distinguish the important from the unimportant ones. These parents were able to relinquish control and not interfere in the other parent's relationship with the child. They were personally flexible and able to accommodate to the needs of the arrangement, the child, and even to the other parent. These were not people who were rigid in their thinking or behavior. There was a capacity to contain their anger and hostility and to divert it away from the children. There was an ability to take responsibility for their part in the break-up and their current life rather than project blame onto their ex-mate. Finally, there was a sense of parity in these coparental relationships. They accepted the premise that they were equally significant to and capable of caring for the children. This meant not only the genuine valuing of the other as a parent in raising the child but, equally as important, it enhanced the parents' own self-confidence. It was important that each parent had a sense of self-esteem as a parent in his or her own right in order to maintain the balance in the co-parental relationship.
>
> These parents were able to separate out their roles and feelings as parents from the marital- and divorce-engendered conflicts. They had rarely argued about the children during the marriage, and were able to maintain a "conflict free" sphere around the children, which they protected through the divorcing process. This capacity was central to a smooth running co-parental arrangement.

Ordinarily the best evidence of compatibility with this criterion will be the past conduct or "track record" of the parties. We recognize, however, that the tensions of separation and litigation will sometimes produce bitterness and lack of ability to cooperate or agree. The trial judge will have to evaluate whether this is a temporary condition, very likely to abate upon resolution of the issues, or whether it is more permanent in nature. Only where the evidence is strong in support of a finding of the existence of a significant potential for compliance with this criterion should joint legal custody be granted. Blind hope that a joint custody agreement will succeed, or that forcing the responsibility of joint decision-making upon the warring parents will bring peace, is not acceptable. In the unusual case where the trial judge concludes that joint legal custody is appropriate notwithstanding the absence of a "track record" of willingness and ability on the part of the parents to cooperate in making decisions dealing with the child's welfare, the trial judge must articulate fully the reasons that support that conclusion.

Willingness of Parents to Share Custody

Generally, the parents should be willing to undertake joint custody or it should not be ordered. We are asked by Appellant, and by the Women's Legal Defense Fund as amicus curiae, to hold that a trial judge may never order joint legal custody over the objection of one parent. They argue, with some force, that unwillingness on the part of one parent to share custody inevitably presages intransigence or inability to cooperate in making decisions affecting the welfare of the child. While we agree that the absence of an express willingness on the part of the parents to accept a joint custody arrangement is a strong indicator that joint legal custody is contraindicated, we are unwilling to fashion a hard and fast rule that would have the effect of granting to either parent veto power over the possibility of a joint custody award. A caring parent, believing that sole custody is in the best interest of the child, may forcefully advance that position throughout the litigation but be willing and able to fully participate in a joint custody arrangement if that is the considered decision of the court.

Fitness of Parents

The psychological and physical capabilities of both parents must be considered, although the determination may vary depending upon whether a parent is being evaluated for fitness for legal custody or for physical custody. A parent may be fit for one type of custody but not the other, or neither, or both.

Relationship Established Between the Child and Each Parent

When both parents are seen by the child as a source of security and love, there is a favorable climate for joint custody. . . .

Preference of the Child

The reasonable preference of a child of suitable age and discretion should be considered. In addition to being sensitive to the possible presence of the "lollipop" or "rescue" syndromes,[12] the trial judge must also recognize that children often

---

[12] The so-called "lollipop syndrome" relates to the situation where one parent in a custody battle may shower the child with gifts and pleasant times, and impose no discipline in order to win the child's preference. The "rescue syndrome" relates to the expression of preference by a child for the parent perceived by the child to be the "weaker" of the two, in the belief that the stronger parent will survive in any event, but the weaker parent needs the child.

experience a strong desire to see separated parents reunited, and this motivation may produce an unrealistic preference for joint custody.

Potential Disruption of Child's Social and School Life

Joint physical custody may seriously disrupt the social and school life of a child when each parent has the child for half the year, and the homes are not in close proximity to one another. In such cases the amount of time each parent has physical custody may be adjusted without interfering with the concept of continued joint custody.

Geographic Proximity of Parental Homes

Parental homes within the same school district offer certain advantages in a joint custody situation. The child may enjoy joint physical custody without changing schools or being required to constantly change a circle of friends, and the parents may find proximity a benefit in discussing the decisions to be made concerning the child. However, distance is not a bar, and when the distance between homes is great, a joint custody arrangement may offer the only practical way to preserve to the child a meaningful relationship with each parent. . . .

Demands of Parental Employment

In some situations, joint physical custody will be appropriate only if the work hours of the parents are different, or there is flexibility in the demands of the employment of each.

Age and Number of Children

The factor of age obviously interrelates with other factors already discussed. The number of children involved may pose practical difficulties to a joint custody arrangement, but on the other hand may be helpful to both parents in bringing about a sharing of the pressures of single family parenting of a number of children. In rare cases, split custody may be preferred over sole or joint custody.

Sincerity of Parents' Request

A number of interested observers have opposed the concept of joint custody absent mutual agreement on the ground that one spouse may interpose a demand for joint custody solely to gain bargaining leverage over the other in extracting favorable alimony, child support or property concessions. Drawing upon the reasoning of King Solomon writers have suggested that a parent truly interested in the welfare of a child will give up almost anything to protect the child, and thus the threat of enforced joint custody can be used to extract unwarranted concessions. While the remedy they suggest — denial of joint custody in the absence of parental agreement — is unnecessarily restrictive, we acknowledge the legitimacy of these concerns and highlight the necessity to carefully examine the motives and sincerity of each parent.

Financial Status of the Parents

Joint physical custody imposes financial burdens upon the parents because of the necessity of maintaining two homes for the child, with separate furnishings and often separate toys, equipment, and clothing. . . .

Benefit to Parents

Although the primary focus is properly upon the best interest of the child, it is also appropriate to consider the salutary effect that joint custody may have on the parents, not only because their feelings and interests are worthy of consideration, but also because their improved self-image as parents is likely to redound to the ultimate benefit of the child.

Other Factors

The enumeration of factors appropriate for consideration in a joint custody case is not intended to be all-inclusive, and a trial judge should consider all other circumstances that reasonably relate to the issue.

IV

In our review of the record to determine whether the trial judge abused his discretion, we are initially confronted with the problem of understanding the exact nature of the custody arrangement he intended. It is clear he intended to perpetuate the arrangement found to exist at the time of trial, which he characterized as "a sort of joint custody." This was basically the arrangement stipulated by the "visitation schedule". . . . The trial judge described the arrangement as follows:

> Both parents teach school. The father's work day is from about 8:30 A.M. to 4:15 P.M. and the mother's 12:30 P.M. to 4:15 P.M. . . . In November 1982 the parties agreed upon a sort of joint custody of the children. Their base is in the father's home but the mother probably sees them more of their waking hours. The mother is in the home with the children Monday to Friday from 7:30 A.M. to 12:30 P.M. The mother has the children in her home from 4:15 P.M. to 8:00 P.M. Tuesday and on alternate [weekends] from 10:00 A.M. Saturday until 8:00 P.M. Sunday. The paternal grandmother babysits Monday to Friday from 12:30 P.M. to 4:15 P.M., i.e. from the time the mother leaves the children until the father gets home. The father pays his mother $29.00 weekly. The mother contributes no money for child support.

It is difficult to determine from an examination of the "visitation schedule" filed by the parties whether they were using "visitation" to mean custody, or whether the agreement assumed custody by Appellee with specific visitation rights reserved to Appellant. The temporary custody order provided for "joint custody," but also established a "visitation" schedule for Appellant. The final order, while perpetuating the existing arrangement with respect to physical care of the children, is silent on the question of legal custody.

We think it likely the trial judge intended to grant joint physical custody, but we would have to speculate concerning his intent as to legal custody. Any uncertainty should be resolved by the trial court, and we shall remand for that purpose. Additionally, we conclude that under the particular facts of this case our remand should mandate full reconsideration of the issue of child custody. This disposition will enable the parties and the trial court to address specifically the issues of physical and legal custody, and to measure the facts of this case against the criteria for joint custody that we have discussed above. Particular attention must be given to the ability and inclination of these parties to effectively communicate with each other, and to agree on those important matters affecting the welfare of the children. Although the record supports the finding of the trial judge that the parties, with the aid of counsel, were able to successfully establish a schedule for the physical care of the children, the record also strongly suggests the presence of considerable hostility between these parents and an inability to effectively communicate directly with each other. We recognize that significant changes may have taken place in the three years that have elapsed since the trial of this matter, and that additional evidence should be received. . . .

Judgment of the Court of Special Appeals vacated. Case remanded. . . .

NOTES ON JOINT CUSTODY

(1) Definition.   As Taylor v. Taylor reveals, the concept of joint custody is beset with "significant semantical problems." An award of custody, in general, encompasses two concepts: legal custody and physical custody. Legal custody involves responsibility for significant and long-range decisions regarding care, upbringing, health, welfare, and education of the child. Physical custody involves decisionmaking regarding the child's daily activities. In an award of joint custody (more accurately termed joint legal custody), each parent shares responsibility for major childrearing decisionmaking irrespective of which parent has physical custody. Courts fashion joint custody awards in varying manners. *Taylor* illustrates that an award of joint physical custody does not always encompass an award of joint legal custody and vice versa.

In *Taylor,* review how joint custody differs from other traditional custodial arrangements. An award of "sole custody" vests one parent with legal control and permanent physical custody; the noncustodial parent has only temporary physical custody during specified visitation periods. "Divided custody," sometimes called "alternating custody," involves a custody order that divides or alternates the legal and physical custody of a child between parents. "Split custody" refers to a situation in which one parent is given sole custody of one or more of the children, while the other parent has sole custody of other children.

(2) Benefits and Criticisms of Joint Custody.   What are the benefits of joint custody — for parents and for children? What are the disadvantages of joint custody for the participants? Are short-range advantages and disadvantages different from long-range ones? The author of one empirical study (involving 24 families who voluntarily selected joint custody) points to the overriding parental benefit of sharing the pleasures and burdens of childrearing compared to the disadvantage of

experiencing a sense of discontinuity of being a part-time parent. Children had a sense of being loved by both parents, recognition that both their parents were making considerable efforts to care for them, and physical access to both parents that mitigated loyalty conflicts. See Susan Steinman, Joint Custody: What We Know, What We Have to Learn, and the Judicial and Legislative Implications, 16 U.C. Davis L. Rev. 739, 743-749 (1983).

On the other hand, the concept of joint custody has many critics. One criticism concerns the unequal bargaining position involved in the joint custody choice that disfavors women.

> Critics argue that joint custody statutes increase men's rights at divorce and their bargaining strength with respect to women, making women more vulnerable to claims and threats made by men. [Citations omitted.] Underlying this critique are the assumptions that women take more responsibility for their children than do men, love their children more than men do, and are more willing than men to sacrifice in order to retain custody of their children. As a result, women will sacrifice their own financial rights, and even those of their children, in negotiations at divorce in order to preserve maximum custody of their children. This distortion in bargaining at divorce occurs, it is claimed, even if men do not really want joint custody of their children or do not intend to exercise their joint custody rights.
>
> Particular forms of joint custody provisions may disfavor women still further. For example, a "friendly parent" provision operates in sole custody disputes to favor the parent who demonstrates the greater willingness to allow the other parent access to the children. This rule may make it too risky for a woman to oppose a father's request for joint custody, even in justifiable circumstances, for to do so might imply that the mother is unwilling to permit the child the greatest access to both parents and thus is less suitable as a custodian. To avoid this implication, the woman may accept joint custody even when she feels it is in neither her nor her child's best interests . . . .[48]

(3) Presumption, Preference, or Option.   In *Taylor,* the appellate court held that trial courts may make awards of joint custody even without express statutory authority. Today, however, almost all states provide for awards of joint custody either by statute or case law. States follow different approaches: Some statutes create a presumption for joint custody, others a preference, and others merely list joint custody as an option. Presumption and preference statutes each accord different weight to joint custody. Preference statutes give joint custody preference over other custodial forms; presumption statutes contain an assumption that joint custody is assumed to be in the child's best interests and will be ordered unless rebutted.

---

[48] Katharine T. Bartlett & Carol B. Stack, Joint Custody, Feminism and the Dependency Dilemma, 2 Berkeley Women's L.J. 9, 19-20 (1986).

Inherent in the first criticism is the suggestion that some men request joint custody to reduce their child support liability. Some states address this issue specifically by providing either that an award of joint custody does not preclude support (see, e.g., Fla. Stat. Ann. §61.13(1)(5) (West 2006 & Supp. 2008); Mo. Stat. Ann. §452.375(12) (West 2003 & Supp. 2008)), or justify modification of a support order.

Some states have retreated from joint custody, removing joint custody presumptions, or precluding joint custody absent an agreement, or simply decreasing the number of joint custody awards. This retreat derives from the belief that joint custody (physical or legal) may not be in the child's best interests, especially when judicially imposed or when there is considerable parental discord. James G. Dwyer, A Taxonomy of Children's Existing Rights in State Decision Making About Their Relationships, 11 Wm. & Mary Bill Rts. J. 845, 911 (2003).

(4) Effect of Parental Agreement. In many states, joint custody will not be awarded unless both parents agree to the arrangement. However, in other states, courts may decree an award of joint custody over the objection of one, or both, of the parents. See, e.g., Kay v. Ludwig, 686 N.W.2d 619 (Neb. Ct. App. 2004) (if parties do not agree, court may award joint custody upon finding of best interests).

There is considerable debate by commentators about whether an award of joint custody is appropriate over the objection of one, or both, of the parents. Consider the following two views:

> Most authorities agree that joint custody is only appropriate and in a child's best interests when both parents agree to such a plan and are capable of joint decision-making regarding the child's welfare. [Citations omitted.] This type of joint custody legislation [joint custody upon request of one party] is antithetical to the above criteria since the court can force joint custody on those parents who are not in agreement or who have not shown themselves capable of co-parenting. Legal edicts cannot force parents to agree on childrearing questions. Nor can the fate of children rest on *the possibility* of success.[49]
>
> A further resistance to joint custody is expressed in the widely held belief that joint custody should never be awarded unless both parents agree. Proponents of this view state that it is not in the "best interest" of the child to be involved in such a shared parenting arrangement because the hostile environment between parents will be perpetuated. . . . First, this position seems to ignore the finding that parents with sole custody orders also experience a period of intense conflict to which the children are witnesses. There is not yet evidence available that, on a daily basis, children in unilaterally desired joint custody arrangements experience *more* hostility, or that the hostility they initially experience would not be balanced by the opportunity to continue their relationship in a meaningful way with both parents. And, in denying joint custody *solely* on the basis of one parent's opposition, the child's wishes and developmental needs are not even being considered as a relevant factor in decision making . . . .[50]

(5) Factors Considered by Courts. *Taylor* mentions several factors that are relevant in determining whether joint custody is appropriate.

a. Parent-Related Factors. Case law emphasizes the necessity for parental cooperation for a successful joint custody arrangement. Although the court in *Taylor* found that the capacity of the parents to communicate and reach shared decisions affecting the child's welfare is the "most important factor" in

---

[49] Joanne Schulman & Valerie Pitt, Second Thoughts on Joint Custody: Analysis of Legislation and Its Impact for Women and Children, 12 Golden Gate L. Rev. 539, 550 (1982).

[50] Joan B. Kelly, Examining Resistance to Joint Custody in Joint Custody and Shared Parenting, in Joint Custody and Shared Parenting (43 Jay Folberg, ed. 1984).

determining the appropriateness of joint custody, many courts do not consider communication difficulties to present an insurmountable obstacle to awards of joint custody.[51]

Among the parent-related factors, the issue of parental cooperation elicits considerable controversy. Critics of joint custody argue that if parents could not agree during marriage, how can they be forced to agree after divorce? Consider the following rebuttal to this argument:

> Another concept contributing to resistance among lawyers, judges, and mental health professionals to joint custody has been the belief that parents who divorce are unable to cooperate about anything, including their parenting after the divorce. This concept actually draws upon two somewhat erroneous and simplistic notions about divorce. The first is that a marriage that fails has done so in every regard, and that the conflict that led to the termination of the marriage permeated child-rearing issues and parental decision making as well. While this is clearly true in some marriages, there is evidence that substantial conflict regarding child-rearing practices is not present in a majority of marriages. Lawyers, in particular, seem to share the belief that if parents could cooperate regarding their children, they would not be divorcing in the first place. Adults divorce for many reasons related to adult needs and dissatisfactions, but dissatisfaction or conflict stemming from the spouse's parental behavior is not among the more prevalent reasons expressed for obtaining a divorce. The second notion is that the anger which attorneys and mental health professionals observe during the divorcing period will remain undiminished during the years following divorce. However, there is evidence that the intense anger between parents diminishes within the first year post-divorce. . . . After two years post-separation, only a small percentage of parents (close to 15%) remain intensely or pathologically enraged. . . .[52]

Another parent-related factor, geographic proximity between parental residences, also has an impact on the appropriateness of joint custody. This is especially true in cases in which parents share joint physical, as well as joint legal, custody. In some cases, courts assume that geographically distant residences lead to too much disruption to make joint custody feasible.[53] Still another parent-related factor is financial resources. Maintenance of two parental residences appropriate for childrearing may place a burden on both parents. Should the inferior financial ability of one party preclude an award of joint custody? Review the discussion of wealth as a factor in custody decisionmaking, pp. 575-576, supra.

b. Child-Related Factors. Among the child-related factors, research has been conducted on the possible disruptive effect of joint custody. One commentator,

---

[51] See, e.g., Van Wieran v. Van Wieran, 858 N.E.2d 216 (Ind. Ct. App. 2006) (refusing to modify joint custody arrangement despite "venomous relationship" between parents); McCarty v. McCarty, 807 A.2d 1211 (Md. 2002).

[52] Schulman & Pitt, supra note [49].

[53] See, e.g., Gray v. Gray, 239 S.W.3d 26 (Ark. Ct. App. 2006) (joint custody was inappropriate when one parent moved several hundreds of miles away, thereby materially altering the parents' ability to cooperate).

reporting on her research, concludes that potential disruption may vary as a function of age:

> A major concern about joint custody is whether switching homes generates confusion and anxiety in the child about where he belongs. Most of the children [in our study] were impressively able to keep their complex schedules in mind and demonstrated a sense of mastery over switching between homes. Twenty-five percent of the children, however, were anxious and insecure about switching homes. They worried about themselves, their parents, possessions, and exhibited an overall sense of instability. . . .
>
> The continuity of school life and friendships was found to be very important to all the children in the study, but particularly to the latency age and adolescent children. They valued the stability of remaining in one school and used school as an anchoring place. The adolescents' age-appropriate involvement in school-based social activities, as well as the loosening of psychological ties to the parents, made the long established dual-home arrangement antithetical to their needs when they became teen-agers. . . .[54]

Another study concurs that the appropriateness of joint custody may depend on the age of the child. It suggests, however, that the preschool child (age three to five) has an even more difficult adjustment than the adolescent.[55] What implication does this finding have for awards of joint custody? Should awards of joint custody be modified automatically when a child reaches adolescence?

c. Contraindicated Factors.   In some contexts, joint custody may be particularly inappropriate. What might those contexts be? Some commentators suggest that joint custody should never be awarded if there is evidence of spousal abuse, because joint custody ensures continued contact with the abuser.[56] Most states now take this factor into account, either specifically in statutes providing for awards of joint custody, or more generally, in terms of determining any custodial arrangement. Can you think of similar situations that would militate against awards of joint custody?

(6) ALI Principles.   The ALI Principles favors joint custody when parents have adhered to it in the past. ALI Principles §2.08(1). The ALI Principles defers to private ordering by requiring all parents who seek to allocate custodial responsibility to file a parenting plan. Id. at §2.05(1). (Recall that the ALI substitutes the term "custodial responsibility" for the former terms "custody" and "visitation" and also uses the term "decision making responsibility" rather than the term "legal custody.") If the parents are unable to agree how to allocate custodial responsibility, the court follows the approximation standard — i.e., the division of parental responsibilities adopted by the parents prior to the divorce. See generally Katharine T. Bartlett, U.S. Custody Law and Trends in the Context of the ALI Principles of the Law of Family Dissolution, 10 Va. J. Soc. Pol'y & L. 5 (2002).

---

[54] Susan Steinman, Joint Custody: What We Know, What We Have Yet to Learn, and the Judicial and Legislative Implications, 16 U.C. Davis L. Rev. 739 (1983).

[55] See Rosemary McKinnon & Judith S. Wallerstein, Joint Custody and the Preschool Child, 4 Behav. Sci. & Law 169 (1986).

[56] See, e.g., Judith G. Greenberg, Domestic Violence and the Danger of Joint Custody Presumptions, 25 N. Ill. U. L. Rev. 403 (2005).

(7) Do parents have a constitutionally protected liberty interest in the joint legal custody of their children upon dissolution? If so, should states protect that right by providing for a rebuttable presumption of joint decisionmaking? Compare Margaret F. Brinig, Does Parental Autonomy Require Equal Custody at Divorce?, 65 La. L. Rev. 1345, 1369-1370 (2005) (expressing concerns over constitutionalizing child custody), with David D. Meyer, The Constitutional Rights of Non-Custodial Parents, 34 Hofstra L. Rev. 1461, 1465 (2006) (arguing that unequal parenting roles are constitutionally permissible).

b.　Standards Regarding the Noncustodial Parent: Visitation

Traditionally, an award of custody to one parent (typically the mother) is accompanied by a grant of visitation rights to the noncustodial parent. A trial judge has considerable discretion to determine the scope and frequency of visitation. Visitation can later be the occasion of disputes and tension because (1) it ordinarily requires the divorced parents to have at least *some contact* with one another; and (2) it may create conflicts of *loyalty* for the child. To avoid judicial intervention in family relationships after a divorce, and to protect the relationship between the child and the custodial parent, Goldstein, Freud and Solnit[57] suggested that "the noncustodial parent should have no legally enforceable right to visit the child," thus giving the custodial parent the full power and responsibility of deciding whether there should be visitation, and if so, when and for how long.

Commentators have been especially critical of this suggestion. For example, the Benedeks have written that

> experience has shown that custodial parents may be motivated to deny visitation by a number of reasons or emotions to which the child's best interests are entirely irrelevant. Ironically, it is the most meaningful relationships between children and noncustodial parents that are frequently the most threatening to custodial parents and, consequently, such relationships would often be in the greatest jeopardy.[58]

Does the Goldstein, Freud, and Solnit proposal raise constitutional problems?

The following section focuses on visitation. First, it explores the issue of the denial of visitation rights. Is it ever appropriate to deny visitation to a parent? If so, in what circumstances? Next, it examines conditions on visitation. Is it ever appropriate to restrict a parent's conduct during visitation periods? If so, in what circumstances? What restrictions are justifiable? Are there any limitations on a court's authority to condition visitation rights? Finally, it examines the rights of third parties to petition for visitation. Do persons such as grandparents, stepparents, and same-sex partners have visitation rights? Should a court be able to undermine a parent's decision to deny visitation to a person who has no legally cognizable relationship with the child? In what instances is such judicial interference in the family appropriate? In what circumstances does it violate the parent's right to raise a child as the parent sees fit?

---

[57] Joseph Goldstein et al., The Best Interests of the Child, supra note [2], at 23.

[58] Elissa P. Benedek & David M. Benedek, Postdivorce Visitation: A Child's Right, 16 J. Am. Acad. of Clinical Psychiatry 256, 263 (Spring 1977).

(1) No Visitation?

Peterson v. Jason
513 So. 2d 1351 (Fla. Ct. App. 1987)

Mills, Judge.

William E. Peterson appeals from a non-final order terminating visitation for non-payment of child support. . . . We reverse.

The parties herein were married in 1980 and produced one child in 1981. The final judgement of dissolution was entered in November 1985, granting primary custody of the child to the wife and visitation rights to Peterson. Based upon his then monthly income of $800.00, Peterson was ordered to pay $150.00 per month in child support, plus $50.00 per month against support arrearages which had accumulated during the period before final judgement was entered.

The ensuing months brought numerous motions for contempt from both parties, the wife alleging failure to pay child support, Peterson alleging wrongful denial of visitation. In November and December 1986, Peterson filed *pro se* motions for modification of his child support obligations based on allegations of illness and inability to pay. These motions were heard in April 1987 after which, despite evidence of Peterson's illness and a reduction in his income from $800.00 per month to $200.00 per month in welfare benefits, the trial court denied Peterson's motions for modification and further held him in "willful contempt" for failure to pay child support.

Despite the stated denial of modification of child support, the order went on to provide that "due to the financial status of petitioner (Peterson), the court will reduce the monthly support obligation from $150.00 to $75.00 per month"; the wife does not challenge this reduction. The order concluded that "visitation would be reinstated" if Peterson paid his May child support payment by 2 May and continued to keep it current. It is not clear if visitation had been terminated orally at the April hearing or by some other written order which does not appear in the record.

On 5 May 1987, the court entered another order noting that Peterson had not paid his child support as required by the first order and stating that "the court hereby stays petitioner's visitation with the minor child until he complies [with the 1 May order]." [R]einstatement of visitation to [occur] at such time as Peterson should appear and show that his child support was current. This appeal followed, on the sole issue of whether the trial court erred in conditioning Peterson's visitation rights on the payment of child support.

It is the general rule that visitation may not be changed or denied based merely on nonpayment of child support. However, there are some cases holding that, while the right to visitation does not terminate upon an *excusable failure* to pay support, in the face of a *willful and intentional refusal* to pay child support which is detrimental to the welfare of the child, the right to visitation may be terminated. [Citations omitted.] Therefore, it appears that a trial court can terminate a parent's right to visitation with a minor child for nonpayment of support only when the nonpayment has been willful and intentional *and* detrimental to the welfare of the child so that termination would be in the child's best interest.

Implicit in a finding of "willful and intentional refusal" to pay support is the ability to pay. . . . In the instant case, although the trial court found Peterson in "willful" contempt for nonpayment of support, withholding visitation until the payments were brought current, at the same time it halved his support obligation from $150.00 to $75.00 per month, specifically based on "the financial status of the petitioner." We cannot hold these equivocal findings sufficient to support the drastic measure of terminating visitation. As has been noted, a court has at its disposal a wide variety of other methods to coerce compliance with a final judgement of divorce.

Reversed.

NOTES AND QUESTIONS

(1) General Rule. The general rule is that the right to visitation and the duty of support are not interdependent variables. That is, visitation may not be conditioned on timely payment of child support. On the other hand, child support may not be withheld because an ex-spouse denies or interferes with visitation rights. See Hastings v. Rigsbee, 875 So. 2d 772 (Fla. Ct. App. 2004) (order conditioning mother's visitation upon payment of support was abuse of discretion). (For a discussion of the Parental Support Obligation, see Chapter 2, section B.)

(2) Exceptions. As *Peterson* reveals, courts are reluctant to impose total denial of visitation. Nonetheless, some situations may result in this "drastic measure." What might be such situations? For example, should a noncustodial parent's lack of interest constitute grounds for denying visitation? Compare J.L.M. v. R.L.C., 132 S.W.3d 279 (Mo. Ct. App. 2004) (denying visitation rights to father who failed to make contact for ten years, despite being financially able to do so), with Jackson v. Jackson, 2004 WL 1299988 (Ky. Ct. App. 2004) (reversing denial of visitation by mother who had not seen child for two years).

What if the noncustodial parent physically abuses the children? Is this a basis to deny visitation? In Painter v. Painter, 688 A.2d 479 (Md. Ct. App. 1997), a father was denied visitation with his son and awarded only limited visitation with his daughter because of the father's severe physical and emotional physical abuse. Similarly, in Stitzel v. Brown, 767 N.Y.S.2d 510 (App. Div. 2003), the father was denied visitation because he committed domestic violence against the mother in the children's presence and injured the youngest child.

Proof of sexual abuse of the child is another ground for denying visitation. See, e.g., Duncan v. Duncan, 843 N.E.2d 966 (Ind. Ct. App. 2006) (upholding denial of visitation to a father who had molested an older sibling); In re Marriage of M.A., 149 S.W.3d 562 (Mo. Ct. App. 2004) (affirming denial of visitation based on father's sexual abuse).

Suppose a parent is incarcerated. Is that sufficient reason to deny visitation? See Wright v. Wooden, 2003 WL 22744370 (Ky. Ct. App. 2003) (holding that visitation should be denied based on a finding of serious endangerment caused by visiting incarcerated father rather than on "best interests" standard). Should the underlying reason for the parent's incarceration be relevant in the determination of that parent's visitation rights? See, e.g., Cal. Fam. Code §3030(b)

(West 2004 & Supp. 2008) (providing a conclusive presumption that an award of custody or visitation to a convicted rapist, when the child was born as a result of the rape, is not in the child's best interests); Cal. Fam. Code §3030(c) (West 2004 & Supp. 2008) (providing a rebuttable presumption against custody or unsupervised visitation with a person who has been convicted of first-degree murder of the child's other parent unless the court finds that there is no risk to the child's health, safety, and welfare).

See generally Deborah Ahrens, Not in Front of the Children: Prohibition on Child Custody as Civil Branding for Criminal Activity, 75 N.Y.U. L. Rev. 737 (2000); Dana Lowy & Mary Redfield, Criminal Histories and Parental Custody and Visitation Rights, 26 L.A. Law. 25 (Oct. 2003); Benjamin Guthrie Stewart, Comment, When Should a Court Order Visitation Between a Child and an Incarcerated Parent?, 9 U. Chi. L. Sch. Roundtable 165 (2002).

(3) Purpose of Visitation Denial.   What purpose does denial of visitation serve in these cases? If the purpose is punishment of the noncustodial parent, is this an appropriate use of punishment? If denial of visitation is based on the best interests of the child, is it ever in the child's best interests to be deprived of all contact with a parent?

(4) Empirical Evidence.   *Peterson* raises the question of the appropriateness of a denial of visitation for failure to pay child support. The relationship of visitation to child support is much debated. Numerous questions arise. What is the incidence of visitation denial by custodial mothers? How often does visitation denial lead to nonpayment of child support? And conversely, how often does nonpayment of support contribute to problems with the exercise of visitation rights? The following article explores the complex relationship between visitation denial and child support, and suggests some areas for reform.

Jessica Pearson & Nancy Thoennes, The Denial of Visitation Rights: A Preliminary Look at Its Incidence, Correlates, Antecedents and Consequences
10 Law & Pol'y 363, 375-379 (1988)

This paper explores the nature and incidence of the denial of visitation rights and the nonpayment of child support. It relies on a secondary analysis of three different longitudinal data sets. . . .

The analysis reveals that visitation denial is a problem with approximately 22 percent of sample mothers reputedly failing to comply with the visitation terms of their divorce decree. This is consistent with reports of [other studies], however, it should be noted that these levels fall far below the reported levels of non-compliance with child support. Only about half of all custodial parents owed child support receive the full amount of support owed to them in any given year. Even fewer custodians receive all the payments on time. [Citations omitted]

Estimated levels of visitation denial also fall below levels of non-contact by absent parents noted in previous research. For example, in their longitudinal study of 1,747 households, Furstenburg and North (1983:10) discovered that in cases involving children living in one-parent families where the non-custodian is believed to be alive, "over a third of the children . . . lost contact altogether with the biological parent living outside the home." Hetherington, et al. (1978) report that two years following the divorce, 30 percent of the children saw their fathers about once a month or less. Luepnitz (1982) reports that in 24 percent of the 34 maternal custody families she studied, all of whom had separated at least two years, the non-custodian parent "never" saw the children. Fulton's (1979) study also notes that after two years, 30 percent of the fathers no longer visit their children. And at the five year follow-up study with their volunteer sample of 60 families, Wallerstein and Kelly (1980) report that only nine percent of the children had no contact with the non-custodian, although another 17 percent were visited only sporadically.

Clearly, it is inaccurate to assume that all of these are cases in which custodians encourage sporadic visitation or deny the non-custodian regular access to the children. Indeed in her study, Luepnitz notes that:

> In half of the cases when the non-custodial father visits rarely or never, it is because the children dislike him and have decided not to see him. But in many other cases, custodial mothers report that their ex had split the scene "in order to evade child support payments" (Luepnitz, 1982:34).

Further investigation of visitation non-compliance reveals that it rarely stands alone as a post-divorce problem and that such allegations are accompanied by a host of other visitation-related complaints. Moreover, for most parents visitation difficulties appear to become established fairly early on and fail to deviate over time.

Couples with visitation problems are decidedly more embittered than their compliant counterparts and their lack of cooperation, conflict and anger are apparent at the earliest interview, well before the promulgation of a divorce decree and are corroborated by independent interviewer ratings. Although non-payment of child support cases do not always involve a visitation problem, the two phenomena are related and cases with visitation problems are substantially more likely to involve child support nonpayment or disputes over support. Both phenomena appear to stem from conflict patterns between the parents, although we were unable to assess causal order in cases that involved both types of non-compliance. In half the cases, visitation preceded child support; in the other half of the cases, the opposite was true. In most instances, both problems were apparent at the time of the first interview and it was impossible to trace problem sequence. . . .

Policy Considerations

These findings inspire several policy recommendations. Minimally, there is a need for reliable record keeping of both child support and visitation arrears. Without reliable record keeping, violations are difficult to prove, make-up policies are impossible to establish or supervise. To date, several states require child support payments to be made through the Clerk of the Court rather than directly to the custodial parent. . . . Objective accounts of visitation denial, however, are harder to come by. One model approach is found in a Michigan law which requires the child support enforcement agency, the Friend of the Court, to keep track of alleged visitation denials (with the custodial parent having an opportunity to contest the allegation) and to supervise make-up visitation orders (Mich. Comp. Laws F25.164 (42) (4)-(5)).

Secondly these findings underscore the importance of interventions with divorcing couples aimed at enhancing their communication skills and reducing levels of anger and hostility. [A] preliminary assessment of relationships between the noncustodial parent and his children reveals that conflict between divorced parents is a good prediction of both child support payment, visitation and other types of involvement (Braver et al., 1985). [I]t appears that neglect of therapeutic elements of the process may vastly diminish its potential effectiveness in reducing post-divorce conflict over visitation and support.

A third conclusion of this research is the need to consider child support and visitation issues concurrently. While there is no evidence to suggest that the two issues should be made contingent upon one another, so that the denial of one should be a remedy for the withholding of the other, policy should reflect the fact that they co-occur and that grievances in both areas should be jointly aired. This conclusion runs counter to current practice. To date most court-based mediation services deal with the issues of contested child custody and/or visitation only. Child support and the other financial issues of divorce are considered to be beyond the purview of the mediation intervention. In the few settings where child support issues are mediated in court settings, they tend to be handled by a separate staff. . . .

For discussion of the relationship between custody and support, see also Ira Mark Ellman, Should Visitation Denial Affect the Obligation to Pay Support?, 36 Ariz. St. L.J. 661 (2004) (contending that the rule of independence of support and visitation should be applied in more narrow range of cases); W Fabricius & S. Braver, Non-Child Support Expenditures on Children by Nonresidential Divorced Fathers, 42 Fam. Ct. Rev. 321 (2003) (arguing that nonresidential fathers incur considerable visitation expenses and that should lead to a reduction in their child support obligations); Irwin Garfinkel et al., Visitation and Child Support Guidelines: A Comment on Fabricius and Braver, 42 Fam. Ct. Rev. 342 (2004) (rebuttal to Fabricius and Braver study).

(5) As aforementioned, Goldstein, Freud, and Solnit in *Beyond the Best Interests of the Child* suggest that the custodial parent be given the power to determine the visitation rights of the noncustodial parent. Putting aside for the moment the constitutional implications of such a proposal, does it constitute sound policy? Consider the following:

Eleanor E. Maccoby & Robert H. Mnookin, Dividing the Child: Social and Legal Dilemmas of Custody
285-287 (1992)

Some children would no doubt benefit from a rule that gave the custodial parent control over the other parent's access. What concerns us, however, is the risk that many other children might well be harmed by such a rule. Our research suggests that a significant if declining portion of parents do remain enmeshed in conflict. For some of these conflicted families, ending visitation might benefit the children. But among the families in our study, the conflicted pattern of co-parenting was not the most common pattern several years after parental separation. Rather, spousal disengagement became the norm as time passed. . . . Our concern is that because of difficulties related to the spousal divorce, a significant number of custodial mothers might put an end to paternal visitation in circumstances where the children would not in fact suffer long-run harm by reason of parental conflict, and where they would receive important long-run benefits from a continuing relationship with their father.

We suggested earlier that children who are primarily residing with their mother can nevertheless receive a variety of benefits — psychological, social, and economic — from a continuing relationship with their father. [T]he evidence in both our study and others makes it clear that there is better compliance with support obligations by fathers who maintain contact with their children. In many states, a father's legal obligation to support his children ends when the child reaches age 18. We think it quite plausible that fathers who remain in contact are more likely to help a child with college expenses after this age. Moreover, in addition to possible economic benefits, we think children can benefit in other ways from a continuing relationship. We have seen that a significant minority of children who start out living with one parent go to live with the other at a later time, at least temporarily. . . . And in cases where the children continue to live with the mother, the relationship with the father — although not nearly so important to a child's development as the relationship with the custodial mother — can nevertheless provide emotional support in times of crisis and possible guidance for the child over the years. . . .

In recent years, there has been considerable debate concerning the wisdom of children's having continuing contact with a non-custodial parent in families where there is a history of domestic violence (Cahn, 1991; Ellis, 1990). We do not doubt that when the *child* has been abused by the non-custodial parent, the court is justified in denying visitation or limiting it to supervised situations. However, in cases of violence between the spouses, the issue is more complex. Incidents of violence (for example, hitting, throwing objects) are quite common at the time a marriage breaks up, and husbands and wives are almost equally likely to engage in violent acts, though women are much more likely to get hurt (Johnston, in press; Straus, Gelles, and Steinmetz, 1981). Further, allegations of physical abuse are common during divorce negotiations (Depner, Cannata, and Simon, in press), and verifying their frequency or severity is difficult indeed. We believe that allegations of violent acts should not be automatic grounds for denying visitation. A history of chronic physical abuse must be taken very seriously, however. While it may not be possible to devise a blanket statutory rule that would be applicable to all cases, we certainly believe that courts should retain the power to eliminate visitation in order to protect mother and children from a physically abusive father.

In families where no abuse has occurred, there are nevertheless some potential risks of maintaining visitation in families in which the parents have disengaged. The child may become the carrier of necessary messages, and may get caught up in parental conflict in the process. Beyond this, children — particularly teenagers — may well be able to weaken the authority of the custodial parent by playing off the two parents against each other. . . .

Despite these potential disadvantages, we are not persuaded that on balance the potential benefits of a general policy giving the custodial parent the legal right to terminate visitation would outweigh the potential costs. Of course, we are constrained by the existing research, which does not allow precise quantification and comparison of the benefits and costs of a legal rule that would give a custodial parent the legal power to end visitation. It is certainly conceivable that research in the future might suggest that on balance the benefits of such a rule would outweigh the costs. But on the basis of existing evidence, and in the absence of a showing of abuse, we are not persuaded this would be so. . . .

(2) Conditions on Visitation

Khalsa v. Khalsa
751 P.2d 715 (N.M. Ct. App. 1988)

GARCIA, Judge.

The parties were married in 1973. At the time, they were Sikhs and believed in and practiced the Sikh religion. In June 1976, the parties' oldest child, Mari Jap Singh Khalsa, was born, and in January 1981, the parties had a second child, Kartar Singh Khalsa. Both children's Sikh names appear on their birth certificates and, while the parties were married, both children were raised as Sikhs. The family observed the requirements of their religion, including the wearing of distinct apparel and turbans, reading from the Guru Granath, the Sikh scriptures, and the assumption of Sikh names. Their adherence to principles and tenets of their faith continued throughout their marriage.

Marital discord ultimately led to the breakdown of their marriage and in December 1982, mother filed an uncontested petition for divorce. Mother was granted the divorce and awarded sole custody of the two children.

In December 1983, mother remarried. Shortly thereafter, mother abandoned the Sikh religion and began discouraging the children from practicing Sikhism. Mother also began calling the children by other than the Sikh names. Father objected to the children not being raised as Sikhs, and the parties' disagreements over religious differences escalated. In May 1984, father filed a motion requesting sole custody of the children or, in the alternative, joint custody.

In violation of father's discovery request, mother failed to timely disclose the names of any expert witnesses whom she planned to call at trial on her behalf. . . . Over father's objections, both witnesses testified.

In December 1986, following a hearing on the merits, the trial court entered its order regarding custody, [and] visitation. . . .

[T]he court ordered that sole custody of the children remain with mother; that father have visitation with the children at his residence for one month each summer; and that the children not participate voluntarily or involuntarily in any Sikh religious activities with father. Father appeals. . . .

Father raised the following . . . on appeal: . . . whether the trial court erred in enjoining father from encouraging his children to practice and participate in the Sikh religion during their visits with father. . . .

This issue presents a matter of first impression. [W]e deem it necessary to give guidance as to the scope of a court's intervention in religious beliefs and practices in child custody disputes.

Without any finding that participation in religious activities was harmful to the children here, the trial court enjoined the parties from freely discussing their religious beliefs with their children. Specifically, the trial court ordered that when the children were with the father, they could not voluntarily or involuntarily participate in any Sikh activity, including any church activity, Sikh camp or Sikh day care center.

It is well established that in child custody matters the best interests and welfare of the children are the primary and controlling considerations. Similarly, where there is a conflict between the parents regarding the religious faith and training of the children, the paramount concern is the welfare of the children.

Courts should proceed cautiously and with circumspection when dealing with religious issues. . . . In Munoz v. Munoz, [489 P.2d 1133 (Wash. 1971)] the court noted:

> The courts are reluctant . . . to interfere with the religious faith and training of children where the conflicting religious preferences of the parents are in no way detrimental to the welfare of the child. The obvious reason for such a policy of impartiality regarding religious beliefs is that, constitutionally, American courts are forbidden from interfering with religious freedoms or to take steps preferring one religion over another.

Thus, the rule appears to be well established that the courts should maintain an attitude of strict impartiality between religions and should not disqualify any applicant for custody or restrain any person having custody or visitation rights from taking the children to a particular church, except where there is a clear and affirmative showing that the conflicting religious beliefs affect the general welfare of the child.

In justifying a prohibition of religious restrictions on visitation rights, physical or emotional harm to the child cannot be assumed, but must be demonstrated in detail. Factual evidence of harm rather than "mere conclusions and speculation" is required.

Thus, a custodial parent's general testimony that the child is upset or confused because of the non-custodial parent's religious practice is insufficient to demonstrate harm. Further, general testimony that the child is upset because the parents practice conflicting religious beliefs is likewise insufficient. Hanson v. Hanson [404 N.W.2d 460 (N.D. 1987)] (mother's testimony that father, a member of the Pentecostal Apostolic church, had told the children, among other things, that the Catholic church believes in cannibalism, which upset the children, was insufficient to prohibit father from taking the children to his church); Munoz v. Munoz [supra] (parent's speculation that six-year-old son, who attended both Mormon services with his mother and Catholic services with his father, was emotionally harmed thereby, was insufficient. The court concluded that duality of religious beliefs, do not, per se, create a conflict upon young minds.)

Although most disputes involve conflicting religious practices between the divorced parents, the same principles apply equally where one parent practices no religion. . . .

A court's reluctance to interfere with the religious upbringing of children, however, is not absolute. Religious restrictions placed upon visitation rights have been upheld where evidence of physical or emotional harm to the child has been substantial. See Funk v. Ossman, 150 Ariz. 578, 724 P.2d 1247 (App. 1986) (court upheld order enjoining noncustodial parent from taking his eight-year-old son to formal Jewish religious training. Evidence presented at trial included the testimony of three psychologists, one of whom testified that child had anxiety problems caused by the religious differences of his parents, which manifested itself in encopresis); Bentley v. Bentley, 86 A.D.2d 926, 448 N.Y.S.2d 559 (1982) (court affirmed order prohibiting non-custodial father from instructing his children in the teachings of the Jehovah's Witnesses. The custodial mother was Catholic and the court found that the children were "emotionally strained and torn" as a result of the parties' conflicting religious beliefs).

Thus, although the courts are reluctant to enjoin a non-custodial parent from practicing his religion with his children, the courts can and will enjoin such practice where the testimony concerning physical or emotional harm to the child is detailed and the best interests of the child will be served through the prohibition. Here, the evidence concerning the impact on the children consisted of testimony by Father Burtner and mother's general testimony that the children appeared upset and disturbed after visitations with father. Because we have held that the trial court abused its discretion in permitting Father Burtner to testify, however, the trial court could not restrict father from practicing his religion with his children based on such testimony. Mother's general testimony alone, however, was insufficient to support the restriction.

In sum, we adopt the view [that] [c]ourts should adhere to a policy of impartiality between religions, and should intervene in this sensitive and constitutionally protected area only where there is a clear and affirmative showing of harm to the children. Restrictions in this area present the danger that court-imposed limitations will unconstitutionally infringe upon a parent's freedom of worship or be perceived as having that effect.

Thus, we hold that, in determining whether a parent involved in a child custody dispute should be restricted from practicing or encouraging the child in a religious belief or practice, the trial court must consider the following:

1. Whether there exists detailed factual evidence demonstrating that the conflicting beliefs or practices of the parents pose substantial physical or emotional harm to the child;

2. Whether restricting the religious interaction between the parent and child will necessarily alleviate this harm; and

3. Whether such restrictions are narrowly tailored so as to minimize interference with the parents' religious freedom.

Here, there was no evidence that either child was harmed by exposure to father's religion. Accordingly, we further hold the trial court's judgment enjoining both parents from freely discussing their religious beliefs with the children, and specifically prohibiting father from encouraging his children to participate in any Sikh activity, to be error. . . .

NOTES AND QUESTIONS

(1) General Rule. In general, the custodial parent has the right to determine the child's upbringing. In some instances the custodial parent can place conditions, which courts will enforce, on visitation between the noncustodial parent and the child. In what situations are courts likely to enforce such restrictions? In what situations will courts refuse? *Khalsa* reveals that one frequent source of contention involves religious differences between parents. Mr. Khalsa wants the children to participate in Sikh religious activities during periods of visitation with him; the mother objects. In this conflict, what are the various interests of the noncustodial father, the custodial mother, and the children? How should the court balance these interests? *Khalsa* reveals that, as a general rule, courts are reluctant to infringe on visitation rights of the noncustodial parent. Visitation will not be restricted because of a noncustodial parent's religious beliefs absent a showing that the child will be harmed thereby.

(2) Constitutional Issues. What constitutional problems are inherent in a court's resolution of visitation disputes between divorced parents? Is visitation a constitutionally protected right of the noncustodial parent? Marsha B. Freedman, Reconnecting the Family: A Need for Sensible Visitation Schedules for Children of Divorce, 22 Whittier L. Rev. 779 (2001).

First Amendment concerns make courts reluctant to become involved in religious disputes. The First Amendment provides that "Congress shall make no law respecting an establishment of religion, or prohibiting the free exercise thereof." U.S. Const. amend. I.[59] The two clauses of the amendment, the Establishment Clause and the Free Exercise Clause, present separate requirements. State action in the form of a judicial opinion that prefers one religion to another may violate both clauses. By favoring one parent over another for religious reasons, judicial action violates the disfavored parent's right to the free exercise of religion. Similarly, favoring a parent for religious reasons also may violate the prohibition against a state's establishing a religion by violating the goals of ensuring separation of church and state and of promoting governmental neutrality toward religion.

(3) Requisite Harm. Courts may not judge the merits of a parent's particular religion. However, courts may properly examine the effect that the particular religion has on the development of the child. See, e.g., Holder v. Holder, 872 N.E.2d 1239 (Ohio Ct. App. 2007). Although courts will condition or refuse visitation rights to a noncustodial parent (or even deny custody to a parent) whose religious practices will harm a child, courts differ on the certainty and amount of harm that must be shown. What harm might result from a child's exposure to different religious beliefs of his or her parents? Courts sometimes look to the amount and intensity of confusion,

---

[59] The amendment applies to the states through the Fourteenth Amendment. In addition, it applies to judicial as well as legislative actions.

frustration, guilt, or anxiety, especially in conjunction with physical manifestations. See, e.g. In re Marriage of Dorworth, 33 P.3d 1260 (Colo. Ct. App. 2001) (impairment of emotional development); Meyer v. Meyer, 789 A.2d 921 (Utah 2001) (tension and severe anxiety). Is a child's confusion about the doctrinal differences between the parents' different religions sufficient harm? See In re Marriage of Minix, 801 N.E.2d 1201 (Ill. App. Ct. 2003).

What evidence is necessary to meet the requisite showing of harm? Is the custodial parent's testimony sufficient? Court conjecture? Or is expert testimony required? *Khalsa* is indicative of cases that require a higher standard of harm: Harm must not be assumed or surmised but rather demonstrated in detail. See also Sagar v. Sagar, 781 N.E.2d 54 (Mass. App. Ct. 2003). What were the allegations of harm in *Khalsa,* and how did the mother attempt to substantiate them? Further, for the necessary showing of harm, must there be actual harm or is the probability of future harm sufficient?[60]

(4) Other Religious Issues.   Suppose that the religious differences between the parents pertain to other issues. For example, should courts reduce or change visitation to accommodate the custodial parent's desires (such as the wish to take the child to Sunday church services or instructional classes)? On the other hand, may a court require the *noncustodial* parent to take the child to church and Sunday school during visitation periods? Compare Johns v. Johns, 918 S.W.2d 728 (Ark. Ct. App. 1996) (father required to take children to church during visitation), with Johnson v. Nation, 615 N.E.2d 141 (Ind. App. Ct. 1993) (contra). May a court condition a mother's taking her child to her church only if she supported the child's attendance at the father's church? See In re Marriage of McSoud, 131 P.3d 1208 (Colo. Ct. App. 2006). See generally Kent Greenawalt, Child Custody, Religious Practices, and Conscience, 76 U. Colo. L. Rev. 965 (2005).

(5) ALI Principles.   The ALI Principles of the Law of Family Dissolution prohibits a court from considering the "religious practices" of either the parent or the child in custody decisionmaking except in the following situations: (a) if the religious practices present "severe and almost certain harm" to the child (and then a court may limit the religious practices only to the minimum degree necessary to protect the child), or (b) if necessary to protect the child's ability to practice a religion "that has been a significant part of the child's life." ALI Principles §2.12(1)(c). For a recent case taking into account the child's religious preference in the custody context, see In re Marriage of Boldt, 176 P.3d 388 (Or. 2008) (finding that 12-year-old's view should be considered regarding whether to be circumcised to convert to Judaism in the determination of the sufficiency of the mother's allegation of a change of circumstances necessary for custody modification).

(6) Conditions on Sexual Conduct and Sexual Orientation.   The issue of judicial enforcement of conditions on visitation also arises in several other contexts, frequently in the area of sexual behavior. For example, a noncustodial

---

[60] See Jennifer Ann Drobac, Note, For the Sake of the Children: Court Consideration of Religion in Child Custody Cases, 50 Stan. L. Rev. 1609, 1631 (1998) (concluding that different courts require actual harm, a substantial threat of harm, or merely some risk of harm although some courts require no showing of harm).

parent's sexual orientation may give rise to conditions on visitation. In many cases involving a gay or lesbian noncustodial parent, courts either award nonovernight visitation or condition visitation on the requirement that the child never be in the presence of the parent's partner. Compare A.O.V. v. J.R.V., 2007 WL 581871 (Va. Ct. App. 2007) (upholding restriction), with Downey v. Muffley, 767 N.E.2d 1014 (Ind. Ct. App. 2002) (invalidating restriction). See also Michael S. Wald, Adults' Sexual Orientation and State Determinations Regarding Placement of Children, 40 Fam L.Q. 381 (2006).

Suppose the noncustodial parent violates the judicially ordered condition. What result? See, e.g., Arms v. Arms, 803 N.E.2d 1201 (Ind. Ct. App. 2004) (affirming transfer of custody).

Do these conditions violate any constitutional rights of the noncustodial parent? Does Lawrence v. Texas, supra p. 571, have any impact on the imposition of such conditions on visitation?

(7) Supervised Visitation. What additional factors might lead to conditions on visitation? Courts have allowed visitation between the noncustodial parent and child in cases of physical or sexual abuse or substance abuse. Usually, however, visitation is strictly supervised.

Supervised visitation often leads to difficulties in framing the order. For example, should supervised visitation begin only after a parent seeks treatment? Completes treatment? Who should supervise visitation — a social worker, mental health professional, relative, friend? Should the child's feelings about the supervisor be taken into account? When should supervised visitation give way to unsupervised visitation?

An increasing number of state laws currently authorize the use of supervised visitation in the child custody context. Statutes vary considerably in terms of the extent of regulation of the practice. Some statutes merely recognize the court's authority to order supervised visitation, whereas others provide specific guidelines for visitation providers. Nat Stern & Karen Oehme, Increasing Safety for Battered Women and Their Children: Creating a Privilege for Supervised Visitation Intake Records, 41 U. Rich. L. Rev. 499 (2007). For a review of research on supervised visitation, see Rachel Birnbaum & Ramona Alaggia, Supervised Visitation: A Call for a Second Generation of Research, 44 Fam. Ct. Rev. 119 (2006).

(3) Third-Party Visitation Rights

What are the rights of third parties (such as grandparents, stepparents, and gay and lesbian partners) to visit with children in the face of parental objection?

Troxel v. Granville
530 U.S. 57 (2000)

Justice O'CONNOR announced the judgment of the Court and delivered an opinion, in which the Chief Justice, Justice GINSBURG, and Justice BREYER join. . . .

Tommie Granville and Brad Troxel shared a relationship that ended in June 1991. The two never married, but they had two daughters, Isabelle and Natalie.

Jenifer and Gary Troxel are Brad's parents, and thus the paternal grandparents of Isabelle and Natalie. After Tommie and Brad separated in 1991, Brad lived with his parents and regularly brought his daughters to his parents' home for weekend visitation. Brad committed suicide in May 1993. Although the Troxels at first continued to see Isabelle and Natalie on a regular basis after their son's death, Tommie Granville informed the Troxels in October 1993 that she wished to limit their visitation with her daughters to one short visit per month.

[Two months later, the Troxels filed this petition for visitation.] At trial, the Troxels requested two weekends of overnight visitation per month and two weeks of visitation each summer. Granville did not oppose visitation altogether, but instead asked the court to order one day of visitation per month with no overnight stay. [T]he Superior Court [ordered] visitation one weekend per month, one week during the summer, and four hours on both of the petitioning grandparents' birthdays. Granville appealed, during which time she married Kelly Wynn. [Before addressing Granville's appeal, the Washington Court of Appeals remanded the case to the Superior Court, which found that visitation was in the children's best interests. Nine months later, Granville's husband adopted the girls. The Court of Appeals reversed the visitation order based on their statutory interpretation that nonparents lack standing unless a custody action is pending.] Having resolved the case on the statutory ground, however, the Court of Appeals did not expressly pass on Granville's constitutional challenge to the visitation statute.

II

The demographic changes of the past century make it difficult to speak of an average American family. The composition of families varies greatly from household to household. While many children may have two married parents and grandparents who visit regularly, many other children are raised in single-parent households. In 1996, children living with only one parent accounted for 28 percent of all children under age 18 in the United States. U.S. Dept. of Commerce, Bureau of Census, Current Population Reports, 1997 Population Profile of the United States 27 (1998). Understandably, in these single-parent households, persons outside the nuclear family are called upon with increasing frequency to assist in the everyday tasks of child rearing. In many cases, grandparents play an important role. For example, in 1998, approximately 4 million children — or 5.6 percent of all children under age 18 — lived in the household of their grandparents. U.S. Dept. of Commerce, Bureau of Census, Current Population Reports, Marital Status and Living Arrangements: March 1998, p. I (1998).

The nationwide enactment of nonparental visitation statutes is assuredly due, in some part, to the States' recognition of these changing realities of the American family. Because grandparents and other relatives undertake duties of a parental nature in many households, States have sought to ensure the welfare of the children therein by protecting the relationships those children form with such third parties. The States' nonparental visitation statutes are further supported by a recognition, which varies from State to State, that children should have the opportunity to benefit from relationships with statutorily specified persons — for example, their grandparents. The extension of statutory rights in this area to persons other than a child's parents, however, comes with an obvious cost. For example, the State's recognition of an independent third-party interest in a child can place a substantial burden on the traditional parent-child relationship. . . .

The liberty interest at issue in this case — the interest of parents in the care, custody, and control of their children — is perhaps the oldest of the fundamental liberty interests recognized by this Court. More than 75 years ago, in Meyer v. Nebraska, 262 U.S. 390, 399, 401 (1923), we held that the "liberty" protected by the Due Process Clause includes the right of parents to "establish a home and bring up children" and "to control the education of their own." Two years later, in Pierce v. Society of Sisters, 268 U.S. 510, 534-535 (1925), we again held that the "liberty of parents and guardians" includes the right "to direct the upbringing and education of children under their control." We explained in *Pierce* that "[t]he child is not the mere creature of the State; those who nurture him and direct his destiny have the right, coupled with the high duty, to recognize and prepare him for additional obligations." Id., at 535. We returned to the subject in Prince v. Massachusetts, 321 U.S. 158 (1944), and again confirmed that there is a constitutional dimension to the right of parents to direct the upbringing of their children. "It is cardinal with us that the custody, care and nurture of the child reside first in the parents, whose primary function and freedom include preparation for obligations the state can neither supply nor hinder." Id., at 166.

In subsequent cases also, we have recognized the fundamental right of parents to make decisions concerning the care, custody, and control of their children [citing Stanley v. Illinois, Wisconsin v. Yoder, Quilloin v. Walcott, etc.]. In light of this extensive precedent, it cannot now be doubted that the Due Process Clause of the Fourteenth Amendment protects the fundamental right of parents to make decisions concerning the care, custody, and control of their children.

Section 26.10.160(3), as applied to Granville and her family in this case, unconstitutionally infringes on that fundamental parental right. The Washington nonparental visitation statute is breathtakingly broad. According to the statute's text, "*[a]ny person* may petition the court for visitation rights at any time," and the court may grant such visitation rights whenever "visitation may serve *the best interest of the child.*" §26.10.160(3) (emphases added). That language effectively permits any third party seeking visitation to subject any decision by a parent concerning visitation of the parent's children to state-court review. Once the visitation petition has been filed in court and the matter is placed before a judge, a parent's decision that visitation would not be in the child's best interest is accorded no deference. Section 26.10.160(3) contains no requirement that a court accord the parent's decision any presumption of validity or any weight whatsoever. Instead, the Washington statute places the best-interest determination solely in the hands of the judge. Should the judge disagree with the parent's estimation of the child's best interests, the judge's view necessarily prevails. Thus, in practical effect, in the State of Washington a court can disregard and overturn any decision by a fit custodial parent concerning visitation whenever a third party affected by the decision files a visitation petition, based solely on the judge's determination of the child's best interests. . . .

Turning to the facts of this case, the record reveals that the Superior Court's order was based on precisely the type of mere disagreement we have just described and nothing more. The Superior Court's order was not founded on any special factors that might justify the State's interference with Granville's fundamental right to make decisions concerning the rearing of her two daughters. To be sure, this case involves a visitation petition filed by grandparents soon after the death of their son — the father of Isabelle and Natalie — but the combination of several factors here compels our conclusion that §26.10.160(3), as applied, exceeded the bounds of the Due Process Clause.

First, the Troxels did not allege, and no court has found, that Granville was an unfit parent. That aspect of the case is important, for there is a presumption that fit parents act in the best interests of their children. [S]o long as a parent adequately cares for his or her children (i.e., is fit), there will normally be no reason for the State to inject itself into the private realm of the family to further question the ability of that parent to make the best decisions concerning the rearing of that parent's children.

The problem here is not that the Washington Superior Court intervened, but that when it did so, it gave no special weight at all to Granville's determination of her daughters' best interests. More importantly, it appears that the Superior Court [adopted a "commonsensical approach [that] it is normally in the best interest of the children to spend quality time with the grandparent," and placing] on Granville, the fit custodial parent, the burden of *disproving* that visitation would be in the best interest of her daughters. . . .

The decisional framework employed by the Superior Court directly contravened the traditional presumption that a fit parent will act in the best interest of his or her child. In that respect, the court's presumption failed to provide any protection for Granville's fundamental constitutional right to make decisions concerning the rearing of her own daughters. In an ideal world, parents might always seek to cultivate the bonds between grandparents and their grandchildren. Needless to say, however, our world is far from perfect, and in it the decision whether such an intergenerational relationship would be beneficial in any specific case is for the parent to make in the first instance. And, if a fit parent's decision of the kind at issue here becomes subject to judicial review, the court must accord at least some special weight to the parent's own determination.

Finally, we note that there is no allegation that Granville ever sought to cut off visitation entirely. Rather, the present dispute originated when Granville informed the Troxels that she would prefer to restrict their visitation with Isabelle and Natalie to one short visit per month and special holidays. . . . The Superior Court gave no weight to Granville's having assented to visitation even before the filing of any visitation petition or subsequent court intervention. . . . Significantly, many other states expressly provide by statute that courts may not award visitation unless a parent has denied (or unreasonably denied) visitation to the concerned third party.

Considered together with the Superior Court's reasons for awarding visitation to the Troxels, the combination of these factors demonstrates that the visitation order in this case was an unconstitutional infringement on Granville's fundamental right to make decisions concerning the care, custody, and control of her two daughters. The Washington Superior Court failed to accord the determination of Granville, a fit custodial parent, any material weight. In fact, the Superior Court made only two formal findings in support of its visitation order. First, the Troxels "are part of a large, central, loving family, all located in this area, and the [Troxels] can provide opportunities for the children in the areas of cousins and music." App. 70a. Second, "[t]he children would be benefitted from spending quality time with the [Troxels], provided that that time is balanced with time with the childrens' [sic] nuclear family." Ibid. These slender findings, in combination with the court's announced presumption in favor of grandparent visitation and its failure to accord significant weight to Granville's already having offered meaningful visitation to the Troxels, show that this case involves nothing more than a simple disagreement between the Washington Superior Court and Granville concerning her children's best interests. The Superior Court's announced reason for ordering one week of visitation in the summer demonstrates our conclusion well: "I look back on some personal experiences. . . . We always spen[t] as kids a week with one set of grandparents and another set of grandparents, [and] it happened to work out in our family that [it] turned out to be an enjoyable experience. Maybe that can, in this family, if that is how it works out." Verbatim Report 220-221. As we have explained, the Due Process Clause does not permit a State to infringe on the fundamental right of parents to make child rearing decisions simply because a state judge believes a "better" decision could be made. Neither the Washington nonparental visitation statute generally — which places no limits on either the persons who may petition for visitation or the circumstances in which such a petition may be granted — nor the Superior Court in this specific case required anything more. Accordingly, we hold that §26.10.160(3), as applied in this case, is unconstitutional. . . .

Because we rest our decision on the sweeping breadth of §26.10.160(3) and the application of that broad, unlimited power in this case, we do not consider the primary constitutional question passed on by the Washington Supreme Court — whether the Due Process Clause requires all nonparental visitation statutes to include a showing of harm or potential harm to the child as a condition precedent to granting visitation. We do not, and need not, define today the precise scope of the parental due process right in the visitation context. [T]he constitutionality of any standard for awarding visitation turns on the specific manner in which that standard is applied. . . . Because much state-court adjudication in this context occurs on a case-by-case basis, we would be hesitant to hold that specific nonparental visitation statutes violate the Due Process Clause as a *per se* matter. . . .

[In separate omitted concurring opinions, Justice Souter upheld the state court's determination of the statute's facial unconstitutionality, and Justice Thomas noted that strict scrutiny ought to apply. In separate omitted dissenting opinions, Justice Scalia declined to recognize unenumerated constitutional rights, and Justice Kennedy reasoned that the best interest doctrine is not always an unconstitutional standard in visitation cases. Justice Stevens's dissent is excerpted *supra*, pp. 81-82.]

NOTES AND QUESTIONS

(1) Background: Common Law. At common law, grandparents had no right to visitation with grandchildren in the face of parental objection. All states now

have third-party visitation statutes that permit grandparents (and sometimes other persons, as *Troxel* reveals) to petition for visitation in certain circumstances.

(2) Background: Biological-Parent Presumption.   A presumption favors biological parents in custody, as opposed to visitation, disputes involving parents versus nonparents. That is, courts apply a rebuttable presumption that custody should be awarded to a biological parent absent evidence of parental unfitness. In a landmark grandparents' rights case, a state supreme court refused to follow that presumption. In Painter v. Bannister, 140 N.W.2d 152 (Iowa 1966), a father left his young son with the maternal grandparents when the boy's sister and mother died in an automobile accident. When the father remarried and requested the return of his son, the grandparents refused. The father brought a habeas corpus action. Refusing to apply the parental presumption, the court held that the child's best interests would be served by remaining with the stable, church-going Midwestern grandparents rather than with the bohemian writer-father. How does a custody dispute between parents and nonparents, such as *Painter,* differ from a visitation dispute such as *Troxel?*

(3) Unconstitutional as Applied.   In *Troxel,* the plurality held that the Washington statute, as applied to Tommie Granville, violated the Due Process Clause. In what way was the application defective? Why did the Court determine that the Washington visitation statute unconstitutionally infringed on the mother's rights? How influential are Meyer v. Nebraska and Pierce v. Society of Sisters in the Court's analysis?

(4) Why is it significant that the Court held the statute unconstitutional as applied rather than facially unconstitutional? How should the Washington state legislature redraft the statute after *Troxel?*

(5) Standard of Review.   In *Troxel,* the Court avoided identifying the appropriate standard of review for evaluating infringements on parental rights. After *Troxel,* should courts apply the strict scrutiny test (out of deference to parental rights) or the rational basis test? See, e.g., Koshko v. Haining, 921 A.2d 171 (Md. 2007) (finding that grandparent visitation statute was subject to strict scrutiny because it imposed a direct and substantial interference with parents' decision regarding visitation). See also Stephen A. Newman, Five Critical Issues in New York's Grandparent Visitation Law after Troxel v. Granville, 48 N.Y.L. Sch. L. Rev. 489, 516 (2003-2004) (pointing out that several state supreme courts post-*Troxel* have adopted strict scrutiny).

(6) Degree of Deference to Fit Parent's Decision.   *Troxel* established that courts must give deference to a fit parent's decision to restrict or deny third-party visitation. However, the Court failed to define the requisite degree of deference. In response, a majority of courts have agreed that the parent's decision regarding visitation is entitled to a rebuttable presumption that the parent is acting in the child's best interests. Solangel Maldonado, When Father (or Mother) Doesn't Know Best: Quasi-Parents and Parental Deference after Troxel v. Granville, 88 Iowa L. Rev. 865, 884-888 (2003). What factors should rebut the presumption?

(7) Showing of Harm.   *Troxel* avoided deciding whether a finding of harm was required before a grandparent may be awarded visitation. Jurisdictions continue to disagree about whether such a finding is required. Compare Rente v. Rente, 915 A.2d 1099 (N.J. Super. Ct. App. Div. 2007) (reversing award of visitation to

grandparents due to their failure to show harm), with Dodd v. Burleson, 967 So. 2d 715 (Ala. Civ. App. 2007) (holding that due process does not require a showing of harm prior to an award of grandparent visitation). Currently, a majority of states hold that the best-interest standard applies to grandparent disputes rather than the more stringent harm standard. Geri L. Dreiling, Grandparents' Rights Survive, 4 ABAJ E-Report (No. 43) 5 (2005), at 5. See generally Lauren F. Cowan, Note, There's No Place Like Home: Why the Harm Standard in Grandparent Visitation Disputes Is in the Child's Best Interests, 75 Fordham L. Rev. 3137 (2007).

(8) Role of Law. What should be the role of the law in the resolution of such private disputes as those between parents and third parties? One commentator criticizes: "[m]any courts, especially trial courts, have little or no concern for the challenges inherent in court-ordered visitation when deciding the appropriateness of granting visitation or in fashioning the order"? Laurence C. Nolan, Beyond *Troxel*: The Pragmatic Challenges of Grandparent Visitation Continue, 50 Drake L. Rev. 267, 270 (2002). What are the stereotypes of grandparents that influence these visitation disputes? To counter these criticisms, should courts always appoint guardians ad litem for the child? See Newman, supra (so arguing).

(9) Stepparent Visitation. Third-party visitation rights also arise in cases involving stepparents, especially in cases of the divorce of a stepparent and the child's biological parent or the death of a child's biological custodial parent who had remarried. In each case, a stepparent who has been actively involved in childrearing wishes to continue the relationship with the child. See, e.g., Riepe v. Riepe, 91 P.3d 312 (Ariz. Ct. App. 2004) (holding that court has authority to award visitation to widowed stepmother pursuant to statutory criteria). In what ways are stepparent visitation disputes similar to, and different from, grandparent visitation disputes? Should stepparent visitation disputes be treated the same as, or different from, grand parent visitation disputes?

Application of the concept of "psychological parent" (as influenced by the views of Goldstein, Freud, and Solnit, supra p. 477) has sometimes led courts to recognize the rights of third parties such as stepparents. Recall, too, that under the ALI Principles, if a stepparent qualifies as a "parent by estoppel" or a "de facto parent," a court would have to recognize that stepparent's right to custody or visitation following the death of a custodial parent or the dissolution of the custodial parent's relationship with the stepparent. ALI Principles §2.03(1)(b) (parenthood by estoppel); §2.03(1)(c) (de facto parent).

After *Troxel,* are stepparent visitation statutes constitutional that allow courts to grant reasonable visitation to a stepparent if the court determines that it is in the child's best interests? See In re Marriage of Engelkens, 821 N.E.2d 799 (Ill. App. Ct. 2004). On stepparent disputes in the adoption context, see supra, pp. 491-492. On stepparents' support obligation, see supra, pp. 189-190.

(10) Second-Parent Visitation Rights. Traditionally, courts have not been receptive to recognition of co-parent's rights to custody and/or visitation after dissolution of a same-sex relationship. In such disputes, courts tend to recognize the biological mother as the sole legal parent and thereby to exclude the same-sex partner as a legal stranger. See, e.g., Nancy S. v. Michele G., 279 Cal. Rptr. 212 (Ct. App. 1991); Alison D. v. Virginia M., 572 N.E.2d 27 (N.Y. 1991).

Currently, many courts continue to deny visitation rights to former same-sex partners. See, e.g., B.F. v. T.D., 194 S.W.3d 310 (Ky. 2006) (affirming finding that partner did not have standing as de facto custodian); A.H. v. M.P., 857 N.E.2d 1061 (Mass. 2006) (same); Janice M. v. Margaret K., 948 A.2d 73 (Md. 2008) (holding that a grant of visitation rights to former same-sex partner required court to find either that mother was unfit or that sufficient exceptional circumstances existed to overcome mother's constitutional right to care, custody, and control of child); Behrens v. Rimland, 822 N.Y.S.2d 285 (App. Div. 2006) (denying visitation to former same-sex partner based on doctrines of equitable estoppel, de facto or psychological parent, and finding failure to establish extraordinary circumstances that would overcome established right of legal parent to choose with whom child could associate); Jones v. Barlow, 154 P.3d 808 (Utah 2007) (rejecting application of in loco parentis, de facto, or psychological parent doctrines to second parent who sought visitation rights).

In contrast, occasional recent cases reflect a greater willingness to recognize lesbian parents' rights. See, e.g., Soohoo v. Johnson, 731 N.W.2d 815 (Minn. 2007) (affirming order of visitation to former same-sex partner and holding that third-party visitation statute did not violate due process); Mason v. Dwinnell, 660 S.E.2d 58 (N.C. Ct. App. 2008) (upholding trial court conclusion that best interest of child permitted permanent joint legal and physical custody to parent and former same-sex partner).

What is the likely impact of Troxel v. Granville on visitation disputes involving gay and lesbian parents? See generally Laura S. Brown, "Relationships More Enduring," Implications of the *Troxel* Decision on Gay and Lesbian Families, 41 Fam. Ct. Rev. 60 (2003); Brooke N. Silverthorn, Notes and Comments, When Parental Rights and Children's Best Interests Collide: An Examination of Troxel v. Granville as It Relates to Gay and Lesbian Families, 19 Ga. St. U. L. Rev. 893 (2003).

(11) Child's Interests.   Do cases addressing second-parent custody and visitation disputes give adequate respect to the child's wishes and interests? See Melanie B. Jacobs, Micah Has One Mommy and One Legal Stranger: Adjudicating Maternity for Nonbiological Lesbian Coparents, 50 Buff. L. Rev. 341 (2002) (arguing that courts fail to take into account the child's perspective). On the context of adoption by second parents, see supra pp. 535-536.

(12) Problem.   Karen and Charles separate after a brief marriage, shortly before the birth of their daughter Emily. Karen moves in with Charles's parents for a week and then moves into a shelter for battered women. She files for dissolution, claiming that Charles was abusive. Karen is granted sole legal and physical custody. Charles is granted supervised visitation. One month later, the paternal grandparents petition for visitation, alleging that Karen has refused them access to Emily. The grandparents want Emily to spend ten days at their home every other month. Karen protests because Emily is still nursing and also because of her concern that Charles was abused as a child by the paternal grandfather. Over Karen's objections, but with Charles's approval, the trial court grants liberal visitation to the grandparents. Several week-long visits occur with the grandparents. Six months later Karen petitions to terminate the grandparents' visitation, alleging that the visits give Emily nightmares and distress her. The state statute provides

that a court may grant reasonable visitation to a grandparent if the court determines that visitation would be in the child's best interests or if there is a preexisting relationship between the grandparent and grandchild that has engendered a bond such that visitation would be in the child's best interests. Karen challenges the statute as unconstitutional on its face and as applied. What result? See In re Marriage of Harris, 96 P.3d 141 (Cal. 2004).

5. Process: What Process Should Be Used to Resolve Disputes?

This section explores the issue of which process should be utilized to settle child custody disputes. Three approaches are presented: (1) the traditional adversarial process; (2) the alternative dispute resolution processes of mediation and collaborative law; and (3) a random process of "coin-flipping." Advantages and disadvantages of each alternative are examined. Finally, this section explores the role of the child in custody decisionmaking: specifically, should the child's wishes be considered in the process?

a. Adversarial Process

Most divorced parents reach private agreements regarding responsibility for childrearing in the postdivorce period. Only a small minority of custody decisions are actually settled by the judicial process. This small percentage of cases, however, involves particularly acrimonious disputes with far-reaching consequences for the participants. Consider the following criticism of the adversarial process:

Donald T. Saposnek, Mediating Child Custody Disputes
7-16 (rev. ed. 1998) (citations omitted)

"The Adversarial Approach"

Traditionally, contested cases had been dealt with exclusively by an adversarial process. For the most part, the adversarial process has proved itself a just and effective approach for discovering the facts and critical issues in criminal and other matters, so that decisions could be made to attribute blame and responsibility or to resolve disputes. However, this same adversarial process, when applied to domestic conflicts, tends to do more harm than good. As Coogler (1978, p. 8) noted, "Whatever may be said in support of the adversarial process for resolving other kinds of controversies, in marital disputes this competitive struggle is frequently more damaging for the marriage partners and their children than anything else that preceded it."

Because divorces and custody decisions were, in the recent past, made on the basis of finding one person at fault, and/or unfit, the adversarial process seemed fully appropriate as the most efficient method for arriving at such decisions. Each contest had a winner and a loser, and the courts assumed that, once the decisions were made, the matter was settled. While the matters of property and the legal dissolution of the marriage were indeed settled, the matters of custody and visitation were very often far from settled. Frequently, in reaction to the humiliation of defeat, the losing spouse would try to get back at the winning spouse by gathering damaging evidence regarding the spouse's unfitness, the quality of care given the children, or the spouse's immorality, and by filing an order to show cause (OSC) petition to reverse the custody decision. Relitigation frequently continued for years beyond the initial decision. . . .

The recent trends toward no-fault divorces and custody decisions based on the best interests of the child rather than on the fitness of the parent have been attempts to reduce the acrimonious nature of such domestic conflicts. Yet the adversarial process by which these new standards are applied inherently breeds acrimony. Moreover, when children are involved in the process, they typically become repeat victims. This victimization can be obvious and publicly painful, as when a child must betray one parent by testifying in court on behalf of the other. Or, it can be more subtle and insidious, as when a parent or lawyer solicits an "evaluation" of, or "treatment" for, the youngster by a child psychologist or psychiatrist as a tactic to help achieve the goal of obtaining custody.

. . . Typically, in such cases, the parent who is about to launch a bid for custody of a child seeks a therapist to help the child deal with the emotional upset manifested in the aftermath of the divorce. However, what that parent often does not tell the therapist until later is that the parent was sent there by the attorney in hopes of documenting some harm that has occurred or will occur to the child as a result of being in the custody of the other parent. If there is no chance of finding harm, the attorney may hope that the therapist, by seeing the one parent and child together, can be enticed into writing a report and perhaps even testifying to the effect that a "strong bond of attachment clearly exists between this parent and the child." . . .

Regardless of whether the request to evaluate the child or child-parent relationship is presented in a straightforward or in an indirect manner, the experience of the child will be nearly the same. The child will be led to consider and/or express a preference for a custodial parent and will be coerced in various ways to participate in discussions that will likely result in the betrayal of one parent. Moreover, when evidence of harm to the child is sought or suspected, the child will feel the intensity of focused probing for pathology. This can cause considerable discomfort in the child. . . .

It is also noteworthy that children who participate in such evaluations occasionally feel betrayed when they find out that a judge made the custody decision based upon what they told the therapist. For in spite of what they may be told to the contrary, they often believe that their conversations will be confidential. . . .

While the adjustment problems that children have following a divorce are commonly attributed by each parent to the quality of caregiving by the other parent, it is much more often the case that they are due to the many stressful changes that children must endure in a parental separation and to the interparental conflict that either begins at separation or continues from the marriage to play out after separation. It has also been found that the adversarial approach exacerbates the effects of these factors. . . .

The adversarial process trains parents, through discussions and modeling, to fight even more effectively, using slander, accusation, defamation, and any other weapons available. Yet such contests are construed as a proper means of achieving the best interests of the child. By any standard of common sense, as well as the accumulated research data showing that children need co-parenting and a cessation of interparental conflict, the adversarial process must rank very low as a method of making satisfactory and lasting postdivorce parenting arrangements. . . .

b. Mediation

Mediation, as an alternative to the formal adversarial process, has a long and varied history. Its roots are found in ancient Chinese, Japanese, African, and even Biblical law.[61] Mediation is a process by which parties to a disagreement, with the aid of a neutral third party, isolate disputed issues to develop options, consider alternatives, and reach a consensual settlement.[62] Many statutes currently provide for mediation in custody disputes: some by mandatory mediation requiring mediation in all disputed custody cases; others by authorizing a court to order mediation in some circumstances;[63] and still others by authorizing mediation only at the request of the parties.

Mediation represents a shift from third-party, external decisionmaking in child custody disputes toward private ordering.[64] In the adversarial process, the law restricts private ordering. That is, the state asserts broad authority not only over the financial aspects of the dissolution, but also over the parties' relationships with their children. With the increasing acceptance of mediation, states confer broad latitude on the divorcing couple to decide for themselves, outside the courtroom, many aspects relevant to the dissolution of their relationship.

Mediation includes many different professionals. Lawyers and mental health professionals comprise a significant percentage of the profession. As a result, mediation is heavily influenced by the diverse orientations of these professions. Given that different professionals are involved, certain issues arise. This section explores several of these issues. First, what is the role of the mediator in a child custody dispute? How do the values and concerns of each profession help define the role of the mediator? Second, how much deference do these different professionals give to the principle of private ordering? That is, what circumstances cause mediators, who are generally neutral, to limit private ordering by questioning custody agreements which the parties accept? Do different professional

---

[61] Jay Folberg & Alison Taylor, Mediation: A Comprehensive Guide to Resolving Conflicts Without Litigation 1-3 (1984); Forest S. Mosten, Institutionalization of Mediation, 42 Fam. Ct. Rev. 292 (2004).

[62] Folberg & Taylor, supra note [61], at 7.

[63] Joan B. Kelly, Psychological and Legal Interventions for Parents and Children in Custody and Access Disputes: Current Research and Practice, 10 Va. J. Soc. Pol'y & L. 129, 138 (2002) (pointing out that 13 states have mandatory mediation and 24 states have statutes conferring discretion on judges to order mediation).

[64] See Robert H. Mnookin & Lewis Kornhauser, Bargaining in the Shadow of the Law: The Case of Divorce, 88 Yale L.J. 950 (1979).

orientations result in different proclivities for intervention? Finally, should the child have a role in the mediation process? If so, what should that role involve?

(1) Roles of the Mediator

Divorce mediation has many forms. "Each form reflects the setting in which the service is being offered, the framework from which the mediator shapes his or her process, and the prior profession of the mediator."[65] Despite these variables, it is possible to identify several models that provide the major frameworks for most mediators.

Commentators have suggested various theoretical models and modes of mediation. For example, Becker-Haven suggests four conceptual frameworks for child custody mediation and the corresponding roles of the mediator derived from each framework.[66] These include:

(a)   the therapeutic framework, with the mediator as healer;
(b)   the educational framework, with the mediator as teacher;
(c)   the rational/analytic framework, with the mediator as strategist;
(d)   the normative/evaluative framework, with the mediator as judge.

In the therapeutic framework, the mediator views an essential part of divorce mediation as addressing the emotional upheaval associated with the divorce (i.e., encouraging the expression of feelings, interpreting behaviors, etc.) to facilitate the resolution of parenting problems. In contrast, the educational mode of mediation places the mediator in the role of a teacher who provides information and builds problem-solving skills to enable the parents to resolve current and future disputes for themselves.

The rational/analytic framework puts the mediator in the role of rational decision manager by helping the parents evaluate options to maximize their values and preferences (i.e., delineating the parameters of decisions, eliciting preferences, generating alternatives, weighing trade-offs, and pointing out flaws in reasoning). The normative/evaluative mode places the mediator in the role of judge by promoting normative prescriptions, sometimes quite forcefully, for decision and inaction into the mediation process. Mediators in this role emphasize giving opinions, directing the parents' attention to the child's interests, acting as advocate for the child, and revealing a potential recommendation if the case were to go to trial.

Mediators may adopt aspects of one or more of the above role(s), depending on their philosophy, value orientation, and the characteristics of the couple and conflict being mediated.[67] In addition, professional background appears to play a role in determining the mode of mediation. Lawyers tend to subscribe to the rational/analytic mode; mental health professionals to the therapeutic mode; counseling

---

[65] Susan M. Brown, Models of Mediation, in Divorce and Family Mediation 49 (James C. Hansen ed., 1985).

[66] See Jane Becker-Haven, Modes of Mediating Child Custody Disputes, Ph.D. Dissertation, Stanford University (1988).

[67] Brown, supra note [65].

psychologists and educators to the educational mode; and juvenile probation workers to the normative/evaluative mode.[68]

(2) Degrees of Intervention

Mediators adopt different degrees of intervention. Some mediators are nondirective, relying instead on the participants' sense of fairness. Other mediators may be quite directive, challenging decisions or agreements reached by the divorcing parties and even refusing to write an agreement that they believe is unfair. An empirical study of mediation concluded that most mediators mix these approaches to balance the values of autonomy and protection. The researchers found no strong association between background characteristics and interventionist approaches, hypothesizing that those practitioners who enter divorce mediation are less committed to either traditional adversarial practice or traditional therapy.[69]

(3) Children's Role in Mediation

Should children have a role in mediation? What might be the advantages to the child for inclusion? The disadvantages? If children should have a role, what should that role be?

First, what might be the benefits to children of their inclusion? One commentator argues that

> [T]here are benefits to be gained by allowing them to observe and participate in negotiation sessions. For many children, this may be the first time in months or years that they actually observe these dynamics between their parents. When the children understand that one of the primary motivations for the parents' mediating is their love and concern for them, it can be very supportive for the children.
>
> Another advantage of having children present during mediation is the potential for positive reinforcement for the existing parenting and caring relationships. . . . This provide[s] the mediator with an opportunity to observe and indicate to the parents how comfortable this child was with both and to commend them for their nurturance of the child's attachment to both parents.
>
> Finally, children's concerns tend to be somewhat more concrete and immediate than those of their parents. They want to know which toys will be in which house, which furniture will be moved, and the exact day and hour that the moves will be made. Their presence in mediation allows them to express these questions and concerns and receive direct responses from parents.[70]

On the other hand, there may be severe disadvantages to children from participating in mediation.

> Including children in sessions also has potentially negative consequences. Parents sometimes express reluctance to expose children to their disagreements

---

[68] Becker-Haven, supra note [66].

[69] Joseph P. Folger & Sydney E. Bernard, Divorce Mediation: When Mediators Challenge the Divorcing Parties, 10 Mediation Q. 5, 11 (1985).

[70] Karen K. Irvin, Including Children in Mediation: Considerations for the Mediator, in Divorce and Family Mediation at 94, 98.

and hostility. [T]hese feelings can make for highly volatile mediation sessions. It is undesirable to expose children to continued accusations, diatribes, and discord if the parents are not progressing toward settlement of the custody issues.

Children tend to display their feelings of sadness, anger, fear and confusion openly. This can become a problem in mediation sessions if the mediator is unwilling or unable to respond to these feelings or if parents blame each other and/or the mediator for the children's emotions. . . .[71]

Just as mediators differ about intervention in the face of an unfair agreement, they also disagree about the role of children in the mediation process. Some mediators believe children should be actively included in the decisionmaking process. On the other hand, in their respect for parental autonomy, other mediators believe that parents alone should make decisions regarding custody, especially when children are young.

For a debate on children's appropriate role in mediation, compare Joan B. Kelly, Psychological and Legal Interventions for Parents and Children in Custody and Access Disputes: Current Research and Practice, 10 Va. J. Soc. Pol'y & L. 129 (2002) (urging greater participation of children) with Robert E. Emery, Easing the Pain of Divorce for Children: Children's Voices, Causes of Conflict, and Mediation, Comments on Kelly's "Resolving Child Custody Disputes," 10 Va. J. Soc. Pol'y & L. 164 (2002) (voicing the fear that inclusion of children inappropriately gives them responsibility for adult decisions).

Efforts by the American Bar Association establishing standards of practice for family mediators also address the role of children in mediation. Standard VIII of the Model Standards of Practice for Family and Divorce Mediation (adopted by the House of Delegates in 2001) provides that children should not participate without the consent of both parents and the children's court-appointed representative except in extraordinary circumstances (VIII.D). In addition, before including children, the mediator should consult with parents and a children's court-appointed representative not only about whether children should participate but the form of their participation (VIII.E) and should discuss the various options (e.g., personal participation, an interview with a mental health professional, the mediator reporting to the parents, a videotape statement) (VIII.F). On the Standards, see generally Andrew Schepard, An Introduction to the Model Standards of Practice for Family and Divorce Mediation, 35 Fam. L.Q. 1 (2001).

Assuming that children's inclusion might be beneficial, what form do you think their participation should take? Should certain circumstances dictate special consideration of children's roles — e.g., if aparent alleges abuse or neglect of the other parent? If so, should children be excluded or included in such cases? Many states provide special protections for the parties in mediation proceedings in cases of domestic violence. See, e.g., Cal. Fam. Code §§3181 (separate sessions), 6303(c) (victim may have support person attend mediation) (West 2003). See also Andrew I. Schepard, Children, Courts, and Custody: Interdisciplinary Models for Divorcing Families 102-104 (2004) (contrasting the different views on

---

[71] Id. at 98.

mandatory mediation in the domestic violence context of the ALI Principles, which reject mandatory mediation, and the ABA Model Standards of Practice for Family and Divorce Mediation, which rejects mediation in inappropriate cases); Nancy Ver Steegh, Yes, No, and Maybe: Informed Decision Making About Divorce Mediation in the Presence of Domestic Violence, 9 Wm. & Mary J. Women & Law 145 (2003).

c. Collaborative Law

Another form of alternative dispute resolution is collaborative law. The collaborative law movement was launched in 1990 by Minneapolis family law attorney Stuart Webb.[72] In such procedures, the parties and their attorneys sign a binding agreement in which they agree to use cooperative techniques without resort to judicial intervention except for court approval of the parties' agreement. Attorneys are prohibited from participating in contested court proceedings for their clients. That is, if the parties are unable to reach agreement through collaborative law procedures, their attorneys must withdraw from representation.

The attorney's role in collaborative law procedures differs from that of the attorney as mediator. The traditional mediation model involves two parties and the neutral mediator; legal services (if any) are provided outside the mediation process (e.g., review of documents). In contrast, collaborative lawyers are advocates for their clients (rather than neutral facilitators). In addition, collaborative lawyers are more directive than traditional mediators in helping their clients realize their goals.[73] Texas became the first state in 2001 to provide, by statute, for resolution of family matters by collaborative law procedures. See Tex. Fam. Code §153.0072 (Vernon 2002 & Supp. 2008).

In 2007, the American Bar Association's ethics committee added its support to the practice of collaborative law. The ABA found that collaborative law did not violate the Model Rules of Professional Conduct, provided that the attorney first obtains the client's informed consent. ABA Standing Comm. on Ethics and Professional Responsibility, Formal Op. 07-447, Aug. 9, 2007.

d. Coin-Flipping

Robert H. Mnookin, Child-Custody Adjudication: Judicial Functions in the Face of Indeterminacy
39 Law & Contemp. Probs. 226, 289-291 (1975)

Random Selection

Assuming that an "intimate" acceptable to both parents cannot be found to make an individualized decision, would not a random process of decision be fairer and

---

[72] Pauline H. Tesler, Collaborative Family Law, 4 Pepp. Disp. Resol. L.J. 317 (2004).

[73] Id. at 329-330. See also Andrew I. Schepard, Children, Courts, and Custody: Interdisciplinary Models for Divorcing Families (2004) (especially Chapter 10, discussing the differences between mediation and collaborative law).

more efficient than adjudication under a best-interests principle? Individualized adjudication means that the result will often turn on a largely intuitive evaluation based on unspoken values and unproven predictions. We would more frankly acknowledge both our ignorance and the presumed equality of the natural parents were we to flip a coin. Whether one had a separate flip for each child or one flip for all the children, the process would certainly be cheaper and quicker. It would avoid the pain associated with an adversary proceeding that requires an open exploration of the intimate aspects of family life and an ultimate judgment that one parent is preferable to the other. And it might have beneficial effects on private negotiations.[254]

Resolving a custody dispute by state-administered coin-flip would probably be viewed as unacceptable by most in our society. Perhaps this reaction reflects an abiding faith, despite the absence of an empirical basis for it, that letting a judge choose produces better results for the child. Alternatively, flipping a coin might be unacceptable for some because it represents an abdication of the search for wisdom. While judgments about what is best for the child may be currently beyond our capacity in many cases, this need not be true in fifty years. Movement toward better judgments implies, however, that judges and decision-makers as a group learn from the process of decision. In the absence of systematic feedback, this is not likely. Indeed, adopting a coin-flip now means neither that at a time when more were known and a consensus existed an adjudicatory system might not be adopted, nor that efforts to discover an adjudicatory standard would cease.

Deciding a child's future by flipping a coin might be viewed as callous. Is it more callous, however, than drafting for the military by lottery? In the same way that a lottery is a social affirmation of equality among those upon whom the government might impose the risks of war, a coin-flip would be a government affirmation of the equality of the parents. In a custody case, however, a coin-flip also symbolically abdicates government responsibility for the child and symbolically denies the importance of human differences and distinctiveness. Moreover, flipping a coin would deprive the parents of a process and a forum where their anger and aspirations might be expressed. In all, these symbolic and participatory values of adjudication would be lost by a random process.

While forceful arguments can be made in favor of the abandonment of adjudication and the adoption of an openly random process, the repulsion many

---

[254] The effect on negotiation would depend on each parent's risk preferences and on how much each wanted the child. Because each parent would face a 50 per cent chance of losing, this might encourage private compromise if both wanted the child and were very risk-averse. But because a coin-flip would be less painful than an adversary proceeding, the threat of holding out for such a resolution might be more frequently and credibly used than the threat of litigation is today by a party who did not much want the child but who was bargaining for advantage with regard to other elements of the marriage dissolution. To avoid these bargaining problems, the state might insist that the coin-flip occur at the time of the marriage. Through state-supervised random process, one of the parents could then be designated as the parent who would have custody (absent a showing of neglect) if the parents should later separate and be unable themselves to decide who should have custody. . . . It is interesting to speculate whether such a rule would affect the loser's emotional commitment to the child or willingness to stay married to avoid losing custody of the child.

would probably feel towards this suggestion may reflect an intuitive appreciation of the importance of the educational, participatory, and symbolic values of adjudication as a mode of dispute settlement. Adjudication under the indeterminate best-interests principle may yield something close to a random pattern of outcomes, while at the same time serving these values, affirming parental equality, and expressing a social concern for the child. Insofar as judges as a group may have value preferences that systematically bias the process and make the pattern less than random, these value preferences may reflect widespread values that have not been acknowledged openly in the form of legal rules. . . .

e. What Role for the Child in Custody Decisionmaking?

(1) Consideration of the Child's Preference

Most states have statutes that call for consideration of the child's wishes. In recent years, an increasing number of states have adopted legislation requiring consideration of children's preferences.[74] States assign different weight to such preferences: (1) some mandate consideration of children's wishes and grant controlling weight to these preferences (sometimes dependent on the age of the child); (2) some mandate consideration of children's preferences based on the judge's discretion; and (3) still others give courts complete discretion to consider a child's preference.[75]

Generally, trial courts treat the wishes of 14- to 18-year-olds as deserving of greater weight or even as dispositive. See, e.g., Reinke v. Reinke, 670 N.W.2d 841 (N.D. 2003); Wheeler v. Mazur, 793 A.2d 929 (Pa. Super. Ct. 2001) (both reversing trial court decisions that failed to give sufficient weight to the preferences of 13- or 14-year olds). On the other hand, trial judges sometimes examine the underlying reasons for a child's preference and refuse to recognize the preference in certain circumstances (e.g., coercion by a parent, sympathy for a parent, or a desire for a more permissive environment).[76] See also Kirkendall v. Kirkendall, 844 A.2d 1261 (Pa. Super. Ct. 2004) (affirming award of paternal custody, and rejecting five-year old's preference for maternal custody as immature). The ALI Principles §2.08 specifies that if the court adopts the approximation presumption (for those parents unable to formulate a parenting plan), one of the factors that shall rebut that presumption is the "firm and reasonable preference" of children of statutorily designated ages (and proposing 11 to 14 years as the range of ages for a uniform rule).

Should courts assign less weight to children's preferences in specific contexts? For example, in cases of domestic violence, children may be pressured to choose

---

[74] Randi L. Dulaney, Note, Children Should Be Seen and Heard in Florida Custody Determinations, 25 Nova L. Rev. 815, 819 (2001) (pointing out that since 1977, the number of states mandating consideration of children's preferences has more than doubled from 16 to 34).

[75] Id. at 823-824. Many states' statutes reflect the influence of UMDA §402, 9A U.L.A. 282, providing that a court shall consider the child's wishes, but the appropriate weight to be accorded to preference is left to the trial judge's discretion.

[76] Barbara A. Atwood, The Child's Voice in Custody Litigation: An Empirical Survey and Suggestions for Reform, 45 Ariz. L. Rev. 629, 640 (2003).

the perpetrator as the custodial parent. Or in custody disputes involving gay and lesbian parents, children may be unduly influenced by their initial negative response to the parent's disclosure of his or her sexual orientation. See Kirsten Lea Doolittle, Note, Don't Ask, You May Not Want to Know: Custody Preferences of Children of Gay and Lesbian Parents, 73 S. Cal. L. Rev. 677, 679 (2000).

(2) Procedures for Ascertaining a Child's Preference

Once it is agreed that the child's preference should be taken into account, the question remains of the proper procedure for learning that preference. Consider the advantages and disadvantages of the following alternatives:

a. having the child testify,
b. having other persons testify regarding the child's preference,
c. having the child's preference recorded in a videotape that is introduced at trial,
d. having the trial judge elicit the child's preference in a private interview in chambers (i) with opposing counsel present or (ii) without counsel present.

An empirical study found that most judges prefer to ascertain children's wishes through court-ordered custody evaluations or party testimony rather than through in-court testimony or an in-camera interview.[77] What do you think explains judges' preferences?

Although in-camera testimony may protect the child from the pain of openly choosing sides, it may present constitutional concerns. Why? See Haines v. Haines, 2007 WL 27112 (Tenn. Ct. App. 2007) (holding that an in-camera interview of children without the presence of parents' attorneys violates due process). Does the Supreme Court's decision in Troxel v. Granville strengthen or weaken parents' claim that procedural due process entitles them to access their children's in-camera statements? See Cynthia Starnes, Swords in the Hands of Babes: Rethinking Custody Interviews after *Troxel,* 2003 Wis. L. Rev. 115. Does a child have a due process right to have a voice in custody decisionmaking? In response to constitutional concerns, many states now require that in-camera interviews be recorded, the record be made available to the parties, and attorneys be present. Although the ALI Principles recommend that judges have discretion to interview children and that parents' counsel should have the right to propose questions that may be asked of the child, the Principles are silent regarding the presence of counsel at the interview and the recording of the interview. See, e.g., ALI Principles §2.14. See generally Patrick Parkinson & Judy Cashmore, Judicial Conversations with Children in Parenting Disputes: The Views of Australian Judge, 21 Int. J.L. & Pol'y & Fam. 160 (2007).

---

[77] Id., at 642. See also Annette Ruth Appell, Representing Children Representing What?: Critical Reflections on Lawyering for Children, 39 Colum. Hum. Rts. L. Rev. 573 (2008).

(3) Counsel for the Child?

The debate about mandatory representation for children in custody and visitation disputes began in the 1960s and 1970s, prompted by the rising rate of divorce (especially concerns about the effects of divorce on children) and the Supreme Court's decision in In re Gault, 387 U.S. 1 (1967) (granting a right to counsel for the child in delinquency proceedings) (supra Chapter 1). Commentators have manifested long-standing support for the appointment of legal representation for the child in custody proceedings.[78] However, virtually all states provide for discretionary appointment.[79]

Should representation for the child in contested custody disputes be mandatory? Or will the court's independent investigative powers and duties ensure protection of the child's interests? One critic of mandatory representation urges judges to be more cautious in appointing counsel for children. Professor Martin Guggenheim argues that the appointment of counsel may actually undermine the nature of the proceedings. Guggenheim believes that children's representatives should be mere fact-finders, ensuring that the process is fair and that judges have sufficient information to make informed decisions about children's best interests. He bases his view on concerns about children's lack of capacity, the undue weight a judge may attach to children's legal advocates, and the invasion of family privacy that may stem from the adversarial nature of the proceedings.[80] Which position do you find persuasive?

In contrast to the widespread discretionary policy on representation in custody proceedings, many jurisdictions now provide for mandatory appointment of counsel in those contested custody cases that involve allegations of abuse or neglect. Why might representation in these proceedings be advisable? Under the Child Abuse Prevention and Treatment Act (CAPTA), 42 U.S.C. §5106a(b)(6) (2000), states are required, to qualify for federal funding, to provide guardians ad litem to all children involved in child protective proceedings. Despite the CAPTA requirement, however, states are not required to appoint attorneys as guardians ad litem. (Guardians ad litem may come from many professions, such as law, social work, psychology, etc.) See Chapter 3, supra pp. 312-313. Should the child's representative be an attorney? Is there a greater need, lesser need, or the same need for legal representation for children in abuse/neglect proceedings compared to contested custody proceedings?

---

[78] See, e.g., Linda Elrod, Counsel for the Child in Custody Disputes: The Time Is Now, 26 Fam. L.Q. 53 (1992); Monroe L. Inker & Charlotte Anne Perretta, A Child's Right to Counsel in Custody Cases, 5 Fam. L.Q. 108 (1971).

[79] Raven C. Lidman & Betsy R. Hollingsworth, The Guardian Ad Litem in Child Custody Cases: The Contours of Our Judicial System Stretched Beyond Recognition, 6 Geo. Mason L. Rev. 255, 262 (1998). Cf. Wis. Stat. Ann. §767.407(1) (West Supp. 2007) (mandatory representation in child custody disputes).

[80] See Martin Guggenheim, The Right to Be Represented but Not Heard: Reflections on Legal Representation for Children, 59 N.Y.U. L. Rev. 76 (1984); Martin Guggenheim, A Paradigm for Determining the Role of Counsel for Children, 64 Fordham L. Rev. 1399 (1996); Martin Guggenheim, Reconsidering the Need for Counsel for Children in Custody, Visitation and Child Protection Proceedings, 29 Loy. U. Chi. L.J. 299 (1998).

If the appointment of a separate representative for the child is preferable in custody proceedings, what role should the representative play? Courts and legislatures often fail to give guidance as to the appropriate role and/or responsibilities of children's representatives. Should the child's representative be an advocate for the child's wishes or advocate the best interests of the child (even if that might differ from the child's wishes)?

Considerable attention has focused recently on the issue of legal representation for children. The ABA promulgated two sets of standards: for abuse, neglect and termination of parental rights cases and also for custody and visitation cases.[81] In response to the adoption by the ABA of these two different sets of standards, the National Conference of Commissioners on Uniform State Laws (NCCUSL) undertook to address the issue of representation of children. The outcome was the Uniform Representation of Children in Abuse, Neglect and Custody Proceedings Act, adopted in 2006.

The purpose of the Act is to improve the representation of children by defining the roles and responsibilities of their representatives. It also provides guidelines to courts in appointment of representatives. The Act addresses the ethical dimensions of the lawyer-client relationship, discretionary versus mandatory appointment, qualifications and duties of the child's representative, the duration of the appointment, access to the child and information relating to the child, and the child's right of action for damages against the representative. Commentators criticize the Act for the extent of judicial discretion that exists in the appointment of a best-interests lawyer (who does not have to follow the child's wishes). See, e.g., Jane Spivak, Simon Takes Three Steps Backwards: The National Conference of Commissioners on Uniform State Laws Recommendations on Child Representation, 6 Nev. L.J. 1385 (2006). For background on the Act, see Barbara Ann Atwood, The Uniform Representation of Children in Abuse, Neglect, and Custody Proceedings Act: Bridging the Divide Between Pragmatism and Idealism, 42 Fam. L.Q. 1 (2008).

6. Postdecree Problems

a. Modification

(1) Traditional Rules and Variations.   For modification of an initial custody decree, a court must determine that a substantial change of circumstances has occurred that warrants an alteration in custody to promote the best interests of the child. Some states follow a stricter rule that further limits modification.[82]

---

[81] See ABA Standards of Practice for Lawyers Who Represent Children in Abuse and Neglect Cases, 29 Fam. L.Q. 375 (1995) ABA Section of Family Law Standards of Practice for Lawyers Representing Children in Custody Cases, 37 Fam. L.Q. 131 (2003).

[82] Some states follow the Uniform Marriage and Divorce Act §409, 9A U.L.A. (pt. II) 439 (1998 & Supp. 2008) (requiring serious endangerment or a two-year period). See, e.g., Ill. Comp. Stat. Ann. (1999 & Supp. 2008), ch. 750, ¶5/610 (2008).

Other states adopt a more liberal test that permits modifications based on the "best interests of the child." The rationale behind the traditional rule is that the child's need for stability militates against relitigation of custody issues.

The usual meaning of the term "changed circumstances" dictates that courts consider only facts that have occurred since entry of the initial decree, as do the general rules of res judicata. However, some states, in the view that the child's welfare outweighs the policy of finality of judgments, hold that custody may be modified for facts existing at the time of that decree if those facts were not presented to or known by the court.

(2) Modification of Agreements. As discussed previously, the majority of custody cases are disposed of by agreement rather than by judicial order. Some courts hold that custody *agreements* may be modified more easily than judicial awards of custody. See, e.g., Elmer v. Elmer, 776 P.2d 599 (Utah 1999). What are the policy reasons behind this relaxation of the traditional modification standard?

(3) Relocation. Special circumstances, such as a parent's relocation, frequently give rise to requests for modification of custody or visitation. A custodial parent might desire to move following the divorce because of better employment or educational opportunities. Some states, by statute or case, regard a move as a sufficient change of circumstances, whereas other states do not. Merle H. Weiner, Inertia and Inequality: Reconceptualizing Disputes over Parental Relocation, 40 U.C. Davis L. Rev. 1747, 1755 (2007).

When faced with an impending move by the custodial spouse, a noncustodial parent may request a custody modification or even a transfer of custody. Statutes vary considerably in their treatment of relocation standards. Some statutes provide specific requirements, whereas others merely authorize the use of judicial discretion. Jurisdictions also vary in terms of their allocation of presumptions and burdens of proof. Some states impose a presumption in favor of the custodial parent, others impose a presumption in favor of the noncustodial parent, and some adopt the best interests standard. Further, some states place the burden of proof on the custodial parent to prove the move is in the child's best interests, whereas in other states, the noncustodial parent has the burden of proving that the move will be detrimental to the child's welfare. Amie J. Tracia, Note, Navigating the Waters of Massachusetts Child Relocation Law: Assessing the Application of the Real Advantage Standard, 13 Suffolk J. Trial & App. Advoc. 139, 143-144 (2008).

Do restrictions on relocation raise constitutional concerns? Compare In re Marriage of Ciesluk, 113 P.3d 135 (Colo. 2005) (holding that the denial of mother's request to relocate unconstitutionally infringed her right to travel), with Meadows v. Meadows, 2008 WL 3582691 (Ala. Civ. App. 2008) (contra); Fredman v. Fredman, 960 So. 2d 52 (Fla. Dist. Ct. App. 2007) (holding that relocation did not violate mother's rights to privacy, travel, or equal protection).

Should the same rules govern interstate and intercountry moves? Several states have enacted statutes addressing international relocations in the context of child abduction. These statutes require courts to consider certain factors in the resolution of these disputes, such as whether the other country is a signatory to the Hague Convention on the Civil Aspects of International Childhood Abduction that would require the return of the child. Lawrence Katz, When the ? Involves an International Move: The Answer May Lie in Retaining U.S. Jurisdiction, 28 Fam. Advoc. 40, 41 (2006).

Relocation restrictions may present significant risks for victims of domestic violence who desire to flee to another state with a child to evade an abusive spouse. See generally Maureen McKnight & Rob Valente, Domestic Violence the Tipping Point: Helping Courts Discern Obstacles to Access from a Desperate Need for Safety, 28 Fam. Advoc. 16 (2006).

In 2006, the National Conference of Commissioners on Uniform State Laws (recently renamed the Uniform Laws Commission) adopted the Uniform Child Abduction Prevention Act (UCAPA). UCAPA, which addresses abduction in both domestic and international custody disputes, authorizes courts to impose "abduction prevention measures" either sua sponte or upon the motion of a parent or child welfare agency. Requests for the imposition of such measures must specify the risk factors for abduction (such as a party's prior arrest or conviction for a crime of domestic violence or child abuse). See generally Patricia M. Hoff, "UU" UCAPA: Understanding and Using UCAPA to Prevent Child Abduction, 41 Fam. L.Q. 1 (2007).

(4) ALI Principles: Relocation.   The ALI Principles permit a parent with primary custody to relocate if he or she acts in good faith and for a "valid purpose." ALI Principles §2.17. According to the Principles, the following reasons constitute valid purposes: proximity to family, employment or educational opportunity, and a desire to be with a spouse or domestic partner or to improve significantly the family's quality of life.

(5) Modification of Joint Custody.   Modification of joint custody decrees poses special problems. In many states, the policy favoring joint custody has eased modifications to joint custody by relaxing the traditional rule to require only that the change to joint custody be in the best interests of the child.[83] Requests for modification from joint to *sole* custody arise for a number of reasons, including a breakdown in cooperation, violation of religious or education provisions of the original joint custody order, relocation, and remarriage. Some courts view parental tension and lack of cooperation as sufficient changes of circumstances to necessitate modification to sole custody.[84] Because joint custody is intended to assure continuing contact with parents, should courts be less willing to permit modification from joint to sole custody on these grounds than modification transferring sole custody from one parent to the other?

(6) Child's Preference.   What role should the child's preference play in modification of custody? The use of the child's preference in modification proceedings raises many of the same problems as in initial custody determinations. See supra, pp. 625-626.

(7) ALI Principles: Modification.   The ALI recommends modification of a parenting plan upon a showing of a substantial change in circumstances (of the child or one or both parents), based on facts that were unknown or that arose since

---

[83] See, e.g., Alaska Stat. §25.20.110 (2006 & Supp. 2007); Mont. Code Ann. §40-4-219 (2007).
[84] See, e.g., White v. Moore, 58 S.W.3d 73 (Mo. Ct. App. 2001); Stanton v. Stanton, 484 S.E.2d 875 (S.C. Ct. App. 1997).

the entry of the prior order and were unanticipated, that makes modification "necessary to the child's welfare." ALI Principles §2.15(1) & (2). Modification based on a more liberal standard is available for consensual changes, minor modifications to the parenting plan, or the attainment of a statutorily designated age for a child who expresses a preference for a custodial change. §2.15, cmt. a. None of the following circumstances justify modification absent a showing of harm: a parent's loss of income or employment, remarriage or cohabitation, or use of day care. ALI Principles §2.15(3).

b. Jurisdiction Over and Enforcement of Custody Decrees

Modification of another state's custody decree raises questions of jurisdiction and sometimes enforcement as well. Modification is permitted subject to the Uniform Child Custody Jurisdiction Act (UCCJA), 9 U.L.A. (pt. IA) 261 (1999 & Supp. 2008), Uniform Child Custody Jurisdiction and Enforcement Act (UCCJEA), 9 U.L.A. (pt. IA) 649 (1999 & Supp. 2008), and the Parental Kidnapping Prevention Act (PKPA), 28 U.S.C. 1738A (2000) (discussed below).

PROBLEM

Heidi and Michael Leyda were divorced in Iowa. They were awarded joint legal custody of their daughter Kim, with physical care entrusted to Heidi. Two years later, the Iowa court modified the decree, as a result of what it believed to be a substantial change of circumstances. Sole custody and care of Kim was awarded to Michael. During these proceedings, Kim lived with Heidi in Florida.

Heidi then filed an action in a Florida trial court requesting that the Iowa judgment granting custody to Michael be declared void or, in the alternative, that the Florida court modify the Iowa judgment to grant custody of Kim to Heidi. An ex parte temporary order was issued by the Florida court to restrain Michael from removing Kim from Florida.

Michael appeared at a hearing before the Florida trial court. He submitted to in personal jurisdiction but challenged the subject matter jurisdiction of the court. Following the hearing, another temporary order was issued that stipulated Michael's challenge and further recited that Florida was the home state jurisdiction under the UCCJA. This order provided that Heidi would have primary physical custody with reasonable visitation rights awarded to Michael. Kim could visit Michael outside of Florida for six weeks during the summer. Furthermore, the order stipulated that the parties both acknowledge that Michael's failure to return Kim to Heidi's custody would be a third-degree felony.

For one month after the temporary order, Michael returned to Iowa with Kim. Then, Heidi filed a petition for a writ of habeas corpus. Does the Iowa court have continuing jurisdiction to resolve this dispute? Or did the Florida trial court act properly in granting the temporary custody order? See In re Marriage of Leyda, 398 N.W.2d 815 (Iowa 1987). The answer lies in an understanding of the UCCJA, UCCJEA, and PKPA.

NOTES AND QUESTIONS ON JURISDICTION AND ENFORCEMENT

(1) UCCJA.   The UCCJA was enacted to avoid jurisdiction competition and confusion and to deter removals of children in order to obtain custody. The Act provides for jurisdiction if

> (1) th[e] State
>> (i) is the home state of the child at the time of commencement of the proceeding, or
>> (ii) had been the child's home state within six months before commencement of the proceeding and the child is absent from th[e] State because of his removal or retention by a person claiming his custody or for other reasons, and a parent or person acting as parent continues to live in th[e] State; or
> (2) it is in the best interest of the child that a court of th[e] State assume jurisdiction because
>> (i) the child and his parents, or the child and at least one contestant, have a significant connection with th[e] State, and
>> (ii) there is available in th[e] State substantial evidence concerning the child's present or future care, protection, training, and personal relationships; or
> (3) the child is physically present in th[e] State and
>> (i) the child has been abandoned or
>> (ii) it is necessary in an emergency to protect the child because he has been subjected to or threatened with mistreatment or abuse or is otherwise neglected [or dependent]; or
> (4)(i) it appears no other state would have jurisdiction under prerequisites substantially in accordance with paragraphs (1), (2), or (3), or another state has declined to exercise jurisdiction on the ground that th[e] State is the more appropriate forum to determine the custody of the child, and
>> (ii) it is in the best interest of the child that this court assume jurisdiction.

The UCCJA applies to both original and modification decrees. Consider whether the Iowa court above had jurisdiction to modify its original decree or whether the Florida court had authority to grant the temporary order. Section 14 of the Act provides that a court cannot modify a foreign custody decree unless (1) the state which rendered the decree does not now have jurisdiction or has declined to assume jurisdiction and (2) the court seeking to modify has jurisdiction.

Under the UCCJA, a court may decline to exercise jurisdiction if the petitioner for an initial decree has wrongfully taken the child from another state or has engaged in similar reprehensible conduct. Consider Michael's knowing violation of Florida's temporary order. Does this preclude further jurisdiction in Iowa? Does it matter that Florida may not have been the home state? Knowing of the action in Iowa, should the Florida court have declined to take action?

(2) PKPA.   The Parental Kidnapping Prevention Act (PKPA) is also relevant in cases involving jurisdiction over child custody determinations. One of its chief

purposes is to avoid jurisdictional competition and conflict between state courts. The Act sets forth jurisdictional criteria for determining which custody decree shall be afforded full faith and credit by a sister court. In addition, the Act assists victimized parents in locating the abductor by making the Federal Parent Locator Service available to state agencies and applying the Fugitive Felon Act, 18 U.S.C. §1073 (2000), to all state felony parental kidnapping cases. Jurisdiction to modify a decree under the PKPA is established if

> (1) such court has jurisdiction under the law of such State; and
> (2) one of the following conditions is met:
>> (A) such State
>>> (i) is the home State of the child on the date of the commencement of the proceeding, or
>>> (ii) had been the child's home State within six months before the date of the commencement of the proceeding and the child is absent from such State because of his removal or retention by a contestant or for other reasons, and a contestant continues to live in such State;
>> (B)(i) it appears that no other State would have jurisdiction under sub-paragraph (A), and
>>> (ii) it is in the best interest of the child that a court of such State assume jurisdiction because
>>>> (I) the child and his parents, or the child and at least one contestant, have a significant connection with such State other than mere physical presence in such State and
>>>> (II) there is available in such State substantial evidence concerning the child's present or future care, protection, training, and personal relationships;
>> (C) the child is physically present in such State and
>>> (i) the child has been abandoned, or
>>> (ii) it is necessary in an emergency to protect the child because he has been subjected to or threatened with mistreatment or abuse;
>> (D)(i) it appears that no other State would have jurisdiction under sub-paragraph (A), (B), (C), or (E), or another State has declined to exercise jurisdiction on the ground that the State whose jurisdiction is in issue is the more appropriate forum to determine the custody of the child, and
>>> (ii) it is in the best interest of the child that such court assume jurisdiction; or
>> (E) the court has continuing jurisdiction pursuant to subsection (d) of this section.

Consider the distinctions in the jurisdictional requirements under the UCCJA and PKPA. Would the Iowa court in *Leyda,* supra, retain jurisdiction to modify its original order under the PKPA? Section 1738A(d) says that if a state has made a child custody determination consistently with the provisions of this section, its jurisdiction continues as long as the requirement of subsection (c)(1) of this section continues to be met and such state remains the residence of the child or of any contestant. Does analysis under the PKPA change the result in the *Leyda* case? Would the result be different had Florida been the jurisdiction where the "best interests of the child" could have best been served?

One author criticizes the PKPA as follows:

> Intrinsically the UCCJA and PKPA involve philosophical differences. The UCCJA deliberately provided for jurisdictional flexibility to insure procurement of its dominant concern, the best interests of children. Some stability and certainty as to child custody jurisdiction was sacrificed where the best interests of the child presumably call[ ] for an assumption of jurisdiction by a state other than the home state. . . . The PKPA, on the other hand, attacks the vice of uncertainty and instability head on. By practically eliminating the "significant connection" alternative for child custody jurisdiction, it vests continuing jurisdiction in the home state alone, except in emergency or vacuum situations.

Henry H. Foster, Child Custody Jurisdiction: UCCJA and PKPA, 27 N.Y.L. Sch. L. Rev. 297, 302 (1981).

(3) Federal Court Jurisdiction?   Suppose different states assert jurisdiction over the same custody matter. May a federal court assert jurisdiction to settle the dispute? Before 1988 a series of decisions interpreted the PKPA to imply federal court jurisdiction when courts of two different states asserted jurisdiction over a custody determination. See, e.g., Flood v. Braaten, 727 F.2d 303 (3d Cir. 1984); Meade v. Meade, 812 F.2d 1473 (4th Cir. 1987). The Supreme Court finally resolved the issue of federal court jurisdiction in Thompson v. Thompson, 484 U.S. 174 (1988), holding:

> The PKPA does not provide an implied cause of action in federal court to determine which of two conflicting state custody decisions is valid. The context in which the PKPA was enacted — the existence of jurisdictional deadlocks among the States in custody cases and a nationwide problem of interstate parental kidnapping — suggests that Congress principal aim was to extend the requirements of the Full Faith and Credit Clause to custody determinations and not to create an entirely new cause of action. The language and placement of the Act reinforce this conclusion, in that the Act is an addendum to, and is therefore clearly intended to have the same operative effect as, the federal full faith and credit statute, the Act's heading is "Full faith and credit given to child custody determinations," and, unlike statutes that explicitly confer aright on a specified class of persons, the Act is addressed to States and to state courts. [T]he PKPA's legislative history provides an unusually clear indication that Congress did not intend the federal courts to play the enforcement role. [Id. at 175.]

The Court rejected the argument that failure to infer a cause of action would render the PKPA nugatory, reasoning that the argument, based on the presumption that the states are either unable or unwilling to enforce provisions of the Act, was one in which the Court was not willing to indulge. What effect will this decision have on a party with two conflicting state decrees?

(4) UCCJEA.   In 1997, the National Conference of Commissioners on Uniform State Laws promulgated the Uniform Child Custody Jurisdiction and

Enforcement Act (UCCJEA), 9 U.L.A. (pt. IA) 649 (1999 & Supp. 2008), to remedy inconsistent application of state laws under the UCCJA and PKPA. The UCCJEA, which is intended eventually to replace the UCCJA, makes several improvements in the UCCJA: "It provides clearer standards for which states can exercise original jurisdiction over a child-custody determination. It also, for the first time, enunciates a standard of continuing jurisdiction and clarifies modification and emergency jurisdiction. Other aspects of the jurisdiction provisions harmonize the law on simultaneous proceedings, clean hands, and forum non conveniens." Linda D. Elrod & Robert G. Spector, A Review of the Year in Family Law: A Search for Definitions and Policy, 31 Fam. L.Q. 613, 619 (1998).

Specifically, the UCCJEA:

(a)   includes a new definition of the term "custody determination" to clarify the custody proceedings that are covered by the Act (all custody and visitation cases with the exception of adoption and issues of tribal custody that remain subject to state determination applicability);

(b)   incorporates the stricter jurisidictional standards of the PKPA by explicitly prioritizing home-state jurisdiction (instead of merely listing the four bases of jurisdiction as did the UCCJA);

(c)   clarifies the meaning and application of "emergency" jurisdiction by providing that emergency jurisdiction may be used to protect the child on a temporary basis until the court issues a permanent order and defines the term to specify the inclusion of domestic violence; and,

(d)   clarifies the meaning of "exclusive continuing jurisdiction" by providing for exclusive continuing jurisdiction in specific situations and facilitates the determination of when a state has relinquished continuing jurisdiction.

In addition, the UCCJEA eliminates a perennial source of confusion in the UCCJA by deleting the term "best interest" from the jurisdictional standards. The UCCJEA explicitly specifies that the Act is not intended to be used to address the underlying merits of a custody dispute or to provide a basis for jurisdiction based on the substantive custody best interests standard. To date, the UCCJEA has been enacted by 46 states and the District of Columbia. See Child Custody Jurisdiction and Enforcement Act, Legislative Fact Sheet, *http://nccusl.org/Update/ uniformact_factsheets/uniformacts-fs-uccjea.asp* (last visited Nov. 11, 2008).

In 1998 Congress amended the Parental Kidnapping Prevention Act with the Visitation Rights Enforcement Act, 28 U.S.C. §1738A (2000). The PKPA now encompasses visitation as well as custody disputes (§1738A(a)), specifies that a court cannot modify the visitation or custody determination of another state unless the other state no longer has jurisdiction (or has declined to exercise it) (§1738A(h)), and revises the definition of "contestant" to include grandparents who claim a right to custody or visitation (§1738A(b)(2)).

(5) Extradition.   Suppose that in the *Leyda* case, Heidi instituted criminal charges against Michael, in the Florida courts, for kidnapping their daughter. Could the Florida court execute an extradition warrant to compel Michael's presence in Florida? Could Michael's home state grant a writ of habeas corpus to block the extradition warrant? See California v. Superior Court of California ex rel. Smolin,

482 U.S. 400 (1987), holding that, under the Extradition Act, "surrender is not to be interfered with by the summary process of habeas corpus upon speculations as to what ought to be the result of a trial in the place where the Constitution provides for its taking place." These issues raise problems of enforcement of custody decrees.

(6) Enforcement Remedies. The traditional method of enforcing custody decrees is a civil contempt proceeding. A defendant is found in contempt if the parent could have complied with the decree yet willfully failed to do so. Because the purpose of civil contempt is to coerce compliance, a conditional punishment (such as a fine, imprisonment, or a temporary custody change) is imposed until the parent complies. If a parent ultimately fails to comply, problems arise in punishing the noncomplying parent. Imprisonment or a permanent custody change, for instance, may be deemed inappropriate as adverse to the best interests of the child.

Some jurisdictions authorize a parent to withhold child support in the face of the other parent's noncompliance with the custody decree. Case law and commentators, however, criticize this remedy because it may impose undue hardship on the child if the custodial parent needs the added support to care adequately for the child. See Carter v. Carter, 479 S.E.2d 681 (W. Va. 1996) for a discussion of diverging case law.

A writ of habeas corpus is another traditional enforcement mechanism. Originally used by prisoners claiming illegal arrest or unlawful detention, the writ is also utilized in child custody cases. Courts are reluctant to use this remedy, however, unless no other means of relief exists. See Hudson v. Purifoy, 986 S.W.2d 870 (Ark. 1999); Amerson v. Iowa, 59 F.3d 92 (8th Cir. 1995).

Complications in enforcement arise when the noncustodial parent leaves the forum state with the child. Because a custody determination is modifiable, it is not a final judgment and therefore not subject to the Full Faith and Credit Clause of Article IV, §1 of the Constitution. This possibility of modification encourages forum-shopping for a favorable decree. The UCCJA, UCCJEA, and the PKPA attempt to limit a state from modifying another state's custody decree. However problems still arise in enforcing that decree. For example, a significant problem may be locating the fleeing parent. Under the PKPA, states have access to the Federal Parental Locator Service to facilitate discovery of the address and employer of the abducting parent. The Act permits such access only to certain parties (e.g., court, state attorney, state or federal law enforcement agency) and not to a custodial parent. See generally Anne B. Goldstein, The Tragedy of the Interstate Child: A Critical Examination of the Uniform Child Custody Jurisdiction Act and the Parental Kidnapping Prevention Act, 25 U.C. Davis L. Rev. 845, 918 M. 335 (1992).

Some states also recognize, by case law or statute, the tort of custodial interference. See, e.g., Matsumoto v. Matsumoto, 762 A.2d 224 (N.J. Super. Ct. App. Div. 2000), *aff'd*, 792 A.2d 1272 (N.J. 2002). However, a minority of jurisdictions refuse to recognize the tort, contending that the action merely increases hostilities for families already suffering from the consequences of divorce. See Zaharias v. Gammill, 844 P.2d 137 (Okla. 1992); Kessel v. Leavitt, 511 S.E.2d 710 (W. Va. 1998). Criminal liability also exists for custodial interference. See, e.g., State v. Wood, 8 P.3d 1189 (Ariz. Ct. App. 2000); Ex parte Jones, 36 S.W.3d 139 (Tex. Ct. App. 2000).

D. CUSTODY AND THE NEW REPRODUCTIVE TECHNIQUES

INTRODUCTORY PROBLEMS

(1) Margaret and Joe Smith have been married for several years but have been unable to have a child because Margaret has damaged fallopian tubes. They would like to have a child who is biologically related to them both. After employing a surrogacy agency, they choose Diane Cady, a 23-year-old graduate student. They wish to enter into a contract with Diane, who would agree to become artificially inseminated using a fertilized embryo consisting of Margaret's ovum and Joe's sperm. The agreement would provide that Diane would give up the child to the Smiths immediately at birth and furnish any necessary consent for the Smiths to adopt the child. The Smiths would pay Diane $50,000 plus medical expenses: $25,000 when she becomes pregnant and $25,000 when the adoption becomes final. Advise the Smiths concerning the applicable law in the following circumstances:

a. All goes according to plan, and Diane delivers a healthy boy whom the Smiths name Sam. Diane relinquishes Sam to the Smiths. In the absence of any dispute, what is the legality of the arrangement? Are the parties subject to criminal liability?

b. After Sam's birth, Diane changes her mind and decides to keep the child. Can the Smiths adopt Sam without Diane's consent? If not, would the Smiths prevail over Diane in a custody fight? Would the contract be specifically enforceable? Does Joe Smith have any support obligation if his efforts at adoption and custody are unsuccessful?

c. Diane gives birth to a mentally disabled child. The Smiths decide they do not want to raise the infant. Neither does Diane. Are the Smiths liable for damages for breach of contract? What are the custody and support obligations of the respective parties?

d. Suppose that before Diane undergoes the implantation, the Smiths' marriage breaks up. At the divorce proceeding, Sally requests that the embryos be distributed to her for implantation. Daniel protests, arguing that he no longer wants to father a child. He wants the embryos destroyed. How should the dispute be resolved? Are the embryos akin to "property" that should be distributed in a divorce proceeding? Or are they "persons" whose custody should be determined according to the best interests of the child?

Would the law's response to the Smith's situation in the preceding examples differ if the ovum were that of Diane? If the genetic material were from anonymous donors?

(2) John and Jim are a gay couple who have been together for ten years. They have undergone a commitment ceremony and list each other in their respective estate planning documents. They live in a state that does not permit same-sex marriage or domestic partnership. John and Jim decide that they would like to raise a child together. They approach Barbara, a friend of Jim's, to ask her if she

would bear their child in return for payment of $50,000 plus medical expenses. When she agrees, they contact a physician who agrees to perform the insemination by commingling both men's sperm and inseminating Barbara. Barbara bears a girl whom she delivers to John and Jim. They name the child Rebecca.

a. What are the parties' custodial rights and support obligations?

b. Would the law's response differ depending on whether Barbara is married or unmarried?

c. Would the law's response differ depending on whether the jurisdiction recognized the validity of John and Jim's same-sex union as a valid "marriage" or "domestic partnership"?

In re Baby M
See pp. 451-460, supra.

NOTES AND QUESTIONS ON *BABY M*

(1) Artificial Insemination.   In the case of artificial insemination (termed "AID") a woman is impregnated with sperm from a third-party donor. AID raises a number of legal issues. Who, for instance, is regarded as the child's father for custody and support purposes? Cases typically arise following a divorce, when the wife refuses the husband visitation rights on the ground that the children conceived by AID are therefore not his children.[85] Or upon separation or divorce, the father of a child conceived by AID alleges he is not liable for child support because there is no child of the marriage.[86]

Case law generally holds that the husband's consent is often decisive in such disputes. That is, by giving consent to the insemination, the husband is entitled to visitation rights and also is estopped from denying liability for support. This result is also dictated by states that follow the original version of the Uniform Parentage Act §5 (1973), 9B U.L.A. 377 (2001 & Supp. 2008). For a recent case in which a husband alleges that he did not consent to donor insemination, see Laura G. v. Peter G., 830 N.Y.S.2d 496 (Sup. Ct. 2007).

What are the rights and responsibilities of the sperm donor? In several states, including those following the original Uniform Parentage Act §5, the sperm donor "is treated in law as if he were not the natural father." Hence, the biological father has no duty of support and no custodial rights. In the absence of legislation, the common law presumption of legitimacy (discussed below) also suggests that the child is the legitimate issue of the woman's husband, rather than of the sperm donor. The UPA was revised in 2000 (and amended in 2002). What are the similarities and differences between the versions?

---

[85] See, e.g., People ex rel. Abajian v. Dennett, 184 N.Y.S.2d 178 (Super. Ct. 1958).
[86] See, e.g., Levin v. Levin, 645 N.E.2d 601 (Ind. Ct. App. 1994).

Uniform Parentage Act (2000, as amended 2002)
9B U.L.A. 355-356 (2001 & Supp. 2008)

[The following provisions are not applicable to children conceived by sexual intercourse or those subject to gestational agreements under Article 8. The latter provisions are presented infra.]

§702. Parental Status of Donor

A donor is not a parent of a child conceived by means of assisted reproduction.

§703. Paternity of Child of Assisted Reproduction

A man who provides sperm for, or consents to, assisted reproduction by a woman as provided in Section 704 with the intent to be the parent of her child, is a parent of the resulting child.

§704. Consent to Assisted Reproduction

(a) Consent by a woman, and a man who intends to be a parent of a child born to the woman by assisted reproduction must be in a record signed by the woman and the man. This requirement does not apply to a donor.

(b) Failure of a man to sign a consent required by subsection (a), before or after birth of the child, does not preclude a finding of paternity if the woman and the man, during the first two years of the child's life resided together in the same household with the child and openly held out the child as their own.

(2) Surrogacy: Background. Surrogate motherhood is the female counterpart of artificial insemination. Whereas artificial insemination addresses problems regarding a man's infertility, surrogate motherhood presents a solution to a woman's fertility problems. Increasingly, surrogacy is also being utilized by gay male couples (discussed later). In surrogacy, a woman (the "surrogate mother") traditionally agrees to be inseminated with the sperm of a man whose wife is unable to conceive or bear a child. Formerly, the ovum used in surrogacy arrangements belonged to the surrogate. However, advances in reproductive technology have now made gestational surrogacy (with the use of the wife's ovum) the norm. Estimates suggest that roughly 25,000 babies have been born as a result of surrogacy since the mid-1970's.[87]

(3) Baby Selling. Baby-selling statutes, which forbid compensation to a surrogate in connection with an adoption or termination of parental rights, raise a number of constitutional problems. For example, do these statutes constitute a denial of equal protection because the surrogate mother is being treated different from the "surrogate father" in artificial insemination? The court in *Baby M* stated: "A sperm donor simply cannot be equated with a surrogate mother." How is the sperm donor analogous to the surrogate mother who donates her egg? How is he

---

[87] Kim O'Brien Root, Family: Surrogate Births: Sister to Make Father out of Brother, Daily Press (Newport News, VA), Feb. 25, 2006, at A1.

different? Further, is the surrogate being paid for a "product" or a "service"? If a product, then why not permit payment, because sperm donors and blood donors are compensated? If a service, then why not allow compensation because wet nurses, nannies, and other child caretakers are compensated for childrearing services?

Baby-selling statutes were also challenged in *Baby M* as violating the constitutional right to privacy. Is the right to hire or serve as a surrogate guaranteed by the constitutional right of privacy — to be free from state interference in the decision to bear or beget a child? If so, can the state interfere nonetheless on the basis of any compelling interests?[88]

The policy underlying baby-selling statutes is to relieve the economic incentive for a mother to give up her child under adverse circumstances. Is the same rationale present in the surrogacy context?

(4) Feminist Concerns. *Baby M*, with its suggestion that surrogate motherhood is "potentially degrading to women," raises a concern about the potential exploitation of the surrogate mother.[89] Do you agree that surrogacy is exploitative? If women desire to enter into such arrangements, it is paternalistic for the law to forbid this conduct? *Baby M* suggests that women may still serve as surrogates if they do so voluntarily and without remuneration. Is this a realistic solution?

(5) Breach of Contract by the Surrogate. As we have seen, the law interposes limits on private ordering in the surrogacy context (e.g., in the form of criminal sanctions in some jurisdictions) even when all parties agree to the arrangement. What happens when disputes arise — either on the part of the surrogate, or on the part of the prospective adoptive parents? In *Baby M*, the surrogate mother breaches by refusing to relinquish the child as she promised. Mr. Stern then attempts to establish his parental rights by enforcement of the surrogacy contract. Is the contract enforceable, according to *Baby M*? If the Sterns are without a contract remedy, one legal recourse that they have is to attempt to proceed with the adoption. Would such an attempt be successful without the biological mother's consent? If, as in *Baby M*, the biological mother refuses consent, what can be done to overcome this obstacle? If adoption is unsuccessful, the couple's next recourse is a custody proceeding based on the best interests of the child standard.

Other possibilities also exist for breach on the part of the surrogate. For example, suppose the surrogate delivers a premature infant who subsequently dies. Or the surrogate wants an abortion. Or, she abuses harmful substances during the pregnancy. What should be the remedy in each case? Are money damages adequate for loss of the couple's "expectation interest"? Could a court order specific performance?

If a gestational surrogate decides to keep the child, must she reimburse the commissioning couple for fees and expenses? See J.F. v. D.B., 848 N.E.2d 873 (Ohio Ct. App. 2006) (upholding the contract and requiring reimbursement), *aff'd*

---

[88] For a prominent proponent of the view that the right to use assisted technologies is inherent in the constitutionally protected procreative liberty, see John A. Robertson, Children of Choice: Freedom and the New Reproductive Technologies (1994).

[89] For classic proponents of this view, see Gena Corea, The Mother Machine: Reproductive Technologies from Artificial Insemination to Artificial Wombs (1985); Robyn Rowland, Living Laboratories: Women and Reproductive Technologies (1992).

in part, rev'd in part, & remanded, 879 N.E.2d 740 (Ohio 2007) (holding that contract does not violate public policy, but remanding on issue of breach and assessment of damages).

(6) Breach by the Commissioning Parent(s). Disputes also arise in the event of breach by the commissioning parent(s). For example, suppose the prospective adoptive parents refuse to accept an infant born with a disability. Such a case arose when surrogate mother Judy Stiver gave birth to a mentally disabled child in Michigan in 1983. The commissioning father (Alexander Malahoff) decided he did not want the child; neither did the surrogate mother. After blood tests revealed that the child was actually fathered by the surrogate's husband, Malahoff sued the surrogate for not producing the child he ordered. The Stivers sued the physician, lawyer, and psychiatrist of the surrogate program. In Stiver v. Parker, 975 F.2d 261 (6th Cir. 1992), the Court of Appeals held that the defendants owed a duty of protection to the mother but that there were jury questions as to negligence and causation (regarding testing the contracting father's semen for a disease she allegedly contracted that led to the child's birth defects).

In another breach by the commissioning parents, suppose that twins are born as a result of the insemination of the surrogate. However, the commissioning parents agree to accept only one of the twins. What remedy, if any, should be available to the surrogate in this situation? See Nick Craven, Dilemma over the Surrogate Twins with No Parents, Daily Mail, May 8, 2000, at 8.

(7) Presumption of Legitimacy. In the biological father's bid for custody, some obstacles stand in his path regarding acknowledgment of his paternity if the surrogate mother is a married woman. The first obstacle is the common law doctrine specifying that a child born of a married woman is presumed conclusively to be fathered by the woman's husband. Thus, in the case of a married surrogate, the woman's husband will be recognized as the child's father rather than the biological father and sperm donor. A second presumption, statutory, rather than common law, presents an additional obstacle to biological fathers seeking to establish paternity of children conceived through surrogacy arrangements. Statutes regulating artificial insemination in many states, modeled after the original Uniform Parentage Act, specify that if a husband consents to artificial insemination of his wife by a third-party semen donor, the woman's husband is presumed to be the father of the resulting child. Such statutes also imply that the married surrogate's husband would be recognized as the child's father rather than the biological father and sperm donor. The purpose of the common law presumption is to protect the rights of the nonmarital child and to preserve family integrity. The purpose of the statutory presumption is to ensure support for the AID child. How relevant are these purposes to surrogacy? What problems do the presumptions evoke in regard to two gay male parents? See generally Susan Frelich Appleton, Presuming Women: Revisiting the Presumption of Legitimacy in the Same-Sex Couples Era, 86 B.U. L. Rev. 227 (2006). Do these difficulties suggest that couples desiring to enter surrogacy arrangements should always select single surrogates? What problems might then arise?

(8) Adoption Consent Statutes. Another obstacle is adoption consent statutes that prohibit prebirth consent. As part of the surrogacy agreement, Mrs. Whitehead

agreed to surrender the child to the Sterns, giving them permanent and sole custody, and to terminate her parental rights. When she breached, she was protected by state laws governing revocation of consent to adoption. All 50 states have legislation prohibiting a mother from granting irrevocable consent to adoption before the child's birth or for some period after birth. The purpose of such laws is to ensure that the mother's consent is knowing, voluntary, and without duress. Should such laws be applicable to the surrogacy context in which the surrogate has considerable time for reflection? One solution to the obstacle of such prebirth consent is a judicial determination of parentage prior to birth. Is this an adequate solution to the problem? See Vanessa S. Browne-Barbour, Bartering for Babies: Are Preconception Agreements in the Best Interests of Children?, 26 Whittier L. Rev. 429 (2004).

(9) Different State Approaches. States adopt a variety of approaches to surrogacy. Some jurisdictions deny enforcement, declaring all surrogacy agreements void. Others prohibit compensation (but permit payment of expenses). Still other states regulate isolated aspects of surrogacy agreements (e.g., by providing exemptions from criminal sanctions for baby selling). Finally, other states permit surrogacy but with significant procedural regulation. See Kelly A. Anderson, Current Development, Certainty in an Uncertain World: The Ethics of Drafting Surrogacy Contracts, 21 Geo. J. Legal Ethics 615, 619-627 (2008) (surveying jurisdictions). See also J.F. v. D.B., 879 N.E.2d 740 (Ohio 2007) (holding surrogacy contracts do not violate state public policy).

(10) Gay and Lesbian Parents. In *Baby M*, the commissioning parents were married. May health care professionals deny reproductive technology to gays and lesbians? To single persons? What constitutional rights and statutory protections are implicated by the limitation of reproductive technology to traditional families? In North Coast Women's Care Medical Group v. San Diego County Superior Court, 189 P.3d 959 (Cal. 2008), a lesbian domestic partner sued health care providers, alleging that their refusal to perform in vitro fertilization on her violated state civil rights legislation (the Unruh Civil Rights Act). Defendants countered that their denial of treatment was based not on her sexual orientation but rather her unmarried state (marital status discrimination was not then prohibited by the state civil rights law). The California Supreme Court subsequently ruled that the defendants' First Amendment right to free exercise does not permit them the right to deny fertility treatment to lesbian patients in violation of state civil rights legislation. See generally Judith F. Daar, Accessing Reproductive Technologies: Invisible Barriers, Indelible Harms, 23 Berkeley J. Gender L. & Just. 18 (2008) (discussing limitations on access to reproductive technology).

Suppose two gay male partners who desire to raise a family decide to commingle the sperm to be used to inseminate a gestational surrogate. The maternal egg is provided by an anonymous egg donor. Must state officials include *both* men's names on the infant's birth certificate? Should it matter if same-sex marriage is recognized in the partners' jurisdiction? See Cunningham v. Tardiff, 2008 WL 4779641 (Conn. Super. Ct. 2008) (reasoning that the parties' names should both be placed on the birth certificate because their marriage was legally recognized in the state and the AID statute required that any child born as a result of the procedure will acquire the status of a legitimate child). If both men's names are placed on the birth certificate, must a "mother's" name be listed? Should it matter if the egg originates from an anonymous donor? See In re Roberto d.B., 923 A.2d 115 (Md. 2007) (ruling that the birth certificate need not name a mother if the sperm donor and gestational surrogate both agree and if the egg is from an anonymous donor).

(11) More Than Two Parents? If nontraditional families may be created with single parents, gay and lesbian parents, or even deceased parents, could (should) families be formed with *more* than two parents for a child? See Jacob v. Shultz-Jacob, 923 A.2d 473 (Pa. Super. Ct. 2007) (finding that a sperm donor was an indispensable party to a proceeding to determine the custody of children born to a lesbian couple who conceived the child through artificial insemination with his sperm). See also Laura Nicole Althouse, Three's Company? How American Law Can Recognize a Third Social Parent in Same-Sex Headed Families, 19 Hastings Women's L.J. 171 (2008). Conversely, is it possible for a child conceived by surrogacy to have *no* legal parents? See In re Marriage of Buzzanca, 72 Cal. Rptr. 2d 280 (Ct. App. 1998) (reversing trial court order determining that the commissioning couple was not the lawful parents of a genetically unrelated child who was born by surrogacy, and terminating the husband's obligation of support).

(12) Model Legislation. Several pieces of model legislation also address surrogate parenting agreements. In 1988, the National Conference of Commissioners on Uniform State Laws (NCCUSL) approved the Uniform Status of Children of Assisted Conception Act (USCACA), 9B U.L.A. 184 (Supp. 1999), with Alternative A that regulates surrogacy by a judicially preapproved adoption proceeding, and Alternative B that makes surrogacy agreements void. A revised Uniform Parentage Act (UPA) replaced USCACA in 2000. Because reproductive technology was in its infancy when the UPA was first enacted in 1973, the original version addressed the issue of legal fatherhood only in the context of artificial insemination (i.e., the rights of the husband versus sperm donor). UPA §5(a).

The UPA was revised substantially in 2000, and amended in 2002, in light of scientific advances in paternity testing and the new reproductive technologies. The revised Act (excerpted later) provides limited regulation of surrogacy. It authorizes "gestational agreements" if validated by a court, permits payment to a surrogate mother, provides that the intended parents may be married or unmarried, and abandons the USCACA requirement that at least one of the intended parents be genetically related to the child. Once the court is satisfied that the requirements are met, the court may issue an order validating the agreement and declaring that the intended parents are the parents of the child. The new UPA provides a mechanism for determining parentage of children in the event that the agreement is not enforceable and also provides for child support in such cases. To date, eight states have enacted the new Act. Uniform Parentage Act, Legislative Fact Sheet, available at *http://nccusl.org/Update/uniformact_factsheets/uniformacts-fs-upa.asp* (last visited Nov. 12, 2008). See generally Mary Patricia Byrn, From Right to Wrong: A Critique of the 2000 Uniform Parentage Act, 16 UCLA Women's L.J. 163 (2007).

In February 2008, the ABA adopted comprehensive model legislation (the Model Act Governing Assisted Reproductive Technology) that offers principles for addressing legal issues involving assisted reproduction technologies (ART). The Model Act provides for parentage status for a participant who provides gametes for, or consent to, assisted reproduction with the intent to be a parent; requires informed consent mental health consultation for participants; mandates disclosures regarding possible disposition of embryos; provides for confidentiality (if desired) for donors except for the provision of medical information; and specifies rules for collection of gametes or embryos from deceased or incompetent individuals. The drafters note that the Model Act is intended to be consistent with, insofar as possible, the new UPA and the Uniform Probate Code. American Bar Association, Model Act Governing Assisted Reproductive Technology, Article 6, Legislative Note, available at *www.abanet.org/family/flq/artmodelact.pdf*. See generally Charles P. Kindregan, Jr., & Steven H. Snyder, Clarifying the Law of Art: The New American Bar Association Model Act Governing Assisted Reproductive Technology, 42 Fam. L.Q. 203 (2008).

(13) International Perspective.   The international response to surrogacy also varies considerably. Some countries ban surrogacy (France, China, Italy, Vietnam). However, many countries now permit private surrogacy arrangements. England, for example, has long recognized private surrogacy agreements (permitting payment for expenses but not services), although it bans commercial surrogacy. Surrogacy Arrangements Act of 1985, ch. 49. See also Human Fertilisation and Embryology Act of 1990, ch. 37 (regulating fertility programs and authorizing courts to declare the infertile couple as the legal parents of a child born via surrogacy). Israel has adopted the most progressive government-supervised approach. The Surrogate Motherhood Agreements Act, 1996, S.H. 1577, establishes a governmental committee to approve all requests for surrogacy, permits payment for services, specifies eligibility criteria, the status of the child (including custody), and the limited conditions under which the surrogate mother may revoke consent. See generally D. Kelly Weisberg, The Birth of Surrogacy in Israel (2005). Because access to surrogacy by same-sex couples is not permitted in Israel, Israeli gay and lesbian partners often hire surrogates from India, where surrogacy was legalized in 2002. Amelia Gentleman, Foreign Couples Turn to India for Surrogate Mothers, Int'l Trib., March 4, 2008, available at *http://www.iht.com/articles/2008/03/04/asia/mother.php*.

Such "reproductive tourism" leads to problems regarding conflicts of law. In such situations, which country's law should prevail — where the contract was signed, where the insemination was performed, where the surrogate or parents are domiciled, or where the child was born? See generally Elizabeth Ferrari Morris, Reproductive Tourism and the Role of the European Union, 8 Chi. J. Int'l L. 701 (2008).

(14) Problem.   You are the legislative assistant to a state legislator who has asked you to draft a statute on surrogate parenting. What do you think the law's response to surrogate parenting should be? At one extreme, should it be a crime to enter into such contracts? At the other extreme, should such contracts be enforceable? Or should the law adopt an intermediate stance? If so, what provisions should this intermediate stance encompass? Should the legislature adopt provisions of the revised Uniform Parentage Act and Model Act Governing Assisted Reproductive Technology (excerpted next)?

Uniform Parentage Act (2000, as amended 2002)
9B U.L.A. 362, 367-369 (2001 & Supp. 2008)

§801. Gestational Agreement Authorized

(a) A prospective gestational mother, her husband if she is married, a donor or the donors, and the intended parents may enter into a written agreement providing that:

(1) the prospective gestational mother agrees to pregnancy by means of assisted reproduction;

(2) the prospective gestational mother, her husband if she is married, and the donors relinquish all rights and duties as the parents of a child conceived through assisted reproduction; and

(3) the intended parents become the parents of the child.

(b) The man and the woman who are the intended parents must both be parties to the gestational agreement.

(c) A gestational agreement is enforceable only if validated as provided in Section 803.

(d) A gestational agreement does not apply to the birth of a child conceived by means of sexual intercourse.

(e) A gestational agreement may provide for payment of consideration.

(f) A gestational agreement may not limit the right of the gestational mother to make decisions to safeguard her health or that of the embryos or fetus.

§806. Termination of Gestational Agreement

(a) After issuance of an order under this [article], but before the prospective gestational mother becomes pregnant by means of assisted reproduction, the prospective gestational mother, her husband, or either of the intended parents may terminate the gestational agreement by giving written notice of termination to all other parties.

(b) The court for good cause shown may terminate the gestational agreement.

(c) An individual who terminates a gestational agreement shall file notice of the termination with the court. On receipt of the notice, the court shall vacate the order issued under this [article]. An individual who does not notify the court of the termination of the agreement is subject to appropriate sanctions.

(d) Neither a prospective gestational mother nor her husband, if any, is liable to the intended parents for terminating a gestational agreement pursuant to this section.

§807. Parentage Under Validated Gestational Agreement

(a) Upon birth of a child to a gestational mother, the intended parents shall file notice with the court that a child has been born to the gestational mother within 300 days after assisted reproduction. Thereupon, the court shall issue an order:

(1) confirming that the intended parents are the parents of the child;

(2) if necessary, ordering that the child be surrendered to the intended parents; and

(3) directing the [agency maintaining birth records] to issue a birth certificate naming the intended parents as parents of the child.

(b) If the parentage of a child born to a gestational mother is alleged not to be the result of assisted reproduction, the court shall order genetic testing to determine the parentage of the child.

(c) If the intended parents fail to file notice required under subsection (a), the gestational mother or the appropriate State agency may file notice with the court that a child has been born to the gestational mother within 300 days after assisted reproduction. Upon proof of a court order issued pursuant to Section 803 validating the gestational agreement, the court shall order the intended parents are the parents of the child and are financially responsible for the child.

§809. *Effect of Nonvalidated Gestational Agreement*

(a) A gestational agreement, whether in a record or not, that is not judicially validated is not enforceable.

(b) If a birth results under a gestational agreement that is not judicially validated as provided in this [article], the parent-child relationship is determined as provided in [Article] 2.

(c) Individuals who are parties to a nonvalidated gestational agreement as intended parents may be held liable for support of the resulting child, even if the agreement is otherwise unenforceable. . . .

NOTE ON IN VITRO FERTILIZATION

In vitro fertilization[90] raises additional provocative legal issues. Early controversy centered around the medical ethics of "experimenting" with human sperm and ova. For example, in Del Zio v. Presbyterian Hospital, 74 Civ. 3588 (S.D.N.Y. 1978), a jury awarded $50,000 to a couple for pain and suffering in regard to a hospital's destruction of the wife's ova and the husband's sperm, created for in vitro fertilization, based on a physician's fear that the procedure constituted experimentation that had not been approved by the hospital ethics committee. Litigation still arises against medical facilities in regard to the care of embryos created by in vitro fertilization. See, e.g., Miller v. American Infertility Group, 897 N.E.2d 837 (Ill. App. Ct. 2008) (holding that state wrongful death act does not permit action for loss of an embryo, created by in vitro fertilization, that has not been implanted); Jeter v. Mayo Clinic, 121 P.3d 1256 (Ariz. Ct. App. 2005) (holding that a couple could sue clinic for negligent loss or destruction of pre-embryos although pre-embryo was not a "person" for purposes of recovery under wrongful death statute).

---

[90] In in vitro fertilization, ova are surgically removed and placed in a laboratory medium together with sperm. After fertilization, the embryo is implanted in the uterus of either the ovum donor or another woman. The procedure enables women with blocked or damaged fallopian tubes to conceive or bear children.

Early statutory law and case law addressed the success rates of infertility clinics that conducted in vitro fertilization (IVF). For example, the federal Fertility Clinic Success Rate and Certification Act of 1992, 42 U.S.C. §§263a-1 to 263-7 (2000), requires that IVF clinics report the number of procedures performed and the resulting number of live births. The Act was enacted to counter claims of inflated success rates by some clinics. Inflated success rates also resulted in consumer protection claims. See, e.g., Karlin v. IVF America, Inc., 712 N.E.2d 662 (N.Y. 1999) (holding that patients who unsuccessfully used services of IVF clinic could assert claims based on alleged fraud and deceptive advertising by clinic).

Two increasingly frequent legal issues arise in conjunction with the disposition of embryos — postdeath and postdivorce. For example, in the case of death or divorce, to whom do the embryos belong? Are they "property" of the respective donors? The issue first arose in March 1981, when a wealthy couple, Mr. and Mrs. Rios, flew to Australia to impregnate the wife through IVF. Three eggs were removed and fertilized from an anonymous donor. An implantation attempt with one of the fertilized eggs was unsuccessful. But, before another attempt, the Rios died in an airplane crash, leaving no instructions regarding disposition of the frozen embryos. Questions arose regarding the disposition of the embryos — should they be discarded or donated to other infertile couples?[91] If a live birth had resulted, do you think the child or children should have inheritance rights to the property of their deceased parents?

In a more recent case that involved a deceased parent, a couple contracted with a medical facility to perform IVF on the wife with the husband's sperm. Before implantation, however, the husband died in a helicopter crash. In the couple's agreement with the medical facility, the husband had provided that in the event of his death or permanent disability, the sperm samples should be discarded. When his widow petitioned for distribution of her deceased husband's frozen sperm to her (based, inter alia, on her fundamental right to procreate), the court of appeals held that the decedent's intent to discard the embryos should control. In re Estate of Kievernagel, 83 Cal. Rptr. 3d 311 (Ct. App. 2008).

Alternatively, what should happen in the event that the couple *divorces* after the fertilization process but before implantation? Should the frozen embryos be distributed to one of the parties as "marital property"? Should they be discarded? Or donated to other infertile couples? If the couple addresses this eventuality in an agreement, will such an agreement be enforceable? Compare In re Marriage of Dahl & Angle, 194 P.3d 834 (Or. Ct. App. 2008) (ordering divorcing couple's frozen embryos to be destroyed, pursuant to couple's agreement and recognizing wife's contractual right as "personal property"); Roman v. Roman, 193 S.W.3d 40 (Tex. App. 2006) (upholding agreement to discard embryos upon divorce, despite wife's contrary wishes); Litowitz v. Litowitz, 48 P.3d 261 (Wash. 2002) (holding that divorcing couple had to petition court for instructions, pursuant to their cryopreservation agreement, when they were unable to agree on disposition of

---

[91] An ethics commission subsequently recommended destruction of the embryos. However, the legislature reversed the recommendation. Ultimately, the embryos were implanted unsuccessfully in the wombs of two women. For an account of the case, see Nicole L. Cucci, Note, The Constitutional Implications of In Vitro Fertilization Procedures, 72 St. John's L. Rev. 417, 432 (1998).

embryos), with A.Z. v. B.Z., 725 N.E.2d 1051 (Mass. 2000) (declining to enforce agreement, upon divorce, to give pre-embryos to wife over husband's objection). See generally I. Glenn Cohen, The Constitution and the Rights Not to Procreate, 60 Stan. L. Rev. 1135 (2008); Jessica L. Lambert, Note, Developing a Legal Framework for Resolving Disputes Between "Adoptive Parents" of Frozen Embryos: A Comparison to Resolutions of Divorce Disputes, 49 B.C. L. Rev. 529 (2008).

How would the ABA Model Act Governing Assisted Reproductive Technology (excerpted next) resolve the preceding issues? Do you agree with that resolution?

American Bar Association, Model Act Governing Assisted Reproductive Technology (2008)

Article 6. Child of Assisted Reproduction

[The following provisions are not applicable to children conceived by means of sexual intercourse or as the result of a gestational agreement as provided in Article 7.]

§603. Parentage of Child of Assisted Reproduction

An individual who provides gametes for, or consent to, assisted reproduction by a woman as provided in Section 604 with the intent to be a parent of her child is a parent of the resulting child.

§604. Consent to Assisted Reproduction

1. Consent by an individual who intends to be a parent of a child born by assisted reproduction must be in a signed record. This requirement does not apply to a donor.
2. Failure of an individual to sign a consent required by paragraph 1, before or after birth of the child, does not preclude a finding of parentage if the woman and the intended parent, during the first two years of the child's life, resided together in the same household with the child and openly held out the child as their own.

. . .

§606. Effect of Dissolution of Marriage or Withdrawal of Consent

1. If a marriage is dissolved before transfer of eggs, sperm, or embryos, the former spouse is not a parent of the resulting child unless the former spouse consented in a record that if assisted reproduction were to occur after a divorce, the former spouse would be a parent of the child.
2. The consent of an individual to assisted reproduction may be withdrawn by that individual in a record at any time before placement of eggs, sperm, or embryos. An individual who withdraws consent under this Section is not a parent of the resulting child.

§607. *Parental Status of Deceased Individual*

Except as otherwise provided in the enacting jurisdiction's probate code, if an individual who consented in a record to be a parent by assisted reproduction dies before placement of eggs, sperm, or embryos, the deceased individual is not a parent of the resulting child unless the deceased spouse consented in a record that if assisted reproduction were to occur after death, the deceased individual would be a parent of the child.

CHAPTER 6

State-Enforced Limitations on the Liberty of Minors

A. INTRODUCTION

In a variety of areas, law constrains the liberty of adolescents more than that of adults. This chapter explores circumstances where, because of age, the freedom of juveniles is limited. The materials in this chapter relate to important aspects of a teenager's life: limitations on their rights to work, drive automobiles, and consume liquor; and the requirements that they attend school and generally be subject to parental controls.

Whether a young person should have the same freedom as an adult is a critical question considered earlier in the book. For example, the *Ginsberg* case, Chapter 1, posed the question of whether a state could prohibit the sale of sexually explicit materials to juveniles in situations in which adult access would be constitutionally protected. The degree of a juvenile's autonomy with regard to medical treatment was a principal concern of Chapter 4. The case of In re Doe, Chapter 1, like Carey v. Population Services International, infra, p. 689, involves the privacy rights of sexually active young persons. There are also parallels between the *Yoder* case, Chapter 1, and the status offender material, infra, p. 713, in that each concerns aspects of the requirement that young people attend school.

Certain common questions should frame your inquiry into the topics that follow:

1. What interests are being served by treating teenagers by different standards from those applying to adults? Is the primary purpose protection of the young person? The enforcement of parental prerogatives? The protection of society?

2. How substantial is the evidence offered to justify limiting the young person's freedom?

3. Are age-based lines appropriate? Are there alternatives? What opportunities are there for standards based on "competence" or "maturity" that would apply irrespective of age? Are the existing age-based lines drawn at the appropriate age?

4. What method is being used to limit the young person's liberty? What are the consequences of a violation? Are sanctions imposed on minors? Their parents? Persons dealing with minors in the marketplace?

5. What role does the young person's family have in enforcement of the constraints on the minor's liberty? To what extent may parents "liberate" their own children?

6. According to Virginia Coigney, "The relationship between the child, his parents, and society is fundamentally a property relationship. . . . Most of the laws relating to children reflect the prevailing attitude that they are the possessions of their parents and/or the state and not very valuable possessions at that."[1] To correct this, she proposes the adoption of "A Child's Bill of Rights," the first right being:

> *The Right to Self-Determination.* Children should have the right to decide the matters which affect them most directly. This is the basic right upon which all others depend. Children are now treated as the private property of their parents on the assumption that it is the parents' right and responsibility to control the life of the child. The achievement of children's rights, however, would reduce the need for this control and bring about an end to the double standard of morals and behavior for adults and children.[2]

Using the topics considered in this chapter,

a. Evaluate critically the extent to which children are treated as the "private property of their parents" or "possessions of their parents and/or the state";

b. Describe and compare the degree to which under present law a minor has "the right to decide";

c. Consider alternative ways in which the law might be changed to broaden the minor's "right to decide" in the relevant areas and then analyze critically the implications of such changes for related areas of the law, for the family, and for society.

B. *CHILD LABOR*[3]

Federal and state laws restrict the ability of young people to work for pay. These laws were the culmination of reform efforts to prevent the exploitation of children, to ensure their education, and to protect them from the hazards of the workplace. But have such laws outlived their appropriateness? The regulation of child labor presents a fascinating context to explore how reform legislation, enacted in an

---

[1] Virginia Coigney, Children Are People Too: How We Fail Our Children and How We Can Love Them 137 (1975).

[2] Id. at 197; Richard E. Farson, Birthrights (1974).

[3] This section on child labor draws on historical source materials reprinted in Children and Youth in America: A Documentary History, Vol. 2, pp. 601-749 (Robert H. Bremner ed., 1971) and vol. 3, pp. 299-518 (Robert H. Bremner ed., 1974) [hereinafter Children and Youth in America].

earlier time to protect young people, may now act as a substantial and unwise constraint on their liberty. Should the state "protect" children from employment or instead encourage young people to gain work experience outside the home? What role should parents have in deciding whether their children should work?

Supporters of child labor laws maintain that the laws protect children from being forced to work at too early an age, for too many hours a day, or in occupations where chances of accident and injury are high. On the other hand, in an era of heightened sensitivity to human rights, both children and their adult spokespersons have objected to child labor laws that pose undesirable restrictions on children's rights to work and deprive them of experience and opportunities beneficial to social development.[4] The following materials explore these issues.

1.   Historical Perspective

Laws restricting the employment of children spring largely from social reform movements of the late nineteenth century. Although work had traditionally been seen as essential to a child's upbringing, the growth of industrialism in America gradually changed the nature of the work and attitudes toward it. Critics suggested that children sent to meet the increasing demand for workers in factories suffered in economic terms: they were no longer being trained in a vocation but typically learned only how to do a small task that was part of a larger process. Children who were taught manufacturing skills at an early age tended to remain in the same jobs at the same factory, and were thus deprived of upward social mobility.[5] More noticeably, work in the factories was physically harmful to children. Often the unhealthiest work was given to the child workers, as concerned reformers pointed out with increasing vividness:

> It is a sorry but indisputable fact that where children are employed, the most unhealthful work is generally given them. In the spinning and carding rooms of cotton and woollen mills, where large numbers of children are employed, clouds of lint-dust fill the lungs and menace the health. The children have often a distressing cough, caused by the irritation of the throat, and many are hoarse from the same cause. In bottle factories and other branches of glass manufacture, the atmosphere is constantly charged with microscopic particles of glass. In the woodworking industries, such as the manufacture of cheap furniture and wooden boxes, and packing cases, the air is laden with fine sawdust. Children employed in soap and soap-powder factories work, many of them, in clouds of alkaline dust which inflames the eyelids and nostrils. Boys employed in filling boxes of soap-powder work all day long with handkerchiefs tied over their mouths. In the coal-mines the breaker boys breathe air that is heavy and thick with particles of coal, and their lungs become black in consequence. In the manufacture of felt hats, little girls are often employed at the machines which tear the fur from the skins of rabbits and other animals. Recently, I stood and watched a young girl working at

[4] 3 Children and Youth in America 299.
[5] Owen R. Lovejoy, Cutting Child Labor Out of the Vicious Circle, 3 Child Lab. Bull. 59 (1914-1915).

such a machine; she wore a newspaper pinned over her head and a handkerchief tied over her mouth. She was white with dust from head to feet, and when she stooped to pick anything from the floor the dust would fall from her paper head-covering in little heaps. About seven feet from the mouth of the machine was a window through which poured thick volumes of dust as it was belched out from the machine. I placed a sheet of paper on the inner sill of the window and in twenty minutes it was covered with a layer of fine dust, half an inch deep. Yet that girl works midway between the window and the machine, in the very center of the volume of dust, sixty hours a week. These are a few of the occupations in which the dangers arise from the forced inhalation of dust.[6]

Increasing awareness of the abuse and exploitation accompanying child labor produced demands for reform. At the beginning of the nineteenth century, industrial working conditions for both children and adults had been largely un-regulated, and there were few legal limitations on child labor. In reaction to this situation, three primary groups pressed for reform. First, from as early as the 1830s, educators began insisting that work not interfere with a child's formal education. Pressure for compulsory education began to grow at the same time as pressure for child labor laws, and the two movements developed alongside in the years from 1830 to 1930. Second, in the late nineteenth century and early twentieth century, increasing numbers of middle-class "progressive" reformers came to oppose child labor as physically dangerous to the child, destructive of family values, and incon-sistent with the child's and society's own long-run interests. Third, in the same period, many in the labor movement, and some economists as well, pressed for child labor laws on the grounds that unregulated child labor depressed wages for adult workers and hindered efforts to organize a strong labor movement through which improvements for adult workers might be won. Labor groups also stressed the humanitarian concerns of the progressive reformers.

State Reform

Efforts for legislative reform began at the state level. The first reform cam-paigns concentrated on ensuring children an education by requiring the factories to set up their own schools or to send the children to school for a specified number of hours each day or for a certain number of months a year. As early as 1813, Connecticut passed a law providing for the education of working children by the proprietors of manufacturing establishments in which children were employed. By 1860, at least five states had laws requiring children under 15 employed in manufacturing establishments to attend school for three months each year, and by 1930 38 states restricted child labor by requiring some kind of educational qualification for children entering employment. Direct regulation of the conditions of employment of children followed a similar pattern, becoming more widespread as knowledge increased of the harmful effects of working conditions on children. By 1860 eight states had laws restricting the number of hours a day that children could work. By 1930 most states had established minimum age requirements for

[6] John Spargo, The Bitter Cry of the Children 175-180 (1906), reprinted in 2 Children and Youth in America 641-642.

the employment of children and had reduced the allowable working hours to eight a day.[7]

Federal Reform

Shortly after the turn of the century, the child labor reform movements shifted their attention from local to national solutions. Although many states had adopted child labor laws, some of the laws were felt to be inadequate, and many states still lacked any regulations. This disparity at the state level was seen as creating an unhealthy economic competition: states with strict child labor laws saw themselves as being at a disadvantage, because they were forced to compete with other states where child labor produced goods of the same quality at a lower cost. States that contemplated adopting child labor laws were vulnerable to threats by manufacturers to move their plants to unregulated states. This unsatisfactory situation prompted reformers to seek national standards.

The first federal legislation passed to regulate child labor, the Keating-Owen bill of 1916, sought to prevent interstate commerce in the products of child labor.[8] In 1918, however, the Supreme Court declared the law unconstitutional on the grounds that (1) by aiming to regulate the production of goods rather than their transportation, the act exceeded the permissible scope of congressional authority over commerce, and (2) in aiming to prevent unfair competition, the act exerted a power as to a purely local matter, over which federal authority has no jurisdiction. Hammer v. Dagenhart, 247 U.S. 251 (1918). Shortly after this ruling, Congress again attempted to regulate child labor, this time by exercising its taxation power and imposing a 10 percent tax on all products of child labor.[9] This act, too, met with constitutional challenges and was repealed.[10] By this time the Supreme Court had also declared it to be unconstitutional on the grounds that because the tax represented a penalty aimed at regulating conduct that constitutionally it was for the states to regulate, the act exceeded the federal taxing power. The Child Labor Tax Case, 259 U.S. 20 (1922).

Frustrated by the Supreme Court's actions, reformers pressed for an amendment to the Constitution to empower Congress to regulate child labor directly. In 1924 Congress approved and submitted to the states for ratification the Child Labor Amendment, authorizing Congress to regulate the labor of persons under age 18.[11] The proposed amendment met with substantial opposition, and by 1931 it had been rejected by 38 states and ratified by only six. In 1933, however, interest in the amendment was rekindled (no doubt by the effects of the Depression and the coming of the "New Deal"), and 14 more states ratified the amendment. Because 12 of these had previously rejected it, their action raised new constitutional challenges and delays.

---

[7] United States Children's Bureau, Child Labor Facts and Figures, Pub. L. No. 197, pp. 4-8 (Washington D.C. 1930), reprinted in 2 Children and Youth in America 666-667.

[8] Child Labor Act of 1916, 39 Stat. 675 (1916).

[9] Child Labor Tax Act, 40 Stat. 1148 (1918).

[10] See 42 Stat. 321 (1921).

[11] 43 Stat. 670(1924).

The questions concerning the proposed constitutional amendment became moot when in 1938 Congress enacted the Fair Labor Standards Act, with its provision relating to "oppressive child labor." In United States v. Darby, 312 U.S. 100 (1940), the Supreme Court upheld the constitutionality of this act, expressly overruling Hammer v. Dagenhart.

Though the Fair Labor Standards Act is a landmark in the regulation of child labor, in its original form it represented only a modest achievement. Because of its broad exemptions (including a total exemption for agricultural employment outside school hours) and the indirectness of its prohibition of the products of child labor, "[i]t is estimated that of the approximately 850,000 children under 16 gainfully employed in 1938, only about 50,000 were subject to the act. Children in industrial agriculture, intrastate industries, the street trades, messenger and delivery service, stores, hotels, restaurants, beauty parlors, bowling alleys, filling stations, garages, etc., were outside the law."[12]

The limitations of the law were further revealed in one of the earliest cases brought under it, Western Union Telegraph v. Lenroot, 323 U.S. 490 (1945). This case involved the question of whether the Western Union Telegraph Company should be restrained from submitting its messages in interstate commerce because it (1) employed some messengers under 16 years of age and (2) permitted messengers between the ages of 16 and 18 to drive motor vehicles. The Court ruled that the legislative history was inconclusive as to the congressional purpose but that the language of the statute providing that "no producer . . . shall ship or deliver for shipment in commerce any goods produced in any establishment" did not apply to the transmission of telegraph messages. As far as its child labor provisions were concerned, the act seems rather to have confirmed a social reality than to have initiated significant reform.

For a historical analysis of the effectiveness of early child labor restrictions, see Adriana Lleras-Muney, Were Compulsory Attendance and Child Labor Laws Effective?, An Analysis From 1915 to 1939, 45 J.L. & Econ. 401 (2002).

2. Contemporary Regulation of Child Labor

Every state now has laws regulating child labor, though they vary considerably in their details. The basic feature of these laws is the minimum age at which a minor can be employed: Typically, the minimum age is 14 for safe work outside of school hours, 16 for work in industrial plants or for work during school hours. Many state laws prohibit or restrict the employment of minors in specified occupations considered hazardous, in specified establishments, or with specified machinery. Most states limit the number of hours and designate the hours between which minors of various ages can work. Many states require minors to have a working permit or educational certificate from either the local school system or from a government

---

[12] Youth: Transition to Adulthood, Report of the Panel on Youth of the President's Science Advisory Committee (Chicago and London: University of Chicago Press, 1972), p. 36.

official to be employed.[13] Further, many state child labor laws are connected to compulsory school attendance laws that proscribe minimum ages for withdrawal from school.[14]

Fair Labor Standards Act
29 U.S.C. §§203, 212 & 213 (2000 & Supp. 2005)

§203(1): Definitions

"Oppressive child labor" means a condition of employment under which

(1) any employee under the age of sixteen years is employed by an employer (other than a parent or a person standing in place of a parent employing his own child or a child in his custody under the age of sixteen years in an occupation other than manufacturing or mining or an occupation found by the Secretary of Labor to be particularly hazardous for the employment of children between the ages of sixteen and eighteen years or detrimental to their health or well-being) in any occupation, or

(2) any employee between the ages of sixteen and eighteen years is employed by an employer in any occupation which the Secretary of Labor shall find and by order declare to be particularly hazardous for the employment of children between such ages or detrimental to their health or well-being. . . . The Secretary of Labor shall provide by regulation or by order that the employment of employees between the ages of fourteen and sixteen years in occupations other than manufacturing and mining shall not be deemed to constitute oppressive child labor if and to the extent that the Secretary determines that such employment is confined to periods which will not interfere with their schooling and to conditions which will not interfere with their health and well-being.

§212: Child Labor Provisions

(a) No producer, manufacturer, or dealer shall ship or deliver for shipment in commerce any goods produced in an establishment situated in the United States in or about which within 30 days prior to the removal of such goods therefrom any oppressive child labor has been employed: *Provided,* That any such shipment or

---

[13] See Sy Moskowitz, American Youth in the Workplace: Legal Aberration, Failed Social Policy, 67 Alb. L. Rev. 1071, 1077-1078 (2004) (reporting that 18 states limit employment of children under age 16; 27 states require parental consent for employment of children of designated ages; 36 states allow children aged 16 and 17 to work 40 hours or more while school is in session). See generally U.S. General Accounting Office, Child Labor: Labor Can Strengthen Its Efforts to Protect Children Who Work (Sept. 2002), available at *http://www.gao.gov/new.items/d02880.pdf* (last visited Jan. 14, 2009).

[14] Most states give parents the right to notice and to consent for children to drop out of school; however, a large number of states allow 16-year-olds to make this decision. Moskowitz, supra note [13], at 1078.

delivery for shipment of such goods by a purchaser who acquired them in good faith in reliance on written assurance from the producer, manufacturer, or dealer that the goods were produced in compliance with the requirements of this section, and who acquired such goods for value without notice of any such violation, shall not be deemed prohibited by this subsection. . . .

(b) The Secretary of Labor, or any of his authorized representatives, shall make all investigations and inspections under section 211 (a) of this title with respect to the employment of minors, and, subject to the direction and control of the Attorney General, shall bring all actions under section 217 of this title to enjoin any act or practice which is unlawful by reason of the existence of oppressive child labor, and shall administer all other provisions of this chapter relating to oppressive child labor.

(c) No employer shall employ any oppressive child labor in commerce or in the production of goods for commerce or in any enterprise engaged in commerce or in the production of goods for commerce.

(d) In order to carry out the objectives of this section, the Secretary may by regulation require employers to obtain from any employee proof of age.

§213: Exemptions From the Child Labor Provision

. . . (c)(1) Except as provided in paragraph (2) or (4), the provisions of section 212 of this title relating to child labor shall not apply to any employee employed in agriculture outside of school hours for the school district where such employee is living while he is so employed, if such employee —
> (A) is less than twelve years of age and
>> (i) is employed by his parent, or by a person standing in the place of his parent, on a farm owned or operated by such parent or person, or
>> (ii) is employed, with the consent of his parent or person standing in the place of his parent, on a farm, none of the employees of which are (because of subsection (a)(6)(A) of this section) required to be paid at the wage rate prescribed by section 206(a)(5) of this title,
> (B) is twelve years or thirteen years of age and
>> (i) such employment is with the consent of his parent or person standing in the place of his parent, or
>> (ii) his parent or such person is employed on the same farm as such employee, or
> (C) is fourteen years of age or older.

(2) The provisions of section 212 of this title relating to child labor shall apply to an employee below the age of sixteen employed in agriculture in an occupation that the Secretary of Labor finds and declares to be particularly hazardous for the employment of children below the age of sixteen, except where such employee is employed by his parent or by a person standing in the place of his parent on a farm owned or operated by such parent or person.

(3) The provisions of section 212 of this title relating to child labor shall not apply to any child employed as an actor or performer in motion pictures or theatrical productions, or in radio or television productions.

(4)(A) An employer or group of employers may apply to the Secretary for a waiver of the application of section 212 of this title to the employment for not more than eight weeks in any calendar year of individuals who are less than twelve years of age, but not less than ten years of age, as hand harvest laborers in an agricultural operation which has been, and is customarily and generally recognized as being, paid on a piece rate basis in the region in which such individuals would be employed. The Secretary may not grant such a waiver unless he finds, based on objective data submitted by the applicant, that —

(i) the crop to be harvested is one with a particularly short harvesting season and the application of section 212 of this title would cause severe economic disruption in the industry of the employer or group of employers applying for the waiver;

(ii) the employment of the individuals to whom the waiver would apply would not be deleterious to their health or well-being;

(iii) the level and type of pesticides and other chemicals used would not have an adverse effect on the health or well-being of the individuals to whom the waiver would apply;

(iv) individuals age twelve and above are not available for such employment; and

(v) the industry of such employer or group of employers has traditionally and substantially employed individuals under twelve years of age without displacing substantial job opportunities for individuals over sixteen years of age.

(B) Any waiver granted by the Secretary under subparagraph (A) shall require that —

(i) the individuals employed under such waiver be employed outside of school hours for the school district where they are living while so employed;

(ii) such individuals while so employed commute daily from their permanent residence to the farm on which they are so employed; and

(iii) such individuals be employed under such waiver (I) for not more than eight weeks between June 1 and October 15 of any calendar year, and (II) in accordance with such other terms and conditions as the Secretary shall prescribe for such individuals' protection.

(d) The provisions of sections . . . 212 of this title shall not apply with respect to any employee engaged in the delivery of newspapers to the consumer or to any homeworker engaged in the making of wreaths composed principally of natural holly, pine, cedar, or other evergreens (including the harvesting of the evergreens or other forest products used in making such wreaths). . . .

NOTES AND QUESTIONS CONCERNING THE CONSEQUENCES OF CHILD LABOR VIOLATIONS

(1) Sanctions. If a young person works illegally, what sanctions should be imposed? A variety of penalties and remedies is often available. The most

commonly employed remedy for a violation of the federal statute is injunctive relief against the employer enjoining future employment of minors. Federal and state child labor laws also provide for criminal sanctions; see 29 U.S.C. §216(a) (2000 & Supp. 2004) (allowing fines of up to $10,000 for a willful violation or imprisonment for not more than one month, or both); civil fines may also be imposed. See 29 U.S.C. §216(e) (2000 & Supp. 2004) and Cal. Lab. Code §§1287-1288 (West 2003).

In 1990 Congress amended the child labor provisions of the Fair Labor Standards Act. The amendments provided for an expansion of civil penalties, that is, increasing the maximum civil penalty for a nonwillful violation from $1,000 to $10,000. 29 U.S.C. §216(e) (2000 & Supp. 2004). Also in 1990, then Secretary of Labor Elizabeth Dole initiated increased federal efforts (termed "Operation Child Watch") to identify violations of the child labor regulations. The Child Labor Protection Act of 2007, currently pending in the Senate, would increase civil penalties for violations of child labor laws. 153 Cong. Rec. H. 6250-6251, 110th Cong., 1st Sess. (2007).

Recent years have witnessed additional attempts to amend the Fair Labor Standards Act regarding child labor. In 1998, Congress passed the Drive for Teen Employment Act to amend the Fair Labor Standards Act for the protection of teenage employee-drivers. The legislation prohibits employees under 17 years of age from driving automobiles or trucks on public roadways except in daylight hours, provided that the automobile or truck does not exceed 6,000 pounds of gross vehicle weight and that the driving is not beyond a 30-mile radius from the employee's place of employment and is occasional and incidental to the employee's employment. Drive for Teen Employment Act, 29 U.S.C. §213(c)(6) (2000 & Supp. 2004).

In addition, Representative Tom Lantos (D.-Cal.) and 57 cosponsors unsuccessfully proposed The Young American Workers' Bill of Rights Act, H.R. 2119, 106th Cong., 1st Sess. (1999). The bill proposed to amend the Fair Labor Standards Act by requiring a minor to obtain certification from the state verifying age, school enrollment, and parental consent; limiting the number of hours per day that a minor can work; and prohibiting minors from working before 6 A.M. and after 10 P.M. while school is in session.

In December 2003, Lantos dedicated another bill (the Youth Worker Protection Act, H.R. 3139) to the memory of Adam Carey, a 16-year-old boy who died as the result of an accident on a golf course where he was illegally driving a golf cart. Lantos cited statistics from the National Institute for Occupational Safety and Health stating than an average of 67 teenagers die annually from employment-related injuries and 230,000 teens are injured each year. 149 Cong. Rec. E. 2501-02, 108th Cong., 1st Sess. (2003). The bill was reintroduced in the House of Representatives in 2005 (H.R. 2870), but never went to a vote. The bill proposed the same minimum age for children in agricultural and nonagricultural employment, a uniform minimum age for all hazardous occupations, and new requirements for notification of work-related injuries, among other changes to the Fair Labor Standards Act.

Finally, Congress has repeatedly considered the Child Labor Deterrence Act (CLDA), first proposed in 1989 (S. 1551, 106th Cong., 1st Sess. (1999)). The

CLDA would prohibit the entry into the United States of goods produced abroad by child labor. The Act provides that any importer of such goods be fined or jailed. It also provides that the Secretary of Labor shall compile an annual report that identifies countries that condone the use of children under the age of 15 in manufacturing or mining to boycott all manufactured articles by that country. Commentators note that the legislation has little chance of passage because of concerns about its effect on international relations. See generally William E. Myers, The Right Rights? Child Labor in a Globalizing World, 575 Annals 38 (2001).

(2) Liability.   Who should be held responsible for violations of the child labor law? The employer? The child? Parents?

a. Employer.   Sanctions are most commonly directed at employers. Should an employer be held responsible for violating the child labor provisions when the employer lacks knowledge that the young person is underage? Must the employer inquire? Compare American Belt Co. v. W.C.A.B., 755 A.2d 77 (Pa. 2000) (employer liable for 50% penalty under state law if it knew or should have known that employee was a minor), with Beard v. Lee Enterprises, Inc., 591 N. W.2d 156 (Wis. Sup. Ct. 1999) (refusing to impose tort liability on employer for minor's negligence unless employer had actual or constructive knowledge of employment relationship with minor).

b. Parents.   In some jurisdictions parents may be subject to criminal sanctions if they permit their child to be employed in violation of the child labor laws. See, e.g., Cal. Lab. Code §1303 (West 2003). Is this consistent with provisions in some child labor laws that allow minors to work under parental supervision in otherwise prohibited or restricted occupations? Should parental consent preempt application of the child labor laws?

c. The Child.   Federal and state laws appear not to contain express provisions subjecting a minor to criminal sanctions for a violation of child labor provisions. Why shouldn't the minor be held responsible, especially in cases where the minor obtains work through misrepresenting age? If a minor accepted a job knowing that the child labor laws were being violated, would this justify a determination by a juvenile court that the minor was a delinquent? See Chapter 7 for a discussion of delinquency. Could a juvenile court take jurisdiction over the young person on the ground that he was "in need of supervision" or "beyond parental control?" See infra p. 733.

(3) Compensation for Injury.   If an illegally employed young person is injured on the job, what recovery is available? Should the child labor violation be sufficient proof of employer negligence to allow tort recovery for the youth's personal injury? Should the employer be able to assert as defenses that the young person "assumed the risk" or was "contributorily negligent," or that the child's parents had consented to the employment? See Fire Ins. Exch. v. Cincinnati Ins. Co., 610 N.W.2d 98 (Wis. Ct. App. 2000) (holding employer strictly liable for violation of child labor law regardless of fault of child employee).

The workers' compensation laws of approximately one-third of the states require employers to pay extra compensation (often double) for a minor who is injured while illegally employed. (See, e.g., Mich. Comp. Laws Ann. §418.161(1)(l) (West 1999 & Supp. 2008).) Some states provide that this additional compensation cannot be covered by insurance, and that the employer must be liable. See e.g., N.J. Stat. Ann. §34:15-10 (2000 & Supp. 2008). See also Dugan v. General Servs. Co., 799 So. 2d 760 (3d Cir. 2004) (workers' compensation is exclusive remedy even though minor was employed illegally). See generally Ronald B. Grayzel, Department Off the Beaten Track: A Primer on Child Labor Torts, 216 N.J. Law. 38 (2002); Annotation, Workers' Compensation Statute as Barring Illegally Employed Minor's Tort Action, 77 A.L.R. 4th 844, 848-849 (1990 & Supp. 2004).

(4) Reexamining Child Labor Laws.   Legal challenges to the Fair Labor Standards Act have been infrequent. Likewise, state child labor laws have gone largely unchallenged or revised. In light of the changing social, economic, and legal status of youth, do these laws represent an undue restraint on children's rights?[15] Should children be treated differently from adults in the area of employment? Can we still justify the restrictions embodied in the child labor laws? Whose rights and what rights are at stake? Examine the following arguments in favor of child labor restrictions:

- Children need to be protected from physical harm.
- Sending children to work at an early age prevents them from securing an education essential for their development.
- Child labor produces harmful effects on society as a whole.

A reexamination of the bases of existing child labor laws suggests several alternatives to the present system. Consider each of the following possibilities and the problems it raises:

- Eliminate all age-based restrictions and give children the same freedom to work as adults, relying on regulations of general applicability to protect both children and adults.
- Maintain the current age-based provisions, but allow a broad exemption whenever parents consent to the employment of their minor children.
- Maintain the current age-based regulations, but allow a broad exemption whenever it can be shown that the minor needs to work to support his or her family.

C. *DRIVING PRIVILEGES*

1. Introduction

Minors are allowed to drive in every state, although age-based limits are universally imposed. The laws relating to driving by minors reflect various social

---

[15] In 2001, approximately 3.7 million youths aged 15 to 17 were employed in the United States. Further, the United States has the highest percentage of employed youth of any developed nation. Cited in id., at 1071.

concerns: the need for protection of the public from unsafe drivers; the need for easily administered rules; the need to hold someone financially responsible for the costs of accidents; and the economic and social importance of transportation to minors, their families, and employers.

In reading through the material that follows, consider these questions: How are power and responsibility for a minor's driving allocated? How are minors treated differently from adults, and why are they so treated? What power and responsibility do minors themselves have? To what extent does the law give the parent responsibility? What special limitations on the minor's liberty does the state impose? What social interests are reflected in the allocation of power?

Age Limits

Every state imposes age restrictions on driving, which vary according to the type of activity involved. The usual practice is to give regular licenses to minors between ages 15 and 17 (usually 16); however, these licenses do not extend to driving for hire, driving oversized vehicles (usually an 18-year-old minimum), or driving a school bus (often a 21-year-old minimum). Special permits are also available for learning to drive. These are sometimes available to persons as young as 14 years old, provided that a parent or certified teacher accompanies the learner.

Many states will give restricted licenses to minors as young as 14 years old if they can show a special need (to go to school or to provide for a needy family) or are employed on a family farm. Such licenses cannot be used for any purpose other than that specified in the restrictions. See, e.g., Cal. Veh. Code §12513 (West 2000).

What should be the minimum driving age, given the existence of competence testing?

Special Rules for Minors Old Enough to Be Eligible for Licenses

Although the states recognize the desirability of giving minors driving privileges, state laws do *not* simply treat minors above the cutoff age exactly like adults. The following are a few examples. What social interests do these rules reflect? Should similar rules apply to adults?

(1) Many states require any driver under 18 to complete driver education (in a classroom) or driver training (behind the wheel). See e.g., Cal. Veh. Code §12509 (West 2000 & Supp. 2008).

(2) Most states make it easier to suspend or revoke the license of minor drivers. In New York, for example, a minor who becomes a ward of the family court as a "youthful offender" may have the license suspended for up to one year (N. Y. Veh. & Traf. Law (Consol.) §510(3)(j) (McKinney 1996 & Supp. 2008)). Colorado uses a point system for all drivers in determining suspensions or revocations. A minor in that jurisdiction loses his or her license after collecting far fewer points than older drivers would have to accumulate (Colo. Rev. Stat. §42-2-127 (West 2004 & Supp. 2007). Many states impose a suspension of license or even impound the car if a minor possesses alcoholic beverages while driving, whether or not the bottle is open. See e.g., Cal. Veh. Code §23224 (West 2000 & Supp. 2004).

(3) Some states have curfew laws affecting young drivers. In Illinois, no one under 17 may be on the streets or highways between 11:00 P.M. and 6:00 A.M. on Sunday to Friday, and 12:01 A.M. and 6:00 A.M. on Saturday and Sunday. However, the statute has two exceptions: minors may be on the streets during curfew hours if they are (1) accompanied by a parent, legal guardian, or other responsible companion at least 18 years of age who has been approved by the minor's parent or guardian; or (2) engaged in some business activity that the law allows them to perform during those hours (Ill. Stat. Ann. ch. 720 ¶555/1(a) (West 2003)). In Massachusetts, a minor under age 18 cannot drive between 12:30 A.M. and 5:00 A.M. unless accompanied by a parent or legal guardian (Mass. Gen. Laws Ann. ch. 90, §8 (West 2001 & Supp. 2008)).

(4) Nearly all states have three-tier *graduated licensing* statutes for minors. Typical statutes specify: (1) minors of a minimum specified age are able to obtain a *learner's permit* provided that they pass vision and knowledge tests, drive at all times with a licensed adult who is at least age 21, never drive while intoxicated, and remain crash- and conviction-free for six months; (2) minors of a minimum specified age are able to obtain a *provisional license* provided that they pass a road test, never drive while intoxicated, drive during night hours only with a licensed adult, and remain crash- and conviction-free for 12 months; and (3) minors are able to obtain a *full license* by completing the previous stage and reaching the specified age. Research reveals that graduated licensing programs reduce automobile accidents significantly, although minors continue to have the highest rate of fatal crashes. Limits on Teenage Drivers Lower Accidents, Data Show, N.Y. Times, Feb. 19, 2003 (data from the National Safety Council reveals a 33% decrease in accident rate in states with such programs). See generally Christine Branche et al., Graduated Licensing for Teens: Why Everybody's Doing It, 30 J.L. Med. & Ethics 146 (2002); Carol Jones, Note: The Unintended Consumer: Protecting Teen Drivers Through Graduated Licensing Laws, 15 Loy. Consumer L. Rev. 163 (2003).

By enacting these statutes, is the state venturing into an area of supervision that is best left to parents? Alternatively, do such statutes violate minors' constitutional rights? See Robert Diaz de Leon, California's Teen Driving Law: Violation of Constitutional Rights?, 21 J. Juv. L. 86 (2000).

2.   The Necessity of Parental Consent and Implied Parental Liability

Jackson v. Houchin
144 S.W.3d 764 (Ark. Ct. App. 2004)

Robert J. GLADWIN, Judge.

On March 15, 1996, appellant Freddie Jackson signed a driver's license application for his cousin, Charles Jackson, who was a minor at that time. Under the provisions of Ark. Code Ann. §27-16-702 (Supp. 1995), appellant was not authorized to sign the application for Charles because the boy's mother was living and appellant did not have custody or guardianship of him. On August 5, 1996, Charles was involved in an automobile accident with appellee David Houchin. Appellee filed a negligence suit, naming appellant as a co-defendant. A jury found for appellee on his complaint against Charles Jackson and appellant Freddie Jackson, and assessed damages in the amount of $11,088.55, plus costs. Appellant contends on appeal that because he was not authorized to sign the application of the minor, he cannot be held liable for the minor's negligent conduct. We affirm.

Arkansas Code Annotated section 27-16-702 (Supp. 1995) provides in relevant part:

> (a)(1)(A) The original application of any person under the age of eighteen (18) years for an instruction permit, driver's license, motor-driven cycle or motorcycle license shall be signed and verified before a person authorized to administer oaths by either the father or mother of the applicant, if either is living and has custody.
>
> (B) In the event neither parent is living or has custody, then the application shall be signed by the person or guardian having custody or by an employer of the minor.
>
> (C) In the event there is no guardian or employer, then the application shall be signed by any other responsible person who is willing to assume the obligations imposed under this subchapter upon a person signing the application of a minor. . . .
>
> (b) Any negligence or willful misconduct of a minor under the age of eighteen (18) years when driving a motor vehicle upon a highway shall be imputed to the person who signed the application of the minor for a permit or license, *regardless of whether the person who signed was authorized to sign under subsection (a) of this section,* which person shall be jointly and severally liable with the minor for any damages caused by negligence or willful misconduct. (Emphasis added.)

In arguing that he cannot be held liable under the above statutory provisions because, under these same provisions, he was not authorized to sign the application, appellant is seeking to benefit from his wrongdoing. The language of the statute makes it clear that even though appellant was not authorized to sign for the minor, once he did sign, he became jointly and severally liable for any damages suffered as a result of the minor's negligence.

Appellant cites two cases to support his contention that he cannot be held liable for the minor's negligence, neither of which is applicable here. The first is Richardson v. Donaldson, 220 Ark. 173, 246 S.W.2d 551 (1952), wherein the father of the minor did not sign an application, but did allow his daughter, who had no driver's license, to drive his vehicle. The court said that negligence could not be imputed to the father under a statutory provision similar to the one in the case now before us because the father had never signed an application. Letting his daughter drive without a license was a misdemeanor, and while violation of the traffic laws was evidence of negligence, it did not establish negligence as a matter of law. The statutory provisions imputing negligence did not apply because Richardson, unlike appellant, had never signed an application at all.

Appellant also cites Jones v. Davis, 300 Ark. 130, 777 S.W.2d 582 (1989). In *Jones,* a vehicle driven by seventeen-year-old Charles Volpert struck a motorcycle driven by Mark Jones. Volpert's mother, Barbara Davis, had signed Volpert's application for a driver's license. Jones contended that Charles Davis, Volpert's stepfather, stood in loco parentis to Volpert; was required to sign Volpert's application; and was liable for his stepson's negligence. The language of the statute in effect at that time required that either parent, if living, sign a minor's application for a driver's license. Only if neither parent was living would anyone else be authorized to sign. Volpert's mother and father were both living, and his mother signed the application. Davis was neither required nor authorized under the statute to sign the application, and had not done so. The court found that Davis could not be held liable under the statute for his stepson's negligence.

The distinction between *Jones* and the case before us is obvious: Davis did not sign an application, while appellant herein did sign the application for his minor cousin. The act of signing the application brought appellant within the purview of the statute, and appellant cannot now say he should be excused from the liability incurred under the statutory provisions because he acted in a manner not authorized by that statute. Affirmed.

NOTES AND QUESTIONS

(1) Parental Consent — Imputed Liability. Most states insist on parental consent before a minor may obtain a driver's license and require parental signatures on the minor's application. This requirement gives the parents control over their children's activities and in many jurisdictions serves as a basis for imputing the child's negligence to the consenting adult(s). The statutes sometimes allow someone other than the parent to consent. In some states, a parent's, guardian's, or employer's signature is sufficient, no matter who has custody. A few states allow a "responsible person" to sign the application if there is no parent, guardian, or employer.

As *Jackson* illustrates, in many states imputed liability for a minor's negligence or willful misconduct while driving is imposed on whoever signs a minor's application for a license. This measure is viewed as a further protection of the public and as an inducement to provide closer supervision of a minor's driving. Is it realistic to expect such supervision?

Suppose the minor's driver's license has been revoked by the state but the minor nevertheless continues to drive. Should this discharge the liability of a parent who signed the license application for the minor's negligence while driving? See Keating v. Hollstein, 557 N.E.2d 1253 (Ohio 1990) (holding that mother's permission automatically terminated upon revocation of her son's driving privileges).

(2) Emancipation. Some statutes allow a parent to withdraw the driving privileges of a minor even if emancipated, despite his or her increased need for independent transportation. Some jurisdictions provide exceptions to imputed liability for married or emancipated minors. Compare Lay v. Suggs, 559 So. 2d 740 (Fla. Dist. Ct. App. 1990) (emancipation terminates signatory's vicarious liability) with State Auto. Ins. Co. v. Reynolds, 32 S.W.3d 508 (Ky. Ct. App. 2000) (holding father liable for negligent acts of emancipated daughter). In California emancipated minors may verify their own applications if they can provide proof of financial responsibility (Cal. Veh. Code §17705 (West 2000 & Supp. 2004)). If a minor, whether or not emancipated, can provide proof of sufficient financial responsibility, why should parental consent be required as a condition for a license?

3. Parental Negligence and Other Special Liability Provisions

Dortman v. Lester
155 N.W.2d 846 (Mich. 1968)

SOURIS, Justice:

This appeal involves two cases brought in behalf of the Dortmans to recover damages from the defendants for injuries suffered by Mrs. Dortman when the car in which she was riding was struck from the rear by a car driven by defendant Barre Lester, the 18-year-old [minor] son of the other defendants. Title to the car Barre Lester was driving was in his name and his mother's. Plaintiffs planted their claim against defendant father on the theory that he was casually negligent in permitting his son to drive a car knowing that the son was an incompetent driver and that the father's negligence and the son's negligence were concurrent proximate causes of Mrs. Dortman's injuries. . . .

. . . The circuit judge granted summary judgments dismissing the actions against defendant father for failure to state causes of action against him. The Court of Appeals affirmed.

Following the Court of Appeals decision in this case, this Court decided Muma v. Brown (1967), 378 Mich. 637, 148 N.W.2d 760. We divided equally on the sufficiency of proofs to support the jury's verdict in favor of plaintiff. The dissenters who voted for reversal considered the crucial legal issue on the appeal to be the applicability of the rule of negligent entrustment to the facts of the case. The Justices who joined in the controlling opinion, on the other hand, like the circuit judge and the Court of Appeals, considered the legal issue to be whether parents are liable for the negligent acts of their children resulting from the parents' negligent failure to exercise parental supervision. See their opinion at [378 Mich. at 644] where it is said that the question was one of first impression. If the question addressed by the Justices who joined in the controlling opinion was a negligent entrustment question, then clearly it was not one of first impression. They were, instead, addressing the issue of parental liability, in a case in which the rules of negligent entrustment would have been adequate to support plaintiffs' claim.

In discussing the issue of parental liability, those Justices who joined in the controlling opinion quite properly did so in the factual context of the *Muma* case, in which the parents happened to own the vehicle with which their child negligently committed atortious injury. The fact of the parents' ownership and control of the vehicle was legally irrelevant to the legal issue of their parental liability, although it would have been legally relevant to their liability under the rules of negligent entrustment. Unfortunately, the controlling opinion's language seems to limit its otherwise valid conclusions regarding parental liability for a child's negligent operation of a motor vehicle only to those situations in which the parents not only can exercise control over the child, but, also can control the availability of the motor vehicle to the child. While I do not believe such limitation is legally justifiable, I concede the case of Muma v. Brown, supra, does not contribute much to our decision herein. We must, instead, look elsewhere for our authority.

Earlier, in May v. Goulding (1961), 365 Mich. 143, 111 N.W.2d 862, this Court cited and applied, among others, the following authorities pertinent to the issue framed by the pleadings in this case of *Dortman:*

1.   Harper and James, Law of Torts, §8.13, p. 662:

Aside from the relationship of master and servant, the parent may be liable for harm inflicted by a child under circumstances that constitute negligence on the part of the parent. This, of course, is not a case of responsibility of a parent for the child's tort, but liability for his own wrong. . . .

2.   Restatement of Torts, §316:

§316. Duty of Parent to Control Conduct of Child

A parent is under a duty to exercise reasonable care so to control his minor child as to prevent it from intentionally harming others or from so conducting itself as to create an unreasonable risk of bodily harm to them, if the parent (a) knows or has reason to know that he has the ability to control his child, and (b) knows or should know of the necessity and opportunity for exercising such control.

4.   Restatement of Torts, §877:

§877. A Person Directing or Permitting Conduct of Another

For harm resulting to a third person from the tortious conduct of another, a person is liable if he . . . (c) controls, or has a duty to use care to control, the conduct of another who is likely to do harm if not controlled, and fails to exercise care in such control. . . .

The theory upon which plaintiffs relied in these cases as against the defendant father is squarely within the above quoted rules of the common law. The motions for summary judgment, therefore, should not have been granted for failure to state causes of action. We reverse and remand to the circuit court for further proceedings. . . .

Kavanagh, Adams and Brennan, JJ., concurred with Souris, J.

O'Hara, Justice.

I disagree with Mr. Justice Souris. First, I am not in accord with his application of Muma v. Brown, 378 Mich. 637, 148 N.W.2d 760 (1967). I regard the case as inapposite.

In *Muma,* we were concerned with an unlicensed and inexperienced minor of the age of 14 driving the family automobile titled in the mother and father jointly. The theory of the plaintiff was that the parents were negligent in leaving the 14-year-old boy at home alone unsupervised for a week end, with a set of keys to the family car in the house.

In the case at bar the minor was 18 years of age. He was a licensed driver. The title to the automobile involved was in his name and the name of his mother. His license to drive was granted him by the State. He was legally entitled to be an owner and he was by the certificate of title a co-owner. His father was a stranger to the title and could not under any statute we have cited have prohibited his son from obtaining title thereto legally, nor legally could he compel his son as co-owner to divest himself of his co-ownership. This is a far factual cry from the situation presented in *Muma*.

With the general principles quoted by Justice Souris I have no basic disagreement. In the pleaded factual context of this case I do not think they control. Plaintiff alleged as to the father only that Barre E. Lester was under 21, and "was subject to the orders, direction and control of his parents." Literally, such a legal conclusion can hardly be challenged. It is little more than a restatement of the parent-child relationship. Such relationship does not per se render a parent liable for the tort of a child. . . .

I would affirm the Court of Appeals. . . .

NOTE: OTHER SPECIAL LIABILITY PROVISIONS

Under the common law parents were not held liable for the consequences of the torts of their minor children solely because of the existence of the parent-child relationship. See 59 Am. Jur. 2d. Parent and Child §116 (1987). Exceptions to this traditional rule were developed when a parent (1) participated in the minor's tort, (2) permitted the tort to occur as the result of the parent's negligent supervision of the minor, or (3) maintained some additional relationship with the child (such as principal and agent) that allowed imputation of the child's negligence.

Apart from imputed liability and parental negligence in controlling their child, most states apply other doctrines (explained below) in certain circumstances to impose responsibility for a minor's negligence on parents or others.

(1) Family Car Doctrine. If a head of household makes his or her auto available to other members of the family, his or her consent is assumed and vicarious liability may be imposed. This does not extend to a car owned by a minor or one provided for the minor and under his or her exclusive control. See, e.g., Aurbach v. Giallina, 753 So. 2d 60 (Fla. 2000); McPhee v. Tuffy, 623 N.W.2d 390 (N.D. 2001).

(2) Expressed or Implied Permission. Most states impose liability on the parents or persons with custody of minors if they give expressed or implied permission to their children to drive in violation of state law. California extends this doctrine to include all parental permission regardless of any violations (Cal. Veh. Code §17708 (West 2000)).

(3) Negligent Entrustment. Any person who negligently and knowingly supplies, entrusts, permits, or lends a vehicle to an incompetent or habitually careless driver may be held liable for negligent entrustment. Such liability arises out of the combined negligence of the owner and the driver—negligence of the owner entrusting the vehicle to the incompetent driver and negligence of the driver in its operation. See Joseph v. Dickerson, 754 So. 2d 912 (La. 2000).

(4) Providing an Unlicensed Minor with a Motor Vehicle. Any person (whether or not a parent) supplying a minor with a vehicle to drive when the minor is not licensed to do so usually faces liability. See State v. King, 620 N.E.2d 306 (Ohio Mun. Ct. 1993).

4. The Minor's Liability: Standard of Care for Adult Activities

Dellwo v. Pearson
107 N.W.2d 859 (Minn. 1961)

LOEVINGER, Justice.

This case arises out of a personal injury to Jeanette E. Dellwo, one of the plaintiffs. She and her husband, the other plaintiff, were fishing on one of Minnesota's numerous and beautiful lakes by trolling at a low speed with about 40 to 50 feet of line trailing behind the boat. Defendant, a 12-year-old boy, operating a boat with an outboard motor, crossed behind plaintiffs' boat. Just at this time Mrs. Dellwo felt a jerk on her line which suddenly was pulled out very rapidly. The line was knotted to the spool of the reel so that when it had run out the fishing rod was pulled downward, the reel hit the side of the boat, the reel came apart, and part of it flew through the lens of Mrs. Dellwo's glasses and injured her eye. Both parties then proceeded to a dock where inspection of defendant's motor disclosed 2 to 3 feet of fishing line wound about the propeller.

The case was . . . submitted to the jury upon instructions which, in so far as relevant here, instructed . . . : (1) In considering the matter of negligence the duty to which defendant is held is modified because he is a child, a child not being held to the same standard of conduct as an adult and being required to exercise only that degree of care which ordinarily is exercised by children of like age, mental capacity, and experience under the same or similar circumstances; (2) "A person guilty of negligence is liable for all consequences which might reasonably have been foreseen as likely to result from one's negligent act or omissions under the circumstances. . . . A wrongdoer is not responsible for a consequence which is merely possible according to occasional experience, but only for a consequence which is probable according to ordinary and usual experience." . . . Several hours after the jury retired it returned and asked for additional instructions with respect to "foreseeable responsibility" and "the responsibility of a youngster compared to a more mature person." The court thereupon repeated the instructions relating to negligence, the standard of care, and proximate cause, including the language quoted above.

The jury returned a general verdict for defendant, and plaintiffs appeal. Plaintiffs contend that the trial court erred in its instruction that a defendant is not responsible for unforeseen consequences of negligence. . . .

The instruction of the trial court limiting liability for negligence to foreseeable consequences was a part of the instruction on proximate cause and, in effect, made foreseeability of a test of proximate cause. . . .

[The court reversed the trial court's judgment because the trial court erred in making foreseeability the test of proximate cause.]

Since the case must be retried, it is appropriate for us to indicate the principles which should govern the submission upon a second trial. . . .

[An] important point involves the instruction that defendant was to be judged by the standard of care of a child of similar age rather than of a reasonable man. There is no doubt that the instruction given substantially reflects the language of numerous decisions in this and other courts. However, the great majority of these cases involve the issue of contributory negligence and the standard of care that may properly be required of a child in protecting himself against some hazard. The standard of care stated is proper and appropriate for such situations.

However, this court has previously recognized that there may be a difference between the standard of care that is required of a child in protecting himself against hazards and the standard that may be applicable when his activities expose others to hazards. Certainly in the circumstances of modern life, where vehicles moved by powerful motors are readily available and frequently operated by immature individuals, we should be skeptical of a rule that would allow motor vehicles to be operated to the hazard of the public with less than the normal minimum degree of care and competence.

To give legal sanction to the operation of automobiles by teen-agers with less than ordinary care for safety of others is impractical today, to say the least. We may take judicial notice of the hazards of automobile traffic, the frequency of accidents, the often catastrophic results of accidents, and the fact that immature individuals are no less prone to accidents than adults. While minors are entitled to be judged by standards commensurate with age, experience, and wisdom when engaged in activities appropriate to their age, experience, and wisdom, it would be unfair to the public to permit a minor in the operation of a motor vehicle to observe any other standards of care and conduct than those expected of all others. A person observing children at play with toys, throwing balls, operating tricycles cycles or velocipedes, or engaged in other childhood activities may anticipate conduct that does not reach an adult standard of care of prudence. However, one cannot know whether the operator of an approaching automobile, airplane, or powerboat is a minor or an adult, and usually cannot protect himself against youthful imprudence even if warned. Accordingly, we hold that in the operation of an automobile, airplane, or powerboat, a minor is to be held to the same standard of care as an adult.

Undoubtedly there are problems attendant upon such a view. However, there are problems in any rule that may be adopted applicable to this matter. They will have to be solved as they may present themselves in the setting of future cases. The latest tentative revision of the Restatement of Torts proposes an even broader rule that would hold a child to adult standards whenever he engages "in an activity which is normally undertaken only by adults, and for which adult qualifications are required." [§238A, comment c] However, it is unnecessary to this case to adopt arule in such broad form, and, therefore, we expressly leave open the question whether or not that rule should be adopted in this state. For the present it is sufficient to say that no reasonable grounds for differentiating between automobiles, airplanes, and powerboats appears, and that a rule requiring a single standard of care in the operation of such vehicles, regardless of the age of the operator, appears to us to be required by the circumstances of contemporary life.

Reversed and remanded for new trial.

5. The Standard of Care for the Negligence of Minors

The Restatement (Third) of Torts §10 (Proposed Final Draft No. 1, Apr. 6, 2005) reads as follows:

(a) A child's conduct is negligent if it does not conform to that of a reasonably careful person of the same age, intelligence, and experience, except as provided in Subsection (b) or (c).

(b) A child less than five years of age is incapable of negligence; and

(c) The special rule in Subsection (a) does not apply when the child is engaging in a dangerous activity that is characteristically undertaken by adults.

The justification for §10(a) is that children, because of their inexperience, have less ability to perceive the probable consequences of their acts or omissions than do adults. Although some courts still generally apply this conventional standard (which allows age and experience to be taken into account), the majority follows that expressed by §10(c) and the court in Dellwo v. Pearson, supra, p. 670, which found that the societal interest in protecting potential victims of negligence requires that there not be an age-based standard of care where a minor is performing an adult activity. See also Summerill v. Shipley, 890 P.2d 1042 (Utah Ct. App. 1995). Do you think the availability of liability insurance to cover people injured by minors should influence the standard of care applied to their behavior?

Traditionally, contributory negligence has been a bar to recovery by plaintiffs even though the defendant was negligent. When children are injured by negligent acts, a question arises concerning the standard to be applied when a minor is contributorily negligent. The so-called Massachusetts standard, which is the majority view, rejects the idea that age is the major factor in determining a child's capacity. The Massachusetts rule on contributory negligence, like the Restatement Rule on negligence, determines the capacity of the child to be contributorily negligent by comparing his intelligence, experience, and discretion with those of other children of the same age, intelligence, and experience, acting under the same or similar circumstances. Other courts, however, have adopted presumptions based on age and have held, for example, that a child below the age of seven cannot be held contributorily negligent.[16] Is it realistic to say that a child seven years old has absolutely no capacity to take care of himself? A majority of jurisdictions apply the "reasonable person of like age" standard to both negligence and contributory negligence. However, a few jurisdictions apply the adult standard of care for a child's negligence but the lesser standard for his contributory negligence. Does this rule make any sense?

Also consider whether it is not somehow inconsistent to apply an adult standard of care to minors who drive, see *Dellwo,* supra, p. 670, and at the same time impose imputed liability on parents who are formally empowered to withdraw a minor's license, see *Dortman,* supra, p. 667.

PROBLEM

On his 16th birthday, Larry Mosk passed his driver's test and received a license to drive. On the same day he purchased a 2004 Toyota from Allen Blum. Larry

---

[16] See generally Lori Rinella, Children and the Law: Children of Tender Years and Contributory Negligence, 63 UMKC L. Rev. 475 (1995). For a critical analysis of the Restatement rule, see John Goldberg & Benjamin Zipursky, Symposium: The Restatement (Third) and the Place of Duty in Negligence Law, 54 Vand. L. Rev. 657 (2001).

found the car from a want ad that Blum had placed in the newspaper. The two of them agreed on a price of $4,200. Larry paid Blum $300 cash and signed a note for the remaining $3,900, secured by a security interest in the car itself.

The day after he purchased the car, Larry was involved in an accident in which the car was seriously damaged and seven-year-old Jessica Finn was injured. It was raining at the time, and Larry was driving 30 miles per hour in a 35 miles per hour zone. After turning a corner, the rear end of the car skidded and "spun out." Because of his inexperience as a driver, Larry turned the steering wheel the "wrong" way — that is, instead of turning into the skid, he turned away from the skid. As a consequence, the car went out of control, smashed into a tree, and then went back into the street, where it hit Jessica who was playing near the curb making mud pies and splashing in puddles. As a result of the accident, Jessica broke her leg and the car was very nearly "totaled." The car's value now is about $550.

Larry obviously needs a lawyer. He reports that he has liability insurance, but no collision coverage for the damage to the car. He asks for your advice concerning the following questions:

1. How likely is it that a court would find Larry's driving to be negligent? Assume that he could show that most beginning drivers do not know which way to turn when there is a skid.
2. What are the chances that Larry could successfully assert that Jessica was contributorily negligent and thus escape liability to her?
3. Larry no longer wants to own a car. Is there any way he can avoid paying the $3,900 to Blum? Can he get his $300 back?

Consider the conceptions of childhood and responsibility underlying (1) the ordinary negligence standard for children, which imposes a standard of care "common to children of like age, intelligence, and experience"; (2) the adult activities exception; (3) the treatment of contributory negligence for children; and (4) the doctrine that contracts entered into by a minor are "voidable" (discussed later). Are these standards consistent?

6. The Power of Minors to Make Contracts and the Defense of Infancy

According to Professor Corbin,

> [a]t common law the contracts of an infant are said to be voidable, but not void. That they are not void is made clear by the fact that the infant can almost always enforce them against the other party. In most cases it is equally true however that the contract cannot be enforced against the infant if he cares to take advantage of his infancy as a defense.[17]

---

[17] Arthur L. Corbin, Contracts §227, at 318 (1952). On the history of the infancy doctrine, see Larry A. DiMatteo, Deconstructing the Myth of the "Infancy Law Doctrine": From Incapacity to Accountability, 21 Ohio N.U.L. Rev. 481 (1994).

Except where changed by statute or case law, this is still the majority rule. Consequently, a minor who purchases goods or services by contract is allowed to disaffirm at any time during minority or even within a reasonable time after reaching majority.[18] Disaffirmance may be accomplished by any act indicating that the minor does not wish to be bound by the contract made during minority.[19]

Three states have changed the common law rule by case law: New Hampshire, Minnesota, and Arizona. Hall v. Butterfield, 59 N.H. 354 (1879); Bergland v. American Multigraph Sales Co., 160 N.W. 191 (Minn. 1916); Worman Motor Co. v. Hill, 94 P.2d 865 (Ariz. 1939). Under the minority view, a minor must make restitution for benefits received. According to the New Hampshire Supreme Court in *Hall*, the infancy defense "is to be used as a shield, not as a sword; not to do injustice, but to prevent it." 59 N.H. at 355.

In states following the majority rule, disaffirmance requires the minor to give back to the seller those purchased goods that remain in his possession.[20] Some courts have allowed a minor to disaffirm when what he gives back has depreciated or is worthless,[21] or even when the goods have been lost or squandered.[22] Moreover, the minor would have no obligation to put the other party back into a position similar to the one existing before the agreement was made.[23] Some courts, however, avoid this extreme result by holding the minor responsible for quasi-contractual damages, requiring the minor to return not only the goods, but also whatever value the minor got from them.[24] Indeed this is always the rule for "necessaries," a term that usually encompasses an actual requirement of food, clothing, shelter, medical aid, or minimal education while considering the particular minor's station in life. (See Chapter 2 p. 158 for a discussion of necessaries.)

The policy behind permitting minors to disaffirm contracts is to protect them from overreaching by unscrupulous adults[25] and from their own inexperience. But the defense of infancy also acts as a constraint on the freedom of minors to contract because the person dealing with the minor will not be certain that he or she can enforce the contract. Although this may not substantially affect the minor's ability to buy for cash, merchants may be very reluctant to sell to them on credit. For instance, unless a parent co-signs a note, a merchant may refuse to sell to a minor on credit. If the practical operation of the rule is to allow young people to buy for cash but require parental cooperation if they are to buy on credit, is this a bad thing?

---

[18] Corbin, supra note [17], at §239. What constitutes a "reasonable time" is a question of fact. See, e.g., Hoblyn v. Johnson, 55 P.3d 1219 (Wyo. 2002).

[19] Corbin, supra note [17], at §234.

[20] See, e.g., Mitchell v. Mitchell, 963 S.W.2d 222 (Ky. Ct. App. 1998).

[21] See, e.g., Dodson v. Shrader, 824 S.W.2d 545 (Tenn. 1992).

[22] See, e.g., Freiburghaus v. Herman Body Co., 102 S.W.2d 743 (Mo. Ct. App. 1937) (depreciation); Bowling v. Sperry, 184 N.E.2d 901 (Ind. Ct. App. 1962) (damage).

[23] See, e.g., Halbman v. Lemke, 298 N.W.2d 562 (Wis. 1980).

[24] Annotation, Infant's Liability for Use or Depreciation of Subject Matter in Action to Recover Purchase Price upon his Disaffirmance of Contract to Purchase Goods, 12 A.L.R.3d 1174 (1967 & Supp. 2004).

[25] See, e.g., McGuckian v. Carpenter, 110 A. 402 (R.I. 1920) (the reason the law allows the infant the privilege of disaffirming is for protection against the immaturity and improvidence that led to making unwise contracts).

In all events, disaffirmance frequently operates inequitably as to the other contracting party, who, having acted innocently, may be compelled to bear the burden of his or her contract without being assured of any of its benefits.

Does the law recognize minors' increasingly important role in current commercial transactions? Teenagers spend billions of dollars annually on clothing, video games, CD players, stereos, and cars.[26] Indeed, in an era of electronic commerce, minors are even more comfortable than adults entering into contracts in cyberspace. Some minors have their own Internet businesses. Does the traditional rule permitting minors to disaffirm contracts serve to "arm minors with a no-accountability shield, allowing them to wreak havoc on the electronic commerce system with little or no legal consequences"?[27]

If a minor misrepresents his or her age to a merchant, can the minor still resort to the protective shield of the disaffirmance doctrine? In such cases, some states treat the minor's misrepresentation as an exception to the rule, holding that the minor can be estopped from asserting the infancy defense.[28]

Several highly publicized cases involve famous adults attempting to disaffirm contracts entered into when they were minors. In Shields v. Gross, 448 N.E.2d 108 (N.Y. 1983), actress Brooke Shields sought damages and injunctive relief to prevent a photographer from using nude photographs taken when she was 10 years old. The New York Court of Appeals held that the plaintiff could not disaffirm the contract because the model's mother effectively had consented on her behalf. The majority reasoned that there was an important need "to bring certainty to an important industry that necessarily uses minors" (id. at 111). On the other hand, the dissent countered that "children must be placed above any concern for trade or commercialism" (id. at 112).

In another famous disaffirmance case, Stephen Barry left royal service after 12 years as Prince Charles' valet. Barry published a book about his experiences with the royal family notwithstanding his pledge of confidentiality when he began service. Barry was able to disaffirm the earlier contract as he was only 17 when he had entered royal service. See Royal Fink? Stephen Barry, Prince Charles' Ex-Valet Slips Through a Loophole and Talks, People Weekly, Apr. 11, 1983, at 124.

There has been a legislative response to the inequities caused by disaffirmance. A student commentator[29] noted six common statutory ways of holding a minor bound to his contract: (1) estoppel by misrepresentation of age, (2) lowering the age of majority on petition to a court, (3) reaching majority status by marriage, (4) holding a minor to his reasonable contracts made while he is engaged in business, or at least putting him under an affirmative duty to warn those with whom he deals about his minority, (5) forcing a restoration of the consideration (or its

---

[26] According to a study by the Rand Youth Poll (a New York City market research firm), 36.7 million teens spent a total of $105.1 billion in 1998. Rand Youth Poll, Teen-Age Personal Spending Continues to Climb, While Youths' Overall Impact on Economy Intensifies (press release available from Rand Youth Poll), undated, at 1-2.

[27] Juana Lowder Daniel, Virtually Mature: Examining the Policy of Minors' Incapacity to Contract, Through the Cyperscope, 43 Gonzaga L. Rev. 239 (2007-2008).

[28] Id. at 248.

[29] H.H.W., Note, The Status of Infancy as a Defense to Contracts, 34 Va. L. Rev. 829, 831-833 (1948).

equivalent) if the contract was made when the minor was 18 or older, and (6) removing disability of a minor veteran so that he can get education loans.

Another commentator[30] would add to this list statutes allowing the infant to make nonvoidable contracts for insurance, for education loans, and for other agreements made pursuant to statute. In addition, in both California and New York special legislation was made applicable to the entertainment industry. Initially, the legislation was prompted by a need to uphold the validity of contracts with minors. Subsequently, state legislatures enacted laws to protect child performers. See generally Jessica Krieg, Comment, There's No Business Like Show Business: Child Entertainers and the Law, 6 U. Pa. J. Lab. & Emp. L. 429 (2004). Do you think this piecemeal approach is an effective means of reforming the infancy rule?

D. DRINKING

INTRODUCTORY PROBLEM

Puerto Rico maintains its minimum legal drinking age of 18 despite the federal government's law that will reduce the amount of federal funding for surface transportation unless the United States territory raises its drinking age to 21. You are the staff director of a federal commission charged with preparing a report that addresses the question of whether the laws should be revised. The commission's charge is to make recommendations on the following issues: (1) Should age-based limitations relating to drinking be continued? (2) If so, should the legal drinking age be raised from 18 to 21? (3) What are the most appropriate means of enforcing age-based limitations on drinking? (4) What exceptions, if any, should be in the new law? (5) What role should parents have?

Your first task is to prepare a research agenda for the commission. Those who are in favor of raising the drinking age rely basically on four arguments: (1) Drinking by minors can lead to increases in juvenile crime and other antisocial behavior; (2) Raising the drinking age to 21 prevents children younger than 18 from experimenting with alcohol and may reduce the incidence of adult alcoholism; (3) Raising the drinking age will reduce the problems of teenage driving under the influence of alcohol; and (4) Drinking is an immoral or socially undesirable activity for adults, and raising the drinking age will emphasize the undesirability of this activity for young people. You should suggest, as part of the commission's agenda, what empirical research might bear on these arguments. You should also spell out what arguments (other than financial) might be made in favor of changing the law and suggest how those arguments might best be evaluated.

---

[30] Robert C. Edge, Voidability of Minor's Contracts: A Feudal Doctrine in a Modern Economy, 1 Ga. L. Rev. 205, 226-227 (1967).

1.   State Controls on Consumption of Alcoholic Beverages by Minors[31]

a. Legal Drinking Age: Background

Prohibitions on the sale of alcohol to youths date from the beginning of the twentieth century.[32] States enacted strict minimum age drinking laws after the repeal of Prohibition. Most state laws set the age of drinking at 21 and made it illegal for any person (including parents) to provide youths with alcoholic beverages. In 1970, in response to the enactment of the Twenty-Sixth Amendment lowering the federal voting age to 18, most states lowered their drinking age from 21 to 18. A few years later, the Supreme Court reviewed the first challenge to minimum age drinking laws when it held that Oklahoma's different minimum age for males and females to drink low-alcohol-content beer was unconstitutional. Craig v. Boren, 429 U.S. 190, 199 (1976).

In 1984, President Reagan's Commission on Drunk Driving recommended age 21 as the uniform minimum legal drinking age, in reliance on statistics showing that a higher drinking age would reduce the number of fatal traffic accidents. In response, Congress enacted the National Minimum Drinking Age Act of 1984 (23 U.S.C. §158(a)(1) & (2)), which requires states to raise their minimum age for the purchase and public possession of alcohol to age 21 or face a reduction in federal highway funds. By 1988, all states had enacted legislation to raise the drinking age.

The United States Supreme Court reviewed another state minimum age law in South Dakota v. Dole, 483 U.S. 203 (1987), upholding the state statute against a challenge that the statute was unconstitutional as an unauthorized use of Congress's spending power. Yet another minimum age law was challenged on the state level in Manuel v. State, 692 So. 2d 320 (La. 1996). In *Manuel,* the Louisiana Supreme Court initially held that the statute constituted age discrimination under the state constitution. However, on rehearing, the state supreme court upheld the constitutionality of the law, reasoning that it substantially furthered the appropriate governmental purpose of improving highway safety.

Critics of the federal minimum age law point to several problems. One major criticism is that society has conferred so many responsibilities of adulthood on 18-year-olds. The frequent argument has been that if 18-year-olds are old enough to drive, vote, marry, and fight in a war, then they are certainly old enough to drink alcohol. What weight should be given to this argument? Do the statistics on fatal traffic accidents involving young drivers under age 21 who have been drinking justify limiting the rights of 18- to 20-year-olds?

---

[31] This section draws on James Mosher, The Prohibition of Youthful Drinking: A Need for Reform (Unpublished), Social Research Group Working Paper No. 29, University of California-Berkeley (1973).

[32] On the history of minimum age drinking laws, see Robin Room, Drinking and Coming of Age in a Cross-Cultural Perspective 654-677, in Reducing Underage Drinking: A Collective Responsibility (Richard J. Bonnie & Mary Ellen O'Connell, eds., 2004).

b. The Variety of Sanctions

(1) Criminal Sanctions Against the Minor

State laws vary concerning what acts by a minor relating to alcoholic drinks constitute a crime. All states prohibit purchase or possession in public of alcoholic beverages by minors, but many do not extend this to possession in a private home. The potential penalties vary considerably. In Arkansas, for example, a judge may impose a fine between $100 and $500 or may require a minor to write an essay on intoxicating liquor, wine, or beer. Ark. Code Ann. §3-3-203 (Michie 2004 & Supp. 2008). In some states, a minor will face only small discretionary fines. In contrast, other states impose a minimum fine of $100, and several others allow for one-year jail sentences and fines up to $1,000. Special provisions with even stiffer penalties are imposed in most states for use of false identification. In addition, many states have "loitering" statutes (a minor is prohibited from entering and remaining on premises in which liquor is on sale). See, e.g., Conn. Gen. Stat. §30-90a (West Supp. 2008).

Minors who violate a drinking statute also subject themselves to juvenile court jurisdiction as delinquents. In California, for example, Cal. Welf. & Inst. Code §602 (West 1998 & Supp. 2008) expressly states that a violation by a person under 18 of any state law defining a crime satisfies the jurisdictional requirement of the juvenile court and gives the court power to make the minor a ward of the court. In states with a 21-year-old drinking age, however, 18- to 21-year-olds are exempt from juvenile court jurisdiction.

(2) Criminal Sanctions Against the Adult Supplier

The adult who supplies a minor with liquor is generally subject to harsher sanctions than the minor, reflecting perhaps a notion that a child is the "victim." Most states distinguish between a "seller" and other suppliers, the former being subject to more severe sanctions. A few states, in fact, have provisions covering only the "sale" of alcoholic beverages. The range of penalties among states varies greatly. Oklahoma, for example, has a felony provision for the first offense with a maximum sentence of five years and/or a $5,000 fine. Okla. Stat. Ann. tit. 37 §538 (West 1999 & Supp. 2008). Arkansas, for a first offense, provides for a fine not to exceed $100. Ark. Code Ann. §3-3-204 (Michie 2004 & Supp. 2008). Most states have misdemeanor statutes with light, discretionary sentences and fines.

Other provisions usually prohibit furnishing a minor with false identification or allowing a minor to remain on premises serving alcohol. There are also sanctions for contributing to the delinquency of a minor. A supplier, after all, is encouraging minors to break state laws and encouraging "immoral" behavior.

(3) Exemptions for Parents Who Supply Liquor to Their Children

Many states have express exemptions in their statutes or case law for supplying liquor to minors under specific circumstances. A number of states have general provisions allowing parents to procure, supply, or give alcoholic beverages to their children. For example, Wisconsin and Texas allow drinking in the presence of a parent. Wis. Stat. Ann. §125.07 (West 1999 & Supp. 2007); Tex. [alcoholic beverages] Code Ann. §106.06 (West 2007). A few states provide for drinking in the parent's home. Several others exempt married minors.

These exemptions and their constriction over time reflect an interesting historical trend toward increasing skepticism concerning family social control. Criminal statutes concerning child drinking first appeared in the second half of the nineteenth century and gave considerable discretionary authority to parents and other adults. For example, at least three states, Georgia, Texas, and Arkansas, allowed a parent to give written permission for their children to drink.[33] Three other states, Michigan, Connecticut, and Pennsylvania, had exemptions similar to the present New York provisions, N.Y. Penal Law §260.20 (McKinney 2000 & Supp. 2008).[34] But in this century the move has been toward greater regulation. Why do you think this has occurred?

(4) *Regulatory and Civil Provisions*

Civil controls against commercial suppliers are widespread and are more likely to be enforced than criminal sanctions. Usually, fines can be assessed and liquor licenses revoked if a bar or liquor store sells to minors. The owners are subject to strict liability in many states; an honest mistake is not a defense.

At common law, a supplier of liquor could not be held liable for injury or death to either a consumer of alcoholic beverages or to a third party who was harmed by the acts of the intoxicated consumer. A majority of jurisdictions have rejected this rule of nonliability by the enactment of "dram shop acts" — legislation that imposes civil liability on vendors under certain circumstances.[35]

In addition, a few state courts have found a cause of action against any adult supplier, not simply commercial sellers. See, e.g., Camp v. Lummino, 800 A.2d 234 (N.J. Super. Ct. 2002); Barnes v. Cohen Dry Wall, Inc., 592 S.E.2d 311 (S.C. Ct. App. 2003). Should courts impose liability on an adolescent host who collects a "cover charge" from other minors at a party and then supplies them with alcohol? See Koehnen v. Dufuor, 590 N.W.2d 107 (Minn. 1999).

See generally Richard Smith, Note: A Comparative Analysis of Dramshop Liability and a Proposal for Uniform Legislation, 25 J. Corp. L. 553 (2003).

---

[33] See, e.g., Gill v. State, 13 S.E. 86 (Ga. 1891); State v. Jarvis, 427 S.W.2d 531 (Ark. 1968).

[34] People v. Bird, 100 N. W. 1003 (Minn. 1904); State v. Hughes, 209 A.2d 872 (Conn. Cir. Ct. 1965).

[35] Angela M. Easley, Note, Vendor Liability for the Sale of Alcohol to an Underage Person: The Untoward Consequences of Estate of Mullis v. Monroe Oil Co., 21 Campbell L. Rev. 277, 285 (1999) (as of 1988, 37 states had such legislation). See also Implementation of the National Minimum Drinking Age Act, Hearing before the Subcomm. on Surface Transportation of the Comm. on Public Works and Transportation, 102d Cong., 2d Sess. 56 (1992) (testimony of Surgeon General Antonia G. Novello) (the ABA recommended in 1985 that all states should enact such statutes).

(5)   *Enforcement*

Although the laws on the books seem formidable, enforcement policies by state and local agencies reflect greater acceptance of youthful drinking. In California, for example, informal interviews suggest that the criminal laws are rarely, if ever, invoked against sellers. Instead, the California Alcoholic Beverage Control Board may bring civil disciplinary action against a store or bar that serves anyone under 21. The initial fines are usually lenient — $500 or less, depending on income. Only if there are repeated, blatant violations will the liquor license be revoked. No "contributing to delinquency" prosecution has been reported in recent years for selling or giving liquor to a minor. The local police do not recall taking any action against a minor unless the youth's drinking is combined with driving or some other crime.

> Police also point out that parents do not like their children arrested for "doing what everyone else does." One official described enforcement of alcohol laws as "a no-win" situation. And another commented, "Local police have another priority — [illicit] drugs. They ignore alcohol."
>
> Frequently, there are only nominal penalties against vendors and minors when they violate these laws. While vendors may have fines or their licenses suspended, license revocations are rare. The penalties against the youth who violate the laws are often not deterrents. Even when strict penalties exist, courts are lenient and do not apply them.[36]

Furthermore, additional constraints on enforcement exist. As James Mosher notes:

> While the ABC [Alcoholic Beverage Control Board] has exclusive authority to revoke or suspend liquor licenses, its ability to effectively carry out its responsibilities is limited by the law of enforcement personnel. The department currently has 198 enforcement agents assigned to approximately 68,000 licensees, a ratio of one enforcement agent for every 343 outlets. As department enforcement capacity has eroded, enforcement responsibilities have increasingly been left to local officials. Yet, the role of local government is severely restricted because the ABC Department retains exclusive authority to conduct disciplinary actions against a business' state liquor license.
>
> To date, the state has failed to expand local control of sales-to-minors laws despite these problems in enforcement and despite overwhelming public support for the action. Yet, it is important for policy-makers to recognize that local control is a linchpin of the environmental approach to prevention because of its emphasis on community norms and practices.[37]

Do these enforcement patterns suggest the laws should be changed to reflect actual practices? Or that there is no need for change because of an informal accommodation of present social mores?

---

[36] Hearing, Implementation of the National Minimum Drinking Age Act, supra note [35], at 55 (testimony of Surgeon General Antonia C. Novello).

[37] James F. Mosher, Preventing Alcohol Problems Among Young People: Californians Support Key Public Policies, Growing Up Well: Focus on Prevention 5 (1998).

2. Teenagers and Alcohol: Research Findings

In 2007, the U.S. Department of Health and Human Services published The National Survey on Drug Use and Health, a study of drug use that included an extensive exploration of alcohol use among minors. The study examined the pattern and frequency of the consumption of alcoholic beverages, including beer, wine, whiskey, brandy, and mixed drinks. The results revealed that 10.8 million people aged 12 to 20 reported drinking alcohol in the past month. Of those who drink, nearly 7.2 million (19.0 percent) were binge drinkers and 2.4 million (6.2 percent) were heavy drinkers. The prevalence of current alcohol use increases with age, from 3.9 percent of youth aged 12 or 13, 15.6 percent at ages 14 or 15, 29.7 percent at ages 16 or 17, and 51.6 percent at ages 18 to 20. The rate reaches a peak of 68.6 percent for persons aged 21 to 25.[38]

A decade and a half earlier, a study conducted by the Office of the Inspector General (OIG), titled Youth and Alcohol: A National Survey, investigated youths' motivations for drinking, the amount of alcohol consumed, and attitudes about drinking and driving. Of those students who drink, their reasons include: 25 percent drink to get high, 25 percent drink when they are bored, 41 percent drink when they are upset, and 31 percent drink alone. When queried about their attitudes about drinking and driving, 92 percent of the youths responded that a person who has been drinking should not drive; however, one-third of the students had driven with a friend who had been drinking. These findings, according to the OIG, indicate a need for increased education and peer approval of designated drivers.[39]

In other research, Patrick M. O'Malley and Alexander C. Wagenaar examined the effects of different minimum drinking ages on the alcohol-related behavior of high school seniors. Their purpose was to explore differences in drinking behavior in states with high versus low minimum drinking ages. Specifically, they compared alcohol consumption of youths in states that changed their minimum drinking age law from 18 to 21 during 1976 to 1987 with that of youth in states that maintained a minimum age of 21 throughout the same period. The authors found that the minimum age of 21 does indeed lead to lower consumption of alcohol by high school seniors and that, surprisingly, the lower rate of drinking appears to continue into early adulthood.[40]

They also noted that increases in the minimum drinking age did not lead to significantly more alcohol consumption by underage persons in private settings such as cars. Nor did increases in the minimum drinking age lead to increased abuse of other illicit substances.

---

[38] U.S. Dept. of Health & Human Servs., Substance Abuse and Mental Health Servs. Admin., Results from the 2006 National Study on Drug Use and Health: National Findings, Pub. No. SMA 07-4293 (2007).

[39] Office of Inspector General, "Youth and Alcohol: A National Survey," reprinted in Hearing, Implementation of the National Minimum Drinking Age Act, supra note [35] at 19-51. See also Catalina Arata et al., High School Drinking and Its Consequences, 38 Adolescence (No. 151) 567 (2003).

[40] Patrick M. O'Malley & Alexander C. Wagenaar, Effects of Minimum Drinking Age Laws on Alcohol Use, Related Behaviors and Traffic Crash Involvement among American Youth, 1976-1987, 52 J. Stud. Alcohol (No. 5) 478, 482, 489 (1991).

The following excerpt (although written before the 1984 federal legislation) presents a provocative analysis of the public policy implications of raising the minimum drinking age.

James Mosher, The History of Youthful-Drinking Laws: Implications for Public Policy

Minimum-Drinking-Age Laws: An Evaluation 26-31 (Henry Wechsler ed., 1980)

Youthful-Drinking Laws and the Prevention of Alcohol-Related Problems

The Symbolic Nature of Youthful-Drinking Laws

Perhaps the most striking characteristic of current youthful-drinking regulations is the gulf that they create between adults and children in the legal availability of alcohol. Until either ages 18 or 21, depending on the jurisdiction, children are legally expected neither to possess alcohol nor to be present in premises where alcohol is the primary product being served. Any attempts by a child to do so may, in theory, lead to serious legal consequences. Adults, including in most cases parents, who aid a child in drinking or permit them in forbidden premises face even stiffer penalties. After the magic age is reached, however, the "new adult" is expected to be a moderate drinker, using alcohol as a pleasant social lubricant in an increasing number of social settings. The new adult is also expected to avoid the serious dangers that alcohol poses to long-term personal health, traffic accidents and fatalities, and other forms of accidents and injuries.

The legal structuring of alcohol availability is obviously not designed as a real guide for actual behavior, as current youthful-drinking patterns strongly suggest. "Learning to drink" involves experimentation that our society actually encourages in many ways. That the law does not provide a guideline for behavior, however, does not necessarily lead to a conclusion that the law needs to be reformed. As Bonnie points out, there are numerous methods for utilizing the law to shape individual behavior. Youthful-drinking laws, in Bonnie's terms, are "symbolic" and "moralistic" prescripts, used to denote the official posture toward youthful drinking — that is, they articulate what is held to be desirable or undesirable behavior. The vast majority of adolescents are not punished for their drinking; the law functions more as a flashing red light, a warning that social norms discourage this form of behavior.

Youthful-drinking laws might also be viewed as vestiges of moral or symbolic prescripts against drinking generally, a flashback to earlier attitudes about alcohol as an evil or undesirable force in our society. In pre-Prohibition times, in fact, youthful-drinking laws served just such a purpose. Drinking was considered dangerous for everyone, but particularly for youth. Laws directed at youths served as a subset for an overall legal strategy of discouragement. The difference today is that while the law provides that drinking is undesirable behavior for youth, it provides a different message to the society generally.

"Moral" or "symbolic" laws aimed at youth that are in conflict with societal norms are not limited to alcohol availability. We tend to act out our moral ambiguities by "protecting" our children. Obscenity law provides the most obvious parallel — as the society has become increasingly permissive about public displays of sexuality, laws concerning youthful exposure to sexually-oriented materials have become stricter. . . .

The problem with subjecting youths to special symbolic laws that are not relevant to adult behavior is the confusion that they create. Youths, after all, do become adults, and to prescribe radically different behavior norms breeds contempt rather than respect for the laws. Perhaps the success that the Temperance movement had in enlisting children to their cause was that the adults themselves passionately believed in the norms the children were expected to follow. By contrast, adolescents today view drinking-age laws with either indifference or contempt. Further, the law not only loses its moral suasion, it also loses its potential for guiding youths toward healthy personal choices through other strategies.

Closing the Gap Between Childhood and Adult Drinking Norms

The destruction of the symbolic value of drinking-age laws points to two possible policy initiatives. The first involves reform in youthful-drinking laws themselves. Stringent, symbolic controls without a real expectation of compliance preclude the use of law as a guidepost for desired behavior. Adolescents are going to experiment with alcohol; the law could serve to regulate the circumstances of this experimentation to deter undesired behavior and consequences.

As the historical analysis shows, there are numerous variables that may be considered. Most obviously, parents could be given explicit permission to regulate their children's drinking behavior. Complete adult availability could be staggered in various ways. Commercial sale could remain prohibited, but non-commercial furnishing could be decriminalized. Civil controls making adult suppliers civilly responsible for harms caused by minors they serve could be expanded. [D]rinking-age laws may be structured in various ways to discourage specific undesired behavior.

For instance, driving laws in this country do use such a strategy. Typically, young drivers are placed under stricter controls than adults. Parental permission to drive is usually required prior to the child's eighteenth birthday. Successful completion of driver education and/or training may be required before licensing, and a young person's license is typically subject to prompter revocation than adults. The law's message is not merely that "driving is dangerous," which would be the case if driving laws were mainly treated symbolically. Rather, it attempts to provide youths with special guidelines for learning to drive and for avoiding harmful consequences. Similar but less stringent deterrents are placed on adults. Thus, the youthful regulations are but a consistent subset of overall driving laws. It is obviously not a perfect system. However, it can be forcefully argued that it provides more guidance than a system that, on the one hand, prohibits young persons under 18 or 21 from driving and, on the other, grants unlimited driving privileges to those over that age.

Driving, unlike drinking, is not a morally ambiguous activity, which accounts at least in part for the difference in legal approvals. There is no innate reason for the differing treatment, however. Permitting increased adolescent responsibility is consistent with recent trends in children's law. Beginning in the 1960s, the U.S.

Supreme Court has expanded recognition of the rights of families and children to resist state intrusion in private decisions concerning religion, schooling, and social protest. . . . Thus, the trend toward increased state power over adolescents, which began in the nineteenth century concurrently with the adoption of strict youthful-drinking laws, is being partially reversed. Adolescence, in the eyes of the law, has become an age of only partial incompetence.

Although these constitutional protections probably do not include a child's right to purchase or consume alcohol, they do provide insights into issues raised by drinking-age laws. Encouraging adolescents to take on increased responsibility for their lives may have a beneficial long-term effect on their ability to learn and manage adult roles. This is particularly important in drinking behavior, which focuses attention on individual restraints and responsibility as the primary mode for discouraging harmful drinking practices.

Promoting increased responsibility among adolescents is limited, however, as shown by the recent reduction in the drinking age. In the present social climate, loosening the symbolic restrictions on youthful drinking may well be interpreted as measures to encourage drinking. Thus, increased youthful experimentation with alcohol should not be permitted without legal attention being given to the second area of legal policy initiatives — the availability of alcohol to adults.

The failure of symbolic youthful-drinking laws can be explained in part by the societal acceptance of alcohol generally and the relative disinterest in controlling its legal use. Today, the law more often serves to encourage rather than discourage drinking. As discussed earlier, federal and state governments and an increasing number of businesses outside the alcohol industry are profiting from alcohol use. The relaxing of availability regulations has been accomplished to increase this profitability. Alcohol advertising is widespread, and, despite recent media campaigns to the contrary, the dominant message remains alcohol's ability to increase life's pleasures and enhance one's social success and sexual appeal. This combination of increased availability and massive advertising appeals has contributed to the integration of alcohol use into an ever-expanding matrix of daily experience. These are particularly potent messages to adolescents, who are expected to experiment with adult behaviors. An adolescent's desire to experiment freely with this seemingly safe and exciting adult product can hardly be taken as surprising.

Those concerned with promoting the public health among drinking minors must examine seriously the laws which promote this positive alcohol environment. The government's economic role in alcohol policy must be balanced more evenly against public health responsibilities. This does not mean that legal prohibition should be reinstituted but rather that the alcohol messages in the mass media, the laws concerning availability of alcohol, and the economic structure of the alcohol market must be examined from a public health perspective. In short, the legal treatment of alcohol as merely another commercial commodity, the chief characteristic of which is its profitability both for the state and for an expanding range of businesses and industries, must be challenged.

Such a reorientation does, inevitably, raise wider, conflicting social policies. As Bonnie points out, using regulation to discourage unhealthy personal choices must be balanced against an individual's right of free choice. However, freedom of choice hardly necessitates a societal encouragement of alcohol use. Clearly, there is much that can be done in this area.

By providing a public health perspective to overall availability, youthful-drinking laws will become more effective. Minors will be given a more consistent message concerning alcohol use and the public health issues involved. The law's symbolic import will be less ambiguous. Most importantly, regulations that limit availability to minors can be more effectively molded to deter harmful drinking and to promote safer experimentation without the appearance of encouraging over-all use.

Conclusion

The controversy concerning drinking-age laws has been notable for its limited scope. It has, for the most part, ignored the complexity of legal issues that form a drinking-age law and has failed to examine them in terms of overall social attitudes toward alcohol consumption and availability. When the trend was to reduce the drinking age to 18 during the 1970s, the primary issue was the abstract, legal rights of 18- to 20-year-olds. No concern was given to the fact that the age reduction placed the contradictions of adult-child drinking norms at a younger, even less mature age. In fact, as Richard Douglass' excellent study shows, alcohol avail-ability in Michigan — particularly Sunday sales, when adolescents would be expected to be drinking — was actually expanded during the same period that the drinking age was lowered. The relationship of the two was not even considered. These policy reforms together provided a clear message of approval to young drinkers.

Today, the move is in the opposite direction. Permitting adult availability to 18- to 20-year-olds has apparently increased consumption and the risk of alcohol problems, particularly driving problems. However, the debate has centered on the age of legal drinking, treating it as an either/or choice and as a problem divorced from the overall alcohol environment.

History suggests that the drinking age in fact includes a number of availability issues and that various forms of youthful experimentation can be encouraged or discouraged through careful use of the variables. It also suggests that youthful drinking must be regulated in such a way as to be consistent with a general alcohol policy.

Drinking/driving problems among adolescents, the most forceful rationale for returning to a drinking age of 21, illustrates these points. Drunk driving is a societal problem, not merely an adolescent problem. That adolescents have particular prob-lems with learning to drink and drive reflects the conflicts of adult roles — adults are expected to drink in a wide range of social settings and to drive to and from those settings. Serious consideration must be given to limiting alcohol availability in situations where driving is likely to occur and to providing safer transportation. Regulation of young drinkers and drivers, which will undoubtedly necessitate stricter controls, can then be set within the overall strategy.

As Douglass suggests, raising the drinking age to deter drunk driving is at best an indirect strategy. It avoids the basic conflict and raises serious policy questions of possible constitutional proportions. No doubt raising the drinking age to 25, 30, or even 50, as one house of the Mississippi legislature recently passed, would also tend to reduce drunk driving. The youngest age group is being chosen as a symbolic gesture because of its political impotence and because, unlike other possible reforms, there are no major economic consequences involved for the state or for the national alcohol industry. It serves to demonstrate our inability to face the hard issues at hand.

The political shuffling of the legal drinking age has also raised serious practical problems for college administrators — problems that legislatures have widely ignored. When drinking ages are raised, college programs to supervise drinking and to integrate younger students into college social settings are disrupted, and colleges' legal responsibilities became clouded. Instead of attempting to regulate college drinking, administrators are forced officially to prohibit most college drinking, which in practical terms leads to ignoring actual student practices. A more careful attempt to regulate youthful drinking could avoid these unintended results.

In sum, a coherent youthful-drinking policy requires careful attention to wider issues. The needs of children and adolescents for learning and experimenting with adult roles in limited ways and the need for a consistent alcohol policy must be carefully examined. . . . Hopefully, a wider debate of youthful-drinking laws will result in effective legal reform.

3. Drinking and Driving Among Teenagers

Perhaps the most serious problem connected with drinking is drunk driving, particularly among teenagers. Teenagers are involved in a disproportionately high percentage of fatal car accidents, and a substantial portion of these involve drinking. Consider that youth between the ages of 15 and 20 years old account for 6.4 percent of the total number of drivers in the United States. Yet 12.9 percent of all drivers involved in fatal crashes are drivers in this age group. Moreover, of these victims, 25 percent were intoxicated at the time of the crash.[41] As a group, teenagers have the least amount of experience with either drinking or driving and thus are more likely to misjudge their abilities and reactions. They are affected by small amounts of alcohol to a greater degree than more experienced drinkers.

There is considerable debate concerning the relationship of increases in the minimum drinking age to the accident rate. Research reveals that the number of teenage deaths decreased after states returned to 21 as the drinking age. One study, conducted in selected states three years before and three years after changes in minimum drinking age laws (based on self-report and crash data) reported a significant decline in single-vehicle night-time (SVN) fatal automobile crashes among drivers of under 21 years of age following increases in the minimum drinking age. "The largest rate change occurred among states whose change in minimum drinking age was 3 years (i.e., from 18 to 21); in these states, there was a

---

[41] National Highway Traffic Safety Admin. (NHTSA), U.S. Dept. of Transportation, Traffic Safety Facts 2006. Motor vehicle crashes are the leading cause of death for 15- to 20-year-olds. Id.

decline of 26.3% in the rate per licensed driver of alcohol-involved SVN fatal crashes involving drivers under 21. . . ."[42]

Do these findings signify that the decrease in alcohol-related deaths is attributed solely to changes in the minimum drinking age laws? This is a difficult question to answer because the number of alcohol-related injuries decreased in all age categories during the same time period. Thus, while the 15- to 20-year-old group witnessed the greatest decline in involvement in alcohol-related fatal crashes, other factors may account for this phenomenon.

For example, independent researcher Mike Males suggests that research overestimates the lifesaving potential of the 21-year-old drinking age because data reveal that increases in minimum drinking age laws merely shift the number of fatal crashes from a lower to a higher age group.[43] In addition, he concludes that "[t]he facile assumption that an increase in age alone correlates with more mature practices toward alcohol — and the exclusion of more important factors such as quality of family supervision, experience and individual learning abilities — may be the deadliest myth of the drinking age debate."[44]

Other critics raise similar questions. Some experts say that the 21- to 24-year-old age group is just as dangerous on the road as the 18- to 20-year-old group. So if "adulthood" is not a factor, then why not raise the drinking age to 25 if the only aim is to reduce the number of traffic accidents caused by drunken driving? Why, too, prohibit home consumption of alcohol for 18- to 20-year-olds?

Another question is: is it fair to limit drinking by women between 18 and 20? Data reveal that, for young drivers, alcohol involvement is higher among males than females. For example, in 2006, 27 percent of the young male drivers involved in fatal crashes had been drinking, compared with 15 percent of young female drivers.[45] However, to limit access to alcohol by males probably would be unconstitutional. In Craig v. Boren, 429 U.S. 190 (1976), the United States Supreme Court held that an Oklahoma law prohibiting sale of low-alcohol-content beer to males under the age of 21 and to females under the age of 18 was a gender-based difference that violated the equal protection rights of males aged 18 to 20.

If it is impermissible to use gender-based restrictions to reduce the number of fatal drunk driving accidents, perhaps a better solution would be to find ways to reduce drunk driving for all age groups, such as enforcing stiffer penalties for drunk driving, adopting stronger controls on sale and distribution of alcohol, adopting stronger controls on driver licensing, or providing special mass transit service to give drivers another option after consuming alcohol.

Another criticism of raising the drinking age to 21 is that to do so is unduly restrictive and/or intrusive and thus unconstitutional. This criticism was voiced not only by commentators but also by courts, when the states began raising the minimum legal drinking age on their own initiative. For example, in Felix v. Milliken, 463 F. Supp. 1360 (E.D. Mich. 1978), the federal district court ruled

---

[42] O'Malley & Wagenaar, supra note [40], at 478, 487.

[43] Mike A. Males, The Minimum Purchase Age for Alcohol and Young-Driver Fatal Crashes: A Long-Term View, 15 J. Leg. Stud. 181, 183 (1986).

[44] Id. at 211.

[45] NHTSA Traffic Safety Facts, supra note [41].

that a state constitutional amendment passed by voters that raised the minimum drinking age from 19 to 21 did not violate parental rights of parents or the right to privacy, based on rational basis review applicable to age-based discrimination (according to Massachusetts Board of Retirement v. Murgia, 427 U.S. 307 (1976)). The district court reasoned that the data showing a strong correlation between lowering the drinking age and the increase in teenage involvement in fatal crashes demonstrated a rational relationship between raising the drinking age and the constitutionally permissible purpose of increasing traffic safety. For similar reasoning, see Manuel v. State, 677 So. 2d 116 (La. 1996) (upholding state minimum drinking age law).

Increases in the minimum drinking age have been followed by a resort to additional methods of enforcement. For example, many states enacted legislation (referred to as "abuse and lose" statutes) providing for revocation or suspension of juveniles' driving privileges on conviction of drunk driving or substance abuse. Other states preclude juveniles from driving while intoxicated by means of their graduated licensing programs (discussed supra, p. 664). Do "abuse and lose" statutes violate equal protection? See R.T.M. v. State, 677 So. 2d 801 (Ala. Ct. App. 1995) (upholding statute as a legitimate state purpose in protecting the public from juvenile substance abusers). See also Freed v. Ryan, 704 N.E.2d 746 (Ill. Ct. App. 1998) (holding that state "abuse and lose" statutes did not violate due process).

In addition, enforcement of laws restricting the sale of liquor to minors coupled with the growing incidence of traffic accidents involving young drivers prompted the National Traffic Safety Board (NTSB) to recommend that states establish lower blood-alcohol content (BAC) levels for youth.[46] In response, Congress enacted the National Highway Safety Designation Act (NHSDA) of 1995, Pub. L. No. 104-59, 109 Stat. 568 (codified as amended in scattered sections of 23 U.S.C.), a coercive measure that withholds federal highway funds to states that do not consider a 0.02 BAC to be "driving while intoxicated" for drivers under the age of 21. Conversely, states that consider a 0.02 BAC (or less) to be "driving while intoxicated" for drivers under age 21 may qualify for drunk-driving-incentive-grant funds under §410 of the Highway Safety Act.[47]

SOME FINAL QUESTIONS ON TEENAGE DRINKING

(1) The sale of liquor to minors is illegal in every state, but most teenagers drink before reaching 18. Does this suggest the need for stricter laws? Repeal? Neither?

(2) Alcoholism and drunken driving are both serious social problems: Do they suggest the need for stricter laws directed at young and old alike? Or better methods of teaching young people good drinking habits?

---

[46] National Transportation Safety Board, Safety Recommendation 15 (Mar. 11, 1993).

[47] National Highway Traffic Safety Admin., U.S. Dept. of Transportation, State Legislative Fact Sheet: Zero-Tolerance Laws to Reduce Alcohol Impaired Driving by Youth (1996).

(3) In a world where some adults consider drinking by adults to be immoral and inappropriate, and other adults consider drinking an acceptable social activity, what role should parents have in the regulation or development of their children's drinking? Is it possible to satisfy parents who want to make it more difficult for their children to drink as well as those who are prepared to allow their children to experiment?

REVIEW PROBLEM: DRINKING, DRIVING, AND OBSCENITY

You will recall that in Prince v. Massachusetts (Chapter 1), the Supreme Court suggested that "streets afford dangers" for children "not affecting adults." The Court further suggested that "this is so not only when children are unaccompanied but certainly to some extent when they are with their parents. What may be wholly permissible for adults therefore may not be so for children, either with or without their parents' presence."

Compare the age-based restrictions relating to driving, drinking, and viewing sexually explicit materials (that would not be pornographic for adults). See pp. 662-689, supra. (1) Analyze whether there are dangers for young people that are different in kind or degree from the dangers for adults in each of these areas. Is it appropriate in each area to give young people less freedom than adults? (2) What power should parents have to teach their children how to drive, to let them drink in their parents' presence, and to permit them to view sexually explicit materials? (3) Are there similarities in the problems of enforcement in the three areas? (4) Compare for each area the possibilities for "licensing" based on "competence" rather than age. Could the licensing procedures used in driving be applied to drinking? Sexual activities? (5) In each area, do the legal prohibitions facilitate a young person's transition into adulthood? Or make it more problematic? Does the law strengthen the role of parents and the family? Or contribute to intrafamily conflict?

E.   CONTRACEPTION

Carey v. Population Services International
431 U.S. 678 (1977)

Mr. Justice BRENNAN delivered the opinion of the Court (Parts I, II, III, and V), together with an opinion (Part IV) in which Mr. Justice STEWART, Mr. Justice MARSHALL, and Mr. Justice BLACKMUN joined.

Under New York Education Law §6811(8) it is a crime (1) for any person to sell or distribute any contraceptive of any kind to a minor under the age of 16 years; (2) for anyone other than a licensed pharmacist to distribute contraceptives to persons over 16; and (3) for anyone, including licensed pharmacists, to advertise or display contraceptives.

[A distributor of mail-order contraceptives challenged the constitutionality of the statute, asserting that it violated the constitutionally protected right to privacy of potential purchasers. The federal district court declared the statute unconstitutional. In omitted portions of the case here, the Supreme Court held that the limitation on distribution only by *licensed pharmacists* served no compelling state interest and also that the prohibition on *advertisement or display* could not be justified as offensive to consumers or as legitimation of sexual activity. Here, the Court examines the prohibition on the *sale or distribution of contraceptives to minors* under age 16.]

Although "[t]he Constitution does not explicitly mention any right of privacy," the Court has recognized that one aspect of the "liberty" protected by the Due Process Clause of the Fourteenth Amendment is "a right of personal privacy, or a guarantee of certain areas or zones of privacy." Roe v. Wade, 410 U.S. 113, 152 (1973). . . . While the outer limits of this aspect of privacy have not been marked by the Court, it is clear that among the decisions that an individual may make without unjustified government interference are personal decisions "relating to marriage, procreation, contraception, family relationships, and child rearing and education [citing Loving v. Virginia, Eisenstadt v. Baird, Meyer v. Nebraska, Pierce v. Society of Sisters, and Roe v. Wade].

The decision whether or not to beget or bear a child is at the very heart of this cluster of constitutionally protected choices. That decision holds a particularly important place in the history of the right of privacy, a right first explicitly recognized in an opinion holding unconstitutional a statute prohibiting the use of contraceptives, Griswold v. Connecticut, 381 U.S. 479 (1965), and most prominently vindicated in recent years in the contexts of contraception and abortion. This is understandable, for in a field that by definition concerns the most intimate of human activities and relationships, decisions whether to accomplish or to prevent conception are among the most private and sensitive. "If the right of privacy means anything, it is the right of the individual, married or single, to be free of unwarranted governmental intrusion into matters so fundamentally affecting a person as the decision whether to bear or beget a child." Eisenstadt v. Baird, supra, 405 U.S., at 453. (Emphasis omitted.)

That the constitutionally protected right of privacy extends to an individual's liberty to make choices regarding contraception does not, however, automatically invalidate every state regulation in this area. [E]ven a burdensome regulation may be validated by a sufficiently compelling state interest. . . .

With these principles in mind, we turn to the question whether the District Court was correct in holding invalid the provisions of §6811(8) as applied to the distribution of nonprescription contraceptives. . . .

IV

A

Appellants contend that [the prohibition on the sale or distribution of contraceptives to minors] is constitutionally permissible as a regulation of the morality of minors in furtherance of the State's policy against promiscuous sexual intercourse among the young.

The question of the extent of state power to regulate conduct of minors not constitutionally regulable when committed by adults is a vexing one, perhaps not susceptible to precise answer. . . . Certain principles, however, have been recognized. "Minors, as well as adults, are protected by the Constitution and possess constitutional rights." Planned Parenthood of Central Missouri v. Danforth, [428 U.S. 52, 74 (1976)]. "[W]hatever may be their precise impact, neither the Fourteenth Amendment nor the Bill of Rights is for adults alone." In re Gault, [387 U.S. 1, 13 (1967)]. On the other hand, we have held in a variety of contexts that "the power of the state to control the conduct of children reaches beyond the scope of its authority over adults." Prince v. Massachusetts, [321 U.S. 158, 170 (1994)]; Ginsberg v. New York, 390 U.S. 629 (1968).

Of particular significance to the decision of this case, the right to privacy in connection with decision affecting procreation extends to minors as well as to adults. Planned Parenthood of Central Missouri v. Danforth, supra, held that a State "may not impose a blanket provision . . . requiring the consent of a parent or person in loco parentis as a condition for abortion of an unmarried mother during the first 12 weeks of her pregnancy." 428 U.S., at 74. As in the case of the spousal consent requirement struck down in the same case, "the State does not have the constitutional authority to give a third party an absolute, and possibly arbitrary, veto," id., at 74, "which the state itself is absolutely and totally prohibited from exercising." Id., at 69. State restrictions inhibiting privacy rights of minors are valid only if they serve "any significant state interest . . . that is not present in the case of an adult." Id., at 75. *Planned Parenthood* found that no such interest justified a state requirement of parental consent.

Since the State may not impose a blanket prohibition, or even a blanket requirement of parental consent, on the choice of a minor to terminate her pregnancy, the constitutionality of a blanket prohibition of the distribution of contraceptives to minors is *a fortiori* foreclosed. The State's interests in protection of the mental and physical health of the pregnant minor, and in protection of potential life are clearly more implicated by the abortion decision than by the decision to use a nonhazardous contraceptive.

Appellants argue, however, that significant state interests are served by restricting minors' access to contraceptives, because free availability to minors of contraceptives would lead to increased sexual activity among the young, in violation of the policy of New York to discourage such behavior.[17] The argument is that minors' sexual activity may be deterred by increasing the hazards attendant on it. The same argument, however, would support a ban on abortions for minors, or indeed support a prohibition on abortions, or access to contraceptives, for the

---

[17] Appellees argue that the State's policy to discourage sexual activity of minors is itself unconstitutional, for the reason that the right to privacy comprehends a right of minors as well as adults to engage in private consensual sexual behavior. We observe that the Court has not definitively answered the difficult question whether and to what extent the Constitution prohibits state statutes regulating such behavior among adults. But whatever the answer to that question, Ginsberg v. New York, 390 U.S. 629 (1968), indicates that in the area of sexual mores, as in other areas, the scope of permissible state regulation is broader as to minors than as to adults. In any event, it is unnecessary to pass upon this contention of appellees, and our decision proceeds on the assumption that the Constitution does not bar state regulation of the sexual behavior of minors.

unmarried, whose sexual activity is also against the public policy of many States. Yet, in each of these areas, the Court has rejected the argument, noting in Roe v. Wade, that "no court or commentator has taken the argument seriously." 410 U.S., at 148. The reason for this unanimous rejection was stated in Eisenstadt v. Baird, supra: "It would be plainly unreasonable to assume that [the state] has prescribed pregnancy and the birth of an unwanted child [or the physical and psychological dangers of an abortion] as punishment for fornication." 405 U.S., at 448. We remain reluctant to attribute any such "scheme of values" to the State.

Moreover, there is substantial reason for doubt whether limiting access to contraceptives will in fact substantially discourage early sexual behavior. Appellants themselves conceded in the District Court that "there is no evidence that teenage extramarital sexual activity increases in proportion to the availability of contraceptives," 398 F. Supp., at 332, and n.10 and accordingly offered none. . . . Appellees, on the other hand, cite a considerable body of evidence and opinion indicating that there is no such deterrent effect. Although we take judicial notice . . . that with or without access to contraceptives, the incidence of sexual activity among minors is high, and the consequences of such activity are frequently devastating, the studies cited by appellees play no part in our decision. It is enough that we again confirm the principle that when a State, as here, burdens the exercise of a fundamental right, its attempt to justify that burden as a rational means for the accomplishment of some significant State policy requires more than a bare assertion, based on a conceded complete absence of supporting evidence, that the burden is connected to such a policy.

B

Appellants argue that New York does not totally prohibit distribution of contraceptives to minors under 16, and that accordingly §6811(8) cannot be held unconstitutional. Although §6811 (8) on its face is a flat unqualified prohibition, Education Law §6807(b), . . . provides that nothing in Education Law §§6800-6826 shall be construed to prevent "[a]ny physician . . . from supplying his patients with such drugs as [he] . . . deems proper in connection with his practice." This narrow exception, however, does not save the statute. As we have held above as to limitations upon distribution to adults, less than total restrictions on access to contraceptives that significantly burden the right to decide whether to bear children must also pass contitutional scrutiny. Appellants assert no medical necessity for imposing a medical limitation on the distribution of nonprescription contraceptives to minors. Rather, they argue that such a restriction serves to emphasize to young people the seriousness with which the State views the decision to engage in sexual intercourse at an early age. But this is only another form of the argument that juvenile sexual conduct will be deterred by making contraceptives more difficult to obtain. Moreover, that argument is particularly poorly suited to the restriction appellants are attempting to justify, which on appellants' construction delegates the State's authority to disapprove of minors' sexual behavior to physicians, who may exercise it arbitrarily, either to deny contraceptives to young people, or to undermine the State's policy of discouraging illicit early sexual behavior. This the State may not do. . . .

Affirmed.

Mr. Justice W\ITE, concurring in part and concurring in the result in part. . . .

I concur in the result in Part IV primarily because the State has not demonstrated that the prohibition against distribution of contraceptives to minors measurably contributes to the deterrent purposes which the State advances as justification for the restriction. . . .

Mr. Justice P\OWELL, concurring in part and concurring in the judgment. . . .

New York has made it a crime for anyone other than a physician to sell or distribute contraceptives to minors under the age of 16 years. This element of New York's program of regulation for the protection of its minor citizens is said to evidence the State's judgment that the health and well-being of minors would be better assured if they are not encouraged to engage in sexual intercourse without guidance. Although I have no doubt that properly framed legislation serving this purpose would meet constitutional standards, the New York provision is defective in two respects. First, it infringes the privacy interests of married females between the ages of 14 and 16, . . . in that it prohibits the distribution of contraceptives to such females except by a physician. In authorizing marriage at that age, the State also sanctions sexual intercourse between the partners and expressly recognizes that once the marriage relationship exists the husband and wife are presumed to possess the requisite understanding and maturity to make decisions concerning sex and procreation. Consequently, the State interest that justifies a requirement of prior counseling with respect to minors in general simply is inapplicable with respect to minors for whom the State has affirmatively approved marriage.

Second, this provision prohibits parents from distributing contraceptives to their children, a restriction that unjustifiably interferes with parental interests in rearing their children [citing Meyer v. Nebraska, Pierce v. Society of Sisters, Wisconsin v. Yoder]. Moreover, this statute would allow the State "to enquire into, prove, and punish," Poe v. Ullman, 367 U.S. 497, 548 (1961) (Harlan, J., dissenting), the exercise of this parental responsibility. The State points to no interest of sufficient magnitude to justify this direct interference with the parental guidance that is especially appropriate in this sensitive area of child development.

But in my view there is considerably more room for state regulation in this area than would be permissible under the Court's opinion. It seems clear to me, for example, that the State would further a constitutionally permissible end if it encouraged adolescents to seek the advice and guidance of their parents before deciding whether to engage in sexual intercourse. The State justifiably may take note of the psychological pressures that might influence children at a time in their lives when they generally do not possess the maturity necessary to understand and control their responses. Participation in sexual intercourse at an early age may have both physical and psychological consequences. These include the risks of venereal disease and pregnancy, and the less obvious mental and emotional problems that may result from sexual activity by children. Moreover, society has long adhered to the view that sexual intercourse should not be engaged in promiscuously, a judgment that an adolescent may be less likely to heed than an adult.

Requiring minors to seek parental guidance would be consistent with our prior cases. In Planned Parenthood of Central Missouri v. Danforth, 428 U.S. 52 (1976), we considered whether there was "any significant state interest in conditioning [a minor's] abortion [decision] on the consent of a parent or person in loco parentis that is not present in the case of an adult." Id., at 75. Observing that the minor necessarily would be consulting with a physician on all aspects of the abortion decision, we concluded that the Missouri requirement was invalid because it imposed "a special-consent provision, exercisable by a person other than the woman and her physician, as a prerequisite to a minor's termination of her pregnancy and [did] so without a sufficient justification for the restriction." Ibid. But we explicitly suggested that a materially different constitutional issue would be presented with respect to a statute assuring in most instances consultation between the parent and child. Ibid., citing Bellotti v. Baird, 428 U.S. 132 (1976). See *Planned Parenthood*, 428 U.S., at 90-91 (Stewart, J., concurring).

A requirement of prior parental consultation is merely one illustration of permissible regulation in this area. As long as parental distribution is permitted, a State should have substantial latitude in regulating the distribution of contraceptives to minors. . . .

Mr. Justice STEVENS, concurring in part and concurring in the judgment.

. . . I also agree with the conclusion that New York's prohibition against the distribution of contraceptives to persons under 16 years of age is unconstitutional, . . . but my reasons differ from those set forth in Part IV of Mr. Justice Brennan's opinion. . . .

There are two reasons why I do not join Part IV. First, the holding in Planned Parenthood of Missouri v. Danforth, 428 U.S. 52, 72-75 [1976], that a minor's decision to abort her pregnancy may not be conditioned on parental consent, is not dispositive here. The options available to the already pregnant minor are fundamentally different from those available to nonpregnant minors. The former must bear a child unless she aborts; but persons in the latter category can and generally will avoid childbearing by abstention. Consequently, even if I had joined that part of *Planned Parenthood,* I could not agree that the Constitution provides the same measure of protection to the minor's right to use contraceptives as to the pregnant female's right to abort.

Second, I would not leave open the question whether there is a significant state interest in discouraging sexual activity among unmarried persons under 16 years of age. Indeed, I would describe as "frivolous" appellee's argument that a minor has the constitutional right to put contraceptives to their intended use, notwithstanding the combined objection of both parents and the State.

For the reasons explained by Mr. Justice Powell, I agree that the statute may not be applied to married females between the ages of 14 and 16, or to distribution by parents. I am not persuaded, however, that these glaring defects alone justify an injunction against other applications of the statute. Only one of the three plaintiffs in this case is a parent who wishes to give contraceptives to his children. The others are an Episcopal minister who sponsors a program against venereal disease, and a mail order firm, which presumably has no way to determine the age of its customers. I am satisfied, for the reasons that follow, that the statute is also invalid as applied to them.

The State's important interest in the welfare of its young citizens justifies a number of protective measures. Such special legislation is premised on the fact that young persons frequently make unwise choices with harmful consequences; the State may properly ameliorate those consequences by providing, for example, that a minor may not be required to honor his bargain. It is almost unprecedented, however, for a State to require that an ill-advised act by a minor give rise to greater risk of irreparable harm than a similar act by an adult.

Common sense indicates that many young people will engage in sexual activity regardless of what the New York Legislature does; and further, that the incidence of venereal disease and premarital pregnancy is affected by the availability or unavailability of contraceptives. Although young persons theoretically may avoid those harms by practicing total abstention, inevitably many will not. The statutory prohibition denies them and their parents a choice which, if available, would reduce their exposure to disease or unwanted pregnancy.

The State's asserted justification is a desire to inhibit sexual conduct by minors under 16. It does not seriously contend that if contraceptives are available, significant numbers of minors who now abstain from sex will cease abstaining because they will no longer fear pregnancy or disease. Rather its central argument is that the statute has the important symbolic effect of communicating disapproval of sexual activity by minors. In essence, therefore, the statute is defended as a form of propaganda, rather than a regulation of behavior.[4]

Although the State may properly perform a teaching function, it seems to me that an attempt to persuade by inflicting harm on the listener is an unacceptable means of conveying a message that is otherwise legitimate. The propaganda technique used in this case significantly increases the risk of unwanted pregnancy and venereal disease. It is as though a State decided to dramatize its disapproval of motorcycles by forbidding the use of safety helmets. One need not posit a constitutional right to ride a motorcycle to characterize such a restriction as irrational and perverse.

Even as a regulation of behavior, such a statute would be defective. Assuming that the State could impose a uniform sanction upon young persons who risk self-inflicted harm by operating motorcycles, or by engaging in sexual activity, surely that sanction could not take the form of deliberately injuring the cyclist or infecting the promiscuous child. If such punishment may not be administered deliberately, after trial and a finding of guilt, it manifestly cannot be imposed by a legislature, indiscriminately and at random. This kind of government-mandated harm, is, in my judgment, appropriately characterized as a deprivation of liberty without due process of law.

Mr. Justice REHNQUIST, dissenting.

Those who valiantly but vainly defended the heights of Bunker Hill in 1775 made it possible that men such as James Madison might later sit in the first Congress and draft the Bill of Rights to the Constitution. The post-Civil War

---

[4] The State presents no empirical evidence to support the conclusion that its "propaganda" is effective. Simply as a matter of common sense, it seems unlikely that many minors under 16 are influenced by the mere existence of a law indirectly disapproving their conduct.

Congresses, which drafted the Civil War Amendments to the Constitution, could not have accomplished their task without the blood of brave men on both sides which was shed at Shiloh, Gettysburg, and Cold Harbor. If those responsible for these Amendments, by feats of valor or efforts of draftsmanship, could have lived to know that their efforts had enshrined in the Constitution the right of commercial vendors of contraceptives to peddle them to unmarried minors through such means as window displays and vending machines located in the men's room of truck stops, notwithstanding the considered judgment of the New York Legislature to the contrary, it is not difficult to imagine their reaction. . . .

No questions of religious belief, compelled allegiance to a secular creed, or decisions on the part of married couples as to procreation are involved here. New York has simply decided that it wishes to discourage unmarried minors in the 14- to 16-years-age bracket from having promiscuous sexual intercourse with one another. Even the Court would scarcely go so far as to say that this is not a subject with which the New York Legislature may properly concern itself.

That legislature has not chosen to deny to a pregnant woman, after the *fait accompli* of pregnancy, the one remedy which would enable her to terminate an unwanted pregnancy. It has instead sought to deter the conduct which will produce such *faits accomplis.* The majority of New York's citizens are in effect told that however deeply they may be concerned about the problem of promiscuous sex and intercourse among unmarried teenagers, they may not adopt this means of dealing with it. The Court holds that New York may not use its police power to legislate in the interests of its concept of the public morality as it pertains to minors. The Court's denial of a power so fundamental to self-government must, in the long run, prove to be but a temporary departure from a wise and heretofore settled course of adjudication to the contrary. I would reverse the judgment of the District Court.

NOTES AND QUESTIONS

(1) State's Interest.   What did the various *Carey* opinions assume about the legitimacy of a state's attempt to deter sexual activity? Note that there are two reasons a state could wish to inhibit teenage sexual activity. One is based on moral justifications: Sexual intercourse outside marriage or by the immature members of our society is wrong. The second relates to the problem of unwanted teenage pregnancies.

(2) Data on Teen Contraceptive Use.   Research reveals that about 75 percent of teenage girls use contraceptives at first intercourse.[48] The two most popular forms of contraception by young men and women are condoms and birth control pills. Slightly more than half of sexually active youth in grades 9 through 12 reported using a condom during their last sexual intercourse, while approximately one-fifth

---

[48] Teenagers in the United States: Sexual Activity, Contraceptive Use, and Childbearing, 2002, available at *www.cdc.gov/nchs/data/series/sr_23/sr23_024FactSheet.pdf* (last visited Dec. 1, 2008).

reported use of birth control pills.[49] However, although more youths are using contraceptives, these youths are likely to practice contraception sporadically.[50] Not surprisingly, the percentage of sexually active youths rises with each subsequent grade. However, condom use among 12th graders is lower than among youths in earlier grades.[51]

(3) Constitutionality of Condom Distribution Programs. Should parental consent be required for the distribution of condoms in schools? If parents are opposed on religious grounds, does the distribution of condoms violate parents' freedom of religion? Does condom distribution interfere with the parents' right to raise a child free from state interference as established in *Meyer, Pierce,* and *Yoder?* These issues were raised in Curtis v. School Committee of Falmouth, 652 N.E.2d 580 (1st Cir. 1995), which held that a condom distribution program that contained no "opt-out" provision did not violate plaintiffs' liberty to raise their children as they saw fit or their right to privacy or to free exercise. See also Parents United for Better Public Schools v. School Dist. of Phila., 148 F.3d 260 (3d Cir. 1998) (holding that condom distribution program did not violate parents' fundamental right to bring up their children without unnecessary governmental interference when participation is voluntary and the program reserves to parents the right to opt out). School-based provision of contraception is primarily limited to condom distribution. Whereas one-fourth of school-based clinics provide contraception nationwide, fewer than 1 percent of these clinics offer prescription contraceptives. The recent decision by a Maine school board to allow a health clinic at a middle school to provide access to prescription contraceptives triggered national attention.[52]

(4) Data on Teens and Sexually Transmissible Disease (STD). Data reveal that about one in four sexually experienced teens acquire an STD each year. Chlamydia is more common among teens than among older men and women. Teens have higher rates of gonorrhea than sexually active men and women aged 20 to 44. Further, teenage girls are more likely to be hospitalized than older women for acute pelvic inflammatory disease (PID) (which is often caused by untreated gonorrhea or chlamydia and can lead to infertility and ectopic pregnancy).[53]

(5) Teen Pregnancy. Studies reveal the high rates of teenage sexual activity and pregnancy as well as the serious implications that pregnancy has for the teenage mother, teenage father, child, and society. The Alan Guttmacher Institute notes the following statistics: only about one in five young people do *not* have intercourse while teenagers, and over half of 17-year-olds have had intercourse. Each

[49] U.S. Dept. of Health & Human Servs., Trends in the Well-Being of America's Children and Youth 2003, Contraceptive Use, 288.

[50] Id.

[51] Id. at 286, 288.

[52] Katie Zezima, Not All Are Pleased at Plan to Offer Birth Control at Maine Middle School, N.Y. Times, Oct. 21, 2007, at 22.

[53] Guttmacher Report, supra note [48]. A recent government study estimated that one in four girls aged 14 to 19 is infected with one of the most common STDs. Centers for Disease Control and Prevention, Nationally Representative CDC Study Finds 1 in 4 Teenage Girls Has a Sexually Transmitted Disease, available at *http: www.cdc.gov/stdconference/2008/mediarelease-11march2008.htm* (last visited Mar. 22, 2008).

year, almost one million teenage women— 10 percent of all women aged 15 to 19 and 19 percent of those who have had sexual intercourse — become pregnant; nearly 4 in 10 of these pregnancies end in abortion. More than three-quarters of teen pregnancies are unplanned and occur outside of marriage.[54]

A national study by the U.S. Department of Health and Human Services elaborates on the societal consequences of teen pregnancies:

> Research indicates that giving birth as a youth can have negative consequences on both mothers and their children. Giving birth at an early age can limit a young female's options regarding education and employment opportunities, increase the likelihood that she will need public assistance, and can have negative effects on the development of her children. Young mothers are less likely to complete high school (only one third receive a high school diploma) and are more likely to end up on welfare (nearly 80 percent of unmarried young mothers end up on welfare). The sons of young mothers are 13 percent more likely to serve time in prison, while their daughters are 22 percent more likely to become young mothers themselves.[55]

Despite these statistics, it is important to note that the rate of teenage pregnancy decreased dramatically during the 1990s (for teens aged 15 to 17 as well as for older teens aged 18 to 19). Current data reveal that the birth rate for women aged 15 to 19 is the lowest recorded in the 65-year period for which data are available.[56] Researchers attribute the decline to a decrease in sexual activity, more effective use of contraceptives, and, to a lesser degree, increased abstinence among teenagers.[57]

(6) Minors' Sexual Privacy.   Could a state pass a law making it a crime for minors to engage in sexual intercourse? Does the Constitution ensure the right to private consensual sexual activity for adults? In Lawrence v. Texas, 539 U.S. 558 (2003), the Supreme Court held that a Texas statute criminalizing homosexual sodomy violated petitioners' due process right to engage in private consensual sexual conduct.

However, in *Carey,* Justice Brennan observed that "our decision proceeds on the assumption that the Constitution does not bar state regulation of the sexual behavior of minors" (p. 691 n. 17, supra). Moreover, the Supreme Court in *Lawrence* differentiated the right of adults to engage in consensual private sexual conduct from that of minors ("[t]his case does not involve minors") (539 U.S. at 578), thereby indicating a reluctance to extend the right to engage in consensual sexual activity to minors.

Some states have "Romeo and Juliet" laws that mitigate the punishment for minors' sexual activity in recognition of the belief that teenage sexual

[54] Id.

[55] Trends in Well-Being, supra note [49] at 30.

[56] Center for Disease Control (CDC), Births: Final Data for 2005, 56 Natl. Vital Statistics Reports (No. 6), at 5 (2007) (the pregnancy rate for teens aged 15-17 fell from 38.6 per 1,000 in 1991 to 21.4 per 1,000 in 2002. The rate for teens aged 18-19 decreased from 94 per 1,000 in 1991 to 69.9 per 1,000 in 2002).

[57] Jacqueline Darroch & Susheela Singh, Why Is Teenage Pregnancy Declining? The Roles of Abstinence, Sexual Activity, and Contraceptive Use 9 (Guttmacher Institute, 1999).

experimentation should not be punished as severely as statutory rape if both parties are close in age. In State v. Limon, 122 P.3d 22 (Kan. 2005), the Kansas Supreme Court ruled that such a statute that punished sodomy between adults and children of the opposite sex less severely than similar same-sex conduct violated equal protection provisions under the federal and state constitutions.

Also, in Kansas, the state attorney general's interpretation of the state mandatory reporting statute to require the reporting of all sexual activity (including consensual sexual activity) involving minors under age 16 was found to violate minors' right to informational privacy. Aid for Women v. Foulston, 427 F. Supp. 2d 1093 (D. Kan. 2006).

Should statutory rape laws be revised to bring them into conformity with changes in sexual behavior? See generally Meredith Cohen, No Child Left Behind Bars: The Need to Combat Cruel and Unusual Punishment of State Statutory Rape Laws, 16 J.L. & Pol'y 717 (2008).

(7) Effectiveness of Regulation. What is the relationship between the state's attempt to regulate access to contraceptives and its attempt to regulate teenage sexual activity? Some people believe access to contraceptives will have *no* effect on the level of teenage sexual activity but will reduce unwanted pregnancies. Others fear that access to contraceptives will encourage more sexual activity and may ironically lead to more unwanted pregnancies, because despite the availability, teenagers are not very good contraceptive users. In *Carey,* the state argued that "significant state interests are served by restricting minor's access to contraceptives, because free availability to minors of contraceptives would lead to increased sexual activity among the young, in violation of the policy of New York to discourage such behavior" (p. 691, supra). The state apparently felt that preventing access to contraceptives would deter teenage sexual activity by "increasing the hazards attendant on it" (p. 691, supra). The state also argued that their restrictions served to "emphasize to young people the seriousness with which the state views the decision to engage in sexual intercourse at an early age" (p. 692, supra). How does the Court treat this argument? Consider Justice Stevens's response (p. 692, supra). Do you agree that prohibiting contraceptives will increase the risk of unwanted pregnancies and venereal disease? Is it really "as though a State decided to dramatize its disapproval of motorcycles by forbidding the use of safety helmets" (p. 695, supra)?

The evidence regarding the deterrent effect of limited contraceptive availability on sexual activity is not conclusive. Critics of family planning services point out that the significant increase in teenage sexual activity in the 1970s was accompanied by a significant growth in the availability of contraceptive services for both adult women and adolescents. Yet some researchers point out that the existence of a causal connection between these trends is not clear; they criticize that prior research does not always control for other factors that might affect levels of sexual activity among different subgroups or different points in time.[58] One study on the effects of condom availability programs in schools on teenage sexual activity found that: "Adolescents in schools where condoms were available were more

---

[58] National Research Council, Risking the Future: Adolescent Sexuality, Pregnancy and Childbearing, vol. I, 165-166 (1986).

likely to receive condom use instruction and less likely to report lifetime or recent sexual intercourse."[59]

Furthermore, the Children's Defense Fund finds:

> Teaching teens about sex has been found to increase their knowledge without increasing their sexual activity, despite assumptions to the contrary. In *No Easy Answers: Research Findings on Programs to Reduce Teen Pregnancy,* the National Campaign to Prevent Teen Pregnancy reported in 1997 that making condoms and school-based health clinics available as part of pregnancy prevention efforts does not increase teens' sexual activity. However, simply providing access to contraception is not enough to prevent pregnancy. The weight of the research evidence indicates that making contraceptives available in school-based clinics — without adding other important program components that address teens' motivations — does not affect teen pregnancy or birth rates. *No Easy Answers* notes that even though abstinence-only programs may be appropriate for many young people, especially junior high and middle school youths, no published scientific research of adequate quality measures whether or not such initiatives actually delay sexual activity. The report's author, Douglas Kirby, cautions that because some young people have sexual relations and others refrain, "programs need to address both abstaining from or postponing sex and using contraceptives."[60]

Abstinence-based sex education programs are discussed infra.

(8) Parental Involvement Laws.   What role should parents have when their teenagers seek access to contraceptives? Currently, fewer than half of the states allow all minors to consent to contraceptive services. Most of the remaining states permit minors to consent to such services only in limited circumstances (married minors, minors who have ever been pregnant, minors facing health hazards, etc).[61]

Federal legislation currently provides confidentiality to teenage clients of federally funded health providers, although reformers have attempted to change that rule. In 1970, Congress adopted Title X of the Public Health Service Act, Family Planning Services & Population Research Act of 1970, 42 U.S.C. §§300 to 300a-41 (2000), to provide family planning and preventive health screening services (e.g., contraceptives, infertility management, prenatal information and counseling, and treatment of STDs, but not abortion) to low-income women by means of grants to private and public health care providers. In 1978, Congress amended Title X to place special emphasis on "preventing unwanted pregnancies among sexually active adolescents."[62] In 1981, Congress amended Title X to require providers to "encourage family participation" whenever minors sought contraceptive

---

[59] Susan Blake et al., Condom Availability in Massachusetts High Schools: Relationships with Condom Use and Sexual Behavior, 93 Am. J. Pub. Health 955, 957 (2003).

[60] Children's Defense Fund, The Status of America's Children: Yearbook 1998: 87 (1998).

[61] Guttmacher Institute, State Policies in Brief: Minors' Access to Contraceptive Services, available at *http://www.guttmacher.org* (last visited Dec. 1, 2008).

[62] Center for Reproductive Rights, Forced Parental Involvement Defeats the Goals of Title X (Jan. 2004), available at *http://www.reproductiverights.org/pub_fac_titlex.html* (last visited Mar. 23, 2008).

services.[63] Although the federal program mandates confidentiality in the physician–patient relationship, the Department of Health and Human Services amended regulations governing the family planning services program in 1983 to require notification of parents of unemancipated minors who receive prescription contraceptives within ten days of receipt (42 C.F.R. §59.5(a)(12)(I)(A)(1983)). Two federal appellate courts invalidated the so-called squeal rule as contrary to congressional intent. New York v. Heckler, 719 F.2d 1191 (2d Cir. 1983); Planned Parenthood Fed., Inc. v. Heckler, 712 F.2d 650 (D.C. Cir. 1983).

Efforts continued to abrogate the confidentiality provision of Title X. In June 2003, Representative Todd Akin (R-Mo.) introduced the Parents' Right to Know Act of 2003 (108th Cong., 1st Sess., H.R. 2444) to require federally funded health care providers to notify a custodial parent or legal guardian of the intent to provide contraceptive drugs or devices at least five business days beforehand and also to secure the written consent of that parent or guardian. Exceptions are provided for emancipated minors and minors who have obtained a judicial waiver of parental consent and notification.

What do you think would be the effect of federal legislation mandating parental involvement before teenagers are permitted to obtain contraceptives? Research reveals that many adolescents would refuse to seek reproductive health care if health care providers insist on parental notification or consent. The first national study of teenagers' attitudes on parental notification (including more than 1,500 female minors in 33 states) found that parental notification requirements would result in only 30 percent of the teenagers continuing to patronize health care providers for contraceptives and that nearly one in five females would stop using contraceptives.[64] See generally Shoshanna Erhlich, From Age of Consent Laws to the "Silver Ring Thing": The Regulation of Adolescent Female Sexuality, 16 Health Matrix 151 (2006).

(9) AIDS Prevention Programs. Youth are at persistent risk for contracting HIV/AIDS. Approximately 13 percent of people receiving a diagnosis of either HIV or AIDS are between the ages of 13 and 24.[65] Indeed, the prevalence of infected youths may be higher than reported because many adolescents fail to get tested for the disease. A key problem in AIDS testing is that most statutes that permit adolescents themselves to consent to medical care for specific conditions (such as substance abuse or sexually transmitted diseases) omit any reference to HIV or AIDS testing.[66]

Is preventing the spread of AIDS a compelling state interest to justify the burden of imposing such educational programs on teenagers' sexual decision making? Currently, 35 states mandate HIV, STD, and/or AIDS education; 20 states and the District of Columbia merely mandate sexuality education.[67]

---

[63] Pub. L. No. 97-35, 95 Stat. 570 §931(b)(1) (codified as 42 U.S.C. §300(a) (1981)).

[64] Diane M. Reddy et al., Effect of Mandatory Parental Notification on Adolescent Girls' Use of Sexual Health Care Services, 288 JAMA (No. 6) 710 (Aug. 14, 2002).

[65] Centers for Disease Control and Prevention, Fact Sheet: HIV/AIDS Among Youth (June 2006), available at *http://www.cdc.gov/hiv/resource/factsheet/youth.htm* (last visited Mar. 24, 2008).

[66] Rhonda Gay Hartman, AIDS and Adolescents, 7 J. Health Care L. & Pol'y 280, 284 (2004).

[67] Guttmacher Institute, State Policies in Brief: Sex and STI/HIV Education (Mar. 2008), available at *http:///www.guttmacher.org/statecenter/spibs/spib_SE.pdf* (last visited Mar. 24, 2008).

(10) Abstinence-Based Sex Education.   As already explained, many states require that sex education programs be offered in the schools. Such programs are known by different labels (e.g., "family life education," "health," "sexual health," etc.) and cover a variety of topics. Most statutes on sex education provide "opt out" provisions for parents who do not want their children taught certain subjects. Moreover, as a result of federal legislation (discussed later), most such statutes emphasize abstinence-only education. Abstinence-based programs generally prohibit discussion of contraceptives and convey the message that premarital sexual activity leads to psychological and physical harm.

Abstinence-based sex education received a boost from federal legislation. The Adolescent Family Life Act of 1981 (AFLA), 42 U.S.C. §§300z(a)(1)-300z(a)(10) (2000), provided funding for abstinence-only education through federal matching grants to the states. In Bowen v. Kendrick, 487 U.S. 589 (1988), the United States Supreme Court upheld the constitutionality of AFLA against a challenge that it violated the Establishment Clause. The Court reasoned that the Act would not lead to excessive government entanglement with religion and did not have a primary effect of advancing religion.

Subsequently, in 1996, federal welfare reform legislation (PRWORA), Pub. L. No. 104-193, §912, 110 Stat. 2105 (1996) (codified in scattered sections of 42 U.S.C.), reaffirmed the federal commitment to an abstinence-only approach. In an effort to reduce teen pregnancy, PRWORA allocated $50 million annually to states that adopted abstinence-only educational programs. 42 U.S.C. §710 (2000 & Supp. 2005). Congress doubled the funding in 2003. The proposed budget for these programs for fiscal year 2009 is $204 million. Despite such federal encouragement, the number of states participating in the program has declined steadily.[68]

Is abstinence-only sex education an effective deterrent to sexual activity? Recent research suggests that such programs are ineffective in delaying teenage sexual activity and reducing unintended pregnancies. In contrast, comprehensive sex education programs are significantly associated with reduced risk of pregnancy.[69] Do abstinence-based sex education programs violate minors' right to privacy? Parents' right to control the upbringing of their children?

F.   JUVENILE CURFEWS

Hodgkins v. Peterson *(Hodgkins II)*
355 F.3d 1048 (7th Cir. 2004)

ROVNER, Circuit Judge. . . .

Shortly after 11:00 P.M. on August 26, 1999, Colin Hodgkins and his three friends left a Steak'n Shake restaurant in Marion County, Indiana where they had

---

[68] Kevin Freking, 28 States Remain in Abstinence-Only Program, S.F. Chron., June 25, 2008, at A4.

[69] Pamela K. Kohler et al., Abstinence-Only and Comprehensive Sex Education and the Initiation of Sexual Activity and Teen Pregnancy, 42 J. Adolescent Health 344, 349 (2008).

stopped to eat after attending a school soccer game. As they left the restaurant, police arrested and handcuffed them for violating Indiana's curfew regulation. The police took Colin and his friends to a curfew sweep processing site where he was given a breathalyser test and escorted to a bathroom where he was required to submit a urine sample to be tested for drugs. Later, both tests were determined to be negative. After the tests, a community volunteer interviewed Colin, asking him various personal questions about his friends and family including whether his family attended church. Two and a half hours later, at 1:30 A.M., a member of the Marion County Sheriff's Department went to the Hodgkins residence to inform Nancy Hodgkins that her son had been arrested and had to be picked up at the local high school. When she arrived to pick up her son, a community volunteer interviewed her and asked her personal questions about the Hodgkins family.

Colin's arrest spurred a series of legal challenges to the constitutionality of the statute. [At the time of Colin's arrest, the Indiana statute (Ind. Code §31-37-3-2) set a curfew of 11 P.M. on weekday nights and 1 A.M. on weekend nights for youth aged 15 to 17 with additional restrictions for those under age 15. Exemptions applied for any child who was accompanied by a parent or guardian or by an adult designated by the parent or guardian; or participating in employment, a school activity, or a religious event.] Pursuant to a challenge by Colin, his mother, and a certified class of minors similarly situated, the district court determined that the statutes were constitutionally flawed as they lacked any exceptions for First Amendment activity. Hodgkins v. Goldsmith, No. IP99-1528-C-T/G, 2000 WL 892964, at *18 (S.D. Ind. July 3, 2000) (*Hodgkins I*). Following this decision, the defendants appealed. While the appeal was pending, the Indiana General Assembly passed the current version of the curfew law, effective May 1, 2001 [which incorporated the prior exceptions to the curfew rule and added a new provision] which, rather than creating an exception for First Amendment activity, created an affirmative defense for those engaged in protected expressive activity. [Plaintiffs again sought to preliminarily enjoin the enforcement of the law in the belief that the statutory revisions did not cure the constitutional defects. The district court denied the plaintiffs' motion.]

Named plaintiff Nancy Hodgkins is a resident of Indianapolis, Indiana, and is the mother of named plaintiffs Colin and Caroline Hodgkins. Ms. Hodgkins would like to allow her children to participate in the activities protected by the curfew law's First Amendment exception, however, she is concerned that if they do so, they will be subject to arrest. Ms. Hodgkins recognizes that if one of her children is arrested while participating in a First Amendment activity she and the child could later use that activity as a defense to the charges. She is nevertheless concerned about the potential expense and time involved in launching such a defense, and, we surmise, she is wary of again placing herself in a position where she will be summoned by the police in the middle of the night to come to a curfew processing center or detention center and of placing her children in a position where they will be subject to arrest, a breathalyser test, urine test, and an intrusive interview. Ms. Hodgkins states that she will certainly consider the risk of arrest when deciding whether to allow her children to participate in First Amendment activities after curfew. Consequently, she asserts that the current statute chills her children's ability to engage in these types of activities.

Furthermore, Ms. Hodgkins wishes to assert her rights as a parent to measure out more privileges and responsibilities to her children as they mature and grow more capable of acting responsibly with additional freedom. She believes that it is part of a parent's job to prepare a child for adulthood by doling out greater freedoms, including the freedom to remain out past curfew without being accompanied by an adult. [Defendants (i.e., the Indianapolis mayor, county sheriff, and county prosecutor)] claim that the curfew law is constitutional and serves the compelling governmental interest in lowering the incidence of drug and alcohol use by youth, decreasing crime committed by and against minors, fostering parental involvement in children's conduct, and empowering parents who wish to set limits on their children's nightime activities. . . .

[J]uvenile curfew laws have existed throughout our nation's history, and state and local governmental attempts at enacting constitutional curfew statutes have met with varying degrees of success. See Ramos v. Town of Vernon, 353 F.3d 171, 172 (2d Cir. 2003) (amended Dec. 19, 2003) (Equal Protection challenge to curfew law). In this case, the plaintiffs are concerned with two burdens that the Indianapolis curfew law imposes: the burden on the First Amendment rights of the youths themselves and the burden on the due process rights of the parents and legal guardians to direct their children's upbringing. . . .

We must begin by exploring the baseline question: Do minors have a fundamental right to freedom of expression worthy of constitutional protection? The Supreme Court answered this question affirmatively in Tinker v. Des Moines Indep. Cmty. Sch. Dist., 393 U.S. 503, 511 (1969). It is oft said that those rights are not coextensive with the rights of adults, at least in the context of the rights of students in public schools. Bethel Sch. Dist. No. 403 v. Fraser, 478 U.S. 675, 682 (1986); Hazelwood Sch. Dist. v. Kuhlmeier, 484 U.S. 260, 266 (1988). The question as to whether a minor's First Amendment rights are diluted outside of the school context is not as clear. *Hazelwood,* 484 U.S. at 266 (noting that student speech which disrupts the educational environment need not be tolerated "even though the government could not censor similar speech outside the school").

The strength of our democracy depends on a citizenry that knows and understands its freedoms, exercises them responsibly, and guards them vigilantly. Young adults, as Judge Tinder [in *Hodgkins I*] pointed out, are not suddenly granted the full panoply of constitutional rights on the day they attain the age of majority. We not only permit but expect youths to exercise those liberties — to learn to think for themselves, to give voice to their opinions, to hear and evaluate competing points of view — so that they might attain the right to vote at age eighteen with the tools to exercise that right. A juvenile's ability to worship, associate, and speak freely is therefore not simply a privilege that benefits her as an individual, but a necessary means of allowing her to become a fully enfranchised member of democratic society. "People are unlikely to become well-functioning, independent-minded adults and responsible citizens if they are raised in an intellectual bubble." [American Amusement Mach. Assoc. v. Kendrick, 244 F.3d 572, 577 (7th Cir. 2001).] In short, minors have First Amendment rights worthy of protection. How we balance those rights against other legitimate governmental interests is, of course, the key question in this case and will be discussed at length below.

The Hodgkins maintain that the revisions to the curfew law have not cured the constitutional defect found in the previous version of the law which was struck down by the district court in *Hodgkins I*. The affirmative defenses added to the revised curfew law, they argue, do not adequately protect minors' First Amendment rights, as the curfew law requires them to subject themselves to arrest — including the possibility of breathalyser tests, urine tests and intrusive questioning about their family life — and then prove at a later time that the activity they were engaging in fell within the affirmative defense for First Amendment activity. They assert that the consequences of violating the curfew law are so burdensome and intrusive that, rather than risk arrest, they will be discouraged from participating in expressive activity during curfew hours. In other words, the plaintiffs claim that the curfew regulation creates a "chill" that imposes on their First Amendment rights. . . .

[Our first task] is to decide through which of the many First Amendment lenses we will analyze the constitutionality of the curfew law. [The court adopts an intermediate level of scrutiny applicable to content-neutral government regulations affecting speech.][5]

These intermediate scrutiny tests can be applied only to governmental regulation of conduct that has an expressive element or to regulations directed at activity with no expressive component but which nevertheless impose a disproportionate burden on those engaged in protected First Amendment activity. The government claims that plaintiffs cannot mount a facial challenge to the curfew law . . . because they have not demonstrated either that the curfew law imposes a disproportionate burden on those engaged in First Amendment activities or that it regulates conduct with an expressive element.

We agree that the Indiana curfew ordinance does not disproportionately impact First Amendment rights. As Colin Hodgkins can attest, it burdens minors who want to attend soccer games as much as it burdens those who wish to speak at a political rally. On the other hand, the curfew ordinance regulates minors' abilities to engage in some of the purest and most protected forms of speech and expression. As Judge Tinder [in *Hodgkins I*] recognized, a wide range of First Amendment activities occur during curfew hours, including political events, death penalty protests, late night sessions of the Indiana General Assembly, and neighborhood association meetings or nighttime events. *Hodgkins I*, 2000 WL 892964, at *10. A number of religions mark particular days or events with late-night services, prayers, or other activities: many Christians, for example, commemorate the birth of Christ with a midnight service on Christmas Eve and the Last Supper with an all-night vigil on Holy Thursday; Jews observe the first night of Shavuot by studying Torah

---

[5] Other courts that have reviewed curfew laws challenged on Equal Protection grounds and the right to travel or to free movement have struggled to decide whether minors' constitutional rights should be subject to strict scrutiny, intermediate scrutiny, or an amalgam of both. See Ramos, 353 F.3d 171, 2003 WL 22989226, at *5-6 (including discussion of the various methodologies courts have chosen to incorporate the status of minors into the Equal Protection framework). We find it unnecessary to reach any conclusion regarding the level of scrutiny minors should receive in Equal Protection cases, as the minor plaintiffs in this case challenge the statute on First Amendment grounds only. As we will discuss further, under this type of First Amendment challenge to a content neutral statute, a level of intermediate scrutiny . . . applies.

all through the night; and throughout the month of Ramadan, Muslims engage in late-evening prayer. Late-night or all-night marches, rallies, and sleep-ins are often held to protest government action or inaction. And it is not unusual for political campaigns, particularly in the whirlwind final hours before an election, to hold rallies in the middle of the night. Thus, during the last weeks of the 1960 presidential campaign, then-Senator John F. Kennedy addressed a group of University of Michigan students at 2:00 A.M. on the steps of the Michigan Union. In unprepared remarks, he asked the students whether they would be willing to devote a few years of their lives working in underdeveloped countries in order to foster better relations between the people of those nations and the United States. The students responded with a petition calling for the creation of the Peace Corps, which came into being the following year. These are but a few examples. The curfew ordinance regulates access to almost every form of public expression during the late night hours. The effect on the speech of the plaintiffs is significant.

Despite this extensive regulation, the State of Indiana argues that the curfew law is a general regulation of conduct and not a regulation of expressive conduct. . . . In this case, however, the government regulation of nonspeech (the nocturnal activity of minors) is intimately related to the expressive conduct at issue. Being out in public is a necessary precursor to almost all public forums for speech, expression, and political activity. Its relationship to expressive conduct is intimate and profound.

. . . The lynchpin questions in this case then are first, whether the curfew law furthers an important or substantial governmental interest and, second, whether the restrictions imposed by the curfew regulation are no greater than are essential to further that interest [— that is] whether the statute is narrowly tailored to serve a significant governmental interest — [and] whether the curfew law allows for ample alternative channels for expression.

The district court found that the curfew law advanced the important governmental interest in providing for the safety and well-being of children and combating juvenile crime. *Hodgkins II,* 175 F. Supp. 2d at 1150. Even the plaintiffs agree that the interests asserted by the government are legitimate (though they stop short of calling the interests substantial or important). And we agree that they are indeed important and substantial.

The question remains, however, whether the nexus between the curfew law and those significant governmental interests is close enough to pass constitutional muster. . . . We look to see whether the curfew law is no more restrictive than necessary to further the governmental interest. . . . The district court in *Hodgkins I* concluded that without the affirmative defense, the curfew ordinance indeed did burden speech more than was necessary to serve the state's legitimate interests. *Hodgkins I,* 2000 WL 892964, at *10-11. After the affirmative defense for First Amendment activity was added, however, the district court concluded that the defense sufficiently protected children's abilities to engage in protected communication during curfew hours. *Hodgkins II,* 175 F. Supp. 2d at 1150-51. After all, the court noted,

> an officer would not have probable cause to arrest children who appear to be under the age of 18 and who also appear to be participating in an early morning protest at

the Governor's residence. Similarly, an officer would not have probable cause to arrest children apparently under the age of 18 attending Midnight Mass at the Cathedral. In those cases, the officer would have knowledge of facts and circumstances which would conclusively establish the First Amendment activity affirmative defense; the officer would not have to conduct any investigation into the defense as it would be readily apparent that the children were engaging in protected activity. [*Hodgkins II,* 175 F. Supp. 2d at 1149.]

But there is no reason to think that the minors whom the affirmative defense will shield from arrest represent most or even many of those who are at risk of being stopped by the police. A police officer has probable cause to arrest when "the facts and circumstances *within the officer's knowledge* . . . are sufficient to warrant a prudent person, or one of reasonable caution, in believing, in the circumstances shown, that the suspect has committed, is committing, or is about to commit an offense." Michigan v. DeFillippo, 443 U.S. 31, 37 (1979) (emphasis ours). Under Indiana law, "[r]easonable suspicion exists where the facts *known to the officer,* together with the reasonable inferences arising from such facts, would cause an ordinarily prudent person to believe that criminal activity has or is about to occur." Baldwin v. Reagan, 715 N.E.2d 332, 337 (Ind. 1999) (emphasis ours). Once a police officer discovers sufficient facts to establish probable cause, she has no constitutional obligation to conduct any further investigation in the hope of discovering exculpatory evidence. A police officer may not ignore conclusively established evidence of the existence of an affirmative defense, but the officer has no duty to investigate the validity of any defense. In fact, both the defendants in this case and the court below, ruling in their favor, conceded that a police officer need not investigate an individual's claim of an affirmative defense to determine facts unknown to the officer. See *Hodgkins II,* 175 F. Supp. 2d at 1147. A legislature can draft a curfew law which specifies that a law enforcement official must look into whether an affirmative defense applies before making an arrest. See Hutchins v. District of Columbia, 188 F.3d 531, 535 (D.C. Cir. 1999) (en banc) (noting that before police officer may detain juvenile for violation of District of Columbia's curfew ordinance, officer must "reasonably believe . . . that an offense has occurred under the curfew law *and* that no defense exists") (emphasis ours); [Qutb v. Strauss, 11 F.3d 488, 490-491] (noting that Dallas curfew ordinance requires police officer to inquire into minor's reasons for being in public place during curfew hours and permits officer to issue citation or make arrest "only if the officer reasonably believes that the person has violated the ordinance *and* that no defenses apply") (emphasis ours). The Indiana Legislature did not impose that requirement.

Thus, a police officer who actually sees a sixteen-year-old leaving a late-night religious service or political rally could not properly arrest the youth for staying out past curfew. But, as Judge Tinder held, the statute's affirmative defenses do not compel the officer to look beyond what he already knows in order to decide whether one of the affirmative defenses applies. *Hodgkins II,* 175 F. Supp. 2d at 1148. Thus, if a police officer stops a seventeen-year-old on the road at 1:00 A.M., and the teen informs the officer that she is returning home from a midnight political rally, the officer need not take the teen at her word nor attempt to ascertain whether she is telling the truth. Lacking first-hand knowledge that the juvenile indeed has been participating in First Amendment activity, the officer is free to arrest her and leave assessment of the First Amendment or any other affirmative defense for a judicial officer. . . . Any juvenile who chooses to participate in a late-night religious or political activity thus runs the risk that he will be arrested if a police officer stops him en route to or from that activity and he cannot prove to the officer's satisfaction that he is out after hours in order to exercise his First Amendment rights.

Consequently, because the defense imposes no duty of investigation on the arresting officer, as a practical matter it protects only those minors whom the officer has actually seen participating in protected activity. This strikes us as a small subset of minors participating in late-night First Amendment activities, and therefore we conclude that the statute reaches a substantial amount of protected conduct. . . .

Furthermore, we think the district court took too narrow a view when determining that the curfew law left open adequate alternative channels of communication. Judge Tinder noted that minors could engage in protected activity during the ample non-curfew hours, during curfew hours under the shield of the affirmative defense, when accompanied by an authorized adult, or within the confines of their home by telephone or through the internet. No doubt many if not most of the participants would find it more convenient to exercise their First Amendment rights other than in the dead of night. It is by no means a coincidence, however, that so many of the expressive activities we illustrated above occur late in the evening. In some instances, the late hour of the activity may be dictated by necessity — as, for example, when citizens wish to observe or influence a legislative session that extends into the late hours, or a down-to-the-wire election postpones a celebration for the winning candidate until the wee hours of the morning. More often, however, the late hour is closely linked with the purpose and message of the activity. Take Back the Night marches and rallies frequently extend to and after midnight in order to protest the crimes that jeopardize the security of women at night. Executions of prisoners on death row often are carried out shortly after midnight or in the early hours of the day, and so are routinely attended by all-night vigils held by those for and against the death penalty. Kristallnacht (Night of Glass) is commemorated with late-night prayers and vigils because it was after midnight one evening sixty-five years ago when Nazi hooligans looted and destroyed Jewish businesses, homes, and synagogues in Germany. In the final days of Ramadan, mosques remain open all night so that Muslims may mark Lailat al-Qadr (Night of Power), the night when the prophet Mohammed first received revelations from the angel Jibra'el (Gabriel), by holding vigil in prayer, Qur'anic reading, and contemplation. And it was after midnight one evening in October 1998 when young Matthew Shepard was beaten, burned, and lashed to a fence, and left for dead outside of Laramie, Wyoming; and so it is that candlelight vigils were and are held in the middle of the night to protest the homophobia that motivated his killers. Thus, to the extent that the curfew prevents a minor from being outside of the home during curfew hours, it does not mean simply that she must shift the exercise of her First Amendment rights to noncurfew hours or to the telephone or internet; it means that she must surrender her right to participate in late-night activities whose context and message are tied to the late hour and the public forum. There is no internet connection, no telephone call, no television coverage that can compare to attending a political rally in person, praying in the sanctuary of one's choice side-by-side with other worshipers, feeling the energy of the crowd as a victorious political candidate announces his plans for the new administration, holding hands with other mourners at a candlelight vigil, or standing in front of the seat of state government as a legislative session winds its way into the night. . . .

Granted, Indiana's curfew does not forbid minors from exercising their First Amendment rights during curfew hours, but it does forcefully discourage the exercise of those rights. The First Amendment defense will shield a minor from conviction, assuming that she can prove to the satisfaction of a judge that she was exercising her First Amendment rights, but, as discussed, it will not shield her from arrest if the officer who stops her has not actually seen her participating in a religious service, political rally, or other First Amendment event. The prospect of an arrest is intimidating in and of itself; but one should also have in mind what else might follow from the arrest [as did occur in this case]. We have no doubt that the authorities are well meaning in administering the drug and alcohol testing and in questioning the minor and his parents about his friends and family life. But these are also rather serious intrusions upon one's personal and familial privacy, and they represent a substantial price for a minor to have to pay in order to take part in a late-night political or religious event. The chill that the prospect of arrest imposes on a minor's exercise of his or her First Amendment rights is patent.

The only way that a minor can avoid this risk is to find a parent or another adult designated by his parent to accompany him. See Ind. Code §31-37-3-3.5(b)(1), (2). But that alternative itself burdens a minor's expressive rights: adults may be reluctant or unable to accompany the minor to a late-night activity; a seventeen-year-old attending college away from home may be unable to recruit a parent or designated adult; and the minor himself may decide that participation is not worth the bother if he must bring a parent or other adult along with him. To condition the exercise of First Amendment rights on the willingness of an adult to chaperone is to curtail them. . . .

In sum, we hold that the curfew law, even with the new affirmative defenses for First Amendment activity, is not narrowly tailored to serve a significant governmental interest and fails to allow for ample alternative channels for expression. . . .

NOTES AND QUESTIONS ON CURFEWS

(1) Background. The central issue in the litigation regarding curfew ordinances concerns their constitutionality. The United States Supreme Court was first presented with the constitutionality of a curfew ordinance in Bykofsky v. Middletown, 401 F. Supp. 1242 (M.D. Pa. 1975), *aff'd,* 535 F.2d 1245, challenged on grounds of vagueness, minors' due process rights, minors' First Amendment rights, the right to travel, parents' rights to direct the upbringing of their children, and minors' right to equal protection. The district court upheld the ordinance with the

exception of a few vague words and phrases, which it deleted. The Third Circuit Court of Appeals affirmed. The Supreme Court denied certiorari, but three Justices (White, Marshall, and Brennan) indicated that they would have granted certiorari and set the case for oral argument. Justice Marshall, joined by Justice Brennan, dissented from the denial of certiorari as follows:

> The freedom to leave one's house and move about at will is "of the very essence of a scheme of ordered liberty," Palko v. Connecticut, 302 U.S. 319, 325 (1937), and hence is protected against state intrusions by the Due Process of the Fourteenth Amendment. To justify a law that significantly intrudes on this freedom, therefore, a State must demonstrate that the law is "narrowly drawn" to further a "compelling state interest." . . . I have little doubt but that, absent a genuine emergency, a curfew aimed at all citizens could not survive constitutional scrutiny. . . .
>
> The question squarely presented by this case, then, is whether the due process rights of juveniles are entitled to lesser protection than those of adults. The prior decisions of this Court provide no clear answer. We have recognized that, "Constitutional rights do not mature and come into being magically only when one attains the state defined age of majority. Minors, as well as adults, are protected by the Constitution and possess constitutional rights." Planned Parenthood v. Danforth, 428 U.S. 52 (1976); see also Tinker v. Des Moines Independent Community School Dist., 393 U.S. 503, 511 (1969). But we also have acknowledged that "the State has somewhat broader authority to regulate the activities of children than of adults." Planned Parenthood v. Danforth, supra; see also Ginsberg v. New York, 390 U.S. 629 (1968); Prince v. Massachusetts, 321 U.S. 158 (1944). Not surprisingly, therefore, the lower courts have reached conflicting conclusions in addressing the issue raised here.
>
> Because I believe this case poses a substantial constitutional question — one which is of great importance to thousands of towns with similar ordinances — I would grant a writ of certiorari. [429 U.S. 964 (1976).]

Federal courts continue to reach "conflicting conclusions" regarding the constitutionality of curfew ordinances. Compare Hutchins v. District of Columbia, 188 F.3d 531 (D.C. Cir. 1999) (en banc); Schliefer v. City of Charlottesville, 159 F.3d 843 (4th Cir. 1998); Qutb v. Strauss, 11 F.3d 488, 492 (5th Cir. 1993) (upholding curfew laws), with Ramos v. Town of Vernon, 353 F.3d 171 (2d Cir. 2003); Nunez v. City of San Diego, 114 F.3d 935 (9th Cir. 1997) (contra). For state court decisions, see State v. J.P., 907 So. 2d 1101 (Fla. 2004); City of Sumner v. Walsh, 61 P.3d 1111 (Wash. 2003) (both invalidating juvenile curfew ordinances).

(2) Applicable Level of Scrutiny.   The success of challenges to juvenile curfew laws often depends on the level of scrutiny applied by particular courts to evaluate juveniles' constitutional rights. Courts differ on the level of scrutiny applicable to juvenile curfew laws. (The level of scrutiny dictates the level of protection given to a constitutional right. Ordinances that infringe upon fundamental rights are given strict scrutiny.) What level of scrutiny did the *Hodgkins II* court apply to invalidate the Indiana curfew ordinance? Note that other courts have applied a higher level of scrutiny based on their perception of the federal or state constitutional right at issue. See Nunez v. City of San Diego, 114 F.3d 935, 944-946 (9th Cir. 1997) (finding juveniles' fundamental rights

implicated and applying strict scrutiny); State v. J.P., supra (applying strict scrutiny to infringement on juveniles' rights to privacy and travel). What level of constitutional scrutiny do you think is appropriate? See generally Calvin Massey, Juvenile Curfews and Fundamental Rights Methodology, 27 Hastings Const. L.Q. 775 (2000) (comparing the different approaches of federal courts of appeal).

(3) Equal Protection. Some courts (e.g., *Bykofsky,* supra; *Hutchins,* supra) have held that curfew laws do not violate minors' right to equal protection, reasoning that minors are subject to greater governmental regulation of their conduct. Other courts have disagreed that the constitutional rights of minors are less deserving of protection that those of adults. See, e.g., Waters v. Barry, 711 F. Supp. 1125 (D.D.C. 1989). The Supreme Court has recognized three reasons to allow courts to treat the rights of minors differently from those of adults: the peculiar vulnerability of youth, their inability to make critical decisions in an informed mature manner, and the importance of the parental role in childrearing. Bellotti v. Baird, 443 U.S. 622, 634 (1979). How applicable is the *Bellotti* rationale, developed for juvenile abortion decision making, to the curfew context? Compare People ex rel. J.M., 768 P.2d 219 (Colo. 1989); Village of Deerfield v. Greenberg, 550 N.E.2d 12 (Ill. App. Ct. 1990) (relying on *Bellotti* rationale to uphold juvenile curfew ordinances) with Johnson v. City of Opelousas, 658 F.2d 1065 (5th Cir. 1981); Waters v. Barry, supra (relying on *Bellotti* rationale to invalidate juvenile curfew ordinances).

(4) Exemptions. Many juvenile curfew laws, like those of Indiana in *Hodgkins,* contain exceptions for various juvenile activities. Second-generation curfew laws are more narrowly drawn than the curfew laws of the 1960s and 1970s (i.e., they contain more exceptions) in an effort to pass constitutional muster. Common exceptions include parental consent or travel for work- or school-related purposes.

Some recent decisions, such as *Hodgkins II,* invalidate curfew laws for failure to include an exception that allows the expression of minors' First Amendment rights. After the district court initially enjoined the statute, the state legislature amended the statute to include a First Amendment exception. Why does the court in the principal case find that the curfew law with its First Amendment exception is still unconstitutional? See also City of Maquoketa v. Russell, 484 N.W.2d 179 (Iowa 1992) (similarly invalidating ordinance on First Amendment grounds). How should the state legislature amend the Indiana statute to shift the burden *from* youth to prove their activity exempts them from the curfew — *to* police to determine that a youth is not engaged in protected First Amendment activities?

(5) Parental Rights. Many courts have considered whether juvenile curfew laws interfere with parental rights by injecting government in the role of childrearing. Do juvenile curfews promote the role of parents in childrearing or infringe on parental rights? How do *Meyer, Pierce,* and *Prince* affect the analysis? Although the holding in *Hodgkins II* rendered it unnecessary to rule on the parents' due process claims, the court did make the following observations on the issue:

> In this case, the exceptions covering a broad variety of circumstances do give parents greater flexibility to allow their children to stay out after hours and in that way minimize the interference with parental autonomy. But the affirmative defenses in the Indiana curfew statute present a risk that a minor will be arrested

whenever the arresting officer lacks direct knowledge that the minor is on an emergency errand, coming from a school sanctioned activity, or engaging in some other activity encompassed by the specified defenses. For that reason, we are not convinced that the affirmative defenses actually do minimize the state's restraint on parental authority in a manner sufficient to overcome a constitutional attack. 355 F.3d at 1065.

In contrast, many courts have held that the curfew laws do not violate parents' constitutional rights. See, e.g., Hutchins v. District of Columbia, supra; Schleifer v. City of Charlottesville, supra; Treacy v. Municipality of Anchorage, 91 P.3d 252 (Alaska 2004); Panora v. Simmons, 445 N.W.2d 363 (Iowa 1989).

(6) Social Interests.   What social interests are served by juvenile curfews, according to the defendants in *Hodgkins II*? Historically, curfews have functioned as a vehicle of social control. Prior to the Civil War, Southern towns enacted curfew ordinances to prohibit the presence of slaves and free blacks on public streets during certain hours. Peter L. Scherr, Note, The Juvenile Curfew Ordinance: In Search of a New Standard of Review, 41 J. Urb. & Contemp. L. 163, 164-165 (1992). Curfew ordinances were enacted in the 1890s to decrease crime among immigrant youth. Later, they were perceived as an effective method of control for parents who were busy helping with the war effort during World War II. Current ordinances have been enacted in response to problems of drugs and/or crime. To the extent that the purpose of juvenile curfew laws is to control juvenile crime, particularly gang activity, why not limit the application of curfew laws to prohibit groups of people on the street late at night? For further issues relating to gangs and juvenile delinquency, see Chapter 7.

Some commentators suggest that juvenile curfews disproportionately target minority youth. See Carol M. Bast & K. Michael Reynolds, A New Look at Juvenile Curfews: Are They Effective?, 39 Crim. L. Bull. 5 (May 2003); Ronald Smothers, Atlanta Sets a Curfew for Youths, Prompting Concern on Race Bias, N.Y. Times, Nov. 20, 1990, at A1. Data also suggest that enforcement of curfew restrictions disproportionately targets females. Howard N. Snyder, Juvenile Arrests 2002, Juvenile Justice Bulletin (Office of Juvenile Justice & Delinquency Prevention, Sept. 2004) at 8.

(7) Deterrent Effect of Curfew Laws.   Do curfew laws prevent crime and victimization? Most studies observe no change in crime rates after implementation of a new or revised curfew law. Whereas some studies note a decrease in certain types of crimes (e.g., criminal mischief), other studies actually report a slight increase in violent crimes and felonies. See Kenneth Adams, The Effectiveness of Juvenile Curfews at Crime Prevention, 587 Annals of Am. Acad. of Pol. & Soc. Sci. 136 (May 1, 2003); Center on Juvenile and Criminal Justice, Impact of Juvenile Curfew Laws in California 1, 3, available at *www.cjcj.org/pubs/curfew* (last visited Mar. 23, 2008) (finding that "[c]urfew enforcement generally had no discernible effect on youth crime"). For further commentary on juvenile curfews, see Deirdre Norton, Why Criminalize Children? Looking Beyond the Express Policies Driving Juvenile Curfew Legislation, 4 N.Y.U. J. Legis. & Pub. Pol'y 175 (2000); Todd Kaminsky, Rethinking Judicial Attitudes Toward Freedom of Association Challenges to Teen Curfews: The First Amendment Exception

Explored, 78 N.Y.U. L. Rev. 2278 (2003); Note, Juvenile Curfews and the Major Confusion over Minors' Rights, 118 Harv. L. Rev. 2400 (2005).

G. *"STATUS" OFFENSES*

> If a man has a stubborn and rebellious son, who will not obey his father or his mother who will not listen to them even when they chastise him, then his father and mother shall lay hands upon him and bring him before the sheikhs of his town at the local gateway, telling the sheikhs of his town, "This son of ours is a stubborn and rebellious fellow who will not obey our orders: he is a spendthrift and is a drunkard." Whereupon all his fellow-citizens shall stone him to death. So shall you eradicate evil from you, and all Israel shall hear and fear. [Deuteronomy 21:18-21.]

1. Status Offense Jurisdiction of the Juvenile Court

In re Walker
191 S.E.2d 702 (N.C. 1972)

On 2 August 1971 Mrs. Katherine Walker, mother of Valerie Lenise Walker, filed a petition in the district court alleging [that Valerie was an "undisciplined child as defined by G.S. §7A-278"]. . . .

The matter came on for hearing before Judge Gentry on 17 August 1971. Valerie was present with her mother and the court counselor, Mrs. Ann M. Jones. Valerie was not represented by an attorney at this hearing. Judge Gentry heard evidence and found (a) that Valerie Lenise Walker . . . is a child under sixteen years of age in the custody and under the supervision and control of her parents . . . ; (b) that Valerie has been regularly disobedient to her parents in that she goes and comes without permission, keeps late hours, associates with persons that her parents object to, and goes to places where her parents tell her not to go; and (c) that Valerie is an undisciplined child and in need of the discipline and supervision of the State. This order was signed on 19 August 1971.

Based on the foregoing findings, it was ordered, adjudged and decreed that Valerie was an undisciplined child within the meaning of the law. She was placed on probation subject to the following conditions:

> 1. That she be of good behavior and conduct herself in a law-abiding manner; 2. That she mind and obey her parents and not leave home without permission and then to go only to places that she has permission to go and return as directed; 3. That she attend school regularly during the school year and obey the school rules and regulations; 4. That she report to the court counselor as directed, truthfully answer questions put to her concerning her conduct, behavior, associates and activities and carry out requests given her concerning such; 5. That this matter be reopened for further orders on March 22, 1972. . . .

Thereafter on 21 September 1971 Ann M. Jones, Court Counselor, filed a verified petition and motion in the cause for further consideration and review of the case, alleging:

> That the said child is a delinquent child as defined by G.S. §7A-278(2) in that the said child has violated Conditions No. 1, 2, and 3 of the probation order dated August 19, 1971, in that the said child continuously disobeys her parents in that she goes and comes as she pleases; keeps late hours; and frequents places not approved by her parents; further, the said child refuses to obey school rules and regulations in that she misbehaves in the classroom and is disrespectful to school officials; further, the said child is beyond the control of her parents.

A juvenile summons was thereupon issued and served upon Valerie and her parents, notifying them to appear in juvenile court for a further hearing. . . .

Prior to the hearing the public defender . . . was appointed to represent Valerie, and the matter came on for hearing before Judge Gentry on 15 October 1971. . . .

Prior to the introduction of evidence, Valerie's counsel moved to vacate the order dated 19 August 1971 finding that Valerie was an undisciplined child and placing her on probation for that she was not represented by counsel at that time and was unable to defend herself on the charge that she was an undisciplined child, resulting in a denial of due process. Her counsel further moved to dismiss the petition and motion in the cause filed 21 September 1971 [because] G.S. §7A-278 violates the Equal Protection Clause of the Fourteenth Amendment in that the statute provides for an adjudication of delinquency when the respondent has violated none of the laws of the State of North Carolina. Both motions were denied and respondent duly excepted.

Katherine Walker, mother of Valerie, testified that she lives with her husband and seven small children, including Valerie; that she and her husband both work and that Valerie is usually not at home when she returns from work; that Valerie fails to do the chores which have been assigned to her, such as cleaning her room, the bathroom, and taking her turn washing dishes; that when Valerie comes home she usually says she has been at Mrs. Cunningham's house with Vanessa Cunningham; that Valerie has been told not to leave home without telling her mother where she is going but she continues to disobey in that respect; that Valerie keeps late hours and sometimes comes in at eleven, twelve, one and two o'clock at night; that Valerie has been to Paradise Inn in violation of parental instructions; that Paradise Inn sells beer and has a bad reputation and is no place for a fourteen-year-old girl; that during Valerie's nocturnal absences her parents do not know where she is.

Mrs. Walker further testified that she is the mother of ten children; that Valerie is lazy and disobedient; that Valerie signed for a registered letter from school officials, addressed to her mother, and then destroyed the letter. Mrs. Walker said: "All I want her to do is to behave like a fourteen year old should."

Howard King, Assistant Principal at Mendenhall Junior High School, testified that Valerie came to his school on September 8, 1971, and was placed in special education with a group of students who had similar defects in adjusting; that . . . he saw Valerie in his office many times on referral from all of her teachers except one for disrupting the class; that he had numerous conferences with Valerie and specifically recalls one problem which arose due to Valerie's refusal . . . to dress for physical education practically every day . . . ; that he could not communicate very well with Valerie because she sucked her thumb, did not talk for a while, "and when she does start talking it's almost impossible to keep her from talking and it doesn't have any meaning to what we're talking about when she comes to the office. . . . It was not something that was relevant."

Mr. King further testified that Valerie was large for her age and as compared to the other children in the class; that Valerie was sent by her teachers to the office practically every day, does not fit into the classroom and disrupts whatever the teachers try to do; that he would have suspended her each day but had no way to get her home; that he simply required her to sit in the office and occasionally she would leave the office without permission; that Valerie does not respond to any methods of discipline available at the school.

The probation officer testified that Valerie had problems at her previous school similar to those described by Mr. King; that her attitude was bad toward her probation officer as well as others and that her behavior has not shown improvement; that Valerie does not have a receptive attitude toward her probation officer or the school or her mother in regard to discipline.

The respondent elected to offer no evidence and moved to dismiss the proceeding at the close of all the evidence. The motion was denied, and under date of 27 October 1971 Judge Gentry signed an order providing in pertinent part as follows:

> The court finds, upon hearing evidence, that the child was before the court on August 17, 1971 and that she was adjudged to be an undisciplined child and placed on probation, one of the conditions of probation being that she be of good behavior and conduct herself in a law-abiding manner; another condition being that she mind and obey her mother and not be away from home without permission. Another condition was that she attend school regularly and obey the school rules and regulations. The court finds that the said child did not obey her parents in that she left home without permission and did keep late hours at night. That she went to places that she was told not to go to by her parents and that she failed to do chores assigned to her by her mother. The court further finds that the child was sent out of the classroom in school a number of times for disobeying the teachers and disturbing the class. That she also refused to dress for her Physical Education classes without giving any reasons for doing so. The court finds that these acts of the child constitute a violation of the conditions of probation and that she is a delinquent child for having violated the conditions of probation and that she is in need of the discipline and supervision of the state. The court further finds that since September 21, 1971, the said child has been a constant behavior problem in school and has not responded to disciplinary actions taken and that she continues to disobey her mother. The court finds that she is in need of more discipline and supervision than can be provided for her within Guilford County.
>
> It is now therefore ordered, adjudged and decreed that Valerie Walker, having been found to be a delinquent child, that the said child is hereby committed to the North Carolina Board of Juvenile Correction and is to be in the custody and under the control and supervision of the officials thereof until discharged. [S]he is to

remain in the temporary custody of the court until she can be delivered to the designated correction school. . . .

B. *Gordon Gentry*
Judge presiding

From the foregoing order respondent appealed to the Court of Appeals which found no error. Respondent thereupon appealed to the Supreme Court . . . asserting involvement of substantial constitutional questions. . . .

Huskins, Justice.

Appellant Valerie Walker contends that she had a constitutional right to counsel at the hearing on the initial petition alleging her to be an *undisciplined* child. We first consider whether the Constitution affords her such right.

In In re Gault, 387 U.S. 1 (1967), the United States Supreme Court held, inter alia, that

> the Due Process Clause of the Fourteenth Amendment requires that in respect of proceedings to determine delinquency which may result in commitment to an institution in which the juvenile's freedom is curtailed, the child and his parents must be notified of the child's right to be represented by counsel retained by them, or if they are unable to afford counsel, that counsel will be appointed to represent the child.

A similar statutory right to counsel for indigent juveniles at a hearing which could result in commitment to an institution is afforded by G.S. §7A-451(a)(8).

The initial petition alleging that Valerie was an *undisciplined* child was heard on August 17, 1971. At that time the 1969 version of Article 23, Chapter 7A of the North Carolina General Statutes (Jurisdiction and Procedure Applicable to Children) was in effect. . . .

> (1) "Child" is any person who has not reached his sixteenth birthday.
> (2) "Delinquent child" includes any child who has committed any criminal offense under State law or under an ordinance of local government . . . or a child who has violated the conditions of his probation under this article. . . .
> (5) "Undisciplined child" includes any child who is unlawfully absent from school, or who is regularly disobedient to his parents or guardian or custodian and beyond their disciplinary control, or who is regularly found in places where it is unlawful for a child to be, or who has run away from home.

G.S. §7A-286(1969) . . . makes the following alternatives available to any judge exercising juvenile jurisdiction: "(4) In the case of any child who is delinquent or undisciplined, the court may: a. Place the child on probation . . . ; or b. Continue the case . . . ; or, *if the child is delinquent,* the court may: c. Commit the child to the care of the North Carolina Board of Juvenile Correction . . . ." (Emphasis added.)

Despite the somewhat awkward structure of G.S. §7A-286 (1969), it is clear that under its terms, no judge exercising juvenile jurisdiction had any authority upon finding the child to be *undisciplined* to commit such child to the Board of

Juvenile Correction for assignment to a State facility in which the juvenile's freedom is curtailed. The statute permitted incarceration of *delinquent* children only.

Therefore, we hold that neither *Gault,* supra, nor G.S. §7A-451(a)(8) afforded Valerie Walker the right to counsel at the hearing on the initial petition alleging her to be an undisciplined child, for under the wording of G.S. §7A-286(4) (1969) that hearing could not result in her commitment to an institution in which her freedom would be curtailed. Nor would there be such a right under the statute as presently written. See G.S. §7A-286(5) (1971).

Appellant would have this Court go further than *Gault* requires. She argues for the right to counsel at the hearing of an *undisciplined child* petition on the theory that such a hearing is a critical stage in the juvenile process since it subjects the child to the risk of probation and since a violation of probation means that the child is *delinquent* and subject to commitment. In such fashion appellant seeks to engraft upon the juvenile process the "critical stage" test used by the United States Supreme Court in determining the scope of the Sixth Amendment right to counsel in *criminal prosecutions.* We find no authority for such engraftment. Whatever may be the proper classification for a juvenile proceeding in which the child is alleged to be undisciplined, it certainly is not a criminal prosecution within the meaning of the Sixth Amendment which guarantees the assistance of counsel. . . .

The right to counsel delineated in *Gault* has not been extended to other procedural steps in juvenile proceedings. Neither this Court nor the United States Supreme Court has ever applied the "critical stage" test to the juvenile process. Accordingly, we hold that counsel is not constitutionally required at the hearing on an *undisciplined child* petition. See In re Gault, supra (n.48) in which it is stated: "[W]hat we hold in this opinion with regard to the procedural requirements at the adjudicatory stage has no necessary applicability to other steps of the juvenile process."

The fact that a child initially has been found to be undisciplined and placed on probation is merely incidental to a later petition and motion alleging delinquency based on violation of the terms of probation. The initial finding can never legally result in commitment to an institution in which the juvenile's freedom is curtailed. It is only the latter petition and motion, and the finding that the child is a *delinquent* child by reason of its conduct since the initial hearing, that may result in the child's commitment. . . .

Appellant's second contention is that G.S. §7A-286 violates the Equal Protection Clause of the Fourteenth Amendment in that it subjects an undisciplined child to probation and the concomitant risk of incarceration when the child has committed no criminal offense, while adults are subjected to probation and incarceration only for actual criminal offenses. . . .

The purpose of the Juvenile Court Act "is not for the punishment of offenders but for the salvation of children." Commonwealth v. Fisher, 213 Pa. 48, 62 A. 198 (1905). The Act treats "delinquent children not as criminals, but as wards, and undertakes . . . to give them the control and environment that may lead to their reformation, and enable them to become law-abiding and useful citizens. . . ." State v. Burnett, 179 N.C. 735, 102 S.E. 711 (1920). The State must exercise its power as "parens patriae to protect and provide for the comfort and well-being of such of its citizens as by reason of infancy . . . are unable to take care of themselves." County of McLean v. Humphreys, 104 Ill. 378 (1882). Thus, juveniles are in need of supervision and control due to their inability to protect themselves. In contrast, adults are regarded as self sufficient.

Therefore, the classification here challenged is based on differences between adults and children; and there are so many valid distinctions that the basis for challenge seems shallow. These differences are "reasonably related to the purposes of the Act." . . . Consequently, the classification does not offend the Equal Protection Clause. [I]t is our view that the desire of the State to exercise its authority as parens patriae and provide for the care and protection of its children supplies a "compellingly rational" justification for the classification.

The conclusion we reach — that G.S. §7A-278 and related statutes do not violate the Equal Protection Clause by classifying and treating children differently from adults — has also been reached in numerous cases upholding juvenile Acts in other states. [Citations omitted]. . . .

Appellant makes the further contention that North Carolina's statutory scheme, G.S. §§7A-278(5), 7A-285 and 7A-286(2) and (4), allowing a child to be adjudged *undisciplined* and placed on probation *without benefit of counsel,* while at the same time requiring counsel before a child may be adjudged *delinquent,* denies equal protection of the laws to the undisciplined child.

This argument has no merit and cannot be sustained. The Equal Protection Clause is offended only if the classifications of "undisciplined" and "delinquent" rest on grounds wholly irrelevant to the achievement of the State's objective. . . . In seeking solutions which provide in each case for the protection, treatment, rehabilitation and correction of the child, it is impellingly relevant to the achievement of the State's objective that distinctions be made between undisciplined children on the one hand and delinquent children on the other. The one may need protection while the other needs correction. . . .

Finally, appellant urges that the trial judge's failure to state in his order that he found "beyond a reasonable doubt" that appellant had violated the conditions of her probation was constitutional error under In re Winship, 397 U.S. 358 (1970).

In *Winship,* the juvenile was accused of stealing $112 from a woman's pocketbook. . . . The juvenile was adjudged delinquent and placed in a training school, subject to confinement for as long as six years. The juvenile judge acknowledged that pursuant to a New York statute his determination of the delinquency issue was based on a preponderance of the evidence. The juvenile, contending that due process required proof beyond a reasonable doubt, carried the case by successive appeals to the Supreme Court of the United States. The Court held that the Due Process Clause requires proof beyond a reasonable doubt in delinquency proceedings wherein the child is charged with an act that would constitute a crime if committed by an adult. Here, Valerie Walker was charged with delinquency by reason of probation violations, none of which violations amounted to a crime. See G.S. §7A-278(2). Therefore, *Winship* does not apply to these findings. . . .

For the reasons stated, the result reached by the Court of Appeals upholding the order entered by Judge Gentry is affirmed.

BOBBITT, Chief Justice (dissenting). . . .

G.S. §7A-285 includes the following: "In cases where the petition alleges that a child is delinquent *or* undisciplined *and* where the child *may* be committed to a

State institution, the child shall have a right to assigned counsel as provided by law in cases of indigency." (Our italics.)

Valerie was found delinquent and committed solely on the ground she had violated certain of the probation conditions imposed when she was adjudicated an "undisciplined child" on August 19th. The adjudication that she was an "undisciplined child" was absolutely essential to a valid commitment for violation of probation conditions. The Court holds that she was entitled to assigned counsel *only at the final hearing* to determine whether the probation conditions had been violated. In my opinion, she was equally entitled to assigned counsel at the earlier hearing to determine whether she should be adjudged an "undisciplined child."

Here a fourteen-year-old girl was brought before the juvenile court upon the complaint of her mother. Absent counsel, she stood alone before the court. In addition to the statutory requirement, it is my opinion that due process required that counsel be assigned to represent her at any hearing which might result in an adjudication prejudicial to her.

For the reasons indicated, I would reverse the decision of the Court of Appeals, vacate Judge Gentry's order of October 27, 1971, and remand the case with direction that a plenary hearing be conducted when Valerie is represented by counsel for de novo consideration and determination of the charge in the original petition that she is an "undisciplined child."

District of Columbia v. B.J.R.

332 A.2d 58 (D.C.), *cert. denied,* **421 U.S. 1016 (1975)**

Yeagley, Associate Judge.

This is an appeal from an order of the Family Division dismissing a petition, as amended, filed under D.C. Code 1973, §16-2301(8)(A)(iii) and 16-2301(8)(B), on the ground that the definition of "children in need of supervision" in that statute (hereinafter CINS) is "unconstitutionally vague" and cannot be saved by reasonable construction. The amended petition alleged that the appellee was a "child in need of supervision in that she is habitually disobedient of the reasonable and lawful commands of her parent and is ungovernable." Appellee was specifically charged with absconding from home in April and October 1969, in June and August of 1972, and on February 26, 1973. The last three abscondances were within the nine months preceding the March 6, 1973, filing of the CINS petition in the trial court.

The pertinent portion of §16-2301 reads as follows: . . . "(8) The term 'child in need of supervision' means a child who — . . . (iii) is habitually disobedient of the reasonable and lawful commands of his parent, guardian, or other custodian and is ungovernable; and (B) is in need of care or rehabilitation." The sole issue on appeal is whether or not this language under attack for vagueness passes constitutional muster. We find that it does.

The Supreme Court in Parker v. Levy, 417 U.S. 733, 752 (1974), recently summarized the due process elements of the "void-for-vagueness" doctrine:

> The doctrine incorporates notions of fair notice or warning. Moreover, it requires legislatures to set reasonably clear guidelines for law enforcement

officials and triers of fact in order to prevent "arbitrary and discriminatory enforcement." Where a statute's literal scope, unaided by narrowing state court interpretation, is capable of reaching expression sheltered by the First Amendment, the doctrine demands a greater degree of specificity than in other contexts. Smith v. Goguen, 415 U.S. 566, 572-573 (1974).

It is difficult to perceive how our CINS statute could violate these requirements when considered in regard to the conduct of the appellee.

Children of ordinary understanding know that to repeatedly abscond from home in defiance of the lawful commands of one's parent is a rather drastic form of disobedience that may well precipitate some disciplinary or punitive action. The statute here gave the appellee adequate warning that to abscond from home five times in four years, three of those times within the nine months preceding the instant petition, would subject her to the sanctions provided for a child who "is habitually disobedient of the reasonable and lawful commands of [her] parent. . . ." Such conduct establishes the "frequent practice or habit acquired over a period of time" required to satisfy the "habitually" element as that term was authoritatively construed under an earlier version of our juvenile statute in In re Elmore, D.C. App., 222 A.2d 255, 258-259 (1966), *rev'd on other grounds,* 127 U.S. App. D.C. 176, 382 F.2d 125 (1967).

When a child's conduct clearly falls within the common understanding of the statutory language, the officials charged with enforcing the CINS statute are not compelled to make arbitrary decisions in applying it to juveniles such as the appellee. If a parent makes reasonable efforts to control a child from running away, it seems clear that the child is "ungovernable" in his present home situation and may be in need of closer supervision than is available at home. Section 16-2301(8) was explicitly designed to provide such supervision.

While it may be said that the wording of the CINS statute is somewhat broad and general, we must recognize, as did the Supreme Court . . . that ". . . there are limitations in the English language with respect to being both specific and manageably brief, and it seems to us that although the prohibitions may not satisfy those intent on finding fault at any cost, they are set out in terms that the ordinary person exercising ordinary common sense can sufficiently understand and comply with, without sacrifice to the public interest." [United States Civil Service Commn. v. National Assn. of Letter Carriers, 413 U.S. 548, 578-579 (1973).]

Our juvenile code, particularly the CINS section, is not a criminal statute in the ordinary sense. Further, language limitations are particularly acute for the draftsmen of juvenile laws designed to implement the broad social policy of reinforcing parents in carrying out their responsibility to support and promote the welfare of their children. To enable parents to carry out this legal obligation, the law gives them the authority to control their children through the giving of reasonable and lawful commands. The CINS statute reinforces this authority and may be invoked when children repeatedly refuse to recognize their obligation to obey such commands.

The court is also mindful that our present CINS statute, adopted in 1970, is the product of highly competent, contemporaneous legal expertise in the drafting of juvenile court statutes. The definition of "children in need of supervision" is substantially identical to those proposed in the Uniform Juvenile Court Act (U.L.A.) §2(4)(1973) and the Legislative Guide for Drafting Family and Juvenile Court Acts §2(p) (Dept. of H.E.W., Children's Bureau Pub. No. 472-1969). The 1970 statute eliminated, inter alia, troublesome language from D.C. Code 1967, §§111551(a)(1)(H) and (1), which gave the juvenile court jurisdiction over children who engaged in "immoral" activities.[3] Neither the lower court nor the appellee has provided us with convincing suggestions for further improvement in our present act. . . .

Our conclusion that the CINS statute is not unconstitutionally vague is supported by the overwhelming weight of authority from other jurisdictions which have considered the validity of juvenile statutes with similar language. [Citations omitted]. . . . Interpretations by sister jurisdictions of statutory language so strikingly parallel to our own cannot be dismissed, as the trial court attempted to do, merely because the language is not "identical" or is a "less-than-perfect fit."

The trial court, in finding the CINS statute unconstitutionally vague, limited itself to an examination of the statute's facial validity without consideration of whether its language gave one such as the appellee fair warning that to repeatedly abscond from home would subject her to CINS sanctions. Appellee attempts to continue this line of reasoning on appeal by anticipating potentially abusive applications of the statute in a variety of hypothetical situations, particularly emphasizing possible infringements upon First Amendment rights of children. But the Supreme Court in Parker v. Levy, supra, 417 U.S., at 759, rejected that approach when it said: . . . "[e]mbedded in the traditional rules governing constitutional adjudication is the principle that a person to whom a statute may constitutionally be applied will not be heard to challenge that statute on the ground that it may conceivably be applied unconstitutionally to others, in other situations not before the Court." [Broadrick v. Oklahoma, 413 U.S. 601, 610 (1973).] . . . "[T]he Court has recognized some limited exceptions to these principles, but only because of the most 'weighty countervailing policies.' " Id., at 611. One of those exceptions "has been carved out in the area of the First Amendment." Ibid. . . .

We find no "weighty countervailing policies" in this case to justify an attack on the facial validity of the CINS statute by one whose conduct clearly falls within its parameters. . . .

Neither the plainly legitimate sweep of the language of the CINS statute nor the facts of this case suggest a substantial infringement upon the constitutionally protected conduct of children so as to merit facial invalidation. The statute reinforces parents as they attempt to discipline their children in the broad ambit of family life. We conclude that the sort of activity that would establish a child as "habitually disobedient of the reasonable and lawful commands of his parent"

---

[3] Similar language in other statutes had been struck down on "vagueness" grounds in several jurisdictions. See, e.g., Gesicki v. Oswald, 336 P. Supp. 371 (S.D.N.Y. 1971) (holding unconstitutional N.Y. Code Crim. Proc. §913-a(5) and (6) which allowed incarceration of children "morally depraved or in danger of becoming morally depraved"). But see A. v. City of New York, 31 N.Y.2d 83, 286 N.E.2d 432 (1972) (upholding the "persons in need of supervision" portion of the same New York juvenile court act which consists of language remarkably similar to our own).

would seldom directly and principally involve First Amendment activity such as expressive conduct or pure speech. . . .

To the extent that First Amendment activities may be infringed when the CINS statute is applied, we suggest that in balancing such infringement against the right and duty of a parent to teach, control, and discipline a child, we are obliged, if we are to accord some recognition to reality, to grant the parent greater latitude in the First Amendment area than is permitted the state. However, such parental authority would be seriously undermined if not given some official support. It strikes us that in applying the First Amendment, the strict enforcement of those rights must be tempered when we consider disciplinary problems involving a parent-child relationship. . . .

Reversed and remanded for further proceedings not inconsistent with this opinion.

NOTE: RUNAWAYS — WHERE DO THEY GO?

Both *Walker* and *B.J.R.* involve young people who ran away from home. Consider what life is like for a runaway. Evidence indicates that most runaways, although they may travel within their own state, stay close to home.[70] According to the National Incidence Studies (NIS) of Runaway and Thrownaway Children, almost 1.7 million youths had a runaway or thrownaway episode in 1999.[71]

(1) Runaway Shelters.   One option for runaways is to seek the shelter and services of a runaway shelter. This is a viable alternative only for those fortunate enough to arrive in a community with one of the relatively small number of runaway houses in the United States. Of the estimated 500,000 to 1.5 million runaways annually, at most 70,000 find shelter in a runaway shelter.[72]

The federal government provides funding for runaway shelters through the Runaway Youth Act.[73] In passing the act in 1974, Congress acknowledged the effectiveness of community-based runaway youth centers to provide shelter and emergency assistance to runaway youth. Federal funds provide support to existing runaway youth centers and help establish new programs in unserved communities. To qualify for federal funding a runaway house must (1) be located in an area accessible to runaway youth; (2) have a maximum capacity of no more than 20 children with an adequate staff-child ratio; (3) develop plans for contacting the child's parents or relatives and assuring the safe return of the child, and for

---

[70] Only 23 percent of runaways travel more than 50 miles from home. Office of Juvenile Justice and Delinquency Prevention, National Incidence Studies (NIS) of Missing, Abducted, Runaway and Throwaway Children, "Runaway/Thrownaway Children: National Estimates and Characteristics," Table 3, at 7 (Oct. 2002).

[71] Id. at 5.

[72] Patricia Montoya (Commissioner, Administration on Children, Youth and Families, Dept. of Health & Human Servs.), Prepared Statement Before the House Education and the Workforce Subcomm. on Early Childhood, Youth and Families, The Reauthorization of the Runaway and Homeless Youth Act, 1999 WL 8086486, Mar. 25, 1999.

[73] Title III of the Juvenile Justice and Delinquency Prevention Act of 1974, 42 U.S.C. §§5700-5702, 5711-5713, 5715-5716, 5731-5732, 5751 (2000 & Supp. 2005).

providing other appropriate alternative living arrangements; (4) develop an adequate plan for assuring proper relations with law enforcement personnel, social service personnel, and welfare personnel and for the return of runaway youths from correctional institutions; (5) develop an adequate plan for aftercare counseling of youth and their parents; (6) develop an adequate plan for establishing or coordinating with outreach programs; (7) keep statistical records profiling the children and their parents while assuring the confidentiality of records; and (8) submit annual reports and budget estimates to the Secretary of Health and Human Services.[74]

In addition to federal funding, some states provide funding to runaway shelters. Runaway shelters offer a variety of services to the youth. All centers provide the basic services required by law, including outreach, temporary shelter, and individual and family counseling services. In addition, the centers furnish aftercare assistance in such areas as health, education, legal, and employment services, either directly or through referrals to other social service agencies.

(2) Profile of Runaway Youth.   According to the NIS Study of Runaway and Thrownaway Children, most runaway youths (68 percent) are older teens, aged 15 to 17. However, a surprisingly large percentage (28 percent) are aged 12 to 14. A considerable number of runaway episodes occur during the summer months, when young people are less constrained by weather and school activities. Although most runaways are gone from home for less than one week (77 percent), 7 percent are away for more than one month. Of the possible reasons for youths to leave home, 21 percent leave due to physical or sexual abuse and 19 percent due to addiction. In addition, 18 percent were in the company of someone known to be abusing drugs; 17 percent were using hard drugs; 11 percent engaged in criminal activity; and 4 percent had previously attempted suicide. Police are contacted to locate less than one-third of runaway or thrownaway youths. The two most common reasons for not contacting police are that the child's caretakers know the child's location or do not believe that police are needed.[75]

Researchers have explored in depth the relationship between running away and adolescent prostitution. The NIS Study reveals that many runaway or thrownaway youths engage in sexual activity in exchange for money, drugs, food, or shelter during the episode.[76] See generally D. Kelly Weisberg, Children of the Night: A Study of Adolescent Prostitution (1985).

In recognition of the large numbers of youth who are homeless because they were throwaways, rather than runaways, Congress reenacted the Runaway Youth Act in 1980 and broadened its scope, renaming it the Runaway and Homeless Youth Act, Pub. L. No. 96-509, 94 Stat. 2750 (codified as amended in scattered sections of 42 U.S.C.). In April 1999, the Senate passed legislation (S. 249, 106th Cong., 1st Sess. (1999)), titled the "Missing, Exploited and Runaway Children Protection Act," which provided funding for the National Center for Missing and

---

[74] 42 U.S.C. §5712(b)(3)-5712(b)(7) (2000).

[75] NIS Studies of Missing Children, supra note [70], Table 3, at 6-7. See generally Adrienne L. Fernandez, Runaway and Homeless Youth: Demographics, Programs, and Emerging Issues, Congressional Research Service Report to Congress (Dec. 2007).

[76] Id. at 6.

Exploited Children and also reauthorized funding for the Runaway and Homeless Youth Act for the years 2000 to 2004. In October 2003, Congress reauthorized programs under the Runaway and Homeless Youth Act and also the Missing Children's Assistance Act (S. 1451, 108th Cong., 1st Sess. (2003)). The Act is scheduled for reauthorization in 2008.

2.   Should Status Offenses Be Abolished?

Randy Frances Kandel & Anne Griffiths, Reconfiguring Personhood: From Ungovernability to Parent Adolescent Autonomy Conflict Actions
53 Syracuse L. Rev. 995, 1002-1003, 1032-1042, 1059-1063 (2003)

. . . Reconfiguration of the rights basis of ungovernability is essential because it remains a resilient populist resource, in the face of more than thirty years of governmental and professional efforts to abolish or curtail it. Ungovernability or PINS ["persons in need of supervision"] jurisdiction is easy to condemn, but it is very hard to kill. Disparaged by such entities as the Department of Justice, the American Bar Association and the Institute of Judicial Administration, ungovernability actions are increasingly seen as a resource by the largely poor and working class families who become caught in the web, often generation after generation.

In 1967, the President's Commission on Law Enforcement and Administration of Justice opined that "serious consideration . . . should be given to complete elimination of the court's power over children for noncriminal conduct." In 1974, during consideration of the major federal juvenile justice overhaul statute, the Juvenile Justice and Delinquency Prevention Act of 1974 (JJDPA), numerous august advisory and standard-setting groups recommended the reduction or elimination of juvenile court status offense jurisdiction and increased reliance on voluntary community-based services. The National Council on Crime and Delinquency issued a policy statement stating that:

> Subjecting a child to judicial sanction for a status offense . . . helps neither the child nor society; instead, it often does considerable harm to both. [It] serves no humanitarian or rehabilitative purpose. It is, instead, unwarranted punishment, unjust because it is disproportionate to the harm done by the child's noncriminal behavior. It cannot be justified under either a treatment or a punishment rationale.

[Nonetheless,] the 1974 version of the JJDPA stopped short of eliminating status offense jurisdiction. . . . The 1992 reauthorization of the JJDPA included a State Challenge Program amendment authorizing grants to states for innovative programming consistent with the Act's goals, including "[d]eveloping and adopting policies and programs to remove, where appropriate, status offenders from the jurisdiction of the juvenile court." Yet, since 1993, ungovernability cases have increased significantly. . . .

An ungovernability finding places the court in the position of enforcer of cultural stasis. . . . First, it places a particular onus on teens whose own personal development may be out of step with the mainstream chronological cultural norm. For example, girls whose physical and sexual maturity comes early may find themselves in foster homes or even institutions, branded as promiscuous merely because in the United States the length of required schooling is relatively long in a global sense, although many of the world's cultures may consider such girls ready for marriage and adult roles.

Second, teens who are considered rebellious in their local communities for violation of their cultural norms may find themselves branded ungovernable, even though, on a global scale, innovation in everything from music to politics often begins with teens, especially because it is a time of risk taking and experimentation. Constraining teens who "act-out" to follow traditional community norms may limit cultural diversity and may change society as a whole in a way which curtails creativity and diversity. As the norms of the legal culture approximate those of the middle class, the dampening of diversity results in an unconscious bias against the mores of lower class communities and ethnic and racial minorities. . . .

[A]dolescence and its constraints are especially prolonged in modern Western society, which requires along, generally expensive, period of post-childhood formal training before entry into the work world as an adult and a relatively high average age for childbirth. Many youths are PINSed because they are or seem to be ready to leave their period of formal school and to begin bearing children at an age that only postmodern technological twenty-first century Western society would find too young. However, this amounts to a class bias because many working class youths who are PINSed come from the kinds of backgrounds where "coming of age" has been relatively early. . . .

I. Summing Up: The Wrongs of Rights

Ungovernability jurisdiction is difficult to rationalize from either a parental rights or children's rights perspective. First, although seemingly buttressed by a conservative policy of enlisting the power and authority of the court in support of parental efforts to control a difficult or disobedient child and to maintain their fundamental liberty to raise their children as "they see fit," PINS jurisdiction . . . often accomplishes the reverse.

In seeking judicial intervention in the raising of their children, parents weaken the presumption that parental custody is in the child's best interests, in practice and effect if not in black letter law. The sad irony is that the court, in its parens patriae role, substitutes for, rather than strengthens, parental control. The initiation of a petition itself suggests an inability to personally and independently perform what the petitioner believes to be his or her parental responsibilities and duties. [T]he probation officer is empowered to prepare an influential report to the judge that details what the probation officer has learned from parents, child, and others and sets forth the probation officer's views about inadequacies or difficulties with the parents as well as the child. The confrontation of working-class and middle class views of rights, protection, and discipline . . . may now become part of the case. . . .

As an ungovernability finding is based only upon the child's behavior (ungovernable, habitually disobedient, beyond the control of custodian or lawful authority) and a disposition after such finding is based only upon the child's best interest, the custodial parent may (however initially willingly) lose custody of the child to a non-parent (the Department of Social Services) without any finding that parental custody is detrimental to the child, the stricter standard most often applied in custody disputes between parent and non-parent. . . .

Second, even if ungovernability jurisdiction did support parents' rights in the strong sense, the justification and rationale for enlisting judicial support in the process of child rearing weakens dramatically in the adolescent and teen years. In conflicts between parents and young children, children's autonomy rights are generally trumped by the custodial parents' fundamental constitutional liberty to control their children and the presumption that fit parents act in their children's best interests. With young children, parental rights, children's interests, and protective rights are tied together through the Gordian Knot of the child's relative immaturity. But the knot unravels in adolescence when people begin to think, choose, and act for themselves along lines that differ from those of their parents. . . .

Third, in ungovernability jurisdiction, the emphasis is almost totally on protective rights, at a developmental stage when the balance should be tipping towards autonomous choice. . . . The rights that [an adolescent] may constitutionally enjoy independently or with parental consent and the privileges that may be extended to her in her own family give way to institutional rules when a PINS is "placed" in a group home or institutional setting. The protective custody given to PINS youths resembles other non-criminal semi-incarcerations, such as detention of undocumented alien children or hospitalization of mentally ill teenagers, at least as much as the protective warmth of a loving parent.

Fourth, the protective emphasis is legitimated in "ungovernability" jurisprudence by the idea that there is something especially wrong, troubled, or at risk about the ungovernable adolescent. The exercise of "protective rights" as used in the PINS action is rationalized by a fuzzy pastiche of quasi-criminal and quasi-psychological-medical discourses that cloak the child and the parents in the context of social and psychological pathology and make it possible to avoid the hard issue of whether or not the PINS child may have good reasons for disobedience. Running away, cutting class, staying out late, "trashing" one's room, "stealing" a sibling's or stepparents' clothes, and defying household rules are often the instrumentalities of rational youths who, as subordinated actors, have no other means to resist unfairness, exercise independence, or influence family dynamics. . . .

Fifth, by definition, "ungovernable" adolescents and teens are neither criminal nor insane, so that it is only by a collaboration and conflation of discipline and therapy . . . that the action can be sustained as a way to provide protective custody and help to "soft" deviants. An entire "behavioral disorder" universe of symptoms and syndromes, such as oppositional/defiant disorder (ODD), has been developed largely for forensic purposes. The diagnostic features of these syndromes parallel the noncriminal behaviors that typify "ungovernable" youths either before or after they are so legally labeled. Diagnosis of syndromes that track legal charges becomes one reason to "place" adolescents and teens "for their own good," just at the age when the mix of rights begins to tip towards the autonomy pole. As the term of an ungovernability placement is renewable and ultimately indeterminate and follows the old juvenile justice rule of "best interests," mere naughtiness, renamed as "ungovernability" and/or "psychopathology" may lead to a longer institutionalization than criminality, and would come close to unconstitutionality in any non parens patriae context.

Sixth, in many situations, the forensic syndromes overtake and swamp the developmental stage of adolescence itself. The terms "ungovernability" and "habitual disobedience" virtually define adolescence as it is culturally understood and celebrated in the United States, and as it is defined in core Western psychological theory as a time of rebellion, turmoil and increasing conflict with parents. The heart of the problem is that adolescence and the teenage years are a time when it is both normal and normative to be deviant and therefore the syndromes, applied broadly, may apply to any adolescent. "[O]ppositional-defiant disorder" is a forensic syndrome with which almost any teenager may be loosely labeled. The jurisdiction is, indeed, an offense of being in a developmental "status."

Seventh, in ungovernability actions, adolescents and teens are at a procedural disadvantage as they are necessarily placed in the role of the quasi-criminal defendant. Substantively, the ungovernability allegation (Is the child ungovernable, habitually disobedient, or out of control?) and the presumption that parental decision-making is in the child's best interests, effectively deny the respondent youth any positive agency, choice, or intelligent wisdom. Either he is following what his parents prescribe, and he is not ungovernable, or he is not following what his parents prescribe, and he is ungovernable, either because he is naughty and willful or because he is diagnosable (e.g. with oppositional-defiant disorder). There is no defense of justification, better judgment, or personal choice and no counterclaim or action, if his parents are not neglectful or abusive but merely arbitrary, authoritarian, or insensitive. Not surprisingly, even respondents with excellent committed law guardians, rarely put on a case. The respondent has no real choice. She may receive protective rights under parental custody or the custody of the state but, unless the youth meets the standards for emancipation, there will not be a considered decision as to whether the respondent is in need of protective rights or entitled to rights of autonomy regarding any issue. . . .

The key question that brings families to the ungovernability court is who should make the decisions about the youth's day-to-day life. Parents PINS their sons and daughters because they believe that they must control and constrain the acts and autonomy of their youths to keep them on the path to productive adulthood, while the youths themselves feel the need to disagree, make defiant choices, do nothing, rebel, or experiment with possibly wild and risky decisions in order to be autonomous and independent adults. These are core questions of liberty, autonomy, and choice that are essentially legal ones, not psychological ones (although like divorce actions, they are intertwined with emotional matters). . . .

We suggest revamping the ungovernability action as a new Parent-Adolescent Autonomy Conflict action [PAAC]. . . . First, rather than a quasi-criminal action that requires a status offense determination to make a specific disposition, the PAAC would be a purely civil action between the parents (or other custodial caregiver) and the adolescent or teen. Both the parents and their son or daughter would have affirmative rights of standing to bring an initial action, assert claims and counterclaims, and to terminate a placement or modify a decision or order. To make the right a reality, adolescents and teens who lacked their own funds would be assigned attorneys.

Without any "status" finding the court would be empowered to determine the rights, responsibilities, obligations, directives, and breaches between the parties regarding specific issues, as in a contract dispute. Alternatively, the allegations might be more general, like a no fault divorce, speaking to the overall tension between a parent who wants to control and an offspring who wants to rebel. In emulation of some Australian juvenile statutes, they might allege "substantial and presently irretrievable breakdown" or "substantial and presently irreconcilable difference" between parent and child. . . .

Second, there would be a change of emphasis from disobedience and psychological dysfunction to disagreement between the parties. Third, there would be a change in emphasis from an exclusively welfare or protective rights rationale to a predominantly autonomy rights rationale. And fourth, at the same time, the essence and gravamen of the action would be to forthrightly address on an individualized case-by-case basis the nuances and tensions that exist in the gray area where parental control gradually slips away as children attain autonomy. In making decisions that cannot be determined by bright line rules, the court would be guided by the principles of legal personhood for adolescents and teens . . . (1) maturing decisional capacity; (2) the affirmative value and normality of experiment, risk, and rebellion; and (3) the standard of the "reasonable teen" as it incorporates context, culture, and class, and subordination as well as psychological and biological development.

[J]ust as adolescents and teens may sometimes be ordered to follow the dictates of their parents, so should parents, who are presumed to be capable of sufficient understanding of diverse personal views and their measurement against social and cultural norms, be charged with the obligation to recognize the independent ideas and decisions of their adolescents, even if they are in disagreement with them, and may be court ordered to respect their adolescent's ideas, behaviors, and decisions at the risk of losing custody of their teens.

Inevitably, the court would have authority to make a broad range of findings and dispositions and be able to open access to a wide range of resources. At one extreme, a court might make a finding of emancipation, enabling the youth to entirely live independently and self-responsibly if the youth meets the requisite criteria of maturity and potential self-sufficiency. At the other extreme, and as a last resort, the court might find, as it now often does, that the youth is truly out of parental control, yet too immature, wild, or unstable to make his or her daily decisions and should be adjudicated ungovernable, taken into the custody of social services, and "placed" in a foster family, group home, or institution.

But more often, the court would use its jurisdiction for intermediate decisions. For example, the court might order the parents to respect certain decisions of their son, not because he is a "mature minor" but because he is "mature enough" to make the decisions at issue, and enforce their custodial obligation to guide him in the expression of autonomy rights.

Adolescents and teens would have the right to assert, by petition or counterclaim, that specific parental demands or controls are unreasonable, and have an affirmative substantive right to petition the court to be removed from their parents because of unreasonable parental constraints or parental inadequacies (even those that do not constitute neglect or abuse). The court would be able to find that the child is a mature minor who is able to make an informed autonomous decision about a change of custody — in other words a rearrangement of residence and custody could be accomplished without a finding that the child is a wrongdoer. Alternatively, if the court found that the child was not a mature minor, the court would be able to arrange a placement on the grounds of irreconcilable parent-child conflict — a no fault decision, analogous to a divorce determination.

Parents or youths should be able to contract for a placement for a specified time through an expansion of respite, emergency, and short-term placements. In situations where an adolescent or teen is removed from the parental home, he or she should have a meaningful right to petition to go home that is not conditioned upon the preferences of the Department of Social Services. By the same token, parents should be able to petition to have their son or daughter temporarily, voluntarily "placed," and then returned without the present elaborate investigations and procedures. . . .

This reconceptualization of the PINS would also . . . require a greater use of mediation and other alternative dispute resolution options, either as mandated by the court or initiated by the parties. [M]ediation or other negotiated solutions might include contracts between parents and children regarding the reciprocal behavior of each, which would be legally enforceable.

Educational and residential alternatives would be needed. . . . Instead of providing only schools and homes that are based on disciplinary and behavior modification techniques, alternative environments that are facilitative of teens' evolving capacities and maturing decisional, emotional, and managerial capacities, and respectful of teens' choices, emotional connections, and developing ethics should be created. Upon a youth's petition, the court would have authority to issue an order permitting a youth, on the basis of the youth's decisional autonomy and against the parents' wishes, to live in an educational, vocational, or cooperative living situation that is facilitative to the youth's interests, and development, and that is "maturity enhancing," and not primarily intended to be correctional, rehabilitative, or therapeutic. . . . [A]lternatives should [facilitate] alternative ways to acquire a basic education, apprenticeships, mentorships and "vacations" from education, which would allow adolescents and teens to take a semester or a year off from school and then return without being labeled as truants or drop outs. Earlier opportunities to obtain the GED should be available so that people who do not want to study further could enter the job market sooner. . . .

In this way the legal system would promote a new approach to dealing with cases of conflict between parent and child, one that is based on a positive view of adolescents' and teens' agency, and an empowering vision of their rights. . . .

3. Status Offenders

NOTES AND QUESTIONS

(1) Justification for Status Offense Statutes. Note that in *Walker* the court suggests that an "undisciplined child" proceeding was "not a criminal prosecution" and that in *B.J.R.* the court says that the "CINS section is not a criminal

statute in the ordinary sense." What are these courts saying? That the state's purpose is rehabilitative, not retributive? Was the young person's liberty constrained substantially as a result of juvenile court jurisdiction in each case? Consider what Professor Francis A. Allen has written:

> Measures which subject individuals to the substantial and involuntary deprivation of their liberty contain an inescapable punitive element, and this reality is not altered by the facts that the motivations that prompt incarceration are to provide therapy or otherwise contribute to the person's well-being or reform. As such, these measures must be closely scrutinized to insure that power is being applied consistently with those values of the community that justify interference with liberty for only the most clear and compelling reasons.[77]

Do you agree?

What are the "clear and compelling" reasons consistent with community values to interfere with the liberty of the young people in *B.J.R.* and *Walker*? Was there any showing that the young person was in danger? Or was endangering others? Is the enforcement of parental controls over children a clear and compelling justification? Why?

Are status offenders substantially similar enough to juvenile delinquents that they should be handled by the same system? Or is the behavior of most status offenders a normal part of growing up and thus unlike the more hardened, deviant behavior of delinquents? Will early court intervention at the point of status offense prevent an escalation into more serious forms of delinquency? Or does juvenile court intervention itself cause escalation by encouraging youth to think of themselves as delinquent and to associate with others who have been similarly identified? For a recent discussion of the research, see Alex R. Piquero et al., The Criminal Career Paradigm, 30 Crime & Just. 359 (2003).

(2) The Procedural Rights of Youth "in Need of Supervision."   Are young people allegedly "in need of supervision" entitled to the same procedural rights, such as the privilege against self-incrimination, as young people accused of a crime? The juvenile justice system differentiates status offenders from delinquents in many ways. For example, the Supreme Court has required proof beyond a reasonable doubt in delinquency cases. In re Winship, 397 U.S. 358 (1970). However, the proof standard is not uniform for status offenses. Many states require only a preponderance of the evidence or clear and convincing evidence. See, e.g., Ark. Stat. Ann. §9-27-325 (Michie 2002 & Supp. 2008); N.C. Gen. Stat. §7B-805 (2004 & Supp. 2007). Some states, however, do require proof beyond a reasonable doubt. See, e.g., N.Y. Fam. Ct. Act §744(b) (McKinney 1999 & Supp. 2008); S.D. Codified Laws Ann. §26-7A-96/87 (2004).

Moreover, it is likely that evidence may be admissible at a PINS hearing that would not be admissible in the trial of a delinquency petition, and some statutes expressly authorize this. See, e.g., Cal. Welf. & Inst. Code §701 (West 1998 & Supp. 2008), providing that admissibility of evidence in a beyond-control case is

---

[77] Francis A. Allen, The Borderland of Criminal Justice: Essays in Law and Criminology 37 (1964).

governed by rules of evidence applicable to trial of a civil case, rather than by rules of evidence applicable to trial of a criminal case that govern in case of delinquency. This, together with the lower standard of proof commonly required, may explain in part why criminal offenses sometimes are dealt with under the PINS or other unruly child rubric.

Should a juvenile be entitled to counsel in status offense proceedings? Recall that *Walker,* supra p. 713, said no (like many jurisdictions). But cf. Mass. Gen. Laws ch. 119 §39F (2003 & Supp. 2008) (conferring right to counsel on status offenders). After *Walker,* the North Carolina legislature expressly provided for a right to representation in all juvenile court proceedings. N.C. Gen. Stat. §7B-2000 (2004 & Supp. 2007). Some courts maintain there is no right to counsel if institutionalization is not authorized. See, e.g., M.J.M. v. Department of Health & Rehabilitation Servs., 397 So. 2d 755 (Fla. Dist. Ct. App. 1981).

(3) Vagueness and Overbreadth. Many commentators have suggested that the statutes conferring status offense jurisdiction are unconstitutionally vague and overbroad.[78] But as *B.J.R.* suggests, appellate courts have generally upheld the constitutional validity of PINS statutes against such attacks. The Supreme Court has not explicitly dealt with these issues, although it summarily affirmed Oswald v. Gesicki, 406 U.S. 913 (1972) without opinion. In Gesicki v. Oswald, 336 F. Supp. 371 (S.D.N.Y. 1971), a three-judge federal district court invalidated a New York youthful offender statute that allowed jurisdiction over a wayward minor, defined as one who was "morally depraved or . . . in danger of becoming morally depraved."

(4) Sex Discrimination. Note that both *Walker* and *B.J.R.* involved teenage girls. Research reveals that status offense jurisdiction is invoked more frequently for girls than for boys. Parents refer girls to the juvenile justice system at a much higher rate than they refer boys, and girls are more likely to be arrested for these offenses. Thus, for example, in 1995, 27.5 percent of all girls' arrests were for status offenses, whereas only 10.5 percent of boys arrested were for status offenses.[79] In addition, whereas females accounted for 15 percent of juvenile offenders in custody in 2003, they accounted for 40 percent of youth in custody for status offenses.[80]

A number of states have set different age levels for the assertion of ungovernability (and sometimes delinquency and neglect) jurisdiction as between girls and boys. Courts, however, have invalidated such different age levels as violative of equal protection. See, e.g., People v. Ellis, 311 N.E.2d 98 (Ill. 1974); In re Patricia A., 286 N.E.2d 431 (N.Y. 1972). Courts that have struck down these laws have rejected the state's reliance on concerns about female pregnancy. Note, however, that in Michael M. v. Superior Court, 450 U.S. 464 (1981), in an equal protection

[78] See, e.g., Al Katz & Lee E. Teitelbaum, PINS Jurisdiction, the Vagueness Doctrine and the Rule of Law, 53 Ind. L.J. 1 (1978); Irene Merker Rosenberg, Juvenile Status Offender Statutes — New Perspectives on an Old Problem, 16 U.C. Davis L. Rev. 283, 294-300 (1983); Patricia M. Wald, The Rights of Youth, 4 Hum. Rts. 13, 21 (1974).

[79] Alecia Humphrey, The Criminalization of Survival Attempts: Locking Up Female Runaways and Other Status Offenders, 15 Hastings Women's L.J. 165, 173 (2004) (citing research).

[80] Howard N. Snyder & Melissa Sickmund, Juvenile Offenders and Victims: 2006 National Report, Office of Juvenile Justice and Delinquency Prevention (Mar. 2006), at 217.

challenge to California's statutory rape law, the United States Supreme Court found that the state's asserted concern about teenage pregnancy was a legitimate interest to justify the gender-discriminatory statute.

See generally Meda Chesney-Lind, The Female Offender (1997); Meda Chesney-Lind & Randall G. Shelden, Girls, Delinquency, and Juvenile Justice (2d ed., 1997); Cheryl Dalby, Gender Bias Toward Status Offenders: A Paternalistic Approach Carried Out Through the JJDPA, 12 Law & Ineq. J. 429 (1994); Laura A. Barnickol, Note, The Disparate Treatment of Males and Females Within the Juvenile Justice System, 2 Wash. U. J.L. & Pol'y, 429, 434 (2000).

(5) Proposed ABA Juvenile Justice Standards. The American Bar Association Juvenile Justice Standards Project has proposed the elimination of the general juvenile court jurisdiction over status offenses in noncriminal juvenile misbehavior. Instead, the standards place primary reliance on "a system of voluntary referral to services provided outside the juvenile justice system."[81]

> It is the position of these standards that the dejudicialization of status offenses and reliance on voluntarily based services will make those services more appropriate to the needs of the youth and his or her family; it is both true and a truism that help that a person elects to receive and in which he or she willingly participates has a better likelihood of success than services imposed at the end of a writ. Removal of the status offense jurisdiction will, it is submitted, encourage more people to get more effective help; stimulate the creation and extension of a wider range of voluntary services than is presently available; end the corrosive effects of treating noncriminal youth as though they had committed crimes; and free up a substantial part of the resources of the juvenile justice system to deal with the cases of delinquency and of abused and neglected children that belong in it.[82]

The proposed standards do not eliminate coercive instruction completely, however. The Introduction to the Standards notes:

> [B]ecause of the particular problems presented by certain kinds of cases — youths who run away, who are in circumstances of immediate jeopardy, who are in need of alternative living arrangements when they and their parents cannot agree, and who evidence a need for emergency medical services — some carefully limited official intervention is preserved, though in all cases wardship as a result of the child's noncriminal behavior or circumstances is precluded.[83]

The standards permit a law enforcement officer to take a juvenile into limited custody for no more than six hours if the juvenile (a) is "absent from home without [parental] consent";[84] or (b) "is in circumstances which constitute a substantial and immediate danger to the juvenile's physical safety."[85] The officer must then notify the child's parent or guardian "as soon as practicable" unless there are

---

[81] American Bar Association, Juvenile Justice Standards for Noncriminal Misbehavior 2(1982).

[82] Id. at 15.

[83] Id. at 2.

[84] Id. at 25.

[85] Id. at 23.

"compelling circumstances why the parent or guardian should not" be notified.[86] If a parent or other responsible person is unavailable, or if the child refuses to go home with the parents, the officer is authorized to take the juvenile to a state licensed "temporary nonsecure residential facility."[87] The juvenile may stay there for no more than 21 days, unless the parent consents or a neglect petition is filed.[88]

If the juvenile chooses not to return home, the juvenile may file a motion to have the juvenile court approve some alternative residential placement.[89] The court is required to approve the placement requested by the juvenile unless the court finds upon a preponderance of the evidence that that placement imperils or would imperil the juvenile — that is, that it "fails to provide physical protection, adequate shelter, or adequate nutrition; or seriously and unconscionably obstructs the juvenile's medical care, education, or physical and emotional development, as determined according to the needs of the juvenile in the particular case; or exposes the juvenile to unconscionable exploitation."[90] In such circumstances the court may direct some alternative "non-secure" placement.

The standards also allow for a juvenile to be taken into "emergency custody" for a period not to exceed 72 hours in limited circumstances that show an "immediate need for emergency psychiatric or medical evaluation and possible care." Beyond that period, however, the standards envision that the juvenile may be held only pursuant to the state's adult procedures for mental health commitments.[91]

4.   Dispositions in PINS Cases

State v. Damian R.
591 S.E.2d 168 (W. Va. 2003)

STARCHER, C.J.

. . . The appellant, D.R., was born on September 4, 1987, and was fourteen years old at the time of the proceedings below. During the 2001-2002 school year the juvenile resided with his mother [a single parent] in Berkeley County, and was enrolled in the seventh grade. The juvenile had truancy and anger management problems at school; in the Fall of 2001 he was expelled from school and the school system offered him alternative educational services on two nights a week after school. A truancy diversion social worker was assigned to work with the juvenile and his family. The juvenile attended some of the alternative education sessions, but missed most of them.

---

[86] Id. at 24.
[87] Id.
[88] Id. at 25.
[89] Id. at 29.
[90] Id. at 29-30.
[91] Id. at 31-34.

In late 2001, the juvenile's mother, seeking further assistance in dealing with her problems with her son,[2] consulted with the Berkeley County Prosecuting Attorney's Office. As a result of this consultation and with the mother's consent, on December 12, 2001, the Berkeley County Prosecuting Attorney filed a petition pursuant to W.Va. Code, 49-5-7 [1998], requesting that the juvenile be adjudged to be a status offender.

A probable cause hearing was held by the circuit court on January 29, 2002, where a truancy diversion social worker and the juvenile's mother testified briefly to the juvenile's misconduct. The social worker testified that the juvenile would benefit from counseling; the mother testified that while the juvenile's behavior had already improved noticeably since the petition was filed, the mother still felt she needed help from the court. The circuit court ruled that probable cause had been established and set a date about one month later for an adjudicatory hearing.

On February 27, 2002, the circuit court held the adjudicatory hearing. There was no evidence presented of any further misconduct by the juvenile since the probable cause hearing. The juvenile's counsel advised the court that the juvenile would admit to the factual allegations in the petition and that the juvenile wished to remain with his mother. The circuit court questioned the juvenile to be sure that he understood his rights and then accepted the juvenile's acknowledgment of the truth of the allegations in the petition.

The circuit court entered an order adjudicating the juvenile as a status offender, based on incorrigibility and truancy. The court referred the juvenile to the West Virginia Department of Health and Human Resources ("DHHR") "for treatment according to statute." The court also ordered a psychological examination of the juvenile. The court cautioned the juvenile that his truancy was unacceptable; that he needed above all to attend school regularly; and that he would face more serious consequences if he did not attend school as required.

After this hearing the juvenile began to attend school again. Then, on March 1, 4 and 7, the juvenile reportedly "acted out" in school, by yelling at a teacher and not following directions. The school contacted the DHHR, and on March 15, 2002 the DHHR filed a petition with the circuit court, briefly describing the reported "acting out" incidents and further alleging that "[t]he Juvenile is not amenable to services in the community because he will not remain in a safe residence long enough for services to be offered nor is there a community service available that can supervise the Juvenile to prevent him from skipping school, being incorrigible, and running away, so therefore it is in the best interest of this fourteen-year-old Juvenile if he is placed in the custody of the Department and placed in a staff secure facility." The DHHR sought an order awarding custody of the juvenile to the DHHR for out-of-home placement.

A hearing on this petition was held on March 25, 2002, following which the circuit court entered an order — without making any specific written findings — granting custody of the juvenile to the DHHR for the purpose of making placement

---

[2] These problems included emotional outbursts, not following household rules, throwing things, not saying where he was going when he left the house, smoking marijuana; and, as previously noted, refusing to go to school.

at a place to be determined, and pending such placement ordering that the juvenile be held at the Romney Child Care Center. . . .

[On appeal, appellant argues] that awarding custody to the DHHR was improper because the DHHR had not even attempted to provide the services that would be a less restrictive alternative than removal from his mother's custody. . . .

The proceedings at issue in the instant case alleged that the juvenile was a "status offender" — i.e., a child whose complained-of conduct would not be a crime if the conduct was engaged in by an adult. . . . [W.Va. Code 49-5-11.] The referral from the circuit court pursuant to W.Va. Code, 49-5-11(d) [1998] triggers a duty by the DHHR to provide services to the juvenile, under the mandate of W.Va. Code, 49-5-11a [1998], which states in part:

> (a) Services provided by the department for juveniles adjudicated as status offenders shall be consistent with the provisions of article five-b of this chapter [49-5B-1] and shall be designed to develop skills and supports *within families* and to resolve problems related to the juveniles or conflicts *within their families.* Services may include, but are not limited to, referral of juveniles and parents, guardians or custodians and other family members to services for psychiatric or other medical care, or psychological, welfare, legal, educational or other social services, as appropriate to the needs of the juvenile and his or her family. (Emphasis added.) . . .

The DHHR's petition for custody in the instant case is grounded in the language in the foregoing-quoted statute authorizing the DHHR to "[i]f necessary . . . petition the circuit court [to] . . . place a [referred status offender] out of home in a non-secure or staff-secure setting, and/or to place a juvenile in custody of the department." Id.

The appellant suggests that as a matter of law and in all cases, in order for the DHHR to seek under W.Va. Code, 49-5-11a(b)(2) [1998] to have custody of an adjudicated status offender transferred from the child's parent to the DHHR — as a quasi-jurisdictional and necessary precursor for such a request, the DHHR must first have provided services to the juvenile and his or her family while the juvenile is in the parent's home and custody, and the DHHR must show that these in-home services have been ineffective, thus rendering a further court order "necessary."

However, such a reading of W.Va. Code, 49-5-11a [1998] is not compelled by the language of the statute, nor would such a reading comport with common sense. Certainly there could be a severe case in which the provision of services to a status offender necessarily requires, in the first instance, an order placing a juvenile out of his or her parents' custody or home in the first instance — such as when a juvenile's parent is gravely ill, for example. Having said this, however, we must emphasize that the entire statutory scheme for status offenders contemplates that removal from the home and/or transfer of custody from a parent be undertaken only when necessary and upon clear and convincing proof that no less restrictive alternative is feasible.

The removal of a juvenile status offender or delinquent from his parent's custody is authorized "only when the child's welfare or the safety and protection of the public cannot be adequately safeguarded without removal . . . ." W.Va.

Code, 49-1-1(a)(12)(b) [1999].[5] While the 1997 revisions to the child welfare statutes "grant courts broader discretion in determining the precise placement for status offenders that will meet the best interests of the juvenile and the community [,]" the requirement of selecting the least restrictive appropriate alternative remains.

In the law concerning custody of minor children, no rule is more firmly established than that the right of a natural parent to the custody of his or her infant child is paramount to that of any other person; it is a fundamental personal liberty protected and guaranteed by the Due Process Clauses of the West Virginia and United States Constitutions. . . .

Based on the foregoing, we hold that the prior actual provision of services by the State Department of Health and Human Resources to a status offender is not in all cases a jurisdictional prerequisite for the filing of a petition seeking an order transferring custody of the status offender to the Department and/or out-of-home placement under W.Va. Code, 49-5-11a(b)(2) [1998]; however, such a petition may only be granted upon a showing by clear and convincing evidence that such a custody or placement order is actually necessary; that the effective provision of services cannot occur absent such an order; and that all reasonable efforts have been made to provide appropriate services without an out-of-home placement and/ or custody transfer; additionally, orders granting such placement or transfer must be based on specific findings and conclusions by the court with respect to the grounds for and necessity of the order.

Applying the foregoing principles to the facts of the instant case, we first note that the DHHR was required upon receipt of the initial referral from the court to establish an individualized plan of rehabilitation for the juvenile. W.Va. Code, 49-5B-4(b) [1999]. No evidence was adduced regarding the establishment of such a plan in the instant case. Moreover, while the DHHR alleged in its post-adjudication petition for custody and transfer that "services were provided to the Juvenile by the Children's Home Society of West Virginia[,]" and that "[t]he juvenile will not remain in a safe residence long enough for services to be provided nor is there a community service available that can supervise the Juvenile to prevent him from skipping school, being incorrigible, and running away . . . [,]" in fact none of these allegations were addressed, much less proven, at the March 25, 2002 hearing.[7] [T]he evidence at the March 25, 2002 hearing did not legally establish the

---

[5] Additionally, W.Va. Code, 49-5-13(b)(4) [1999], which applies to delinquents and not status offenders, requires the court to determine whether the Department made reasonable efforts to prevent an out-of-home placement before such a placement may be ordered. Certainly there is no less of a requirement for status offenders.

[7] Additionally, no evidence showed that the DHHR had, prior to filing its post-adjudication petition for custody and placement, attempted to implement any less restrictive alternative. A lecture from a trial judge and "fear of consequences" is not the provision of rehabilitative services that the DHHR is required to deliver to status offenders. In the instant case, the DHHR had a responsibility after adjudication to promptly meet with the juvenile and his parent and to discuss how to implement a home-based services plan. Certainly, after the first reported incident at school of March 1, 2002, the DHHR was on notice of a pressing need to immediately begin to work with the juvenile to try to avoid further incidents in school — or to return to an effective alternative education plan. Nothing in the record demonstrates any such attempt.

necessity — for the protection of the juvenile or the public — of transferring legal custody of the juvenile to the DHHR and removing him from his home.

For this reason, the circuit court's order removing the juvenile from his parent's custody and transferring it to the DHHR and placing him out of his home must be reversed. . . .

NOTES AND QUESTIONS

(1) Statistics. In 2004, 159,400 status offense cases were formally disposed of by juvenile courts nationwide. The number of petitioned status offense cases processed by juvenile courts rose 39 percent between 1995 and 2004, including a 69 percent increase in truancy cases, a 38 percent increase in ungovernability cases, and a 17 percent increase in liquor violations. The rate for curfew violation cases increased 66 percent between 1995 and 2000 before declining 17 percent between 2000 and 2004.[92]

(2) Deinstitutionalization Movement. No state has adopted the ABA Juvenile Justice Standards that eliminate general juvenile court jurisdiction over noncriminal juvenile behavior.[93] However, there has been an important movement to deinstitutionalize status offenders.[94] The deinstitutionalization movement began in the 1970s as concerns were raised about incarcerating juveniles for noncriminal behavior. The federal government facilitated the movement by enacting in 1974 the Juvenile Justice and Delinquency Prevention Act (JJDPA), 42 U.S.C. §§5601-5751 (2000 & Supp. 2005). Prior to the JJDPA, most states provided for secure detention for status offenders. However, the JJDPA discouraged the practice of commingling status offenders and delinquents, encouraged the diversion of status offenders from the juvenile justice system whenever possible, and encouraged alternatives to the traditional juvenile detention and correctional facilities. The JJDPA required states to remove all status offenders from secure institutions to be eligible for federal funds.

Juvenile Justice and Delinquency Prevention Act
42 U.S.C. §5633 (2000 & Supp. 2005)

State Plans

(a) Requirements

In order to receive formula grants under this part, a State shall submit a plan for carrying out its purposes applicable to a 3-year period. [S]uch plan . . .

---

[92] Office of Juvenile Justice and Delinquency Prevention, U.S. Dept. of Justice, Juvenile Court Statistics 2003-2004, at 70 (2007).

[93] See John Murray, Status Offenders: A Sourcebook 28 (table 8) (1983).

[94] "Deinstitutionalization" refers to the removal of status offenders from secure detention or correctional facilities or preventing their placement in such facilities. (In contrast to secure facilities, nonsecure facilities permit greater freedom of movement by the juvenile, offer minimal supervision by staff, and generally have no locked areas.)

(11) shall, in accordance with rules issued by the Administrator, provide that—

(A) juveniles who are charged with or who have committed an offense that would not be criminal if committed by an adult [with some exceptions, such as youths who knowingly possess a handgun or ammunition, who have committed a violation of a valid court order, etc.] shall not be placed in secure detention facilities or secure correctional facilities; and

(B) juveniles—

(i) who are not charged with any offense; and

(ii) who are [aliens or alleged to be dependent, neglected, or abused];

shall not be placed in secure detention facilities or secure correctional facilities;

(12) provide that—

(A) juveniles alleged to be or found to be delinquent or juveniles within the purview of paragraph (11) will not be detained or confined in any institution in which they have contact with adult inmates; . . .

(13) provide that no juvenile will be detained or confined in any jail or lockup for adults except—

(A) juveniles who are accused of nonstatus offenses and who are detained in such jail or lockup for a period not to exceed 6 hours—

(i) for processing or release;

(ii) while awaiting transfer to a juvenile facility; or

(iii) in which period such juveniles make a court appearance;

and only if such juveniles do not have contact with adult inmates. . . .

(B) juveniles who are accused of nonstatus offenses, who are awaiting an initial court appearance that will occur within 48 hours after being taken into custody (excluding Saturdays, Sundays, and legal holidays), and who are detained in a jail or lockup—

(i) in which—

(I) such juveniles do not have contact with adult inmates; and

(II) there is in effect in the State a policy that requires individuals who work with both such juveniles and adult inmates in collocated facilities have been trained and certified to work with juveniles; and

(ii) that

(I) [is located outside a metropolitan area and has no existing acceptable alternative placement available]; or

(II) [is located where travel conditions do not allow for court appearances within 48 hours]; or

(III) [is located where adverse conditions of safety exist (such as adverse weather conditions)]

(14) provide for an adequate system of monitoring jails, detention facilities, correctional facilities, and non-secure facilities to insure that the requirements of paragraphs (11), (12), and (13) are met, and for annual reporting of the results of such monitoring to the Administrator, except that such reporting requirements shall not apply in the case of a State which is in compliance with the other requirements of this paragraph, which is in compliance with the requirements in paragraphs (11) and (12), and which has enacted legislation which conforms to such requirements and which contains, in the opinion of the Administrator, sufficient enforcement mechanisms to ensure that such legislation will be administered effectively. . . .

Subsequent amendments changed the deinstitutionalization (DSO) requirements. The Juvenile Justice Amendments of 1977, Pub. L. No. 95-115, 91 Stat. 1054 (1977), revised the timetable by adding two years to the three-year limit within which states must comply. In addition, the amendments defined what was required for substantial compliance with the JJDPA — "achievement of deinstitutionalization of not less than 75 per centum of such juveniles." The Juvenile Justice Amendments of 1980, 42 U.S.C. §5633(a)(12) (2000), contained additional revisions that authorized the confinement of status offenders who had violated a valid court order. Further, states are still eligible for grants if their failure to comply is "de minimus," according to a legal opinion of the Law Enforcement Assistance Administration Office of General Counsel.[95]

(3) Compliance Data. The Office of Juvenile Justice and Delinquency Prevention (OJJDP) is the agency responsible for administering JJDPA funds. In regard to states' compliance with deinstitutionalization requirements, OJJDP notes that as of December 31, 2003, five states and territories were in compliance with the deinstitutionalization of status offenders provision of the JJDPA, 46 states and territories were in full compliance with de minimis exceptions (fewer than 29.4 violations per 100,000 persons under age 18 in the state), and three states and territories were not in compliance. With regard to the provision in the JJDPA requiring separation of juveniles and adult offenders, 41 states and territories were in full compliance, ten states were in compliance based on regulatory exceptions, and three jurisdictions were not in compliance. Nine states and territories were in compliance with the jail and lockup provision of JJDPA, stipulating that juveniles cannot be detained in any adult jail or lockup. Forty-three states and territories were in full compliance with de minimus exceptions, and two jurisdictions were not in compliance.[96]

These statistics, however, do not reveal the full picture. To meet governmental requirements to comply with the JJDPA, many states did prohibit the secure

---

[95] Cited in Robert W. Sweet, Jr., Deinstitutionalization of Status Offenders: In Perspective, 18 Pepperdine L. Rev. 389, 408 (1991).

[96] Office of Juvenile Justice and Delinquency Prevention, U.S. Dept. of Justice, Annual Report 37-38 (2004).

detention of status offenders. However, states then were torn between satisfying governmental funding requirements and popular demands to respond to the many problems of status offenders. In response to this dilemma, as commentators explain, states developed certain tactics to circumvent the JJDPA's requirements: "(a) referring or committing a status offender to a secure mental health facility (public or private), (b) alleging juvenile delinquency instead of status offense in petition to permit detention in juvenile hall, (c) developing "semi-secure" facilities which would technically comply with the JJDPA definition but which operated as secure in fact, and (d) using the court's contempt power to "bootstrap" a status offender into a delinquent."[97]

(4) The "Re-Institutionalization" Movement.   Subsequent to the JJDPA, the wisdom of the deinstitutionalization movement was called into question, particularly in regard to runaway children. The U.S. Attorney General Advisory Board on Missing and Exploited Children issued a report recommending that both federal and state legislatures amend their laws to allow the institutionalization of runaways. OJJDP America's Missing and Exploited Children: Their Safety and Their Future 19-20 (March 1986). Some authorities who worked with runaway prostitutes believed that police officers should be able to place the youth in secure facilities at least for short periods. This would keep the youth safe from pimps, as well as facilitate both rehabilitation services and criminal investigation.

In response to calls for reform, in 1995 the Washington state legislature passed "Becca's Bill," Wash Rev. Code §13.32 (West 2004), to provide for the detention of status offenders in secure facilities for at least 24 hours and up to five consecutive days. (A more stringent provision, to hold habitual runaways in secure facilities for up to six months, was vetoed by the governor.) The bill was passed in response to the murder of a 13-year-old runaway prostitute. Following her death, her adoptive parents sought legislation to address the frustration caused by the fact that police could detain runaways only for a short time and only in unsecured facilities.[98] Do Becca's Bill detention provisions, which place runaways in secure facilities, violate juveniles' due process rights? See Carrie A. Tracy, Note, A Proposal to Bring the Becca's Bill Runaway-Detention Provisions into Compliance with Juvenile's Procedural Due Process Rights, 75 Wash. L. Rev. 1399 (2000) (so arguing).

(5) Policy Arguments.   What are the arguments in support of, and in opposition to, the institutionalization of status offenders? Is it fair to lock up children who have done nothing criminal? Will exposure to delinquents be harmful to status offenders? Is it wasteful to spend juvenile court resources on noncriminal youth? What light does *Damian R.* shed on this issue?

(6) Some commentators argue that deinstitutionalization results in the practice of relabeling or in the phenomenon of a "hardening of the record." Often minors

---

[97] Bruce J. Winick et al., "Wayward and Noncompliant" People with Mental Disabilities, 9 Psychol. Pub. Pol'y & L. 233, 240 (2003).

[98] On the history of the legislation, see Tiffany Zwicker Eggers, The "Becca Bill" Would Not Have Saved Becca: Washington State's Treatment of Young Female Offenders, 16 Law & Ineq. 219, 219-225, 230-235 (1998).

commit two offenses — a status offense and a delinquent offense. Before the dein-stitutionalization movement, the system would have labeled the juvenile a status offender to avoid the stigma of delinquency. However, after the deinstitutional-ization requirements, the child would have to be relabeled a delinquent or mentally ill to become eligible for services or to provide for detention. See Status Offender Incarceration Decreases Partly Offset by Relabelling, Net Widening, 12 Crim. Just. Newsletter 1 (April 27, 1981). Is this a result of the prohibition against placing children in secure facilities or of a systems failure elsewhere?

(7) Bootstrapping. May a status offender be institutionalized as a delinquent for violating a court order (for instance, to attend school regularly or not run away)? "Bootstrapping" refers to the practice of using the court's contempt power to change a "status offender" into a "delinquent." Initially, the Juvenile Justice and Delinquency Prevention Act, 42 U.S.C. §§5601-5751 (2000), prohibited incar-cerating status offenders after elevating them to delinquency status for failure to comply with a court order. However, as explained earlier, §5633(a)(12)(A) of the Act was amended in 1980 to permit the incarceration in secure facilities of status offenders, who violated valid court orders. Courts have split over the question of whether they can use their contempt power to place children in secure facilities. Note the ease with which the West Virginia Department of Health and Human Services in the principal case requested that Damian be placed in a secure facility for violating the court order that he attend school regularly. Most states have affirmed their courts' use of the contempt power to order the secure detention of contemptuous status offenders, despite an expression of legislative intent gen-erally banning such detention. Bruce J. Winick et al., "Wayward and Noncom-pliant People" with Mental Disabilities, 9 Psychol. Pub. Pol'y & L. 233, 242 (2003). But cf. Commonwealth v. Florence F., 709 N.E.2d 418 (Mass. 1999) (disapproving the practice).

(8) Juvenile Diversion Programs. Many states offer juvenile diversion pro-grams by which status offenders (and sometimes, first-offender delinquents) are diverted out of the juvenile court and channeled to community-based treatment-oriented programs. As Professor Franklin Zimring explains, diversion "has been an important motive in juvenile justice from the beginning, and became the dominant purpose of a separate juvenile court after In re Gault in 1967."[99] As mentioned previously (supra, p. 737), the federal government gave such programs a boost when the JJDPA emphasized the need to establish programs "to divert juveniles from the traditional juvenile justice system and to provide critically needed alternatives to institutionalization." Juvenile diversion programs have several benefits:

> By maintaining the youth's ties with his family and the community, diversion avoids the potential effect of a formal delinquent label which could adversely affect his self-image and contribute to subsequent delinquent behavior. Studies show that diversion programs are reducing the number of repeat offenders.

---

[99] Franklin E. Zimring, The Common Thread: Diversion in Juvenile Justice, 88 Cal. L. Rev. 2477, 2479 (2000).

> In addition, in the long run, diversion programs are cheaper than expanding juvenile police, courts, and corrective functions. Diversion offers the possibility of reallocating funds and resources to community programs that may satisfy a more rational public policy than traditional static juvenile corrections programs.[100]

Professor Zimring concludes that "The past thirty years have been the juvenile court's finest hour as a diversion project; the rate of juvenile incarceration has been stable, while incarceration of young adults has soared."[101]

(9) Anti-Truancy Reforms. The juvenile in *Damian R.* came to the attention of the juvenile justice system because of truancy. School districts increasingly are enacting tough new measures to curb truancy. Many states now punish *parents* with fines and imprisonment if their children are habitually truant. The definition of "habitually truant" varies considerably (e.g., 15 unexcused absences within 90 days in Florida; 6 unexcused absences in Oakland, California). Punishments also vary. For example, parents in Florida face fines of $500 and 60 days in jail compared to fines of $2,500 and a year in jail for parents in Kern County, California.[102] Moreover, in some jurisdictions, parents of truant children can be made to attend parenting class and are subject to prosecution for contributing to the delinquency of a minor.[103] Is this approach likely to be effective? Is it sound policy?

5. Should Children Be Able to Divorce Their Parents?

In re Snyder
532 P.2d 278 (Wash. 1975)

EN BANC.
HUNTER, Associate Justice.

Paul Snyder and Nell Snyder, petitioners, seek review of the King County Juvenile Court's finding that their daughter, Cynthia Nell Snyder, respondent, was an incorrigible child as defined under RCW 13.04.010(7). . . .

Cynthia Nell Snyder is 16 years old, attends high school, and has consistently received above average grades. Prior to the occurrences which led to this action, she resided with her parents in their North Seattle home. The record shows that as Cynthia entered her teen years, a hostility began to develop between herself and her parents. This environment within the family home worsened due to a total breakdown in the lines of communication between

---

[100] S'Lee Arthur Hinshaw II, Juvenile Diversion: An Alternative to Juvenile Court, 1993 J. Disp. Resol. 305, 312-313 (1993).

[101] Zimring, supra note [99], at 2479.

[102] Julian Guthrie, Parents Face Jail Time if Kids Miss Class, S.F. Examiner, Sept. 19, 1999, at A1.

[103] Jennifer Radcliffe, Warning Issued on Truancy, Consequences Spelled out for Offenders, L.A. Daily News, Dec. 2, 2004, at N4.

Cynthia and her parents. Cynthia's parents, being strict disciplinarians, placed numerous limitations on their daughter's activities such as restricting her choice of friends, and refusing to let her smoke, date, or participate in certain extracurricular activities within the school, all of which caused Cynthia to rebel against their authority. These hostilities culminated in a total collapse of the parent-child relationship. This atmosphere resulted in extreme mental abuse to all parties concerned.

On June 18, 1973, Mr. Snyder, having concluded that the juvenile court might be able to assist him in controlling his daughter, removed Cynthia from the family home and delivered her to the Youth Service Center. As a result, Cynthia was placed in a receiving home. On July 19, 1973, in an attempt to avoid returning home, Cynthia filed a petition in the Juvenile Department of the Superior Court for King County, alleging that she was a dependent child as defined by RCW 13.04.010(2) and (3), which provide:

> This chapter shall be shown as the "Juvenile Court Law" and shall apply to all minor children under the age of eighteen years who are delinquent or dependent, and to any person or persons who are responsible for or contribute to, the delinquency or dependency of such children.
>
> For the purpose of this chapter the words "dependent child" shall mean any child under the age of eighteen years: . . .
>
> (2) Who has no parent, guardian or other responsible person; or who has no parent or guardian willing to exercise, or capable of exercising, proper parental control; or
>
> (3) Whose home by reason of neglect, cruelty or depravity of his parents or either of them, or on the part of his guardian, or on the part of the person in whose custody or care he may be, or for any other reason, is an unfit place for such child; . . .

On July 23, 1973, Cynthia was placed in the temporary custody of the Department of Social and Health Services and an attorney was appointed to be her guardian ad litem. On October 12, 1973, the juvenile court held that the allegations attacking the fitness of Cynthia's parents were incorrect, at least to the extent that they alleged dependency, and that Cynthia should be returned to the custody of her parents. Cynthia did return to the family residence, where she remained until November 16, 1973. At that time, following additional confrontations in her home, Cynthia went to Youth Advocates, a group which assists troubled juveniles, who in turn directed her to the Youth Service Center. On November 21, 1973, Margaret Rozmyn, who was in charge of the intake program at the center, filed a petition alleging that Cynthia was incorrigible as defined under RCW 13.04.010(7), which provides:

> For the purpose of this chapter the words "dependent child" mean any child under the age of eighteen years: . . .
>
> (7) Who is incorrigible; that is, who is beyond the control and power of his parents, guardian, or custodian by reason of the conduct or nature of said child; . . .

A hearing was held on December 3, 1973, to determine temporary custody. The court limited the proceedings to arguments of opposing counsel and ultimately decided that Cynthia should be placed in a foster home pending the outcome of the fact-finding hearing. This hearing was held on December 10 and 11, 1973. At that time, Commissioner Quinn found that Cynthia was incorrigible and continued the matter for one week in order for the entire family to meet with a counselor. Originally, the commissioner indicated that he was inclined to have Cynthia return home, while at the same time being placed under supervised probation. However, on December 18, 1973, Commissioner Quinn upon hearing the comments and conclusions of the counseling psychiatrists chosen by the parents, decided that Cynthia was to be placed in a foster home, under the supervision of the probation department of the juvenile court, and that she and her parents were to continue counseling, subject to subsequent review by the court. The parents immediately filed a motion for revision of the commissioner's decision, which was denied by the Superior Court for King County in August of 1974.

This court assumed jurisdiction of the case upon our issuance of the requested writ of certiorari.

The sole issue presented by these facts is whether there is substantial evidence in the record, taken as a whole, to support the juvenile court's determination that Cynthia Nell Snyder is incorrigible. Her parents contend that Cynthia is not incorrigible, as a matter of law, since the only evidence to support such a finding is their daughter's own statements. We disagree.

A child is incorrigible when she is beyond the power and control of her parents by reason of her own conduct. RCW 13.04.010(7). In reviewing the record in search of substantial evidence, we must find "evidence in sufficient quantum to persuade a fair-minded, rational person of the truth of a declared premise." Helman v. Sacred Heart Hospital, 62 Wash. 2d 136, 147, 381 P.2d 605, 612 (1963). In applying this criteria for review, we are mindful that our paramount consideration, irrespective of the natural emotions in cases of this nature, must be the welfare of the child. . . . When the questions of dependency and incorrigibility arise, "we have often noted what we think is a realistic and rational appellate policy of placing very strong reliance on trial court determinations of what course of action will be in the best interests of the child." In re Todd, 68 Wash. 2d [587] at 591, 414 P.2d [605] at 608. In reviewing the record, we find no evidence which would indicate that Commissioner Quinn acted unfairly, irrationally, or in a prejudicial manner in reaching his conclusion. Therefore, we must give "very strong" credence to his determinations. We feel it is imperative to recognize that the issue of who is actually responsible for the breakdown in the parent-child relationship is irrelevant to our disposition of this case. The issue is whether there is substantial evidence to support a finding that the parent-child relationship has dissipated to the point where parental control is lost and, therefore, Cynthia is incorrigible. It is for this reason that Cynthia's conduct, her state of mind, and the opinion of Doctor Gallagher, the psychiatrist chosen by Mr. and Mrs. Snyder, are of such paramount importance. This child has established a pattern of refusing to obey her parents and, on two occasions, has, in effect, fled her home by filing petitions in the juvenile court in order that she might be made a ward of the court. Cynthia's adamant state of mind can be best understood by considering her *clear* and *unambiguous* testimony in response to her attorney's direct examination.

Q. Your petition alleges that you absolutely refuse to go home and obey your parents, is that correct?

A. Yes.

Q. You are under oath today, of course, and is that the statement you would make to the Court today?

A. Yes.

Q. Cindy, do you understand the consequences of filing a petition of this nature?

A. Yes.

Q. Did we discuss this matter?

A. Yes.

Q. Have we discussed this on several occasions?

A. Yes.

Q. What is your understanding of what might be the consequences of this type of petition?

A. I could be put in the Youth Center or I could be put in another institution of some kind or I could go into the custody of the Department of Social and Health Services.

Q. So you understand it is conceivable that you might not be able to go back home, is that correct?

A. Yes.

Q. In spite of all that, is it still your statement today that at the time of the petition anyway you refused to go back home?

A. Yes.

Q. Is that your position right now?

A. Yes.

Q. The position then, why don't you state that for the Court?

A. I refuse to go back there. I just won't do it.

MR. SANDERS [Attorney for parents]. I object to the whole line of testimony. I think it is irrelevant whether she refuses to go back home. That is not an issue in the case.

THE COURT. Overruled.

A. *I just absolutely refuse to go back there. I can't live with them.* (Italics ours.)

In addition, the parents and the older sister, by their testimony, admitted that a difficult situation existed in the home. The court also considered the testimony of the intake officer from the Youth Service Center as to the attitude of Cynthia. Finally, the court considered the opinion of Dr. Gallagher, who met with Cynthia and her parents, and reported that counseling would not be beneficial until all of the individuals concerned backed away from the hard and fast positions they now held in regard to this matter, which, in his opinion, was the cause of the tension which resulted in overt hostility. In other words, the finding of incorrigibility is not supported solely by Cynthia's testimony and her refusal to return home. But in addition thereto, the commissioner's opinion finds support in the testimony of other individuals who are familiar with the situation, either from a personal or a professional standpoint. . . .

Having found the juvenile court's finding of incorrigibility, as defined in RCW 13.04.010(7), to be supported by substantial evidence within the entire record, we are constitutionally bound to affirm the juvenile court's decision.

The parents also contend that RCW 13.04.010(7), is unconstitutionally vague. Our recent upholding of this statute in Blondheim v. State, 84 Wash. 2d 874, 529 P.2d 1096 (1974), is dispositive of this issue, and no further discussion is warranted.

It is implicit in the record that the petitioner parents believe the juvenile court has given sympathy and support to Cynthia's problems in disregard of their rights as parents, and that the juvenile court has failed to assume its responsibility to assist in the resolution of the parents' problems with their minor child. We find this presumption of the petitioners to be unsupported by the evidence.

The record clearly shows that numerous attempts were made by the juvenile court commissioner to reconcile the family differences, as evidenced by its unsuccessful attempt at sending Cynthia home subsequent to the disposition of the first petition, the attempt to gain assistance through professional counseling, and the numerous and extensive exchanges between Commissioner Quinn and the Snyder family during the proceeding. The avenues for counseling were to remain open and counseling of both parties was to continue, which was interrupted by the interposition of the application by the parents for our review. In view of our disposition of this case, we are satisfied that the juvenile court, in exercising its continuing jurisdiction, will continue to review the progress of the parties to the end of a hoped for reconciliation.

The decision of the juvenile court for King County is affirmed.

NOTES AND QUESTIONS

(1) As applied to the facts in the case, does the incorrigibility statute violate parental prerogatives that *Prince, Meyer,* and *Yoder* (Chapter 1) suggest may have constitutional dimensions?

(2) Epilogue.   In 1979, a jury awarded Mr. and Mrs. Snyder $140,000 against the State of Washington and King County for alienation of the affections of their child. The award was affirmed on appeal by a Washington state appellate court without opinion. Cynthia Snyder never returned home. (Richard Sanders, attorney for the parents, telephone conversation, May 13, 1987.)

Snyder is analyzed and discussed in Comment, Status Offenses and the Status of Children's Rights: Do Children Have the Legal Right to Be Incorrigible? 1976 B.Y.U. L. Rev. (No. 3) 659.

(3) Emancipation.   Emancipation is the process by which a minor becomes free from parental authority. An emancipated minor is considered an adult for legal purposes. At common law, a minor could be emancipated by marriage or service in the armed forces. Today, most states have statutes regulating emancipation. For example, according to California law, the petitioner must be at least 14 years old, willingly live separate and apart from his or her parents or legal guardian with their

consent, have a legal source of income and manage his or her own financial affairs; and emancipation must not be contrary to the minor's best interest. Cal. Fam. Code §7120 (West 2004 & Supp. 2008).

Minors seek emancipation for several reasons. Some are unmarried parents who want custody of their children, to qualify for government assistance, or to engage in such activities as obtaining a lease and consenting to medical care. Other youths seek to leave abusive homes. Kristine Alton, Rights of Children: Emancipation in San Diego County, 11 J. Contemp. Legal Issues 662, 662 (2000). One empirical study of 90 cases reported, surprisingly, that in many cases, parents initiate the idea of emancipation to abdicate their caretaking responsibilities (e.g., child support duty). Carol Sanger & Eleanor Willemsen, Minor Changes: Emancipating Children in Modern Times, 25 U. Mich. J.L. Ref. 239 (1992).

(4) Another interesting case, like *Snyder,* in which a PINS statute was used in an attempt to gain a minor's freedom from his parents was In re Polovchak, 454 N.E.2d 258 (Ill. 1983). Two children (12-year-old Walter and his 17-year-old sister Natalie) ran away from home when their parents, who had recently immigrated to the United States, decided to return to the Soviet Union. After the police found the children, the juvenile court determined that both Natalie and Walter were minors in need of supervision. The parents appealed, and the appellate court reversed. When Walter appealed, the state supreme court affirmed, concluding that "Walter should have been released to the custody of his parents, who were in the courtroom requesting permission to take their son home." Id. at 263. The court determined that Walter was not "beyond control." By the time the litigation concluded, however, Walter had turned 18 and was free to remain in the United States on his own. For a discussion of the case, see Irene Merker Rosenberg, Juvenile Status Offender Statutes — New Perspectives on an Old Problem, 16 U.C. Davis L. Rev. 283, 300-310 (1983).

(5) Several additional cases also involve a child's right to "divorce" his or her parents. Kimberly Mays was mistakenly switched at birth and sent home with a couple who were not her biological parents. The biological parents (the Twiggs) learned of the mistake ten years later when blood tests were taken while their daughter was dying of a congenital heart condition. Although the Twiggs agreed not to seek custody of Kimberly, they did seek visitation rights. The court denied the request for visitation, finding that such contact would be detrimental to the child. Twiggs v. Mays, 543 So. 2d 241 (Fla. Dist. Ct. App.), *aff'd,* 1993 WL 330624 (Fla. Cir. Ct. 1993). Kimberly (then 14) told the judge at first that she wanted nothing to do with her biological parents but subsequently changed her mind and moved in with the Twiggs. William Booth, Tangled Family Ties and Children's Rights, Teen's Change of Mind Revives Debate, Wash. Post, Mar. 11, 1994, at A3.

In another highly publicized case, Gregory K. was placed in foster care after his mother abandoned him. At age 11, he filed a petition in the juvenile division of the circuit court for termination of his mother's parental rights (his father died during the proceedings). The trial court ruled that Gregory had standing to initiate the action even though he was an unemancipated minor. The appellate court, however, ruled that a minor did not have the capacity to bring a termination of parental rights proceeding in his own right but that the error was rendered harmless by the fact that separate petitions for termination were filed on his behalf by other parties (i.e., his foster parents, who filed for adoption). Kingsley v. Kingsley, 623 So. 2d 780 (Fla. Ct. App. 1993).

Subsequently, a 14-year-old Massachusetts boy, Patrick Holland, petitioned to terminate his father's parental rights. The father had murdered the boy's mother and left the boy, then eight years old, to find her body. After the mother's death, Patrick went to live with his mother's best friend and her husband, who wanted to adopt him. Before the matter came to trial, the father (who is serving life in prison without parole for first-degree murder) agreed to relinquish his parental rights. James Compton, Couple Wanting to Adopt Son of Killer Dad Are Called into Court, Patriot Ledger, Nov. 29, 2004, at 1.

The case inspired proposed legislation in Massachusetts (called "Patrick's Law") that would provide for termination of parental rights in cases when a person is convicted of first- or second-degree murder of the other parent unless the child refuses or if the surviving parent (i.e., the perpetrator) was the victim of domestic violence. State News in Brief, Providence J., Dec. 7, 2004, at C3. The bill is currently pending in the Massachusetts legislature.[104] See also Katherine B.T. v. Jackson, 640 S.E.2d 569 (W. Va. 2006) (holding that a minor may file a petition for a protective order against his or her parents even when such order will result in removal from parental custody).

(6) Does *Snyder* suggest that young people may now themselves initiate governmental intervention into the family to diminish parental prerogatives? Do you think a likely legacy of *Snyder,* and the cases of *Gregory K.,* and Kimberly Mays, will be "kids . . . suing their parents for being told to do their homework or take out the trash?" Mark Hansen, Boy Wins "Divorce" from Mom: Critics Claim Ruling Will Encourage Frivolous Suits by Dissatisfied Kids, 78 A.B.A.J. 16 (1992).

Bruce C. Hafen, Children's Liberation and the New Egalitarianism: Some Reservations About Abandoning Youth to Their "Rights"
1976 B.Y.U. L. Rev. (No. 3) 605, 656-658

The individual tradition is at the heart of American culture. Yet the fulfillment of individualism's promise of personal liberty depends, paradoxically, upon the maintenance of a set of corollary traditions that require what may seem to be the opposite of personal liberty: submission to authority, acceptance of responsibility, and the discharge of duty. The family tradition is among the most essential corollaries to the individual tradition, because it is in families that both children and parents experience the need for and the value of authority, responsibility, and duty in their most pristine forms. When individualism breaks loose from its corollaries, however, its tendency to destroy personal fulfillment and human relationships is

---

[104] Candy Chan & Neil Mirochnick, Holland Pleads Case, Promotes Bill to Allow Children to Cut Ties with Killer Parent, Patriot Ledger, Jan. 25, 2008, at 1. See also Jessica G. Gray, Note, De-Sensationalizing the Child "Divorce": A Jurisdictional Analysis of a Child's Role in Terminating Parental Rights, 39 Suffolk U.L. Rev. 489 (2006).

exposed. This result was anticipated in the infancy of the American democratic experiment by Alexis de Tocqueville:

> As social conditions become more equal, the number of persons increases who, although they are neither rich nor powerful enough to exercise any great influence over their fellows, have nevertheless acquired or retained sufficient education and fortune to satisfy their own wants. They owe nothing to any man, they expect nothing from any man; they acquire the habit of always considering themselves as standing alone, and they are apt to imagine that their whole destiny is in their own hands.
>
> Thus, not only does democracy make every man forget his ancestors, but it hides his descendants and separates his contemporaries from him; it throws him back forever upon himself alone, and threatens in the end to confine him entirely within the solitude of his own heart.[159]

Perhaps it is no coincidence that the recent period of expansive egalitarianism is also the period of the most widespread loneliness and alienation Western culture has known. It may also be that the tendency of democracy to make men forget both their ancestors and their descendants is causing some adults to seek the liberation of children as a way of liberating themselves from the duties, the ambiguities, and the self-denial that are necessarily required of parents and communities committed to the pattern of family life.

But individualism must remain embedded in the context of its corollary obligations to family and community if the individual tradition itself is to survive in a meaningful form. Family life, rather than subjecting the young to the permanent disadvantages caused by certain unfair discriminations against other classes, has served to nurture children's readiness for responsible participation in the individual tradition. The natural need to prepare children for entry into the fray of individualism, with its risks and obligations as well as its opportunities, has, until the last decade, kept children within the walls of the family tradition. We may now be on the verge of seeing a rejuvenated egalitarian movement break down those walls. To date, however, there is no serious evidence that society has outgrown the need for the preparatory role of the family tradition, nor has industrial society discovered substitute institutions or relationships adequate to fulfill the functions historically performed by the family.

Because of its preparatory role, maintenance of the family tradition is in fact a prerequisite to the existence of a rational and productive individual tradition. John Locke concluded his discussion of the role of children in the individual tradition with this statement: "And thus we see how natural freedom and subjection to parents may consist together and are both founded on the same principle."[161] The principle upon which both freedom and subjection to parents is founded has to do with the most fundamental human processes of learning. Locke believed that parents were obliged by "Nature" to "nourish and educate" children in developing the minimal capacities one must possess before the liberty to make binding choices can be meaningful. The related obligation of children is to submit to some

---

[159] A. de Tocqueville, Democracy in America 194 (R. Heffner ed., 1956).

[161] J. Locke, The Second Treatise of Government §55 (1952).

degree of parental authority; otherwise, little significant learning can take place. In his important work on the development of individual knowledge, philosopher Michael Polanyi has pointed out that neither basic nor sophisticated skills can be learned without the kind of personal master-apprentice relationship Locke saw as existing between parents and children:

> An art which cannot be specified in detail cannot be transmitted by prescription, since no prescription for it exists. It can be passed only by example from master to apprentice. . . . To learn by example is to submit to authority. You follow your master because you trust his manner of doing things even when you cannot account in detail for its effectiveness. By watching the master and emulating his efforts in the presence of his example, the apprentice unconsciously picks up the rules of the art, including those which are not explicitly known to the master himself. These hidden rules can be assimilated only by a person who surrenders himself to that extent uncritically to the imitation of another. A society which wants to preserve a fund of personal knowledge must submit to tradition.[162]

It is more than coincidental that for the ancient Greeks and Romans, as well as for Western society in the post-1500 period, a strong commitment to the idea of childhood and lasting family relationships grew parallel with a strong commitment to the idea of education. Childhood, as a time of life and as a frame of mind, is intimately related to educational development.

Ardent advocates of children's rights may believe that "in this society . . . we are not likely to err in the direction of too much freedom,"[164] but too much freedom can undermine and finally destroy the most fundamental processes and the human relationships that sustain them. To the extent that these relationships and processes are undetermined, it is ultimately the tradition of individual liberty that will be damaged.

WRITTEN REVIEW PROBLEMS

(1) Legislative Proposal to Give Teenagers the Vote.   A state senator introduces a bill, titled "Training Wheels for Citizenship," to amend the Blackacre state constitution to give youths a partial vote in statewide elections. According to the bill, youths aged 16 and 17 would receive a fractional vote equal to one-half of an adult; and youths aged 14 and 15 would have a fractional vote equal to one-quarter of an adult. The senator who sponsored the legislation claims that the proposal would boost voter participation, which has hit historic lows. He argues that the modern teenager is much better informed than youths in the past because of the technological innovations such as the Internet, cell phones, and multichannel television. Ken McNeill, Proposed Amendment Would Reduce Minimum Age from 18 to 14, Daily Review (Hayward, CA), Mar. 9, 2004 (describing similar legislative efforts by California state senator John Vasconcellos). The senator adds that lowering the voting age would develop youths' sense of responsibility

---

[162] M. Polanyi, Personal Knowledge: Towards a Post-Critical Philosophy 53 (1964).
[164] R. Farson, Birthrights 2 (1974).

while at the same time their fractional representation would recognize that they are not yet fully mature. John M. Hubbell, Partial Vote for Teenagers Proposed, S.F. Chron., May 6, 2004, at A10.

Supporters of the bill explain that some countries allow youths younger than age 18 to vote (e.g., Austria and Germany allow 16-year-olds to vote; Israel allows 17-year-olds to vote). McNeill, supra. A delegation of local high school youths lobby the state legislature to adopt the bill by arguing that teenagers contribute to the state economy (by means of their employment, income taxes, and sales tax) and therefore should have the right to decide how their taxes are spent. Hubbell, supra. On the other hand, one lobbyist contends that teens do not have the life experience to be voters and that teenage voters would be "susceptible to peer pressure, even a rock or a rap song." Id. Additional opponents point out that the proposal would create a "logistical nightmare" in tallying an election. Id. In addition, an African American legislator opposes the proposal, by "allud[ing] to a time in history when blacks were viewed as three-fifths of a man in determining representation." Id.

You are the legislative intern to the state senator in Blackacre who is sponsoring the legislation. Please write a memorandum explaining your opinion of the proposal. In your memorandum, consider the following: the various age-based limitations on the liberty of minors, the issue whether young persons should have the same rights as adults, the interests that are served by treating youths by different standards, and the appropriateness of age-based lines generally and as applied to the voting context.

(2) Parent-Child Divorce.   A husband and wife have some legal power to change their marital status. They may go to court and secure a judicial determination of whether and how the marriage should be dissolved or modified. Write an essay on the legal ability and desirability of allowing young people aged 14 to 18 to divorce themselves from their parents. You may use the law of your own state.

a. First consider the case in which the parents and young person agree that they wish to change their legal relationship and have the young person assume more adult responsibilities. Under existing law, what legal impediments lie in the way of such emancipation? Put another way, are there limits under existing law to the power of young people and their parents to change consensually their legal relationship? What would you advise them? Consider this question, in light of parental support obligations, parental rights and duties to discipline, parental duties with regard to the child's torts and contracts, and the young person's ability to secure medical treatment, a job, a driver's license, a car, and the control of his or her own property; and to make decisions about his or her education. Does the state have an independent interest if the young person and the parents agree? Would you change their power to modify their relationship in any of these areas? Why? How? If young people "run away," and the parents do ask for them back, is this a different situation?

b. Now consider the situation if the parents and the young person do not agree — the young person wants to emancipate himself or herself and the parents will not consent. Briefly describe those areas (if any) where the young person can assert autonomy under existing law before reaching 18. Should the law be changed to allow a young person to invoke the judicial process to change the legal relationship with his or her parents? Should there be a proceeding (analogous to a contested divorce?) in which young people can "free" themselves or modify the legal relationship with their parents? What difficulties do you see with such an approach? If there were such a judicial inquiry, what factors would be relevant to the decision — what legal standards and process would you suggest? Describe those areas, if any, where you think such an approach would be appropriate.

c. Finally, consider whether there is a need for a uniform statutory emancipation of minors act. If so, how should the act take into account the following issues: (1) the minimum age for emancipation, (2) the proper court of jurisdiction, (3) the specific standards by which the court may judge the petition, (4) whether the minor needs parental consent before the court may grant the petition, (5) the purposes for which the minor may be considered emancipated? See generally H. Jeffrey Gottesfeld, Comment, The Uncertain Status of the Emancipated Minor: Why We Need a Uniform Statutory Emancipation of Minors Act (USEMA), 15 U.S.F.L. Rev. 473 (1981) (explaining how modern statutes generally address these issues).

CHAPTER 7

Juvenile Delinquency

A. *INTRODUCTION*

How are juvenile offenders treated differently from adult offenders? To what extent should they be? These questions, closely related to the general issues in this book, provide the focus for this examination of delinquency.[1]

As background for these questions, the various purposes of criminal punishment (rehabilitation, deterrence, incapacitation, and retribution) are examined to analyze whether delinquents and adult offenders should be treated differently. Introductory materials are provided next concerning juvenile crime and the juvenile court: its history, philosophy, and bureaucratic context. Then, the jurisdictional and dispositional authority of the juvenile court are examined.

Next, various procedures governing the juvenile delinquency process and the adult criminal process are compared in light of the questions presented earlier: whether delinquents and adult offenders are and should be treated differently. The final section of the chapter concerns the role of the lawyer in the juvenile court process. Again, the core question examined is whether a lawyer's professional responsibility is different with a juvenile, rather than an adult client, who is accused of a criminal act.

Throughout the chapter, consider how the difference between the juvenile delinquency process and the adult criminal process is affected by or should be affected by:

1. the parent-child relationship,
2. the young person's possible lack of maturity and competence, and
3. the rehabilitative goals of the juvenile court.

---

[1] For additional materials on the procedural and substantive law concerning the juvenile court's delinquency jurisdiction, see generally Robert Agnew, Juvenile Delinquency: Causes and Control (2d ed. 2005); Dean John Champion, The Juvenile Justice System: Delinquency, Processing, and the Law (5th ed. 2006); Joseph G. Weis et al., Juvenile Delinquency: Readings (2d ed. 2001).

INTRODUCTORY PROBLEM

Thirteen-year-old Tony is a member of the Jets, a loose gang of boys who are mostly 15 to 17 years old. As his initiation into the Jets, Tony was told he must mug an old lady. Two days later Tony knocked down a 73-year-old woman as she was leaving a grocery store and snatched her purse. The woman was hospitalized with a broken hip. A bystander recognized Tony, and reported the incident to the police.

(1) Should Tony be held responsible for his act? How? Should he be adjudicated a delinquent? If so, should he be sent to a training school? Put in foster care? Put on probation? What information would be relevant to these decisions? What criteria should be used to decide?

(2) Suppose the day after the mugging, the police went to Tony's home where his parents allowed the police to search his room. The police find the victim's purse under Tony's bed. Is the search valid?

(3) Suppose the police ask Tony's parents to be allowed to question Tony. Tony's parents agree. The police then question Tony in the family's living room for 30 minutes with his parents present. Is Tony entitled to his *Miranda* rights? Is he entitled to counsel? Does it matter if the interrogation takes place at the police station instead? If the questioning lasts three hours? May the police exclude Tony's parents from the interrogation despite their request to be present?

(4) Suppose Tony at first denies involvement but then confesses to the police after his father threatens to beat him if he doesn't tell the truth. Should Tony's confession be admissible as evidence?

(5) A delinquency petition is filed against Tony, and you are appointed to represent him. Tony tells you he wants to "beat the rap" and not be adjudicated a delinquent. Most of all, he doesn't want to be sent to training school. Suppose the probation officer offers to put Tony on informal supervision without his being adjudicated a delinquent, provided Tony agrees to cooperate with the police in their investigation of the Jets? Tony says that he doesn't want to "rat" on his friends, but that he is afraid of his parents' reaction if he refuses to cooperate. How would you advise him?

(6) Would it be appropriate to hold Tony's parents financially responsible for his actions? To what extent? Suppose $500 of the victim's medical bills was not paid for by her health insurance. Should Tony's parents be made to pay?[2] Would your opinion change if the victim does not have medical insurance and her bills total $25,000?

(7) If Tony were 18 instead of 13, would any of your answers be different? From a policy perspective, is there a single age that defines an appropriate cutoff point for distinguishing youth crime from adult crime?

---

[2] For a discussion of parents' civil liability for acts committed by their minor children, see James H. DiFonzo, Parental Responsibility for Juvenile Crime, 80 Or. L. Rev. 1 (2001); Pamela K. Graham, Parental Responsibility Laws: Let the Punishment Fit the Crime, 33 Loy. L.A. L. Rev. 1719 (2000).

B. BACKGROUND

1. The Purposes of Punishment and Juvenile Justice

Various justifications have been offered for punishing adult criminal conduct: (a) rehabilitation; (b) deterrence, special and general; (c) incapacitation; and (d) retribution. Is each a legitimate purpose with regard to delinquents?

a. Rehabilitation

Treatment and rehabilitation traditionally have served as *the* justification for the juvenile justice system. As Professor Herbert Packer has written: "The most immediately appealing justification for punishment is the claim that it may be used to prevent crime by so changing the personality of the offender that he will conform to the dictates of the law; in a word, by reforming him."[3] In theory, delinquency proceedings allowed a benevolent judge to provide the necessary help and guidance to a young person who might otherwise travel further down the road of crime. This rehabilitative ideal had several important consequences for the juvenile court process: Because the underlying justification was prevention, not punishment, proof that a youth in fact committed a particular crime was traditionally thought less relevant than the youth's need for rehabilitation; judges were given broad discretion with regard to dispositions; and the length of sentences was typically indeterminate, so that "treatment" could continue as long as it was thought appropriate.

In re Gault (discussed infra p. 798) and its progeny imposed procedural safeguards intended to ensure an adequate factual determination concerning a past criminal act. Nevertheless, the rehabilitative premises of the juvenile court still have important consequences that remain open to question: judges and corrections personnel still have broad discretionary power with regard to disposition. Once jurisdiction is established, the disposition does not typically depend on the seriousness of the crime proven. "The murderer was as eligible for the indeterminate commitment as was the beggar."[4] Indeed, notwithstanding the criticisms of the rehabilitative ideal that have become increasingly vociferous since *Gault,* the juvenile justice system remains largely wedded to this purpose; McKeiver v. Pennsylvania, infra p. 815, suggests as much.

With regard to rehabilitation, should children be treated differently than adults? Are children easier to rehabilitate than adults? Or more difficult to treat? Two behavioral assumptions underlie claims that rehabilitation is more relevant for youthful offenders than for adult criminals: (1) juvenile offenders will become adult offenders unless they are treated, (2) youthful offenders are particularly amenable to rehabilitative treatment. Available social science evidence fails to establish either assumption.[5]

---

[3] Herbert L. Packer, The Limits of the Criminal Sanction 53 (1968).

[4] Sanford J. Fox, Philosophy and the Principle of Punishment in the Juvenile Court, 8 Fam. L.Q. (No. 4) 373, 377 (1974).

[5] See generally Anna Louise Simpson, Comment, Rehabilitation as the Justification of a Separate Juvenile Justice System, 64 Cal. L. Rev. 984 (1976).

In terms of the first assumption, it appears that most adolescents at one time or another engage in unlawful conduct. But most do not go on to pursue a life of crime. This necessarily implies that many young people who have committed a criminal act "do not graduate to criminal careers."

There have been several studies that followed, over an extended period of time, the careers of juvenile offenders. The most important of these traced the arrest histories of males born in Philadelphia in 1945. See Marvin E. Wolfgang et al., Delinquency in a Birth Cohort (1972). Of the 9,945 cohort subjects, about 35 percent were involved with the police at least once to the extent that an official recording of the act resulted. Of these offenders, 54 percent were recidivists and 46 percent were one-timers. About 18 percent of the offenders were categorized as "chronic offenders" — they each committed more than four violations. As a group, the chronic offenders committed over one-half of all the juvenile offenses recorded. Id. at 244-248.

Subsequently, the Wolfgang study was replicated with surprisingly similar results. See Paul E. Tracy et al., Delinquency in Two Birth Cohorts, Executive Summary, U.S. Dept. Justice, Office of Juvenile Justice and Delinquency Prevention (Sept. 1985). In the later study, of 13,160 male cohort subjects, about 33 percent were involved with the police at least once, to the extent that an official record ensued. Of these offenders, 58 percent were recidivists, and 42 percent were one-timers. About 23 percent of the recidivists were termed "chronic offenders" (with more than four violations). A comparison of the two birth cohorts revealed an enduring effect regarding the chronic offenders' share of offenses. That is, compared to the earlier study in which 18 percent of the chronic delinquent subset committed 52 percent of the delinquent acts, in the later group 23 percent of the chronic delinquents committed 61 percent of the delinquent offenses. Id. at 5, 9, 10. It must be remembered, of course, that this study, like most of the empirical research bearing on rehabilitation, is based on subsequent arrest records — such records are obviously an imperfect measure of subsequent criminal behavior.

Analysis is complicated by the fact that youthful offenders tend to commit somewhat different sorts of crimes than older offenders. The more serious offenses are more likely to be committed by older delinquents.[6] To the extent that the young tend to commit different sorts of crimes, does this in itself justify greater reliance on rehabilitation? Does it imply that a 16-year-old who steals a car is more likely to be rehabilitated than a 16-year-old who commits aggravated assault? The earlier Wolfgang study (referred to previously) suggested that "the choice of the type of the next offense is only very slightly related to the type of the prior offense or offenses." Wolfgang et al., Delinquency in a Birth Cohort, supra, at 254.

As imperfect as our knowledge today is, it nevertheless appears that ". . . the clearest finding from the statistics on the age distribution of offenders and the studies following the later lives of juvenile offenders is that the probability of offenses decreases with age. There is no generally accepted explanation of this decrease."[7]

---

[6] Paul E. Tracy et al., Delinquency in Two Birth Cohorts, Executive Summary, U.S. Dept. Justice, Office of Juvenile Justice and Delinquency Prevention 15 (Sept. 1985).

[7] Simpson, supra note [5], at 984-985.

The second assumption, that juvenile offenders are more amenable to rehabilitative treatment than adult offenders, also finds little support in the evidence:

> Despite the evidence that juvenile and adult offenders share important characteristics [with regard to moral reasoning, decision making, and control of impulses] the supposition that juvenile offenders, because less fixed in their ways, are more amenable to rehabilitative treatment than adults, might make the special treatment of juveniles appropriate. But there is little evidence to support this simple and popular view. Maturational reform is not evidence of greater amenability to rehabilitative programs; the reform associated with age appears to occur whether or not the offender is apprehended. Apparently, variables that account for maturational reform are not influenced by treatment programs. The evidence does not lead to the conclusion that all rehabilitative programs should be eliminated; rather, it suggests that an emphasis on rehabilitative treatment for juveniles is not justified by the assumption that juveniles are especially amenable to rehabilitative treatment.[8]

In a thoughtful essay on delinquency prevention, Professor Frank Zimring cautions against primary reliance on rehabilitation and "people programs" that treat young offenders:

> A treatment emphasis is particularly risky given the track record of the great number of such programs that have been evaluated. Most programs have had no measurable impact on the criminality of their clientele. In a few cases, programs have apparently produced some improvement in some subjects. Overall, there is no present treatment technology that appears capable of substantially reducing recidivism, and there is no reason to suppose that we are approaching a breakthrough.[9]

Some critics go beyond simply doubting the efficacy of rehabilitation within the juvenile justice system. They suggest that, particularly for youthful offenders, intervention may increase the probability of future criminal conduct. If intervention were more likely to affect adversely recidivism for the young, then should not youthful offenders become "priority targets for non-intervention"?[10] See generally Edwin M. Schur, Radical Non-Intervention (1973).

Even if existing evidence does not demonstrate that juveniles are especially amenable to rehabilitation, does this necessarily imply that rehabilitation should be abandoned as the primary goal of the juvenile justice process? After all, in the last century rehabilitation has become an increasingly important goal for adult offenders.

Consider the institutional consequences of the rehabilitative ideal for the juvenile justice system. Some commentators have suggested that the rehabilitation rationale provides extraordinarily broad discretion to correctional personnel and "is to some extent a smokescreen to satisfy an ambivalent public, which sometimes feels guilty at merely punishing; and is primarily a managerial device to make it

---

[8] Id. at 1012-1013.

[9] Franklin E. Zimring, Dealing with Youth Crime: National Needs and Federal Priorities 8 (Sept. 1975) (unpublished policy paper prepared for the Federal Coordinating Council for Juvenile Justice and Delinquency Prevention).

[10] Id. at 23.

easier to manipulate prisoners in ways that minimize administrative problems."[11] On the other hand, might the abandonment of rehabilitation as the primary goal of the delinquency process make the juvenile justice system less humane? For example, at the present time, social workers and probation officers assume primary responsibility for delinquents. Are their attitudes different from those of prison guards? Is it not possible that juvenile institutions, because of the rehabilitation ideal, are, on average, better facilities than adult prisons? Put another way, even if we do not know how to rehabilitate, is it not possible that the goal nevertheless makes the custodial arrangements for young people better than they would be if rehabilitation were abandoned?

b. Deterrence

The classical utilitarian justification for punishment is that it has an inhibiting effect on the future conduct of those who might otherwise commit crimes. Punishing a youthful offender may thus serve as a threat that deters others from committing crimes ("general deterrence"). It may also deter the youth being punished from future criminal conduct because of increased sensitivity to threatened punishment in the future ("intimidation" or "special deterrence").[12]

From the victim's perspective, and probably from society's as well, the fact that a criminal act has been committed by a young person rather than by an adult hardly makes it of *less* social concern. To the victim of a mugging the age of the attacker is not of primary concern. If the short-run undesirable consequences of a criminal act do not depend on the age of the offender, is not deterrence (both general and special) as valid a purpose with regard to youthful offenders as for adult offenders?

Deterrence has been criticized by psychologists on the ground that the behavioral model underlying deterrence "assumes a perfectly hedonistic, perfectly rational actor, whose object it is to maximize pleasure and minimize pain." To such an actor contemplating the possibility of a criminal act, the decision is based on a calculus: "How much do I stand to gain by doing it? How much do I stand to lose if I am caught doing it? What are the chances of my getting away with it? What is the balance of gain and loss as discounted by the chance of apprehension?"[13] Some psychological critics suggest that a person's behavior is largely determined by unconscious drives that impel actions, which are therefore not rationally based. Such critics reject the notion that punishment will deter future behavior.

The high recidivism rate for juvenile offenders who are punished is often cited as evidence that special deterrence or intimidation does not in fact work. Indeed, it might be argued that

---

[11] Caleb Foote, quoted in Leigh, Corrections and the Courts: A Plea for Understanding and Implementation, Resolution (1974) at 23.

[12] It should be noted that special deterrence is not unrelated to rehabilitation. Both aim to curb future criminal misconduct of the person being "punished" or "treated." Special deterrence is based on a model that punishment will reduce the commission of future crimes by the individual being punished, specifically by causing that individual to realize that the consequences outweigh the benefits of future criminal acts. See generally Packer, supra note [3].

[13] Packer, supra note [3], at 40-41.

the corrupting influence of criminal associations in prison with the feelings of bitterness, hatred, and desire for revenge that are engendered by inhumane treatment in a backward prison may well produce a net loss in crime prevention. Whatever feelings of intimidation are produced on the prisoner by the severity of his punishment may be outweighed by the deterioration of his character in prison. His punishment may contribute to the effect of deterrence on others, but in the process he is lost to society.[14]

It should be pointed out, however, that "we do not know how much higher the recidivism rate would be if there had been no criminal punishment in the first place."[15] Moreover, threats of punishment may be more effective in curbing some types of crimes than others. For example, intuition suggests that it might be easier to deter economic crime (such as income tax evasion) than certain assaultive crimes (e.g., rape or murder).[16] It appears that much juvenile delinquency occurs as a result of group activities. There has been a considerable amount of sociological research relating to the juvenile gang. Unfortunately, no empirical research has been specifically directed at examining the degree to which group pressures within juvenile gangs may affect deterrence. To the extent that more juvenile crime is a result of group pressures than adult crime, it is certainly possible that deterrence has a differential effectiveness. In all events, empirical studies to date do not establish the differential effects on compliance with criminal law resulting from changes in particular sanctions. Still less do they disclose the differential effect of deterrence on young people as opposed to adults. See generally Franklin E. Zimring, American Youth Violence (1998); Franklin E. Zimring & Gordon J. Hawkins, Deterrence: The Legal Threat in Crime Control (1973).

Consider the implications of accepting deterrence as a valid purpose for imposing sanctions on juvenile offenders. If deterrence is adopted as a goal, this necessarily implies that we are prepared to punish a young person not because we necessarily believe it will help that particular youth but because we believe it may help society by altering the behavior of others. In other words, the state is *using* this young person to achieve state objectives. This, of course, is an accepted feature of the adult criminal process. But is it consistent with the claim that intervention is occurring to serve the child's "best interests"? If the juvenile justice system is premised in part on deterrence, is there any justification for denying juveniles the full range of due process protections afforded adults, including a jury trial? See *McKeiver* and the materials that follow, infra.

Acceptance of deterrence as a goal has other implications as well. For deterrence to be effective, potential offenders must be made aware of the probable consequences of their conduct. A threat must be communicated, and sanctions must be imposed. If in fact the sentences meted out by the juvenile process today are typically less severe than those imposed on adults, even insubstantial, then deterrence will suffer, at least if one assumes that juveniles are susceptible to threats and have learned that the sanctions are light. There does exist anecdotal evidence that the insubstantiality of the sanctions imposed by the juvenile justice

[14] Id. at 47.
[15] Id. at 46.
[16] Id. at 46-47.

process may affect behavior. For example, a New York Times article suggested that "thousands of Harlem drug runners, [aged] 9 to 16, find the rewards are high, the risks low." The article goes on to suggest:

> Arrests are commonly viewed as minor inconveniences. The youths are treated as juvenile delinquents and released to the custody of a parent or guardian. Sometimes they are back on the street dealing before the sun rises and sets. Under the present law, the maximum sentence a juvenile can receive is 18 months.[17]

c. Incapacitation

Past misconduct may lead to the belief that in the future if permitted to remain at large in society, the offender will in all likelihood commit further crimes. By putting the offenders somewhere where they can no longer endanger members of society at large, the streets have thereby been made safer by being rid of troublemakers.

Is incapacitation as valid a purpose for youthful offenders as it is for adult criminals? As suggested earlier, "statistics on the age distribution of offenders and the studies following the later lives of juvenile offenders" demonstrate that "the probability of offenses decreases with age" and that by 25 or 30 most criminal careers will end.[18] Consider the implications of this social science finding. If most youthful offenders "grow out" of their delinquency, why not incapacitate a delinquent found guilty of several offenses during the years when it is likely he will commit further crimes and release him only when he reaches an age that makes further criminal behavior unlikely — say, 25 or 30?

Various criticisms of incapacitation have been made. For one thing, keeping someone locked up is quite expensive. In California in 2004-2005, for example, the Youth Authority indicated that it cost $71,700 annually to keep a delinquent in a secure facility.[19] Second, long-term incarceration may make successful reintegration of the offender into the community more difficult when he or she finally is released. In addition, incapacitation may often offend notions of proportionality. Note that it would imply that a young offender (whose potential criminal career had more years remaining) would be given a more severe sentence than an older offender, even though their past conduct was largely identical. Finally, how confident are we about the implicit prediction that a youthful offender who has been convicted for several offenses will in all probability have a long criminal career? In this sense, incapacitation poses the same problems as *preventive detention.*

---

[17] Lena Williams, Thousands of Harlem Drug Runners, 9 to 16, Find the Rewards Are High, the Risks Low, N.Y. Times, Apr. 21, 1977, at B1.

[18] Simpson, supra note [5], at 1005, 1010-1013.

[19] Telephone interview with Nancy Lungren, Chief Information Officer, California Youth Authority, Sacramento, California (Feb. 10, 2004).

d. Retribution

By imposing a sanction on persons who engage in serious misconduct, society can express a sense of injury and moral outrage at the conduct and give the criminals their commensurate deserts. Punishment is "the deserved infliction of suffering on evildoers."[20]

It has been suggested that two different theories explain retribution. One is "revenge theory." A society pays a criminal back for his bad conduct, and punishment is a desirable community expression of hatred and fear aroused by the criminal's act. The second theory, "expiation theory," rests on the idea that through suffering the criminal expiates sin. This theory focuses on the demands that the offender should make on himself. Punishment represents an external expression of condemnation that usefully reinforces or creates an adequate sense of guilt on the part of the offender.

In recent years, the legal response to crime, in general, and juvenile crime, in particular, has shifted from rehabilitation to an increased emphasis on retribution (as the following excerpt illustrates). Justifications for this shift to punishment include: (1) punishment will deter juveniles from committing future offenses, (2) punishment will incapacitate juvenile offenders and thereby prevent the commission of future offenses, and (3) punishment satisfies the societal desire for accountability. Consider whether retribution is a valid goal of punishment with regard to juvenile offenders. Implicit in notions of retribution is the idea that people are responsible for their actions. Are juveniles as "responsible" for their own conduct as adult offenders? Is it fair to hold young people accountable for their actions? Consider again the notions of responsibility underlying the legal treatment of young people in other contexts, such as the decision to have an abortion (Chapter 1), to secure medical treatment (Chapter 4), as well as the various topics considered in Chapter 6.

Recent scientific research reveals that the adolescent brain processes information differently from that of an adult. Studies that used modern scientific techniques (e.g., magnetic resonance imaging) and that focused on the causes of attention deficit hyperactivity disorder (ADHD) and autism, in fact, led to discoveries about adolescents' cognitive development that have relevance to juvenile justice. Research has demonstrated that certain characteristics of adolescents (e.g., their impulsivity, disregard of consequences, irresponsibility, vulnerability to peer pressure, and tendency to take risks) are products of their neurological immaturity rather than symptoms of deviance. Based on such evidence, are you convinced that juvenile offenders are less culpable than they are often thought to be?

For a review of this research and a discussion of its implications, see Barry Feld, Competence, Culpability, and Punishment: Implications of *Atkins* for Executing and Sentencing Adolescents, 32 Hofstra L. Rev. 463 (2003) (arguing that the psychological characteristics that were recognized by the Supreme Court in Atkins v. Virginia, 536 U.S. 304 (2002), as rendering mentally retarded offenders less blameworthy, also characterize adolescents and should therefore lead to a prohibition on their execution); Elizabeth Scott & Laurence Steinberg,

---

[20] Packer, supra note [3], at 36.

Blaming Youth, 81 Tex. L. Rev. 799 (2003) (analyzing the culpability of juvenile offenders within the framework of criminal law doctrine and theory to enlighten lawmakers about how to assign criminal responsibility); Robert E. Shepherd, The Relevance of Brain Research to Juvenile Defense, 19 Crim. Just. 51 (2005) (arguing that an understanding of the neurological basis of adolescent functioning is essential for lawyers who represent youths).

Andrew R. Strauss, Note, Losing Sight of the Utilitarian Forest for the Retributivist Trees: An Analysis of the Role of Public Opinion in a Utilitarian Model of Punishment
23 Cardozo L. Rev. 1549, 1571-1581 (2002)

*Public Opinion at Work in the Criminal Law: Rehabilitation and
the Evolution of the Juvenile Justice System*

Since the early 19th century, a system of juvenile justice has existed largely independently of the system of adult justice. The original premise behind the separateness of the juvenile justice system was that the juvenile is "unable to comprehend the wrongness of his acts and needs to be treated as though he were ill, instead of being punished like a criminal." Juvenile courts were to be guided by the best interests of the child rather than by the protection of society. In the past thirty years, however, the juvenile justice system has seen a shift in philosophy away from rehabilitation and towards retribution. . . .

C. The Fall of the Rehabilitative Ideal

[The author points out that the juvenile justice system "began its convergence towards the adult system" during the "due process revolution" of the 1960s and 1970s, consisting of cases such as Kent v. United States, In re Winship, and In re Gault (all discussed infra), which recognized procedural safeguards in delinquency proceedings.]

[Subsequent] events occurred that caused the rehabilitative ideal to lose favor with the public. First, the arrest rates for juveniles increased dramatically: between 1962 and 1972, the number of arrests of juveniles increased almost one hundred percent. This led the public to believe that juvenile delinquency was a major problem. Secondly, several studies were published that suggested that rehabilitation did not work. The most influential of these studies was the work conducted by Robert Martinson and his colleagues in the mid-1970s. This work consisted of a review of over two hundred studies of rehabilitation programs conducted from 1945 to 1967. Although some of these programs proved to be effective, the overall conclusion drawn by Martinson and his colleagues was that rehabilitation in general was an ineffective strategy for controlling juvenile crime. Soon after, the National Academy of Sciences commissioned a further study of the issue and came to similar conclusions. Both of these studies were used to support the "nothing works" philosophy, which claimed that the rehabilitative ideal was ineffective and should be scrapped.

Around the same time as the due process cases and the publication of Martinson's work, the book *Struggle for Justice* was published. This document, prepared for the

American Friends Service Committee, presented an extremely harsh and compelling attack on rehabilitation. The authors argued that the rehabilitative model was a product of a class society, and that it resulted in a two-tiered system of criminal justice that gave preferential treatment to upper- and middle-class criminals. *Struggle for Justice* was extremely influential because it combined a political critique of rehabilitation based on inequality with empirical studies demonstrating the failure of rehabilitation. This document was subsequently cited by other, less radical, commentators who also advocated reform of the criminal justice system.

Also around the same period, the Joint Commission on Juvenile Justice Standards, a collaboration between the Institute of Judicial Administration and the American Bar Association, initiated a study of the juvenile justice system called the Juvenile Justice Standards Project. The fundamental working principle of the study was to create standards "to establish the best possible juvenile justice system for our society, not to fluctuate in response to transitory headlines or controversies." This ten-year study culminated in the publication of a twenty-three-volume report, which included a set of ten principles that a juvenile justice system should follow and which would impose more of an adult criminal law-like structure and emphasis on the juvenile system.

Although the Joint Commission founded these principles on the "idealized design of the family court as the centerpiece of [an] idealized juvenile justice system," it rejected the need for treatment as the basis for the court's jurisdiction. Instead, influenced by the In re Gault decision [discussed infra], it adopted "a due process model governed by equity and fairness."

D. The Political and Legislative Response

The shift in public opinion away from rehabilitation and towards greater punitive policies has had a significant effect on politics and state legislatures over the last thirty years. The politicization of crime and juvenile justice policies began in the 1960s, when conservative Republicans began to use crime control as an issue to distinguish themselves from Democrats. Political candidates such as Richard Nixon, Gerald Ford, and George Wallace ran "law and order" and "get tough" campaigns. Public statements about the "crime issue" by these politicians "who 'ought to know' contributed to the collective public perceptions that there was a 'crime problem,' and, in turn, contributed to the election of those who were making the statements." Since then, politicians have avoided running on platforms that can be characterized "soft on crime."

More importantly, public opinion has also prompted significant state legislative activity that has greatly altered the way in which juvenile crime is handled. Much of this activity has consisted in the increased use of waiver, which allows prosecutors, under certain circumstances, to try juveniles as adults in criminal court, and in the increased use of mandatory minimum sentences that depend on the seriousness of the offense. These changes reflect the shift in philosophy from rehabilitation to retribution, from individualized justice to just deserts, from offender to offense. This shift is also seen in state juvenile codes, which have increasingly used the language of accountability, responsibility, punishment, and public safety rather than the best interests of the child. . . .

2. The Problem of Juvenile Crime

Howard N. Snyder, Juvenile Arrests 2004,
Office of Juvenile Justice and Delinquency Prevention, Juvenile Justice Bulletin (Dec. 2006), pp. 1, 6-10

In 2004, law enforcement agencies in the United States made an estimated 2.2 million arrests of persons under age 18. According to the Federal Bureau of Investigation (FBI), juveniles accounted for 16 percent of all arrests and 16 percent of all violent crime arrests in 2004. The substantial growth in juvenile violent crime arrests that began in the late 1980s peaked in 1994. In 2004, for the tenth consecutive year, the rate of juvenile arrests for Violent Crime Index offenses — murder, forcible rape, robbery, and aggravated assault — declined. Specifically, between 1994 and 2004, the juvenile arrest rate for Violent Crime Index offenses fell 49 percent. As a result, the juvenile Violent Crime Index arrest rate in 2004 was at its lowest level since at least 1980. From its peak in 1993 to 2004, the juvenile arrest rate for murder fell 77 percent.

These findings are derived from data reported annually by local law enforcement agencies across the country to the FBI's Uniform Crime Reporting (UCR) Program.

In 2004, 30 Percent of Juvenile Arrests Involved Females

Law enforcement agencies made 658,000 arrests of females under age 18 in 2004. Between 1995 and 2004, arrests of juvenile females decreased less than male arrests in most offense categories; in some categories, female arrests increased while male arrests decreased.

Juvenile Arrests Disproportionately Involved Minorities

The racial composition of the juvenile population in 2004 was 78 percent white, 17 percent Black, 4 percent Asian/Pacific Islander, and 1 percent American Indian. Most Hispanics (an ethnic designation, not a race) were classified as white. Of all juvenile arrests for violent crimes in 2004, 52 percent involved white youth, 46 percent involved Black youth, 1 percent involved Asian youth, and 1 percent involved American Indian youth. For property crime arrests, the proportions were 69 percent white youth, 28 percent Black youth, 2 percent Asian youth, and 1 percent American Indian youth. Black youth were overrepresented in juvenile arrests.

The Violent Crime Index arrest rate (i.e., arrests per 100,000 juveniles in the racial group) in 2004 for Black juveniles (746) was more than 4 times the rates for American Indian juveniles (173) and white juveniles (182) and almost 10 times the rate for Asian juveniles (78). For Property Crime Index arrests, the rate for Black juveniles (2,288) was about double the rates for American Indian juveniles (1,300) and white juveniles (1,198) and 4 times the rate for Asian juveniles (557). Over the period from 1980 through 2004, the Black-to-white disparity in juvenile arrest rates for violent crimes declined. In 1980, the Black juvenile Violent Crime Index arrest rate was 6.3 times the white rate; in 2004, the rate disparity had declined to 4.1. This reduction in arrest rate disparities between 1980 and 2004 was primarily the result of the decline in the disparity for robbery (from 11.5 in 1980 to 8.4 in 2004), because the disparity for aggravated assault changed little (3.2 vs. 3.1).

Murder

- Between 1980 and 2004, the juvenile arrest rate for murder peaked in 1993. In that year, there were an estimated 3,790 arrests of juveniles for murder.
- From the mid-1980s to the peak in 1993, the juvenile arrest rate for murder more than doubled.
- With one minor exception, the juvenile arrest rate for murder fell each year after 1993, so that by 2004 it was 77 percent below the peak 1993 rate. In 2004, there were an estimated 1,110 arrests of juveniles for murder.

Forcible Rape

- Following the general pattern of other assaultive offenses, the juvenile arrest rate for forcible rape increased from the early 1980s through the early 1990s and then fell substantially.
- Over the 1980-2004 period, the juvenile arrest rate for forcible rape peaked in 1991, 44 percent above its 1980 level.
- After 1991, with minor exceptions, the juvenile arrest rate dropped annually through 2004. By 1999, it had returned to its 1980 level. By 2004, the juvenile arrest rate for forcible rape had fallen to a point 22 percent below the 1980 level, and to its lowest level in more than a generation.

Robbery

- Unlike the juvenile arrest rates for other violent crimes, the rate for robbery declined through much of the 1980s, reaching a low point in 1988, 30 percent below its 1980 level.
- The growth in the juvenile arrest rate for robbery between 1988 and 1994-95 moved the rate above the 1980 level, a pattern found in each of the other Violent Crime Index offenses.
- Like the other Violent Crime Index offenses, the juvenile arrest rate for robbery declined substantially after its mid-1990s peak, falling 62 percent from 1995 through 2004 — to a point 55 percent below its 1980 level and 35 percent below its previous low point in 1988.

Aggravated Assault

- The juvenile arrest rate for aggravated assault doubled between 1980 and 1994. As with the other crimes in the Violent Crime Index, the juvenile arrest rate for aggravated assault fell from the mid-1990s to 2004; for aggravated assault, the decline from 1994 through 2004 was 39 percent.
- Unlike the juvenile arrest rates for other crimes in the Violent Crime Index, the rate for aggravated assault in 2004 was not at its lowest level in the 1980-2004 period. The juvenile arrest rate for aggravated assault in 2004 was, in fact, 23 percent above its 1980 level.

Burglary

- Unique in the set of Property Crime Index offenses, the juvenile arrest rate for burglary declined almost consistently and fell substantially between

1980 and 2004. In 2004, the juvenile arrest rate for burglary was less than one-third of what it was in 1980, down 70 percent.

- This large fall in juvenile arrests between 1980 and 2004 was not replicated in the adult statistics. Between 1995 and 2004, the number of juvenile burglary arrests fell 39 percent, while adult burglary arrests dropped just 10 percent. In the prior 10-year period, the juvenile and adult patterns were the same; between 1986 and 1995, both juvenile and adult arrests for burglary fell 18 percent.

Although It Increased Slightly from 2002 to 2004, the Juvenile Arrest Rate for Weapons Law Violations in 2004 Was Still About Half Its 1993 Peak

- Between 1980 and 1993, the juvenile arrest rate for weapons law violations increased more than 140 percent. Then the rate fell substantially, so that by 2004, the rate was 30 percent above the 1980 rate.
- Between 1980 and 1993, the arrest rates for weapons law violations for both white juveniles and Black juveniles increased substantially (116 percent and 214 percent, respectively). Then both fell substantially, so that by 2004, both rates were about one-third above their 1980 levels (29 percent and 35 percent, respectively).

The Juvenile Arrest Rate for Drug Abuse Violations Was Relatively Constant in the 1980s but Rose Considerably in the 1990s

- Between 1990 and 1997, the juvenile arrest rate for drug abuse violations increased 145 percent. The rate declined somewhat between 1997 and 2004 (down 23 percent), but the 2004 rate was still almost double the 1990 rate.
- Over the 1980-2004 period, the white juvenile arrest rate for drug abuse violations peaked in 1997 and held relatively constant through 2004 (down 9 percent). In contrast, the Black rate peaked in 1995 and by 2004 had fallen 44 percent from its peak level.

Two economists have proposed a novel and controversial theory to explain the decrease in crime rates over the past few decades. Professors John J. Donohue III and Steven D. Levitt posit a relationship between the legalization of abortion and the reduction in the crime rate. The authors theorize, "Crime began to fall roughly eighteen years after abortion legalization. The five states that allowed abortion in 1970 experienced declines earlier than the rest of the nation, which legalized abortion in 1973 with Roe v. Wade. States with high abortion rates in the 1970s and 1980s experienced greater crime reductions in the 1990s. . . . Legalized abortion appears to account for as much as 50 percent of recent drop in crime." John J. Donohue III & Steven D. Levitt, The Impact of Legalized Abortion on Crime, 116 Q. J. Econ. 379 (2001). Donohue and Levitt speculate that, as a result of legalization of abortion, fewer unwanted children were born to mothers in straitened circumstances — children who would have been more likely to grow up to be criminals.

NOTE: YOUTH GANGS AND ANTI-GANG LEGISLATION

Despite evidence of a decline in violent youth crime, gang crimes have become an increasing social problem. In the past decade, national concern with youth gangs has escalated. Nearly 24,000 gangs having 760,000 members were active in the United States in 2004, according to the Department of Justice. The highest concentration of gangs is found in Los Angeles and Chicago, Illinois.[21] Moreover, modern street gangs are manifesting heightened levels of violence and, increasingly, are injuring innocent bystanders by their criminal activities.[22]

Stemming from these concerns, many states have enacted anti-gang measures. In 1988 California became the first state to pass anti-gang legislation. The Street Terrorism Enforcement and Prevention Act (STEP) (Cal. Penal Code §§186.20-186.28 (West 1999 & Supp. 2008)) was modeled after the federal Racketeer Influenced and Corrupt Organizations Act (RICO), 18 U.S.C. §1962(c) (2000). STEP creates a new crime of participation in criminal street gang activity by specifying that "any person who actively participates in any criminal street gang with knowledge that its members engage in or have engaged in a pattern of criminal gang activity, and who willfully promotes, furthers, or assists in any felonious criminal conduct by members of that gang" is guilty of a criminal offense (§186.22(a)). STEP also provides for sentence enhancements of one to three years for felonies committed in conjunction with gang activity (§186.22(b)), enhancements of two to four years for felonies committed in or near occupied schools (id.), forfeiture of weapons that are in the possession of gang members (§186.22(e)(1)), and criminalizes gang recruitment of a minor by means of violence or threats of violence ((§186.22(a)). STEP has withstood constitutional challenges on the basis of overbreadth, vagueness, and violations of due process and freedom of association. See People v. Gardeley, 59 Cal. Rptr. 2d 356 (Cal. 1996); People v. Green, 278 Cal. Rptr. 140 (Ct. App. 1991).

The California statute served as an important influence on other states' responses to street gang criminal activity. Some states, however, adopted provisions that went beyond STEP by penalizing gang intimidation, gang recruitment not only by force but also by mere encouragement, and gang drive-by shootings; and providing for broad forfeiture of gang assets as well as broad definitions of gang membership.[23]

Legislators and law enforcement have turned to other anti-gang remedies as well. Federal prosecutors began using RICO to prosecute urban street gangs in the 1980s. Congress enacted RICO in 1970 to eradicate the infiltration of organized crime, especially the Mafia. RICO statutes give prosecutors several advantages: use of more severe penalties, prosecution of *groups* of criminals and gang leaders, use of evidence of related crimes, and encouragement of witnesses' testimony

---

[21] Arlen Egley, Jr. & Christina E. Ritz Highlights of the 2004 National Youth Gang Survey, U.S. Department of Justice, Office of Juvenile Justice and Delinquency Prevention (2006).

[22] Id. See also Fox Butterfield, Guns and Jeers Used by Gangs to Buy Silence, N.Y. Times, Jan. 16, 2005, at 11 (juvenile gang homicides have increased by 25 percent since 2000).

[23] See Beth Bjerregard, The Constitutionality of Anti-Gang Legislation, 12 Campbell L. Rev. 31, 32-33 (1998); Carol J. Martinez, Note, The Street Terrorism Enforcement and Prevention Act: Gang Members and Guilt by Association, 28 Pac. L.J. 711, 714 (1997) (discussing statutes).

because witnesses are likely to feel less threatened when groups of members are prosecuted.[24]

Some states target gangs by means of such civil remedies as injunctions that apply general nuisance statutes to gang members' conduct. Civil injunctions prohibit gang members from engaging in *legal* as well as illegal activities. "In addition to barring gang members from gathering in public, some injunctions prohibit them from wearing gang colors or symbols and possessing everyday items like cellular phones, pagers, tools, and spray paint cans — objects they typically use to conduct drug sales or vandalize property."[25]

California courts have granted preliminary injunctions against gangs on behalf of other citizens living in the neighborhood. The California Supreme Court upheld the constitutionality of such anti-gang injunctions in People ex rel. Gallo v. Acuna, 929 P.2d 596 (Cal. 1997) (holding that anti-gang injunctions do not violate freedom of association and are not vague or overbroad).

Some jurisdictions have also passed anti-loitering measures that are directed at gangs. For example, Chicago passed a "gang loitering ordinance" that allowed Chicago police officers who reasonably believed they saw a gang member loitering in any public place with one or more persons to order the group to disperse. Failure to comply with the officer's order to leave the area gave the police power to arrest. In City of Chicago v. Morales, 697 N.E.2d 11 (Ill. 1995), the Illinois Supreme Court invalidated the ordinance as unconstitutional. Affirming, the United States Supreme Court held that the ordinance was unconstitutionally vague (reasoning that the statutory definition of "loiter" would not enable the ordinary citizen to confirm his or her conduct to the law). 527 U.S. 41, 60 (1999).

Some states address gang-related violence by expanding the circumstances that evoke the death penalty to include gang-related murders. See H. Mitchell Caldwell, Stalking the Jets and the Sharks: Exploring the Constitutionality of the Gang Death Penalty Enhancer, 12 Geo. Mason L. Rev. 601, 603 (2004) (identifying four states with these provisions).

Congressional concerns with juvenile gang violence led, in part, to enactment of the Violent Crime Control and Law Enforcement Act of 1994 (VCCLEA), Pub. L. No. 103-322, 108 Stat. 1796 (codified in scattered sections of U.S.C.), which imposes federal criminal liability for participation in street gangs. 18 U.S.C. §521(d) (2000). In addition, a juvenile's role in gang activity may serve as a factor in the judicial decision to transfer a youth to adult criminal court. 18 U.S.C. §5032 (2000 & Supp. 2005).

Congress is presently considering the Criminal Gang Abatement Act (CGAA) (S. 1236, 107th Cong.), first introduced in 2001 by Senators Dianne Feinstein (D-Cal.) and Orrin Hatch (R-Utah). The CGAA encourages creation of regional task forces composed of local, state, and federal agencies to fight gangs, criminalizes gang recruitment of minors, increases funding to law enforcement for fighting

---

[24] Janice A. Petrella, Note, Equal Protection — What Is in a Name? Sign? Symbol? Gang Members and RICO Considered: State v. Frazier, 649 N.W.2d 828 (Minn. 2002), 34 Rutgers L.J. 1237, 1257 (2003).
[25] Julie Gannon Shoop, Gang Warfare: Legal Battle Pits Personal Liberty Against Public Safety, Trial, Mar. 1998, at 12.

gangs, enhances sentences for gang-related crimes, and creates a new federal crime of interstate witness intimidation.[26]

Commentators voice concerns about the constitutional shortcomings of the various anti-gang measures.[27] Nonetheless, most courts that have reviewed anti-gang legislation have rejected challenges on grounds of overbreadth or vagueness.[28] Aside from constitutional concerns, some commentators criticize anti-gang civil injunctions for their negative social connotations for minority youth.[29]

3. The Early Juvenile Court: Historical Origins and Philosophy

a. Historical Origins of the Juvenile Court[30]

The Invention of the Juvenile Court

Juvenile Justice Philosophy: Readings, Cases and Comments 550-557 (Frederic L. Faust & Paul J. Brantingham eds. 1974)

Historical analysis of the origin of the juvenile court is in flux. Two separate interpretations of juvenile court history — agreeing only on the year 1899 as the formal date of founding — have currency. . . .

The orthodox interpretation of the founding of the juvenile court is a tale of humane impulse merging with social science through a legal catalyst to replace the barbarous and vengeful cruelties of the criminal law with something better. At common law, and in the American criminal laws formed under the influence of classical criminology during the course of the 19th century, all persons capable of mature reasoning were held criminally accountable for their actions. Built into that general rule was the ancient common law exception of *doli incapax* which held children under the age of seven years legally incapable of criminal intent and hence crime. Children aged seven to fourteen years were presumed incapable of mature reasoning and so not criminally punishable. But the state could rebut the presumption. Where the presumption was successfully rebutted, children were held to answer in criminal court. Children above the age of 14 were treated as adults by

---

[26] For an explanation and criticism of CGAA, see Andrew E. Goldsmith, Criminal Gang Abatement Act, 39 Harv. J. on Legis. 503 (2002).

[27] See, e.g., Kim Strosnider, Anti-Gang Ordinances After City of Chicago v. Morales: The Intersection of Race, Vagueness Doctrine, and Equal Protection in the Criminal Law, 39 Am. Crim. L. Rev. 101 (2002); Matthew Mickle Werdegar, Note, Enjoining the Constitution: The Use of Public Nuisance Abatement Injunctions Against Urban Street Gangs, 51 Stan. L. Rev. 409 (1999) (suggesting anti-gang injunctions are unconstitutional).

[28] Bjerregaard, supra note [23], at 41-42.

[29] See, e.g., Gary Stewart, Note, Black Codes and Broken Windows: The Legacy of Racial Hegemony in Anti-Gang Civil Injunctions, 107 Yale L.J. 2249, 2250 (1998); Toni Massaro, The Gang's Not Here, 2 Green Bag 2d 25, 32 (1998).

[30] A great deal has been written on the origins of the juvenile court. Two examples of the traditional, orthodox view are Herbert H. Lou, Juvenile Courts in the United States (1927) and Julian W. Mack, The Juvenile Court, 23 Harv. L. Rev. 104 (1909). See also Sanford Fox, The Early History of the Court, in the Future of Children: The Juvenile Court 29 (Packard Foundation, 1996); Anthony M. Platt, The Child Savers: The Invention of Delinquency (2d ed. 1977); Margaret K. Rosenheim, A Century of Juvenile Justice (2002).

the criminal law. The result was that children were arrested and jailed with adults, were tried under the same grueling procedures used for adults, and could be sentenced to the same punishments as adults. The orthodox histories of the juvenile court cite examples of children being hung, tortured, transported and imprisoned to make their point. In the orthodox interpretation, the founders of juvenile courts were first and foremost searching for a way to save children from the scourges of criminal law and prison discipline. The founders sought a humane and beneficial method for controlling offensive conduct and alleviating juvenile misery.

During the latter part of the 19th century nascent social science made its first impact on penology. The American version of positive criminology suggested that the causes of delinquency could be found in the heredity, and social and physical environments of the individual offenders. Where the causes could be identified, the medical analogy suggested that cures could be found and administered. Beyond that, the religious-humanistic child-saving movement, which dated from 1825, offered support and guidance for the positive school conclusions: children were infinitely malleable, the best possible subjects for the new social sciences to work wonders upon; and the source of most troubled children's problems could be identified in the social environment in the home created by irresponsibly indulgent or incompetent parents.

But to work its wonders, social science had to have early access to children, before they were molded into a life of depravity. . . . What was needed was a legal bridge between the troubled child and the agencies of amelioration. That legal bridge was found in the informal procedures of equity jurisdictions; in the doctrine of parens patriae. American ingenuity extended the parens patriae concept — the idea that the state was the ultimate parent — from its traditional role as guardian of the persons and property of wealthy orphans to a new and nobler role as guardian of all children. Suddenly the state took up the burden of parenthood and stood between all children and the manifest dangers of parental laxness and urban temptation. At the same time, equity procedure protected children from the stigma of criminality and the horrors of prison discipline. Parens patriae doctrine became the legal catalyst necessary to the formal foundation of the juvenile court. . . .

The revisionist interpretation of the founding of the juvenile court rejects orthodox history as both self-serving and ingenuous. The juvenile court was not a major departure in legal process, but rather an evolutionary culmination of at least a half-century's developments in penology and legal practice. The juvenile court was a steel fist of social control — fired in a blast furnace of class conflict and women's liberation and tempered in the fluid doctrines of positive criminology.

In the revisionist retelling of the creation of the juvenile court, it is no more than the last in a series of institutions created by 19th century Americans to deal with troubled and troublesome urban children. . . .

By the 1890s there was general agreement on reformatory theory. Anthony M. Platt has identified and articulated a nine-point statement of the ideal reformatory scheme: (1) segregation of young deviants from adult deviants; (2) removal of deviant children from unsound environments to reformatories for their own good; (3) denial of need for trial or due process legal trappings in the removal process because reformatories helped rather than hurt; (4) indeterminate commitments; (5) denial of sentimentality and resort to punishment where it became a necessary means to reform; (6) military drill, physical exercise, labor, and constant supervision to protect reformatory inmates from idleness and indulgence; (7) cottage plan physical plants in rural locations; (8) tripartite school program based on elementary education, industrial and agricultural training, and religious education; and (9) constant training in the value of sobriety, thrift, industry, prudence, realistic ambition, and life adjustment.

[T]he civil poor laws — marked by informal legal procedures and biased against the social environment implicit in pauper homes — were expanded and used to break up pauper families and direct pauper children into reformatory institutions. Penal theory made little distinction between delinquent and dependent children. As the 19th century progressed, courts came to blur the distinctions between delinquents and dependents in the same way penal theory did and to move toward use of the informal procedures of the poor laws as the most efficient method for delivering troubled and troublesome children to the child savers. On the eve of its founding, the revisionist interpretation concludes, all of the elements of the juvenile court existed in well-developed form. The Illinois juvenile court act merely codified extant practice.

The revisionist interpretation also rejects the orthodox history's analysis of the motives of the founders of the juvenile court. Far from seeing the founders as humanitarians, the revisionist interpretation sees them as members of social and political interest groups: a socio-economic elite manipulating the juvenile laws to hold the impoverished and immigrant lower classes in their places; professional child savers seeking protection and expansion of their careers; and middle-class feminists seeking both political power and socially acceptable careers outside the home. . . . The juvenile court gave a patina of respectability to and a rationale for the destruction of lower-class families. Deviance was a product of biology and environment. The juvenile court allowed the child savers to identify and save children by painlessly substituting healthy environments for sickly environments. It was all so scientific.

b.   Philosophy of the Early Juvenile Court

Rehabilitative Ideal

The early juvenile court acts promised a new brand of justice for the child. Although this justice was to be dispensed in a court proceeding, the goals of the proceeding were investigation, diagnosis, and prescription of treatment, rather than adversary determination of facts and impositions of punitive sanctions. Rehabilitation, rather than deterrence and retribution, was to be emphasized. These objectives were set out by the court in Commonwealth v. Fisher, 62 A. 198 (Pa. 1905):

> The act is not for the trial of a child charged with a crime, but is mercifully to save it from such an ordeal, with the prison or penitentiary in its wake, if the child's own good and the best interests of the state justify such salvation. . . . The act is but an exercise by the state of its supreme power over the welfare of its children. . . .
>
> The design is not punishment, nor the restraint imprisonment, any more than is the wholesome restraint which a parent exercises over his child. . . . There is no probability, in the proper administration of the law, of the child's liberty being unduly invaded. Every statute which is designed to give protection, care, and training to children, as a needed substitute for parental authority and performance of parental duty, is but a recognition of the duty of the state, as the legitimate guardian and protector of children where other guardianship fails. No constitutional right is violated.

Procedural Informality

Judge Julian Mack, writing of the early twentieth century juvenile court, depicted a benevolent and paternalistic institution in which legalistic formalities would be not only inappropriate, but counterproductive:

> The child who must be brought into court should, of course, be made to know that he is face to face with the power of the state, but he should at the same time, and more emphatically, be made to feel that he is the object of its care and solicitude. The ordinary trappings of the courtroom are out of place in such hearings. The judge on a bench, looking down upon the boy standing at the bar, can never evoke a proper sympathetic spirit. Seated at a desk, with the child at his side, where he can on occasion put his arm around his shoulder and draw the lad to him, the judge, while losing none of his judicial dignity, will gain immensely in the effectiveness of his work.[31]

Individualization

Justice for children was to be personalized, individualized. Mack describes the court's obligation as one of determining the child's need for treatment and writing out the correct prescription, rather than adjudicating criminal conduct:

> The problem for determination by the judge is not, Has this boy or girl committed a specific wrong, but what is he, how has he become what he is, and what had best be done in his interest and in the interest of the state to save him from a downward career. It is apparent at once that the ordinary legal evidence in a criminal court is not the sort of evidence to be heard in such a proceeding. A thorough investigation, usually made by the probation officer, will give the court much information bearing on the heredity and environment of the child.[32]

Separation of Juvenile and Adult Offenders

The juvenile court movement sought to ensure that children were not incarcerated with adults to protect children from being physically brutalized or taught criminal habits by hardened adult offenders. Indeed this goal of establishing separate and specialized juvenile detention facilities had been pressed by reformers with occasional success much earlier in the nineteenth century — New York City founded a House of Refuge for children only in 1825. Building on this tradition, juvenile court acts typically prohibited a court from committing a delinquent child to a correctional facility that also housed adult convicts.

4.   The Juvenile Justice System Today: The Bureaucratic Process

The juvenile court is one part of a larger juvenile justice system that includes police and correctional agencies. The number of children who actually go through the

---

[31] Mack, supra note [30], at 120.
[32] Id. at 119-120.

court's adjudicatory process and are placed in institutions represent a small fraction of those children who come in contact with some part of the total system. Most juveniles who appear in juvenile court are sent there by the police. However, some youths may also be sent to juvenile court by social agencies or parents.

Howard N. Snyder, The Juvenile Court and Delinquency Cases
The Future of Children: The Juvenile Court 53, 55-58 (1996)

The Juvenile Court's Response to Delinquency Cases

In general, the juvenile court process can be conceptualized as a series of decision points. . . . All juvenile justice systems contain the same series of decision points; however, who performs these tasks (for example, police, prosecutor, court clerk, judge, or probation officer) may differ from jurisdiction to jurisdiction.

Diversion

Once a juvenile is arrested and the case is referred to court intake, an intake official (for example, a juvenile probation officer with intake responsibility or a prosecutor) decides if the referral should be processed by the court. The intake official's first consideration is the case's legal sufficiency — whether there is enough evidence to prosecute the matter successfully. If not, the case is dismissed. If the intake official decides that the case has legal sufficiency, the case may either go to the court or be diverted for handling outside the formal court process. Cases are likely to be diverted if the youth admits to the act, if it is the youth's first referral, if the charge is not serious, and if the victim is satisfied with the agreed-upon outcome such as the level of restitution. [A]pproximately one quarter of all delinquency cases [are] either dismissed or diverted to community agencies at the intake level.

Preadjudicatory Detention

At the time of referral to court intake, it is often the intake official who determines if the juvenile should be placed in a secure detention facility prior to the court's first hearing on the case. The intake official typically is employed by the detention center or by the intake department of the court. Detention may be ordered if the juvenile is a threat to the community, to ensure the juvenile's appearance at court hearings, or for the juvenile's own safety. State statutes require that, if detention is ordered, a judge must review the detention decision within a short period of time (generally 24 to 71 hours). Juveniles may also be detained later in the processing of the case if the court believes it is necessary. [I]n about one in five delinquency cases, the juveniles [are] securely detained for some period between the date of intake and the date of court disposition. . . .

Informal versus Formal Processing

If there is sufficient reason to believe the youth committed the delinquent act and it is determined that the matter requires some form of court intervention, the intake officer must then decide if the case should be handled informally or formally. In many jurisdictions, the youth must admit that he or she committed the act before informal processing is permitted. If the case is handled informally, the juvenile *voluntarily agrees* to serve a period of informal probation, to pay victim restitution, to pay a fine, to perform community service, or to submit to some other sanction. If the youth successfully adheres to this informal agreement, the case is then dismissed. If the youth fails to abide by the agreement, the case can then be reassessed and in most instances, handled formally. . . .

Transfers to Juvenile Court

There are three basic pathways for a juvenile to be tried in a criminal court: statutory exclusion, prosecutorial discretion, and judicial waiver or transfer. Statutes in many states exclude from juvenile court jurisdiction certain cases involving a person who by age alone would be classified as a juvenile and require that they be processed in a criminal court. Along with statutory exclusions, some states give prosecutors the discretion to file certain types of cases in either the juvenile or criminal court. The criteria for statutory exclusion and prosecutorial discretion normally involve factors of age, seriousness of the offense, and prior record. The third pathway enables juvenile court judges to waive the juvenile court's jurisdiction over a case and send the matter to criminal court. In addition to the factors mentioned above, the judge's decision is influenced by the juvenile's amenability to treatment in the juvenile justice system. . . .

Adjudication

Instead of a transfer petition, a petition may be filed asking the court to find (adjudicate) the youth to be delinquent. [Juveniles are] adjudicated delinquent in nearly three of every five, or more than 2 million, of these cases. In nearly two-thirds of those cases in which the youth was not found delinquent, the case was dismissed. In the other nonadjudicated cases, the youth *voluntarily agreed* to some form of probation, restitution, or other sanction(s).

Court-Ordered Dispositions

Once a youth is found to be delinquent, the judge can place the youth on formal probation, order the youth to a residential facility, invoke other sanctions such as restitution, fines, or community service, or dismiss the case in consideration of actions already taken. . . . When juveniles are placed in residential facilities, a variety of options are available to the court ranging from large state training schools with hundreds of beds to small, 30-bed, community-based facilities, to residential group homes for fewer than six youths. It is not uncommon for juveniles to move through different levels of security within a single institution or through more than one type of facility before completing their court-ordered disposition. . . .

Although there is some variation, in most states the juvenile court may keep juveniles in a residential placement or on probation until their 21st birthdays. Courts in a few states lose jurisdiction at age 18. . . .

C.   JURISDICTION AND DISPOSITION IN THE JUVENILE COURT

1.   Who Is Subject to the Delinquency Jurisdiction of the Juvenile Court?

In re Michael B.
118 Cal. Rptr. 685 (Ct. App. 1975)

FLEMING, J.

Nine-year-old Michael B. appeals the order of the juvenile court declaring him a ward of the court under Welfare and Institutions Code section 602.[1] The court based its order on a finding that Michael committed a burglary in violation of Penal Code section 459.

Richard Lewis testified that on 16 April 1974 he parked and locked his 1967 Mercedes Benz automobile in the parking area of his apartment building on North Maltman Avenue in Los Angeles. On his return to the automobile he found the outside rearview mirror broken off, the antenna bent, and the windwing pried open. Lewis gave no one permission to enter his automobile.

Police Officer John Murphy testified that on 16 April 1974 he was searching for a missing juvenile, Michael B., in the area of Bellvue Park, where Michael had been seen riding a purple, girl's bicycle. Murphy saw Michael hiding behind a shed in the park and asked him for his name and the whereabouts of the bicycle he had been riding. The boy showed the officer the bicycle in the bushes. Murphy took Michael into custody and advised him of his constitutional rights to silence and to counsel. Michael said he had heard his rights before and understood them, he did not want counsel, and he wanted to talk. At the police station, Murphy asked Michael where he had been the night before. Michael said he had been with friends, and they had gone into three or four cars on Maltman Avenue near the park. He then took Murphy to Richard Lewis' Mercedes Benz, told him he had broken off the rearview mirror so he could get his hands in to pry open the windwing and that when he had done so, one of his friends reached inside and unlocked the door. They took a package of cigarettes, the only thing they could find of value.

Murphy asked Michael if he knew right from wrong, if he knew it was wrong to break into cars and steal. Michael said yes. Murphy asked Michael how he would feel if someone took something that meant a lot to him. Michael said he never had anything that meant a lot to him, so it really didn't matter.

Penal Code section 26, which applies to proceedings under Welfare and Institutions Code section 602 (In re Gladys R., 1 Cal. 3d 855, 862-867), provides in pertinent part: "All persons are capable of committing crimes except those belonging to the following classes: One — Children under the age of 14, in the absence of clear proof that at the time of committing the act charged against them, they knew

---

[1] Section 602 provides in pertinent part: "Any person who is under the age of 18 years when he violates any law of this state . . . defining crime . . . is within the jurisdiction of the juvenile court, which may adjudge such person to be a ward of the court."

its wrongfulness." The Supreme Court declared in In re Gladys R., at page 867: "Only if the age, experience, knowledge, and conduct of the child demonstrate by clear proof that he has violated a criminal law should he be declared a ward of the court under section 602." The evidence here falls far short of that necessary to establish "clear proof" that Michael knew the wrongfulness of his acts.

The only evidence on that issue was the brief statement of the police officer that Michael said yes when asked if he knew the difference between right and wrong. Penal Code section 26 requires more substantial evidence than that to clearly prove that a nine-year-old boy, no more than a third-grade pupil, harbored the necessary capacity to commit a serious criminal offense. No such substantial evidence was presented here, nor do the nature and circumstances of the crime itself furnish that clear proof of knowledge of the wrongfulness of the conduct that is required by the statute. We think nine-year-old Michael was improperly adjudicated a ward of the court under Welfare and Institutions Code section 602.

In re Gladys R., 1 Cal. 3d 855, suggests alternative procedures under Welfare and Institutions Code sections 600 or 601 for disposition of cases involving, as here, a child too young to appreciate the wrongfulness of his acts (at p. 867):

> Section 601 provides that a child who disobeys the lawful orders of his parents or school authorities, who is beyond the control of such persons, or who is in danger of leading an immoral life may be adjudged a ward of the court. Section 601 might clearly cover younger children who lack the age or experience to understand the wrongfulness of their conduct. If the juvenile court considers section 601 inappropriate for the particular child, he may be covered by the even broader provisions of section 600. . . . Section 602 should apply only to those who are over 14 and may be presumed to understand the wrongfulness of their acts and to those under the age of 14 who clearly appreciate the wrongfulness of their conduct.

While Michael may be receiving the same care and treatment as a ward under section 602 that he would be receiving if a ward under section 600 or 601, disposition under section 602 carries a stigma of criminal conduct which is not justified by the record in this case.

The judgment (order) is reversed, and the cause is remanded to the juvenile court for further proceedings consistent with this opinion.

NOTE: JURISDICTIONAL REQUIREMENTS

From the outset, delinquency jurisdiction of a juvenile court has included young persons whose conduct would constitute "a crime if committed by an adult" (Or. Rev. Stat. §419.C453 (2003)) or who violated "any law . . . defining crime" (Cal. Welf. & Inst. Code §602 (West 1999 & Supp. 2008)). In other words, the jurisdiction is defined in terms of age and in terms of violation of a criminal law.[33]

---

[33] As indicated in Chapter 6, young people who violate curfews, are truants, or are ungovernable may also be subject to the delinquency jurisdiction in some states, although the tendency in modern juvenile statutes is to create a special category for them.

(1) Minimum Age.   Most jurisdictional statutes do not establish a minimum age for persons to be subject to the original jurisdiction of the juvenile court.[34] There are exceptions, however. For example, 11 states set the minimum age at ten years old; 1 state sets the minimum age at eight; and 3 states set it at seven; North Carolina has the lowest statutory minimum age: six years.[35] In In re Michael B., note that California Welfare & Institutions Code §602 does not itself establish a jurisdictional lower limit. Instead, the court's ruling that nine-year-old Michael was not a delinquent turned on the statutory provision that excludes from the category of persons "capable of committing crimes" those children under 14, at least "in the absence of clear proof that at the time of committing the act charged against them, they knew its wrongfulness." That case suggests, however, how an infancy defense or the mens rea requirement may, as a practical matter, exclude younger children from being adjudicated delinquents. See also infra, In re S.H.

(2) Maximum Age.   The majority of state statutes provide that persons 17 and younger are subject to the jurisdiction of the juvenile court. Ten states set the maximum age for juvenile court jurisdiction at 16. Only three states set it even younger, at 15.[36] In addition to the variations in the maximum ages, statutes differ in terms of whether that age limit applies to the time when the alleged *crime* took place, or the age when *proceedings* are brought. States are split on this issue, and even among those states that set the age limit at the time when proceedings are brought, numerous interpretations of the standard exist.[37]

Although very young children might not be adjudicated as delinquents, a juvenile court may nevertheless assume jurisdiction over children because they are "neglected" or are beyond parental control. As a practical matter, what difference does this make? Is it less stigmatizing? Are the consequences for the child less severe?

(3) Violation of a Criminal Statute.   Every state incorporates "in some form and with various exceptions the criminal law applicable to adults as the dominant source of substantive rules governing the behavior of juveniles."[38] Precise limits of this incorporation vary substantially from state to state. Many states specifically exclude traffic offenses as a basis for delinquency. See, e.g., Colo. Rev. Stat. Ann. §§19-2-104(1)(a)(I) & (1)(a)(II) (West 2005). Questions can arise as to whether

[34] Melanie King & Linda Szymanski, State Juvenile Justice Profiles: National Overviews (2006), available at *http://www.ncjj.org/stateprofiles/* (last visited May 19, 2008).

[35] Id.

[36] Id.

[37] H.D. Warren & C.P. Jhong, Annotation, Age of Child at Time of Alleged Offense or Delinquency, or at Time of Legal Proceedings, as Criterion of Jurisdiction of Juvenile Court, 89 A.L.R.2d 506 (2007).

[38] American Bar Association, Juvenile Justice Standards, Standards Relating to Juvenile Delinquency and Sanctions 18 (1980). In 1971 the Institute of Judicial Administration, a private nonprofit research and educational organization at N.Y.U. School of Law, began a Juvenile Justice Standards Project to address juvenile justice issues. The ABA became cosponsor of the project in 1973. More than 30 scholars undertook the task of writing standards and accompanying commentary. Their efforts culminated in tentative drafts. An executive committee was formed to review individual volumes. Twenty of the 23 volumes subsequently were approved by the ABA House of Delegates. The result is a set of standards and commentary intended to serve as a compilation of current thought and guidelines for action at local, state, and federal levels.

municipal ordinances, regulations concerning fish and game laws, and various other regulatory laws that allow the imposition of a fine satisfy the jurisdictional requirement that the conduct would be criminal if committed by an adult.

The Juvenile Justice Standards advocate the following:

2.2 Offense

A. The delinquency jurisdiction of the juvenile court should include only those offenses which are:

> 1. punishable by incarceration in a prison, jail, or other place of detention, and
>
> 2. except as qualified by these standards, in violation of an applicable federal, state, or local criminal statute or ordinance, or
>
> 3. in violation of an applicable state or local statute or ordinance defining a major traffic offense.[39]

(4) Mens Rea and the Infancy Defense.   Most crimes require that a mental element — mens rea — be proven for conviction. Mens rea focuses on whether an accused possesses the specific state of mind required to commit a blameworthy act. The required state of mind varies with the crime: often, but not always, fault (not simply an unhappy result) must be shown.[40] Responsibility for criminal acts also involves the issue of capacity — whether the accused has the capacity to understand wrongfulness. In a sense, capacity is a prerequisite to mens rea — an individual must have the capacity to be culpable, that is to know wrongfulness, to maintain a specific mens rea. The criminal law permits the accused to prove defects in capacity, in the form of defenses such as insanity, mistake, or justification, to show that the accused is not a proper object of criminal sanctions.

In cases in which the accused is a minor there are additional complexities. Several questions can be posed. *First*, should age sometimes be a complete defense to a crime? An infancy defense did exist at common law: It centered on the question whether a child had sufficient maturity or capacity to know right from wrong. Special rules existed concerning the capacity of children to commit crimes. Children under seven were conclusively presumed to lack capacity to commit a crime. Children between seven and 14 were presumed to be without capacity, but this presumption could be rebutted. Finally, children 14 and above were held to the same standards as adults.[41]

In only a few jurisdictions today is a defense based on infancy available. When a general defense based on infancy is unavailable, a *second* and separate question concerns whether the minor had the requisite mens rea for the particular crime alleged. For example, a 15-year-old accused of the theft of a book would not at common law have an infancy defense available, but might nevertheless avoid

---

[39] Id. at 4.

[40] Professors LaFave and Scott have written: "Crimes may be classified according to their mental aspects into (1) crimes requiring subjective fault, (2) crimes requiring objective fault, and (3) crimes imposing liability without fault. The principal types of mental culpability in crimes requiring fault are (1) intention, (2) knowledge, (3) recklessness, and (4) negligence." Wayne R. LaFave & Austin W. Scott, Jr., Criminal Law 191 (1972).

[41] Id. at 399-403.

conviction if there was insufficient proof that he had intentionally taken the book knowing it was not his book but belonged to some other student.

Francis McCarthy has suggested that

> The principles of criminal liability at common law applied equally to both adults and children. In both instances the criminal sanction was imposed only upon proof of the commission of an offense and all the requisite elements, including mens rea, of that offense. The only difference between the child and the adult was that the former was aided by a presumption which had the same force for those children between ages seven and 14 as that which would be occasioned by a prima facie showing of insanity by an adult. If this obstacle to prosecution were overcome, the principles of criminal responsibility for adults and children were identical.[42]

A *third* set of questions concerns whether and how the creation of a juvenile court (and its delinquency jurisdiction) changed, if at all, these common law notions of children's criminal responsibility. Does an infancy defense exist in juvenile court? Must there be proof of the mens rea element of the crime on which delinquency is to be based?

A number of state courts have considered whether the infancy defense is applicable to juvenile court proceedings. The traditional view, based on the rehabilitative ideal on which the juvenile court was founded, is that because the juvenile court is not penal, children do not need to be protected from its jurisdiction by presumptions of incapacity.[43] As one commentator has described:

> Because parens patriae theory depends on the notion that the child is being helped and thus is not being tried for a crime and punished as a criminal, there was no need to determine whether the child had the capacity to act in a culpable fashion. Indeed, assertion of the defense could be viewed as wrongfully precluding treatment for those very children most susceptible to the benefits of intervention. . . .[44]

Only a small number of jurisdictions hold that the infancy defense is applicable to juvenile proceedings.[45] One commentator suggests that the shift in focus of the juvenile court to a punishment-based rationale calls forth a new consideration of the infancy defense:

> Since 1992 all but 10 of the states have greatly liberalized the ability of the state to try juveniles as adults, a number of them at earlier ages than previously. In addition, public and law enforcement access to juvenile court records has broadened considerably. In more than half the states juveniles may be transferred to

---

[42] Francis B. McCarthy, The Role of the Concept of Responsibility in Juvenile Delinquency Proceedings, 10 U. Mich. J.L. Ref. 181, 187 (1977).

[43] Lara A. Bazelon, Exploding the Superpredator Myth: Why Infancy Is the Preadolescent's Best Defense in Juvenile Court, 75 N.Y.U. L. Rev. 159, 161 (2000).

[44] Andrew Walkover, The Infancy Defense in the New Juvenile Court, 31 UCLA L. Rev. 503, 516-517 (1984).

[45] Bazelon, supra note [43], at 161 n. 7 (pointing out that only four states apply the infancy defense in juvenile court proceedings).

criminal court by judicial waiver, prosecutorial waiver, or statute for certain serious offenses committed prior to their fourteenth birthday, with a significant number of these jurisdictions permitting adult treatment for children of any age for at least some offenses.

Even those youths retained in the juvenile or family court for handling as delinquents are increasingly exposed to sanctions that focus more on accountability than treatment, and they may be deprived of their liberty for longer periods of time pursuant to serious offender statutes. Juvenile court adjudications may be utilized more freely to enhance subsequent adult sentences under three-strikes laws or pursuant to sentencing guidelines in both the federal and criminal justice systems. In other words, the once large gulf between juvenile or family court rehabilitation and treatment and adult criminal court handling has narrowed considerably, if it has not disappeared entirely. In light of these major developments, the defense of infancy deserves a new look and fresh consideration by those involved in the juvenile justice process.[46]

Few reported cases explicitly consider whether mens rea must be shown in delinquency proceedings. However, most commentators, as well as the ABA Standards, have suggested that the state should have to prove the same mental element of the underlying crime for delinquency as in adult proceedings.[47] The ABA Juvenile Justice Standards require the state to prove mens rea — or the appropriate culpable mental state — in all cases in which it would be required if an adult were accused of the underlying crime. In addition, the Standards provide for a "reasonableness defense" for risk-creating conduct (that the juvenile's conduct conformed to the standard of care that a reasonable person of the juvenile's age, maturity, and mental capacity would observe in the juvenile's situation) and an "insanity defense" (that as a result of mental disease or defect, the juvenile lacked substantial capacity to appreciate the criminality of conduct or to conform conduct to the requirements of the law).[48]

(5) Fitness Hearings, Waiver, and Transfer for Trial in Adult Criminal Court. There are circumstances in which a minor may be tried for a crime in adult criminal court rather than juvenile court. The possibility of transfer or waiver has been a feature of the juvenile court system since its inception, and nearly every state allows for it. The recent "get tough on crime" movement has resulted in an increasing number of youths being transferred to criminal court. Juveniles may be transferred from the juvenile court to the adult criminal court in three ways: judicial waiver, legislative waiver, or prosecutorial discretion.

First, juvenile court judges may transfer cases to adult criminal court following a hearing. Common judicial waiver provisions allow a juvenile court judge to transfer a juvenile to criminal court if the judge determines that

---

[46] Robert E. Shepherd, Jr., Juvenile Justice, 12 Crim. Just. 45, 45 (1997). See also Andrew M. Carter, Age Matters: The Case for a Constitutionalized Infancy Defense, 54 Kan. L. Rev. 687 (2006) (arguing that the infancy defense is constitutionally mandated); Barbara Kaban & James Orlando, Revitalizing the Infancy Defense in the Contemporary Juvenile Court, 60 Rutgers L. Rev. 33 (2007) (arguing that the infancy defense is consistent with delinquency proceedings).

[47] See, e.g., McCarthy, supra note [42]; Sanford J. Fox, Responsibility in the Juvenile Court, 11 Wm. & Mary L. Rev. 650 (1970).

[48] American Bar Association, Juvenile Justice Standards, supra note [38], at 5-6.

the youth is not a "fit and proper" subject for juvenile court processing or that the youth "cannot benefit" from the "guidance" or "treatment" available in the juvenile court system."[49]

In Kent v. United States, 383 U.S. 541 (1966), the United States Supreme Court mandated certain procedural safeguards for judicial waiver (a hearing, representation, access by counsel to social and probation records, and a statement of reasons justifying the transfer). In an attempt to provide guidelines for the exercise of judicial discretion, the Court enumerated certain factors that should be considered in the waiver determination — that is, seriousness of the offense to the community, manner in which the offense was committed (violence or premeditation), person-based or property-based offense, sufficiency of the evidence, desirability of trying the offense in one court, maturity of juvenile, record and previous arrest history of juvenile, protection of public, and likelihood of rehabilitation of juvenile by use of juvenile court procedures. Id. at 566-567. *Kent* required that judges make explicit findings based on individualized determinations of amenability to treatment or dangerousness to the community.

The ABA Juvenile Justice Standards also attempted to limit judicial discretion by requiring the following findings for transfer:

2.2 Necessary Findings

A. The juvenile court should waive its jurisdiction only upon finding:

1. that probable cause exists to believe that the juvenile has committed the class one [punishable by more than 20 years or the death penalty] or class two [punishable by 5 to 20 years] juvenile offense alleged in the petition; and

2. that by clear and convincing evidence the juvenile is not a proper person to be handled by the juvenile court.

B. A finding of probable cause to believe that a juvenile has committed a class one or class two juvenile offense should be based solely on evidence admissible in an adjudicatory hearing of the juvenile court.

C. A finding that a juvenile is not a proper person to be handled by the juvenile court must include determinations, by clear and convincing evidence, of:

1. the seriousness of the alleged class one or class two juvenile offense;

2. a prior record of adjudicated delinquency involving the infliction or threat of significant bodily injury, if the juvenile is alleged to have committed a class two juvenile offense;

3. the likely inefficacy of the dispositions available to the juvenile court as demonstrated by previous dispositions of the juvenile; and

4. the appropriateness of the services and dispositional alternatives available in the criminal justice system for dealing with the juvenile's problems and whether they are, in fact, available.

---

[49] See, e.g., Cal. Welf. & Inst. Code §707(c) (West 1998 & Supp. 2008), which creates a presumption that a juvenile who commits certain felonies defined under §707(b) is not a fit and proper subject to be dealt with under juvenile court jurisdiction unless the court finds that the minor "would be amenable to care, treatment and training programs available through facilities of the juvenile court."

Expert opinion should be considered in assessing the likely efficacy of the dispositions available to the juvenile court. A finding that a juvenile is not a proper person to be handled by the juvenile court should be based solely on evidence admissible in a disposition hearing of the juvenile court and should be in writing, as provided in Standard 2.1E.

D. A finding of probable cause to believe that a juvenile has committed a class one or class two juvenile offense may be substituted for a probable cause determination relating to that offense (or a lesser included offense) required in any subsequent juvenile court proceeding. Such a finding should not be substituted for any finding of probable cause required in any subsequent criminal proceeding.[50]

Fitness hearings result in a considerable amount of litigation and introduce substantial complexity into the juvenile justice process. For example, Breed v. Jones, discussed infra p. 822, posed a double jeopardy issue because a juvenile court transferred a case to adult court *after* the adjudicatory hearing in juvenile court. After *Kent*, supra, recurring issues regarding waiver included the following: (1) Does a minor have a right to counsel at the waiver hearing? (2) Does the minor and/or minor's parents have a right to notice of the transfer hearing? (3) Are the rules of evidence applicable at the hearing, especially the admissibility of hearsay? (4) What is the standard of proof at the hearing? (5) Is the privilege against self-incrimination applicable, especially the admissibility in subsequent proceedings of incriminating statements? (6) Does a right of appeal exist?

Judicial waiver practice received considerable criticism in the years following *Kent*. Such criticisms triggered statutory reforms focusing on an offense-based system. In this second form of waiver, "legislative" or "automatic waiver," many state statutes exclude certain crimes or chronic offenders from juvenile court jurisdiction. For example, juvenile court jurisdiction is automatically precluded in some states when the child is charged with an act that would be a capital crime or an extremely serious felony (e.g., murder, kidnapping, rape, armed robbery, crimes committed with a firearm). Some states include drug offenses and felonies committed in furtherance of gang activities. In the past few years, many states revised their transfer statutes to facilitate transfers to adult court — by reducing the minimum age for transfer,[51] expanding the list of transferable offenses, and eliminating some of the factors that must be considered (such as no longer requiring that the juvenile must first be found "unamenable to treatment").[52]

Finally, in the third form of waiver, prosecutors in some states may file certain cases involving juveniles directly in either juvenile or adult criminal court. Unlike judicial waiver, prosecutorial waiver of juveniles to criminal court is unreviewable

[50] American Bar Association, Juvenile Justice Standards, Standards Relating to Transfer Between Courts, at 10-11 (1980).

[51] Richard E. Redding, Juveniles Transferred to Criminal Court: Legal Reform Proposals Based on Social Science Research, 1997 Utah L. Rev. 709, 714. All states have lowered the minimum age for transfer to age 14 or younger. The federal transfer statute, the Violent Crime Control and Law Enforcement Act, 18 U.S.C. §5032 (2000 & Supp. 2005), permits juveniles as young as age 13 to face federal prosecution for some offenses.

[52] Redding, supra note [51], at 714.

and final.[53] In addition, the prosecutor's decision is made without the benefit of a hearing at which information about the juvenile can be presented.[54] Furthermore, prosecutorial discretion is subject to political pressure.[55]

Formerly, judicial waivers constituted the most popular form of transfer of juveniles to adult court. However, today, prosecutorial and legislative waivers are considerably more common. For example, in one multijurisdictional study of adult courts in 18 large urban counties in 1998, 45 percent of all transfer decisions were made by prosecutors and 40 percent were made by legislatures, rather than judges.[56] The increasing use of transfer raises questions regarding juvenile justice policy. For example, commentators disagree about the effectiveness of transfer. Some suggest that transfer is worthwhile for its symbolic value (as a statement that juvenile crime is taken seriously), its deterrent value (to deter juveniles from criminal behavior), or its protective function (to provide due process protections conferred on adults).[57] Other commentators claim that research findings do not substantiate the belief that transfer reduces the rate of reoffending by juvenile offenders.[58] Furthermore, questions arise about who should make the initial decision about waiver — the prosecutor, the judge, or the legislature — and how much discretion should be permitted.

Other commentators criticize the trend of expanding waiver that results in the transfer to adult court of juveniles at increasingly younger ages.[59] A highly publicized example of this trend is the Florida case of 12-year-old Lionel Tate, who killed a 6-year-old friend while he was practicing professional wrestling moves that he saw on television (Tate v. Florida, 864 So. 2d 44 (Fla. Dist. Ct. App. 2003)). Prosecutorial waiver resulted in Lionel being tried as an adult. After the boy was convicted of first-degree murder (carrying a mandatory sentence of life in prison without the possibility of parole), public outcry led to his being granted a retrial and, subsequently, his acceptance of a plea bargain with a reduced sentence. See generally Mike Clary, Teen's Life Sentence Sparks Juvenile Punishment Debate, Chi. Trib., Mar. 21, 2001, at 11.

One commentator, who analyzed transfer decision making with reference to empirical research on offending and recidivism patterns, points out additional problems with transfer practice: (1) immature and incompetent juveniles are being transferred to be tried as adults, (2) older juveniles are being transferred to ensure their incarceration past the age of majority, (3) transfer laws often target

---

[53] Janet Ainsworth, The Court's Effectiveness in Protecting the Rights of Juveniles in Delinquency Cases, in The Future of Children: The Juvenile Court 64, 68 (Packard Fdn. 1996).

[54] The Juvenile Court: Analysis and Recommendations, in The Future of Children: The Juvenile Court 4, 10 (Packard Fdn. 1996).

[55] Id. at 10.

[56] Cited in Stephen A. Drizin & Allison McGowen Keegan, Abolishing the Use of the Felony-Murder Rule When the Defendant Is a Teenager 507, 539 (2004).

[57] The Juvenile Court: Analysis and Recommendations, supra note [54], at 9.

[58] Id.

[59] See, e.g., David O. Brink, Immaturity, Normative Competence, and Juvenile Transfer: How (Not) to Punish Minors for Major Crimes, 82 Tex. L. Rev. 1555, 1557 (2004); Marcy R. Podkopacz & Barry Feld, The Back-Door to Prison: Waiver Reform, "Blended Sentencing," and the Law of Unintended Consequences, 91 J. Crim. L. & Criminology 997, 999 (2001).

first-time violent offenders although repeat offenders are more likely to be recidivists, and (4) transfer decision making is highly variable and arbitrary. In
response to these problems, the author suggests the following reforms: abolish
mandatory transfer laws, provide explicit transfer decision making guidelines
for judges, require a competency evaluation before the transfer hearing, and extend
juvenile court jurisdiction to allow it to impose adult sentences.[60] What do you
think of these proposed reforms?

For commentary on juvenile waiver, see Jeffrey Fagan & Franklin Zimring,
The Changing Borders of Juvenile Justice: Transfer of Adolescents to the Criminal
Court (2000); David L. Myers, Boys Among Men: Trying and Sentencing Juve-
niles as Adults (2005); Jennifer Park, Note, Balancing Rehabilitation and Punish-
ment: A Legislative Solution for Unconstitutional Juvenile Waiver Policies, 76
Geo. Wash. L. Rev. 786 (2008).

2. Disposition and Treatment

Juvenile court delinquency proceedings have two aspects: (a) the adjudicatory or
jurisdictional phase, in which the court must decide whether the young person's
conduct warrants juvenile court jurisdiction; and (b) the dispositional phase, in
which the judge is faced with the task of deciding what to do with a youth over
whom jurisdiction has been established. Basically the dispositional choices (apart
from a possible fine) are (1) allowing the young person to remain living at home,
under the supervision of a probation officer or the court; (2) placement of the child
in the home of a relative or foster parent; (3) placement of the child in a "group
home," often under the supervision of a child care agency; or (4) placement in a
state or local institution — typically a "training school" or a juvenile "ranch."

State juvenile court acts typically give the judge the same dispositional power
over all delinquents: it makes no difference whether the judge is dealing with a
first-time shoplifter or a fourth-time armed robber. Statutes *do not* set out punishments according to the offense. In this respect, the disposition power of a juvenile
court differs from adult penal sanctions, which are often graduated in proportion to
the specific violation. The statutes themselves typically give the judge extraordinarily broad discretion in making the dispositional decision, often subject to the
best-interests-of-the-child standard.

Judge Ketcham commented on the problems flowing from giving such vast
discretion to judges:

> The high degree of autonomy which the juvenile court judge typically enjoys has
> the corollary effect of focusing upon him virtually the total responsibility for a just
> adjudication and an astute disposition. In a great majority of jurisdictions,
> however, he is hampered not only by his own lack of training in the necessarily
> specialized skills demanded by his job and by overloaded calendars, but also by

[60] Redding, supra note [51], at 716. For recent criticism of the policy of transferring juveniles to
adult criminal court, see Brink, supra note [59]; Joshua T. Rose, Innocence Lost: The Detrimental
Effect of Automatic Waiver Statutes on Juvenile Justice, 41 Brandeis L.J. 977 (2003); Marissa Slaten,
Juvenile Transfers to Criminal Court: Whose Right Is It Anyway?, 55 Rutgers L. Rev. 821 (2003).

administrative duties and essential extracurricular activities far beyond those demanded by judges in other courts. His task is further complicated in many jurisdictions by intake and probation staffs that are overworked, underpaid, and poorly trained.[61]

The judge typically receives information on which to base his or her decision from a *social study* prepared by the probation officer who has investigated the child's circumstances. The report often contains evidence that would not be legally admissible during the adjudicatory hearing. For this reason many statutes prohibit the judge from seeing any predisposition study before jurisdiction is established, e.g., N.Y. Fam. Ct. Act §750(1) (McKinney 1999 & Supp. 2008), and courts have held it reversible error for a judge to consider the report prior to a jurisdictional finding. E.g., In re Gladys R., 464 P.2d 127 (Cal. 1970).

To aid in the court's effort to provide "individualized justice," the report may contain (1) facts concerning the family background, the child's past and present behavior in the home and community, and his or her medical and social history; (2) the views of interested third parties, such as teachers, social workers, and court-appointed clinicians; (3) the probation officer's estimate of the nature and seriousness of the child's "problem"; and (4) the probation officer's recommendation as to the appropriate treatment. While many juvenile court statutes are silent on the question of what access the juvenile and his or her attorney have to the report, "denial of access to these materials may constitute a denial of the right to the effective assistance of counsel and, therefore, be a mistake of constitutional dimensions."[62] Cf. Kent v. United States, 383 U.S. 541 (1966).

The judge is not bound by this social study. The report does, however, furnish the bulk of the information that influences the dispositional decision. In the majority of cases the probation officer's recommendation is followed. One of the problems with this system was pointed out by Judge Polier:

> The value of diagnostic studies and recommendations is too often reduced to a paper recommendation. In shopping for placement, probation officers are forced to lower their sights from what they know a child needs to what they can secure. Their sense of professional responsibility is steadily eroded. The judge, in turn, becomes a ceremonial officer who in many cases approves a disposition which he knows is only a dead end for the child.[63]

The Supreme Court has never considered what procedural requirements the Constitution imposes with regard to the dispositional phase of the juvenile court proceeding. Indeed, in In re Gault (discussed infra p. 798), the Court stated in a footnote:

> The problems of pre-adjudication treatment of juveniles, and of post-adjudication disposition, are unique to the juvenile process; hence, what we hold in this opinion

---

[61] Orman W. Ketcham, The Unfulfilled Promise of the Juvenile Court, 7 Crime & Delinq. 97, 104(1961).

[62] Sanford J. Fox, The Law of Juvenile Courts in a Nutshell 224 (3d ed. 1984).

[63] Justine Wise Polier, A View from the Bench 30 (1964).

with regard to the procedural requirements at the adjudicatory stage has no necessary applicability to other steps of the juvenile process. [387 U.S. 1, 31 n.48 (1967).]

Nevertheless, it seems clear that because the disposition stage is "critical" and because many juvenile court statutes provide for a right to counsel for disposition, e.g., N.Y. Fam. Ct. Act §741 (McKinney 1999 & Supp. 2008), the right to counsel is firmly established.

How long may a juvenile who is adjudicated a delinquent be supervised under probation or required to stay in an institution? As a general rule, juvenile court statutes allow commitment or probation until a juvenile reaches majority. Lowering the age of majority from 21 to 18 automatically reduced in some states the term of a possible commitment. Some states still provide by statute that probation or commitment can continue until the 21st birthday. See, e.g., Cal. Welf. & Inst. Code §607 (West 2004); Minn. Stat. Ann. §260B.193(5)(b) (2007). In many states, although commitment normally ends at 18, it is possible for an extension until the age of 21 to be authorized by the juvenile court on an appropriate request from the institution. See, e.g., Me. Rev. Stat. Ann. tit. 15, §3316 (2003 & Supp. 2007).

Because commitment may typically extend until the child reaches the age of majority, some children may possibly serve longer terms at institutions than an adult convicted for violating the same law. Several cases have challenged this on equal protection grounds, but no court has held that the possibility of a longer term violates equal protection. Courts have typically sustained the juvenile court's dispositional authority by refusing to equate delinquency adjudication with criminal proceedings. See, e.g., In re A.M.H., 447 N.W.2d 40 (Neb. 1989); In re J.K., 228 N.W.2d 713 (Wis. 1975).

However, departing from the traditional mode of analysis, the United States Supreme Court decided United States v. R.L.C., 503 U.S. 291 (1992). The case involved a juvenile offender who was originally sentenced for a longer period of time (three years) for involuntary manslaughter (i.e., an automobile accident on an Indian reservation) than a similarly situated adult would have received pursuant to the United States Sentencing Guidelines (21 months). The United States Supreme Court affirmed the court of appeals' opinion, thereby opting for the lesser sentence under the federal sentencing guidelines.

Justice O'Connor, joined by Justice Blackmun, dissented, arguing that

> [r]equiring a district court to calculate a Guideline maximum for each juvenile imports formal factfinding procedures foreign to the discretionary sentencing system Congress intended to retain. Juvenile proceedings, in contrast to adult proceedings, have traditionally aspired to be "intimate, informal [and] protective." McKeiver v. Pennsylvania, 403 U.S. 528, 545 (1971). One reason for the traditional informality of juvenile proceedings is that the focus of sentencing is on treatment, not punishment. The presumption is that juveniles are still teachable and not yet "hardened criminals." S. Rep. No. 1989, 75th Cong., 3d Sess., 1 (1938). . . . As a result, the sentencing considerations relevant to juveniles are far different from those relevant to adults. [503 U.S. at 314.]

(Note that the Court's decision in *R.L.C.* was based on statutory rather than constitutional grounds.)

Some statutes have established a maximum term of juvenile commitment; see, e.g., N.C. Gen. Stat. §7B-2513 (2004 & Supp. 2007) (definite term of commitment restricted to two years), or established a schedule of maximum detention terms based on the seriousness of the delinquent act. See, e.g., N.J. Stat. Ann. §2A:4A-44(d) (West 1987 & Supp. 2008).

Several states allow either juvenile courts to impose adult criminal sanctions, or criminal courts to impose juvenile sanctions through the use of "blended sentencing," also known as extended jurisdiction.[64]

The United States Supreme Court's recent pronouncements on adult sentencing policy have also influenced juvenile sentencing policy. For example, in Apprendi v. New Jersey, 530 U.S. 466 (2000), the Court invalidated a state statute that allowed judges to add sentence enhancements, holding that any fact that increases a penalty beyond a prescribed statutory maximum must be submitted to a jury and proven beyond a reasonable doubt. Several courts have considered whether the fact that waiver to adult court would result in the possibility of increasing a juvenile's sentence should require that the waiver issue be submitted to a jury and proven beyond a reasonable doubt. Most federal and state courts have ruled that *Apprendi* does not apply to such hearings on whether to prosecute a juvenile as an adult. See, e.g., United States v. Miguel, 338 F.3d 995 (9th Cir. 2003); In re Welfare of J.C.P., 716 N.W.3d 664 (Minn. Ct. App. 2006); Texas v. Lopez, 196 S.W.3d 872 (Tex. App. 2006); In re Hegney, 158 P.3d 1193 (Wash. Ct. App. 2007).

The ABA Juvenile Justice Standards recommended a rather radical restructuring of the dispositional authority of the juvenile courts. The Standards generally require a determinate sentence to be established at the time of the adjudication. The maximum confinement would be 36 months, and the maximum probation would be 36 months. These would apply only to "class one" offenses, which would for adults be punishable by sentences in excess of 20 years or the death penalty. For "class five" offenses, on the other hand, which for an adult could result in imprisonment of six months or less, a juvenile may be committed to a "nonsecure facility or residence for a period of two months" if the juvenile has a prior record, or "conditional freedom for a period of six months" if the juvenile does not have a prior record.[65]

3. Segregation of Juvenile Offenders from Adult Offenders

Are there special dangers if young people are committed to the same correctional institutions as adults? Do these dangers justify treating youthful offenders differently from adult offenders?

---

[64] Patrick Griffin, Trying and Sentencing Juveniles as Adults: An Analysis of State Transfer and Blended Sentencing Laws, National Center for Juvenile Justice 13 (2003) (pointing out that 15 states allow juvenile courts to impose such sanctions and 17 states allow criminal courts to do so). For criticism of blended sentencing, see Marcy R. Podkopacz & Barry C. Feld, The Back-Door to Prison: Waiver Reform, "Blended Sentencing," and the Law of Unintended Consequences, 91 J. Crim. L. & Criminology 997 (2001); Christian Sullivan, Juvenile Delinquency in the Twenty-First Century: Is Blended Sentencing the Middle-Road Solution for Violent Kids?, 21 N. Ill. U. L. Rev. 483 (2001).

[65] See American Bar Association, Juvenile Justice Standards, Standards Relating to Juvenile Delinquency and Sanctions, supra note [38], at 7-9.

As earlier noted, an important goal of the original movement to create juvenile courts was to ensure that juvenile offenders were kept separate and apart from adult offenders. Most juvenile court acts today do not permit a juvenile court at the time of the original disposition to commit a delinquent child to a correctional facility that also houses adult prisoners. Section 223(a)(14) of the Juvenile Justice and Delinquency Prevention Act (Pub. L. No. 93-415 (1974), codified at 42 U.S.C. §5600 et seq.) specifically provides that no juvenile will be detained or confined in any jail or lock-up for adults. Subsequent implementing regulations clarify this requirement by providing that brief and inadvertent contact in nonresidential areas is not a violation. Regulations also exempt those juveniles who are transferred from a juvenile institution to an adult one, such as those juveniles who are being tried for felonies or who have been convicted as felons.[66]

According to the Bureau of Justice Statistics' Annual Survey of Jails, an estimated 7,600 youths younger than 18 were being held in adult jails on June 30, 2000. These inmates account for 1.2 percent of the total jail population.[67] Most jail inmates younger than 18 (80%) were convicted or awaiting trial as adult criminal offenders — some who were transferred to criminal court and others who resided in states where all 17-year-olds (or all 16- and 17-year-olds) are considered adults for purposes of criminal prosecution.[68]

Commentators highlight an additional problem of intermingling juveniles and adult offenders that is caused by the Immigration and Naturalization Service's failure to segregate nondelinquent alien juveniles (those who enter the country unlawfully) in facilities with either serious juvenile offenders or adult offenders. See generally Devon A. Corneal, On the Way to Grandmother's House: Is U.S. Immigration Policy More Dangerous Than the Big Bad Wolf for Unaccompanied Juvenile Aliens?, 109 Penn St. L. Rev. 609 (2004); Lara Yoder Nafziger, Protection or Prosecution?: The Detention of Unaccompanied Immigrant Children in the United States, 28 Hamline J. Pub. L. & Pol'y 357 (2006).

To what hazards are juveniles exposed if committed to the same facilities as adults? One commentator explains:

> Foremost is the increased exposure of these children to emotional and physical abuse from other prisoners and, sadly, sometimes from the jail employees themselves. . . . The hard facts are most dramatically illustrated in a simple statistic compiled by the Community Research Center. The suicide rate for juveniles placed in adult jails and lock-ups is nearly eight times greater than for juveniles placed in separate, secure juvenile detention centers.
>
> But there is a more generalized, less dramatic harm. Adult jails are simply not designed, intended, equipped, or staffed to supervise juveniles, nor are they required to provide the counseling, educational, recreational, and other ancillary services to the same extent as are secure juvenile detention facilities. . . .[69]

---

[66] Melissa Sickmund, Juveniles in Corrections, Office of Juvenile Justice and Delinquency Prevention 18 (June 2004).

[67] Id.

[68] Id.

[69] Gordon Raley, Removing Children from Adult Jails: The Balance of Legislation, 3 Children's Legal Rts. J. 4, 6 (1982).

4.   Capital Punishment for Persons Who Commit Crimes as Juveniles

Roper v. Simmons
543 U.S. 551 (2005)

Justice KENNEDY delivered the opinion of the Court.

... At the age of 17, when he was still a junior in high school, Christopher Simmons, the respondent here, committed murder. . . . There is little doubt that Simmons was the instigator of the crime. Before its commission Simmons said he wanted to murder someone. In chilling, callous terms he talked about his plan, discussing it for the most part with two friends, Charles Benjamin and John Tessmer, then aged 15 and 16 respectively. Simmons proposed to commit burglary and murder by breaking and entering, tying up a victim, and throwing the victim off a bridge. Simmons assured his friends they could "get away with it" because they were minors.

The three met at about 2 A.M. on the night of the murder, but Tessmer left before the other two set out. (The State later charged Tessmer with conspiracy, but dropped the charge in exchange for his testimony against Simmons.) Simmons and Benjamin entered the home of the victim, Shirley Crook, after reaching through an open window and unlocking the back door. Simmons turned on a hallway light. Awakened, Mrs. Crook called out, "Who's there?" In response Simmons entered Mrs. Crook's bedroom, where he recognized her from a previous car accident involving them both. Simmons later admitted this confirmed his resolve to murder her. Using duct tape to cover her eyes and mouth and bind her hands, the two perpetrators put Mrs. Crook in her minivan and drove to a state park. They reinforced the bindings, covered her head with a towel, and walked her to a railroad trestle spanning the Meramec River. There they tied her hands and feet together with electrical wire, wrapped her whole face in duct tape and threw her from the bridge, drowning her in the waters below. . . .

... The State sought the death penalty. As aggravating factors, the State submitted that the murder [involved] depravity of mind and was outrageously and wantonly vile, horrible, and inhuman. [As a mitigating factor, Simmons's attorneys argued that he had no prior criminal record.]

During closing arguments, both the prosecutor and defense counsel addressed Simmons' age, which the trial judge had instructed the jurors they could consider as a mitigating factor. Defense counsel reminded the jurors that juveniles of Simmons' age cannot drink, serve on juries, or even see certain movies, because "the legislatures have wisely decided that individuals of a certain age aren't responsible enough." Defense counsel argued that Simmons' age should make "a huge difference to [the jurors] in deciding just exactly what sort of punishment to make." In rebuttal, the prosecutor gave the following response: "Age, he says. Think about age. Seventeen years old. Isn't that scary? Doesn't that scare you? Mitigating? Quite the contrary I submit. Quite the contrary." . . .

Accepting the jury's recommendation, the trial judge imposed the death penalty. [The defendant; unsuccessfully petitioned for postconviction relief, claiming ineffective counsel; i.e., during sentencing, counsel should have established Simmons's immaturity, impulsivity, susceptibility to being influenced, difficult home environment, and negative associations with other youths. After the United

States Supreme Court decided Atkins v. Virginia, 536 U.S. 304 (2002), Simmons brought a new petition for postconviction relief.] We granted certiorari, and now affirm.

The Eighth Amendment provides: "Excessive bail shall not be required, nor excessive fines imposed, nor cruel and unusual punishments inflicted." . . . By protecting even those convicted of heinous crimes, the Eighth Amendment re-affirms the duty of the government to respect the dignity of all persons.

The prohibition against "cruel and unusual punishments," like other expansive language in the Constitution, must be interpreted according to its text, by considering history, tradition, and precedent, and with due regard for its purpose and function in the constitutional design. To implement this framework we have established the propriety and affirmed the necessity of referring to "the evolving standards of decency that mark the progress of a maturing society" to determine which punishments are so disproportionate as to be cruel and unusual. Trop v. Dulles, 356 U.S. 86, 100-101 (1958) (plurality opinion).

In Thompson v. Oklahoma, 487 U.S. 815 (1988), a plurality of the Court deter-mined that our standards of decency do not permit the execution of any offender under the age of 16 at the time of the crime. The plurality opinion explained that no death penalty State that had given express consideration to a minimum age for the death penalty had set the age lower than 16. The plurality also observed that "[t]he conclusion that it would offend civilized standards of decency to execute a person who was less than 16 years old at the time of his or her offense is consistent with the views that have been expressed by respected professional organizations, by other nations that share our Anglo-American heritage, and by the leading members of the Western European community." Id., at 830. The opinion further noted that juries imposed the death penalty on offenders under 16 with exceeding rarity; the last execution of an offender for a crime committed under the age of 16 had been carried out in 1948, 40 years prior.

The next year, in Stanford v. Kentucky, 492 U.S. 361 (1989), the Court, over a dissenting opinion joined by four Justices, referred to contemporary standards of decency in this country and concluded the Eighth and Fourteenth Amendments did not proscribe the execution of juvenile offenders over 15 but under 18. The Court noted that 22 of the 37 death penalty States permitted the death penalty for 16-year-old offenders, and, among these 37 States, 25 permitted it for 17-year-old offenders. These numbers, in the Court's view, indicated there was no national consensus "sufficient to label a particular punishment cruel and unusual." Id., at 370-371. . . .

The same day the Court decided *Stanford,* it held that the Eighth Amendment did not mandate a categorical exemption from the death penalty for the mentally retarded [because there was not sufficient evidence of a national consensus to ban the practice]. Penry v. Lynaugh, 492 U.S. 302 (1989). . . . Three Terms ago the subject was reconsidered in *Atkins.* We held that standards of decency have evolved since *Penry* and [that] the execution of the mentally retarded is cruel and unusual punishment. . . .

The evidence of national consensus against the death penalty for juveniles is similar, and in some respects parallel, to the evidence *Atkins* held sufficient to demonstrate a national consensus against the death penalty for the mentally retarded. When *Atkins* was decided, 30 States prohibited the death penalty for the mentally retarded. . . . By a similar calculation in this case, 30 States prohibit the juvenile death penalty, comprising 12 that have rejected the death penalty altogether and 18 that maintain it but, by express provision or judicial interpretation, exclude juveniles from its reach. *Atkins* emphasized that even in the 20 States without formal prohibition, the practice of executing the mentally retarded was infrequent. . . . In the present case, too, even in the 20 States without a formal prohibition on executing juveniles, the practice is infrequent. Since *Stanford,* six States have executed prisoners for crimes committed as juveniles. In the past 10 years, only three have done so: Oklahoma, Texas, and Virginia. . . .

There is, to be sure, at least one difference between the evidence of consensus in *Atkins* and in this case. Impressive in *Atkins* was the rate of abolition of the death penalty for the mentally retarded. . . . By contrast, the rate of change in reducing the incidence of the juvenile death penalty, or in taking specific steps to abolish it, has been slower. [However, any difference] between this case and *Atkins* with respect to the pace of abolition is thus counterbalanced by the consistent direction of the change. . . .

As in *Atkins,* the objective indicia of consensus in this case — the rejection of the juvenile death penalty in the majority of States; the infrequency of its use even where it remains on the books; and the consistency in the trend toward abolition of the practice — provide sufficient evidence that today our society views juveniles, in the words *Atkins* used respecting the mentally retarded, as "categorically less culpable than the average criminal." 536 U.S., at 316.

. . . Because the death penalty is the most severe punishment, the Eighth Amendment applies to it with special force. Capital punishment must be limited to those offenders who commit "a narrow category of the most serious crimes" and whose extreme culpability makes them "the most deserving of execution." *Atkins,* supra, at 319. . . .

Three general differences between juveniles under 18 and adults demonstrate that juvenile offenders cannot with reliability be classified among the worst offenders. First, as any parent knows and as the scientific and sociological studies respondent and his amici cite tend to confirm, "[a] lack of maturity and an underdeveloped sense of responsibility are found in youth more often than in adults and are more understandable among the young. These qualities often result in impetuous and ill-considered actions and decisions." [Johnson v. Texas, 509 U.S. 350, 367 (1993).] It has been noted that "adolescents are overrepresented statistically in virtually every category of reckless behavior." Arnett, Reckless Behavior in Adolescence: A Developmental Perspective, 12 Developmental Review 339 (1992). In recognition of the comparative immaturity and irresponsibility of juveniles, almost every State prohibits those under 18 years of age from voting, serving on juries, or marrying without parental consent.

The second area of difference is that juveniles are more vulnerable or susceptible to negative influences and outside pressures, including peer pressure. This is explained in part by the prevailing circumstance that juveniles have less control, or less experience with control, over their own environment. See Steinberg & Scott, Less Guilty by Reason of Adolescence: Developmental Immaturity, Diminished Responsibility, and the Juvenile Death Penalty, 58 Am. Psychologist 1009, 1014

(2003) (hereinafter Steinberg & Scott) ("[A]s legal minors, [juveniles] lack the freedom that adults have to extricate themselves from a criminogenic setting").

The third broad difference is that the character of a juvenile is not as well formed as that of an adult. The personality traits of juveniles are more transitory, less fixed. See generally E. Erikson, Identity: Youth and Crisis (1968).

These differences render suspect any conclusion that a juvenile falls among the worst offenders. The susceptibility of juveniles to immature and irresponsible behavior means "their irresponsible conduct is not as morally reprehensible as that of an adult." *Thompson,* supra, at 835. Their own vulnerability and comparative lack of control over their immediate surroundings mean juveniles have a greater claim than adults to be forgiven for failing to escape negative influences in their whole environment. The reality that juveniles still struggle to define their identity means it is less supportable to conclude that even a heinous crime committed by a juvenile is evidence of irretrievably depraved character. From a moral standpoint it would be misguided to equate the failings of a minor with those of an adult, for a greater possibility exists that a minor's character deficiencies will be reformed. Indeed, "[t]he relevance of youth as a mitigating factor derives from the fact that the signature qualities of youth are transient; as individuals mature, the impetuousness and recklessness that may dominate in younger years can subside." *Johnson,* supra, at 368; see also Steinberg & Scott 1014 ("For most teens, [risky or antisocial] behaviors are fleeting; they cease with maturity as individual identity becomes settled. Only a relatively small proportion of adolescents who experiment in risky or illegal activities develop entrenched patterns of problem behavior that persist into adulthood"). In *Thompson,* a plurality of the Court recognized the import of these characteristics with respect to juveniles under 16, and relied on them to hold that the Eighth Amendment prohibited the imposition of the death penalty on juveniles below that age. We conclude the same reasoning applies to all juvenile offenders under 18.

Once the diminished culpability of juveniles is recognized, it is evident that the penological justifications for the death penalty apply to them with lesser force than to adults. We have held there are two distinct social purposes served by the death penalty: " 'retribution and deterrence of capital crimes by prospective offenders.' " *Atkins,* 536 U.S., at 319. As for retribution, we remarked in *Atkins* that "[i]f the culpability of the average murderer is insufficient to justify the most extreme sanction available to the State, the lesser culpability of the mentally retarded offender surely does not merit that form of retribution." 536 U.S., at 319. The same conclusions follow from the lesser culpability of the juvenile offender. Whether viewed as an attempt to express the community's moral outrage or as an attempt to right the balance for the wrong to the victim, the case for retribution is not as strong with a minor as with an adult. Retribution is not proportional if the law's most severe penalty is imposed on one whose culpability or blameworthiness is diminished, to a substantial degree, by reason of youth and immaturity.

As for deterrence, it is unclear whether the death penalty has a significant or even measurable deterrent effect on juveniles. [Here], the absence of evidence of deterrent effect is of special concern because the same characteristics that render juveniles less culpable than adults suggest as well that juveniles will be less susceptible to deterrence. In particular, as the plurality observed in *Thompson,* "[t]he likelihood that the teenage offender has made the kind of cost-benefit analysis that attaches any weight to the possibility of execution is so remote as to be virtually nonexistent." 487 U.S., at 837. To the extent the juvenile death penalty might have residual deterrent effect, it is worth noting that the punishment of life imprisonment without the possibility of parole is itself a severe sanction, in particular for a young person.

In concluding that neither retribution nor deterrence provides adequate justification for imposing the death penalty on juvenile offenders, we cannot deny or overlook the brutal crimes too many juvenile offenders have committed. Certainly it can be argued, although we by no means concede the point, that a rare case might arise in which a juvenile offender has sufficient psychological maturity, and at the same time demonstrates sufficient depravity, to merit a sentence of death. Indeed, this possibility is the linchpin of one contention pressed by petitioner and his amici. They assert that even assuming the truth of the observations we have made about juveniles' diminished culpability in general, jurors nonetheless should be allowed to consider mitigating arguments related to youth on a case-by-case basis, and in some cases to impose the death penalty if justified. A central feature of death penalty sentencing is a particular assessment of the circumstances of the crime and the characteristics of the offender. The system is designed to consider both aggravating and mitigating circumstances, including youth, in every case. Given this Court's own insistence on individualized consideration, petitioner maintains that it is both arbitrary and unnecessary to adopt a categorical rule barring imposition of the death penalty on any offender under 18 years of age.

We disagree. The differences between juvenile and adult offenders are too marked and well understood to risk allowing a youthful person to receive the death penalty despite insufficient culpability. An unacceptable likelihood exists that the brutality or cold-blooded nature of any particular crime would overpower mitigating arguments based on youth as a matter of course, even where the juvenile offender's objective immaturity, vulnerability, and lack of true depravity should require a sentence less severe than death. In some cases a defendant's youth may even be counted against him. In this very case, as we noted above, the prosecutor argued Simmons' youth was aggravating rather than mitigating. While this sort of overreaching could be corrected by a particular rule to ensure that the mitigating force of youth is not overlooked, that would not address our larger concerns.

It is difficult even for expert psychologists to differentiate between the juvenile offender whose crime reflects unfortunate yet transient immaturity, and the rare juvenile offender whose crime reflects irreparable corruption. As we understand it, this difficulty underlies the rule forbidding psychiatrists from diagnosing any patient under 18 as having antisocial personality disorder, a disorder also referred to as psychopathy or sociopathy, and which is characterized by callousness, cynicism, and contempt for the feelings, rights, and suffering of others. American Psychiatric Association, Diagnostic and Statistical Manual of Mental Disorders 701-706 (4th ed. text rev. 2000); see also Steinberg & Scott 1015. If trained psychiatrists with the advantage of clinical testing and observation refrain, despite diagnostic expertise, from assessing any juvenile under 18 as having antisocial personality disorder, we conclude that States should refrain from asking jurors to issue a far graver condemnation — that a juvenile offender merits the death penalty. When a juvenile offender commits a heinous crime, the State can exact forfeiture of some of the most basic liberties, but the State cannot extinguish his life and his potential to attain a mature understanding of his own humanity.

Drawing the line at 18 years of age is subject, of course, to the objections always raised against categorical rules. The qualities that distinguish juveniles from adults do not disappear when an individual turns 18. By the same token, some under 18 have already attained a level of maturity some adults will never reach. For the reasons we have discussed, however, a line must be drawn. The plurality opinion in *Thompson* drew the line at 16. In the intervening years the *Thompson* plurality's conclusion that offenders under 16 may not be executed has not been challenged. The logic of *Thompson* extends to those who are under 18. The age of 18 is the point where society draws the line for many purposes between childhood and adulthood. It is, we conclude, the age at which the line for death eligibility ought to rest. . . .

Justice O'CONNOR, dissenting.

[T]he rule decreed by the Court rests, ultimately, on its independent moral judgment that death is a disproportionately severe punishment for any 17-year-old offender. I do not subscribe to this judgment. . . .

Seventeen-year-old murderers must be categorically exempted from capital punishment, the Court says, because they "cannot with reliability be classified among the worst offenders." That conclusion is premised on three perceived differences between "adults," who have already reached their 18th birthdays, and "juveniles," who have not. First, juveniles lack maturity and responsibility and are more reckless than adults. Second, juveniles are more vulnerable to outside influences because they have less control over their surroundings. And third, a juvenile's character is not as fully formed as that of an adult. Based on these characteristics, the Court determines that 17-year-old capital murderers are not as blameworthy as adults guilty of similar crimes; that 17-year-olds are less likely than adults to be deterred by the prospect of a death sentence; and that it is difficult to conclude that a 17-year-old who commits even the most heinous of crimes is "irretrievably depraved." . . .

It is beyond cavil that juveniles as a class are generally less mature, less responsible, and less fully formed than adults, and that these differences bear on juveniles' comparative moral culpability. But even accepting this premise, the Court's proportionality argument fails to support its categorical rule.

First, the Court adduces no evidence whatsoever in support of its sweeping conclusion, that it is only in "rare" cases, if ever, that 17-year-old murderers are sufficiently mature and act with sufficient depravity to warrant the death penalty. The fact that juveniles are generally less culpable for their misconduct than adults does not necessarily mean that a 17-year-old murderer cannot be sufficiently culpable to merit the death penalty. At most, the Court's argument suggests that the average 17-year-old murderer is not as culpable as the average adult murderer. But an especially depraved juvenile offender may nevertheless be just as culpable as many adult offenders considered bad enough to deserve the death penalty. Similarly, the fact that the availability of the death penalty may be less likely to deter a juvenile from committing a capital crime does not imply that this threat cannot effectively deter some 17-year-olds from such an act. Surely there is an age below which no offender, no matter what his crime, can be deemed to have the cognitive or emotional maturity necessary to warrant the death penalty. But at least at the margins between adolescence and adulthood — and especially for 17-year-olds such as respondent — the relevant differences between "adults" and "juveniles" appear to be a matter of degree, rather than of kind. It follows that a legislature may reasonably conclude that at least some 17-year-olds can act with sufficient moral culpability, and can be sufficiently deterred by the threat of execution, that capital punishment may be warranted in an appropriate case. Indeed, this appears to be just such a case. . . .

The Court's proportionality argument suffers from a second and closely related defect: It fails to establish that the differences in maturity between 17-year-olds and young "adults" are both universal enough and significant enough to justify a bright-line prophylactic rule against capital punishment of the former. The Court's analysis is premised on differences *in the aggregate* between juveniles and adults, which frequently do not hold true when comparing individuals. Although it may be that many 17-year-old murderers lack sufficient maturity to deserve the death penalty, some juvenile murderers may be quite mature. Chronological age is not an unfailing measure of psychological development, and common experience suggests that many 17-year-olds are more mature than the average young "adult." In short, the class of offenders exempted from capital punishment by today's decision is too broad and too diverse to warrant a categorical prohibition. Indeed, the age-based line drawn by the Court is indefensibly arbitrary — it quite likely will protect a number of offenders who are mature enough to deserve the death penalty and may well leave vulnerable many who are not.

For purposes of proportionality analysis, 17-year-olds as a class are qualitatively and materially different from the mentally retarded. "Mentally retarded" offenders, as we understood that category in *Atkins,* are defined by precisely the characteristics which render death an excessive punishment. A mentally retarded person is, "by definition," one whose cognitive and behavioral capacities have been proven to fall below a certain minimum. Accordingly, for purposes of our decision in *Atkins,* the mentally retarded are not merely less blameworthy for their misconduct or less likely to be deterred by the death penalty than others. Rather, a mentally retarded offender is one whose demonstrated impairments make it so highly unlikely that he is culpable enough to deserve the death penalty or that he could have been deterred by the threat of death, that execution is not a defensible punishment. There is no such inherent or accurate fit between an offender's chronological age and the personal limitations which the Court believes make capital punishment excessive for 17-year-old murderers. Moreover, it defies common sense to suggest that 17-year-olds as a class are somehow equivalent to mentally retarded persons with regard to culpability or susceptibility to deterrence. Seventeen-year-olds may, on average, be less mature than adults, but that lesser maturity simply cannot be equated with the major, lifelong impairments suffered by the mentally retarded.

The proportionality issues raised by the Court clearly implicate Eighth Amendment concerns. But these concerns may properly be addressed not by means of an arbitrary, categorical age-based rule, but rather through individualized sentencing. . . .

[The separate dissenting opinion of Justice Scalia, with whom Justices Rehnquist and Thomas join, is omitted.]

NOTES AND QUESTIONS

(1) Background.   The issue of the appropriateness of capital punishment for minors is raised initially upon waiver — that is, the decision whether to transfer a juvenile from the juvenile justice system to the adult system. If tried as an adult, the juvenile is subject to the same range of punishments, including capital punishment, imposed on adults. (Waiver is discussed, supra p. 780.) Before *Roper* was decided, a total of 78 persons were on death row for crimes committed as juveniles. All of these offenders were either 16 or 17 at the time of their offenses. Victor L. Streib, The Juvenile Death Penalty Today: Death Sentences and Executions for Juvenile Crimes, Jan. 1, 1973-Feb. 28, 2005, at 11, available at *http://www.law.onu.edu/faculty-staff/ faculty-profiles/victorstreib* (last visited May 19, 2008).

As the *Roper* case explains, the Supreme Court previously explored the constitutionality of capital punishment for juveniles in Thompson v. Oklahoma, 487 U.S. 815 (1988) (declaring the death penalty unconstitutional for defendants who were 15 years old at the time of the offense), and Stanford v. Kentucky, 492 U.S. 361 (1989) (upholding the imposition of the death sentence for offenders who were at least 16 years old at the time of the offense). Why did the Supreme Court decide these two cases differently?

(2) Sniper Case.   A highly publicized series of murders focused renewed interest in the juvenile death penalty. In October 2002, Lee Boyd Malvo was arrested in connection with the Washington, D.C., area "sniper slayings," a series of 13 random shootings that terrorized residents in Virginia, Maryland, and Washington, D.C. Malvo was the triggerman in the murder spree that was masterminded by 41-year-old John Allan Muhammad. Malvo's attorneys argued that the impressionable teen was brainwashed by Muhammad, and that Malvo's susceptibility to Muham mad's influence resulted from Malvo's troubled background (an absent father and abusive mother). Malvo was tried initially in Virginia (a state that permits the imposition of the death penalty on juveniles) and received a sentence of life imprisonment. Muhammad received the death penalty. See generally Joseph W. Goodman, Overturning Stanford v. Kentucky: Lee Boyd Malvo and the Execution of Juvenile Offenders, 2003 Mich. St. DCL L. Rev. 389.

(3) Eighth Amendment.   The debate over the juvenile death penalty centers around the application of the Eighth Amendment's prohibition on cruel and unusual punishment. Because the Supreme Court has interpreted the Eighth Amendment to require an evaluation of the punishment in terms of "the evolving standards of decency that mark the progress of a maturing society," an analysis is required of these standards and their evolution. According to *Roper*, what factors are relevant in that analysis?

(4) Purposes of Punishment.   Does the death penalty serve valid penological purposes when applied to juveniles, according to *Roper*? Review the material supra pp. 755-762 on the purposes of punishment and juvenile justice. In terms of retribution, is it appropriate to punish juveniles with the same degree of severity as adults? In terms of deterrence, does capital sentencing send a message to other potential juvenile offenders? Are there inherent characteristics of youth that might prevent this message from being received? Do juveniles modify their actions rationally so as to avoid crime and punishment? Do age-based lines make sense in light of these penological purposes?

(5) Arguments Pro and Con. Professor Victor Streib, who has written extensively on the juvenile death penalty, summarizes the policy debate. Streib, supra, at 13-14. Assess the following arguments he identifies in favor of the imposition of the death penalty on juveniles: (a) the incidence of violent juvenile crime, particularly homicide, is higher in America than in other countries; (b) juvenile homicide rates increased substantially until the mid- to late 1990s and, although they are on the decline, public fear of juvenile homicide remains very high; (c) juvenile murders seem to be particularly brutal and senseless; (d) political leaders advocate harsher punishments for violent juvenile crime; and (e) correcting the societal conditions that contribute to violent juvenile crime is an impossible task. Opposing arguments include: (a) almost all serious juvenile offenders have had troubled childhoods; (b) research indicates that brain maturation does not occur until the late teens or early twenties, with impulse control developing last; (c) the threat of capital punishment does not deter teenagers, who tend to see themselves as immortal; (d) the retribution rationale is less weighty if the offender is a child; and (e) harsh punishment for violent juvenile offenders is an ineffective solution to the problem of juvenile crime because society should address the causes (environments, neighborhoods, schools, and societal structures).

(6) Who Should Decide? The debate over the juvenile death penalty raises the issue of the state and legislature's traditional role in determining appropriate punishments. In an omitted dissent, Justice Scalia notes: "Today's opinion provides a perfect example of why judges are ill equipped to make the type of legislative judgments the Court insists on making here." 543 U.S. at 616. Given the test of the evolving standards of decency, should the determination of the permissibility of the juvenile death penalty be made more appropriately by state legislatures rather than the federal judiciary?

(7) Are Juveniles Analogous to the Mentally Retarded? In *Roper,* the United States Supreme Court analogizes the juvenile offender to the mentally retarded defendant. Do the reasons supporting the unconstitutionality of the death penalty for mentally retarded defendants apply with equal force to the execution of juvenile offenders? How does Justice O'Connor in her dissent distinguish juvenile offenders from the mentally retarded? Do you find her arguments persuasive? See also Robin M. A. Weeks, Comparing Children to the Mentally Retarded: How the Decision in Atkins v. Virginia Will Affect the Execution of Juvenile Offenders, 17 BYU J. Pub. L. 451 (2003).

(8) Equal Protection. Consider that a substantial number of juveniles who are executed are African Americans and that a similar high percentage of offenders on death row who committed offenses as juveniles are African American. See General Accounting Office, Death Penalty Sentencing: Research Indicates Pattern of Racial Disparities 5 (Feb. 1990) (discussing data). Is the imposition of the death penalty on these offenders a violation of equal protection, a form of racial discrimination?

(9) Supreme Court's Treatment of Maturity in Different Contexts. In his omitted dissent, Justice Scalia highlights the Court's inconsistent treatment of the issue of minors' maturity. He points out that several psychological studies reveal that many minors are mature enough to make the abortion decision without parental involvement. 543 U.S. at 617. How does consideration of the issue of maturity differ in the contexts of abortion and capital punishment? That is, how can a minor

be sufficiently mature to make the abortion decision but not mature enough to be subject to the death penalty? See generally Nicole A. Saharsky, Consistency as a Constitutional Value: A Comparative Look at Age in Abortion and Death Penalty Jurisprudence, 85 Minn. L. Rev. 1119 (2001).

(10) Extension of **Roper** *to Juvenile Sentencing Practices.*   Should the reasoning of *Roper* be extended to other juvenile sentences, such as life without parole and lengthy sentences without the possibility of parole?[70] Following *Roper*, lawsuits were filed in several states challenging life without parole sentences for offenders who committed crimes as young teenagers.[71] The Supreme Court has declined to review an Eighth Amendment challenge to the sentence of Christopher Pittman, who was 12 years old when he killed his grandparents and was sentenced to 30 years without possibility of parole. State v. Pittman, 647 S.E.2d 144 (S.C. 2007), *cert. denied*, 128 S. Ct. 1872 (2008). See generally Barry C. Feld, A Slower Form of Death: Implications of Roper v. Simmons for Juveniles Sentenced to Life Without Parole, 22 Notre Dame J.L. Ethics & Pub. Pol'y 9 (2008).

(11) International Consensus.   In an omitted portion of *Roper,* the majority asserts that various international human rights documents (U.N. Convention on the Rights of the Child, the International Covenant on Civil and Political Rights) and the law of other countries support the abolition of the juvenile death penalty. In his omitted dissent, Justice Scalia contends that consideration of international human rights law and foreign law should play no role in the determination of the constitutionality of the death penalty. 543 U.S. at 622-628. Which view do you find more persuasive and why? See generally Youngjae Lee, International Consensus as Persuasive Authority in the Eighth Amendment, 156 U. Pa. L. Rev. 63 (2007).

D. PROCEDURAL DIFFERENCES BETWEEN THE DELINQUENCY PROCESS AND THE ADULT CRIMINAL PROCESS

In re Gault
387 U.S. 1 (1967)

Mr. Justice FORTAS delivered the opinion of the Court.

This is an appeal . . . from a judgment of the Supreme Court of Arizona affirming the dismissal of a petition for a writ of habeas corpus. The petition sought the release of Gerald Francis Gault, appellants' 15-year-old son, who had been

---

[70] As of 2005, 42 states allowed juveniles to be sentenced to life without parole, and at least 2,225 individuals were serving sentences of life without parole for crimes committed while under the age of eighteen. Amnesty International and Human Rights Watch, The Rest of Their Lives: Life Without Parole for Child Offenders in the United States 1, 18 (2005), available at *http://www. amnestyusa.org/countries/usa/clwop/report.pdf* (last visited May 19, 2008).

[71] Adam Liptak, Lifers as Teenagers, Now Seeking Second Chance, N.Y. Times (Oct. 17, 2007).

committed as a juvenile delinquent to the State Industrial School by the Juvenile Court of Gila County, Arizona. The Supreme Court of Arizona affirmed dismissal of the writ. . . . We do not agree, and we reverse. . . .

I

On Monday, June 8, 1964, at about 10 A.M., Gerald Francis Gault and a friend, Ronald Lewis, were taken into custody by the Sheriff of Gila County. Gerald was then still subject to a six months' probation order which had been entered on February 25, 1964, as a result of his having been in the company of another boy who had stolen a wallet from a lady's purse. The police action on June 8 was taken as the result of a verbal complaint by a neighbor of the boys, Mrs. Cook, about a telephone call made to her in which the caller or callers made lewd or indecent remarks . . . of the irritatingly offensive, adolescent, sex variety.

At the time Gerald was picked up, his mother and father were both at work. No notice that Gerald was being taken into custody was left at the home. No other steps were taken to advise them that their son had, in effect, been arrested. Gerald was taken to the Children's Detention Home. When his mother arrived home at about 6 o'clock, Gerald was not there. Gerald's older brother was sent to look for him at the trailer home of the Lewis family. He apparently learned then that Gerald was in custody. He so informed his mother. The two of them went to the Detention Home. The deputy probation officer, Flagg, who was also superintendent of the Detention Home, told Mrs. Gault "why Jerry was there" and said that a hearing would be held in Juvenile Court at 3 o'clock the following day, June 9.

Officer Flagg filed a petition with the court on the hearing day, June 9, 1964. It was not served on the Gaults. Indeed, none of them saw this petition until the habeas corpus hearing on August 17, 1964. The petition . . . made no reference to any factual basis for the judicial action which it initiated. It recited only that "said minor is under the age of eighteen years, . . . [and that] said minor is a delinquent minor." It prayed for a hearing and an order regarding "the care and custody of said minor." . . .

On June 9, Gerald, his mother, his older brother, and Probation Officers Flagg and Henderson appeared before the juvenile judge in chambers. . . . Mrs. Cook, the complainant, was not there. No one was sworn at this hearing. No transcript or recording was made. . . . Our information about the proceedings of the subsequent hearing on June 15, derives entirely from the testimony of the Juvenile Court Judge, Mr. and Mrs. Gault and Officer Flagg at the habeas corpus proceeding conducted two months later. From this, it appears that at the June 9 hearing Gerald was questioned by the judge about the telephone call. There was conflict as to what he said. His mother recalled that Gerald said he only dialed Mrs. Cook's number and handed the telephone to his friend, Ronald. Officer Flagg recalled that Gerald had admitted making the lewd remarks. Judge McGhee testified that Gerald "admitted making one of these [lewd] statements." . . . Gerald was taken back to the Detention Home. . . . On June 11 or 12, after having been detained since June 8, Gerald was released. . . . There is no explanation in the record as to why he was kept in the Detention Home or why he was released. At 5 P.M. on the day of

Gerald's release, Mrs. Gault received a note signed by Officer Flagg. It was on plain paper, not letterhead. Its entire text was as follows:

> Mrs. Gault:
> Judge McGhee has set Monday, June 15, 1964 at 11:00 A.M. as the date and time for further Hearings on Gerald's delinquency.
>
> /s/ Flagg

At the appointed time on Monday, June 15, Gerald, his father and mother, Ronald Lewis and his father, and Officers Flagg and Henderson were present before Judge McGhee. Witnesses at the habeas corpus proceeding differed in their recollections of Gerald's testimony at the June 15 hearing Mr. and Mrs. Gault recalled that Gerald again testified that he had only dialed the number and that the other boy had made the remarks. Officer Flagg agreed that at this hearing Gerald did not admit making the lewd remarks. But Judge McGhee recalled that "there was some admission again of some of the lewd statements. He — he didn't admit any of the more serious lewd statements." Again, the complainant, Mrs. Cook, was not present. Mrs. Gault asked that Mrs. Cook be present. . . . The juvenile judge said "she didn't have to be present at that hearing." The judge did not speak to Mrs. Cook or communicate with her at any time. Probation Officer Flagg had talked to her once — over the telephone on June 9.

At this June 15 hearing a "referral report" made by the probation officers was filed with the court, although not disclosed to Gerald or his parents. This listed the charge as "Lewd Phone Calls." At the conclusion of the hearing, the judge committed Gerald as a juvenile delinquent to the State Industrial School "for the period of his minority [that is, until 21], unless sooner discharged by due process of law." . . .

No appeal is permitted by Arizona law in juvenile cases. [A] petition for a writ of habeas corpus was filed with the Supreme Court of Arizona and referred by it to the Superior Court for hearing.

At the habeas corpus hearing on August 17, Judge McGhee was vigorously cross-examined as to the basis for his actions. He testified that he had taken into account the fact that Gerald was on probation. He was asked "under what section of . . . the code you found the boy delinquent?"

His answer is set forth in the margin.[5] In substance, he concluded that Gerald came within ARS §8-201, subsec. 6(a), which specifies that a "delinquent child" includes one "who has violated alaw of the state or an ordinance. . . ." The law which Gerald was found to have violated is ARS §13-377 [which] provides that a person who "in the presence or hearing of any woman or child . . . uses vulgar, abusive or obscene language, is guilty of a misdeameanor. . . ." The penalty

---

[5] Q. All right. Now, judge, would you tell me under what section of the law or tell me under what section of — of the code you found the boy delinquent?

A. Well, there is a — I think it amounts to disturbing the peace. I can't give you the section, but I can tell you the law, that when one person uses lewd language in the presence of another person, that it can amount to — and I consider that when a person makes it over the phone, that it is considered in the presence, I might be wrong, that is one section. The other section upon which I consider the boy delinquent is Section 8-201, Subsection (d), habitually involved in immoral matters.

specified in the Criminal Code, which would apply to an adult, is $5 to $50, or imprisonment for not more than two months. The judge also testified that he acted under ARS §8-201, subsec. 6(d) which includes in the definition of a "delinquent child" one who, as the judge phrased it, is "habitually involved in immoral matters."

Asked about the basis for his conclusion that Gerald was "habitually involved in immoral matters," the judge testified, somewhat vaguely, that two years earlier, on July 2, 1962, a "referral" was made concerning Gerald, "where the boy had stolen a baseball glove from another boy and lied to the Police Department about it." The judge said there was "no hearing, . . . because of lack of material foundation." But it seems to have remained in his mind as a relevant factor. The judge also testified that Gerald had admitted making other nuisance phone calls in the past which, as the judge recalled the boy's testimony, were "silly calls, or funny calls, or something like that."

[The Superior Court dismissed the writ of habeas corpus. The Arizona Supreme Court affirmed.]

II

The Supreme Court of Arizona held that due process of law is requisite to the constitutional validity of proceedings in which . . . a juvenile . . . has engaged in conduct prohibited by law, or has otherwise misbehaved with the consequence that he is committed to an institution in which his freedom is curtailed. This conclusion is in accord with the decisions of a number of courts under both federal and state constitutions.

This Court has not heretofore decided the precise question. In Kent v. United States, 383 U.S. 541 (1966), we considered the requirements for a valid waiver of the "exclusive" jurisdiction of the Juvenile Court of the District of Columbia so that a juvenile could be tried in the adult criminal court of the District. Although our decision turned upon the language of the statute, we emphasized the necessity that "the basic requirements of due process and fairness" be satisfied in such proceedings. [383 U.S. at 553.] [I]n Haley v. State of Ohio, 332 U.S. 596 (1948), [t]he Court held that the Fourteenth Amendment applied to prohibit the use of the coerced confession [of a 15-year-old boy]. [T]hese cases . . . unmistakably indicate that, whatever may be their precise impact, neither the Fourteenth Amendment nor the Bill of Rights is for adults alone.

We do not in this opinion . . . consider the entire process relating to juvenile "delinquents." For example, we are not here concerned with the procedures or constitutional rights applicable to the pre-judicial stages of the juvenile process, nor do we direct our attention to the post-adjudicative or dispositional process. We consider only . . . proceedings by which a determination is made as to whether a juvenile is a "delinquent" as a result of alleged misconduct on his part, with the consequence that he may be committed to a state institution. As to these proceedings, . . . the Due Process Clause has a role to play. The problem is to ascertain the precise impact of the due process requirement upon such proceedings.

From the inception of the juvenile court system, wide differences have been tolerated—indeed insisted upon—between the procedural rights accorded to adults and those of juveniles. In practically all jurisdictions, there are rights granted to adults which are withheld from juveniles. [F]or example, it has been held that the juvenile is not entitled to bail, to indictment by grand jury, to a public trial or to trial by jury. It is frequent practice that rules governing the arrest and interrogation of adults by the police are not observed in the case of juveniles.

The history and theory underlying this development are well known. . . . The Juvenile Court movement began in this country at the end of the last century. From the juvenile court statute adopted in Illinois in 1899, the system has spread to every State in the Union, the District of Columbia, and Puerto Rico. The constitutionality of juvenile court laws has been sustained in over 40 jurisdictions against a variety of attacks.

The early reformers were appalled by adult procedures and penalties, and by the fact that children could be given long prison sentences and mixed in jails with hardened criminals. . . . They believed that society's role was not to ascertain whether the child was "guilty" or "innocent," but "What is he, how has he become what he is, and what had best be done in his interest and in the interest of the state to save him from a downward career." The child — essentially good, as they saw it — was to be made "to feel that he is the object of [the state's] care and solicitude," not that he was under arrest or on trial. The rules of criminal procedure were therefore altogether inapplicable. The apparent rigidities, technicalities, and harshness which they observed in both substantive and procedural criminal law were therefore to be discarded. The idea of crime and punishment was to be abandoned. The child was to be "treated" and "rehabilitated" and the procedures, from apprehension through institutionalization, were to be "clinical" rather than punitive.

These results were to be achieved . . . by insisting that the proceedings were not adversary, but that the state was proceeding as parens patriae. The Latin phrase proved to be a great help to those who sought to rationalize the exclusion of juveniles from the constitutional scheme; but its meaning is murky. . . . The phrase was taken from chancery practice, where, however, it was used to describe the power of the state to act in loco parentis for the purpose of protecting the property interests and the person of the child. . . .

The right of the state, as parens patriae, to deny to the child procedural rights available to his elders was elaborated by the assertion that a child, unlike an adult, has a right "not to liberty but to custody." He can be made to attorn to his parents, to go to school, etc. If his parents default in effectively performing their custodial functions — that is, if the child is "delinquent" — the state may intervene. In doing so, it does not deprive the child of any rights, because he has none. It merely provides the "custody" to which the child is entitled. On this basis, proceedings involving juveniles were described as "civil" not "criminal" and therefore not subject to the requirements which restrict the state when it seeks to deprive a person of his liberty.

Accordingly, the highest motives and most enlightened impulses led to a peculiar system for juveniles, unknown to our law in any comparable context. The constitutional and theoretical basis for this peculiar system is — to say the least — debatable. And in practice, as we remarked in the *Kent* case, supra, the results have not been entirely satisfactory. Juvenile Court history has again demonstrated that unbridled discretion, however benevolently motivated, is frequently a poor substitute for principle and procedure. In 1937, Dean Pound wrote: "The powers of the Star Chamber were a trifle in comparison with those of our juvenile courts. . . ." The absence of substantive standards has not necessarily meant that children receive careful, compassionate, individualized treatment. The absence of procedural rules based upon constitutional principle has not always produced fair, efficient, and effective procedures. . . .

Failure to observe the fundamental requirements of due process has resulted in instances, which might have been avoided, of unfairness to individuals and inadequate or inaccurate findings of fact and unfortunate prescriptions of remedy. Due process of law is the primary and indispensable foundation of individual freedom. It is the basic and essential term in the social compact which defines the rights of the individual and delimits the powers which the state may exercise. . . . But, in addition, the procedural rules which have been fashioned from the generality of due process . . . enhance the possibility that truth will emerge from the confrontation of opposing versions and conflicting data. . . .

It is claimed that juveniles obtain benefits from the special procedures applicable to them which more than offset the disadvantages of denial of the substance of normal due process. [I]t is important, we think, that the claimed benefits of the juvenile process should be candidly appraised. . . .

[T]he high crime rates among juveniles . . . could not lead us to conclude that the absence of constitutional protections reduces crime, or that the juvenile system, functioning free of constitutional inhibitions as it has largely done, is effective to reduce crime or rehabilitate offenders. We do not mean by this to denigrate the juvenile court process or to suggest that there are not aspects of the juvenile system relating to offenders which are valuable. But the features of the juvenile system which its proponents have asserted are of unique benefit will not be impaired by constitutional domestication. For example, the commendable principles relating to the processing and treatment of juveniles separately from adults are in no way involved or affected by the procedural issues under discussion. Further, we are told that one of the procedural benefits of the special juvenile court procedures is that they avoid classifying the juvenile as a "criminal." The juvenile offender is now classed as a "delinquent." There is, of course, no reason why this should not continue. . . .

Beyond this, it is frequently said that juveniles are protected by the process from disclosure of their deviational behavior. [T]he summary procedures of Juvenile Courts are sometimes defended by a statement that it is the law's policy "to hide youthful errors from the full gaze of the public and bury them in the graveyard of the forgotten past." This claim of secrecy, however, is more rhetoric than reality. Disclosure of court records is discretionary with the judge in most jurisdictions. [M]any courts routinely furnish information to the FBI and the military, and on request to government agencies and even to private employers. . . .

Further, it is urged that the juvenile benefits from informal proceedings in the court. The early conception of the Juvenile Court proceeding was one in which a fatherly judge touched the heart and conscience of the erring youth by talking over his problems, by paternal advice and admonition, and in which, in extreme situations, benevolent and wise institutions of the State provided guidance and help "to

save him from a downward career." [R]ecent studies have, with surprising una-
nimity, entered sharp dissent as to the validity of this gentle conception. They
suggest that the appearance as well as the actuality of fairness, impartiality and
orderliness — in short, the essentials of due process — may be a more impressive
and more therapeutic attitude so far as the juvenile is concerned. For example, in a
recent study, the sociologists Wheeler and Cottrell observe that when the
procedural laxness of the "parens patriae" attitude is followed by stern disciplining, the contrast may have an adverse effect upon the child, who feels that he has
been deceived or enticed. They conclude as follows: "Unless appropriate due
process of law is followed, even the juvenile who has violated the law may not
feel that he is being fairly treated and may therefore resist the rehabilitative efforts
of court personnel."[37] . . . While due process requirements will, in some instances,
introduce a degree of order and regularity to Juvenile Court proceedings to determine delinquency, and in contested cases will introduce some elements of the
adversary system, nothing will require that the conception of the kindly juvenile
judge be replaced by its opposite. . . .

Ultimately, however, we confront the reality of that portion of the Juvenile
Court process with which we deal in this case. A boy is charged with misconduct.
The boy is committed to an institution where he may be restrained of liberty for
years. It is of no constitutional consequence — and of limited practical meaning —
that the institution to which he is committed is called an Industrial School. The fact
of the matter is that, however euphemistic the title . . . an "industrial school" for
juveniles is an institution of confinement. . . . His world becomes "a building with
whitewashed walls, regimented routine and institutional hours. . . ." Instead of
mother and father and sisters and brothers and friends and classmates, his world
is peopled by guards, custodians, state employees, and "delinquents" confined
with him for anything from waywardness to rape and homicide.

In view of this, it would be extraordinary if our Constitution did not require the
procedural regularity and the exercise of care implied in the phrase "due process."
Under our Constitution, the condition of being a boy does not justify a kangaroo
court. The traditional ideas of Juvenile Court procedure, indeed, contemplated that
time would be available and care would be used to establish precisely what the
juvenile did and why he did it — was it a prank of adolescence or a brutal act
threatening serious consequences to himself or society unless corrected? Under
traditional notions, one would assume that in a case like that of Gerald Gault, where
the juvenile appears to have a home, a working mother and father, and an older
brother, the juvenile judge would have made a careful inquiry and judgment as to
the possibility that the boy could be disciplined and dealt with at home, despite his
previous transgressions.[41] Indeed, so far as appears in the record before us, except

---

[37] Juvenile Delinquency — Its Prevention and Control (Russell Sage Foundation, 1966),
p. 33. . . .

[41] The juvenile judge's testimony at the habeas corpus proceeding is devoid of any meaningful
discussion of this. He appears to have centered his attention upon whether Gerald made the phone call
and used lewd words. He was impressed by the fact that Gerald was on six months' probation because
he was with another boy who allegedly stole a purse — a different sort of offense, sharing the feature
that Gerald was "along," and he even referred to a report which he said was not investigated because
"there was no accusation" "because of lack of material foundation." . . .

for some conversation with Gerald about his school work and his "wanting to go to . . . Grand Canyon with his father," the points to which the judge directed his attention were little different from those that would be involved in determining any charge of violation of apenal statute. The essential difference between Gerald's case and a normal criminal case is that safeguards available to adults were discarded in Gerald's case. The summary procedure as well as the long commitment was possible because Gerald was 15 years of age instead of over 18.

If Gerald had been over 18, he would not have been subject to Juvenile Court proceedings. For the particular offense immediately involved, the maximum punishment would have been a fine of $5 to $50, or imprisonment in jail for not more than two months. Instead, he was committed to custody for a maximum of six years. If he had been over 18 and had committed an offense to which such a sentence might apply, he would have been entitled to substantial rights under the Constitution of the United States as well as under Arizona's laws and constitution. The United States Constitution would guarantee him rights and protections with respect to arrest, search, and seizure, and pretrial interrogation. It would assure him of specific notice of the charges and adequate time to decide his course of action and to prepare his defense. He would be entitled to clear advice that he could be represented by counsel, and, at least if a felony were involved, the State would be required to provide counsel if his parents were unable to afford it. If the court acted on the basis of his confession, careful procedures would be required to assure its voluntariness. If the case went to trial, confrontation and opportunity for cross-examination would be guaranteed. So wide a gulf between the State's treatment of the adult and of the child requires a bridge sturdier than mere verbiage, and reasons more persuasive than cliche can provide. . . .

We now turn to the specific issues which are presented to us in the present case.

III. Notice of Charges

Appellants allege that . . . the proceedings before the Juvenile Court were constitutionally defective because of failure to provide adequate notice of hearings. No notice was given to Gerald's parents when he was taken into custody on Monday, June 8. On that night, when Mrs. Gault went to the Detention Home, she was orally informed that there would be a hearing the next afternoon and was told the reason why Gerald was in custody. The only written notice Gerald's parents received at any time was a note on plain paper from Officer Flagg delivered on Thursday or Friday, June 11 or 12, to the effect that the judge had set Monday, June 15, "for further Hearings on Gerald's delinquency."

A "petition" was filed with the court on June 9 by Officer Flagg, reciting only that he was informed and believed that "said minor is a delinquent minor and that it is necessary that some order be made by the Honorable Court for said minor's welfare." The applicable Arizona statute provides for a petition to be filed in Juvenile Court, alleging in general terms that the child is "neglected, dependent or delinquent." The statute explicitly states that such a general allegation is sufficient, "without alleging the facts." There is no requirement that the petition be served and it was not served upon, given to, or shown to Gerald or his parents.

The Supreme Court of Arizona rejected appellants' claim that due process was denied because of inadequate notice. It stated that "Mrs. Gault knew the exact nature of the charge against Gerald from the day he was taken to the detention home." . . . It held that the appropriate rule is that "the infant and his parents or guardian will receive a petition only reciting a conclusion of delinquency.[51] But no later than the initial hearing by the judge, they must be advised of the facts involved in the case. . . ."

We cannot agree. . . . Notice, to comply with due process requirements, must be given sufficiently in advance of scheduled court proceedings so that reasonable opportunity to prepare will be afforded, and it must "set forth the alleged misconduct with particularity." . . . The "initial hearing" in the present case was a hearing on the merits. Notice at that time is not timely; and even if there were a conceivable purpose served by the deferral . . . it would have to yield to the requirements that the child and his parents or guardian be notified, in writing, of the specific charge or factual allegations . . . at the earliest practicable time, and in any event sufficiently in advance of the hearing to permit preparation. Due process of law requires notice of the sort we have described. . . . It does not allow a hearing to be held in which a youth's freedom and his parents' right to his custody are at stake without giving them timely notice, in advance of the hearing, of the specific issues that they must meet. Nor, in the circumstances of this case, can it reasonably be said that the requirement of notice was waived.[54]

IV. Right to Counsel

Appellants charge that the Juvenile Court proceedings were fatally defective because the court did not advise Gerald or his parents of their right to counsel, and proceeded with the hearing, the adjudication of delinquency and the order of commitment in the absence of counsel for the child and his parents or an express waiver of the right thereto. The Supreme Court of Arizona pointed out that "[t]here is disagreement [among the various jurisdictions] as to whether the court must advise the infant that he has a right to counsel." It noted its own decision . . . to the effect "that the *parents* of an infant in a juvenile proceeding cannot be denied representation by counsel of their choosing." (Emphasis added.) It referred to a provision of the Juvenile Code which it characterized as requiring "that the probation officer shall look after the interests of neglected, delinquent and dependent children," including representing their interests in court. The court argued that "The parent and the probation officer may be relied upon to protect the infant's

---

[51] No such petition was served or supplied in the present case.

[54] Mrs. Gault's "knowledge" of the charge against Gerald, and/or the asserted failure to object, does not excuse the lack of adequate notice. Indeed, one of the purposes of notice is to clarify the issues to be considered, and as our discussion of the facts, supra, shows, even the Juvenile Court Judge was uncertain as to the precise issues determined at the two "hearings." Since the Gaults had no counsel and were not told of their right to counsel, we cannot consider their failure to object to the lack of constitutionally adequate notice as a waiver of their rights. Because of our conclusion that notice given only at the first hearing is inadequate, we need not reach the question whether the Gaults ever received adequately specific notice even at the June 9 hearing, in light of the fact they were never apprised of the charge of being habitually involved in immoral matters.

interests." Accordingly it rejected the proposition that "due process requires that an infant have a right to counsel." It said that juvenile courts have the discretion, but not the duty, to allow such representation. . . . We do not agree. Probation officers, in the Arizona scheme, are also arresting officers. They initiate proceedings and file petitions which they verify, as here, alleging the delinquency of the child; and they testify, as here, against the child. . . . The probation officer cannot act as counsel for the child. . . . Nor can the judge represent the child. There is no material difference in this respect between adult and juvenile proceedings of the sort here involved. In adult proceedings, this contention has been foreclosed by decisions of this Court.[57] A proceeding where the issue is whether the child will be found to be "delinquent" and subjected to the loss of his liberty for years is comparable in seriousness to a felony prosecution. The juvenile needs the assistance of counsel to cope with problems of law, to make skilled inquiry into the facts, to insist upon regularity of the proceedings, and to ascertain whether he has a defense and to prepare and submit it. The child "requires the guiding hand of counsel at every step in the proceedings against him." [Powell v. Alabama, 287 U.S. 45, 69 (1932).]

We conclude that the Due Process Clause of the Fourteenth Amendment requires that in respect of proceedings to determine delinquency which may result in commitment to an institution in which the juvenile's freedom is curtailed, the child and his parents must be notified of the child's right to be represented by counsel retained by them, or if they are unable to afford counsel, the counsel will be appointed to represent the child. . . .

Child has a right to counsel

V. Confrontation, Self-Incrimination, Cross-Examination

Appellants urge that the writ of habeas corpus should have been granted because of the denial of the rights of confrontation and cross-examination in the Juvenile Court hearings, and because the privilege against self-incrimination was not observed. The Juvenile Court Judge testified at the habeas corpus hearing that he had proceeded on the basis of Gerald's admissions at the two hearings. Appellants attack this on the ground that the admissions were obtained in disregard of the privilege against self-incrimination. . . .

Our first question, then, is whether Gerald's admission was improperly obtained. . . . For this purpose, it is necessary briefly to recall the relevant facts.

Mrs. Cook, the complainant, and the recipient of the alleged telephone call, was not called as a witness. Gerald's mother asked the Juvenile Court Judge why Mrs. Cook was not present and the judge replied that "she didn't have to be present." So far as appears, Mrs. Cook was spoken to only once, by Officer Flagg, and this was by telephone. The judge did not speak with her on any occasion. Gerald had been questioned by the probation officer after having been taken into custody. The exact circumstances of this questioning do not appear but any admissions Gerald may have made at this time do not appear in the record. Gerald was also questioned by the Juvenile Court Judge at each of the two hearings. . . . There

[57] Powell v. State of Alabama, 287 U.S. 45, 61 (1932); Gideon v. Wainwright, 372 U.S. 335 (1963).

was conflict and uncertainty among the witnesses at the habeas corpus proceeding — the Juvenile Court Judge, Mr. and Mrs. Gault, and the probation officer — as to what Gerald did or did not admit.

... Neither Gerald nor his parents were advised that he did not have to testify or make a statement, or that an incriminating statement might result in his commitment as a "delinquent."

The Arizona Supreme Court rejected appellants' contention that Gerald had a right to be advised that he need not incriminate himself. ...

In reviewing this conclusion of Arizona's Supreme Court, we emphasize again that we are here concerned only with a proceeding to determine whether a minor is a "delinquent" and which may result in commitment to a state institution. Specifically, the question is whether, in such a proceeding, an admission by the juvenile may be used against him in the absence of clear and unequivocal evidence that the admission was made with knowledge that he was not obliged to speak and would not be penalized for remaining silent. In light of Miranda v. State of Arizona, 384 U.S. 436 (1966), we must also consider whether, if the privilege against self-incrimination is available, it can effectively be waived unless counsel is present or the right to counsel has been waived.

It has long been recognized that the eliciting and use of confessions or admissions require careful scrutiny. ...

The privilege against self-incrimination is, of course, related to the question of the safeguards necessary to assure that admissions or confessions are reasonably trustworthy, that they are not the mere fruits of fear or coercion, but are reliable expressions of the truth. The roots of the privilege are, however, far deeper. They [insist] upon the equality of the individual and the state. In other words, the privilege has a broader and deeper thrust than the rule which prevents the use of confessions which are the product of coercion because coercion is thought to carry with it the danger of unreliability. One of its purposes is to prevent the state, whether by force or by psychological domination, from overcoming the mind and will of the person under investigation and depriving him of the freedom to decide whether to assist the state in securing his conviction.

It would indeed be surprising if the privilege against self-incrimination were available to hardened criminals but not to children. The language of the Fifth Amendment, applicable to the States by operation of the Fourteenth Amendment, is unequivocal and without exception. ...

Against the application to juveniles of the right to silence, it is argued that juvenile proceedings are "civil" and not "criminal," and therefore the privilege should not apply. It is true that the statement of the privilege in the Fifth Amendment ... is that no person "shall be compelled in any *criminal case* to be a witness against himself." However, it is also clear that the availability of the privilege does not turn upon the type of proceeding in which its protection is invoked, but upon the nature of the statement or admission and the exposure which it invites. ...

It would be entirely unrealistic to carve out of the Fifth Amendment all statements by juveniles on the ground that these cannot lead to "criminal" involvement. In the first place, juvenile proceedings to determine "delinquency," which may lead to commitment to a state institution, must be regarded as "criminal" for purposes of the privilege against self-incrimination. To hold otherwise would be to disregard substance because of the feeble enticement of the "civil" label-of-convenience which has been attached to juvenile proceedings. [C]ommitment is a deprivation of liberty. It is incarceration against one's will, whether it is called "criminal" or "civil." And our Constitution guarantees that no person shall be "compelled" to be a witness against himself when he is threatened with deprivation of his liberty. . . .

In addition, . . . there is little or no assurance in Arizona, as in most if not all of the States, that a juvenile apprehended and interrogated by the police or even by the Juvenile Court itself will remain outside of the reach of adult courts as a consequence of the offense for which he has been taken into custody. In Arizona, as in other States, provision is made for Juvenile Courts to relinquish or waive jurisdiction to the ordinary criminal courts. In the present case, when Gerald Gault was interrogated concerning violation of a section of the Arizona Criminal Code, it could not be certain that the Juvenile Court Judge would decide to "suspend" criminal prosecution in court for adults by proceeding to an adjudication in Juvenile Court.

It is also urged, as the Supreme Court of Arizona here asserted, that the juvenile and presumably his parents should not be advised of the juvenile's right to silence because confession is good for the child as the commencement of the assumed therapy of the juvenile court process, and he should be encouraged to assume an attitude of trust and confidence toward the officials of the juvenile process. This proposition has been subjected to widespread challenge on the basis of current reappraisals of the rhetoric and realities of the handling of juvenile offenders.

In fact, evidence is accumulating that confessions by juveniles do not aid in "individualized treatment," as the court below put it, and that compelling the child to answer questions, without warning or advice as to his right to remain silent, does not serve this or any other good purpose. In light of the observations of Wheeler and Cottrell, and others, it seems probable that where children are induced to confess by "paternal" urgings on the part of officials and the confession is then followed by disciplinary action, the child's reaction is likely to be hostile and adverse — the child may well feel that he has been led or tricked into confession and that despite his confession, he is being punished.

Further, authoritative opinion has cast formidable doubt upon the reliability and trustworthiness of "confessions" by children. . . .

We conclude that the constitutional privilege against self-incrimination is applicable in the case of juveniles as it is with respect to adults. We appreciate that special problems may arise with respect to waiver of the privilege by or on behalf of children, and that there may well be some differences in technique — but not in principle — depending upon the age of the child and the presence and competence of parents. The participation of counsel will, of course, assist the police, Juvenile Courts and appellate tribunals in administering the privilege. If counsel was not present for some permissible reason when an admission was obtained, the greatest care must be taken to assure that the admission was voluntary, in the sense not only that it was not coerced or suggested, but also that it was not the product of ignorance of rights or of adolescent fantasy, fright or despair.

The "confession" of Gerald Gault was first obtained by Officer Flagg, out of the presence of Gerald's parents, without counsel and without advising him of his right to silence, as far as appears. The judgment of the Juvenile Court was stated by the judge to be based on Gerald's admissions in court. Neither "admission" was reduced to writing, and, to say the least, the process by which the "admissions" were obtained and received must be characterized as lacking the certainty and order which are required of proceedings of such formidable consequences. Apart from the "admission," there was nothing upon which a judgment or finding might be based. There was no sworn testimony. Mrs. Cook, the complainant, was not present. The Arizona Supreme Court held that "sworn testimony must be required of all witnesses including police officers, probation officers and others who are part of or officially related to the juvenile court structure." We hold that this is not enough. No reason is suggested or appears for a different rule in respect of sworn testimony in juvenile courts than in adult tribunals. Absent a valid confession adequate to support the determination of the Juvenile Court, confrontation and sworn testimony by witnesses available for cross-examination were essential for a finding of "delinquency" and an order committing Gerald to a state institution for a maximum of six years. . . .

VI. Appellate Review and Transcript of Proceedings

Appellants urge that the Arizona statute is unconstitutional under the Due Process Clause because, as construed by its Supreme Court, "there is no right of appeal from a juvenile court order. . . ." The court held that there is no right to a transcript because there is no right to appeal and because the proceedings are confidential and any record must be destroyed after a prescribed period of time. Whether a transcript or other recording is made, it held, is a matter for the discretion of the juvenile court.

This Court has not held that a State is required by the Federal Constitution "to provide appellate courts or a right to appellate review at all." In view of the fact that we must reverse the Supreme Court of Arizona's affirmance of the dismissal of the writ of habeas corpus for other reasons, we need not rule on this question in the present case or upon the failure to provide a transcript. [T]he consequences of failure to provide an appeal, to record the proceedings, or to make findings or state the grounds for the juvenile court's conclusion may be to throw a burden upon the machinery for habeas corpus, to saddle the reviewing process with the burden of attempting to reconstruct a record, and to impose upon the juvenile judge the unseemly duty of testifying under cross-examination as to the events that transpired in the hearings before him. . . .

Judgment reversed and cause remanded with directions.

[The separate concurring opinions of Justices Black, Harlan, and White are omitted.]

Mr. Justice STEWART, dissenting.

The Court today uses an obscure Arizona case as a vehicle to impose upon thousands of juvenile courts throughout the Nation restrictions that the Constitution made applicable to adversary criminal trials. I believe the Court's decision is wholly unsound as a matter of constitutional law, and sadly unwise as a matter of judicial policy. Juvenile proceedings are not criminal trials. . . .

The inflexible restrictions that the Constitution so wisely made applicable to adversary criminal trials have no inevitable place in the proceedings of those public social agencies known as juvenile or family courts. And to impose the Court's long catalog of requirements . . . is to invite a long step backwards into the nineteenth century. In that era . . . a child was tried in a conventional criminal court with all the trappings of a conventional criminal trial. So it was that a 12-year-old boy named James Guild was tried in New Jersey for killing Catharine Beakes. A jury found him guilty of murder, and he was sentenced to death by hanging. The sentence was executed. It was all very constitutional [State v. Guild, 5 Hals. 163, 10 N.J. L. 163, 18 Am. Dec. 404 (1828)].

[D]ue process may require that some of the same restrictions which the Constitution has placed upon criminal trials must be imposed upon juvenile proceedings. For example, I suppose that all would agree that a brutally coerced confession could not constitutionally be considered in a juvenile court hearing. But it surely does not follow that the testimonial privilege against self-incrimination is applicable in all justice proceedings. Similarly, due process clearly requires timely notice of the purpose and scope of any proceedings affecting the relationship of parent and child. But it certainly does not follow that notice of a juvenile hearing must be framed with all the technical niceties of a criminal indictment.

In any event, there is no reason to deal with issues such as these in the present case. The Supreme Court of Arizona found that the parents of Gerald Gault "knew of their right to counsel, to subpoena and cross examine witnesses, of the right to confront the witnesses against Gerald and the possible consequences of a finding of delinquency." 407 P.2d 760, 763. It further found that "Mrs. Gault knew the exact nature of the charge against Gerald from the day he was taken to the detention home." 407 P.2d, at 768. And, as Mr. Justice White correctly points out, no issue of compulsory self-incrimination is presented by this case.

I would dismiss the appeal.

NOTES AND QUESTIONS

(1) **Gault:** *Wellspring for the Rights of Children.* *Gault* has served as a wellspring for the development of the constitutional rights of minors. Although the holdings were limited to the adjudicatory stage of juvenile court delinquency proceedings where a young person risked incarceration, the principles underlying the decision and the approach taken by the court have broader implications for delinquency proceedings, for other sorts of juvenile court proceedings, and for the rights of children generally. *Gault* represented the first unequivocal holding that young people, as individuals, have constitutional rights of their own: "[W]hatever may be their precise impact, neither the Fourteenth Amendment nor the Bill of Rights is for adults alone." Moreover, the Court displayed a willingness to base its decision on what it perceived as the realities of the juvenile justice system. Neither the high motives and "enlightened impulses" of state officials, nor the parens patriae power of the state were accepted as sufficient justifications for the denial of procedural rights to a young person.

The cases considered in Chapter 1, *Roe, Meyer, Pierce, Prince,* and *Yoder,* all reflect the tension between two principles: (a) The family has a broad range of authority over the child, and the parent-child relationship itself has a constitutional dimension; and (b) the state has legitimate interests in childrearing, and need not treat children like adults. *Gault* established a third principle: Young people may have rights of their own, some of which are of constitutional dimension. *Gault*'s principle thus represents a third point in the triangular relationship between the child, the family, and the state.

(2) **Gault:** *Implications for Juvenile Delinquency.*   Consider the following questions:

a. Due Process v. Equal Protection.   Does *Gault* suggest that a juvenile accused of criminal conduct must be treated in all respects like an adult accused of criminal conduct? Are society's interests with regard to juvenile offenders any different from those with regard to adult offenders? What significance do you attach to the fact that *Gault* was decided on the basis of the Due Process Clause and not the Equal Protection Clause?

b. Post-Gault *Constitutional Developments.*   Does the Court's approach in *Gault* suggest that a juvenile accused of delinquency must have all the procedural rights constitutionally guaranteed for an adult accused of a crime? Since *Gault,* the Supreme Court has considered whether delinquents are entitled to the "beyond a reasonable doubt" standard of proof, In re Winship, 397 U.S. 358 (1970) (discussed infra p. 819); jury trials, McKeiver v. Pennsylvania, 403 U.S. 528 (1971) (discussed infra p. 815); protection against double jeopardy, Breed v. Jones, 421 U.S. 519 (1975) (discussed infra p. 822); certain interrogation-related rights, Fare v. Michael C., 442 U.S. 707 (1979) (discussed infra p. 855); the right not to be detained prior to trial, Schall v. Martin, 467 U.S. 253 (1984) (discussed infra p. 825); and unreasonable search and seizure, New Jersey v. T.L.O., 469 U.S. 325 (1985) (discussed infra p. 827).

c. Parental Role.   What does *Gault* suggest concerning the question of the role of a young person's parents in a delinquency proceeding? Why did the court say that "the child *and his parents* must be notified of the child's right to be represented by counsel retained by them, or if they are unable to afford counsel, that counsel will be appointed to represent the child"? (Supra p. 807.) Even if a young person is notified of the charges against him, and his right of counsel, would the Constitution be violated if his parents were not notified? Should a young person be able to insist that his parents *not* be notified? Who should be able to waive the youth's right to counsel, the young person or his parents? Neither alone? See generally p. 868.

d. Procedural Safeguards.   Consider the implications of a youthful offender's possible immaturity. Because *Gault* implies that young persons are entitled to certain procedural safeguards that adults also have, does this imply that young people should be held responsible for their criminal misconduct like adults? Is it possible that certain procedural safeguards that may be adequate for an adult offender, may not sufficiently protect a young person who is immature? Can a 13-year-old give a "knowing and informed" waiver of his constitutional rights?

Do you think it is more important for a young person than for an adult to be encouraged to "tell the truth" and confess to a misdeed? What message is a

12-year-old receiving when he is told that he has a right to remain silent and not confess to a crime? In everyday childrearing, how do you think most parents would feel if they were required to tell their child that he or she had a right to remain silent when asked about involvement in possible misdeeds? How is the delinquency process different?

(3) **Gault:** *Implications for Procedural Due Process in Contexts Other Than Delinquency Proceedings.*   *Gault* has had implications far broader than the delinquency process itself, and has provided the foundation for arguments in a variety of contexts that a young person is constitutionally entitled to various procedural safeguards because of the Due Process Clause. In applying the Due Process Clause, the Supreme Court has generally indicated that a two-stage analysis is necessary; first, the court must determine whether the individual's interests involved in a particular case are encompassed within the Fourteenth Amendment's protection of "life, liberty, or property." Although these concepts are hardly self-defining, the court has made plain that only if protected interests are implicated does the Constitution require procedural safeguards. Second, assuming protected interests are implicated, the court must then decide what procedures in a particular context constitute "due process of law."

In *Gault,* the young person obviously had a "liberty" interest at stake: He was charged with misconduct and risked commitment to an institution for a period of years. Because the possible consequences for a youth are so akin to those of an adult accused, *Gault* and its progeny have interpreted due process to require a highly adversary and formal process in a delinquency proceeding: These include the right to counsel, a right to confront witnesses, a high standard of proof, etc. See infra p. 807. In other contexts, however, the Court has determined that the Due Process Clause is satisfied with fewer procedural safeguards, or none at all. See infra pp. 133-135.

The following questions suggest the variety of contexts in which procedural due process claims might be made on behalf of a young person.

a. Juvenile Court Cases Involving Alleged Noncriminal Misconduct.   A juvenile court may assume jurisdiction over a young person based on allegations that the youth is in need of supervision, has been a truant, is a runaway, or is engaged in other noncriminal misbehavior. As a consequence, the young person's liberty can be constrained. What does the Due Process Clause require in such cases? See Chapter 6.

b. Child Neglect Cases.   What procedural safeguards should be required before the state may coercively remove a young person from parental custody on the grounds that the parent is neglecting or abusing the child? Must there be a hearing before an initial removal? Must there be counsel for the parents? Independent counsel for the child? See Chapter 3. Are more substantial safeguards necessary if the court is considering termination of parental rights to free the child for adoption?

c. Divorce Proceedings.   Should the child have independent counsel in all cases where parents are divorcing? All disputed cases? Only in cases where custody is disputed? Divorce-related custody issues are considered in Chapter 5.

d. Commitment to State Mental Hospital.   Must there be a hearing, and must the child be represented by independent counsel before his or her parents can commit him or her to a state mental hospital? See Parham v. J.R., supra p. 393.

e. Due Process Rights in Schools.   Is a young person constitutionally entitled to a hearing before being expelled from school? Before being suspended from school for a short period? See supra pp. 133-135. Before being subjected to corporal punishment for disciplinary purposes? See supra p. 239. If a hearing is required, what sort of hearing?

(4) Social Science Evidence.   Notice how the court in *Gault* relies on various types of social science evidence in reaching its conclusion. Do you think this is a firm basis for the result reached? Consider the following elements.[72]

a. Increase in Crime.   The Court suggests that juvenile crime has increased since the juvenile court was established. Is this relevant? Does the Court mean to imply that this demonstrates the failure of the juvenile court? Does the Court address the question of how much crime there would be under an alternative scheme that was of a more adversary nature? Is it possible that crime rates may have been even greater without juvenile courts? Was there a "control" that would allow the Court to evaluate what difference having the juvenile court made?

b. Stigma.   The Court suggests that the information that a juvenile has been adjudicated a delinquent could be stigmatizing if the information became available, and the Court suggested that in fact this information often did become available. Does guaranteeing counsel in the delinquency proceeding in any way limit access to the information that a juvenile has been adjudicated a delinquent? Does it keep that information more secret? Is not the problem raised by the Court the illegitimate use of juvenile records? If this is the problem, are there alternative procedures, quite apart from representation by counsel, that might attack this problem directly?

c. The Juvenile's Perception of the System's Fairness.   The majority opinion sharply questions the value of informality as a molder of desirable views of justice. Citing Juvenile Delinquency: Its Prevention and Control, the Court suggested that "recent studies" indicated that the essentials of due process "may be a more impressive and more therapeutic attitude so far as the juvenile is concerned." But the primary study cited by the Court was described by its own authors as a "brief overview of major problems, issues, and developments in the field of juvenile delinquency," *not* a report of actual findings. Moreover, as Stapleton and Teitelbaum write,

> Recent studies on the attitudes of juvenile offenders suggest that, for many, there is little understanding of the system or perception of "unfairness." In addition, data from an as yet unreleased portion of this study indicate that relatively few juveniles processed through [juvenile] courts regard the system as "unjust." Generally, therefore, it may be said that the theories connecting juveniles' perceptions of justice with the court's processes are little more than current and provocative, but untested, ideas, and that the Supreme Court's evaluation rested on intelligent guesswork rather than empirical data. [William V. Stapleton & Lee E. Teitelbaum, In Defense of Youth: A Study of the Role of Counsel in American Juvenile Courts 171 (1972).]

d. Punishment and Loss of Liberty.   The final empirical observation on which the Court's decision rests seems to be the punitive nature of the sanctions. Indeed,

---

[72] The questions that follow in the text are suggested by William V. Stapleton & Lee E. Teitelbaum, In Defense of Youth: A Study of Counsel in American Juvenile Courts (1972).

this may be the critical aspect. The Court emphasized that a juvenile sent to a "home" or "school" was deprived of his liberty, and was, in effect, incarcerated. Does *Gault* require counsel when there is no possibility of incarceration? For example, could a state establish informal proceedings without the various procedural safeguards in circumstances in which the minor did not risk incarceration, and the only issue concerned the conditions of his probation? See In re K., 554 P.2d 180 (Or. Ct. App. 1976) (holding that due process required fewer guarantees when child is not subject to incarceration).

McKeiver v. Pennsylvania
403 U.S. 528 (1971)

Mr. Justice BLACKMUN announced the judgments of the Court and an opinion in which The Chief Justice, Mr. Justice STEWART, and Mr. Justice WHITE join.

These cases present the narrow but precise issue whether the Due Process Clause of the Fourteenth Amendment assures the right to trial by jury in the adjudicative phase of a state juvenile court delinquency proceeding. . . .

II

[W]e turn to the facts of the present cases:

No. 322. Joseph McKeiver, then age 16, in May 1968 was charged with robbery, larceny, and receiving stolen goods (felonies under Pennsylvania law) . . . as acts of juvenile delinquency. At the time of the adjudication hearing he was represented by counsel. His request for a jury trial was denied. . . . McKeiver was adjudged a delinquent upon findings that he had violated a law of the Commonwealth. Pa. Stat. Ann., Tit. 11, §243 (4) (a) (1965). He was placed on probation. . . .

It suffices to say that McKeiver's offense was his participating with 20 or 30 youths who pursued three young teenagers and took 25 cents from them; that McKeiver never before had been arrested and had a record of gainful employment; that the testimony of two of the victims was described by the court as somewhat inconsistent and as "weak" . . .

[Edward Terry, age 15, was charged with assault and battery on a police officer and conspiracy (misdemeanors under Pennsylvania law) for hitting a police officer who broke up a fight that Terry and others were watching. Barbara Burrus was one of the 45 African-American children, ages 11 to 15, whose charges arose from their participation in a series of demonstrations regarding school assignments and a school consolidation plan. The request for jury trial in each case was denied. The cases were consolidated. On appeal, the Supreme Court of North Carolina affirmed the appellate courts' delinquency adjudications and denials of the right to jury trial. In re Burrus, 169 S.E.2d 879 (N.C. 1969).]

IV

The right to an impartial jury "[i]n all criminal prosecutions" under federal law is guaranteed by the Sixth Amendment. Through the Fourteenth Amendment that

requirement has now been imposed upon the States "in all criminal cases which —
were they to be tried in a federal court — would come within the Sixth Amendment's guarantee." This is because the Court has said it believes "that trial by jury
in criminal cases is fundamental to the American scheme of justice." . . .

This, of course, does not automatically provide the answer to the present jury
trial issue, if for no other reason than that the juvenile court proceeding has not yet
been held to be a "criminal prosecution," within the meaning and reach of the
Sixth Amendment, and also has not yet been regarded as devoid of criminal aspects
merely because it usually has been given the civil label.

Little, indeed, is to be gained by any attempt simplistically to call the juvenile
court proceeding either "civil" or "criminal." The Court carefully has avoided this
wooden approach. Before *Gault* was decided in 1967, the Fifth Amendment's
guarantee against self-incrimination had been imposed upon the state criminal
trial. . . . So, too, had the Sixth Amendment's rights of confrontation and cross-
examination. . . . Yet the Court did not automatically and peremptorily apply those
rights to the juvenile proceeding. A reading of *Gault* reveals the opposite. And the
same separate approach to the standard-of-proof issue is evident from the carefully
separated application of the standard, first to the criminal trial, and then to the
juvenile proceeding, displayed in *Winship.* [397 U.S. 358, 361, 365.]

Thus, accepting "the proposition that the Due Process Clause has a role to
play," *Gault,* 387 U.S., at 13, our task here with respect to trial by jury, as it was in
Gault with respect to other claimed rights, "is to ascertain the precise impact of the
due process requirement." Id., at 13-14.

V

~~The Pennsylvania juveniles' basic argument is that they were tried in proceedings~~
~~"substantially similar to a criminal trial."~~ They say that a delinquency proceeding
in their State is initiated by a petition charging a penal code violation in the conclusory language of an indictment; that a juvenile detained prior to trial is held in a
building substantially similar to an adult prison; . . . that counsel and the prosecution engage in plea bargaining; that motions to suppress are routinely heard and
decided; that the usual rules of evidence are applied; that the customary common-
law defenses are available; that the press is generally admitted in the Philadelphia
juvenile courtrooms; that members of the public enter the room; that arrest and
prior record may be reported by the press (from police sources, however, rather
than from the juvenile court records); that, once adjudged delinquent, a juvenile
may be confined until his majority in what amounts to a prison and that the stigma
attached upon delinquency adjudication approximates that resulting from conviction in an adult criminal proceeding.

The North Carolina juveniles particularly urge that the requirement of a jury
trial would not operate to deny the supposed benefits of the juvenile court system
[flexible sentencing permitting emphasis on rehabilitation]; that realization of
these benefits does not depend upon dispensing with the jury; that adjudication
of factual issues on the one hand and disposition of the case on the other are very
different matters with very different purposes; that the purpose of the former is
indistinguishable from that of the criminal trial; that the jury trial provides an

independent protective factor; that experience has shown that jury trials in juvenile courts are manageable; that no reason exists why protection traditionally accorded in criminal proceedings should be denied young people subject to involuntary incarceration for lengthy periods; and that the juvenile courts deserve healthy public scrutiny.

VI

All the litigants here agree that the applicable due process standard in juvenile proceedings, as developed by *Gault* and *Winship,* is fundamental fairness. As that standard was applied in those two cases, we have an emphasis on factfinding procedures. The requirements of notice, counsel, confrontation, cross-examination, and standard of proof naturally flowed from this emphasis. But one cannot say that in our legal system the jury is a necessary component of accurate factfinding. There is much to be said for it, to be sure, but we have been content to pursue other ways for determining facts. Juries are not required, and have not been, for example, in equity cases, in workmen's compensation, in probate, or in deportation cases. Neither have they been generally used in military trials. . . .

We must recognize, as the Court has recognized before, that the fond and idealistic hopes of the juvenile court proponents and early reformers of three generations ago have not been realized. The devastating commentary upon the system's failures as a whole, contained in the President's Commission on Law Enforcement and Administration of Justice, Task Force Report: Juvenile Delinquency and Youth Crime 7-9 (1967), reveals the depth of disappointment in what has been accomplished. Too often the juvenile court judge falls far short of that stalwart, protective, and communicating figure the system envisaged. The community's unwillingness to provide people and facilities and to be concerned, the insufficiency of time devoted, the scarcity of professional help, the inadequacy of dispositional alternatives, and our general lack of knowledge all contribute to dissatisfaction with the experiment. . . .

Despite all these disappointments, all these failures, and all these shortcomings, we conclude that trial by jury in the juvenile court's adjudicative stage is not a constitutional requirement. We so conclude for a number of reasons:

1. The Court has refrained, in the cases heretofore decided, from taking the easy way with a flat holding that all rights constitutionally assured for the adult accused are to be imposed upon the state juvenile proceeding. . . .

2. There is a possibility, at least, that the jury trial, if required as a matter of constitutional precept, will remake the juvenile proceeding into a fully adversary process and will put an effective end to what has been the idealistic prospect of an intimate, informal protective proceeding.

3. The Task Force Report, although concededly pre-*Gault,* is notable for its not making any recommendation that the jury trial be imposed upon the juvenile court system. This is so despite its vivid description of the system's deficiencies and disappointments. . . .

4. The Court specifically has recognized by dictum that a jury is not a necessary part even of every criminal process that is fair and equitable. . . .

5. The imposition of the jury trial on the juvenile court system would not strengthen greatly, if at all, the factfinding function, and would, contrarily, provide an attrition of the juvenile court's assumed ability to function in a unique manner. It would not remedy the defects of the system. . . .

6. The juvenile concept held high promise. We are reluctant to say that, despite disappointments of grave dimensions, it still does not hold promise, and we are particularly reluctant to say, as do the Pennsylvania appellants here, that the system cannot accomplish its rehabilitative goals. . . . We are reluctant to disallow the States to experiment further and to seek in new and different ways the elusive answers to the problems of the young, and we feel that we would be impeding that experimentation by imposing the jury trial. . . . If, in its wisdom, any State feels the jury trial is desirable in all cases, or in certain kinds, there appears to be no impediment to its installing a system embracing that feature. That, however, is the State's privilege and not its obligation. . . .

10. Since *Gault* . . . the great majority of States, in addition to Pennsylvania and North Carolina, that have faced the issue have concluded that the considerations that led to the result in those two cases do not compel trial by jury in the juvenile court. . . .

12. If the jury trial were to be injected into the juvenile court system as a matter of right, it would bring with it into that system the traditional delay, the formality, and the clamor of the adversary system and, possibly, the public trial. . . .

13. Finally, the arguments advanced by the juveniles here are, of course, the identical arguments that underlie the demand for the jury trial for criminal proceedings. The arguments necessarily equate the juvenile proceeding — or at least the adjudicative phase of it — with the criminal trial. Whether they should be so equated is our issue. Concern about the inapplicability of exclusionary and other rules of evidence, about the juvenile court judge's possible awareness of the juvenile's prior record and of the contents of the social file; about repeated appearances of the same familiar witnesses in the persons of juvenile and probation officers and social workers — all to the effect that this will create the likelihood of pre-judgment — chooses to ignore, it seems to us, every aspect of fairness, of concern, of sympathy, and of paternal attention that the juvenile court system contemplates.

If the formalities of the criminal adjudicative process are to be superimposed upon the juvenile court system, there is little need for its separate existence. Perhaps that ultimate disillusionment will come one day, but for the moment we are disinclined to give impetus to it.

Affirmed.

[The separate concurring opinions of Justice Harlan and Justice White have been omitted.]

Mr. Justice DOUGLAS, with whom Mr. Justice BLACK and Mr. Justice MARSHALL concur, dissenting.

These cases from Pennsylvania and North Carolina present the issue of the right to a jury trial for offenders charged in juvenile court and facing a possible incarceration until they reach their majority. I believe the guarantees of the Bill of Rights, made applicable to the States by the Fourteenth Amendment, require a jury trial. . . .

Conviction of each of these crimes would subject a person, whether juvenile or adult, to imprisonment in a state institution. In the case of these students the possible term was six to 10 years; it would be computed for the period until an individual reached the age of 21.

[W]here a State uses its juvenile court proceedings to prosecute a juvenile for a criminal act and to order "confinement" until the child reaches 21 years of age or where the child at the threshold of the proceedings faces that prospect, then he is entitled to the same procedural protection as an adult. . . .

Just as courts have sometimes confused delinquency with crime, so have law enforcement officials treated juveniles not as delinquents but as criminals. . . .

In the present cases imprisonment or confinement up to 10 years was possible for one child and each faced at least a possible five-year incarceration. No adult could be denied a jury trial in those circumstances. Duncan v. Louisiana, 391 U.S. 145, 162. The Fourteenth Amendment, which makes trial by jury provided in the Sixth Amendment applicable to the States, speaks of denial of rights to "any person," not denial of rights to "any adult person". . . .

NOTES AND QUESTIONS

(1) **McKeiver's** *Role in the Due Process Revolutions.*   During the years following *Gault,* the Supreme Court decided a number of cases that raised questions concerning the constitutional requirements of delinquency proceedings. Among *Gault's* Supreme Court progeny, *McKeiver* stood alone in denying a constitutional safeguard to children accused of delinquency. Another of *Gault's* progeny, In re Winship, 397 U.S. 358 (1970), alluded to in *McKeiver,* held that the standard of proof beyond a reasonable doubt was constitutionally required during the adjudicatory stage of a delinquency proceeding. Is *McKeiver* consistent with *Gault, Winship,* and *Breed* (holding that the Double Jeopardy Clause attached to juvenile waiver proceedings)?

(2) *Premise: Reliability of Judicial Fact Finding.*   *McKeiver* is based in part on the premise of the reliability of judicial fact finding. Specifically, the plurality in *McKeiver* asserts that the use of a jury "would not strengthen greatly, if at all, the factfinding function [of the juvenile court]" (supra p. 818). Is the premise correct that judicial fact finding is as reliable as jury fact finding?

In response to this question, Professors Martin Guggenheim and Randy Hertz concluded (based on their empirical study of bench versus jury trials) that judges are more likely to convict alleged delinquents on insufficient evidence, to lean unduly in the prosecution's favor when appraising the evidence, to be less likely to subject police officers' testimony to critical evaluation even when their accounts seem dubious, and to be biased by highly incriminating evidence that would be inadmissible at trial and would be kept from a jury. Martin Guggenheim & Randy Hertz, Reflections on Judges, Juries, and Justice: Ensuring the Fairness of Juvenile Delinquency Trials, 33 Wake Forest L. Rev. 553 (1998). In contrast, the authors claim that the use of juries (by drawing on the experiences and perspectives of many persons from diverse backgrounds) "increases the likelihood that witnesses' credibility will be assessed accurately and facts correctly found" (id. at 576), and that "salient facts will not be overlooked or forgotten" (id. at 578). See also Recent Cases, Constitutional Law — Right to Jury Trial — Eighth Circuit Holds an Adjudication of Juvenile Delinquency to Be a "Prior Conviction" for the Purpose of Sentence Enhancement at a Subsequent Criminal Proceeding — United States v. Smalley, 294 F.3d 1030 (8th Cir. 2002), 116 Harv. L. Rev. 705, 709 (2002) (pointing out that the *McKeiver* plurality's assertion of the reliability of judicial fact finding is "belied by empirical evidence the Court itself has accepted").

Professors Guggenheim and Hertz suggest that certain procedures should be adopted by legislatures and judges in jurisdictions that deny juveniles the right to jury trial. First, they advocate guarding against the juvenile court judge's exposure to prejudicial information in all pretrial matters (e.g., detention hearings, transfers to adult court, and hearings to suppress evidence) by having a judge different from the one who will preside over the trial. Second, they suggest that juvenile court judges should make a routine practice of discussing cases with other judges before rendering a verdict to improve the quality of judicial decision making. Guggenheim & Hertz, supra, at 583-585. What do you think of the proposed reforms?

(3) Premise: Need for Special Characteristics of Juvenile Court. Another premise of *McKeiver* was that the introduction of jury trials would erode the unique characteristics of the juvenile court system, in particular its paternal approach to the juvenile offender. Does the recent criminalization trend of the juvenile justice system undermine this assumption? Several commentators have argued that it does. For example, one student commentator writes:

> Even admitting that the juvenile justice system had fallen short of its ideal of rehabilitating juveniles in a noncriminal context, the *McKeiver* plurality was "reluctant to say that, despite disappointments of grave dimensions, [the system] still does not hold promise." The plurality was therefore wary of any reform that would "place the juvenile squarely in the routine of the criminal process" — implicitly assuming that the juvenile process had not already done so. Whether or not there was a great practical distinction — beyond the procedural protections at issue — between the criminal and juvenile justice systems of 1971, the systems have since converged to the point that *McKeiver*'s idealistic conception of the juvenile justice system is hard to sustain. Whereas early juvenile courts emphasized flexibility in order to serve the best interests of individual offenders, today states increasingly use fixed or mandatory-minimum sentences in defining punishments for juvenile delinquents. Some states even allow juvenile courts to impose "blended" sentences that include incarceration in both juvenile and adult correctional facilities. . . . One juvenile justice scholar summarizes: "Within the past three decades, judicial decisions, legislative amendments, and administrative changes have transformed the juvenile court from a nominally rehabilitative social welfare agency into a scaled-down, second-class criminal court for young offenders that provides neither therapy nor justice." The increasing convergence of the juvenile and criminal courts undermines one of *McKeiver*'s key reasons for denying juries to juveniles — preservation of the unique aspects of the juvenile system — as the system loses the unique aspects the Court wanted to preserve. . . . [Recent Cases, supra, at 711-712.]

Do you agree?

(4) Effects of Denial of Jury Trial. How does denial of the right to jury trial hurt juveniles? Possible ways include the following:

> First, and foremost, juries acquit more readily than do judges, so juveniles are more likely to be convicted than if they could opt for jury trial. [The author speculates that because juvenile court judges hear so many cases, they are less careful in weighing the evidence and more cynical in evaluating juveniles' credibility.] In addition, the parties in a jury trial have an opportunity to exclude jurors whose personal biases may prevent them from fairly trying the case. . . .
>
> [Finally,] [d]enial of the right to jury trial disadvantages juveniles even after the fact-finding stage. In a jury trial, jurors must be explicitly instructed in the law to be applied in the case by the trial judge through written jury instructions. Any error of law can be later reviewed by an appellate court. However, when a judge sits without a jury, she need not expressly articulate her understanding of the law; therefore, the appellate court has no way of determining whether the juvenile court judge misunderstood or misapplied the law to the juvenile's detriment. Thus, depriving juveniles of jury trial puts them at a double disadvantage compared to adult defendants: they are more likely to be convicted at trial and are less likely to be able to demonstrate an error of law on appeal.[73]

(5) Implication of the Right to Jury Trials for Juvenile Courts. One commentator elaborates on the reasons that the majority of states deny the right to a jury trial in juvenile court, including: juvenile court proceedings would become adversarial; jury trials would result in considerable delay in juvenile court proceedings and complicate the rehabilitative process.[74] If *McKeiver* required a jury trial in delinquency adjudications, would this have jeopardized the long-range survival of a separate system for juvenile offenders? Would pressure have increased for the abolition of the juvenile justice system, with young offenders simply treated the same as adult offenders?

(6) Effects of Denial of Jury Trial on Sentence Enhancements. Denial of the right to jury trial in juvenile proceedings has other ramifications in terms of the offender's subsequent processing by the criminal justice system. Several federal courts recently have wrestled with whether a juvenile adjudication may be considered a prior conviction for subsequent sentence enhancement purposes. Traditionally, juvenile delinquents' "adjudications" were not considered "convictions," from a semantic point of view, because of the differences between the juvenile and adult criminal courts. Nonetheless, in United States v. Smalley, 294 F.3d 1030 (8th Cir. 2002), a district court enhanced the sentence of a convicted felon based on his two adjudications of delinquency for violent crimes involving firearms. The Eighth Circuit affirmed, counting the juvenile adjudications toward sentence enhancements. But cf. United States v. Tighe, 266 F.3d 1187 (9th Cir. 2001) (holding that judge's use of defendant's prior, nonjury juvenile adjudication

---

[73] Ainsworth, supra note [53], at 67-68.

[74] Korine L. Larsen, With Liberty and Juvenile Justice for All: Extending the Right to a Jury Trial to the Juvenile Courts, 20 Wm. Mitchell L. Rev. 835, 862-866 (1994). See also Kerrin C. Wolf, Note, Justice by Any Other Name: The Right to a Jury Trial and the Criminal Nature of Juvenile Justice in Louisiana, 12 Wm. & Mary Bill Rts. J. 275, 299 (2003) (discussing advantages and disadvantages of juries for the juvenile justice system).

to increase the statutorily mandated maximum punishment to which he was exposed violated due process). Does the use of juvenile adjudications for sentence enhancement purposes strengthen or weaken the argument for the right to a jury trial in delinquency proceedings? See generally Barry C. Feld, The Constitutional Tension Between *Apprendi* and *McKeiver*: Sentence Enhancements Based on Delinquency Convictions and the Quality of Justice in Juvenile Courts, 38 Wake Forest L. Rev. 1111 (2003).

(7) State Provisions for Jury Trials for Delinquents. While holding that the federal Constitution did not require a jury trial in delinquency proceedings, *McKeiver* also indicated that a state could allow them in some or all cases. Nine states provide for jury trial in delinquency cases as a right, and an additional 11 states provide juveniles with jury trials under limited circumstances.[75]

(8) Public Trial. Typically, delinquency proceedings are not open to the public. Most closure statutes provide that the public and press will be excluded from juvenile proceedings unless the juvenile judge finds that such persons have a "direct" or "proper" interest in the matter. Stephan E. Oestreicher, Jr., Note, Toward Fundamental Fairness in the Kangaroo Courtroom: The Due Process Case Against Statutes Presumptively Closing Juvenile Proceedings, 54 Vand. L. Rev. 1751, 1755 n. 13 (2001). This policy is usually rationalized as a means of safeguarding the privacy of the youth.

Beginning in the 1990s, the "get tough on crime" attitude resulted in many states abrogating their closure statutes and mandating that delinquency proceedings be open to the public. See id. (pointing out that 12 states reverse the traditional presumption by providing that juvenile proceedings are presumptively open unless the juvenile judge finds good cause for closing them; 15 other states provide that juvenile proceedings shall be closed in the case of minor offenses but open if the offense would be a felony or other serious crime under the state criminal code). Does the closure policy still serve the rehabilitative ideal of the juvenile court? Or do presumptive closure statutes violate due process? See id. (so arguing). Does this trend signify yet another reason to grant juvenile delinquents the right to a jury trial?

(9) Note on Double Jeopardy. In Breed v. Jones, 421 U.S. 519 (1975), the Supreme Court held that the protections of the Double Jeopardy Clause applied to juveniles. In that case, a 17-year-old, accused of armed robbery, was adjudicated a delinquent by a juvenile court at a jurisdictional (or "adjudicatory") hearing. Two weeks later, having not yet decided on the youth's sentence or disposition, the juvenile court determined at a "fitness" hearing that the youth was not "amenable" to juvenile court "care, treatment, and training" and ordered that the youth be prosecuted as an adult. At a subsequent trial in adult court, the youth was convicted of first-degree robbery. The Supreme Court held that the juvenile had been put in jeopardy at the original adjudicatory hearing in which jurisdiction was established and that the Double Jeopardy Clause had been offended by his subsequent criminal trial for the same offense.

---

[75] Linda A. Szymanski, Juvenile Delinquents' Right to a Jury Trial (2005 Update), NCJJ Snapshot 11(1) (2006).

The Court distinguished *McKeiver* in a single sentence: "We deal here, not with the 'formalities of the criminal adjudicative process' [citing *McKeiver*], but with analysis of an aspect of the juvenile court system in terms of the kind of risk to which jeopardy refers." Id. at 531. Chief Justice Burger, for a unanimous court, wrote:

> We believe it is simply too late in the day to conclude . . . that a juvenile is not put in jeopardy at a proceeding whose object is to determine whether he has committed acts that violate a criminal law and whose potential consequences include both the stigma inherent in such a determination and the deprivation of liberty for many years. [I]n terms of potential consequences, there is little to distinguish an adjudicatory hearing such as was held in this case from a traditional criminal prosecution. [Id. at 529-530.]

The Court rejected the state's argument that applying "the constitutional protection against multiple trials . . . will diminish flexibility and informality to the extent that those qualities relate uniquely to the goals of the juvenile court system." Id. at 535. The Court in *Breed* recognized that its decision "will require, in most cases, that the transfer decision be made prior to an adjudicatory hearing" and that "where transfer is considered and rejected there may be some added burden on juvenile courts by reason of duplicative proceedings." Id. at 536. Nevertheless, the Court concluded:

> [T]he burdens that [the state] envisions appear to us neither qualitatively nor quantitatively sufficient to justify a departure in this context from the fundamental prohibition against double jeopardy.
>
> A requirement that transfer hearings be held prior to adjudicatory hearings affects not at all the nature of the latter proceedings. More significantly, such a requirement need not affect the quality of decisionmaking at transfer hearings themselves. [Id. at 537.]

Gault and its immediate progeny narrowed the differences between the adult criminal process and the juvenile process. Nevertheless, *McKeiver* and subsequent Supreme Court decisions (e.g., Schall v. Martin, New Jersey v. T.L.O., Roper v. Simmons) are doctrinal reminders that the requirements imposed by the Constitution are not identical for delinquents and adult criminals.

This lack of identity is not surprising for several reasons. First, as *McKeiver* suggests, the traditions of the juvenile court and the values of informality and flexibility still may carry weight. Second, a youth accused of a crime will often have a parent or guardian who generally has certain legal powers and responsibilities with regard to the youth. Because minors are involved, various questions necessarily arise in the delinquency process about the appropriate parental role. Finally, the Court has not repudiated the notions, broadly reflected in a variety of other areas of the law, that young people are less able to make mature and responsible decisions and perhaps more susceptible to coercion or undue influence. Therefore, it is not surprising that in the delinquency context courts have considered age relevant as to a number of issues, such as determining the voluntariness of a confession or the validity of a waiver of constitutional rights.

The materials that follow suggest some of the ways the parent-child relationship and concept about the relationship between age, maturity, and competence create procedural differences between the juvenile process and the adult criminal process.

1. Arrest

Generally, the same substantive standards apply to juveniles and adults concerning the legality of an arrest. In some states, however, a youth may be arrested for delinquency even though the youth came to the attention of law enforcement for an act that would be a misdemeanor or noncriminal conduct for an adult. See D.L.C. v. State, 298 So. 2d 480 (Fla. Dist. Ct. App. 1974) (upholding a conviction for possession of marijuana based on a search incident to an arrest for curfew violation and drinking alcohol).

The United States Supreme Court subsequently let stand a similar California case upholding a search incident to an arrest of a youth for truancy. James D., a youthful looking 17-year-old, was spotted by police walking on a sidewalk at 10:30 A.M. on a school day carrying a book bag. The officers stopped and questioned the youth for allegedly violating a provision of the California Education Act mandating full-time school attendance for youths between ages 6 and 16. While conducting the truancy investigation, they proceeded to search the youth and discovered LSD. James D. subsequently was charged in juvenile court with possession of a controlled substance. In the petition for certiorari, his attorneys argued, "California has chosen to afford greater Fourth Amendment protection to individuals suspected of crimes than to youthful appearing persons. . . ." James D. v. California, 741 P.2d 161 (1987).

At common law, law enforcement personnel could arrest an individual only after obtaining a warrant from a court having jurisdiction (except where the gravity of the offense justified an immediate arrest or the crime was committed in the officer's presence). Linda J. Collier & Deborah D. Rosenbloom, Warrant Requirement, 5 Am. Jur. 2d Arrest §11 (2004). However, some states allow arrest of juveniles without a warrant, even though a warrant would be required in the arrest of an adult in the same circumstances. See Garcia v. State, 661 S.W.2d 754 (Tex. Ct. App. 1983) (statute authorizing the taking of a juvenile into custody does not violate equal protection by not requiring arrest warrant). But see In re Martin S., 429 N.Y.S.2d 1009 (Fam. Ct. 1980) (standard of probable cause governing adult arrest is applicable to instances when children under the age of 16 are taken into custody without a warrant).

Further, whereas some states require police to offer an arrested juvenile the opportunity to telephone parents, other states do not explicitly grant this protection. Compare Cal. Welf. & Inst. Code §308(b) (West 1998) (minors ten years of age or older shall be advised within one hour of being taken into custody that they have a right to make at least two telephone calls, one to a parent or responsible relative and one to an attorney) with People v. Stachelek, 495 N.E.2d 984 (Ill. Ct. App. 1986) (no requirement that police officer spontaneously offer a suspect the opportunity to telephone parents). See also Federal Juvenile Delinquency Act, 18 U.S.C. §5033

(2000) (requiring parental notification whenever juvenile is taken into custody for act of delinquency that violates federal law).

Should juveniles receive protections in addition to those provided adults? Special provisions exist allowing for the arrest records of juveniles to be sealed or expunged in some circumstances. In what circumstances should courts allow expungement? Are there some circumstances when juvenile records should be sealed but not expunged? See Commonwealth v. Gavin G., 772 N.E.2d 1067 (Mass. 2002) (holding that juvenile court lacks authority to order expungement of probation records of juveniles wrongfully accused of criminal conduct given alternative statutory remedy for sealing records). See also Luz A. Carrion, Note, Rethinking Expungement of Juvenile Records in Massachusetts: The Case of Commonwealth v. Gavin G., 38 New Eng. L. Rev. 331 (2004). On the gradual erosion of the confidentiality standard for juvenile records, see Kristin Henning, Eroding Confidentiality in Delinquency Proceedings: Should Schools and Public Housing Authorities Be Notified?, 79 N.Y.U. L. Rev. 520 (2004).

2. Pretrial Detention

Two types of youth are generally eligible for pretrial detention: (1) those who might run away and (2) those who might commit another offense. Does the Due Process Clause require that adult standards should govern the pretrial detention of a youth accused of delinquency?

In Schall v. Martin, 467 U.S. 253 (1984), the United States Supreme Court upheld the constitutionality of pretrial detention for juveniles detained after arrest but prior to a determination of guilt. (The statutory provision at issue, New York Family Court Act §320.5(3)(b), permits pretrial detention based on a finding of a "serious risk" that an arrested juvenile may commit a crime before his return date.) The Supreme Court concluded that preventive detention of juveniles does not violate due process because it does not constitute punishment, but rather serves a legitimate governmental objective of protecting the community and the juvenile from the hazards of prehearing crime.

At the time of the case, no comparable authority existed for the pretrial detention of adults charged with crimes. Subsequent to *Schall,* a provision of the Bail Reform Act of 1984,18 U.S.C. §3142 (2000 & Supp. 2005), permitted federal judicial officers to consider dangerousness in pretrial release decisions; the provision was upheld in United States v. Salerno, 481 U.S. 739 (1987).

The majority in *Schall* bases its holding in part on tradition: Prediction of future criminal conduct forms a basis for decisions involving capital sentencing, parole-release determinations, parole revocations, and sentencing of dangerous special offenders. In holding that pretrial detention for juveniles does not violate due process, the Court explains that it previously rejected the contention "that it is impossible to predict future behavior and that the question is so vague as to be meaningless" [*Schall,* supra, at 279]. How accurate are predictions of future criminal conduct in general? Are predictions of juveniles' future dangerousness more or less likely to be speculative than predictions of adults' behavior? Many studies reveal that a large number of offenders predicted to be dangerous are erroneously labeled. A few studies that examine the accuracy of such predictions for juveniles report a significantly higher rate of false positives for juveniles. See Jeffrey Fagan & Martin Guggenheim, Preventive Detention and the Judicial Prediction of Dangerousness for Juveniles: A Natural Experiment, 86 Crim. L. & Criminology 2 (1996); Stephen E. Schlesinger, The Prediction of Dangerousness in Juveniles: A Replication, 24 Crime & Delinq. 40 (1978).

The Court gives additional justifications for its conclusion that pretrial detention of juveniles comports with due process: (1) every state allows such detention, and some state courts have expressly upheld state statutes permitting it; (2) any risk of erroneous deprivation of a juvenile's liberty interest is small because "juveniles, unlike adults, are always in some form of custody" [467 U.S. at 265]; and (3) any risk of unnecessary deprivation of a juvenile's liberty interest is reduced by procedural safeguards (notice of charges, record of proceedings, the right of representation, subsequent probable cause hearings, right to habeas corpus review).

What do you think of these rationales? Is the existence of uniform state practice persuasive evidence to support the view that preventive detention conforms with due process? Can parental custody properly be compared to institutional custody? Do you agree that preventive detention does not constitute "punishment"? The Court reaches this last conclusion in part because confinement for juvenile detainees is either in nonsecure facilities or else in separate secure facilities for juveniles. Is a juvenile who is detained after arrest likely to view such detention other than as punishment? Do *postdetention* safeguards provide adequate protection against "erroneous and unnecessary deprivations of liberty"? [Id. at 254.]

What hazards are posed by pretrial detention of juveniles? A recent study concluded that pretrial detention has deleterious effects on juvenile's mental and physical well-being, education, and employment, and may actually increase recidivism.[76]

Additional questions arise in the context of what pretrial procedures are due a juvenile. First, do detained juveniles have a right to bail? Most states conclude that they do not because juveniles do not have contractual capacity to enter into bail agreements and because statutory criteria often favor release to parents. Ellen Marrus, Best Interests Equals Zealous Advocacy: A Not So Radical View of Holistic Representation for Children Accused of Crime, 62 Md. L. Rev. 288, 306 n. 95 (2003). But cf. Cal. Welf. & Inst. Code §207. 1(c) (West 1998 & Supp. 2008) (mandating right to bail for juveniles who have been transferred to adult court); Minn. Stat. Ann. §260B.176 (West 2007) (allowing reasonable bail).

Second, how long may minors be detained pending a hearing? Although the length of time varies by jurisdiction, the remedy is the same. See In re McCall, 438 N.E.2d 1269 (Ill. Ct. App. 1982) (proper remedy for 36-hour rule is to release the juvenile from custody prior to the adjudicatory hearing).

Third, what is the appropriate evidentiary standard for pretrial detention decisions in juvenile court? See Julia Colton-Bell & Robert J. Levant, Clear and

---

[76] Barry Holman & Jason Ziedenberg, The Dangers of Detention: The Impact of Incarcerating Youth in Detention and Other Secure Facilities 2-3 (Justice Policy Institute 2006). See also National Juvenile Defender Center, The Use and Abuse of Juvenile Detention, Jan. 2004 at 1, available at *http:///www.njdc.info/pdf/factsheetdetention.pdf* (last visited May 19, 2008).

Convincing Evidence: The Standard Required to Support Pretrial Detention of Juveniles Pursuant to D.C. Code §16-2310, 3 D.C. L. Rev. 213 (1995) (arguing for a clear-and-convincing standard).

Fourth, what criteria should govern decision making regarding pretrial detention of juveniles? See Facilities Review Panel v. Coe, 420 S.E.2d 532 (W. Va. 1992) (adopting objective standards based on the type of offense, judicial findings of dangerousness, whether juvenile is an escapee from commitment or has a record of failure to appear in juvenile court, and whether less restrictive method has been tried).

Fifth, where may the juvenile be detained? Section 10.2 of the Juvenile Justice Standards Relating to Interim Status (1977) states a prohibition against the detention of juveniles in any facility also used to detain adults. See also Segregation of Juvenile Offenders from Adult Offenders, supra, p. 787.

Finally, do juveniles who spend time in pretrial detention have the right to receive credit against time spent in postadjudication confinement? Adults generally receive credit on their sentences for time served in detention (commonly known as "jail credit"). In Jonah R. v. Carmona, 446 F.3d 1000 (9th Cir. 2006), the Ninth Circuit held that a juvenile incarcerated under the Federal Juvenile Delinquency Act was entitled to receive credit for time spent in detention. The Court noted that "[w]e can think of no sensible reason why Jonah's liberty, which he lost for almost three years before his culpability was adjudicated, is worth less than a similarly-situated adult's." Id. at 1011. But cf. Reginald D. v. State, 333 N.W.2d 181, 187 (Wisc. 1995) (contra).

3.   Searches

Does the law compel public school students to submit to searches that would be unconstitutional as applied to adults?

New Jersey v. T.L.O.
469 U.S. 325 (1985)

Justice WHITE delivered the opinion of the Court. . . .

I

On March 7, 1980, a teacher at Piscataway High School in Middlesex County, N.J., discovered two girls smoking in a lavatory. One of the two girls was the respondent T.L.O., who at that time was a 14-year-old high school freshman. Because smoking in the lavatory was a violation of a school rule, the teacher took the two girls to the Principal's office, where they met with Assistant Vice Principal Theodore Choplick. In response to questioning by Mr. Choplick, T.L.O.'s companion admitted that she had violated the rule. T.L.O., however, denied that she had been smoking in the lavatory and claimed that she did not smoke at all.

Mr. Choplick asked T.L.O. to come into his private office and demanded to see her purse. Opening the purse, he found a pack of cigarettes, which he removed from the purse and held before T.L.O. as he accused her of having lied to him. As he reached into the purse for the cigarettes, Mr. Choplick also noticed a package of cigarette rolling papers. In his experience, possession of rolling papers by high school students was closely associated with the use of marijuana. Suspecting that a closer examination of the purse might yield further evidence of drug use, Mr. Choplick proceeded to search the purse thoroughly. The search revealed a small amount of marijuana, a pipe, a number of empty plastic bags, a substantial quantity of money in one-dollar bills, an index card that appeared to be a list of students who owed T.L.O. money, and two letters that implicated T.L.O. in marijuana dealing.

Mr. Choplick notified T.L.O.'s mother and police, and turned the evidence of drug dealing over to the police. At the request of the police, T.L.O.'s mother took her daughter to police headquarters, where T.L.O. confessed that she had been selling marijuana at the high school. On the basis of the confession and the evidence seized by Mr. Choplick, the State brought delinquency charges against T.L.O. in the Juvenile and Domestic Relations Court of Middlesex County. Contending that Mr. Choplick's search of her purse violated the Fourth Amendment, T.L.O. moved to suppress the evidence found in her purse as well as her confession, which, she argued, was tainted by the allegedly unlawful search. [The Juvenile Court denied the motion to suppress, found T.L.O. to be a delinquent, and sentenced her to a year's probation. The appellate court affirmed. The New Jersey Supreme Court reversed.]

Although we originally granted certiorari to decide the issue of the appropriate remedy in juvenile court proceedings for unlawful school searches [i.e., the appropriateness of the exclusionary rule as a remedy], our doubts regarding the wisdom of deciding that question in isolation from the broader question of what limits, if any, the Fourth Amendment places on the activities of school authorities prompted us to order reargument on that question.[2] Having heard argument on the legality of the search of T.L.O.'s purse, we are satisfied that the search did not violate the Fourth Amendment.[3]

II

In determining whether the search at issue in this case violated the Fourth Amendment, we are faced initially with the question whether that Amendment's

---

[2] . . . [Courts have] split over whether the exclusionary rule is an appropriate remedy for Fourth Amendment violations committed by school authorities. The Georgia courts have held that although the Fourth Amendment applies to the schools, the exclusionary rule does not. Other jurisdictions have applied the rule to exclude the fruits of unlawful school searches from criminal trials and delinquency proceedings.

[3] In holding that the search of T.L.O.'s purse did not violate the Fourth Amendment, we do not implicitly determine that the exclusionary rule applies to the fruits of unlawful searches conducted by school authorities. The question whether evidence should be excluded from a criminal proceeding involves two discrete inquiries: whether the evidence was seized in violation of the Fourth Amendment, and whether the exclusionary rule is the appropriate remedy for the violation. Neither question is logically antecedent to the other, for a negative answer to either question is sufficient to dispose of the case. Thus, our determination that the search at issue in this case did not violate the Fourth Amendment implies no particular resolution of the question of the applicability of the exclusionary rule.

prohibition on unreasonable searches and seizures applies to searches conducted by public school officials. We hold that it does.

[T]he State of New Jersey has argued that the history of the Fourth Amendment indicates that the Amendment was intended to regulate only searches and seizures carried out by law enforcement officers; accordingly, although public school officials are concededly state agents for purposes of the Fourteenth Amendment, the Fourth Amendment creates no rights enforceable against them.

[T]his Court has never limited the Amendment's prohibition on unreasonable searches and seizures to operations conducted by the police. Rather, the Court has long spoken of the Fourth Amendment's strictures as restraints imposed upon "governmental action" — that is, "upon the activities of sovereign authority." Accordingly, we have held the Fourth Amendment applicable to the activities of civil as well as criminal authorities. . . .

Notwithstanding the general applicability of the Fourth Amendment to the activities of civil authorities, a few courts have concluded that school officials are exempt from the dictates of the Fourth Amendment by virtue of the special nature of their authority over schoolchildren. Teachers and school administrators, it is said, act in loco parentis in their dealings with students: their authority is that of the parent, not the State, and is therefore not subject to the limits of the Fourth Amendment.

Such reasoning is in tension with contemporary reality and the teachings of this Court. We have held school officials subject to the commands of the First Amendment; see Tinker v. Des Moines Independent Community School District, 393 U.S. 503 (1969), and the Due Process Clause of the Fourteenth Amendment; see Goss v. Lopez, 419 U.S. 565 (1975). If school authorities are state actors for purposes of the constitutional guarantees of freedom of expression and due process, it is difficult to understand why they should be deemed to be exercising parental rather than public authority when conducting searches of their students. . . . Today's public school officials do not merely exercise authority voluntarily conferred on them by individual parents; rather, they act in furtherance of publicly mandated educational and disciplinary policies. . . . In carrying out searches and other disciplinary functions pursuant to such policies, school officials act as representatives of the State, not merely as surrogates for the parents, and they cannot claim the parents' immunity from the strictures of the Fourth Amendment.

III

To hold that the Fourth Amendment applies to searches conducted by school authorities is only to begin the inquiry into the standards governing such searches. Although the underlying command of the Fourth Amendment is always that searches and seizures be reasonable, what is reasonable depends on the context within which a search takes place. The determination of the standard of reasonableness governing any specific class of searches requires "balancing the need to search against the invasion which the search entails." On one side of the balance are arrayed the individual's legitimate expectations of privacy and personal security; on the other, the government's need for effective methods to deal with breaches of public order.

We have recognized that even a limited search of the person is a substantial invasion of privacy. . . . A search of a child's person or of a closed purse or other bag carried on her person,[5] no less than a similar search carried out on an adult, is undoubtedly a severe violation of subjective expectations of privacy. . . .

The State of New Jersey has argued that because of the pervasive supervision to which children in the schools are necessarily subject, a child has virtually no legitimate expectation of privacy in articles of personal property "unnecessarily" carried into a school. This argument has two factual premises: (1) the fundamental incompatibility of expectations of privacy with the maintenance of a sound educational environment; and (2) the minimal interest of the child in bringing any items of personal property into the school. Both premises are severely flawed.

Although this Court may take notice of the difficulty of maintaining discipline in the public schools today, the situation is not so dire that students in the schools may claim no legitimate expectations of privacy. We have recently recognized that the need to maintain order in a prison is such that prisoners retain no legitimate expectations of privacy in their cells, but it goes without saying that "[t]he prisoner and the schoolchild stand in wholly different circumstances, separated by the harsh facts of criminal conviction and incarceration." Ingraham v. Wright, supra, at 669. We are not yet ready to hold that the schools and the prisons need be equated for purposes of the Fourth Amendment.

Nor does the State's suggestion that children have no legitimate need to bring personal property into the schools seem well anchored in reality. Students at a minimum must bring to school not only the supplies needed for their studies, but also keys, money, and the necessaries of personal hygiene and grooming. In addition, students may carry on their persons or in purses or wallets such nondisruptive yet highly personal items as photographs, letters, and diaries. Finally, students may have perfectly legitimate reasons to carry with them articles of property needed in connection with extracurricular or recreational activities. In short, schoolchildren may find it necessary to carry with them a variety of legitimate, noncontraband items, and there is no reason to conclude that they have necessarily waived all rights to privacy in such items merely by bringing them onto school grounds.

Against the child's interest in privacy must be set the substantial interest of teachers and administrators in maintaining discipline in the classroom and on school grounds. Maintaining order in the classroom has never been easy, but in recent years, school disorder has often taken particularly ugly forms: drug use and violent crime in the schools have become major social problems. . . .

How, then, should we strike the balance between the schoolchild's legitimate expectations of privacy and the school's equally legitimate need to maintain an environment in which learning can take place? It is evident that the school setting requires some easing of the restrictions to which searches by public authorities are ordinarily subject. The warrant requirement, in particular, is unsuited to the school environment: requiring a teacher to obtain a warrant before searching a child

---

[5] We do not address the question, not presented by this case, whether a schoolchild has a legitimate expectation of privacy in lockers, desks, or other school property provided for the storage of school supplies. Nor do we express any opinion on the standards (if any) governing searches of such areas by school officials or by other public authorities acting at the request of school officials.

suspected of an infraction of school rules (or of the criminal law) would unduly interfere with the maintenance of the swift and informal disciplinary procedures needed in the schools. . . .

The school setting also requires some modification of the level of suspicion of illicit activity needed to justify a search. Ordinarily, a search — even one that may permissibly be carried out without a warrant — must be based upon "probable cause" to believe that a violation of the law has occurred. However, "probable cause" is not an irreducible requirement of a valid search. The fundamental command of the Fourth Amendment is that searches and seizures be reasonable, and although "both the concept of probable cause and the requirement of a warrant bear on the reasonableness of a search, . . . in certain limited circumstances neither is required." Thus, we have in a number of cases recognized the legality of searches and seizures based on suspicions that, although "reasonable," do not rise to the level of probable cause. . . .

We join the majority of courts that have examined this issue in concluding that the accommodation of the privacy interests of schoolchildren with the substantial need of teachers and administrators for freedom to maintain order in the schools does not require strict adherence to the requirement that searches be based on probable cause to believe that the subject of the search has violated or is violating the law. Rather, the legality of a search of a student should depend simply on the reasonableness, under all the circumstances, of the search. Determining the reasonableness of any search involves a twofold inquiry: first, one must consider "whether the . . . action was justified at its inception"; second, one must determine whether the search as actually conducted "was reasonably related in scope to the circumstances which justified the interference in the first place." Under ordinary circumstances, a search of a student by a teacher or other school official[7] will be "justified at its inception" when there are reasonable grounds for suspecting that the search will turn up evidence that the student has violated or is violating either the law or the rules of the school.[8] Such a search will be permissible in its scope when the measures adopted are reasonably related to the objectives of the search and not excessively intrusive in light of the age and sex of the student and the nature of the infraction.

---

[7] We here consider only searches carried out by school authorities acting alone and on their own authority. This case does not present the question of the appropriate standard for assessing the legality of searches conducted by school officials in conjunction with or at the behest of law enforcement agencies, and we express no opinion on that question.

[8] We do not decide whether individualized suspicion is an essential element of the reasonableness standard we adopt for searches by school authorities. In other contexts, however, we have held that although "some quantum of individualized suspicion is usually a prerequisite to a constitutional search or seizure[,] . . . the Fourth Amendment imposes no irreducible requirement of such suspicion." United States v. Martinez-Fuerte, 428 U.S. 543, 560-561 (1976). Exceptions to the requirement of individualized suspicion are generally appropriate only where the privacy interests implicated by a search are minimal and where "other safeguards" are available "to assure that the individual's reason able expectation of privacy is not 'subject to the discretion of the official in the field.' " Delaware v. Prouse, 440 U.S. 648, 654-655 (1979). Because the search of T.L.O.'s purse was based upon an individualized suspicion that she had violated school rules, . . . we need not consider the circumstances that might justify school authorities in conducting searches unsupported by individualized suspicion.

This standard will, we trust, neither unduly burden the efforts of school authorities to maintain order in their schools nor authorize unrestrained intrusions upon the privacy of school children. By focusing attention on the question of reasonableness, the standard will spare teachers and school administrators the necessity of schooling themselves in the niceties of probable cause and permit them to regulate their conduct according to the dictates of reason and common sense. At the same time, the reasonableness standard should ensure that the interests of students will be invaded no more than is necessary to achieve the legitimate end of preserving order in the schools.

IV

There remains the question of the legality of the search in this case. We recognize that the "reasonable grounds" standard applied by the New Jersey Supreme Court in its consideration of this question is not substantially different from the standard that we have adopted today. Nonetheless, we believe that the New Jersey court's application of that standard to strike down the search of T.L.O.'s purse reflects a somewhat crabbed notion of reasonableness. Our review of the facts surrounding the search leads us to conclude that the search was in no sense unreasonable for Fourth Amendment purposes. . . .

Reversed.

[The separate concurring opinion of Justice Powell has been omitted.]

Justice BLACKMUN, concurring in the judgment.

I join the judgment of the Court and agree with much that is said in its opinion. I write separately, however, because I believe the Court omits a crucial step in its analysis of whether a school search must be based upon probable cause. The Court correctly states that we have recognized limited exceptions to the probable-cause requirement "[w]here a careful balancing of governmental and private interests suggests that the public interest is best served" by a lesser standard. I believe that we have used such a balancing test, rather than strictly applying the Fourth Amendment's Warrant and Probable-Cause Clause, only when we were confronted with "a special law enforcement need for greater flexibility." Florida v. Royer, 460 U.S. 491, 514 (1983) (Blackmun, J., dissenting). I pointed out in United States v. Place, 462 U.S. 696 (1983):

> While the Fourth Amendment speaks in terms of freedom from unreasonable [searches], the Amendment does not leave the reasonableness of most [searches] to the judgment of courts or government officers; the Framers of the Amendment balanced the interests involved and decided that a [search] is reasonable only if supported by a judicial warrant based on probable cause.

Only in those exceptional circumstances in which special needs, beyond the normal need for law enforcement, make the warrant and probable-cause requirement impracticable, is a court entitled to substitute its balancing of interests for that of the Framers.

[Blackmun gives examples of stops that are permitted based on less than probable cause in cases of "stop and frisks" when the police believe a crime has occurred or is about to occur, and for border stops.] The Court's implication that the balancing test is the rule rather than the exception is troubling for me because it is unnecessary in this case. The elementary and secondary school setting presents a special need for flexibility justifying a departure from the balance struck by the Framers. As Justice Powell notes, "[w]ithout first establishing discipline and maintaining order, teachers cannot begin to educate their students." Maintaining order in the classroom can be a difficult task. A single teacher often must watch over a large number of students, and, as any parent knows, children at certain ages are inclined to test the outer boundaries of acceptable conduct and to imitate the misbehavior of a peer if that misbehavior is not dealt with quickly. Every adult remembers from his own schooldays the havoc a water pistol or peashooter can wreak until it is taken away. Thus, the Court has recognized that "[e]vents calling for discipline are frequent occurrences and sometimes require immediate, effective action." Goss v. Lopez, 419 U.S. 565, 580 (1975). Indeed, because drug use and possession of weapons have become increasingly common among young people, an immediate response frequently is required not just to maintain an environment conducive to learning, but to protect the very safety of students and school personnel.

Such immediate action obviously would not be possible if a teacher were required to secure a warrant before searching a student. Nor would it be possible if a teacher could not conduct a necessary search until the teacher thought there was probable cause for the search. A teacher has neither the training nor the day-to-day experience in the complexities of probable cause that a law enforcement officer possesses, and is ill-equipped to make a quick judgment about the existence of probable cause. The time required for a teacher to ask the questions or make the observations that are necessary to turn reasonable grounds into probable cause is time during which the teacher, and other students, are diverted from the essential task of education. . . . The special need for an immediate response to behavior that threatens either the safety of schoolchildren and teachers or the educational process itself justifies the Court in excepting school searches from the warrant and probable-cause requirement, and in applying a standard determined by balancing the relevant interests. . . .

Justice STEVENS with whom Justice MARSHALL joins, and with whom Justice BRENNAN joins as to Part I, concurring in part and dissenting in part.

. . . The Court embraces the standard applied by the New Jersey Supreme Court as equivalent to its own, and then deprecates the state court's application of the standard as reflecting "a somewhat crabbed notion of reasonableness." There is no mystery, however, in the state court's finding that the search in this case was unconstitutional; the decision below was not based on a manipulation of reasonable suspicion, but on the trivial character of the activity that promoted the official search. The New Jersey Supreme Court wrote:

> We are satisfied that when a school official has reasonable grounds to believe that a student possesses evidence of *illegal activity or activity that would interfere with school discipline and order,* the school official has the right to conduct a reasonable search for such evidence.

In determining whether the school official has reasonable grounds, courts should consider "the child's age, history, and school record, *the prevalence and seriousness of the problem in the school to which the search was directed,* the exigency to make the search without delay, and the probative value and reliability of the information used as a justification for the search." [State in Interest of T.L.O., 463 A.2d 934, 941-942 (N.J. 1983).]

The emphasized language in the state court's opinion focuses on the character of the rule infraction that is to be the object of the search. In the view of the state court, there is a quite obvious and material difference between a search for evidence relating to violent or disruptive activity, and a search for evidence of a smoking rule violation. . . .

Like the New Jersey Supreme Court, I would view this case differently if the Assistant Vice Principal had reason to believe T.L.O.'s purse contained evidence of criminal activity, or of an activity that would seriously disrupt school discipline. There was, however, absolutely no basis for any such assumption — not even a "hunch."

In this case, Mr. Choplick overreacted to what appeared to be nothing more than a minor infraction — a rule prohibiting smoking in the bathroom of the freshmen's and sophomores' building. It is, of course, true that he actually found evidence of serious wrongdoing by T.L.O., but no one claims that the prior search may be justified by his unexpected discovery. As far as the smoking infraction is concerned, the search for cigarettes merely tended to corroborate a teacher's eye-witness account of T.L.O.'s violation of a minor regulation designed to channel student smoking behavior into designated locations. Because this conduct was neither unlawful nor significantly disruptive of school order or the educational process, the invasion of privacy associated with the forcible opening of T.L.O.'s purse was entirely unjustified at its inception.

A review of the sampling of school search cases relied on by the Court demonstrates how different this case is from those in which there was indeed a valid justification for intruding on a student's privacy. In most of them the student was suspected of a criminal violation; in the remainder either violence or substantial disruption of school order or the integrity of the academic process was at stake. Few involved matters as trivial as the no-smoking rule violated by T.L.O. The rule the Court adopts today is so open-ended that it may make the Fourth Amendment virtually meaningless in the school context. Although I agree that school administrators must have broad latitude to maintain order and discipline in our classrooms, that authority is not unlimited. . . .

Board of Education v. Earls
536 U.S. 822 (2002)

Justice THOMAS delivered the opinion of the Court.

. . . The city of Tecumseh, Oklahoma, is a rural community located approximately 40 miles southeast of Oklahoma City. The School District administers all Tecumseh public schools. In the fall of 1998, the School District adopted the Student Activities Drug Testing Policy (Policy), which requires all middle and high school students to consent to drug testing in order to participate in any extracurricular activity. In practice, the Policy has been applied only to competitive extracurricular activities sanctioned by the Oklahoma Secondary Schools Activities Association, such as the Academic Team, Future Farmers of America, Future Homemakers of America, band, choir, pom-pom, cheerleading, and athletics. Under the Policy, students are required to take a drug test before participating in an extracurricular activity, must submit to random drug testing while participating in that activity, and must agree to be tested at any time upon reasonable suspicion. The urinalysis tests are designed to detect only the use of illegal drugs, including amphetamines, marijuana, cocaine, opiates, and barbituates, not medical conditions or the presence of authorized prescription medications.

. . . Respondent Lindsay Earls was a member of the show choir, the marching band, the Academic Team, and the National Honor Society. Respondent Daniel James sought to participate in the Academic Team. Together with their parents, Earls and James brought a Rev. Stat. §1979, 42 U.S.C. §1983, action against the School District, challenging the Policy both on its face and as applied to their participation in extracurricular activities. They alleged that the Policy violates the Fourth Amendment [and] requested injunctive and declarative relief. . . . [The district court rejected respondents' claim that the school policy was unconstitutional and granted summary judgment to the School District. The Tenth Circuit Court of Appeals reversed, holding that the policy violated the Fourth Amendment.]

The Fourth Amendment to the United States Constitution protects "[t]he right of the people to be secure in their persons, houses, papers, and effects, against unreasonable searches and seizures." Searches by public school officials, such as the collection of urine samples, implicate Fourth Amendment interests. We must therefore review the School District's Policy for "reasonableness," which is the touchstone of the constitutionality of a governmental search.

In the criminal context, reasonableness usually requires a showing of probable cause. The probable-cause standard, however, "is peculiarly related to criminal investigations" and may be unsuited to determining the reasonableness of administrative searches where the "Government seeks to *prevent* the development of hazardous conditions." Treasury Employees v. Von Raab, 489 U.S. 656, 667-668 (1989). The Court has also held that a warrant and finding of probable cause are unnecessary in the public school context because such requirements " 'would unduly interfere with the maintenance of the swift and informal disciplinary procedures [that are] needed.' " [Vernonia School Dist. v. Acton, 515 U.S. 646, 653 (1995) (quoting New Jersey v. T.L.O., 469 U.S. 325, 340-341 (1985).]

Given that the School District's Policy is not in any way related to the conduct of criminal investigations, respondents do not contend that the School District requires probable cause before testing students for drug use. Respondents instead argue that drug testing must be based at least on some level of individualized suspicion. It is true that we generally determine the reasonableness of a search by balancing the nature of the intrusion on the individual's privacy against the promotion of legitimate governmental interests. But we have long held that "the Fourth Amendment imposes no irreducible requirement of [individualized] suspicion." United States v. Martinez-Fuerte, 428 U.S. 543, 561 (1976). "[I]n certain limited circumstances, the

Government's need to discover such latent or hidden conditions, or to prevent their development, is sufficiently compelling to justify the intrusion on privacy entailed by conducting such searches without any measure of individualized suspicion." *Von Raab,* supra, at 668. Therefore, in the context of safety and administrative regulations, a search unsupported by probable cause may be reasonable "when 'special needs, beyond the normal need for law enforcement, make the warrant and probable-cause requirement impracticable.' " Griffin v. Wisconsin, 483 U.S. 868, 873 (1987) (quoting *T.L.O.,* supra, at 351 (Blackmun, J., concurring in judgment)).

Significantly, this Court has previously held that "special needs" inhere in the public school context. See *Vernonia,* supra, at 653; *T.L.O.,* supra, at 339-340. While schoolchildren do not shed their constitutional rights when they enter the schoolhouse, see Tinker v. Des Moines Independent Community School Dist., 393 U.S. 503 (1969), "Fourth Amendment rights . . . are different in public schools than elsewhere; the 'reasonableness' inquiry cannot disregard the schools' custodial and tutelary responsibility for children." *Vernonia,* 515 U.S., at 656. In particular, a finding of individualized suspicion may not be necessary when a school conducts drug testing.

In *Vernonia,* this Court held that the suspicionless drug testing of athletes was constitutional. The Court, however, did not simply authorize all school drug testing, but rather conducted a fact-specific balancing of the intrusion on the children's Fourth Amendment rights against the promotion of legitimate governmental interests. Applying the principles of *Vernonia* to the somewhat different facts of this case, we conclude that Tecumseh's Policy is also constitutional.

A

We first consider the nature of the privacy interest allegedly compromised by the drug testing. As in *Vernonia,* the context of the public school environment serves as the backdrop for the analysis of the privacy interest at stake and the reasonableness of the drug testing policy in general. [Citing *Vernonia*] ("Central . . . is the fact that the subjects of the Policy are (1) children, who (2) have been committed to the temporary custody of the State as schoolmaster"); see also id., at 665 ("The most significant element in this case is the first we discussed: that the Policy was undertaken in furtherance of the government's responsibilities, under a public school system, as guardian and tutor of children entrusted to its care"); ibid. ("[W]hen the government acts as guardian and tutor the relevant question is whether the search is one that a reasonable guardian and tutor might undertake").

A student's privacy interest is limited in a public school environment where the State is responsible for maintaining discipline, health, and safety. Schoolchildren are routinely required to submit to physical examinations and vaccinations against disease. Securing order in the school environment sometimes requires that students be subjected to greater controls than those appropriate for adults. See *T.L.O.,* 469 U.S., at 350 (Powell, J., concurring) ("Without first establishing discipline and maintaining order, teachers cannot begin to educate their students. And apart from education, the school has the obligation to protect pupils from mistreatment by other children, and also to protect teachers themselves from violence by the few students whose conduct in recent years has prompted national concern").

Respondents argue that because children participating in nonathletic extracurricular activities are not subject to regular physicals and communal undress, they have a stronger expectation of privacy than the athletes tested in *Vernonia*. This distinction, however, was not essential to our decision in *Vernonia*, which depended primarily upon the school's custodial responsibility and authority.

In any event, students who participate in competitive extracurricular activities voluntarily subject themselves to many of the same intrusions on their privacy as do athletes. Some of these clubs and activities require occasional off-campus travel and communal undress. All of them have their own rules and requirements for participating students that do not apply to the student body as a whole. For example, each of the competitive extracurricular activities governed by the Policy must abide by the rules of the Oklahoma Secondary Schools Activities Association, and a faculty sponsor monitors the students for compliance with the various rules dictated by the clubs and activities. This regulation of extracurricular activities further diminishes the expectation of privacy among schoolchildren. We therefore conclude that the students affected by this Policy have a limited expectation of privacy.

B

Next, we consider the character of the intrusion imposed by the Policy. Urination is "an excretory function traditionally shielded by great privacy." Skinner v. Railway Labor Executives' Assn., 489 U.S. 602, 626 (1989). But the "degree of intrusion" on one's privacy caused by collecting a urine sample "depends upon the manner in which production of the urine sample is monitored." *Vernonia*, supra, at 658.

Under the Policy, a faculty monitor waits outside the closed restroom stall for the student to produce a sample and must "listen for the normal sounds of urination in order to guard against tampered specimens and to insure an accurate chain of custody." The monitor then pours the sample into two bottles that are sealed and placed into a mailing pouch along with a consent form signed by the student. This procedure is virtually identical to that reviewed in *Vernonia*, except that it additionally protects privacy by allowing male students to produce their samples behind a closed stall. Given that we considered the method of collection in *Vernonia* a "negligible" intrusion, the method here is even less problematic.

In addition, the Policy clearly requires that the test results be kept in confidential files separate from a student's other educational records and released to school personnel only on a "need to know" basis. Respondents nonetheless contend that the intrusion on students' privacy is significant because the Policy fails to protect effectively against the disclosure of confidential information and, specifically, that the school "has been careless in protecting that information: for example, the Choir teacher looked at students' prescription drug lists and left them where other students could see them." Brief for Respondents 24. But the choir teacher is someone with a "need to know," because during off-campus trips she needs to know what medications are taken by her students. Even before the Policy was enacted the choir teacher had access to this information. In any event, there is no allegation that any other student did see such information. This one example of alleged carelessness hardly increases the character of the intrusion.

Moreover, the test results are not turned over to any law enforcement authority. Nor do the test results here lead to the imposition of discipline or have any academic consequences. Rather, the only consequence of a failed drug test is to limit the student's privilege of participating in extracurricular activities. . . .

Given the minimally intrusive nature of the sample collection and the limited uses to which the test results are put, we conclude that the invasion of students' privacy is not significant.

C

Finally, this Court must consider the nature and immediacy of the government's concerns and the efficacy of the Policy in meeting them. This Court has already articulated in detail the importance of the governmental concern in preventing drug use by schoolchildren. The drug abuse problem among our Nation's youth has hardly abated since *Vernonia* was decided in 1995. In fact, evidence suggests that it has only grown worse.[5] As in *Vernonia,* "the necessity for the State to act is magnified by the fact that this evil is being visited not just upon individuals at large, but upon children for whom it has undertaken a special responsibility of care and direction." Id., at 662. The health and safety risks identified in *Vernonia* apply with equal force to Tecumseh's children. Indeed, the nationwide drug epidemic makes the war against drugs a pressing concern in every school.

Additionally, the School District in this case has presented specific evidence of drug use at Tecumseh schools. Teachers testified that they had seen students who appeared to be under the influence of drugs and that they had heard students speaking openly about using drugs. A drug dog found marijuana cigarettes near the school parking lot. Police officers once found drugs or drug paraphernalia in a car driven by a Future Farmers of America member. And the school board president reported that people in the community were calling the board to discuss the "drug situation." We decline to second-guess the finding of the District Court that "[v]iewing the evidence as a whole, it cannot be reasonably disputed that the [School District] was faced with a 'drug problem' when it adopted the Policy" [115 F. Supp. 2d 1281, 1287 (W.D. Okla. 2000)].

Respondents consider the proffered evidence insufficient and argue that there is no "real and immediate interest" to justify a policy of drug testing nonathletes. We have recognized, however, that "[a] demonstrated problem of drug abuse . . . [is] not in all cases necessary to the validity of a testing regime," but that some showing does "shore up an assertion of special need for a suspicionless general search program." Chandler v. Miller, 520 U.S. 305, 319 (1997). The School

---

[5] For instance, the number of 12th graders using any illicit drug increased from 48.4 percent in 1995 to 53.9 percent in 2001. The number of 12th graders reporting they had used marijuana jumped from 41.7 percent to 49.0 percent during that same period. See Department of Health and Human Services, Monitoring the Future: National Results on Adolescent Drug Use, Overview of Key Findings (2001) (Table 1).

District has provided sufficient evidence to shore up the need for its drug testing program.

Furthermore, this Court has not required a particularized or pervasive drug problem before allowing the government to conduct suspicionless drug testing. For instance, in *Von Raab* the Court upheld the drug testing of customs officials on a purely preventive basis, without any documented history of drug use by such officials. In response to the lack of evidence relating to drug use, the Court noted generally that "drug abuse is one of the most serious problems confronting our society today," and that programs to prevent and detect drug use among customs officials could not be deemed unreasonable. [489 U.S. at 674]; cf. *Skinner,* 489 U.S., at 607, and n. 1, 109 S. Ct. 1402 (noting nationwide studies that identified on-the-job alcohol and drug use by railroad employees). Likewise, the need to prevent and deter the substantial harm of childhood drug use provides the necessary immediacy for a school testing policy. Indeed, it would make little sense to require a school district to wait for a substantial portion of its students to begin using drugs before it was allowed to institute a drug testing program designed to deter drug use.

Given the nationwide epidemic of drug use, and the evidence of increased drug use in Tecumseh schools, it was entirely reasonable for the School District to enact this particular drug testing policy. . . .

Respondents also argue that the testing of nonathletes does not implicate any safety concerns, and that safety is a "crucial factor" in applying the special needs framework [to override the usual protections of the Fourth Amendment]. Respondents are correct that safety factors into the special needs analysis, but the safety interest furthered by drug testing is undoubtedly substantial for all children, athletes and nonathletes alike. We know all too well that drug use carries a variety of health risks for children, including death from overdose.

We also reject respondents' argument that drug testing must presumptively be based upon an individualized reasonable suspicion of wrongdoing because such a testing regime would be less intrusive. In this context, the Fourth Amendment does not require a finding of individualized suspicion, and we decline to impose such a requirement on schools attempting to prevent and detect drug use by students. Moreover, we question whether testing based on individualized suspicion in fact would be less intrusive. Such a regime would place an additional burden on public school teachers who are already tasked with the difficult job of maintaining order and discipline. A program of individualized suspicion might unfairly target members of unpopular groups. The fear of lawsuits resulting from such targeted searches may chill enforcement of the program, rendering it ineffective in combating drug use. In any case, this Court has repeatedly stated that reasonableness under the Fourth Amendment does not require employing the least intrusive means, because "[t]he logic of such elaborate less-restrictive-alternative arguments could raise insuperable barriers to the exercise of virtually all search-and-seizure powers." [United States v. Martinez-Fuerte, 428 U.S. 543, 556-557, n. 12 (1976).]

Finally, we find that testing students who participate in extracurricular activities is a reasonably effective means of addressing the School District's legitimate concerns in preventing, deterring, and detecting drug use. While in *Vernonia* there might have been a closer fit between the testing of athletes and the trial court's finding that the drug problem was "fueled by the 'role model' effect of athletes' drug use," such a finding was not essential to the holding. *Vernonia* did not require the school to test the group of students most likely to use drugs, but rather considered the constitutionality of the program in the context of the public school's custodial responsibilities. Evaluating the Policy in this context, we conclude that the drug testing of Tecumseh students who participate in extracurricular activities effectively serves the School District's interest in protecting the safety and health of its students. . . .

[Omitted are the concurring opinion of Justice Breyer as well as the separate dissenting opinion of Justice O'Connor in which Justice Souter joins.]

Justice GINSBURG, with whom Justice STEVENS, Justice O'CONNOR, and Justice SOUTER join, dissenting.

Seven years ago, in Vernonia School Dist. v. Acton, 515 U.S. 646 (1995), this Court determined that a school district's policy of randomly testing the urine of its student athletes for illicit drugs did not violate the Fourth Amendment. In so ruling, the Court emphasized that drug use "increase[d] the risk of sports-related injury" and that Vernonia's athletes were the "leaders" of an aggressive local "drug culture" that had reached " 'epidemic proportions.' " Id., at 649. Today, the Court relies upon *Vernonia* to permit a school district with a drug problem its superintendent repeatedly described as "not . . . major," to test the urine of an academic team member solely by reason of her participation in a nonathletic, competitive extracurricular activity — participation associated with neither special dangers from, nor particular predilections for, drug use.

"[T]he legality of a search of a student," this Court has instructed, "should depend simply on the reasonableness, under all the circumstances, of the search." New Jersey v. T.L.O., 469 U.S. 325, 341 (1985). Although " 'special needs' inhere in the public school context," see *ante,* at 2564 (quoting Vernonia, 515 U.S., at 653), those needs are not so expansive or malleable as to render reasonable any program of student drug testing a school district elects to install. The particular testing program upheld today is not reasonable; it is capricious, even perverse: Petitioners' policy targets for testing a student population least likely to be at risk from illicit drugs and their damaging effects. I therefore dissent. . . .

NOTES AND QUESTIONS ON *T.L.O.* AND *EARLS*

(1) Attenuation of the Fourth Amendment.   The trilogy of juvenile search cases *(T.L.O.,* Vernonia v. Acton, and *Earls)* reflects a gradual attenuation of Fourth Amendment protection as applied to schoolchildren. According to *T.L.O.,* school officials may conduct a warrantless search provided that they have reasonable suspicion (a lower standard than probable cause) that a student violated a school rule or a criminal law. The Court applied a balancing test (discussed later) to test the reasonableness of the search. However, *T.L.O.* left unresolved whether the "reasonableness" standard for school searches requires individualized suspicion (see footnote 8). Because Vice Principal Choplick had individualized suspicion that T.L.O. had violated school rules, the Supreme Court did not consider the validity

of school searches in the absence of individualized suspicion. *Vernonia,* in sustaining random drug testing for student athletes, subsequently answers that question by rejecting the need for individualized suspicion. *Earls* carries *Vernonia* further by extending random warrantless searches beyond athletes to participants in extracurricular activities.

Should the Court in *T.L.O.* have lowered the standard as it did? In an age of drugs and crime, do public school officials function in a manner similar to law enforcement officers? As such, should they be subject to the same standard of probable cause, especially if the purpose of their search is to uncover evidence of a crime (e.g., drug use, possession of a dangerous weapon)? In refusing to adopt the probable cause standard, the Court was concerned with the desire to spare school officials the necessity of educating themselves about the requirements of probable cause. Is such solicitousness appropriate, given that school officials have to educate themselves about legal requirements for many other purposes, such as immunizations, child abuse, and neglect reporting?

(2) Nature of School Setting and Special Needs Doctrine. *T.L.O.* holds that the Fourth Amendment applies in the public school context; as a result, a search in a school setting must be "reasonable." The Supreme Court then applies a balancing test to determine the reasonableness of the particular search. The test involves a two-pronged inquiry: (a) whether the action was justified at its inception (i.e., was likely to turn up evidence of a violation of the law or school rule) and (b) whether the actual search was reasonably related in scope to the circumstances (i.e., it was not overly intrusive in light of the age and sex of the student and the nature of the infraction).

Subsequently, *Vernonia* upheld the reasonableness of a school policy that required athletes to submit to random, warrantless drug tests based on the "special needs" of the school environment. The determination of reasonableness in *Vernonia* (and later *Earls*) was based on the "special needs" doctrine as derived from a statement in Justice Blackmun's concurring opinion in *T.L.O.* in which he asserts that the requirements of a warrant and probable cause may be dispensed with when exigent circumstances make these requirements impracticable (see supra p. 832). The *Vernonia* Court found the existence of such "special needs" in the need to secure order in the educational setting and to deter drug use in the schools.

In *Vernonia,* the Court balanced (a) the student athletes' legitimate expectations of privacy (finding that athletes have lower expectations of privacy than other students); and (b) the character of the intrusion (finding that the invasion of privacy caused by a urinanalysis test was minimal); against (c) the nature of the governmental concern and the efficacy of the chosen method of meeting that concern (finding that the concern was the deterrence of drug use, and the means was efficacious because athletes serve as role models and also because drugs pose a particular danger to them and to others due to the risk of sport-related injuries). How does the Court in *Earls* apply this balancing test to a similar search of student participants in extracurricular activities? How do the majority and dissent in *Earls* differ on the issue of whether the drug testing of participants in extracurricular activities was justified?

As *Earls* explains, the Supreme Court previously applied the "special needs" doctrine to probationers and railroad employees. How is the public school context similar and/or different? What special characteristics of the school setting justify such a limitation, according to the Court? Do you agree with the Court's assessment? How is the school's mission, as characterized by the Court in *T.L.O.* and *Earls,* similar to or different from that previously characterized by the Court in *Tinker, Hazelwood,* and *Bethel*? See generally Bernard James & Joanne E.K. Larson, The Doctrine of Deference: Shifting Constitutional Presumptions and the Supreme Court's Restatement of Student Rights After Board of Education v. Earls, 56 S.C. L. Rev. 1, 35-37 (2004) (discussing changing views of schools' mission).

What criteria does the Court in *Earls* use to determine whether a given need is "special"? Do you think Justice Blackmun, whose concurring opinion in *T.L.O.* was the basis for the special needs doctrine, would agree with the application of the doctrine in *Earls*? That is, does *Earls* represent one of "those exceptional circumstances [like "stop and frisks" during the commission of crimes or border patrol stops] in which special needs, beyond the normal need for law enforcement, make the warrant and probable-cause requirement impracticable," (supra p. 833) such that a court is entitled to substitute its balancing for the view of the Framers [of the Constitution]?

The special needs doctrine has received its share of scholarly criticism. See Robert D. Dodson, Ten Years of Randomized Jurisprudence: Amending the Special Needs Doctrine, 51 S.C. L. Rev. 258, 274 (2000) ("More disturbing is the fact that the Court has never invalidated a law under the special needs balancing test"); Irene Merker Rosenberg, The Public Schools Have a "Special Need" for Their Students' Urine, 31 Hofstra L. Rev. 303, 307 (2002) (criticizing the "special needs" doctrine for its lack of fixed or objective criteria and also for its "double counting" of the governmental interest — once to determine if the need is special, and then again in the balancing of governmental vs. private interests).

(3) Striking the Balance: Weighing Minors' Privacy Rights.   As explained earlier, *T.L.O.* set forth a two-prong test of reasonableness to evaluate the constitutionality of a particular search: whether the search was justified at its inception and whether it was reasonably related in scope to the circumstances (i.e., not overly intrusive in light of the age and sex of the student and the nature of the infraction). In *T.L.O.*, was the vice principal's search justified at its inception? Was it reasonably related to the objectives of the search? How intrusive was the search in light of the age and sex of the student and the nature of the infraction? In *Earls,* the Court similarly dismisses the privacy concerns of the participants in extracurricular activities who must submit to urinanalysis tests. Consider the following comments regarding the privacy interest at issue in the urinanalysis testing of students:

> The unfortunate consequence of [the Court's] finding [of a negligible invasion of privacy] is that it completely minimizes the horrors of adolescence — the time when male junior high students begin growing pubic hair and become self-conscious of their genitalia and the new and, often, uncomfortable bodily responses that accompany puberty. Likewise, junior high is often the time when female students begin menstruating. Imagine the humiliation and embarrassment of a menstruating junior high student required to provide school officials with a urine sample that will possibly reveal that she is taking birth control pills, is

HIV positive, is on medication for depression, or perhaps suffers from a sexually transmitted disease. To assert that providing a urine sample during these formative and agonizing years presents only a "negligible" privacy violation denies a very real fact of adolescence — every little act or action is generally amplified and overwhelming. It is disingenuous to suggest that taking a state-compelled urine sample from an adolescent does not invoke the most intimate of privacy interests. [Meg Penrose, Shedding Rights, Shredding Rights: A Critical Examination of Students' Privacy Rights and the "Special Needs" Doctrine After *Earls,* 3 Nev. L.J. 411, 435 (2002/2003).]

In *Earls,* the Court analogizes the level of intrusion of a urinanalysis to that of physical examinations and vaccinations. Do you agree?

Was the character of the intrusion mitigated, as the Court suggests, by the nature of the specimen collections and the limited uses to which the test results are put? Are you reassured by the Court's assertion that the results of the drug test would remain confidential? See Aaron Marcus, Comment, Beyond the Classroom: A Reality-Based Approach to Student Drug Testing, 3 Whittier J. Child & Fam. Advoc. 365, 390 (2004) (claiming that the Court undervalued the intrusiveness of the disclosure of students' private medical information and suggesting that schools will break confidentiality by informing parents); Dodson, supra, at 277 (pointing out that prosecutors frequently use evidence obtained in school searches in criminal prosecutions and delinquency proceedings).

(4) Limits of **Earls.** Both *Vernonia* and *Earls* upheld limitations on the Fourth Amendment rights of *some* public school students. *Vernonia* applies to student athletes, who, according to the Court, have lowered expectations of privacy because of their practice of dressing and undressing in communal locker rooms. *Earls* applies to participants in competitive extracurricular activities. Do you agree with the Court's characterization that the latter students "voluntarily subject themselves to many of the same intrusions on their privacy as do athletes"?

Does the Court recognize *any* limits to the ability of a school to conduct random warrantless searches? That is, do *Vernonia* and *Earls* permit the random suspicion-less testing of all public school students? See Jacob Brooks, Note, Constitutional Law — Suspicionless Drug Testing of Students Participating in Non-Athletic Competitive School Activities: Are All Students Next? Board of Education v. Earls, 4 Wyo. L. Rev. 365 (2004); Penrose, supra, at 412 (*Earls* "seemingly limitless breadth . . . sounds the death knell of the assurance that students do not shed their Constitutional rights at the school house gate"); Brad Setterberg, Note, Privacy Changes, Precedent Doesn't: Why Board of Education v. Earls Was Judged by the Wrong Standard, 40 Hous. L. Rev. 1183, 1202 (2003) (so arguing). Does the governmental interest in deterring drug use justify such a significant expansion of schools' investigative authority? In its reliance on the policy justification of the drug epidemic, has the Supreme Court "supplemented a concern for safety with rhetoric of fear"? Marcus, supra, at 395.

Some state courts reject *Earls* based on state constitutional provisions. See, e.g., York v. Wahkiakum Sch. Dist., 178 P.3d 995 (Wash. 2008) (state right to privacy); Theodore v. Delaware Valley Sch. Dist., 761 A.2d 652 (Pa. Commnw. Ct. 2000), *aff'd*, 836 A.2d 76 (2003) (state version of Fourth Amendment).

(5) Unanswered Questions.   *T.L.O., Vernonia,* and *Earls* left several unanswered questions.

a. Should the exclusionary rule apply to exclude evidence illegally seized by public school officials?   In *T.L.O.,* the state originally appealed to the United States Supreme Court on the issue of whether the exclusionary rule should bar consideration in delinquency proceedings of evidence that was illegally seized by school officials without the involvement of law enforcement officials. However, the Court decided to address only the threshold Fourth Amendment issue (see supra p. 828 and footnote 3). Since *T.L.O.,* a majority of states have held that the exclusionary rule applies to delinquency proceedings. See Irene Merker Rosenberg, A Door Left Open: Applicability of the Fourth Amendment Exclusionary Rule to Juvenile Court Delinquency Hearings, 24 Am. J. Crim. L. 29, 58-59 (1996).

If the exclusionary rule applies, should evidence be excluded from school disciplinary proceedings as well as delinquency proceedings? Compare Juan C. v. Cortines, 647 N.Y.S.2d 491 (App. Div. 1996) (holding that the exclusionary rule should apply in suspension hearing), *rev'd on other grounds,* 679 N.E.2d 1061 (N.Y. 1997), with Thompson v. Carthage Sch. Dist., 87 F.3d 979 (8th Cir. 1996) (rejecting application of exclusionary rule in disciplinary hearing). See also Dodson, supra, at 286 (advocating exclusion of illegally seized evidence from criminal prosecutions and delinquency proceedings); Mai Linh Spencer, Note, Suppress or Suspend: New York's Exclusionary Rule in School Disciplinary Proceedings, 72 N.Y.U. L. Rev. 1494 (1997).

b. What standard should apply if school officials conduct the search "in concert with" or "at the behest of" law enforcement?   *T.L.O.* left this question unresolved (see footnote 7) because Vice Principal Choplick acted alone in searching T.L.O.'s belongings. In setting the standard, case law makes distinctions regarding whether (1) the law enforcement officer is responsible to a law enforcement agency (applying the probable cause standard) or the school (applying reasonable suspicion standard); (2) the law enforcement officer initiates the search in furtherance of the school's mission to maintain a proper educational environment (applying reason able suspicion); (3) the purpose of the search is to uncover evidence that violates a school rule (applying reasonable suspicion) or to uncover evidence pertaining to a potential criminal violation (applying probable cause); and (4) the situation is potentially dangerous — for example, involving firearms (applying reasonable suspicion). See Michael Pinard, From the Classroom to the Courtroom: Reassessing Fourth Amendment Standards in Public School Searches Involving Law Enforcement Authorities, 45 Ariz. L. Rev. 1067, 1083-1088 (2003) (analyzing different standards and suggesting reforms).

(6) Constitutionality of Other School Searches.   Another question unanswered by *T.L.O., Vernonia,* and *Earls* is what standard should apply to searches of students' personal belongings in lockers and automobiles parked on school grounds and to canine searches (see footnote 3). The trilogy of cases seems to imply that "searches in areas previously deemed murky, involving metal detectors, dogs, and other devices, [henceforth will] be subject to fewer Fourth Amendment challenges." James & Larson, supra, at 51.

a. Locker Searches.   Many courts have held that lockers are school property and therefore students have no legitimate expectation of privacy therein.

Rebecca N. Cordero, No Expectation of Privacy: Should School Officials Be Able to Search Students' Lockers Without Any Suspicion of Wrong Doing? A Study of In re Patrick Y. and Its Effect on Maryland Public School Students, 31 U. Balt. L. Rev. 305, 316 (2002). In these jurisdictions, random locker searches are permissible without the necessity of individualized suspicion. See, e.g., In re Patrick Y., 746 A.2d 405 (Md. 2000); Shoemaker v. State, 971 S.W.2d 178 (Tex. App. 1998); In re Isiah B., 500 N.W.2d 637 (Wis. 1993). Other courts have held that students do have legitimate expectations of privacy in their lockers. See, e.g., State v. Jones, 666 N.W.2d 142 (Iowa 2003) (holding that, despite student's legitimate expectation of privacy, search was permissible because it was conducted as part of routine annual cleanout of lockers). Some courts base their decisions on whether the schools have an explicit policy and give notice of it. See, e.g., Commonwealth v. Snyder, 597 N.E.2d 1363 (Mass. 1992) (existence of school policy established legitimacy of students' expectation of privacy).

Jurisdictions holding that students have no expectation of privacy in school lockers adopt one of the following rationales: (1) students' expectation of privacy is diminished because school officials have a master key; (2) lockers are school property; and (3) the expectation of privacy is diminished because lockers are located in public areas. Cordero, supra, at 317. On the other hand, those jurisdictions that support students' expectation of privacy take the position that lockers are for students' exclusive use and also that the lock indicates restricted entry. Id. at 318.

b. Automobile Searches on School Grounds. Analogizing car searches to locker searches, many courts hold that students do not have a legitimate expectation of privacy in cars that are parked on school premises. Christine Pedigo, Protecting Students' Fourth Amendment Rights: Alternatives to School-Mandated Urinalysis, 4 U.C. Davis J. Juv. L. & Pol'y 175, 193 (2000). See also J. Bates McIntyre, Note, Empowering Schools to Search: The Effect of Growing Drug and Violence Concerns, 2000 U. Ill. L. Rev. 1025,1046 (2000) (suggesting that students enjoy a lowered expectation of privacy in their automobiles, especially if a school requires them to sign a parking agreement in which students agree to abide by school rules and policies). This view is in accordance with the general rule that permits warrantless searches of an automobile if police have probable cause to believe the car contains contraband or evidence of criminal activity (based on the rationale of the inherent mobility of an automobile). Annual Review of Criminal Procedure, Note, Search Incident to Valid Arrest, 91 Geo. L. J. 54, 85 (2003).

c. Metal Detectors. In the wake of increasing incidents of school violence in the 1990s, school officials became increasingly concerned about the presence of weapons on school grounds. As a result, Congress enacted the Safe School Act of 1994, 20 U.S.C. §§5961, 5962 (2000), which permits school districts with high crime rates to compete for federal grants for violence prevention. The Act provides that federal funds may be used for the purchase of metal detectors to prevent weapons from being brought to school (id. at §5965(a)(13)). In response, the use of metal detectors in schools increased significantly.

Most courts hold that the use of metal detectors in schools does not violate the Fourth Amendment. For example, in In re F.B., 726 A.2d 361 (Pa. 1999), the Pennsylvania Supreme Court upheld the constitutionality of a search that confiscated a Swiss army knife. Applying the reasonableness test of *Vernonia,* the court reasoned: (1) students have a limited privacy interest; (2) the particular student suffered a minimal invasion of privacy by the scanner passing over his clothing; and (3) the government had a strong interest in keeping weapons out of the schools. Do you agree that the standard by which to assess the constitutionality of metal detector searches should be "reasonable suspicion" because such searches do not constitute police action? See, e.g., People v. Pruitt, 662 N.E.2d 540 (Ill. App. Ct. 1996) (upholding the constitutionality of a metal detector search directed by a school official although carried out by police). Are metal detectors an effective means of reducing school violence? See Robert S. Johnson, Metal Detector Searches: An Effective Means to Help Keep Weapons Out of Schools, 29 J.L. & Educ. 197, 200-201 (2000) (so arguing).

The United States Supreme Court has also addressed the issue of weapons in schools. In United States v. Lopez, 514 U.S. 549 (1995), a high school student was arrested, on the basis of an anonymous tip, for bringing a 38-caliber handgun to school. The student (Lopez) was carrying the unloaded gun and five bullets for another person who planned to use the weapon in a gang war. Lopez was prosecuted for violating the federal Gun-Free School Zones Act of 1990, 18 U.S.C. §922(q)(1)(A)-2(A) (1994), prohibiting possession of a firearm within 1,000 feet of a school zone. The Supreme Court held that Congress exceeded the scope of its authority under the Commerce Clause in enacting the Act, concluding that bearing weapons near schools does not substantially affect interstate commerce. Congress subsequently reauthorized the Gun-Free School Zones Act pursuant to the Spending Clause (codified at 20 U.S.C. §7151). Also, many states now have zero-tolerance laws modeled after the federal Act.

d. Dog Sniffs.   School searches are sometimes conducted by specially trained canine units. To what extent does "dog sniffing" violate a student's constitutional rights? Most courts hold that a dog sniff of a student's *property* is not a search within the meaning of the Fourth Amendment, in line with Supreme Court authority. See United States v. Place, 462 U.S. 696 (1983) (holding that dog sniffings of luggage are not subject to the Fourth Amendment). However, searches of a minor's *person* have engendered more disagreement. James & Larson, supra, at 51. How intrusive is dog sniffing according to the "reasonableness" factors set forth in *Vernonia* and *Earls:* (1) the privacy interest, (2) the nature of the intrusion, and (3) the nature and immediacy of the governmental concern and the efficacy of the means used? In Horton v. Goose Creek Independent School District, 690 F.2d 470 (5th Cir. 1982), *reh'g denied,* 693 F.2d 524 (5th Cir. 1982), the Fifth Circuit Court of Appeals held a canine search unconstitutional, based in part on the fact that the search was unjustified because of the student's strong interest in bodily integrity and the lack of individualized suspicion. Is *Horton* valid after *Vernonia* and *Earls*? See James & Larson, supra, at 51 (speculating that "dog sniffs as part of a random, suspicionless search policy enjoy a presumption of validity after *Earls*"). In a recent Canadian case, the Supreme Court of Canada held that evidence obtained through the use of drug-sniffing dogs in a public high school was inadmissible under the Canadian Charter of Rights and Freedoms. R. v. M. (A.), [2008], 1 S.C.R. 569 (Can.).

e. Strip Searches.   Courts have upheld the constitutionality of strip searches of school children. Rosemary Spellman, Comment, Strip Searches of Juveniles and the Fourth Amendment: A Delicate Balance of Protection and Privacy, 22 J. Juv. L. 159, 161 (2001/2002). Some courts exempt school officials from liability based on the doctrine of qualified immunity. See, e.g., Thomas ex rel. Thomas v. Roberts, 323 F.3d 950, 951 (11th Cir. 2003); Doe v. Renfrow, 475 F. Supp. 1012 (N.D. Ind. 1979), *aff'd in part, remanded in part on other grounds,* 631 F.2d 91 (7th Cir. 1980), *reh'g denied,* 635 F.2d 582 (7th Cir. 1980). Only six states (California, Iowa, Oklahoma, South Carolina, Washington, and Wisconsin) expressly prohibit strip searches by school officials. Dana Ingrassia, Note, Thomas ex rel. Thomas v. Roberts: Another Photo Finish Where School Officials Win the Race for Qualified Immunity, 26 Whittier L. Rev. 621, 622 (2004).

Some courts that uphold strip searches of students insist on individualized suspicion. See, e.g., Holmes v. Montgomery, 2003 WL 1786518 (Ky. Ct. App. 2003) (reversing summary judgment against parents in school officials' strip search of middle school students and identifying prior case law that upholds such searches of students based on individualized suspicion). Other courts find reasonable those strip searches that are intended for the purpose of finding weapons or drugs. See, e.g., Cornfield v. Consolidated High Sch. Dist., 991 F.2d 1316 (7th Cir. 1993); Williams v. Ellington, 936 F.2d 881 (6th Cir. 1991).

In addition, some juvenile detention facilities have routine policies that permit strip searches. See, e.g., Cuesta v. School Board of Miami-Dade County, 285 F.3d 962 (11th Cir. 2002) (holding that strip search of juvenile in pretrial detention facilities does not require probable cause because of security danger). But cf. Smook v. Minnehaha County, 353 F. Supp. 2d 1059 (D.S.D. 2005) (holding that detention center policy of strip searching juvenile nonfelon detainees violates Fourth Amendment). For a critique of strip searches at juvenile detention facilities, see Jessica R. Feierman & Riya S. Shah, Protecting Personhood: Legal Strategies to Combat the Use of Strip Searches on Youth in Detention, 60 Rutgers L. Rev. 67 (2007).

In Redding v. Safford Unified School District, 504 F.3d 828 (9th Cir. 2007), *vacated on rehearing en banc*, 531 F.3d 1071 (9th Cir. 2008), public middle school officials unsuccessfully strip-searched a 13-year-old honor student for prescription-strength ibuprofen. The search, based on a self-exculpatory uncorroborated tip from another student, took place in a nurse's office in front of two women. Embarrassed and humiliated, the student brought a §1983 action against the school district and school officials, alleging that the search violated her Fourth Amendment rights. Initially, the district court granted summary judgment for the defendants, and the court of appeals affirmed. However, upon rehearing en banc, the Ninth Circuit Court of Appeals ruled that the strip search was not justified at its inception and was not reasonably related in scope to the circumstances because no information pointed to the conclusion that the pills were hidden under the student's panties or bra, and there was no immediate danger to students posed by the possession of prescription-strength ibuprofen pills. The U.S. Supreme Court granted certiorari. Safford Unified Sch. Dist. v. Redding, 2009 WL 104299 (2009). The Court will address the constitutionality of the search as well as the school officials' liability for damages.

What is the harm suffered by juveniles as a result of strip searches? Is a strip search analogous to rape? Are strip searches more damaging to juveniles than to adults? Research on strip searches of juveniles concludes that lower courts fail to take into account the nature and potential impact of the strip search or the significance of the child's age. Steven F. Shatz et al., The Strip Search of Children and the Fourth Amendment, 26 U.S.F. L. Rev. 1 (1991). Should strip searches of children be per se unconstitutional? See Scott A. Garnter, Note, Strip Searches of Juveniles: What Johnny Really Learned in School and How Local School Boards Can Help Solve the Problem, 70 S. Cal. L. Rev. 921 (1997) (so arguing).

(7) Other Search-Related Issues. The issue of minority is relevant with regard to other aspects of the law of search and seizure. For example, there are circumstances that permit the valid arrest of a child, thus allowing a search incident to an arrest, in circumstances in which an adult could not be arrested. See James D. v. California, 741 P.2d 161 (Cal. 1987) (discussed supra p. 824). In addition, if a youth has acquiesced in or consented to a search, presumably the determination of the "voluntariness" of the consent may take into account the factor of the youth's age. See In re Williams, 267 N.Y.S.2d 91 (Fam. Ct. 1966) (15-year-old's submission to authority does not constitute consent to search). Indeed, the American Law Institute's Model Code of Pre-Arraignment Procedure (§240.2(1)(a)148 (1975)) would go much further and require parental consent to search if a youth is under age 16.

The parent-child relationship is also relevant in other ways in the context of searches. May parents consent to a warrantless search directed against a child living at home? A number of courts have so held. See, e.g., United States v. Evans, 27 F.3d 1219 (7th Cir. 1994); State v. Rodriguez, 828 P.2d 636 (Wash. Ct. App. 1992). On the other hand, may children consent to a warrantless search directed against a parent in the home? Do children have the same access and control to the family's living space? Are children as cognizant of the implications of their consent and their ability to refuse consent? See generally Matt McCaughey, Note, And a Child Shall Lead Them: The Validity of Children's Consent to Warrantless Searches of the Family Home, 34 U. Louisville J. Fam. L. 747 (1995-1996).

(8) Problem. School officials from several Indiana high schools, concerned about drug and alcohol use, formulate a new policy, which is adopted by the school board. In addition to permitting testing for students on the basis of individualized suspicion, the policy requires a drug and alcohol test for any student who (1) possesses or uses tobacco products; (2) is suspended for three or more days for fighting; (3) is habitually truant; or (4) violates any other school rule that results in at least a three-day suspension. Test results are disclosed only to parents. Although students are not punished, they may be expelled if they refuse to participate in a drug education program. Students who refuse to undergo a test are considered to have admitted unlawful substance use.

James Willis, a freshman, is suspended for fighting with a fellow student. On his return to school, James is informed that he will be tested for drug and alcohol use. He refuses and is suspended again. He is then advised that if he refuses again to submit to a urinanalysis test, he will be deemed to have admitted unlawful drug use and will be expelled. James files suit, claiming that the policy violates the Fourth and Fourteenth Amendments. Although no school official observed James using drugs or alcohol at any time, the school contends that the fight itself was enough to create a reasonable suspicion that James was using an illegal substance and also claims that students who use illegal substances are "more than twice as likely to get into physical fights." What result? See Willis by Willis v. Anderson Community Sch., 158 F.3d 415 (7th Cir. 1998).

4. Notice of Charges

You will recall that *Gault* required that "the child *and* his parents or guardian be notified, in writing, of the specific charge or factual allegations. . . ." 387 U.S. 1, 33 (1967) (emphasis added). Obviously, this notice requirement does not apply to adults who are accused of a crime and thus distinguishes delinquency proceedings. Consider the purposes served by giving notice to a youth's parents. Whose rights are violated by the failure to give the parents notice? The youth's? The parents'? Both? Does the omission amount to a constitutional violation? Compare McDonald v. Black, 820 F.2d 260 (8th Cir. 1987); United States v. Doe, 155 F.3d 1070 (9th Cir. 1998) (both holding that juvenile defendant was not deprived of due process by lack of parental notification) with In re J.P.J., 485 N.E.2d 848 (Ill. 1985) (adequate notice to minor and his parents is a requirement of due process).

May a parent waive various procedural rights, such as notice requirements, on behalf of his child? If the minor has notice, but his parents are not given adequate notice, does this necessarily vitiate the juvenile court's jurisdiction? See United States v. Watts, 513 F.2d 5 (10th Cir. 1975) (parental notice is a prophylactic safeguard but not a "separate and independent" constitutional requirement); State v. Whitter, 245 So. 2d 913 (Fla. Dist. Ct. App. 1971) (when parent has actual notice, failure to comply with statutory notice requirement does not render a judgment void).

Suppose the juvenile's parents are divorced. Must a state use due diligence in finding and serving the noncustodial parent? Compare In re J.P.J., supra (service of process adequate although divorced father not served and father's whereabouts unknown) with In re T.M.F., 508 N.E.2d 1160 (Ill. App. Ct. 1987) (rule of In re J.P.J. not applicable when mother's whereabouts are known). Does failure to provide the required notice deprive a court of subject matter jurisdiction? See In re T.B., 382 N.E.2d 1292 (Ill. App. Ct. 1978) (juvenile court lacked jurisdiction when a state did not exercise due diligence in trying to find mother's address and failed to give mother proper notice).

Following *Gault,* Congress amended the Federal Juvenile Delinquency Act, 18 U.S.C. §5033 (2000), to provide for parental notification whenever a minor is taken into custody for a federal offense. The arresting officer must immediately notify the parents that the juvenile is in custody and explain to the parents both the juvenile's rights and the nature of the juvenile's offense. However, the Act does not clarify the meaning of "immediately" or specify which of the juvenile's rights must be explained to the parents (i.e., whether notification that the minor is in custody also requires notification of the minor's *Miranda* rights).

The Ninth Circuit Court of Appeals addressed many of these gaps. See, e.g., United States v. Juvenile (RRA-A), 229 F.3d 737 (9th Cir. 2000) (holding that a border agent did not "immediately" advise juvenile of her rights by waiting four hours to give *Miranda* warnings and also that he violated notification provision by failing to personally contact the Mexican consulate when unable to reach minor's parents by phone and by failing to wait a reasonable amount of time to begin interrogation); United States v. Doe (*Doe III*), 170 F.3d 1162 (9th Cir. 1999) (holding that parental notification of the juvenile's *Miranda* rights must be given contemporaneously with the parental notification of custody). For those juveniles whose parents live outside the United States, the government may notify the relevant foreign consulate in the United States if it is not feasible to provide parental notification (e.g., if the parents do not have a phone). United States v. Doe, 701 F.2d 819, 822 (9th Cir. 1983).

May juveniles waive their right to parental notification (e.g., if they do not want their parents to know of their arrest)? See United States v. L.M.K., 149 F.3d 1033 (9th Cir. 1998) (holding that parental notification requirement is nonwaivable by the minor).

5. The Voluntariness of Juvenile Confessions

The admissibility of a juvenile's confession has been frequently litigated. In two cases decided before *Gault,* the Supreme Court held that the confession of a juvenile was not "voluntary" and that its admission as evidence therefore violated the juvenile's due process rights under the Fourteenth Amendment. In each case, the Court made plain that the age of the accused was a relevant factor in applying the voluntariness test.

The first of these cases, Haley v. Ohio, 332 U.S. 596 (1948), involved a 15-year-old who confessed after police questioning from midnight to 5 A.M. Writing for a plurality of the Court, Justice Douglas stated:

> What transpired would make us pause for careful inquiry if a mature man were involved. And when, as here, a mere child — an easy victim of the law — is before us, special care in scrutinizing the record must be used. Age 15 is a tender and difficult age for a boy of any race. He cannot be judged by the more exacting standards of maturity. That which would leave a man cold and unimpressed can overawe and overwhelm a lad in his early teens. This is the period of great instability which the crisis of adolescence produces. A 15-year-old lad, questioned through the dead of night by relays of police, is a ready victim of the inquisition. Mature men possibly might stand the ordeal from midnight to 5 A.M. But we cannot believe that a lad of tender years is a match for the police in such a contest. He needs counsel and support if he is not to become the victim first of fear, then of panic. He needs someone on whom to lean lest the overpowering presence of the law, as he knows it, crush him. No friend stood at the side of this 15-year-old boy as the police, working in relays, questioned him hour after hour, from midnight until dawn. No lawyer stood guard to make sure that the police went so far and no farther, to see to it that they stopped short of the point where he became the victim of coercion. No counsel or friend was called during the critical hours of questioning. A photographer was admitted once this lad broke and confessed. But not even a gesture towards getting a lawyer for him was ever made. [332 U.S. at 599-600.]

The second case, Gallegos v. Colorado, 370 U.S. 49 (1962), involved a 14-year-old boy's formal confession. Writing the opinion for the Court, Justice Douglas stated:

> The fact that petitioner was only 14 years old puts this case on the same footing as Haley v. Ohio, supra. There was here no evidence of prolonged questioning. But the five-day-detention — during which time the boy's mother unsuccessfully tried to see him and he was cut off from contact with any lawyer or adult advisory — gives the case an ominous cast. The prosecution says that the boy was advised of his right to counsel, but that he did not ask either for a lawyer or for his parents. But a 14-year-old boy, no matter how sophisticated, is unlikely to have any conception of what will confront him when he is made accessible only to the police. That is to say, we deal with a person who is not equal to the police in knowledge and understanding of the consequences of the questions and answers being recorded and who is unable to know how to protect his own interests or how to get the benefits of his constitutional rights.
>
> The prosecution says that the youth and immaturity of the petitioner and the five-day detention are irrelevant, because the basic ingredients of the confession came tumbling out as soon as he was arrested. But if we took that position, it would, with all deference, be in callous disregard of this boy's constitutional rights. He cannot be compared with an adult in full possession of his senses and knowledgeable of the consequences of his admissions. He would have no way of knowing what the consequences of his confession were without advice as to his rights — from someone concerned with securing him those rights — and without the aid of more mature judgment as to the steps he should take in the predicament in which he found himself. A lawyer or an adult relative or friend could have given the petitioner the protection which his own immaturity could not. Adult advice would have put him on a less unequal footing with his interrogators. Without some adult protection against this inequality, a 14-year-old boy would not be able to know, let alone assert, such constitutional rights as he had. To allow this conviction to stand would, in effect, be to treat him as if he had no constitutional rights. [Id. at 53-55.]

The United States Supreme Court examined issues surrounding juvenile confessions in two subsequent cases (Fare v. Michael C., 442 U.S. 707 (1979), and Yarborough v. Alvarado, 541 U.S. 652 (2004)). In *Fare,* the Court adopted the totality-of-the-circumstances test to evaluate the voluntariness of a juvenile's confession. In prior case law, the Court had emphasized that "special care" must be taken when assessing the voluntariness of a juvenile's confession; however, in *Fare,* the Court applied the adult totality standard. This test considers factors such as age, intelligence, previous experience with police officers, and the circumstances surrounding the interrogation (e.g., length of the interrogation, etc.). Following *Fare,* a majority of states adopted this standard for juvenile offenders. (*Fare* is discussed in more detail infra p. 855.)

However, dissatisfaction with *Fare* led some states to adopt a per se rule that treats interrogations of juveniles with more care. Although there is some variation in states' per se tests, the most common test is the "interested adult" rule, which requires courts to consider whether the juvenile had an opportunity to consult (before or during the interrogation) with an interested adult before waiving the privilege against self-incrimination.

Several highly publicized cases focus attention on the voluntariness of juvenile confessions. In Chicago in 1999, police arrested two boys, ages 7 and 8, on charges of murdering an 11-year-old girl for her bicycle. The boys confessed to the crime, but police dropped the charges when investigators discovered semen in the victim's underpants that matched that of a known sex offender. See Robyn E. Blumner, Children Confess Whether They Did It or Not, St. Petersburg Times, May 2, 1999, at D6. In another case, an 11-year-old confessed to murdering a toddler at her grandparents' day care center. Evidence subsequently suggested that the toddler was battered by her mother's boyfriend prior to arriving at the day care center. In re L.M., 933 S.W.2d 276 (Tex. Ct. App. 1999). Also, in San Diego, a 14-year-old boy confessed to killing his 12-year-old sister, who was stabbed to death in her bedroom. DNA evidence eventually linked a transient in the neighborhood to the slaying. See Nashiba F. Boyd, Comment, "I Didn't Do It, I Was Forced to Say That I Did": The Problem of Coerced Juvenile Confessions, and Proposed Federal Legislation to Prevent Them, 47 How. L.J. 395, 395-396 (2004).

Psychological research substantiates juveniles' propensity for false confession under police pressure. Data suggest that youths are apt to make choices that result in their complying with adult authority figures, such as confessing to police, rather than remaining silent.[77] Children often fail to understand the long-term implications of their confessions, often thinking that if they confess they will be allowed to go home. Moreover, children are especially likely to confess falsely when they are confronted with police pressure in the form of tactics presenting false evidence of their guilt.[78]

In response to the problems of juvenile confessions, commentators have proposed various reforms. Some commentators suggest that parental presence is a necessary but not sufficient condition and that police should videotape custodial interrogations. See Lawrence Schlam, Police Interrogation of Children and State Constitutions: Why Not Videotape the MTV Generation?, 26 U. Tol. L. Rev. 901 (1995); Welsh S. White, False Confessions and the Constitution: Safeguards Against Untrustworthy Confessions, 32 Harv.-C.R.-C.L. L. Rev. 105, 153 (1997). Another commentator proposes federal legislation to create the role of "juvenile justice officer" to explain *Miranda* warnings to juveniles, alert the court about improper police tactics, and notify parents of custodial interrogations. What do you think of these suggestions?

6. *Miranda* Rights

In Miranda v. Arizona, 384 U.S. 436 (1966), the Supreme Court held that a person in custody must be informed that (1) he has a right to remain silent; (2) anything he

---

[77] Thomas Grisso & Laurence Steinberg, Juveniles' Competence to Stand Trial: A Comparison of Adolescents' and Adults' Capacities as Trial Defendants, 27 Law & Hum. Behav. 333, 353-356 (2003). See also Barry C. Feld, Police Interrogation of Juveniles: An Empirical Study of Policy and Practice, 97 J. Crim. L. & Criminology 219 (2006); Christine S. Scott-Hayward, Explaining Juvenile False Confessions: Adolescent Development and Police Interrogation, 31 Law & Psychol. Rev. 53 (2007).

[78] Allison D. Redlich & Gail S. Goodman, Taking Responsibility for an Act Not Committed: The Influence of Age and Suggestibility, 27 Law & Hum. Behav. 141, 151-152 (2003).

says can be used against him; (3) he has the right to consult with an attorney and to have an attorney with him during an interrogation; and (4) an attorney will be appointed for him if he cannot afford one. When *Miranda* requirements are applied to juveniles in custody, special issues arise.

a. When Is a Juvenile in Custody in Order to Trigger *Miranda* Warnings?

The United States Supreme Court has explored the requirements that trigger a pre-interrogation *Miranda* warning for a juvenile suspect. In a case focusing on the availability of federal habeas corpus relief, the Court had occasion to consider the relevance of age in the determination of whether a suspect is in "custody" for *Miranda* purposes. According to the traditional rule, all "custodial" interviews require a pre-interrogation *Miranda* warning. The determination of whether a suspect is in "custody" is an objective test considering the totality of the circumstances: how a reasonable person in the suspect's situation would perceive the circumstances.

In Yarborough v. Alvarado, 541 U.S. 652 (2004), a police detective asked the parents of 17-year-old Michael Alvarado to bring him to the police station for questioning. There, Alvarado confessed to his role in an attempted robbery and murder (i.e., his participation in the robbery and concealment of the gun) during an interrogation that was conducted without his being advised of his *Miranda* rights. The boy later claimed that his parents had asked to be present during the two-hour interview that led to his confession, but police refused. At trial, Alvarado was convicted after unsuccessfully attempting to suppress his statement on *Miranda* grounds.

The appellate court affirmed the conviction, contending that Alvarado had not been in custody during the interview so that no *Miranda* warning was required. The state supreme court denied review, and Alvarado filed a petition for a writ of habeas corpus in federal court. The federal district court agreed with the state court that Alvarado had not been in custody for *Miranda* purposes. However, the Ninth Circuit Court of Appeals reversed. In holding that Alvarado should have received *Miranda* warnings because the interview was "custodial," the court took into account the factors of age and experience in the determination of whether an interrogation is "custodial." Alvarado v. Hickman, 316 F.3d 841 (9th Cir. 2002). The case was appealed to the United States Supreme Court.

Because *Alvarado* involved a plea for habeas corpus relief, federal law applied (i.e., the Antiterrorism and Effective Death Penalty Act of 1996 (AEDPA), Pub. L. No. 104-132, 110 Stat. 1214 (2000) (codified in scattered sections of 18 U.S.C. and 28 U.S.C.)). Under AEDPA, a federal court may grant an application for a writ of habeas corpus on behalf of a person held pursuant to a state-court judgment if the state-court adjudication resulted in a decision that was "contrary to, or involved an unreasonable application of, clearly established federal law, as determined by the Supreme Court." 28 U.S.C. §2254(d)(1) (2000). Although the Ninth Circuit ruled that the state court unreasonably applied clearly established law in holding that Alvarado was not in custody for *Miranda* purposes, the United States Supreme Court disagreed. The Supreme Court held that the California court's application of the law was reasonable because, in Justice Kennedy's words, "fair-minded jurists could disagree over whether Alvarado was in custody" (541 U.S. at 664). In so ruling, the Court did not establish guidelines regarding when a minor is in "custody" for purposes of *Miranda* warnings. Nonetheless, the *Yarborough* majority implied that a suspect's age and experience are irrelevant in the determination.

> [B]y labeling the test [for whether an interrogation is custodial] "objective" when it clearly contains a subjective element, the Court implied that a suspect's age is irrelevant in determining whether an interrogation is custodial. And it conclusively confirmed that a suspect's past experience with the police should never be a part of the equation. [Craig M. Bradley, Supreme Court Review on 'Custody,' 41 Trial 58, 59-60 (Feb. 2005).]

However, Justice Breyer in his dissent (and Justice O'Connor in her concurring opinion) asserts that age could be a relevant factor in the determination of whether an interrogation is "custodial" for *Miranda* purposes. Contending that a juvenile suspect in Alvarado's position would have believed that he was in "custody," Breyer argues:

> What reasonable person in the circumstances — brought to a police station by his parents at police request, put in a small interrogation room, questioned for a solid two hours, and confronted with claims that there is strong evidence that he participated in a serious crime, could have thought to himself, "Well, anytime I want to leave I can just get up and walk out"? If the person harbored any doubts, would he still think he might be free to leave once he recalls that the police officer has just refused to let his parents remain with him during questioning? Would he still think that he, rather than the officer, controls the situation? There is only one possible answer to these questions. . . .
>
> The fact that Alvarado was 17 helps to show that he was unlikely to have felt free to ignore his parents' request to come to the station. And a 17-year-old is more likely than, say, a 35-year-old, to take a police officer's assertion of authority to keep parents outside the room as an assertion of authority to keep their child inside as well. . . .
>
> Common sense, and an understanding of the law's basic purpose in this area, are enough to make clear that Alvarado's age — an objective, widely shared characteristic about which the police plainly knew — is also relevant to the inquiry. Unless one is prepared to pretend that Alvarado is someone he is not, a middle-aged gentleman, well-versed in police practices, it seems to me clear that the California courts made a serious mistake [in ruling that he was not in custody so that no *Miranda* warning was required. 541 U.S. at 670-671, 676.]

b. Parental Role

Miranda has been interpreted to mean that if either a child or the child's parents ask for a lawyer, questioning by officials must stop. What if the youth asks for his parents? Must questioning stop? See People v. Burton, 491 P.2d 793 (Cal. 1971):

> In this case we are called upon to decide whether a minor's request to see his parents "reasonably appears inconsistent with a present willingness on the part of

the suspect to discuss his case freely and completely with police at that time."
[People v. Randall, 464 P.2d 114 (Cal. 1970).] It appears to us most likely and
most normal that a minor who wants help on how to conduct himself with the
police and wishes to indicate that he does not want to proceed without such help
would express such desire by requesting to see his parents. For adults, removed
from the protective ambit of parental guidance, the desire for help naturally
manifests in a request for an attorney. For minors, it would seem that the desire
for help naturally manifests in a request for parents. It would certainly severely
restrict the "protective devices" required by *Miranda* in cases where the suspects
are minors if the only call for help which is to be deemed an invocation of the
privilege is the call for an attorney. It is fatuous to assume that a minor in custody
will be in a position to call an attorney for assistance and it is unrealistic to
attribute no significance to his call for help from the only person to whom he
normally looks — a parent or guardian. It is common knowledge that this is the
normal reaction of a youthful suspect who finds himself in trouble with the law.

About a dozen states require the presence of a parent or other "interested adult"
during the police interrogation of a juvenile as a condition of the youth's valid
waiver of *Miranda* rights.[79]

Are there situations in which a youth's request for an adult other than his
parents should be treated as an invocation of his *Miranda* rights? Suppose the
youth's parents are unavailable? Or the youth asks for another adult from fear
of facing a parent as a result of his crime (for example, if the crime was patricide
or matricide)? See State v. Oglesby, 648 S.E.2d 819 (N.C. 2007) (holding that
16-year-old's aunt, who played a major role in raising him and whose presence
defendant requested, was not a "guardian" or "custodian" who he had a right to
have present during police questioning).

In Fare v. Michael C., 442 U.S. 707 (1979), the Supreme Court considered
whether a 16-year-old's request to see his probation officer was, in effect, a request
for an attorney. The Court, in a 5-to-4 decision, held that it was not. Writing for the
majority, Justice Blackmun noted:

We . . . believe it clear that the probation officer is not in a position to offer the type
of legal assistance necessary to protect the Fifth Amendment rights of an accused
undergoing custodial interrogation that a lawyer can offer. The Court in *Miranda*
recognized that "the attorney plays a vital role in the administration of criminal
justice under our Constitution." [384 U.S. at 481.] It is this pivotal role of legal
counsel that justifies the per se rule established in *Miranda,* and that distinguishes
the request for counsel from the request for a probation officer, a clergyman, or a
close friend. A probation officer simply is not necessary, in the way an attorney is,
for the protection of the legal rights of the accused, juvenile or adult. He is significantly handicapped by the position he occupies in the juvenile system from serving
as an effective protector of the rights of a juvenile suspected of a crime.

The California Supreme Court, however, found that the close relationship
between juveniles and their probation officers compelled the conclusion that a

[79] Feld, Police Interrogation of Juveniles, supra note [77], at 226.

probation officer, for purposes *of Miranda,* was sufficiently like a lawyer to justify extension of the perse rule. . . . The fact that a relationship of trust and cooperation between a probation officer and a juvenile might exist, however, does not indicate that the probation officer is capable of rendering effective legal advice sufficient to protect the juvenile's rights during interrogation by the police, or of providing the other services rendered by a lawyer. [An extension of the per se rule to include requests for probation officers] would impose the burdens associated with the rule of *Miranda* on the juvenile justice system and the police without serving the interest that rule was designed simultaneously to protect. If it were otherwise, a juvenile's request for almost anyone he considered trustworthy enough to give him reliable advice would trigger the rigid rule *of Miranda.* [442 U.S. at 722-723.]

How explicit must be a juvenile's request to speak with a parent or a lawyer? Suppose that during a police interrogation, and after being advised of his *Miranda* rights, a 14-year-old asks the police officer, "Do I need a lawyer?" Is the youth's question an assertion of his right to counsel that would require questioning to stop? See In re Christopher K., 810 N.E.2d 145 (Ill. App. Ct. 2004) (upholding voluntariness of juvenile's confession to murder, reasoning that juvenile offender should have manifested a more positive assertion of his desire for an attorney to invoke his privilege against self-incrimination).

c. *Miranda* and the Possibility of Transfer to Adult Court

Must children be specifically advised that a confession may be used against them in an adult criminal proceeding if the juvenile court waives jurisdiction? Several courts, although a minority of those that have faced the issue, have held that such a warning is required. See, e.g., State v. Benoit, 490 A.2d 295 (N.H. 1985):

> Many juveniles are aware of the special mechanisms of the juvenile justice system. A child, in making a statement, may reasonably believe that the statement will be used only in the protective and rehabilitative setting of juvenile court. The lack of knowledge on the part of a child concerning the possibility of felony criminal treatment of his offense cannot be allowed to induce the giving of a statement. Hence, to insure a truly knowing and intelligent waiver of the privilege against self-incrimination, the child must be advised of the possibility of prosecution in superior court as an adult.

Following *Benoit,* however, several states criticized its reasoning and declined to follow its lead. See State v. Perez, 591 A.2d 119, 124-125 (Conn. 1991); State v. Campbell, 691 A.2d 564, 567 (R.I. 1997). See also State v. Callahan, 979 S.W.2d 577 (Tenn. 1998) (holding that juvenile need not be informed of the possibility of waiver into adult court as a constitutional prerequisite to waiver of *Miranda* rights).

d. Additional *Miranda* Issues

What should be the specific style and content of the *Miranda* warning when juveniles are involved? In addition to the four basic *Miranda* warnings, should children be told that they have the right to stop the interrogator's questioning at any time? Compare State v. Nicholas, 444 A.2d 373 (Me. 1982), with Romans v. District Court, 633 P.2d 477 (Colo. 1981).

7.   Waiver of a Juvenile's Rights

Should youths be able to waive their constitutional rights? For adults, *Miranda* made clear that accused persons may waive their rights so long as such "waiver is made voluntarily, knowingly, and intelligently." 384 U.S. at 444. Should the same standard be applicable to juveniles? Consider the approaches suggested by In re S.H. and the Juvenile Justice Standards.

In re S.H.
293 A.2d 181 (N.J. 1972)

PROCTOR, J.

A juvenile delinquency complaint in the Mercer County Juvenile and Domestic Relations Court charged that the appellant, S.H., age 10, caused the drowning of B.R., age 6, by pushing him into a canal. The court found that the appellant was a juvenile delinquent. However, it reserved decision as to whether the offense would be manslaughter or second degree murder had the act been committed by a person of the age of 18 or over until it received the report of the Menlo Park Diagnostic Center to which it committed S.H. for 90 days for examination. Upon receipt of the report the court determined the act would be second degree murder if done by an adult and committed S.H. to the State Home for Boys for an indeterminate period of time. S.H. appealed to the Appellate Division, and before argument there upon defendant's application the proceedings were certified to this Court.

. . . On March 17, 1970, three boys, E.J., age 7, W.W., age 8, and B.R. were returning to school in Trenton after lunch. A short distance from the school S.H. approached the boys, accused them of beating up his sister, and asked for some money. The boys denied beating up his sister and refused to give him any money. S.H. then punched W.W. in the face and took B.R. by the coat into an adjacent alley. The two other boys continued to school. B.R. did not return to school or to his home that evening.

The following day, March 18, the Trenton Police Department began a missing person's investigation of B.R. That morning Sergeant John Girman, along with two patrolmen, went to the school S.H. attended. At 11:00 A.M. in the presence of the vice-principal they spoke to S.H. He was not a suspect at this time, as the police did not know whether or not B.R. was the victim of foul play. S.H. was being questioned because the police had information that he was one of the last persons to see B.R. S.H. told the police that he had seen B.R. on Brunswick Avenue with W.W. and E.J. He said they were approached by a boy named Leroy who hit one or both of the older boys and took B.R. away with him. S.H. said he then went to school. After the questioning S.H. returned to class.

That same day, after speaking to W.W. and E.J., the police returned to S.H.'s school at 1:00 P.M. and asked to see the boy again. They questioned him as to the identity of Leroy. After describing Leroy, S.H. suddenly began to cry and said Leroy threw B.R. into the canal. He agreed to show the police the place where Leroy had thrown the boy. Shortly thereafter the police and fire departments along with S.H. went to the canal and he showed them the place where Leroy pushed B.R. into the water. He also told them B.R. floated down the canal, and he pointed out the spot where he last saw him go under. At 3:30 P.M. B.R.'s body was discovered about 300 feet from where S.H. said he saw Leroy push the boy into the water.

After the body was found, S.H. told the police he would take them to Leroy's house. They arrived at the address S.H. gave them about 4:45 P.M., where he identified a certain boy as Leroy. Investigation showed that the boy was not named Leroy, was in school at the time of the episode and was in no way involved.

Thereafter, at about 5:00 P.M., the police took S.H. to the first precinct Trenton Police Station. After discussing the matter with other policemen, Sergeant Girman concluded a homicide had occurred, and S.H. was a prime suspect.

When S.H. arrived at the police station, his father was already there. However, the police told Mr. H. he was not needed at that time, and he left the station and went home.

Sergeant Girman turned S.H. over to Detective Purdy of the Juvenile Bureau of the Trenton Police Department. The detective took the boy to a room on the second floor usually used to interrogate adults. Alone in the room with S.H., the detective read the boy his *Miranda* rights from a card, explaining what they meant as he went along. According to the detective, he spent about 10 minutes explaining the *Miranda* rights. The following colloquy adduced at the hearing shows the nature of the explanation and the extent of S.H.'s understanding of it:

> THE COURT: Well, what were his responses to your (explanation of the *Miranda* warnings)?
> MR. PURDY: And he would say yes and no to me in answer; along with the yes and no's he would also shake his head. And I would move on because I felt that he did know, what the answer was that he was giving me. When he said yes, I would move on. And when he said no, then I would explain to him further.

The entire interrogation lasted about 90 minutes.

About 6:30 P.M., after the interrogation was completed, the police picked Mr. H. up at his house and brought him to the station house. He was taken to a second floor room where he found four policemen. S.H. was brought in by Detective Purdy from the adjoining room where the questioning had taken place. The detective then asked S.H. to tell his father what he had told him during the interrogation. The boy complied.

At the hearing the State called Mr. H. and asked him what S.H. had told him in the presence of the police. Defense counsel objected to the State's use of the father to testify against his son. The objection was sustained. The State then put Detective Purdy back on the stand to relate what S.H. told his father. Purdy told the court that S.H. said, "I walked the boy down by the railroad crossing. And we got by the creek (canal) and, I mean by the water, and I pushed him in." . . . This testimony was admitted over defense counsel's objection.

The State rested, and after motions of defense counsel were heard and denied the defense rested without calling any witnesses.

On this appeal appellant contends his confession was the product of police coercion, and therefore its admission into evidence violated the due process clause of the Fourteenth Amendment. In a juvenile case where a serious offense is charged, before the confession of an accused can be received in evidence against him the State has the burden of establishing that the accused's will was not overborne and that the confession was the product of a free choice. We are not satisfied the State has borne its burden of proving that this confession was voluntarily made and that the fundamental fairness requirement of due process has been met.

The circumstances under which the station house interrogation was conducted showed a complete disregard for the well-being of the accused juvenile. Placing a young boy in the "frightening atmosphere" of a police station without the presence of his parents or someone to whom the boy can turn for support is likely to have harmful effects on his mind and will. Not only was S.H. interrogated in the police station, but he was isolated in a room with a detective for a period of 90 minutes. The State's proofs account for only 10 minutes of this period, that used to give and explain the *Miranda* warnings. There is nothing in the record to show what occurred during the remaining 80 minutes except Detective Purdy's testimony of what the boy told him about the episode (the same story which he told his father in the presence of the police). More significant is the action of the police in sending the father away from the police station before questioning the boy. We emphasize whenever possible and especially in the case of young children no child should be interviewed except in the presence of his parents or guardian. [In re Carlo, 225 A.2d 110 (N.J. 1966)]; Standards for Specialized Courts Dealing With Children (Children's Bureau, Department of Health, Education and Welfare, 1954) at 39. That the police allowed Mr. H. to be present immediately after the interrogation in order to secure a separate confession in no way detracts from our conclusion. This second confession was merely a reprise of what the boy told Detective Purdy when he was secluded alone with him in the room and at best was nothing more than the tainted product of the coercion which produced the first confession. See Wong Sun v. United States, 371 U.S. 471 (1963). The conduct of the police in sending Mr. H. home from the police station when he had appeared in the interest of his son without more may be sufficient to show that the confession was involuntary. In light of the other circumstances, however, we need not pursue this point.

In reaching our conclusion as to the voluntariness of the confession, we have taken into consideration that the police gave S.H. the *Miranda* warnings and that he purportedly waived his rights. We think this factor, however, was of little or no significance in the present case. Recitation of the *Miranda* warnings to a boy of 10 even when they are explained is undoubtedly meaningless. Such a boy certainly lacks the capability to fully understand the meaning of his rights. Thus, he cannot make a knowing and intelligent waiver of something he cannot understand. However, questioning may go forward even if it is obvious the boy does not understand his rights if the questioning is conducted with the utmost fairness and in accordance with the highest standards of due process and fundamental fairness. See State v. In the Interest of R.W., 115 N.J. Super. 286, 295-296, 279 A.2d 709 (App. Div. 1971), *aff'd o.b.*, 61 N.J. 118, 293 A.2d 186 (1972). Such was not the case here.

Upon a consideration of the totality of the circumstances under which the appellant's confession was obtained, we cannot say it convincingly appears that his confession was voluntarily made. In view of the appellant's age, the oppressive environment of the police station where the questioning was conducted, the lengthy period of interrogation (the nature of which is only partially explained) and the cavalier treatment of the father in sending him home when his boy most needed him, we cannot say the State has met its burden of proving the confession of appellant was obtained by methods consistent with due process. We therefore hold that his confession was improperly admitted in evidence.

A new trial, however, is not necessary. A juvenile hearing is not a criminal case; it is a civil proceeding, tried without a jury, and conducted in the interest of the juvenile and for the welfare of society. In such a case our Constitution and rules permit us to exercise such original jurisdiction as may be necessary to the complete determination of the cause on review. N.J. Const., Art. 6, Sec. 5, para. 3; R. 2:10-5; see State v. Taylor, 38 N.J. Super. 6, 21, 118 A.2d 36 (1955). In exercising that jurisdiction we have examined the undisputed evidence other than that contained in the inadmissible confession and find there from beyond a reasonable doubt that S.H. committed the act set forth in the charge and that he therefore requires rehabilitative treatment. . . .

A review of the admissible evidence completely satisfies us that S.H. pushed B.R. into the canal. S.H.'s description of Leroy's actions in stopping the three boys and taking B.R. away was shown, at the hearing, to be in reality the very actions of the appellant. S.H. was the only one who knew B.R.'s body was in the canal. He was the only one who knew the location of the body. And more significantly, he sought to place the blame on an innocent boy. These facts leave no doubt in our minds that the appellant caused the death of B.R.

We are not convinced, however, that appellant's act would constitute murder if committed by an adult rather than manslaughter. Malice differentiates murder from manslaughter. Ordinarily, proof of an intent to kill or to do grievous bodily harm is necessary to establish malice. We are not satisfied on the record before us that this 10-year-old boy had the intent to kill or to do grievous bodily harm. The diagnostic report later furnished the trial court in connection with the disposition of the juvenile discloses that S.H. had an I.Q. "within the mild defective range of intelligence," and that he was "functioning severely behind the norm for his chronological age." This report supports our doubt of the existence of the mens rea required for murder. It shows that S.H. was physically 10 but mentally much younger. Under the circumstances the finding should be that the homicide is involuntary manslaughter.

The judgment of the trial court is modified in accordance with this opinion.

ABA, Institute of Judicial Administration, Juvenile Justice Standards Project, Pretrial Court Proceedings (1980)

Part VI: Waiver of the Juvenile's Rights; The Role of Parents and Guardians ad Litem in the Delinquency Proceedings

Waiver of the Juvenile's Rights

6.1 Waiver of the juvenile's rights in general

A. Any right accorded to the respondent in a delinquency case by these standards or by federal, state, or local law may be waived in the manner described below. A juvenile's right to counsel may not be waived.

B. For purposes of this part:

1. A "mature respondent" is one who is capable of adequately comprehending and participating in the proceedings;

2. An "immature respondent" is one who is incapable of adequately comprehending and participating in the proceedings because of youth or inex perience. This part does not apply to determining a juvenile's incapacity to stand trial or otherwise participate in delinquency proceedings by reason of mental disease or defect.

C. Counsel for the juvenile bears primary responsibility for deciding whether the juvenile is mature or immature. If counsel believes the juvenile is immature, counsel should request the court to appoint a guardian ad litem for the juvenile.

D. A mature respondent should have the power to waive rights on his or her own behalf, in accordance with Standard 6.2. Subject to Standard 6.3, the rights of an immature respondent may be waived on his or her behalf by the guardian ad litem.

6.2 Waiver of the rights of mature respondents

A. A respondent considered by counsel to be mature should be permitted to act through counsel in the proceedings. However, the juvenile may not personally waive any right:

1. except in the presence of and after consultation with counsel; and

2. unless a parent has first been afforded a reasonable opportunity to consult with the juvenile and the juvenile's counsel regarding the decision. If the parent requires an interpreter for this purpose, the court should provide one.

B. The decision to waive a mature juvenile's privilege against self-incrimination; the right to be tried as a juvenile or as an adult where the respondent has that choice; the right to trial, with or without a jury; and the right to appeal or seek other post-adjudication relief should be made by the juvenile. Counsel may decide, after consulting with the juvenile, whether to waive other rights of the juvenile.

6.3 Waiver of the rights of immature respondents

A. A respondent considered by counsel to be immature should not be permitted to act through counsel, nor should a plea on behalf of an immature respondent admitting the allegations of the petition be accepted. The court may adjudicate an immature respondent delinquent only if the petition is proven at trial.

B. The decision to waive the following rights of an immature respondent should be made by the guardian ad litem, after consultation with the respondent and coun sel: the privilege against self-incrimination; the right to be tried as a juvenile or as an adult, where the respondent has that choice; the right to a jury trial; and the right to appeal or seek other postadjudication relief. Subject to subsection A of this standard, other rights of an immature respondent should be waivable by counsel after consultation with the juvenile's guardian ad litem. . . .

The Role of Parents and Guardians ad Litem in the Delinquency Proceedings

6.5 The role of parents

A. Except as provided in subsection B,

1. the parent of a delinquency respondent should have the right to notice to be present, and to make representations to the court either pro se or through counsel at all stages of the proceedings;

2. parents should be encouraged by counsel, the judge, and other officials to take an active interest in the juvenile's case. Their proper functions include consultation with the juvenile and the juvenile's counsel at all stages of the proceedings concerning decisions made by the juvenile or by counsel on the juvenile's behalf, presence at all hearings, and participation in the planning of dispositional alternatives. Subject to the consent of the mature juvenile, parents should have access to all records in the case. If the juvenile does not consent, the court should nevertheless grant the parent access to records if they are not otherwise privileged, and if the court determines, in camera, that disclosure is necessary to protect the parent's interests.

B. The court should have the power, in its discretion, to exclude or restrict the participation of a parent whose interests the court has determined are adverse to those of the respondent, if the court finds that the parent's presence or participation will adversely affect the interests of the respondent.

C. Parents should be provided with necessary interpreter services at all stages of the proceedings.

6.6 "Parent" defined

The term "parent" as used in this part includes:

A. the juvenile's natural or adoptive parents, unless their parental rights have been terminated;

B. if the juvenile is a ward of any person other than a parent, the guardian of the juvenile;

C. if the juvenile is in the custody of some person other than a parent, such custodian, unless the custodian's knowledge of or participation in the proceedings would be detrimental to the juvenile; and

D. separated and divorced parents, even if deprived by judicial decree of the respondent juvenile's custody.

6.7 Appointment of guardian ad litem

A. The court should appoint a guardian ad litem for a juvenile on the request of any party, a parent, or upon the court's own motion:

    1. if the juvenile is immature as defined in Standard 6.1 B.2;

    2. if no parent, guardian, or custodian appears with the juvenile;

    3. if a conflict of interest appears to exist between the juvenile and the parents; or

    4. if the juvenile's interests otherwise require it.

B. The appointment should be made at the earliest feasible time after it appears that representation by a guardian ad litem is necessary. At the time of appointment, the court should ensure that the guardian ad litem is advised of the responsibilities and powers contained in these standards.

C. The function of a guardian ad litem is to act toward the juvenile in the proceedings as would a concerned parent. If the juvenile is immature, the guardian ad litem should also instruct the juvenile's counsel in the conduct of the case, and may waive rights on behalf of the juvenile as provided in Standard 6.3. A guardian ad litem should have all the procedural rights accorded to parents under these standards.

D. The following persons should not be appointed as a guardian ad litem:

    1. the juvenile's parent, if the parent's interest and the juvenile's interest in the proceedings appear to conflict;

    2. the agent, counsel, or employee of a party to the proceedings, or of a public or private institution having custody or guardianship of the juvenile; and

    3. an employee of the court or of the intake agency.

E. Courts should experiment with the use of qualified and trained non-attorney guardians ad litem, recruited from concerned individuals and organizations in the community on a paid or volunteer basis.

6.8 The parent's right to counsel

A. A parent should receive notice of the right to counsel when he or she receives the petition or the summons and also, if the parent appears without counsel, at the start of all judicial hearings. The notice should state that the juvenile's counsel represents the juvenile rather than the parent, that if the parent wishes, he or she has a right to be advised and represented by his or her own counsel, to the extent permitted by Standard 6.5, and that a parent who is unable to pay for legal assistance may have it provided without cost.

B. A parent's counsel may be present at all delinquency proceedings but should have no greater right to participate than a parent does under Standard 6.5.

6.9 Appointment of counsel for parent unable to pay

A. The court should appoint counsel for a respondent's parent who does not waive that right and who is unable to obtain adequate representation without substantial hardship to the parent or family. . . .

6.10 Waiver of the parent's rights

A. Any right accorded to a parent by these standards or under federal, state or local law may be waived. A parent may effectively waive a right only if the parent is fully informed of the right and voluntarily and intelligently waives it. The failure of a parent who has the right to counsel to request counsel should not of itself be construed to constitute a waiver of that right.

------

a. Competence to Waive a Juvenile's Rights

Do you think it possible for a youth to "voluntarily, knowingly, and intelligently" waive a constitutional right? How likely is it that a 14-year-old, without parental advice or the advice of counsel, will know and understand his or her *Miranda* rights and the consequences of a waiver? Empirical studies suggest that although nearly all youths voluntarily waive their *Miranda* rights (in the sense of not having been coerced), a significant number fail to understand those rights and the consequences of a waiver.[80] Grisso summarizes his findings thus:

> [W]e saw in the study employing empirical measures of *Miranda* comprehension that about one-half of juveniles of ages 10-16 demonstrated inadequate understanding of at least one of the four *Miranda* warnings. Understanding of the *Miranda* warnings was significantly poorer among juveniles who were 14 years of age or younger than among 15-[to] 16-year-old juveniles or adult offenders and nonoffenders. . . .
>
> Further deficiencies in juveniles' competence to waive rights were found in the study of their ability to understand the function and significance of the rights to silence and legal counsel. . . . Of special concern was that about one-third of the juveniles misperceived the intended nature of the attorney-client relationship. . . .[81]

If understanding of *Miranda* rights varies as a function of age, then Ferguson and Douglas's findings are illuminating: 96 percent of a sample of 14-year-olds

------

[80] See A. Bruce Ferguson & Alan C. Douglas, A Study of Juvenile Waiver, 7 San Diego L. Rev. 39 (1970); Thomas Grisso, Juveniles' Waiver of Rights: Legal and Psychological Competence (1981); Barry C. Feld, Juveniles' Competence to Exercise *Miranda* Rights: An Empirical Study of Policy and Practice, 91 Minn. L. Rev. 26 (2006); Steven A. Drizin & Greg Luloff, Are Juvenile Courts a Breeding Ground for Wrongful Convictions?, 34 N.Y. L. Rev. 257 (2007).

[81] Grisso, supra note [80], at 192.

failed to understand fully their *Miranda* rights and the consequences of a waiver.[82]

Should the court be required to assist a juvenile in understanding the consequences of a waiver in order for the waiver to be valid? Is the court under a greater responsibility to assist a juvenile in this regard than to assist an adult? See In re W.M.F., 349 S.E.2d 265 (Ga. Ct. App. 1986):

> [A]ppellant contends that she did not make a knowing and intelligent decision to proceed without counsel. We agree. Since the referee did not warn the appellant or her mother of the danger of proceeding without counsel or of the consequences of an affirmative finding or admission of the charge enumerated in the petition, we find that appellant and her mother did not stand before the court with open eyes, knowing the danger and consequences of proceeding without the benefit of legal representation. . . . This is reversible error.

See also In re Montrail M., 589 A.2d 1318 (Md. Ct. Spec. App. 1991) (court must admonish a juvenile who intends not to deny the state's allegations of the nature and possible consequences of such an action, even if the juvenile is represented by counsel).

Should evidence of previous occasions when a juvenile offender was given *Miranda* warnings be admissible to prove that the juvenile understood the *Miranda* warnings on the occasion in question? See State ex rel. Juvenile Dept. v. Charles, 779 P.2d 1075 (Or. Ct. App. 1989).

b. Applicable Standard

What standard should be applied to waivers by juveniles of such rights as the right to counsel and the right to remain silent? Should it be the standard articulated in *Miranda* — a knowing, intelligent, and voluntary waiver "under the totality of the circumstances"? Or, should it be another stricter standard — perhaps, a per se requirement that a juvenile waiver is invalid unless a parent or guardian is present and informed of the youth's rights? (Under the totality approach, the presence or absence of a parent or guardian is only one factor bearing on the validity of the juvenile's waiver.)

As explained previously, the Supreme Court in Fare v. Michael C., 442 U.S. 707 (1979), adopted the "totality of the circumstances" test as the constitutional standard for determining the voluntariness of a juvenile waiver. The totality approach is currently employed in a majority of jurisdictions. Although the per se rule has received almost unanimous support from commentators,[83] it has been adopted in the form of "interested adult" rules in only a few jurisdictions.

---

[82] Ferguson & Douglas, supra note [80].

[83] See American Bar Association, Juvenile Justice Standards, Standards Relating to Counsel 98 (1980); Grisso, supra note [80], at 192.

Are there special reasons to apply the per se rule to mentally disabled juveniles? Compare J.G. v. State, 883 So. 2d 915 (Fla. Ct. App. 2004) (holding that 13-year-old emotionally disabled youth did not voluntarily waive his *Miranda* rights), with Otis v. State, 217 S.W.3d 839 (Ark. 2005) (holding that 14-year-old with functional age of 9-12-year-old boy voluntarily waived his *Miranda* rights).

What constitutes a request for a parent to be present? In In re Shawn B.N., 497 N.W.2d 141 (Wis. Ct. App. 1992), a 13-year-old was accused of first-degree murder of a police officer. He was interrogated in a squad car by a policeman in plain clothes, who "removed Shawn's handcuffs, read him his *Miranda* rights and asked him if he understood." Id. at 148. The youth said that he did. When the waiver provisions were read to him, the youth did not reply, but assented in writing. In the course of the interrogation, Shawn asked whether he would ever be able to see his mother again. Subsequently, the appellate court, reasoning that Shawn had not asked to see his mother immediately, applied a totality of the circumstances test to hold that Shawn voluntarily waived his *Miranda* rights.

Should a parent or other interested adult be able to waive *Miranda* rights for the child? Compare In re Ewing, 350 S.E.2d 887 (N.C. Ct. App. 1986) ("[T]he finding that respondent's [a 10-year-old's] mother freely, under standingly, and knowingly waived respondent's juvenile rights is not equivalent to a finding that respondent knowingly and understandingly waived his rights."), with M.R. v. State, 605 N.E.2d 204, 207 (Ind. Ct. App. 1992) (although juvenile's mother brought him to the police station, she was considered merely "a loving parent, obviously concerned about her son and his future," without an interest adverse to the juvenile, and thus could lawfully waive the juvenile's constitutional rights).

Who may serve as an "interested adult"? Any relative, if the parents are unavailable? See Commonwealth v. Hogan, 688 N.E.2d 977 (Mass. 1998) (grandmother); Commonwealth v. Escalera, 868 N.E.2d 493 (Mass. App. 2007) (foster mother). The Supreme Judicial Court of Massachusetts set forth a legal standard for determining whether the "interested-adult" standard was satisfied in Commonwealth v. Philip S., 611 N.E.2d 226 (Mass. 1993). The court explained that the situation must be viewed from the perspective of the officials conducting the interrogation as to whether the accompanying adult has the capacity to appreciate the situation and give advice or, instead, is antagonistic to the juvenile.

Does a parent's advice that the child confess interfere with a valid waiver? See Harden v. State, 576 N.E.2d 590 (Ind. 1991) (father's advice that son confess did not invalidate son's waiver).

With regard to waiver, is parental presence or concurrence an adequate safeguard? Two assumptions run through case law in terms of the value of parental presence: (1) parents' presence will be a mitigating force to reduce the likelihood of abusive coercion by officers or will reduce the pressures that are inherent in the status and power differences between the juvenile and the police, and (2) parents will be able to provide advice about matters that the juvenile may not be able to comprehend (such as waiver of constitutional rights and an understanding of the consequences of such waiver).[84] Are parents likely to be substantially more knowledgeable concerning the wisdom of waiver than the youth? Is it a safeguard at all when the parents want the child to plead guilty or confess? Consider the results of Grisso's study:

> The results of [our research] indicated that parents generally cannot be relied on to provide juveniles with explanations of the rights and their significance. In addition, a majority of the parents were negatively predisposed to juveniles' right to withhold information from police officers.
>
> In the discussion of these results, we concluded that the weight of the evidence from our studies clearly supported the [opinion] that "we cannot equate physical presence of a parent with meaningful representation." This conclusion has an important implication for judicial decisions concerning the validity of a juvenile's waiver of rights and the admissibility of a subsequent confession as evidence. Judges should not be influenced in their decisions by the mere fact that parents were present. They should weigh, in addition, the evidence concerning the parents' role in the preinterrogation waiver proceedings and evidence suggesting that the parents were or were not capable of providing the advice and protection which many juveniles need. Included in this deliberation should be a consideration of the parents' probable understanding of the rights and their potential significance, their attitudes toward these rights in juvenile cases, the parents' emotional and motivational states during the waiver proceedings, and the nature of the relationship between the parents and their child.[85]

c. Incompetence as a Matter of Law

As mentioned previously, virtually all courts treat age as one of several factors to be considered in analyzing a child's waiver. Should children below a certain age (what age?) *as a matter of law* be considered incapable of providing a knowing and intelligent waiver? Some state variations of the "per se" rule adopt this approach. Note how In re S.H., supra, and the ABA Standards deal with this question. On the basis of empirical research, Grisso concludes that special protections are necessary for youth aged 14 and younger. He writes:

> As a group, juveniles who were 14 years of age or younger consistently fell short of the research definitions of the legal standards for competence to waive rights. . . . We believe that the research results support the need for extraordinary protections for juveniles at ages 14 and below. Legislation to provide blanket exclusion of confessions, or to provide automatically for effective

---

[84] Grisso, supra note [80], at 166.
[85] Id. at 199-200.

counsel to these juveniles prior to police questioning, would afford the type of protection which our results suggest that these juveniles need.[86]

d. Mandatory Counsel

Is compliance with *Miranda* adequate to ensure that the juvenile has made a free and informed choice, particularly when the youth has waived counsel? Or when a confession in violation of *Miranda* is used for dispositional purposes alone? Should consultation with an attorney be a prerequisite to a valid waiver by a juvenile? Consider the following:

> If youths are considered more susceptible to pressure when the question is the voluntariness of a confession, then why does this conception not carry over to *Miranda* issues with the result, for example, that a juvenile may not waive the right to counsel unless first advised by counsel? Moreover, if it is important that juveniles act voluntarily and with knowledge of the possibly adverse consequences of giving preadjudication information, then why is it not equally important that the juvenile act similarly when giving information relevant to disposition? After adjudication, however, juveniles not only have no protection regarding interrogation relating to disposition — even questioning as to unadjudicated offenses — it is expected that they will cooperate. Given the fact that such information can influence the disposition, the juvenile's full awareness of the consequences must be equally important at this stage.[87]

Various commentators, as well as the ABA Standards, have recommended that the juvenile's right to counsel be nonwaivable.[88] Grisso, on the basis of his empirical research, concluded that the right to counsel be nonwaivable for some juveniles: "[c]ompared with that of adults, the comprehension of [the *Miranda*] rights of younger juveniles is so deficient as to mandate a per se exclusion of waivers made without legal counsel by these juveniles."[89] Few states go so far. However, some states insist on additional safeguards for a juvenile's waiver of the right to counsel. See, e.g., Ark. Code Ann. §9-27-317 (Michie 2004 & Supp. 2008) (providing that juvenile's waiver of the right to counsel be accepted only if knowing and voluntary *and* the parent has agreed with the child's waiver of the right to counsel); Tex. Fam. Code Ann. §51.09 (Vernon 2005 & Supp. 2007) (providing that waiver of right to counsel must be made ordinarily by the child and the attorney for the child).

---

[86] Grisso, supra note [80], at 202.

[87] J. Lawrence Schultz & Fred Cohen, Isolationism in Juvenile Court Jurisprudence, in Pursuing Justice for the Child 20, 26 (Margaret Kenney Rosenheim ed., 1976).

[88] See authorities cited supra note [80].

[89] Thomas Grisso, Juveniles' Capacities to Waive *Miranda* Rights: An Empirical Analysis, 68 Cal. L. Rev. 1134, 1166 (1980).

E. THE ROLE OF THE LAWYER IN THE JUVENILE COURT PROCESS[90]

Is the role of a lawyer representing a juvenile accused of a delinquent act identical to that of a lawyer representing an adult accused of a crime? In an adult criminal proceeding, once the case is accepted by a lawyer, it is the attorney's responsibility "regardless of his personal opinion as to the guilt of the accused, . . . to invoke the basic rule that the crime must be proved beyond a reasonable doubt by competent evidence, to raise all valid defenses and, in the case of conviction, to present all proper grounds for probation or mitigation of punishment."[91] The lawyer is, of course, an "officer of the court." This imposes a duty of "candor and fairness," but it is generally assumed that the criminal defense attorney's responsibility to the client is in no way inconsistent with responsibility as an "officer of the court." The lawyer need not provide information suggesting the guilt of his client to the court and indeed is generally thought to have a duty to obtain an acquittal for the client, using all means short of fraud on the justice system. Is a juvenile delinquent proceeding any different?

Three issues are particularly important: (1) Do the possible inexperience and immaturity of the minor inevitably and appropriately require the lawyer to have a different role? (2) Should the often stated (if now somewhat tarnished) rehabilitative goal of the juvenile proceeding affect the lawyer's role? (3) What peculiar problems are created for the lawyer representing a juvenile client by reason of the child's parents and their desires for the child? The problem that follows offers an opportunity to explore these issues. Various perspectives are found in the subsequent materials.

PROBLEM

A delinquency petition has been filed against 16-year-old Ted Blanda, accusing him of armed robbery arising from a holdup of a gift shop. The only evidence against Ted consists of his identification by the shop owner. Based on a preliminary and incomplete description, the police arrested Ted and put him in a lineup, where he was identified by the victim. The lineup took place under circumstances that would violate the Supreme Court's decision in United States v. Wade, 388 U.S. 218 (1967), and Kirby v. Illinois, 406 U.S. 682 (1972), because it took place after a delinquency

---

[90] See generally Mary Berkheiser, The Fiction of Juvenile Right to Counsel: Waiver in the Juvenile Courts, 54 Fla. L. Rev. 577 (2002); Jim Lewis, The Aftermath of the Lionel Tate Case: A Child and a Choice, 28 Nova L. Rev. 479 (2004) (discussing the attorney's role in representing a juvenile murder defendant who is offered a plea bargain); Wallace J. Mlyniec, In re Gault at 40, The Right to Counsel in Juvenile Court — A Promise Unfulfilled, 44 No. 3 Crim. Law Bulletin 5 (May-June 2008); Robert E. Shepherd, Jr., Still Seeking the Promise of *Gault:* Juveniles and the Right to Counsel, 18 Crim. Just. 23 (Summer 2003); Suzanne M. Bookser, Comment, Making *Gault* Meaningful: Access to Counsel and Quality of Representation in Delinquency Proceedings for Indigent Youth, 3 Whittier J. Child & Fam. Advoc. 297 (2004).

[91] American College of Trial Lawyers, A Code of Trial Conduct, 36 N.D. L. Rev. 175, 176 (1960).

petition had been filed against Ted, and yet there had been no counsel present at the lineup. Although it appears likely that you will be able to exclude from evidence the lineup identification of the youth by the victim, the victim will nevertheless make an in-court identification. That testimony will be admissible so long as it is shown to be based on a recollection independent of the tainted lineup identification. Because the complaining witness is old and rather easily confused, however, it is your judgment that by very vigorous cross-examination, the victim's credibility might be sufficiently impeached to avoid an adjudication of delinquency.

Although Ted has made no statement to the police, he did admit to you that he committed the offense. During your initial interview with Ted, he told you that he hates juvenile hall (where he has been detained for three weeks since his arrest) and that he is going crazy being locked up. He suggested that what he cares most about is being with his friends on the street.

From police records, you learn that Ted has been arrested 11 times before, mostly for purse snatching, petty theft, and minor property crimes. On nine of these occasions no juvenile court petition was filed. In the other two, a delinquency petition was filed and sustained, but Ted was put on probation. He lives with his mother, who is an alcoholic, in a chaotic home situation. His father is unknown. Neither the youth nor his 14-year-old brother nor 18-year-old sister go to school or work. Their three-room apartment is badly overcrowded and filthy, and the youth spends all his time on the street. When you interview the youth's mother, she tells you that the boy is a "pain in the ass" and that she wishes he would be "locked up" somewhere to get him out of her hair.

On further inquiry you learn that before Ted dropped out of school at age 15, his academic performance had been very bad. He tells you that because of headaches he was unable to concentrate in class. He suggests that he has had episodic ringing in his ears for the last two years. The probation report relating to one of his earlier arrests indicates that his performance on an IQ test was about 85 and that a psychiatric examination made six months ago had suggested that he had serious, but undefined emotional difficulties. The school district has no special program for a 16-year-old boy with your client's difficulties.

(1) Under the circumstances of this case, once your client tells you that he does not want to be adjudicated a delinquent but instead wants to go back to the street, must you pursue that goal? Suppose that it is your honest opinion that Ted might be better off if the court took jurisdiction, provided he were sent to a particular juvenile "ranch," where he would receive reasonable medical attention, live in a more structured environment, and possibly benefit from an educational program aimed at youth with severe reading difficulties.

(2) Do you have the responsibility to express to Ted what you think is best for him? To try to persuade him to your view? If he disagrees, should you resign from the case? May you act on what you believe is best for him despite his wishes? What are your social responsibilities? Suppose that you also believe that the juvenile's conduct has become increasingly violent and that it is probable that if he is sent back home, he will commit a more serious crime. Is this hunch relevant? Are your responsibilities different during the adjudicatory stage, as opposed to the dispositional stage of the proceedings?

(3) Suppose Ted's mother asks you whether Ted in fact robbed the shop. May you tell her that Ted confessed to you?

DISCUSSION

The *Gault* decision, supra p. 798, extended the Sixth Amendment guarantee of counsel to the delinquent juvenile. *Gault* mandated representation at the adjudicatory stage of a delinquency proceeding in which the juvenile faces a penalty of possible confinement in a juvenile institution. Although most states have now codified *Gault*'s guarantee of legal counsel, empirical research suggests that many juvenile offenders still are not represented.[92]

Several questions arise in the wake of *Gault*. First, does the right to counsel attach at other stages in the proceedings? If not, should it? Second, does the presence of parents affect the right to counsel? And third, what should be the appropriate role of counsel for the minor in the delinquency proceeding?

(1) Stage at Which Right to Counsel Attaches.   *Gault* clearly specified that the right to counsel attaches only at that stage in the proceedings in which "a determination is made as to whether a juvenile is a 'delinquent'" [387 U.S. at 13]. The Court said, "we are not here concerned with the procedures or constitutional rights applicable to the pre-judicial stages of the juvenile process, nor do we direct our attention to the post-adjudicative or disposition process." Id. Nevertheless, many states have expanded the right to counsel beyond that contemplated by *Gault*. Legislation in these states typically directs that the right to counsel attaches at "every stage of the proceedings."[93] See, for instance, Cal. Welf. & Inst. Code §633 (West 1998 & Supp. 2008). The Juvenile Delinquency Act, 18 U.S.C. §5034 (2000), requires counsel at "critical stages" of the proceedings. These statutes leave open the question of whether the right attaches, for example, during a custodial interrogation by the police (including the lineup in the Introductory Problem) and at an intake hearing.

According to the ABA Standards, the right should attach "as soon as the juvenile is taken into custody by an agent of the state, when a petition is filed against the juvenile, or when the juvenile appears personally at an intake conference, whichever comes first."[94] The Commentary to the Standards suggests that mandatory representation is necessary to protect the juvenile and to assist the court in handling cases efficiently. Early representation is intended to "relieve pressures on overcrowded detention facilities by speeding the release of juveniles whose continued incarceration there is unnecessary."[95] The Standards also require prompt communication to the juvenile of the right to counsel. They provide that as soon as the right to counsel attaches, authorities should advise the juvenile of the right and that counsel will be retained if he or she, or the parents, are unable to pay. Notification should be in the juvenile's dominant language and, if necessary, an interpreter's services should be used to convey this message.[96]

---

[92] Mlyniec, supra note [90] (discussing research).

[93] See Tory J. Caeti et al., Juvenile Right to Counsel: A National Comparison of State Legal Codes, 23 Am. J. Crim. L. 611, 628 (1996) (19 states include a statutory requirement that a juvenile has the right to counsel at "all stages" or "every stage" of the proceedings against them).

[94] American Bar Association, Juvenile Justice Standards: Standards Relating to Pretrial Court Proceedings, Rule 5.1, 89 (1990).

[95] Id. at 94.

[96] Id. at 95.

A few jurisdictions significantly expand on *Gault*'s requirements. Courts in these jurisdictions have held that the right to counsel continues through various postadjudicative proceedings (e.g., restitution hearings, sentencing). One study of the right to counsel for juveniles concludes that (a) the right to counsel at intake is a rarity; (b) the right to counsel at detention hearings is becoming more widespread; (c) in most jurisdictions assigned counsel represents the child at both the adjudicatory and dispositional hearings; (d) few jurisdictions grant counsel at juvenile probation revocation proceedings; (e) few states assign counsel at placement review proceedings; and (f) many states fail to recognize a right to appointed counsel on appeal for juveniles. Ellen Marrus, Best Interests Equals Zealous Advocacy: A Not So Radical View of Holistic Representation for Children Accused of Crime, 62 Md. L. Rev. 288, 303-312 (2003).

(2) Parental Right.   What effect does the presence of parents have? Do parents have a separate right to counsel? *Gault* specified that "the child and his parents must be notified of the *child's right* to be represented by counsel . . . ." 387 U.S. at 41 (emphasis added). This implies that the right to counsel is personal to the child. However, a few statutes do confer this right on parents. See, for example, Ill. Comp. Ann. Stat. ¶405/1-5(1) (West 2004). More often, statutes fail to address this issue. Statutes stating that a "party" to the proceeding is entitled to representation, e.g., N.D. Cent. Code §27-20-26 (2006 & Supp. 2007), leave open the question as to whether representation is permitted for parents as well.

The fact that parents are involved raises perplexing issues concerning payment of counsel fees. For adults to have court-appointed counsel, the defendant must be financially unable to retain counsel. When the client is a juvenile, the issue becomes more complicated. The Commentary to the ABA Standards raises several questions: Whose financial resources should be considered in evaluating a juvenile's eligibility — the juvenile's or the parents? If counsel is appointed, should the parent or juvenile be liable to reimburse the court for the costs? Suppose the parents are financially able to retain counsel but refuse to do so. Should the court appoint counsel and declare the parents liable to reimburse the court for the costs thereof?[97]

Finally, imagine a parent is financially able to and does retain counsel for the juvenile but that subsequently the parent's interests conflict with the juvenile's interests. Because the parent is paying, to whom does counsel have a duty?[98]

(3) Appropriate Role for Counsel.   Although *Gault* extended a fundamental protection to juveniles in delinquency proceedings, it did not elaborate on the appropriate role for counsel in those proceedings. Three alternative models have been suggested for counsel: (a) the role of guardian, (b) the role of amicus curiae, and (c) the role of advocate. What duties do these roles encompass? Which role do

---

[97] Juvenile Justice Standards, supra note [94], at 96. See State ex rel. Gordon v. Copeland, 803 S.W.2d 153 (Mo. Ct. App. 1991) (child is indigent if he has no funds, even though his parents may have funds; courts cannot require parents to hire a lawyer, and if parents in fact do not hire a lawyer, child is entitled to public defender).

[98] Juvenile Justice Standards, Standard 5.3C, supra note [94], at 95.

you think is appropriate for the attorney representing a juvenile client accused of a criminal act?

The Commentary to the ABA Standards, infra p. 874, defines the roles of guardian and amicus curiae and also rejects those roles in favor of the role of advocate. On what basis does the Commentary reject those roles? Do you agree that the role of advocate is appropriate in light of the inexperience and immaturity of the client? In your determination, consider carefully the responsibilities of an advocate, especially taking into account the ABA Model Code of Professional Responsibility and the ABA Model Rules of Professional Conduct (below). The ABA House of Delegates adopted the Model Code of Professional Responsibility in 1969, and subsequently, in 1983, adopted the more recent statement of professional standards, the Model Rules of Professional Conduct. Currently, most jurisdictions follow the recent Model Rules; however, some jurisdictions still follow the earlier Model Code. How do the ABA's ethical responsibilities apply when the client is a minor?

The Code of Professional Responsibility dictates generally in Canon 7 that "a lawyer should represent a client zealously within the bounds of the law." American Bar Association, Code of Professional Responsibility 32 (1978). Two ethical considerations (EC 7-11 and EC 7-12) suggest that a lawyer has special responsibilities when the client is not fully competent.

ABA, Model Code of Professional Responsibility (1978)

EC 7-11

The responsibilities of a lawyer may vary according to the intelligence, experience, mental condition or age of a client, the obligation of a public officer, or the nature of a particular proceeding. Examples include the representation of an illiterate or an incompetent, service as a public prosecutor or other government lawyer, and appearances before administrative and legislative bodies.

EC 7-12

Any mental or physical condition of a client that renders him incapable of making a considered judgment on his own behalf casts additional responsibilities upon his lawyer. Where an incompetent is acting through a guardian or other legal representative, a lawyer must look to such representative for those decisions which are normally the prerogative of the client to make. If a client under disability has no legal representative, his lawyer may be compelled in court proceedings to make decisions on behalf of his client. If the client is capable of understanding the matter in question or of contributing to the advancement of his interests, regardless of whether he is legally disqualified from performing certain acts, the lawyer should obtain from him all possible aid. If the disability of a client and the lack of a legal representative compel the lawyer to make decisions for his client, the lawyer should consider all circumstances then prevailing and act with care to safeguard and advance the interests of his client. But obviously a lawyer cannot perform any act or make any decision which the law requires his client to perform or make, either acting for himself if competent, or by a duly constituted representative if legally incompetent.

Note that under EC 7-11, the responsibilities "may vary according to the intelligence, experience, mental condition or age of a client, . . . or the nature of a particular proceeding." Indeed, EC 7-12 suggests that the attorney may at times "be compelled in court proceedings to make decisions on behalf of the client"; EC 7-12 rather unhelpfully indicates that when the lawyer must act in behalf of the client, the lawyer should "consider all circumstances" and act to "safeguard and advance the interests of his client." How should a lawyer go about deciding whether the client's age, experience, or mental condition is such as to require broader and more active responsibility? Moreover, in such cases, how does the lawyer define the interests of the client? By what standards? Normally the lawyer asks the client what his or her interests are. Is this sufficient when the client is a juvenile?

ABA, Annotated Model Rules of Professional Conduct 215 (3d ed. 1996)

Client Under a Disability

Rule 1.14

(a) When a client's ability to make adequately considered decisions in connection with the representation is impaired, whether because of minority, mental disability or some other reason, the lawyer shall, as far as reasonably possible, maintain a normal client-lawyer relationship with the client. . . .

How is a lawyer supposed to "maintain a normal client-lawyer relationship" with a child? How is representation of a minor similar to that of a mentally disabled person? How is it different?

ABA, Institute of Judicial Administration, Juvenile Justice Standards, Standards Relating to Counsel for Private Parties 1-9 (1980)

Juvenile Representation and the Principle of Advocacy

There has always been sharp controversy regarding the propriety and role of counsel in juvenile court proceedings. Traditionally, cases involving children were considered "nonadversarial" with respect to both the relationship of the parties and the forms of procedure employed. The child's interest in the proceeding was assumed to be identical with that of the state, which claimed to seek only the child's welfare and not his or her punishment. There did not exist, accordingly, that adversity of interest among the parties which characterizes other civil or criminal proceedings. Given this premise, modes of trial and methods of protecting legal rights designed for cases involving frankly conflicting interests seemed inappropriate. Juvenile hearings were viewed not as a contentious process but as a therapeutic one. Informality and direct communication between judge and child replaced demonstration by ordinary rules of procedure and evidence as vehicles for eliciting needed information concerning the child's circumstances and, as well, for imparting to children, or sometimes their parents, a sense of social responsibility.

It is not surprising that, in such a forum, legal representation was thought unnecessary and even undesirable. . . . Broad recognition of the importance of representation was not achieved until the Supreme Court in In re Gault, 387 U.S. 1 (1967), held it a matter of constitutional right for delinquency proceedings.

With *Gault,* however, expressions of good intention and references to parens patriae could no longer justify denial of access to counsel to juveniles. Legal assistance was necessary, the Court held, to allow the respondent to "cope with problems of law, to make skilled inquiry into the facts, to insist upon regularity of the proceedings, and to ascertain whether he has a defense and to prepare and submit it." No less than an adult faced with felony charges, "The child requires the guiding hand of counsel at every stage in the proceedings against him." Id. at 36. *Gault* thereby established the importance of legal representation in delinquency matters, while at the same time extending to juvenile respondents the privilege against self-incrimination and rights to notice of charges and confrontation of witnesses. The case did not, however, entirely clarify the nature of juvenile court proceedings nor the role of counsel participating in them. . . .

The post-*Gault* effort to accommodate traditional juvenile court theory and the requirement of counsel resulted, for some, in a fundamental redefinition of counsel's function. Many have suggested that attorneys for children abandon the sharply defined role of the advocate for a "guardianship" theory of representation. As a "guardian," counsel is primarily concerned with ascertaining and presenting the plea and program best calculated to serve the child's perceived welfare. E.g., Isaacs, The Role of Counsel in Representing Minors in the New Family Court, 12 Buffalo L. Rev. 501, 506-507 (1963). Others have urged an "amicus curiae" function, in which counsel acts largely as an intermediary between the participants and explains the significance of proceedings to the client. See Cayton, Relationship of the Probation Officer and the Defense Attorney After *Gault,* 34 Fed. Prob. 8, 10 (1970). See also Skoler & Tenney, Attorney Representation in Juvenile Court, 4 J. Fam. L. 77 (1964); [W. Stapleton & L. Teitelbaum, In Defense of Youth: A Study of the Role of Counsel in American Juvenile Courts 64-65 (1972).] It is apparent that both guardianship and amicus curiae approaches involved radical modification of the rules governing a lawyer's professional role. At the very least, either approach places on counsel responsibility for decisions ordinarily allocated to the client. For example, whether to admit or contest the charges may become a matter to be determined by the attorney, perhaps in consultation with probation staff and parents, rather than by the respondent.

E.g., Edelstein, The Duties and Functions of the Law Guardian in the Family Court, 45 N.Y.S.B.J. 183, 184 (1973). Either of these approaches may also shift from client to counsel responsibility for the exercise of the privilege against self-incrimination, as suggested by the statement, "A sensitive lawyer, like a sensitive judge or a sensitive social worker, knows when confession is good for the soul." Coxe, Lawyers in Juvenile Court, 13 Crime & Delinq. 488, 490 (1967). Moreover, a lawyer who seeks to block presentation of complete and accurate information to the court through, for example, a motion to suppress illegally obtained evidence might be accused by proponents of this redefined role of frustrating the court's proper functioning. See Kay & Segal, The Role of the Attorney in Juvenile Court: A Non-Polar Approach, 61 Geo. L.J. 1401, 1412-1413 (1973). It has further been suggested that counsel is affirmatively required to disclose any information, including that derived from a confidential communication, which bears on the child's need for treatment. See NCCD, Procedure and Evidence in Juvenile Court 43 (1962); Steinfeldt, Kerper & Friel, The Impact of the *Gault* Decision in Texas, 20 Juv. Ct. Judges J. 154 (1969).

The standards set forth in this volume generally reject both guardianship and amicus curiae definitions of counsel's role and require instead that attorneys in juvenile court assume those responsibilities for advocacy and counseling which obtain in other areas of legal representation. Accordingly, counsel's principal function is a derivative one; it lies in furthering the "lawful objectives of his client through all reasonably available means permitted by law." ABA, Code of Professional Responsibility DR 7-101(A). Generally, determination of those objectives — whether to admit or deny, to press or abandon a claim, and the like — is the responsibility of the client whose interests will be affected by the proceeding. Attorneys may urge one course or another, but may not properly arrogate the final decision to themselves. Id. at EC 7-7, 7-8. Once the objective has been chosen by the client, the lawyer is bound by that choice, and must take care to conduct all phases of his or her professional activity, even those largely committed to counsel's discretion, in a manner consistent with the client's instructions in the matter. Id. at EC 7-9.

Reliance on the generally accepted standards of professional conduct in legal representation is justified and indeed demanded by the purposes for which those standards were created. The lawyer's role is defined by a set of rules for behavior which are thought desirable because they advance certain fundamental values or goals of the legal process. These goals are generally shared, with some variations, by all elements of the American justice system, including that of the juvenile court. . . .

The Relevance of the Client's Youth

It has sometimes been suggested that all or most of a juvenile court lawyer's clientele is not sufficiently mature to instruct counsel in any usual sense and that counsel must, therefore, usually act as guardian or amicus curiae. The proponents of this view often tend, however, to equate competence with capacity to weigh accurately all immediate and remote benefits or costs associated with the available options. In representing adults, wisdom of this kind is not required; it is ordinarily sufficient that clients understand the nature and purposes of the proceedings, and its general consequences, and be able to formulate their desires concerning the proceeding with some degree of clarity. Most adolescents can meet this standard, and more ought not be required of them. To do so would, in effect, reintroduce the identification of state and child by imposing on respondents an "objective" definition of their interests.

It is, of course, true that "the responsibilities of a lawyer may vary according to the intelligence, experience, mental condition or age of a client . . . or the nature of the particular proceeding." ABA, Code of Professional Responsibility EC 7-11. Attorneys will sometimes be required, by reason of their clients' youth and inexperience, to take special pains in explaining the nature and potential results of the action and to investigate formal and informal dispositional alternatives in their clients' interests. See, e.g., §§6.2, 8.1 and 9.3, infra. And, particularly where counsel represents a very young client (ordinarily but not always in connection with a child protection, custody or adoption matter), it will in some cases happen that the client is incapable of rational consideration regarding the proceeding. Where this is true, attorneys may be required to abandon their role as advocate. See §3.1(b), infra. However, the occasions for doing so are rare — particularly in delinquency and supervision cases — and may not properly be extended through manipulation of the general standard for competence.

The Lawyer as Counselor

Adoption of an advocacy role for purposes of juvenile court proceedings does not imply that lawyers should limit their concern or activity to the legal requirements of those proceedings. They not only may, but ordinarily should, be prepared to assume responsibility for counseling the client and, in some cases, the client's family with respect to legal and nonlegal matters independent of pending or contemplated litigation. The existence of such a role for an attorney has long been recognized in a variety of kinds of practice [e.g., commercial law, tax counseling, and family law].

Recognition of the attorney's function as counselor seems particularly appropriate for juvenile court representation. In most instances, neither clients nor their families will be familiar with the juvenile court or its procedures, goals and powers. It will, ordinarily, fall to the lawyer to understand and allay their spoken and unspoken fears about the situation in which they find themselves. In addition to his or her capacity as interpreter of specific procedures and rules, the attorney may also become "the first law figure who has performed a helpful function" for the client. Paulsen, The Expanding Horizons of Legal Services: II, 67 W. Va. L. Rev. 267, 276 (1965). As such, counsel has a unique opportunity to explain legal and social propositions in an acceptable fashion to clients whose feelings are often colored by hostility to authoritarian figures and rules. Counsel should also attempt to ascertain whether nonlegal services are needed by the client and the client's family and to assist them in taking advantage of such services if they are available. Performance of these duties will not, it should be emphasized, involve compromise of the obligation to advocate the client's interests before the court, so long as the distinction between counseling and ultimate determination of interest in the matter is observed. See ABA, Code of Professional Responsibility EC 7-3.

———————————

Following *Gault,* several studies highlighted various shortcomings in the quality of representation for juvenile offenders (see discussion supra p. 868). Congress addressed some of these concerns when it reauthorized the Juvenile Justice and Delinquency Prevention Act in 1992 by authorizing the Office of Juvenile Justice and Delinquency Prevention to fund a project to improve representation in delinquency proceedings. The ensuing report of the ABA Juvenile Justice Center called for representation by competent counsel who was knowledgeable about juvenile justice issues for every child accused of a crime. See ABA Juvenile Justice Center, A Call for Justice: An Assessment of Access to Counsel and Quality of Representation in Delinquency Proceedings (Dec. 1995). The report not only uncovered evidence of inadequate representation (e.g., frequent waiver of the right to counsel, high caseloads, inexperienced advocates, lack of representation before detention, scant pretrial preparation, rare appeals, and infrequent resort to other postdispositional remedies), but also made recommendations to improve the quality of legal services. Following that report, the ABA Juvenile Justice Center conducted additional state assessments of legal services to delinquents.

Subsequently, the ABA Juvenile Justice Center helped create the National Juvenile Defender Center (NJDC) in 1999 to improve the quality of representation for children in the justice system. NJDC separated from the American Bar Association in 2005 and became an independent organization. NJDC provides services to public defenders, appointed counsel, law school clinical programs and nonprofit law centers in urban, suburban, rural, and tribal areas. The organization offers services such as training, technical assistance, advocacy, and networking. NJDC also publishes reports, training guides, and practice-oriented fact sheets.

One commentator describes the impact of NJDC by pointing to their vision statement:

> [NJDC's Web site] vision statement says:
>
> > The National Juvenile Defender Center works to create an environment in which: children are treated with respect, dignity and fairness; juvenile courts are knowledgeable, sensitive and responsive to the needs of children; excellence is routine in juvenile defense; juvenile defenders have the capacity to fully protect children's rights, including adequate resources and compensation, manageable caseloads, and sufficient access to investigation, expert and other ancillary and administrative support; juvenile defenders have resources and pay parity with juvenile prosecutors; the representation of children is specialized and adequate opportunities exist for juvenile defenders to fully exercise and enhance their legal, political, organizational, research and advocacy skills. [See *www. abanet.org/crimjust/juvjus/jdc.html.*]

These statements clearly reinforce what the American Bar Association articulated more than two decades earlier in the IJA-ABA Juvenile Justice Standards on Counsel for Private Parties.

... [L]egal services in the juvenile courts must be backed up with interdisciplinary support services and particularized training in youth development and juvenile law, among other more generic trial advocacy and negotiation skills. There must be lower caseloads to allow for earlier representation of juveniles at detention hearings and, in some instances, during intake, and to allow for more time to develop a well-thought-out dispositional plan, perhaps in conjunction with a dispositional specialist. Attorneys need to spend more time with their youthful clients developing trust and simply explaining the legal process in developmentally appropriate terms. The lawyer in juvenile court needs to develop expertise in the range of educational and mental health disabilities of young people, and the laws that define the special rights of those who are so disabled. These skills delineated are just the tip of the iceberg, but they may serve to illustrate that keeping the promise of *Gault* may go well beyond simply heeding the clarion call of *Gideon.* [Robert E. Shepherd, Jr., Still Seeking the Promise of *Gault*: Juveniles and the Right to Counsel, 18 Crim. Just. 23, 27 (2003).]

F.   THE FUTURE OF THE JUVENILE COURT

A heated debate concerning the future of the juvenile court has been in progress for a number of years.[99] The debate took on added significance at the hundredth anniversary of the juvenile court. Some commentators argue for the abolition of the juvenile court. Consider the following excerpt in light of the materials, supra, on the purposes of the juvenile justice system and the procedural differences between the adult and juvenile justice systems.

Barry C. Feld, The Transformation of the Juvenile Court
75 Minn. L. Rev. 691, 723-724 (1991) (citations omitted)

... As juvenile courts converge procedurally and substantively with criminal courts, is there any reason to maintain a separate court whose only distinctions are procedures under which no adult would agree to be tried?

The juvenile court is at a philosophical crossroads that cannot be resolved by simplistic formulations, such as treatment versus punishment. In reality, there are no practical or operational differences between the two. Acknowledging that juvenile courts punish, imposes an obligation to provide all criminal procedural safeguards because, in the words of *Gault,* "the condition of being a boy does not justify a kangaroo court." [387 U.S. 1, 28 (1967).] While procedural parity with adults may sound the death-knell of the juvenile court, to fail to do so perpetuates

---

[99] See, e.g., Janet E. Ainsworth, Re-Imagining Childhood and Reconstructing the Legal Order: The Case for Abolishing the Juvenile Court, 69 N.C. L. Rev. 1083 (1991); Barry C. Feld, The Juvenile Court Meets the Principle of Offense: Punishment, Treatment, and the Difference It Makes, 68 B.U. L. Rev. 821 (1988); Barry C. Feld, The Transformation of the Juvenile Court, 75 Minn. L. Rev. 691 (1991); Katherine Hunt Federle, The Abolition of the Juvenile Court: A Proposal for the Preservation of Children's Legal Rights, 16 J. Contemp. L. 23 (1990); Irene Merker Rosenberg, Leaving Bad Enough Alone: A Response to the Juvenile Court Abolitionists, 1993 Wis. L. Rev. 164.

injustice. To treat similarly situated juveniles differently, to punish them in the name of treatment, and to deny them basic safeguards fosters a sense of injustice that thwarts any efforts to rehabilitate. Abolishing juvenile courts is desirable both for youths and society. After more than two decades of constitutional and legislative reform, juvenile courts continue to deflect, co-opt, ignore, or absorb ameliorative tinkering with minimal institutional change. Despite its transformation from a welfare agency to a criminal court, the juvenile court remains essentially unreformed. The quality of justice youths receive would be intolerable if it were adults facing incarceration. Public and political concerns about drugs and youth crime foster a "get tough" mentality to repress rather than rehabilitate young offenders. With fiscal constraints, budget deficits, and competition from other interest groups, there is little likelihood that treatment services for delinquents will expand. Coupling the emergence of punitive policies with our societal unwillingness to provide for the welfare of children in general, much less to those who commit crimes, there is simply no reason to believe that the juvenile court can be rehabilitated.

Without a juvenile court, an adult criminal court that administers justice for young offenders could provide children with all the procedural guarantees already available to adult defendants and additional enhanced protections because of the children's vulnerability and immaturity. The only virtue of the contemporary juvenile court is that juveniles convicted of serious crimes receive shorter sentences than do adults. Youthfulness, however, long has been recognized as a mitigating, even if not an excusing, condition at sentencing. The common law's infancy defense presumed that children below age fourteen lacked criminal capacity, emphasized their lack of fault, and made youthful irresponsibility explicit. Youths older than fourteen are mature enough to be responsible for their behavior, but immature enough as to not deserve punishment commensurate with adults. If shorter sentences for diminished responsibility is the rationale for punitive juvenile courts, then providing an explicit "youth discount" to reduce adult sentences can ensure an intermediate level of just punishment. Reduced adult sentences do not require young people to be incarcerated with adults; existing juvenile prisons allow the segregation of offenders by age.

Full procedural parity in criminal courts coupled with mechanisms to expunge records, restore civil rights, and the like can more adequately protect young people than does the current juvenile court. Abolishing juvenile courts, however, should not gloss over the many deficiencies of criminal courts such as excessive case loads, insufficient sentencing options, ineffective representation, and over-reliance on plea bargains. These are characteristics of juvenile courts as well. . . .

See also Barry C. Feld, A Century of Juvenile Justice: A Work in Progress or a Revolution That Failed, 34 N. Ky. L. Rev. 189 (2007).

Table of Cases

Principal cases appear in italics.

A. v. United Kingdom, 237
A.A. v. B.B., 188
A.C., In re, 37
ACLU v. Mukasey, *90*, 97,
   99–101, 103
Adar v. Smith, 536
Adoption of _____. See party name
Aguero v. Aguero, 200
A.H., In re, 318
A.H. v. M.P., 188, 616
Aichele v. Hodge, 169
Aid for Women v. Foulston, 699
Akron, City of v. Akron Ctr. for
   Reproductive Health, 143
Alabama & Coushatta Tribes of Tex. v.
   Trustees of Big Sandy Indep. Sch.
   Dist., 131
Alison D. v. Virginia M., 615
Alvarado v. Hickman, 853
Amenson v. Iosa, 636
American Acad. of Pediatrics v.
   Lungren, 146
American Amusement Mach. Assn. v.
   Kendrick, 97, 104, 114
American Belt Co. v. W.C.A.B., 661
American Library Assn.,
   United States v., 132
Americana Health Care v. Randall, 191
A.M.H., In re, 786
Anonymous, Ex parte, 144, 145
Anonymous, In re, 143
A.O.V. v. J.R.V., 570, 571, 609
Apprendi v. New Jersey, 787, 822
Armijo v. Wagon Mound Pub. Sch., 434
Arms v. Arms, 609
Ashcroft v. American Civil Liberties
   Union, 99
Ashcroft v. Free Speech Coalition, 105
Atkins v. Virginia, 286, 291, 761, 797
Aurbach v. Giallina, 669
Ayotte v. Planned Parenthood of N. New
   England, 143, 147
A.Z. v. B.Z., 648

Baby Boy Doe v. Mother Doe, 36
Baby Boy K., Matter of, 409
Baby Boy L., In re, 545
Baby Girl Clausen, In re, 514
Baby Girl H., In re Adoption of, 169
Baby Girl U., In re, 515
Baby M, In re, *451*, 460, 461, 469, 470, 476,
   638, 640, 642
Baker v. Owen, 135, *239*, 243
Barber v. Barber, 202
Barber ex rel. Barber v. Dearborn Pub.
   Sch., 131
Barnes v. Cohen Dry Wall, 679
Barr v. Lafon, 128
B.C., In re, 144
Beal v. Doe, 23
Beard v. Lee Enter., 661
Becker v. Mayo Fdn., 256
Bednarski v. Bednarski, 576
Beene v. Beene, 579
Behrens v. Rimland, 616
Bellotti v. Baird, 136, 141–143, 711
Benoit, State v., 856
Benson v. Patterson, 200
Bergland v. American Multigraph Sales
   Co., 674
Bethel v. Fraser, 126, 133, 842
Bethley v. Louisiana, 290
B.F. v. T.D., 616
B.G.C., In re, 514
Bird, People v., 679
Bird, United States v., 30
Bivens ex rel. Green v. Albuquerque Pub.
   Sch., 131
Board of Educ. v. Earls, *834*,
   840–848
Board of Educ. v. Pico, 132
Bobbijean P., In re, 77
Boerne, City of v. Flores, 69
Boldt, In re Marriage of, 608
Bolton, Doe v., 12
Bonner v. Moran, 445
Boone v. Ballinger, 169

Boroff v. Van Wert City Board
of Educ., 131
Bottoms v. Bottoms, 569
Bouchard v. Frost, 176
Bowen v. Kendrick, 702
Bowers v. Pearson, 516
Bowling v. Sperry, 674
Bradley, People v., 298
Breed v. Jones, 812, 819, 822
Brian C. v. Ginger K., 169
Brigman, State v., 298
Brookbank v. Gray, 177
Brown v. Board of Educ., 57
Brown, State v., 255, 290
Buda, State v., 301
Burton, People v., 854
Burton v. Richmond, 354
Bush v. Holmes, 56
Butler v. Michigan, 84, 102
Buzzanca, In re Marriage of, 643
Bykofsky v. Middletown, 709, 711

Caban v. Mohammed, 504, 505, 513
Califano v. Boles, 177
California v. Superior Ct. of Cal. ex rel.
Smolin, 635
Callahan, State v., 856
Callender v. Skiles, 169
Camp v. Lummino, 679
Campbell, State v., 856
Canadian Fdn. for Children, Youth &
Law v. Canada, 237
Carey v. Population Servs. Intl.,
689, 698, 699
Carney v. Carney, 577
Carter v. Carter, 636
Caudillo v. Lubbock Indep. Sch.
Dist., 128
Chambers v. Chambers, 198
Charlie H. v. Whitman, 354
Charpentier v. Charpentier, 570
Chen v. Chen, 198
Chicago, City of v. Morales, 768
Child Labor Tax Case, 655
Children, Youth & Families Dept., State
ex rel., 367
Christopher K., In re, 856
Ciesluk, In re Marriage of, 629
Circle Schools v. Pappert, 68
City of. See name of city

Clark v. Jeter, 173
Clark v. Madden, 577
C.L.J., Ex parte, 544
Coe v. Cook County, 45
Coker v. Georgia, 290
Cole v. Arkansas, 536
Comino v. Kelly, 169
Commonwealth v. _____. See name of
opposing party
Cook v. Cook, 571
Cornfield v. Consolidated High
Sch. Dist., 847
Cox v. Florida Dept. of Health &
Rehabilitative Servs., 534
Coy v. Iowa, 301, 302
Craig v. Boren, 677, 687
Craig, Maryland v., 301
Crawford v. Washington, 293, 298,
299, 301
Crocker, In re, 197
Cruzan v. Director, Mo. Dept. of
Health, 35
Cuesta v. School Board of Miami-Dade
County, 847
Cunningham v. Tardiff, 642
Curtis v. Kline, 197
Curtis v. School Comm. of Falmouth, 697
Cutter v. Wilkinson, 70
Cuyler v. United States, 256
Cyberspace Commun. v. Engler, 103

Dahl & Angle, In re Marriage of, 647
Damian R., State v., *733*, 740
Danielson v. Evans, 201
Dansby v. Dansby, 583
Darby v. United States, 656
Davidson v. Time Warner, 112
Davis v. Washington, 298
Dawn D. v. Superior Court, 169
Day v. Heller, 189
DeArriba v. DeArriba, 200
Deborah G., In re, *314*, 318
Deerfield, Village of v. Greenberg, 711
Dellwo v. Pearson, *670*, 672
Del Zio v. Presbyterian Hosp., 646
Denver Area Telecomms. Consortium,
Inc. v. FCC, 110
Department of Human Servs. & Child
Welfare Agency Review Bd. v.
Howard, 536

DeShaney v. Winnebago County Dept. of
    Soc. Servs., 264, 265
Dial Info. Servs. v. Thornburgh, 108
Dickens v. Ernesto, 544
Dietrich v. Northampton, 48
District of Columbia v. B.J.R., *719*, 722,
    729–731
D.L.C. v. State, 824
Dodd v. Burleson, 615
Dodson v. Shrader, 674
Doe, In re, *135*
Doe, In re Adoption of, 347, *528*, 534,
    535, 537
Doe v. See name of opposing party
Doe, United States v., 849, 850
Doe ex rel. Doe v. Yunits, 131
Doncer v. Dickerson, 492
Doninger v. Niehoff, 129
Dortman v. Lester, *667*
Dorworth, In re Marriage of, 608
Downey v. Muffley, 609
Dubay v. Wells, 46, 176
Dugan v. General Servs. Co., 662
Duncan v. Duncan, 599
Dupuy v. Samuels, 264

E.C., In re, 570
E.H., In re, 298
Eisel v. Board of Educ. of Montgomery
    County, 434
Elisa B. v. Superior Court, *178*, 187, 188
Elk Grove Unified Sch. Dist. v. Newdow,
    67
Ellis, People v., 731
Elmer v. Elmer, 629
Emiliano M., In re, 346
Employment Div. v. Smith, 69
Engelkens, In re Marriage of, 615
Entertainment Software Assn. v.
    Swanson, 114
Erznoznik v. Jacksonville, 103
Etimani, United States v., 302
Evans v. United States, 848
Ewing, In re, 866
Excalera, Commonwealth v., 866
Ex parte _____. See name of party

Fare v. Michael C., 812, 851, 855, 865
F.B., In re, 845

FCC v. Pacifica Fdn., 99
Felix v. Milliken, 687
Ferguson v. City of Charleston, 39
Fetus Brown, In re, 36
Findaya W. ex rel. Theresa W. v.
    A.-T.E.A.M. Co., 177
Finley v. Astrue, 212
Finstuen v. Crutcher, 536
Fire Ins. Exch. v. Cincinnati Ins. Co., 661
Fish v. Behers, 168
Fisher, Commonwealth v., 771
Flood v. Braaten, 634
Ford, In re Marriage of, 200
Ford v. Browning, 56
Frazier, State v., 768
Fredman v. Fredman, 629
Freed v. Ryan, 688
Freiburghaus v. Herman Body Co., 674

Gallegos v. Colorado, 851
Gallo, People ex rel. v. Acuna, 768
Gambla, In re Marriage of, 583
Garcia v. State, 824
Gardely, People v., 767
Garska v. McCoy, 560
Gault, In re, 627, 755, 785, *798*, 811–815,
    819, 871–875
Gavin G., Commonwealth v., 825
Gay-Straight Alliance of Okeechobee
    High Sch. v. School Board, 128
Gibson v. Gibson, 237
Gibson v. Merced County Dept. of Human
    Res., 347
Gigante, United States v., 301
Gill v. State, 679
Gillett-Netting v. Barnhart, 49,
    207, 212, 213
Gillman ex rel. Gillman v. School
    Board, 128
Ginsberg v. New York, 2, *83*, 97, 99–101,
    103, 108, 126, 651
Gladys R., In re, 785
Globe Newspaper v. Superior Ct., 303
Glona v. American Guar. & Liab.
    Ins. Co., 171, 177
Gonzales v. Carhart, *13*, 21, 25–29, 92, 93
Gonzalez v. Gallo, 711, 768
Goodridge v. Department of Pub.
    Health, 571
Goodson v. Castellanos, 535

Gordon, State ex rel. v. Copeland, 872
Goss v. Lopez, 133, 135, 242, 246
Green, People v., 767
Greer v. Greer, 579
Grimes v. Kennedy Krieger Inst., *442*, 448
Grittman, In re Marriage of, 197
Grumet v. Cuomo, 69
Grumet v. Pataki, 69

Haines v. Haines, 626
Halbman v. Lemke, 674
Haley, In re, 575
Haley v. Ohio, 850, 851
Hall v. Butterfield, 674
Ham v. Hospital of Morristown, *252*
Hamilton v. Hamilton, 583
Hammer v. Dagenhart, 655, 656
Hammers v. Hammers, 575
Harden v. State, 866
*Harmon v. Department of Soc.
    Servs.*, *184*, 189
Harris, In re Marriage of, 617
Harris v. McRae, 23
Hart v. Brown, 445, 449
Hastings v. Rigsfee, 599
Hathaway v. Hathaway, 197
Hazelwood v. Kuhlmeier, 126, 127, 129,
    130, 842
Heart of Adoptions v. J.A., 517
Heatzig v. MacLean, 571
Hegney, In re, 787
Heidibreder v. Carton, 513
Hermesmann, State ex rel. v. Seyer, 189
Hewellette v. George, 237
H.G., In re, 367
Hill v. Colorado, 30
Hinkle v. State, 230
Hodgkins v. Peterson, *702*, 710, 711
Hodgson v. Minnesota, 143
Hogan, Commonwealth v., 866
Holder v. Holder, 607
Hollon v. Hollon, *564*
Horton v. Goose Creek Indep.
    Sch. Dist., 846
Hubbard v. Hubbard, 176
Hudson v. Purifoy, 636
Hughes, State v., 679
Humphries v. County of Los Angeles, *258*
Hutchins v. District of Columbia,
    710, 711, 712

Idaho v. Wright, 300
Ikerd, State v., 35
Infant Doe, In re, 409, 416, 417
Infant Doe v. Bloomington Hosp., 416, 417
Information Providers' Coalition v.
    FCC, 108
Ingraham v. Wright, 135, 245, 246
In re _____. See name of party
In re Estate of _____. See name of party
In re Guardianship of _____. See name
    of party
In re Marriage of _____. See name
    of party
In re Parentage of _____. See name
    of party
Inscoe v. Inscoe, 583
International Union, UAW v. Johnson
    Controls, 39
Interstate v. Dallas, 108
Isiah B., In re, 845

Jackson v. Bishop, 242
Jackson v. Houchin, *664*, 666
Jackson v. Jackson, 599
Jacob v. Schultz-Jacob, 188, 643
Jacobson, In re, 198
Jacobson v. Massachusetts, 385
Jacoby v. Jacoby, 569, 583
James v. Meow Media, 114
James D. v. California, 824, 848
Janice M. v. Margaret K., 616
J.C.P., In re, 787
J.D.S. v. Department of Children and
    Families, In re Guardianship of, 36
*Jefferson v. Griffin Spalding County
    Hosp. Auth.*, *31*, 36, 37, 41
Jesusa V., In re, 169
Jeter v. Mayo Clinic, 646
J.F. v. D.B., 640, 642
J.G. v. State, 866
Jimenez v. Weinberger, 217
J.K., In re, 786
J.L.M. v. R.L.C., 599
J.M., People ex rel., 711
J.M.F., Ex parte, 570
J.M.K., In re Parentage of, 189
John Doe, In re Petition of, 514
John R. v. Carmona, 827
Johns v. Johns, 608
Johnson v. Nation, 608

Johnson v. City of Opelousas, 711
Jonathan L. v. Superior Ct., 69
Jones, Ex parte, 636
Jones v. Barlow, 616
Jones, State v., 845
Joseph v. Dickerson, 669
J.P., State v., 710
J.P.J., In re, 849
J.S. ex rel. H.S. v. Bethlehem Area Sch. Dist., 126
Juan C. v. Cortines, 844
Juvenile v. United States, 849
Juvenile Dept., State ex rel. v. Charles, 865
J.W.T., In re, 169

Karlin v. IVF Am., 647
Katherine B.T. v. Jackson, 748
Kay v. Ludwig, 594
Keating v. Hollstein, 666
Kelsey S., Adoption of, 517
Kennedy v. Louisiana, 283, 289
Kennedy, State v., 290–292
Kenny A. ex rel. Winn v. Perdue, 312, 354
Kent v. United States, 781, 782, 785
Kerrigan v. Commissioner of Pub. Health, 187, 571
Kessel v. Leavitt, 517, 636
Khalsa v. Khalsa, 604, 607, 608
K.I., In re, 400, 405
Kievernagel, In re Estate of, 647
Kilmon v. State, 49, 255
King, State v., 669
Kingsley v. Kingsley, 748
Kirchner, In re Petition of, 514
Kirkendall v. Kirkendall, 625
Kirkland ex rel. Jones v. Greene County Board of Educ., 246
Kiryas Joel Vill. Sch. Dist. v. Grumet, 69
Klein, Matter of, 46
K.M. v. E.G., 189
Koehnen v. Dufuor, 679
Kohring v. Snodgrass, 197
Kolacy, In re Estate of, 212
Kopp, United States v., 30
Koshko v. Haining, 614
Kovacs v. Kovacs, 575

Lacey v. Laird, 373
Lalli v. Lalli, 172

L.A.M. v. B.M., 570
Lambert v. Wicklund, 143
Landeros v. Flood, 253
Laney v. Farley, 133
LaShawn v. Dixon, 354
Lassiter v. Department of Soc. Servs., 312, 369
Lau v. Nichols, 55
Lauga, Succession of, 211
Lavine v. Blaine Sch. Dist., 130
Lawrence v. Texas, 29, 102, 292, 571, 584, 609, 698
Lay v. Suggs, 666
Layshock v. Harmitage Sch. Dist., 129
Layton Phys. Therapy Co. v. Palozzi, 159
Lehr v. Robertson, 505, 513, 515, 516
Levy v. Louisiana, 171, 177
Leyda, In re Marriage of, 633, 635
Limon, State v., 699
Lisa Diane G., In re, 521
Litowitz v. Litowitz, 647
Little v. Little, 199
L.M., In re, 852
L.M.K. v. United States, 850
Locke v. Davey, 56
Lofton v. Department of Children & Family Servs., 347, 534
Lomholt v. Iowa, 302
Lopez v. United States, 133, 846
Loyd A., In re Marriage of, 578
L. Pamela P. v. Frank S., 189
Luke, In re Adoption of, 535
L.W. ex rel. L.G. v. Toms River Regl. Sch. Board of Educ., 435
L.W.K. v. E.R.C., 211
Lynch v. Dukakis, 354
Lynch v. King, 354

M.A., In re Adoption of, 536
M.A., In re Marriage of, 599
Mahaffey ex rel. Mahaffey v. Aldrich, 133
Maher v. Roe, 23, 25
Manuel v. State, 677, 688
Maquoketa, City of v. Russell, 711
Marlow v. Marlow, 570
Marriage Cases, In re, 187, 571
Martin S., In re, 824
Martinez, State v., 49
Maryland v. Craig, 301, 302
Mason v. Dwinnell, 616

Massachusetts Board of Ret. v. Murgia, 688
Mathews v. Lucas, 177
Matsumoto v. Matsumoto, 636
Matta v. Matta, 577
McCall, In re, 826
McCallum v. Salazar, 516
McCarty v. McCarty, 595
McCorvey v. Hill, 30
McDonald v. Black, 849
McGriff v. McGriff, 571
McGuckian v. Carpenter, 674
McKeiver v. Pennsylvania, 755, 759, 812, 815, 819–823
McKnight v. State, 49
McKnight, State v., 38, 49, 255
McPhee v. Tuffy, 669
McSoud, In re Marriage of, 608
Meade v. Meade, 634
Meadows v. Meadows, 629
Meyer v. Meyer, 608
Meyer v. Nebraska, 49, 53–55, 496, 614, 697, 711, 746, 812
Michael B., In re, 775, 777
Michael H. v. Gerald D., 161, 168, 169, 172, 173
Michael M. v. Superior Court, 731
Miguel, United States v., 787
Miller v. American Infertility Group, 646
Miller v. California, 98, 99
Miller v. Pfizer, 415, 435
Miller ex rel. Miller v. HCA, 400, 409, 410
Mills v. Habluetzel, 173
Minix, In re Marriage of, 608
Minor, In re Adoption of, 522
Mintz v. Zoernig, 189
Miramax Films Corp. v. Motion Picture Assn. of Am., 109
Miranda v. Arizona, 852, 853–857
Mississippi Band of Choctaw Indians v. Holyfield, 544
Mitchell v. Helms, 56
Mitchell v. Mitchell, 674
M.J.M. v. Department of Health & Rehab. Servs., 731
Moe, In re, 145
Morse v. Frederick, 120, 126–131, 133
Mortimore v. Wright, 157
Moss v. Rishworth, 373
M.R. v. State, 866
M.S., In re, 370
M.W. v. Department of Children & Family Servs., 269

N.A.H. v. S.L.S., 168
Nancy S. v. Michele G., 615
National Cas. Co. v. Northern Trust Bank of Fla., 48
National Family Planning & Reproductive Health Assn. v. Gonzales, 24
N.B., In re, 544
New Jersey v. T.L.O., 812, 823, 827, 840–848
New Jersey Div. of Youth & Family Servs. v. B.R., 369
New York v. Ferber, 104, 105
New York v. Heckler, 701
Nguyen v. INS, 177
Nicholas, State v., 857
Nicholson v. Williams, 257
Nickerson, Commonwealth v., 373
North Coast Women's Care Med. Group v. Benitez, 642
North Fla. Women's Health & Counseling Servs. v. State, 141
Northland Family Planning Clinic v. Cox, 27
Norton v. Ashcroft, 30
Nunez v. City of San Diego, 710

Oakley, State v., 77
Occean v. Kearney, 349, 351
O'Connell v. Kirchner, 514
Ohio v. Roberts, 295
Olivia Y. ex rel. Johnson v. Barbour, 354
Oregon v. Mitchell, 2
Osborne v. Ohio, 105
Oswald v. Gesicki, 731
Otis v. State, 866

Painter v. Bannister, 614
Painter v. Painter, 599
Palmore v. Sidoti, 543, 580, 582, 583
Panora v. Simmons, 712
Parents United for Better Pub. Sch. v. School Dist. of Phila., 697
Parham v. J.R., 393, 398, 399, 813
Parker v. Parker, 583
Patricia A., In re, 731
Patrick Y., In re, 845
Pelman v. McDonald's Corp., 436
Pemberton v. Tallahassee Regl. Med. Ctr., 37

People v. _____. See name of opposing party

People ex rel. See name of related party

People United for Children, Inc. v. City of New York, 264

Perez, State v., 856

Peterson v. Jason, *598*, 599

Philip S., Commonwealth v., 866

Phillip B., Guardianship of, *461*, 469, 470, 477

Phillip B., In re, *388*, 392, 464, 467

Pickett v. Brown, 173

Pierce, In re Adoption of, 345

Pierce v. Pierce, 579

Pierce v. Society of Sisters, *51*, 53–55, 66, 67, 614, 697, 711, 812

Pikula v. Pikula, 560

Pittman, State v., 798

Place v. United States, 846

Planned Parenthood Fedn. of Am. v. Heckler, 701

Planned Parenthood of Blue Ridge v. Camblos, 147

Planned Parenthood of Cent. Mo. v. Danforth, *40*, 44, 142

Planned Parenthood of Cent. N.J. v. Farmer, 146

Planned Parenthood of Columbia/ Williamette v. American Coalition of Life Activists, 30

Planned Parenthood of Ind. v. Carter, 145

Planned Parenthood of Kan. & Mid-Missouri v. Nixon, 142

Planned Parenthood of Minn., N.D., S.D. v. Rounds, 26

Planned Parenthood of N. New England v. Heed, 146

Planned Parenthood of S.E. Pa. v. Casey, 25–27, *40*, 44, 46, 142

Planned Parenthood of Wis. v. Doyle, 46

Planned Parenthood, Sioux Falls Clinic v. Miller, 147

Playboy Ent. Group, United States v., 111

Plyler v. Doe, 57

Poelker v. Doe, 23

Polovchak, In re, 747

Ponce v. Socorro Indep. Sch. Dist., 130

Potts, In re Marriage of, 200

Pratt v. Davis, 373

Preschooler II v. Clark County Sch. Board of Trustees, 246

Preston v. Meriter Hosp., 409, 415

Prince v. Massachusetts, *58*, 62, 65, 67, 241, 449, 496, 689, 711, 746, 812

Procopio v. Johnson, 347

Prost v. Green, *578*

Pruitt, People v., 846

Pusey v. Pusey, 560

Quilloin v. Walcott, 503–505, 513

Qutb v. Strauss, 710

R. v. M. (A.), 846

R. v. Swan, 237

Rachel L., In re, 69

Rainey v. Cheever, 172

Raleigh Fitkin-Paul Morgan Meml. Hosp. v. Anderson, 37

Ramos v. Town of Vernon, 710

Randy A.J. v. Norma I.J., 168

Raquel Marie X, In re, 518

Rebecca B., In re, 578

Redding v. Safford Unified Sch. Dist., 847

Reginald D. v. State, 827

Reinke v. Reinke, 625

Remy v. MacDonald, 48

Renfrow, Doe v., 847

Reno v. ACLU, 99

Rente v. Rente, 614

Rex v. Brasier, 304

Richmond v. Tecklenberg, 578

Richmond Med. Ctr. for Women v. Herring, 27

Riehm v. Engelking, 134

Riepe v. Riepe, 615

Riggs, In re Marriage of, 492

Riggs v. Riggs, 198

Rine v. Chase, 257

Rinehart v. Board of Educ., 244

Rivera v. Minnich, 174

R.L.C., State v., 176

R.L.C. v. United States, 786

Robert O. v. Russell K., 515

Roberto d.B., In re, 643

Rodriguez v. McLoughlin, 347

Rodriguez, State v., 848

Roe v. Conn, *305*, 310, 311

Roe v. Doe, 197

Roe v. Wade, *4*, 12, 21, 27, 28, 30, 766, 812

Roger S., In re, 397

Roman v. Roman, 647
Romans v. District Court, 857
Roper v. Simmons, 291, *789*, 796, 798, 823
Ross v. Louise Wise Servs., 522
Rouse, United States v., 302
R.T.M. v. State, 688
Rust v. Sullivan, 25

Sable Commun. v. FCC, 107
Safford Unified Sch. Dist. v. Redding, 847
Sagar v. Sagar, 608
Salerno, United States v., 825
Sampson, In re, 391
San Antonio Indep. Sch. Dist. v.
    Rodriguez, 57, 242
Sanders v. Acclaim Ent., 114
Sanjivini K., In re, 346
Santosky v. Kramer, 368, 369, 492
Scarpetta v. Spence-Chapin Adoption
    Serv., 521
Schall v. Martin, 812, 823, 825
Scheidler v. National Org. for Women, 30
Schliefer v. City of Charlottesville, 710, 712
Scofield v. Sibley, 148
Scruggs, State v., *429*, 434
Sees v. Baber, 521
S.F. v. State ex rel. T.M., 189
S.H., In re, 777, *857*
Shawn B.N., In re, 866
Shields v. Gross, 675
Shoemaker v. State, 845
Short v. Klein, 46
Sims v. Sims, 570
Sistare v. Sistare, 202
S.J.L.S. v. T.L.S., 535, 536
Smalley v. United States, 820, 821
Smith v. Novato Unified Sch. Dist., 126
*Smith v. Organization of Foster Families
    for Equality and Reform*, *334*, 346,
    347, 352
Smith v. Soligon, 516
Smook v. Minnehaha County, 847
Snowden v. State, 294, 299
Snyder, In re, *742*, 746, 748
Snyder, Commonwealth v., 845
Soohoo v. Johnson, 616
Soundgarden v. Eikenberry, 112
South Dakota v. Dole, 677
Spencer v. Spencer, 197
Stachelek, People v., 824

Stanley v. Illinois, *495*, 498, 499
Stanton v. Stanton, 630
State v. _____. See name of opposing
    party
State Auto Ins. Co. v. Reynolds, 666
State ex rel. See name of related party
Stenberg v. Carhart, *28*
Stephanie L. v. Benjamin L., 405
Steven W. v. Matthew S., 169
Stitzel v. Brown, 599
Stiver v. Parker, 641
Strauss v. Horton, 571
Strunk v. Strunk, 445, 449
Succession of _____. See party name
Sullivan v. Zebley, 217
Summerill v. Shipley, 672
Sumner, City of v. Walsh, 710
Suter v. Artist M., 354
Swopes v. Lubbers, 109

T.A., In re, 238
Taft v. Taft, 37
Tara Marie Pearce, In re Custody of, *572*,
    575, 576, 580
Tate v. Florida, 783
Taylor v. Taylor, *584*, 592, 593, 594
T.B., In re, 849
Terry, Succession of, 211
Texas v. Lopez, 787
Texas Dept. of Family & Protective
    Servs., In re, 314
Theodore v. Delaware Valley Sch.
    Dist., 843
Thomas ex rel. Thomas v. Roberts, 847
Thompson v. Carthage Sch. Dist., 844
Thompson v. Thompson, 634
Tighe v. United States, 821
*Tinker v. Des Moines Indep. Community
    Sch. Dist.*, *114*, 126–133, 242, 842
T.M.F., In re, 849
Tran v. State, 290
Treacy v. Municipality of Anchorage, 712
Trimble v. Gordon, 172
Troxel v. Granville, 54, 81, *609*, 614, 615, 626
Twiggs v. Mays, 747
Ty M., In re, *361*

United States v. _____. See name of
    opposing party

Valmonte v. Bane, 264
Vance v. Judas Priest, 113
Vernonia v. Acton, 840, 841, 843–844, 846
Vest, In re Adoption of, 516
Video Software Dealers' Assn. v. Schwarzenegger, 114
Video Software Dealers Assn. v. Webster, 110
Vigil, People v., 292, 297–299, 302
Village of. See name of village
Vincent M., In re, 544
Vito, Adoption of, 538
Vogelsberg v. Wisconsin, 301

Waddell v. Waddell, 194, 197
Wagner v. Wagner, 192, 197
Wakeman v. Dixon, 188
Walker, In re, 713, 722, 729–731
Waller v. Osbourne, 113
Wallis v. Smith, 181
Warford v. Warford, 583
Waters v. Barry, 711
Watts v. United States, 134
Watts, United States v., 849
Watts v. Watts, 560
Weber v. Aetna Cas. & Sur. Co., 177
Weber v. Stony Brook Hosp., 417
Webster v. Reproductive Health Servs., 23, 25
Western Union Tel. v. Lenroot, 656
Wheeler v. Mazur, 625
Wheeler v. United States, 304
Wheeler v. Wheeler, 535
White v. Illinois, 301, 302
White v. Moore, 630
White v. Thompson, 570
Whitter, State v., 849

Williams, In re, 848
Williams, In re Adoption of, 489
Williams v. Baptist Health Sys., 159
Williams v. Ellington, 847
Willis v. State, 228, 235
Willis ex rel. Willis v. Anderson Community Sch., 849
Wilson, State v., 290
Winship, In re, 730, 812, 819
Wisconsin v. Yoder, 55, 63, 67, 78
Wisniewski v. Board of Educ. of Weedsport Cent. Sch. Dist., 134
W.M.F., In re, 865
Wood, State v., 636
Wood v. Wood, 198
Woodward v. Commissioner of Soc. Sec., 210
Worman Motor Co. v. Hill, 674
Wright v. Wooden, 301, 599

X-Citement Video, United States v., 105
X, Y, and Z v. Sweden, 237

Yale Diagnostic Radiology v. Estate of Fountain, 154
Yarborough v. Alvarado, 851, 853
Yates, United States v., 301
Yoder, State v., 67–69, 81, 83, 697, 746
York v. Wahkiakum Sch. Dist., 843
Young v. Hector, 578
Yuan v. Rivera, 264

Zaharias v. Gammill, 636
Zelman v. Simmons-Harris, 56
Zoski v. Gaines, 373

Index

ABA
Juvenile Justice Standards, 732–733
Model Act Governing Assisted
Reproductive Technology, 213,
644, 648
Model Code of Professional
Responsibility, 873–874
Model Rules of Professional
Conduct, 874
Standards of Practice for Family and
Divorce Mediation, 622–623
Standards of Practice for Lawyers Who
Represent Children in Abuse and
Neglect Cases, 312–313, 628
Abandonment
as child neglect, 313
as grounds for adoption/termination of
parental rights, 488
Abduction of children in custody disputes,
632–634, 636
international abduction, 629–630
Parental Kidnapping Prevention Act,
632–634, 636
Abortion. *See also* Fetus; Pregnancy
adolescents, 135–148
bypass procedure, 143–145
clinic violence, 29–30
conscience clauses, 23–24
consent
informed, 25–26
of minor, 376–378
parental consent requirements,
142–143
spousal consent, 39–46
waiver in medical emergencies,
146–147
constitutional guarantees, 4–5, 146
counseling and referral, 24–25
as crime, 4–7
crime rates and, 766
father and, 39–46
fetal pain laws, 25, 26, 27
fetal rights, 22
fundamental right to, 8
funding, public, 23

gag rule on counseling, 24–25
gender discrimination and, 22–23
husbands and, 39–46
informed consent, 25–26
legal history, 6–7
liberty interest, 7
maternal health and, 6–7, 11–13,
16–17, 27
"mature minor" concept, 377–378
medical emergencies, waiver of
parental consent or notification
in, 146–147
morality and, 29
notice
medical treatment of minor, 379
natural father's right to, 505–512
parental notification prior to minor's
abortion, 135–148, 379
parental consent requirements, 142–143
partial-birth abortion, 13–20, 28
physician's role and restrictions, 12, 28
post-*Roe* abortion regulation, 23–26
privacy rights, 5, 7–10, 20–21
public abortion funding, 23
religious views, 10
RU-486, 28–29, 146
sex discrimination, 22–23
spousal consent and notification, 39–46
technological advances, 28–29
trimester framework, 11–12, 14–15
"undue burden" standard, 26–27, 45
viability of fetus
compelling state interest, 21–22
defined, 10
Abuse. *See* Child abuse; Sexual abuse
Adolescents
abortion and, 135–148. *See also*
Abortion
contraception and. *See* Contraception
contractual rights and liabilities,
673–676
criminal behavior. *See* Juvenile courts;
Juvenile delinquency
curfews. *See* Curfews
delinquent. *See* Juvenile delinquency

Adolescents (*continued*)
 depression and antipsychotic drugs,
  436–437
 drinking and, 676–689
 driving and, 662–676
  child labor laws, 658–659
 emancipation. *See* Emancipated minors
 freedom of expression, 702–709
 liability when engaging in adult
  activities, 670–671
 "mature minor" concept. *See* Mature
  minors
 minor's medical care, 427–437
 negligence, liability for, 671–672
 noncriminal misbehavior. *See* Status
  offenders
 parental consent
  regarding abortion. *See* Abortion
  regarding marriage, 153
 post-minority support for, 191–198
 pregnancy, 223, 697–698
 procedural rights in schools, 133–135
 research findings on drinking and,
  681–682
 right to counsel. *See* Right to counsel
 right to initiate court intervention,
  751–752
 runaways, 722–724, 740
 sexual activity, 689–696
 sexually transmitted diseases
  (STDs), 697
Adoption, 487–547
 access to information about origins,
  526–527
 Adoption and Safe Families Act. *See*
  Adoption and Safe Families
  Act (ASFA)
 adult adoptions, 467–469
 agency vs. independent, 518–520
 as "babyselling," 453–456, 523–526
 best interests test, 491–492, 508
 biological parent
  consent by, 491–492
  father's rights, 500–503
  misrepresentation of biological
   father, 514
  objection to, 489–491
 "black market," 520
 confidentiality concerns, 526–527
 consent, 471–472, 488, 495, 498

  by biological parent, 491–492
  father's consent, 495, 498
 defined, 518–519
 empirical research on, 518
 ethnicity, role of, 544
 failure, 520–522
 false information that baby died,
  513–514
 grandparents
  effect on rights of, 492–493
  visitation, post-adoption, 493–495
 gray market, 519
 ignorance of pregnancy, 515
 independent vs. agency adoption,
  518–520
 inheritance rights of child, 493
 notice to father, 505–512
 "open adoption," 493–494, 527
 opportunity to develop relationship,
  507–509, 515–517
 over biological parent's objection,
  505–512
 parental visitation following, 493–494,
  527
 proceeding to vacate, 521–522
 race. *See* Race
 religion, role of, 543–544
 screening of potential parents, 71
 sexual orientation, role of. *See* Sexual
  orientation
 stepparent, by, 493–494
 support, 493
 surrogate parenting agreements and,
  451–460
 termination of parental rights and,
  471–472, 503, 513
 unknown whereabouts of mother, 513
 unwed father and, 495–518
 visitation following, 493–494
 "weak" adoptions, 493
Adoption and Safe Families Act (ASFA)
 biological bonds disparaged by, 357–359
 criticism of, 355–361
 foster care and, 346–347, 353
 mischaracterization of foster care
  problem, 357
 proposals for reform, 355–361
 race and, 357–359
Adoption Assistance and Child Welfare
  Act, 352–355

AIDS
  child welfare system and, 333
  custody/visitation, 576–577
  pregnant women, 36
  prevention programs, 701
  screening newborns for, 387
Aid to Families with Dependent Children
        (AFDC), 203, 218, 382
Alcoholism. *See* Substance abuse
Alcohol laws. *See* Liquor laws
ALI
  abortion, 12
  approximation standard, 561, 596
  child's preferences, 626, 630
  child support, 494–495
  corporal punishment, 232–233
  "custodial responsibility," 596
  custody, 190, 494–495
    day care as factor, 579
    domestic violence as factor,
        561–562
    gender as factor, 560
    race as factor, 583
    religion as factor, 579
    sexual conduct as factor, 571
    sexual orientation as factor, 571
  custody modification, 579, 630–631
  "decisionmaking responsibility," 596
  de facto parent, 190, 494–495, 615
  minor's tort liability, 232–233
  parent by estoppel, 190, 494–495, 615
  parenting plans, 626, 630–631
  relocation, 630
Aliens, right to education of, 57
Alternative dispute resolution
  collaborative law, 623
  mediation. *See* Mediation
Amish, 63–70, 78–80
Antipsychotic drugs, depression in
        adolescents and, 436–437
Aristotle, 10
Arrests
  juvenile delinquents, 765–766, 824–825
  search and seizure incident to,
        824–825, 848
  warrants, 824–825
Artificial insemination. *See* Assisted
        reproduction
ASFA. *See* Adoption and Safe Families
        Act (ASFA)

Assault and battery
  battery defined, 372
  medical context, 372–374
Assisted reproduction. *See also* Surrogate
        parenting agreements
  child support, 187–188
  consent, 639
    father's consent as taking
        responsibility, 638
  custody and, 637–638
  father's obligation for custody and
        support purposes, 178–181, 638
  homosexual parents, custody and
        visitation rights of, 642–643
  inheritance by posthumous children,
        212–213
  in vitro fertilization. *See* In vitro
        fertilization
  nonmarital children, 170
  Uniform Parentage Act. *See* Uniform
        Parentage Act
Autism, link to childhood vaccines, 386

Baby Jane Doe case, 416–420
Babyselling
  adoption as, 453–456, 523–526
  surrogate parenting agreements. *See*
        Surrogate parenting agreements
Bail, right to, 802, 826
Bankruptcy, child support and, 206
Battered child. *See* Child abuse
Battery. *See* Assault and battery
Best interests of child standard
  child's wishes, 477–478
  custody decisions, 562–584
  in incorrigibility cases, 742–746
  legal standards, 563
  medical decisions, 41–42, 400–405
  psychological best interests test, 474
  psychological investigations, 475–476
Biological parent. *See* Adoption
Biomedical research. *See* Medical
        experimentation
Birth control. *See* Contraception
Blackstone, William
  duties of children, 153–154
  duties of parents, 149–154
  legitimate children, 150
  nonmarital children, 160–161
  parental power, 152–153

Blood donation
    minor's consent to, 405–406
Blood transfusions
    parental refusal, 391
    refusal on religious grounds, 32, 36–37,
        384, 391
"Bong hits for Jesus" case, 120–126
Bullying in schools, legislation to address,
    434–436

California
    dependency statute, 318–321
    Street Terrorism Enforcement and
        Prevention Act, 767
Capital punishment
    child rape, 283–292
    cruel and unusual punishment,
        789–791, 796
    deterrence effect on juveniles, 792,
        794–795
    equal protection, 797
    international consensus, 798
    mentally retarded and, 791, 797
    pros and cons, 797
    psychological research regarding,
        761–762
    purposes of, 796
    "sniper slayings" of 2002, 796
    Supreme Court's treatment of maturity
        issues, 797–798
Censorship. *See also* Freedom of speech
    in school libraries, 132
Cesarean section, forced, 31–34
Child abuse. *See also* Corporal
        punishment by parent;
        Sexual abuse
    Baby Does, 416–420
    "Baby Moses" statutes, 313
    caregiver characteristics and, 249–250
    central registry in state, 257–263
    child abandonment as neglect, 313
    child characteristics and, 250
    child rape
        adult rape compared, 290
        data, 289
        recidivism, 289–290
        standards of decency, 291–292
    clergy privilege and sex abuse scandal,
        256–257
    contraception, mandatory, 77–78
    counsel for abused child, 312–313

custody decision, as factor in, 579–580
defining, 248–249
disabled infants, withholding of care,
    416–420
early intensive home visitation, 359–360
emotional maltreatment, 311–312
employment screening and, 257–263
equal protection challenges, 264
expungement of records when
    unsubstantiated or false, 264
factors associated with abuse and
    neglect, 249
failure to protect, 257
family preservation, 360–361
federal legislation, 279, 281
federal regulations, 419–420
fetal abuse, 49
freedom of religion defenses of parents,
    227–228
prevention and treatment of, 312
psychological abuse, 78
purpose of, 255–256
rape, capital punishment for, 283–292
reforms, 265–269
removal from home. *See* Foster care
reporting laws, 252–269
    central registry of reported cases,
        257–263
    failure of state to act after report,
        264–265
    failure to report, liability for, 256
    immunity for erroneous reports, 257
    mandatory, 255–256
    protection for failure to report, 256
sanctions for parent's failure to protect,
    257
schools and, 135, 228, 238–243
scope of problem, 247
sexual abuse. *See* Sexual abuse
socioeconomic characteristics and, 250
stages of intervention, 310–311
standards of proof, 257–263
summary seizure, 305–310
threshold for removal, 311
visitation rights, effect on, 599, 609
Child Abuse Prevention and Treatment Act
    (CAPTA), 248, 279, 281, 312
Child care providers, employment
    screening of, 257–263
Child Custody Protection Act, 142
Child Labor Deterrence Act, 660

Child labor laws, 652–662
  actors or performers, 658
  alternatives to present system, 662
  Amish and, 70
  Child Labor Deterrence Act, 660
  Child Labor Protection Act of
    2007, 660
  constraints on freedom to work, 652–653
  driving regulations, 658–659
  exemptions, 658–659
  Fair Labor Standards Act, 70, 657–659
  farm work, 64–65, 658–659
  historical perspective, 653–656
  history in United States, 653–656
  Jehovah's Witnesses and, 58–62
  oppressive child labor defined, 657
  oppressive conditions in, 657–658
  parental consent to, 661
  reforms, federal, 655–656
  state laws, 654–657
  violations and penalties, 659–661
  work-related injuries, 661–662
  Young American Workers' Bill of
    Rights, 660
Child Labor Protection Act of 2007, 660
Child neglect. *See* Child abuse; Neglected
  children
Child Online Privacy Protection Act,
  105–106
Child Online Protection Act (COPA),
  90–96, 98
Child placement. *See also* Foster care
  care defined, 475
  delinquency proceedings, 784
  "least detrimental alternative" test, 475
Child pornography. *See* Pornography
Child Pornography Prevention Act, 105
Child Protection and Obscenity and
  Enforcement Act, 105
Child rape, 283–292
Children. *See also* Adolescents;
    Emancipated minors; Mature
    minors
  abused. *See* Child abuse; Sexual abuse
  adopted. *See* Adoption
  consent. *See* Abortion; Medical care;
    specific types of care or
    activities
  contraception, 381
  custody. *See* Custody
  disabled. *See* Disabled children

  duties to parents, 153–154
  education. *See* Education; Schools
  financial liability of, 158
  foster care. *See* Foster care
  illegitimate. *See* Nonmarital children
  infants. *See* Infants
  labor. *See* Child labor laws
  medical care. *See* Medical care
  medical experimentation. *See* Medical
    experimentation
  "minimums" related to children's
    care, 3
  neglected. *See* Neglected children
  newborn. *See* Infants
  parents and. *See* Parent and child
  as "property," 53–54, 523–526, 652
  religious rights of, 78–80
  rights as pupils, 114–126
  socialization of, 1–4
  "sovereignties" of childhood, 4–5
  visitation rights. *See* Visitation
Children in need of supervision (CINS),
  83, 719–722
Children's Internet Protection Act (CIPA),
  132
Child's Bill of Rights, 652
Child sexual abuse. *See* Sexual abuse
Child Sexual Abuse and Pornography
  Act, 105
Child support. *See* Support
Child Support Enforcement Act, 203
Child Support Enforcement Amendments,
  195, 203–204
Child Support Recovery Act, 204–205
Child Victims' and Child Witnesses'
  Rights Act (CVCWR), 302–303
Clergy privilege, child abuse reporting
  requirements and, 256–257
Collaborative law and attorney's role, 623
Commission on Obscenity and
  Pornography, 96, 99–100, 106–107
Commitment of children
  to mental hospitals, due process rights,
    393–400
  status offenders, 716–719
Communicable diseases. *See*
    Immunizations
Communications Decency Act, 95, 98
Compelling state interest
  abortion, 8, 11, 138–140
  contraceptive laws, 689–696

Compelling state interest (*continued*)
  corporal punishment in schools,
    240–243
  maternal health, 11–12
Compulsory education, 51–53, 63–70,
    78–80
Compulsory medical care, 31–39
Confessions
  improperly obtained, 850–852, 857–860
  "interested adult" rule, 851
  Miranda rights, 853–860, 864–867
  parental presence, 850–852, 857–860,
    865–867
  probation officers, confessions to,
    855–856
  psychological research on propensity
    for false confessions, 852
  voluntariness of, 850–852, 857–860,
    865–867
Confidentiality. *See also* Privacy
  in adoption, 526–527
  juvenile court records, 814
Confrontation, right to
  juvenile's rights, 807–811, 815–816
  sexual abuse cases, 292–297
Consent. *See* Abortion; Medical care;
    specific types of care or activities
Conservatorships for disabled adults, 468
Constitutionality. *See also* Confrontation,
    right to; Cruel and unusual
    punishment; Due process; Equal
    protection; Freedom of
    association; Freedom of religion;
    Freedom of speech; Privacy
  child labor laws, 655–656
  spousal consent, 39–46
Contraception, 689–702
  adolescent pregnancy, 697–698
  adolescent use of, research on,
    696–697
  birth control, 28–29
  compulsory, 70–77
  condom distribution programs,
    constitutionality of, 697
  confidentiality for teenage clients,
    698–699
  distribution to minors, generally,
    689–696, 698–699
  "Lock" scenario in future, 72–74,
    76–77
  minor's consent for, 381

parental consent to condom
    distribution, 700–701
  in schools, 697
  right to privacy and, 689–696, 698–699
  support obligation and
    misrepresentation in use of,
    181–183, 189
  teen sexual activity, laws as deterrent
    to, 689–696, 698–699
Contracts
  foster care as contractual relationship,
    345
  minor's right to disaffirm, 214,
    673–676
  surrogate parenting, 451–460, 639–644
Convention on the Rights of the Child, 237
Corporal punishment by parent, 227–246
  authority for, decision on, 243
  as cruel and unusual punishment, 240,
    245–246
  due process, 243, 246
  effectiveness of, 244
  international law, 234–237
  Model Penal Code, 232–233
  nationwide trend, 245
  North Carolina post-*Baker*, 244–245
  over parental opposition, 239–243
  parental privilege to discipline, 228–238
  parental tort immunity doctrine,
    237–238
  permission vs. preclusion, 244
  reasonable vs. excessive, 236
  Restatement (Second) of Torts, 233
  in schools, 135, 228, 238–246
  Swedish law on, 234–237
Council of Europe Convention on Human
    Rights and Biomedicine,
    439–440
Court-appointed special advocates
    (CASAs), 333
Courts. *See also* Juvenile courts
  abortion for minor, authorization of,
    376–378
  courtroom closure for sexual abuse
    victims, 303
  function, child protection vs. dispute
    resolution, 473
  joint custody, authority to award,
    586–587
  obstetrical intervention orders, 32–39
  parental agreements, review of, 559

removal powers
    history, 329–330, 470–471
    jurisdiction, 330–331
    sexual abuse victims and, 277, 303
Crime prevention by deterrence
    generally, 758–760
    pretrial detention and, 825–827
    through rehabilitation, 755–758
Criminal Gang Abatement Act, 768
Criminal liability
    failure to support, 201, 204–205
    fetal death or injury, 38–39
    fetal homicide laws, 47
    liquor laws and, 678–679
    postpartum psychosis defense, 47
    sexual abuse, 276–277
    withholding care from disabled
        infant, 422
Cross-examination, juvenile's right to,
    807–810
Cruel and unusual punishment
    capital punishment, 789–791, 796
    mentally retarded, 791, 797
Curfews, 702–713
    applicable level of scrutiny, 710–711
    constitutionality, 702–713
    deterrent effect on crime and
        victimization, 712–713
    exemptions for specific juvenile
        activities, 711
    parental rights, 711–712
    social interests served by, 712
Custody, 451–649
    adversarial process, 617–619
    age of child and, 556–557
    alternative dispute resolution, 549–550,
        619–623
    best interests of child standard, 562–584
    breastfeeding, 579
    child's right to counsel, 627–628
    child's role, 574–575, 625–626
    child's wishes, 477–478
    collaborative law, 623
    custodial responsibility standard, 561
    day care, 579
    delay in resolving disputes, 469–470
    dispute resolution, 549–550, 619–623
    "divided" custody, 592
    effects of divorce on children, 550–554
    emotional ties of parent and child, 567
    empirical research, 550–552

employment, 566
enforcement of decrees, 631–636
equally fit or unfit parents, 580
factors affecting decision, 561, 579–580
fitness, 580
frozen embryos, 647
guardianship distinguished, 472–473
history, 562–564
interstate cases, jurisdictional and
    enforcement problems, 631–636
in vitro fertilization and embryo
    transfers, 646–649
joint. *See* Joint custody
jurisdiction over decrees, 631–636
least detrimental alternative, 475
"legal" vs. "physical" custody, 586, 592
maternal preference, 555–556, 560, 563
mediation, 619–623
mentally disabled children, 461–469,
    478–479
mentally disabled parents, 573,
    576–577
modification of agreements, 578,
    628–631
moral fitness, 567–568
neglect, 574–575, 579–580
number of children in family and, 557
overnight stays, 555–556
parental agreements, effect of, 559, 561
"parental alienation syndrome,"
    475–476
parenting skills, 566
paternal preference, 562–563
physical and mental health and age of
    parents, 566
physical custody, 555–557
physical illness or disability, 576–577
primary caretaker presumption,
    560–562, 564–565
private dispute settlement, 472–473,
    479–480
probability of outcome decisions,
    481–484
process, decisionmaking adversarial,
    617–619
psychological evidence, 474–476
"psychological parent" concept and,
    477–479
race, 580–584
random selection (coin-flipping),
    623–625

Custody, (*continued*)
    religion, 573, 577–578
    reproductive technology and, 637–649
    residential arrangements, 556–557
    sex of child and, 556
    sexual abuse, 579–580
    sexual orientation, 569–571
    siblings, 562
    smoking by parent, 579
    "sole" custody, 592
    "split" custody, 592
    stability of home environment and
        employment, 568
    state paternalism and, 486
    by stepparents, 491–492
    substance abuse, 579–580
    surrogate parenting agreements and.
        See Surrogate parenting
        agreements
    third-party, 477
    time spent with child, 578
    unwed fathers' rights, 495–498
    visitation, 559, 597–599, 604–609
    wealth, 572–575
    weight of parental agreements, 559
Custody decrees
    enforcement, 631–636
    jurisdiction, 631–636
    modification of, 628–631

Day care, custody after divorce and, 579
Deadbeat Parents Punishment Act, 205
Death row, juveniles on. *See* Capital
        punishment
Defenses to crime
    infancy, 778–780
    mens rea lacking, 777, 778–780
Delinquents. *See* Juvenile delinquency
Dependent children. *See also* Child
        abuse; Neglected children
    California statute, 318–321
    delinquents distinguished from,
        769–771
    incorrigible children, 742–746
Depression in adolescents, antipsychotic
        drugs and, 436–437
Detention, pretrial, 773, 825–827
Dial-a-porn, 107–108
Dietary control for pregnant women, 36
Disabled children
    infants, 409–427

parental custody decision, 576–577
post-majority support, 198
Supplemental Security Income (SSI)
        program, 217
Discipline. *See* Corporal punishment by
        parent
Discrimination
    based on disability, 416–418
    based on gender. *See* Gender
        discrimination
Divorce. *See also* Custody; Support
    parental notification in cases of,
        849–850
    parent-child divorce, 751–752
    support and, 192–200
Dog sniffs in public schools,
        846. *See also* Search
        and seizure
Domestic violence
    abortion and, 41–42
    custody decision, as factor in, 561–562,
        579–580, 596
    visitation rights, effect on, 599,
        602–604
Double jeopardy, transfers to adult court
        and, 782, 822–824
Drinking. *See* Liquor laws; Substance
        abuse
Driving by minors, 662–676
    age restrictions, 663
    child labor laws, 658–659
    drunk driving problem, 686–688
    minor's liability, 670–671
    negligent entrustment, 667–669
    parental consent, 664–666
    parental liability, 666
    special rules for minors, 663–664
    standards for care, 671–672
Drugs
    depression in adolescents, antipsychotic
        drugs and, 436–437
    medical experimentation. *See* Medical
        experimentation
    substance abuse. *See* Substance abuse
Due process. *See also* Confrontation, right
        to; Right to counsel
    anti-gang legislation, 767
    child abuse and
        children's rights, generally, 810–811
        inclusion in child abuse registry,
            257–263

commitment of minors, 393–400
   confessions in juvenile proceedings,
      857–860
   corporal punishment, 228, 243, 246
   family integrity, right to, 307–308
   hearings
      commitment to mental hospital,
         396–397
      foster parents' rights, 334–345
      pretrial detention, 826
      transfers to adult court, 780–784
   judicial waivers, 781
   juvenile court proceedings, 785–786,
      825–827
   juvenile delinquency cases, 798–811
   juvenile proceedings other than
      delinquency, 813–814
   notice of charges, 849–850
   paternity, establishment of, 161–167
   pretrial detention, 825–827
   student punishment for expressive
      activity, 133
   summary seizure, 308
   unwed fathers' rights, 496–498,
      505–512
   "void-for-vagueness" doctrine,
      719–722
   wage withholding to enforce support
      obligation, 206

Earnings of minor, parents' common
   law rights to, 158
Education. *See also* Schools
   alien children's right to, 57
   Amish attitudes, 63–70, 78–80
   child's views considered, 78–80
   compulsory, 51–53, 63–70, 78–80
   constitutional right to, 57
   foreign language, 49–51, 54–55
   funding of, 56–57
   government indoctrination and, 54–55
   Hasidic community and, 69
   home schooling, 55, 68–69
   parental rights movement, 57–58
   parent's duty to educate, 152
   Pledge of Allegiance, 67–68
   pluralism in, 55
   post-minority support issues, 192–198
   public and private discussed, 51–58
   religious views, disagreement of
      parents, 67–68

sex education. *See* Sex education
state's duties and limitations, 57, 63–65
voucher program, 56–57
xenophobia and, 54–55
Elderly parents and filial responsibility
   laws, 191
Electronic benefits transfer systems, 218
Emancipated minors
   child's emancipation petition, 751–752
   consent for medical care, 376, 380, 406
   contraception, 689–696
   driving, parent's consent, 666
   medical treatment, 376, 380, 406
   parent-child divorce, 751–752
   post-minority support, 191–198
   proposed uniform statute, issues to be
      addressed in, 752
   rights and duties of parent,
      effect of, 158
   voting rights, 750–751
Embryo transfers, 45–46, 646–649. *See
      also* Surrogate parenting
      agreements
Emergencies, medical
   minor's consent for treatment,
      378, 380
   parental consent, 400
   payment for care, 154–157
Emergency Assistance for Needy Families
      Program, 221–222
Employment programs
   food stamp recipients, 218
   "responsible fatherhood" proposed
      legislation, 206
Employment screening for child abusers,
      257–263
Equal protection
   adoption by same-sex partners, 532–533
   capital punishment, 797
   child abuse reporting laws, 264
   curfew laws, 711
   education, right to, 57
   juvenile offenders, 810–811
   nonmarital children, 167
   paternal rights, 457–458
   race and, 581
   religious freedom and, 62
   status offenders, 714, 717–718
   support laws and, 158
   surrogate mothers and, 639
   unwed fathers, 495–498, 505–512

Ethnicity as consideration in
    adoption, 544
European Convention for the Protection of
    Human Rights and Fundamental
    Freedoms, 237
Euthanasia of disabled newborns,
    421, 423–424
Experimentation on humans. *See* Medical
    experimentation
Expungement
    of records of child maltreatment when
        unsubstantiated or false, 264

Fair Labor Standards Act, 70,
    657–659
Family autonomy, government
    intervention and, 54
Family courts. *See* Juvenile courts
Family Entertainment and Copyright Act
    (FECA), 104, 111
Family expense statutes, 191
Family integrity
    adoption by same-sex partners, 528–533
    children's rights and, 746–748
    custody laws and, 486
    fundamental right to, 307–308
Family Movie Act, 104, 111
Family planning. *See* Contraception
Family Support Act, 195, 204
Farm Bill, 218
Farm Security and Rural Investment
    Act, 219
Fathers. *See also* Parent and child;
        Paternity
    abortion and, 39–46
    adoption and. *See* Adoption
    custodial preference, 562–563
    custody rights, 495–498
    notice of adoption to, 505–512
    partial-birth abortion, legal standing to
        challenge state ban on, 46
    termination of rights, 513
    unwed
        adoption, consent to, 495, 498,
            505–512
        presumption of unfitness,
            495–498
FECA. *See* Family Entertainment and
        Copyright Act (FECA)
Federal Refusal Clause, 24
Federal Trade Commission, 112–113

Fertility Clinic Success Rate and
    Certification Act, 647
Fetus. *See also* Abortion; Pregnancy
    actions for death, 48
    criminal sanctions for failure to protect,
        38–39
    custody of, 32
    father's interest in, 44–45
    fetal homicide legislation, 47
    fetal protection policies, 39
    guardians for, 46
    health as state's responsibility, 6–7,
        32–39, 49
    legal rights of, 10–11
    medical care of, 36
    as "person," 8–9, 47
    prenatal abuse and neglect, 32, 38–39,
        49
    prenatal genetic testing, 36
    state's compelling interest, 32–39
    surgery on, 36, 46
    viable defined, 10
Filial responsibility laws, 191
Financial responsibility. *See also* Support
    lawyers' fees in delinquency
        proceedings, 872
    for minor's medical care, 378–382
Firearms. *See* Weapons
First Amendment rights. *See* Freedom of
        expression; Freedom of religion;
        Freedom of speech
Food stamp program, 217–219, 223
Foster care, 328–361
    aging out of older foster children, 349–
        352
    average length of stay, 331–333
    child welfare system, 333–334
    coercive vs. voluntary placements,
        328–329, 346
    as contractual relationship, 345
    court-appointed special advocates
        (CASAs), 333
    criticisms and proposals for reform,
        355–359
    criticisms of Adoption and Safe
        Families Act, 355–359
    current state of, 331–333
    empirical research, 321–323
    foster family, removal from, 334–345
    foster parents' rights due process,
        334–345

gays and lesbians as foster parents, 535
government-sponsored, 329–330
grounds for removal, 320–321
kinship care, 346
legal claims by foster children,
    352–353
limited, 330–331
litigation's role in, 354–355
New York system critique, 334–345
older foster children, aging out of,
    349–352
placement, 330–331
pre-removal procedures, 330
principles for governing, 331
psychological impact, 321–323
psychological parent and, 345–346
race and, 357–359
reform of, 352–361
removal of child from foster family,
    334–345
sexual orientation, 347
sibling relationships, child's rights
    regarding, 345
statutory, 352–353
subsidies for children with special
    needs, 346–347
theory of temporariness, 322
voluntary placement, 346
Foster Care Independence Act, 352
Freedom of Access to Clinic Entrances
    Act, 30
Freedom of association
anti-gang legislation and, 768
Freedom of expression, 128–135
children in need of supervision and, 722
curfew laws, 702–709
dress codes, 131–132
Internet-based, 134
invasion of rights test, 129–130
parental role, 127–128
political speech by students, 114–128
punishment of students for expressive
    activity, 133–135
school-related speech, 128–129
sexual orientation, 131
Tinker test, 126
"true threat" doctrine, 134
viewpoint discrimination, 129–130
Freedom of religion
Amish children, 78–80
child labor laws and, 58–62, 70

compulsory education vs., 63–70,
    78–80
compulsory medical care and, 31–39
custody decision, religion as factor in,
    577–578
generally applicable law, religious
    exemption, 69–70
Hasidic community, 69
Jehovah's Witnesses, 58–62
Pledge of Allegiance, 67–68
public funding of religious
    schools, 56–57
visitation, religious issues in, 604–607
Freedom of speech. *See also* Freedom of
    expression
dial-a-porn, 107–108
movie ratings, 108–111
music labels, 111–113
obscenity and, 83–90
parental role, 127–128
restricting minor's access in modern
    era, 106–114
Tinker test, 126
video games, 113–114
violent materials and, 106–114
Full Faith and Credit for Child Support
    Orders Act, 204–205

Gag rule (abortion counseling), 24–25
Gangs
anti-gang legislation,
    767–769
Criminal Gang Abatement Act, 768
effect on deterrence, 758–760
transfer of cases to adult court, 782
Gender discrimination
abortion laws as, 22–23
fetal protection employment
    policies, 38
status offenders, 731–732
Genetic testing for paternity
prenatal, 36
PRWORA and, 223
Gore, Tipper, 112
Government income transfer programs,
    216–221
Grandparents
post-adoption, 492–495
support obligation of, 206
visitation rights of, 81–82,
    493–495, 609–617

Guardian ad litem
  for abused child, 312
  in custody disputes, 627
  juvenile court proceedings, 863
  unborn children, representation
      of, 10, 36
Guardians
  child's choice of, 478–479
  child's estate, 214–215
  custody law, 472–473
  institutionalized children, 461–469
  lawyer as juvenile's guardian in court,
      875–876
  unborn children, representation of, 46
Gun-Free School Act, 133
Guns. *See* Weapons

Habeas corpus, 582, 636, 798–801
Hague Convention on the Civil Aspects
    of International Childhood
    Abduction, 629
Hasidism, 69
Health care. *See* Medical care
Health insurance, post-minority support
    and, 194
HIV. *See* AIDS
Homelessness, 218
Home schooling, 55, 68–69
Homicide
  abortion as, 47
  mens rea element required for, 860
  withholding care from disabled
      infant, 422
Homosexuality. *See* Sexual orientation
Human experimentation. *See* Medical
    experimentation
Hunger Prevention Act, 218
Hyde Amendment, 23

Illegitimate children. *See* Nonmarital
    children
Immigration, status of nonmarital children
    and, 177–178
Immunizations
  compulsory, 385–386
  federal funding, 385–386
  history of, 439–441
  minor's consent for, 378
  religious exemptions, 385–386
Improving America's Schools Act, 132
Incarceration. *See* Prisons and prisoners

Income transfer programs, government,
    216–221
Incorrigible children, 742–746
Indian Child Welfare Act, 544
Indians, ritual drug use by, 69–70
Infancy defense
  common law, 880
  contract law, 673–676
  juvenile delinquents, 778–780
Infanticide, 421
Infants
  care review committees, 417, 420
  clearly beneficial therapies, 424–425
  disabled, 409–427
  euthanasia and, 427
  family's ability to cope, 420–422
  federal legislation, 416–420, 426–427
  futile therapies, 424–425
  Groningen Protocol, 427
  Infant Doe case, 416–422
Informed consent in abortion cases,
    25–26
Inheritance
  children's rights, 207–213
  child support obligations and, 212
  disinheritance of children, 151,
      210–212
  family protection statutes, 212
  guardianship, 214–215
  intestate share for a child, 210
  nonmarital children, 161, 167,
      172–173
  parent's right to inherit from, 172
  posthumous children, 212–213
  stepchild's rights, 493
  termination of parental rights and, 472
  trusts, 215
  unborn child's rights, 10, 49
In loco parentis doctrine, 127, 190
Institutionalization. *See* Commitment of
    children; Mental hospitals
Inter-Ethnic Adoption Act, 543
International law
  ban on corporal punishment of children,
      234–236
  capital punishment, 798
  child abduction, 629–630
  death penalty for juveniles, 292, 798
  human research and experimentation,
      438–442
  surrogacy, 644

Internet
    child pornography on, 90–96, 98
    constitutionality of punishment for
        Internet-based expressive
        activity, 134
    filtering technologies, 92–95, 132
    indecent or offensive materials on,
        92–95, 98
    restricting access of minors, 92–95, 98
Intestacy. *See* Inheritance
In vitro fertilization
    early controversies, 646–649
    embryo disputes, post-divorce, 647
    ethics issues, 646–649
    posthumous use, 647

Jehovah's Witnesses, 58–62, 384
Job Opportunities and Basic Skills (JOBS)
    program, 222
Joint custody, 584–597
    approximation standard, 596
    authority to award, 586–587
    benefits of, 587–589, 591
    criticisms of, 587
    defined, 585–586, 592
    factors affecting decision
        age and number of children, 590
        child's preference, 589–590
        demands of parental
            employment, 590
        disruptive effect, 590, 595–596
        financial considerations, 591, 595
        fitness, 589
        geographic proximity, 590, 595
        parental cooperation, 587–589,
            594–595
        parent-child relationship, 589
        spousal abuse, 596
    modification of agreements, 630
    parental agreements, effect of, 594, 596
    presumption, preference or option,
        593–594
    shared parenting, 555–558
Jury trial. *See* Trial by jury
Juvenile courts
    abolition, proposed, 879–880
    adjudicatory proceedings, 774–776
    California dependency statute, 318–321
    as "civil" not "criminal," 808
    delinquency cases, 83, 773–776
    delinquents' views, 814

    dispositional proceedings, 774,
        784–787
    due process, 785–786, 798–811
    future of, 879–880
    goal as protective and rehabilitative,
        771–772
    historical origins, 801–805
    infancy defense, 778–780
    judge's discretionary power, 784–785
    jurisdiction
        age limits, 777
        delinquency, 83, 678, 755, 774,
            776–778
        incorrigible child cases, 742–746
    lawyers' role in proceedings, 869–879
    need for counsel in proceedings, 875
    neglect cases, 83, 388–392, 400–405,
        470–471
    orthodox theory, 769–770
    procedural differences between
        delinquency vs. criminal process,
        772, 798–868
    public trial, 822
    records, 803, 810, 814
    revisionist theory, 769–771
    similarities to adult court, 879–880
    status offender cases, 83, 713–733
    transcript of proceedings, 810
    transfers to criminal courts, 780–784
    trial by jury, right of, 815–819
    unborn children, 31–34
Juvenile delinquency, 753–880
    adolescent brain research, culpability of
        juvenile offenders and, 761–762
    age distribution, 756, 760
    arrests, 765–766, 824–825
    capital punishment. *See* Capital
        punishment
    case study of court process, 753
    causes of delinquency, generally,
        769–771
    due process rights, 798–811, 825–827,
        857–860
    female, 764
    gangs, 767–769, 775–776, 778–780
    involving minorities, 764
    pretrial detention, 773, 825–827
    recidivism, 755–762, 784
    records, 756
    rehabilitation, 755–758, 762–763,
        771–772

Juvenile delinquency (*continued*)
  right to counsel, 786, 806–807, 868,
      871–872
  separation from adult offenders, 772,
      787–788, 827
  statistics, 756
  status offenders as, 740
  treatment after adjudication hearings,
      784–787
  by type of crime, 765–766
Juvenile justice
  adult criminal law compared, 717–718,
      753, 780–781
  bureaucratic process, 772–773
  capital punishment. *See* Capital
      punishment
  deterrence justification for punishment,
      758–760
  notice of charges, 849–850
  politicization of crime, 763
  pretrial detention, 773, 825–827
  proposed reforms, 879–880
  public opinion and, 762–763
  purposes of, 755–762
  rehabilitation model of, move toward
      punitive policies from, 762–763
  retribution, punishment as, 761–762
  sentencing, 798, 879–880
  transfer to adult court, 768, 774, 780–
      784, 856, 879–880
  waiver of jurisdiction
    judicial waiver, 780–784
    "legislative" or "automatic" waiver,
        782
    prosecutorial discretion, 782
  waiver of rights, 857–860, 864–868
Juvenile Justice and Delinquency
      Prevention Act, 724, 737–740, 788
Juvenile Justice Standards
  defenses to juvenile crime, 781–782
  detention with adults, 787
  jurisdictional requirements of juvenile
      courts, 778
  medical care, 379–381
  proposed, 732–733
  right to counsel, 868
  role of parents and guardians ad litem,
      862–864
  sentencing guidelines, 787
  transfers to adult court, 781–782
  waiver of rights, 861–864

Keeping Children and Families Safe Act,
      248
Kidnapping. *See* Abduction of children in
      custody disputes
Kinship care, 346

Lawyers. *See also* Right to counsel
  advocacy role, 875–879
  "amicus curiae" function, 875
  as counselors, 877–878
  duty to client, 869
  as guardians of juveniles in court,
      875–876
  professional responsibility, 869,
      872–874
  role in juvenile proceedings, 861–862,
      869–879
  Standards of Practice. *See* ABA
Legal paternalism, 31–39
Legitimacy
  artificial insemination, child conceived
      by, 638
  defined, 150
  effect on consent to adopt, 495
  English common law, 165
  obligation to provide for legitimate
      child, 150–151
  presumption of, 161–167
Libraries, censorship of, 132
Licenses, tracking child support
      obligations and, 206
Life sentences for juveniles, 798
Life support
  disabled infants, 409–427
  for pregnant woman, 46
Liquor laws, 676–689
  adolescents and alcohol, research
      findings on, 681–682
  criminal sanctions
    adult suppliers, 678
    minors, 678
    parental exemption, 678–679
  enforcement, 680
  liability of suppliers, 678
  minimum age laws, 681–689
    alternatives to, 682–686
    drunk driving and, 686–688
    enforcement, 688
    minors' drinking habits, effect on,
        681–682
    parent's role, 689

societal norms, conflict with,
682–686
as symbolic of social norms, 682–686
Locke, John, 749–750
Locker searches in public schools,
844–845. *See also* Search and
seizure

Maintenance. *See* Support
Marriage
parental consent to adolescent
marriage, 153
same-sex marriage, 187–188
adoption and, 536–537
Uniform Marriage and Divorce Act,
194–195, 199
Maternal health
compulsory prenatal care, 36
state's interest, 7–8, 13–17, 21, 27,
31–34
Mature minors
consent for abortion, 377–378
consent for medical care, 381, 406
waiver of rights, 861–862
Mediation
children's role in, 621–623
of custody disputes, 549–550
mediator's role in, 619–623
Medicaid
abortion funding, 23
coverage of children, generally,
220, 382
older foster care children and, 352
Medical care, 371–449. *See also*
Abortion; Mental hospitals
adolescents, 427–437
child's view considered, 383–385
commitment to mental hospital,
393–400
competency to consent, 407–408
contraception. *See* Contraception
disagreement between parents,
384–385, 400–405
drinking. *See* Liquor laws
emergency, 154–157, 378, 380, 400
exceptions and limitations, 406
financial responsibility for minor's,
154–159, 378–382
immunizations. *See* Immunizations
institutionalized children, 461–469
minor's consent, 374–381, 405–408

neglect limitation, 388–400
obesity, 436–437
parental consent, 372–374, 379
pregnant women, 32–39
sexually transmitted diseases, 701. *See
also* AIDS
state-imposed requirements, 385–388
suicide, 428–436
Medical experimentation
consent, 437–449
federal regulation (Common Rule), 440
guidelines for research on children,
439–441
history, 439–441
need for, 441
Nuremberg Code, 439–441
orphans and foundlings, 439
parental consent, 437–449
potentially hazardous nontherapeutic
research, 442–448
procedures not undertaken for treatment
of child in question, 442–448
reproductive research, 646–649
sample problems, 437–438
Medical screening
for HIV, 387
newborns, 387
in schools, 387
Mens rea element in criminal conduct,
778–780, 860
Mental health
as factor in best interests test, 573,
576–577
minor's consent for treatment,
381, 406
of parent, in custody decision, 573,
576–577
Mental hospitals
due process in commitment
proceedings, 393–400
"transinstitutionalization," 399
"voluntary" commitment by parents,
393–400
Mentally disabled
capital punishment, 791, 797
guardianship of, 461–469, 478–479
lawyer's representation of, 874
medical care, 388–390, 393–400
newborns, care decisions, 416–418
waiver of rights in juvenile
proceedings, 866

Metal detectors in public schools,
    845–846. *See also* Search and
    seizure
Mickey Leland Childhood Hunger Relief
    Act, 218
Mill, John Stuart, 1–2
Minors. *See* Adolescents; Children;
    Emancipated minors; Mature
    minors; Property of minor
Miranda rights, 852–860
    parental role, 854–856
    possibility of transfer to adult court
        and, 856
    requirements triggering juvenile,
        853–854
    right to counsel, 853–857, 868
    waiver of, 857–860, 864–867
Missing, Exploited and Runaway Children
    Protection Act, 723–724
Missing Children's Assistance Act, 724
Model Act Governing Assisted
    Reproductive Technology
    (ABA), 213, 644, 648
Model Code of Professional
    Responsibility (ABA), 873–874
Model Penal Code, 232–233
Model Rules of Professional Conduct
    (ABA), 874
Movies
    controlling minors' access to, 108–111
    Family Movie Act, 111
    rating of, 108–111
    sexual content in, 108–111
    violent content in, 108–111
Multiethnic Placement Act, 543
Music labeling, 111–113

National Highway Safety Designation
    Act, 688
National Parent Teachers Association of
    America, 111
National Research Act, 440
National School Lunch Act, 219
National Vaccine Injury Compensation
    Act of 1986, 386
Native Americans, ritual drug use by,
    69–70
Natural Death Act, 415
"Necessaries" doctrine, 158–159
Neglected children, 305–352. *See also*
    Child abuse

California dependency statute, 318–321
case study, 323–328
class bias suggested, 318
custody decision, neglect as factor in,
    574–575, 579–580
defined, Alabama law, 305, 308–309
disabled infants, withholding of care,
    418–420
early intensive home visitation,
    359–360
emotional neglect, 311–312, 474
family preservation, 360–361
home "fitness" decision, 308–309,
    314–317
medical considerations, generally, 384,
    388–392, 400–405
race as factor, 309–310
removal from home, 496. *See also*
    Foster care
right to counsel, 309, 312–313, 390
social services as alternative to
    removal, 318
summary seizure, 305–310
termination of parental rights, 471–472
Negligence
    medical, 372–374
    minor's standard of care, 671–672
    parental negligence in allowing minor
        to drive, 667–669
    prenatal injuries, 48
Newborns. *See* Infants
New York system of foster care,
    334–345
No Child Left Behind Act, 56–57, 134
Nonmarital children. *See also* Paternity
    adoption, father's rights and, 495, 498
    custody of, 495–498
    defined, 160, 168–171
    demographic data for United States, 171
    dependency benefits, 176–177
    English common law, 160–161, 167–168
    equal protection and, 167
    immigration status, 177–178
    inheritance rights, 161, 167, 172–173
    legal status, 161
    legitimation, 170–171
    support obligation for, 160–161, 167,
        171–174
    unwed teen mothers, welfare
        benefits, 223
    visitation by father of, 162–164

Notice
    abortion
        natural father's right to, 505–512
        parental notification prior to minor's
            abortion, 135–148, 379
    charges against juvenile, 849–850
    juvenile court proceedings, 805–806,
        810–811
    right to counsel, 864, 871
Nuremberg Code, 439–441

Obesity in children and adolescents,
    436–437
Obscenity. *See also* Pornography
    child-related legislation, 83–90,
        96–104
    children's and adults' rights
        differentiated, 83–90, 97–101
    children's First Amendment rights,
        103–104
    "community standards" criterion,
        91, 99
    defined, 87–88
    effectiveness of parental regulation,
        101–103
    effects of, 85–87, 96, 99–101
    First Amendment protection, 83–90
    on Internet, 90–96
    pictorial vs. written, 89, 96
    protection of parents' rights, 101
    state's role in regulating, 97–101
    "variable obscenity" concept, 84–85,
        97–101
Old Age Survivors and Disability
    Insurance Program (OASDI),
    216–217
Overbreadth. *See* Vagueness

Parens patriae, 82, 389, 391, 403, 405,
    770, 804
Parental Kidnapping Prevention Act,
    632–634, 636
Parental termination. *See* Termination of
    parental rights
Parent and child
    abuse by parent. *See* Child abuse;
        Sexual abuse
    attachment theory, 322
    authority to rear, 53–55, 59–60
    Blackstone's view on, 149–154
    child as victim, 71

child's services and earnings, parent's
    right to, 158
child's standing to sue for personal
    injuries, 48
commitment of children. *See*
    Commitment of children
conflicting interests of, rights of child
    and, 81–82
control of child's property, 213–216
duties of children, 153–154
education as parent's duty, 152
emancipation of. *See* Emancipated
    minors
foster care. *See* Foster care
juvenile court proceedings, issues in,
    857–860, 862–867, 872
limitation on parental rights, 2–3
marriage, parent's consent to, 153
property, child as, 53–54, 523–526,
    652
protection as parental duty, 152
"psychological parent" concept,
    345–346, 465–466, 477–479
religious upbringing, parental control
    over, 66
Roman law, 152
schools, parent's right to choose, 53–55
support obligations. *See* Support
surrogate parenting agreements, rights
    to child under, 455–458
termination of relationship. *See*
    Termination of parental rights
traditional roles, 746–748
truancy, punishing parents for, 742
unwed father's relationship with child,
    515–517
Parenthood licensing, 70–78
Parents' Music Resource Center, 112
Partial-birth abortion, 13–20, 28
Paternity
    assisted reproduction, child of, 639
    conduct, establishment by, 175
    disestablishment, 176
    establishment, 161–167, 223
    genetic testing and, 174, 223
    interstate paternity establishment,
        175–176
    limitation period for establishing,
        173–174, 204
    presumption of, 161–167
    proceedings, 173–176

Paternity (*continued*)
   Revised Uniform Parentage Act, 500
   in surrogate parenting situations, 641
   Uniform Adoption Act, 515
   voluntary acknowledgment
      programs, 223
   voluntary paternity establishment, 174
Personal Responsibility and Work
      Opportunity Reconciliation Act
      (PRWORA)
   paternity establishment, 223, 500
   provisions on paternity, 205–206,
      221–225, 358, 382
   sanctions, 223–225
   sex education, funding of abstinence-
      based, 702
   unwed teenage mothers, 223
   work requirements, 222–223
Persons in need of supervision (PINS),
      719–722, 724–731, 733–742. *See*
      also Status offenders
Physicians
   abortion, role in decisionmaking,
      12, 145
   liability for treating minor without
      parental consent, 375–376
   responsibilities regarding disabled
      infants, 423–424
Political speech by students, 114–128
Poor laws, 157–158, 167, 770–771
Pornography. *See also* Obscenity
   child, 90–96, 98, 104–106
   commercial distribution to children,
      regulation of, 96
   Commission on Obscenity and
      Pornography, 99–100, 106–107
   "community standards" criterion, 91
   dial-a-porn, 107–108
   on Internet, protection of minors
     from exposure to, 90–96
     parents' role, 96
   protection of children from sexual
      exploitation, 104–106
   telephone, 107–108
Posthumous children
   inheritance rights of, 212–213
   posthumously conceived, 49, 207–210,
      212–213
Postpartum psychosis defense, 47
Pregnancy. *See also* Abortion; Fetus
   autonomy vs. equality, 37–38

cesarean section, forced, 31–34
criminal sanctions for failure to protect
   fetus, 38–39
discrimination and, 38
fetal protection policies, 39
HIV-infected mothers, 36
justification for intervention, 35
medical treatment, 32–39
minor's consent for medical care,
   375–378, 381, 405–406
mother's conduct during, 36, 38–39
refusal of treatment during, 32–39
religious belief, refusal of treatment, 37
standard for intervention, 37
substance abuse during, 36, 38–39
teenage, 697–698
terminal illness, 37
unwed mothers, welfare benefits, 223
Prisons and prisoners
   incapacitation as goal of
      punishment of, 760
   parental termination, incarceration as
      grounds for, 367–368
   segregation of juveniles from adults,
      787–788
   visitation rights, effect on, 599–600
Privacy
   abortion, 5, 7–10, 20–21
   adoption by gays and lesbians, rights of
      privacy and, 528–533
   consensual sexual activity and right to,
      698–699
   contraception and, 689–696
   medical treatment and, 405–406
   school searches and, 829–832, 842–843
   surrogate parenting agreements
      and, 640
Probation
   dispositional decisions for juvenile
      delinquents, 785
   request to meet with probation officers
      under *Miranda* rights, 855–856
   violation of as juvenile delinquency,
      713–719
Professional responsibility
   lawyer's, in juvenile court proceedings,
      869, 872–874
   probation officers, 785
Property, children as, 53–54, 523–526, 652
Property of minor
   guardian of child's estate, 214–215

held in minor's name, 214–215
management and control, 213–216
parent's rights, 213–216
trusts for children's property, 215
Uniform Transfers to Minors Act,
215–216
Prostitution, runaways and, 723
Protect Children from Video Game Sex
and Violence Act
(proposed), 114
Protection of Children Against Sexual
Exploitation Act, 104–105
Protection of Children Against Sexual
Predators Act, 105–106
PRWORA. *See* Personal Responsibility
and Work Opportunity
Reconciliation Act (PRWORA)
Punishment. *See* Corporal punishment by
parent; Cruel and unusual
punishment; Juvenile justice

Race
adoption
empirical research, 542–543
federal legislation, 543
opposition to, arguments in, 545–547
post-adoption visitation by natural
parent, 541
race-matching policies, background
of, 541–542
relevance of race to, 537–547
transracial, 357–359, 537–547
custody decision, as factor in,
580–584
neglect and, 309–310
Racketeer Influenced and Corrupt
Organizations Act (RICO),
767–768
Rape of child
capital punishment for, 283–292
Recidivism
child rape cases, 289–290
juvenile delinquency, 755–762, 784
Recording Industry Association of
America, 111–112
Reformatories, origins of, 770–771
Rehabilitation Act, 416–419
Religion, role of
abortion and, 10
in adoption, 543–544
in custody, 573, 577–578

pregnant women, refusal of
treatment, 37
in visitation, 604–607
Religious freedom. *See* Freedom of
religion
Religious Freedom Restoration Act,
69–70
Religious Land Use and Institutionalized
Persons Act, 69–70
Removal of children. *See* Child abuse;
Foster care; Termination of
parental rights
Reproductive technologies. *See* Assisted
reproduction
"Reproductive tourism," 644
Restatement (Second) of Torts,
233, 236, 239
Restatement (Third) of Torts, 671–672
Retarded children. *See* Mentally
disabled
Revised Uniform Reciprocal Enforcement
of Support Act (RURESA), 202
Right to counsel
custody disputes, children in, 627–628
delinquency proceedings, 806–807,
810–811, 871–872
juvenile court proceedings, 390, 786
Miranda rights, 853–857, 868
neglect cases, children in, 309, 312–313
parental termination, 369–370
parent's rights, 863–864, 872
stage of proceeding at which right
attaches, 871–872
status offender cases, 714,
716–719, 731
waiver of, 861–862, 864, 868
RU-486, 28–29, 146
Runaway and Homeless Youth Act, 724
Runaways
institutionalization of, 740
profile of, 723–724
prostitution, 740
shelters, 722–723
street life, 723–724
Runaway Youth Act, 722–724

Same-sex marriage, 187–188, 536–537
Schools. *See also* Education; Truancy
antibullying legislation, 435–436
attendance requirements for welfare
benefits, 223–224

Schools (*continued*)
   child abuse and, 135, 228, 238–243
   dress codes, 131–132
   educational mission, 130
   libraries, censorship and, 132
   in loco parentis, 829
   medical screening, 386–387
   parent's right to choose, 53–55
   political expression, students' rights to,
      114–126, 128
   school-related speech, 128–129
   search and seizure. *See* Search and
      seizure
   violence in
      Columbine incident, 107
      First Amendment and, 130–131
      procedural rights and, 133–135
      weapons in, 133–134
   voucher program, 56–57
   zero-tolerance policies, 133–135
Search and seizure, 824–849
   incident to arrest, 824–825
   public schools, 827–849
      automobile searches on school
         grounds, 845
      in concert with or at behest of law
         enforcement, 844
      consent to, 848
      dog sniffs, 846
      drug testing, 834–840
      exclusionary rule, 844
      incident to arrest, 848
      locker searches, 844–845
      metal detectors and weapons,
         845–846
      privacy interest, 842–843
      probable cause standard, 832–834,
         840–841
   reasonableness requirement, 840–841
   "special needs" doctrine, 841–842
   strip searches, 846–848
   warrant requirement, 831, 848
Second Amendment, 434
"Second-parent adoptions," 535–536
Self-incrimination, juvenile's rights and,
      730–731
Sentencing, 786–787, 879–880
Separation agreements and post-minority
      support, 198
Sex discrimination. *See* Gender
   discrimination

Sex education
   abstinence-based, 702
   AIDS, 702
   parental rights, 57–58
Sexual abuse, 269–283
   anatomically correct dolls, 302
   background, 301
   child rape
      adult rape compared, 290
      capital punishment, 283–292
      data, 289
      recidivism, 289–290
      standards of decency, 291–292
   child victim as witness, 292–304
   constitutionality of, 303
   custody decision, as factor in, 579–580
   definitions, 272–273
   determination of necessity, 301–302
   excited utterances or spontaneous
      declarations, 300
   federal legislation, 302
   hearsay evidence, 299–300, 488
   impact of, 274–275
   in-court procedures for child victim,
      292–297
   intervention, coordination of, 277
   legal policy information, 277–283
   marital privilege, abrogation of, 304
   medical diagnosis and treatment
      exception, 300
   mental health professionals, role of,
      277–283
   out-of-court statements, 297–298
   prevalence of, 273–274
   prevention, 275–277
   punishment vs. treatment, 275–277, 283
   "tender years" hearsay statutes, 299,
      304
   victims, protective mechanisms for
      testimony of, 303–304
Sexual activity
   minors, 689–696
   right to privacy in consensual sexual
      conduct, 698–699
Sexually transmitted diseases (STDs),
      375–378, 381, 405–406, 697
   AIDS. *See* AIDS
   data on teens and, 701
Sexual orientation
   adoption, 528–537
      equal protection, 532–533

family integrity, right to, 528–533
  foster parenting bans, distinguished
    from, 535
  interstate recognition, 536
  private sexual intimacy, right to,
    528–533
  right to privacy, 528–533
  same-sex marriage and, 536–537
  "second-parent adoptions," 535–536
  social science data on impact of gay
    parenting, 537
  state restrictions, 534
  stereotypes and, 534
  Uniform Parentage Act, 537
  visitation rights and, 608–609
child support, same-sex couples and,
  187–188
  as factor in custody, 569–571, 642–643
  foster care, 347, 535
  "second-parent" visitation rights,
    615–616
Shared parenting, 555–558
Smoking, pregnant women and, 36
Social agencies
  as alternative to court jurisdiction in
    status offender cases, 732–733
  central registries of child abuse cases,
    257–263
  home services as alternative to
    removal, 318
  intervention in sexual abuse cases, 277
Social Security Act
  nonmarital children, benefits
    for, 177, 203
  provisions for dependents, 221
Special Supplemental Nutrition Program
    for Women, Infants, and
    Children, 219–220
Sperm donors. *See* Assisted reproduction
Spousal abuse. *See* Domestic violence
Standards of proof
  juvenile court proceedings, 817–820
  medical care decisions, 400–405
  neglect cases, 389–390
  parental termination, 368–369
  status offenses, 730
State Children's Health Insurance
    Program, 22, 47, 221
State paternalism, custody law and, 486
Status offenders, 713–752
  arguments for and against, 740–741

compliance rate, 739–740
criticisms of, 740–741
deinstitutionalization, 737
dispositions in PINS cases, 733–742
equal protection, 714, 717–718
federal legislative efforts, 737–739
incorrigible children, 742–746
justification for statutes, 729–730
juvenile court jurisdiction, 713–733
juvenile diversion programs, 741–742
movement toward, 737
persons in need of supervision,
    719–722, 724–731, 733–742
procedural rights, 730–731
proposed elimination of, 724–725,
    732–733
right to counsel, 714, 716–719, 731
runaways, 722–724, 740
secure detention, 737–740
sex discrimination, 731–732
truants, 742
ungovernability, moving toward parent-
    adolescent autonomy from,
    724–729
vagueness of statutes, 719–722, 731
Statute of limitations
  sexual abuse cases, 304
  testimony, closed circuit television,
    301–302
STDs. *See* Sexually transmitted diseases
    (STDs)
Stepparents
  adoption by. *See* Adoption
  de facto parent, 494–495
  "parent by estoppel," 494–495
  support obligations. *See* Support
  visitation rights, 493–494, 615
Street Terrorism Enforcement and
    Prevention Act (California), 767
Students. *See* Education; Schools
Substance abuse. *See also* Liquor laws
  contraception, mandatory, 77–78
  drug testing in schools, 834–841
  as factor in custody decision,
    579–580
  juvenile arrests for, 766
  minor's consent for medical care,
    375–378, 381, 405–406
  by pregnant women, 36, 38–39
Substituted judgment standard for medical
    care, 400–405

Suicide
  adolescent, 428–436
  in detention centers, 788
  juveniles placed in adult lockups, 788
Summary seizure, 305–310
Supplemental Security Income (SSI)
      program, 217
Support, 178–206. *See also* Financial
      responsibility
  abortion rights and, 46
  adult disabled children, 198
  ALI Principles, 198
  assisted reproduction, child conceived
      by, 178–181, 187–188, 638
  biological relationship to child, based
      on, 187–188
  child's economic contributions, 159
  common law rules on, 150–151
  conduct, conditioning on, 197–198
  constitutional issues, 197
  contraception, misrepresentation as to,
      181–183, 189
  criminal nonsupport proceedings, 201
  definition of "educational
      expenses," 197
  discretionary standards, 194–196
  disinheritance and, 210–212
  divorce cases, 199–200
  duty of parents, 150–151
  educational expenses, post-minority,
      192–194, 196–198
  empirical research, 198
  enforcement, 194–196, 199–206
  failure to make support payments,
      studies of, 200–201
  gamete donors, 188–189
  government programs, 216–225
  guidelines, enforcement, 194–196
  health insurance, post-minority, 194
  interception of income tax refunds to
      enforce, 204
  interstate enforcement, 201–203, 204
  judgments, sequestration and
      attachments to enforce, 201
  legitimate children, 150–151
  modification of agreements, 199–206
  mother's refusal to enforce, 188
  nondischargeable in bankruptcy, 206
  nonmarital children, 160–161, 167,
      171–174
  overlap of child support and, 193–194

  parent-child relationship, 193
  parenthood by contract, 178–181
  paternity establishment and, 223
  poor laws, 157–158
  post-minority, 191–198
  removed children, 471–472
  reproductive technology and, 637–638
  "Responsible Fatherhood" bill, 206
  room and board expenses, 193–194
  same-sex couples and, 187–188
  schedules or guidelines for, 185, 204
  separation agreements requiring, 198
  state registries and directories, 206
  stepparent's obligation, 184–191
      ALI Principles, 190
      federal legislation, 190
      financial resources of stepparent and
          parent's obligations, 190
      during marriage, 190
      post-divorce, 190
      relative responsibility, 191
      temporal limitations on, 193–194
  visitation conditioned on, 599–602
  wage withholding to enforce, 206
  withholding, for failure to comply with
      custody decree, 8
Surrogate parenting agreements. *See also*
      Assisted reproduction; Embryo
      transfers; In vitro fertilization
  as "baby selling," 453–456, 639–640
  breach of contract, 451–460, 640–641
  constitutional issues, 457–458, 639–640
  custody issues, 451–461, 639–644
  as exploitation of women, 640
  international perspective, 644
  model legislation, 643–644
  public policy considerations, 455–456
  Revised Uniform Parentage Act, 643
  state approaches to, 642
  termination of parental rights and,
      451–460
  validity and enforcement, 451–460
  visitation and, 459–460
Swedish Parenthood and Guardianship
      Code, 234–235

TANF. *See* Temporary Assistance for
      Needy Families (TANF) program
Technology. *See also* Internet
  birth control, 70–77
  contraception. *See* Contraception

reproductive, 460, 637–649. *See also*
    Assisted reproduction
Teen pregnancy. *See* Pregnancy
Telecommunications Act of 1996,
    110–111
Television
    sexual abuse victims, testimony by
        closed circuit television,
        301–302
    V-chip, 110
    violence, 110
Television Program Improvement Act
    of 1990, 110
Temporary Assistance for Needy Families
    (TANF) program
    criticisms of, 223–225
    free meals, 219
    funding, 222
    Medicaid and, 221–222, 382
    paternity establishment, 223
    unwed teen mothers, 223
    work requirements, 222–223
Terminal illness
    parent's consent to medical care,
        384–385
    pregnant women, 37
Termination of parental rights
    adoption and, 471–472, 503, 513
    child's right to terminate, 751–752
    disabled newborns, 423–424
    duration in foster care as
        ground for, 367
    exceptions to, 367
    fathers' rights, 496
    incarceration as ground for, 367–368
    for neglect, 305–310
    procedural safeguards, 361–370
    reasonable efforts requirement,
        361–370
    right to counsel, parental, 369–370
    standard of proof, 368–369
    surrogate parenting agreements and,
        451–460
    time-limited services, 367
    voluntary, 491–492
Testimony by child witness
    sexual abuse cases, 292–304
    Uniform Child Witness Testimony
        by Alternative Methods Act,
        302–303
Title X, 700

Torts
    battery or negligence, 372–374
    corporal punishment, 227–228,
        237–238
    justifiable use of force, 233, 239
    negligence, minor's standard of care,
        671–672
    parental liability, 667–669
    parental tort immunity doctrine,
        237–238
    prenatal injuries, 10, 48
    reasonable force rule, 233
    violent video games, 113–114
    wrongful life, wrongful birth, 48–49
Trial by jury
    judicial factfinding, reliability of,
        819–820
    juvenile courts, right in, 815–819
    sentence enhancements, effect of denial
        of jury trial on, 821–822
    special characteristics of juvenile
        court, 820
    waiver of rights to, 861–864
Truancy, 742, 824
Trusts, child's estate, 215

Unborn Victims of Violence Act,
    22, 47
UN Convention on the Rights of the
    Child, 237
Undisciplined children as status offenders.
    See Status offenders
Undue burden standard, 26–27
Unemployment insurance, 216
Uniform Adoption Act, 488, 494,
    515, 527
Uniform Child Abduction Prevention Act
    (UCAPA), 630
Uniform Child Custody Jurisdiction Act,
    631–632
Uniform Child Custody Jurisdiction and
    Enforcement Act, 634–635
Uniform Child Witness Testimony by
    Alternative Methods Act,
    302–303
Uniform Gifts to Minors Act, 215
Uniform Interstate Family Support Act,
    175–176, 202–203
Uniform Juvenile Courts Act, 721
Uniform Marriage and Divorce Act,
    194–195, 199

Uniform Parentage Act
  assisted reproduction, 639
  conduct, paternity established by, 175
  "gestational agreements," 643,
      645–646
  paternity and, 500–503
  same-sex couples, 187–188
  same-sex custody and adoption
      cases, 537
Uniform Probate Code, 212
Uniform Putative and Unknown Fathers
      Act, 499
Uniform Reciprocal Enforcement of
      Support Act (URESA), 202
Uniform Representation of Children in
      Abuse, Neglect and Custody
      Proceedings Act, 628
Uniform Status of Children of Assisted
      Conception Act, 499, 643
Uniform Transfers to Minors Act,
      215–216
Unwed fathers. *See* Fathers
U.S. Agency for International
      Development (USAID), 25

Vaccines. *See* Immunizations
Vagueness
  abortion statutes, 5, 12
  anti-gang laws, 768
  neglect laws, 309, 318
  status offense statutes,
      719–722, 731
V-chips, 110
Venereal disease. *See* Sexually
      transmitted diseases (STDs)
Video games, violence and minors' access
      to, 113–114
Videotaping testimony of sexual abuse
      victims, 303
Viewpoint discrimination, 129–130
Violence. *See also* Domestic violence
  restricting minors' access to sexually
      explicit and violent materials,
      106–114
  in schools. *See* Schools
  on television, 110
Violent Crime Control and Law
      Enforcement Act, 768
Visitation
  abusive parent, 599
  benefits to child, 602–604

conditions on homosexual parent,
      608–609
grandparents' rights, 81–82,
      493–495, 609–617
jurisdiction, interstate cases, 635
nonmarital children, 162–164
physical or sexual abuse, 609
religious disputes between parents,
      604–607
"second-parent" rights, 615–616
stepparents' rights, 493–494, 615
support, conditioned on, 599–602
surrogate parenting agreements and,
      459–460
third parties, rights of, 609–617
Visitation Rights Enforcement Act, 635
Voting rights, 750–751
Voucher programs for schools, 56–57

Waiver
  age of juvenile as consideration,
      867–868
  competence to waive, 857–860,
      864–865, 867–868
  counsel, right to, 868
  juvenile's rights in delinquency
      proceedings, 857–860,
      864–868
  parental rights in delinquency
      proceedings, 864
  by parent or other interested adult,
      865–867
Warrants
  juvenile arrest, 824–825
  search and seizure, 831, 848
Wealth as factor in custody decision,
      572–575
Weapons
  child access prevention (CAP)
      laws, 434
  metal detectors in schools and,
      845–846
  zero tolerance policies in schools,
      133–134
Web. *See* Internet
Weldon Amendment, 24
Welfare. *See* Aid to Families with
      Dependent Children (AFDC);
      Food stamp program; Personal
      Responsibility and Work
      Opportunity Reconciliation Act

(PRWORA); Temporary
Assistance for Needy Families
(TANF) program
Witness, child as. *See* Testimony by child
witness
Workers' compensation, 177, 206, 216,
661–662
Wrongful birth, recovery for, 48–49
Wrongful death
nonmarital child, 176–177

preembryos, negligent loss or
destruction of, 646
recovery for, generally, 48
stillbirth, 10
Wrongful life actions,
48–49, 415

Youth Worker Protection Act, 660

Zero tolerance policies, 133–135